EXPOSITION
OF THE
PARABLES

SERIES ONE

EXPOSITION
OF THE
PARABLES

SERIES ONE

BENJAMIN KEACH

Foreword by

Herbert Lockyer

KREGEL PUBLICATIONS
Grand Rapids, Michigan 49501

Exposition of the Parables: First Series, by Benjamin Keach. © 1991 by Kregel Publications, a division of Kregel, Inc., P. O. Box 2607, Grand Rapids, MI 49501. All rights reserved.

Cover Design: Don Ellens

Library of Congress Cataloging-in-Publication Data

Keach, Benjamin, 1640-1704.
    [Exposition of the parables and express similitudes of our Lord and Saviour Jesus Christ]
    Exposition of the Parables / by Benjamin Keach.
        p.   cm.
    Reprint, with new introduction. Originally published: An exposition of the parables and express similitudes of our Lord and Saviour Jesus Christ. London: W. H. Collingridge, 1865.

    1. Jesus Christ— Parables — Early works to 1800.   I. Title.

BT374.K4   1991   226.8'066—dc20   90-22767
                                                                                          CIP
ISBN 0-8254-3055-0 —First Series (paperback)
ISBN 0-8254-3056-9 —Second Series (paperback)

5 6 7 8 9 Printing/Year 95 94 93 92 91

FOREWORD

Not only Baptists, but believers throughout the Christian world, should know and revere the witness and work of Benjamin Keach since few men ranked higher in the period in which this famous Baptist preacher lived. Born in 1649, he was immersed on the confession of his faith in Christ at the age of 15, and began to preach at 18. In 1668, at the age of 28, he became the Pastor of the Baptist Church, Horsleydown, London, the center from which he exercised a very wide influence. He died in 1704 at the age of 68. A striking fact of his later years was his severe illness in 1689, when the physician despaired of his life. His beloved friend, Hanserd Knollys, another famous Baptist worthy of that time, knelt by Keach's bedside, and fervently prayed that God would add to his life the time granted to Hezekiah. Rising from prayer he said, "Brother Keach, I shall be in Heaven before you." Both the prayer and the prediction were honoured to the letter—Knollys died 2 years later and Keach lived for another 15 years.

Read

In 1686, Elias Keach, son of Benjamin Keach of noble memory, went to America and settled at Pennepek. But when Elias arrived in Pennsylvania, he was a wild youth of 19, and for sport dressed like a minister of that time. Because of his honored name and appearance as a young divine from London, invitations to preach reached him. When a crowd gathered this wayward young man felt that the bravest thing to do was to preach, but he suddenly stopped short in his sermon. The vision of his saintly father and mother came before him and conviction seized him. To those gathered he confessed his imposture. Later on, he went forth as an Evangelist, and after a while founded a Church at Pennepek, Pennsylvania, where he preached with great power. He married the daughter of Chief Justice Moore, of Pennsylvania. In 1689, he returned to London and organized a Church in Ayles Street and preached to great crowds of people. Like his remarkable father, Elias Keach published several books, among them being *Grace of Patience*. He died in 1701, at the age of 34.

To Benjamin Keach, a man of great faith in God, the Church owes its hymn singing. This warrior was the one who first introduced the practice of singing hymns in worship. Baptists and Independents revolting against the singing of some of the translations of the Psalms the Presbyterians used, irreverently called them "Geneva Jiggs." The first time hymns were used was at a communion service in 1673. In 1691, Keach published his book of 300 hymns called *Spiritual Melody*. Hardly any of these hymns have survived. Those who argued against the principle of hymn singing condemned many of Keach's hymns as doggerel, as these specimens seem to be—

Our wounds do stink and are corrupt,
Hard swelling do we see;
We want a little ointment Lord,
Let us more humble be.

V

* * * *

> *Repentance like a bucket us*
> *To pump the water out;*
> *For leaky is our ship, alas,*
> *Which makes us look about.*

However, Benjamin Keach will ever be remembered as a prolific author, some 43 different works coming from his most gifted pen.

It was for one of these, a small work on fundamental Baptist principles, that he was indicted in 1664, and brought before Chief Justice Hyde whose treatment of the prisoner was harsh and unjust. To all charges Keach pleaded "not guilty." Although the jury found a technical error in the indictment, the court, despite the law, forced a verdict of "guilty." The judge sentenced him to prison for two weeks, and to stand in the pillory in the Aylesbury market place with a paper over his head inscribed, "For writing, printing and publishing a schismatical book entitled, *The Child's Instructor* or *A New and Easy Primmer.*" Keach was also commanded to pay a fine of £20, a great sum in those days, and to give sureties for his appearance at the next assize, to recant his doctrines, and to have his book burned before his eyes while in the pillory.

Usually, those whose feet and hands were in stocks would be pelted with eggs and rotten fruit and hooted at. But the crowd treated Keach with great respect when he was in the pillory and listened eagerly as he preached to the people. The enraged Sheriff threatened to gag him, but he continued to exhort the people out of the Bible. The following Saturday as he stood in the pillory at Winslow his book was burned. No copy of that edition was preserved but Benjamin Keach lived to rewrite and republish it, just as Jeremiah, through Baruch, rewrote and republished his own burned prophecies. This stalwart for the faith was often in prison for preaching the Gospel. After the Declaration of Indulgence of 1672, the people were no longer forced to meet in private houses. Then the followers of Keach built their first house of worship, which was frequently enlarged until it would hold a thousand people.

Among his printed works, *Preaching from the Types and Metaphors of the Bible* and *Exposition of the Parables in the Bible* are now very difficult to secure. *Kregel Publications* are to be complimented for the reissue of these classics for the benefit of preachers and teachers of this generation, when sound Biblical exposition is so greatly needed. After preaching the Word for over 60 years, I am not ashamed to confess how deeply in debt I am to these most substantial studies of this renowned expositor.

No preacher will be short of messages if he lives in *The Metaphors* and in *The Parables* and weaves into his personal treatment recently discovered facts and features on some of the natural objects dealt with in these monumental homiletical works. In his original *"Preface"* to *Preaching from the Types and Metaphors of the Bible* Keach quotes Augustine as saying that the Scripture seemed rude, and unpolished when compared with Cicero's adorned style, because he did not understand their beauty. But once his mind was illuminated to understand the Scriptures then no writing appeared so wise or even eloquent. In a most remarkable way, Keach understood the inward beauty of Bible symbols and expounded them in a most unique way.

To all Pastors who decide to take their people through the parables in the Bible with the aid of dear old Benjamin Keach, we can promise them happy and effective preaching. Chrysostom said, "Read all the prophetic books without seeing Christ in them, and what will you find so insipid and flat? See Christ there, and what you read becomes fragrant." Is this not the experience of all who endeavour to rightly divide the Word of Truth? A perusal of the volume now before you will convince you of the affirmation of Isaac Williams in the lines—

> Through every page the universal King
> From Eden's loss unto the end of years,
> From East to West, the Son of Man appears . . .
>
> Truth through the sacred volume hidden lies,
> And spreads from end to end her secret wing,
> Through ritual, type, and storied mysteries.

—Herbert Lockyer

NOTE TO THE READER

Because of the unfamiliarity of most of us today with the Roman numeral system used throughout this book, the following conversion table may offer welcome assistance to many readers:

i	1	xxii	22
ii	2	xxiii	23
iii	3	xxiv	24
iv	4	xxv	25
v	5	xxvi	26
vi	6	xxvii	27
vii	7	xxviii	28
viii	8	xxix	29
ix	9	xxx	30
x	10	xl	40
xi	11	l	50
xii	12	lx	60
xiii	13	lxx	70
xiv	14	lxxx	80
xv	15	xc	90
xvi	16	c	100
xvii	17	cx	110
xviii	18	cxx	120
xvix	19	cxxx	130
xx	20	cxl	140
xxi	21	cl	150

CONTENTS

PUBLISHER'S PREFACE

A reviewer for *The Presbyterian Journal* had good things to say about Benjamin Keach's monumental *Exposition of the Parables:*

"Keach gives exhaustive treatment to forty-eight of Christ's similitudes and parables, mostly taken from Matthew and Luke. Among them is salt—'Have salt in yourselves' (Mark 9:50). Writing 300 years before our present era of mushrooming scientific knowledge, he well applied what he knew about salt, showing remarkable understanding of psychology and, most of all, knowledge of the Bible. . . . His biblical exposition is challenging . . . rich.

"Even where one may not agree entirely with his interpretations, Keach gives such varied and Scriptural arguments that this book on Jesus' parables provides abundant dividends to the diligent reader. I commend it to every Bible student."

Kregel Publications is happy to make this new two-volume edition of *Exposition of the Parables* available to a new generation of readers. Series One includes the first twenty-eight expositions and Series Two covers expositions twenty-nine through forty-eight. Each volume is carefully indexed and provides the reader with a wealth of expository material on the parables of our Lord recorded in the New Testament.

KREGEL PUBLICATIONS

PREFACE

THE officers who were sent to take or apprehend our blessed Lord, being demanded why they had not brought him, answered, "Never man spake like this man;" that is, as to the matter or depth of divine wisdom, and with that authority and evidence of truth. But when we consider that almost all which our Lord spake to the multitude, he spake in parables, (and in them being hid the rich treasure of his heavenly doctrine, or such things that had been kept secret from the foundation of the world, that it might be fulfilled which was spoken by the prophets) it may seem strange that none of our learned modern divines, nor others, have been stirred up to write an exposition upon all the parables and similitudes spoken by our blessed Lord in the four evangelists. Though it is true, some of them have most excellently written upon, and opened a few of them ; but no one author (as I can learn) hath in one or more volumes written upon them all, if the greatest part, nor any exposition as I can meet with of many of them : yet what large and learned expositions have they written upon divers books of the Old and New Testament ! So that what is here presented to your view, hath not been done by any before ; and it might have been wished, that some now better capable than I am, had been stirred up to have undertaken it. And (considering that the parables contain the substance of our Saviour's ministry, and the profound mysteries couched therein,) the sense of my great weakness, or inabilities to manage so great a work, hath caused me not to undertake it without tremblings of heart, and many prayers and cries to God, that my heart, tongue, and pen, might be influenced and guided by the divine Spirit : though the want of those attainments that some have arrived at, beyond what I pretend to, hath been no small discouragement to me. Though I am persuaded I have not been left without the gracious assistance of the Spirit of Truth ; nor have I omitted searching into what authors I could meet with, who have either written upon the parables, and on the customs of the Jews, to which in many things contained in them our Saviour doth refer. Moreover, I have had regard to those four rules mentioned by the learned in opening of the parables, viz., their Properties, Qualities, Effects, Operations. And that with special respect to their constitution, natural, civil, or moral, and have laboured to draw forth suitable propositions, which are raised and prosecuted from the scope or principal matter contained in one or another parable ; though perhaps I may vary from the directions given by one or two authors (I have met with) about opening of and drawing propositions from parables, who insinuate as if no propositions nor answerable applications ought to be made, but from the general scope of the parable Now in this I am not of their opinion, for some things that may (perhaps) not so clearly appear to lie in the direct scope, may contain in them much instruction, and profitable truths may be raised therefrom, and improved. I remember one very learned author (Mr. H. Knollys), gave direction or allowance that in opening metaphorical or parabolical Scriptures, we may enlarge so far as there is a clear analogy of faith ; yet all authors agree, that parables run not always upon all four ; that is, there are in parables some great disparities, some things being brought in or mentioned for illustration sake, which cannot be spiritually applied parallelwise. Indeed, some I find who have written on some parables, have given such a general exposition of the sum and scope of some, as renders their exposition quite different from the exposition our blessed Lord gave himself of those he unfolded unto his disciples : see Matt. xiii. about the Sower, and that of the Wheat and Tares, in which he opens every particular part, and applies it. Now can any directions given by learned men be so safe a rule to follow in expounding the parables, as that rule our Saviour hath left in the way taken by himself.

One saith to this purpose, speaking of the parables ; viz., who will or ought to force from an author such things which he himself never dreamed of ? To which I answer,

1. Who knows directly how far the intentions of our Lord in his parables do or may extend, in many words, and parts of a parable, besides the general main scope thereof ?

2. I would know whether he that draws propositions from a parabolical text, may not be allowed the same liberty others take in preaching upon any other Scriptures (that may not be tropical or parabolical) provided he keeps to the true analogy of faith? And pray do not some ministers preach from one or another text of Scripture almost all the whole Gospel, and in doing so are they certain the Sacred Author, I mean the Holy Ghost, directly intended or comprehended in those texts (as his main scope and design) all those things which they drew therefrom ; and perhaps very safely and profitably. I must confess I perceive that some men render many things (spoken by our Lord in many parables) very insignificant or to little or no purpose mentioned by him, and so not to be improved by us to our spiritual profit ; which to me seems to cast a kind of contempt upon the ministry of our Lord Jesus Christ, as well as it clearly contradicts his own exposition of those parables He Himself explained.

Moreover, I think those expositions of the parables of some men, who only (or principally) improve them to instruct people into practical duties, or rather only how they should live, than how they should believe, are worthy of blame ; as if our Saviour chiefly designed by speaking so many parables, to teach us how to lead our lives, and not so much to open to us the great doctrine of the Gospel, or to show us the necessity of faith in himself, or to instruct us into doctrinal truths ; whereas the latter seeming directly to be the main scope of our Lord in most of his parables. As is clearly held forth in these words recorded by the Evangelist St. Matthew, chap. xiii. 34, 35, " I will open my mouth in parables, I will utter things which have been kept secret from the foundation of the world." Were the duties of morality, or the rules of a godly life, kept secret from the foundation of the world, until our Saviour came ? No, certainly, for the law of the Lord is perfect in that great case ; but they were the mysteries of the Gospel, or the mysteries of our salvation by our Lord Jesus Christ, which He mainly designed to instruct us in, by speaking his parables.

Certainly nothing is more necessary to understand the Scripture (whether metaphorical or parabolical, or not) than the help, teachings, and influences of the Holy Spirit, which some of late (as well as formerly) as it seems to me, have cast contempt upon, to the dishonour of God, his Blessed Spirit, and to the scandal of our sacred religion, intimating as if without the knowledge of the tongues or school-divinity no men are capable, truly and profitably, to preach the Gospel nor understand the Scripture. I must confess I think it a great blessing God hath raised up learned men among us, and readily grant the knowledge of the tongues is very useful, but not of necessity in a minister, nor of such great use in order to understand the Scripture (as some talk of), provided it be granted that the sacred Bible be truly translated (which none dares deny,) and also if a man stores himself with all such books that open in English, the different reading of many of the Hebrew and Greek texts, which are extant, particularly those Bibles that have best quotations or marginal notes. Sirs, the knowledge of the tongues is none of the qualifications laid down of one that is to be chosen an overseer, or pastor of a church, 1 Tim. iii., and Tit. i. Besides, how ignorant of the doctrine of the Gospel, and of the Holy Scriptures, are some learned men ! " For what man knoweth the things of a man, save the spirit of a man that is in him ; even so the things of God knoweth no man, but the Spirit of God," 1 Cor. ii. 11. Men by the knowledge of the tongues and other human arts, may understand the things of a man, or attain to more clear knowledge of things that are merely human ; but none have a true and saving knowledge of Christ, the Gospel, or of spiritual things, but by the Spirit of God. " Which things we speak, not in the words which man's wisdom teacheth, but which the Holy Ghost teacheth, comparing spiritual things with spiritual," ver. 13.

Let men take heed how they cry up man's wisdom, though the simple knowledge of the tongues none will or can deny to be useful. Therefore it is that stress which is by some laid upon it, rendering it essential in a Gospel minister, that gives the offence. Pray, see what our learned annotators observe, viz., That they do not preach or argue philosophically, like an Athenian philosopher, but use a familiar, plain style, giving forth the naked truths of God, without any paint or gaudy phrase.

Moreover, I think it not amiss to recite here what a late bishop of the church of England hath written upon the knowledge of the tongues, viz.,

" There hath not (saith he) been a greater plague to the Christian religion than school divinity, where men take upon them the liberty to propose new questions, make nice distinctions, and rash conclusions of divine matters, tossing them up and down with their tongues like tennis balls; and from hence proceeded all the dangerous heresies, and cruel bickerings about them, falling from words to blows. The first divinity school we read of, was set up at Alexandria, by Pantænus, and from thence soon after sprang up that damnable heresy of the Arians, which overran all Christendom, and was the cause of the destruction of so many millions of Christians, both of body and soul; which before this were so gross and sensual, that none took them up but dissolute or frantic people, and soon vanished. But after this school, subtle way of arguing was brought into Christianity, heresy grew more refined, and so subtle, that the plain and pious fathers of the church knew not how to lay hold of it; the school distinctions and evasions baffled them; and so those sophisters proud of their conquest, triumphed, and carried away a specious appearance of truth as well as learning, or rather cunning, insomuch that many godly persons were deluded and fell into them, and many of their heresies continue unto this day."

I would advise all Christians who are so bigotted to human learning, so as to think none ought to be allowed to preach but such who have been trained up in schools or universities, and have the knowledge of the tongues, to read Rev. Dr. Owen on the Hebrews, chap. v, who shows, that teachers were trained up in the primitive churches only, as being endowed with grace and ministerial gifts by the Lord Jesus, every church being then the great seminary for preachers. Also let them read Mr. Crandon's answer to Mr. Baxter's Aphorisms, who tells us human learning is of no force to decide, judge, and conclude any questions merely evangelical; and that no men have done more mischief or hurt to the church of God, than learned men, by their nice scholastic and philosophical distinctions. Indeed, by this wisdom the Apostle shows that the world knew not God, nor can they know thereby the Lord Jesus Christ, nor the great doctrine of justification by his righteousness; for this lies above the art and wisdom of man, let his knowledge of the tongues, or other human learning, be what it will. Moreover, he gives several arguments to prove that God hath not ordained philosophical learning to be instrumental for the promoting of the Gospel, and also shows by such learning many heresies came into the church, and were defended to such a degree, that unlearned men were hard beset to confute them.

But further he shows how the Holy Ghost slighteth, and uttereth invective terms against human learning or man's wisdom, 1 Cor. i. 18, 21, &c. And also how God blessed the preaching of the Gospel by the unlearned, and blasted such who have used (or rather say I, abused) philosophicial learning: he also shows how the Gospel spread in the next ages after the Apostles, when most, if not all gospel ministers were unacquainted with human learning.—Yet let none think I speak against grammar learning, or the knowledge of the tongues, for certainly the usefulness thereof (as I hinted) is considerable: and what cause have we to bless God, that he raised up such learned men in the church, as Dr. Owen, and multitudes more I might mention, to defend the great fundamental truths of Christ against heretics; and let us be thankful that we have still such who are considerably learned amongst us, and I wish that worthy young men, to whom God hath given ministerial gifts, might be furnished with such learning, which some others want. What I have here said, is because some lay too great a stress upon human learning, and cry against all such ministers who have it not. But yet I must say, that it is very evident, that the allwise God chose some men, who were counted "foolish and base things of the world, to confound the wise, &c., that no flesh should glory in his presence," 1 Cor. i. 7—30.

Moreover it ought to be noted, how Paul looked upon the use of the tongues in the church, though they were those tongues that were the extraordinary gifts of the Spirit, to capacitate the Apostles and first ministers to preach the Gospel to the people of divers languages; "I thank God I speak with more tongues than you all, yet in the church I had rather speak five words with my understanding, than ten thousand words in an unknown tongue," 1 Cor. xiv. 18, 19. The truth is, in preaching, to speak in a language the people understand not, it seems to serve for nothing, unless it is that the preacher would let them know he is a scholar. How ready is man to glory in his human attainments! therefore Christ made use of very few, if any, who were learned in the primitive time; I know none, except Luke and the Apostle Paul; yet, on the other hand, it ought to be the care of our churches to see that none but such men are allowed to preach, to whom God hath given competent gifts, and such also who are able to speak proper English, for the contrary exposeth the Gospel to contempt.

But to say no more to this, reader, I shall not in this epistle speak much as to the nature and usefulness of the parabolical and metaphorical Scripture, because I have spoken to it in the introduction, being the substance of a sermon preached upon that account ; only let me add, what Mr. Caryl hath said concerning parables ; he saith, the original word signifies to rule or govern, as a prince whose righteous precepts and commands his people ought to obey, viz., (Caryl on Job 27. 1. p. 6, 7, 8).

Speeches or sentences full of wisdom and of truth are called parables, for a threefold reason.

" 1. Because a wise sentence rules over the spirits of men,—Parables carry convincing light, and so great authority, &c.

" 2. Parables are so called, because such speeches came usually from the mouths of princes and great persons.

" 3. Because whether men will submit to such speeches and truths, or not, yet their judgments, actions, and opinions must be tried and ruled by them. Parables are as touchstones of truth, they are rules, and therefore ought to rule.

" Moreover, he (with other learned men) says, that parables are similitudes, because they resemble and bear (as it were) the express image of their wisdom, gravity, modesty, and truth, who spake them. All words should be the image of the mind, and parables are the beautiful image of a beautiful mind.—A parable is taken several ways in Scripture.

" 1. For any divine maxim, axiom, or principle.

" 2. A Parable is a dark and hard saying, and is opposed to a plain speech ; ' I will open my mouth in a parable. I will utter dark sayings of old,' Psal lxxviii. 2."

3. A man's judgment or opinion in any case, is his parable, &c. As to the power and efficacy a parable hath upon a man's heart when understood, evidently appears in David's case, when he understood Nathan's parable : and touching the nature and usefulness of them, read the introduction.

Reader, thou art here presented with the labours of near twelve years, not that I preached every Lord's day in the morning upon the parables ; no, but generally for so long time I so did ; and I hope not without some gracious success. You will find I have enlarged much upon some of them more than on others. Moreover, but short enlargements upon most particular heads, which make the sermons short ; and if I had not done so, it would have swollen to another volume as big as this. Also you will find many great Gospel truths improved in one parable, which are also mentioned with some alterations or additions in another. And, now, to close with this epistle, I cannot expect to escape the censure of many in writing upon the parables. Many men so much differ from others in respect of the sense and meaning of our Lord in divers things contained therein, but generally in the main I hope all will receive satisfaction, that the Lord hath helped me in opening of them, to whose most gracious blessing I shall commit these and all poor labours of mine.

BENJAMIN KEACH

INTRODUCTION

All these things spake Jesus in parables, and without parables spake he not unto them;
That it might be fulfilled which was spoken by the prophets, I will open my mouth in para-
bles, I will utter things which have been kept secret from the foundation of the world.—
Matt. xiii. 34, 35.

IN these words the ministry of our blessed Saviour, in speaking in parables, is magnified, i. e., they fully discover, that in his parables are contained the profound and deep things or mysteries of the Gospel; and therefore the opening of them by the help of the divine Spirit, must needs be of no small profit unto the souls of God's people. Now my purpose at this time, is not to speak to the distinct parts of these words, nor to raise any doctrinal truths therefrom; but to speak something of parables in general, as an introduction to the great work before me.

1. I shall show you the difference between typical and tropical Scriptures.

2. Show what a parable is.

3. Show what advantages we have by parables, above what we have by some other Scriptures.

4. Lay down some rules, to know tropical Scriptures from Scriptures that are to be taken literally.

5. Show you why our Saviour might speak so much in parables.

First, Types suppose the verity of some real history, as to matter of fact; as the first Adam was a type or figure of Jesus Christ: so was the high-priest, and many other persons under the law. Jonas being in the whale's belly, was a type or figure of our Saviour's lying three days in the grave. *The difference between typical and tropical Scripture.*

2. Types look only to matter of fact, or things done under the law; to matter of fact, or things under the Gospel; as Sarah and Hagar, Isaac and Ishmael, the paschal-lamb, &c.

3. Types are only historical, as such, the truth agreeing with the Antitype makes them up, and fulfils them as to the design of God therein; as the brazen serpent in its perfect signification was fulfilled, when Jesus Christ was lifted up upon the cross; the like in respect had unto the rock that was pierced in the wilderness, was (as to its signification fully completed), when our Lord was pierced on the cross. *See my Key to open Scripture Metaphors.*

4. Types in the Old Testament respect only some persons and things, with their proper antitypes under the gospel; as Christ, the gospel, and gospel-church, together with the spreading of the gospel; and nature of the grace, blessings, and privileges of the members thereof.

2ndly. Tropical Scriptures, as parables, metaphors, allegories, and simili-tudes, do not require such a necessary supposition as to matter of fact. (1.) As that of the rich man and Lazarus; there is no necessity to conclude, it intends or shows there were two such particular persons; but by the rich man, may any ungodly rich man, that is of such an evil temper, be held forth, and such to be his state at death: and by Lazarus, may be showed, the state and condition of such that are very poor and afflicted ones, that are truly godly; and that at death their souls go all to heaven, or into the bosom of Jesus Christ the true Abraham. See more in the exposition of that parable. *How to know figu-rative Scrip-tures.*

2. Parables and allegories take in words, sentences, and doctrines, containing matter of faith and manners; and are used for illustration-sake, to open and explain some hidden mystery that lies covered in them; which would be hard to be understood unless so opened.

3. Therefore parables, &c., in their main scope and design, intend not matter of fact

1

(as types do), but are principally doctrinal, and are brought to open the mind of God the better to our weak capacities, move upon our affections, and convince the conscience, as the parable of Nathan in David's case.   That parables do not always (if ever) contain matter of fact, is evident in respect of Jotham's parable of the Trees going to choose a King, &c.

4. And whereas types in the Old Testament respect only some persons and things, (as I said before) and their antitypes; so they are such persons and things, which none but whom God himself made use of as types; men are not to frame, or make types, nor ought any to attempt once so to do; for after that rate men may turn all historical Scriptures into allegories, as some will have Pharaoh a type of the devil.   I am satisfied that all persons and things that were types under the Old Testament, God hath somewhere or another given us grounds to believe, that they were types or figurative.

But now as to parables, allegories, &c., they take in almost every thing, that belongs either to doctrine, instruction, faith, and practice.   Moreover, a minister may use other parables and similitudes of his own framing, besides what are mentioned in the Scriptures for illustration sake; which is found by experience very useful to the hearers: (yet what are they to Christ's parables and similitudes?) so that tropical Scriptures, and the use of parables, are more extensive and comprehensive in their use, meaning, and application, than typical Scriptures are: so much as to the first thing propounded.

What a pa-   Secondly, I shall show you what a parable is, and the nature thereof.
rable is.   1. A parable signifies no more than a similitude, which is to make use of natural things by way of allusion or comparison, to open spiritual things, the better to our understanding; "If I have told you of earthly things, and ye believe not, how shall you believe if I tell you of heavenly things?" John iii. 12.   That is, if I should without using earthly things and similitudes, speak of the sublime nature of heavenly things, how would you understand them?

Take what you have in our Key to open Scripture Metaphors: a parable is called ϖαρατω παραϐαλλειν, which beside other significations which the subject is unconcerned in (for it signifies *objicere, conjicere, detorquere, committere, appropinquare, transmittere,* &c.) denotes conferring, comparing, or the collocation of different things.

Jerome calls it a similitude, Παραϐολ, because as a previous shadow of truth, it represents it; it answers to the Hebrew mashal.   Properly and strictly it signifies an artificial narrative of a thing done, to signify another thing.   So Glassius.

2. In parables, it is not necessary that all the actions of men mentioned in them should be just actions: I mean morally just and honest, for the unjust Steward is not mentioned by our Saviour to justify his injustice; but to show his care and wisdom in providing for the future time.

3. Therefore in parables, if we would understand the mind of God in them, we must always take care to consider the main design and scope of them; or which way the sacred story tends, or what our Lord chiefly designs therein.

"For parabolical texts one cannot well explain them (saith a French minister) but he must remark and observe attentively, the proper scope unto which the parable tendeth; there must be great care, especially in handling them well, to consider what the parable aimeth at principally, and less principally, or primarily and secondarily; for there may be divers ends, one general and principal, and others particular and subalternate.

"Then, secondly, when the scope is discovered, we must narrowly observe what the parable is taken from, and what it tends unto the general end, and what unto the particular; examining how far every thing in the parable tendeth and serveth; for though there are some things which are principally of the end of the parable, and others which are not expressed, but serve only to enrich and beautify the parable; nevertheless we must not in examining the principal things, neglect the other; as in the study of the law, so of a parable; we must make the things which are of the greater importance the main of our labour and application, yet we must not neglect or leave out the lesser, &c.

"There are some parables prophetical, as that of the ten virgins; Mat. xxv. But commonly they are dogmaticals, and therefore are so to be handled; but it must be done in the light of the similitude, for the matter of parables have these advantages.

"And though (saith our French author) in the explanation of parables, nothing is to be mentioned, but that which is properly of the end and scope of them; yet in the application we may enlarge these reports more particularly."

4. I know (as he and others observe) such that handle the parables of our Saviour, ought to have the knowledge of natural, moral, and civil histories, and consult classic

authors, &c.; which so far as I am capable I have endeavoured; together with the customs and practice of the Jews and the eastern countries, also their plants, seeds, &c., some of which differ from ours.

5. Moreover, the main scope or design of a parable, is commonly to be under- *How the main scope of a parable may be understood.* stood, either from our Saviour's more general or more particular exposition of it, or else from his main and principal design, which may be gathered from the preface to it, or else from the conclusion thereof. As for example, in the parable of the Vineyard let out to husbandmen; Mat. xxi. 33. See what precedes and what succeeds in that parable, so also in the parable of the rich man.

6. It is not always to be expected, that every particular thing, passage, or action, mentioned in a parable, should be answered by something in the explication thereof. Some for want of considering this, run into many errors, and say the soul hath a tongue, because in the parable of the rich man, Luke xvi. When his soul came to lie in hell, he speaks of his tongue, and wanted a little water to cool it. Yet that may afford much instruction; it may be that that ungodly man (or such that are represented by him) had greatly offended with his tongue, either by swearing, blaspheming, or railing on the poor; or reproaching the godly, or by lying; and therefore that member is mentioned, as being grievously tormented in those flames.

7. Though the scope of a parable be the chief thing we should attend upon, yet more generally many other things may be made use of to the advantage of the hearers; even so far as it bears a clear analogy of faith, as in metaphorical Scriptures; as is showed in my Key to open Scripture-metaphors.

Thirdly, we have by parables divers advantages above what we have by some other Scriptures. *The profitableness of parabolical Scripture.*

1. They greatly tend to help the memory; we are more apt to remember stories, than other things delivered in a sermon. Besides, people when they see these natural things before their eyes, which the Holy Ghost makes use of to explain heavenly things by, they presently are the better enabled to call to remembrance what they have heard; as when they see a sower sow his seed, and the like.

2. They greatly help the mind and thinking faculty, to study the meaning of what they have so heard delivered unto them.

3. They are profitable to stir up, or to excite the affections, and to awaken the conscience; as when hell in a parable is set out by a furnace of fire, and conscience by a gnawing worm; and heaven and glory above, is represented by a glorious kingdom, and by a crown of glory.

4. Also to inform the judgment of the weak; indeed what could any of us do, to understand the deep things of God, if they were not thus opened and explained unto us? Yet parables have one great disadvantage to some who hear them, that they being not explained to them, understand them not; as it was in our Saviour's days, it being not given unto all to know the mysteries of the kingdom of heaven; therefore it must needs be no small blessing to have those parables of our blessed Lord opened unto us; so that we may be helped rightly to understand them.

Fourthly, I shall add here some rules, how you may know tropical and parabolical Scriptures from Scriptures that are to be taken literally.

How to know figurative scriptures. 1. When it is directly called a parable, "He spake a parable," &c. Yet because some scriptures are to be taken parabolically or figuratively, that are not directly called parables or similitudes. Therefore,

2. Know and be assured, that all Scriptures are to be taken figuratively or parabolically, when the literal sense would be absurd; as when Christ says, "This is my body," and when he said, "I am a Door, a Vine," &c., John xv., and when it is said, "And that Rock was Christ," 1 Cor. x. 4. As also when our Lord saith, "Unless ye eat the flesh of the Son of man, and drink his blood, you have no life in you," John vi. 53. Also those sayings, "Pluck out thy right eye, and cut off thy right hand." Should these Scriptures be taken literally, how absurd would they seem to all!

3. When the literal sense would not reach to the great design of edification, as when Christ speaks of sowing; certainly, none can suppose, our Lord went about to instruct them in husbandry, but in higher matters.

4. Those Scriptures must be taken figuratively, when the literal sense would obtrude clear falsities upon the sacred texts: As for example, "Destroy this temple, and in three days I will raise it up again;" "Unless ye eat the flesh of the Son of man," &c.

5. When the literal sense would not agree with, but be repugnant unto other Scriptures;

as when we are bid to heap coals of fire on the heads of our enemies; seeing it is said, "Revenge not yourselves," &c.

6. When the literal sense would render the Holy Ghost to speak impertinently; as when John Baptist says, "Now is the axe laid to the root of the trees, every tree therefore that brings not forth good fruit;" compared with Luke xiii. 7, "Cut it down, why cumbers it the ground?" Those texts refer to unfruitful persons under the means of gospel-grace, not of external trees; therefore should such places of the holy Scriptures be taken literally, it might seem to all an impertinent way of speaking.

Why Christ spake in parables. But to proceed to the last thing propounded,

Fifthly, Why did our blessed Saviour speak in parables?

Answ. 1. I answer, because some persons (as the Jews in our Saviour's days) were so averse to divine knowledge, and they having contemned the means of grace, God in judgment gave them up to blindness of mind. "And the disciples came and said unto him, why speakest thou unto them in parables? He answered and said unto them, it is given unto you to know the mysteries of the kingdom of heaven, but unto them it is not given; therefore speak I unto them in parables, because they seeing, see not, and in hearing, hear not, neither do they understand," Matt. xiii. 10—13.

There is a twofold knowledge of divine things: One notional, the other an effective and experimental knowledge. Now some men only hear the mysteries of the gospel, out of curiosity to fill their heads with knowledge : this sort therefore attain to as much knowledge as they desire and covet after; they do not improve to their spiritual profit what they hear; therefore "in hearing they hear not, and in seeing they see not." But unto others it is given to understand, and embrace the truth, in the love and saving mystery and power thereof. When a people have despised the knowledge of God's word in its spiritual efficacy, and so sin against knowledge; they find the Gospel as a sealed book to them, and many truths are delivered unto them in parables, which they either seek not after the true knowledge of, or else think their own wisdom and learning, to be sufficient to unfold the mysteries of them; and God, for their great wickedness in contemning the more clear and visible appearances of truth, (as the Jews did, who contemned those mighty works our Saviour wrought) it caused him to speak to them in parables, without affording them the help of his Spirit, in opening them to their understanding. "Unto you it is given to know the mysteries of the kingdom of heaven; but unto them that are without, all things are done in parables," Mark iv. 11. Unto them that are without the pale of the church, or are not in the election of grace, or who are without any saving knowledge of God, or desire to attain thereunto, all things seem riddles, paradoxes, or empty notions, or fruitless parables.

2. Christ might speak often in parables, because he would have men be studious and industrious to search out profound wisdom, like as Sampson, who, to try the wisdom of the Philistines, put forth his riddle. For as nothing is more difficult and hard to understand than a parable, until it is opened and explained, so nothing is more clear, when it is fully understood. A parable is like a golden mine, you must dig and search with all pains and diligence, that would find the true vein thereof.

3. It may be to discover the great need men have of the teachings of the Holy Spirit to understand divine truths; notwithstanding their greatest human learning, or clearest natural or acquired parts, "For what man knoweth the things of a man, but the spirit of a man that is in him? so the things of God knoweth no man, but the Spirit of God," 1 Cor. ii. 11. God has revealed some things concerning himself more plainly, but there are deep things of God, or great mysteries in the Scripture; and many such are contained in these parables, which, until the Spirit of God hath revealed them unto men, they understand them not. To what a degree of light and true spiritual knowledge, did the disciples of Christ attain, by the teachings of the Holy Ghost (who were but "fishermen or unlearned and ignorant persons,") John vii. 47, 48, Acts iv. 13, above what the learned Scribes and Pharisees arrived at, that contemned the Holy Spirit's teachings.

4. No doubt but our blessed Lord spake so often in parables, to illustrate and open sacred truths in the mystery of them, to the understandings of those that are spiritually wise. Because (as you have heard) heavenly things are, in their own primitive and sublime nature, so hard to be understood.

5. Moreover, one reason why our Lord spake in parables, was to fulfil the prophecy of Scripture, Psal. lxxviii. 2, compared with Matt. xiii. 34, 35. "Without a parable spake he nothing; that it might be fulfilled, which was spoken by the prophet, I will open my mouth in parables," &c.

6. And lastly, It may be, that the Lord's own people might the better improve all natural things unto their spiritual advantage, as to instance in some few particulars; viz.

1. As when you light a candle, and put it into a candlestick, say within thyself, thus must God by his Word and Spirit, light my dark heart; and thus must not my light be hid, but shine forth to the profit of others. And thus of like benefit to the world, is the church and people of God. Also,

2. When you taste things unsavoury for want of salt, say, O how unsavoury are such Christians or professors, whose words and conversations are not as becometh the Gospel; or when you taste things very sweet and savoury, say, O how savoury should I be in my life, or in all my words and actions! Also, O how good is grace, to season my heart and life!

3. When you see men dig deep, to lay the foundation of a house upon a rock, say, O how careful should I be, to see that my soul is built upon that rock, Jesus Christ, whom God hath laid in Zion.

4. When you, good women, leaven your bread, and you see in a little time the whole lump is leavened; say, thus will the true grace of God, if I receive it into my soul, leaven my heart and every faculty in me, and never cease until I become a new lump.

5. When you dig up new ground for to turn it into a garden, and find there much filth, stones, worms and vermin of the earth; say within thyself, thus naturally, in me and in all men, there was much filth and abominable corruption, and loathsome vermin undiscovered, until God by his Spirit, by powerful convictions, ploughed up the fallow ground of my heart.

6. When you see weeds, for want of care and pains, to grow up in your garden, which spoil your herbs and choice flowers; say within thyself, how will the weeds of sin and unbelief, spoil the growth of the good seed of grace in my soul, if I by faith, repentance and godly care, do not daily strive to weed them out, or get these base weeds up by the roots.

7. When you see the fire burn the wood, or consume all combustible matter; say within thyself, thus will the Spirit of God, when it hath kindled in my soul, burn up and consume every sin in me; as pride, vain-glory, the inordinate love of this world, wrath, envy, malice, revenge, undue passion, slavish fear, unbelief, hypocrisy, and all things that are of a carnal and combustible nature.

8. And when you see one coal kindle and enliven another, and the fire to burn more fervently by stirring it up; say within thyself, O what a mercy is it to be in the company of, and daily to converse with lively Christians! How doth their zeal heat, and warm, and enliven my soul; and O what need have I to stir up that grace and gift of God that is in me, by fervent prayer, fresh acts of faith and holy meditation.

9. When you see the wind blows, by which means the ship you behold before your eyes sail swiftly before a prosperous gale, say within thyself, thus shall I sail swiftly along through the troublesome sea of this world, when the wind of the Spirit blows upon my soul.

When you see the sun in the spring, to cause the grass, herbs, trees, and flowers put forth and smell fragrantly, say within thyself, thus it will be with my soul, if Jesus Christ draws near to me by the powerful influences of his Spirit, all grace will put forth, bud, and blossom in me; so that I shall become fruitful to God in righteousness and true holiness, and be of a fragrant scent in his nostrils, to the delighting the heart of Jesus.

10. When you see a great shower of rain fall on the earth, say within thyself, O how fruitful would this world be if God would send that great shower of the Spirit upon the souls of men, promised to be poured forth in the latter days! And when you see a small and gentle rain fall upon the tender herb, which softens the mould, and causes the flowers and herbs to sprout forth and smell sweetly, say to God, O send the sweet rain and dew of thy Spirit upon thy word, people, and ordinances, and upon my soul; so shall we grow and flourish in thy courts.

11. When you see the sun to shine bright and clear, and dispel all fogs and thick clouds, say within thyself, what glorious times will they be, when the Sun of righteousness will break forth in all nations, and disperse all the dark clouds of Popery, errors, heresy, Paganism, and Mahometanism, which now cover all kingdoms and people, making it is a dismal world. And when you see the sun to shine bright and clear into your house, whereby you discern what dust and filth is therein; say within yourself thus, when Jesus Christ began to shine into my heart by his Spirit, I came to see the filth and the abominable evils, and pollution of my heart, which humbles my soul, and lays me mourning at his feet.

12. When you go to bed (death being compared to our going to rest,) say within thyself, it will be but a little while, before I shall lie down in the grave, and rest there until the morning of the resurrection.

13. When you rise in the morning, say within thyself, over a little time I shall arise out of my grave, and meet Jesus Christ in the air.

14. When your dearest friend is displeased with you, and comes not to visit you as in former times, say, ah! what have I done? Oh! how sad is it, that my dear Jesus has hid his face, and withdrawn himself from my poor soul!

15. When you are in a dark night, or in a dark room, say, O how dismal will the blackness of darkness be, to the ungodly for evermore! O Lord, let me never be shut up in eternal darkness.

16. When you see a furnace of fire, or a hot oven, think of hell or the lake of fire, into which the wicked shall be cast; and admire God's free grace in Christ, who hath saved thee from that burning lake.

17. When you see a man or woman very crooked, deformed, and full of filthy sores running on them, say, such a crooked, filthy, and loathsome creature was I, before God changed my heart, and cleansed and healed all the stinking sores which were in my soul; which rendered me more loathsome in the sight of God, than this deformed and loathsome person before mine eyes is.

Lastly, When you see a sower sowing his seed, and some of it falls on the highway side, and some on stony places, and some among thorns, and some upon good ground, that is well ploughed and manured; call to mind what our Lord speaketh in the parable of the sower; and say within thyself, O how few hear the word, and bring forth the fruit thereof unto eternal life. O Lord, prepare my heart to receive thy word, that it may be like the good ground, or I shall be undone for ever. Let my heart be broken up and prepared by thy plough. O that I may have a good, an upright and sincere heart. Thus parables and metaphorical Scriptures may be improved every day, by each particular Christian, to his great profit and spiritual advantage.

APPLICATION

1. I infer from hence, of what great use parables are: behold, my brethren, take notice and ponder well what has been said.

2. This also justifies such ministers, who labour with what wisdom God hath given them, to open and explain the truths of the gospel unto the people, hid in these parables and similitudes spoken by our Lord Jesus Christ. Nay, and it justifies those who, in their preaching, do make use of apt similes to illustrate the matter they are upon, to affect the hearts of the people; yet it greatly concerns them all to see they use fit and proper allusions, lest they darken counsel with words without knowledge; and so instead of giving more light, expose the gospel and name of God to reproach.

3. It also tends to reprove those, who turn literal, plain, or historical Scripture into allegories; as well as it reproves such, who, like the Papists, take figurative Scripture literally; as when Christ saith, "This is my body;" they say, he speaks of his real body, and not figuratively. Moreover, all such who through their gross ignorance affirm, God is in the form of a man, because eyes, ears, a mouth, hands, and feet, are attributed to him.

4. Exhort. Learn to be studious, search into the spiritual meaning and mysteries of allegorical and parabolical Scripture. O be wise and experienced hearers, and be sure you do not despise men's preaching on these parables, since the substance of our Saviour's ministry to the world is contained in them.

5. Yet let us all take heed (which I shall endeavour to do), that we strain no metaphors or parables, beyond their due bounds, beyond the clear analogy of faith. But so much shall serve, as to the nature of similes and parables in general.

1. EVERY VALLEY SHALL BE FILLED

I

Every valley shall be filled, and every mountain and hill shall be brought low; and the crooked shall be made straight, and the rough ways shall be made smooth;
And all flesh shall see the Salvation of God.—Luke iii. 5, 6.

THE evangelist Matthew, Mat. iii. 3, hath the same passage, but he speaks more briefly unto it; " The voice of one crying in the wilderness, prepare ye the way of the Lord, make his paths straight."

Saint Luke repeats the words of the prophet Isaiah, almost word by word, it being a clear prophecy of John the Baptist; " The voice of him that crieth in the wilderness, prepare ye the way of the Lord; make straight in the desert, a highway for our God. Every valley shall be exalted and every mountain and hill shall be made low; and the crooked shall be made straight, and the rough places plain; and the glory of God shall be revealed together, and all flesh shall see it," Isa. x. 3.

For the better coming to open these words take notice,

1. We have the time of John's ministry.

2. His call unto his office, " The word of God came unto John," Luke iii. 2.

3. An account of the places where he preached: " He came into all the country round about Jordan," preaching, &c. ver. 3.

4. The subject-matter of his preaching, viz. " The Baptism of repentance for the remission of sins," ver. 3.

5. The occasion which might prompt him to enter on his ministry, viz., the ancient prophecy of Isaiah; Isa. xl. 3. The Holy Ghost, no doubt, bringing this into his mind, and discovering it to him, that he was the person there prophesied of, and that it was now in him to be fulfilled.

6. The end and grand design of his preaching, which was, " To prepare the way of the Lord;" and make a people ready to receive our Lord Jesus Christ, and to make known what great things our Saviour should do: viz., level mountains, and exalt valleys, &c.

From the main scope of these words, and design of John's ministry, it ap- The scope pears that he was an harbinger to Jesus Christ, and was to proclaim his near of the words opened. approach, &c.

From hence we may note, that this clearly showed to all, that Jesus Christ is a most glorious person, yea, a great and an almighty Prince; in that he had such a renowned person and prophet as John Baptist was, to be his harbinger, to usher him into the world: (Though our Lord vailed his glory at his first coming, that he might, in the days of his humiliation, the better accomplish the great work he came to do.) For our Saviour speaking of John, saith, that among all them born of women, there had not risen a greater prophet than John the Baptist; and that he was more than a prophet: He said more than any of the prophets could do; viz., that the Messiah was come, pointing to him, said, this is He.

2. From the whole matter contained in these symbolical expressions, we may clearly gather that the way of our Lord and Saviour, in order to the doing of the great work he came about, was rough and untrodden, even like a way through a wildernesss; and that he must fill up vallies, and bring down mountains, and make crooked things straight, and rough ways smooth; that so the glory of God might be revealed.

7

3. John was ministerially to signify these things must be done, but not that he was able to do them ; no, no ; but saith he, every valley shall be filled, and every mountain and hill shall be brought low, &c. Meaning that the Lord Jesus Christ should do these wonderful things ; and he was to give warning to the people, and tell them the Messiah was come, who should do these things, and so prepare them the better to look for him, and endeavour to find out the mighty things our Lord was to perform.

Therefore, they who call John the Baptist a pioneer to Jesus Christ ; or, one that was to fill up ditches, and throw down hills, &c. certainly greatly mistake the meaning of John in those metaphorical expressions. Could John level mountains, and fill up or exalt vallies ? no no ; it was to discover what our Lord Christ should do. Other ministers may as soon accomplish such mighty works as John Baptist ; as will appear, in opening what may, and doubtless is meant, by " Every valley being exalted, and every mountain and hill being brought low, and the crooked made straight, and the rough ways made smooth," viz.

1. And that I may come to speak hereunto, no doubt these things more generally signify, the removing of all those obstacles, difficulties, impediments, and stumbling-blocks out of God's way unto sinners, in order to their peace and reconciliation ; and also all obstacles and stumbling-blocks out of the sinner's way unto God : " Make straight a highway for our God, every valley shall be exalted," &c. For in both these respects there was such mountains of difficulties in the way, which none but Christ Jesus could remove ; but unless all those things were done of which John speaks, sinners could not be saved, nor the glory of God (personally considered) and also in all his attributes, be revealed. For evident it is this was the end and design of God ; in and by Jesus Christ as Mediator, by his " Levelling mountains and exalting vallies, " viz. " That the glory of God might be revealed."

Therefore let not any once think, that the bare opening the scope of these metaphorical Particular things in similitudes and Parables to be opened words is enough (and so in other symbolical and parabolical Scriptures) and that it favours more of wit than any solid judgment, to attempt to show, what may rationally be thought to be meant by mountains, hills, vallies, crooked things and rough ways.

1. Because it would render the Holy Ghost to multiply terms and words to no purpose. For why might not John rather have said all impediments or obstructions shall be removed out of God's way of saving of sinners, and not have told us of mountains, hills, and vallies ?

2. And also, that our Saviour himself used needless allusions in all those mysterious similitudes and parables he uttered, and indeed in which the greatest part of his ministry to the world did consist. It is not sufficient to open only the chief scope and design of our Lord in speaking of every parable ; for any so to say, it doth doubtless cast great contempt upon his sacred preaching.

3. Moreover, did not our blessed Saviour in all those parables and similitudes which he was pleased to expound unto his own disciples, open every part of them, as being significant ? See the " Parable of the sower," Mat. xiii., and that of the wheat and tares.

4. Consider what St Matthew saith about Christ's speaking in parables, similitude, &c. " All these things spake Jesus in parables, and without parables spake he not unto them ; that it might be fulfilled which was spoken by the prophet, I will utter things which have been kept secret from the foundation of the world," Matt. xiii. 34, 35. By this it appears, that under our Saviour's parables and symbolical allusions, that those mysteries of the gospel which were hid from the beginning of the world, are comprehended ; and therefore ought to be opened.

5. There are in parabolical Scriptures (as tropical writers observe) three things to be considered.

1. The root.
2. The bark.
3. The sap or fruit.

1. The root is the scope to which parables tend. (2.) The bark is the similitude itself. And, (3.) The sap or fruit ; is the mystical sense, &c.

Now according to these learned men some would have us to be contented with the root, and bark, without the fruit ; as if those fruitful trees were barren, dry, and sapless.

See the introduction. In opening parables, or such like dark Scriptures, we ought (I say again) well to eye the scope and drift of the Holy Spirit, which may be known from foregoing or subsequent things mentioned ; and we cannot err much, if our exposition of them agrees with the analogy of faith.

6. Though we readily grant, as the proverb is, metaphors and parables do not always

run on all four ; also, in some parables there are disparities ; as, when Christ's coming is compared to a thief, not like a thief unrighteously to rob and steal, &c. So much I thought good to premise, to make my way the easier in speaking to this dark similitude, or these metaphorical expressions.

2. I shall endeavour (God assisting) to open all theparts of these words, not The parts opened. straining any thing beyond the analogy of faith, though I will not presume to affirm every thing I may observe, is the direct meaning of the Holy Spirit, nor dare others in their expounding Scriptures less doubtful ; yet so that none shall see just cause to conclude, it is not the mind or sense of the Spirit.

3. I shall observe some propositions, or points of doctrine, from some of the chief parts contained therein.

1. But before I proceed, let it be considered (as I conceive) that the grand obstructions or obstacles which lie in the way of God's being reconciled to sinners, and of sinners' reconciliation unto him, are comprehended by these metaphorical expressions.

2. And that John foretels what our Lord Jesus Christ came to do ; " every valley shall be exalted, and every mountain and hill shall be brought low ;" that is, it shall be done by him (as if John should say) whose way I came to prepare.

3. Now what doctrine did John the Baptist preach, as Christ's forerunner ? Did it not end to exalt God's mercy to penitent believers ? Some poor sinners lay under The doctrine of John Baptist the apprehension of God's severe justice, and they could not see mercy raised up, but that divine justice was so magnified, that they saw not any ground to expect forgiveness by the mercy of a gracious God ; he declaring the soul that sinneth shall die, and they saw that they had sinned, and were become guilty before God ; and he saith, he will in no wise clear the guilty.

Every valley shall be filled ; that the people might know what our Lord would do, to exalt the mercy of God to undone sinners, who, like vallies, lay very low under despondency of spirit ; John bid them repent, which the law did not admit of : this word repent is a most sweet word, and tends to advance mercy and God's free-grace, and so to fill up those vallies, I mean despairing and desponding sinners. When God sends a messenger to rebels, and commands them to repent and believe, a sweet pardon be sure is A desponding sinner is a valley. comprehended therein ; and this tends to fill up or exalt two vallies.

1. The lowly and desponding soul.

2. The mercy of God is exalted, which was one grand design of God in sending of his Son to satisfy divine justice ; for mercy, and divine goodness, could not be raised to run level with justice, until our Saviour had made a complete satisfaction for our sins.

Every mountain and hill shall be brought low. Certainly by mountains and hills may be meant,

1. The haughty Jews and Pharisees, who were swelled with pride ; yea, like lifted up high mountains and hills ; how did the Pharisee glory, " God, I thank thee, I am Self-Righteous persons mountains not as other men, nor as this Publican ?" How did they boast of their own righteousness ; they not understanding the purity and holiness of the law, it never being opened unto them in the spirituality of it, they sought justification thereby ; " They being ignorant of God's righteousness, went about to establish their own righteousness." Rom. x. 3. Paul tells us, he was alive once without the law ; that is, when he was a pharisee. How without it ? had he not the law in the letter of it ? Yea, he had the law in that sense, and was not without it ; but he means, he was without the true knowledge of the law : I thought (as if he should say) I was safe enough, and a justified person, because I had not broken the law in the letter thereof, being no swearer, drunkard, adulterer, extortioner, &c. But now he saw every sinful thought and lust of the heart, was a breach of the law, and laid the soul under God's wrath and curse. And that no righteousness save the righteousness of God, can justify a sinner before him : but this the " Jews and pharisees saw not, but thought themselves righteous, and condemned others," Luke xviii. 9 ; and from hence were like lofty hills and mountains in their conceit : and these mountains John showed should be brought low, either in a way of mercy, as Paul was ; or else in a way of judgment, as the Jews and Pharisees who believed not.

2. They were like mountains, in respect had to their legal privileges, being God's covenant people, boasting " They had Abraham to their father, and never were in bondage," John viii. 33. John Baptist in his ministry strove to level these mountains, when he saw them coming to his baptism, " O generation of vipers, who hath warned you to flee from the wrath to come ? think not to say within yourselves, we have Abraham to our father "—— " Now is the axe laid to the root of the tree," Matt. iii. 7, 8, 9. He strives to cut them off

by the root ; namely, from having any spiritual advantages by the covenant with Abraham, as they were his natural offspring, as such.

Cotton on the
Covenant,
p. 21, 22. Mr. Cotton, speaking of John Baptist, saith, " The ministry of John the Baptist did burn as an oven, and left them neither the root of Abraham's covenant, nor the branches of their own good works ; he cutteth them off from the covenant of Abraham, and by cutting them off from the root, he leaveth them no ground to trust to."

Thus he says, God hath cut us off from the righteousness of our parents, and from boasting of his ordinances.

This John Baptist declared, and thus he laboured to prepare the way of the Lord ; who indeed utterly threw down these hills and mountains of the Jews' confidence, in their glorying of their legal covenant and birth-right privileges.

For, my brethren, what became of these mountains and hills, who were lifted up (by pride and vain boasting, that they were the church of God, the only people of God) when our Lord at his death took away that legal covenant and covenant-privileges ; utterly dissolving their national, legal, and typical church-state, and in its room erected his gospel-churches, his congregational churches ? These hills and mountains were then brought low, and that people were levelled with the Gentiles, who before were as vallies, but by our blessed Lord were filled up, and exalted, and made fellow-heirs of the same grace, that the Jews that believe partook of.

3. The Jews and Pharisees might be compared to mountains and hills, in that they boasted they had the key of knowledge, and were the only teachers and masters of Israel, and that all besides themselves were ignorant and foolish persons. Do but read what holy Paul speaketh of them, to bring them down level with the ground ; " Behold thou art called a Jew, and restest in the law, and makest thy boast of God. And knowest his will and approvest things that are excellent, being instructed out of the law. And art confident thou thyself art a guide of the blind, a light of them which are in darkness, an instructor of the foolish, a teacher of babes, which hast the form of knowledge, and of the truth of the law," Rom. ii. 17—21. See here how they were lifted up, and what mighty confidence they had of their knowledge and learning : but how low did our Lord bring these mountains and hills, and what contempt bring upon them, by his leaving lawyers, and pharisees, and learned Rabbins to themselves, and to the carnal confidence of their vain and fleshly minds, in rejecting of them, and not choosing one of them to be a disciple of his, and choosing poor fishermen, toll-gatherers, and such that were accounted unlearned and ignorant men ? " And when they perceived that they were unlearned and ignorant men, they marvelled, and they took knowledge of them, that they had been with Jesus," Acts iv. 13. No men who have not been with Jesus, or have not received ministerial gifts and graces from the Lord Jesus, is a true minister of the Gospel. My brethren, who were more ignorant of Christ, and of the mysteries of the Gospel, than the learned rabbins among the Jews ? " Nay, God hath hid these things from such, and hath revealed them to babes," Matt. xi. 25. And thus Christ brings low the mountains and hills, and exalts babes and contemptible persons (who are like vallies) to the honour of being his great ambassadors, and stewards of his sacred gospel mysteries. " Ye see your calling, brethren, how that not many wise men after the flesh, not many mighty, not many noble are called ; but God hath chosen the foolish things of the world to confound the wise," &c. 1 Cor. i. 26, 27. And thus Jesus Christ exalts the low, the humble person, who is like a valley, and brings the proud and haughty, (like mountains and hills) low ; making good or fulfilling the prophecy of Isaiah, " The lofty looks shall be humbled, and the haughtiness of men shall be bowed down. And the day of the Lord shall be upon every one that is lifted up, and he shall be brought low : and upon all the high mountains, and upon all the hills that are lifted up," Isa. ii. 11—14. See here how the Holy Ghost compares proud and haughty men to hills and mountains.

Secondly, sin (as Mr. Caryl notes, speaking of this very text) may be also meant by Our   sins
and   unwor-
thiness a
mountain. these mountains. Our sins and unworthiness, which is as a mighty mountain in our sight, when God opens our eyes ; nay, the mountain of our sins reached to heaven, calling for wrath and divine vengeance : yet our Lord Jesus Christ hath levelled this mountain, and hath thrown it into the sea. " Thou wilt cast our sins into the depths of the sea," Mich. vii. 19.

1. Jesus Christ hath removed the guilt of our sins, by bearing them upon his own body on the tree ; this part of this hill is brought low in our justification and free pardon. Oh, what a mountain of guilt lay upon us ! 1 Pet. ii. 24.

2. He hath also removed the filth of our sins in sanctification, by which he hath washed us by the operations of his Spirit, and by sprinkling of the virtue of his own blood upon our consciences. So that our sins and unworthiness (though like to great mountains) cannot.hinder us, nor any poor sinner that comes to Christ, to doubt of pardon, justification, and eternal life.

Thirdly, By mountains here also may be meant, or refer unto those great oppositions our Lord Jesus met withal, in his working out our salvation. (1.) From men. (2.) From the devil. These stood in his way like mighty mountains, like as Sanballet stood as a mountain in the way of Zerubbabel (a type of Christ) "And who art thou, great mountain? Before Zerubbabel, thou shalt become a plain," Zech. iv. 7. *Men and devils are like mountains in Christ's way, but are brought low.*

Fourthly, As vallies may refer to despairing sinners, so mountains and hills may refer to haughty and presumptuous sinners; I speak not here of self-righteous persons, but of profane and ungodly persons, who, though they are ungodly wretches, loving and living in sin, being swearers, drunkards, covetous persons, and idolaters, yet boast and glory in the mercy of God; that since Christ died for sinners, they say, they doubt not of being saved. These are swelled with a faithless confidence, a fond credulous presumption, arising from a groundless persuasion of the mercy of God and the merits of Christ. Yet, it may be joined with some sense, and convictions of sin and the dangerous consequences thereof; but presently all is salved with the common air and breath of a promise misconstrued, and falsely applied; they not experiencing the nature of the faith of God's elect, but are such whom God denounceth wrath and eternal death against.

Therefore this is more a fancy than faith, or a sure hope; and but a vain imagination that deludes them into a belief and expectation of that, which they are in no likelihood of enjoying; for that promise that gives us Christ, gives us also a new heart, but they find no thorough change in them; Christ came to save his people from their sins, not in their sins; or to "Redeem us from all iniquity," Tit. ii. 14, 1 Pet. i. 18, and from a vain conversation: but they are not thus redeemed; therefore they are but as mountains lifted up, or presume their state is good, and that they shall be saved, when they are at present in a state of death and wrath; and these mountains Christ came to bring low, and will level them with the ground, if ever he manifest his love and favour to them. They say, they are Christians, they believe in God the Father, and in his Son Jesus Christ, and rest on him; but yet are swearing Christians, lying Christians, drunken and whoring Christians, which is a direct contradiction. A Christian is one that is like Christ, a disciple of Christ; but they are more like the devil than Jesus Christ; yet nevertheless, though they are so notorious in sin and wickedness, doubt not of their salvation, but " Say in their hearts they shall have peace, though they add drunkenness to thirst," Deut. xxix. 19, 20. But see what God saith, and how he will bring these hills down, " The Lord will not spare him, but then the anger of the Lord and his jealousy shall smoke against that man," &c.

Fifthly, Vallies may refer to the low estate of mankind, or of God's elect, as considered dead in the first Adam, or as under the law and curse thereof: and mountains may refer to Satan, or those evil spirits, who were filled with pride, and were exalted on high in their hellish and diabolical power and kingdom over mankind. *Mankind naturally like a valley.* These spirits had man down under their feet by reason of the fall and their natural pravity, weakness, and inability that is in them, to withstand the force of this prince of the power of the air, who rules in all the children of disobedience, and hath all men naturally in his chains and fetters. O how high are devils exalted by means of our sin, over us naturally; and how low are we laid thereby! What dominion have the evil angels over all mankind until renewed! But now our blessed Lord came to bring these " Cursed mountains and high hills low;" i. e., to divest them of all their power, rule, and authority, which they have in the hearts of God's elect, while they abide in their natural state. " For this purpose was the Son of God manifested, that he might destroy the works of the devil," 1 John iii. 8. This was the end of the Son of God, or one design of his, in taking our nature and becoming Mediator betwixt God and man; viz. To pull down these lofty and haughty mountains and hills, or utterly to destroy the power of the devil, and the very basis and whole frame of his kingdom, and that " By his making an end of sin, and by bringing in an everlasting righteousness," Dan. ix. See what Paul saith, "And having spoiled principalities and powers, he made a show of them openly, triumphing over them in it, that is, by the blood of his cross," Col. ii.15. By this means he hath brought these mountains and hills low, he hath Satan and all evil spirits under his feet; Jesus Christ hath absolutely conquered, and disarmed all the whole infer- *Devils like hills and mountains.*

nal lake, or vanquished the power of all these cruel enemies of our souls. "By death he hath destroyed death, and him that hath the power of death, which is the devil; and delivered them who through fear of death, were all their life-time subject to bondage," Heb. ii. 14, 15. And as these mountains are brought low, so poor man, (I mean God's elect, or all that believe in Jesus, who were like to vallies) are filled or exalted: how high are the lowly, nay, poor fallen men and women, lifted up and exalted?

(1.) From a state of wrath to a state of grace.

(2.) From a state of death to a state of life.

(3.) From a state of condemnation to a state of justification.

(4.) From God's fearful curse, or curse of the law, to be blessed with all spiritual blessings in heavenly things in Jesus Christ.

(5.) From being the children of Satan, or children of wrath; to become the children of God, sons and daughters of God.

(6.) They being under the power of Satan, are brought into the kingdom of God's dear Son.

(7.) And being obnoxions to the wrath of God in hell, they are made heirs of eternal life, and of eternal glory in heaven.

Sixthly, mountains and hills may refer to every lofty imagination and high thought, that exalteth itself in believers, or that magnifieth itself against the knowledge of God, 2 Cor. 10. These mountains Christ doth and will bring low, and all those dejected spirits, who by reason of sin, and sense of their unworthiness, think themselves not worthy of the least bit of bread; and can hardly lift up their heads, being so oppressed and afflicted with the plague of inward corruption, or by means of that body of sin and death that is in them, they like low vallies shall be filled and exalted. "When men are cast down, then thou shalt say, there is a lifting up; and he will save the humble person," Job xxii. 29. "Let the brother of low degree rejoice in that he is exalted," Jam. i. 9; and such who were in a lowly condition are lifted up. By being in Christ he is a brother, and equal now in dignity and spiritual honour with the highest, and most noble, and richest Christian in the world, nay, if the poorest saint hath more grace, is most like Christ, he is lifted up higher than that brother who is rich in the world, that hath not arrived to his attainments. "But let the brother of high degree rejoice, in that he is made low," ver. 10; not made low as to his worldly riches, but low and humble in spirit. Riches make wicked men proud and haughty, they are like mountains, but when Christ comes and changes their hearts, though they be rich, yet are humble and lowly minded.

Seventhly, I might add, that mountains, &c., may in a remote sense refer to the proud and haughty monarchs of the earth, or to tyrannical kings and princes, whom the Lord Jesus will in the latter days bring low, and divest of all their power and kingdoms, and will lift up poor Sion, or exalt his church and people, who have been a long time as low vallies: "The mountains of the Lord's house shall be established in the top of the mountains, and shall be exalted above the hills," &c., Isa. ii. 2. They that are now in the valley, or are like vallies, shall then be like mountains, they shall be exalted; or such who are now like mountains and hills, shall then become vallies: God will turn the world upside down, Isa. xxiv. 1, 2; the wicked shall then be the tail, and the saints the head. The government of the world shall be in Christ's hand, and the people of the saints shall take and possess the kingdom to the end; yea, and all the kingdoms under the whole heaven shall be given unto them, Dan. vii. 27. So much as to vallies being exalted, and mountains and hills brought low.

"The crooked things shall be made strait."

What is meant by crooked things. 1. Crooked may refer to men's crooked opinions: they speak not right of God; they do not judge according to the straight and equal glory of all the perfections of God's holy nature; nor according to the strait rule of his holy law, but magnify the glory of his mercy, to the eclipsing the glory of his justice: and of this crooked opinion are the Socinians, and all that magnify the pardoning grace of God, without having respect to a plenary satisfaction, made to the justice and law of God by Jesus Christ. 2. The strait rule of the law is, that "He that doth those things shall live in them;" i. e., he only that never sinned, nor doth sin, shall be justified; so that none can be justified by the works of the law. But the Scribes and Pharisees, though their righteousness lay not even, or in a straight line with the law of God; but was crooked, sometimes much short on one hand, and wide on the other. For in many things they did not what the law required, and in other things they did what the law forbid, or commanded not; yet they thought none (in their opinions and lives) were more straight and even than they, when indeed none were more crooked: but these Pharisees, who were in opinion, principles, and practices, very crooked, Christ came to make straight; and such of them that believed, were set straight, both in faith and practice by him.

2. Crooked things may refer to those false and crooked ways of worship which many walk in ; ways which Christ never instituted or appointed: the word of God is the only rule for worship, and administration of ordinances ; now all pretended ordinances and divine worship, that doth not exactly agree with this rule, but vary in matter or manner from it, are crooked ways.

3. Crooked may refer to the lives and conversations of men, the law of God (as it is in the hand of Jesus Christ,) and the glorious gospel, is the only rule of our lives ; and all whose lives and conversations do not agree with that rule, are crooked ways. Therefore in all these respects, we should lay men's opinions, their doctrine, their worship and lives to the line and plummet ; and if they agree not, or lie not strait with the rule, line, and plummet, they are crooked things. Sin is a missing the mark, an erring from the rule, or transgressing God's law ; and so sinful ways are crooked ways. And as the gospel also is our rule in respect of our conversations, in its precepts, so also in what it holds forth. (1). In that hatred God thereby shows against sin, in punishing it in his own blessed Son. (2). In God's infinite love : O how are we taught of God to love him and one another, by the love of God to us in the gift of his Son ! (3). In pity and bowels of compassion to one another, when in want, sorrow, and afflictions ; for what pity and bowels of compassion doth the gospel hold forth was in God, to such who were in distress, want, and misery ! (4). In humility : what condescension and humility hath the Son of God showed ! " Who was in the form of God, and thought it not robbery to be equal with God, yet took upon him the form of a servant, and became obedient unto death even the death of the cross :" Phil. ii. 6, 8. Hence he says, " Learn of me, for I am meek and lowly in heart," &c. Matt. xi. 29. (5). In holiness : the gospel holds forth the infinite holiness and righteousness of God's nature ; in that without a perfect and complete righteousness no man can be justified in his sight ; as also in sending of his Son to wash away all our sins and filthiness in his own blood ; and in that the gospel also shows, that without regeneration, sanctification, and holiness, no man can enter into the kingdom, nor see his face. (6). In forgiveness : the blessed God hath laid down a rule in the gospel (in his free pardon and forgiveness of great sinners) for us ; that we might learn, how to forgive them that trespass against us : I might proceed to many other things ; and as what things the gospel holds forth, should be a rule to us how to walk in this world, towards God and man ; so the life of Christ and his apostles, is our pattern. And all men, whose lives and conversations do not accord, or agree with the precepts of the law in Christ's hand, nor according to what the Gospel holds forth, nor according to our holy pattern, they walk in their own crooked ways ; and Christ came to make men's lives straight, and that they might leave all their own crooked ways.

4. Crooked may also refer unto men's crooked spirits ; how cross and uneven are some men's hearts and spirits to the word and will of God. " The carnal mind is enmity against God, it is not subject to the law of God, neither indeed can be," Rom. viii. 7. But Jesus Christ, by the power of his Spirit, makes their hearts and spirits to lie straight and even with the word and will of God.

" And rough ways shall be made smooth."

Rough ways may denote, or set forth, those many obstructions and stumbling-blocks that are in the sinner's way ; their paths are rough, many obstacles and stumbling-blocks being in their way, in coming to Christ, and in closing with his church and people ; which Christ by his word, gospel-ministry, and by the operations of his Spirit, removes, and so makes their way smooth and even. " Cast up, cast up, prepare the way, take up the stumbling-blocks out of the way of my people, Isa. lvii. 14 ; which words may refer to the ministry of John Baptist, and to gospel ministers.

My brethren, God caused the ways to the cities of refuge under the law, to be very smooth, plain, and easy, for the man-slayer ; and ordered all stumbling-blocks to be taken up, and rough ways to be made plain ; which was a type of Christ's making the way of sinners easy in coming to him, and to the Father by him.

" And all flesh shall see the salvation of God."

This is the design of God in his levelling mountains, and filling or exalting valleys, and in making crooked things straight, and rough ways smooth. viz.

O that all flesh, that is, all men that believe, may, 1. See the glory of God's wisdom in his contriving the way of our salvation by Jesus Christ.

2. The glory of his infinite love, mercy, and divine goodness.

3. The glory of his infinite justice and holiness, in that his justice is as much exalted in and by Christ, as his love and mercy.

4. The glory of God's power, and his Almighty arm ; "Christ is the power of God, and the wisdom of God," 1 Cor. i. 24. All the divine attributes being united, or meeting together in sweet harmony in Jesus Christ; how Almighty is God in him to save lost sinners !

5. The glory of his truth and faithfulness.

6. The glory of his free grace, being exalted alone in our salvation, and sorry man utterly debased and laid low.

7. The glory of the holy law of God ; how is the law magnified and made honourable in Christ, who was born under it, and came to perform all that righteousness and obedience which it required of us, and in dying for us, to satisfy for our breach thereof !   Thus in respect of all the glorious attributes of God, the glory of God is in and by Jesus Christ revealed.

Secondly, take the glory of God here, for his glory personally considered, (1).   How doth the glory of God the Father shine forth herein, or what revelation is there of it in the gospel ! (2).   How is the glory of God the Son revealed also ! and, (3).   How is the glory of God the Holy Ghost likewise revealed and magnified !   And all this is done and displayed in Jesus Christ the Mediator.   And all flesh shall see it ;   that is, not the Jews only, but also the Gentiles, or all nations; i. e., some in all nations ; nay, the whole world at last.

From the opening these metaphorical expressions, two or three propositions or points of doctrine may be raised.

The Doctrine raised.   1. Doct. That there are many obstructions, stumbling-blocks, or difficulties that Jesus Christ must remove, to make the way of sinners plain and smooth unto everlasting life.

2. Doct. That the grand design of Christ in coming into this world, was to discover, reveal, and manifest the glory of God.

To fill every valley, and bring low every hill and moun-tain, &c.   I shall begin with the first of these propositions.

First, I shall show you further concerning those obstacles, difficulties, and stumbling-blocks, which lie in the sinner's way in respect to their justification before God and eternal life, which render the way rough, &c. Also show how the Lord Jesus Christ doth remove these stumbling-blocks.

First. As to the Jews, there were several stumbling-blocks in their way, as there are also now in the way of many persons in respect of their justification before God, and of eternal life, which tend to make the way rough.

The law and justice of God a mountain of difficulty,   1. The law and justice of God was as an obstacle in the sinner's way : Who could get over it ? Mount Sinai was a burning mountain, from whence proceeded fire and smoke, blackness, and darkness, and tempest, Heb. xii. 18, shadowing forth the terrible storms of God's wrath and indignation; which pursued the breakers of that law, to the lowest hell ; which made " Moses ex-ceedingly to fear and quake," verse 21.

But Jesus Christ by his obedience to the law, and, in bearing that wrath, punish-ment and curse due to us for the breach thereof, hath removed this stumbling-block or diffi-culty out of the way.

But the Jews did not (as many now a-days do not) see how this obstacle is removed, but they thought it possible to get over this mount, and it seemed to them but as a mole-hill, they thinking by their external conformity to the letter thereof, and so by their own legal righteousness, to be justified; not knowing that it required a perfect or sinless obedience, and that one sinful or evil thought was a breach thereof.

This was their ignorance, viz., they understood not the end, purpose, and design of God, in giving forth that ministration of the law upon Mount Sinai ; which was not given to the Jews (nor others) after sin entered, for life, to justify them before God.   But,

1. To make " sin appear exceeding sinful," Rom. vii. 13, and to discover how they (who were under that law) as well as the Gentiles, by violating the law, or works of the law, written in their hearts, were found guilty before God.   " Now we know that what-soever the law saith, it saith unto them that are under the law, that every mouth might be stopped, and all the world become guilty before God," Rom. iii. 19.

2. To show the need and absolute necessity of a perfect righteousness, which every way answered the strict requirement of the moral law ; and by the types and sacrifices of the ceremonial law, God showed the necessity of a sin-atoning sacrifice : " For it was

impossible that the blood of bulls and goats could take away sin, as to the conscience," Heb. ix. 13.

3.   Therefore the law in both respects served as a school-master, to lead sinners to Christ ; but neither of these they understood, but sought to be justified by their own imperfect righteousness.   And that the law was a stumbling-block to them, is evident by what Paul saith, " But Israel that followed after the law of righteousness, hath not attain-ed to the law of righteousness, Rom. ix. 31.   Wherefore ? Because they sought it not by faith, but as it were by the works of the law, for they stumbled at thatstumbling-stone," ver. 32.

Whosoever seeks justification or righteousness to justify them, by doing or by working in obedience to the law, or any law, and not by Christ's righteousness alone, in a way of believing, stumble ; the law is a stumbling-block to them, being ignorant of the righteous-ness of God, as the Jews were.   " For they being ignorant of God's righteousness, and going about to establish their own righteousness, have not submitted themselves to the righteousness of God," Rom. x. 3.   It is, as I have often told you, when the conscience of a sinner is awakened, and he sees his horrid guilt ; O then he seeks for help and relief by his prayers, tears, reformation of life, and not in and by Jesus Christ ; and at this stumb-ling-block many stumble and perish, this makes the sinner's way rough, which Christ in the ministry of the gospel makes smooth ; telling all both Jews and Gentiles, that by the " works of the law shall no flesh be justified," Rom. iii. 20.   " For had there been a law," (any law) " that could have given life, verily righteousness should have been by the law," Gal. iii. 21. Again, he saith, " If righteousness came by the law, then Christ is dead in vain," Gal. ii. 21.

Secondly, Jesus Christ himself was a stumbling-block to the Jews. " But we preach Christ crucified, unto the Jews a stumbling-block," 1 Cor. i. 23, not intentionally ; Christ is not the cause of their stumbling, but the object at whom they stumbled.

Quest. How came this to pass ?

Answ. 1.   They thought, that the Messiah when he came, would appear in great out-ward grandeur, as a mighty temporal prince, to save them from all their earthly enemies ; they not knowing, they needed a Christ to come to die for them, to save them from their sins, wrath, and all their spiritual enemies ; yet it was said in Daniel, the Messiah should be cut off.

2. And as they stumbled at his person, so also at his shameful and ignomi- The person nious death ; they could not believe nor once imagine, that they could be justi- of Christ a fied from sin by the obedience and righteousness of Christ, or by a person that block to the they hanged on a tree ; they could not see how their sins should be laid upon Jews. another, or one in the sinner's stead.

The Scripture saith, that the soul that sins shall die ; so that they could not see, how another should die in the stead, or room of the guilty criminal, or that God would accept of a surety, the just for the unjust.

Thirdly, the word of faith was another stumbling-block to the Jews, " Even The word of them that stumble at the word ;" (1 Pet. ii. 8.) or at the preaching of the Gospel : faith a our Lord told them, " That unless a man eat his flesh and drink his blood, he block. hath no life in him ——And when they heard this, they said, This is a hard. saying, who can hear it ?" (John vi. 53, 60).   By this eating, the Jews thought our Saviour meant a corporal eating ; " How can this man give us his flesh to eat ?" (ver. 52.) The papists say, it refers to a sacramental eating his flesh, of which our Lord speaks not ; men may eat of that bread, and drink of that cup in the sacrament, and perish ; but this eating is a believing in Jesus Christ, or apprehending, or receiving of him by faith, who only is the object of that faith, which is called justifying faith ; but this believing to righ-teousness, and justification, was a mere stumbling-block to the Jews ; and so it is to many in our days, who would eat their own bread, and drink their own drink, and wear their own apparel.

Fourthly, sin is another grand stumbling-block in the sinner's way, which Sin is a makes their way rough : O my sins are great, my sins are many, I am a vile stumbling-and a polluted wretch ; were I a righteous, a holy, and spiritual person (saith an the way to ungodly man) I could believe I might be justified. If I had a holy heart, and a salvation. holy life, or were I truly humbled, and broken for my sins, then I could venture my soul upon Christ.

Answ. 1.   Now to remove this stumbling-block, and to make the sinner's This stum-way smooth, Jesus Christ shows us in his word, that original sin, Adam's first sin, removed.

brought wrath and condemnation upon all mankind, or " Judgment came to all men unto condemnation, and so death passed upon all men," Rom. v.

2. Moreover, that the least actual sin is enough to damn the soul for ever ; yea, one evil thought, as well as ten thousand of the greatest sins, it being a breach of God's law.

3. Nay, If a sinner could live and not commit one sin, yet he could not be justified there-by ; for " I know nothing of myself, yet am I not thereby justified ;" or if Paul should say, admit I did not know any sin was in me, or now lived and sinned not ; yet my old sins, my former sins would condemn me, without I have the righteousness of Christ to stand in before God.

Sirs, all our sins, original and actual, before grace and after grace ; small sins as well as great sins, were laid upon Jesus Christ ; he bore the sins and punishment due for all the sins of God's people, both past, present, and to come ; all the whole debt is paid for God's elect, and this thou must believe, God in Christ is reconciled and pacified towards all that be-lieve in Jesus : and this is the way, by which he makes the sinner's way smooth, and re-moves this stumbling-block out of his way, 2 Cor. v. 18, 19 ; Rom. v. 10.

4. Sinners must not believe, that their forgiveness lies in their repentance and sorrow for sin, nor in their inherent holiness. I mean, it is not for the sake of their repentance, nor for the the worth of their faith, nor that their inherent holiness is any part, or matter of their justifying righteousness before God ; or for the sake and worth of which they are pardoned and justified ; but only by the active and passive obedience of Christ. " Be it known unto you therefore, that through this man is preached unto you the forgiveness of sins, and by him all that believe are justified from all things," Acts xiii. 38, 39.

5. Consider that repentance, sorrow for sin, and humiliation, faith itself, are the effects of Christ's death and merits ; and that all sense of sin, and such a believing or confidence, which an ungodly person may have, before he obtains a vital union with Christ, are but dead works, and profits no man to justification ; and know also, that true repentance, &c., is the immediate product of saving faith, though faith itself is a fruit of God's Spirit, Gal. v. 22. The sense of divine love in free forgiveness, works brokenness of heart, and true sorrow for sin. Can a malefactor be melted into tears, for his treason and rebellion against his lawful sovereign, when he sees he is condemned to die ? No, no, he is rather hardened against him ; but when he hears that there is a proclamation come forth of a free pardon for all his rebellion and abominable treasons, then he is melted and falls down at the feet of his gracious sovereign. So it is here.

6. To make the way yet more smooth and easy, God pronounceth a free pardon to the rebellious and stout-hearted ones who look unto him, " Hearken unto me, ye stout-hearted, that are far from righteousness ; for I bring my righteousness near unto you," Isa. xlvi. 12. Yea, such that are not only void of righteousness, but enemies to true righteousness and holiness of life, that despise God's counsel, and hate instruction and the knowledge of God. Sure this may tend to remove this stumbling-block, or raise these vallies, and level this mountain.

7. The blessed God is so gracious in Jesus Christ, that though he afflict thee for thy sins, and thou art never the better, but rather worse ; yet his free grace comes leaping over this mountain, and all impediments and unworthiness in us whatsoever. " For the iniquity of his covetousness I was wroth, and I smote him, and hid me, and was wroth," Isa. lvii. 17, 18. Well, and was he humbled ? No. " And he went on frowardly in the way of his heart ;" and what will God do now with him ? Will he not pour forth his anger, and con-sume him for ever ? No, no. " I have seen his ways, saith the Lord, and will heal him, and restore comfort to him." Ay, but saith a poor believer, I cannot pray, I have almost given quite over praying ; such a temptation thou mayest be under, and so it was with some of God's people of old : nay, and they were also weary of God's ordinances and holy worship ; yet see how God's free grace levels this mountain and removes this stumbling-block. " But thou hast not called upon me, O Jacob, but thou hast been weary of me, O Israel. Thou hast not brought me the small cattle of thy burnt-offerings, neither hast thou honoured me with thy sacrifices. I have not caused thee to serve with an offering, nor wearied thee with incense. Thou hast bought me no sweet cane with thy money, neither hast thou filled me with the fat of thy sacrifices ; but thou hast made me to serve with thy sins, and hast wearied me with thine iniquities," Isa. xliii. 22, 23. 24. Thou hast (as if Christ should say) made it necessary for me to take upon me the form of a ser-vant, that I might bear the weight and carry away the load of thy sins ; see how our

Lord aggravates the sins of his people, not to magnify his justice, but to exalt his mercy in his free pardon. " I, even I, am he that blotteth out thy transgressions for my own Name's sake, and will not remember thy sins," v. 25.

9. O what promises hath God made to great and notorious sinners ! " Though your sins be as scarlet, they shall be as white as snow ; though they be red like crimson, they shall be as wool," Isa. i. 18.

" I say unto you, all manner of sins and blasphemy, against the Father and the Son, shall be forgiven unto men," &c. Matt. xii. 31.

" Let the wicked forsake his way, and the unrighteous man his thoughts," or the man of iniquity, " the vilest man, and let him return unto the Lord, and he will have mercy upon him, and to our God, and he will abundantly pardon," Isa. lv. 7.

Let him believe in Jesus Christ, for there is no other way to return to God ; and then all their wicked, unbelieving, presuming, or despairing and blasphemous thoughts, shall be forgiven, and all acts of gross transgressions whatsoever.

10. What horrid and vile sinners hath God in a way of free grace through Christ pardoned! What a sinner was Manasses, Mary Magdalene, the Jews that cried, " let his blood be on us, and on our children," and who murdered the Lord of life and glory ! Paul, who persecuted the saints to death ; nay, what a sinner was Adam ? and yet was pardoied. What did God do for him ? what power had he to withstand all temptations ! *The greatness of* what a common head was he made to all his whole offspring ! what a stock *Adam's* had he in his hand ! and what ruin did he bring upon the whole world, as *first sin opened.* well as on his own soul ! what a God did he disbelieve, contemn and despise ! what a holy and blessed image did he deface ! what a vile devil did he obey, and set on his hellish throne ! And what a curse did he by his sin bring upon the whole Creation ! Moreover, what were some of the Corinthians ? 1 Cor. vi. 10, 11.

11. And lastly, what kind of sinners are invited to come to Christ, or to fly to God in him ? Such who are heavy laden with sin and horrid guilt, Matt. xi. 28. Backsliders from God, and such that had done as evil things as they could, Jer. iii. 5. And why is all this, but to magnify free-grace without works ; and to fill up vallies, and bring mountains low, and remove all stumbling-blocks out of the sinner's way, that the glory of God might be revealed ? But no more at this time.

II

Every valley shall be filled, and every mountain shall be brought low, and the crooked shall be made straight, and rough ways shall be made smooth.—Luke iii. 5.

THAT there are many mountains of difficulties that Jesus Christ must remove, and several stumbling-blocks which he must take up, to make the sinner's way smooth unto eternal life.

I have spoken already of four things, which are as mountains of difficulty or stumbling-blocks in the sinner's way, and have showed how Jesus Christ doth remove them. I shall now proceed,

Fifthly, there is another stumbling-block which must be removed, or as a great impediment, taken out of the sinner's way ; and that is, despair of the pardoning grace of God in and by Jesus Christ. *Despair like a deep valley, or a*

1. I shall show what despair is. *great stumbling block.*

2. Discover from whence it is, that this stumbling-block comes to lie in the sinner's way.

3. Show the great evil and danger thereof.

Note, despair, I have intimated, in opening these metaphorical expressions, is like a valley, and presumption as a mountain ; so it may be considered as a stumbling-block in the sinner's way.

2. Despair of any sufficiency in ourselves, of any worth, power, and strength of our own, is a holy despair ; and this valley of humility and self-abasement must never be

filled up; we must by no means allow of self-exaltation. " No flesh must glory in his presence," 1 Cor. i. 29. This I do not mean.

Despair of God's pardoning grace in Christ is that I speak of, which is either (1.) Private, a total privation of the habit of faith or hope; or, (2.) Negative, a cessation of the act or exercise of faith and hope, at least for a time, in the sense and discerning of the soul itself, arising through temptation, or weakness of grace, or from the want of the exercising of faith and hope in God. It is despair in this sense, I chiefly purpose to speak to.

1. Despair refuseth all manner of comfort, or hope of mercy, under those strong convictions the sinner hath of sin, wrath, and misery; he urging the sentence of the law, not considering the greatness of the grace of God in Christ; whereas faith and hope have to do with the promises.

2. Utter despair takes off the soul from inclining to embrace the free favour and rich grace of God in Jesus Christ; Faith and hope take hold of it, knowing " Where sin hath abounded, grace hath much more abounded." Rom. vi.

3. Despair sees more sin in the soul, than there is grace and pardon in Jesus Christ; but faith sees more virtue in Christ's blood, and favour through him in the heart of God, to justify and save the soul, than there is demerit in sin, to damn and destroy it.

4. Despair always pores upon sin, or on the disease of the soul; and sees not the cure; faith and hope eyes the Lord Jesus Christ, as that full and blessed remedy. " They said there is no hope," Jer. xviii. 21.

Despair (as one observes) is very peremptory and positive in concluding against itself; it is resolved upon nothing but death, sin he thinks being greater than can be forgiven to a lost and undone creature; as in the highest degree of faith and hope, there is assurance of salvation, so in despair there is a dismal and uncomfortable apprehension and persuasion of eternal damnation. But hope, though it may be accompanied with many fears and doubts, yet hath some grounded expectation of future happiness, and therefore in a patient and felicitous manner waits on God in the use of means for it.

Secondly, I shall show you from whence this stumbling-block comes to lie in the way of sinners.

From whence despair arises. 1. It ariseth from a sense that the sinner hath of the breach of God's holy law, and his severe sentence against all men thereupon, who saith, he will by no means clear the guilty. Now to remove this, consider, that the guilt of our sins was charged upon Christ as our Surety, and he hath made a full satisfaction to the law and justice of God; so that every soul that believes, shall be acquitted in a way of justice and righteousness, as well as in a way of grace and mercy.

2. But, saith the despairing sinner, I find naturally such pravity, such inward filth and corruption in my heart, that I may see there is no hope for me.

The woful state of sinners by nature.

Clarkson, p. 75.

Answ. 1. It is true, there is in all unrenewed persons a privation of power, an absence, a total privation; an absence not in part but in degrees; it is not only a suspension of acts, as may be in a man that is asleep, but in a man that is dead, when we were without strength; Nay, without life; not as an absence of power, as in sickness, but a total privation or absence of power. Also (as one notes) not only a total privation in the respect of power, but it is universal in respect of the subject of power, every part, every faculty is impotent, and depraved, yea, wholly deprived of power to act, do, stir or move, in a true spiritual manner; the will, the understanding, the affections, memory, conscience, &c.

3. Nay, and the soul is uncapable in a natural way to receive power as a branch that is cut off from a tree, and is withered, is incapable to become fruitful; it is such an incapacity as are in stones to become children unto Abraham; or that in dry bones to live, to be joined together, and to be animated, and made instruments of vital acts; nothing but infinite power can bring them together: regeneration is a new creation, it is God's workmanship.

It is not (as worthy writers observe) 2 Cor. v. 17; Eph. iv. 24, only a physical want of power; but a moral privation, a want of will, both unable and unwilling to be able, and also unable to be willing, without infinite power incline the will, and make it willing; " Ye will not come to me," John v. 40.

Life must be given before a sinner can breathe, stir, or move, in a spiritual manner; either to believe, repent, love God, subdue sin; faith, repentance, and love to God, &c., are given to a sinner. Sinners are in a wretched state. " Their thoughts are only evil, and that continually," Gen. vi. 5; their lusts have power over them, they have eyes full of adultery, that cannot cease from sin. Moreover, they are all in Satan's chains, he hath them under his feet. But what of all this? Is there no hope? Must a sinner despair because he cannot help himself, quicken himself, renew himself, and change his own heart? Though he may change his outward course of life, yet his heart will remain vile and filthy still. Yet sinners ought not to despair. For,

1. Consider, is not God able to put a principle of life into thee? Cannot he quicken thee, and put a new spirit into thee? **How this stumbling-block is removed.**

2. And hath he not promised to take away the heart of stone, and give a heart of flesh?

3. Were not·such who have got a new heart, and are renewed and do believe, once in the same condition thou art in, being dead, blind, depraved, filthy, carried away with folly and vanity as thou art?

Object. You say right, saith the despairing soul, I do not only want power, and am prone to all evil, but I find that I love vanity, and my vile lusts; and I find in me an indisposition to that which is good, and this stumbles me: sin is sweet, the world is pleasant, carnal company desirable. But I find no propensity, no desire, no love to, nor any delight in spiritual things; nay, and not only an indisposition to good, but also an averseness, a hatred thereunto; " There is enmity in my carnal mind against God and spiritual things," Rom. viii. 7; so that such things are wearisomeness to me, therefore I give up all hope, and cannot believe.

Answ. To answer this, suppose thou art as bad as sin and the devil can make thee. **Encourage-ment to sin-ners to be-lieve in Christ.**

1. Yet is not God able to change that vile heart of thine? Cannot he destroy that enmity that is in thee, and cause thee to love him, and hate all sin?

2. Were not those St. Paul speaks of, as bad as thou art? viz., " Thieves, covetous, drunkards, revilers, extortioners, idolaters, adulterers, effeminate persons, abusers of themselves with mankind : and such were some of you, but ye are washed, but ye are sanctified, but ye are justified," 1 Cor. vi. 9, 10, 11.

3. You can be but sinners, and not worse than the chiefest of sinners, and Jesus Christ came into the world to save such. This is a " saying worthy of all acceptation, that Christ Jesus came into the world to save sinners, of whom I am chief," 1 Tim. i. 15. But why, Paul, didst thou obtain mercy? see ver. 16, " That in me first Jesus Christ might show forth all long-suffering for a pattern to them, which hereafter should believe on him to everlasting life. Were not his sins as great as thine, and his heart as much depraved, his will as rebellious? O then look up to God for help, and cry for faith to believe, and resolve to venture on the Lord Jesus Christ. I told you the last day, what great sinners (besides Paul) found mercy.

4. God hath sent me to you in this place, to treat with you as a poor despised ambassador, and to offer peace to you, though you have been long rebellious against him, and what though you " Have spoken and done as evil things as you could?" Jer. iii. 5. So had they God offered mercy to, Jer. iii. 5. " Now then we are ambassadors for Christ, as though God did beseech you by us, we pray you in Christ's stead, be you reconciled to God," 2 Cor. v. 20. The ministration of the gospel is ordained to that end, that sinners might believe; and God hath promised it shall accomplish that for which he hath sent it, Isa. lv. 11. It shall come to some in " power and not in word," only, 2 Thes. i. 4, 5. And why not so to you? Cannot you say with the poor man in the gospel, " Lord, I believe, help thou my unbelief," Mark ix. 24. The more impotent you are, the more need to look to Christ for help: " For without him you can do nothing," John xv. 5.

5. If ye perish, it is not only because you are great sinners (though sin is the procuring cause thereof) but it is because you refuse to look to Christ, or refuse to accept of Jesus Christ, or despair of God's mercy in him, even as they perished in the wilderness, who refused to look up the brazen serpent; " If ye believe not that I am he, ye shall die in your sins," John viii. 24. What, neither believe God, when he saith there is life in his Son? Not believe Christ, who saith, " Whosoever cometh to me I will in no wise cast them out," John vi. 37; nor believe his ambassadors? But what cause or reason have you to conclude there is no Christ, no grace, no faith for you? Is there not less cause or ground for you to despair or to doubt, than the Jews had that put our Lord to death, and many others I have mentioned?

6. Consider how soon God was reconciled to Adam; and whose sin was worse than his? Who was made ruler and lord of this nether creation; who had no spot, no stain of sin, nor inward pollution in him, who had power to stand; he was a free-willer indeed, and none but he had power of himself to will and do that which was good; he was set up as a common head of all his posterity. If thou sin, thou dost but murder thyself, or destroy

thine own soul; but he by his first sin murdered millions of millions, even the whole world; yet he believing the free promise of God in Christ, was pardoned.

7. That God should be reconciled in Christ, fully reconciled; so that all his wrath is over, and "No fury in him" (Isa. xxvii. 4,) to all that fly to Jesus Christ, who hath borne all God's vindictive wrath and justice. God is not in Christ only reconcileable, (as some speak) but he is reconciled; if it were not so, what can reconcile him, or what can appease his anger? Can any thing but a sacrifice? And is there any other sin-atoning and wrath-appeasing sacrifice, to be offered up to God? Can men's believing, repenting, or obedience, reconcile God to sinners? Doth Christ's obedience make God reconcileable, and sinners' obedience reconcile him? Which then ought to have the greatest glory, Christ, or sinners? Come, a free pardon is offered to you once again, upon your acceptance of Jesus Christ; for God is so reconciled in his Son, that he doth discharge, pardon, and acquit all those that believe in him, without a satisfaction made by sinners to his law and justice, and without any foreseen faith or obedience (to any such end or purpose) done by them, and without anything wrought in them: faith does not make the obedience and death of Christ satisfactory unto God, it adds no worth to Christ's merits. Oh! admire free grace, what love and favour is this!

Should a sinner lie a thousand years in hell, and bear a part of God's vindictive justice, and yet then through Christ's blood and satisfactory sacrifice, be discharged and redeemed out of it; all must say that would be great grace; but such that believe, bear no part of his vindictive wrath; we pay not one farthing of that debt (nor were we able) which we owed to God's justice: no, Christ hath borne it all, he hath paid all that we stood charged with.

8. God is reconciled for ever to such that believe, and no new war shall ever arise between God and them; the league and covenant of peace can never be dissolved, never be broken, "Sion's warfare is accomplished, her sins are pardoned, for she hath received double for all her sin," Isa. xl. 1, 2. Christ's satisfaction was a double payment, nay, (as Mr. Caryl notes) it was an hundred-fold more than enough, considering the infiniteness of the worth of his person. Our comfort is this, our warfare is ended, and the fruits of Christ's death is not only pardon of all our sins, but a double favour; not only a discharge from hell, but grace, adoption, sonship; nay, a marriage with Christ, and glory in heaven for evermore.

Thirdly. It is not only from the sense of God's law being broken, or their sins very great, and their state deplorable, that some despair, "But by reason they have found all

Some stumble and despair because the means of grace hitherto have been ineffectual to them.

means of grace hitherto ineffectual, or insufficient to them, to this very day." I have (saith a doubting and despairing sinner) heard many most excellent sermons, I have sat under a powerful ministry, and yet I find I cannot believe, I am still in my sins, and as bad as ever: nay, I have had strong convictions sometimes, but they are gone off; I have sinned against light, promises, and solemn covenantings with God, when under his rod, &c.

Answ. To take up this stumbling-block.

1. May be thou comest to hear men, and not Christ, speak to thee; or hadst too great an eye upon the instruments by whom the gospel is administered; alas! what means this great noise that is abroad, of crying up one, and crying down another free-grace preacher? The people of this age are carnal: one is for Paul, and another for Apollos. Sirs, the efficacy of the word lies not in the gifts, learning, eloquence, or abilities of ministers, but alone in the agency of the Holy Spirit; "We have this treasure in earthen vessels, that the excellency of the power may be of God, and not of us," 2 Cor. iv. 7.

2. Or may be, you looked for the efficacy and divine power to lie in the bare word; alas, the Word is like Christ's flesh, without the Spirit it quickeneth no man, it profiteth no man. John vi.

3. Or may be, you have heard the word out of curiosity, or to feed your heads only with notions and speculative knowledge.

4. Or (perhaps) never prayed to God before you came to hear, that he would bless the word to your conversion; for though God will do all that he hath promised, yet he will be sought unto by poor creatures, that he may do it for them. "I will cry unto God most high, to God that performeth all things for me," Psal. xxxvii. 2. Or,

5. May be, the day of God's power was not, is not yet come: you must wait (as the poor man did) at the pool though it be thirty-eight years; the time of healing may come at last. "In the day of God's power," John v. 2, 3, 4, 5; Psal. cx. 3; conviction shall never finally go off.

Fourthly. Despair may arise from Satan's temptations, he hath many **Despair arises from Satan's suggestions.** ways to cause doubts and fears to rise in the mind of a poor sinner, and be sure all despairing thoughts that rise in the heart are from Satan.

1. May be thou dost believe and hast hope, but because thy faith is small and weak, the devil will call it despair; he would make thee believe a little grace is no grace; he will argue from thy weakness in grace, thy total want of it; as he persuades some that are strong in faith, that their confidence is nothing but presumption.

2. Consider all true faith is mixed with some doubts; is our faith, our love, our patience, our humility perfect? Who can say he believes, and has no unbelief, and has no want of love to God and Jesus Christ? Who is so meek, that never was angry, or so patient, that he never did unduly complain, or so humble, that he never had one high thought of himself? I shall now proceed to the next thing proposed.

Secondly, viz. speak a little to that great evil and danger of despair and unbelieving thoughts.

I. Consider, that despair casteth contempt upon the word of God, and upon **The end and danger of despair.** the ministers of Christ; for both declare how ready, able, and willing God is to embrace and save all that come to him by Jesus Christ; such that despair, render the word and ministers of Christ liars, and not to be regarded in what they say and testify.

II. But this is not the worst, for despair and unbelieving thoughts cast contempt upon God himself, and on most of his holy attributes. (1.) On his mercy in Christ, which is infinite. (2.) On his justice, which is fully satisfied, towards all them that believe. (3.) On his power, who is able to do more abundantly than we can conceive or think. " He is able to save to the uttermost all that come unto God by him," Heb. vii. 25; and the like might be said in respect of his wisdom, love, truth, and faithfulness.

III. Despairing and unbelieving thoughts, cast contempt upon that fulness that is in Jesus Christ, on the fulness of his merits and righteousness, and upon the efficaciousness of his blood; also it casteth contempt upon the faithfulness and gracious promises of our Lord Jesus Christ.

IV. The evil of despairing and unbelieving thoughts are aggravated by the clearness and fulness of that testimony God hath given of the freeness of his grace, in the pardon of sin to all that believe.

1. The Father bears witness.

2. The Son bears witness.

3. The Holy Ghost bears witness, that whosoever cometh to Christ, " Believes in Christ, shall not perish, but have everlasting life," Mark xvi. 16, John iii. 16.

4. And Christ's faithful ministers bear witness also, how ready God is to receive all such.

V. Despair is aggravated, by God's gracious performance of his free promises to the greatest sinner, to thousands of sinners; yes, to every individual sinner that ever threw himself upon his mercy, believing in Jesus Christ; multitudes have tried God's faithfulness in his promises, and have found his word a sure word, a tried word; who had no other ground to believe but what you have: if never any sinner who cast himself upon God in Christ in a right manner, missed of pardon and free justification, what a sin is it for any to say, as to me, there is no hope?

VI. The evil and danger of despair is also aggravated, in that those very persons will and can believe mortal men, who are faithful in respect of their promises; and yet will not believe and trust a faithful God, and the ever-blessed Redeemer, who cannot lie; so that the credit and reputation of God (it seems) is gone with these persons; men in this case are greatly enraged and wounded, *i. e.*, if they cannot be believed nor trusted, who are both able and faithful persons.

VII. Such that despair, or believe not, give more credit to Satan, or believe the devil more than God : Satan puts these despairing and unbelieving thoughts (as you heard) into their hearts. O sinner, sinner, will you believe the Devil, rather than the most high and faithful God of heaven and earth ?

VII. Despair exposeth a sinner (as it hath many a one) to destroy both body and soul for ever; how many in despair have destroyed themselves, by self-murder, by hanging, drowning, and by cutting their own throats ?

IX. It renders preaching vain, as to them " The word preached did not profit them, not being mixed with faith in them that heard it. Can God spread a table in the wilderness ? " Can God, or will he pardon my sins ? Such that believe not, profit not under the word.

X. Despair upholds and strengthens Satan's kingdom in the sinner's heart, and in the world, and binds the guilt of all sin, the curse of the law, and the wrath of God, upon the unbelieving and despairing person.

To remove this stumbling-block, I shall but add one or two things more.

The greatest sinner is allowed to believe on Christ. 1. Consider, O sinner, that thou art allowed, or admitted to believe in Jesus Christ, whosoever thou art. If meat be set upon a nobleman's table, with a free admittance of all that come to eat ; certainly, no hungry man need to fear, but fall on and fill his belly : why should he say, I shall perish with hunger, when he is come to such a plentiful banquet ?

He is invited to come and eat. 2. And not only are all allowed to eat and spare not, but they are invited by this great God, to come and feed on his dainties.

Nay, commanded to believe. 3. Nay, which is more, they are not only allowed to eat, and invited to this feast, but commanded to eat, and drink abundantly : if thou art a sinner, thou art commanded to believe, commanded to eat; "This is his commandment, that ye believe on his Son Jesus Christ," 1 John iii. 23.

4. And thy refusing to eat, or to come to Christ, or to believe on him, will grieve him ; and know it is the greatest sin not to believe on Christ.

5. Besides you must eternally perish if you do not believe, therefore endeavour to come, labour to believe ; at your utmost peril, see you do not refuse to do it. Do not say you cannot believe, but exercise such a faith as you can, or are able to do.

How a weak christian may be relieved. Secondly, as to such who do not utterly despair, but are attended with doubts and fears, or who are betwixt hope and despair. I shall add a word or two by way of direction to them.

1. Consider, it is not the degree of grace, but the truth of grace to which salvation is promised : therefore,

2. Put a just value upon the lowest degree of faith, and let it not seem contemptible in thy sight ; let it not appear as nothing, though it be as small as a grain of mustard-seed, for it is of more worth than the whole world.

3. Labour to distinguish between the weakness of grace, and grace itself under that weakness ; and whilst you are mourning under one, be sure that you rejoice in the other. Do **See the Parable of the lost groat.** not cast away a bit of bread because thou hast no more, nor throw away one corn with the chaff; if it be but a lost groat, do not sweep it up with the dust behind the door. Christ came to seek a lost groat.

4. Consider the many promises, which are made to the weakest degree of grace ; Jesus Christ will not quench the smoking flax, nor the bruised reed. If there be in thy heart a hatred of sin, and a sense of the want of righteousness, thou being taken off from resting on any thing short of Christ, thou hast no cause to doubt.

5. Consider, to deny the least degree or measure of grace in us, against clear demonstrations and evidences brought to convince us of it, is to be cruel to our own souls ; nay, and (as one observes) it is a kind of denying of Jesus Christ. I have (saith he) sent in provision into such a soul, and have often bid him eat ; and he says, there is nothing before him. Is not this an affront put upon the Lord Jesus ?

6. Christ will make weak grace victorious, all the devils of hell cannot quench the least degree, smallest spark of true grace in the soul ; and it shall in due time become strong and mighty through God.

7. All graces are mixed (as I have often told you) with their contraries ; no faith but is mixed up with some unbelief at first ; no hope without some kind of despair ; nor humility without some pride ; no grace is perfect ; that which is perfected, is not yet come : because thou hast a weak eye, wilt thou say thou art quite blind. And to accept of a small favour, is the way to receive a greater.

USE

1. Let us dread all despair and unbelieving thoughts, about God's mercy, free grace, justification, and pardon in Christ ; since the evil and danger of this sin is so great.

2. We infer also, that God is infinite in his patience and forbearance towards sinners in preserving of such, and calling to them, and in crying after them who cast such horrid contempt upon him ; yea, and upon his goodness, power, truth, and faithfulness.

3. Admire the grace and goodness of God, in his continuance and renewal of the offers of pardon, to such unbelieving and desponding sinners ; also admire the love of Jesus Christ, who is come to fill the vallies, and level the mountains; and to remove all obstacles and stumbling-blocks out of the sinner's way.

4. O what encouragement is here for great sinners, old sinners, backsliding sinners, Jer. iii. 12, to believe in Christ ! What though thou art the worst of men, the greatest of sin-

ners, and under matchless guilt ; let it be so, and thou art under the blackest character, yet there is hope ; " Thy scarlet sins shall be made as white as snow," Isa. 1, 18. i. e. they shall be washed away in Christ's blood that very moment that thou believest in him. What though thou art without Christ now, without God, and without hope ; so were they Paul speaks of, Eph. ii. 12. Christ is offered to sinners as sinners, he came to call sinners. The whole need not a physician, but they that are sick ; and such that believe not, sin grievously.

5. Let all tremble who believe not, because their sins are so great, and they are not humbled enough, as they say ; such are digging up the foundation of God's free grace, as much as lieth in them ; the greater your sins are, the more need you have of a Saviour : the more polluted, the more need you have to go to the fountain to be washed ; the sicker thou art, the more need thou hast of a physician.

6. You can have no true and well-grounded hope, until you believe in Christ, or come to him ; nothing can secure you from God's divine wrath and vengeance ; no, not your praying, not your hearing, not your sorrow for sin, not your tears, not the reforming your lives ; all is vain, until you believe in Christ, or rest on him.

Lastly, you that do believe, strive for a greater faith ; some see not, and yet believe : O give all the glory unto God, and to Christ ; let us assume none of it to our selves, nor ascribe it to faith ; but to him, who is the Object and Author thereof.

III

Every valley shall be filled, and every mountain shall be brought low, &c.—Luke iii. 5.

DOCT. That there are many mountains of difficulties that Jesus Christ must remove, and several stumbling-blocks taken out of the way of sinners, to make their way smooth to eternal life.

The last day I spoke of despair, which is a great stumbling-block in the way of some sinners, and showed how the Lord Jesus removes that.

Presumption is a stumbling-block in the sinner's way.

Fifthly, presumption is another mountain Christ came to bring low ; or, as it is a stumbling-block, to take up out of the sinner's way.

Some are so far from despairing, that they are very confident of their salvation, and doubt not, but pretend they wholly rest upon Jesus Christ, and yet go on in a wicked course of life ; are earthly, covetous, proud, loose, vain, and carnal ; find no change of heart, no regeneration, no sanctification ; yet say, they doubt not of being saved : and it may be, there are more that stumble here than fall into the ditch or valley of desperation : though Christ says, " Except a man be born again, he shall not enter into the kingdom of heaven," John iii. 3. And " that without holiness, no man shall see the Lord," Heb. xii. 14 ; which consisteth in a spiritual conformity to God, and is peculiar to all God's elect that are called ; is the result and quintessence of all the graces of the Spirit, and effects of the death and resurrection of Jesus Christ, and fruits of true faith, and of our union with Christ. Moreover, as the body without the Spirit is dead, so faith without proper fruits is dead also. See the opening of the words, page 11.

I shall here speak of this stumbling-block, I mean presumption ; in respect had to four sorts of people, besides them I have mentioned.

1. Some like the Jews (of whom I have spoken) presume on their own righteousness ; and what is that ? Why, a sober and moral life, doing to all men as they would be done unto ; or by living up to the light and dictates of natural conscience ; this is good, but such that depend on this, trust to this, make faith void, and intimate that Christ is dead in vain. To this sort I may add and rank all those, who pretend to a Christ within ; they give a new name, a blasphemous name to this inward light ; but their whole religion is no more than that of a sober moral man's (and some of them have not that) yet presume and boast of an absolute perfection in themselves, by the light within, casting See Pen's contempt on a Christ without, and on his imputed righteousness in justification. Sandy Foundation Shaken.

Moreover, there is among these, another sort near of kin to them (who are like mountains lifted up, that God in due time will bring low) who magnify natural religion, light and knowledge of Christ crucified, and like the Greeks of old, call it The deist foolishness ; nay, decry all revealed and supernatural religion. They pretend condemned.

to own and acknowledge a God, but deny he is such a God as his holy word declares him to be ; viz., one infinite, simple, and entire essence, subsisting in three distinct Persons ; they deny Christ and the Holy Spirit, to be God equal with the Father ; and also affirm, that God is made up wholly of mercy and goodness, and that they believe not, that justice is such a property of his very being, that he cannot, will not pardon sins, as a simple act of mercy, without a satisfaction to his law and justice.

Yet they seem to commend moral virtue, like the old heathen, saying, God will reward it here with inward serenity of mind ; nay, and will also eternally, seeing it so well suits with his goodness and benignity : but that it doth not suit with his goodness nor justice, to punish sin with eternal torments.   Because (say they) there is no proportion between temporal guilt and eternal punishment, they neither consider the na- ture of God, against whom sin is committed ; nor the nature of the soul of man, who offends and sins against this God ; nor will they give credit to the testimony of his unerring word.

How could God then in justice af- flict and pun- ish his own Son for our sins, in his body and soul ?

And from hence these wretched persons, who are swollen up with pride and presumption, intimate that wicked men need not fear any hell, but only an in- capacity for heaven, thinking that natural religion is a sure title for it, and that which makes men meet for it also ; so that according to them, the vilest sinner can but only expect a sentence of being eternally annihilated, or cease for ever to be, or lose their beings ; and thus they open a door to all profaneness, by exempting sin- ners from hell flames, and strokes of God's divine vengeance.

These men boast of human reason, and will believe nothing but what they can compre- hend, or give a reason of ; and say that there is no mystery contained in the gospel, though the Holy Ghost testifies that " without controversy, great is the mystery of godliness, God manifested in the flesh," 1 Tim. iii. 16, &c.   And strange it is, that they should affirm they will believe nothing in divine things, that is above their reason and compre- hension ; and yet are forced to confess, that there are many things in nature they cannot, nor could any mere man comprehend, or give a reason of.

Above reason (as one notes), is an equivocal expression, and signifies two things.

Mr. Peter Brown.

1. It signifies a thing which does not exceed our powers of understanding ; but is concealed from us, and lies out of our reach, by some accidental impedi- ment or obstruction, which is impossible for us to remove.   And in this sense, it is above our reason to know certainly what is the centre of the earth, or the cause of the flowing and ebbing of the sea, or the true motion of the heavenly bodies, and what order they ob- serve amongst themselves, and the different configuration of the little parts of matter, &c. That which makes those things above our reason, is not something essential to them, but it is that ignorance that is in us ; therefore our knowledge of them is improved by the help of glasses, &c., so that we may say they were above our reason, before such helps were found out.

2.   Things may be above our reason in their own nature, exceeding our capacities, and are no proper objects of those faculties of knowledge, which we are now endued withal : and in this sense the nature and being of God, Father, Son, and Spirit, in one entire and individual essence ; the mystery of the union of the two natures in the person of Christ, and that of the incarnation, and the manner of the operation of the Holy Ghost ; as also the mystery of the resurrection, and many other things, are more properly above our rea- son, than earthly things are ; as eternity than time ; a spirit than a body ; the joys of hea- ven, than sensual pleasures ; the eternal generation of the Son, than the ordinary procrea- tion of man ; the operations of the Holy Spirit, than the nourishment of our bodies : there is as yet no proportion between these objects and faculties of knowledge. Our intellectual powers are not get formed and so adapted to them, as they are for those things in nature ; and though the Spirit reveals to believers greater knowledge than any mere natural man hath of them, yet St. Paul himself saith, " He knew but in part, and saw darkly, as through a glass," 1 Cor. xiii. 12. " What man knoweth the things of a man, save the Spirit of a man that is in him ? even so the things of God knoweth no man, but the Spirit of God," 1 Cor. ii. 11. " For the natural man receiveth not the things of God, for they are foolishness to him ; neither can he know them, because they are spiritually discerned," ver. 14. From hence it appears, these mere natural men are ignorant of gospel mysteries, and being under Satan's influences, they speak thus, and fain would overthrow the whole of the Christian religion ; but their folly is made manifest, and these mountains and hills Christ will bring low. " They professing themselves to be wise, they become fools," Rom. i. 22.

II.   There is another sort, who have greater light and knowledge, as touch-   Baxterian-ism condemned.
ing the Christian religion, and the necessity of Christ's obedience, and dying
to satisfy divine justice ; yet conclude Jesus Christ having made a full compen-
sation for the breach of the law of works, or the law of perfect obedience, hath abrogated
that law, and taken it away, and hath merited a mild law of faith and sincere obedience ;
so that faith in the largest sense, viz., faith, repentance, and sincere obedi-
ence, through Christ's merits, is that righteousness which justifies us before God,   See Mr. Sam. Clark of Wickham's Scripture Justification.
even so far as we have attained ; for they declare that justification is imperfect,
as well as inherent sanctification, until death.

Thus these men presume upon their own inherent righteousness, and so go
about to overthrow the doctrine of free justification by the righteousness of God.   To level
these mountains, the Holy Ghost declares,

1.   That the righteousness that justifies a sinner, is a free gift ;   " But the free gift is
of many offences to justification.   They which receive abundance of grace, and of the gift
of righteousness," &c. Rom. iv. 16, 18.   How can a righteousness wrought out by us, be
a free gift ?

2.   It is the righteousness of one, not of many, not every man's own righteousness;
" For as by one man's disobedience, many were made sinners ;   so by the obedience of
one, shall many be made righteous," ver. 19.   Adam's sin was counted to us, or imputed
to all men, as he was a common head of all his seed ; so Christ's righteousness is counted
to us, or imputed to all his seed, as he is their common head.

3.   That righteousness that justifies a sinner in God's sight, is imputed, not inherent
in us, but put upon us, counted or imputed ;   " Blessed is the man to whom God imputeth
righteousness," &c., Rom. iv. 6.   And that righteousness might be imputed to them.   Also
" He was made sin for us who knew no sin, that we might be made the righteousness of God
in him," 2 Cor. v. 21.   Now Christ was not inherently a sinner, but by imputation of the
sins of the elect to him;   even so that righteousness by which we are justified, is not inherent
in us, but imputed to us.

4.   That righteousness that justifies us is called the righteousness of God, in contradiction to the inherent righteousness of a mere man :   it is called the righteousness of God,
because Christ is God as well as man ; it is not the essential righteousness of God, but the
meditorial righteousness of God-man, Christ Jesus :   " They being ignorant of God's righteousness, went about to establish their own righteousness, and have not submitted themselves to the righteousness of God," Rom. x. 3.   Though these swelling mountains would,
yet " Paul would not be found in his own righteousness, but in the righteousness of God,"
Phil. iii. 8, 9.

5.   That righteousness that justifies a sinner, is a righteousness without works ;   works
are works, whether legal or evangelical.   " Even as David also describeth the blessedness
of the man, to whom God imputeth righteousness without works :   to him that worketh
not, but believeth on him that justifies the ungodly, his faith is counted for righteousness,"
Rom. iv. 5, 6 ; that is, Christ's righteousness received by faith, faith objectively, not subjectively taken.

6.   The righteousness that justifies a sinner is a perfect righteousness, answering to
the pure nature of God, and his holy law ;   but our inherent righteousness is imperfect
and as filthy rags ;   therefore must these mountains be brought low.   A new law !   Why
did not God give this law of faith and sincere obedience at first ?   And so have saved the
precious blood of his Son from being shed, to purchase a law of imperfect obedience ; but
pray did the law of perfect obedience only result from the sovereignty of God ; and not
rather from the rectitude of his holy nature ? if from the first they may conclude, God
repenteth he gave such a severe law, the removing of which cost him so dear.

Take what a learned man speaketh on this occasion, " Could not man keep   Mr. Cross—the new Law detected.
the law of works ?   Then it seems, the first law was too strict ; this reflecteth
upon the wisdom and justice of God : it must be granted, that perfect man
could observe a perfect law, had God given him grace and assistance sufficient to his state
and necessity ; and so there was no need the law should be altered, and the obedience,
the condition of it changed from perfect to imperfect.   For if perfect man could not keep
the law of perfect obedience, with sufficient grace, how should sinful man perform the law
of sincere obedience, having no more than sufficient grace to assist him ?   Did not God
foreknow that man would break the law of works, and so was necessitated to make a
new and more easy law ?   Or, did not God both foreknow and permit the fall of man,
or could he not have hindered it ?   Why then should he give way to the abrogating the

command of perfect obedience, to bring in that of imperfect. Surely (as Augustine saith) God is so just, that he can allow of no evil; and so good, that he can permit no evil; except it be with a design to bring greater good out of it. If God permitted the first covenant to be broken, that thereby he might abase man, and magnify his own grace and his Son; in bestowing heaven freely on him, and in bringing him thither by the continued power of pardoning and sanctifying grace; hereby God indeed doth advance his own glory, by changing of the covenants.

" But that the condition of perfect obedience, being broke by man's sin, the law therefore should be disannulled, and a new way of treating with man set up, wherein still man should be something, and his works bring about his own salvation, and God be contented with few and very imperfect acts of obedience; this certainly is a prejudice to his honour; nor doth this make it up, *i. e.*, that our obedience is accepted for Christ's sake; for Christ only made way for removing the old covenant (say they) and the granting a new, but he did not obey in our stead; nor doth add any worth to our obedience; unless they will say, that we are justified by our own sincere obedience, the righteousness of Christ making up the defect of it; and so our own righteousness will be a co-ordinate cause of our justification with the righteousness of Christ."

7. We are justified by grace alone, or by such a righteousness that man should not boast, nor have any ground or cause to boast; but the way that these men speak of, *i. e.*, that we are justified by our sincere obedience, makes way for boasting. " Being justified by his grace, through the redemption that is in Christ Jesus. Whom God hath set forth, &c. To declare his righteousness, that God might be just, and the justifier of him that believeth in Jesus," Rom. iii. 24—26. That he may appear just, or that we may know the purity, justice, and holiness of his nature; that no righteousness, but that which is perfect, can justify us before him. Where is boasting then? It is excluded. By what law? Of works? Nay, but by the law of faith.

If it be by grace we are justified, it is not of works, any kind or sort of works whatsoever, either wrought in us or done by us, either to the law or Gospel; But it is of grace, &c. " And if it be grace, then it is not of works, otherwise grace is no more grace; but if it be of works, then it is no more of grace, otherwise work is no more work," Rom. xi. 6. There is no mixing God's grace and our works together; for one of these will destroy the other, it must be by works alone, or by grace alone; by Christ's righteousness only, without ours, or else by our righteousness alone, without his, and then we may glory in ourselves, and not in our Lord Jesus Christ.

And thus these bold presumptuous, or high and lofty mountains, are brought down.

Alas! Sirs, the law of perfect obedience remains the same in Christ's hand, as firm as ever; though it is abrogated as a covenant of work; yet it abides as a perfect rule of obedience. For it is still our duty to love God with all our hearts, souls, and strength, and our neighbour as ourselves; yea, to be perfect as our Father in heaven is perfect. Though this perfection we have only in Christ to justify us before God; yet notwithstanding, it is our duty to press after it, and not to obey sincerely only.

A third sort of persons carried away by presumption.   III. There is another sort of presumptuous sinners, who are lifted up with a mighty conceit of their faith, and persuasion that they are in Christ, believe and doubt not of their salvation.

1. Some of this sort are they, that tell you they believe the whole revelation of God's Word and Gospel of Christ, and do not deny one truth contained therein, such is the assent of their understanding.

2. And not only so, but they conform to all the external rules, commands, and precepts of Jesus Christ, and are brought into a visible profession of religion, and so walk that all true Christians take them for sincere believers; they are baptised, break bread, give to the poor, &c.; of this sort were the " foolish virgins," Matt. xxv. 1—3: who presumed their state was good, but had not one dram of saving grace in their hearts, but only had a form of godliness without the power thereof; now some of these empty professors may perhaps be more confident than many true believers.

1. Because they have but little to do with their own hearts, but labour to wash clean the outside of the cup and platter; or keep their outward conversation as spotless as they can; so that men may see no just cause to suspect them, and thus they go on and doubt not.

2. Because Satan does not disturb and perplex them as he doth sincere Christians, he having (as a curious observer) found all their religion is but in show or appearance only; they harbouring the love of the world, or some sin or another in their hearts.

3. Because perhaps good men, nay, pious ministers, take them for sincere Christians ; nay, may be, a whole congregation ; and this tends to deceive them, and make them conclude all is well, when indeed Satan hath them in his chains.

4. They never look to God for converting grace (as great sinners are forced to do, when awakened) because they think they are renewed already, and thus they are lifted up, or exalted, like hills and mountains, which Christ in due time, will one way or another bring low ; as those under despair are like vallies who shall be exalted, though the work is difficult on either hand, *i.e.*, it is as hard to fill up vallies, as it is to level hills and mountains.

Pray note, that either ignorance of God's nature and of his law, or the The causes ignorance of the Gospel, and the design of God therein, or else ignorance of tion in men. the state men are in, are the causes of presumption ; together with self-love, and that good opinion men are too apt to have of themselves.

Therefore (as one well observes) " a faithless confidence, a fond credulous presumption, ariseth from a groundless over-easy persuasion of the mercy of God towards us." To which I might add, also it riseth from mistaken apprehension about the death of Christ, and the extent thereof ; and from ignorance of the nature of true faith and regeneration. Sirs, if it be a difficult thing ; nay, impossible for us to pursuade a profane person, to believe his state is bad, how much harder and more impossible is it to persuade a Pharisee, or a zealous professor, and self-righteous, and a self-deceived man or woman, to believe that their condition and state is as bad, if not worse ?

But to proceed a little further, to open the nature of presumption, and to bring these hills and mountains down, if Christ will put his hand to it.

1. Presumption in most persons is, I say, no more than a strong fancy or The nature vain imagination, that carries them away into a belief of the goodness of their tion open-present condition, without any true ground thereof. They assure themselves ed. of that which they possess not, nor God ever gave to them, crying, peace, peace ; when God hath not spoken peace to them in such a state.

2. They do not rightly distinguish between the working of conscience, and We must dis-natural afflictions towards that good propounded in the Gospel, and the real tween the and efficacious actings of faith in Christ, in order to the obtaining of it ; they working of may find some sense of sin, and the dangerous consequents of it, but the pro- science and mises are misapplied. true faith.

3. They catch at the promises with a presumptuous faith in their own sense, A man that like as did the Jews in another case ; we have " Abraham to our father," John does but viii. 39 ; not considering that the promise ran to the spiritual seed of catch at the Abraham only. Thus they cry we are God's elect, I believe Christ died for me, concluding that faith is nothing but a confident persuasion that they are elected, and that Christ died for them ; Jews should have counted from their having Christ, they were Abraham's seed, and not his seed because by natural generation they proceeded from his loins ; so these persons do not regard the effects and nature of true faith, nor the fruits and effects of God's " everlasting love," Jer. xxxi. 3 ; election, nor of the death of Jesus Christ.

One that

4. Presumption in these persons fastens on some promises only, and little, presumes is or not at all on others, viz., the promises, and privileges of pardon of sin some parti-and justification, and freedom from condemnation, and eternal life. But mind mises. not, (or very little) the promises of " A new heart, a new spirit, grace, and sanctification," Ezek. xxxvi. 25—27. Now it is much if the pressing of such promises be not called by them a legal doctrine.

5. Presumption in them, is so strong and so sweet, that it gives them no Sin not bit-taste of the bitterness of sin, as true faith always doth ; true faith makes sin sumptuous bitter to the soul, and causeth us to loath, and abhor ourselves in the sight of sinner. God ; thus did Job, (Job xlii. 5), and thus did Isaiah (Isa. vi. 5), and holy Paul, (Rom. vii. 18, 24) ; and thus God saith shall all do when he hath taken hold of them. " And then ye shall remember your own evil ways, and your doings that were not good, and you shall loath yourselves," Ezek. xx. 41. And again he saith, " That thou mayest remember, and be confounded, and never open thy mouth any more, because of thy shame, when I am pacified towards thee, for all that thou hast done, saith the Lord," Ezek. xvi. 63. This all those do who have true faith ; because of the nature of sin as it is against God. Shall we not bewail ourselves for our sins, because Christ hath borne it, borne the guilt and weight thereof, for us ? Yes, they do it the more upon that account, " They shall look up

unto him whom they have pierced, and shall mourn, and be in bitterness because of him," Zech. **x.** 12, considering what sorrow he underwent. But these presumers and self-confident persons, look upon sin as a small thing, and speak slightingly of repentance, though it was the first doctrine John preached, Matt. iii. 1, and the first that our Saviour preached, Matt. iv. 17, and the first doctrine that St. Peter preached upon his receiving that great measure of the Spirit, Acts ii. 37. But alas these seem above repentance ; " They are rich, and increased in goods, and have need of nothing, and know not that they are wretched, miserable, poor, blind, and naked ;" Laodicean-like, Rev. iii. 17.

6. Such who have this presumptuous confidence, are chiefly set upon comfort ; they are for cordials, when indeed corrosives are more proper for them ; they cry up the free grace of God in justification, and pardon, more than the free grace of God in regeneration, faith, and new obedience ; whereas the former more refers to our good, to our happiness, and to our title to heaven ; they are wonderfully affected with such things, but the latter refers more directly to the glory of God. True, the glory of God is wonderfully raised by Jesus Christ in our free and eternal justification, but in regeneration, holiness, and new obedience, we by the Spirit show forth the praises of his glory ; and hereby we bear his likeness, and magnify the nature of grace, and bring forth the fruits of the Spirit. " Hereby is my Father glorified, that you bring forth much fruit," John xv. 8. " This people have I formed for myself, they shall show forth my praise," Isa. xliii. 21. And this it appears is the end of God in creating us anew in Christ Jesus ; nay, to this end were we chosen, "that we might be holy," Tit. ii. 14. And to this end we were also redeemed.

A person carried away by presumption is most for comfort.

These people think that the riches of free grace appears only in justification, or at least-wise they are most affected with that ; but see what Paul saith, " And the grace of our Lord was exceeding abundant with faith and love," 1 Tim i. 14. Our vocation and sanctification, our faith and love, doth abundantly set forth the free grace of God; and this all true believers as much admire, which these persons take but little notice of.

7. Presumption is easy ; it is no hard thing to presume on the mercy of God, and on the death and merits of Christ ; Satan will help them here, and not any ways hinder them ; but to believe truly in Christ, this is a hard and difficult thing. Satan labours to oppose us in resting in a right manner on Jesus Christ ; faith is not easily had ; no, but after much crying to God, and beating down a man's own self ; no man believes, but self dies ; sinful self, and religious self also. Faith is the death of sin, the death of the old man ; but sin and self too, live in a presumptuous person. Unbelief is contrary to faith, and makes head against it ; despair is contrary to faith, and makes head against it ; and also presumption is contrary to faith, and makes head against it. Sin is opposite to faith, and a man's own legal heart is opposite to faith, and self is opposite to it, and Satan is the grand enemy to it ; therefore it is no easy thing to believe.

That presumption is easy.

8. Such who are carried away with this presumptuous confidence are commonly very negligent in the use of the means God directs unto, in order to the obtaining of saving faith, as prayer, hearing of the word, &c. They are little concerned about praying, they do not say, Lord, I believe, help thou my unbelief. Mark ix. 24. Alas, they have no doubts, no unbelief ; that faith that is attended with godly fear or doubtings, it may be contemned by them, but if there are no true believers but such who have a full persuasion, or full assurance that Christ is theirs, then there is no little, or small faith, nor any weak believers, no babes in Christ, Matt. vi. 30, Heb. v. 12. Nor indeed can there be any further growth in faith. What is a higher degree of faith then a full assurance ? Moreover, to press the duties of religion upon men's consciences, is a very unpleasant doctrine with these men.

A presumptuous sinner little in prayer or other duties.

9. Such who have this presumptuous confidence, talk much of what Christ has done for them, but very little of what he hath wrought, and done in them. A true believer is as much affected with the work of the Holy Spirit, in renewing him, as with the love of the Father in electing him, or as with the love of the Son in redeeming him. For there is equal love and grace in all the three Persons of the blessed Trinity ; nor indeed can we know that we were elected by the Father, and redeemed by the Son, until we are effectually called, and renewed by the Holy Spirit. Therefore they love, adore, and admire the grace and goodness of the Holy Ghost, without whose divine operations the death of Christ is not, cannot be made effectual or efficacious to them. It is Christ in us the hope of glory, Col. i. 27. To depend upon Christ for life and salvation by his righteousness, and yet never feel, nor experience the effects of his death, is but a bold piece of presumption.

A presumptuous person more affected with what Christ has done for him than what he has wrought in him.

10. Faith is grounded upon the promises of God by the Spirit rightly applied to a proper subject; a lost, undone, a sick, and wounded sinner: not only lost in himself, but absolutely lost in the first Adam, and a child of wrath, even as others. Presumptuous sinners have no such promise by the Spirit applied to them, and perhaps think their state was as good before their pretended calling, as after, though they did not know it, and never were indeed children of wrath in their conceit, though the Holy Ghost asserts the direct contrary, Eph. ii. 3.

A presumptuous person doth not rightly apply the promises.

11. Those who are carried away with a presumptuous confidence, do not love to be tried by the marks, and characters of true faith; no, they cannot endure such a doctrine that comes so close to their consciences; though this was Christ's doctrine. " A good tree brings forth good fruit," Matt. vii. 17. And Paul's doctrine, " They that are after the Spirit mind the things of the Spirit," Rom. viii. 5. " If any man be in Christ, he is a new creature," 2 Cor. v. 17. " They that are Christ's have crucified the flesh, with the affections and lusts," Gal. v. 24. And this was James's doctrine, " Shew me thy faith without thy works, I will shew thee my faith by my works," Jam. ii. 18. And this also was John's doctrine, " We know that we are passed from death to life, because we love the brethren," 1 John iii. 14. Moreover, how often are we required to try our selves, prove our selves, and to examine our own selves? Now which way can we do this, if all signs or marks of a true believer must be decried, and by no means regarded?

A presumptuous person loves not to be tried by signs of grace.

Fourthly, There are another sort of presumptuous sinners, who, like hills and mountains, Christ will bring low, and they are such who glory that they are true to the church, and abide in that religion in which they were born, and in which their forefathers walked, who are zealous perhaps for such rites, ceremonies, or modes of worship that are nowhere found in God's word, nor were indeed instituted by Jesus Christ.

Formal protestants like hills and mountains lifted with a presumptuous confidence.

Not but that there are many good Christians amongst this sort; but O the vain confidence of the most of them; they believe in God the Father, and in Jesus Christ his only-begotton Son, and in the Holy Ghost; this is very good, were their faith the faith of God's elect. Nay, more, they in their baptism are (they say) made the children of God, members of Christ, and inheritors of the kingdom of heaven; and being then (as they are taught to believe) regenerated and born again, they presume they shall be saved, though never brought indeed under a real change, but live in sin, serve sin, and the devil, and hate all such who are truly religious; they are Protestants, they say, and good Christians, yet many of them are guilty of all gross immoralities; and yet presume through God's mercy and the death of Christ, by saying their prayers, and coming to church, they shall be saved. But the time will come when Christ will bring down these mountains, and remove all these stumbling-blocks out of the way of these sinners, and all others I have mentioned.

APPLICATION

This may serve to awaken all sorts of persons to consider what a state and condition they are in; and to take heed their hope at last prove not as the spiders' web.

The application.

2. Moreover, it may inform us what a subtle devil we have to do with; O how many ways hath he to deceive and eternally ruin poor sinners; some by their despairing of God's mercy in Christ, and others by a vain and faithless confidence that their state is good, when it is very bad and dangerous.

3. It may also serve to stir up all true Christians to praise the blessed God, who hath helped them over all these stumbling-blocks, and hath made their way smooth and plain before them.

4. It may likewise be a caution to all to take heed what principles they do embrace, and to pray they may not swerve to the right hand nor the left; it also shows what a blessed thing it is to be found in the true apostolical doctrine, and to have true faith and a holy life.

5. Happy are they who sit under a clear gospel ministry, and understand how Christ doth fill up, or exalt every valley and bring low every mountain and hill; making the crooked straight, and rough ways smooth; so that the glory of the Lord may be revealed.

6. Know assuredly that the levelling of mountains, is the raising up of valleys; and that when man is abased, God's free grace, and the believing soul is exalted.

7. Also, when all mountains, all obstructions are finally removed out of the way of believers, then they shall arrive to a perfect state, and be glorified; which will not be effected in this life; for we shall meet with some obstructions from within and from without, whilst we are in this body.

IV

And the glory of the Lord shall be revealed. —Isa. xl. 5.

DOCT. That the grand design of Christ coming unto this world, and in exalting every valley, and in bringing low every hill and mountain, and making that which was crooked straight, and rough ways smooth, was to discover, reveal, or manifest the glory of the Lord.

My brethren, in my opening of these words, I showed you what I understood by the revelation of the glory of the Lord.

I shall now insist a little further upon the opening of it. And the glory of the Lord shall be revealed, and all flesh shall see it : the design of Christ in his filling every valley, and in bringing low every mountain and hill, it was to reveal the glory of Jehovah ;

1. In all his blessed attributes.

2. The glory of all the three sacred Persons in the blessed Trinity.

3. I shall speak to both these, and briefly apply it, and so conclude with this metaphorical text.   The great God designed from eternity to magnify his glory, in permitting the fall of man, and in bringing in a Saviour, but it was never so fully *(The glory of the wisdom of God revealed by Christ's undertakings.)* and clearly revealed, until Jesus Christ came, and removed all those mountains of difficulties, and takes all stumbling-blocks out of his and our way. I say, the supreme end of God in the contriving of our salvation, was chiefly and principally his own glory. 1. In all the perfections of his nature, and more particularly the glory of his wisdom.   2. The subordinate end was the recovery of lost sinners, and the overthrow of Satan and his kingdom.   The glory of God's wisdom is revealed in his works of creation and providence : " The heavens declare the glory of the Lord," Psal. xix. 1. but not so conspicuously, not so in every one of his attributes, nor so resplendently in any of them, as in the work of redemption is revealed, and· wrought out by our Lord Jesus Christ.   And,

I. The misery of fallen man was great, and mercy pities him, and was ready to restore him ; but justice, like a high mountain interposed, and requires satisfaction ; and whatsoever plea mercy had, justice had every way as great.   Mercy might say, shall such an excellent creature as man was, who was created in the image of God, be lost, and mercy and divine goodness in God be veiled and eclipsed ? Justice might say, shall not such guilty criminals be punished, and shall not God be just ?   Shall holiness and justice be vailed and eclipsed, and lose their glory ?   Now divine wisdom is manifested, in finding out a way to reconcile infinite mercy and infinite justice, that they might meet in sweet harmony, and the glory of both be equally magnified.   Divine goodness and mercy is exalted to the wonder of men and angels, for the divine justice receives double for all the injury the sin of man hath done to it ; considering the worth and dignity of the person that wisdom found out to bear our sin, and pay our debts.

II. The wisdom of God is revealed in and by Christ in an astonishing manner, in taking occasion from the sin of man, to bring so great glory to God ; sin it is true, in its own nature, hath no tendency to the glory of God, but is most hateful to him, and the greatest dishonour is thereby done to him imaginable ; but O see the wisdom of God.   God can bring good out of sin and the fall, the highest glory to his name : he therefore permitted man to fall,

III. That we might see the glory of God's wisdom, in restoring of poor sinners, and his mercy, which was hid before, (there being no proper object that the sovereignty of God was resolved to let it towards) until his wisdom suffered man to fall under misery to a lamentable degree.

My brethren, the lower man was fallen, the higher is wisdom and divine goodness exalted, in raising of him up again. " God's wisdom is seen (saith a worthy writer) in *(Mr. Charnock on the Attributes. p. 359.)* bringing good to the creature out of sin ; he hath ordered sin to such an end as man never dreamed of, and the devils never imagined, and sin in its own nature could never attain ; sin in its own nature tends to no good, but that of punishment, it hath no relation to the creature's good in itself, but to his mischief ; but God by an act of infinnite wisdom, brings good out of it to the creature, as well as glory to his own name ; contrary to the nature of the crime, the intention of the criminal, and design of the tempter.   God willed sin, that is, he willed to permit it, that he might communicate himself to the creature in the most excellent manner.   He willed the permission of sin as an occasion to bring forth the mystery of the incarnation and passion of our Saviour ;

as he permitted the sin of Joseph's brethren, that he might use their evil to a good end. Because of his holiness ;—he never willed sin as an end, but in regard of his wisdom, he willed to permit it as a means and occasion. And thus to draw good out of those things which are in their own nature contrary to good, is the highest act of wisdom.

And thus, my brethren, from the occasion of sin, God brings the greatest glory to himself, and the highest good to lost creatures, that ever any were blessed with.

Some measures of wisdom were given out in creation and providence, but the infinite treasures of it are opened in redemption, or revealed in Jesus Christ ; and hence he is called " the wisdom of God," and the gospel is called the wisdom of God, yea, " the hidden wisdom," 1 Cor. i. 24 ; that is so called, because it reveals God's glorious wisdom that was long hid as to its clearest discovery.

IV. The wisdom of God is revealed in and by Christ, or in that glorious contrivance of his in the after disappointment and overthrow of the design, and work of the devil, in drawing man into sin to his undoing ; no doubt Satan read his own fall in the first promise, the seed of the woman shall break the serpent's head, though he know not what seed God intended thereby ; he is conquered by that nature he had cast undern [Charnock] wrath and the curse. The flesh of old Adam infected us, and the flesh of the second Adam cures us.

Secondly, The glory of the divine goodness, love, and mercy, is revealed in and by Jesus Christ.

1. Mercy and goodness was the spring of our redemption ; it was that which stirred up wisdom to contrive the way, that goodness and mercy might flow forth. *The glory of mercy, love, and goodness, revealed.*

2. It is called the riches of mercy and goodness ; God who is rich in mercy.

3. It was free and undeserved goodness, there was no obligation lay on God to pity fallen man.

4. It was sovereign goodness, why should God show his love and mercy to fallen man, and not to fallen angels ?

5. It is infinite and incomprehensible love, mercy, and goodness ; what, save a vile rebel, to give his own Son ! could God show a greater love ? certainly no greater demonstration of love and goodness could be manifested, considering who the Redeemer is, what he suffered, and for whom, and what we are delivered from, and what raised unto, by this blessed Redeemer ; it was greater love and goodness (saith one) than was for a time manifested to Christ himself ; " God so loved the world, that he gave his only-begotton Son," John iii. 16.

Thirdly, The glory of divine justice is hereby also revealed, in that man is not raised out of this lapsed state, as a simple act of love and mercy ; but to the highest exaltion of his justice, in that blessed satisfaction Christ hath made by his active and passive obedience to the law and justice, in doing and suffering what we were to have done and suffered. Mercy might plead, if man be ruined for ever, the creation is in vain, and that sweet property of God's nature, divine mercy and goodness, for ever covered and remained obscure to any created being. Justice might plead, if man be not sentenced, the law is in vain, and God appears not just nor true, in his threatening : grace abets mercy, that pity might be showed, yet justice will be injured if man be not punished ; now in Jesus Christ the plea of justice is answered in punishing, and the plea of mercy in pardoning. Justice (saith one) shall not complain for want of punishment, nor mercy want in pardoning sins ; the love, grace, and goodness of God in Christ, is to the honour of God's truth and justice ; he preserves " the righteousness of his law, and the counsel of his mercy, not by changing the sentence against sin, but the person ; laying that upon his Son as our Surety, which by the rigour of the law we were to endure in our own persons ; whereby God appears just, and justice is satisfied with the punishment due to the sinner, and mercy is satisfied with the merit due to our Saviour, and the truth of God preserved in the execution of the sentence pronounced."

Fourthly, The glory of divine power is also revealed in and by Jesus Christ, who is called " the power of God, and the arm of the Lord," 1 Cor. i. 24, Isaiah liii. 1. *Glorious power revealed.*

1. " In that all the divine attributes are united, and meet in sweet harmony, in and by the Lord Jesus, and thus God is said to be made strong, by the man of his right hand ;" not that Christ added any strength to the essential power of God ; no, that could not be ; but hereby he exerts or puts forth his united and wonderful power.

2. His power is revealed in the incarnation of Jesus Christ, who was born without sin, and yet partook of our nature ; he did not take the person of any man into union with his own divine person, but the nature of man.

3. His power is revealed in his divesting, and utterly destroying the power of Satan, and the power of sin, both for us and in us.

4. In his vanquishing of death by the death of his own Son, that " through death he might destroy him that had the power of death, and deliver them who through fear of death were all their life-time subject to bondage," Heb. ii. 14, 15.

5. His power is revealed in his bringing low and removing of all those mountains of difficulty and stumbling-blocks that were in the way of God's being reconciled unto us.

6. In his quickening of all his elect " who were dead in sins and trespasses," Ephes. ii. 1; and in preserving grace in them, which though it be but as a small spark of fire, yet no enemies within, nor devils without, can finally quench or extinguish it; and in raising those who are fallen so low, to a higher, and more firm state, and to greater glory and happiness than man had before he fell. These things are ascribed to God's almighty power, 2 Thess. i. 11, Eph. i. 19, Isa. xii. 1.

7. And in raising the dead at the last day.

Glorious holiness revealed.   Fifthly, The glory of the holiness of the Lord is revealed in our Lord Jesus Christ.

1. No judgment, no punishment which God ever brought on the wicked in this world, no, not that burning wrath in the consciences of any, nor the torments and groans of the damned in hell, discovereth the glory of divine holiness, like that marred countenance, bloody agony, bleeding sides, and dying groans of the blessed Jesus, considering who he was, or the dignity of his person, the eternal Son of God, or the only-begotten of the Father.

2. The glory of holiness is revealed in God's infinite hatred of sin, not only in punishing of his Son standing in our law-place, but in his justifying of us by the righteousness of him who " is God over all, blessed for evermore," Rom. ix. 5. By a righteousness far exceeding that of Adam's in innocency, or that the holy angels; for Adam's holiness and righteousness was but the righteousness of a mere creature, and so is the holiness and righteousness of angels, is the righteousness of mere creatures; but this of God-man.

3. In his glorious design in sending of Jesus Christ to redeem us, which was not only to satisfy justice, and magnify mercy, but it was also to exalt his infinite holiness, in purging away both the guilt and filth of all sin, by the blood of his own Son. The same grace that inclined God to send his Son to die for us, to bear our sins, hath purchased the Holy Spirit, and sends it to us to renew us, and to live in us, that we being regenerated, and having his own image stamped on us, might be capable to enjoy communion with him here, and eternally hereafter : and as faith apprehends Jesus Christ to our justification by God's ordination, so the same faith purifies our hearts through the Spirit to our inherent sanctification and holiness, by its own divine operations.

4. In that his design is to present all his elect at last in Jesus Christ, absolutely holy, perfect, and without spot and blemish, Ephes. v. 27.

The glory of God's sovereignty revealed in the Gospel   Sixthly. The glory of God's sovereignty and dominion over his creatures, is revealed in and by Jesus Christ.

1. In that he was not obliged to save any of the lost sons of Adam, by any necessity arising from his nature, any more than he was the fallen angels.

2. In that he did not send his Son with a purpose to save all men, but only such whom he foreknew and predestinated, and gave to him from everlasting, Rom. viii. 29; The whole gospel is but a declaration of his sovereign pleasure concerning Christ and his elect, in him; it is therefore called, the mystery of his will, and the purpose of his will; " Who hath saved us, and called us with an holy calling, not according to our works, but according to his own purpose and grace given us in Christ Jesus before the world began," Eph. i. 9; 2 Tim. ii. 9; Tit. iii. 5.

And thus the glory of the Lord is revealed in respect to his glorious attributes and perfections of his nature.

Secondly, I shall show how the glory of God is revealed in the gospel, personally considered; or the glory of all the three Persons of the ever-blessed Trinity.

Pray let it be considered, that though God is often called a Father in the Old Testament, yet how hard is it without the help of the gospel to find out where he is so called, or taken in distinction from the Son and the Holy Spirit, sith, father (as many divines observe) in some places of Scripture respects all the three Persons ; and hence the Jewish Rabbins, (who allow not of the New Testament) manifestly declare their ignorance touching this great truth of the Trinity, though it may in part be imputed to that judicial blindness they are left under, yet it must be granted, that there is in the gospel a more clear and discovery of this glorious mystery, then there is in the law or Old Testament. O how plainly, and by manifold testimony, is this borne witness unto !

1. By the angels, " He shall be great, and shall be called the Son of the highest," Luke i. 32.

2. By the Father himself from heaven, "And lo, a voice came from heaven, saying, this is my beloved Son, in whom I am well pleased," Matt. iii. 17. St. Peter saith, mentioning this passage, " He received from God the Father honour and glory, when there came such a voice from the excellent glory, this is my beloved Son, in whom I am well pleased," 2 Pet. i. 17.

3. By the testimony of Christ himself, " I thank thee, O Father; even so Father—— the Father sent me——the Father hath not left me alone; I and my Father are one," Matt. xi. 25. It is observed, he calls God Father near an hundred times in the gospel.

4. By the testimony of the Holy Ghost, in and by the apostles; so that the very personality of the Father is here fully revealed.

First, the glory of the Father is hereby revealed; my brethren, the Father in magnifying his Son, did not design to vail or eclipse his own glory, but to magnify it, though all are to honour the Son, as they honour the Father; but how did our Lord endeavour to the utmost to glorify the Father. " My doctrine is not mine, but the Father's that sent me," John vi. 57. " As the living Father sent me, and I live by the Father——I honour my Father," John xiv. 29. " I have glorified thy name, O holy Father," John xvii., &c. *(The glory of God the Father revealed in the Gospel.)*

5. In that whatsoever belief, succour, and saving benefit we receive, all primarily is ascribed to God the Father.

(1). To the wisdom of the Father, in contriving the way of our redemption.
(2). To the love, mercy, and goodness of the Father.
(3). That all might redound to the glory of God the Father.

All things are of God, who hath reconciled us to himself by Jesus Christ. The Father, he is the first Person, and he is also the first in order, in all the divine operations.

1. The Father chose Christ to be our Surety and Saviour.
2. He accepted of him in our stead.
3. He sent him into the world.
4. He anointed him.
5. He upheld him.
6. He raised him from the dead, and justified him, and God the Father justifies us in him.
7. Our union is of the Father: " Of him are ye in Christ Jesus, who of God is made unto us," &c.—that is, God the Father.

Secondly, The glory of the Son our blessed Redeemer, is also herein revealed, and all flesh shall first or last see it.

1. The glory of his person, who is God essential with the Father; " I and my Father are one." He thought it not robbery to be equal with God. See " pearl of great price," Phil. ii. 6.

2. His glory is revealed in his glorious offices, which indeed He executed from the beginning under the Old Testament; but the nature and exercise of his offices never were so fully and clearly revealed, as in the gospel, when he was actually anointed and proclaimed King, Priest, and Prophet, and gave forth laws, taught his people, and suffered for their sins.

3. In the glory of his works, in what he did in obedience to the law, and in those wonderful miracles which he wrought; and in his death, glorious resurrection, and ascension into heaven. *(The glory of God the Son revealed in the Gospel.)*

4. The glory of Christ is revealed in respect of those glorious names or titles that are given to Him, and in respect had to what he is made of God unto all them that believe on him, i. e., to them indeed he is all, and in all. For,

5. Christ is all with God, he is all to God, and he is all from God; we have no acceptance but in him, we only come to God by him, and receive all from God through him; he is all in redemption, all in satisfaction, reconciliation, justification, union and communion, and in regeneration and sanctification, in pardon, peace, and in all glorification. Christ is the foundation on which we are built, the fountain in which we are washed, the bread of life with which we are fed, and the water of life of which we drink. In a word, he is our life, our light, our strength; he is made every thing to our souls that we need. He is the power of God; Christ is the great repository of all sacred truth, and of all grace; and Christ is the great out-let or conduit-pipe of all that grace and goodness we receive from God also. Thus is the glory of the Son of God revealed.

Lastly, his glory is revealed in that great victory and conquest he hath obtained over all his, and our enemies.

Thirdly, The glory of the Holy Ghost is hereby also revealed.

The glory of the Holy Ghost is re-vealed also.

1. In that manifestation of his distinct personality from the Person of the Father and the Son, i. e., that he is an eternal divine, existing substance or essence with the Father and the Son, or an intelligent voluntary divine agent; he knoweth, worketh, he willeth, &c., and therefore an intelligent agent.

Now his being a distinct Person from the Father and the Son, and yet the same God in essence, sets forth the glory of the Holy Ghost.

1. He is called God.

2. The Saints are called the temple of God, because the " Holy Ghost dwells in them." Acts v. 3, 4; 1 Cor. iii. 10.

3. We are baptized in the name of the Father, Son, and Holy Spirit, and therefore the Spirit is the same God; and we are thereby obliged to worship him, and live to him.

4. He is called the Comforter, which is a personal appellation, John xiv. 26.

5. He is the voluntary Author of all divine operations, i. e., he cherished the creation, moved upon the waters; yea, he made and formed them, Gen. i. 3. Psal. xxiii. 6, Job xxvi. 13.——" The Spirit of God (saith Job) hath made me;" he spake by the prophets, he enlightened, renewed, regenerates, sanctifieth, teacheth, and guideth us.

6. We may grieve him, nay, vex him; and so we cannot be said to do to a mere divine quality or operation; grief denotes or belongs to a person, Ephes. iv. 30.

7. He is said to appoint overseers, or give pastors, and send them forth; " The Holy Ghost said, separate me Paul and Barnabas, for the work whereunto I have appointed them," Acts xx. 28; Acts xiii. 2.

II. The glory of the love of the Holy Ghost is in the gospel, revealed in removing all those mountains of difficulties, that lie in the way of the conversion of sinners. (1). All that the Father elected, the Son redeemed, the Holy Spirit renewed and sanctifieth; the love of the Father, and of the Son, and of the Holy Spirit, is the same in nature, and of like extent; the Father prepared the matter of which the garment of Christ's righteousness is made; he prepared the body of Christ, the Son wrought that garment, by his active and passive obedience, and the Holy Spirit puts it upon us. (2). Our union with Christ is by the Spirit. (3). All graces in us are the fruits of the Holy Spirit.

III. The glorious power of the Holy Spirit is also herein revealed. (1). In quickening us. And (2). In forming Christ in us. (3). Raising us from the dead, in his enabling us to mortify sin. (4). And to repel all Satan's temptations, and to overcome the world. (5). Likewise in helping of us to bear all manner of trials, torments, and sorrows, with an undaunted courage. (7). In his helping us to perform all holy duties, and to exercise all our spiritual graces, and in his preserving us in a state of grace to the end, and in perfecting of that work in our souls.

APPLICATION

1. We may infer from hence, that the grand design of God in sending his Son, &c., is to abase man, and wholly to advance and magnify his own name and glory.

2. That salvation is alone of God's free grace.

3. This may tend also sharply to reprove all those who are lifted up in pride and vain glory, and such that ascribe part of that glory which belongs unto God, to sorry man, or to the will, or power, or righteousness of the creature.

4. By it likewise we may learn to give equal honour to the Father, and to the Son, and to the Holy Ghost, they being all but one and the same God. " These Three are one," one in essence.

5. Let all the ministers of the gospel learn from hence to exalt the Holy God, and his free grace in our salvation.

6. From hence also, I infer that such who have not the gospel, are ignorant of God, in respect of his chiefest glory, and of their own good.

7. And that the knowledge of Christ and the gospel, is the way to be truly wise, Christ being the wisdom of God, and the gospel a declaration of the depth of God's wisdom; " the wisdom of God in a mystery," which is hid from most men: those that would be truly wise, must learn to know Jesus Christ. And this wisdom also will enrich the soul, even to make such who understand it " wise unto everlasting life." It makes not only knowing heads, but knowing and gracious hearts, and thus I close with these words.

2. THE AXE LAID TO THE ROOT OF THE TREES

And now also the axe is laid to the root of the trees, every tree therefore that bringeth not forth good fruit, is hewn down and cast into the fire.—Matt. iii. 10.

In speaking to this symbolical text, I shall,

1. Open the scope and coherence thereof.
2. Explain the parts and terms therein contained.
3. I shall observe one or two points of doctrine therefrom.
4. Improve the whole by way of application.

First, From the scope and coherence of the place, it is evident, that John The scope of Baptist endeavours to take off the Jews, particularly the Pharisees and Saddu- these words opened. cees, from the external and legal covenant God made with Abraham and his fleshly-seed, or offspring. See verse 7. "But when he saw many of the Pharisees and Sadducees come to his baptism, he said unto them, O generation of vipers, who hath warned you to flee from the wrath to come !"

Historians tells us, That there were three more eminent religious sects amongst the Jews, the first were called Essenes, of whom we do not read in the holy scripture ; their main doctrine was fate ; they (say our annotators) ascribed all things to it. Secondly, the Sadducees were directly opposite to the Essenes, they ascribed nothing to fate, but asserted the liberty and power of man's will, in the largest sense, or in the most extravagant height ; they denied the immortality of the soul of man, the resurrection, angels, &c., all which the Pharisees owned. See Act. xxiii. 8.

Thirdly, The Pharisees, who were outwardly a very zealous sort of people ; and, though they were tainted with that false opinion of the freedom of man's will to do good, yet they ascribed much to the providence and grace of God ; they were interpreters of the law, and separated themselves from others ; they spent much time in fasting and prayer. 1. They held, nevertheless, a righteousness by the works of the law, by which they thought they were justified and accepted of God, " And so stumbled at that stumbling-stone," Rom. ix. 32. 2. They gave a very corrupt interpretation of the law. 3. They held many unwritten traditions of equal force with the law of God ; by which means, they made void the commandments of God. 4. They were a mere hypocritical sort of men in their practices, being very strict and zealous for the smaller matters of the law, and neglected the weightier things thereof.

Whether these Pharisees and Sadducees came with an intention to be baptized, or only out of curiosity, is hard to be resolved, since it is said, " They rejected the counsel of God against themselves, being not baptized by John," Luke vii. 30.

John, however, sharply treats them both, calling them " a generation of vipers," a sort of serpents ; of whom it is said, they make way into the world through the bowels of their dam. It may be upon this account, he gave them that name, or so called them, who thought through the bowels (as I may so say of their ancestors) or being the seed of Abraham, or the offspring of godly progenitors, to come to heaven; " who hath warned you to flee from the wrath to come ? What is the reason that you come to my baptism ? Whereas some of you think there is no resurrection, no heaven, no hell, no angels, no spirits ; or, you, who think you are so righteous, as you need no repentance, and so need fear no wrath to come. From whence comes this to pass, that you seem to fear, or to be afraid of future wrath, and the vengeance of an angry God ? " Bring forth therefore fruits meet for repentance," ver. 8.

O come now, and put yourselves among the crowd of poor sinners, and godly penitent persons ; repent of your false doctrines you have taught ; repent of the corrupt and wicked notions and opinions you hold, and of the vain and hypocritical lives you have led, and think not that a bare profession of this will do neither ; for you must bring forth fruits of true repentance, fruits of true holiness, from a thorough change of heart that must be wrought in you.

But, (as if he should say) I know your thoughts, I have heard what a belief you are of. You think you are in covenant with God, and so are federally holy, and in a saved and safe condition, because you have Abraham to your father. You conclude, that the covenant God made with Abraham, and his natural or fleshly seed, was the covenant of grace ; and so the promise is sure to you : and therefore, he adds, ver. 7, " And think not to say within

35

yourselves, We have Abraham to our Father: for I say unto you, that God is able of these stones to raise up children to Abraham."

You promise good to yourselves, because you are the natural offspring of believing Abraham, you rest upon your descent from him. The very same plea we find they made to our blessed Saviour, Job viii. 33, "We be Abraham's seed, and were never in bondage to any man. How sayest thou, ye shall be made free?" We were never under the bondage of sin, as others are; that covenant made with Abraham being the covenant of grace, we are thereby set at liberty, and no man shall by his doctrine make us believe the contrary. We are a free people, in respect of our souls and spiritual privileges, (for they could not mean otherwise, because they had often been in bondage to men, in respect of external liberty and freedom: first to Pharaoh king of Egypt, and then to Nebuchadnezzar, and now were so in bondage under the Romans). I know (saith our Saviour) that ye are Abraham's seed, (John viii. 37;) according to the flesh, they were his offspring; but that was no spiritual advantage to them; though it did give them right to legal privileges and ordinances under the law, yet it signified nothing now, it would not profit them under the gospel dispensation, they must be the spiritual seed of Abraham, and do the works of Abraham, and walk in his steps; which they did not; and therefore the Lord Jesus told them, " Ye are of your father the devil, and the lusts of you father you will do."

John Baptist intimates the same thing, when he called them a generation of vipers; though they entitled themselves to the covenant of grace, (like as some do now a-days) upon that, in Gen. xvii., extended to Abraham's seed, as well as to himself, and concluded, they were members of God's church, then on earth, and could not therefore be denied any privilege, or ordinance, that of right belonged to covenant children. But this great prophet knew how blind and deceived they were, not understanding that there were two covenants made with Abraham; and also a two-fold seed (viz.), a natural, and a spiritual seed: they thought that promise of God, made with Abraham, must be made of none effect, if they should not be owned or allowed to be the seed of Abraham. But, (saith the Baptist) God is able of these stones, to raise up children to Abraham. If he should turn stones into men and women, who have Abraham's faith, they would be certainly the true seed of Abraham, and not such as they were, though they naturally proceeded from his loins, according to the flesh; or, God could of the Gentiles raise up children to Abraham, and so make good his promise to him, who said, " In thy seed shall all the nations of the earth be blessed," Gen. xii. 3.

And now farther to convince them, and so to take away, for ever, all their hope and pretences of right to gospel-ordinances, and church-membership, by virtue of the covenant made with Abraham; or, from the consideration of their being his natural or fleshly seed, he in the words I first read to you, says, " and now also the axe is laid to the root of the trees, therefore every tree which bringeth forth not good fruit, is hewn down and cast into the fire," ver. 10.

Now, this now refers to time in this place, sometimes it refers to the matter, or occasion of what is spoken. " Now the axe is laid to the root of the trees;" this is certain, the axe was not till now, or until this time so laid, or thus laid to the root. We cannot understand what the Holy Ghost intends hereby, unless we observe, and well consider, the scope and coherence of the text, which does clearly unfold the whole drift and purport of the Baptist. He shewed them before in the context, that their plea to gospel baptism, was not good nor pleadable, i. e., " We are Abraham's seed;" they might object and say,

What is meant by the axe being (now) laid, &c.

Obj. All the seed of Abraham were taken into covenant with God, and all that sprang from his loins were members of the visible church; and had right to the external rites, ordinances, and privileges thereof.

Ans. This John Baptist seems to grant, i. e., that it was so from Abraham's time until these days, or under the law or old covenant-dispensation; they had, he denies not, a right to Jewish church-membership and legal ordinances: but what of that, " now the axe is laid to the root of the trees;" that is, as Abraham was the root, or common covenanting-father, as concerning the flesh, out of which root, all the Jews, his natural offspring, sprang; and, upon which foundation, they and their natural church-state was founded: yet, now the axe is laid to this root, i. e., to this covenant, i. e., the legal, or external covenant made with Abraham; and down must the building fall, when the foundation is removed; down goes the trees, when the root (out of which they grew) is cut down. So much as to the scope and coherence of words.

Secondly, I shall explain the terms and parts of the text:

1. Show farther what is meant by the root.
2. What is intended by the trees.
3. What is meant by the axe.
4. What by laying the axe to the root of the trees, and by cutting down.
5. What by the fire, and casting into the fire.

First, by the root is meant, that which bears up the branches, and on which *The terms and parts opened.* the trees and branches stand and grow ; and it is from hence, from this allusion, the Baptists makes use of these words and expressions. Now the root, whereof he speaks (as I conceive) was that covenant God made with Abraham, and his natural seed, or off-spring ; which covenant did in a mystical sense, as clearly bear up the national *What is meant by the root.* church of Israel, and all the trees, i. e., members or branches thereof, as common natural root doth the tree, or trees that grow out of it.

2. And as by root may be meant that covenant made with Abraham, and his natural seed, as such (from whence the national policy, and church of the Jews, sprang, and was borne up, and from whence it grew and was to abide) until the gospel dispensation came in, and was established ; so also by the root may be intended the foundation of all their hopes, confidence, and outward privileges ; for that they (I mean the natural offspring of Abraham), had great confidence in the flesh, by means of that legal or external ministration they were under, cannot be denied, and had many outward rights and privileges also, above all people then in the world ; and if so (I mean if this be granted, which I am sure cannot be denied), then it follows there was some root, ground, or foundation, which they had, and upon which they built, and laid claim to those outward ecclesiastical and civil rights and privileges ; and that the ground, root, or foundation of all this, was that covenant God made with Abraham and his natural seed, is apparent to all who are not willingly blind. For before those covenant transactions with Abraham, we read not that the people, from whom Abraham sprang, had any such rights or privileges granted to them, and what outward privileges God promised them afterwards by Moses, it is signified in divers places to be upon the account of the covenant made with Abraham, &c. And according to the exact time, told by the Lord to Abraham, God brought his natural seed out of the land of Egypt.

This, from the scope and coherence of the words therefore, I must affirm, is primarily, and chiefly intended by the root of the trees in this place : but,

Thirdly, by root, in a more remote sense, may be meant the state and standing of every ungodly, unbelieving, and impenitent person ; let their hopes, expectation, and confidence, be what it will ; if he be not a good tree, a believing and true penitent person, his root, or foundation on which he builds, let it be what it will, cannot secure him, for down he must go with all his vain hopes, works, expectation, and confidence whatsoever with him, for " now is the axe laid to the root of the trees."

Secondly, by trees are meant men and women, but chiefly the seed of the stock *What is meant by trees.* of Abraham, according to the flesh; of whom the national church of the Jews was made up, and did consist ; as also, all wicked and unbelieving persons whatsoever, who embrace not the offers of grace in the gospel, or believe not in Jesus Christ. For, as the Church of God is compared to a good tree, and godly men in particular, are called good trees, so is the adulterated church of the Jews compared to an evil tree ; and wicked and ungodly persons, called, " Evil and corrupt trees," Matt. vii. 17. Yet it might be here noted, that they are in this place compared to fruit trees, though to such that bring not forth good fruit, as (by the Prophet) the Jewish church is compared to a vine, and an olive tree, though she brought forth sour grapes, Isa. v. 1, 2, 4.

Thirdly, as to the axe, we all know an axe is that instrument used by men to cut down trees, at the pleasure, or for the profit of the owner thereof ; by the axe here, may be intended divers things, by which God may be said to cut down impenitent sinners, or unfruitful churches, or bodies and souls of men. For cutting down may refer,

1. To the souls of men, &c.
2. To their outward rights and privileges.
3. To their bodies and souls both.
4. To their external, fleshly and corrupt church-state.

First, to the souls of sinners, which is done by an act of God's justice, when *What is meant by cutting down the trees.* he cuts off, from profiting by the means of grace, giving them up to unbelief and hardness of heart : and thus he in judgment dealt with the Jews, by giving them up to blindness of mind, when they have ears, and hear not ; eyes, and see not ; hearts, and understand not ; God utterly leaving them to a seared conscience, or gives them up to their own heart's lusts, and to walk in their own counsel. Then they, in respect of their souls, may be said to be cut down in wrath for ever.

2. Or, when he takes away the kingdom of God from them, *i. e.*, the dispensation of the gospel. "Therefore shall the kingdom of heaven be taken from you, and given to another people," &c. Matt. xxi. 43.

Secondly, it may refer to the cutting down their religious and civil rights and privileges.

1. When God takes away all the external and spiritual immunities, blessings, and favours, a people once enjoyed.

No gospel more preached to them, no ministers to preach it, the hedge of protection and preservation plucked up, and ravenous beasts let in to devour them ; like as God threatened the national church of Israel, Isa. v. The sun to shine upon them no more, nor the clouds to rain upon them. This is a dismal cutting down.

Thirdly, their bodies left to be destroyed by merciless enemies, or cut down by famine, sword, or pestilence, as this very people were dealt with, when God brought the Romans upon them, and their souls cut off for their final unbelief and impenitency. Also,

Fourthly, It may refer to the cutting down of their church-state, sacrifices, priesthood, sabbaths, temple, and all taken away and overthrown ; and another people, another seed, and more spiritual church, constituted and established in the room thereof. And thus God dealt with this people, *i. e.*, the church of the Jews they were broken off, or cut down, and the Gentiles were grafted in, as the apostle shows at large, Rom. xi.

The axe, by which they are cut down, may be,

What is meant by the axe First, the dispensation of God's providence, or time. Time is pictured with a scythe ; but then man is compared to grass, but it may be pictured with an axe, since men are compared to trees ; a scythe is no fit instrument to cut down trees. Men, as you have heard, are here compared to trees, and when once the time set for the Jewish church to stand, or abide in the world, was expired, time, or the dispensation of God's providence, like an axe, cut it down for ever ; and so will the prefixed time appointed by the Lord, when it is come, even cut down at the root, the bloody idolatrous church of Rome ; when the beast, forty-two months are expired, down she shall go with vengeance, and unless time lays the axe at her root, and at the root of all other corrupt churches, there will be no cutting them down, nor will there be any then able to save her or them. The standing of all human and ecclesiastical states and constitutions, are determined by the Almighty, who works all things according to the counsel of his own will.

2. The axe also may refer to the gospel : the word of God is an axe to hew and square some persons for God's spiritual building, and to cut down others also, as trees that are rotten, and bear no good fruit ; "Therefore (saith the Lord) I have hewn them by the prophets ; and what follows, mark it, "I have slain them by the words of my mouth," Hos. vi. 5. The word of God either kills or cures ; it is either a savour of life unto life, or the savour of death unto death, 2 Cor. ii. 16. Like as sweet-meats are to some pleasant and comfortable, and to others pernicious and deadly.

The abuse of gospel grace cut the Jews down, and so it will all others who slight and contemn it ; the word either softens or hardens, like as the sun, which shining on the wax, it softens that ; but shining on the clay, it hardens that. When the word comes in judgment, then it is like an axe in the hand of God's justice. I find one learned man speaking thus on this place, viz., the Word of God, which is a spiritual axe, cutteth down spiritually wicked men, and hypocrites, like rotten and barren trees. This is it, which is elsewhere meant by plucking up, destroying, hardening, &c. Some, (saith he) expound this, not of spiritual judgments, threatened in his word against impenitent sinners, but of the power of the Romans, which were the instruments of God, to destroy utterly the unfaithful and wicked generation of the Jews. The former is (saith he) the best exposition, but I conceive it may refer to both.

The axe is cutting down may refer to judgment. 3. The axe may refer to men, whom God makes use of, as instruments in his hand, to cut down and destroy a wicked and God-provoking people : hence wicked rulers and kings, whom God raises up as instruments in his hand, to chastise and cut down a rebellious people, are called " his sword, and the rod of his wrath and indignation," Psal. xvii. 14. "Arise, O Lord, disappoint him, cast him down, deliver my soul from the wicked, which is thy sword." And thus the Assyrians were an axe in God's hand, to use, as he pleased, and the Romans afterwards, to the Jews likewise.

Moreover, God's Israel is called his axe "Thou art my battle-axe and weapons of war ; with thee I will break in pieces the nations, and with thee will I destroy kingdoms." God's people, in the last days, which are now very near, shall be his axe, by whom, as instruments in his hand, he will destroy Babylon, Jer. li. 20, 24. "And I will render unto Babylon, &c., all the evil they have done to Sion, in your sight, saith the Lord. Reward her as she hath rewarded you, double to her double," Rev. xviii. 6. Give her blood to drink, for she is worthy. " The stone cut out of the mountains without hands, shall break to pieces all the powers of the earth, that oppose Christ's kingdom, or that stand in the way of its establishment," Dan. iii. 34, 44.

4. By the axe, may in general be meant God's wrath; however it is, or may be executed, or upon whom, wrath will sooner, or later, cut down all the ungodly, both false churches, and tyrannical powers of the earth, and all who continue in unbelief and in rebellion against God. *The axe may mean God's wrath.*

The axe laid at the root may refer to final cutting down of sinners.

The laying the axe to the root, discovers the final fall and ruin of sinners, whether considered as a church, or as particular persons ; dig up, or cut down the root, and down falls the body, and all the branches of the tree.

Fifthly, and lastly, " therefore every tree that bringeth not forth good fruit, shall be hewn down and cast into the fire." Now he draws a necessary inference and conclusion from the premises.

Every tree, that is, every man and woman, or every corrupt church, be they who they will, either Jew or Gentile, Babylonian or Christian ; if not plants of God's planting, if not fruitful to God, if they answer not his 'design and end, if they bring not forth good fruit, they shall be hewn down and cast into the fire of external and eternal wrath. A fire, saith the Lord, is kindled in my anger, and it shall burn to the lowest hell. Wrath seizes, and shall seize on them here ; but at last they shall be cast into hell-fire, " where the worm dies not, and the fire is not quenched," Mark ix. 46.

1. The words being thus opened and explained, I shall take notice of two points of doctrine.

1. Doct. Now the dispensation is changed. To be of the natural root, or of the national church of the Jews, or the seed of Abraham, according to the flesh, as such, is no ground of church-membership; or it is no argument for such to be admitted into the gospel church, or to gospel baptism.

2. Doct. Now in the times of the Gospel, God is, and will be, severe with all ungodly, unbelieving, and impenitent sinners ; he strikes at their root, at the root of all their hopes, false faith, or fleshly confidence whatsoever.

These propositions I shall not prosecute now, but shall make some brief use of what I have said.

1. Caution. Take heed on what you build your hopes of justification and salvation, what is that which bears up your spirits : for if you are trees that grow not out of the true root, Jesus Christ, and the covenant of grace ; if you have not union with the Lord Jesus, or are not built on that foundation, or corner-stone, God hath laid in Sion, down you fall ; for " now the axe is laid to the root of the trees."

2. Enquiry. Is not morality, a civil and honest life, doing to all as you would be done unto, the ground or foundation of your hopes ? Do you build upon this ? If it be so, tremble : remember Christ saith, " Except a man be born again, he cannot see the kingdom of God," John iii. 3.

If you have no other ground of hope, but from your own moral righteousness, when death comes with his axe, down you will go, and be cast into the fire.

3. Consider, all you profane and ungodly ones, what is that which bears your hopes up, what do you build upon ; is it not on the mere mercy of God, or death of Christ ? God (say you) is gracious, slow to anger, and we therefore have hopes, and do trust to that : Christ died for sinners, &c. You say right, God is merciful; but what then ? Will you therefore presumptuously go on in ungodly and wicked courses ? Oh ! know he is just as well as " gracious, and will in no wise clear the guilty," Exod. xxxiv. 7. " Except ye repent therefore, ye shall all likewise perish," Luke xiii. 3, 5. Shall the goodness of God, which should lead you to repentance, be thus evilly improved ; i. e., to strengthen your hands, and encourage you to sin against him, and provoke him ? It is, I fear, with you as Solomon speaks, " Because sentence against an evil work is not executed speedily, therefore the hearts of the sons of men are fully set in them to do wickedly," Eccles. viii. 11.

Christ, it is true, died for sinners, but you have no true faith in him ; he died to save sinners from their sins, and that they live to him. See my text, " now the axe is laid to the root of the trees ;" if you believe not on Christ, if you are not made new creatures, 1 Cor. v. 17, the axe will cut you down, and with vengeance and wrath, will at last cast you into the fire. You must learn to know the way of salvation, and how the mercy of God shines forth in a Mediator. Christ hath satisfied his justice, and by him you must come to God ; out of Christ, he is a consuming fire. Abused mercy, O sinner ! will be turned at last into fury. Except you obtain an interest in Jesus Christ, you are undone ; " for the wrath of God is revealed from heaven against all ungodliness and unrighteousness of men," Rom. i. 18.

3. Or are you self-righteous persons ? Do you build on your own righteousness, like the Jews and hypocritical Pharisees ? You, may be, think your state's good, because you are not swearers, drunkards, &c., May be, you do read, pray, and hear sermons, and give to the poor, and do much good ; but if you build your hopes of heaven on these things ; down this axe will cut you also ; " Except your righteousness exceed the righteousness of the Scribes and Pharisees, you shall in no wise enter into the kingdom of heaven," Matt. v. 20. Nay, you must be found in the righteousness of Christ ; " all ours is but dung," Phil. iii. 8, 9. You must, in a word, bring forth good fruit, every soul of you, or perish ; and this you cannot do, till your hearts are changed, and so you become good trees. Make the tree good, and then the fruit will be good ; "an evil tree cannot bring forth good fruit," &c. All works of regenerate persons, yea, their religious duties, are but dead works, not good fruits ; nor can they bring forth good fruits, unless they are planted by faith into Jesus Christ. Nay, I must tell you, that gospel-holiness will not save us ; it must be the righteousness of God by faith.

3. THE FAN IN HIS HAND

Whose fan is in his hand, and he will thoroughly purge his floor, and gather the wheat into his garner, but the chaff he will burn up with unquenchable fire.—Matt. iii. 12.

OUR text is metaphorically, and as touching the main scope and coherence of it, it is one and the same with the 10th verse of this chapter, I have already spoken unto.

John the Baptist endeavoureth to take off the Jews from their pretended privileges, of having Abraham to their father, or their being his natural seed, or offspring ; and so considered in covenant with God, and thought their state and condition good. Which he strove to convince them was a mistake, and this he doth by that tropical expression in ver. 10, " Now also is the axe laid to the root of the trees." And in this 12th verse, " whose fan is in his hand," &c. As if he should say, you shall ere long see yourselves deceived, for all your great confidence in the flesh, touching your external, federal, relative holiness, and legal privileges : for Christ with his axe will now quickly cut you down : and with his fan, fan you away as chaff, if you have no better right to church-membership on earth, and to the glory in heaven, than that which is derived to you from the account whereof you boast, viz., having Abraham to your Father. So much only shall now serve as to the scope and coherence of the words.

1. I shall proceed to give you the parts of this symbolical text.
2. Open the terms hereof.
3. Note two or three points of doctrine therefrom.
4. Apply the whole.

First, we have the person speaking, and that is, John the Baptist.

Secondly, the person spoken of, and that is Jesus Christ.

Thirdly, The predicate, or what is spoken of Christ, *i. e.*, whose fan is in his hand, &c.

John the Baptist was a great prophet, yea, " the greatest prophet that was born of woman ;" having greater light and knowledge of the Messiah than any of them that went before him, in that he could tell them this is he. He was sent to prepare the way of the Lord, as his great messenger or harbinger. He therefore was well instructed into the nature and excellency of his Master's kingdom, which was suddenly to be set up, upon the removal of the old Jewish church, and church membership ; this John was he that the prophet Malachi spoke of, that God would send as his messenger, to prepare the way of the

Lord, as also how he would do this, even by a spirit of burning, that should consume that people, and leave them neither root nor branch, *i. e.*, burn up all their hopes in respect of their root, viz., that external covenant, God made with Abraham, on which they stood, and of which they boasted: as also all that confidence they had in their own good works, and inherent righteousness. And this, John's ministry, clearly held forth, and thereby discovered the grand effect and glorious design of Christ's doctrine, and nature of his spiritual kingdom, which was near at hand.

Secondly, As touching Jesus Christ, who is the person John speaks of. I shall not now treat of his office, power, dignity, and glory, which are more fully hinted at in the context. "Whose shoes I am not worthy to bear, he shall baptize you with the Holy Ghost and with fire," ver. 11.

But I shall pass by that, and shall explain the terms.

1. Show you what is intended by floor.
2. What by the fan in Christ's hand.
3. What is meant by the chaff.
4. What by the wheat.
5. What are we to understand by Christ's garner.
6. And lastly, what is meant by the fire, and by burning up the chaff.

First, Thoroughly purge his floor. No doubt by floor the Holy Ghost alludes to that, which, in common acceptation, is well understood by husbandmen, *i. e.*, a floor is a heap of corn that is threshed out of the straw, and laid in a barn, wheat and chaff together; this usually is called a floor. **What is meant by the floor.**

By floor here, is doubtless intended more directly and immediately the Jewish church, but in a more remote and comprehensive sense, any spiritual community of Christians, church, or body of people, professing religion.

1. The Jews were then God's floor (or God's people), as God himself is called a husbandman; and they were a great heap, a mighty floor. But almost all chaff; loose, vain, empty, carnal, and unbelieving men and women. A more profane and ungodly generation was hardly ever in the world; and but a very few godly ones among them, but a very little wheat, viz: few sincere or believing persons in all that floor, who waited for Christ's coming, and did when he came, in truth receive him.

But now the Lord Jesus was come, with his fan in his hand, to separate the wheat from the chaff, and not let them remain any longer together on that floor in that old barn, *i. e.*, in the legal Jewish church-state, according to the external covenant of peculiarity God made with Abraham, and his natural seed as such: which had stood near its full period of time prefixed by the Almighty, but now must be pulled down, Jesus Christ being come, and just going to build a new spiritual garner, or Gospel church, to put all his choice grain or wheat into; viz., all believing and true penitent persons; this primarily I am satisfied, is intended by floor. For the Jewish church was not to abide or continue any longer than till the death and resurrection of Jesus Christ; it being a typical church. When the Antitype was come, that must needs vanish away.

Whose fan is in his hand. A fan is a certain instrument which the husbandman uses to cleanse, or purge his corn from the chaff, evil seeds, and all filth whatsoever. And this instrument he holds in his hands, and uses upon his knees, by which he tosses up the wheat and chaff together, and then shakes it to and fro, moving all at once, by which a wind is made, and the chaff is blown away, and the wheat separated and purged from it. Now John Baptist alludes to such an instrument as this. **What is a fan.**

1. By Christ's fan is meant his word, his holy Gospel, especially the doctrine thereof; it is by this he cleanses and purges his floor. "Now you are clean through the word I have spoken unto you." Now the unclean person, the traitor Judas, is gone out from you, Through my word, *i. e.*, through my doctrine, you believing in me, and receiving me by faith for righteousness and eternal life. It is said "Christ gave himself for his church, that he might sanctify and cleanse it with the washing of water by the word," Ephes. v. 26. Cleansing here imports the means by which it is wrought, or the instrument, namely the word of the Gospel, especially the promise of free justification and sanctification by Christ. Sirs, this was, and still is, Christ's fan, namely, the glorious doctrine of God's free grace through the redemption that is in Christ's blood; and it was by this fan Christ cleansed that Jewish floor, to which my text primarily refers. For the Jews were his floor, and now Jesus Christ was come with his fan in his hand, to purge this floor; and evident it is, his holy doctrine severed or separated the wheat from the chaff; and by this means was the wheat gathered into Christ's gospel-garner, and the chaff blown **What Christ's fan is.**

away; for as chaff cannot endure the wind of the fan, so could not those unbelieving Jews, and hypocritical Pharisees, endure Christ's holy and heavenly doctrine, see John vi. 52, to ver. 60. "How can this man give us his flesh to eat?" They thought he spake of a natural eating of his flesh, as we eat the flesh of beasts or fish: his doctrine was not understood by them. "Then Jesus said unto them, Verily, verily I say unto you, except you eat the flesh of the Son of man, and drink his blood, ye have no life in you," ver. 53. The eating of Christ's flesh, and drinking of his blood, is no other thing than the receiving Jesus Christ by faith for righteousness and eternal life. "Believing in Christ, coming to Christ, looking to Christ, leaning, trusting, or staying on Christ, receiving of Christ, and eating of Christ," imply one and the same thing. It is our going out of ourselves to him, or feeding by faith on him, or resting, or relying on his merits, on his obedience in his life, and in his death, for justification and eternal life, without any works done by us, or any righteousness wrought in us, as the Apostle speaks, "But to him that worketh not, but believeth on him that justifies the ungodly, his faith is counted for righteousness," Rom. iv. 5.

But this mysterious and sublime doctrine the Jews could not bear, but it was such a fan as fanned them all away that believed not, "For they being ignorant of God's righteousness, going about to establish their own righteousness, have not submitted themselves to the righteousness of God," Rom. x. 3. They thought their own personal inherent righteousness was that by which they must be justified, accepted, and eternally saved: they had meat of their own to eat, and therefore saw no need to go to their neighbours' door for it; they were full, and increased in goods, and thought they had need of nothing. And hence the doctrine of justification by the righteousness of Christ alone was rejected by them, it was not understood by them: that "Christ's flesh should be meat indeed, and his blood drink indeed," was a strange doctrine in their apprehensions; they could not conceive how such things could be, (as Nicodemus spake of regeneration,) John iii. 9. Nor can any man whatsoever, who will receive no point of faith, but what his natural reason can comprehend. And thus this doctrine of our Lord Jesus was a fan in his hand, and it fanned away all the chaff of that mighty Jewish floor, who believed not in Christ.

The dispensation of God was a fan in Christ's hand. Second place, Jesus Christ hath another fan also, and that is (I doubt not likewise intended here. The dispensation of God's providence: for this was also a fan in Christ's hand, by which he fanned away those unbelieving Jews, and so purged his floor; I mean, the time was now come that their national, legal, and external church-state must be pulled down and dissolved, the dispensation was changed, the priesthood changed, and right of church-membership changed. Their having Abraham to their father, or being the seed of professing parents, would do them no good, nor avail them any thing, because the covenant of peculiarity God made with him and his natural seed as such, as to the date or duration thereof, was now run out and expired, the axe being now laid to the root of the tree, ver. 10. So that unless they receive Christ, believe in Christ, and are found gracious persons, fit wheat for Christ's spiritual garner or gospel-church (which is built up of lively stones) as chaff the gospel-dispensation like a fan purges them out, as indeed it did, and blew them all away: and we are not alone in respect of this great truth, for many of our worthy brethren (who in some things differ from us) assert the same; particularly the Rev. Mr. Cotton, who speaking of this text, Matt. iii. 10, saith, "The first is the root of Abraham's covenant, which this people much trusted upon, and of that it is which John Baptist speaketh, 'Now is the axe laid to the root of the tree, think not to say within yourselves, we have Abraham to our father,' so that all their confidence that they had in Abraham's covenant, temple, and tabernacle, and such things are burnt up, and so they have no root left them to stand upon, and this is one thing intended by the root.

"Secondly, There is (saith he) something more in it; the Lord by the power of his Spirit doth cut us off from any power of our natural gifts and parts, and spiritual gifts also; or from any confidence of our own sufficiency; the Lord hath cut us off from any hope in the righteousness of our parents, and from boasting of ordinances. And again, he saith, 'This we read of,' Mal. iv. 1. It is spoken of the ministry of John the Baptist, which did burn as an oven against all the Scribes and Pharisees, and left them neither the root of Abraham's covenant, nor the branch of their own good works. He cutteth them off from the covenant of Abraham, &c. And by cutting them off from the root, he leaveth them no ground to trust on." Thus Mr. Cotton on the covenant, p. 177, and p. 21, 22. Now evident it is, that nothing but the dispensation of God's providence, or the expiration of that period of time determined by the Almighty for the standing of the church of Israel, could cut the Jews off as a nation, from being a church and peculiar people unto God; I mean in respect of that legal covenant. (I deny not but that the covenant of grace God made with Abraham, and with his true spiritual seed, stands firm for ever and ever, and none in that covenant can be cut off, nor fanned away.) For the Jewish priesthood, church-state, and church-membership, and all their church-privileges were to remain until Christ came; or until the time of reformation; that is, till the gospel days and gospel-dispensation took place and no longer. But now that time being come, and they not seeing an end put to the old covenant-church, as it was made with the natural offspring of Abraham, and that their right to legal ordinances and church-membership, could not give them any right to gospel ordinances, nor gospel-church-membership; and they not believing in Christ, not accepting of the terms of the gospel, were all of necessity purged out, or fanned away by the fan of the New Testament dispensation, and so were no longer a people in any sense in covenant with God.

Thirdly, Christ hath also another fan in his hand, viz., the fan of church discipline. And many persons falling into sin, are purged like chaff out of his floor thereby. 1. Sometimes some evil and corrupt persons, who get among God's people (or into his church) and pass a while for wheat, i.e., for gracious persons, yet in time God suffers them to fall into one temptation or another, by which means they are fanned away. The holy Jesus by his wise providence making a discovery of them, and their evil tempers and dispositions.

2. Others, whom Christ would have purged out of his church, may be suffered to such in some evil, corrupt, and dangerous principle, or errors in fundamentals, like that of " Hymeneus and Alexander," 1 Tim. i. 20; whose errors being discovered, are purged uot.

3. Also many fall into notorious and scandalous sins, and are purged out by this fan, Also.

4. Some who are chaff, or unsound Christians, may be suffered to take up undue offences against the church, or churches to whom they do belong, and by giving way to temptation, they may become unreconcileable, magnifying their own wisdom and self-conceitedness, so by a secret hand of God be discovered and purged out. But it must be considered that the use and exercise of the keys or rules of church discipline, is appointed by Christ, as the proper fan by which those sorts of persons last mentioned, and some others, are to be purged out of the church, or congregation of the saints.

I told you that this fan of discipline takes hold of, are such that suck in heresies or capital errors; these after the first and second admonition (Tit. iii. 10), ought to be " rejected and delivered up to Satan, that they may not learn to blaspheme," 1 Tim. i. 20.

5. Such also who refuse to hear the church after the case (in which they have offended) is regularly brought in against them, according to the rule contained in Matt. xviii. 17. The offence at first may be against one brother, and the offended party is first to tell him his fault between himself and his brother or sister that hath offended him, alone : whom if he can bring to see and acknowledge his evil, it is to proceed no further; but if he cannot, then he is obliged by the holy law of Christ, to take one or two more, and go to him, and strive to convince him, and bring him to a sight and sense of his iniquity; but if he cannot do it, then it ought to be brought to the church, and if he will not hear the church, then the fan of excommunication is to be used in the name of Jesus Christ, and he purged out.

Fourthly, Jesus Christ hath also another fan in his hand to purge his floor, or cleanse his wheat from the chaff, filth, and defilement of sin, namely the Holy Spirit ; and by this means he cleanses and purifies, in a gracious manner, the souls of his own people: " Such were some of you ; but ye are washed, but ye are sanctified, but ye are justified in the name of the Lord Jesus, and by the Spirit of our God," 1 Cor. vi. 11. What filthy creatures were those Corinthians, before the Lord Jesus by his Spirit had purged and sanctified them.

Faith, of the operation of God, is a most excellent grace ; it is by faith in the blood of Christ that we come to be purged from the guilt of sin ; faith applying his merits and righteousness unto the soul in justification ; and such is the nature thereof, that it makes holy the hearts and lives of all such persons in whom it is by the Spirit wrought or infused in sanctification ; " And hath put no difference between them and us, purifying their hearts by faith," Acts xv. 9. Yea, it cleanseth them " From all filthiness of flesh and spirit, that they may perfect holiness in the fear of God," 2 Cor. vii. 1.

But let me tell you that the Spirit and grace of Christ, in this respect, is as a fan, and rather to cleanse the saints, by purging out the chaff of corruption, which naturally is in their hearts and lives, than to purge hypocrites and false professors out of the church, and to that I principally refer here.

Fifthly, moreover Christ hath the fan of persecution, or the sufferings of the cross, and all other afflictions which he brings upon his people, which he uses to purge and purify their souls, and his churches too.

And from hence afflictions are compared to a refiner's fire : " He shall sit as a refiner's fire, and purifier of silver." He, that is, the Messiah, i.e., our Lord Jesus Christ ; this his work, viz., to purge his people, who in this place are compared to silver and gold, that is refined : as in my text they are likened unto wheat. In this he is compared to a refiner, and hath his furnace ; in the other to an husbandman, and so hath his fan. Both these texts allude to the same thing, and doing the same work, namely, to sever and separate the clean from the unclean, the gold from the dross, the chaff from the wheat. And evident it is, that persecutions, trials, and afflictions, commonly make a great discovery who are wheat or pure gold, viz., sincere believers : and who drossy and chaffy professors. If wheat, persecution purges and purifies them : but if they are chaff, it usually fans them away. But he that receiveth the seed in stony places, the same is he who heareth the word, and with joy receiveth it : " Yet hath he not root in himself, but endureth for a while ; for when tribulation or persecution ariseth, because of the word, by and by he is offended," Matt. xiii. 20, 21. Thus the fan of persecution purges these chaffy professors out of Christ's spiritual floor, or rather his garner : by the spirit of judgment and by the spirit of burning. The rod of affliction, or furnace of persecution, cannot purge out the filth of sin that is in the Lord's people without the operations of the Holy Spirit ; the Spirit is called a Spirit of burning, because like fire it burns up and consumes the filth, chaff, and dross, that is in us. Before trials and persecution come, Christ seems to have a very great floor, a great heap, or much corn ; but when he comes to try them with his fan in his hand, one great part thereof is found mere chaff, and the wind drives it away. So much shall suffice as to the fan in Christ's hand by which he purges his floor.

Quest. What is meant by the chaff ?

Answ. I answer the chaff may be understood to be twofold.

1. Men and women who get into God's church, or among his people, but are not wheat, but vile hypocrites, pretending to be that which in truth they are not ; thus all that are of Israel are not Israel. Though they bore his name, were called Jews, called saints, yet were unsound at heart, and graceless souls, or mere chaff, in God's sight.

2. By chaff may also be intended sin, or that filth and corruption which cleaveth ofttimes to the best of God's people, which Christ must and will purge out.

Quest. Why are hypocrites or ungodly persons in the church compared to chaff ? And how may they be known ?

Answ. I answer, hypocrites and ungodly men in the church are compared to chaff ;

1. Because chaff, before it is separated from the wheat, cleaveth close to it, and it is hard to sever it from the wheat, and it also seems like unto it : even so some carnal and hypocritical professors cleave to the church, and seem to love and embrace the godly in their arms, and to lay them in their hearts ; they walk in company, nay in outward fellowship and church communion with them ; they pray, and break bread with them, as if they were really gracious, and are not known to their brethren to be otherwise : and as it is hard to discern them from the godly, so it is hard to separate such from them. Chaff is so much like to the wheat, that some have taken it at first view to be wheat ; so are these taken to be saints, and there may be no severing them from the congregation of the Lord, till Christ comes with his fan to purge his floor.

2. They may be compared to chaff, in regard of the great pains that is and must be used to separate it from the wheat : the wheat must be threshed and fanned ; nay, fanned again and again, before all the chaff can be severed from it. So unsound professors, or some hypocrites in the church, seem to cleave so close to the godly, and are in such seeming union and oneness with them, that the Lord sees there is no other way to sever them from each other, but by threshing his wheat with the flail of persecution, and then the chaff flies away by the wind of this fan.

3. Chaff is of very little worth or value unto wheat ; " What is the chaff unto the wheat, saith the Lord ?" Jer. xxiii. 28. One peck of good wheat is worth many bushels of chaff. So ungodly men and women are of little worth in God's sight ; a wicked man to him is loathsome," Prov. xiii. 5, as Solomon shows, and that which is loathsome and hateful in our sight, we value not, but cast away. The prayers of the wicked are abominable to the Lord, because their persons are not accepted in Christ. Whatsoever the ungodly do, or whatsoever show they

make of religion, let them pray, hear, read, preach, or give to the poor, it is not regarded nor accepted of the Lord ; one godly person is more to him, than a multitude of unsanctified and hypocritical persons. The tongue of the just is as choice as silver, the heart of the wicked is but of little worth. The best part of a child of God is his heart, though he thinks that is the worst of all. Saints are wheat, hypocrites chaff ; the one is gold, the other dross in God's esteem. Hence the Lord saith, " Since thou wast precious in my sight, thou hast been honourable, and I have loved thee : therefore will I give men for thee, and people for thy life : I will give Egypt for thy ransom, Ethiopia and Seba for thee." Isa. xliii. 3, 4. God so little values graceless persons, that he will sacrifice thousands of them in love and mercy to his faithful ones.

4 Chaff is light and airy, it is no ponderous thing, therefore the wind carries it this way, and that way, at every turn : nay, every small breath of wind moves it to and fro ; whereas wheat stirs not, moves not, but abides in its place, it being a weighty and ponderous thing. Even so all hypocritical and unsound professors, whatsoever they seem to be at some times, (by making a show of religion, and pretending to piety) yet they are in God's sight as light as vanity ; they are like chaff, not serious, weighty, and ponderous, they are but a flash, a shadow, and no substance, having mere dry, barren, and empty souls. And their lightness appears and shows itself in many respects.

1. It appears sometimes by their light, frothy, and airy talk and discourse. They may sometimes seem serious ; but if watched they will be discovered, their tongues will betray them, by their foolish and vain words, and communication. " They setting no watch before the door of their lips, and bridle not their tongue, therefore their religion is vain," James i. 26, as the apostle James shows.

Christians, if you would not be found chaff at the great day, take heed of a reviling tongue, lest you deceive yourselves, and all your religion and profession be vain. " He either deceiveth his own heart (saith our Annotators) in thinking himself religious, when indulging himself in things contrary to religion ; or else deceiveth his own heart, being blinded with self-love, and lifted up with self-conceit, which is the cause of his railing, censuring, and speaking evil of others. Their religion is vain, empty, and to no purpose, having no reality in itself, and bringeth no benefit to them.

O what a reproach doth the talkative and prating person bring on the name of God. This man, this woman, say they, is a member of such or such a church, and see what vain talk, frothy words, and frivolous discourse proceed from their lips ? But much more evil is in such who backbite, revile, and defame others (as was hinted before.) This I say may discover such to be but chaff.

2. They appear to be chaff, not only by their light, vain, idle, and back-biting tongues, but also by their light behaviour ; for the lightness of the heart is as much discovered by a loose and airy deportment, as by loose and vain words ; their wanton looks, and rolling eyes, or other unseemly and uncomely carriage, show in part what they are ; they being not of a grave, sober, and serious spirit, but behave themselves as if they had no sense of the omnisciency of God upon their hearts, nor of his holiness ; not setting the Lord always before them, gives cause to all to fear they are but chaff.

3. Their light, empty, and airy attire, dresses, and antic fashions, which they wear and take delight in, doubtless too much discovers the lightness, vanity, and emptiness of their spirits. I am persuaded these high and shameless head-dresses which some women appear in, that come into Christian assemblies, are but as tell-tales of the vanity, pride, emptiness, and haughtiness of their hearts ; who but they that sell wine will put forth a bush ? I cannot see how a sober serious Christian woman should be satisfied to wear such antique dresses. Their souls sure must needs blush at the thoughts of them ; when they consider whose eyes behold them, viz., God.

4. Such are chaff that only have the husk or shell of Christianity. Chaff is the husks of wheat. Many professors please themselves with the external part of religion, having a form of godliness, but are strangers to the life and power thereof. Like the foolish virgins, they have lamps, but no oil ; a name, but want the nature of true believers ; can talk and discourse of religion, of the covenant of grace, and excellency of Christ. They may have, I grant, clear notions in their heads of the mysteries of the Gospel, and defend it too against opposers, yet their hearts are unsanctified, and never felt nor experienced the work of faith with power ; they have the outside of the true Christian, the shell of the wheat, but if tried and searched there is nothing but chaff, no kernel in them, they want the root of the matter. All true believers have passed through the pangs of the new birth ; they found they were once dead, but are now alive ; once blind, but now they see ; once

lost in their own eyes, but now found ; once carnal, but now spiritual ; once had their affection set on things below, but now on things above. Sin was once sweet and pleasant to them, but now it is bitter and loathsome in their eyes, because they see it is so in the sight of God. Their judgments are informed, their understandings savingly enlightened, Christ and heavenly things are valued and esteemed above all things here below, yea, above ten thousand worlds, by them ; and their understandings are not only brought to assent to the truth of Christ, to the glory and beauty of Christ ; but their wills also are subjected to him ; they are brought to consent and yield themselves to the Lord ; they believe and love, believe and obey, believe and suffer reproach, taking up the cross, putting on the yoke of Christ ; their affections are so changed, and under divine influences, that what they loved once, they hate ; and what they once hated, or liked not, they dearly love and approve of now. But thus it is not with chaffy professors. They may be changed from open profaneness to an outward reformation of life, but their hearts are not changed, sin is not crucified in them, self is not subdued ; that enmity that was naturally in their hearts, or dislike to the life and power of strict godliness, is not removed ; they act only from common illuminations of the Spirit, and so they put a force upon themselves when found in religious duties : and find not a natural inclination and sweet propensity in their hearts to heavenly things. And this shows they are no more than chaff.

5. And lastly, chaff I told you is light, and every breath of wind will move it, this way, and that way ; and if it rises high, it will, may be, blow it quite away, there being no kernel in it, whereas the wheat abides.

So chaffy and vain professors are startled at every small blast of persecution, and presently begin to move out of their place, and shun assembling themselves with God's people. Nay, every wind of corrupt doctrine is ready to blow some of this sort away ; they are unsettled persons, that want weight, or are not rooted in the truth, wanting a good understanding, and a principle of saving grace in their hearts. " Be not carried about with divers and strange doctrines, for it is good to have the heart established with grace, and not with meats," Heb. xiii. 9.

This sort are soon corrupted from the simplicity of the gospel, by the cunning craftiness of men, being ready to receive any strange notion, or close in with a new scheme of religion, some turning to Judaism and add Moses to Christ, or join to the gospel their own works. They are commonly corrupt, either in principles or practices, or in both ; making a stir about the mint, annise, and cummin. i. e., about the smaller matters of religion, as concerning meats and observation of days, as if in such things lay the great stress of Christianity. How many are there who like those false teachers, and deluded people in the primitive times, plead for justification some other way than by faith only, and bring in their own inherent holiness and sincere obedience, and add that to the merits of Christ, in point of justification before God ; or exalt the power and will of the creature, to the eclipsing the doctrine of free-grace.

Sin is likened to chaff,
Matt. iii. 3.

Secondly, By chaff may also be meant, sin, filth, and corruption, which cleaveth to the hearts and lives of true believers, which Christ by the fan of his Word, Spirit, and afflictions, as you have heard, purges out. " He shall purify the sons of Levi, and purge them as gold and silver, that they may offer unto the Lord an offering in righteousness." This is spoken of Jesus Christ, whose fan is in his hand. It shows his work and office, namely, to refine and fan his people, not only members but ministers also, signified by the sons of Levi, that they all may offer acceptable sacrifice unto God. Besides, our Lord Jesus sometimes makes use of wicked men as a fan in his hand to purge his people, and he did of old fan Israel by the Babylonians, and by the Assyrians ; " I will send unto Babylon fanners, as I have sometimes fanned and scattered my people by them ; so will I fan them by the Medes and Persians, who shall empty the land of them," Jer. lix. 2. After Christ hath fanned or purged away the chaff and filth of the daughter of Zion, he will fan their enemies, and they being all chaff, the wind of his indignation will drive them away. Let this be noted, that Christ hath many ways to fan and purge his people, yet still it is for their good ; and they shall lose nothing but their chaff, their sin and corruptions thereby.

" And gather his wheat into his garner." The saints are here called wheat.

1. Wheat is a choice grain, the best grain ; so true believers are a choice people in Christ's sight. " The righteous is more excellent than his neighbour," Prov. xii. 26. They are called " the excellent in all the earth," Psal. xvi. 3. " God calls his people his jewels, or choice treaure ;" Matt. iii. ult. They are men of a high and heavenly birth, of

high, sublime, and excellent spirit; they are espoused, by an excellent person act, and are influenced by excellent principles; and have glorious ends and aims in all they do. And from hence may be compared to wheat. See the parable of the wheat and Tares, Matt. xiii. 24.

2. Wheat hath its chaff, cleaving ofttimes close it, it will stick and cleave so to it, that it is not easily separated. Where the nature of wheat is largely opened.

So it is with Christ's spiritual wheat; the filth or chaff of internal corruption is very subject to cleave to them, and hard it is for them to get rid of it. " When I would do good, sin is present with me; for the good I would, I do not; but the evil which I would not do, that do I," Rom. vii. 21—24.

Oh! wretched man that I am, who shall deliver me from the body of this death? I am (as if he should say) even wearied with continual combating. I cannot get rid of this dead body, this inward filth and corruption, the remainders of sin in my flesh; this chaff cleaves to all Christ's wheat.

3. Wheat is threshed with the flail, to sever it from the straw or chaff, by the husbandman; so God, to sever the wheat, i. e., the godly from the chaffy professor, and free them of the filth and corruption of their own hearts, brings his flail of affliction and persecution upon them.

4. Wheat is also fanned, to cleanse it; and it is to be noted, that the fan in the hand of the husbandman tosses up the wheat and chaff together, and then he shakes it to and fro, this way, and that way, on his knees.

So the Lord Jesus with his spiritual fan tosses the godly and hypocritical professor, by the same afflictions, trials, persecutions, and temptations. And O what hurryings, tossings and tumblings to and fro in their spirits, have some Christians met with in the late times, and still daily meet withal. They have their ups and downs, this affliction and the other temptation; this loss, and the other cross: but yet, nevertheless, they are not tossed out; whilst Christ's wheat is refined, they abide fanning, (as I hinted before), but so doth not the carnal and light professor: " They are offended," Matt. xiii. 21, through this means, as our Saviour shows, and are ready to say with that wicked man of old, " this evil is of the Lord, why should I wait upon him any longer?" 1 Kings vi. 33. Believers know God doth it not for his pleasure, but for their profit, that they might be partakers of his holiness," Heb. xii. 10. Hence it is said, that " they endure chastening, and faint not when they are rebuked of the Lord."

" And gather the wheat into his garner."

Christ hath a two-fold garner.

First. His Church is his garner.

1. A garner is prepared on purpose to retain, and safely to secure the wheat in a heap together, where it is carefully to be looked after. So is the Church of God appointed and prepared to receive and secure his faithful people together; it is not built for chaff and tares, and great care and pains is required of Christ's servants in looking to, and taking care of his spiritual wheat in his Church.

Yet through want of care, or weakness, or want of knowledge in Christ's ministers and servants, in discerning who are sincere Christians, and who are not: many unsound and chaffy professors are let into the church or churches of Jesus Christ, which is displeasing unto him, because they spoil the beauty and glory thereof, and cause many to reproach his faithful ones; as it also renders them in the sight of the carnal world not to be God's people.

Therefore, Christ with the fan of persecution oftentimes fans his people, to purge out the loose and profane from among them.

Secondly, By the garner is meant heaven itself, into which all the elect shall be put at the last day, and into this garner shall none come but pure wheat: " And there shall in no wise enter into it any thing that defileth, neither whatsoever worketh abomination, or that maketh a lie, but they which are written in the Lamb's book of life." Rev. xxi. 27. Heaven is Christ's garner.

" But he will burn up the chaff with unquenchable fire."

By burning up the chaff with unquenchable fire, is meant the direful wrath of God, which sometimes seizes on ungodly persons in this world, and shall eternally take hold of all the chaff in the world to come. The wrath of God is often compared to fire in the Scripture. " There went up a smoke out of his nostrils, and a fire out of his mouth devouring; coals were kindled by it," Psal. viii. 8. So in another place it is said, " A fire goeth before him," Psal. xc. 3, &c. " Shall thy wrath burn like fire?" Psal. lxxxii. 46. " His fury is poured out like fire, and the rocks are thrown down by him," Nah. i. 7. What meant by burning up the chaff.

1. Fire is a terrible and a most amazing element, especially when it breaks forth like a masterless enemy, and none can stop it ; so is the wrath of God very terrible, when he poureth it forth in his greatest fury. O what a frightful cry doth a dreadful fire that breaks out in a town or city cause ! what a wringing of hands ! men tremble, women miscarry oftentimes, children screech out, it frightens the very fowls of the air, and beasts of the earth, and turns all faces into paleness ! How amazing were the flames of Sodom, and how terrible is the burning of mount Ætna ! The wrath of God, when it furiously breaketh forth upon a people and nation, or particular person, causeth dreadful horror, it maketh the stoutest heart to quake, and the strongest hands feeble : " At his wrath the earth shall tremble, and the nations shall not be able to abide his indignation," Jer. x. 10. His fury is poured out like fire, and the mountains are thrown down before him. Can thy heart endure, or thy hands be strong, in the day when I contend with thee ? " Who can stand before his indignation ?" Nah. i. 6. O how will the wicked fly into holes, quiver like a leaf, " and cry to the rocks and mountains to fall upon them, and hide them from the face of him that sitteth upon the throne, and from the wrath of the Lamb," Rev. vi. 16.

2. Fire breaks out sometimes very suddenly, when none think of it, but all are, as they judge, safe and secure ; yet in a moment how are they surprised, when nothing but the horror and cry of, fire, fire, fire, is heard in their ears. So God's wrath, like a dreadful and unexpected fire, breaks out sometimes suddenly upon the ungodly. How surprising were the flames of Sodom, and the amazing hand-writing on Belshazzar's wall, when he was drinking wine in bowls ! immediately the " king's countenance was changed, and he was troubled in his thoughts, so that the joints of his loins were loosed, and his knees smote one against the other : Dan. v. 5, 6. " When they cry peace and safety, then sudden destruction cometh, as travail upon a woman with child, and they shall not escape," 1 Thess. iii. 3.

3. A fire sometimes breaks forth in the night, when men are asleep : so God comes upon men many times in the night of ignorance and unbelief, while they lie on their beds of ease and carnal security, by amazing judgments, or by suddden death. How secure was the old world, and the rich man in the gospel, to whom God said, " this night thy soul shall be required of thee ?"

4. A consuming fire destroys, wastes, and devours exceedingly ; as Sodom found, and London also, by woeful experience. So God when he breaks forth in his wrath and fury, he makes most lamentable desolation. " The Lord shall swallow them up in his wrath, and the fire shall devour them," Psal. xxi. 9, 10. The wrath of God is compared to a consuming fire : " For our God is a consuming fire," Heb. xii. ult.

5. A consuming and raging fire spares none, the palace of the prince, no more than the cottage of the peasant ; the mighty oaks, as well as the lowest shrubs, are devoured by it. So the wrath of God seizeth, and will seize on all wicked men ; on the mighty and honourable of the earth, as well as the poor and contemptible ones ; the king on his thrones, as well as the beggar on the dunghill. " His wrath shall be on every one that is proud and lifted up, and he shall be brought down ; upon all the cedars of Lebanon, and upon all the oaks of Bashan," Isa. ii. 12—16. " He will come upon princes as upon mortar, the whole earth shall be devoured by the fire of his jealousy, neither their gold nor silver shall be able to deliver them in the day of the Lord's wrath," Zeph. i. 18.

6. Wood, hay, stubble, chaff, and tares, are fit fuel for the fire to seize upon, and such things that are combustible make it to burn the more vehemently. And if strong towers cannot stand before a consuming fire, how is it possible for briars and thorns ? Some sinners are like stubble fully dry : they are fit fuel for the wrath of God, like fire, to take hold of. O what horrid guilt lies upon some men's consciences ! Just like a great heap or pile of wood, well dried, or cart loads of straw, or dry stubble : " What if God will to show his wrath, and make his power known, endured with much long suffering, the vessels of wrath fitted to destruction ?" Rom. ix. 22.

A long course in sin, custom in sin, resisting the grace of God, slighting convictions, hardening the heart against reproof, stifling the accusations of conscience, and abusing the patience and long suffering of God, fits men for the fire of his wrath ; " Whilst they are folden together as thorns, and whilst they are drunken as drunkards, they shall be devoured as stubble full dry," Nah. i. 10.

7. A dreadful fire, when it breaks out, turns all joy into sorrow, and makes a day of mirth a day of mourning : so the consuming wrath of God, whether it seizes on the consciences of men only whilst alive in the body, or on body and soul both here, or on the

soul at death, it turns all joy into sorrow. O what extremity of misery do such feel! ask Judas or Spira, they could tell you.

8. Fire is a most cruel and dreadful tormentor; if a man be cast into a fire, what intolerable pain and anguish doth it put him to; but alas, alas, that is nothing to the wrath of God, when God kindles it in the consciences of men, nor to hell fire. You will say, O it is a fearful thing to fall into a furious fire, into a burning furnace; but, O sirs, how much more dreadful it is to fall under the wrath of God! " It is a fearful thing to fall into the hands of the living God: for our God is a consuming fire," Heb. ii. 12. If it be terrible to have a finger, a foot, or a hand to be burned off, or to have the whole body cast into a furnace of boiling oil, (as some of the holy martyrs were) how then can sinners, who are as chaff, bear the thoughts of God's wrath and vindictive vengeance, which is far more intolerable than any fire into which any mortal was ever cast? For,

1. Other fire burns only the external part, or temporal, or corporal matter; but the fire of God's wrath burns and torments the spirit, the soul, the invisible part.

2. Elementary fire is seen, but internal wrath is only felt inwardly, it cannot be seen.

3. The fiercest fire that ever was kindled hath been overcome, and by engines or instruments put out; but the fire of God's wrath, when kindled, and the soul thrown into hell, cannot be put out, nor be extinguished; it is unquenchable fire. Though the burning of mount Etna and other burning mountains is impossible for man to extinguish, yet doubtless they shall not burn always, they will be put out; but wrath shall burn for ever. So much as to the explanation of our text. From hence we may observe divers propositions or points of doctrine.

1. Doct. The old floor is gone, it is removed, viz., the old Jewish Church, or national Church of Israel, the wheat that was in it being taken into Christ's gospel garner, and the chaff, or all graceless persons, " or unbelievers, are fanned away," Eph. ii. 16. Now Christ hath removed the partition-wall that was between Jew and Gentile, and hath reconciled both unto God in one body, 2 Cor. v. 17. Now there is no knowing men after the flesh, fleshly privileges, i. e., being the seed of Abraham, or being the seed of believers as such, gives no right to spiritual, saving, and eternal blessings. Both those two people, Jews and Gentiles, that believe, of twain are made one, i. e., one new man, or one Christian or Gospel Church. And this is done by Jesus Christ, who by his fan, or dispensation of the New Testament, hath abolished the old covenant right of church-membership; not the fleshly seed, but the spiritual seed of Abraham, are to be received into Christ's Gospel garner; " Ye as lively stones are built up a spiritual house," 1 Pet. ii. 5., &c. But this I shall not prosecute.

2. Doct. Jesus Christ would have none but pure wheat be gathered into his garner; not the fleshly and spiritual seed, not the believer and the unbeliever, not godly ones and ungodly ones, not the chaff and the wheat, as it was under the law, in the national church of the Jews. Not whole parishes, or whole nations; no, no, none but true Christians, or holy persons, sanctified and sincere, and truly gracious souls.

3. Doct. Christ's great work and office is to purge his people, to cleanse them, and make them holy, and to sever the wheat from the chaff, the pure from the impure; or to separate hypocrites from his church, and purge his saints from all their inward filth and corruption: he would have no chaff there, none that are false-hearted and unsound, such will he first or last purge out; and he will make them that are good to be much better, more clean, more holy, more pure, he will purge out the chaff of hypocrites, unbelief, pride, passion, covetousness, vain-glory, carnality, and all manner of corruption whatsoever that is in them. He sits as a refiner and purifier of silver, and he will throughly " purge away their dross, and take away all their tin," Isa. i. 25. The time draws near in which " the sinners in Zion shall be afraid, fearfulness shall surprise the hypocrites: who amongst us shall dwell with devouring fire? who amongst us shall dwell with everlasting burnings?" Isa. xxxiii. 14.

4. Doct. All true believers, or all Christ's wheat, shall be saved, shall be received into heaven, or be gathered into his glorious garner above, and into which place no wicked person, no false-hearted professor, no hypocrite, no carnal and self-deceived gospeller, shall come. Though some of this sort get into the church militant, they shall not get into the church triumphant; though they may get a seeming place in his garner below, yet they shall have no place in his glorious barn or garner above. Sirs, you that seem to take delight in the company of the saints, and seem to feed and lie down with Christ's sheep, yet know you shall one day be separated as goats from the sheep, as foolish virgins from the wise,

as chaff from the wheat, and as dross from the gold ; all you that are not sincere must go to your place ; and those that shall be set at Christ's right-hand, shall receive the kingdom prepared for them, and all that shall be on his left-hand, must go into " everlasting fire, prepared for the devil and his angels," Matt. xxv. 41.

5. Doct. A discrimination day will come, a day of severing the good from the bad, &c.

6. Doct. The wrath of God is like fire, it is intolerable ; or the misery and torments of the damned, or of all hypocrites and unbelievers, will be dismal and amazing ; or there is no expressing how fearful their condition is and will be, who fall under the vindictive wrath and vengeance of an angry God. I shall not speak now to either of these propositions, but at present I shall close with a word or two by way of use.

The wrath of God, whether internal or external, is intolerable.

APPLICATION

1. Caution. Take heed you are not chaff, or prove not chaff, when the fanner comes to fan you. O see you are not loose, carnal, and empty professors ; if you have only a form of godliness, the name of Christ only, or lamps, and no more, sad will it be with you ; if you are not solid, weighty, and ponderous Christians. If you experience not the divine power of godliness, the sin-killing, the soul-quickening, the heart-transforming, and God-exalting power of Christ's Spirit, you are undone.

Take a few motives to stir you up to take heed.

1. The fanner is coming with his fan in his hand : A providence may be near, yea, such a providence and dispensation which you little think or dream of. I might have showed you that the whole earth is but Christ's common floor, and he is now about to fan this mighty floor ; he hath many fans to do this. What are his fearful judgments but as a fan in his hand, whether it be war, pestilence, or famine, or other strange judgment, it is and will be but as a fan to purge the earth, and consume the ungodly, or blow them away as chaff.

What amazing earthquakes have there been lately in divers places. Have not we in England, in London, felt some of it, (as well as most nations in Europe) though not like to that in Jamaica, and some other places ? Are not these fearful tokens and signs of God's wrath and indignation ? Are they not harbingers and presages of what is coming upon the world, and of the end thereof ? Look to it, there is great wrath at the door. I am afraid thousands will be suddenly surprised, and paleness of face take hold of them. God is certainly about to shake and toss the earth to and fro : the seven vials of his wrath will quickly now begin to be poured out : expect all of you to be tossed and fanned, as wheat and chaff is tossed and shook together : " The lion hath roared, who will not fear ? the Lord hath spoken, who can but prophesy ?" Amos iii. 8. There is a worse earthquake near, as the wicked shall find it ; yea, such an earthquake that will make all their hearts to tremble, which will shake down the foundations of mystery Babylon, and all false states ; it will be such a one that never was since the world began ; these which have been of late, may be but signs and forerunners of that. In the earthquake which is near, the tenth part of the great city shall fall, and seven thousand of the names of men, or names given to religious men, that were never given to them by Jesus Christ, mere antichristian names, shall be no more, strange will be the effects of it no doubt. O what will you do in the day of God's wrath if ye are chaff, or but counterfeit Christians ? If not sincere, if not in Christ, " Thou shalt be visited of the Lord in earthquakes and a great noise," &c., Isa. xxix. 6. Great changes, commotions, mutations, and revolutions, will suddenly come from the Lord of hosts : " He will make the earth empty, and turn it up-side down, and it shall be as with the people, so with the priest," Isa. xxiv. 1. He will fan, shake, and tumble the people together ; you will find distress of nations, and perplexity with a witness, in a short time ; nay, no doubt, but the day of judgment and end of the world, or coming of Christ ; is very near ; for he hath foretold these things as signs thereof " that there shall be great earthquakes in divers places," Matt. ii. 4.

2. If you be chaff among the wheat, you spoil the beauty and glory of the wheat ; you bring a reproach upon the saints and upon the church ; the ways of God are evil spoken of through your means ; your pride, your covetousness, your back-biting and detracting tongue, and unjust dealing, hinders the propagation of the gospel ; your formality, deadness, slighting and neglecting of the worship of God, and want of zeal, and love to Christ and to his

people, have bitter effects on the unbelieving world, as well as it will have on your own souls.

3. If you are chaff, you shall ere long be separated or severed from the wheat : there is a time near that will discover all, and make a full discrimination " between the righteous and the wicked, between him that serveth the Lord, and him that serveth him not," Mal. iii. 18. There shall not (ere long) be a Canaanite in the house of God any more.

4. Nay, and (remember) the chaff shall be burned with unquenchable fire ; into hell at last all false-hearted, light, and loose professors, shall be thrown. O take heed for your soul's sake, that you rest not upon a bare profession, or on a name of Christian.

5. This may inform us also, that Christ hath a gracious end in bringing persecutions and trials on his people ; it shows us why he uses the fan, as severe providences, judgments, and afflictions : it is, you have heard, to purge, to purify them, and to separate the chaff from them. O do not then think it strange concerning fiery trials, as if some strange thing had befallen you.

Exhort. Let me exhort you to see to it in time, that you be not deceived, and to prove chaff, and vain persons, empty and foolish virgins at last.

Motives. 1. O how far may men go, and yet be but almost Christians ! remember this.

2. Many when Christ comes shall have great confidence, and go forth to meet him, and yet be found foolish ones: some deceive their own hearts, and others have hearts deceived them, by trusting in them, and never examine how matters are between God and their own souls.

3. Men may preach and prophesy, yea, speak as if they had the tongue of men and angels, 1 Cor. xiii. 1, 2, and cast out devils in Christ's name, and yet be nothing ; they may preach, no doubt, to the conversion of others, and yet may not be converted themselves.

4. Wheat is commonly weighed, to know the goodness of it ; so God weighs the actions of men : thou art weighed in the balance, and art found wanting : weighed in a balance, alluding to the weighing of gold or goods exactly in scales. God tries men and women, that all may know he will proceed justly and righteously with them ; he weighs them in the balance of the sanctuary, or tries them by the touch-stone of his word, and if found full weight, or pure gold, then he declares that they are his, and he owns them as his people, as his wheat ; but if too light, or hold not weight, but are greatly wanting, there being no worth in them, but are dross, chaff, light, and empty persons, unsound and unsanctified ones, then he rejects them as none of his, but are as reprobate silver, false coin, people of no value with him.

As he weighs men, so he weighs their works, their graces, their duties, to see whether they hold weight, whether true and righteous or not ; whether their grace be true grace, special grace, not common grace, and their gifts counterfeit gifts, or mere natural gifts, or only human and acquired gifts. Some boast of false gifts, which as Solomon tells us, is like clouds and wind without rain. What a stir doth a vain person make of a strong memory, crying it up as if it was a spiritual gift, and as if none were true ministers but such who have a great memory, and can deliver all they have got by their study, by the strength of their memory. Alas, all men of any sense know, that is but a natural gift, which some wicked men have, as well as some good men ; but let him know, God knows what men's hearts are, what their ends and designs are, as well as what the matter of their worship is, which they perform to God ; that is, whether it hath his image stamped upon it ; or is of his authority, his own appointment, his own institution, or but human inventions : he also weighs the manner how they perform all divine worship towards him, from what principle, life, power, end, and design ; whether it is from a changed heart, from unfeigned faith and love to Christ, in sincerity, with zeal, and to glorify God ; if not, he will discover them, weigh them, and they will be found wanting, and be found no better than chaff at last. Though they may seek ways to hide and cover their wickedness, and false spirits, and base designs, yet let them know, he that weighs the hill in scales, and the mountains in balances, doth and will weigh them, and find out all their cursed deeds, their pride, their malice, and put a rebuke upon their backsliding and detracting tongues : " Talk (saith Hannah) no more so exceeding proudly, let not arrogancy come out of thy mouth ; for God is a God of knowledge, and by him actions are weighed," 1 Sam. ii. 3. Thou Peninnah (as our annotators note) "speak no more so insolently and reproachfully of me as thou hast done ; he knoweth thy heart, and all that pride, envy, and contempt of me, which thy own conscience knows, and thy perverse carriage towards me : God pondereth, and trieth all men's thoughts and actions, as a just judge, to give to every one according to their works.

Oh what a motive should this be to us all ! God weighs our persons, our graces, our gifts, our duties, and all our services, in scales : take heed you are not found too light, found wanting, as be sure you will, if you be found chaff, when put into the balance of the sanctuary.

Directions to try ourselves. Direction. 1. If you would not be found chaff, try and weigh your spirits, your persons, your faith, your love : see if it holds weight by the king's standard, see on what foundation you are built : have you dug deep, and laid your foundation on a rock ? What love have you to Christ ? Is He precious to your souls, the chiefest of ten thousand ? What love have you to the children of God ? How do you carry it at home and abroad ? Do you feed the hungry, visit the sick, and clothe the naked ? Is Christ's family, Christ's servants, Christ's poor, more in your esteem, love, and affections, than sons and daughters, than brethren and sisters, that are not his children ? If you do not love Christ more than father and mother, son or daughter, you may justly fear whether you are wheat or no ! And if it be so, that you do so love him, and his saints, ministers and people, it will appear whilst you live : and when you come to die, you will not forget Christ then, his people and interest then. O think on this !

2. And to you, sinners, if you would be found wheat in the day of Christ, then receive Christ's true doctrine, labour to distinguish between truth and error; beware of that strange and new scheme that darkens the free-grace of God, and tends to destroy the covenant of grace ; remember to exalt Christ alone in your salvation. How do some turn the gospel of God's free-grace into a law, by the performance of which, as the conditions of life and justification, tell thee, thy salvation doth depend. See what subtle opposers (of the clearest gospel) are risen up amongst us, and labour to avoid them; though their tongues should seem to be tipped with silver, yet their doctrine is copper.

3. Be sure build on Christ alone, and see that that faith thou hast in him, be the faith of God's elect, which sanctifies both heart and life, and is attended with good fruits ; you must work from life, and not for life.

Consolat. 1. Lastly, by way of comfort and consolation : be not afraid, O child of God, though thou art in Christ's fan, and art tossed up and down with temptations, trials, and afflictions. Know that his design is wholly herein for thy good; it is but to purge out thy chaff, that thou, as pure white wheat, mayest shine the more bright and clear in grace and gospel-holiness, for sin and corruption spoil thy beauty to all that behold thee. No doctrine tends to promote gospel-holiness, like the doctrine of God's free-grace : " Shall we sin because grace hath abounded ?" God forbid. Rom. vi. 1.

2. O what a mercy of mercies it is that God's wrath is appeased towards you. Christ's blood has quenched this dreadful fire, as to you who believe, and indeed nothing else could do it. O bless God for Christ, and for that river of water which proceeds from him, to the extinguishing this flaming fire ; he hath borne it, and allayed it, nay, quite put it out, so that you shall never feel the burning or tormenting nature thereof.

3. Thou shalt at last, whosoever thou art, if wheat, be gathered into his garner ; viz., into heaven itself, for Christ will not lose one grain of his spiritual wheat, not one sheep of his shall perish; " He that has begun that good work in thee, will perform it to the day of Christ," Phil. i. 6.

He will gather his wheat into his garner, but the chaff he will burn up with unquenchable fire.

4. DISCIPLES THE SALT OF THE EARTH

Ye are the salt of the earth, but if the salt hath lost its savour, wherewith shall it be salted? Thence it is good for nothing but to be trodden under foot of men.—Matt. v. xiii.

THESE words are metaphorical, they were spoken by our blessed Saviour, and in them are contained three parts.

The parts opened. 1. Something asserted, " ye are the salt of the earth."

2. A supposition, or something supposed ; " but if the salt hath lost its savour," &c.

3. Taking that which is supposed to be granted ; the third thing containeth a necessary conclusion ; " it is thenceforth good for nothing," &c.

The persons here spoken of, are the disciples of Christ.
1. Considered as true Christians.
2. As ministers, who are compared to salt.
1. I shall show in what respect they may be compared to salt.
2. Why called the salt of the earth.
3. Observe one or two points of doctrine from hence.
4. Apply the whole.

1. They may be compared to salt, in respect of the grace of God given to them, for naturally they are not salt, nor savoury, any more than others; but grace is compared to salt, "every sacrifice shall be salted with salt," Mark ix. 49.

2. Saints and true ministers of the gospel may be compared to salt, in respect of their holy and savoury doctrine, those seasonable principles, and blessed truths, professed and preached by them, tend to salt the world; as false doctrine is called corrupt doctrine, so true doctrine, savoury and pure doctrine to the souls of men, is like savoury meat well and fitly seasoned for the body. *In what respect the saints are compared to salt.*

What would become of the world, was it not for that holy doctrine and savoury truths that Christ's ministers preach? Even all the earth, and souls of men, would putrefy, and like corrupt flesh (for want of being salted) stink and become good for nothing; what hath corrupted the Popish and Mahometan world, but false and corrupt doctrine? Moreover, what a multitude among us, for not being salted with good doctrine, are corrupted and stink in the nostrils of God?

3. The saints, &c., may be compared to salt in respect of their savoury words; "Let your speech be always with grace seasoned with salt, that ye may know how ye ought to answer every man," Col. iv. 6. Hence, in another place, the same apostle saith, "Evil communication corrupteth good manners," 1 Cor. xv. 33. Our words should not be tinctured with gall; put gall on meat, you spoil it. Brethren, a vile and malicious tongue is like gall, it is of a poisonous and embittering nature; so also is a frothy and profane tongue, a filthy and unclean tongue, tends to corrupt youth; nay, all that are pleased and delighted in such ungodly talk, but sweet, gentle, heavenly and savoury words, season all company, and tends to preserve the souls of men in this loose and licentious age. "A mild answer turns away wrath," Prov. xxix. 8.

4. The saints are compared to salt, in respect of their holy and savoury conversation: they by their pious deportment, just and holy life, and Christian behaviour, do put a curb upon the lusts of men, they are the salt of the earth, by their good example, this way they season others.

Secondly, Why are the saints and ministers of Christ compared to salt.

Answ. Upon the consideration of the excellent properties or qualities of salt.

1. Salt is very profitable, it keeps and preserves meats, and other things from putrefaction, which would soon stink and perish, were it not salted with salt. *Note, the nature of salt is opened, as it refers to grace, in those words, Mark 9.*

So the godly are a people very profitable unto the world, in preserving of it from corruption and spiritual pollution.

1. They are a means to keep the earth from being totally corrupted by evil and pestilent errors and damnable heresies; they are helped to correct and confute bold heretics, and to defend the holy truths of Christ from their poisonous notions; and observable it is to see how God hath this way in every age, had some salt, I mean some most excellent instruments to stand up to preserve and defend his blessed truth against prevailing errors, which otherwise to all appearance would have totally corrupted the earth. *Every sacrifice shall be salted with salt, to which I refer the reader.*

2. They are like unto salt, to preserve the earth and the souls of men, from being spoiled by profaneness and hellish debauchery; they are helped by their doctrine and holy lives to put a check to that over-spreading wickedness that threateneth every age in which they live; the world this way would soon become so filthy and abominable, that it would stink so in the nostrils of God, that he would tread it down under his feet, were it not for the godly.

2ndly. A little salt seasons much meat, and so prevents its perishing: so a little of this spiritual salt, I mean, a few godly persons, seasons much people, and prevents their perishing: what a little of this salt, for some time kept off or prevented God's wrath from being poured forth upon Sodom. Brethren, Lot was the salt of Sodom, whilst he was in it, and had there been but a little more of that salt in that city, even but ten righteous ones therein, it had not perished. In like manner may we not say in our days, as the prophet said of old, "Except the Lord of Hosts had left us a very small remnant, we should have been as Sodom, and been like unto Gomorrah," Gen. xviii. 32, Isa. i. 9.

3rdly. Salt draws putrefying matter out of meat, by which means it appears it is of a purging quality; so gracious Christians, by their doctrine and holy example (especially ministers) draw out rottenness and filth out of the hearts, tongues, and lives of men, even as God's Spirit accompanies their word and example.

4thly. Salt seasons, and makes meats and other things savoury. So godly Christians and ministers season the minds of men (as instruments in God's hand, by the operation of the word and Spirit) with savoury thoughts, meditations, and discourses and practices.

5thly. Salt is of a hot and fiery nature, being cast into the fire, it sparkles and burns furiously. So the saints by the Holy Spirit are made holy, fervent, and zealous for God and his truth; how holy was David, who could say, "The zeal of thy house hath eaten me up:" and by their doctrine, how zealous are others also made, as were those we read of; "Many also of them which used curious arts, brought their books together, and burned them before all men, and they counted the price of them, and found it fifty thousand pieces of silver," Acts xix. 19. Coals that burn but slowly, yet by laying them close together, and blow upon them, will soon burn vehemently, so the saints of God heat one another; one live coal or lively Christian (if God doth but please to blow upon them,) causes many to kindle in zeal for God, and in love to God.

6thly. Salt stirs up thirst in them that receive it; so a godly minister by his heavenly doctrine, when his word is received, causeth all such to thirst after Christ, and after a likeness to him; as also when some hear them speak of their experiences, and of what sweetness they find in God's ways, and in his love and favour.

7thly. Salt makes meat fit for food, and meet to be received by such who want it; so a holy and good life and conversation in those who profess the gospel, makes the word savoury, fit and meet to be received by poor sinners. It is this which commends the gospel and doctrine thereof to a blind and deceived world; but how unsavoury is a good doctrine in the mouth of a wicked man, (or one that is scandalous in his life). What little relish hath the word that comes forth out of such unholy and unsanctified lips.

8thly. Salt may lose its saltness in a great degree, nay, may quite lose it, and become good for nothing.—So may a sincere Christian become unsavoury in his life, or decay in grace and piety; also such who never were sincere, may utterly lose that seeming grace and savour they once had, or seemed to have.

9thly. If salt hath lost its savour utterly, it is good for nothing, (flesh that is corrupt and not good for men to eat, may yet be good to feed dogs) but salt that has lost its savour is good for nothing: naturalists tell us, that salt which hath lost its savour, if it be laid upon land causeth barrenness. So hypocrites, or unsavoury professors, that once seemed holy, religious, and devout persons, and exemplary to others, when they apotatize finally and totally, they are the worst of mortals, neither fit to live nor die; they also make the church barren, or by their wicked example hinder the increase thereof, causing the good ways of the Lord to be reproached, and his people contemned; and God will at last tread all such under foot in his wrath, to their fearful ruin and damnation in hell, for ever and ever. But so much as to the second thing proposed.

Doct. The saints of God, and the faithful ministers of the gospel, are a great blessing to the world, or the true interest of the nations in which they dwell. The world is not worthy of them, yet they receive marvellous benefit by them; they are not unfitly called " the pillars of the earth;" the earth would sink were it not for God's elect ones; it would soon be so loathsome, were it not for this salt, God would presently destroy it; and indeed no sooner are all God's elect gathered to him, but he will consume the world by the flames of his incensed wrath. Was not Noah the interest of the earth in his days, for not so much as a small seed had (doubtless) been spared, had not he been found righteous in that generation? And was not Lot the true interest of Sodom, while he dwelt among them? "I cannot do any thing till thou come thither," Gen. xix. Was not Jacob the true interest to Laban? Was not he blessed for Jacob's sake? The like I might speak of Joseph to his master, and to the whole land of Egypt.

The saints a great blessing to the world.

APPLICATION

1. From hence also I infer that grace is a most excellent thing.

2. It appears that there is a vast difference between God's people and others; but what hath made this difference? All naturally are alike; it is only grace that makes some men to excel others; "The righteous is more excellent than his neighbour," Prov. xii. 26.

3. From hence we may see what the cause is that some places are more vile, filthy, and abominable than others; it is because they have no salt, to season them, or but a little; i. e., but few gracious men, and godly ministers among them.

4. From hence also we may infer, that the earth is naturally unsavoury; they are loathsome in God's sight. All are as unsavoury meat, and things not salted, until they receive the true grace of God, and have gracious persons among them.

5. This shows what the duty of the saints is, and what true ministers should do. They should season the place, the town, the city, the family where they dwell. 1. They should season them by savoury words, savoury discourse, and communication; such words that may administer grace to the hearers. Spiritual discourse becomes the children of God in all company, and at all fit and proper seasons, and to put a rebuke upon profane and idle talk; for in this it will appear they are the salt of the earth. 2. And not only by their words, but also by their works, and savoury behaviour, and holy conversation.

6. It therefore affords also sharp reproof and reprehension to such professors who would be looked upon to be the salt of the earth, who themselves need salting. O how unsavoury are some professors, nay, church-members! Instead of preserving sinners by their holy instruction and precious example, they rather corrupt them, and harden them in their evil ways. Some can be as vain, as foolish, as wanton, as proud, as others are; do not many of them pursue the world as eagerly as most carnal people? And are not others ready to get into every foolish and idle fashion! What are these but like unsavoury salt?

7. Moreover, this may serve to discover the sad and fearful state of all false and unsavoury Christians; they are like salt that hath lost its savour, which is henceforth good for nothing; they are worse, and do more hurt to religion, than the vilest people on the earth. Others cannot render the ways of God so reproachful, nor cause the name of God to be blasphemed as these do. Let therefore these unholy and unsavoury professors tremble, for God will suddenly in his wrath tread them under his feet, nay, cast them to the dunghill; I mean to hell, where all such like unsavoury and filthy creatures are, and must lie for ever.

8. Let me exhort all Christians, especially ministers, to see that they are savoury in doctrine and conversation: ministers should preach savoury and wholesome doctrine; not law, but gospel; not Moses, but Christ; not error, bnt sound truth; not men's traditions, but Christ's holy and plain institutions; and to deliver the gospel in sound and wholesome words and expressions with all gravity, that it may appear savoury food to all that hear them; and let all take heed of scandalous sins, for by these the name of the Lord is blasphemed: religion brought to contempt and reproach: the hearts of all that are sincere, greatly grieved, and the conversion of sinners hindered, and the damnation of many souls furthered.

9. It may be matter of comfort to the godly. O what use are they of to the world! By them the world is preserved, that is, God preserves it for their sakes, they keep the earth from such horrid pollution, as instruments in God's hands, that it doth not stink in the nostrils of God to such a degree, as to provoke him to destroy it; their holy and savoury lives make good men lift up their heads with boldness; though unjustly reproached, it tends to stop the mouths of the wicked, and to put to silence the ignorance of foolish men, nay, it often proves not only a means of conviction, but of the conversion of sinners, even of such that will not be won by the word. It also gives great evidence to their own consciences of their uprightness when unrighteously charged, as Job and others were; " Whose ox have I taken, or whose ass, or of whose hands have I received a bribe?" 1 Sam. xii. 3.

10. This also may discover the folly and blindness of wicked men that strive to root the godly out of the earth; it may well be said that the world is not worthy of them, since they receive so many great benefits and blessings from them, and yet they would not have them live among them.

Lastly, it may serve to deter and caution all professors against apostacy; our Lord bids us remember Lot's wife, she for not being savoury, or for looking back, was turned into a pillar of salt, nay, into a standing and an abiding pillar, that all may take warning by her; and might not one reason of this be to show that one example of God's severity upon her, might tend to be sufficiently to salt or season all Christians to the end of the world against the sin of apostacy. No doubt but our Saviour in this similitude refers to that horrid sin; " If any man draws back, my soul shall have no pleasure in him," Heb. x. 38. Nay, he will be so far from taking delight or pleasure in him, that his soul will abhor him; he is so highly displeased with his sin, that his very soul abominates his person, and takes pleasure in his misery and fearful damnation; the Lord help all therefore that profess the Gospel, to remember that they should be as salt, and tremble at the thoughts of being unsavoury, either in life or doctrine.

5. DISCIPLES THE LIGHT OF THE WORLD

Ye are the light of the world; a city set on a hill cannot be hid.—Matt. v. 14.

In these words our Lord makes use of a two-fold simile.

1. The saints are compared to light.

2. To a city set upon a hill. " Ye are the light of the world." Before he told them they were the salt of the earth ; ye that are my disciples, but especially ye that are my apostles, my ministers, who preach my Gospel, " ye are the light of the world." The method I shall take in speaking unto this fruitful similitude, shall be,

1. To give you the various acceptations of this word, [light.]

2. To show you in what respects the saints and ministers of the Gospel are called the light of the world.

3. Observe two or three points of doctrine from hence.

4. Apply the whole.

1. Light is taken sometimes for a thing of little value ; our souls loathed this light bread," Numb. xxi. 5 ; they esteemed it as a light or small thing, they did not value it ; he that setteth light by his father is accursed.

2. Sometimes it refers to loose persons. " Abimelech hired vain and light persons," Judg. ix. 4. But these things are remote to that which is intended by the word in this place.

3. Light is that which is opposed to darkness ; there is a three-fold light. (1.) Natural. (2.) Artificial. (3.) Eternal and spiritual.

1. Natural light is that of the sun, moon, and stars, by which our natural eyes are lighted.

2. Artificial light, is that of a candle, lamp, &c.

3. Eternal and spiritual light.

1. God is light, he is that eternal and uncreated light ; he is that original of all natural and spiritual light, and like as the light of the moon and stars proceeds from the sun, so all spiritual light proceeds from God ; he is the fountain of all light, yea, that wonderful light that is in Christ, considered as Mediator, proceeded from God ; though Christ considered as God, is the same original light, and fountain of light.

2. Christ is called light, yea, the light of the world. " In him was life, and the life was the light of men," John i. 4. " That was the true light that lighteth every man that cometh into the world," Verse 9. This denotes his having light in himself, as considered. The eternal Word, or ever-blessed God, he hath lightened with the light of reason and understanding, every man that cometh into the world ; or if it be taken for divine light, then it signifies no more but only those who are spiritually enlightened by him, for no man hath any true light but what he hath received from Jesus Christ ; but because the Holy Ghost in this place speaketh of Christ considered as God or Creator, I cannot see he refers to any other light here, but that light which is said to be in the Gentiles, viz., the light of natural conscience, which is materially the same with the moral law of God that was given to Israel. Jesus Christ is called " the light of the Gentiles, and the sun of righteousness," Mal. iv. 2. Christ is the great Sun of the world ; look what use the sun in the firmament of heaven is of to this visible world ; such is Christ to mankind in a spiritual sense, especially to all believers, and to the church of God ; this Sun giveth light to all who have the eyes of their understanding opened, or true faith infused into their souls.

3. The word of God is also called light, " Thy word is a lamp to my feet, and a light to my paths," Psal. cxix. 105. The word of God like unto light, hath a directive quality in it. It is that unerring rule or infallible guide in all matters of religion, both in respect of faith and practice.

4. The doctrine of the Gospel is called light, " Lest the light of the glorious Gospel of Christ should shine upon them," 2 Cor. iv. 4, 6. *Lux est claritas seu splendor in corpore luminoso, vel extra a corpore luminoso exiens*, the Gospel is as light, a clarity brightness or splendour in a luminous body ; such glory doth proceed from it, that the brightness of the blessed God, in all his glorious attributes or perfections of his nature, shines forth therein.

5. The saints and ministers of Christ are called light or lights; John the Baptist is called a burning and shining light; and saith Paul, speaking unto the saints, " Ye are light in the Lord," Eph. v. 8. They have not only received light, or have the light of grace in them, but are a light to others ; " Ye are the light of the world."

6. And lastly, light sometimes refers to the blessedness of heaven, or light of eternal glory ; " Who hath made us meet for the inheritance of the saints in light," Col. i. 12. So much as to the first thing proposed.

Secondly, I shall show you in what respects the saints may be called the light of the world.

1. Negatively. 2. Positively.

1. Negatively, not in themselves, for Christ only is the light of the world as considered simply in himself : saints in themselves are but dark bodies, (as astronomers tells us the moon is) but they are such who have received great light from the Sun of righteousness ; they, like a candle being lighted, give light to all in the house. *How the saints are not the light of the world.*

2. Not that they can give or communicate the light of saving grace to others ; no, no, all light of grace and of saving knowledge, is from Jesus Christ ; therefore in this sense, he only is the light of the world. The wise virgins could not give of their oil unto the foolish ; a minister though he may have much grace in his own soul, yet he cannot communicate one drachm of it to his poor unbelieving wife or children, though he should see her or them ready to drop into hell.

3. The saints are not such a light as to be the only rule or guide by which others should walk ; no, no, whether you take them as they are a body united together, I mean a church, or as particular persons ; and though such that excel others, as Paul and Peter, &c. The saints, ministers, nor the church, are a light to the world in this sense : they are not the rule of our faith and practice, for woe to the world, had God left us no better rule to walk by than they, because the best of men, yea, the best of ministers, and the best of churches, may, and doubtless do err in many things. True, this had been the pretence of the blind Papists, and that by which they have deceived the world ; they assert the church is the rule, or the Pope, or church and Pope, (they are at a loss where to fix their pretended infallibility) yet they say we first must find the church, and then take the scriptures from her, because she is the only rule. O beware of this delusion : all good Protestants ever have abominated this cursed doctrine (as they have cause to do) and affirm that the word of God alone is that rule which he hath left us, and by it we are to find out the true church, that is, know the true church by the Scriptures, and not the Scriptures by the church ; Paul himself would not have any to follow him any further then he followed Christ. *The church nor ministers are the rule of our faith and practice.*

4. The saints and ministers of the Gospel are not so a light, as that there is no darkness, no ignorance, no error, no sin at all in them. Brethren, in this sense none but God and Christ is Light ; " in him is light and no darkness at all," 1 John i. 5 ; every Christian may say with David, " who can know his errors ?" " If we say we have no sin, we deceive ourselves, and the truth is not in us," 1 John i. 8, And doth not Paul say, that " he knew but in part ?" 1 Cor. xiii. Besides, did he not cry out, " Oh wretched man that I am—When I would do good, evil is present with me ?" Rom. vii. 24. Sirs, the best of men are but so, the light of the world, as in every thing they may preach or practice, they ought to be followed. But to proceed,

Secondly and positively, the saints and ministers of Christ have much light and knowledge communicated unto them from Christ, by which means (as they are savingly enlightened) they are a light to the world ; like as the moon and stars, receive their light from the sun to give light to the earth in the night ; hence Christ's ministers are called stars, they are the light of the world, as compared to stars, " the seven stars are the angels of the seven churches," Rev. i. 20, and these Christ holds in his right hand, ver. 16. Which shows that great honour and dignity he hath conferred on them, as also their blessed safety, security, and protection. This may put a rebuke upon those who slight and despise Christ's poor ministers. Now they may be compared to the stars upon divers considerations, and so the light of the world. *In what sense saints are the light of the world. Ministers are the light of the world, as they are compared to stars.*

1. As the stars receive their light from the sun, so the saints and ministers of Christ do receive their light of grace and knowledge from Christ. " What hast thou which thou hast not received ? And of his fulness have all we received, and grace for grace," John i. 16.

2. Stars are placed by the Lord in the firmament of heaven, to give light to the earth ;

and so in like manner, are the ministers of Christ placed in the church, (which is often-times called heaven) to give light to the world, which is in darkness and in the night of sin, of ignorance, and error.

3. The stars are a great ornament to the heavens ; they sparkle and shine there as so many rare and glorious jewels or diamonds. Even so the ministers of Christ are, or ought to be, a great and glorious ornament unto the church, and to shine therein like the stars of the first magnitude in grace, gifts, and true holiness.

4. The stars sometimes are obscured : the clouds shadow them, and they shine not ; they give very little or no light at all.

So it is sometimes with the ministers of Christ, they fall through Satan's temptations ; and by reason of the corruptions of their own hearts into sin, as David and Peter did, and are thereby brought under great obscurity and darkness, that they shine not until they get out of those dark clouds.

5. Stars differ in glory, some appear not so bright and splendent as others ; all are not stars of the first magnitude : even so the ministers of Christ, and saints of God, greatly differ in respect of that grace, and those spiritual gifts which they have received from Jesus Christ. Some have great parts, they excel in wisdom and knowledge, like as Paul, who was a glorious light, and outshone many of Christ's ministers ; moreover, we have had in latter days, some that have been like stars of the first or greatest magnitude. What a light was blessed Luther in the last age. And what great lights have we had in this age ? Though none shone more splendidly (in my judgment,) in our days, than renowned Dr. Owen, but, considering all circumstances, I think Bunyan should not be thought a very small star, he having not those human improvements, in respect of learning, &c., as others have, yet shone very bright and outdid many others.

Luther was a great light,

Owen a great light also.

6. Stars give their light only in the night. So Christ's ministers and holy people only give light unto the world, whilst the night of this world shall last, which now is far spent, and the day of Christ's coming is near, when those stars shall be all fixed in the highest heavens, and shall be no more of use to give light to the earth. O brethren ! let us long for the morning of that eternal day, when all these stars shall be transfixed in other orbs above, and not dart down their light any more for the use of men ; but let us bless God for that little light these stars do give, whilst the dark night of this world abides.

7. Stars have good and evil influences upon all natural bodies, and things on earth, as astronomers observe.

So the ministers of Christ have by their lives and doctrine, also good and evil influences upon the souls of men ; to some they are " the savour of life unto life, and to others, the savour of death unto death," 2 Cor. ii. 16. The gospel in its ministration hath hardening influences on some, as well as softening influences on others ; yet as God orders all the influences of the stars as he pleaseth, so it is he that gives all success to the ministry of the word.

2ndly, As the saints and ministers of Christ are compared to stars, and are the light of the world in that respect, so also they are compared to candles, their light is compared I say, to the light of a candle ; " Neither do men light a candle and put it under a bushel, but put it into a candlestick, and it giveth light unto all that are in the house," Matt. v. 15.

Ministers the light of the world, as compared to a candle.

Though the light of the stars be far greater than the light of a candle, yet all know a candle gives much more light to such that are in that house where it is lighted and set up in the night than the stars do ; though the stars give a more extensive light, yet their light is but dim as to us, by reason of their vast distance from us.

1. A candle gives no light until it is lighted, it is until then a dark body. So the saints give no light until they are enlightened with the Spirit of God, or have received divine grace and spiritual gifts.

2. A candle must be put into a candlestick, that so it may the better give light to all the house. So ministers ought to be set or placed orderly in the church which is compared to a golden candlestick, Rev. i. 8. Such preachers ought to be disowned, who are not set in a due and orderly manner in some regular church or candlestick, the light must shine in and from Zion. " Out of Zion, the perfection of beauty God hath shined," Rev. i.

3. A candle, or lamp, that it may give the better light, ought to be often snuffed and trimmed, for else by means of the ashes, the light will be but very dim. So the saints and ministers of the Gospel, should like the wise virgins, trim their lamps, Matt. xxv. 7 : that is, they should get all that deadness and earthliness from their spirits by

the quickening operations of grace. A worldly spirit spoils the light, it is like ashes, that hinders the candle from burning clear, also they should get rid of their remaining ignorances of divine truths. Some candles give but a very dim light by this means, and others want topping; they are swelled in pride and haughtiness to such a degree, that they give hardly any light at all, so that men by these means stumble: the candle gives them not light to see their way, or find out that filth and corruption that is in their house, (I mean their hearts.)

4. A candle wasteth itself by giving light unto others. So poor ministers, especially some of them, spend their strength, and bring their bodies to utter weakness, by their hard studies, and painful and laborious preaching, to the profit of others.

5. A candle is not to be hid or put under a bushel or bed: no more ought a servant of Christ, to whom God hath given ministerial gifts, being able to edify the church, and give the light of knowledge to the world, to hide those gifts, or refuse to exercise them, but ought to be set up in the pulpit as a candle in a candlestick, to give light to all.

Thirdly, In what respects are the saints and ministers of Christ, the light of the world?

1. I answer, By that holy and glorious doctrine which they have received and preach unto the world, in this they are the light of it. How dark are those nations and regions of the earth where there is no knowledge of the gospel, or where there are no gracious Christians and ministers to hold forth the light of saving truth? Was not famous Luther the light of the world in his time upon this account? For like as when light breaketh forth, darkness is thereby expelled: even so by the rising of that glorious star, and by virtue of that doctrine he preached of free justification by the righteousness of Christ alone, how was Popish darkness vanquished?

2. They are the light of the world by their holy and heavenly lives. "Let your light so shine before men, that they may see your good works, and glorify your Father which is in heaven," Matt. v. 16 ; that is, let the light of your doctrine, which you have received from me, and the light of your holy conversations, so shine before men ; but by the following words, it is the latter which I conclude is principally meant. The saints should not do good works to be seen of men for their own glory, or for vain glory sake, (as hypocrites do,) yet they should do good works, and let them be seen, that God may be glorified. " Herein is my Father glorified, if you bear much fruit," John xv. 8. Not that we can add any thing to the essential glory of God, but we are to manifest or declare hereby his glory: nay, it doth tend to excite and stir up others who see our holy lives and good works, to praise and glorify God, from whom all grace, by which all good works are performed, doth proceed. This shows, that all acceptable services are done by the help and influence of special efficacious grace required from God, otherwise (I mean, if we do good works by the mere power and liberty of our own wills,) it would rather tend to our own glory than to the glory of God.

Brethren, as the candle ought not to be hid, but to be seen, that so it may give light to all that are in the house; so ought not Christians to hide their convictions of sin or of duty, they must not quench the Spirit, or put out that spark of divine fire, which God hath kindled in them, but let it be seen, and not conceal their religion, or those convictions they are under out of shame or fear of reproach ; nor neglect prayer, reading, hearing, or heavenly converse under any pretence whatsoever: yet they should see rightly to time everything, and labour to avoid hypocrisy, and shun all just occasions which may cause them to be suspected as guilty of it.

1. Doct. The world is in darkness, they are in the night, else there would be no need of light, or to set up candles.

2. Doct. God is pleased out of his infinite grace and mercy to the world, to afford light unto it.

3. Doct. The people of God, and ministers of the gospel, are as lights to this world where they are, whilst darkness or the night doth continue.

I shall only speak a little to the first of these propositions.

1. Prove it.

2. Show their woful condition thereby.

1 That the world is in darkness or in the night, appears by the testimony of divers scriptures, " for they that sleep, sleep in the night, " 1 Thess. v. 7 ; by their sleeping in sin and ignorance, they show that they are in the night, or are in darkness ; " for ye were sometimes darkness, but are now light in the Lord," Ephes. v. 8. Yea, the saints of God who are the the children of the day, were once in darkness as well as others : nay, were darkness ; works of sin, are from hence called works of darkness, " have no fellow-

ship with the unfruitful works of darkness," Ephes. v. 11.   This further appears, because the saints are said to be " delivered out of the power of darkness," Col. i. 13; that is, out of the world in whom the prince of darkness rules and tyrannizes, and keeps all the ungodly of the earth in his bonds and chains of darkness ; the devil is called " The prince of the darkness of this world," Ephes. vi. 12.   Jesus Christ was sent " to give light to them that sit in darkness," Luke i. 79.

Secondly, Their misery upon this account is great.

1. Darkness is uncomfortable ; so it is to be in spiritual darkness.   How uncomfortable was it to the Egyptians to be in that thick darkness that might be felt, so what comfort can a poor sinner have that is in spiritual darkness, " Who walk in the valley of the shadow of death."

2. Darkness is dangerous, especially when a man's way lies among pits, snares, and where there are lions and devouring creatures.   So it is dangerous to be in spiritual darkness, because sinners pass through a howling wilderness ; this world is full of dangerous pits and snares, where devils and hellish deceivers lie in wait to prey upon them, nay, they walk upon the brink of the bottomless pit.

3. Darkness is fearful, we read of the horror of darkness ; so the state of spiritual darkness, or to be in the state of nature, is fearful ; terrors attend such on every side, both from within, and from without, an unconverted sinner is a Magor Misabid, like as was Pashur, Gen. xv. 12.

1. Is it not a fearful thing to be led by the devil, left to the power of the devil, to the will and power of the God of this world ? they know not whither they go, Ephes. ii. 2, 3.

2. Is it not a fearful thing to fall into the hands of the living God, or to lie under his wrath and curse ? Heb. xii. ult.

3. Is it not a fearful thing to lodge in the next room to hell ?

4. Is it not a fearful thing to have the guilt of sin charged on their souls; but so it is with all that are in darkness, or in an unrenewed state ?

5. Is it not a fearful thing to be without God, without Christ, and without hope in the world ? Eph. ii. 12.

6. Is it not a fearful thing to be condemned to die, to die eternally, always a dying, yet cannot die?   Now all unconverted sinners are condemned to die such a death.

APPLICATION

1. I infer, it is a dangerous thing to be led by this blind and dark world, or by them that walk according to the course of this world, or to follow the multitude in their ways and sinful practices, this is to walk in darkness.

2. I infer, what great folly is in the people of the world, they hate the saints and ministers of Christ, who are appointed by the Lord to be a light to them.   How many of the world would, if they could, destroy the saints and ministers of Christ, it is because they love darkness and hate the light.

3. They may teach all to prize Christ's ministers, from whom they receive so much good ; they by their divine doctrine enlighten the earth ; " I send thee to open their eyes, (that is the Gentiles) and to turn them from darkness to light," &c., Acts xxvi. 17, 18.

4. Let ministers also learn from hence to discharge their work and office in all faithfulness, that they may be lights where they live; it behoves them to see they preach the gospel clearly without errors, and plainly without obscure terms and words which the people understand not.   I am sure in so doing, they are not a light to the world ; it may be also a caution to them to take heed how they live ; we must live religion, live Christ as well as preach Christ ; our conversations must give light as well as our doctrine.

5. Let all take heed what ministers they are led by, that they be disciples of Jesus Christ, and ministers of his making.   All ministers are not the light of the world ; no, none but the true ministers of Christ, and they are known three ways.   1. By their call to the ministry.   1. They are regenerated men, and have received grace and ministerial gifts of Christ.   2. They are regularly called, and empowered to preach by the church with whom they are members ; they also take not up the ministry for filthy lucre's sake, but in love to Christ preach freely, and as freely the people should minister to them in all good things.   3. They preach Christ, Jesus Christ is the sum and substance of their ministry ; they preach not Moses, nor the traditions of men, nor magnify the righteousness of man, but their whole design is to abase the creature, and exalt Jesus Christ ; they preach not themselves, " but Jesus Christ the Lord ;" they preach a whole Christ, and nothing but Christ, and so are the light of the world.

6. Pray that your ministers may have much light, much clear knowledge, since they are the light of the world, and that they may not at any time be clouded.

7. Lastly, Bewail the loss of faithful ministers ; oh what a sad loss it is to lose any of our glorious lights ! how many are gone, and how few raised up in their stead !

6. AGREE WITH YOUR ADVERSARY QUICKLY

I

Agree with thine adversary quickly, whilst thou art in the way with him, lest at any time thy adversary deliver thee to the judge, and the judge deliver thee to the officer, and thou be cast into prison. Verily I say unto thee, thou shalt by no means come out thence, until thou hast paid the uttermost farthing,—Matt. v. 25, 26.

I WILL not deny but that our Saviour may design by these words to advise such who are fallen into the hands of an external adversary (whom they have provoked) to endeavour to agree with him, whilst they are in a way to do it, from the consideration of The occasion the temporal danger which (otherwise) may follow, especially when they are in of our Lord speaking the hands of such who stand upon acts of strict justice. Yet certainly he had these words. in uttering of these words higher and more important matter in his mind ; so that besides the literal, there is a mystical sense, which we ought to search into ; indeed our late annotators, after they speak of the first, they also allude to the second or metaphorical signification, viz. " Let my disciples who have been, or may be overtaken with great The annotfaults, by repentance, and faith in me, make their peace with God in this life, ators sense lest dying in impenitency, they be under the eternal displeasure and wrath of of the words. God, from whence they shall never be delivered." Also Marlorate saith, that these words, " Lest at any time thy adversary deliver thee to the judge," &c. That some expound it metaphorically, and that the similitude very aptly refers to God, &c. 2. Besides we find our Saviour uttered the same words in substance, without respect had to what St. Matthew speaks of, as antecedent to them, St. Luke xii. 58. 3. Also how often do worthy ministers refer to it, as a symbolical or parabolical allusion ; especially in respect to the last clause ; " Verily, I say unto thee, thou shalt not come out thence until thou hast paid the utmost farthing." What man stands so upon strict justice, that he will not forgive the least part of a debt, but will have every farthing paid ? God is indeed not only just, but justice itself, and therefore forgives no man, without a full satisfaction made to his justice ; and therefore, I. I conclude our Lord refers chiefly to the holy God. 1. This therefore may be one main scope and design of this similitude. 2. The great danger all unreconciled sinners are in of falling into the hands of the living God, who is a The scope worse adversary, if an adversary, than any mortal man can be. 3. To show of the words opened. to sinners there is a way found out by which they may attain to peace and reconciliation with God. 4. And that they should not delay in the use of all means to endeavour after it, whilst the day of grace lasteth, or " before the things of their peace be hid from their eyes ;" for it is evident, our Lord did not preach this sermon to his disciples only, but to the multitude also, ver. 1. Even to such who were not in a reconciled state, so that he seems to take an occasion from what precedes (about offending a brother) to instruct them about a higher concernment, i. e., that such who have God for their adversary, should above all things labour to obtain peace and reconciliation with him ; and this indeed on other occasions was his frequent practice, that he might improve temporal things, to the spiritual profit and advantage of his hearers. So much as to the scope hereof.

Secondly, I shall proceed to open the parts of this simile.

1. By the adversary, I understand, as I have hinted, the holy and just God The parts is meant, who is set out often in the Scriptures to be an adversary to all un- opened. godly men.

2. The persons he directs his advice or counsel to, are all unreconciled sinners, who have not laid down their arms, but remain in a state of rebellion against God.

3. By the judge may be meant the Lord Jesus Christ, Acts xvii. 31, who is appointed, and ordained the judge of the quick and the dead : " The Father judgeth no man, but hath committed all judgment to the Son," John v. 12.

4. By the officer (some read it, jailor,) may be meant death, or divine justice ; death as a sergeant, may be said to arrest a guilty sinner, when Christ the judge gives him a commission to seize him, or cut him down.

5. By the prison, no doubt is meant hell, out of which there is no redemption ; were it not this prison, why should our Lord use this great asseveration, " Verily I say unto you,

he shall not come out thence, until he hath paid the utmost farthing." He doth not use such an expression certainly to confirm small matters, or things only of a temporal concernment : besides men commonly, though provoked, do not always stand upon severe justice, so as not to release a prisoner without the payment of the whole debt ; justice and mercy are not essentials of man's nature, but only qualities (or virtues) ; and severe justice in men may be, and sometimes is, mere cruelty, but God's nature is just, he is essentially and absolutely just : yea, justice itself, as well as he is love, holiness, goodness, truth, &c. These are not qualities in God, but they are his attributes, or essential properties, so that he can as soon cease to be God, as cease to be just, righteous, and good.

Thirdly, In the words we have.

The parts opened.   1. An exhortation, or a duty enjoined ; " agree with thine adversary."

2. The time expressed, when, quickly, or now presently, or without delay.

3. We have a threefold motive, to excite, or to stir men up to this.

(1). Is taken from the consideration of the means of grace God affords, whilst thou art in the way with him ; or whilst he calls and extends mercy and means of reconciliation to the sinner.

(2). From the consideration of the uncertainty of the continuation of the mercy and forbearance of God, lest at any time, or before thou art aware.

(3). From the fearful consequence of delay, and of the punishment that will unavoidably follow ; He delivers thee to the judge, that is, God delivers the sinner into Christ's hand, not as a Saviour, but as an offended and just judge, who will deliver him up also into the hands of death and divine justice, and so his soul is sent to hell. From the words thus opened and explained, I shall take notice of several propositions or points of doctrine.

Doct. 1. That God is an adversary to all unbelieving and impenitent sinners.

Doct. 2. That it is the great duty of guilty or unbelieving sinners, to labour after peace and reconciliation with God, or accept of the offers of his grace and favour, in and by Jesus Christ.

Doct. 3. That sinners ought to seek peace and reconciliation with God presently or without delay.

Doct. 4. That a person who is not reconciled to God, is at all times in danger of wrath and divine vengeance, or of being sent to hell.

Even this very day, this morning, this night, or at any time ; or if he lives until tomorrow, one day, one week, one month, or one year longer, it may be then O how uncertain is the life of a poor sinner ! And how uncertain are the means of grace also ! Whether persons are young or old, rich or poor, strong or weak, male or female, in health or sickness, they are in danger, if not reconciled to God, at any time of being delivered up into the hands of an offended judge, and of being thrown into hell. I shall speak a little to the first of these propositions, viz., that God is an adversary to sinners, &c.

And 1. I shall show how God became an adversary to man.

2. How it appears he is an adversary to sinners.

3. Show what a kind of adversary God is.

How God became man's enemy.   First. Let this be considered, i. e., God was a friend to man, and took delight in him whilst he abode in the state of innocency, but by sin and disobedience : in eating of the forbidden fruit, God cast him off, and became an enemy unto him : man rebelled originally against God, and God cannot but be an adversary to rebellious sinners. " They rebelled, and vexed his Spirit, therefore he was turned to be their enemy, and he fought against them," Isa. lxiii. 10. By original and actual sin, the hearts of men are set against God ; resisting his authority, crossing his will, and violating his holy law: and from thence he became their adversary.

Secondly, It appears many ways that God is an adversary to sinners.

1. By declaring his wrath and anger against them : " God judgeth the righteous, and he is angry with the wicked every day. The wrath of God is revealed from heaven against all ungodliness and unrighteousness of men, Rom. i. 18.

2. By whetting of his sword, he appears to be an adversary to all unbelieving sinners ; " He will whet his sword, he hath bent his bow and made it ready : he hath prepared for him the instruments of death," Psal. vii. 12. What can more clearly discover God to be an enemy to sinners than this, to prepare war against them ?

3. By his fearful threatenings and pronunciation of his anger against them ; every where in this word, it evidently appears, that he is an adversary to them : " upon the wicked he shall rain snares, fire and brimstone, and an horrible tempest, this shall be the portion

of their cup," Psal. i. 16. " Except ye repent, ye shall all likewise perish," Luke xiii. 3, 5.

4. By his abhorrence of them, some say that God only abhors the sins of some wicked men, but not their persons, but this is not true; " The wicked (saith the Psalmist) boasteth of his heart's desire, and blesseth the covetous, whom the Lord abhorreth," Psal. x. 2. He abhorreth not their sin only, but their persons also. " Three shepherds also I cut off in one month, and my soul loatheth them, and their souls also abhorred me," Zech. xi. 8. Every ungodly person, as sinners, God abhorreth.

5. By his laying the whole race of sinful mankind under his wrath, curse, and sentence of condemnation, and in that state all abide : that is, under his wrath, whilst they continue in unbelief: " He that believeth not the Son hath not life, but the wrath of God abideth on him," John iii. 36. Every man in the world was a child of wrath by nature," Ephes. ii. 3; and God is an enemy unto them all, without distinction there is no difference.

Thirdly, I shall show you what an adversary God is to all unbelievers.

1. God is an enemy with just cause, not without good reason he became an adversary to sinners ; he was provoked and stirred up by acts of highest treason and rebellion ; how was man honoured at first ! What dignity and glory did God confer upon him, in creating him in his own image, and in making him a prince and ruler over all things and creatures on earth ! And how abominably did he revolt from God, and conspire with the devil against his Maker !

2. God is a strong and an invincible adversary, who is a match for him ? Or who can stand before his indignation ? " God is jealous, and the Lord revengeth and is furious, the Lord taketh vengeance on his adversaries, and he reserveth wrath for his enemies, the elect themselves are his enemies before called; the mountains quake at him, and the hills melt, and the earth is burnt at his presence, yea, the world, and all that dwell therein. Who can stand before his indignation, and who can abide in the fierceness of his anger; his fury is poured out like fire, and the rocks are thrown down by him ?" Nahum i. 2. 5, 6. Man can stand no more before the wrath of this terrible God, than stubble can stand before a devouring fire : " Who would set briars and thorns against me in battle ? I would go through them, and burn them together," Isa. xxvii. 4. He is an adversary clothed with might, power, terror, and majesty, he hath made mighty kings as stubble to his bow, and emperors as chaff before the whirlwind.

3. God is a wise and skilful adversary, he knows how to marshal his host, and set his battle in array, and how with ease to revenge himself of his enemies : " He is wise in heart, and mighty in strength," Job ix. 4. There is no device, no policy, nor crafty counsel against this adversary, the Lord of Hosts.

4. God is an incensed enemy, wrath hath been long kindling in his heart: and at last if sinners lay not down their arms, it will be poured forth like fire upon them.

5. God is a victorious and a prevailing adversary : when he rises up he devours at once ; he shall cry, " He shall roar, he shall prevail against his enemies," Isa. xliv. 19.

6. Yet he is a forbearing and long-suffering adversary, he seeks not all advantages to destroy and avenge himself of his enemies. O how willing is he to put an end to that fearful war that is between him and poor sinners ; he sends his ambassadors to offer peace, and to intreat them to be reconciled ; he puts out his white flag to draw them, and to allure them to lay down their arms, and to accept of mercy and free pardon, before the bloody flag is put up.

7. In Jesus Christ he is reconciled ; though he is an enemy to all sinners who have not Christ's satisfaction applied to them, his wrath is appeased in Christ, or by the sacrifice of his Son, and fury is not in him towards any that are in Jesus Christ, or who plead the satisfaction he has given, and that atonement he hath made by his blood ; yet to such, I say, who stand out and refuse to come in, or accept of this atoning sacrifice, or to believe in Jesus Christ, or who seek by some other ways to make their peace with God ; his frightful and soul amazing wrath will overtake and devour with dreadful vengeance and fury.

Fourthly, I shall endeavour to prove or to demonstrate, that it is the duty and highest concernment of sinners to accept of terms of peace with God.

1. Because the sinner first broke with God, the breach was not made by the holy Creator, but by man the wretched creature. God made man upright, but he hath sought out many inventions. Man first began this fearful war, he took up arms against his Maker, and therefore it is his duty and interest to accept of peace while he is in the way, or may be received into favour with God.

2. Because it is an unjust and unreasonable rebellion ; shall the subject strive to dethrone his sovereign, and set up a sworn traitor in his place ? Or shall the creature contemn and raise up war against his glorious Creator, who not only gave him his being, but feeds, clothes, and preserves him contiuually O what a rebel is sorry man, and what ground and reason is there why he should strive to be at peace and reconciled unto God !

3. Because if they do not speedily take hold of peace, the mischief and wrong will fall upon themselves : what hath the sinner already suffered ? and what may he further expect to meet with, if he continues in his rebellion and enmity against God? how poor and wretched hath this war already made him ; and how miserable will he be in the end ; and, yet will he not be convinced of this his madness and folly ; their swords will turn back into their own bowels, and pierce their own souls.

4. What cost and charge hath God been at to reconcile sinners to himself? God has sacrificed his own Son to procure their peace and reconciliation ; this is the way he took, this is the way by which his wrath is appeased, and his offended justice satisfied ; " All things are of God, who hath reconciled us unto himself by Jesus Christ," 2 Cor. v. 18, 19. Our blessed Jonah was thrown into the sea of God's wrath, to lay that dreadful storm our sins had raised ; the honour of God's justice, and sanctification of the law, must be vindicated ; we have not peace with God, as a simple act of mercy, but in a way of satisfaction to injured justice ! but such who do not accept of this Christ, this succour, and fly to God by him, God will have war with for ever. It is indeed to abuse infinite wisdom, justice, love, goodness, and mercy, for sinners any other way to seek peace and reconciliation with God, or to refuse this way.

5. Because you are not able to deal with, or to stand against this adversary : are you a match for him ? will you run upon the bosses of his buckler ? He is a God of influences and authority, he commands all. The frogs invade Pharaoh, the stars fight against Sisera, an angel destroyed a whole army of Assyrians in a night, the watchers cut down Nebuchadnezzar, and sent him to graze with oxen, and tosses Belshazzar from the throne ; and dost thou think to escape his awful frowns? can any by strength prevail? or will thy riches profit thee in the day of wrath ? Or canst thou out-wit infinite wisdom ? He taketh the wise in their own craftiness, and by power shall none prevail. " He is of one mind, and who can turn him ?" Job xxiii. 13. " His counsel shall stand, and he will do all his pleasure," Isa. xl. 10. " Whosoever hardeneth his heart against him and prospered ?" Job. ix. 4 ? Wilt thou resolve to go on in thy sinful course, let God say what he will, ministers say what they will, and godly parents say what they will ; nay, and thy conscience never so often and severely rebuke thee and terrify thy soul ? And yet for all this wilt thou swear, lie, be drunk, and commit uncleanness ; nay, " Add drunkenness to thirst, and say thou shalt have peace ? O hear what God saith and tremble, the Lord will not spare him, but then the anger of the Lord and his jealousy shall smoke against that man, and all the curses that are written in this book shall be upon him, and the Lord shall blot out his name from under heaven," Deut. xxix. 19, 20. Thou hardenest thy heart against him, when thou dost delay to close with Christ, and dost stifle those convictions thou mayest be under of sin and danger ; every act of sin hardens the heart against God ; what, shall neither the word nor the rod break thy heart ?

6. Now peace may be had with God : this is the time, the things of thy peace are not yet hid from thine eyes ; mind the words, " whilst thou art in the way with him." Oh wonder that thou art out of hell, or that the day of grace is not yet ended ; believe God is willing to be at peace with you, he is ready to pardon, and thou mayest not live until to-morrow, therefore it is thy wisdom to accept of peace to-day.

7. Christ's ambassadors do offer peace to you in their great Master's name ; what answer will you give them ? He will call them home in a short time. " Now then we are ambassadors for Christ, as though God did beseech you by us, we pray you in Christ's stead be ye reconciled to God," 2 Cor. v. 20. What, doth God and Jesus Christ entreat and beseech you to be reconciled, and dare you refuse ? Nay, is God in Christ reconciled, and will you reject this Christ, and that peace he hath made by his own blood ?

8· Moreover, you may have peace on easy terms, your sins are the plague and sores of your souls ; no man but would be cured of the plague, or of a mortal disease ; are you not willing to throw your filthy rags away, to be clothed with a glorious robe, or to accept of a plaister to heal your wounds ? Would a man wounded with a spear, not have it pulled out of his side ? You are polluted, and it was to wash and be clean. What poor virgin would think it a hard thing, to yield to be espoused to a glorious prince, when courted by him ? Doth not Christ deserve your choicest love and affections ?

True, to the flesh the terms are hard, it is like pulling out a right eye, &c.   But the Spirit of God makes it easy to the soul ; it is but to believe and be saved, and that faith God is also ready to give to thee.

9. If you refuse peace to-day, your adversary may deliver you to the judge to-morrow, and the judge to the officer, and you be cast into hell ; and what will you do then ? Verily you shall not come out thence, until you have paid the utmost farthing you owe to God's justice.

10. It is peace with God, the mighty God, he will become thy friend, and thou wilt see in Christ all his wrath is over for ever.

11. Thou hereby shalt see thou art actually brought into the bonds of the covenant, and in a league of lasting peace and real friendship ; so that God's enemies will be thy enemies, and such that are his friends, will be thy friends, his strength will be engaged for thee, to help and succour thee at all times, both of afflictions and temptations.

12. Thou wilt have soul-peace, peace within, as well as peace with God ; " Great peace have they that love thy law," Psal. cxix. 165 ; it is indeed, " Peace that passeth all understanding," Phil. iv. 7.   O what is it to have peace with God ?   It is perfect peace, " Thou wilt keep him in perfect peace," Isa. xxvi. 3 ; and this peace opens a blessed trade, even free access to God, thou shalt have communion with him, and enjoy many other high and glorious privileges also, therefore it is thy wisdom and interest, and the interest of all sinners, quickly to accept of peace with God.

USE

This may serve to reprove such who say God is no adversary to the persons of the elect, whilst in their sins, and unbelievers, though they are swearers, blasphemers, drunkards, whoremongers, murderers, &c., because in his Son he is reconciled, or Christ hath satisfied the justice of God for all their sins.   Cannot they distinguish between the satisfaction of Christ, or that atonement he hath made for sinners, and the application of it to the sinner's person and conscience ?   Sure they are ignorant of the holy nature of God, and do not believe the truth of his word, or the record thereof.

Object. 1.   God is (say these men) unchangeable, and therefore how can his elect be at one time under his wrath, and another time in his love ?   Can such ever be children of wrath, and God an enemy to them whom he loved from eternity ?   Thus they argue.

Answ.   You look upon God as upon man ; as if love and hatred were but qualities in God ; that which we call love, and that which we call hatred, in God is all $\quad$ On reconciliation, p. 19.
one, saith Reverend Jer. Burroughs, but in us they are two things, two acts ;
one while God acts in a way of love, and at another time in a way of wrath,
but the change is not in God, but in those objects towards whom his love or wrath is
manifested.   God himself (saith he) is one pure act, one in his own holy na- $\quad$ How God may be said to love. and
ture, though in his acting towards creatures, he seems to us as it were divided,
when all is but the several ways of the manifestation of his own infinite es- $\quad$ yet hate the same person.
sence.   Pray did not God love the angels that fell when they were holy and
pure creatures ?   And yet now they are become devils, and doth he not hate them ?   Yet is there from hence any change in God ?   We must distinguish between what God is in himself, and his actings and manifestations of himself to creatures.   Man in a state of innocency was, as it were (saith Mr. Burroughs) white glass, and God shined thereon in a way of love and goodness to man ; the same man falls, and is dyed red by his sin, and let him now be presented unto God, and the ways of God are bloody, and appear full of wrath ; let this man be converted, and then again the glass is changed, and God presenteth himself another way, i.e., in love and sweet complacency : but he is still the same God, only according to the several ways of the creature, so are his several actings ; whose ways to us are past finding out : therefore those that would speak of God, as he is in himself, who is but one act, lead people into abundance of errors, because they are not able to manage their apprehensions of him as he is in himself, page 20.   We converts (saith the Apostle), were the children of wrath as well as others, in that respect there was no difference between us and others.   I will put this to these men, i.e., was not there a time when Christ was under God's wrath ?   Yet God loved his Son from all eternity.   Sirs, that wrath of God due to us under which the elect were fallen, Christ came under, and from hence we may see that the elect were under wrath, and God acted as an enemy to them, and yet he loved them, as he saw them in his Son from eternity, and also acted in a way

of love, pity, and good-will towards them from everlasting, Jer. xxxi. 3.   God, saith another author, hates no man's person, simply considered as his creature, but he hates them as ungodly or wicked persons, and so he could not but hate elect sinners, as well as he hates their sins, and sinful state ; and he hates them also, so as to withhold (for a time) the effects of his love from them.   We call (saith he) the effects of God's grace, grace ; and the effects of his wrath, wrath ; as God is said to repent when he causes the effects of anger to cease ; God was in Christ reconciling the world to himself ; the meritorious and wrath-appeasing sacrifice is paid once for all, but it is in Christ for us, and not applied to any adult person, until they believe ; we must be in Christ, if God be reconciled to us, and we to him ; in him only is God well pleased, that is, with none else but them that are in Jesus Christ.

2.   Bewail the state of all unbelievers, all who are in a state of enmity and rebellion against God.   O what a fearful thing is it to have God for an adversary, and to fall into the hands of the living God !

3.   Here is great encouragement for sinners to fly to God by Jesus Christ, God being in his Son well pleased and reconciled, though he is not well pleased, nor actually reconciled to the person of any wicked, ungodly, and unbelieving sinner ; and such who assert the contrary, speak not that which is right of the holy God, but contradict the testimony of the word of truth.   Let no sinner therefore once imagine God can be at peace with him, delight in him, or be reconciled to his person, whilst he is an unbeliever, or lives in, and love his horrid sins and abominable lusts ; but let him lay hold of God's free offers of peace, and strive to obtain the grace of God, and faith in Christ, to change and purify both his heart and life.

4.   Terror.   This may be for a use of terror to all such, as resist and fight against God, and slight all the offers of his grace and free pardon, in and through Jesus Christ ; what will they do in the day of his fierce anger ?   " He will then speak to him in his wrath, and vex them in his sore displeasure," Psa. ii. 5.   Yea, he will thunder out of heaven against them, and break them all to pieces, who is able to gather heaven up in the folds as a curtain, and roll it together as a scroll of parchment, and break up the fountain of the great deeps of his wrath, and open the windows of heaven, and drown them in a deluge of his divine vengeance, and affright them by rattling peals of thunder, or cut them to pieces with thunderbolts, and amazing hail, fire, and brimstone.   Quake, ye haughty, and God-contemning infidels, whither will you fly ?   Or where can you find a place to hide yourselves from this incensed adversary when he rises up to the prey, and his hands takes hold of judgment ?

5.   But sing, ye saints, rejoice ye righteous ; this terrible God is your Father, your Friend, he is at peace with you, and will plead your cause against your enemies ; and he will hide you in the day of his wrath, and be your refuge when he comes forth in flames and flashes of fire, to burn up the earth, and to consume the proud and all the wicked like unto stubble. " The Lord also shall roar out of Zion, and utter his voice from Jerusalem, and the heavens and the earth shall shake ; but the Lord will be hope of his people, and the strength of the children of Israel," Joel iii. 16.

II

Agree with thine adversary quickly, &c.—Matt. v. 25, 26.

I SHALL proceed to the next proposition, &c.

Doct. 3.   That sinners ought without delay, quickly, presently, to seek peace and reconciliation with God.

1.   I shall show you what is necessary for sinners to know and to do, in order to their being reconciled unto God.

2.   Give you the purport of this word " quickly."

3.   Give you the reasons why they should agree with their adversary quickly, or without delay.

1.   It is absolutely necessary that such sinners who would have peace, do know the blessed God, or what a God he is ; that he is a holy God, his nature is holy ; that he is originally and essentially holy, yea infinitely holy, and hateth all sin and wickedness, and all that live in sin and rebellion against him.

2.   And they ought also to know the holiness and purity of his blessed law, which lays unbelieving sinners under wrath and the curse.

3. They ought to know the justice of God, who will not acquit any guilty sinner, but will implead mercy, unless the sinner can plead a full satisfaction is made for his sins to the injured law and justice of God.

4. Sinners ought to know the mercy of God is exceeding great, and that love and good-ness are as absolutely the essential properties of God's nature as holiness and justice.

5. They ought to know the channel in which mercy, love, and goodness, only runs down like a mighty stream, or the way by which God displays his mercy and pardoning grace to sinners, which infinite wisdom found out, which is that way, and that way alone, by which his divine wrath is appeased, and infinite justice is satisfied; viz., by the sacrifice and obedience of Jesus Christ, who was offered up in our stead; the just for the unjust, that he might bring us to God, or make our peace by the blood of his cross.

II. Sinners ought to know the insufficiency of all other ways and means whatsoever, in order to their obtaining peace and reconciliation with God.

1. That no other sacrifice can appease the wrath of God; no, though a sinner should offer a thousand rams, or ten thousand rivers of oil, or give his first-born, the fruit of his body for the sin of his soul, Mich. vi. 7. Much less the sacrifice of bulls and goats.

2. That his repentance cannot satisfy divine justice, no, though he could shed tears of blood.

3. Nor his leaving off his sins; no, though he could live and sin no more, because his former sins, the old score, would cast him into hell; will not running into God's debt any more, satisfy for sin and debts committed, or contracted in times past?

4. No more ought the sinner to think his faith. either as a habit or a gracious act, can satisfy divine justice, or appease God's anger for his sins; for faith is imperfect, through his sin cleaving to it; who can say his faith is perfect, or any other grace? No, our faith needs a Saviour, or rather that unbelief that cleaves to our faith. Sirs, faith subjectively taken, justifies us not, or makes not our peace with God; but objectively considered; I mean, it is Christ that faith apprehends: Jesus Christ, the object of faith. Doth faith make the obedience and death of Christ satisfactory unto God? Doth that pay our debts and satisfy divine justice, because that way the atonement is received or applied to us?

5. Nor is it our inherent righteousness, nor our religious duties that can make our peace with God; all our own righteousness is but unrighteousness in the eye of severe justice. Hence it is compared to " filthy rags or dung," Phil. iii. 8, in comparison of the righte-ousness of God. Therefore sinners ought to know that regeneration and sanctification cannot make their peace with God, or satisfy for their sins; for *A new piece* although no man can enter into the kingdom of heaven that is not born again, *of cloth put to an old* and made inherently holy, yet neither of these doth, or can atone for sins, *garment.* nor appease God's wrath; therefore do not think, though you become new creatures, that regeneration can procure or purchase your peace, or make reconciliation with God; it doth indeed make us meet for heaven, but it gives us no right or title to it. Grace in us is but a creature, and regeneration is but in part; whilst we are in this world, there is much sin and corruption remaining in the best of saints.

III. Therefore sinners must know that it is Christ's obedience only, his blood *Our peace is* and merits, his sin-atoning sacrifice that makes our peace. O it is a most dan- *only made by* gerous thing for any to build their hopes of God's favour and peace with him *Jesus Christ.* upon any thing wrought in them, or done by them. Moreover, it is not your pleading God's mercy that will avail you anything, unless you eye the way in which he lets his mercy run forth. God's mercy will not acquit a sinner to the eclipsing the glory of his justice and holiness. Mercy indeed moved infinite wisdom to find out the ransom, but to plead for pardon without respect to Christ's bloody sacrifice, is the way to turn mercy into fury. Shall a condemned criminal sue to his sovereign for pardon upon the simple score or account of mercy, after the king had sacrificed his own son, to satisfy the law and justice for those his horrid offences; this would but enrage his abused sovereign. Might he not say, Thou ignorant wretch, did I not sacrifice my son to make thy peace? why dost thou not plead the merits of his blood, in which my mercy and justice are both magnified? He that would have pardon and peace with God, ought well to consider these things. They must despair of help or relief any other way, therefore seek it by Jesus Christ alone. We must die to our own righteousness, as St. Paul did, and count all that is gain to us as loss for Christ, that we may be found in him, and clothed with his righteousness only, Phil. iii. 8, 9, if we would have peace with God; or else the law will let fly his killing arrows against us, and divine justice will throw us into hell. Woe to such who build upon their own inhe-ent righteousness, or boast of a state of perfection in themselves, or place their title to heaven on their inherent sanctification, or mix works with Christ's merits in point of justification, reconciliation, and peace with God.

IV.   Such sinners who would have peace with God, must resolve to lay down their arms, and fight against God no more. Dare a condemned rebel approach the throne of his incensed sovereign, to beg pardon with his sword in his hand, as if he would sheath it in the bowels of his prince ?

1.   Resolve not to sin any more, whether God will pardon thee or not ; do not hug any idol in thy heart.

2.   Be convinced that this world in its riches, honours, and sensual pleasures, is a cursed enemy to thy soul, and while it smiles upon thee, it secretly and unawares cuts thy throat ; do not be fond of a name amongst men ; self is a grand idol, self-love, self-interest, self-righteousness ; beware of human applauses, and vain glory.

3.   Take heed thou dost not love husband, wife, children, or estate, above Christ, and so in love to them neglect to seek peace with God through Jesus Christ.

4.   Take heed of resting on that knowledge, and upon those outward privileges thou hast attained ; I may say to thee, alluding to that passage, 2 Kings ix. 18, " Is it peace ? and Jehu said, what hast thou to do with peace ? turn thou behind me," ver. 22.   " And it came to pass when Joram saw Jehu, that he said, is it peace, Jehu ? And he answered and said, what peace, so long as the whoredoms of thy mother Jezebel, and her witchcrafts are so many ?" O put away your idols, your strange gods ; let no trust, no relation, no duty, no attainment be your idol, if you would have peace with God ; what peace so long as men love the world above God ?   What peace whilst thou art a swearer, a drunkard, a liar, a back-biter, a whoremonger ? What peace so long as pride, covetousness, and other abominable lusts, reign and predominate in the sinner's heart.

Sinners must accept of peace presently.   V.   Agree you must with your adversary quickly, accept presently of the free offers of grace in Christ, and be united to him by the Holy Spirit ; it is only to them in Christ : I say again, that God is reconciled in Christ, and therefore cry to God to give thee his Spirit, to bring thy soul to accept, espouse, and unite thee to the Lord Jesus, and so to enable thee to believe in him, John iii. 36, Mark xvi. 16 ; for he that believeth not, God's wrath abides upon, and such shall perish.   " He that believeth not shall be damned ;" nay, he " that believeth not is condemned already," and abides condemned, because he believes not in the Lord Jesus Christ.

VI.   You must be born again, if you ever come to have peace with God, for though regeneration does not reconcile God to us, (as you have heard) yet we must have the old nature, that evil nature changed, and that enmity that is in our minds against God removed. God will ever have war with the old nature, and with all such in whom that old enmity remains ; therefore marvel not that Christ says, " ye must be born again ;" you cannot love God till then, nor the things of God, nor enjoy communion and fellowship with God and Jesus Christ, nor delight in him, until you find a new heart, or partake of the divine nature. God hath promised to circumcise our hearts to love him, and to give us a new heart.   O plead his absolute promises, take hold of his absolute promises, and observe the proclamation of peace and reconciliation God hath sent out, and daily makes in the ministry of his word ;

Sinners must know the power of Christ to save.   lay hold of the first summons, do not delay, your life lies at stake.

VII.   You must know the power of God in Christ to save to the uttermost, all that come unto him ; and also how ready and willing he is to pardon all your sins, though never so many, or never so great, Heb. vii. 25.

What encouragements sinners have to believe.   Object. But I am not sure that God will pardon me, and be at peace with me.

Answ. 1. Observe this well, our Lord hath said, " That whosoever cometh unto me, I will in no wise cast him out," John vi. 36, 37, that is, I will receive him, he shall be pardoned, and have peace ; never did any come to God by Christ, but found acceptance, and therefore thou shalt if thou dost come unto him.

2.   Thou hast as much ground to believe that God will pardon thee, and be at peace with thee, as any of those sinners had, who have found mercy, and now have peace with God ; they could not find their names in the proclamation, no more than you can, but the promise to sinners, to all that see themselves lost, and undone sinners.

3. Many as bad, nay perhaps worse sinners than you, have found mercy, and been received into favour with God.

4. If thou canst not believe, cry to God to help thy unbelief ; he will give faith to thee, if thou dost but cry to him, and wait on him in the use of all means he hath ordained.

5. Hath not God sent his ambassadors to offer peace to you, and doth not he command

you to believe in his Son, and tells you that he will abundantly pardon all that turn to him: " though their sins be as red as scarlet, he will make them as white as snow," Isa. i. 18. What would you have more ?

Secondly, I shall show you what this word quickly doth denote ; " agree with thine adversary quickly."

1. It is to do a thing with great haste, make ready three measures of fine What quick-meal quickly, that is, make haste ; "Abraham made haste to fetch a calf, he ply, ran unto the herd—and he hasted to dress it," Gen. xviii. 7, so such who would have peace with God, must make great haste, and speed to do it.

2. The word signifies utmost diligence : " Thou shalt go down quickly, and come to the place," 1 Sam. xx. 19. Sinners should endeavour after pardon and peace, by closing with Christ with the uttermost care and diligence imaginable.

3. It denotes the doing of a thing without the least delay or lingering. " Take thy bill, and sit down quickly, and write fifty," Luke xvi. 6. So here ; this great work must not be delayed one moment, nor be deferred until to-morrow.

Thirdly, I shall give you the reasons of this and so confirm this proposition by arguments.

I. Because it is business of the highest concernment in the world : Can you eat, drink, or sleep, whilst God is your enemy, and his wrath abides upon you ? Will you Why sinners play with your souls, and trifle about things of an eternal concernment ? Were must quickly you not sent into this world to seek after God ? he is accounted a foolish man peace. that neglects his seed-time, his market, or exchange-time : Doth our Lord say in vain, " Strive to enter in at the strait gate ?" Luke xiii. 24. What, are there none here that will stir up themselves to take hold of God ? Will you all plead excuses ? Your blood then be upon your own heads. I have given you warning this day, to agree with your adversary now speedily, and without delay.

II. Because the present time is the very season in which God commands you to seek him, and be at peace with him, " To-day if you will hear his voice, harden not your hearts," Heb. iii. 15. " Behold, now is the accepted time, now is the day of salvation," 2 Cor. vi. 2. Behold, take notice of it, would you have pardon, be accepted, and have peace with God ? Behold this is the time, the accepted time, the day of salvation ; but if you do not now lay hold of Christ, it may be the day of your damnation ; It is not the time you like or approve of, sad ! that God's time should not be your time : Is it meet you should choose the proper time, or God ?

III. Because the neglect of the present time, is to neglect the time of your visitation : " O that thou hadst known, at least in this thy day, the things that belong to thy peace," Luke xix. 42. If you stay till to-morrow, you may never have another offer of peace made to you : the proclamation is, that you rebels lay down your arms, and kiss the Son, submit yourselves to his mercy this very day, if you would have pardon and peace with God.

IV. Because the day of your lives it is but short and very uncertain ; nay, and the day of God's patience, or the day of grace, may be but short also, as it is very uncertain. We know how many hours are in a natural day, but we know not the number of the days of our lives : and we are bid " not to boast ourselves of to-morrow, because we know not what a day may bring forth," Prov. xxvii. 1. We know not also how long God's may be, this I say, brethren, the time is short ; O make haste, what you do, do quickly : doth not God say now, Christ says quickly ? " Acquaint now thyself with him, and be at peace," Job xxii. 21. If you remain ignorant of God, or know not God in Christ, you can expect no peace : or if you think to acquaint yourselves with him hereafter, it may not do ; you must do it now : shall God say now, and you say no, not now, not to-day, but to-morrow ? If God's now be not regarded, and Christ not closed with this day, thy soul may be in hell to morrow ; " This night shall thy soul be required of thee." Dare you disobey God's calls, and refuse his now ? is it not an act of the greatest folly as well of rebellion ? why do you delay ? would a condemned criminal when sent to by his prince to haste and come quickly to him, even to-day, say no, I'll defer it till to-morrow ? All would say he was out of his wits should he so do : Alas, saith he, if I go not to-day, execution-day may be to-morrow. Consider, sinner, what thou doest, thou that sayest thou wilt turn to God to-morrow, or art not resolved to do it to-day ; thy purpose it appears is to be wicked to-day, such sin with full resolution : and what if God says, thou shalt have thy choice, thy lusts to-day, thy pleasures to-day, thy carnal delights and profits to-day, and be damned to-morrow ; thou shalt be hardened to-day, and be cast into hell to-morrow. Were your house on fire to-day, would you say you will endeavour to quench it to-morrow ? or had you a child fallen into the river to-day, would you say you would pull it out to-morrow ? *Seneca*, though a heathen, condemns many that call themselves Christians ; it is the folly of a man (saith he) to think to live, when a thousand to one but he will be dead and rotten ! O what folly is it in men to think of closing with Christ, and get peace with God when they are old ! whereas thousands are cut off while young. Let me ask you a few questions.

1. Is not peace with God worth seeking ? is it not absolutely necessary ? can you be happy without it ? I know you will say nothing is more needful, why do you not then quickly seek after it ?

2. Did Jesus Christ out-bid himself in dying for us who were enemies to God ? was he unwise to die to make our peace, or was it worth the price of his most precious blood, and is it not worth your serious thought, prayers, and tears, and greatest diligence to seek after the merits and blessing thereof ?

3. Or do you think God will be better pleased with the dregs of your days, than with the chief and prime of your days ? You will say no, why then do you reserve them and waste the best of your time, days, and strength, in the service of sin and Satan ?

4. Or do you think that you shall be in a better capacity to mind heavenly things hereafter, when sickness, pain, and anguish seize on you, and when God's Spirit perhaps will be withdrawn from you, or strive no more with you ?

5. Or is it fit for a servant to say, to-morrow I will go and work in thy vineyard, when his master says go to-day ? O will you deal with the holy God, as you would not be dealt with yourself ?

God as an act of sovereignty may at any time cut down a sinner. — V. Mind these words well, lest at any time the adversary deliver thee to the judge. Thy times are in God's hand ; he may act when he pleaseth in a way of sovereignty, i. e., at any time he may give thee up into the hands of divine Justice and cut thee off ; death may seize on thee this day, this night, or at any time, even before you are aware. Man knows not his time.

VI. When once the Judge delivers thee to the Officer, and thou art cast into prison, how dismal will thy state be for ever ? There is no redemption out of hell. Could sinners satisfy divine justice by suffering, though they lay in torments ten thousand years, they might come out thence ; but, because the sufferings of a finite creature cannot satisfy infinite justice, who demands the uttermost farthing, they must lie in those flames to an endless eternity. For though Christ satisfied for all the sins of the elect, or paid the uttermost farthing in a short space of time, yet the sinner cannot ; sinners in hell sin eternally, and therefore must suffer eternally. Christ, saith one, endured the penal death of men, not the spiritual death of men : and that in the nature of it, not in the continuance, not in the despair and moral evils that follow upon it. Such sins as the damned are guilty of, are not essential to the nature of the punishment, but arise from the inherent unrighteousness of the person suffering ; neither is the eternal duration of the punishment essential to its nature, but ariseth from the infinite nature of the suffering creature, which renders a commensurate satisfaction from him impossible. But the infinite holiness of Christ's nature was a bar against the sins which are committed by others under wrath ; and the infinite satisfaction he made, by means of the grandeur and dignity of his Person, was a bar against the eternal duration of the punishment.

APPLICATION

Our peace with God is a mystery. — From hence I infer, that the sinner's peace and reconciliation with God, is a great mystery ; Christ did not plead with the Father, pray and intreat the Father only to be at peace with us ; no, but he bled, he died, to procure our peace. " We speak the wisdom of God in a mystery, even the hidden wisdom which God ordained before the world began, to our glory," 1 Cor. ii. 7.

2. That our peace and reconciliation with God, is alone of his free grace. It is free to us, though Christ paid dear for it : sinners could not make their own peace with God, neither do anything to reconcile God to them, or them to God ; no, God alone is the Author of it, and it flows from him as an act of infinite love, grace, and favour. He found out the great Peace-maker, he sent him into the world, he accepted him as our Surety in our stead ; he anointed him, upheld him, and raised him up from he dead ; he, by the power of his Spirit, changes our hearts, bows our wills, draws our affections, and makes us yield to receive the Lord Jesus Christ, and to accept of that peace he made by his blood.

3. We also infer from hence, that God the Father, who is the Author of our peace

and reconciliation, ought to receive equal glory with our Lord Jesus *The Father is the Author of our peace.* Christ, who hath made our peace; and that we ought equally to exalt the Holy Ghost, who applies this peace to us, and who works out all that enmity which was in our hearts against God; and so makes the blood of atonement efficacious to our souls.

4. That it is a certain, a sure, and an abiding peace; " The covenant of my *It is sure peace.* peace shall not be removed, saith the Lord who hath mercy on thee." This peace is according to God's eternal counsel: it is founded upon his unalterable decree and purpose in Jesus Christ, and it is confirmed by the blood of his Son, and the oath of God, Heb. vi. 17—19. Shall any of them miss of peace and reconciliation with God, for whom Christ died, and to whom this peace is applied? No, no, that is impossible. " Let God be true, and every man a liar."

5. We may infer that Christ as Mediator doth the whole work, or all for *Christ alone is the Reconciler.* us, about our peace: he reconciles God to us, and us to God, so lays his hands upon both.

6. We also may infer from hence, that he that would agree with God (who *The Spirit is a great Agent in our peace, Isa. vi. 37.* is an enemy to sinners whilst they remain in their sins) and have peace with him, must receive the Holy Spirit, and so be united to Jesus Christ, and must believe in him, receive him by faith, or perish for ever. And all that the Father gave to his Son, shall be thus united to him; they shall believe, or come to Christ, John vi. 37.

7. We may infer, that to reject Jesus Christ, or not to receive him who *The evil of rejecting peace with God.* hath made our peace, is an abominable evil, the worst sin any soul can be guilty of. Hath God done all this, Christ done all this, for sinners' peace, and shall any wickedly refuse to accept it? Or shall they think of getting peace with God some other way, even by their own works, reformation of life, or by their righteousness, repentance, and sincere obedience? Let such fear of falling into hell, and so perish for ever. " For there is no other name given under heaven whereby we must be saved, if ever we are saved," Acts iv. 12.

8. We infer from whence it is that we are made accepted in the sight of God, *i. e.*, it is in the beloved; and by this means also we have free access to God; our peace being made, and we justified, we may come with boldness to the throne of grace, by the blood of Jesus.

9. We infer also, that God is reconciled to sinners upon honourable terms; *Gospel-peace upon honourable terms.* God every way is magnified, and suffers not in any of his blessed attributes. Had we only been pardoned as an act of simple mercy, perhaps the devil would cry, where is now the glory of thy justice, the glory of thy truth and holiness, and the sanction of thy law?

10. This may serve to abase man, humble man: here is peace made with- *Man hated the way of his peace.* out sorry man's seeking, or man's procuring, nay, and without any desert of mankind? Did we deserve this favour, such love, such a Saviour? What did Christ die for us when we were enemies? " Where is boasting then?" " All things are of God," &c., that man might be nothing, but cry out, O the riches of God's grace! who works all our works in us and for us.

Exhort. O sinners, sinners! make haste, and quickly agree with your *Sinners exhorted to accept of peace by Christ Jesus.* adversary, *i. e.*, embrace Jesus Christ, labour to know and receive the atonement, and the things of your peace, lest they are hid from your eyes, or before you are given up to hardness of heart, &c., or into the hands of your righteous Judge, whose lamb-like nature will be turned into fury, and like a lion will tear you in pieces. And O let the sight of a bleeding Jesus upon the cross, *What is sin?* move you into tears, and melt your hearts to think that no other ways you could have peace and reconciliation with God. What is sin? O what a kind of breach did it make between God and us, that nothing but the blood of his own Son could make up that breach?

Comfort. What consolations here to all that are reconciled to God; there will never any more be a breach between God and you; he is your Father in Jesus Christ, he will defend your cause, and take care of your persons, and fight against and subdue all your enemies; and keep your souls in perfect peace whose minds are stayed upon him.

7. HEARING CHRIST'S SAYINGS

I

*Therefore whosoever heareth these sayings of mine, and doeth them, I will liken him
unto a wise man that built his house upon a rock.*
*And the rain descended, and the floods came, and the winds blew, and beat upon that
house, and it fell not, for it was founded upon a rock.*—Matt. vii. 24, 25.

**1 Sermon
preached
July 2.
1693.** THIS is an express similitude, (and as my purpose is to open and explain all
the parables contained in the four Evangelists) so likewise all the principal
similitudes which our blessed Saviour made use of.

The method I shall take shall be as followeth :

First, open every part of this similitude.

Secondly, I shall take notice of the chief points of doctrine that lie therein.

Thirdly, apply the whole.

First, Christ's sayings may comprehend his whole doctrine.

**What is
meant by the
sayings of
Christ.** 1. The doctrine of faith and repentance, for in these two things did part
of his sayings consist, nay, the first and chief of them. This doctrine on
these sayings, he began to offer just after he was baptized, when he first
entered on this ministry. " Saying, the time is fulfilled, and the kingdom of
God is at hand, repent ye and believe the Gospel," Matt. i. 10—15.

2. The doctrine of regeneration. " Verily, verily, I say unto thee, except a man
be born again, he cannot see the kingdom of God," John iii. 3.

3. The doctrine of self-denial.

Then said Jesus to his disciples, " If any man will come after me, let him deny
himself, and take up his cross and follow me," Matt. xvi. 24.

But more particularly, that doctrine, and those saying of his, which he uttered in
the mount, Matt. v. ; to which these of my text, particularly refer.

1. Wherein he presseth a holy life, and openeth the nature and spirituality of the
moral law.

2. The doctrine of righteousness, showing that we must have a righteousness that exceeds that of the Scribes and Pharisees, Matt. v. 20.

Quest. What was the righteousness of the Pharisees ?

**What the
righteousness
of the Phari-
sees was.** Answ. I am not ignorant that some affirm it was only a formal hypocritical
righteousness, because many of the Scribes and Pharisees were charged by
our Lord with horrid hypocrisy.

And this they would have here meant, to bring in man's own inherent
righteousness, or our sincere obedience to the precepts of the law and Gospel, to be that
righteousness which exceeds the righteousness of the Scribes and Pharisees ; thereby to
exclude the imputed righteousness of Jesus Christ, to be intended by our blessed Lord.

Now, though we deny not but that some of the Scribes and Pharisees were guilty of
abominable hypocrisy, and consequently all their righteousness was but in show, and outward appearance ; also mixed with many vain rites, ceremonies, and traditions : yet evident it is, all of them were not of this sort, but some might act out of moral sincerity :
and can we think that our Saviour alluded to that righteousness that was in the grosser
and courser sort of the Pharisees, and not to the righteousness of those of them that
acted in moral uprightness towards God, as Paul did whilst he was a Pharisee, as he testified before the counsel ; " Men and brethren, I have lived in all good conscience before
God until this day," Acts xxiii. 1. That he acted in uprightness, or morally in all good
conscience towards God, in obedience to the law while a Pharisee ; I think there is no
doubt to be made of this ; Saul certainly was no hypocrite, though misled, and ignorant
of that justifying righteousness that is in Christ only ; which when he came to believe, he
so valued, " That his own righteousness he accounted but dung," Phil. iii. 8, 9, 10, in
comparison of it.

2. So that it appears, the righteousness of the Scribes and Pharisees was a self-righte-

72

ousness, a legal righteousness, an inherent righteousness, or righteousness of works. A righteousness in conformity to the letter of the law, not to the perfection or spirituality of the law.

Our Lord shows, that our righteousness, if we enter into heaven, must exceed the very best that any of the Pharisees had, (viz.)

1. It must be a perfect righteousness, a spotless righteousness; viz., the righteousness of God through faith in Jesus Christ, for our justification.

2. He may also comprehend that sincere, inherent righteousness that is in believers, that flows from faith, and union with Christ, and right principles, which tends to sanctify and cleanse both our hearts and lives.

But such who preach the righteousness our Lord speaks of, (as exceeding the righteousness of the Scribes, &c.,) to be only a sincere, inward, and outward conformity to the rules and precepts of the Gospel, no doubt are mistaken. For should a man gain an inherent righteousness, that exceeds the righteousness of the Scribes and Pharisees, will that justify him at God's bar; or give him a title to, and an entrance into the kingdom of heaven?

Certainly, whosoever he be that obtains the highest degree of an inherent righteousness, and resteth on that, thinking that will save him, he is blind and deceived, and in danger to fall into hell; for all works either done by us, or wrought in us, are utterly excluded in point of justification.

Christ's righteousness only is our alone title to eternal life, without any of ours being joined with it, (though by the operations of the Holy Spirit, and blessed effects of faith, and union with Christ) we are made meet, or fit for that glorious "inheritance of the saints in light," Col. i. 12.

It was not Abraham's nor David's own inherent righteousness that justified and saved them, though theirs did far exceed the righteousness of any of the Scribes or Pharisees, because it was the effects of faith and union with Christ.

"Abraham believed, and it was counted to him for righteousness," Rom. iv. 3, that is, by faith he saw Christ and believed on him; Christ's righteousness to apprehend, justified him. "Now to him that worketh not, but believeth on him that justifieth the ungodly, his faith is counted for righteousness," Rom. iv. 5. "Enter not into judgment (saith David) with thy servant, for in thy sight shall no flesh living be justified," Psal. cxliii. 2. All our righteousness (saith the prophet) is but as filthy rags; therefore our Saviour by his sayings, doth not put us upon doing, or working for life; no, no, though we exceed therein the Scribes and the Pharisees; but to show that we must look out for a perfect righteousness to another; that is, look by faith to Christ, believe in him for righteousness; "Believe on the Lord Jesus, and thou shalt be saved," Acts xvi. 31. "If ye believe not that I am he, ye shall die in your sins," John viii. 24. "When ye have done all, say ye are unprofitable servants." Heaven is not a reward of debt, but of grace.

3. Our Lord alludes to those sayings of his, of heart purity; not only, not to commit the act of adultery, but also, not to look upon a woman to commit adultery with her, Matt. v. 28.

4. To cut off a right-hand lusts, and pull out a right-eye lusts. Also,

5. Not to be angry with our brother without cause; showing that we may be guilty of murder without committing the overt-act of murder; thereby to convince us that it is impossible for us to keep the holy law of God, and to be justified thereby, and so to lead us to rely, and depend upon his perfect obedience unto it, in our nature and stead: likewise to those sayings of his about abstinence and secret prayer; also to "agree with thine adversary quickly," Matt. v. 25, that is, to plead the atonement he hath made for our sins; and to that satisfaction he hath given to the law and justice of God. Moreover, what he said about mourning for sin, labouring after poverty of spirit, to be meek, and "hunger and thirst after righteousness, to bear reproaches and persecution patiently for his sake; to be the salt of the earth, and light of the world," Matt. v. 3—13; as also to be "merciful, as our Father that is in heaven is merciful and perfect," ver. 48; that is, to labour after the implantation of grace, and to obtain an impress of God's image upon our souls, or to experience the same holiness, as to its nature and quality (though we cannot arrive to the same in respect to degrees thereof.) So much as to what those sayings of Christ my text refers to.

Secondly, What is meant by hearing of Christ's sayings?

Answ. 1. To hear his word and sayings with attention, to hear in hearing;

What it is to some will not hear at all, they will not come where Christ's doctrine and
hear Christ's sayings are preached ; others do not regard what they hear, but hear carelessly.
sayings.

2. To hear his sayings and holy doctrine, as it is his word, not as the word of man, but as it is indeed the Word of God. Thus those in Thessalonica heard it, and received it, which becomes effectual in all that believe.

3. They hear Christ's sayings with holy trembling. Thus the good king Josiah heard the book of the law. " Princes (saith David) persecuted me without a cause, but my heart standeth in awe of thy word," Psal. cxix. 161.

If they heard the words of Moses with such trembling and holy awe, who was but the servant, and but a man as we are ; with what fear and awe should we hear Christ's word, who is the Son of God, the Lord from heaven ; we certainly should give the more earnest heed to the things he says ; " To this man will I look that is poor, and that trembleth at my word," Isa. lxvi. 2.

S. To hear Christ's sayings and heavenly doctrine believingly ; " Who hath believed our report ?" Isa. liii. 1. Many that heard our Saviour's sayings did not believe ; they did not give that credence to his doctrine which they gave to such that came in their own names to deceive them : yet it is one thing to believe Christ's sayings to be true, and another thing truly to believe in him, and receive him, and rest upon him, for life and salvation.

5. To hear with understanding ; many hear but remain ignorant of their state, do not understand the purport of the word, which is to convince them of the evil of sin, and of their woful and undone condition thereby, and of the necessity of a Mediator, or of a Saviour ; as also of the excellency of that blessed Saviour, together with that mighty power and ability that he is clothed with to save. They hear and understand, that there is an absolute necessity of faith in Christ, of receiving him, resting and relying upon him for salvation ; these are they that rightly hear the word and sayings of Jesus Christ ; " But he that receiveth seed into good ground, is he that heareth the word, and understandeth it which also beareth fruit," &c., Matt. xiii. 23.

6. The wise hearer hears Christ's sayings and retains them, he is not a forgetful hearer ; he sees the excellency of the word ; likes and approves of the sayings and doctrine of Jesus Christ ; he is like to Mary who pondered, " And kept all these sayings in her heart." These persons, with holy David, love God's word above gold, yea, above fine gold ; " therefore I esteem all thy precepts concerning all things to be right, and hate every false way," Psal. cxix. 127, 128.

7. It is a hearing of Christ's word and sayings subjectively ; such hear and come to Christ. " Whosoever cometh to me, and heareth my sayings, &c. Luke vi. 47. In coming to Christ they hear, and in hearing, come, that is, then believe, and receive Jesus Christ.

What is it to   Thirdly, what is meant by doing Christ's sayings ?
do Christ's   Answ. 1. It is to believe whatsoever is matter of faith ; and to do
sayings.   and practise whatsoever is matter of practice and duty.

2. He may be said to do what Christ saith that hath his whole trust and dependence upon him, or that resteth wholly upon Christ's merits and righteousness for justification and eternal life ; " This is the work of God that ye believe on him whom he hath sent." Brethren, this is one of the sayings of Christ ; you are for working, for doing, (as if Christ should say) I will therefore resolve and answer our question, " What shall we do to work the work of God ?" Ver. 28. That which God would have you do, or is his work, i.e., that which he had commanded you to do, is, that you believe on him whom he hath sent. Sirs, none do Christ's sayings but such that believe on him.

3. To do Christ's sayings is to yield ready and hearty obedience to the precepts he hath given forth in the Gospel ; some will not hear what Christ says ; others will hear, but they hear carelessly ; others hear but do not. " If I am your Lord and Master, why do ye not what I say ? Not every one that saith unto me, Lord, Lord, but he that doeth the will of my Father which is in heaven," Matt. vii. 21.

4. They that uprightly do Christ's sayings, do them sincerely, in truth, not out of by-ends and aims ; neither for loaves, not for self and carnal profit, nor for self-applause. " Verily, verily, I say unto you, ye seek me not because ye saw the miracles, but because ye did not eat of the loaves, and were filled," John vii. 26. Some have low, carnal, and base ends in hearing and doing Christ's sayings ; but such who are truly wise, act as those St. Paul speaks of : " But ye have obeyed from the heart, that form of doctrine that was delivered unto you :" Rom vii. 17. The divine doctrine hath great efficacy on the hearts of these persons ; the word makes an impression upon their souls, so that with joy and delight they obey it.

5. They do Christ's sayings from right principles, from a principle of life, from faith in, and love to Christ: if ye love me, keep my commandments; that obedience which proceeds not from faith and love, is not regarded, nor accepted of by Jesus Christ.

6. They are such that do all Christ's sayings; " Ye are my friends if ye do whatsoever I say," John xv. 14. Nothing more clearly declares, or expresses our love to Christ, than our obedience to all his precepts, or our universal obedience to him; " Then shall I not be ashamed when I have respect unto all thy commandments," Psal. cxix. 6.

7. Such continue in doing Christ's sayings; they abide in their obedience, they obey always, or continue in well doing.

Fourthly, What is meant by his house? He is like to a man that built his house, &c.

1. I answer, By this house is, doubtless, meant his hope of salvation; " Whose hope shall be cut off, and whose trust shall be as the spider's web," Job. viii. 14. He shall lean on his house, but it shall not stand.

1. A house is that which we rest in, and where we take our repose ; a true believer resteth on Christ, he builds his house, i. e., his hope, his soul, and all he doth, on Christ ; he that hath a right hope, a true faith, he hath a firm and well-built house, where he reposeth himself, or resteth continually.

2. A house is a place of shelter to us, in a tempestuous or stormy season, when rain, hail, snow, thunder, &c., are like to annoy us ; so this man that builds his hope in Christ, is secured and safe, when Satan raises storms of temptations upon him; he is safe also from the thunderings of mount Sinai, or the thunderbolts of the law and of the wrath of God, which all unbelievers lie open to.

3. A house is often assaulted by thieves, and if not firm and strong, may be broke up, and all that dwell in it may be robbed, nay murdered; so is the hope of a Christian often attacked by Satan, and if his faith and hope was not built upon Christ, he was certainly in danger of losing all he hath ; nay, his precious soul for ever.

Fifthly, What is meant by the Rock?

I answer, by the rock is no doubt meant Jesus Christ ; he is often called a What is meant by the rock on which this man builds. rock ; " The Lord is my rock and my fortress." Psal. xviii. 1. " Who is a rock save our God ?" O Lord, my rock be not silent," verse 31. Psal. xxviii. 1. " Upon this rock will I build my church," Matt. xvi. 18 ; 1 Cor. x. 4.

Jesus Christ may be fitly compared to a rock ;

1. A rock is a firm and immovable thing, therefore good for a foun- Christ is as firm as a rock. dation; that which is built on a rock, stands sure ; so Christ is a firm and sure foundation ; " Upon this rock I will build my Church, and the gates of hell shall not prevail against it," Matt. xvi. 18.

2. Christ may be compared to a rock, in regard that in ancient times people built their houses in rocks, as well as built upon them; " they hewed out houses, or habitations in rocks," Isa. xxii. 16. Christ is a believer's spiritual habitation; " they, like the dove, make their dwelling in the clifts of the rock," Psal. xc. 1. " He that dwelleth in love, dwelleth in God," 1 John iv. 16.

3. A rock in Locus Excelsus, an high place; though it hath its bottom Christ a high rock. deep, yet is the top high and the towering, far above the surface of the earth : so Jesus Christ, though in his humiliation he was laid low, that we might build upon him, yet in the dignity of his person, he being God, the most high God, as well as man, he is high, far above all conceptions of our hearts ; as the Mediator he is also exalted at God's right hand, far above all heavens; and in his power and sovereign authority he is lifted up, having absolute dominion over angels, devils, and men.

4. Rocks are strong, and were made use of for places of defence ; no Christ is a strong rock. fortifications like some rocks, they are impregnable : David for security fled into a rock ; in this respect Christ may also be compared to a rock, because he is our refuge from the wrath and vengeance of God, the curse of the law, and rage of wicked men, sin, and devils ; a believer in Christ is safe, his dwelling place is impregnable.

5. Rocks being high, or eminent places for height, are useful to take a Christ is a blessed prospect. pleasant prospect; from hence a person may see afar off; he that by faith ascends to the top of this spiritual rock, may take a survey of heaven, yea, of the glory of God, in all his attributes, to the joy of his soul.

6. Rocks are durable, permanent, and lasting; Jesus Christ hath the Christ is a durable rock, stability of a rock, he is the same yesterday, to-day, and for ever ; hence he is called, the Rock of Ages.

7. Rocks yield the purest water; most pleasant springs come from them; no water is so clear as that which comes percolated through rocks; " Brethren, all our springs are in Christ, and flow from him; the Spirit proceeds from the throne of God and the Lamb," Rev. xxii. 1. He was also the antitype of the rock smitten in the wilderness, from whence waters flowed to refresh the Israelites, till they came to Canaan; all our divine consolations and comforts flow from a smitten and crucified Saviour, till we come to heaven; we live upon this rock, as well as build upon him.

8. And as a rock affords sweet refreshing shadow for weary travellers; Jesus Christ is that rock whose shadow is good; he is as the shadow of a great rock in a weary land; it is he that keeps off all the hot scorching beams of God's wrath.

Christ a rock of offence to some.

6. Rocks are dangerous to stumble at, or to fall from; Jesus Christ is called a rock of offence, many stumble at his person, some at his doctrine and ordinances; some fall on him, and others fall from him, whose state of all is the worst; after they have made a high profession, and have attained great speculative knowledge, they fall, and all they built upon him; and down they go to the lowest hell.

O brethren, how should we prize our rock, out of whom flows precious water, honey, and oil. He is a rich, a living rock, a high rock, a strong rock, an invincible rock, a feeding and fattening rock; he is (as it were) as a rock of pearls and diamonds; yea, and an eternal rock: he converts all that build rightly upon him unto precious stones, and communicates life to them; so do no rocks; he far excels all rocks; " Their rock is not like our rock."

This wise builder is said to " dig deep, and lay his foundation on a rock," Luke vi. 48. As St. Luke notes, he never gives over searching and digging into the word of God, and his design and purpose, until he finds good ground, or a good bottom and foundation to build upon. Which I propose further to open in the prosecution of one point of doctrine from hence.

II

Therefore whosoever heareth these sayings of mine, and doeth them, I will liken him unto a wise man.—Matt. vii. 24, 25.

THIS similitude I have already explained, and now shall note one or two points of doctrine therefrom. viz.

Doct. 1. That every godly man is a wise man, a wise builder.

I purpose, in speaking to this proposition, to do these three things.

First, Show and prove that every godly man is a wise man, or why so called.

Secondly, Show you wherein his wisdom doth consist, according to the purport of this similitude.

Thirdly, Apply it.

First, He is a wise man, because he prefers the good of his soul before all things in this world.

A wise man prefers religion above temporal good.

1. He prefers the good of his soul, before the temporal good of his body, and this certainly demonstrates him to be a wise man, considering how precious a thing the soul is, as shall God willing be opened.

A wise man prefers religion above a name.

2. He prefers religion itself above a bare name of being religious. Alas! how many are there who content themselves with the notion of divine truth, or with an empty vessel. " The foolish virgins took lamps, but took no oil; but the wise took oil in their vessels," Matt. xxv. 3. 4; and for thus doing, they are wise virgins.

3. Because they prefer the approbation of God, above the approbation of men. They value not that honour that comes from men, they regard not the applause of men, so that they can but have the praise of God, and be accepted by him.

4. Because a godly man considers his future well being. " And the Lord commended

the unjust steward, because he had done wisely," &c. Luke xvi. 8. *He eyes his future state chiefly.* Brethren, our blessed Saviour doth not commend the unjust steward for his honesty; He calls him an unjust steward; honesty he had not; but he commends him for his policy, in providing for himself for the time to come, or a future state. We cannot wrong our blessed Master, whilst we improve his goods, his grace, and all spiritual or external gifts given to us, to our utmost advantage and profit; we are allowed to contrive our own good; he that is wise, is wise for himself. Servants among men who study their own interest, and convert their master's money to their own use, do abominably, and God will plague them for their injustice; but believers may, nay, ought to put all that grace they have into exercise to their own profit here, *A believer is* and to their own eternal advantage, or future happiness; and all that thus do, are *godly or* accounted faithful servants. Nay, and in this thing lies the difference there is be- *righteous for himself.* tween a sincere Christian and an hypocrite, the one trades for himself that he may be happy here in this world; the other only eyes the glory of God, and his own future profit, his future honour and happiness; a foolish man he is that chiefly minds his present good; the other a wise man, he seeks his own future well being. Brethren, do not mistake me, while we seek our own eternal profit, and well being, we bring glory to God, nay, God hath no honour from any but from such who so wisely lay out their Lord's goods, or those talents he hath intrusted them with, as to provide for their future estate, for by this means we do what God commands, and answer his end in bestowing spiritual gifts and grace upon us, " They are given for every man to profit withal," 1 Cor. xii. 7; and by bringing forth fruit thus to ourselves for ever, God is glorified. In this lay the wisdom of the unjust steward, viz., in providing for himself for the future time, and for this our Lord commended him. Now, beloved, if he is counted wise, that provides for an after time that is uncertain, and at most not a moment when compared to eternity, how wise are they who take care to live everlastingly in glory, possessed of all true joys and delights!

1. A godly man ponders well all future dangers.

2. All future safety and security, how he may avoid and escape the one, and enjoy the other. If he builds not with wisdom, he foresees the danger that will follow, for his soul will fall into hell.

Brethren, if there was no greater evil than earthly or temporal evil, nor any greater good than earthly or temporal good; then the men of this world would appear to all, to be the wisest men, and the godly would be the greatest fools of all men. But alas, alas! what is the greatest sorrow or torment here to the torments of hell? Or the greatest joy, and worldly riches and glory, to the glory of heaven?

3dly. A godly man may be looked upon to be wise, because he so consults *He is a wise* matters, that he may not suffer the loss of all his labour and cost; such who *man that sees he suf-* hear Christ's sayings and do them not, that do not believe in him, nor obey *fers no loss* his precepts; though they may make a visible profession, and do many things, *now by building.* and give to the poor, and suffer much external loss, yet all their labour, pains, and costs, and future hopes, will be utterly lost; but a true Christian is so wise as to close savingly with Christ, and obey his precepts, by which he knows his labour will not be in vain in the Lord.

4. A godly man is a wise man, because he complies with, and approves of that *A wise man* great and glorious design, and purpose of God in Jesus Christ; it being the *is carrying on the same* contrivance of his infinite wisdom, this way only to restore and save lost man: *design God* Now seeing a true Christian accepteth of Christ alone, and builds upon him as *carries on in* the only foundation, it shows he is a wise man. *the world.*

5. Because he seeks the honour of his blessed Lord and Master, and there- *A wise man* by keeps in his love and favour; it is not his own good only, but Christ's glory *chiefly seeks* which he seeks, and this is a great point of wisdom. " Why call ye me Lord, *the honour of Christ.* Lord, and do not what I say? It is not every one that saith to me, Lord, Lord," Luke. vi. 46. Is he a wise man that hath a good prince to be his master, and yet never regards his master's interest nor honour, nor values his love and special favour, but rather doth expose his prince to great reproach and shame; now a godly man by doing what Christ says, honours him, and so abides in his love. "If ye keep my commandments, ye shall abide in my love, even as I have kept my Father's commandments, and abide in his love," John xv. 10. A father commands his child to do this or that which he knows will be for his own good; now, if he doth it not, as the child suffers, so his Father hath shame and contempt cast upon him thereby also. " A wise son makes a glad father, but a foolish son causeth shame."

" A son honoureth his father, and a servant his master," Mal. i. 6 ; that is, every wise and obedient son and servant.

6thly. Because nothing but God, and an interest in him, and the eternal enjoyment of this God, will satisfy his soul ; if God be the chief good, then to place all our hope and happiness in him, and to enjoy him, must needs be a part of high- est wisdom. " He that keepeth his commandments, dwelleth in God, and God in him," 1 John. iii. 24, This man hath God to be his God ; O what man is wise, save this man only ? Others have the shell, but this man hath the kernel : others have the cabinet, and that contents them, but this man hath also the jewel.

A wise man prefers the chiefest good.

7thly. Because these men are the declared friends of Jesus Christ, and only favourites of heaven : " Ye are my friends, if ye do whatsoever I command you," John. xv. 14. What can be a greater part of wisdom than to obtain the favour and friendship of Jesus Christ ? I do not say, by doing of Christ say- ings, we purchase or procure Christ's love and friendship : no, no, his favour cannot be bought, but he doth freely vouchsafe this blessing to his chosen, who obey his word : it is hereby we are assured of his love : " He that hath my commandments and keepeth them, he it is that loveth me, and he that loveth me, shall be beloved of my Father." A man may have Christ's commandments in his Bible, and in his head, and in mouth, and in the notion of them : he may know what his commands be, but he may not have them in his heart, he may not keep them, or be subject to them : but a godly man loves them, ap- proves them, and sincerely keeps them, and reaps the benefit and blessings of them, and therefore is a wise man.

He is a wise man that has Christ for his friend.

8. He is a wise man, because he is resolved to keep a good conscience : bre- thren, conscience is a tender thing, and to offend it is a piece of greatest folly; it is for a man to arm himself to murder his own soul, or kill himself; better to have all men in the world against us, and to reproach us, than to have our own consciences to accuse and reproach us. Moreover, nothing more fully evinceth, or is a clearer evidence of a man's integrity, than when he keepeth a conscience void of offence towards God, and towards men : hence holy Job saith, " My integrity I hold fast, and I will not let it go : my heart shall not reproach me as long as I live." That man certainly is an hypocrite, that doth not impartially all the commands of Christ, according to his light, or doth not whatsoever he says : universal obedience is a mighty proof of sincerity. " Then shall I not be ashamed, when I have respect to all thy commandments," Psal. cxix. 6. An hypocrite will do some things, but he faulters and declines to do every thing, which he is convinced to be his duty : " Now I know that thou fearest me," Gen. xxii. 16. Why so? because he did not refuse to obey God in the hard- est and most difficult thing, even in offering up his son Isaac, whom he so dearly loved.

He is a wise man that keeps a good conscience.

9thly. A godly man who keeps Christ's sayings, is a wise man, because he departs from iniquity: " The fear of the Lord is the beginning of wisdom : and to depart from evil, that is understanding," Job xxviii. 28. Now to keep Christ's sayings, is to depart from evil : " For obedience is better than sacrifice, and to hearken than the fat of lambs : But rebellion is as the sin of witchcraft, and stubbornness as ini- quity and idolatry," 1 Sam. xv. 22, 23.

True wisdom is to part from iniqui- ty.

Certainly, if it be the greatest folly to disobey God's precepts, it must be great wisdom, sincerely, and from right principles to keep them. " My son, forget not my law, but let thine heart keep my commandments: for length of days, and long life, and peace shall they add to thee," Prov. iii. 1, 2, 3. This is the way of peace here, and of eternal peace and honour hereafter : " Keep therefore, and do them, for this is your wisdom and your understanding," Deut. iv. 6.

And as they who keep Christ's word, are wise, so such that keep them not, are fools. " They have rejected the word of the Lord, and what wisdom is in them?" Jer. viii. 9.

They only are wise that are wise to salvation.

He is a wise man, because he is wise unto salvation ; all others are only wise to get this world, in heaping up earthly riches ; such things that are uncertain, and which cannot profit in the day of wrath; they do but load themselves with thick clay, and weary themselves for very vanity : but a godly man is not satisfied with earthly riches, earthly honours and pleasures, but he is for the riches and glory of heaven : it is a crown of glory that is in his eye, nothing but God himself will satisfy him. This man, brethren, is under a clear promise of eternal life : I mean, he that obeys Christ and keepeth his sayings.

" And being made perfect, he became the Author of eternal salvation unto all that obey him," Heb. v. 9. These persons have a declared right to future glory which Christ hath purchased, and that God hath promised. "Blessed are they that do his commandments, that they may have right to the tree of life, and may enter in through the gates into the city," Rev. xxii. 14. Even into that city is so glorious, the foundations of which are laid with precious stones, and the city pure gold.

APPLICATION

I. If these things be so, we infer, that all wicked men, though never so wise with the wisdom of this world, are the worst of fools. Ungodly men think the saints are guilty of folly in contemning all earthly riches, honours, and pleasures, for Christ's sake. But the saints of God know all carnal and graceless persons are fools, Christ called the covetous rich man a fool. " Thou fool, this night thy soul shall be required of thee, then whose shall those things be which thou hast provided?" But more as touching their folly, when I come to speak to the next verse.

II. Be exhorted to enquire what the commands or sayings of Jesus Christ are?

Now understand they are of two sorts.

1. Precepts that are purely moral, which contain our duty to God, and our duty to man.

2. Such precepts that are merely positive, and those also are of two sorts.

First, Such that are essential to salvation, as faith in Christ ; this is one of Christ's commands.

2. Repentance, self-denial, taking up our cross, and following him, and leading of a holy and godly life, prayer, &c.

3. Duties of charity, and acts of bounty, and all other divine graces, though they are Christ's gift, yet he hath enjoined us to labour after them, and to strive to increase and abound in them.

Secondly, There are also precepts that appertain to the worship of God, and the discipline of the church, as preaching and hearing the word of God, and the holy ordinances of the Gospel, as baptism and the Lord's Supper, and church-fellowship ; and there are also some sayings of Christ that appertain to the disciplining of the church, which are mentioned in Matt. xxviii. All which sayings and holy precepts, all true Christians should with great care and faithfulness, observe and keep.

CAUTION

Let sinners know it behoveth them to see they rest not satisfied in their obedience thinking by that way to obtain the love and favour of God ; for no obedience Caution 2. can make your state good : I mean, you should not think that any obedience, either to moral or positive precepts, while you abide unbelievers, will, or can profit you anything.

Your first business is to labour after true faith, to believe in Jesus Christ, and obtain union with him ; your persons must be first accepted, before any duty of obedience can be accepted. All works of obedience before faith and regeneration, please not God, nor profit the creature ; you must first come to Christ, (as his sayings direct you,) and then "take his yoke upon you, and learn of him," Matt. xi. 28, 29. The tree must be first made good, before the fruit can be good. "An evil tree cannot bring forth good fruit," Luke vi. 43.

God had first a respect to Abel, and then to his offering : obedience follows true faith, as the fruit of it.

REPROOF

This may also serve to reprove all those Christians, that content themselves in doing some of Christ's sayings, and never enquire after all things, whatsoever he hath commanded them.

2. Also it may reprehend such, who, when convinced of a duty or ordinance, yet delay to obey Jesus Christ in it. " I made haste and delayed not to keep thy precepts ;" " Arise (saith Ananias to Paul) and be baptized, why tarriest thou ?" It may call into question the truth of your grace and sincerity, when you are convinced of an ordinance, and you delay or refuse to yield obedience unto Christ in it ; you may fear that your house will not stand the winds of Satan's temptation, nor the floods of persecution, if you do not all the sayings of Jesus Christ.

This also may yield much comfort to sincere Christians, and be an evidence of their uprightness, when they are universal in their obedience to Christ. He that says he loveth God, and keepeth not his commandments, is a liar. " By this we know, that we love the children of God, when we love God and keep his commandments: this is love, that we keep his commandments, and his commandments are not grievous," 1 John v. 2, 3. David, by this means, came to have an evidence of his sincerity. "Then shall I not be ashamed, when I have respect to all thy commandments."

2. This tends to show that your love is true love, and your faith is true faith. Satan may get strong advantages against such persons who are partial in their obedience to Jesus Christ; such do, as it were, put a sword into their enemy's hand.

3. Hereby also you come under the clear promise of eternal life, and have grounds to hope you shall stand, "when the winds blow, and the floods come and beat against your house." But so much at this time.

III

Therefore, whosoever heareth these sayings of mine, and doeth them, I will liken him to a wise man that built his house upon a rock, &c.—Matt. vii. 24, 25.

Sermon 3., preached in July, 1693.
Doct. 1. Every godly man is a wise man, and a wise builder.

I. I have shown you why he is called a wise man.

I shall proceed to the next thing.

II. Show you wherein his wisdom doth consist.

I have done with the first, and shall speak to the second head, viz., show wherein his wisdom doth consist.

1. A godly man's wisdom doth consist in his thoughtfulness of his soul.

True wisdom consisteth in the care of the soul.
Should a man have treasure of great value committed to his trust, and he take no care of it, or not regard what becomes of it; would not all say such a one is a fool or a mad-man, especially if lost, the loss would be his own, it would wholly fall upon himself.

Now the soul of man is of great worth, yea, of an inconceivable value; and every man hath this precious soul committed to his charge. And that the soul is of great worth or value, see what our blessed Saviour saith, "What is a man profited if he gain the whole world, and lose his own soul," Matt. xvi. 26. It appears that it is such treasure, such a jewel, that it is more worth than all the world. Should a man, to get the world, lose his life, what would be his profit he? Much more, should he lose his body and soul too, or lose his natural life here, his everlasting life hereafter. Such certainly would be looked upon by all to be fools, but wicked men are far greater fools, because they lose their souls for less than the ten thousandth part of the world; perhaps for the gain of one shilling, nay, may be of a groat; for what do they less who are unjust in their dealings; and for a very small matter of gain, will cheat and wrong their neighbour. Nay, for the sake of some base and filthy lusts that perhaps tend to ruin the body as well as the soul, do expose both to eternal flames.

But further, to demonstrate the great worth and preciousness of the soul, consider these things following.

The preciousness of the soul.
I. The soul was originally made in the image of God; it was made capable to bear an impression of the divine and holy image of the blessed God; in which consisteth the nature and substance of it, for the soul bears some likeness or resemblance of God, being spiritual, invisible, immortal, &c.

II. In its powers and faculties, being endowed with reason of understanding, and freedom of choice, as it came out of God's hands.

III. In respect of these singular endowments, wherewith God hath adorned it, as knowledge, righteousness, and true holiness, 1 Cor. i. 30, Eph. iv. 24, in which chiefly, the apostle shows the image of God consisteth; and though that impression of God's image was lost, marred, and spoiled by sin, or defaced by the fall, yet it is capable by the work and operations of the Spirit, to receive a second and new impression of the same image again.

2. The soul is capable of divine contemplation on God, and on the works of God. "My spirit made diligent search," Psal. lxxvii. 6, saith David. Again he saith, "I am fearfully and wonderfully made, and that my soul knoweth right well," Psal. cxxxix. 14. The soul can find out the glory and greatness, infinite power, and wisdom, of the blessed Creator;

by searching into, and contemplating on the rareness, greatness, and wonderfulness of his works, and operations of his hands; which no other creature on earth is able, or capable to do: and this is only from the excellency of the nature and faculties of the soul.

3. The soul is capable of divine union with God. "He that is joined to the Lord is one spirit," 1 Cor. vi. 17. The soul is not essentially, but mystically one with Christ; our spirit is united to Christ, and by virtue of this union of the soul, the body is brought into the same union also, for the body and soul, jointly considered, is the member of Christ. And from hence Paul takes his argument, to deter the saints from the sin of uncleanness; but were it not from the excellent nature of the soul, man could not have partaken of this high and glorious privilege.

4. The soul is capable of divine inspiration. In this the glory of man excels all other creatures on earth. "There is a spirit in man, and the inspiration of the Almighty giveth him understanding," Job xxxii. 8. No doubt the text refers to the reasonable soul, or those vessels in which natural reason hath its seat and exercise, as a worthy divine notes, "Surely there is a spirit in man," an excellent soul in man that is Caryl on Job, cap. 32, 3. capable, when God pleaseth to breathe upon it, to receive spiritual life and light, and high discoveries or inspirations of the Almighty. Man's soul is like a glorious house that requires suitable furniture. The soul of man I may compare to the moon, it is a light capable to shine gloriously, when the Sun of Righteousness shines upon it.

There is a light of acceptation. Such a light is the spirit of man; and there is a light of information: such a light is Christ, or the Spirit of Christ.

5. The price that bought or redeemed the soul, shows the great worth and A great price paid to redeem the soul. value of it. God the Father gave his own begotten Son to ransom our souls from sin, wrath, and hell. Jesus Christ gave himself, poured forth his own precious blood to redeem the soul. "We were not redeemed with corruptible things, as silver and gold from a vain conversation; but with the precious blood of Christ, as of a Lamb without spot," 1 Pet. i. 18, 19.

6. Moreover, the food the soul liveth upon, which is the flesh and blood of Jesus Christ, shows the nature and worth of it; as also the clothes that God puts upon The soul lives on spiritual food, therefore is precious. it, or that one glorious robe, namely the perfect righteousness of Christ, which is of infinite worth, together with those rich ornaments with which God adorns it, sets out the excellencies of it, which are the graces of the Holy Spirit, they being all in the sight of God, of great price.

7. The communion it is capable of enjoying with God, even with the Father and his Son Jesus Christ, demonstrates its transcendant excellency; "Truly our fellowship is with the Father, and with his Son Jesus Christ," 1 John i. 3; and that unwearied endeavour of Satan to destroy it, and that continual care of God to preserve, keep, and defend it, shows the value of it; moreover, it appears, in that all wise men ever preferred the worth of their souls above all things on earth; these things to show the soul, it is a very precious jewel.

8thly and lastly, its immortality mightly evinceth this great truth; the soul The soul is immortal. is precious, it cannot die, nor be annihilated.

Secondly, The wisdom of a believer, or of a godly man, consisteth in his care to provide a house, or in building a house for his precious soul.

Some will provide a house for this son, and that daughter, and every one takes A wise man builds a house for his soul. care to get a house to put their heads in; but oh! how few are there who have so much wisdom as to provide a house to shelter, secure, and preserve their precious and immortal souls! Now a good man doth not only provide a house for his soul, but also a firm house while it is in the body, and also when it leaves this body. "For we know that if our earthly house of this tabernacle were dissolved; we have a house not made with hands, eternal in the heavens," 2 Cor. v. 1. The soul is the inhabiter, and the body is here called a habitation or a tabernacle, which will soon be dissolved. But such is the care and wisdom of every true Christian, that he sees to provide a better house for his soul at death; that his soul may not then be naked, or without a dwelling-place. "In my Father's house are many mansions," John xiv. 2, saith our Saviour. Many stately dwelling-places, of which "the spirits of just men made perfect," are now possessed. Wicked men are such fools, that they build houses for the body only, none for their souls, and they are such houses that are of short duration, in which they know not they shall dwell one day; but a godly man is so wise as to build an house that will stand for ever. The souls of unbelievers, at death, shall be turned out of their bodies naked, or have no safe dwelling-place to go unto; and since they provide for their souls no house, God in his wrath hath provided a dwelling for all such, a house indeed that they will not like. It will be an uneasy and troublesome habitation. "Who among us shall dwell with devouring fire? Who among us shall dwell with everlasting fire?" Isa. xxxiii. 14.

A wise builder builds on a firm foundation, so doth a wise Christian.   III. A godly man's wisdom consisteth in building his house upon a good and safe foundation.

A foolish person either builds his house on the sand, on a false foundation, or else without a foundation. "He that heareth these sayings of mine and doeth them not, is like a man, that without a foundation, built an house upon the earth," Luke vi. 49.

1. Brethren, some persons build their house or hope of heaven upon God's outward **Some build their hopes of God's favour on external blessings.** favours or external blessings, which he is pleased to bestow upon them; as riches, honours, and earthly prosperity. They conclude from hence, they are in a good condition, and that God loves them; and since he gives them such a large portion of earthly blessings, he will not deny them the blessings of heaven, But, alas, they mistake! Some men will be rich, they value earthly riches above a portion in God, or an interest in Jesus Christ. Therefore God, in wrath and judgment, may give them the desire of their hearts, and, like an offended and displeased father, (who cuts off his disobedient children by his last will and testament with a shilling, or some small matter) so God, I say, may cut off these with a portion only in this life, therefore our Lord pronounces a woe to this sort of people. "Woe unto you that are rich, for ye have received your consolation," Luke vi. 24. Not because they were rich, but because they desired no better riches; they prized earthly riches as their portion, and chiefest good. Was not the rich glutton blessed with abundance of the good things of this world? Yet when he died, he went to hell for all that, Luke xvi. 19. Is it an argument that the great Turk is in the special favour of God, and many other proud tyrants, because they have so great a portion of earthly riches and honours bestowed upon them?

Some build on birth-privilege,   2dly. I told you the last day, that some build their hopes of heaven on external birth-privileges, because they are the children of godly parents, thus the Jews built. "We have Abraham to our Father," Matt. xxxix. 10. When our Saviour endeavoured, by his doctrine, to bring them to believe in him: they answered "We be Abraham's seed, and were never in bondage to any man, how sayest thou ye shall be made free?" John viii. 33. What doth this privilege signify? "The children of the flesh, these are not the children of God," Rom. ix. 8. All are born children of wrath by nature. We read of one of Abraham's seed, according to the flesh, crying out in hell, as he said, "Father Abraham, have mercy on me, and send Lazarus that he may dip the tip of his finger in water, and cool my tongue, for I am tormented in this flame," Luke xvi. 2.

Some build on common justice or morality.   3. Some people build their hopes of heaven on morality, or principles of common justice and civil honesty; doing to all men as they would be done unto, which Christianity teacheth all to do; but if this could save the soul from wrath and hell, Christ is dead in vain, and faith utterly made void. But the truth is, we have such teachers in these days, that strive to subvert the gospel, and establish the old pagan religion, contemning the mysteries of the cross of Christ, and justification by his imputed righteousness.

Some build on learned men.   4. Others build on their learning, and on learned men, like them, who, of old, said, "Have any of the rulers or the Pharisees believed on him? but this people who know not the law are cursed," John vii. 48, 49. Is it a good argument that popery is true Christianity, because Bellarmin was, and many papists and Jesuits are, learned men; evident it is, the "World by wisdom knew not God," 1 Cor. i. 21, that is, by their own wisdom, by all their human arts and sciences; nor "are many wise men after the flesh called," 1 Cor. i. 26.

Some build on their church.   5. Some build on their church, they believe as the church believes; thus the papists, and too many common Protestants at this day; as if the church was the only rule, and not God's word; and as if we were to try the word of God by the doctrine of the church, and not the doctrine of the church by the word of God.

Some build on inherent graces.   6. Others build their house or hope of heaven on their own inherent graces, holiness, and righteousness, with Christ's merits, that is to say, their inherent righteousness is part of the matter of their justification before God; Christ having, by his merits, purchased such a mild law of grace (and by his obedience, removed the rigid and severe law of perfect righteousness) that our faith and sincere obedience is the material cause of our justification: which dangerous error I have lately detected when I was upon Rom. iv. 5.

7. Some build their hope on their duties : they hear sermons, read God's Some build their house on their duties. word, pray often, both in their closets and families, and are very charitable to the poor ; this is good, but it is a bad foundation to build our house or hope of heaven upon. Brethren, our duties ought to be performed from right principles, and to a right end : O ! say some, if that man that is so just, so holy, so charitable, do not go to heaven, Lord, have mercy upon us : though they know not what his faith is, his principles are, or what his aims or ends be. Some of the Jews and Pharisees were very devout persons, as Paul before converted, yet they stumbled at that stumbling-stone, "they being ignorant of God's righteousness ;" Rom. x. 3, by that means perished for ever. I have mentioned all these, to show they are but foolish builders.

But a true believer, he lays a better foundation ; he builds on a rock, his wisdom appears in that : " he builds on that foundation with God hath laid in Sion," Isa. xxvii. 16. " And other foundation can no man lay than that which is laid, which is Jesus Christ," 1 Cor. iii. 11. He builds only upon Christ, wholly upon Christ, or on Christ, and nothing else ; he doth not mix his own works with Christ's merits, nor his own inherent holiuess, and sincere obedience, with the complete and perfect righteousness of Jesus Christ, and in this his wisdom cometh.

IV. The wisdom of a true Christian consisteth in digging deep : (I hinted at this in the explanation) but I shall now speak more fully to it, you know the allusion ; if it be a great and famous building, some magnificent fabric which a man designs to build, he will dig deep to lay a firm and sure foundation, he digs until he comes to a rock, or sound bottom : now it is a great and glorious fabric that a Christian is to build, a building that is to stand for ever, and endure all storms and assaults of Satan, and all other enemies of the soul. Besides, pardon of sin, justification, and eternal life, are great things ; and the soul being so excellent, so precious, the house that is to be built for it, ought to bear some proportion unto it ; also Jesus Christ the prince of kings of the earth, designs to dwell with the soul, so that it may be truly said to be a house for the great king ; therefore, on all these respects, it behoveth us so dig deep, aud to lay a safe and sure foundation.

Quest. What doth this digging deep, denote, or into what may the soul be said to dig?

Answ. 1. I answer, the soul of a believer digs deep into the nature of What digging deep doth denote, God, to find out what righteousness will comport and suit with the righteousness and infinite holiness of God.

1. He digs and searches into the divine nature and perfections of God, or consults his attributes, to see whether God forgives sin, as a pure or mere act of his sovereign mercy, without a satisfaction to his offended justice, or not.

2. Whether it is consistent with the glory of his infinite wisdom, in the salvation of sinners, to raise the honour of one of his glorious attributes, to darken or eclipse the glory of others ; and they find out by searching or digging, that God cannot, will not impeach the attribute of his justice, to magnify the attribute of his mercy. Justice is a property of his nature, or of the divine essence, as well as mercy.

3. He finds out by digging, or by diligent search, that no righteousness can comport with God's infinite holiness, to the justification of a sinner, but that which is perfect, or a sinless righteousness ; and this leads him to build on the righteousness of Jesus Christ alone. That is to say, he finds out that a man must either be in himself, naturally and inherently, and absolutely perfect, without sin, or else have the perfect and sinless righteousness of Christ imputed to him, if ever he be justified at God's bar.

4. He finds that a sinner is made righteous, accounted righteous, declared and pronounced righteous in the righteousness of another, (that is, in the righteousness of Christ) and that this only comports with the wisdom, holiness, and justice of God.

2ndly. He digs deep into the nature and tenour of the holy law of God ; and he finds that in point of justification, the law doth require a perfect righteousness, it being a written impression of God's holy nature ; and denounceth wrath, death, and the curse upon all and every particular soul " that continueth not in all things that are therein written, to do them," Gal. iii. 10.

Hence he finds that the law must be perfectly kept, and a full satisfaction must be made for the breach of it by man, or by his surety ; and this leads him to Christ, and wholly to build upon him. Since no man can either answer the precepts thereof, in point of perfect righteousness, nor make an atonement for the breach thereof; thus " by the deeds or works of the law, no flesh can be justified in the sight of God."

He digs into the decrees and purpose of God. 3dly. He digs deep into the mysteries of God's eternal purpose, design, and council of saving lost man by Jesus Christ; that man might be utterly abased, and God, in a way of free and sovereign grace, might be exalted: "Who hath saved us, and called us with a holy calling, not according to our works; but according to his own purpose and grace, which was given us in Christ Jesus before the world began." "By grace ye are saved, through faith," &c., 2 Tim. i. 9, Eph. ii. 8. And lest man, in any respect, should boast or ascribe any part of salvation to his own power, or to the will of the creature, the apostle adds (though we cannot have actual interest in Christ, and salvation by Christ without faith) that "Faith is not of ourselves," nor the fruit or product of our natural power, but "it is the gift of God." And thus (as it was foretold by the prophet) man is abased; "And the loftiness of man bowed down, and the haughtiness of man made low, and the Lord alone exalted," Isa. ii. 17.

He digs deep into the depravity of human nature. 4thly. The wisdom of a godly man doth consist in his digging into the pravity of human nature, and abominable evil of original sin, and treacherousness of their own vile hearts; there being naturally in us a propensity to all evil, though not an equal propensity in all to every sin, yet it is so in all more or less; the seed of every sin being in every man and woman that comes into the world: "As all men are said to be in the first man virtually, in primo cuncti fuimus patræ; so may all sins, in respect to this propensity in all, be said to be in the first sin, the sin of our birth and nature," (Clarkson's, p. 3.)

Hereby man also became miserable, by being obnoxious to the wrath of God, and utterly unable to deliver himself from sin, and that just and deserved vengeance due to it; being "by nature dead in sins and trespasses." Brethren, this sin he sees is worse, and more sinful than the most grievous actual sin, that ever hath, or can be committed.

The evil of original sin. 1. For no man was an actual sinner before he was born, but by original sin all were sinners in their mothers' womb.

2. Actual sin is the fruit, but this is the root of all sin.

3. Actual sin only breaks the law in being, the very time it is in acting; but this is a continual violation of the law, without any interruption, or least intermission, from that instant of the soul's conjunction with the body to the hour of our dissolution.

4. It is the cause of all actual sin, it is the egg that produceth the cursed cockatrice.

5. It is a contagion that hath spread over the whole man, and hath corrupted the soul in all its faculties, and the body in all its members, making both soul and body a lump of filth, and cursed pollution.

6. It is so habitual and so rooted in all, that nothing but the infinite power of God can conquer it; nothing but Almighty Power can subdue its prevailing strength; common improvements of natural light and abilities, may much overcome, or restrain all gross acts of sin; but nothing but saving grace infused, can overcome these vicious habits.

7. It hath defaced in us the image of God, rendering us averse to all that is spiritually good; in this evil nature the devil reigns and keeps his court, and all is subject to his will and lusts.

8. It renders all men naturally brutish, nay, far worse; their reason being lost or corrupted, they are like bears, swine, lions, dogs, from whence it is that the Scripture compares wicked men to such animals; nay it was by this sin that the whole creation came to be corrupted, and the creatures brought into bondage and misery; yea, the very ground was, for this sin, cursed for man's sake.

9. He digs deep into the fulness, (as well as into the freeness) of God's grace in Christ: O what blessed digging is here! I may allude to that passage in Job; "Surely there is a vein for silver, and a place for gold, where they find it; there is a path which no fowl knoweth, and the vulture's eye hath not seen," Job xxviii. 1. But this wise man discerneth this precious vein of heavenly treasure, whilst he digs into the depths of divine love, and that fulness that is in Christ; he finds, (as there is no light but in this sun, nor any water but in this fountain) so there is an infinite fulness of all grace, and whatsoever any sinner or believer needs in Jesus Christ.

VI. The wisdom of a godly man consisteth in building his house of proper and fit materials; others build with corrupt and deceitful matter; whether carnal worldlings, or hypocritical professors. In which their folly doth consist (as shall, God willing, be showed in its place) but this man builds with gold, silver, and precious stones, for so may the doctrine, ordinances, and truths of the gospel, be called; being all pillars of God's hewing.

VII. His wisdom consisteth in building by rule, i. e., according to the exact rule of God's word, and according to the pattern left for all good and gracious men; he builds by faith, and according to the rule of the new creature; he doth not build upon faith, but by faith only, upon the object of faith, Jesus Christ; as Abraham and all the faithful ever did. *True wisdom consists in building by the rule of God's word.*

VIII. His wisdom doth consist in building in the proper time. He doth not defer building his soul on Christ to another day, which he foresees is uncertain; but he takes the present time, whilst it is called to-day, not knowing what to-morrow may bring forth.

IX. His wisdom consisteth in setting down to account the cost. Which our Lord intimateth, is necessary in all that will build: "For which of you intending to build a tower, sitteth not down first, and counteth the cost, whether he have sufficient to finish. Lest haply after he hath laid the foundation, and is not able to finish it; all that behold it mock him, saying, this man began to build, and was not able to finish," Luke xiv. 28 29.

He therefore counts all the charge and cost he must be at from first to the last. *In a fit and proper time.*

1. What the digging up the old foundation will cost him.

2. What old habits must be changed, and what right-eye sins must be pulled out, and what right-hand sins must be cut off.

3. What old companions must be forsaken, and what enticements must be withstood and resisted.

4. What reproaches for Christ's sake must be borne, and what external losses and persecutions must be endured.

5. He counts his own weakness and inability to do any of these things, and so consults the power, faithfulness, and promises of Christ, on which he solely and wholly depends, and thereby knows and is sure he cannot fail; he doth not begin nor go on in his own strength, but sees his riches and strength is in Jesus Christ, and therefore strengtheneth himself in that grace that is in him, which is sufficient for him, as Paul was told after he had begun to build, when assaulted by the messenger of Satan.

6. He accounts what temptations must be withstood, from Satan, from his carnal relations, and from the corruptions of his own heart.

7. And what reproaches and persecutions must be endured.

APPLICATION

From hence we may infer, that many men are greatly mistaken about true wisdom; some think that chief wisdom consisteth in being wise, to gain the world, in heaping up gold and silver, or to attain to earthly honour and grandeur among men.

But alas! it lies not in these things, but in providing for another world, to get a true title of the crown of glory, to have an everlasting house for the soul when this life is ended.

Others think it is wisdom enough to hear God's word, or the sayings of Christ, and to be esteemed godly men, or to have a name to live: but such do but deceive themselves; for true wisdom, it appears, consisteth in getting true faith in Christ, such faith that works by love, which leads the soul to yield obedience, yea, universal obedience to all the commandments of Jesus Christ.

Quest. A question might here be propounded, viz., What is the nature of true obedience, or whose obedience is accepted?

Answ. I answer, divers things are to be considered, if a full resolution be given to this question.

1. The person must be one that is accepted of God; it is not our obedience that can make our persons accepted of God, but our persons must be first accepted in Christ, for out of him there is no acceptation; God had first a respect to Abel, and then to his offering: no unbeliever, let him do what he will, is regarded by the Lord.

2. In true obedience, the matter of it must be considered, and that is, the sayings of Christ, which are twofold.

1. All moral precepts.

2. All mere positive precepts; the first are agreeing to the light of nature. The second are contained in the New Testament, given forth by Christ as Mediator.

3. True obedience consisteth in right principles, from whence it proceedeth; all true obedience must and doth proceed from a principle of faith and love.

4. We must also consider the pattern of true obedience; that our pattern is our Lord Jesus; he hath left us an example, what, and how to obey.

5. True obedience must be considered as to the manner of it; it must be sincere, hearty, or from the heart.

6. It must be universal, all Christ's sayings.

7. It must be done by the Spirit, or in Christ's strength.

8. True obedience consisteth in a right timing of it, it must be done presently, or as soon as the soul is convinced of its duty, not delayed.

9. True obedience consisteth in a right end, i. e., that God may be glorified, or to glorify God; not out of self-ends.

10. True obedience is constant; we must obey always without intermission or growing weary.

11. In true obedience, the rule must be considered, which is the word and will of God, not the traditions of men, but the commands of God in his word.   Only,

12thly, and lastly. It must be pure obedience, not mixed; everything Christ hath commanded or doth require, and nothing else.

IV

And every one that heareth these sayings of mine, and doeth them not, shall be likened to a foolish man that built his house upon the sand, ver. 26. And the rain descended, and the floods came, and the winds blew, and beat upon that house, and it fell, and great was the fall of it.—Matt. vii. 26, 27.

OUR text doth afford us several other points of doctrine besides what I have mentioned, viz.:

Doct. 1.   That it is not enough to hear what Christ says, or to be hearers of the word only.

Doct. 2.   That it is dangerous to build our hope of heaven on the sand, or without a sure foundation.

Doct. 3.   That as such who hear Christ's sayings and do them not, are foolish builders, so the time will come to try their house or hope, and the fall of all such builders will be great and dreadful.

It is the last of these I intend to speak to at this time, and so conclude with all I shall say.

1. Show you what times they are, that will try the house or hope of these foolish builders.

2. Give you the causes or reasons why the house of these builders will fall.

3. Show you wherein the greatness of their fall doth and will appear, or why it is said the fall is great.

1. Times of temptations that will try the hope of these professors, and all others. Temptations may be,

  1. From God.
  2. From Satan.
  3. From the world.
  4. At death.
  5. At judgment.

1. From God.   Thus God tempted Abraham; that is, he tried him, God
God tries the   tried his faith, tried his love, tried his sincerity; the winds of temptations
building.   came, and his house stood, for he did what God said to him, though it was
hard to offer up his only son Isaac, whom he so dearly loved.   Another whose heart was not right with God, could not have stood such a temptation, such a trial as this was, he would doubtless have argued after this manner, viz.:

1. Lord, wilt thou have me be guilty of murder? nay, murder my own son?

2. Will not this bring shame and reproach upon me, and open the mouths of the wicked?

3. Besides, is he not the child of promise?   Shall thy promise be frustrated? Besides,

4. My wife Sarah will think me a bloody husband, and a most cruel Father, should I do it.

5. Also he is Sarah's child as well as mine, and the son of her old age ; she hath equal right to him, and interest in him ; if she will consent that I should slay him, and make her childless, I may the better do it.

6. But, Lord, it may break her heart, should I do this thing.

Sirs, that man whose heart is not sincere, when God calls for his beloved Isaac, it will discover it at such a time, and his house will shake. Thus God also tried Job ; certainly, had not he built his hope well, that storm that came upon him had blowed it down ; but he stood. God is said to visit man every morning, and to try him every moment, Job vii. 18.

God doth many ways try professors.

What way God tries builders.

1. He brings some men into a state of poverty to try them ; he takes away all their substance, to see whether they can trust in him, and depend upon him at such a time, and live by faith on the care and providence of God. " Thy God led thee these forty years in the wilderness, to humble thee and to prove thee, to know what was in thy heart, whether thou wouldest keep his commandments or no, ver. 2. And he humbled thee, and suffered thee to hunger, &c. And fed thee with manna, which thou knewest not, neither did thy fathers know ; that he might make thee know, that man doth not live by bread alone, but by every word that proceedeth out of the mouth of the Lord, doth man live," ver. 3. Deut. viii. 2, 3.

2. He, to try their graces, or sincerity, ofttimes sets objects of charity before them who are rich, to see whether they will feed or clothe them or not ; God doth not only bring some persons into a state of want and poverty to try them, but also to try others : " The poor ye have always with you :" there shall be objects of charity to the end, that grace in his people may come under trial. " I was hungry, and you fed me, thirsty, and you gave me drink," &c., Matt. xxv. 35. Rich men are but stewards of what they have, and must distribute and give forth of their treasure, or have in their possession, as their Lord directeth them ; and if they do not, it will be found they are unfaithful stewards ; many persons little think what the end and design of the Lord is, in giving them the riches of this world ; they see not it as a trial of their love to him, for what they give to the poor saints, Christ takes it as given unto himself ; " Inasmuch as you have done it unto one of the least of these my brethren, you have done it unto me," Matt. xxv. 40.

3. God sometimes bringeth those who profess the Gospel into the wilderness, or into a bewildered state, to try them, to see whether they can trust in the Lord, and stay themselves upon their God, when they walk in darkness, and have no light, Isa. l. 10. Some in such an hour fall, and utterly despair of God's mercy. Walking in darkness sometimes denotes outward calamities and afflictions, but principally it signifies the want of comfort or inward peace, being under terror of conscience : a false professor may have some seeming peace and comfort, though it commonly doth arise from what he possesseth of riches, outward peace or applause from men, and if these fail, his heart dies within him.

Now God may stop up these springs of false comfort, to show him the rottenness and baseness of his heart, and unsafeness of his condition ; that it is not God that he liveth upon, it is not his love, his favour, that is the joy of his soul, but it is self which he aimeth at in all he doeth. But now if a man be sincere, though God takes away all his outward comforts, and suffers him to fall under the frowns of men, to such a degree that they slight and disesteem him ; and also withholds the comforts of his Spirit, or hideth his face from him, yet he bears it, and says, " I will bear the indignation of the Lord, because I have sinned against him," Mich. vii. 9. He is not offended, but still holds fast his integrity, as Job did ; he endures this trial, and hath hope still in God : " I will wait on the Lord that hideth his face from the house of Jacob, and I will look for him," Isa. viii. 17.

Quest. Wherefore doth God try his saints ?

(1). Answ. God doeth this to show us, that the spring of all true comfort lies in himself, and that we are depending creatures, and that he himself keeps the key of his own treasury, and hands forth unto us as he seeth good.

(2). That we may have a trial and proof of our faith, and of all other graces ; " Ye are in heaviness through manifold temptations ; that the trial of your faith being much more precious than gold which perisheth, being tried in the fire, may be found to glory, praise, and honour," 1 Pet. i. 7.

4. God, to try men, suffers them sometimes to fall into evil company, to see whether they will stand or fall in such an hour ; thus was Peter tried when he was in the high-priest's hall ; " A damsel came unto him, and said, Thou also wast with Jesus of Galilee,

Matt. xxvi. 69. See how he faltered at this time, who had made such a bold and brave confession of Christ before this. Trial he could not bear. " But he denied before the mall, saying, I know not the man : and when he was gone out into the porch, another maid saw him, and said unto them that were there, This fellow was also with Jesus of Nazareth. And again he denied it with an oath, I do not know the man," Matt. xxvi. 70—72. When God leaves his dear children to their own strength, they fall immediately : some persons who have made a profession of the Gospel, and showed much zeal for God, when they have fallen into the company of wicked men, such who are scoffers, they have faltered and fallen abominably, so that this way they have been tried, and overcome ; though all sincere Christians, with Peter, have been recovered again ; God would not cast out all the Canaanites, but left them to try his people Israel.

5. God brings sometimes a flood of tribulation and persecution upon his people to try them ; and then ofttimes the foolish builder falls : " Yet hath he not root in himself, but endureth for awhile ; for when tribulation or persecution ariseth, because of the word, by and by, he is offended," Matt. xiii. 21. This storm beateth down their house. " Who is wise, and he shall understand these things ? prudent, and he shall know them ? for the way of the Lord is right, and the just shall walk in them, but the transgressors shall fall therein, Hos. xiv. 9..

Secondly, Satan is suffered also to try and tempt men.

Satan will tempt and try the house we have built. 1. God lets him raise up a storm of trouble upon his people, as in Job's case, that the devil and wicked men may see the uprightness and sincerity of their hearts ; nay, and that they may have the clearer evidence of it themselves, for we know not our own hearts, nor the strength of our graces so fully, until we come to be tried.

2. Satan is suffered to tempt us to sin, and violate God's holy precepts, as he tempted our first parents ; he presents his golden baits of pleasure or profit, to allure our souls. Tush, saith he, you may do it and have repentance as Peter had ; many good men have done as bad things as this is, or that is ; thus was Achan tempted by the devil and his own evil heart, to covet a wedge of gold, and a goodly Babylonish garment, Josh. vii. 21 ; many false professors and foolish builders, fall by this trial, and with the dog, turn to their own vomit, and with the swine to their wallowing in the mire.

3. Satan also tempts men, whose hearts are not right with God, to presume, and though in their sin, and under the power of unbelief, yet to rely on the mercy of God, and merits of Christ.

4. Others he tempts to despair, and utterly to doubt of the pardoning grace of God, through the blood of Jesus Christ ; he tells them that their sins are so great, God will not forgive them, or else, that their day of grace is past.

5. Others he tempts to delay the work of their salvation. Says he, It is time enough yet, God will accept of you if you come to him at the eleventh hour ; you may be a young saint and an old devil, if you begin so soon you will not hold out to the end.

6. He tempts others to trust to their own doings, their own works of righteousness ; by this means some thousands fall into hell, and are never convinced of the need of the righteousness of Christ, but remain ignorant of the way to the Father.

7. Others he tempts to neglect the means of grace ; not to hear the word, or to hear it carelessly, also wholly to neglect prayer and reading, or to rest upon these duties.

Thirdly, The world also doth and will try all sorts of professors. I am persuaded

The world will try us and our building also. great numbers are, by this means, shaken, and their house thrown down ; it may said of the world, as it is of the harlot, or adulterous woman ; " She hath cast down many wounded, yea, many strong men have been slain by her," Prov. vii. 26. Some, by the riches of the world, fall short of heaven. The young man's hope and house which he had built of legal materials, fell with one blast from this quarter; " he went away very sorrowful, for he had great possessions." The love of this world also overthrew Demas, he could not stand that storm of temptation that he met

See the parable of the sower. Matt. xiii. withal. And, as riches, honours, and the sinful pleasures of the world overthrow many on the one hand, so do the cares of the world on the other hand ; poverty may prove as fatal as riches ; it is the cares of this life as well as riches that choke the word ; how good then is it to cry with Agur, " Give me neither poverty nor riches," &c.

Fourthly, But if these trials, and at such times cannot prevail, or do not prevail to beat down the hope and house of foolish builders, yet there is another hour and enemy that will do it, and that is death. If the hypocrites' house doth not fall in the day of temptation, nor persecution, yet down it goes at the hour of death; if his hope should abide whilst he lives, yet it will fail when he comes to die; "For what is the hope of the hypocrite, though he hath gained, when God taketh away his soul?" John xxvii. 8. Though he hath gained many gifts, much riches, a name and great applause among men, yet death puts an end, and quite cuts off all his hope; when he dies all his hopes die. "And the hypocrite's hope shall perish, whose hope shall be cut off, and whose trust shall be as the spiders' web," ver. 14. "He shall lean upon his house, but it shall not stand; he shall hold it fast, but it shall not endure," Job viii. 14, 15. He builds his house of rotten and false materials, his house or hope is built with worldly or earthly materials, or else with counterfeit or false spiritual materials, as moral or inherent righteousness, or on spiritual or acquired gifts, or on vain glory, and a name among men.

Death will be as a storm against the house or hope we build.

Fifthly and lastly, At the day of judgment his hope and house shall fall for ever; all his cries, his pleading then will do him no good, nor avail him any thing: "Lord, have we not prophesied in thy name? And in thy name done many wonderful works?" Down goes his house, his hope, with body and soul, to hell, and he shall perish for ever. So much as to the first thing proposed.

The judgment day the great time of trial.

Secondly, I shall show you the cause and reasons of the fall of his house.

1. It is because he never attained to a work of true saving grace; he never truly believed in Jesus Christ, and so built not his house on a rock; let a man build his house never so high and strong in his own conceit, that never dug so deep as to know what his state was by nature, his house will fall.

The cause of the fall of the foolish builder's house.

2. Because he was blinded by the god of this world, the devil, and his own deceitful heart were too hard for him; he builds his house with such materials that could not bear the shock and storm that comes upon him.

3. Because his heart was never changed, he hath no meetness for heaven; he is unholy, unsanctified, and no unholy thing can enter into the kingdom of heaven, therefore down he falls into hell.

4. The enemy can throw down that house, spoil that hope that is not fixed on Christ, and the sinner has no power to help himself, he cannot keep his house up; such strong enemies come against him, who are clothed with such power, to throw him down, which he cannot withstand: besides, he is alone and hath none to help him, neither friend nor brother; God will not, Christ will not, nor can he stand before the accusing and sin-condemning law, that lets fly its bitter curses against him; much less can he stand against the dreadful and incensed wrath of an offended God. If divine mercy and infinite goodness plead against him for contemning of Jesus Christ, whither will he fly for refuge? Who can stand before God's indignation? it is from hence, and for these causes, his house, his hope, and his soul must fall.

Thirdly, I shall show you wherein the greatness of the fall of these persons doth appear; "and great was the fall of it."

The greatness of the fall of the house built by a foolish builder.

1. It is because it is the fall of their souls as well as their house they had built; the more excellent a thing is, the more great is the loss of it. As life is precious; now if a house falls and kills those who live it, that fall is accounted a sad and dismal fall; or if a king falls in a battle, that is esteemed a great fall, because he is worth many thousand common soldiers. Now the soul is of great worth; what is the whole world to the precious soul which God hath given to us? What is the worth of our natural lives, when compared to our immortal souls? If your souls perish when your hope perishes, the fall of your house be great; other houses may fall, yet the lives of the people who dwelt therein may be saved, but it is not so here.

2. The fall of such will be great, because great was their expectation; they were elevated in their thoughts, doubted not perhaps of a blessed eternity; concluded, with the Jews, their state was good, because they were Abraham's seed; it is therefore an unexpected fall, and so a great fall, like that of Haman's, who thought of nothing less than of the highest exaltation, but sad news came that he must be hanged on the gallows which he had made for Mordecai, Est. vii. 8, 9. It is as when a man thinks he hath found a precious stone of a great value, and is wonderfully elevated thereby, and concludes he is made for ever by it, but when it is tried, it proves but a mere counterfeit. O how is he disappointed, and ashamed of his vain boast! or as when a man thinks he is an heir to a crown, and mighty kingdom, and seems not to doubt of his title; but when his right and title comes to be examined, it is no such matter, he did but deceive himself, and as a false traitor, hath his head cut off; how great is his fall! So it is here, some

men think they have grace, think they are heirs of glory, but when they come to die, they find themselves mistaken ; hence their fall will be great.

3. Because they had built their house so high in their own conceit, that the top of it reached almost up to heaven, this makes the fall of their house the greater : perhaps some of them were not far from the kingdom of heaven, as our Saviour told the young man, " Thou art not far from the kingdom of God," Mark xii. 35. When a merchant with a very rich ship is come almost home, and quite in sight of his port, is suddenly cast away; oh how great is his loss ! Some are exalted to heaven in respect of the means of grace, light, and knowledge, and yet fall at last ; their fall is therefore great : " And thou, Capernaum, that art exalted unto heaven, shalt be brought down to hell," Mat. xi. 23.

They fall very low, anon into hell   4. Because the fall of their house, and hope of heaven, is a falling down to hell ; when they thought of being saved, they, alas ! are damned ; instead of being blessed for ever, they are cursed for ever ; instead of dwelling in heaven, they see they must dwell in everlasting fire. This shows the fall of their house will be great.

Their house can never be built again, it will be an eternal fall.   5. Because their house can never be built again. When London fell by fire, 1666, it would have been a far greater fall, if it could have been built no more for ever ; but lo, a new city, and far more glorious, is raised out of its ashes, and ruins : but there is no building a house again for the fallen soul, that is in hell ; no Christ for them, no faith, no hope there ; there is no redemption out of hell, they are lost, yea, lost to eternity. This will be the fate and fall of Babylon, and therefore her fall will be great. " And Babylon, &c.—shall be as when God overthrew Sodom and Gomorrah," Isa. xiii. 19. And thus it will be with those foolish builders, who lose their souls and bodies, it will be a final loss, yea, an eternal loss there is no hope for the damned, therefore their fall is and will be great.

APPLICATION

1. Tremble all ye foolish builders, who hear Christ's sayings, but do them not, that hear his word, but do not believe ; who are reformed perhaps in your lives, but not changed in your hearts.

2. Be exhorted to try yourselves, examine your hearts, see with what materials you have built your house, I mean your hope for heaven ; if it be not upon Jesus Christ, if it be on the sands of your own works, or inherent righteousness, or on your duties, or upon your external privileges, or on gifts, parts, or knowledge, or traditions ; pull down your house and new build it, build it on the only and sure foundation. " Other foundation can no man lay than that which is already laid, which is Jesus Christ," 1 Cor. iii. 11.

3. Let all professors prepare for a storm ; the winds will blow, the rain will fall, and the floods will come ; you shall all be tried ; God will try every man's work. If temptations of Satan, if tribulation and persecution from men, do not beat down your house and hope, yet death will.

4. We infer from hence, that the state of false professors, or all such who are no more than bare hearers of the word, is very sad and deplorable, their hope will be as the spider's web.

5. Sinners, doubtless you have got some house, or hope, or another ; but any hope will not serve your turn. O how near may you be to a storm, death may be at the door, and then your hope will perish, and your souls be lost.

6. What comfort is here for believers, they are safe !

8. THE BLIND LEADING THE BLIND

And he spake a parable unto them, Can the blind lead the blind ; shall they not both fall into the ditch ?—Luke vi. 39.

Our late annotators on this place say by a parable, " Here is to be understood, a proverbial saying, which hath some darkness in it, as being brought to express or signify more than the words naturally do express ; proverbial speeches are applicable to more cases than one," &c. I find that tropical writers, as Azorius, Gillius, Morton, &c., say, That a parable is a continued metaphor, or an allegory of words, λἰξεως, which is a continuation of tropes, especially metaphors. Though learned Glassius seems to differ from them. A parable, according to Jerome, is a comparison made of things different in nature: others say, A parable is a comparison or a similitude: hence Marloret, in his exposition of St. Matthew, Every where when we read Christ spake a parable, he saith a similitude, a *parœmia*, a proverb, or an adagy, with respect to its obscurity, and is called *Ænigma*, or a riddle, as Delaun notes. However, this saying is called a parable (i. e.,) a dark saying. Our Saviour, referring to something else than what the literal sense denotes, viz., from one that is blind or without bodily sight, leading such that Sacra, p. 204, are blind, he shows the danger of men who are led by blind preachers, or teachers, viz., such that understand not the mysteries of God, Christ, and the gospel, or who are spiritually blind, and without the light of saving knowledge, and the true teachings of the Spirit of God. And evident it is, that our blessed Saviour applied these words more directly to the Scribes and Pharisees, the Jewish leaders, and Rabbins, or those guides amongst them, who, notwithstanding all their great human literature, natural reason, and philosophical learning, were ignorant of Christ, and of the only way of salvation by him; therefore, as Justin Martyr excellently shows, *Infelix est sapientia extra verbum Dei sapere*, &c. That it is not the formality of academical degrees, nor philosophical dexterity, which is to be exercised in the things that may be known by the light of reason, or variety of languages, that qualifies a preacher. And true it is, for a man may understand all languages, and all human arts, and sciences, and yet be but a blind leader, or one that is ignorant of Christ; hence Paul saith, "That the world by wisdom knew not God;" and from most of these was the gospel, and the "Mysteries of the kingdom of heaven," hid, as our Lord shows, Matt. xi. 25. The occasion of these words (as it seems to me) may rise from what our Lord said of the Pharisees and Jewish doctors, in respect to their false interpretations of the law, as St. Matthew shows more clearly, Matt. v. Our Lord called them blind guides: "Ye blind guides, which strain at a gnat," &c. So that his design herein is to forewarn all people to take heed they are not led by blind guides, or by teachers who are not inspired, or illuminated with the Spirit of God, or endowed with saving knowledge, being not ministers of Christ's making, having not received true grace, nor those ministerial gifts, which Jesus Christ gave when he ascended on high.

The words contain a twofold interrogation. 1. "Can the blind lead the blind?" 2. "Shall they not both fall into the ditch?" Eph. iv. 8, 11, 12, 13. That is, can they safely, securely lead them? This interrogation hath in it a strong negation, (i. e.) they cannot safely, wisely, or securely lead the blind who are blind themselves; "shall they not both fall into the ditch?" This question contains the highest affirmation; yea, "they shall both fall," &c., that is, both perish; signifying, that such people, that are led by blind, ignorant, or false teachers, shall fall into hell at last. The words being thus briefly opened, I shall observe one or two propositions from hence.

Doct. 1. That some men, who pretend to be leaders or teachers of the people, are spiritually blind, as they also are that are taught by them. The doctrine raised.

Doct. 2. That such teachers or ministers, who are spiritually blind, and all those blind people, who are taught by them, are in danger of perishing eternally together.

I shall speak briefly to both these points of doctrine. As to the first I shall,

1. Show in what respect men may be said to be blind in a spiritual sense.
2. Run the parallel.
3. Shall show who they are that are blind leaders of the blind.
4. Apply it.

There is a threefold spiritual blindness. 1. Such that are in their natural All men naturally are blind, spiritually blind. state, being never savingly enlightened; and in this sense all are blind, ignorant, or without the true knowledge of God naturally, or as they came into the world; by nature as all are dead, dead in sin and trespasses, so they are all spiritually blind. "And knewest not that thou art miserable, poor, and blind."—"And the eyes of the blind shall see." Hence our Saviour was sent "to open blind eyes," Rev. iii. 17, Isa. xxix. 18, Isa. xlii. 7. The eyes of their understanding is darkened, and when they receive the Holy Spirit, their eyes are opened, and never till then, Eph. i. 18.

2. Some men are not only naturally in a spiritual sense blind, but judicially blind. God in judgment smites them with spiritual blindness, so that they shall never see, never understand: "In seeing they shall not see, neither perceive: for judgment I am come into this world, that they that see not might not see, and that they that see might be made blind," John ix. 39, (i. e.) some who are spiritually blind with the rest of mankind, I am come to give sight unto, or to open their eyes; but others who think they see, and are able to lead

such that are blind. I am come to make them blind, or this will be the effect, or event of my ministry and doctrine, viz. through their perverseness, and unbelief, and contempt of me, I will give them up to utter blindness of mind, and hardness of heart; " But now ye say we see, therefore your sin remaineth," ver. 41. Some are sensible of their blindness, they are blind in their own sight, none are worse blind, or darker in their own apprehension, than such whose eyes Christ hath opened, or than believers; by reason that some darkness remains in them, they cry out of their woful ignorance, and blindness, declaring they see but in part, and know but in part; nay, know nothing as they ought to know.

Secondly, I shall run a parallel betwixt such who are blind in a literal sense, and they who are spiritually blind.

Sinners are born blind.
1. Some are born blind, never saw; so all men (as I hinted) were born blind, (i. e.) they come into the world under the power of of sin, and spiritual blindness, for as they are under a privation of spiritual life, so it follows that they are also blind.

Sin hath put out the eyes of sinners.
II. Some men are blind casually, by some accident, or through age. Adam before the fall could see; man's eye-sight was good originally, he was created in knowledge, he bore the Image of God; but sin put out his eyes, he lost (and all mankind in him) the true knowledge of God, when he lost God's Image, and so came short of the glory of God.

They know not whither they go.
III. Blind men know not whither they go, nor where they are, nor the danger they are in; may be upon the brink of a deep pit, or just entering into a lion's den, or on the edge of a dangerous river, or fearful lake, &c. So those that are spiritually blind, they know not the way they take or go in, neither in respect of their worship and principles of religion; nor the way of their lives and evil practices. They may think they are in the way of God, and that their false notions are the truths of Christ, when indeed they are abominable errors. They being given up to the delusions of the devil, and have their understanding darkened; moreover, they may be just upon the brink of ruin, and ready to fall into hell, and yet may not know anything of their eternal danger, nor know they are in Satan's snares or den, and paw of that lion.

Ungodly sinners never saw the sun.
IV. Let the sun shine never so bright, yet a blind man sees it not; it is all one to him as if it was midnight. So though the Gospel be preached never so clearly and powerfully, yet wicked men, or such as are left to spiritual blindness, see not. They know not truth from error, light from darkness, until the eyes of their understandings are enlightened; and this is the grand evil and misery of all mere natural men.

Sinners know not what spiritual light is.
V. A man born blind never knew, nor can he know what light is, but only by imagination, or, as he is told, he knows it not by experience. So those that are spiritually blind never knew what the light of God's countenance is, the saving light of Christ, or illuminations of the Holy Spirit are; nor can they know this, until the eyes of their minds and understanding are opened. True, they may be told how raising, how pleasant, and sweet, divine light is, or the knowledge of Christ is, the enjoyment of the love and favour of God is; but they know not any of these things by experience, and therefore all they can know or speak of them, is but what they have read, or heard others declare, or make known of them.

Blind men cannot discern, nor see Christ's beauty.
VI. They that are blind, can discern neither the beauty that is in one object that stands before them, nor the deformity of another. So such who are without the saving light or knowledge of God in Jesus Christ, see no beauty, no glory, either in God himself or in Jesus Christ; though he be the most amiable and most glorious object in heaven and earth. For as no blind man can be affected, or smitten with earthly beauty, so can no blind sinner be affected with the loveliness, glory, and beauty of the person of Christ, or with the preciousness of divine things. It is by reason the eyes of our souls are enlightened to behold the Sun of Righteousness, that we cry out with the spouse, " He is the chiefest among ten thousand,—and is altogether lovely," Cant. v. 10, 16. " For the light is sweet, and it is a pleasant thing for the eyes to behold the sun," Eccl. xi. 7. So is spiritual light to believers, whose eyes behold the Sun of Righteousness.

Blind sinners cannot discern things that differ.
VII. They who are in darkness, or utterly blind, cannot discern things that differ, nor judge of colours. So men spiritually blind cannot discern nor know the things of God, " For what man knoweth the things of a man, save the spirit of a man which is in him? even so the things of God knoweth no man but the Spirit of God;" that is, no man but he whose eyes are enlightened by the

Spirit of God. "For, (saith the apostle,) we have not received the spirit of the world, but the Spirit which is of God, that we might know the things that are freely given us of God— But the natural man receiveth not the things of the Spirit of God, for they are foolishness unto him; neither can he know them, because they are spiritually discerned," 1 Cor. ii. 11, 12, 14. By a natural man is meant such a one that is in the state of nature, and hath not received the Spirit of God, and the divine illuminations thereof, and so is spiritually blind.

VIII. It is the greatest folly in the world for a man that is blind, to choose a blind person to lead him, he being thereby exposed equally to dismal dangers with his guide. So what greater folly can any be guilty of, than for such who are spiritually blind, or wholly ignorant of Christ, and of the only **The folly of choosing a blind guide.** way to eternal life, to choose such to guide or lead them, who are as blind and as ignorant as themselves, in respect of Christ, and of salvation by him. But, O what a multitude of such foolish and ignorant persons are there in the world. And this brings me to the next thing proposed to be opened.

Thirdly, Who are blind teachers, or blind guides, or how may they be known? **Who are blind leaders of the blind.**

Now blind guides may be either considered absolutely, or comparatively. (1.) Such preachers are blind guides, who are utterly in darkness, or without any saving grace and knowledge of Christ. Or (2ndly,) Such who, though they may be savingly enlightened, and have the true knowledge of Jesus Christ, yet in respect to some others, who have received much greater knowledge, abilities, and experience, they may be said to be blind, or ignorant teachers; for all that have grace, and true spiritual knowledge, so as to be renewed, and become truly gracious persons, are not fit to be preachers or teachers of others; yet it is better to be led by a man who hath a dim sight, than by one that is utterly blind. But to proceed, and speak first of such spiritual guides who are totally, or utterly blind and ignorant, as to saving knowledge.

I. He that is not a converted man, a renewed man, having not received the Holy Spirit to enlighten his dark mind and understanding, if he take upon him to be a teacher or a guide to the blind, he himself is to be sure a blind leader of the blind. Yet some of this sort may have knowing heads, though they are blind in their hearts, or without the saving knowledge of God and Jesus Christ themselves; and know not by experience what it is to be born again, neither ever tasted nor know how good God is, and how precious Jesus Christ is. Yet there may not be such danger to be led by some of this sort, as there is in being led by others, whose hearts and heads too are dark, or without the knowledge of the Gospel; (yet having received spiritual gifts and clear heads, or much light and knowledge as to the doctrine of the Gospel,) are not blind guides in that sense, and should therefore be acquitted of this name of blind leading of the blind. They are blind as to their state, but as teachers they are not blind; but were this sort known, they ought not to be admitted to be ministers of the Gospel. Unto the wicked, God saith "What hast thou to do to declare my statutes, or that thou shouldst take my covenant into thy mouth?" Psal. l. 16. 'None are true ministers of Christ but such only, which he approves of, or who are gracious men, that truly love him, and can tell what God hath done for their souls, who by their own experience are able to open the nature of true faith, and regeneration. The ministration of the Gospel ought to be committed to faithful men.' "And the things that thou hast heard of me among many witnesses, the same commit thou to faithful men, who shall be able to teach others also," 2 Tim. ii. 2.

(II.) Such are blind leaders that know not who the true Christ of God is, that know not the true Messiah, and yet take upon them to be preachers and teachers of the people. The Scribes and Pharisees knew not that Jesus Christ was the true Saviour, the true Messiah, and yet pretended they were instructors of the foolish guides to the blind, and a light to them that were in darkness, Rom. ii. 18—20. So all such now who pretend they are guides and instructors of the people who deny the Lord Christ, or Jesus of Nazareth, to be God, of the **All those teachers that know not who, or what the Person of Christ is, are blind guides.** essence of the Father, and truly man of the substance of the blessed Virgin, they know not who, or whom the true Messiah is, and therefore are blind guides, false teachers, and deceivers. For what can betray greater ignorance than this? What, preach a false Christ? Err about the object of worship? If Jesus of Nazareth was not the most high God, but a mere man, he was, as they said, a blasphemer, and so a deceiver; for he bore witness that he and the Father were one, that is, one in essence, and was the only-begotten Son of God; Christ is the Son of God by an eternal generation. Moreover, was he not so the Son of God, he could not be our Saviour, because we have no Saviour but God only, none that can save us from sin and eternal wrath. "I am God, and there is none else, besides me there is no Saviour," Isa. xliii. 11.   And then also, it is idolatry to give the same divine worship to him that belongs to God only; but this worship is given, and ought to be given to Jesus Christ, as Mediator. "All the angels are required to worship him," Heb. i. 6.

Therefore the Arians, Socinians, and the Caffionites, are blind guides. More-over, such teachers that deny the true Saviour is truly man of our nature, without us, now in heaven, and in respect of his human nature can be but in one place at one time, are blind guides. For Christ died as con-cerning the flesh, but had he not been man as well as God, he could not have died; that Christ therefore that never died, nor could die, is a false Christ; or who is not "Bone of our bone, and flesh of our flesh." And from hence it appears, the Quakers, who pretend to be teachers, are false teachers, or blind leaders of the blind; for none but he that was the seed of the woman, is or can be the true Saviour. "He was made of a woman, and was of the seed of David according to the flesh.—He took on him the seed of Abraham," Gen. iii. 15, Acts ii. 30, Gal. iv. 4, Heb. ii. 16. But the Quakers say, Christ was never seen of fleshly eyes, and reproach them that say he is a man, consisting of the same nature with us (though glorified) now in heaven. One told me, he knew not where that body is, that rose from the dead.

The Arians, Socinians, Caffionites, and Quakers blind leaders of the blind.

(III.) All legal teachers are blind leaders. I mean such that preach justification by the works of the law, or by the righteousness of man in conformity to the law. This doctrine the Scribes and Jewish doctors taught, whom our Saviour called blind leaders of the blind, they preached justification by doing, or by a man's own righteousness, and not by Christ, or by his righteousness alone. "They being ignorant of God's righteousness, and going about to establish their own righteousness, have not submittted themselves to the righteous-ness of God," Rom. x. 3. "They sought it not by faith, but as it were by the works of the law," Rom. ix. 32. These men pervert the Gospel of Christ; nay, preach another Gospel than that which Christ and his apostles preached: and hence Paul told the Galatians, "They were removed to another Gospel, by these blind and false teachers, whose doctrine they had too far adhered unto, Gal. i. 6. "For if righteousness came by the law, then Christ is dead in vain," Gal. ii. 21. and this is to frustrate the grace of God; therefore whoever they are that bring in men's own inherent righteousness to justify them before God, are blind leaders of the blind.

Legal preachers, false guides.

(IV.) Such who preach up morality, or a sober moral life to be sufficient to justify and save the souls of men; or do not strive to take people off from any thing that they can do, or from depending upon any good works of their own, or to trust in any thing, save upon Jesus Christ alone, are blind leaders of the blind, and will all fall into the ditch at last, unless God in mercy opens their eyes; for this sort are as blind as the Jews and Jewish Rabbins were: for had there been a law (any law) that could have given life, verily righteousness had been by the law, Gal. iii. 21. While Paul was a Pharisee, no doubt but he was a good moral man, and had as much legal righteousness as any have now in our days. For he says, he had walked in all good conversation, even until that day, Acts xxiii. 1; and as touch-ing the righteousness which is of the law, he was blameless, Phil. iii. 7, 8; but all this he counted but dung, when his eyes were truly opened, and he believed in Jesus Christ. " Except your righteousness exceed the righteousness of the Scribes and Pharisees, you cannot enter into the kingdom of heaven," Matt. v. 20.

Such that preach mor-tality, justifi-tion to save men are blind guides.

(V.) Such teachers that preach for doctrine the commandments of men, or traditions, and inventions of men, or that call devised worship, divine wor-ship, or precepts of men to be the institutions of Christ, and would impose such rites and superstitions upon the consciences of men, are blind leaders of the blind. These things our blessed Saviour charged the Scribes and Pharisees with, whom he called blind leaders of the blind, " teaching for doctrine the commandments of men," Matt. xv. 9; and such who have made void the commandments of God through their traditions.

Such that preach mens tradition are blind leaders of the blidd.

(VI.) All that preach not justification, and salvation by Jesus Christ alone, or that preach not that holy doctrine delivered by Christ and his apostles, and which was con-firmed by miracles, are blind guides.

(VII.) Such that deny the written word to be the Word of God, and the only rule of faith and practice.

APPLICATION

1. Infer. Sin is a mischievous evil. O what hath man done in sinning against God! he is become blind thereby, sin hath put the eyes of his understanding. See the parable of the rich man and Lazarus.

2. O what a deplorable state are all men in naturally! O how grievous a thing is it, to be blind, born blind, and never to see the sun.

3. I infer, that sinners are punished with the worst of blindness. (1.) Because it is the blindness of the soul; what is natural blindness to spiritual blindness? Many who have lost their natural sight, are happy, have blessed divine light in their souls, being savingly enlightened. (2.) Others know they are blind, such I mean that have lost their natural sight; but sinners know not, will not believe they are blind. (3.) And such who are deprived of their bodily sight, are glad to accept of one to lead them : but some blind sinners desire not any guide, and others choose blind guides to lead them. (4.) Others that are blind, bewail their blindness, mourn for being dark, and having no sight; but sinners never bewail their want of sight, or mourn in being spiritually blind. (5.) Poor blind men and women would account it no small mercy to have their sight restored to them, but sinners love darkness rather than light. (6.) Such who are naturally blind, are willing and ready to take warning when in danger of falling into a ditch, or into the fire, or into a river. But blind sinners contemn all warning given to them of, or falling into the deep ditch of God's eternal wrath, or into the lake of eternal fire and brimstone. Oh there is no blindness like spiritual blindness.

4. I infer, No man can by any power of his own arrive to true spiritual sight; no, it must be God that opens the eyes of such that were born blind, it requires almighty power. Conversion work is a miraculous work, it raises the dead, and opens the eyes of the blind.

5. Learn from hence to pity the blind, such blind that pity not themselves.

6. Be exhorted to praise God for the Gospel, which is sent to open blind eyes. But if sinners come to see, they must have their eyes also opened. The blind see not the sun though it shines in its strength. O pray for the Spirit to open your eyes, to see the Sun of righteousness.

7. You that see, have a twofold cause to praise God, 1. For the light of information : 2. For the light of acceptation.

8. Terror, why wretched sinners, what do you mean to choose, to be led by blind guides? Whither will you, and they that lead you, fall at last? Take heed who you are led by.

9. You that see, praise and admire infinite grace, and walk as children of the light.

10. Bewail them most of all, that are smitten with spiritual blindness. For as God smote the Sodomites with natural blindness, so hath he smote many with spiritual blindness, in a way of judgment. Some are left to hardness of heart, and blindness of mind, and others in wrath left to believe a lie, or given up to " strong delusions, that they might be damned, because they received not the truth in the love of it, that they might be saved," 2 Thess. ii.

11. Trial. By this all may know, whether they see or not. O what a vast difference is there between being utterly blind, and having clear eye-sight. " One thing I know (said the man that Christ opened his eyes) that whereas I was blind, I now see," John ix. 25. Can you say so? Be sure if you see, you can remember how woful blind and ignorant you once were, and also do know, when and by what means you came to see ; and do also not a little admire infinite grace, that God should open your blind eyes, or give you the saving knowledge of himself, in the face of Jesus Christ, and O how sweet is the light of saving knowledge to your souls! Also what wonderful things do you see in God's law, and in Christ, and in the blessed Gospel, what dangers do you see, and know how to avoid them ; and what do you experience of a change, that is wrought in you, to what your state was once! And how do you prize the light, and hate darkness, the darkness of sin, and all errors.

12. Bewail them that are blind ; are not some of your children and friends blind, stone blind, and know it not? O mourn over them, and cry to God, to open their eyes. Also bewail a blind and dark world, and that is led and resolved to be led by blind leaders. Cry that God would enlighten the earth, and send more leaders, who have clear sight and knowledge of God, Jesus Christ, and of the salvation he hath wrought out.

9. BUILDING A TOWER

*For which of you intending to build a tower, sitteth not down first, and counteth the cost,
whether he have sufficient to finish it,*
*Lest haply after he hath laid the foundation, and is not able to finish it, all begin to mock him,
saying, this man began to build, and was not able to finish.*—Luke xiv. 28, 29, 30.

This parable was spoken by our blessed Saviour, to the multitude, as it is expressed in
ver. 25. And there went great multitudes with him, and he turned and said unto them,
" If any man come unto me, and hate not his father, and mother, and wife, and children,
and brethren, and sister, and his own life also, he cannot be my disciple," ver. 26. " And
whosoever doth not bear his cross, and come after me, cannot be my disciple," ver. 27.
And then it follows. " For which of you intending to build," &c. So that the main design
and scope of this and the parable immediately following, of going to war, are to put all
persons upon considering, and weighing well, (before they take upon them the profession
of religion, or give themselves up to be members of his Church) what it will cost them,
what pains, and what loss, or what they must do, and expect to meet withal for his sake.

In this parable the work of a Christian is compared to a building, in the other to a
warfare ; and to both these things frequently in the Scripture, the work and business of a
Christian professor and a holy life are compared, both by our Lord himself, and his apostles : in Matt. vii. 24, a true believer is likened to a wise builder : and a hypocrite to
a foolish builder, that built his house on the sand ; which I have opened.

" Which of you intending to build a tower ;" he that builds, puts what was in his thoughts,
A builder
puts his pur-
pose into ex-
ecution. intention, and purpose, into execution : he first designs, or resolves within
himself, that he will build, &c. So every person, before he takes upon him the
profession of the Gospel, or becomes a disciple of Christ, first thinks upon it,
ponders, and weighs well the matter in his mind, and then fully resolves that he will do
it. And he that is wise, will also consider well, what cost, and what pains, or labour he
must be at, in building of such a tower, or house. (1.) He considers, what cost, and
pains, the digging up the old foundation may be to him, and the removing all the rubbish,
It will cost
much pains
to dig deep
to lay the
foundation, for removing the rubbish of the old Temple, cost the Jews much pains and
cost ; so every sinner should consider, what the digging up the old foundation
of nature, and the covenant of works, will cost him, and also the rooting
out of all evil habits of sin.

It will cost
great pains
to remove
an old foun-
dation. 2. What pains it will cost him to dig deep, to lay the foundation of a high
tower. For that must be done, or his building may soon fall. So every spiritual builder should consider, what it will cost him, to lay the foundation
stone, Jesus Christ, at the bottom of all his building, which he cannot do, but
he must dig deep into the eternal counsel and purpose of God, and also into the covenant,
and blessed compact between the Father and the Son from all eternity, and this will cost
him much wisdom and pains also.

To build a tower. Certainly, our Lord, on purpose, mentioned a tower, rather than any
other building, and perhaps to signify, that the top of our spiritual building must reach up
to heaven, or otherwise it will be vain to build : for though the builders of Babel were
fools, to think that they could build a tower to save them from the deluge of God's wrath,
or that way to get up to heaven ; yet he that builds in a right manner upon Christ, shall
find, and that when he hath finished his building, or received the end of his faith, he shall
reach heaven, so that an entrance into it shall be ministered abundantly unto him, (i. e.)
he shall receive the salvation of his soul.

" Sitteth not down first, and counteth the cost :" If he be wise, he will not rashly undertake so great a work ; so every sinner ought deliberately, not hastily, rashly, or inconsider-
ately, to enter into a visible profession of religion, or become a disciple of Jesus Christ ; but
count the whole cost, viz., that he must part with all his sins, though never so sweet, pleasant, or profitable to him in times past ; and that he must not only deny, or part with sinful self, but with religious self also, or with all his own righteousness, in point of trust, or
dependance, yea, and with natural self likewise, wife, children, brethren, sisters, and his
own life also ; he must part with all, when Christ calls for it ; nay, he must hate all these
presently ; that is, he must have a lesser love to any of these relations, and to his own life,

than to the Lord Jesus Christ : a lesser love is in the scripture called, a hatred. Leah is said to be hated by Jacob, because he loved Rachel better than she : "And when the Lord saw, that Leah was hated, he opened her womb," &c., Gen. xxix. 31. Moreover, he must consider, that his name wi'l be reproached, vilified, and despised by the men of the world, if he begins once to cleave to Jesus Christ, and become a member of his visible church, and a professor of the gospel ; and be accounted every day as a sheep for the slaughter--"They shall put you out of the synagogue : yea, the time cometh, that whosoever killeth you will think he doeth God service," John xvi. 2. Now these things our Lord made known, and spake this parable on purpose also, that all persons, who seem inclined to follow him, should consider well of, even ponder in their minds, what it will cost them ; he would have us know the worst that can befal us in following of him, that when troubles rise, none might be offended, nor have cause to say, I was not told of these things before I began to build.

"Whether they have to finish it." We readsufficient, but that is a supplement, whether they have enough, or that which is sufficient to finish the whole work, or to hold out in your Christian course to the end. Now I conceive our blessed Saviour intended by these words to discover the insufficiency, or that great weakness, and inability that is in every person, considered as in himself, to go on to perfect the great building, or salvation of his own soul, that so he might put every one upon considering in whom his sufficiency alone lies, or who it is that is his strength, before he begins to profess the Lord Jesus. Brethren, he that thinks (when he begins to build) he hath in himself sufficient wisdom, strength, grace, and courage to finish, hath neither sat down to count what he hath, nor what it will cost him to begin and finish the building of this tower. But he that counts Christ's righteousness his righteousness, and the strength of Christ, his strength, and that grace that is in Christ, to be treasured up in the Lord Jesus for him, and as he builds on Christ the whole of his salvation, so trusteth alone upon him for supportation, or for whatsoever he sees needful, or necessary for him, in order to finish this spiritual building, certainly he hath wisely sat down, and counted the cost, and knows where he may have sufficient supply, at all times to perfect the whole work : "For I know whom I have believed, and am persuaded, that he is able to keep that which I have committed to him, against that day," 2 Tim. i. 12. Our Lord would have us know, that without him we can do nothing, John xv. 5 ; and this we should consider, and know at first, and so count our own weakness, and yet find out that great mine of riches which we have in Jesus Christ, that so we may be able to say with Paul, "I can do all things through Jesus Christ that strengtheneth me."

No man is sufficient of himself to build this tower.

"Lest haply after he hath laid the foundation, and is not able to finish ; all that behold it begin to mock him," &c. Parables, as I have told you, do not run always on all four ; the scope of this parable chiefly should be observed: a man may lay a foundation of a house well, and yet may not be able to finish it, but expose himself to shame and reproach ; but he that lays Christ as the foundation of his faith, hope, and salvation, or begins in a true and right manner to build, having saving faith in Jesus Christ, shall be enabled to finish. But some lay the foundation of their building on the sand, or build not rightly on Christ, (i. e.) not upon his merits, on his righteousness, on his power, on his wisdom, on his promises, and on his faithfulness, they build not on Christ, but rather upon their own righteousness, on their own power, and on their sufficiency, they glory in themselves ; and these, when they have begun, or have laid a foundation thus, are not able to finish, and so men begin to mock them ; for suffering some losses in professing of Christ, yet after all fail in their profession : a high tower had need to have a good and firm foundation, for else it may fall before it is finished.

Our Lord here compares the faith and work of a Christian, to a man's building of a tower, and from hence note,

Doct. A Christian is, or may be compared to a man that builds a tower, a noble building, not a cottage, and therefore should count the cost.

1. I shall show you what a tower or building it is, or why it is called a tower.
2. I shall show you why a Christian is said to build a tower.
3. That every believer should consider so well the matter as to count the cost.
4. Apply it.

1. In opening those words of our Lord Matt. vii. (He that heareth these saying of mine and doeth them, &c.) I have showed that every true Christian is compared to a builder, and therefore shall pass by that here, and show you why he is said to build a tower.

1. A tower is no small building, but a noble structure, one of the chiefest of buildings : so a believer's spiritual building is a most noble building. This appears,

1. Upon the consideration of the contriver of it, which was the great God, by his own eternal wisdom : O what a kind of tower is this, a building is this, that infinite wisdom was the contriver, viz. To build us up in Jesus Christ ; " but ye, beloved, building up your selves on your most holy faith," &c. Every believer is a builder, but God contrived the building, and also gives directions how to build ; the foundation, the materials, and the skilful putting all together, was found out, ordained, or appointed by Almighty God.

2. It is a noble building, because the Lord Jesus Christ is the foundation of it, and was also first laid by the Father, in his eternal decree and purposes. (2.) Christ laid himself for this foundation. (1.) In and by that holy doctrine he taught. (2.) By his own actual obedience, and by what he suffered. (3.) In the holy example of his life, as our pattern.

3. The Apostles also laid Christ for the only foundation of this noble tower and structure, by their doctrine and practice, I have laid the foundation, &c.

4. Every believer also lays Christ for a foundation, by believing, resting, or relying alone upon him.

II. It is a noble building, or a famous tower, because the design of it is to preserve the soul from all its enemies, and from all dangers whatsoever, to eternal life.

III. This spiritual building may be called a tower, because a Christian is a soldier, and this building is to be his fortress, and if he builds on Christ or rightly upon the only foundation, he need not fear all the gun-shot of satan, sin, the flesh, and the world, though he must expect to be battered severely by these enemies.

IV. It may be called a tower, because the top of it must reach up to heaven : he builds for another world, and must gradually proceed until he come to heaven ; he hath not finished this tower until then, not till an entrance be administered to him into the everlasting kingdom of our Lord and Saviour Jesus Christ.

Secondly, why is a Christian said to build this tower ?

May be fitly called a building upon Christ. I. Because he is to believe in Jesus Christ ; faith is required of him, or believing in Christ ; that which we build upon, we trust in it, or rely upon. So in this sense we build on Christ ; that is, we trust in him, venture our souls on him, we build our faith, our hope, expectation, and eternal life on Jesus Christ ; and so may be said to build this famous tower of our salvation.

But pray note, it is God that finds all the materials, our " Faith is not of ourselves, it is the gift of God," Eph. ii. 8. So our hope is not only in God, but also of God ; he also gives strength, skill, and courage ; and is at all the charge of the whole building ; but as we are required to work out our own Salvation, so we are commanded to ; " building up yourselves in your most holy faith," Jude 20 ; by trusting in God through Jesus Christ, or by exercising faith in his word and promises, and adding unto our faith virtue, and unto virtue knowledge, and unto knowledge temperance, &c. And thus he may be said to build, and still make a further progression, until he have finished the building, or receive the end of his faith, the salvation of his soul.

Thirdly, that every believer should consider so well the matter, as to count the cost.

1. I shall note here what he should consider :

2. Why count the cost.

I. He should consider well what foundation he builds this tower upon, because there is but one ; " Other foundation can no man lay then that which is laid, which is Jesus Christ," 1 Cor. iii. 11.

Because if he builds his hopes of salvation upon any other foundation, his tower will fall, though he build never so high, or never such a glorious profession of religion in the sight of men.

II. He should consider and ponder well what he should build upon this foundation, viz. His faith, his hope, his soul, his justification, his redemption, his sanctification ; in a word his soul, every thing, even all his whole salvation must be built upon Christ alone, and upon nothing else.

III. He should consider when he should build, and that is presently ; he must not delay building one hour, for he is in danger of falling into hell every moment : " I made haste and delayed not, to keep thy precepts," saith David.

IV. He should consider, how he must build, viz., that is by faith, or by believing, by trusting in, or relying upon Jesus Christ only : not by working, not by doing, no, but by believing : not on Christ's righteousness, and on his own inherent righteousness together :

but on Christ's merits and righteousness alone, exclusive of all things, either as wrought in him, and done by him; not on his own sincere obedience, but on Christ's obedience; not on his faith, but on the object of his faith, the Lord Jesus Christ; and the blessed God and Father, in, and by Christ Jesus.

Quest. Why should he sit down and count the costs?

1. Because it will be a very costly building to him. (1.) He must give up all his cursed sins and lusts, though as dear to him in times past, as a right hand, or a right eye. (2.) He must expect it will cost him the loss of whatsoever he once accounted gain. (3.) He must part with all his former companions, and expect they will mock and deride him (as I hinted before) and may be his own life also. *Why a poor sinner should sit down and count the cost first.*

2. Because great storms may rise, and floods come, and beat upon his high tower: and he should count the damage he may sustain in such storms.

3. Because he is not able either to begin, nor to build, or lay one stone by his own strength; and if he knows not this, or doth not utterly despair of any power, or ability of his own, he will never be able to finish, and then men will mock him, and say, " This man begun to build, but was not able to finish."

4. He must account, how rich, how strong, and able he is in Jesus Christ; and if he knows, that Christ is his strength, (as well as his righteousness,) he counts the cost aright; and if he depends wholly, constantly, he need not fear, but he shall have wherewith to finish this famous tower, (*i. e.,*) the salvation of his precious soul.

APPLICATION

1. This reprehends all rash and inconsiderate persons, who through some sudden slash of zeal (which may prove like a land flood) set out in a visible profession of Christ and the gospel. Alas, sirs, though men should not delay in closing with Christ, and flying from the wrath to come, yet they should do nothing rashly, or without weighing the matter deliberately. Some young people I fear have showed no small folly this way. *Reproof.*

2. This may inform us of the reason, there are so many who grow cold, and soon falter, and fall off, or decline in their zeal, and seeming love to Christ, his truth and people, they counted not the cost, what corruptions they must mortify, what temptations they must withstand, and what reproaches they must expect to meet with, and what enemies they may find, and what relations they may enrage, and stir up against them. *Inform.*

3. Let all from hence be exhorted, who have it in their hearts, to begin to build, or to come forth into a visible profession of Christ, to count the cost, and not expose themselves by their inconsiderateness to the reproach of men, either to the grief of the godly, or to the contempt and scorn of the wicked. *Exhort.*

4. Yet let none from hence be discouraged, or decline closing with Christ, or with his people; for if they are sincere and gracious persons, they will understand, that the almighty power of God is engaged to help them. O what promises hath he made to all who truly believe in him, and rest upon him, though they have no might, no riches, nor strength in themselves; yet they may say with the psalmist, " My flesh and my heart faileth, but God is the strength of my heart, and my portion for ever," Psal. lxxiii. 26. There are none that have cause to fear, but false professors, or such whose hearts are not right with God; therefore let such lay to heart what hath been said. *Encouragment.*

5. Count also all the external charge, which a visible profession of religion may expose you to; for the interest of Christ, and the charge of his church, must be borne: I do not call this loss, for it will be none in the end. For by casting their bread upon the waters, they shall find it again after many days. But yet nevertheless this ought to be considered, and reckoned up, before a man begins to build this tower.

6. How great is the work of a Christian; building is not only costly work, but a very laborious work also, especially to build a strong and mighty tower: therefore know it is no lazy life, no, such must work hard: we read of the " work of faith, and labour of love," &c., Heb. vi. 10. *Inference.*

7. Let all learn, on what foundation to build, and not refuse the chief corner stone, for what foundation soever they lay besides Christ, let them be assured, they will not be able to finish; but shall come to shame, and be mocked at last. O depend wholly upon God in Jesus Christ; you must know his money pays for all: yet you shall not miscarry for want of money to finish, if in all your wants you go to him, by faith, and *Direction.*

prayer! and you that build on him, or on this rock, the gates of hell shall never prevail against you.

Your tower will stand firm, and endure all the battering rams, and roaring cannon Satan lets fly against it; neither need you fear any mines, for your tower is built upon such a hard rock, that the cunning miner, Satan, cannot pierce it, no pick-axe of the devil can enter into this rock, nor can the enemy storm your strong tower; for besides its strength the Lord of hosts dwells therein, and Jesus Christ is always within the walls thereof: your tower is also fenced round with salvation, which God had prepared for walls and bulwarks. For as it is thus with Sion in general, so the same fortification has every believer, " Walk about Zion, and go round about her, tell the towers thereof, mark well her bulwarks, consider her palaces, that ye may tell it to the generations following; for this God, is our God for ever and ever; he will be our God even unto death," Psal. xlviii. 12, 13, 14.

Moreover, the enemy cannot starve you, or cut off your provision, " for he shall dwell on high, his place of defence shall be the munitions of rocks, bread shall be given him, and his waters shall be sure," Isa. xxxiii. 16.

O what comfort is here for you that wisely build on the Lord Jesus, whose faith stands in the wisdom and power of God; though others are not able to finish, yet you shall, but so much to this parable.

10. GOING TO WAR

Or what king going to war against another king, sitteth not down first, and consulteth whether he be able with ten thousand to meet him that cometh against him with twenty thousand?

Or else, while the other is yet a great way off, he sendeth an ambassage, and desireth conditions of peace.

So likewise, whosoever he be of you, that forsaketh not all that he hath, he cannot be my disciple.—Luke xiv. 31, 32, 33.

THE design and purport of this parable is the same with that which precedes about building a tower, &c., which I have opened according to that small light received.

The scope of this parable.   Both being to put all men that purpose to become disciples of Christ, first to count the cost, as to what they must part with, the difficulties they must run, and what oppositions they must expect to meet withal in their Christian warfare.

Though probably this may have more in it than the former: may not the king that comes with twenty thousand refer in a remote sense to the great God?

A sinner here is compared to a King, though he hath lost his kingdom, and is abdicated: all the glory and regal power he had in his first state, is gone; he also is an enemy to God, and while he remains in his unconverted state wars against his Maker; though his men (I mean) all his noble faculties, are corrupted, and have deserted and gone over to his enemy, the devil; and now the mighty king, the dreadful God, is coming out against him, who is more than twenty thousand strong, nay, more than ten thousand times ten thousand stronger than he. O what millions of millions of angels hath God, or what mighty armies hath the Lord of hosts! but alas he needs not any of them; himself alone is clothed with infinite power, might, and majesty, and can crush in a moment like a moth all the numberless numbers of men and devils; therefore a sinner had best sit down, and consult whether or no he is a match for this mighty and terrible king, the Lord of hosts: which alas he may soon understand he is not, though he had all the powers and armies on earth, and devils of hell at his command, to assist him: and therefore it his wisdom, before the great God comes too near towards him in a way of divine wrath, and vengeance, to lay down his arms, and accept of an embassage of peace, offered to him in and by Jesus Christ.

Indeed the sinner ought to send to treat first, and submit himself upon any terms to the great God of heaven and earth; but this the Lord foresaw man could not, would not do, and therefore out of his infinite love, bowels and pity, he sends his ambassadors to persuade him to submit himself, and be reconciled to his offended Creator: this holds a good analogy of faith: but by considering the scope and design of the parable, this is not chiefly (if at all) intended here, and therefore I shall pass this by, and speak to the parts briefly, by way of exposition.

"Or what king going to make war," &c. That is, what man or what sinner going to war against sin, the world, the flesh and the devil: Our Lord seems here to put some seeming honour upon sorry man, by comparing him to a king; he was so at first, even the king of this nether creation, all things were put into his hand.

Going to war, "sitteth not first and consulteth whether he is able," &c. A sinner ought to consult his own strength, and consider that he with all the powers of his soul, is but ten thousand, and all deceitful and treacherous soldiers too.

"Whether he be able with ten thousand to meet him that comes against him with twenty thousand." Satan hath more than two to his one, nay, more than ten to his one.

1. He hath all the whole hosts of the infernal lake, all the evil spirits, or many legions of fallen angels in his army, and all expert soldiers, and filled also with rage, against the poor, weak, and impotent sinner. *Satan stronger than sinful man, nay than saints as in themselves.*

2. The world in all its cursed snares and allurements its riches, honours, and pleasures, Satan has no muster up, as another mighty army.

3. This black king hath also hath got great strength in the poor sinner's own house, or small isle, viz., inbred corruption, who have corrupted to his party all the strength and powers of his soul. Now is it not necessary for him to *Satan has a party in our own house.* consult his own strength, and despair by any force or might of his own to prevail, in this great enterprize? Certainly he must desist and yield himself overmatched, or else look out for some assistance from some other prince, who may espouse his quarrel, and help him; and one also that is every way able to repel and vanquish the powerful prince of darkness, with all his forces and mighty hosts; especially, considering that the king that comes out against him, is a most subtil enemy, that ever drew sword against God or sinners, and as he is crafty, and full of subtilty, and mighty strong and powerful, so also is filled full of rage, enmity, and malice against every poor mortal, that is resolved to desert his service, and return to the Lord Jesus Christ. Moreover, he is well armed, being called the strong man armed, Luke xi. 21.

What now should a poor sinner do? He cannot once suppose himself able to make head against all the powers of darkness, that are both within and without. And if he enters again into a covenant of peace, with sin, Satan, and the world, he is *No peace must be made with sin nor Satan.* undone, (the parable runs not so far on all four as to allow him to do that) no, no league must the sinner make either with sin, the devil, or this world.

From hence note,

Doct. 1. The work or life of a Christian is a warfare.

Doct. 2. That a sinner who designs to close with Christ, and become his disciple, should first consult matters well, and then take courage, and not fear any enemy, but resolvedly pursue his great and good design.

It is the last of these I purpose briefly to speak to or open.

By consulting he may know, that he hath one with him, that will assist him, so that he need not fear, nor desist his design and purpose, though his enemy be a hundred thousand strong, and he hath no strength, nor power of his own, to withstand so great a force. And no doubt this our blessed Lord chiefly designed to instruct all his followers in, by speaking this parable, or in making use of this allusion.

The Philistines were greedy to know wherein Sampson's great strength lay, which when his Delilah knew, she, by cutting of his hair, destroyed his strength; but no Delilah, no sin, no devil, can spoil or rob a true believer of his strength, which, though it lies not in his hair, yet it lies in his head (I mean) in Jesus Christ, who is the head of the body, the Church and every member thereof, and this he that begins to go forth on the spiritual warfare, ought to know, and should sit down, and consult; and hereby he will see, that he is able to maintain a war, and be a victor over sin, the flesh, the world, and the devil, though never so weak in himself; and without Christ can do nothing, John xv. 5. But what of this? Yet through Christ's strength, or in the power of his might, we can do all things, and therefore need not fear, but through the Lord Jesus Christ we shall be able to meet the black prince, though he comes forth against us with all his hellish forces.

But to speak more distinctly to this proposition, I shall

1. Show particularly, what a poor sinner, who designs to enter upon this war, should consult.

2. Show, why he should first sit down, and consult with himself, &c.

3. Apply it. *Sinners should consult the charge of the war.*

1. He should consult the charge of this war: no war can be carried on without charge and expense, no more can this spiritual war, and this is

hinted in the precedent parable. Building is costly as well as war ; we must resolve to lose all things, that we may call our own, or expend all, give up all that we once counted gain to us, for Christ's sake. He that spares one beloved lust, will be worsted, and lose the field ; or is not willing to part with all he hath.

II. He should consult what great hardship he must undergo. A soldier's life is attended with hardship many ways. (1.) He must not expect to lodge always on beds of down, but to lie on the cold ground. (2.) Also sometimes to fare hard. (3.) And not have that rest and sleep which others have. (4.) And likewise be exposed to cold and bitter storms in winter, and to hot scorching heat in summer. (5.) And to tedious and weary marches, as well as to the dangerous assaults of his enemy : so the Christian soldier must expect to endure great hardship. Hence Paul (speaking to Timothy) saith, "Thou therefore endure hardness as a good soldier of Jesus Christ," 2 Tim. ii. 3 ; as a Christian, and much more as a minister, he must look to meet with hardships; the life of a Christian is no easy life ; what hardships have the people of God in every age met withal ! like soldiers, they some-times have no certain dwelling place, as Paul saith, and as many poor French Protestants at this very time experience ; we are strangers and pilgrims on earth. "I beseech ye, as strangers and pilgrims, abstain from fleshy lusts, which war against the soul," 1 Pet. ii. 11. (2.) Sometimes also they meet with days of famine, and years of drought, when the bread of their souls seems to fail, there being no open vision, but seek the food of their souls with the peril of their lives. Nor do they always live on the fat things of God's house, but may want the light of God's countenance, and be ready to say, their hope is cut off. (3.) Besides they must not sleep as others do, but always be on their watch ; watch and pray always, &c. "Give not sleep to thine eyes, nor slumber to thine eyelids, deliver thyself as a roe from the hand of the hunter, and as a bird from the hand of the fowler. (4.) Moreover, what cold blasts and storms of affliction, and temptations do be-lievers frequently meet with ! and also what scorching heat of persecution, which some faint hearted soldiers cannot endure. (5.) And sometimes by this means they are forced to long marches, even to fly from one city to another, nay, from one kingdom to another, and that they may do by the directions their Captain hath given them. "When they per-secute you in this city, fly ye into another," &c. Matt. x. 23.

III. They should consult the cause of the war, and absolute necessity thereof. Sometimes there is such necessity to take up arms, that if it be not done, a kingdom may be lost : the justness and goodness of the cause, and necessity of a war, are to be considered well.

The cause of war against sin and Satan must be consulted. So likewise every soul that would be a soldier of Jesus Christ, should con-sider, and carefully consult the righteousness, and justness of the war against sin, and the devil, &c. As also the necessity of it, they must take up arms, and fight, or else perish for ever : for these enemies design the murder of every soul, if possible, and put all to the sword. Sin and Satan are grand and merci-less tyrants, and such that we must resist, and take up arms against, and never have peace with, or otherwise remain declared rebels and traitors to the great God and King of hea-ven and earth.

IV. They should also consult the length, or duration of the war. Whoever takes up arms, and lift themselves under the command of Jesus Christ, must resolve to abide his soldiers as long as they live ; this spiritual war will last all our days. "And, we must re-sist unto blood, (if called to it) striving against sin," Heb. xii. 4.

V. They must consider, at whose charge the war is to be carried on, and maintained. for if any think they are rich enough themselves to bear the expense thereof, they will certainly fail, and be soon overcome. The whole charge is borne by the Lord Jesus Christ, whose riches and treasure is infinite ; and therefore inexhaustible, so that we need not fear want of any thing needful for us ; "For the Lord God is a Sun and a shield, he will give grace and glory, and no good thing will be withhold from them that walk uprightly," Psal. lxxxiv. 11.

The time must be con-sidered, when to be listed under Christ. VI. They should consult, or well consider the manner and time, when they must list themselves under this glorious General, the Lord of Hosts, and know also, what armour they must put on, and what the armour is. For if they consult the excellency of the spiritual armour, they need not fear the force, power, and craft of the King that comes forth against them ; it is armour of proof. As to the time of lifting themselves, it is just when Christ calls them, that is to-day, "while it is called to-day," Heb. iii. 13. Many are called at the third hour, that is in youth ; these are always readily entertained : "I love them that love me, and they that seek me early, shall find me," Prov. viii. 17. They are lifted into some of Christ's companies, in and by baptism, where they must keep rank and file, and learn all the art of order, and spiritual discipline. The armour is, (1.) Their loins girt about with truth, Eph. vi. 14, 17; being sincere, and always kept in the bounds of truth; and, (2.) Their feet shod with the preparation of the Gospel of peace; (3.) Also they must take the shield of faith; they must strive for due preparedness to every work and duty, with purpose of heart to cleave to the Lord; and by faith as with a shield resist all the fiery darts of the devil; (4.) For an helmet take the hope of salvation, and (5.) Always have the sword of the Spirit in their hand, which is the word of God; and with skill use it to the wounding all their enemies. (6.) Praying always, and watching thereunto with all perseverance.

VII. They must consult the strength, policy, wrath, and cruelty of Satan, and other enemies, which I have already hinted something about. *We must consult the strength of our enemies.*

VIII. They must consult, and be sensible of their own weakness, and never engage in their own names, nor in their own strength; but always "be strong in the Lord, and in the power of his might;" as David came out against Goliah. So through God we shall do valiantly; "My flesh and my heart faileth, but God is the strength of my heart, and my portion for ever," Psal. lxxiii. 26. To be strong in the Lord, &c., is always to trust in him, and rely upon him for wisdom, power, and aid at all times; we must not trust in that grace we have already received, nor in any of our own inherent grace, but in the grace that is in Christ Jesus.

IX. They must consult the power, and irresistible strength of their Captain, the Lord Jesus Christ.

They must know, (1). That he is almighty; and also have a firm persuasion of this. (2). Also act faith in him.

(3). And know that he hath engaged himself, by his faithful promises, to help them, and fight for them at all times, "And that he will never fail them, nor forsake them," as he did not Joshua of old, Josh. i. 5. "Fear not, worm Jacob, I will help thee, saith the Lord. Fear thou not, for I am with thee, be not dismayed, for I am thy God," Isa. xli. 10, 13, 14.

X. They must consult the covenant of peace, the oath and promises of God the Father, unto Christ as Mediator, and in him to all believers. Moreover, how in that covenant all the elect are put into Christ's hand, not only to redeem them, to renew them, but also to aid, help, and assist, and to fight for them, yea, and to strengthen and support them, as likewise that the cause is his, and our enemies his enemies.

XI. They must consult that relation they stand into their Captain, he hath espoused and marries them for ever that list themselves to fight under his banner, and that his love is an everlasting and an unchangeable love, so that they need not fear his leaving them to war alone, or suffer their enemies to prevail; who is a match for them, for no sin, no world, no devil, no enemy, but he can subdue and vanquish in a moment.

XII. They should also consult and know, that all their enemies are already conquered; the king that comes forth against him, is a slain or conquered enemy, our blessed Captain hath led "him captive, and hath triumphed over principalities and powers, and made a shew of them openly." Sirs, believers are more than conquerors through Jesus Christ, Col. ii. 15. Because other warriors know not assuredly that they shall conquer, but all Christ's faithful soldiers are assured of the victory; they have it already in their head, and they shall have it actually in their own persons, "they shall never perish, neither shall any pluck them out of my hand," &c. John x. 28.

XIII. They should consult the honour of God, and the honour and exaltation, and glory of their blessed Captain, and prefer that above their lives. While we seek glory, he will seek our good; should we be worsted, the dishonour would fall on our Lord Jesus Christ.

XIV. Moreover, they should consult the nature of the crown for which they fight. Every saint, every soldier, shall be crowned with a crown of glory. "Be thou faithful unto death, and I will give thee a crown of life," Rev. ii. 10.——"I have fought the good fight, I have kept the faith." Well, what of this? "Henceforth there is laid up for me a crown of righteousness, which God the righteous Judge will give to me in that day," 2 Tim. iv. 7, 8. Aye, but Paul he was a nonsuch, a champion for Christ. Pray read the next words, "And not to me only, but to all them also that love his appearing." And not only a crown but they shall sit on his throne. "He that overcometh will I grant to sit with me in my throne, even as I also overcame, and am sat down with my Father in his throne," Rev. iii. 21.

Now if thou consultest all these things, thou wilt not be afraid to go forth in this war-fare against that king that comes against thee with his twenty thousand, though thou art

weak, and not one hundred strong, provided thou art well armed, a man born of God, and
Why a sin- united to Jesus Christ, and in covenant with him.
ner ought to   Secondly, I shall give you one or two reasons, why sinners should sit down
sit down and
consult. and consult these things, before they enter into these wars.

1. Because man is naturally a self-confident creature, and thinks he can do wonderful things by his own strength, but did he know how weak he is, and how deceitful his heart is, and all the powers of his soul, he would not pride it so in himself, nor ever venture to go forth in his own strength, against one who is so much stronger than he. Is sinful man a match for Satan? or can he destroy and overcome sin who lies dead, or slain, at the feet of sin and the devil already? No, for a man renewed, one quickened, one that is also well armed, is no more able to vanquish his spiritual enemies, without Christ's special and immediate assistance, than a child is able to encounter with a giant.

2. Becaue all that ever engaged these enemies, not consulting their own weakness, but went out in their own strength, were put to flight and utterly beat and spoiled. When Peter did, thus, he came off with broken bones, " Though all deny thee, yet will not I." He should first have sat down and consulted better, for none indeed denied his Lord so basely as he did, and it was through self-confidence, or through trusting to his own strength, or not consulting his own impotence without special assistance.

3. Because our Lord would have none of his soldiers be surprised, either by the power, wrath, malice, or subtilty of the enemy ; he hath therefore given us warning of the danger, and discovered what all his disciples may, nay, must look to meet with, that so when troubles come, persecution and trials come, none of them might be offended in him.

4. It is that we might be ready prepared for the worst that can come. Fore-warned, fore-armed ; and that we might be much in prayer, and in the exercise of faith at all times of need, and utterly despair of our own abilities. " We had the sentence of death in ourselves, that we should not trust in ourselves, but in God that raiseth the dead," 2 Cor. i. 9.

APPLICATION

Information. 1. This informs us, that the work of a Christian is no easy, but a very hard and difficult work. What is a harder undertaking, or attended with greater trouble than that of a soldier ?

2. Moreover it may inform us, what the reason is, that so many professors who seemed zealous in times of peace and liberty have deserted in an hour of trial and persecutions. Alas, they did not sit down and consult what a mighty force, or what troops of temptation, &c., troops of opposition from without, and from within, they should meet withal.

3. It may be of use to all poor convinced sinners that purpose to follow Jesus Christ, first of all to ponder and well weigh the nature, troubles, and difficulties of a Christian life, as I hinted under the foregoing parable.

4. It also may tend to convince us of the great strength and power of Satan and other enemies of our souls, and the need we have to be well armed, and to stand always upon watch, and never give way to self-confidence. We (saith Paul) have no confidence in the flesh. My brethren, to trust in ourselves is to depart from the Lord, and yield ourselves up into the hands of our enemies. For whom we (as considered in ourselves) are no match ; for if Satan can meet with us alone, or not in the strength and power of Christ, down we go.

Terror. 5. It shows also the woeful condition of such who are in a state of unbelief, who have not the power of Christ to help and assist them. Is it any wonder to see the devil (who rules and reigns in the hearts of the children of disobedience) taken captive by him at his will, and led away into all manner of sins and cursed abominations ? there is a multitude of this sort; what can a naked man do to oppose, or vanquish a strong man armed ?

6. It may likewise be improved by way of encouragement and comfort to all sincere believers. For,

Comfort. (1). From hence they may see what a good cause they are engaged in ; a good cause greatly animates pious soldiers in the face of all difficulties.

(2). They may also see, that though they are weak in themselves, and the enemy stronger than they, yet that in the Lord they have such strength, that the powers of hell and darkness cannot withstand. For, 1. The eternal God is on their side, the Father of our Lord Jesus Christ. 2. Jesus Christ the Mediator, their victorious Captain, commands and heads them ; he leads them on and encounters with all their enemies, whom none can withstand, and who is not only a powerful Captain, but wise also, even the wisdom of God, and can outwit Satan in all his devices. 3. The Holy Spirit is always at hand to assist, aid, and influence them in all attempts and just enterprises, who in power, &c., is equal with the Father and the Son. 4. They have all the heavenly hosts, I mean the holy angels, on their side, and to fight for them, who like horses and chariots of fire, are continually round about them, as they were about the prophet Elisha. "And when the servant of the man of God was risen early and gone forth, behold an host compassed the city both with horses and chariots, and his servant said unto him, Alas! master, how shall we do? And he answered, fear not, for they that are with us are more than they that are against us. And Elisha prayed and said, Lord, I pray thee, open his eyes, that he may see, and the Lord opened the eyes of the young man, and behold the mountain was full of horses and chariots of fire round about Elisha," 2 Kings vi. 15, 16, 17. Thus the angels of the Lord are employed to save and defend all the people of God ; they encamp round about them that fear him, and that fight under the banner of the Lord Jesus Christ. 5. They have also all the prayers of the Lord's people continually for them ; there is not one believer, but hath the constant prayers of the universal church for him, and against his enemies, whose prayers are always most prevalent with God. This was that fire which went out of the mouths of the two witnesses. "And if any man will hurt them, fire proceedeth out of their mouths, and devoureth their enemies," Rev. xi. 5. Their prayers are like fire to burn and destroy ; for as none can stand before consuming fire, so none can stand before the prayers of the saints of God, when God fires their prayers with his Spirit. Now all these things being considered, what little cause have any poor believers to fear what force of hell comes against them ? besides, they are sure of victory. But so much as to this useful parable.

11. THE NEW PIECE OF CLOTH

I

No man putteth a new piece of cloth into an old garment, for that which is put to it to fill it up, taketh from the garment, and the rent is made worse, Matt. ix. 16, 17.
Neither do men put new wine into old bottles, &c., Mark ii. 21. *No man also seweth a piece of cloth to an old garment,* &c.
And he spake also a parable unto them : no man putteth a new piece of a garment upon an old.
—Luke v. 36, 37.

OUR annotators think that our Saviour refers here in these two parables to what precedes immediately the two verses before our text, about his disciples not fasting : viz. "It is not (say they) yet a time of mourning for my disciples, yet do not envy them, there will shortly come a time, when as to my bodily presence I shall be taken away from them ; then they shall mourn. The second thing (say they) he illustrateth by a two-fold similitude,—viz. Should I impose upon them the severe exercises of religion, it might discourage them, and be a temptation to them to look back.—This is a portion of Scripture, which much commendeth prudence to ministers in teaching their people as they are able to bear, &c. Though I have a great value for these learned men, in many things they have said upon several dark texts, yet I cannot agree with them as to the design of our Saviour in these two parables, (there being nothing in my judgment, in what they say, that is correspondent with the design of our Saviour herein) for could not the disciples of Christ bear the duty of fasting, &c., without being put upon temptation to leave their Master ? Strange ! had not they a principle of grace in them sufficient to bear them up in discharge of that duty ? or had our Lord not power to strengthen them in it, if he had seen good to have enjoined it upon them ?

2. Were the disciples' garments old garments, or such that needed a new piece of cloth to mend them, or were they like old bottles that would not hold new wine ? and where are hard duties of religion, I pray, compared to wine ? No doubt the reason why Christ's disciples did not fast, was from the reason he gives, ver. 15, "Because the Bridegroom was yet with them :" but he doth not allude to that matter in these two symbolical allusions ; for from that foot of an account these similies bear no correspondent signification, but must allude to something else of a quite different nature.

Pool's Annotations.

The scope of the words opened.

The reason why Christ's disciples did not then fast.

1. Therefore I shall give you (as I understand) the main scope and coherence of these parabolical allusions, or the drift and design of our Saviour in them.

2. Explain all the terms and parts herein contained.

3. Take notice of such truths or propositions that necessarily arise therefrom.

4. And apply the whole.

The scope of this parable. First, I conclude that our Lord rather alludes in these similies to what he said in ver. 12, 13, 14. The Pharisees were offended with him, because he ate with publicans and sinners : " Why eateth your Master with publicans and sinners ?" ver. 11. They were so righteous in their own eyes, that they despised others. And this made our Lord say, that God " will have mercy and not sacrifice ; for I am come, not to call the righteous but sinners to repentance, " ver. 13. The Pharisees thought that the whole of religion lay in the discharge of duties, in sacrifices, prayer, fasting, and other like performances ; and upon this the disciples of John came and asked him, why they and the Pharisees fasted often, and his disciples fasted not at all, ver. 14.

Now, to convince them of the unprofitableness of all duties of religion performed by unrenewed persons, he brings in these two parables : the Pharisees, as if he should say, think themselves holy and righteous persons, and they pray, and fast, but it is all in vain, whilst they remain in their old nature. For all their own righteousness is but as filthy rags, or like an old rotten garment, which cannot be mended by any acts of obedience, as sacrifices, prayer, fasting, &c.

And (2) they are like old broken bottles, that cannot hold new wine, but will let it all out.

So much shall suffice as to the scope hereof.

Secondly, We shall open and explain the parts and terms contained in this two-fold parable.

1. Show what is meant by the old garment.

2. What is meant or intended by the new piece of cloth put to the old garment.

3. What by the rent being made worse.

4. Show what is intended by old bottles.

5. And what by new wine.

6. What by putting in new wine.

" No man putteth a new piece, a new garment, on an old," verse 16.

Why a man's own righteousness is compared to a garment. 1. By an old garment, I understand is meant a man's own righteousness : the righteousness of an unrenewed person may be compared to an old garment.

1. Because it is as old as Adam ; it is that righteousness which we derived from him in his fallen estate, that garment which is near six thousand years old, must needs be looked upon to be very old.

2. Because it is worn out, being rotten, rent, and torn, and abominably defiled, filthy, polluted, so that it stinks in the nostrils of God, and renders such who have it upon them, loathed also in his sight, as an old filthy garment doth render a person in the sight of men.

3. An old garment pre-supposeth that it was once a new, a firm, and a good garment ; and so was man's own righteousness in the state of innocency, a new and beautiful garment ; our first parents were curiously clothed, as they came out of God's hand, before they sinned, and fell from that state ; but now that clothing or garment which should cover their souls, is rotten, and torn, and good for nothing.

4. An old garment needs mending if it can be mended ; so such that know not how to buy them a new one, strive to piece and patch their old. Thus many sinners strive (as did the Pharisees) to mend their old garment, and patch it together with their duties, as prayers, fasting, and giving to the poor ; as some now in our days strive to patch their old garment, by putting a piece of a new garment to it, viz., part of Christ's righteousness to their own ragged righteousness, which is, alas, so rotten that it will not hold together to cover their nakedness in the sight of God, nor will it bear a piece of Christ's righteousness ; many sinners are ignorant that Christ's righteousness cannot be parted, nor their own bear mending ; these cannot mix together ; neither will they beg, or seek to him for a whole new garment that hath it ready for them ; but unless they can purchase a garment with their own money, they are so proud that they will rather wear their old one : nor do they see any need of a new one, but only to have the old mended with a piece of Christ's righteousness.

Quest. But why is righteousness compared unto a garment ?

Answ. 1. I answer, Because a garment is to cover nakedness, so a man sees that he is naked in the sight of God without a righteousness, since the fall, and therefore, like Adam, he goes about to sew fig-leaves together: I mean, he labours to get a righteousness of his own making to cover him. *Righteousness compared to a garment.*

2. Because a garment is that which covers the shame of mankind: now sin, or the horrid guilt of a profane and debauched life, is the shame of any soul; as Solomon saith, " Sin is the shame of any people." And to cover *A garment covers our shame.* this shame some poor wretches pray, fast, read the word of God, and give alms, and do many other religious duties, which like a garment is to hide or prevent that shame or reproach their sins they think otherwise will expose them unto; though others like to mere brutes commit all manner of wickedness and are not ashamed; but are like such as the prophet complains of; " Were they ashamed when they committed all abominations ? nay, they were not ashamed, neither would they blush," Jer. viii. 12.

3. Righteousness may be compared to a garment, because of the usefulness of it.

A garment is good to keep off piercing heat, or the scorching beams of the sun in summer

Even so men need a spiritual garment to keep off the scorching beams of God's wrath, though no garment of our own making can do this. No, no, none but the complete robe of Christ's righteousness.

Because our righteousness cannot answer all the demands of God's holy law. Neither doth it suit with the purity of God's nature, nor can it satisfy his offended justice.

4. Righteousness may be compared to a garment, in respect of ornament; if it be a fair and rich robe, it renders the person that hath it on very comely to all that see him.

So doth a perfect and complete righteousness render the soul that hath it on very comely in the sight of God.

But if it be a ragged and filthy garment it renders the person that wears it to be poor and contemptible; and so doth a man's old rotten and filthy robe of his own righteousness render him odious in God's sight.

5. Righteousness may be compared to a garment, because we judge of the honour, greatness, nobleness, and grandeur of a person, by the garment he wears; " Those that are clothed in soft raiment are in king's houses," Matt. xi. 8; Luke vii. 25.

Such who are clothed with the rich robe of righteousness are persons of no mean quality; they are more honourable than their brethren, or more excellent than their neighbours. Believers are king's children, and are allowed to dwell in his house, and to be richly clothed; they are the most excellent in all the earth, though they are contemptible ones in the sight of the ungodly of the earth.

6. Righteousness may be compared to a garment, because a garment tends to keep a man warm in the winter.

So a perfect and complete righteousness tends to keep the soul warm, such have divine heat in them, they are warm in the winter of afflictions, and in cold storms of tribulation; and in the sharp time of Satan's temptations; it is the righteousness of Christ in justification, also inherent holiness and sincerity in sanctification, keeps believers warm. It is the thoughts of these, the knowledge of these, that comforts and cherishes the souls of true Christians in such a time, like as a garment comforts and cherishes the body in a cold and bitter frost and snow.

7. A garment preserves the body of him that hath it on from thorns and briers, as he passeth though a wilderness, or the like. So the righteousness of God preserves the soul from Satan's darts, and from those pricking thorns of divine wrath; and the scratching briers of a wounded and accusing conscience. *A garment preserves from wounds. So doth Christ's righteousness preserve the soul.*

But an old rotten ragged garment, as a man passes through briers and thorns will not, cannot preserve him from wounds or sore scratches he may meet withal; for such a garment cannot preserve itself, but will be torn to pieces thereby.

So the righteousness of the creature, or our own righteousness, that sorry old garment, cannot preserve the soul from the piercing thorns of divine vengeance, nor of Satan's temptations; nay, but justice, the law, and divine wrath *An old garment can preserve the body.* will soon tear that garment to pieces, nor can it preserve us from Satan's fiery darts; for notwithstanding this covering, these thorns will soon wound the soul to death.

If otherwise, then both the new maketh a rent, &c.

Quest. What is meant by the rent, or as St. Mark saith, made worse ; " And the new agreeth not with the old," Mark ii. 21, according to St. Luke ?

What is meant by the rent made worse.   1. *Answ.* I answer, it may represent the state of all self-righteous persons, who seek to patch their old garment by that they call new obedience, or by Christ's merits or righteousness added to their own righteousness : for by this means their state is rendered worse than the state of the profane, or ungodly sinners, or that of Publicans and Harlots, as our Saviour shows, the Pharisees made their proselytes " twofold more the children of the devil than they were before," Matt. xxiii. 15, a greater rent makes the garment worse. So patching our old spiritual garment after this manner, makes the state of the soul worse, (i. e.,) it causes a greater wound, or their state to be more dangerous, and they more unlikely to be cured, or brought to believe, and wholly to rely upon Christ.

How the rent is made worse.   1. Made worse, because such, like the pharisees, think their state is better, and that the breach between them and the great God is now made up ; whereas it is no such thing ; by patching their old garment with duties, or with part of Christ's righteousness, they conclude all is well, and hence they are called such that are whole, and that think they need no Physician : what said the proud pharisee, " God I thank thee I am not as other men, nor as this publican," Luke xviii. 11.

2. Their state is worse, or the wound or rent is worse, because through this means they see no need to look out for a garment, no, they have, they conclude, so well patched up their old one, they have no occasion for a new garment ; " They being ignorant of God's righteousness, went about to establish their own righteousness, and have not submitted themselves to the righteousness of God," Rom. x. 3.

3. A worse rent, because the old garment will not, cannot mix together with this new piece of righteousness, nor the new with that ; the old is so rotten it will not hold sewing ; our Saviour refers to such an old garment that is good for nothing, it is eaten of moths, or rotten. Cannot grace be joined to works ? grace and works, my brethren, will not mix or hold together ; " And if by grace, then it is not by works, otherwise grace is no more grace ; but if it be of works, then it is no more of grace, or otherwise work is no more work," Rom. xi. 6. There is no mixing of the works of the creature with the free grace of God : the righteousness of Christ will not mix with our righteousness in our justification before God. For one of these tends to destroy the other ; for whatsoever comes free is of grace alone, and it is free ; but that which is of works is a debt, or else grace is not grace, or work is not work.

Yet we have some in our days, like those in the Apostles' time, who strive to mix these two together, and this will in time make a greater rent in their consciences, if ever God be pleased to open their eyes, or they will have greater condemnation ; sad it is to see how some Christians seek justification by Christ, and by their own faith and sincere obedience.

" Neither do men put new wine into old bottles."

Quest. What is meant by old bottles ?

Answ. I answer, the old heart, the carnal and unrenewed heart. "I am like a new bottle," &c., that is, my heart. Why is the old unrenewed heart compared to an old broken bottle?

Why the heart is compared to a bottle.   1. I answer, because a bottle is a proper receptacle of liquor, as of oil or wine, &c., so is the heart of man a proper receptacle of divine knowledge, grace, joy, peace, comfort, and the like.

2. Because a bottle of itself, is an empty thing, it must be filled, or have liquor put into it, before there is, or can be any in it ; so is the heart of man of itself naturally empty of whatsoever is truly good, spiritually good ; grace must be put into it before one drop will be there ; all naturally are without God, " without Christ, and without hope," Eph. ii. 12.

3 Because a broken bottle cannot hold new wine ; no more can an old and unrenewed heart hold or retain saving peace, joy, and comfort, but the heart must be made new.

Quest. Why doth our Saviour say men do not put new wine into old bottles, for some old bottles will hold new wine as well as such that are new, and not break nor spill the wine.

Why new wine is not put into some old bottles.   *Answ.* I answer, our blessed Lord it is evident refers to bottles that are cracked or broken bottles, or such bottles that are very old and rotten ; and the old heart, the unregenerate heart, is like to such a broken, cracked, or old rotten bottle, that will not hold or retain the wine of divine consolations, or the wine of heavenly comfort, if it were put in; unless at the same time the heart was renewed, it would all presently run out again like a leaky vessel; Heb. ii. 1; nay, grace itself (was not the heart renewed) should it be put into the heart, would be utterly lost; but grace put into the heart, new makes it in an instant. A cracked or broken bottle must be new made, or if it be a glass bottle, it must be by the glass-maker be melted down; so must the old unrenewed heart, like a cracked bell, or cracked glass bottle, melted down by the divine Spirit, and be new cast or new made, before God will pour in the wine of heavenly consolation, the heart must be melted in the fire of God's Spirit, there is no mending of it. Some strive to amend the old garment, and the old bottle, but it cannot be done; we must have a whole new garment, the righteousness of Christ for our justification, and a new heart through the Spirit's operation, for our sanctification.

" Puts new wine," &c.

Quest. 5. What is meant by the new wine?

Answ. By the new wine here may be meant all those choice blessings which are the concomitants of grace. *What meant by new wine.*

Wine being put in scripture for all sorts of choice things; " buy wine and milk," &c., Isa. lv. 1. Peace, inward joy, or those consolations of God that are not small, may be here intended; and this wine is only put into new bottles, *(i. e.,)* into renewed or regenerated hearts.

1. Wine is a choice thing, the choicest of drink; so inward joy, peace, and spiritual consolation, are most choice things.

2. Wine is the fruit of a good tree, or of a precious plant. So inward joy, peace, and spiritual consolations, are the fruits of the true wine Jesus Christ, or of the Holy Spirit, and grace thereof, John xv. 1. *Why the consolations of God are compared to wine.*

3. Wine is highly esteemed for its most excellent virtue; it hath a pleasant taste, and strengthens decayed nature.

So the comforts and consolations of God are highly prized, or esteemed by every true believer; they taste most sweet to a regenerate heart, and also greatly tend to strengthen the soul in times of weakness; " The joy of the Lord is your strength," Nehemiah viii. 10.

4. Wine makes glad the heart of man, so these spiritual consolations rejoice the new creature. " Thou hast put gladness into my heart, more than in the time that their corn and wine increased," Psal. iv. 7. He that drinks of this wine, though sad before, will forget his sorrows. Note also, that

1. " No man having drunk of old wine," viz., Luke v. 39; the delights of the flesh, carnal pleasures, or earthly comforts, straightway desireth new, that is true spiritual joy and consolation; no, he cannot straightway, or presently upon drinking the old, tasting the seeming sweetness of that, loving and relishing of that, before he is changed, or has got a new heart, desire those joys, and spiritual consolations of Christ and of the Holy Ghost.

" Putteth new wine into new bottles."

6. Quest. What may be meant by putting new wine into new bottles?

Answ. I answer; it may be intended or meant, Christ putting divine consolations into a new heart; at that very time the Spirit brings the soul into union with Christ, and the heart is changed, and so receives and retains those spiritual comforts and consolations; God makes the heart new, or gives a new heart, and then fills it with his precious wine of joy and peace.

Thus I have opened all the parts of this parable; and should proceed to raise one or two propositions from hence, but shall say no more at this time.

II

No man putteth a new piece of cloth to an old garment. Or as *Luke* reads it, *No man puts a piece of a new garment upon an old.*—Luke v. 36.

I HAVE already opened all the terms and parts of this parable, and I shall now observe one or two points of doctrine from hence.

Doct. 1. That such who would be saved and accepted of God, must not think to patch their old garment, by putting of a part or piece of Christ's righteousness, or his merits unto it, but must throw it quite away in point of justification; or that Christ and his righteousness, as a whole new garment, must be put on, before they, or any of their duties, prayer, fastings, &c., can be accepted of God.

1. This I shall endeavour to prove.

2. And then apply it.

Why the old garment must not, cannot be a-mended.   I. Because grace and works will not, cannot mix together, they being directly of a quite different nature, the one will destroy the other, like as a piece of a new garment would destroy an old, rotten, moth-eaten garment (or make the rent worse) but because I opened this the last day, in the exposition of the terms, I shall pass it by now.

II. Because all the saints of God have ever esteemed or looked upon all their own righteousness, in point of justification, as filthy rags; " But we are all as an unclean thing, and all our righteousnesses are as filthy rags," Isa. lxiv. 6.

Some perhaps will say, that these persons that the prophet speaks of, were not believers, nor such who had arrived to faith and sincere obedience, but were ungodly persons, hypocrites, or such like people. I answer, They were such who could call God Father, see ver. 8. " But now, O Lord, thou art our Father." Moreover, the prophet includes himself amongst the rest; though it is true, at that time they were under great declensions, yet by comparing this text with others, it appeareth very clear, that all the inherent righteousness of the best of saints, when compared to the righteousness of Christ, is but as filthy rags, or as mere dung." See what the holy apostle Paul saith; " Yea, doubtless, and I

Gospel obedience, or the saints' inherent righteousness as filthy rags, when compared to the righteousness of God.   account all things but loss, for the excellency of the knowledge of Christ Jesus my Lord, for whom I have suffered the loss of all things, and do count them but dung, that I may win Christ," Phil. iii. 8. He did not only disesteem all his Jewish privilege, and legal righteousness, which he had before converted, and counted them as dung, in respect of his justification before God, but also he shows he did not ascribe his being accepted and justified in God's sight to his own obedience, or to that inherent righteousness which he had attained unto after he was renewed, and had so many years served God in his apostolic office and ministry; he puts in all, both what he had attained before grace, and after grace; " Yea doubtless I account," I do now account of all things which I have now been helped to do, or is wrought in me, as dung in comparison of Christ, and the righteousness of God in him. But know, Paul did not thus account of his own inherent holiness, &c., simply considered in itself; no, no, for as so considered, sanctification being the work of the Spirit, is to be highly valued; but in respect had to his trusting in that, or dependance upon it, touching his justification and acceptance with God, or in comparison of the righteousness of Christ, which alone (without his inherent sanctification) justified him at the bar of God, or in God's sight.

III. Because to mix works and grace together, or our own righteousness with the righteousness of Christ, is directly opposite to the design of God in the gospel (or in the glorious contrivance of our salvation by a Mediator) and it tends to eclipse the doctrine of free grace, and so to take off the crown from Christ's head; " By grace ye are saved, through faith, and that not of yourselves, it is the gift of God," Eph. ii. 8. It is alone of the free favour of God, from the first to the last, wholly of grace, exclusive of anything of the creature; that so God might have all the glory unto himself; " Not by works of righteousness which we have done, but according to his mercy he saved us," &c., Tit. iii. 5. " That being justified by his grace, we should be made heirs according to the hope of eternal life," ver. 7. No works either ceremonial or moral, have any hand in our justification in God's sight.

IV. Because to join any thing of the creature's with Christ's merits or obedience, is to let in boasting, or to make way for men to glory in themselves; " Where is boasting then? it is excluded; by what law? law of works; nay, but by the law of faith," Rom. iii. 27. If my own old, or new personal and inherent righteousness, is joined with the merits of Christ, or through the virtue of his merits it justifies me, then I have room to boast: as the apostle speaks of Abraham, " If Abraham were justified by works, he had whereof to glory, but not before God," Rom. iv. 2. But according to the doctrine that some men preach, a man's own righteousness is that which covers him, or, that hides his nakedness; and Christ's righteousness is but to amend a hole, or to patch their old garment: nay, and it is their own hand also that puts this new piece to their old garment. For the Spirit of God will not piece their old garment, he only seeks Christ's honour;

" He shall glorify me, for he shall receive of mine and show it to you," John xvi. 14. Will the Holy Ghost give part of the glory of our salvation to the creature; Now the tendency of their doctrine is this, viz. That I may be saved, I may thank God, (Christ has made God reconcilable) but if I am saved, I may thank myself, for my diligence in acting faith, and yielding sincere obedience to the gospel procures it; for they affirm, God doth no more for the salvation of them that are saved, than he doth to save them that perish; the will of man being left to determine the whole issue of the ministry of the gospel; not that the Holy Spirit inclines or bows the will, but he leaves the will to act according to its own natural powers, and so this must needs open a door to boasting. But were it thus, certainly not one soul would ever be saved, because the will of all men naturally is so depraved, corrupted, and carried away to sin and vanity, that nothing but the mighty power of God put forth by the Spirit, can remove that averseness, prejudice, and enmity which is in it, to God, and the things of God.

V. Because such a garment is a dishonourable and a contemptible garment, for believers to be clothed with. Doth it, my brethren, become king's children to be clothed with a patched coat? Shall saints, who are the sons and daughters of the God of heaven and earth, the true heirs of glory, be clothed with their old over-worn rags of their own righteousness, pierced with part of Christ's righteousness? What a dishonour would it be to Christ, to work out a righteousness to no other purpose, or end, than to piece our old garment. Brethren, the robe with which the spouse, the king's daughter, is said to be clothed with, is all made of " Wrought gold, and raiment of needle-work," Psal. xlv. 9, 13, which shows the curiousness, richness, and most excellency of it ; and how contrary is this to an old rotten garment pieced, and patched together with a new piece of cloth. Would a man patch an old garment with a new piece of cloth of gold? *The saints have no patched garment on to justify them.* *No man will patch an old garment with a piece of cloth of gold.*

Object. " The king's daughter is all glorious within," therefore this must refer to her own inherent righteousness, Psal. xlv. 13.

Answ. I answer, we deny not but that may refer to the glory of the new creature, and so to the sanctification of the Holy Spirit; but pray observe the very next words, " her clothing is wrought gold;" this is not that righteousness wrought in her, no, but that righteousness, or that robe which is put upon her. As it is said in another place, " He hath clothed me with the robe of righteousness," Isa. lxi. 10; hence it is called "righteousness unto all, and upon all them that believe," Rom. iii. 22. Our justifying righteousness is not a righteousness inherent, a righteousness wrought within us, but a righteousness wrought without us by the active and passive obedience of Jesus Christ, and put upon us, or imputed to us by the Lord.

VI. Because our justifying righteousness hath no flaw, no rent, no seam, no spot in it ; but it is all glorious, holy, and pure ; now to add any part of Christ's new robe, to our old garment, cannot change that which is ours; no, ours would still be sinful and abominable as ever, in the sight of God's most pure and piercing eyes. Brethren, what think you, can a king delight in his bride, to see her clothed in an old patched garment, though it should be " spangled with pearls, and rich diamonds?" See Isa. lxii. 4, 5.

VII. Because that righteousness by which we are justified, is said to be the "righteousness of God," Rom. x. 3; nor the essential righteousness of God. But

1. It is called " the righteousness of God," Phil. iii. 9, in contradistinction to the righteousness of a mere creature. *Why Christ's righteousness is called the righteousness of God.*

2. Because it is the righteousness which God requires (viz. a perfect and complete righteousness) in order to our justification in his sight.

3. Because it is that righteousness which comports, and every way suits with the holiness, justice, and all other blessed attributes of God ; God's infinite justice and holiness cannot find the least flaw, spot, or defect in the righteousness of Christ; but his holiness and justice would soon espy it (the old garment, though never so well pieced) very vile, defective, and abominable, so as to be abhorred by him, and him that trusteth to it, or has it on, how firmly soever it be patched.

4. Because it is that righteousness which the wisdom of God hath found out, and none but he could find it ; none could buy it or procure it with gold or silver, nor any other ways ; no, neither men nor angels.

5. Because it is a righteousness which answereth all the demands of the holy moral law of God, not only the penal part thereof, (as these men preach) but also the preceptory part thereof ; excluding the active obedience of Christ from being any part of that righte-

ousness, which is imputed to us, and where is the sanction of the law ; or how is the law made glorious by Christ's obedience to our justification. " The Lord is well pleased for his righteousness' sake, he will magnify the law, and make it honourable," Isa. xlii. 21.

Brethren, do we who assert justification by Christ's active and passive obedience make void the law ; is the law violated ? The apostle's answers, " God forbid, we establish the law," Rom. iii. 31, inasmuch that we attain through faith to a perfect righteousness, by being interested in the most perfect and complete righteousness of Christ, in respect of the preceptory and penal part thereof.   And in that also because hereby every type is fulfilled, and particularly those that disallow of all mixtures, as the ploughing with an ox and an ass, or to wear a garment of linen and woollen, or to cause beasts to gender of divers kinds ; clearly intimating that nothing of the creature must be put to, or mixed with the righteousness of Christ in our justification before God (as well as all mixtures in divine worship) are here forbidden.

6. It may also be called the righteousness of God, because it is such a righteousness which wholly tends to exalt the glory of God, and his own free and undeserved grace and favour, and also doth abase the creature.

7. Because it is that righteousness which God hath ordained, instituted, and appointed to justify us in his sight.

VIII. Christ's righteousness alone must be put on, as a whole new garment pieced and patched with it, because that righteousness by which we are justified, is a righteousness without the law, and without works : " But now the righteousness of God without the law is manifested, &c., that is, without their own personal obedience to the moral law, or any other law whatsoever.   " But to him that works not, but believeth on him that jusfieth the ungodly, his faith is counted for righteousness," Rom. iv. 5.   Were it by works, or by our own righteousness, salvation would be of debt, as Paul affirms.   " Now to him that worketh is the reward not reckoned of grace, but of debt," Rom. iv. 4.   Though we are not taken off of doing works of righteousness by the free grace of God, yet we are taken off of it as to that end, purpose, and design, some speak of, (i.e.,) it is not that we may be justified thereby, nor is it a condition that procures our interest in Christ, or that gives us a right and title to eternal life ; but it is to glorify God, and to demonstrate our faith in, and thankfulness unto God in Jesus Christ.

IX. Because, had our own righteousness any part or share in clothing us in our justification, how could the righteousness of another be said to be imputed to us, or Christ be said to be the " Lord our righteousness, or be made of God unto us wisdom, righteousness, sanctification, and redemption," 1 Cor. i. 30. As Christ was not made sin for us by any sin inherent in him, so neither are we made righteous by any righteousness inherent in us, but by the righteousness of Christ imputed to us.

X. Because then also it would not be by the righteousness of one man that we are clothed or justified : " Therefore as by the offence of one judgment came upon all men to condemnation ; even so by the righteousness of one the free-gift came upon all men unto justification of life," Rom. v. 18.   That is, as all the seed of the first Adam were brought into a state of condemnation by the imputation of his first sin unto them : even so the free gift of righteousness came upon all the seed of the second Adam by the imputation of his righteousness to their justification, unto eternal life.   And as all in Adam died, so in Christ, or all in him, are made alive. Now I say, were it every man's own righteousness, through Christ's merits, that which clothes and justifies them, then it could not be said to be alone done by the righteousness of one, which the apostles asserts it is.   " For as by one man's disobedience many were made sinners, so by the obedience of one shall many be made righteous," Rom. v. 19.   Adam as a public person brought death on all his posterity, whom he represented : so Christ as a public person, brought life to all whom he representeth, viz., all the elect, or such that are given to him for his seed.

XI. Christ and his righteousness, as a whole new garment, must be put upon us, &c., and not an old garment patched with part of a new one.

1. Because " all things are become new," 2 Cor. v. 17 ; wholly new, a new covenant, a new priesthood, a new Church-state, and new church membership, and a new right to that membership : so a new robe of righteousness, to clothe all that are to be members of this new Gospel Church.

Argu. If all things in the new covenant are new, wholly new, then a whole new robe to clothe us, and not an old one pieced with Christ's new garment, or by his passive obedience or merits ?

Obj. It is for our new obedience we contend ; we do not plead for the righteousness of the old law.

Answ. I answer, what though this be so, that you do not plead for the old garment, as you perceive it is rent, or torn before conversion ; yet you plead for it as it is pieced or amended by the Spirit's operations. It is but the old one new vamped, it is the first Adam's still, (I mean) the righteousness of mere sinful creatures, though wrought by him by the Spirit's assistance, or patched by the help of divine grace. We will grant them, that the righteousness of sanctification is a new garment, yet that is not without spot, or stain ; besides that needs daily to be amended ; but if they intend this by the new garment, then they confound justification with sanctification, and also then no believer is complete, or without sin in point of justification in this life, nor until he hath his sanctification perfect, or complete. But how then can Christ's spouse be said to be undefiled, and to have no spot in her ?

APPLICATION

First I infer from hence that mankind, or all men and women naturally are **1 Inference.** blind and wofully ignorant of God's righteousness, in that they go about to establish their own, as the Jews of old did, Rom. x. 3 ; they think by amending their ways, by their faith, repentance, and reformation of life ; by their prayers, tears, and good deeds, to be accepted and justified with God ; which, alas, all they who so do, (i.e.,) rest upon these things, or that trust to these duties, or thus seek to piece their old garment ; they will certainly perish for ever, as the Jews did.

2. Yet let none conclude, that I hereby discourage any persons from en- **2 Inference.** deavouring after a reformation of life, or to amend their lives ; no, God forbid ; the light of natural conscience doth excite all who hearkens unto it, to cast off all acts of sin, and to live sober and moral lives, as well as the word of God presses this upon their consciences. But the purport of what I have laboured to do, is to take all men off from resting upon, or trusting unto such amendment of life for justification, or salvation : nay, and to show the danger such are in, who think to piece and patch their old garment by holy and religious duties, or inherent righteousness, or in joining their own works, faith and obedience, with Christ's merits, or by walking up to the gospel rule as a new and mild law of evangelical holiness.

3. We also infer, that new obedience, and a holy conversation, though it be **3 Inference.** part of our sanctification, yet it is no part of our justification ; and that all such that differ from us here, do but go about to patch the old garment, though it be done by the assistance of grace, or the Spirit of God.

4. Moreover we infer, that justification and sanctification are two distinct **4 Inference.** things, and ought not to be confounded together ; and that sanctification as a garment may be amended, or become more perfect ; but that justification is always one and the same, and is complete ; it being the perfect righteousness of Jesus Christ imputed to all that do believe.

5, That for any to trust to a reformed life, &c., is nothing else than for **Information.** a man to endeavour to piece his old garment, as the Pharisees did ; and that no duties, as prayer, givings alms, fasting, and the like, can render any man to be in a good condition, or in a saved state. Because his own personal righteousness cannot satisfy the justice of God, for the sins he committed in times past, nor can he live (let him do his utmost) without sin, for the time to come : by which means it follows, that all he doth, the justice and holiness of God, and his just and righteous law will find so much sin and filth to cleave unto him, that God will abhor him and all his righteousness, and condemn him to everlasting flames. Besides, it is to mix God's pure gold with the sinner's filthy dross ; or to sow Christ's glorious robe of righteousness to his filthy rags, or to put a choice jewel on a swine's snout.

6. By way of exhortation, sinners, be persuaded to cast off, and throw **Exhort.** away all your own righteousness, in point of justification, that so you may be clothed with the whole, perfect, and complete garment of Christ's righteousness.

You must come naked to Jesus Christ : " And knowest not that thou art poor, miserable, wretched, and naked," Rev. iii. 17. Some pride it in their own old and filthy rags, as Laodicea did, and think they want nothing, but will trust to their duties, prayers, and repentance, faith and reformation of life ; and wherein these seem to be defective, they will fly to Christ, to make up that which is wanting.

1. Direction. Study the nature of God, consider his infinite holiness and **Direction.** justice, though he be gracious, merciful, &c., yet " he will by no means clear the guilty," Exod. xxxiv. 6.

2. Study the purity of God's law, that condemns all to eternal vengeance who are not clothed with a perfect and sinless righteousness.

3. Study to understand the end and design of Christ in his taking our nature on him, being made of a woman, made under the law ; and in his perfect obedience to the law, and bearing the penalty or punishment due to us for our breaking of it, as our blessed head, and Representative.

4. Attend upon the preaching of the gospel : " For therein is the righteousness of God revealed," Rom. i. 17, and by it is faith wrought.

Comfort.   For comfort and consolation to you, that have seen all your own righteousness as old rotten rags, and have cast it away, and count it but dung that you may win Christ. O happy souls ! blessed are your eyes ! for you see. O how richly are you clothed, what a noble robe have you on, the hardest duties to you are easy.   You act out of love, knowing you are accepted in Christ, and always are in a safe state, being ever justified ; you shall not be found naked, now nor at death, or in the judgment-day, nor to eternity. For in a righteousness excelling that of the holy angels you shall shine for evermore, Amen.

12. THE NEW WINE

Neither do men put new wine into old bottles.—Matt. ix. 17.

3 Predic,   I CLOSED with the former part of this parable the last time.
Decemb.
19. 1697.   There is one proposition I purpose to open from the latter, and so conclude
                with both, viz.

Doct.   The heart of man must be made new, or there is an absolute necessity of regeneration, before any person can receive the wine of true spiritual consolation.

1.   I shall prove it.

2.   I shall apply it.

My brethren, as sin brought a change upon mankind in Adam, from that state they were in by creation, so must a change pass upon all that would be saved from that state of corruption, in which naturally all remain, by reason of the fall.

A two-fold   1. A relative change.
change pass-
eth on belie-   2. A real change.
vers.   The first is a change of state.

The second is a change of heart, or disposition.

The first is made in justification.

The second is made in, and by regeneration.

It is this change I am to speak to, and open, it being that which our Lord (as I conceive) doth here refer to.

And though the first of these, viz., the relative change, may precede in order of nature, yet not in order of time.   For a person as soon as he is in a justified state, he is at that very instant of time also regenerated.

But to proceed to prove the proposition, that there is an absolute necessity that the heart of man be new made.

I.   In respect of Gospel revelation, (God's word I mean) fully shows this must be ; " Marvel not that I say unto thee, that ye must be born again," John iii. 7.   Ye must, ye that are Jews, ye doctors and masters in Israel, ye that are sober and religious persons, ye that pray, fast, give alms, pay tithes, ye that are legally righteous, and learned men, ye must be born again as well as pagans, publicans and harlots, or profane persons. " Verily, I say unto you, except a man be born again he cannot see the kingdom of God," John iii. 3. There is no obtaining the kingdom of heaven without the new birth, or a spiritual and saving renovation of the whole man, soul and body.

II.   This is the unchangeable decree of God, as it is revealed in the Gospel. " Therefore if any man be in Christ, he is a new creature," 2 Cor. v. 17, or of the new creation, which, as our annotators observe, argues the greatest change imaginable, and such a one can be wrought in the soul by no other power than the almighty power of God.

Old things are passed away, old affections, passions, notions, &c. He hath the same soul, but new qualities, new apprehensions, and new light in his understanding, new desires, new inclinations, in his will, new thoughts, counsels, and designs, as well as he hath got new clothing, a new robe of righteousness. What signifieth (as if our Saviour should say) all those things which the Pharisees do ? though they pray oft, &c., will this avail them any thing, whilst they are in a state of nature, and their hearts are carnal, nay, like old broken bottles ? the wine of heavenly consolation my Father will not put into such men's hearts, he hath decreed that all that are saved shall be regenerated.

III.   The carnal heart of man must be changed or new made, because until then it cannot hold the new wine, should God put it in, it would all run out, (to follow the meta- phor ;) what saith the apostle, " The natural man receiveth not the things of God ; nei- ther can he perceive them, because they are spiritually discerned," 1 Cor. ii. 14. He cannot receive them, because his heart is full of other things, full of sin and filthiness; which like pitch cleaves to the bottle, but put in pure water or wine, it will run all out. The carnal heart is like a sieve which will hold chaff or bran, but it will hold no water or wine.

The heart of a sinner is leaky, like a broken vessel, it is no proper receptacle for spiri- tual things.

IV.   Wisdom teacheth men not to put choice wine into a cracked or broken bottle ; so the wisdom of God is such that he will not put his costly and most precious new wine into an unrenewed heart, he will not lose it ; for should he do so, both the bottle and wine would perish ; for, as I hinted in the explication, if it was possible for grace to be put into a car- nal heart, and the heart not changed thereby, grace itself would be utterly lost, as wine put into a sieve or broken bottle. Though it is true, the Holy Spirit is infused into a sinner's heart, but at that very instant that it is infused or put into the soul of a sinner, it works a blessed change therein ; and so it retains the wine of heavenly consolation.

V.   The heart of man must be new made, or changed, because the carnal heart cannot please God, nor be subject to the law of God. Brethren, the state of sin is a state of en- mity against God ; will a prince take a swine into his embraces, or will he hang pearls or diamonds upon a filthy stinking old garment ?   No sure, no more will Christ take a vile rebellious and filthy sinner into his spiritual embraces ; now this cursed enmity which is in the sinner's heart naturally, cannot be removed till the heart is changed or new made.

1.   True, the nature of men may be restrained from acts of gross wickedness by com- mon grace, or by the prosecution of severe human laws, or by the terrors of God's divine law ; but yet neither of these can change their hearts.

2.   Neither can good education do it.   For no doubt but Ishmael had as good educa- tion as Isaac ;   certainly Abraham was not wanting in his duty to him, what saith the blessed God concerning him ?   " I know him that he will command his children and his household after him, and they shall keep the way of the Lord," &c. Gen. xviii. 19.

Yet for all this his son Ishmael was an ungodly child, and one that scoffed at religion and true piety.   So no doubt but Esau had as good education as Jacob, Isaac gave him the same good counsel and instruction which he gave to Jacob ;   but Esau still continued a profane person notwithstanding, and retained his old evil nature and disposition still, and became no new man.   Education may restrain from acts of sin, but cannot change the heart from the love of sin.

VI.   The heart of man must be new made, or changed, because there is in all unre- newed persons, an unfitness, an unwillingness, and an utter inability to do any thing that is truly and spiritually good.

1.   There is in them an unfitness ; as a fool or ignorant man is unfit to be made a judge, so a man that knows not God is unfit to judge of spiritual things, or to be trusted with them, or to have communion with him ; he knows not what they are, he cannot re- lish or favour the things of the Spirit, " for they are foolishness unto him," 1 Cor. ii. 14.

2.   There is an unwillingness in all unrenewed persons to receive these spiritual things. A natural man is like a wild ass-colt.   " Vain man would be wise, though man be born like a wild ass's colt," Job. xii. 12. He is born so, it is natural, and hereditary, and there- fore common to all men ; they are not only ignorant and weak, but also wilful, stubborn, heady, and rebellious.

No beast is more wild and brutish than man in respect of spiritual things, until he is changed. A man, saith Mr. Caryl on Job, cap. 11, 12, is like a beast, for wantonness, lust, and vanity.   And in regard of stubbornness, every wicked man is " a son of Belial, a son without a yoke ; " " Ye will not come to me that ye might have life," John v. 40. You are unwilling, you have no will this way, to be saved in believing in me, to cleave to me, to build all your hopes of heaven upon me ; no, you have other ways, you think to be saved by your reading the law, and conforming your lives to the external precepts of that, your hearts are carnal, your wills are rebellious ; now from hence it is that the heart must be changed.

3.   There is in all men naturally not only an unwillingness to that which is spiritually good, but also an utter inability or want of power ; and this must needs be so.

1.   Because man before grace is spiritually dead ; can a dead man act or do any natural or moral acts ? You will say, no, that is impossible; even so no man that is spiritually dead can perform any true spiritual acts of obedience unto God. True, he may do that which is naturally and morally good, but not that which is spiritually good. "You hath he quickened that were dead in sins and trespasses," Eph. ii. 1, 2, 3. Beloved, every creature acts according to that principle he hath, or according to his nature.

As a mere sensitive creature acts only according to sense, and rational creatures according to mere rational principles. Hence it is some men in these days, because they have received no higher principles, do decry all revealed religion, and are for no other than mere natural religion, which they can comprehend by their natural reason.

But now a true spiritual man acts and doth every thing by that spiritual vital principle he hath received ; he goes out of himself by acts of faith, and believes that which he cannot comprehend by mere natural reason.

2.   Can a blind man judge of colours, or see the beauty of an object to delight in it ? Or can a swine delight in the glory of a king's palace ? All men naturally are in a spiritual sense, blind, and cannot see the beauty of Christ, to fall in love with him ; they can see no beauty in holiness; no, it is good for nought in their sight ; and as a dead man must be quickened before he can breathe, hear, see, act, and walk ; so must a sinner be spiritually quickened before he hath any spiritual power or ability to do anything that is spiritually good. "Without me you can do nothing," John xv. 5 ; that is, without union with me, or life from me.

VII. Because (as it appeareth from hence,) all men are naturally, wholly depraved and corrupted, like cracked and broken bottles, there is no amending of them, they must (as you heard) be melted down and new made ; their understanding is darkened, nay, they are darkness. "Ye that were sometimes darkness," Ephes. v. 8 ; darkness in the abstract. Their wills rebellious, their affections carnal, "Their minds and consciences are defiled," Tit. i. 15. Now as there is an universal depravation, so there must be an universal renovation.

VIII. Because God doth not, will not, nay, cannot accept of any service but what is spiritual. "God is a Spirit," John iv. 24. Service therefore must be suited or proportioned to his holy nature and being. "We must pray in the Spirit, and sing in and with the Spirit, not only with our spirits, but also with the Spirit of God. Therefore it followeth that we must be spiritual persons, this must be before we can perform spiritual service or taste of spiritual comforts. Some of the kings of Judea did that which was right in the sight of God, but not with perfect hearts ; they did it not from a renewed heart, and so not in sincerity of heart. It was right as to the matter of it, i. e., it was that which God commanded, but not performed from right principles, and also not to a right end. "They have not cried to me with their hearts, when they howled on their beds," Hos. vii. 14. The prayers of unrenewed persons is but as the howling of a dog, in the ears of God, hence said to be an abomination unto him.

IX. The heart of man must be made new, because God accepteth of no service but what is done freely, voluntarily, and not by the mere force of natural conscience, or for fear of hell. But now the old heart hath in it an aversion to any thing that is spiritually good ; none act freely (as well as they act not in love to God, and to glorify him,) but such only who have received a new heart. Holy duties are a great burthen to an unsanctified spirit ; a carnal heart can find no sweetness in divine consolations. "What fellowship hath light with darkness ?" Do but call to mind what conceptions you had of the things of God before your conversion ; was the word sweet to you ? Did you delight in prayer, or in heavenly communication, or were not such things rather bitter and unpleasant to you ? Carnal men love not to hear of spiritual converse or discourse, therefore their hearts must be changed.

X. Because the old heart, or the hearts of all men unrenewed, are full of hypocrisy ; they may profess religion, but it is from false principles, and to wrong ends. Self is in the bottom of all. "Ye fasted not to me, even to me, saith the Lord."

Read Charnock on regeneration.

Brethren, there is an artificial, as well as a natural motion. Take off the weights of a clock, and it will presently stand still. So if a mere natural man or a hypocrite, loses his ends in his profession of religion, he presently draws back or grows cold and heartless; but a natural motion continues or abides, because of that life which is the cause of its moving; but so it is not with an artificial motion; the sole of your shoe will soon wear out, but so will not the sole of your foot; no, but they will grow more hard every day if you go directly upon them, because the one is artificial, and the other natural. " The righteous shall hold on his way, and he that hath clean hands, shall grow stronger and stronger," Job xvi. 9. But all unconverted persons, or mere natural men, will either die in hypocrisy, or perish in apostacy. Though they seem never so zealous for God, and religion, " They do all to be seen of men," Matt. xxiii. 5.

XI. Because, until a man is renewed, they can take no delight in God, nor can God take delight in them; they are only earthly, have earthly and carnal hearts, and therefore earthly and sensual things are their chiefest delight. "They that are after the flesh, mind the things of the flesh," Rom. viii. 5. Either they mind such things that are absolutely evil, as "the lusts of the flesh," Gal. v. 19—21; or else such things as are occasionally evil, as riches, honours, pleasures, &c. These are the things of the flesh, and such things as all carnal and unregenerate persons, favour, affect, and take delight in. And it is only the new nature, the renewed heart, that makes the soul to delight in God as the chief good. Interest in God, adoption and regeneration, go always together in the same subject; he that is a child of God, hath the image of God stamped upon his soul. I say, it is the new heart only, which is capable to enjoy communion with God; a likeness in nature is a spring of fellowship. A man will never espouse a beast, as we have a parable, " Birds of a feather will flock together."

XII. And as it is thus absolutely necessary (in respect to a state of grace,) that the heart be made new; so, as revered Charnock shows, it is also in respect to a state of glory; for as an unsanctified, or an unrenewed person can take no delight in God, or find any consolation in Christ in this world, having no grace; so they could not find any joy, or comfort, were they in heaven, for heaven is no place of sensual pleasure. What should carnal men do in heaven? They cannot taste of the joys that are there, because they are all spiritual, and their hearts are carnal; they love not God, nor the things of God, while they are here on earth, nor the saints and people of God, their company is hateful to them, their heavenly converse is grievous to such, and death will not change their hearts; and as they die in a state of enmity against God, so that enmity will evermore remain in them. But, brethren, I do not say that the new nature, or new heart, doth give us a title to heaven; no, it is Christ's righteousness alone that is our title to glory above; but it is regeneration which gives us a meetness for it. " Who hath made us meet to be partakers of the inheritance of the saints in light," Col. i. 12. And, as without this new heart, and new nature, heaven could be no heaven to us; so no unrenewed person can perform, or discharge the duties of heaven, as the same author excellently shows.

1. They cannot attend upon God, who is holy; they cannot come near him, but be consumed, for unto such, God is as a consuming fire. God's presence would be very terrible to such.

2. They cannot contemplate on God, nor be ravished with the glory of his holiness, grace, and infinite goodness.

3. They cannot love God, nor make him the object of their affections. Love is a grace that remains for ever.

4. Nor can they sing the praises of God for what they received from him while on earth; the song of the saints will be sweet in remembrance of his redeeming love, and regenerating grace and love, but they never knew what either of these things were, and therefore cannot sing that song.

5. They cannot love the saints in heaven (were they there) who are all made perfect in holiness; evident it is, that wicked men hate the saints of God here, because of their holiness, and of that likeness there is in them to God; and if this makes the ungodly contemn the saints, who do but in part resemble the Holy God, while here; how much more would they hate them, were it possible for them to be with those glorified saints in heaven, who are all made completely perfect in holiness.

APPLICATION

1. We infer from hence, that the ignorance of men is exceeding great, about the nature and excellency of the new birth. They, alas! know not what it is, but are ready to say

with Nicodemus, "How can these things be?" John iii. 9.   The natural man receiveth not the things of God.

2.   We infer, that saving and regenerating grace is of infinite worth and value.   What must that cause be which hath such most blessed and glorious effects? that is precious seed which produceth such excellent fruit.

3.   We also infer, that all those duties, as prayer, fasting, &c, which many (like the Pharisees) rest upon, and trust in, are but vain and fruitless things; for if the duties and inherent holiness of sanctified persons, are comparatively but as dung, what are the duties and pretended righteousness of such who were never regenerated?   "No man putteth new wine into old bottles."   God will not put in the wine of heavenly joy and consolation into carnal and unrenewed hearts.

4.   Moreover, how fruitless and insufficient is all that speculative knowledge which men unrenewed have attained.   Knowledge puffs up: what is human learning, or arts and sciences, which those have and glory in, who never knew the nature and power of the new-birth?   Are such men fit to be preachers of the Gospel?   Can they open the nature of regeneration by experience, who are wholly ignorant of it, or know not what it is?

5.   How blind are they that take reformation for regeneration; who think, because a profane man hath left his swearing, his drunkenness, his whoring, cheating, or thieving, &c.; and now lives a sober life, therefore he is a new creature.   Brethren, a man may be reformed that is not renewed, though a man can be renewed but he is reformed? a man may have a changed life, that hath not a changed heart; he may with king Saul, become another man, but not become a new man.

6.   This also shows that morality can save no person.   The heathen (many of them I mean,) were excellent moralists, and multitudes amongst us, think their state is happy upon this account, and yet are in the gall of bitterness.

7.   Moreover we infer, that all such who rest on a presumptuous faith, who boast that they rely on Christ, trust in the righteousness of Christ, and yet were never changed or born again, but are under the delusion of the devil, and in a fearful condition.

8.   Also what signifies all that an unrenewed person doth, though he reads, prays, is baptized, breaks bread with God's people, and is called a saint? alas, perish he must for all this, if he be not born again.

II.   Examine and try yourselves; are you such who have got the new wine in new bottles?   Are you such who have passed through the pangs of the new birth?   What hatred have you of sin, as it is sin?   What love have you of true godliness?   Can you taste how sweet pardon of sin and peace with God if?   Is this world as a wilderness to you, are you dead to it?   Are the riches of grace prized by you above gold and silver? Are your hearts changed, and lives changed?   What light is there in your understandings? are your wills bowed to the will of God, and to a loving and liking of the work of holiness, as well as to a loving the reward of holiness?   Are your affections changed, your desires, your fears, your passions? what object doth your love run out to?

III.   You that find that you have got new hearts, what cause of joy, what consolation may this administer unto you!   True, you may be born again, and yet for some time may not know it; all have not arrived to the faith of assurance; yet O how sweet and comfortable is it to know we are in Christ, and born of God.

1.   Such who have new hearts, new bottles, shall have the new wine poured into them, and they shall taste how sweet and pleasant it is first or last; and such will not say the old wine of earthly comforts is best, but rather look upon it as ditch or kennel water. Brethren, because you are children, you shall have the best things of your Father's house; you shall be clothed as king's children, and be fed as king's children.

2.   Moreover, being children, you are heirs; " if children, then heirs, heirs of God, and joint heirs with Christ," Rom. viii. 17.

3.   And being children, begotten and born of God, you shall ever be children; for you know we must be children of such parents, and have their nature who begot us; we cannot cease being their children; believers may be disobedient children, and break his laws, &c.   But if so, he will but chasten us, as a father; we shall be his children still; children we must be and in his love, for this relation will abide for ever.

Lastly, One word of exhortation, and I have done.

1.   Bless God for the gospel, you that are sinners, and for the ministration thereof; for by preaching God is pleased to sow that seed, by which your hearts may be renewed; the word of God is the seed of regeneration.   I do not say the bare word is the seed; no, but

as the Spirit does accompany the word : " being born again, not of corruptible seed, but of incorruptible, by the word that liveth and abideth for ever," 1 Pet. i. 23.

Where the gospel comes in word only, there no change is wrought; but there is, my brethren, a divine power that goes along with the gospel, where it is made effectual to any poor soul.

2. Highly honour and esteem the Holy Spirit, for it is by his special agency alone that regeneration is wrought; hence it is said, that believers are " born of the Spirit," John iii. 5, 6 ; and so are Spirit, or spiritual.

3. Attend daily upon the word, neglect no opportunity, because you know not when, whether by this, or by that sermon, the Spirit may work upon your souls : " The wind blows where it listeth," John iii. 8; so the Holy Spirit is a free agent, and works when and how he pleaseth.

4. Cry mightily to God to send the Spirit to work in, and by the word on your souls; and be sure, see you do not grieve nor quench the Holy Spirit of God, nor weary out the Holy Spirit.   God told the old world,   " That his Spirit should not always strive with man," Gen. vi. 3.

5. Do not trust to your own power, or once think you can become new creatures when you please ; no, no, doth the child begotten in the womb contribute anything to its own being, or to its conception ?   O abominate the evil notion of free-will, and strive to exalt God's free-grace.

C A U T I O N.

Take heed of the notion that some promote, i. e., as if your state may be good, or you under a relative change, that have not passed under a real change; for know assuredly, you remain children of wrath, until you have the Spirit infused into your souls, and remain condemned in the first Adam.   Nay, and the Holy Spirit will convince you this is your condition, if ever he thoroughly works and operates in your hearts.   The Holy Ghost convinceth all whom he takes hold of, that their state is bad and miserable before special vocation.   O therefore wait for the Spirit, who both works conviction and regeneration; to whom with the Father, and the Son, be glory for evermore. Amen.

13. THE SOWER

I

And he spake many things unto them in parables, saying, Behold a sower went forth to sow.
—Matt. xiii. 3,—23.

My Brethren, in the opening of this parable, I shall proceed in that method   The year of which I purpose to take in speaking generally unto them all, viz.   Christ's life, 31.

First, Give an account of the main design of our blessed Lord, in his speaking of this parable, or give the scope thereof.

Secondly, explain (according to what our Saviour himself hath done) every part thereof.

1. More generally.

2. More partcularly, open some things which our Lord hath not.

Thirdly, I shall raise some propositions, or points of doctrine from the chief or principal parts, and prosecute them in my usual method with the necessary improvements.

First, One great design of this parable (as I conceive), is to show the ex-   The scope cellent nature of the word of God, in that it is the seed of all grace in the   of the para- hand of the Spirit; or as it is by the influences of the Spirit, received into an   ble. heart prepared by the convictions of the Holy Ghost.

Secondly, (Considering the great multitudes that were gathered together to hear the word of God at that time, as the second verse shows) It is evident, that one   Year of reason or main design of Christ's speaking this parable, was to convince them,   Christ's that it is not enough or sufficient to hear the word of God preached, but that   ministry. many may hear it, who are never effectually wrought upon by it, but shall eternally perish.

Thirdly, It might be the design of our Saviour, also hereby to show, that but few comparatively, prove right hearers of the word.   Three sorts of ground proving bad, and only but one in four good ground ; intimating, but very few hearers have their hearts broken up, or prepared by the convictions of the Holy Spirit, to receive Jesus Christ.

Fourthly, Another main design of this parable, might be to show that grace is not of ourselves, or from nature; but that is a supernatural work or blessing flowing from the Lord Jesus Christ. The heart must be first dug up, or be ploughed up by the Holy Ghost, that it may become like good tillage, before the seed of the word will take root and bring forth fruit unto perfection, which three sorts of hearers never experience.

The year of Christ's ministry, 2.

Fifthly, Also it might be to discover the cause of men's damnation, or of their final apostacy, viz., Because their hearts were never right with God.

Sixthly, Also to discover that some men who never were sincere or upright Christians, might nevertheless go very far in a profession of the gospel, as is signified by the stony and thorny ground. So that most evident it is, that this blessed parable gives us to understand the different effect, or success the preaching of the gospel hath upon those that hear it. So much as to the design and scope of the parable.

The parts opened.

Secondly, Take our Lord's general exposition of the several parts of the parable. For he, upon the desire, and humble request of his disciples, opened it.

" Hear ye the parable of the sower," ver. 18. Mark addeth somewhat more, which seems to be in the nature of a gentle reproof: " Know ye not this parable, how then will ye know all parables ?" Mark iv. 13. That is, the sense and meaning of them; considering that God hath graciously opened your eyes, or given you to understand the mysteries of the kingdom of heaven; but if it be so, you as yet understand it not; hear and consider, that I by this parable, do discover unto you the different effects the preaching of the gospel or word of God hath upon the hearts of the sons of men.

" A sower went out to sow," ver. 3. The sower is the Son of Man; his word it is, " Thou hast the words of everlasting life," John vi. 68. The Gospel is not the word of men, but the word of God. But more comprehensively, the faithful ministers of the gospel; they that preach the word, may be said to sow the seed, but indeed it is our Lord Jesus that is more properly the sower; he it is that sows the seed of the word by them, they are but Christ's seedsmen.

" And when he sowed, some fell by the way-side, and the fowls came and devoured them up," ver. 4. Our Saviour explaineth this: " When any one heareth the word of the kingdom, and understandeth it not, then cometh the wicked one, and catcheth away that which is sown in his heart; this is he which received the seed by the way-side," ver. 19. By the wicked one is meant the devil.

Highway-side-ground.

Doct. Satan is the wicked one, or is called the wicked one.

1. By way of eminency, Satan is that wicked one, or may be so called, because he hath utterly lost his original purity, or holy nature.

2. Because he is universally wicked, filthy, and abominable, and so remains, and will abide for ever.

3. Because all wickedness is originally from the devil, as all holiness is from God.

4. Because the devil continually tempteth, enticeth, or draws men to commit wickedness; from these reasons, and many others, Satan may be called the wicked one, 1 John v. 18, in whom all ungodly sinners are said to lie. The gospel is called the word of the kingdom, Mat. xiii. 19, because it is the instrument by which Christ raiseth up his spiritual church, or kingdom in this world; or bringeth men and women into his kingdom on earth, and also prepareth them for the kingdom of glory. The seed is the word of God. By the several sorts of ground is meant the several sorts of hearers, or the natural state of their hearts.

" And some fell upon stony places, where they had not much earth, and forthwith they sprung up, because they had no deepness of earth; and when the sun was up they were scorched, and because they had no root they withered away," ver. 5, 6. What Matthew calls stony ground, Luke calls a rock, Luke viii. 13. Our blessed Saviour explaineth this in ver. 20, 21. " But he that receiveth the seed into stony places, is the same which heareth the word, and anon with joy receiveth it. Yet hath he no root in himself, but endureth for awhile; for when tribulation or persecution ariseth because of the word, by and by he is offended," Luke viii. 13. By the sun rising up, &c., our Saviour shows is meant tribulation or persecution, which Luke calleth a time of temptation, because such times are times of great trials or temptations, as shall (God willing) be opened, when I come more particularly to this sort of ground. Our Lord showeth two causes of such hearers falling away.

1. Internal.

2. External.

And the former (as our worthy annotators show) is the cause of the latter: by " not having depth of earth," and so wanting root, &c., I conceive is meant the want of thorough conviction; their rocky or stony hearts were never broken by the hammer of the word; and by wanting root, no doubt is meant a principle of true grace in their hearts, which is elsewhere called the " root of the matter," Job xix. 28. They never were savingly united to Jesus Christ, they had not the true faith of God's elect, nor ever sincerely loved the Lord Jesus, they were never born of God, because the seed remained not in them. There was some seeming work began upon them, 1 John iii. 9; perhaps their affections might be stirred up with some flashes or warmth, and transient joy, but it was but like a land flood; they had self in their eye in all they did, either self-interest, self-honour, &c., they could not lose their estates, liberty, and lives, for the sake of Jesus Christ.

" And some fell among thorns, and the thorns sprang up and choked them," ver. 7.

Our Lord opened this part of the parable also, ver. 22, " He also that receiveth seed amongst the thorns is he that heareth the word, and the cares of this life, and the deceitfulness of riches choke the word, and he becometh unfruitful." Mark adds, " And the lusts of other things entering, choke the word," Mark iv. 19. Luke saith, " And that which fell among thorns are they, which when they have heard, go forth, are choked with cares, and riches, and pleasures of this life, and bring forth no fruit unto perfection," Luke viii. 14.

What is meant by thorns, or by the cares of this life, and by the deceitfulness of riches, I shall endeavour to open more particularly when I come to speak to this sort of ground, or hearers of the word; these no doubt went a great way, and made a profession of the gospel, were church-members, or not profane in their lives and conversations; but seemed to bid fair for the kingdom of heaven, like as the foolish virgins did. They might for a great while attend upon the word, and ordinances of Christ; and seem devout persons, but their hearts were never crucified to the love of this world.

" But other fell into good ground, and brought forth fruit, some an hundred-fold, some sixty-fold, and some thirty-fold. Who hath ears to hear, let him hear," ver. 8, 9, 10.

See our Saviour's general exposition of the good ground, ver. 23; " But he that received seed into the good ground, is he that heareth the word and understandeth it, which also beareth fruit, and bringeth forth some an hundred-fold, some sixty, and some thirty." Luke addeth, " But that on the good ground are they which in an honest and good heart having heard the word, keep it, and being forth fruit with patience," Luke viii. 15.

Here an objection might be made.

Obj. How can any man before grace is infused, be said to be good? are not all the hearts of men evil naturally?

Ans. I told you in the introduction the last time, that no parable ought to be strained beyond the analogy of faith. Therefore here is more included than is expressed. This must be received as an undeniable truth, that no man naturally can be said to have a good and honest heart. " All are gone out of the way, there is none righteous, no not one. There is none that understandeth, there is none that seeketh after God," Rom. iii. 11, 12. " All are dead in sins and trespasses, all (even the elect themselves) by nature are children of wrath as others," Eph. ii. 1, 2, 3.

Therefore we are to understand, that what one parable, or simile, or place of Scripture, doth not so fully open or explain, another doth.

2. It is God's grace, or the work of his Spirit only, which makes the heart good; it is he that gives this good understanding. The heart is evil and not good, until it is changed or new made; which none can do but God himself. He therefore hath promised " to take away the heart of stone, and to give a heart of flesh;" all have rocky, stony, and thorny hearts by nature, and so abide, until they are new made.

3. There is a two-fold work of the Spirit. (1.) A work of conviction, this is called " a ploughing up the fallow ground of our hearts," Hos. x. 12.

(2.) A work of renovation, and of sanctification; and both these works of the Spirit tend to the making the heart good; though in order of nature the first passes on the soul before the second.

It appears from this parable, that all believers or sincere Christians do not bring forth the like quantity of fruit to God; some bring forth a hundred, some sixty, and some but thirty-fold, yet all is fruit of the same nature or quality. All have not received the same gifts, the same number of talents, nor the same degree of grace; all are not in the same places, offices, and stations in the church; and so are not in a capacity to bring forth fruit (as to the degree) either of profit to the church (or the members thereof,) nor to the souls of men, and to the glory of God.

2. All have not the same time allowed unto them to continue in this world; the same length of time to grow and to do service for God, and therefore it is not to be expected all should bring forth the same quantity or measure of spiritual fruit.

So much as to the more general exposition of this parable.

I shall proceed to a more particular opening and explication of this parable.

" A Sower went out to sow."

There are three things to be noted in the words.

1. The agent, a sower, Jesus Christ.

2. His action, he went forth.

3. His design, purpose, or end in going forth, viz., to sow his seed.

1. Note, That the hearts of men and women are Christ's spiritual hus-
The hearts
of men
Christ's
husbandry. bandry. The whole world is his, he hath power to dispose of all creatures as he pleaseth, either to till, plough, manure; and sow every sort of ground, or to let what part of mankind to lie barren, untilled, and unsown, as seemeth good in his sight; " The earth is the Lord's, and the fulness thereof." An husbandman may do what he will with his own land.

Quest. But some may say, Are not mimisters sowers? what difference is there between Christ's sowing, and ministers sowing the seed of the word?

1. Ans. I answer, Jesus Christ is the principal sower, the master sower; ministers are his servants, who have the honour to be " Workers together with him," 2 Cor. vi. 1: " If we have sown unto you spiritual things," &c., 1 Cor. ix. 11.

2. Christ sows his own by creation, considered as God; his by redemption and purchase, considered as Mediator, and by the free donation of the Father, " knowing the Father had given all things into his hand," John xiii. 3. Ministers themselves are his, their hearts are Christ's tillage, he sows the seed of grace in them, they are not their own. Therefore the ground that they sow is none of theirs; also Jesus Christ sows his own seed; a sower went forth to sow his seed. Ministers have no seed of their own, their doctrine, and the words which they preach, is the word of Christ.

3. Christ is a most wise and skilful Sower, he hath a perfect knowledge of all sorts of ground. So have not his ministers; they know not men's hearts.

4. Christ is a universal Sower; all the seed of the word that ever was sown, was sown by him. A minister sows but a small quantity of seed, and but on a little ground.

5. Jesus Christ is an efficacious Sower; he can speak to men's hearts, and cause the seed which he sows to take root, and bring forth fruit. But so cannot a minister. Christ can cause the rain to fall upon the seed that he sows; nay, he is the Sun of righteousness, that must and doth shine upon the souls of men, to cause the seed to grow: " Thou blessest the bud of the earth, thou crownest the year with goodness, and thy paths drop fatness," Psal. lxv. 16. But ministers can do none of this; what says the apostle? " Paul may plant, and Apollos water, but God gives the increase," 1 Cor. iii. 6.

II. We have the action of this sower: " A sower went forth to sow."

Brethren, Jesus Christ may be said to go forth to sow three manner of ways.

1. In his own person, thus he went forth to preach (as soon as he was baptized) or to sow the seed of his word in Judea, Jerusalem, and all the regions round about.

2. In the ministry of his servants Christ may be said to go forth to sow, (for as he is said to baptize when his disciples did it by his authority) so he may be said to preach, or sow the seed of the gospel, when his ministers do it in his name, in his stead, or by his authority, John iv. 1, 2.

3. He may be said to go forth to sow his seed by his Spirit, and this only is his more effectual and efficacious way: the seed never takes root until it is thus sown in the heart; for though the word is called the seed, yet doubtless the Spirit more properly or primarily is the seed; seeing all the power, virtue, and efficacy of the word, lies in the Holy Spirit; the gospel coming to a sinner in word only, never works a change, no man is born again by the word without the Spirit accompanies it.

III. Consider the end and purpose of the sower sowing his seed, which is, the conversion of sinners by preaching the Gospel: " He began to preach, saying, repent and believe he Gospel," Mark i. 15; and this is his design by employing of his servants, or in sowing the seed, or in preaching the Gospel. His seed, not cunning devised fables, not the traditions of men, not decrees and canons of general counsels, but his own holy and heavenly doctrine: " My doctrine is not mine, but his that sent me," John vii. 16: Christ received his seed, (i.e.,) his doctrine from his Father; " The things that I have heard of my Father, those speak I in the world," John viii. 26.

Doct. 1. The preaching of the word is the sowing of the divine seed in the hearts of men ; or as the word is compared to seed, so the preaching of it is the sowing of that seed, and ministers are Christ's seeds-men. For Minister Christ's seedsmen.

1. They like seeds-men must sow the seed in its proper season, as Christ himself did ; " I must work the work of him that sent me, while it is day,"—" Now is the accepted time." 2 Cor. vi. 2.

2. They must sow their seed, let it be what weather it will, a time of peace, or a time of persecution.

3. They must sow no seed of their own, but what is Christ's seed, his doctrine ; " Thou shalt not sow thy vineyard with divers sorts of seed," Deut. xxii. 9.

4. Ministers must sow or preach all Christ's seed : as he showed them all things he had received of the Father, so they must preach the whole counsel of God.

5. Constantly, as long as the seed-time lasteth : " In the morning sow thy seed, and in the evening withhold not thine hand," Eccl. xi. 6.

6. They sow, but the whole success is of God, and though they see but little fruit, yet they must preach.

Secondly. I shall show you, why the word is compared to seed. Why the Word is compared to seed.

1. Seed springs not out of the ground naturally : no, but before it can grow and bring forth fruit, it must be sowed ; for naturally no ground brings forth wheat, barley, herbs, or choice flowers, until it is first sown, or planted. So mankind can bring forth no spiritual or sacred fruit unto God, before they sit under the word, or have thee seed of grace infused, or sown in their hearts ; it is true, nature improved may produce that which is naturally and morally good ; but not that which is truly spiritually good ; the heart must be made good, before the fruit can be good : " A corrupt tree cannot bear good fruit," Matt. vii. 17. As the earth naturally of itself produceth nothing but weeds, grass, nettles, briers, and thorns ; so all men before grace is sowed or infused into their hearts, bring forth nothing but sin, or the fruits of depraved and corrupt nature, or that which is natural.

Therefore the product of natural conscience, or natural light improved, is not the fruit of divine grace ; much less is it the Christ of God, which the Quakers boldly affirm it is.

2. Seed, let it be of wheat, or barley, or seed of herbs or flowers, or whatsoever else, it is the choicest of each sort respectively.

If it be of wheat, it is the best of wheat ; or if barley, it is the best of barley.

So in like manner the seed of the word, which is called " the incorruptible seed, by which believers are born again," is the best of all seeds ; the word of God, and true grace, is of an excellent nature.

3. Until seed is sown, there will be no increase, the ground must receive it : so the heart of man must take in, or sinners by faith receive the word of Christ, or the choice seed of grace ; or there will be no spiritual increase : as bread feeds no man until he eat it, so Jesus Christ is of no spiritual profit, nor his word efficacious and effectual unto a sinner, until it is by faith received, or Christ spiritually fed upon. " Except ye eat the flesh of the Son of man, and drink his blood, ye have no life in you," John vi. 53.

4. Seed, sometimes which is sown, lies a considerable time in the ground, before it springs up, or visibly appears, it must have time to take root.

Even so and in like manner the Word of God, which is sown in the heart of a sinner, sometimes doth not presently appear, though it be not always so ; for as some ground that is more rich, or by the rain that falls upon it, and the most powerful influences of the sun produceth the visible growth thereof quickly ; so by the divine and more strong and efficacious influences of the Spirit of Christ, some seed sown in some sinners' hearts, presently, or in a very short time, its rooting, its growth appeareth, as it did in those three thousand that Peter preached to, Acts ii. 37, 40, 44.

5. Clods of the earth being not broken, oft-times obstruct or hinder the springing up of seed, or it is from thence it appears not to have taken root so soon as in some other ground ; so likewise through the power of Satan's temptations, or the inward filth and corruption of the heart, the seed of the word is for a time obstructed, or hindered from rooting, and springing up in some souls of men and women.

6. A husbandman observes the proper time and season of sowing his seed : so doth Jesus Christ and his faithful ministers ; " I must work the work of him that sent me, while it is day," John ix. 4. " Behold now is the accepted time, behold now is the day of salvation," 2 Cor. vi. 2. The spiritual seed-time will not last always.

7. Men are not sparing in sowing their seed, but scatter it abroad plentifully, though they expect not that all the seed which is sown, should take root, and bring forth.

So our Lord Jesus plentifully, and in a most gracious manner disperseth the seed of the Word; the Gospel is preached to multitudes, although he knows all the seed which is sown will not take rooting in all sinners' hearts, and bring forth the fruit thereof. Here is but one sort of ground of four, which produceth the desired effects.

8. A husbandman sows his seed on what ground he pleaseth, some he lets lie barren, and never ploughs it up, nor tills or manures it; and who shall blame him if he doth thus?

Christ sows his seed on what ground he pleases. So likewise Jesus Christ is pleased to send his Word and blessed gospel to one nation and people, and not unto another. Some regions of the earth, he lets lie barren, without the knowledge of the gospel, or knowledge of salvation, they never had the word preached unto them. Moreover, many people in those nations, to whom the gospel is sent, never had it preached unto them, in the power and purity of it, but they are left like unto fallow or unploughed and untilled ground: yet who can say unto God, "Why dost thou do thus," Matt. xx. 15? May not I do what I please with my own? As he himself intimateth in another parable; shall he not have the same power and prerogative to do in this matter, as every husbandman hath?

9. No storms nor bad weather hinder a husbandman from sowing his seed. "He that regardeth the wind shall never sow," Eccl. xi. 4.

So and in like manner Christ's ministers must see that they preach the word in season, and out of season, at all times: even in days of persecution as well as in times of peace and liberty.

10. It is observed that the earlier seed is sown, the better it is rooted, and made capable to endure the sharpness of the winter.

So the word, or seed of grace, the sooner, or earlier it is sown in the hearts of young people, and they receive it in the love thereof, they being renewed, and sanctified thereby, even in the flower of their days; the more firmly are they confirmed in the truth, and having longer experience, it tends the better to root them in grace and holiness.

11. And lastly, some seed (as it is showed in this parable) falls on the highway-side, and some on stony and thorny ground: but none but good ground bringeth forth fruit.

So it is with the seed of the word: yet the fault lies not in the seed, nor in the sower; but in the ground, viz., it is from the evil heart, the unbelieving heart, that the seed of the word brings forth no fruit; "the word preached did not profit them, it being not mixed with faith in them that heard it," Heb. iv. 2.

Quest. Why are the hearts of men compared to ground?

Why the hearts of men are compared to ground. Answ. I answer, for many reasons: (1.) Ground is sometimes bought or purchased before the husbandman will manure it. So Jesus Christ bought or purchased all his elect ones, and because he loved and purchased them, therefore he ploughs up the fallow ground of their hearts, tills and sows the seed of grace in their souls.

2. Ground is the proper soil for seed to grow in: so are the hearts of men the proper soil for the seed of the word.

3. Ground nevertheless must be first ploughed up, or be well manured (as hath been hinted) before it is sowed, or the seed will not take root, and for want of this oft-times the seed becomes unprofitable. So likewise must the hearts of men and women be dug or ploughed up by convictions of the Holy Spirit, or be throughly broken by the plough of the gospel, or the seed of grace can take no root. "Break up the fallow ground, sow to yourselves in righteousness, reap in mercy," Hos. x. 12.

Brethren, this one cause, why the highway-side ground, the stony and thorny ground brought forth no fruit to perfection. Had the hearts of all those persons signified hereby, been throughly broken, ploughed up and manured, why might not they have brought forth fruit, as the good ground did? what is it that makes barren, thorny, or stony ground good, which naturally is bad? Is it not that cost and pains which the husbandman taketh in manuring, dunging, &c.? Can the ground make itself better? no surely.

So it is that pains and cost the Lord useth (who is called the good Husbandman) John xv. 1) upon the hearts, the evil and barren hearts of sinners, which makes them good. No man hath any skill or power of his own to change those evil and vicious habits of his own heart: but such is the pride of men naturally, they think they have power of themselves to believe in Christ, to repent, and convert, or turn to God, and so never seek to him, or look unto him to do it. And how just is it in God utterly to leave such creatures unto themselves.

If God therefore did not put forth his almighty power in a way of sovereign grace upon the hearts of some men, he would have no right and lasting fruit from any creatures, but all would remain barren, notwithstanding the sowing the seed, or preaching of the Gospel. Nor is God obliged any more to put forth this power upon all that have the word preached unto them, than he is to send the Gospel into the dark heathen nations of the earth. It is infinite mercy in God he is pleased to make any men's hearts like good ground, since he first made man upright, yea, very good, but he by his many inventions hath made his heart so vile and abominable.

4. Ground is not known of what nature it is, until it be dug or plowed up; it may perhaps seem good to the sight, but when it is broken up, stones, and evil roots, and much nauseous filth appear. *The heart not known until it by ve--tions is plow ed up.*

Even just thus it is with the hearts of men; until God by his Spirit searcheth them and breaks them into pieces, by the powerful operations of his own Spirit, and discovers the filth of them; they alas do not know their own hearts. Those Jews Peter preached to, (Acts ii.) did not know what abominable wretches they were, until they were pricked at the heart, or broken to pieces under the word, as it was an instrument of God's power, in the hand of the Spirit. The like also I might mind concerning the woman of Samaria, who, when Christ's word reached her heart by powerful convictions, she cried out, " Come see a man that told me all that ever I did, is not this the Christ?" John iv. 29. Christ's word laid all her sins before her eyes, which made her to know he was the Christ; and also to loathe and abhor herself. Brethren, the plough makes deep gashes, or pierceth into the ground : so doth the Spirit of God pierce the hearts of poor sinners, causing deep wounds in their souls and consciences.

5. Husbandmen find it hard and difficult to break up some ground, it is so stony and rocky.

So Christ lays on blow after blow by the hammer of his word, in the hand of his Spirit, before some sinner's hearts are broken and made fit soil for the seed of grace. " Is not my word like fire, and like a hammer, to break the rock in pieces," Jer. xxiii. 29.

The best ploughing is when the earth is softened and mollified with showers of rain from heaven ; the hearts of men may be compared to ground upon the same account; for the gospel, or word of God, never works so kindly and *The divine rain of the Spirit softens hard hearts.* effectually, for the mollifying, and ploughing up the fallow ground thereof, until God lets the divine rain of his Spirit come down upon them. " I will pour upon the house of David and upon the inhabitants of Jerusalem, the Spirit of grace, and of supplication, and they shall look upon him whom they have pierced, and they shall mourn for him as a man mourneth for his only son, and shall be in bitterness as one is in bitterness for his first born," Zech. xii. 10. The Holy Spirit is like to rain that falls upon the earth, it makes the heart fit to receive the heavenly seed. This makes that great difference there is between ground and ground ; I mean between one man's heart and another. The Holy Spirit causeth a poor sinner to look upon Jesus Christ, whom his sins pierced, and to weep bitterly.

7. Like as that ground is not well ploughed up, where the plough jumps or skips over some part thereof; so the heart of a sinner is not savingly and effectually wrought upon, when any faculty of the soul is not reached, or under a thorough change by the divine influences of the Spirit. Some have their consciences ploughed up or awakened, and their understandings somewhat enlightened, (as it was with Balaam) and yet their wills and affections may not at all be touched. The divine plough as it were, jumps over the rugged and rebellious will, that bows not, yields not to Jesus Christ, nor are their affections renewed, and set upon him as the chiefest object ; hence, notwithstanding that light Balaam had received into his understanding, (who spake of God, and of the glory of Jesus Christ, and of the happiness of the people of Israel at such a rate, or in such a raised and elegant manner, as if he had been a true believer) yet how fain would he have cursed Israel, which shows the vileness and rebelliousness of his will ; and also it is expressly said, that " he loved the wages of unrighteousness," 2 Pet. ii. 15.

8. New ground is easier broken up than that which hath lain a long time barren and unploughed.

So the hearts of young people are soonest and easier broken and wrought upon, than the hearts of old and hardened sinners, though it is true if God will work, all are alike to him, to whom nothing is hard. *The whole heart must be manured.*

9. Some ground (it is observed) continueth bad, after all the pains that an husbandman uses, or cost laid out upon it, nay so bad that it is neither good for tillage, nor pasture, and therefore he lets it alone, and bestows no pains more upon it. Thus it is also with the hearts of some people (as it was of old with the peo- *Young people, soonest wrought upon.*

ple of Israel,) God plants some people by a river, and they grow and thrive like to willows, but others are like miry places. "And it shall come to pass, that everything that liveth which moveth, whithersoever the river shall come shall live, but the miry places thereof, and the marshes thereof shall not be healed," Ezek. xlvii. 9. This river may signify the doctrine of the Gospel. Yet these waters do not heal the miry places and marshes; earth and water mixed together makes a miry place, so when the word is preached, and the corruptions of men's hearts mixed with it, instead of the word being mixed with faith, these mens' hearts become miry places, and so like ground that is good for nothing; they may hold some truths of God, or receive divine truths into their heads, but retain the love of sin in their hearts, and their hearts cast up nothing but "mire and dirt," Isa. lvii. 19, 20. Brethren, it is observed, the longer the water stands on some ground the worse it is; so the longer some men sit under the word, and means of grace, the worse they are, even the more filthy, worldly, and unbelieving, until God says of them as of Ephraim, "Let them alone;" or as our Lord of the barren fig-tree, "Never fruit grow on thee henceforth for ever," Matt. xxi. 19.

Some ground never made good,

Great skill required in ploughing, and so in preaching.

10. Ground that is to be sowed, is with great skill and care ploughed up; the plough must not go too deep, lest the seed be buried too low; nor too shallow, lest there be not earth enough to cover it from the danger of the fowls of heaven; nor have that depth of earth proper for it to take good root. So the word of God, through the convictions of the Spirit upon the spirits of sinners, is guided by the wisdom of God. So that the plough of the gospel doth not go too deep, lest it drive the soul into despair, nor too shallow; but that it may break up the whole heart, or effectually work (in conviction) upon every faculty thereof.

11. An husbandman, by his pains and cost, can restore lost land, such that was very barren, and unlikely ever to become good and fruitful.

Even so the blessed God can by the work of his word and Spirit, restore barren and fruitless souls, such that were very unlikely ever to become good and gracious Christians: and as an husbandman strives to root out the weeds, and destroy the vermin; and by carrying out his compost to fatten it, he makes the ground good; so God by the efficacious operations of his Spirit, he destroys the weeds of sin, and corruptions of the heart, and so makes the heart good, and gracious, that it is with such souls as it is with a barren tree which Job speaks of: "For there is hope of a tree, if it be cut down, that it will sprout again, and that the tender branch thereof will not cease," Job xiv. 7. "Though the root thereof wax old in the earth, and the stock thereof die in the ground;" ver. 8, "Yet through the scent of water it will bud and bring forth boughs like a plant," ver 9.

II

When any one heareth the word of the kingdom, and understandeth it not, then cometh the wicked one and catcheth away that which was sown in his heart; this is he which receiveth the seed by the way side."—Matt. xiii. 19.

Brethren, I shall endeavour to do three things in opening this part of the parable.

First, I shall show you the nature of the high way ground.

Secondly, I shall show you how the devil may be said to catch away the word out of the hearts of this sort of hearers.

Thirdly, Give you the causes or reasons of it, and also show you why devils are compared to the fowls of heaven.

The nature of the high-way ground opened.

1. High-way side ground is very hard, or such ground which is not ploughed up.

So these persons' hearts are very hard, not only by nature; but also by a continued custom in sin. Hence they are said to make their hearts as hard as the nether mill-stone. Moreover, these were never ploughed up, by the convictions of the Spirit of God, nor mollified by heavenly rain.

II. The ground by the high-way side, commonly beareth no grass, or but very little, nothing but weeds, or being wholly barren.

Even so this sort of men bring forth, hardly so much as the grass of morality, the common product of nature; nothing proceedeth from them but horrid wickedness, or the filthy weeds and corruptions of sin, or fruits of the flesh, they are the worst of men, most ungodly and profane persons that are signified hereby.   Such who make no profession of religion.

III. High-way ground, or ground by the high-way side, is oftentimes very unprofitable, hence called king's waste. Though perhaps a poor man's cow, may now and then get a mouthful or two of grass on such ground.

So these persons are very unprofitable in their lives unto God and his people ; they neither bring forth fruit to the honour of God, nor to the good and benefit of men ; no spiritual increase or sacred fruit can be expected from these persons, though perhaps now and then they may be a little helpful to the poor, by giving them a mouthful or two of bread, or giving them some small matter when they die ; they may show, though very wicked some small neighbourly kindness.

IV.   Every foot treads upon the highway ground, the common path of travellers lies there.   Other ground is fenced in to keep them out, as also to prevent the breaking in of mischievous beasts ; but the highway lies open and common to all.

1.   So in these persons hearts every lust, filthy corruption, and cursed co- *What travellers tread on the highway ground.* gitation, hath a free passage ; In them is the way of evil.   Brethren, every evil habit, or wicked custom in sin, is like a common road or beaten path. A way of sin is far worse than to be overtaken by the power of temptation, with some evil action, or deed of darkness.   " Therefore David desired, that God would search him, to see whether there was in him a way of evil," Psal. cxxxix. 23.   That is, some evil habit of sin that was never changed ; it is, my brethren, this which discovers a man's state to be naught, or that he is not renewed.

2.   This sort of men is the way of earthly or worldly thoughts, they pass to and fro every moment as travellers on the highway.

3.   These persons hearts also is the highway of a worse traveller, namely, the devil, for, like as God is said to walk in his people, " I will dwell in them, and walk in them," 2 Cor. vi. 16, so the devil walks up and down by his evil suggestions, and filthy motions in the hearts of these ungodly ones.

4.   Moreover, these people are not by God's care and providence fenced *Highway ground not fenced in.* in, to keep Satan out; the careful eye of God is like a hedge to a holy person, and his Spirit is as a strong fence to repulse and keep Satan out ; from spoiling and devouring them and theirs.   " Hast thou not made a hedge about him, and about all he hath on every side ?" Job i. 10.   Believers are like a field, or garden enclosed, to prevent the danger they are from this watchful traveller ; but thus it is not with this sort of men, for they, like the highway, lie open to Satan's temptations.

V.   The seed which falls on the highway-side, is either trodden by the feet of travellers, or else caught up, and devoured by the fowls of the air.   Even so, and in like manner, the word that is either trodden down by the cursed feet and power of lusts, and love of this world, or temptations, and suggestions of Satan, or else the wicked one catcheth it out of their hearts ; by which means they bring forth no fruit of the word, but lose all the profit others receive thereby.

Secondly, I shall show you what ways and devices Satan hath to catch the word out of these persons' hearts.

They received the word ; this implies some kind of notional reception of it, but it is as our Lord told the unbelieving Jews, his word had no abiding in them.   But, *How the devil catches the word out of men's hearts.*

1.   To proceed, no sooner do they hear the word, but Satan darts in evil and hurtful thoughts, perhaps such as these following.

1.   Why should I regard what this minister says ?   he is but a man, he tells me, " I must be born again, or I shall never see the kingdom of God," John iii. 3.   " and that if I do not believe in Christ, I shall be damned," Mark xvi. 16.   It is but his opinion, his thoughts, he may be mistaken ; for if this be so, what will become of the most of men in the world ?

2.   In another of this sort he raises up prejudice against the preacher ; perhaps some have unjustly reproached him, as they did of old vilify the prophet Jeremiah ; report, say they, and we will report ;   and by this means the devil may catch the word out of his heart.   Brethren, by this device the devil caught the word out of the hearts of many persons who heard our Saviour preach, i. e., by rendering him odious unto the people by his cursed instruments which he employed, calling him a " gluttonous person, a wine-bibber ; a friend of publicans and sinners," Matt. xi. 19.

3.   To another Satan may suggest such thoughts as these, i. e., it is evident I am a

Christian, a member of Christ, and an inheritor of the kingdom of heaven ; I was born of Christian parents, and am in covenant with God, and so in the pale of the church, and therefore in a good and safe condition. I was regenerated by my baptism, when an infant, what doctrine is this ? " Must I be born again twice ?" Matt. iii. 9, 10, 11, 12, After this manner, or by this subtle snare, the devil deceived the Jews of all the benefit of the word. " We are Abraham's seed," John. viii. 33.

4. Saith Satan to others, " If you hearken to such doctrine which these men preach, you will become a mere mome, and then farewell to all the sweet comforts of this world ; for you will be mad, or else fall certainly into desperation ; and so become utterly uncapable to follow your employment, by which means your family will be brought to beggary." And unto these suggestions these adhere, and so the devil catches the word away that was sown upon their heart, for into their heart it never entered."

5. Other of this sort of hearers, Satan fills full of earthly thoughts ; so that as soon as he hath heard a word which greatly concerns him, it is presently lost in a crowd of worldly cogitations ; perhaps the person is poor, and he is thinking where to borrow a little money ; or having met with some losses, or disappointments the week past, this so perplexeth his mind, that he can think of nothing else. Or may be he has some bad debts, and his thoughts are taken up about them. Also another having a good trade the week before, he is thinking how much he hath gained, and by that means the devil catcheth away the word which he newly heard. Or possibly some body hath injured him, and he is thinking how to right himself ; or being defamed, he is so disturbed, that he cannot hear (to his profit) what the minister says, or least wise not retain it in his mind, by which means the devil catcheth the word out of his thoughts, and it becomes unprofitable. Or if a young person, it may be he is in love, and while he is hearing of the word, he is consulting how to act, in order to obtain the person he hath set his heart upon. And this man is by Satan, so filled with these thoughts, that he catches away the word. Or, perhaps the devil fills others of this sort which disquieting thoughts about the times, deadness of trade, and dearness of corn, and by that way he catches away the word they hear preached. Or, says Satan to others (by his inward suggestions) "Thou art young, and these things belong to aged people, who are going out of the world ; it will be time enough to mind the con- The subtilty cernments of thy soul many years hence ;" and so the devil catches the word of Satan. out of their hearts. Or, if the person be old, and is brought under the word, and begins to lay what he hears to heart, the devil presently injects such thoughts into his heart as these, i.e., " Thou wast called formerly, and thou didst slight that call, and offer of God's grace, and didst stifle those convictions thou hadst then ; that was the day of thy visitation ; but now it is too late, thy day is gone," and so the devil catcheth the word out (or rather) off of his heart. Another, Satan persuades to rest on the performance of du- ties ; perhaps they read and pray, and though they are very ungodly, will swear, lie, be drunk ; yet soon upon it they seem troubled, and get upon their knees and pray, and make promises to reform, but yet are again overcome with the same evils ; but then by being troubled, and by praying again, they think all is well ; they apply these duties to heal their sinful souls, and by that means the devil catcheth the word from them, so that they are never renewed, but perish in their sins. Satan suggesteth in others, that if they re- gard the word which they hear, so as to become religious, they will be reproached, and de- rided ; nay, may sometime or another be persecuted and thrown into prison, and be utter- ly undone ; and the thoughts of such things they cannot bear ; and by this means Satan also catcheth the word away from these. Moreover, Satan strives to deceive them, by telling them that many find repentance at last when they come to lie upon a death-bed ; and from thence, saith a sinner, this is, no doubt, a truth therefore why may not I ? many have taken their fill of all the delights and pleasures of this world, and have been happy for ever in heaven also ; and I hope so may I, and thus Satan catches the word out of their hearts, before it had taken any root therein. Furthermore, the devil tells them, that their condition is as good, as the condition of many thousands in the world. I shall therefore (saith the poor deluded soul) speed as well as they ; as if it were any relief to a poor con- demned criminal, that great numbers are like to suffer the shameful death with him- self. These and many other ways the devil hath to catch the word out of the hearts of them that hear it.

Thirdly, I shall show you what the reason is why the devil hath such power to catch the word out of the hearts of this sort of hearers.

1. It is because their hearts being hard, and never mollified, the word can have no

rooting in them, what seed can take root in ground that is so trodden upon, that is as hard almost as a rock.

2. It is because God, as a just and fearful judgment, leaves them unto their own hearts' lusts, they being so in love with sin, and the vanities of this evil world, esteeming earthly riches, honours, and pleasures of sin, above Jesus Christ.

Quest. Why are the devils compared to the fowls of heaven ?

Answ. 1. Some fowls are fowls of prey, ravenous fowls ; the devils are compared unto such fowls, because they are of a destructive nature, seeking how they may prey upon poor innocent Christians, and daily devour unwary and ignorant sinners ; like as some fowls live upon their prey, so those evil spirits live (as it were) upon preying upon, and destroying the souls of sinners.

2. Some fowls of prey have a quick and piercing eye, as the eagle : even so these evil spirits have a very quick and piercing sight ; if any sinner seems to be secure, they will soon on a sudden prey upon him : for as eagles with all diligence and subtilty watch for their prey, so do these evil and wicked spirits to destroy men's souls.

3. The fowls of prey, especially eagles, have their residence in the air, they love the upward regions ; and by that means have the greater advantage and opportunity to prey upon creatures below ; even so these wicked spirits have their residence in the air ; hence the devil is called " the prince of the power of the air," Eph. ii. 2, 3 ; and also by this means poor mortals are in the greater danger, they having much advantage of us by being above us, and find hereby an opportunity to devour such that are not aware of them.

4. The fowls of the air are great destroyers of seed, when it is newly sown ; and therefore the husbandman appoints his servants to drive them away : so these evil spirits are very busy in the time when the spiritual seed of the word is newly preached, to catch it up out of the hearts, or out of the mind and thoughts of all such that hear it, and hence the blessed God gives strict charge to all to resist them, and by faith and prayer, with a promise Satan shall fly from us.

5. Fowls come down upon their prey on a sudden, as a kite in a moment catches up a chicken.

So the devil here is said to catch the seed of the word out of these peoples' hearts ; which denote a quick and speedy motion. Satan sees there is need for him to do what he doth, (as it were with a jirk) he sees it is not safe for him to let sinners muse and contemplate upon the word, nor on their own dangerous condition ; lest the seed should begin to root in their hearts, (i.e.) get into their understandings, and into their affections.

It is said, when Abraham had killed his beasts, (viz.,) " an heifer of three years old, and a she-goat of three years old, and a ram of three years old, and a turtle-dove, and a young pigeon, the fowls came down upon the carcasses, and Abraham drove them away," Gen. xv. 10, 11 : even so these evil fowls, or wicked spirits, come down to disturb and disquiet the saints, when they are in the discharge of holy duties ; or are offering up spiritual sacrifices unto God, which they ought to drive away by a stout resistance of them in all their temptations, through the assistance of the Spirit of God. Moreover,

6. Where the seed is newly sown, thither it is observed oft-times great multitudes of evil and hurtful fowls will resort, so that sometimes the ground is covered with them.

So no doubt where the word of God in the assemblies of his people is powerfully preached, there are multitudes of those evil spirits, who strive to catch up the seed, thereby to make a prey of the souls of such they may destroy.

APPLICATION

1. O with what care and diligence should sinners attend upon the word, and lay it up in their hearts ! This was David's care : " Thy word have I hid in my heart," &c., Psal. cxix. 9. This is the way to prevent Satan from catching it up.

2. Let all that hear the word beware, what thoughts they adhere to, or entertain ; least they are ensnared by the evil spirits.

3. This also may inform all persons, how it behoveth them to find out, and not to be ignorant of Satan's devices : moreover it appears from hence, what the cause is, that so few in the world, who hear the word of God, do receive it in the love of it ; for certainly there are many more people comprehended by the highway-side ground than of any, if not more than of all the other three sorts, I mean such that remain openly wicked, and are never brought into any visible profession of religion.

4. From hence we also may infer, that there is a necessity of sowing the seed of the word. Ministers must preach, as husbandmen must sow ; if they sow not, they cannot expect to reap : so if ministers preach not, they cannot expect any souls should be converted by them ; he shall reap no harvest that sows no seed.

2. So he that sows sparingly, or but a little seed, shall reap sparingly, or have but a thin harvest.

3. A seeds-man (you heard) must not regard the cold, neither the wind, nor storms . so a minister must not fear reproaches nor persecution.

5. Terror ; this may afford terror to careless hearers, such that regard not how they hear. Take heed how you hear. The word of God is to this sort of hearers the savour of death unto death ; if the word softens not, it hardens ; if men hear not to their salvation, they hear to their damnation. The word of God is like a sword with two edges, if it do not kill their sins, it will kill their souls. If it tends not to fit them for heaven, it will fit them for hell.

6. Careless hearers are the worst of all hearers : as the highway ground is the worst of all sorts of ground ; there is no hope, that ever the seed of the word should take root in these men's hearts : true, the seed may fall upon such ground, but it cannot fall into it ; the stony and thorny ground was bad, but yet nevertheless they are said to receive the seed ; it seemed to be covered, but these tread it under their feet, they despise the word, and let the devil catch it up, or take it off of their hearts : our Saviour, as Gregory saith, *Non indiget expositione, sed admonitione.* Christ hath expounded this to our hand. The word hath no abiding in these persons, they hear, but resolve to continue in their evil and wicked courses, these have certainly the mark of reprobation up:n them ; they hear, but understand not, it is a mark of a child of God to understand the word : " To you it is given to understand the mysteries of the kingdom of heaven," Luke. viii. 10.

1. They desire not after knowledge, but are wise in their own conceit, and know as much as is sufficient, as they think to salvation.

2. Such hear negligently, or remissly, and are in a worse condition than those that never had the gospel, their sin is more heinous, and their state is more desperate ! " If I had not come and spoken unto them, they had not had sin," John xv. 22 ; that is, they had not sinned with such severe aggravations, " but now they have no cloak for their sin," 2'Chron. xxxvi. 15, 16. They of old that despised the word, and abused God's prophets, wrath came upon them, until there was no remedy ; the higher persons are lifted up to heaven in respect of the means of grace, the lower they will fall into hell.

The gospel, according as it is heard, is either the greatest blessing, or mercy, or the greatest judgment. It is either a blessing, or else a curse ; it either binds us with cords of love to God, or with the bonds of wrath and death ; it either softens or hardens.

3. Such persons are left inexcusable, they are hereby prepared for judgment, and judge themselves unworthy of eternal life ; such are justly rejected of God, because they despise and neglect the means of their cure ; the preaching of the gospel is to them that believe " the power of God unto salvation," Rom. i. 16. Let me caution all that hear the word to beware of Satan ;

Then cometh the wicked one.

Quest. Whither comes he ?

I answer, he comes into the assemblies of God's people, he comes where the good seed is sown. Many devils or wicked spirits attend and wait to catch the word out of the men's thoughts and hearts, whilest it is preached. O take heed of those ravenous fowls.

Quest. When doth Satan come ?

Answ. When any begin to hear, and diligently to attend upon the word of God ; " Whensoever any man heareth the word of the kingdom," Matt. xiii. 19 ; he fears no person, noble nor ignoble, old or young ; though you see him not, he being a spirit, yet he is by you, he stands among the children of God : Satan, my brethren, comes always to church, he is one of the first that comes, and the last that goes from thence ; when any word that suits the state of a sinner, falls from the mouth of the preacher, then comes the wicked one to catch it away.

Quest. How doth Satan come ?

1. I answer, he comes by darting into the heart, roving, and wandering thoughts, to take the hearer's mind quite away from that which concerns his everlasting welfare ; he comes by putting vain and idle cogitations into his heart and mind.

2. He comes to see if he can rock the hearer of the word asleep, or make him drowsy or heavy under the word : what is the cause, think you, that people are so subject to fall

asleep under the word? nay, more ready then to take a nap, than when they are else-where? Alas, it is from Satan. I have heard of a woman that chose to go to the place of God's worship, or where, and when the word was preached, that she might have a sound sleep; she found at such times she could sooner sleep, than at any other time or place.

3. He comes by many inward suggestions (as I have showed you) to stir up their na-tural corruption, and fill them with prejudice against the word.

Quest. Why doth Satan thus come? What end hath he in it?

Answ. No good end, you may be sure.

1. He comes as thieves comes to rob and steal; his end and design is to steal the word out of the heart. The devil is a great thief, he is not a pocket-picker, but a heart-picker; he comes not to get away your gold or silver, but that which is of far greater value, viz., the word.

2. His end is to hinder all that hear the word, (if possible) from believing; he is not so great an enemy to the hearing of the word, as he is to the believing and right applying of it; he never loses the sinner, until the sinner believes, and truly takes hold of Jesus Christ. Christ prays for all his elect, that they may believe; faith ruins Satan's design, and spoils his kingdom; faith unites the soul to Christ, therefore it is no wonder the devil is such an enemy to believing: faith is that shield whereby we quench all Satan's fiery darts; it is that by which we resist him, and overcome him.

3. He comes to hinder sinners from considering, knowing, and understanding the word; none receive it truly, but such that understand it; that know the necessity and excellency of God's word.

4. He comes to obstruct and hinder sinners of salvation, and so to blind men's minds that they may be lost for ever.

Quest. But why? to catch the word out of the heart?

Answ. Because if he can get it out of the heart, he knows it can do no soul any good; he cares not how much of the word a man gets into his mouth, or into his head, so that he can keep it out of his heart, or catch it out of that. *Why Satan strives to catch the word out of the heart.*

2. Because if once the heart truly receives the word, Satan knows it will soon take root there, and cause the soul to bring forth fruit.

3. Because the word rightly received into the heart, is like to leaven that will quickly leaven the whole lump.

4. Because if once the word of God be hid in the heart, he knows he cannot steal it away; David well understood this, and therefore he says, " Thy word have I hid in my heart," Psal. cxix. 11.

5. Because he knows when the word is truly received into the heart, Christ is at that time received also, and the soul is happy for ever. O then a stronger than he comes, and binds the strong man armed.

6. And lastly, Because the devil knows if he can but hinder the word from brooding and rooting on, or in the heart, the best sermon that can be preached will be ineffectual to that person. No wonder then that Satan strives to catch the word out of the hearts of sinners; he doth, it is true, what he can, to hinder a man from hearing the word, for fear he should not be able to prevent its being received; for it must be took into the ear before it can be received (as it is preached) into the heart.

O see what ground your hearts are, examine yourselves; for according to *Trial.* the nature of the ground, will the success of the seed that is sown be; are your hearts well ploughed up, or has the Spirit of God, by convictions, broken and pierced your hearts, so that you, like them of old, are made to cry out, " Sirs, what shall we do?"

And be sure do not think it enough to hear the word, content not yourselves to come to hear, lest Satan's coming prevents thy profiting by it. From hence we may learn that Satan hath more knowledge of the nature of the word, than many sinners have. For,

1. Satan knows that the preaching of the word tends to the ruin of his interest and kingdom in this world.

2. Satan knows the preaching of the word is an instrument in God's hand to the con-version and salvation of sinners.

3. Satan knows that faith comes by hearing, and that a bare hearing of the word can profit no person to the salvation of their souls. Moreover it informs us, that we can come to no meeting of the godly to hear God's word, but we may expect to meet with Satan there. O watch him, ye poor unwary hearers! have a godly jealousy, lest it is he that

keeps you sometimes at home, and also causes you to be sleepy and drowsy under the word when you do come; or that raiseth such thoughts and wanderings in your hearts, or that fills you with prejudice either against the word or the preacher thereof. Let nothing hinder thee from hearing the word of God; nor let a simple hearing of it satisfy thee. So much to the first sort of ground, viz., the highway-side-ground.

III

But he that receiveth the seed in stony places,—Matt. xiii. 20, 21, 22.

THREE things are to be considered in these words.

1. The nature of the ground; some fell in stony places.

2. The success of the seed; for a time it sprang up, but in the end it withered.

3. The cause and reason why and wherefore it withered, and brought not forth fruit unto perfection. I shall begin with the first of these, viz., the nature or quality of the ground.

The nature of the stony ground.   I. Stony ground wants breaking up; let rocky or stony ground be but well broken up, and mollified and mixed with earth, seed will grow, and bring forth fruit unto perfection.

So these persons enter into a profession of religion, before their hearts were thoroughly broken in the sense of sin; they never saw the baseness and hardness of their hearts; true faith works contrition and godly sorrow only in those hearts where the seed of the word takes root, and who continue fruitful unto the end. But these remain hardened in their sin; their wills being stubborn and rebellious, though they seem to be affected with the word; their consciences may be somewhat awakened and enlightened, and their affections suddenly raised, before they were brought under a true sense of sin: the natural hardness of their hearts remains, of which they are ignorant.

2. Stony ground is cold; what is colder than a stone? So these persons abide without any divine warmth, or spiritual heat in their souls, because they are without a vital principle, they have not the life of true grace in them, from whence all spiritual heat flows; the Sun of righteousness never enlivened them, though they might experience the common illuminations of the Spirit, as the apostle shows elsewhere. Heb. vi. 4.

3. Their hearts may be compared to stony ground, from the heaviness or lumpishness of their spirits; a stone is heavy and not easily removed out of its place; the earth is its proper centre; you may perhaps by your strength cast a heavy stone up a little way into the air, but down it falls again; so these hearers are heavy and lumpish, and not soon removed out of their evil course, but by the improvement of natural powers, or strength of common light and knowledge, they may be somewhat raised in their desires and affections towards heavenly things; but in a short time they cleave again to the earth their own proper centre, still they remain earthly and carnal inwardly.

4. Stony or rocky ground doth not drink in the rain that falls from heaven; it is observed that the rain glides off a rock, and very little of it soaks in: perhaps there may be a little earth, and in that some seed may take some small rooting.

So this sort of hearers do not receive with the word, the Holy Spirit, but do resist the more effectual influences and operations thereof; we read of the former and latter rain, which God's elect receive.

Where is the former and latter rain of the Spirit.   1. The former rain mollifies or softeneth their hearts, and so tends to root the divine seeds, and maketh it to sprout; and the latter rain ripeneth the soul for the harvest of glory, by bringing forth the fruits of the Spirit, and of a holy life. But these wanted the mollifying power and operations of the Holy Ghost; they never experienced the Spirit's rooting influences; the apostle prays for the saint to whom he writes; " that Christ might dwell in their hearts by faith, that they might be rooted and grounded in love," Eph. iii. 17. My brethren, faith roots the seed of the word by the Spirit in the understanding, and in the will; for the rooting of the seed in the heart, chiefly consisteth in the assent of the understanding, and consent of the will, and this is done by the Holy Spirit in its first workings and operations. But these professors who have rocky hearts, taking not in the spiritual rain in either of those respects, Christ is not received, nor doth he dwell in their hearts. And from hence they are not rooted in love; they seem to have some love to Christ, but as it is not sincere, so it abides not; they are not rooted in love. The former rain, by rooting the seed of grace in believers, infuseth divine habits; whom whence all gracious acts proceed, as the effect from the cause. And the latter rain strengthens those habits, and enables the soul from right principles, and to a right end, to discharge all holy duties, acts of piety, and gospel obedience.

But these stony-ground professors have not the habits of grace, and therefore they continue not in holy duties, but for want of oil in their vessels, their lamps go out. "Why persecute we him, seeing the root of the matter is found in him," Job xix. 28. By the root of the matter here, is doubtless meant the truth of grace, *i. e.*, The saving habit of faith, and love; he was a sincere and upright man, but this root is not found in these persons mentioned in my text.

5. All the hearts of men are naturally hard, stony, and like a rock, yet the hammer of the word can, and doth oft-times break it to pieces: "Is not my word like fire and like a hammer, that breaks the rock in pieces," Jer. xxiii. 29; therefore it evidently follows, that these persons' hearts were never changed, notwithstanding they become professors of the gospel, and seem to be disciples of Christ. *The hearts of all men naturally bad.*

6. Stony ground seems to be the fruit of the curse for man's sin, and it renders that part of the earth barren, and hinders the seed that is sown upon it from bringing forth fruit.

So these persons seem still to be under the curse; for by the stonyness and hardness of their hearts, the seed of the word is rendered as unfruitful as any stony-ground doth, or can render the natural seed to be, that is sown upon it.

7. Stony ground by reason of the little earth that is found there, it bringeth forth only the blade of the corn, it never comes to a kernel, nor to bring forth fruit for him that sowed it.

So these professors for want of deepness of earth, or for want of a sound judgment, a broken heart, and a good understanding, they only bring forth the externals of religion; they get a name, and an outward profession, and discharge external duties and ordinances, or no more than the stalk or blade of a Christian profession, or form of godliness, without the power thereof; no fruit of saving-grace, no inward sanctification, nor gospel holiness: and though they promised fair for awhile, and when they first set out or began to be religious, many thought them sincere, yet they continue not long in their course of a visible profession.

8. Stony ground, when the sun rises high and begins to shine hot upon it, the scorching beams thereof soon causeth the blade to wilk and wither away.

So these professors when persecution ariseth because of the word, they fade and wither, they cannot bear the trials of the cross, nor stand in a day of persecution.

Now the cause of their decay is two-fold.

1. Internal, in themselves, for want of root, or depth of earth, this is the chief cause.

2. External, from the scorching sun of persecution, temptation, and tribulation. From hence they wither.

1. Their hearts are not good nor upright with God, may be aim at self in all they do, or have not inward sincerity, perhaps get a profession to make that as a bridge to carry them to heaven, but cannot wade through the waters of temptations, nor swim through the floods of persecution and tribulation; they cannot bear bitter reproaches, scoffs, and jeers for Christ, nor loss of goods, estates, and life for his sake; when they see they cannot hold their profession without being in danger of losing their names, liberties, estates, places of profit, pleasures, or honours, and lives, they are presently offended.

Thus having showed why the hearts of some sort of hearers are compared to stony ground,

I shall observe from hence one or two points of doctrine.

Doct. 1. Stony or hard-hearted hearers may go a great way in the profession of the Christian religion, and yet be lost for ever.

1. I shall show you how far this sort may go.

2. Show you from whence it is they go so far.

3. Show you the cause or reason why they go no farther. 4. Apply it.

First, They may hear the word of God with diligence, these are not like to the high-way side ground, these do not scoff at the word, nor despise the ministers of the gospel; moreover they do not let Satan steal it away as soon as they hear it preached, but it hath some short abiding in them. *Stony ground hearers go a great way in a profession.*

II. They may be zealous hearers, or be very forward to hear, nay, hear it with gladness, as Herod heard John the Baptist.

III. They may receive the word into their hearts, they may suddenly receive it ; "anon receiveth it," that is, (saith a noted writer) immediately, they hear Christ died for sinners, and the doctrine pleaseth them, they are affected with these tidings and catch hold of the word, and receive it into their thoughts, and their affections are somewhat raised by it to such a degree, that they seem transported by it.

IV. From hence it is said that they received it with joy. The word is received into their affections, more than it is into their judgments and solid understandings. They did not count the cost, nor did they esteem the word above the love of the world ; our Saviour saith of some of John's hearers, " ye rejoiced in the light for a season," John v. 35.

V. It is said they believed for awhile, they are a sort of believers, though not true be- lievers ; many of the Jews believed in Christ, " But he did not commit himself unto them," John ii. 24.

They had no saving union with the Lord Jesus, he did not take them into his bosom, he knowing that their hearts were not sincere ; these give credit to the truth of the gos- pel, they arrive to the faith of credence, or a dogmatical faith, like many in our days ; they do not doubt of the truth of the Christian religion, of the truth of the Protestant re- ligion ; these are said " to believe for a while," Luke viii. 13, but not with a true saving faith ; they believe not with the faith of God's elect ; " Simon Magus believed," Acts viii. 13. There is mention made in the Scripture of divers sorts of faith.

True faith unites the soul to Christ, in our understanding, will, and affections, and wherever it is, it purifies the heart, therefore that faith which any unrenewed or ungodly persons have, is not true saving faith. Act. xv. 9.

The nature of the faith that is not saving.   This faith therefore being but a temporary faith is not of the right kind, it is not the faith of the operation of God ; true faith never faileth : " I have prayed for thee that thy faith fail not ," Col. ii. 10, Luke xii. 32 ; though it may fail in the act, yet it cannot fail in the habit.

2. It is a general faith, or a common faith ; it lies I mean in the general and common love of God to all, it comprehendeth a belief of the Scriptures, not a special and particular application of the object of justifying faith, Jesus Christ in the promises.

The devils no doubt believe the truth of the Scriptures, as well as they believe there is a God.

3. This faith is only seated in the understanding, but not in the will ; there is an assent of the one, but not a consent of the other ; this sort of hearers may believe all the attri- butes of God, i. e., that God is just, holy, wise, faithful, good, and gracious, almighty, &c., and yet never are brought to trust in him, and rest upon him ; they do not make him the object of their souls' affections, holy fear, and dependence ; they may have believing heads, but not believing hearts ; they believe God is good, but never tasted how good he is ; be- lieve he is able to save, but never threw their souls upon him in Jesus Christ, to be saved : it is, my brethren, a faith without experience, they believe the truth of the word, but never felt the power of it upon their own souls ; they believe the truth of the promises, but never tasted the sweets of the promises.

4. This is a faith without true brokenness of heart, their hearts (notwithstanding they are said to believe) abide hard and stony. True Christians " look up to him that they pierced, and mourn," Zech. xii. 10.   That is, they believe in Christ and are broken, they have soft hearts, but these do not so believe ; therefore it is not true faith they have.

5. This faith doth not change or transform them into the image of Christ, nor cause them to abide fruitful ; it makes them professors, but not true believers, they believe a man must be a new creature that would be saved, but they are not made new creatures that they may be saved ; they believe (as one observes) they must be changed, but are not changed by believing.

What obedi- ence is not true obedience   VI. The stony ground hearers may yield obedience to all external duties or ordinances ; they may read, pray, give to the poor, attend frequently upon the word, nay, may be baptized, as Simon the sorcerer was, Act. viii.

I do not say they may obey gospel ordinances, and perform gospel duties from right principles, nor to a right end, they may be right in the matter of their obedience, but not in the manner of it.   They may do that which is right in the sight of God, (as some of the kings of Juda did) but not with a perfect heart ; though evident it is, these sort of per- sons do not whatsoever God commandeth them ; some of the hardest things which he re- quireth of them they do not ; they do not " Pull out their right eye lusts, nor cut off right hand lusts, they do not deny themselves, take up their cross, and follow Christ whithverso- ever he goeth," Matt. xvi. 23, 24, 25.

They are not universal in their obedience, nor is their obedience evangelical, neither constant and abiding; they do not "Obey always even unto the end." Their obedience is not right in the spring of it, the motive of it, nor rule of it; a man may obey the law, and yet not love the law; "if ye love me keep my commandments," John xv.; but they do some of his commandments, and yet sincerely love him not.

VII. The stony ground hearers may become members of a visible church of Christ, and break bread with the church, and be owned for faithful brethren, like as the foolish virgins were, and no doubt the wise took them to be good Christians; they were not known to be unsound to them.

VIII. They may have a great zeal for all the externals of religion, as the Pharisees had; "I bear them record that they have a zeal of God," saith the apostle concerning the Jews, but it was not according to knowledge," Rom. x. 2; commonly the zeal of this sort of professors, appears in their conformity to the smaller matters of religion, as the Pharisees were extremely zealous in payment of tithes of mint, annis, and cummin; but neglected the weightier things of the law, as justice, mercy, faith, and the love of God. Besides their zeal, as it is partial so it is inconstant; their zeal doth not burn long, it is but for a time, they quickly cool in their zeal. Moreover, it is commonly a selfish zeal; "Come, (saith Jehu) and see my zeal for the Lord of Hosts," 2 King x. 16; when, alas, it was a zeal for his own glory and interest.

IX. The stony ground hearers may leave all gross acts of sin, as swearing, lying, drunkenness, uncleanness, and the like; but for all this they may not hate those sins which they leave. Sin may seem to be out of their conversation, but not out of their affections. They are other creatures, but not new creatures; they are changed in their lives, but not in their hearts. Nor let this seem strange to any, for pray to what a degree of outward reformation did many of the Heathens attain unto, by the improvement of the dark light of nature, as touching all gross sins. Nay, in subduing of many of the unruly passions of their hearts. Now those persons who sit under the hearing of the gospel, have far greater advantages by the means of common light and knowledge, than those Heathens ever had; besides, they have more powerful motives, by hearing of that future reward God hath promised to the truly godly, and the fearful punishment of all that are ungodly, that live and die in their sins.

X. And lastly, They may have some inward joy, as to the hopes they have of heaven; it is said of this sort, "They take delight in approaching to God," Isa. lviii. 2. I do not say, they rejoice in the word, or delight in it, because of the purity of it; no, that no hypocrite can do; but because of the profit of it, or because of the future reward it promiseth; or their delight in the word may arise from the eloquence of the preacher, it pleaseth their ears; "It is as a very lovely song of one that hath a pleasant voice, and can play well on an instrument," Ezek. xxxiii. 32. These men have hopes to be saved, but it is not built upon a sure foundation. We read of the hope of the hypocrite, and of his leaning upon his house, but because it is not well built, it shall fall for all that; perhaps they ground their hopes upon that external change that hath passed upon them, or upon those external duties they have performed: men of no grace, may be men of great hope; it is not a hope in Christ that riseth from faith and union with him, or from what he hath done for them, but from what they have done; "We have prophesied in thy name," &c. Heb. vi. 16—18. We have fasted, say they; the hope of a true Christian is both sure and steadfast, it is built upon Christ alone, and on the covenant of grace, promise, and oath of God, and the excellent nature of it is known by its effects: "Every man that hath this hope in him purifieth himself even as he is pure," 1 John iii. 3; he that is not in Christ, is without any sure hope of heaven. This was that mystery Paul preached among the Gentiles, "which is Christ in you the hope of glory," Col. i. 27. Such that have Christ dwelling in their hearts by faith, have a certain and sure hope of eternal life: but so had not the stony ground hearers; but because the thorny ground hearers go further than these, I shall say no more unto this head now.

Secondly, from whence is it, that the stony ground hearers go so far?

1. These hearers go so far in a way of profession, and performance of duties of religion, from those common illuminations of the word and Spirit of God; hence they are said "once to be enlightened," Heb. vi. 4, 5, they are brought by the light of the word to see the state of man by nature is very wretched and deplorable; how was hard-hearted Balaam enlightened in this respect; he knew the condition of such that died unrenewed was sad; therefore cried out, "let me die the death of the righteous, let my last end be like his." Natural conscience being enlightened, convinces these persons, that they are sinners,

and in a lost and woful condition, and therefore they cannot rest in the present state they are in, and therefore strive to step out of it into a profession of religion : no doubt Felix was under great convictions, and Herod also, who upon those convictions did many things, and heard John the Baptist gladly.

2. It may be from the effects of that faith they had ; for though they had not the faith of God's elect, yet their temporary faith was not wholly without some product; the seed sprang up, there was the stalk or blade of a visible profession, they reformed their ways, and left their old course of life ; as the product of that faith, which they had obtained through hearing of the word ; a temporary faith will bring forth some kind of temporary fruit.

3. It may arise from a heat of love and affection to some ministers, that this sort of hearers do go so far. One observes, curiosity and novelty goes a great way with this sort of people ; a new preacher, that hath a fluent tongue, and an elegant way of delivery, takes with them exceedingly ; O how will they run after him, and croud to hear such an one : you must know they are much raised in affections, but weak in judgment.

Affection to some ministers.

4. Self-respect and honour may cause them to go far, merely to get a name, may be they will largely contribute to such a minister they do affect, and seem very zealous for a time, that they may be taken notice of to be men that love religion ; many persons greatly affect a name among men, and it is not a little way that this will carry them.

5. It may be self-profit: so long as this sort of hopes of receiving any thing by Christ, they will follow him: how earnestly and zealously did some follow Christ, they took shipping to follow him, but what was the cause, saith our Saviour; " Verily, verily, I say unto you, ye seek me not because ye saw the miracles, but because ye eat of the loaves and were filled," John vi. 28; but when there is no more profit, no loaves, they cease following of Christ ; this sort will adhere to Christ, as Demas did, until they meet with greater advantages or earthly profit, then they leave him, as he did, out of love to this present evil world,

6. It may arise from that seeming sweetness and satisfaction they meet with from within themselves, whilst they continue in the profession of religion, and in the discharge of spiritual duties; hence they are said to " taste of the good Word of God," Heb. vi. 5, 6 ; it is but a taste of it, they feed not upon it, nor digest it, yet nevertheless that taste they have (though it be but like a cook's licking his fingers) helps them to go forward, and do many things.

7. It may be from a desire they have of being saved ; there is a natural desire in all men to be delivered from that which is evil, and hurtful to them, and to enjoy that which is good ; now they believe there is a future state of blessedness to be had, and therefore go far in the way of a profession to obtain it. The young man cried out, " Good Master, what good thing shall I do that I may inherit eternal life ?" This sort know there is an eternal life to be had, and they think it is to be had by doing ; something they conclude they must do for it ; they no doubt seek it by their own righteousness, as the Jews did, and this spurs them on to do much, and to go far in the ways of doing and obedience.

8. It may arise from that consideration of that shame and reproach (they conceive) all such that lie under that are openly wicked and profane ; an ungodly person is one that exposeth himself to the contempt of all mere moral and civilized people.

9. Moreover, slavish fear, or a dread of hell and eternal damnation, may be the cause why these persons go so far in the way of Christianity ; they seem to fly from the wrath to come.

Be sure it is from Satan's subtilty, or the delusions of the devil ; for no doubt some of this sort may think they are saints, or true believers, and under the promises of eternal happiness ; their hearts deceive them, or Satan deceives them, concluding they are in the ready way to heaven ; yet perhaps some of them may deceive their own hearts, for so do all those whose conscience condemn them for hypocrisy, yet not to such a degree, but sometimes they may have hopes their state is good.

Thirdly, from whence is it that the stony ground hearers go no further in the ways of God ?

From whence it is these professors go no further.

1. Answ. I answer, it may arise from that great ignorance that is in them ; the god of this world hath blinded their minds, and hence it is they go no further ; being persuaded they have received the grace of God, because of that great light and knowledge they have attained unto in the mysteries of the Gospel. Gifts are like grace, and because they have the one, they conclude

they have received the other also ; if a man thinks, or is persuaded he hath got a sure title to such or such an estate, he will trouble himself no further to search records, nor employ lawyers to that purpose ; I mean that so he may make such an estate more sure unto him : because they are so much in duties, so constant in performance of prayer, so frequent under the word, give so much to the poor saints, they do not doubt but all is well with them, and that they need not go further to search their hearts, though they see they have many sins cleaving unto them ; yet what of that ? they see all men, yet the best of saints are not without manifold infirmities ; in many things we offend all : who say they are without sin ? Thus they seem to " make themselves rich, when (as Solomon observes) they have nothing," Prov. xiii. 7. It is a very dangerous thing for a man to think he is rich, and increased in goods, and hath need of nothing ; for many of these " know not that they are wretched, and miserable, and poor, and blind, and naked," Rev. iii. 17. It is lamentable for a man to think himself something, when he is nothing.

2. It ariseth from the unsoundness of their hearts, the ground is not good, and therefore cannot bring forth more fruit, or better fruit than it doth. Our Saviour shows in my text, that their hearts are stony, or rocky, that is, very hard ; yet in them there is some earth, though not depth of earth, sufficient for the rooting of the seed. Now what doth this denote, but that there is a work upon one faculty, and not upon another. Their understanding is somewhat enlightened, and their conscience a little touched, and in those two faculties the seed seems to be received ; though the work upon those faculties is not efficacious, there is no depth of earth, that is, no thorough and effectual convictions passeth upon them, and as to their wills they are still stubborn, hard, rebellious, stony, and like a rock, being never mollified, bowed, nor broken to pieces ; and their affections are as carnal as ever ; and from hence it is they go no further. And

3. From hence it appeareth, that it riseth from the deceitfulness of the heart, that these persons go no further, as their hearts are divided, so they are deceitful, as every natural man's heart is ; " The heart is deceitful above all things, and desperately evil, who can know it ?" Jer. xvii. 19. Many things are deceitful ; we read of the deceitfulness of beauty, of a deceitful tongue, of the deceitfulness of riches, of friends, of the deceitfulness of sin, and of the deceitfulness of the devil, Psal. lii. 4, and Job. vi. 15 ; but the heart is said to be deceitful above all things. Was not the heart of man very deceitful, Satan could not deceive him. O, says some, I thank God, I have a good heart . though I do not make such a show of religion, now these are be sure most fearfully deceived, for where true grace is in the soul, the heart appears to such a one, most filthy and loathsome above all things ; " He that trusteth in his own heart is a fool," Prov. xxviii. 26.

4. This sort of hearers go no further by reason of their abominable pride : " God, I thank thee I am not as other men are, &c., not as this publican." Tell these professors that they have cause to doubt of the goodness of their state, their hearts will rise at you, and their spirits will swell with pride and self-conceitedness : look to yourselves, trouble not yourself with me, I know my condition ; thus perhaps they will retort upon you ; a fool rageth and is confident.

5. They go no further, because they never had real union with Christ, they had no vital principle in them, they act rather from an artificial principle, than from a principle of life.

6. These stony-ground hearers go no further because there is some lust, or secret sin or another hid in their hearts ; there is no hypocrite but he hath some Delilah, some beloved lust, that he harbors and lodges in his bosom ; though such may go far, yet they will not hold out to the end ; the young man that came running to Christ, bid fair for heaven, but one sin he hugged in his breast, and would not part with, and that was the sin of covetousness, his heart was set upon his earthly riches ; " He went away sorrowful, because he had great possessions."

7. Another reason may be through a sad mistake, they being not able to discern between the nature of special and common grace ; I am persuaded this is the ruin of many professors. There is, my brethren, a great resemblance between these two ; many are cheated, you know, by counterfeit money ; they take it for current coin ; a man may pass under a great change, and yet not pass through a saving change. He may become another man, but not be a new man. He may (as one observes) take a work of conviction and reformation, for a work of regeneration ; because he is become a religious and a great professor, he thinks he is a true believer, but (as the proverb is) all is not gold that glitters, so there may be an outward sanctification, where there is no inward renovation ; the Pharisees " made clean the outside of the cup and platter," but inwardly were very vile, filthy, and unclean.

8. No doubt, but one cause these professors signified by the stony ground, go no further in their pretended zeal and Christianity, may be, because they were never brought under the convictions of the Spirit, or the application of the law of God to their hearts and consciences; they never saw themselves slain or dead, by the power of the killing letter; " I was alive without the law," Rom. vii. 9. That is, without the true sense of the spirituality and severity of the law. I saw not that I was condemned, and slain by it, by reason every lust or evil thought of the heart, is a breach of the holy law of God, and lays the soul under God's wrath, and the curse; he was for a time without the law, that is, without the knowledge of the law, he was not without the letter of the law, but spiritually he was without it, he felt not the soul-killing efficacy of it upon his own heart, convincing him of his lost and undone condition. " But when the commandment came sin revived, and I died;" that is, when the word or law of God came with power upon his soul, it broke his stony heart to pieces, it was set home so effectually upon his conscience, that then he saw his estate was desperate, and that all his own righteousness was but filthiness, or as dogs' meat; by reason he could not answer all the precepts of it, so as to live and not sin; and that nothing but a perfect righteousness could justify him at the bar of God's justice. But, alas! the stony-ground hearers were never thus broken, slain, and dead; they were never made sensible of their own wretched and deplorable state by original sin, and by reason of their actual breach of God's holy law, but take up with some sudden flashes of joy by hearing the glad tidings of the gospel. But when they find they must forsake all for Christ's sake, persecution and tribulation, because of the world rising upon them, they are offended, and fall away. But no more at this time.

IV

But he that received the seed in stony places, &c.,—Matt. xiii. 20.

" THEY on the rock, are they which when they hear, receive the word with joy, and these have no root, which for a while believe, and in time of temptation fall away," Luke viii. 13.

1. I have showed you that the stony ground professors may go a great way in their religious course.

2. Also from whence it is they go so far. And,

3. Why they go no further.

I shall now make some improvement of what I have said.

1, Infer.   1. Infer. From hence we may infer, that many professors may be, and doubtless are greatly deceived as to their eternal state; a man may be taken for a saint on earth, that is no saint in heaven, I mean in God's sight; he may strive to enter into heaven, but shall not be able; people may be forward hearers, and zealous professors, and yet fall short of God's eternal rest.

2. Infer.   2. That it is not an easy thing to be saved, the " way is narrow, and the gate straight, that leadeth to life, and few there be that find it," Matt. vii. 14. Though Christ hath opened a door to salvation, and made the way easy by shedding his own blood, yet sin makes it very hard to find; in respect of sinners themselves, it is very hard and difficult to be saved, they are so in love with their lusts, and with the carnal things of this world. Regeneration is a very narrow way, to believe and not to work for life, is a paradox to corrupt mortals.

3. Infer.   3. This being so, what will be the end of such that never hear the word at all, who never tread one step in the way of a visible profession, if so many perish that go so far, certainly their state is very sad who never made any beginning in religion? if professors may perish, what will become of the profane?

2. Exhort.   The second use shall be by way of exhortation to try ourselves.

1. Do not slightly pass over the work of self-examination, nor take up with a bare profession, or with an empty name.

2. Do you see a stony ground hearer receive the word with joy? what will become of thee, that takes no delight in hearing of it? if the sermon be but an hour long, thou art weary, and tired out? O! doubtless, thou art in the gall of bitterness.

3. If an unsound heart may find some sweetness in the word, what wilt thou do, that finds none, that cannot relish it at all, that never tasted of the good word of God?

4. If such that attain to great light and knowledge of the things of God, and truths of the gospel, may be damned, what will become of all ignorant people, such who are without understanding; " They are a people without understanding, therefore he that made them will not save them; and he that formed them will show them no favour," Isa. xxvii. 11.

5. O how dangerous a thing is it to lay a false foundation, and build our salvation upon it? If a man be not right in the main, if he build not upon Jesus Christ, if the root of the matter be not in him, if he miss in the fundamental work, if he be without true grace in his heart, he is a lost man.

6. Beware your hearts deceive you not, trust not your own hearts. O how many deceits are there! because many see they have great gifts, they think that they have true grace; others, because they are reformed persons, they think they are converted persons.

7. Know God will try you at one time or another; " Every man's work shall be tried by fire." When the sun was up, these stony-ground professors withered away; the sun of persecution may rise and scorch men severely, and that quickly too.

8. Moreover, know Satan will try you, he will come with his sieve to sift you; as well as Christ with his fan to fan you.

However, death will try us all, and if deceived when death comes, down to hell such must go.

No man can receive any hurt or injury, by searching his own heart and state; it is be sure a bad sign a man is ready to break, that is not willing to cast up his books, or leastwise he fears things are bad, so it is a bad sign thy heart and state is naught, if thou art afraid to be tried or searched thoroughly; a true Christian cries with David, " Search me, O Lord, and know my heart, try me, and know my thoughts, and see if there be any evil way in me," Psal. cxxxix. 23, 24.

Examine thyself, was thy heart ever thoroughly broken? did sin ever   Examin. revive by the force and strength of the law, and thou died? didst ever cry out as being pricked at the heart? Is there no secret sin, or way of sin, in thy soul allowed and indulged? Hast thou no Delilah lying in thy bosom? What are thy ends and aims? O look well to them; is not thy end in thy making of a profession, to get a name? is it not self-interest, self-profit, or applause? or is it not merely to get heaven, or to be happy? is not happiness more in thy eye than holiness? O then fear, examine thyself about the nature of thy inward joy; doth thy joy rise from that sense thou hast of God's love, and light of his countenance? Is it in the word, because of the purity of it? Is it holy joy? Is it in God and Jesus Christ? " We rejoice in Christ Jesus, and have no confidence in the flesh," Phil. iii. 3. Not in what we have done, or in what is wrought in us, but in what Christ hath done for us, and is made to us. Even wisdom and righteousness, sanctification and redemption; is God himself, Jesus Christ himself, thy joy, and chiefest delight? Doth thy joy continue? the joy of an hypocrite is but for a moment, his joy soon abates. Canst thou rejoice in being abased, reproached, and persecuted for Christ's sake? joy in tribulation? Rejoice in the Lord when all outward comforts fail thee? " Although the fig-tree shall not blossom, neither shall fruit be in the vine; the labour of the olive shall fail, and the field shall yield no meat, and the flock shall be cut off from the fold, and there shall be no herd in the stalls," Hab. iii. 17. " Yet will I rejoice in the Lord, I will joy in the God of my salvation," ver. 18. Is thy heart low when thy condition in the world is advanced? Canst thou abase thyself before God, and mourn most for those sins before God, that appear least before men? Dost thou bring forth all the fruits of the Spirit? these stony ground professors bring forth but the blade, or stalk of external duties, not the graces of the Spirit; not faith, love, meekness, humility, long-suffering, temperance, charity, and patience. Doth thy fruit remain? Dost thou not cease bearing fruit in times of drought? if so, no fear of the goodness of thy state.

1. " And some fell upon stony places, where they had not much earth; verses 5, 6. " And forthwith they sprung up because they had no deepness of earth."

" And when the sun was up they were scorched, and because they had no root, they withered."

We shall consider the cause and reason of the withering of the stony ground hearers more distinctly.

But before we speak of that, observe,

Doct. Persecution and tribulation upon the account of the cross, is compared to the sun's scorching beams, or the burning heat and influences thereof, when the sun is up.

By the sun our Saviour shows, is meant persecution and tribulation, ver. 20, 21.

I. The sun when it is risen high, towards noon, scorcheth such things that want rooting in the earth. So persecution scorcheth those professors that want grace, or the root of the matter in them.

2. The sun so scorcheth such things that they soon hang their heads, and wither. So unsound professors do soon hang down their heads, and wither in their seeming zeal and holiness, as soon as persecution rises high.

3. Though the sun shines never so hot and scorching, yet that seed and tender blade that is well rooted, and daily watered, grows and flourishes the more. So all sincere Christians, though persecution may be never so hot, they being well rooted in Jesus Christ, and watered with divine showers of God's Spirit, do grow and flourish the more in grace and heavenliness. "The more Israel was oppressed, the more he multiplied." It is observed that the saints never thrived, and grew more, than in the times of the ten hot persecutions. See the different effects persecution hath on sincere and false professors.

4. The hot beams of the sun tends to tan or make black those persons that are much under the influences of it; so the sun takes away all that seeming spiritual beauty that was in unsound professors. Common grace is like an artificial beauty, or a natural beauty improved by art, but when the sun of persecution is up, and scorcheth them sore, this beauty vanisheth away; and they seem to be the same persons they were before they made any profession of religion.

5. The sun of persecution makes sincere Christians black also, externally in the sight of men. Yet they are then comely in God's sight. "I am black but comely, because the sun hath looked upon me," Cant. i. 5, 6. Most men judge of blackness and comeliness by a mere sensual eye. Job seemed black when he sat upon the dunghill; and thus all the godly in the sight of carnal persons (when they are blackened and villified by their cruel persecutors) seem black.

6. Many find some shadowy place at noon, when the sun shines most hot: so believers find a shadowy place in the hottest time of persecution. "Tell me, O thou whom my soul loveth, where thou feedest, and where thou makest thy flock to rest at noon," &c., Cant. i.

7. Jesus Christ refreshes their souls in such times by his blessed presence, promises, and ordinances; he is unto them "as a shadow of a great rock in a weary land," Isa. xxxii. 2. Thus we see the sun hath quite different effects upon some things it shineth hot upon, to what it hath on other things; and those different effects arise from the nature of those things upon which it shines; and so likewise hath the sun of persecution different effects upon professors of the Gospel; for such who are sincere, it tends to quicken them, to revive them, and to cause such to take the deeper root.

But the unsound and hypocritical professor is soon scorched thereby, and withereth away; but the cause is in the persons, or in the matter on which this metaphorical sun shineth; this brings me to the next thing I promised to speak to, viz., to show you the cause of the withering of these professors, signified by the stony ground.

"And as soon as it sprung up, it withereth away, because it lacked moisture," Luke viii. 6.

Doct. Withering is the fearful fate of all stony ground hearers. I shall speak to this withering and spiritual barrenness.

1. As to the evil or badness of the cause that produces such evil effects.

2. As to the evil or badness of the effects produced by such evil causes.

First. As the badness of the evil cause or causes of withering, and spiritual barrenness.

1. The principal and positive cause of the withering of these professors is the stonyness of their hearts.

2. Privative cause.

1. Want of moisture.

2. Want of earth.

3. Want of taking root.

Before I proceed, let me premise one or two things.

1. That there is a partial decay, or a partial withering.

There is some degree of hardness of heart also attending the best of saints, but I am to speak of a total and final withering, of such that are never renewed again, and of such hardness of heart, that cleaves only to unsound and unmortified professors. And now, I say, the principal and positive cause of this total and final withering, is the stonyness or hardness of these men's hearts, like as this seed fell upon a rock, some ground, though very stony, or full of stones, (we daily see by experience) brings forth fruit to perfection; but if seed falls upon a rock, though there may be a little earth; yet that seed never brings forth fruit to the harvest. Now these men's hearts were all of one piece, as it were; all a rock, and nothing but a rock; the little earth that was found there (as I conceive) was nothing but natural conscience, somewhat enlightened, or awakened by the preaching of the word, all the other faculties remain under the power of their natural hardness, and original pravity. I say, all the earth that seems to be in these men's hearts (in which the seed seemed to take some small root) was in their consciences only; their understandings being not savingly enlightened, nor their wills brought over to receive Christ; but remained rebellious, and their affections earthly and carnal, no effectual change having passed upon them.

2. A rock will resist the plough, and the strokes of the hammer; so the stony heart is not pierced, nor is it proper soil for the seed to take root in. " Their heart is as the nether mill-stone, or like the leviathian," Job xli. 15. Now this is the evil cause of that barrenness, and withering that is in these men's souls.

To bring forth fruit (you have heard) the ground must be soft, the soil must be mellow; but how can a stone or rock be made soft? These men under the word, or under the means of softening, become more hard; that which *A rock cannot bring forth fruit.* tends to soften others, hardens these; in them is not only a natural, but also an acquired hardness. "He stretcheth out his hand against God; and strengtheneth himself against the Almighty," Job xv. 25. "Pharaoh hardened his heart before the Lord, and would not let Israel go," Exod. v.

Let me give you the characters of a hard-hearted person, or the properties of a stony and hard heart.

1. When a sinner sits under the powerful preaching of the word, or under a ministry, where the nature of sin and the law, in its killing and condemning *Signs of a hard heart.* power is opened, and the woful state of all men by nature, is clearly evinced; and yet the man is not stirred, nor in the least measure awakened, but concludes all is well with him; this shows his heart is hard, it is a rock.

2. When a minister openeth the infinite love of God to undone sinners, in the gift of Christ, as also the nature of Christ's sufferings in his name, in his *The love of God breaks not a rocky heart.* body, and in his soul, which may be enough (as some think, to break a heart of stone) yet this and that man regards it not, he melts not, mourns not, or thinks not of the evil of his sins, which thus exposed the Son of God to bear divine wrath, and the pangs of hell for sinners.

3. It is a sign of a hard and rocky heart, in those who sitting under such a sermon or ministry, where many are broken into pieces; but the word toucheth them not, they are not wrought upon, though the hammer of the word is lifted up, and blow after blow laid on, but no impression is made on their hearts. This shows that their hearts are as a rock. "Is not my word like fire, and as a hammer that breaks the rock in pieces?" Jer. xxii. 29. It appears some rocky hearts are broken by the hammer of the word, but others are so hardened they are not broken thereby.

4. When all that impression which the preaching of the word doth make on a man's heart is chiefly on his conscience, that may yield a little, and give way, and the affections be stirred somewhat up, but the will of the person remains obstinate and rebellious as ever. This is a sign of a stony-hearted professor; many of the Jews that heard our Saviour, were touched in their consciences, or much convinced under his preaching, and seemed to have some love and affections to him, insomuch that it is said, they believed on him. "But Jesus did not commit himself unto them," John ii. 24. Because he knew their hearts remained carnal and hard still, and therefore he told them, "They were the servants of sin, and of their father the devil," John viii. 34, 44.

5. When men, though they hear of the nature of God's justice and holiness, as it is displayed both in the law and Gospel; yet presumptuously rely upon his mercy, and remain without dread or fear of the wrath and majesty of God; these men's hearts are not only hard, but they persist to harden themselves against God more and more.

6. When a person sees the patience of God in his delaying of his judgments, and it makes him rather worse; because God is slow to wrath, he is swift to *The goodness and patience of God hardens some sinners.* sin; if the execution of judgment are not at the heels of sin, they conclude there is no danger. It is with them as Solomon observes, "Because sentence against an evil work is not executed speedily, therefore the hearts of the sons of men are fully set in them to do evil," Eccl. viii. 11.

7. When a man hath been often reproved for this and that sin, and yet he hardeneth his neck; it is not the preaching and lamentations of ministers, nor their tears, nor the tears

of their godly parents, or other relations, that will melt them, or work upon them ; this is a sign their hearts are hard.

8.   When all the effects, the word and Spirit of God hath upon a man, is only to change his course, or causeth him to leave only the gross acts of sin, or to reform his life, and so to take upon him the profession of religion, but never changed his heart, or infused new habits therein, but that he still remains unregenerate, harbouring this and that lust in his bosom, it is a sign he is a stony-hearted professor.

A professor may be a stony hearted hearer.

9. When a person, though a professor, is told of his pride, passion, covetousness, or worldly mindedness, or of the neglect of his duty to God, or to the poor saints ; he shall fly in the face of the reprover, and may be reflect on him, and become his enemy ; it is a sad sign he is one of the stony ground professors ; you know if you sometimes strike at a stone it will rebound, and perhaps fly in your face, and wound you ; even just thus do these persons oft-times blemish, or wound a faithful minister, or friend, that reproves them : Whereas a true Christian takes reproof kindly ; " Let the righteous smite me, it shall be a kindness ; and let him reprove me, it shall be an excellent oil, which shall not break my head ; for yet my prayer also shall be in their calamities," Psal. cxli. 5.   He that is sincere is far from being offended with him that in love reproveth him ; he will rather bless God for the faithfulness, and kindness of his friend, he will the more pray for such in their trouble and afflictions, and not insult over them that pity and pray for them.

10. When a man's conscience shall often reprove him for evils he lives in, or for neglect of duties, and yet he turn a deaf ear to the checks and rebukes thereof, and will not lay his sin to heart, and return to God, but stifles those motions of his conscience ; this is another sign of one of those stony ground professors.

Now this is the direct cause of barrenness and withering : it is, I say, the direct, the inward, and positive cause thereof.

The privative cause of withering.

I shall now proceed to the inward privative cause, as they are laid down by both the Evangelist, viz., want of moistness, earth, and root, or rooting.

Now all these proceed from the former cause, viz., the hardness of their hearts, for the heart being hard and stony underneath (as a worthy divine observeth) affords neither earth, or rooting, or moisture to the seed.

Taylor

The words do not intimate as if there was no earth, or nothing in their hearts for the seed to fasten upon, but there was no depth of earth, or but a slight rooting in the conscience, and affections only, no depth of judgment, small understanding, nor any rooting in the will, ἐλίγχε πολλυι, as Mark notes, not much earth.

For want of earth, by which I understand the want of saving knowledge, or an enlightened judgment, and a true understanding ; the word rather was received into their heads, than into their hearts : some slight convictions, and some sudden flashes of joy, from the seeming heat of their affections they might have, or such may have ; but they take up with a general notional knowledge of divine truths, they taste the good word of God, Heb. vi. 5, but do not feed upon it, nor thoroughly digest it ; they taste some sweetness in the word, but receive not strengthening and soul-saving nourishment by it : all the fruit that they bring forth, are but the effects of natural conscience, or work of common grace. They never digged deep enough in their own hearts and state by nature, nor tried and examined themselves, nor did they dig deep into the truths and mysteries of the gospel, to make by saving faith an application of Christ's merits unto their own souls ; and from hence in a short time they wither away, like as seed doth that is sown upon the top of a rock.

" They had not root in themselves," Matt. xiii. 6, not the root of the matter in them, viz., no saving faith, no true love to Christ, nor any other special grace of the Spirit ; faith cannot take root in these, because there is no ground in the will and understanding for it ; grace hath its chief rooting in these noble faculties, so that ignorance is a cause of their barrenness and withering : ignorance of themselves, I mean of their own woful condition, ignorance of God's holy nature and blessed law : ignorance of Christ ; they never had a true spiritual knowledge of the Lord Jesus, he was never received by faith into their hearts ; see how Paul prayeth for the saints, " That Christ may dwell in their hearts by faith ; that ye being rooted and grounded in love," &c.   And to know the love of Christ, which passeth knowledge, that ye might be filled with all the fulness of God," Eph. iii. 17.   But in these men there is no rooting, no ground for faith, and love, to take root in.

So that it also appeareth, that unbelief is a grand cause of their withering ; what work soever passeth upon a man, if he does not truly believe in Christ, or hath not the work of faith with power passeth on him, the seed of the word can have no rooting in such a one, and though he may seem a lively Christian, and zealous for the external parts of religion for awhile, and many may think there is some greenness on his branches, yet he will wither in an hour of temptation, or tribulation, and fall away : they have, it is true, some kind of faith ; it is said they believed, but their faith was but a temporary faith, they did not believe to the saving of the soul, as the apostle speaks, Heb. x. 39 ; they had the faith of credence, a historical, or dogmatical faith, but the faith of God's elect they had not, for that never fails in the seed, or habit of it ; I have prayed for thee, that thy faith fail not. It is only, brethren, the fruit of such a faith that is not saving these men have, and all the fruit they bring forth, is but the external duties of obedience, and their care is more for the blade and stalk, than for the root that should bear it ; their unsettled faith riseth from an unconstant and wavering principle, and not from a sound inward apprehension of Christ ; and as is the cause, such is the effects ; (i.e.,) they are as changeable as their faith, and every wind of doctrine, and waving, and wheeling of times of providence, carry them about, and they come to nothing.

" It withered, because it lacked moisture," Luke viii. 6.

(1.) By moisture I understand the Spirit of God is meant. The Holy Spirit is compared to water often in the Scripture, and it is the Spirit that causeth that moisture, softness, and tenderness of our hearts ; and evident it is, as without rain or moisture no seed will grow and bring forth fruit to perfection, so without the Spirit of Christ the word will be barren, and such that hear it will bring forth no fruit unto eternal life. So that the evil cause of these men's withering, is for want of the Spirit, and the effects of it, viz., the moisturing, softening, and fructifying influences thereof. Brethren, pray remember that as the seed which is sown in the earth takes root, grows, and brings forth fruit by the continual showers that fall upon it ; even so the seed or word of God is rooted, grows, and brings forth spiritual fruit, by the acts and influences of the Spirit ; " without me ye can do nothing," John xv. 5 ; that is, without union with Christ, and a continual supply of the Spirit from Christ, no soul can bring forth fruit. *What is meant by the lack of moisture.*

2. By moisture may also be meant, that special effect of the Holy Spirit upon the soul, viz., compunction, there is not the moisture of godly sorrow for sin in these professors, they want effectual mortification, they never (as some of the saints have) " watered their couch with tears," Psal. vi. 6 ; these waters, these tears of true repentance, they are utter strangers unto ; the hardness of their hearts hinder the descent of water from above, as to its abiding upon them : and also the ascent of water from below ; it is too great pain for them to afflict their souls, their tears were soon dried up, and the rain that falls from heaven perhaps for a while might lie on their spirits, but it was just as the rain that falls on a rock ; there may be some moisture, and the small earth that is thereon, makes it take it in, but when the sun is up, it is dried away : so the common influences of the Spirit may be in these men, and natural conscience for awhile receives it, and there seems to spring up the green blade of external holiness and obedience ; but when the sun of temptation and tribulation is up, they wither away. *Mr. Tho. Taylor.*

Thus I have showed you the badness of the cause that produceth such evil effects ; viz.

1. Hardness of heart.

2. The want of deepness of earth ; viz., the want of saving knowledge, a good judgment, or a right understanding, much ignorance abiding in them.

3. Want of rooting, viz., the want of faith, union with Christ, and love to him.

4. The want of the Spirit, from whence all spiritual moisture flows, or all saving graces.

Secondly, I shall now show you the badness of those effects that proceed from such evil causes.

1. Barrenness ; this is the fruit of the curse, and, as I hinted, it denotes that these men are still under the curse of the law ; there can be no true fruit to God without union with Christ ; we are said to be " married to him that God hath raised from the dead, that we might bring forth fruit to God," Rom. vii. 4 ; but these men were never married to Jesus Christ, they not savingly believing in him, nor partaking of his Spirit.

2. Another evil effect that attend these professors, is earthliness, or worldly-mindedness, their hearts being not changed, they still mind earthly things ; as they cannot bring forth the fruits of the Spirit, because not made spiritual, so they bring forth the fruits of the flesh, being carnal and unregenerate; and no doubt but it is partly this sort of professors that expose the name of God, and religion to reproach, and make so much trouble in churches. *Earthly mindedness an effect of a withering.*

Lukewarm-
ness an effect
of withering.

3. Lukewarmness in religious duties, or that great neglect and remissness in the performance of them, is also the effect of the badness of these men's hearts; what liveliness of spirit can be expected from such who are dead, or without a principle of spiritual life? they discharge all religious duties by the help of natural conscience, or by the power of the common gifts of the Spirit, and not by the grace and special influences of the Spirit.

Pride ano-
ther effect.

4. Pride, conceitedness, or haughtiness of heart, is likewise the effects of this evil cause, or causes; viz., it flows from hardness of their hearts, their want of grace, of faith, and the indwelling of the Spirit of Jesus Christ; a tender heart is an humble heart; faith causes a man to think soberly of himself, or shows him his own emptiness and poverty, and that nothingness that is in himself.

But unbelief is attended with pride, and vain glory, and haughtiness of heart; no doubt but many in the Church of the Laodiceans were but stony ground professors, and how rich, full, and proud were they! O how conceited, and confident of their good estate! "Because thou sayest, I am rich, and increased with goods, and have need of nothing," Rev. iii. 17.

Uncharita-
bleness an
effect of
withering.

5. Another bad effect that is produced by these evil causes, is that great uncharitableness and envy which are in this sort of professors; they being barren of grace, and so wanting particularly that precious grace of love, are filled with prejudice and enmity against such that are far better than themselves. It is, beloved, the character of an hypocrite, to spy the mote that is in his brother's eye, but sees not the beam that is in his own eye," Matt. vii. 3, 4; they will mark every slip, or every blemish of others, and represent them as in a magnifying glass, but cannot endure to be told of their own faults; such that are frequently abroad and seldom at home, may be suspected to be stony-ground professors; had they not hard hearts, they could not grieve the souls of their poor brethren, and afflict and trouble those churches, where they are members, as sometimes they do; if they cannot have their will, or what they would have done, woe to them that oppose them; for they will endeavour to render them odious to all, or cast dirt enough, besure, thinking some perhaps may stick; "Wrath is cruel, and anger outrageous, but who can stand before envy?" Prov. xxvii. 4. Uncharitableness and envy is worse than wrath or anger, because sudden wrath or anger may soon be gone, but envy is more lasting; wrath or anger also may be caused by some great provocation, or injury done to a person; but envy and an uncharitable and censorious spirit may not rise from any such cause, but rather from the pride of the person's own heart, and that malignity of his mind, being grieved for another man's happiness, or that honour and respect others may have above himself. Envy is also more deeply rooted in the heart, and implacable; whereas the other passions are soon allayed. Moreover, this vice has more hurtful and mischievous effects; such care not if they ruin the person they malign and envy. It may be a question, whether envy is consistent with grace, or a gracious heart, or not?

Contention
another ef-
fect.

6. Contention is another evil effect of these bad causes, and the immediate fruit of envy and malignity. What contention do some professors make in their families, and amongst their neighbours, and between one member and another? nay, what strife and contention in churches, which is worst of all, do they too often make? A sower of discord among brethren, is one that the Lord hates; he hates both the sower, and the seed he sows.

Strife and contention sometimes ariseth from pride and a Diotrepheous spirit, occasioned by such that love to have the pre-eminence amongst churches, saith John, speaking of that evil person, "I will remember his deeds which he doth, prating against us with malicious words," 3 John x. This hath of late times too much appeared in some persons, which gives just cause to fear they are but stony-ground professors.

Schism and
division
another ef-
fect,

7. Sedition, schism, and divisions in churches, is also the evil effects that flows from these stony-ground professors, tearing and rending congregations to pieces, to gratify their own lusts and horrid pride; were not these men void of the true grace, or not hard-hearted persons, could they act so much like the devil as they do? Sure they would rather let their own names and reputation suffer, than disturb, divide, and break to pieces the church, or churches of Jesus Christ; I know a gracious man may be overcome with grand and grievous temptations, but it may be feared most of this sort are ill persons. For this fruit is too much like that which stony-ground, or a rock beareth, viz., briars and thorns; you may perhaps see thorns and briars grow on a rock; so nothing seems more like to thorns and briars than contention, sedition, and divisions. O these are grievous pricking and piercing thorns, wounding all gracious and tender-hearted Christians, and making whole churches to bleed.

8. Inconstancy, unsettledness of mind, or waveringness of heart, is likewise the effects of a stony heart; they being not well rooted in the truth, or not receiving the truth in the love of it, are often left to delusions; "And are carried away by every wind of doctrine by the sleight of men, and cunning craftiness, whereby they lie in wait to deceive," Eph. iv. 14. That tree, or plant, that is not well rooted, is soon shaken down, or rooted up. What is the cause, think you, that Quakerism hath carried away so many professors? Alas, you may soon come to a solution in the case, they generally may be such, and I am persuaded are, that never had the root of the matter in them, they were not men well rooted in Christ, had no true faith in, nor love to Christ, nor were they men of a good, solid and settled judgment, but rather led by affections, and something they call heat and warmth of heart, as if that was the way to judge who were in the right way, and who in the wrong: how easy is it for Satan to transform himself into an angel of light, and fill deluded souls with false joy, and pretended raptures! A comet, or false star, may make a great blaze, and give more light than a true natural star may.

Inconstancy another effect.

9. Decay of love to God, to Christ, to religion, and to the truth of God, and people of God, is another effect produced by these evil causes. Love may decay, it is true, in sincere Christians, but those decays are but partial, but in this sort it is total. O how soon is their zeal for God, and love to God and his truth and people, quite gone, the interest of Christ may stand or fall, sink or swim for them, they care not; their hard and stony hearts will not be moved, by all the arguments poor ministers may use, they will not stretch out their hand to preserve it; they will not part with their money, though ministers want necessaries, and the poor starve; sure this must needs be the fruits, and effects of an hard and rocky heart; the tears of ministers, nor cries of the church, and of the poor saints, will not melt them, nor move them to love and pity. They are like Ephraim, their "Goodness is as the morning cloud, and as the early dew it goeth away," Hos. vi. 4. Their zeal for God, his name, honour, worship, and interest, and seeming piety, is soon gone; it is not the zeal of God's house, but for their own house, which eateth them up.

Decay of love a sign and effect of witherings.

10. Moreover, that fearful neglect of the worship of God, in attendance upon his public ordinances, is an effect of these evil causes. Brethren, as they neglect, or are remiss in private duties, a small matter will keep them from hearing the word, and the holy table of the Lord; thus their blade and leaves wither, they cannot keep up an honourable profession of religion; as they have not true faith, so they hold not fast a profession of faith, it is no marvel they bear not fruit, when their very leaves are withered. The blessed man the Psalmist says, "His leaf shall not wither," Psal. i. 3; he shall be green and flourishing in his profession, and fruitful in his conversation.

Fearful neglect of God's worship another effect.

11. Backbiting, whispering, and a detracting tongue is also another effect, that attends these evil causes in these men. It is no wonder they will reproach their brethren, when their hard hearts stick not at a worse evil; viz., to expose the holy name of God to contempt, by their pride, carnality, covetousness, and earthly-mindedness, and other evils, they are found guilty of. All these things are the fruit, the sad fruit of a stony and hard-hearted professor; "He that backbiteth with his tongue, and taketh up a reproach against his neighbour, shall not ascend God's holy hill," Psal. xv. 3.

Apostacy an effect of decay or of witherings.

12. Apostacy is also another sad effect: brethren, none of the stony ground hearers, but they either die in hypocrisy, or perish by apostacy.

1. Their apostacy at first may be but partial, but it doth not always so end; this apostacy in them, ariseth for the want of union with Christ, or not having a vital principle in them; and it may be considered under four general heads.

1. In judgment.
2. In affection.
3. In practice.
4. In respect of means.

1. Many of them decline, or let go the true orthodox faith, as to some of the main fundamental principles thereof; and either sucking in Socinian errors, or Baxterian errors, or some as bad as they; being sadly corrupted in, and about the doctrine of justification; some of them, as at this day, assert, that unbelievers and vile ungodly sinners, may be actually justified, and in a good estate. Others make faith and obedience a part of the matter of our justification; this I call a partial apostacy, in respect of judgment, though it may extend to more principles than these I here mention.

Apostacy. 1. In judgment.

2 In affec-
tion. 2. They fall from their first love ; I mean that seeming love which they pretended to have at first. They appearing once fervent in spirit, and most devout in maintaining of religion, but afterwards cool and become indifferent.

3 Apostacy
in practice. 3. They grow careless and carnal, and walk like other men, conforming to the base and odious fashions and customs of the world, and are light and wanton in their words and gestures ; they seemed once to be like the Galatians, (*i. e.*) could pull out their eyes for their ministers, or thought nothing too much to part with which they wanted or stood in need of ; but now it is quite otherwise, they draw off, and may be stick not to violate, and break their own covenant with the church and ministers thereof.

3 As to the
use of means. 4. Moreover, as to the use of that means God hath left for the preservation of the soul in life and liveliness ; that there may be greenness on our branches, and no withering ; they fall off and forsake the assembling of themselves with that church with which they solemnly covenanted to walk, and to attend upon the ordinances and ministry therein, Heb. x. 25 ; may be, formerly, the word seemed sweet to them, but now perhaps it is like dry bread to them, or light manna ; they forsooth cannot profit by that ministry, under which they pretended they received their new birth.

Others may be formerly prayed much or very often, and read the word of God, and with some seeming fervour of spirit discharged those duties ; but may be now pray but little, or very seldom, and that with a cool and flat spirit ; their hand grows heavy, that (as one observes as in Moses' case) Aaron and Hur have much ado to support them ; may be some of their families were once praying families, but now prayerless families. And so by degrees they decay until they become nothing, but cleave wholly to the world, and perish in apostacy. But no more at this time.

V

But he that receiveth the seed into stony places, &c., Matt. xiii. 20, 21. *They on the rock,* &c., Luke viii. 13.

Doct. Withering is the fearful fate of the stony-ground professors. They all fall away from that grace and holiness they seemed to have.

1. I have opened the badness of the cause, or causes, that produceth such evil effects.

2. I have also showed the badness of those effects produced by such an evil cause or causes.

3. I shall now proceed to show the great danger and fearful condition of such that thus wither and fall away.

4. Give you the signs of withering.

5. I shall apply the whole, and so conclude with this sort of professors.

1. Such seem to disappoint the holy God of his expectation (to speak after the manner of men) for properly God is not, cannot be disappointed ; but like as a man when he hath taken pains with a piece of ground, and hath sowed it with good seed, he expecteth that it should bring forth fruit answerable to that cost and pains he lays out ; so the Lord is said to look for, or expect fruit from such persons, he by his ministers takes pains with in order to their fruitfulness in grace and holiness ; " Wherefore when I looked that it should bring forth grapes, brought it forth wild grapes," &c., Isa. v. 4.

The fearful
state of
apostates
opened. 2. These persons are hateful to God, in that they seem to declare to all the world, there is not that good to be found in God, and in his ways, which the blessed word, ministers, and all sincere Christians do affirm there is ; nay, and this also upon a taste and trial they have made of the ways and things of God. For by their cleaving to their former lusts, and to the love of this world, after they have made a profession of religion, they hereby clearly intimate, that the pleasures of sin, the riches and honours of this world, are better than whatsoever good can be found in God, or in his Son Jesus Christ, and in his ways and ordinances. For like as a good man in renouncing all the ways of sin, and vanities of the world, for Christ's sake, and (like Moses esteems reproaches of Christ better than all the glory of Pharaoh's court) do thereby cast contempt upon the devil, his works, ways, and kingdom ; so these men on the other hand by forsaking God and his holy truth, do thereby cast contempt upon God, Christ, and his ways, works, and kingdom, which must needs be hateful to the blessed God, and to our

Lord Jesus Christ. For they like the evil spies of old, bring up an evil report upon the good land.

Secondly, The danger and evil of withering is further demonstrated by considering the evil effects of it, in respect of the church of God, and gracious Christians. The evil effects of withering in respect of the church of God.

1. They bring an horrible scandal upon the church, on the saints, and on all that dwell in heaven, by their forsaking the good ways of God; this tends to bring the Lord's people into reproach, to the grief of strong Christians, and the stumbling and offence of the weak.

Thirdly, In respect of the world these men's sin, and danger is also aggravated; " Woe to the world because of offences—But rather woe to him by whom the offence cometh," Matt. xviii. 7. The wicked are hereby stumbled, and their mouths opened to blaspheme God, his ways, and people; and many of them are hereby confirmed and hardened in their evil ways. You see, say they, what they are, they are a company of hypocrites, and deceivers.

Fourthly, In respect of this sin itself, no sin is more odious, and dangerous.

1. We commonly say, relapses are far more dangerous than the disease. Also,

2. Satan, when he returns to his former house, and finds it empty of grace (however it had been seemingly swept and garnished) "takes with him seven more wicked spirits than himself."

3. This sin of withering and barrenness is commonly punished with other sins, viz.

1. With blindness of mind.

2. With judicial hardness of heart.

3. With a seared conscience.

4. And with final impenitence; " So I gave them up to their own hearts' lusts, and they walked in their own counsels," Psal. lxxxi. 12.

5. It leads them to sin the unpardonable sin; it is none but this sort, and those comprehended under the thorny ground, that sin the sin against the Holy Ghost; " They are such that have been once enlightened," Heb. vi. 4, 5, 6.

Fifthly, The evil and danger of such is great in respect to themselves, who thus decline, wither, and fall away. And thus appears,

1. It is an evident sign, that they are hypocrites, and were not such they seemed to be; for the good ground brings forth fruit to eternal life; no sincere person can finally fall away; " The righteous shall hold on his way, and he that hath clean hands, shall grow stronger and stronger," Job. xvii. 9.

2. They are near unto cursing. That ground that is barren and unfruitful, " is nigh unto cursing," Heb. vi. 8; nay, under the curse already, barrenness is a fruit of the curse.

3. They by turning with the dog to his vomit again, and with the sow to her wallowing in the mire, " show their latter end to be worse than the beginning," 2 Pet. ii. 20.

4. Their end will be burning, as they are nigh unto cursing, so their end is to be burned, what, alas, remains for this sort, who finally fall away? " But a certain fearful looking for of judgment and fiery indignation, which devour the adversaries," Heb. x. 27.

Quest. How may it be known that a man is in a withering, decaying, and dying condition?

1. Self-confidence. When a person resteth in a general hope of his good estate, without searching, trying, or examining himself, this is a sign his condition is naught, and that he is in a decaying state; a lively Christian will not take up with a fancied hope, but does try himself, and search his own heart, and cries to God also to search and try him. Self-confidence a sign of withering.

II. When a man doth not love, nay, he cannot bear a trying, nor a searching doctrine, it is another sign of withering; he is like to a tradesman, that fears he runs behind in the world, but lothe to cast up his books, lest he should find things worse than he perhaps hopes they are; or he is like a man, that hath a sore skinned over, and because he is in no great pain, he hopes it is near cured; but if you lay your hand hard on it, he cries out, being not able to bear it.

III. When a man's conscience is not so tender as it once was, now he can talk vainly, frothily, and in other things, as to his garbs, gestures, and behaviour allow him or herself that liberty, which once their conscience would not suffer them to do; this doubtless is a sign he or they are going back, or in a withering estate; strictness of life, and holy and circumspect walking, is a good sign of a growing in grace, and the contrary of spiritual decay. When the conscience is not tender.

When pray-er is neglected.   IV. When a man's prayers are short, or prays but seldom, and that with some difficulty too, being hardly able to bring his heart to it; this is another sign. As you know it is a sign, that a person is in a languishing condition as to his body, when he fetches his breath short, or breathes with difficulty.

V. When corruptions of the heart, especially that sin that doth so easily beset a man, gets strength, or prevails more and more; this is a sign he is in a decaying and in a withering condition.

When a man falls in an hour of temptation.   VI. When a man cannot stand in an hour of temptation, but is overcome, it may be a sign of his withering condition; for pray observe the words in my text, " In times of temptation they fall away." This is what the apostle James shows, " For the sun is no sooner risen with burning heat, but it withereth the grass, and the flower thereof faileth," Jam. i. 11. It is the grass, observe it well, that which is the product of nature, the sun doth not cause the wheat to wither; now these professors bring forth only the fruit of natural conscience, not the fruit of saving grace. And hence it is that they cannot stand in an hour of trial and temptation; " Blessed is the man that endureth temptation," ver. 12.

When there is a gnawing worm at the root, sometimes the seed though it be come up, yet the blade is observed to wither; and yet the cause is not soon discerned, but when the husbandman comes, and searches the root, he finds a worm there, that has spoiled it, which made it hold down its head. So in these there is a worm at their root, and they wither; I mean some secret sin allowed and lived in, and conscience upon this gnaws them, an accusing conscience, a condemning guilty conscience, shows such are in a withering and dying condition.

VII. When sweet showers that fall from heaven, and blessed shinings cause others to thrive, fructify, and flourish; and yet these thrive not, grow not; it is a dangerous sign of withering.

So when a man sits under a fruitful ministry, that God is pleased to own, and graciously to bless it to the growth of many souls; but some that sit under it grow not, or receive no spiritual profit by it, it is a sign of their withering; and it must needs be so, when the chief means of growth in grace is wholly ineffectual to them.

VIII. Feebleness of knees, or lameness, is a sign of decay in grace; how many are found to halt between hope and despair, they halt perhaps between two opinions, between truth and error, and know not which to choose; one while they seem to take up a resolution to abide in the truth which they have received; and at another time that resolution is near gone, and they are ready to resolve, to cleave to some other new and strange notions, and thus they halt and are ready to be turned out of the way; or may be they halt between God and mammon; one while they seem to be for God and religion, but at another time grow cold God-ward, and set their hearts upon the vanities of this world; now this is a great sign they are in a decaying and withering state.

Deadness a sign of decays.   IX. Deadness of spirit is another sign of withering; when a man is cold and dead, and without a heart, or not so lively and brisk in spirit as he was formerly; he has a prize in his hands, but hath no heart to improve it, Prov. xvii. 18; spiritual discourse was once more sweet to him than it is now, the word more sweet than it is now, he had more sense and feeling in him than he hath now; now small sins are no sins with him, and great sins but small and little; he can do that which once he could not, but his conscience would fly in his face. No heart to attend on the word, no heart to cherish convictions, no heart to obey Christ's precepts, nor apply his promises, no heart to do good, and to communicate, no heart to plead for God and his people; no, he is grown dead and cold to all these things.

Slothfulnes a sign of decays.   X. Sleepiness, love to sleep, and will not be roused up, though the man hears that wrath is just ready to be poured forth on the whole land, nay, on the whole earth, and many are awakened, and get upon the watch tower; but no warnings, no thunderings, either by the word or works of God, will awaken these; this is a sign they are in a dying and withering condition. They are both insensible of their sins and of their estates, and also of their dangers, neither grieve for their own iniquities, nor for the sins and iniquities of others.

XI. When the blade of corn is weak and sickly, it is a sign it is in a decaying and withering condition.

So when a professor seems weak, and can hardly hold up his head in his external profession, but it is in a sickly state of soul, weak in knowledge of divine things, weak in his affections, weak in his purposes and resolutions, it is a sign he is in a decaying state.

XII. Blasting is a sign of withering; sometimes corn looks well and hopeful, promising fair, but on a sudden the husbandman sees it is blasted, which makes him fear he shall reap no crop there.

So some professors for a time seem to promise fair, and are very hopeful: but God for just cause (as a judgment upon them) blasteth them in their gifts and seeming graces, and presently they decay and wither away; many times it is observed, it is thus with some men: God has sent a blast and a mildew upon their souls, that they are not like the persons they seemed a little before to be; and this is another sign of withering.

APPLICATION

Infer. From hence I infer, that it is no certain sign a man is a child of **Infer.** God, and shall be saved, because he hears the Word of God preached, or loves to hear sermons, or makes a visible profession of religion, and becomes a church member, and does many things that are commendable, or praiseworthy, for all these things are common to reprobate or unsound professors as with elect ones; nay, though a man holds out in religious practices for many years unsuspected, yet afterwards he may decay and wither.

Be exhorted to take heed lest you wither away, as the stony ground **Exhort.** hearers do; " Take heed, brethren, lest there be in any of you an evil heart of unbelief, in departing from the living God," Heb. iii. 12. Unbelief, though it is in itself but a denial to assent to, or to rely on God in Christ according to the revelation of his will in the gospel; yet it is the rise or spring of all other sins; and the seeming womb (as one observes) from whence issueth all unrighteousness, hardness of heart, and it is the root of withering, and oft-times of final apostacy.

Quest. What should we do to prevent withering?

1. *Answ.* Never rest until you do arrive to some good and certain demon- **What we** strations of your union with Christ; for if a man be not grafted into Christ **must do to** by the Spirit, he will not abide long in a profession of the Gospel, before he **prevent** withers and decays in his profession, zeal, and seeming piety: " Abide in me, **withering.** and I in you, as the branch cannot bear fruit, except it abide in the vine: no more can ye except ye abide in me," John xv. 4. No man can abide in Christ, that was never grafted into him; true he may be externally in him, by a visible profession, or in the vine the Church, that sometimes bears Christ's name; and such are said to be in Christ. But without our being spiritually or internally in him, we can bring forth no fruit to perfection: " We are married to Christ, that we might bring forth fruit to God," Rom. vii. 4.

2. Be sure see you are truly regenerated, or born again; the tree must be made good, before the fruit can be good, as to the nature of it, as well as to the abiding or duration of it. It is the good ground that brings forth fruit to eternal life: now no man's ground (I mean his heart) is naturally good, it is grace only that makes the heart good.

3. Be sure, see that your faith is of the right kind, or is the faith of the operation of God. True faith is always attended with good fruits, yea such fruit that remains; true believers shall not cease bearing fruit: " Blessed is the man that trusteth in the Lord, and whose hope the Lord is; for he shall be as a tree planted by the water, and that spreadeth out her roots by the river, and shall not see when heat cometh, but his leaf shall be green, and shall not be careful in the year of drought, neither shall cease yielding fruit," Jer. xvii. 7, 8.

Trusting in God, and believing truly in God through Jesus Christ, is one and the same thing; such always draw saving or divine virtue from Christ, which keeps them alive, and prevents their withering; a temporary faith is not the faith of God's elect, they that believe but for a time, will bring forth fruit but for a time; such cannot bear the heat when it cometh; nor stand in the year of drought.

4. Labour to have a sound judgment, to discern between truth and error; this is commonly obtained by sitting under a sound true Gospel ministry; if we would not wither, we must be grounded, and built upon the foundation of the prophets and apostles: it is for want of a good understanding that some fall into errors, and so wither and die away.

5. Get also a sound and steadfast persuasion of the truth thou professest; be not satisfied with having the truth in thy bible, nor in thy head, or mouth, to talk of it, or dispute for it; but get it into thy heart, see thou hast an experimental knowledge of the nature, and power of divine truth, in thy own soul. Many do not receive the truth in the love of it: and they are such that wither and fall away; either by being carried away by the craftiness of deceivers into detestable errors and heresies, or else are overcome with the love of this present evil world, as Demas was.

If a man hath tasted how good and gracious the Lord is, and of Christ's love, and his merits, he will never totally wither, and fade away; sincerity will preserve him.

If you experience how sweet the favour of God is, the love of Christ is, you will find it stronger than death; no waters can quench it, nor can the floods drown it; you will not hang down your head, nor remain in a doubtful suspense of your salvation, nor ever wither away and come to nothing.

6. See that thy heart and conscience is always kept tender, making strait steps for thy feet, and do not give way to the sin, or any time to the neglect of thy duties; it is for want of tenderness of heart many wither; the stony ground is hard, therefore brings no fruit forth unto perfection; inward guilt will be like a worm at the root; if we allow ourselves in any known sin, or regard iniquity in our hearts, in vain do we pray for grace and the influences of the Spirit, to keep us alive; for God will not hear thy prayers, as David shows, if we regard iniquity in our hearts.

7. See that you daily attend upon the word, and ordinances of God, and be much in meditation. " They that wait on the Lord shall renew their strength; they shall mount up with wings as eagles, they shall run and not be weary, they shall walk and not faint," Isa. xli. 31; This will be an excellent means to prevent withering, and decaying in grace and holiness. Can a man expect to be strong that forsakes his food, or will not eat? if once our appetite is gone, our strength will soon be gone; now the word and ordinances of God are the food of the soul, it is that which tends to strengthen our hearts: I mean, God thereby doth in a gracious manner strengthen us; "Wait upon the Lord, be of good courage, and he shall strengthen thy heart; wait I say on the Lord," Psal. xxvii. 14. But do not only wait on the Lord in hearing of his word, and in the Lord's Supper, and in meditation; but also in prayer; be much in prayer, cry often, and mightily to God, if you would not wither, and decay in grace; a man may live that cannot breathe, or without breathing, as well as a Christian may live, and be lively without praying; for prayer, spiritual prayer, is the breath of the new creature; two things are absolutely necessary in order to spiritual growth.

First, our being born again, or getting a changed heart.

Secondly, our being fed, and daily nourished with the food of the word: " As new-born babes desire the sincere milk of the word, that you may grow thereby," 1 Pet. ii. 2.

8. See that you daily keep close to God in the holy fellowship and communion of the saints, in receiving and communicating with them, and let not small things impede or hinder thee from thy indispensible duty herein, if thou wouldest not decay and wither: nay, abide constantly in that place and fellowship where thou art a member; let not thy place be empty at any time, if thou art able to go thither. " Tell me, O thou whom my soul loveth where thou feedest, and where thou makest thy flock to rest at noon," Cant. i. 7. At noon, that is when the sun is up, and shines very hot, i.e., when persecution rises because of the word: it is to be feared, the stony ground hearers did not take care when the sun was up to get among the saints, under the shadow of Christ, in his house, but abode alone, abroad in the word; and so they were scorched. " Not forsaking the assembling of ourselves together, as the manner of some is, but exhorting one another daily, so much the more as we see the day approaching."

9. Think often of the shortness of your lives; many think they shall have time enough to recover themselves hereafter; whereas did they but look upon themselves just a going to die, or that death was at the door, they would act and live otherwise; that is to say, be more serious and careful in watching their hearts, and ways. "Be ye also ready, for in such an hour as you think not, the Son of Man will come," Matt. xxiv. 44. We know not how short our lives may be, therefore should be always on our watch. " Watch therefore, for ye know not what hour your Lord will come." This doubtless (as we find by experience) will be a great help to our leading of a sober, and heavenly life, and so prevent withering.

10. Add one grace to another. " Besides this, giving all diligence add to your faith virtue, and to virtue knowledge, and to knowledge temperance, and to temperance patience, and to patience godliness, and to godliness brotherly kindness; and to brotherly kindness charity," 2 Pet. i. 5—7. Faith being in exercise it will set all other graces on work; " For if these things be in you and abound, they make you that ye shall neither be barren, nor unfruitful in the knowledge of our Lord and Saviour Jesus Christ," ver. 8. Nay, more, they will make us active, lively, green, and flourishing in our profession, and blessed knowledge of Christ; and that to such a degree, that we shall never wither nor decay in grace and holiness.

11thly. If you would not decay or wither, you must see that you early weed your own hearts; you know that weeds oftentimes choke the seed, and cause it to be weak, and so to wither; therefore you will weed your corn and your gardens. So must we weed our hearts day by day, or else one sin or corruption or another, will spoil the seed of grace that is sown in them. We must weed out that pride, that inordinate love to the world, that passion, that unbelief, that carnality of our affections, and that hypocrisy, and deadness out of our hearts that remain; this we must do, if we would not wither and decay in our souls, as the stony-ground professors did. *Our hearts must be daily weeded, to prevent witherings.*

12. See that you are never offended at the word, as the counterfeit Christian sometimes is. "When tribulation and persecution ariseth because of the word, by and by he is offended." Men may be offended three ways.

1. When the word puts them to this choice, *i. e.*, whether they will have Christ or the world; whether they will have Christ and forego their trades, their goods, their friends, their liberty, and their lives for Christ; or forego Christ, forsake Christ for these things. *Men are offended three ways because of the word.* Now when this choice was put to the young man in the Gospel, rather than he would part with his possessions, he bids Christ farewell; he was offended and went away sorrowful. This choice hath offended many in our days, and therefore some have cleaved to the false church, and to human rites and ceremonies, rather than be exposed to suffer loss and want in the world, and bear persecution for Christ's sake.

2. When the doctrine of Christ is too hard for their understanding, or because it lies above their own human reason, they are by and by offended. They will have no religion that wholly depends upon the revelation of God's word, but only that which comports with their natural reason, and natural knowledge. They must do something for to save themselves, must work for life, to believe for righteousness, to trust to and depend upon another's righteousness, this doctrine they are offended at. Hence in these days what dangerous books are published, asserting that there is nothing in the Gospel which is above our own human reason to comprehend. Thus the Jews that heard our blessed Saviour say, "That unless a man eat his flesh, and drink his blood, he had no life in him," John vi. 60. They were offended, and went their way.

3. When the word pursues them close, and follows them home to their consciences, telling them that every secret sin and lust, though never so pleasant or profitable, must be parted with; they are offended when it tells them their right eye must be pulled out, and their right hand must be cut off, or begins once to touch or meddle with their Herodias, their bosom sin, they are offended, and they wither away. Now a true believer takes Christ for better or worse, whithersoever he goes, he will follow him, though it be to the cross. Whatsover he commands us to do, we must obey him, though it be to offer up our own beloved Isaacs, if we would never wither or decay in grace and holiness.

13. Resolve to endure any hardness for Jesus Christ: the design of Christ in persecution and tribulation is to try his people, that it may be seen and known who are sound and sincere, and who are not. A mighty wind many times shakes down an old rotten house, and floods overthrow houses built upon the sands: a weak and feeble person cannot go up a mighty hill; also a tender and sickly man cannot bear to lie all night in the field, on the cold ground, in a frosty and bitter season. So none but such whom grace fortifies and enables to endure hardness, trouble, and persecution, can abide to the end in their holy profession under trials.

4. From hence we may infer, from whence it is that so many professors fall away in a time of persecution. Alas, their hearts were not right with God, their hearts were hard and stony.

VI

And some fell among thorns, and the thorns sprang up with it, and choked it.—MATT. xiii. 7.

Verse 22, our Lord opens this part of the parable, and shows what are meant by thorns. "He also that receiveth the seed among thorns, is he that heareth, and the cares of this world, and the deceitfulness of riches choke the word, and it becometh unfruitful."

Thorns, by what our Lord here declares, do signify or mean two things.

1. The cares of the world, which refer to the poorer sort.

2. The deceitfulness of riches, which refer to the richer sort; both the poor and rich are in danger by these thorns to be undone for ever.

1. I shall show you the nature of thorny ground.

2. Show why the cares of this world are compared to thorns.

3. Why the riches of this world are so compared also ; and likewise why they are called deceitful riches.

To begin with the first of these.

What sort of ground thorny ground is.

1. Thorny ground wants ploughing up and manuring, "For thus saith the Lord to the men of Judah and Jerusalem, Break up the fallow ground, and sow not among thorns," Jer. iv. 3. The meaning is, they should take care about their hearts, and labour to root out the thorns, *i. e.*, the inordinate love of this world, and not let either worldly cares, nor the deceitfulness of riches, hinder the rooting of the word, or the grace of God in their souls.

2. The plough must go deep to reach the roots of every thorn. So the root of every sin, particularly unbelief, the inordinate love of the world, and cursed hypocrisy, the immoderate love of, and cares about the things of this life, are not easily rooted out.

3. Thorns choke the seed ; they spread this way and that way, so that the seed cannot spring up but the thorns spring up with it. So unbelief and sinful cares spread themselves into many branches, which choke the word and make it unprofitable and unfruitful.

(1.) Pride. This is one evil branch ; they know enough, yea, as much as the preacher (in their own conceit) they are rich in their own eyes, and have need of nothing.

(2.) Self-confidence. Who were more confident as touching the goodness of their condition than the Jews ? see Rom. ii. 17, 18. Faith makes the soul very diligent to try and search the heart, but unbelief makes a man careless ; he regards not his own heart, not doubting but Christ is his, and his state is safe. "I went by the field of the slothful, by the vineyard of the man void of understanding, and so it was all grown over with thorns, and nettles had covered the face thereof," Prov. xxiv. 30, 31.

4. From hence immoderate cares spring up, they have no time to pray, no time to hear with diligence the word of God, no time to meditate ; no, all their time is little enough to get bread, and to think how to get out of debt, or how to improve what they have, or increase and keep their worldly riches.

5. Thorns hinder the influences of the sun from causing the seed to take root. So the evils of these men's hearts, particularly the cares of the world, and the deceitfulness of riches, hinder serious meditation ; by which means the influences of the Spirit are obstructed, also they quench the Spirit's motions, and the common operations thereof, nay, resist the Holy Ghost in this respect.

6. All the showers of heaven cannot make the thorny ground to bring forth fruit, until the thorns are rooted up. No, though the rain falls upon it very often. So such who are filled full of earthly cares, and set their hearts upon the riches of this world, though the divine rain falls often upon them, yet their hearts are never the better, they bear nothing but thorns and briers. Heb. vi. 7.

7. It is a very unpleasant sight to see a field of wheat run over with thorns, briers, and nettles, and it greatly grieves the husbandman to see it. So it is grievous to Christ, and to a faithful minister, to see his hearers so earthly, worldly, and carnal ; they cannot attend upon the word timely, nor with holy diligence, the world has got so much room in their hearts,

8. That ground that brings forth thorns and briers is rejected, and is near unto cursing ; so those men who bring forth no fruit to God, though the heavenly rain falls often upon them, yet nothing but thorns appear ; all their talk is about the world, either bewailing their losses, or speaking of the badness of the times, nothing of the badness of their hearts ; "These persons are rejected, and are nigh unto cursing, whose end will be burning," Heb. vi. 7, 8.

Why the cares of the world are likened to thorns.

Secondly, why are the cares of the world like unto thorns ?

1. As thorns have their rooting in the earth, or ground that is naught ; so the cares of the world have their rooting in an evil and carnal heart.

2. Thorns and briers, as one observes, are dens for serpents, and receptacles for poisonous and hurtful worms. So the cares of the world, unmortified lusts, and an earthly spirit, is a fit den and receptacle for Satan, that old serpent, and the gnawing worm of an accusing conscience, there this worm is bred and nourished.

3. Thorns are every way (as it were) armed and ready to wound and tare him that meddles with them ; so they that give way to the inordinate cares of the world, and will be rich, labour to be rich, fall into many "hurtful lusts which drown men in destruction and perdition, and pierce themselves through with many sorrows," 1 Tim. vi. 9, 10.

4. Thorns are unprofitable things; the fruit they bear is of little worth, but commonly tends to feed the fowls of the air ; so the cares of the world and an heart set upon riches, are good for nothing but to feed the devil and a devilish sensual heart. " Who by taking care can add one cubit to his stature," Matt. vi. 27.

5. Thorns quite cover some ground, and eat up the heart of the land where they grow. So cares and the love of worldly riches overspread some men's hearts, and eat up all their time and thoughts, that should other ways be employed about their precious souls.

6. And as thorns at last are cast into the fire, and are burned ; so should we cast all inordinate cares and covetous desires into the flames of the divine fire, that the Holy Spirit may burn them up, and utterly consume them.

7. Thorns must be rooted out of land if ever it be made good tillage; so must all worldly cares be rooted out of our hearts if ever they become good soil for the seed of the word.

8. A man that lies upon thorns can have no sweet rest. So he that gives way to the cares of the world, or that sets his heart upon deceitful riches, shall never have inward peace, joy, and comfort in Jesus Christ; nay, many cannot by the means of worldly cares takes their natural rest, their troublesome thoughts hinder them from bodily repose and quiet sleep.

Doct. The cares of this life and love of riches are very sinful and dangerous, or lawful things, by an inordinate thoughtfulness about them, and love to them, are pernicious to the soul.

1. I shall prove this proposition.

2. Apply it.

1. What hath been said, makes this truth very clear ; but consider further, that these hearers appear better than the former, their hearts are not so hard ; there is somekind of tenderness in these; the seed of the word seems *The curses of this life and riches dangerous.* to have some deeper rooting in these than in the stony ground hearers, they hear with more joy, and stand longer in their profession ; but yet their hearts retaining an inordinate love to the world, after all, they fall utterly away, and perish eternally.

2. These cares choke the word, and make it unfruitful, therefore most dangerous and pernicious to the soul.

3. The stony ground hearers no doubt did allow themselves in such sins, that this sort could not, may be these cast off all gross acts of immorality, while the other lives in some secret course of wickedness, though hid from the world ; yet these lose their souls by overloving, or setting their hearts upon the lawful things of this world. And from hence we may see what a mischievous thing it is to become a professor without a changed heart, or being renewed.

4. That which is the root of all evil, must needs be a most dangerous thing; but the love of money is the root of all evil. And the inordinate love of any earthly thing, or enjoyment, is idolatry; the Apostle positively saith, "that covetousness is idolatry," Col. iii. 5. That which a person chiefly sets his heart upon, or loves with a superlative love, is his god, whether husband, wife, child, gold, silver, house, land, or his own belly. No notorious and open acts of wickedness, is more hateful to God than this ; it is as bad as to fall down before a graven image. Moreover, in vain are all those directions that some worthy men give to sinners to get rid of these cares, and love of the riches, honours, and pleasures, of the world, unless first they obtain union with Christ, and feel the efficacious operations of the Spirit in true regeneration. " For they that are after the flesh mind the things of the flesh," Rom. viii. 5, 6, 7. And will until they are born of the Spirit.

True the blade of a visible profession, may spring up, but the seed of the word that should be rooted in the soul, is choked by these thorns.

They may receive the word into their understanding in some measure, but their wills are never brought over to a full and hearty consent, to love and embrace the Lord Jesus Christ, or to receive the truth in the love of it ; the word of God hath no abiding in these; it is not hid in their hearts.

The thorns sprung up and choked it. Note, that not only unlawful things, but the abuse of lawful, do shut men out of the kingdom of heaven. It is not only whoredom, adultery, drunkenness, swearing, murder, lying, or stealing, *The sad effects of abusing of lawful things.* that tend to choke the word, but the abuse of lawful profits, lawful cares, and lawful desires ; the old world (as one observes) eat and drank, built and planted, married and were given in marriage ; why all these things were lawful, but they abused these things. What is more lawful than to purchase a farm, or a yoke of oxen, or to marry a wife. But if men will in doing these things refuse to come to Christ, or prefer it above a marriage with the Lord Jesus, the Lord saith, they shall never taste of my supper.

Eating and drinking may become a snare. Eating and drinking is lawful, but when men feed without fear, or eat and drink to make provision for the flesh, it is not only unlawful, but a damning evil; to put on apparel decently, to cover our nakedness is very lawful, but they that dress themselves in immodest apparel to tempt unto uncleanness, or in new, strange, and fantastical attire, that exposeth religion to reproach, such putting on of apparel is abominable, or when people can spare pounds to deck and adorn their body, and can hardly afford a poor child of God a shilling, or will have fine clothes, and yet cannot pay their debts, it is hateful to God, or take more care to adorn their bodies, than their souls.

Marriage may become a snare. What is more lawful than marriage? but when men marry the portion rather than the person, or marry such that they like and never regard the divine precept, in the Lord, and to please his wife, casteth off his profession; or when the husband or wife is more beloved than Jesus Christ; or the marriage-bed becomes a snare, or is defiled, it is abominable, or when a man abuses his wife, and makes her life uncomfortable to her, or takes no due care to provide either for wife or children. How is marriage, though a lawful thing, abused!

What is more lawful than company or society with men? but when a man shall choose evil company, and be a companion of drunkards, it is abominable.

Or what is more lawful than for a man to take care to get bread, and to provide for his family, and in an honest way to keep or get out of debt? but if men neglect the worship of God, or be in their shops when they should be in the Church, or to get bread will take unlawful courses, or to enrich themselves, pinch or grip the poor, or labour more for the "meat that perishes, than for that meat which endureth unto everlasting life," John vi. 27, or when carking and distractful cares fill their heads and hearts so that they forget God, and take his name in vain, or steal, it is abominable.

A trade may become a snare. What is more lawful than for a man to follow his trade and employment? And if God bless him, so that he grows rich, he may comfortably enjoy what he hath, but if he in trading over-reaches his neighbours, and tells a company of lies, praising goods beyond what he ought and knows of them, or minds his particular calling more than his general, or neglects the poor, and all acts of bounty, this lawful and necessary thing, is abused. Or what is more lawful than a feast, but if men or women will eat and drink to excess, such feasts are abused.

APPLICATION

1 **Inference.** See what ways Satan hath to ruin the souls of men, and to hinder the blessed effects the word of God should have on their hearts.

2. If lawful things when abused may destroy the soul, and be as piercing thorns, what venom and poison is there in those things, the very bare use of which is unlawful or a palpable breach of God's law, what thorns and snares do such walk upon. Our Lord speaking of the people of the "old world in the days of Noah," Luke. xvii. 28, makes no mention of their more beastly sins, as pride, uncleanness, sodomy, &c. And this might be (as 2 **Inference.** Taylor observes) to show what fearful plagues such vile enormous courses bring upon men, when lawful things immoderately used were punished with the vengeance of God.

1 **Exhort.** 3. Take heed you offend not, exceed not in the use of lawful things, although you venture not upon things unlawful in themselves, it is bad sleeping upon a bed of thorns; but how then do such wound themselves, saith one, that dare venture over a hedge of sharp and fearful curses by which God hath fenced and hedged his law. O that bold sinners, shameless harlots, whoremongers, debauched, drunkards, blasphemers, and profaners of the Lord's day, would lay these things to heart!

2 **Exhort.** 4. Do not go to the out-side, or top of your liberty; it is better to pinch thy carcase than pamper the flesh, and so wound the Spirit. Take St. Paul's counsel: This I say, brethren, the time is short; it remaineth that both they that have wives be as though they had none; And they that weep, as though they wept not, and they that rejoice, as though they rejoiced not; and they that buy, as though they possessed not. And they that use the world as not abusing it, for the fashion of the world passeth away," 1 Cor. vii. 29, 30, 31. In the use of the earthly things learn to find out the profit and sweetness of spiritual things; whilst thou cherishes and feeds thy body, think how thou shouldst have food and refreshment for thy soul, and in labouring for bread, think what great pains thou shouldst take for the bread of life; and in thy enjoying of lawful pleasures, remember the joys and pleasures of heaven, that are at God's right hand for evermore,

that have no snare attending them, but are satisfying and eternal. This (saith one) is an holy alchimy, to draw gold out of lead, heaven out of earth, and grace out of nature.

5. When you enjoy peace and plenty, take heed your hearts do not forget God or grow wanton like to Jesurun of old, " who waxed fat, and kicked against the Lord—and lightly esteemed of the God of his salvation," Deut. xxxii. 15. How abominable is it whilst God loads us with his mercies, we should load him with our iniquities, or whilst we receive his wages we should do the devil's work; when God raiseth our states highest, let us strive to have our hearts lowest.

" And the cares of this world, and the deceitfulness of riches choke the word, and he becometh unfruitful," ver. 22.

These two things undo the thorny ground hearers.

(1.) The cares of this world.

(2.) The deceitfulness of riches.

A little farther to both these, as to cares.

1. They are cares about the things of this life. (1.) What we shall eat, what we shall drink, or wherewith we shall be clothed.

2. Care how to get out of debt, or fear of want, or lying in a prison.

3. Care about the times, or what will become of us or our children, such dismal days being expected.

4. Being perplexed about losses, badness of trade and disappointments, they are of this nature.

Quest. But are all earthly cares sinful, and unlawful?

Answ. " Be careful for nothing," Phil. iv. 6; that is, solicitously, or anxiously careful, or be not overwhelmed with inordinate cares, they are these cares which choke the word; for not all kind of care is unlawful.

1. For we may take notice of our outward condition, we may take notice of what we have, and what we have lost; yet be content with our present state. *All kind of cares not unlawful.*

2. Every one ought to have a moderate and provident care of his own worldly concerns, and follow his business so as to eat his own bread, and provide for his family, or he is worse in that than an infidel.

3. We may be affected also with our outward losses, though not to distress our minds, but lay it so to heart, as to enquire why it is thus? Have we not sinned?

4. If we are prosperous in the world, we should be so thoughtful, as to remember what our state was once, and how God has blessed us; " With my staff I came over this Jordan, and now lo I am become two bands," said good old Jacob.

5. How in a lawful way to repair our losses, and how all we have may be employed to the glory of God, and good of his people.

6. Lawful cares may be attended with moderate fear, hope or joy; such that ariseth from the sense of the little worth of all earthly things; our fear or joy should be according to the nature of those things, our thoughts are let out about.

7. Moderate joy for the good things received, or moderate grief for the evils we lie under, are both lawful.

Quest. How may a person know when his care is excessive, inordinate, and sinful?

1. When the mind is wholly, or almost altogether taken up about earthly things, there being hardly any room for better thoughts in our hearts; our thoughts being too many, &c., too frequent running out to these things. *When cares are sinful.*

2. When we let our thoughts and care run out on earthly things in an unseasonable time, as when we are in God's holy worship; the Jews on their sabbath day, were not to think their own thoughts; what shall we present our bodies before the Lord, and let the world, nay, sin and the devil, have our hearts? God looks at our hearts, sees and observes our thoughts when we are in his service; " their hearts go after their covetousness."

3. When cares or earthly thoughts hurry, and hale our souls and spirits into disorder, or when they throng and crowd in upon our minds, that we find inward commotion, and our souls like the restless sea, be sure then your care exceeds all due bounds.

4. When worldly cares and thoughts are perplexing and vexatious, so that we cannot sleep quietly, by reason of our thoughtfulness about the things of this life, the soul being filled with pain and great sorrow.

5. When our care is more to get the riches of this world, than the riches of grace and the riches of glory; more about earth than heaven, more on time than on eternity; " While we look not on things that are seen," 2 Cor. iv. 18. Alas! but all do not thus; some look on things that are seen, and but little on things that are eternal, or not seen; some take

more care to make sure an estate than to make their calling and election sure; more thought-ful to get bread, or heap up gold and silver, than to get eternal life, or the meat which perishes not, "Labour not for the meat that perishes," that is, not chiefly, John vi. 27.

6. When our cares and careful thoughts hinder us from enjoying what we have, or eats up all the comfort of what we do profess; when a man lies in his bed, as if he lay upon thorns. Earthly cares (as you have heard) are of a pricking and piercing nature, they embitter the soul, wound the soul.

7. When so disquieting, that they indispose us to holy duties, so that we cannot break through the crowd of careful thoughts, to converse with God; or if we do it, it is but sel-dom, and with much difficulty.

(1.) Perhaps rarely think of the soul, or what that wants.

(2.) Nor on what God has done for our souls.

(3.) Nor can we meditate but little on spiritual things and objects; the mind is so filled with earthly cogitations.

8. When through worldly cares and thoughtfulness we forgot the time of God's holy worship (as some say) alas I forgot the hour when such a meeting was to begin, my thoughts were so hurried with many things. O what abominable a thing is this! certainly they do not forget their dining-time, nor their supper-time, they forget not to feed their bodies, but forgot to feed their souls.

9. When distracting cares have got the ruling and predominating power over a poor creature, so that he cannot recal them, but they carry him away captive; they cannot say as Abraham did (in another case) to his servants; "stay you here while I and the lad go up yonder to worship."

10. When your cares and thoughts are unbelieving and distrustful, and take the heart off depending upon God, you cannot rely upon his promises and faithfulness, or when they carry a man into a lawful way and means, either to get bread, or increase their substance, or in a way that is doubtful, or whether lawful or not. Perhaps it is an unlawful trade, or it is to live upon extortion or unlawful use for money, or by selling of goods for unlaw-ful gain or profit; or above what they may be had'for of others, or by pinching the labourer, or forcing a man to sell his goods cheaper than he can afford them, and so feed on his ne-cessities.

Lastly. When we care more for earthly things than for the things of God, "The un-married careth for the things of the Lord," &c., 1 Cor. vii. 32.

USE

Exhort. O be exhorted to fly all sinful and perplexing cares!

MOTIVES

I. It is a breach of God's holy precept; "Take no care what you shall eat, or what you shall drink, nor yet for you bodies, what you shall put on," Matt. vi. 25, 26; will you violate Christ's command or holy precept?

The sinful-ness of in-ordinate cares.   II. The sinfulness of these inordinate thoughts and distracting cares are further aggravated.

1. It argues that such are not contented with their present state, which every one is commanded to be; "content with such things as you have;" not what others have, or what you had once.

2. It argues, such like not God's providential government of the world; they seem to arraign the wisdom of God at their bar, as if they knew better than God, what was best for them; O, say they, what abundance of riches have some, and I am poor, and want bread! why is this thus? they have much health, and I am always weak, sickly, and in pain! sirs, God knows that sickness is better than health for you; and may be the riches that some have, are given them in judgment, to their hurt, and not for their good, or per-haps it is all they shall have, it is their portion; and would you then change your condition and estate for theirs?

III. Consider, all your perplexing cares are vain and fruitless; "Who by taking care can add one cubit to his stature?" Matt. vi. 27, this is not the way to get bread. It is vain to rise up early, and sit up late, and to eat the bread of carefulness. It is the worst food you can feed on; care will never fill your bellies, nor your purses; no, it will sooner break your hearts.

IV. Because there is no need of it; one is enough to take care, if he be one that is able to supply all our wants, and willing and faithful also. Breth-ren, Christ takes care of us; "Cast your care upon him, for he cares for you," No need of their anxi-ous cares.

1 Pet. v. 7, Again he saith, " In nothing be careful," &c., Phil. iv. 6. Nay, Christ does not only take care of us, but the Father also ; " Your heavenly Father knoweth you have need of all these things," Matt. vi. 32. Can you not trust God with all your concernments ?

V. To give way to these inordinate cares, is to act below a rich man's child, the child, may be, hath but a little or nothing in his own possession, perhaps, no money at all ; but what of that, saith the child, my father is a rich man, he hath many thousands, I shall have what he sees I need ; so he takes no care. O learn wisdom by such a child, is not your Father very rich ? " is not the earth the Lord's, and the fulness thereof ?" What, though you and I have but a little in our own keeping, our Father is the King of heaven and earth, and shall any of his children fear they shall want any good thing ; but we must leave him to judge in the case. David saith, " The Lord is my Shepherd, I shall not lack ;" but he might have said, the Lord is my Father, I shall not lack. The relation of a child is nearer than that of a sheep to the shepherd.

VI. It is a reproach, and scandalous to religion ; it shows (1.) As if you cannot find satisfaction in God, without the creature. (2.) Nay, it is a sign you are carnally minded, and that you have not your dependence and trust in God, or doubt of his care and faithfulness. (3.) That you are not well taught, or else ill proficients ; you have not " learned in whatsoever state you are, therewith to be content," Phil. iv. 11. This was a lesson that Paul had learned : moreover, it shows you have not seen that all earthly things are vanity. See, saith the ungodly, how this man, this woman, who are professors, and boast of a part in Christ, and know how good God is, how uneasy he is, because he wants the riches of this world, or enjoys no more health, or meets with losses and crosses in his temporal affairs ; what faith has he more than other men ? is this the man that makes his boast of God ?

VII. They are very sinful, because they hinder better thoughts, they thrust all good thoughts and heavenly care out of the heart ; nay, thrust Christ out, who should dwell in our hearts, in our minds and thoughts, continually, but there is no room for him in this house.

VIII. It is heathenish, and it is a sign you are no better than others, and Mr. Dodd. have no higher dependence on God than heathens have ; nay, that you are like them. " After all these things do the Gentiles seek," Matt. vi. 32.

IX. That it is hurtful to your own souls, further appears.

1. May it not disoblige Christ from taking care of you, to take his work out of his hand, and take care for yourselves.

2. It hinders the efficacy of the word and ordinances of God ; " The cares of this world, and the deceitfulness of riches, choke the word," Matt. xiii. 22. No wonder you profit not under the word ; may be your thoughts are on the world when you sit under the preaching of the gospel.

X. It hinders us from preparing for Christ's coming ; " Take heed to yourselves, lest at any time your hearts be overcharged with surfeiting and drunkenness, and the cares of this life, and so that day come upon you unawares."

XI. It shows that the hearts of such are naught.

1. That they are earthly, and mind carnal things.

2. That their wills are not bowed to the will of God, but that much unmortified lusts remain in you.

3. And that you do not first, chiefly, and above all things, " seek the kingdom of heaven," Matt. vi. 33.

Quest. How shall we get rid of sinful care ? How to be rid of distracting cares.

1. Ans. Consider the evil of them, and how dishonourable it is for you thus to let your hearts run after earthly things.

2. Consider the relation you stand in to God, and that you are his children. O remember what a Father you have.

3. Live by faith upon the promises ; " Trust in the Lord and do good, and verily thou shalt be fed," Psal. xxxvii. 3 ; " They that fear the Lord, shall want no good thing," Psal. xxxiv. 10.

4. Believe in the all-sufficiency of God ; " I am God Almighty," Gen. xvii. 1 ; this is enough. Thus Abraham was supported.

5. Consult the wisdom of God, so you will be content with the portion he gives you, or what things you have, not what others have, or what you have had, but what you now have ; " Having food and raiment, therewith be content," Heb. xiii. 5.

6. Remember God is faithful, who hath promised that he will help you, and never leave or forsake you.

7. Call to remembrance your former experience, how in former straits he helped you, and appeared for you. Thus David was relieved, when in fears and straits.

Lastly, Live much on the thoughts of death; a little will serve our turn while we are here.

VII

And thorns sprung up and choked them.—Matt. xiii. 7.

SEE our Saviour's exposition, ver. 22, "And the cares of this world, and the deceitfulness of riches, choke the word, and he becometh unfruitful."

1. By thorns are meant

(1.) The cares of this life, and that I have spoken to.

(2.) The deceitfulness of riches.

Mr. Taylor. How riches are like thorns. Wealth (saith one) in *spina purigens;* pricking thorns, full of molestation. "They that will be rich pierce themselves through with many sorrows," 1 Tim. vi. 10, will be rich; they pursue after riches, whether God please to give them in a way of mercy or not, yet their hearts are set upon wealth, though they prove like pricking thorns to him; as a man walking through thorns is pricked on every side, before him and behind him." So saith my author, a man greedy of gain, the craving thoughts of getting, the labour and toil of increasing, the fear of losing, the sorrow of leaving, prick him on every side.

2. Thorns are choking. So it was riches that choked Demas, he loved this present evil world, he would cast off Christ and sacrifice to an idol, before he would miss of riches. Riches choked also the young man in the gospel, so that he could not swallow down Christ's holy doctrine, of selling all, and giving to the poor; multitudes have been this way choked in every age of the church.

3. Thorns, when the blossom is upon them, are deceiving, they seem pleasant to the sight, but let men touch them with their tender hands, they soon wound him. So riches are deceitful things, they smile in a man's face, and secretly pierce his heart; also a man thinks he has fast hold of them, but lo, on a sudden "They take themselves wings, and fly away like an eagle to heaven," Prov. xxiii. 5.

Doct. Riches are dangerous, deceitful, and hurtful things.

1. Negatively, they are not evil nor hurtful in themselves.

2. But in the affirmative, through the evil of men's hearts, and the temptations of Satan, they are hurtful, evil, and deceitful. Riches to a godly man, who hath a heart to use them to the glory of God, are a great blessing, but to most men they prove a plague and a curse.

I shall endeavour to do two things.

1. Show the evils and snares that attend riches.

2. Show they are deceitful.

3. Apply it.

1. The evils that attend riches, are expressed by our blessed Saviour, viz., "They choke the word;" like as thorns choke good seed where it is sown.

How riches choke the Word. 1. They tend to choke the word by filling the thoughts of such men to such a degree, that the word can have no room in the hearts of such persons to take root; they mind earthly things. They take up room (saith one) where the seed should root and grow. The inordinate love of the world stuffs the **Taylor.** heart with worldly desires and motions, so that they cannot think of any of their spiritual wants.

II. They are in their love and affections to such a degree that they are the rich man's god; they prefer riches above Christ. The young man in the gospel left Jesus Christ rather than he would part with his great possessions. And Demas, for the love to the riches of this present evil world, cast off Christ and the Christian religion; "Demas hath forsaken me, having loved this present world,". 2 Tim. iv. 10. Not that riches are the cause of carrying away the heart; no, but are as an occasion; the cause is not in them, but in the evil heart of man, that is so prone naturally to be set upon them, they so suit and agree with the corruptions and natural inclination of men's evil hearts.

III. The evil of riches appears from what our Saviour saith, viz., " It is as as hard for a camel to go through the eye of a needle, as it is for a rich man to enter into the kingdom of heaven," Matt. xix. 24. He never saith thus of poor men, or that a poor man shall hardly enter into the kingdom of heaven ; no, but saith he, " the poor received the gospel." So that it appears, though poverty has many snares attending it, yet riches have more and greater ; but not that it is impossible for those who are rich, to be saved ; (no, all things with God are possible :) but it is exceeding hard and difficult, to speak after the manner of men, they are so great a snare and obstruction to them who have their hearts set upon them.

IV. The evil of riches lies in their bewitching nature ; they have a strange influence upon men's hearts. *Riches are of a bewitching nature.*

1. This appears by that greedy desire men have after them, when they see them coming ; O how restless are they, to add heap to heap, join house to house, and land to land ; a little will not serve their turn, Job. v. 5.

2. By the great pains, they take, and amazing dangers they run, to grow rich and great in the world, " He putteth forth his hand upon the rock ; he overturneth the mountains by the roots," Job. xxviii. 9. If rocks stand in his way of finding gold or silver, he will batter those rocks ; or if mountains do hinder him, he will undermine them, or cut through them ; what hazards do they run by sea, and what perils and dangers by land, to get riches and honours : they will venture their lives for them, and sooner lose their lives than part with them. The reasons may be these why they thus prize riches.

1. Because they are connatural unto man : man is (saith Mr. Caryl) a kin unto the earth, and the things of the earth ; he was made of the earth, or of the dust, and what is gold but yellow earth, or the dust of the ground ? *Why men so highly prize and esteem riches.* He whose original is of the earth, and hath obtained no other birth, seeketh the earth : " He is of the earth, and speaketh of the earth," John iii. 31, and minds earthly things.

2. Earthly things, gold and silver glitter, or have a shining beauty or glory in them, and so are a bewitching or ensnaring object of the eye. I saw a wedge of gold, and a goodly Babylonish garment ; Well, and what then ? I coveted them ; my eye was smitten with them, and my heart desired them ; covetousness is called the lust of the eyes, 1 John ii. 16 ; it is that which the eye lusteth after, and earthly men walk by the sight of their eyes, they only look at things that are seen ; they have no spiritual sight, they cannot see eternal things : and gold, silver, and earthly treasure, are best of all things their eyes can see or look upon.

3. Because they find the continual need and great usefulnes of these things : money is a defence, Eccl. vii. 12. Nay, money answereth all things, Eccl. x. 19. What may not a man have of all desirable things here, that has abundance of money ? It answers beauty, gallantry, nobility, and what not ?

4. It raiseth men up in repute and honour in the world : estimation and grandeur flow in with riches : poverty bringeth contempt ; the poor are trod upon, and despised, but the rich have many friends. Such who are of low and base birth, if once they grow very rich, they may be made knights, earls, lords, &c. Money procures great titles, and great places : poor men are not made rulers, and governors of towns and cities, &c., no, they are the rich.

5. Because riches deliver men from many outward evils, and supply men with all earthly comforts ; when the poor suffer want, and are in necessities.

V. Riches are evil in respect had to many temporal dangers, they expose men's lives : how many have lost their sweet lives for the sake of their money ! the son has murdered the father, the heir the prince, out of love to riches and honour, to get their estates, crowns, and kingdoms : and we might fill a volume of stories of this kind. " Come cast in thy lot with us, let us lie in wait for blood ; we shall find all precious substance, we shall fill our houses with spoil," Prov. i. 13, 14. *Riches evil in respect of temporal dangers.*

VI. Riches are evil and pernicious things, because multitudes of men for the love of them, have pierced themselves through with many sorrows : " they fall into temptation, and a snare, and into many foolish and hurtful lusts," &c., 1 Tim. vi. 9, 10. Again, he saith, " While some have coveted after, they have erred from the faith, and have pierced themselves through with many sorrows." Some by outward losses have run distracted ; others have laid violent hands upon themselves, and many have wounded their own consciences. *Riches evil because they expose to many snares?*

VII. Many by the love of riches have lost their precious souls ; and this our Saviour showeth in this place, in respect of some of these hearers. Therefore riches are evil and dangerous things.

Secondly, riches are deceitful things.

Riches are deceitful.

1. In respect of what things they deceive men of.

2. In respect of the way by which they do deceive.

I. Riches deceive men of the blessings of the word of God; they are by the love of wealth cheated of, and have lost those convictions which they have had in their hearts, of the evil of sin, and of the need of Christ.

What riches deceive men of.

II. Riches deceive men of their time, cheat and rob them of those seasons they might have had of hearing the word: what opportunities by the inordinate love of the world have many been deceived of! They must attend their trades, their shops, or see to get in their debts, or tell their money, when they should have been at a meeting, or in hearing the word of God.

III. Riches deceive men of profiting under the word when they come to hear it; their hearts run after their covetousness, they can give no account of what the minister said, their heads and hearts were so filled with other things; perhaps they are thinking of what is owing them, or what they have got by this or that bargain, or how to lay out their money to their further advantage, when they should hear, and labour to receive the word of God into their hearts.

IV. Riches, or the love of the world, deceive men of Christ, or of espousing of Jesus Christ; when they are bid to come to the marriage, one hath " brought three yoke of oxen, and he must needs go to try them; another hath bought a farm and he must go and see it; and another hath married a wife, and he cannot come," Matt. xxii. 5; no doubt it was a wife that was an enemy to religion and godliness, but perhaps she was fair, or had a great store of money; however, these outward things, or riches were so in their heart, that Christ is slighted, these men make light of those great things of another world.

V. Riches deceive them of eternal life, they cannot part with their money for Christ's sake; a place in God's house would be too chargeable for them: what give so much to the pastor, and so much to the poor? and may be, saith a rich man, troubles may come, and I may lose all I have at once: therefore he will rather lose his soul and heaven, than expose his estate to such hazard.

VI. Riches deceive men of the love of God; " for if any man love the world, the love of the Father is not in him," 1 John i. 15. And as men by the love of riches are deprived of God's love, so hereby they incur his wrath; some bless the covetous whom the Lord abhorreth, Psal. ciii. 3. God hates a covetous person, and no wonder, since he is an idolator, Col. iii. 5.

Secondly, in what way, how or after what manner doth riches deceive wicked men?

How riches deceive.

1. By its promises (1.) They promise peace, satisfaction, and content to his mind, but the poor wretch is deceived, he finds none, for these satisfy not. " He that loveth silver, shall not be satisfied with silver," &c., Eccl. v. 10. We see this true by daily experience, let men get many thousands, yet they covet after more, and are never satisfied.

2. Riches promise security; the man thinks when once he hath got them he shall hold them, keep them, and be for ever sure of them; but, lo, on a sudden they fly away; for " Riches certainly make themselves wings, and fly away as an eagle towards heaven," Prov. xxiii. 5. Which denotes two things. (1.) That riches sometimes fly away swiftly, they are soon gone. (2.) That they often fly away irrecoverably, there is no recalling them; they are lying riches they promise to continue with the owner, but deceive him, and may be called lying vanities; yet they are not deceitful objectively, as sin and the devil are, but by means of the evil of men's hearts that trust in them, man deceives himself by them: they are only deceitful through the deceit of the heart.

(3.) They promise safety in times of trouble, and in this respect they deceive men also; " for riches profit not in the day of wrath," Prov. xi. 12. " Your silver and your gold shall not deliver you," Ezek. vii. 9, neither in the day of conscience, when God that way lets out his wrath; nor in the days of outward calamity, nor at the hour of death, nor at the day of judgment, yet the rich man's wealth is his strong tower, (i. e.) he trusteth in it.

VII. Riches do not only deceive the possessor, but the poor also. Perhaps a poor man hath a rich brother or sister. O, saith he, I shall not want, nor be exposed to beg, because my brother is worth thousands: but riches are so got into his brother's heart, that there is no love, no pity, no charity to be found in him to so near a relation, the poor man is deceived : many have lain in prison for debt, who have had rich relations; many times a stranger is a better friend than a brother.

VII. They deceive a man's own heart : O, saith a poor man, had I but the riches of such, or such men, what good would I do ? but sometimes when God hath raised such to great riches, they have proved as niggardly and as covetous as those which before they condemned upon that account ; such deceitful things riches are to a carnal heart.

Quest.   Who are they that are deceived by riches ? how may they be known ?

1. Such who through love to riches will not attend upon the word, but pre- Who are
deceived by
riches, fer the world above the word, the present good more than future good.

2.   Such who desire more after the riches of the world than after grace : many say, " Who will shew us any good ?" Psal. iv. 6; and but few say, " Lord, lift up the light of thy countenance upon us." Many thirst more for gold, than for God or Jesus Christ.

3.   Such are deceived, who look upon riches and other earthly things of this world, as the chiefest things or business they have to mind, or seek after while they are here.

4.   Such who will run themselves into great snares or temptations for the sake of wealth and riches.   What hazards will some men run, though they are told of the snares of such a trade, of such an office, of such a company ; yet because it is gainful, nothing can change their minds, but they proceed in it, and will not be dissuaded from it.

5.   Such that clog themselves with too much business, so that their hearts are almost distracted ; alas, they allow themselves no time for holy duties, no leisure for the service of God, neither pray morning nor night ; they regard neither the public nor private wor- ship of God, they have no time to meditate on the word, or on what they perhaps hear on the Lord's day, and so the word is choked by these thorns.

6.   You may know who are deceived by riches, by their talk, their speech betrayeth them.   " Out of the abundance of the heart their tongues speak, they are of the world, therefore speak of the world."   No sooner do they go from hearing of a sermon but (if you observe them) they are discoursing of worldly things, not a word of what they heard.

7.   Such who place their chief delight, content and happiness in the things of this world, when riches flow in upon them, that is their greatest joy, and if they lose, or go behind hand, and fear their estate declines, that is their chiefest and greatest sorrow and grief.

8.   Such who do that which is unjust to increase their wealth, even dig down to hell, or fall down before the devil as it were, to get riches, they care not who they wrong or ruin, so that they can but augment their riches, and go off with it without danger from men, or from the law of the land.

9.   Such whose hearts are earthly, where your treasure is there is your heart also. Now some men show that the riches of this world are their chiefest treasure, because there their hearts are.   " They that are after the flesh mind the things of the flesh," Rom. viii. 5.   These men will be rich, that is, their resolution and all their study and contriv- ance, their hearts are fully set upon the world, let who will take heaven, they are for a present portion, they are for a heaven here, though they lose their souls for ever.

These are they that the riches of the world deceive, and by these thorns the word is choked.

10.   Such that hear the word, and make a profession of it, and are counted saints, who nevertheless retain the love of the world in their hearts to such a degree, that they give but a little to the poor saints, nor to support the ministry, and that grudgingly also, it is more too out of fear they should be suspected, or out of shame, than from love to Christ, or to the poor saints and faithful ministers.   May be a man that gets his bread by his hard labour, will give more than these persons, though they may be have hundreds, but that is for their children, or relations, not for Christ, not to uphold his sinking interest, no, let that stand or fall, they lay it not to heart, may be when they die, they will give hundreds to this son, or to that daughter, but five or ten pounds they think enough, nay, a great deal, to give to the poor, or to support the Church or ministry where they were members, thus they also are deceived by the riches of this world, and prove themselves part of the thorny ground.

APPLICATION

I.   Look upon riches as dangerous things, and learn from hence to pray Inference. as Agur did,   " Give me neither poverty nor riches," &c. Prov. xxx. 8.   O how few pray against riches.

II. If riches increase, take heed of your hearts, and as David saith, " Set not your heart upon them," Psal. lxii. 10. They tend to steal the heart away from God.

III. Happy are they who are in a middle state, neither rich nor poor, these men are in the best condition of all others, therefore let such be content, though they never grow rich.

Inference.   IV. I infer that, such men who are rich, and yet good, great, and yet gracious, have great cause to praise God ; riches to such are a great blessing. O what a mercy is it to a church to have many of this sort among them ! they give liberally according to their abundance.; riches to them are given in mercy to themselves, and to others also.

V. Do not take undue ways to be rich. O beware of that, follow no unlawful calling or ways to get riches, or to get a livelihood, but choose honest trades, and beware of extortion.

VI. Let such that are rich, labour to be rich in good works, and to be humble, for riches are apt to puff men with pride.

VIII

But the other fell into good ground, and brought forth fruit, &c.—Matt. xiii. 8

But he that received the seed into good ground is he that heareth the word, and understandeth it, and beareth fruit, and bringeth forth some an hundred-fold, some sixty, some thirty, ver. 23.

But that on the good ground, are they which with an honest and good heart having heard the word, keep it, and bring forth fruit with patience.—Luke xviii. 15.

THIS is the fourth sort of ground, and that only which is good ; all the other three was very bad and unfruitful.

First, there are five things mentioned concerning this good ground, or those who are honest hearers.

1. They hear the word.
2. They understand it.
3. They keep it.
4. They bring forth fruit (though not all to the same degree).
5. They bring forth fruit with patience. Though all do not bring forth the same quantity of fruit, yet all have good and honest hearts, and it is the same fruit in quality.

Doct. Some ground is good, or some hearers are sincere and honest-hearted persons.

In speaking to this,

1. I shall show you, how this ground came to be good.
2. Show what a good and honest heart is.

All ground naturally bad.   1. Negatively, there is no ground naturally good, but all is alike evil and barren. " Every imagination of men's hearts (yea, the hearts of men) are evil, and that continually," Gen. vi. 5. All by nature are children of wrath, there is none that understandeth, &c. Eph. ii. 3. " All are gone out of the way, there is none that doeth good, no not one, there is no difference, &c. Rom. iii. 11, 12, 13. Jews and Gentiles, the elect and reprobate, are all alike by nature.

2. Therefore in the affirmative, the difference is of God's making ; as he makes one Christian to excel another in gifts and graces, so he only it is that makes the difference between some hearers and others.

(1. Good ground pre-supposeth a previous work of the Holy Spirit, to prepare it and make it fit to receive the seed, at, or before the sowing of it, which is showed by another metaphor ; the Word of God is compared to a plough ; " He that sets his hand to the plough, &c." Luke ix. 62. The plough is the Gospel, and he that setteth his hand to it, is one that professeth the Gospel. Plough up the fallow-ground, and sow not among thorns, that ground that is not well ploughed and manured before the seed is sown, is bad. Every man's heart naturally lies barren, stony or thorny, until by the convictions of the word and Spirit it is prepared or ploughed up. This way only the heart of a sinner is made good. God breaks the hard and rocky heart to pieces, and makes soft and tender ; " He takes away the heart of stone and gives a heart of flesh," Ezek. xxxvi. 26. Not that this is done be-

fore the seed of the word is sown, or grace is infused, but it is at one and the same time ; the same word is as a plough, and also seed to these hearers, yet the first work of the Spirit on God's elect in order of nature, as to its operation, is that of conviction. " He shall convince the world of sin," &c. John xvi. 7, 8.   And then follows regeneration, a new heart, in which heart the seed of the word (i. e.,) true holiness springs up, and such only brings forth fruit.   The tree must first be made good.   No man can make his own evil heart good, he. cannot make himself a new heart, no, that is the work of the Holy Spirit. " Create in me a clean heart," Psal. li. 10 ; it is done by Almighty power, it is a creating operation, " A new heart will I give them," &c. Ezek. xxxvi. 26.   The same seed that produceth faith in the soul, doth by powerful convictions melt and mollify the heart, and also purges and purifies it, and so the ground becomes good.   And this work is done at once, in a moment. God works not as man works, man first ploughs, and then sows ; but God doth both together by the seed of the word, and workings of his Spirit on the soul.

1.   There is therefore first the grace of preparation in order of nature, the ground is ploughed up ; i. e., every faculty of the soul is effectually wrought upon ; the work of the plough, (saith one) is but *opus ordinabile*, a preparative work ; in order to sowing the seed, the ground must be well ploughed ; there must be no baulks, all the thorns, briars, and nettles must be turned up by the roots.   So the Holy Spirit works upon the whole heart, and changes every faculty as to its evil quality, both the conscience, judgment, understanding, the will and the affections.

How the heart comes to be good.

2.   Then the new heart follows, or the renovation of the whole soul appears.

3.   There are also the heavenly influences ; the seed is watered by sweet showers, and by the shinings or fructifying influences of the sun : so God causes the dew and showers of his grace, and the shinings and fructifying influences of the Sun of righteousness, to descend upon the hearts of these hearers ; the Spirit sprinkles daily the blood of Christ, or applies the virtue thereof to their souls, and that causes them to grow and bring forth much fruit : and as it is observed, the blood of beasts, applied to the root of trees, makes them very fruitful ; so the heart, I say, becomes fruitful through the virtue of Christ's blood applied by faith.

Secondly, I shall show you what kind of a heart a good heart is, or in what respect it may be called a good heart.

How to know a good heart.

I. A good heart is a new heart, and regenerated heart.

II. It is a heart united to God and to Jesus Christ : union with Christ makes the heart good ; it is a heart that loves Christ, delights in Christ, that cleaves to him in all cordial affections ; it is not divided between Christ and sin, nor between Christ and the world.

III. It is a believing heart ; such believe with all their heart, or with a whole heart, trusting in Christ, resting on Christ alone, and on nothing else, for righteousness, justification, and eternal life, Acts viii. 37.   They that have a good and honest heart, rejoice in Christ Jesus, and have no confidence in the flesh, Phil. iii. 3 ; such account all things but as dung in comparison with Jesus Christ ; he is most dear and precious to them ; they suffer the loss of all things for the excellency of the knowledge of Jesus Christ, Phil. iii. x, 9 ; whatsoever they did before, with Paul, account gain to them, is parted with for Christ.

IV. A good and honest heart is a humble heart, a tender and contrite heart, Hab. ii. 4 ; it is not a heart lifted up ; " Behold his soul, that is lifted up, is not upright in him."

Quest. What is it to have a heart lifted up ?

1. Answ.   To be strongly conceited of themselves, as to their parts and attainments above others, because of their learning, natural or acquired parts, or spiritual gifts, casting a slight and contempt upon others, as if they were not worth regard, in comparison of themselves ; some men glory in their knowledge of the tongues, and cast all others under reproach, that have not human learning, magnifying that above the Spirit's teachings, or the gifts and graces thereof; " Be not wise in thine own eyes," Prov. iii. 7 ; there is more hope of a fool than of him.   A humble Christian thinks he knows nothing, or has not the knowledge of a man ; thus Agur ; " Sure I am more brutish than any man, and have not the understanding of a man," Prov. xxx. 2 : but a proud person is puffed up with a conceit of his own understanding.

2. Such who think others can teach them no more than they know already.

3. Such who are so conceited of their own wisdom, that when they have sucked in a principle, wherein they differ from the whole body of the godly, and have no arguments to defend it from God's word ; yet will go on and maintain it, and though they have no answer, yet will not hold their peace.

4. When the thing is of small moment (perhaps the observation of a day), yet they will lay great stress upon it, and disturb the peace of a whole congregation about it ; this shows they are proud and conceited.

5. Such who when they have proselyted others to their notion, glory in it, whereas he should keep it to himself, and not seek to ensnare weak and unwary persons, who are ready to be tossed about with every wind of doctrine.

6. When men aim at self-applause, or are vain-glorious, the souls of such are lifted up.

7. When a man's notions are directly against plain and express Scriptures, and such that cast reproach upon religion, and upon the office and operations of the Holy Ghost : some say the elect were in as good a state and a condition before effectual calling as afterwards, and so a vital union with Christ, and regeneration, is rendered as a small thing ; or such who glory in their own strength, or magnify the power of the creature, and will of man.

8. Or when a man endeavours to make others little to exalt himself.

9. Or such who are uneasy under the providences of God, and foolishly in their hearts condemn the wisdom of God, and are impatient under his hand, or seek undue ways to deliver themselves, have a heart lifted up : this is a dangerous thing ; " Pride goes before destruction, and a haughty spirit before a fall," Prov. xvi. 18.——God has made no promise to such ; no, " He resisteth the proud, but gives grace to the humble ; God abhorreth the proud," Prov. xvi. 5. And such Paul shows, " Know nothing, but doting on questions and strifes of words, whereof cometh envy, strife, railing, and evil surmisings," 1 Tim. vi. 4.

V. An honest and a good heart is an understanding heart ; he heareth the word, and understandeth it.

1. He understandeth it is not the word of man, but the word of God.

2. He receives it not from the eloquence of the preacher, nor because it affects his ears, but because it reacheth his heart.

3. Not from the love he has to the minister, but in love to Christ, whose word it is.

4. He receives it into his understanding, or believes it not barely with the faith of credence or human faith, but with a divine faith, a faith wrought in Him by the Holy Ghost, or with the faith of the operation of God, he doth not receive the word into his head only, but into his heart also.

5. He understands the worth of the word, he sees it is rich treasure, he knows that Christ is hid in this field.

6. He understands the doctrine of the Gospel, and the word of righteousness, and it is so called.

7. He understands the power and efficacy of the word ; he experienceth " that the word is like fire, and a hammer that breaks the rock in pieces ;" and that it works physically on his soul.

VI. A good and honest heart is a perfect heart, a sincere or upright heart (i.e.), he wants no essential part of a true Christian, as a perfect man-child hath all the parts, and wants no limb, no member, or no essential part of a man : he follows Christ not for loaves, nor for profit or applause ; he is the same in private as in public, and no changes change him ; he is for the work as well as for the wages, for the cross as well as for the crown.

VII. It is an obedient heart ; he follows Christ whithersoever he goes ; he will do whatsoever Christ saith, because he loves the Lord Jesus ; such " obey from the heart the form of doctrine, Rom. vi. 17 : his obedience is evangelical, universal, and continual ; he obeys from right principles, he obeys Christ in every command, yea, in the hardest thing, and continues to obey to the end.

VIII. It is a faithful heart, will do everything as God requires it to be done, that, and no more ; neither diminish from the commission Christ hath given, nor make any alteration, nor add thereunto ; " Beloved, thou doest faithfully all thou doest," &c., 3 John v. Abraham, Moses, and all the godly, acted in all truth and faithfulness in their obedience to God.

IX. It is a jealous heart ; such take great heed lest their hearts should deceive them, or not be right with God ; " Search me, O Lord, and know my heart," Psal. cxxxix. 23 ; " try me, and know my reins ;——make my heart found in thy statutes, that I may never be ashamed," Psal. cxix. 80. They know the heart is deceitful, therefore are jealous over it.

X. It is a fruitful heart.

Thirdly, What fruit does a good heart bring forth ?

1. Fruits of holiness.

2. It brings forth the fruits of the Spirit, the fruits of faith, love, and meekness.

3. The fruit of mercy, and charity.

4. Justice : Lo, half my goods I give to the poor ; such also will (if able), if they have wronged any man, make restitution ; " If I have taken away from any man by false accusation, I restore him fourfold."

5. They bring forth much fruit, some an hundred-fold, some sixty, and some thirty-fold : all do not bring forth the like quantity ; some have not so great a measure of grace, nor like gifts ; one receiveth two talents, another five, and each brings forth fruit according to the degrees or measure of grace and gifts received.

6. They bring forth ripe fruit, and fruit in due season ; it is good fruit, and it is fruit also according to the cost and pains God is at with us ; " What could I have done more for my vineyard than I' have done ?" Isa. v. 4. Some answer not the charge and cost Christ is at with them ; if a man lays out more cost on some ground than on others, he expects more fruit from that ground : so doth Jesus Christ.

7. They bring forth fruit with patience. They continue in well doing, and wait on God for all the good which he hath promised ; they bear up under trouble and afflictions with patience. " He that believes shall not make haste :" they endure sharp providences, like as the wheat endures sharp frosts, and also abide fruitful in years of drought, Jer. xvii. 8.

APPLICATION

I. Infer. From hence we may infer, that the cause why many that hear the Word are unfruitful, and profit not, is by reason of their corrupt, barren, and evil hearts ; it is impossible that an unconverted person, or a carnal heart, should bring forth good fruit : a bitter fountain may as well send forth sweet water, or a fig-tree bear olive berries, or a thorn bear figs.

II. That God accepteth of no religious duties, which are performed by an unrenewed person, though he may preach, read, hear, give to the poor, yet being all done by a man void of grace, or by one whose person is not accepted, his duties are not accepted, but are rather an abomination unto the Lord ; neither can anything which sinners can do, bring them into a state of acceptation with God ; none are accepted but only in Christ ; " who hath made us accepted in the Beloved," Eph. i. 6.

III. That the hearts of all men naturally are evil, or like bad ground, bring forth only evil and corrupt fruit.

IV. That God alone prepares the heart for the seed ; it is he that makes the ground good ; no ground can make itself good, no, it is the work of the husbandman ; the sinner is wholly passive in the work of regeneration, grace works physically on the heart.

V. That the reason why some men fall away from the profession they make of religion, is because their hearts were never right in the sight of God, or were never changed.

VI. That no sincere believer doth, or can fall away totally and finally, so as to perish ; all who received the work into good and honest hearts, brought forth fruit unto eternal life, they hold out to the end. " We are not of them that draw back unto perdition, but of them that believe to the saving of the soul," Heb. x. 39. Apostates are of another sort, i. e., either of the stony or thorny *Sincere believers cannot totally and finally fall away.* ground, and indeed of all either of those sort of hearers fall into apostacy, or perish in hypocrisy. But good and honest hearted professors hold out to the end. This being a great and comfortable truth, though denied by many persons (and some of which I hope are good Christians, whose experiences I am persuaded contradict their principles) I shall here give some reasons or arguments to prove they who are true believers cannot totally and finally fall away.

1. Arg. Because they are elected or chosen to eternal life, all that are *1. Argu.* elected do truly believe in Christ, and they are ordained to be saved as well as to be sanctified ; if it be impossible for the elect finally to be deceived by false prophets, then it is impossible for the elect totally and finally to perish ; but it is impossible for the elect finally to be deceived, *ergo.* See what our Saviour saith, " If it were possible they should deceive the very elect," Matt. xxiv. 24. Our Saviour by these words shows, it is impossible for the elect finally to be deceived ; though they may fall, yet they shall rise again.

2. Arg. If the elect are not ordained only to be saved, but also to be fruitful, and

that their fruit shall remain, then they cannot totally and finally perish. But the elect are not only chosen to be saved, but to be fruitful, and that their fruit should remain, *ergo*. See the words of our Lord, " Ye have not chosen me, but I have chosen you, and ordained you that you should go and bring forth fruit, and that your fruit should remain," John v. 16. It is worthy of our noting, that our Saviour in these words anticipates his disciples as to a doubt that might rise in them; he having just before told them, that some branches that were in him by an outward profession, or externally in him, might wither and be cut off, and be cast into the fire. From hence they might say, Lord, if this be so, we may also become unfruitful, and as withered branches be cut off and perish for ever. ————Now to prevent any such doubt, he brings in these words, pray observe the scope and rise of what our Lord here said, and then will appear to you the exposition of what he spoke in the beginning of this chapter, which many bring as an argument to prove, that such who are in Christ, may utterly perish; whereas he shows, he does not there refer to his elect, or such who obtain a vital union with himself, but to such believers as the stony and thorny ground hearers were.

O, it is a mighty word, " Ordained you that you should go and bring forth fruit." Can the absolute decree and purpose of God be made of none effect? Nay, and " that your fruit should remain," Jer. xvii. 8; that is, that you shall not cease to bear fruit, as the prophet speaks,

Some shall bring forth good fruit to the end, the reasons showed thereof.

3. Arg. The covenant of grace secures them from final falling; Christ has engaged in that holy compact for all the elect, to preserve them unto eternal life; the Father hath put them as sheep into his hand, as their Surety and Shepherd: ———— " They shall never perish, nor can any pluck them out of my hand," John x. 28. Moreover, God hath sworn to Christ the true David in this covenant, " that his seed shall endure for ever." His seed are all true believers; all that are born of God; this covenant is " ordered in all things and sure," 2 Sam. xxiii. 5; it cannot be dissolved nor broken; it is made with Christ for us, who is obliged to perform all the conditions that were agreed unto between the Father and Himself, before the world began; which was to die for us, to renew us, and to preserve us to eternal life.

If the love of God be unchangeable, and everlasting, if the covenant between God the Father and God the Son as Mediator cannot be broken, if God hath sworn that the seed of Christ shall endure for ever; if Christ hath undertaken to preserve us by his almighty power to salvation, and hath said none of his sheep shall perish; if none, i. e., neither sin, Satan, the world, nor any thing else, can pluck them out of his hand, or separate them from the love of God; then true believers can never totally and finally perish; but all these things are so: *ergo*.

4. Arg. Is taken from the death, resurrection, ascension, and intercession of Jesus Christ. If Christ in the room and stead of all his elect, and hath borne all God's vindictive vengeance for them, and God is for ever reconciled to them by the death of his Son; if they were all virtually quickened and raised from the dead in him, and they did representatively also all ascend in him who was their Head, and are all virtually now glorified in him in heaven; if Christ intercedes for all his elect, or prays that their faith may never utterly fail, if he prays that they may be kept from all evil that is damnable, and may all be with him where he is; then no true believer can fall totally and finally from a state of grace, so as to perish. But all these things are undoubtedly so, as I could abundantly prove: *ergo*.

5. Arg. Our union with Christ is an indissolvable union, and this secures all true believers from final falling. It is like the union that is between the Father and Jesus Christ as Mediator; " I in them, and thou in me, that they may be made perfect in one," John xvii. 23, or into one; into this union Christ prayed all that believe may be taken; " Neither pray I for these alone, but for them also, which shall believe on me through their word, that they all may be one, as thou, Father, art in me, and I in thee, that they also may be one in us," &c., John xvii. 20, 21.

If the union between the Father and Jesus Christ can never be dissolved or broken, and believers are brought into as firm a union, then believers can never finally fall, but the former is true, *ergo*.

6. Arg. My next argument is taken from the indwelling or cohabitation of the Holy Spirit in all believers; the Spirit hath taken up his abode in them for ever; " He dwelleth in you, and shall be in you,—that he may abide with you for ever," John xiv. 17, verse 16. If the holy Spirit dwells in believers, and shall abide in them, to uphold, guide, lead, strengthen, support, confirm, and preserve them to the end of their days, they can never finally fall. But this I have, and might more abundantly prove, *ergo*.

Lastly. If all that receive the word into good and honest hearts, do bring forth fruit unto eternal life ; then none of them shall finally fall : but this our Lord doth positively affirm, *ergo*.

VII. We infer, that the Word of God is not understood as to its worth, excellency, power, or efficacy by many hearers ; they feel not, know not, experience not the worth and virtue thereof ; no, none but sincere Christians experience this.

Exhort. 1. O, prize the Word of God ; esteem it above your necessary food ; value it more than much fine gold ; it is with the Spirit the immortal seed, by which an immortal babe is begotten, and fed to everlasting life.

2. Show you are good ground by your fruitfulness, in holiness, in grace, in all the graces and fruits of the Spirit, and in all good duties, good deeds, and good works.

MOTIVES

That I may press you to labour after fruitfulness in grace and holiness :

1. Consider you were chosen to be holy, or ordained to go and bring forth fruit, &c. You cannot know you are God's elect, unless you are holy and fruitful persons.

2. You are united and married to Christ, that you should bring forth, Rom. vii. 4.

3. God hath made your hearts like good ground, to the end you should be a holy and fruitful people.

4. God hath bestowed much cost and pains on us, that we might be made fruitful Christians, and as the effects thereof, he looks and expects we should be fruitful.

5. He gives us fruitful seasons, fruitful showers, and fruitful shinings, and all to this end and purpose.

6. It is our fruitfulness in grace and holiness that is the glory of believers, and that which commends religion to the blind and barren world.

7. This tends also to the glory of God ; " Hereby is my Father glorified that you bear much fruit, and so shall ye be my disciples," John xv. 8.

8. If after all the showers that fall from heaven, any remain like evil and bad ground, " bring forth briers and thorns, such are near to cursing, and whose end is to be burned," Heb. vi. 7, 8.

9. We are created in Christ Jesus to good works, and ordained to walk in them, Eph. ii. 10.

10. No man's faith is known to be true, but by its fruits or good works, though holiness and good works cannot justify our persons, yet they justify our faith, and render us justified persons before men, and to our own consciences also.

Obj. If believers cannot fall away, what need is there to press them to lead an holy life ?

1. Answ. To glorify God : besides they are as much ordained to holiness as they are unto happiness, or to use the means, as well as to enjoy the end.

2. It is in well-doing we are to seek eternal life : " to them who by a patient continuance in well-doing, seek for glory and honour, and immortality, eternal life," Rom. ii. 7.

Quest. Why are there so many cautions and take heeds, given to us in epistles the apostles wrote, lest we fall, if believers cannot finally fall so as to perish ?

1. Answ. The epistles were wrote to the churches, and all were not true Christians that were got into the churches of the saints ; therefore there was need to caution all to abide steadfast, and to take heed, lest some appeared to be but false professors.

2. Because believers may fall foully, though they cannot fall finally, they may through Satan's temptations, and the evil that remains in them, wound their own souls, and greatly dishonour God ; and therefore there is need of those cautions and take-heeds. But if they are sincere, they cannot finally fall ; " if they had been of us, no doubt but they would have continued with us." Therefore those in Heb. vi. 4, 5, who tasted of the good word of God, &c., and fell away, were not true believers, as Paul in ver. 9, shows, they had not those things which accompany salvation, or do always accompany or attend true grace.

And thus I shall close with this parable.

14. THE PEARL OF GREAT PRICE

I

Again the kingdom of heaven is like unto a merchantman seeking goodly pearl, who when he had found one pearl of great price, went and sold all that he had, and bought it.—Matt. xiii. 45, 46.

The year of Christ. 32. In speaking unto this parable, I shall in my usual method.

1. Open what the design or chief intention of our blessed Lord is, in speaking of it.

2. Open the parts thereof.

3. Raise one or two points of doctrine therefrom, and in our usual method prosecute them.

The design and scope of the parable opened 1. Doubtless our blessed Saviour in this parable designeth two things.

(1.) To set forth the excellency of the gospel dispensation, there lying in it a precious pearl, which they that are truly wise will seek, and part with all to purchase.

(2.) To set forth the transcendent worth and excellency of the pearl of great price.

What is meant by the kingdom of Heaven. This I conceive is the main scope and design of our Lord in this parable. 2ndly, I shall explain the parts thereof.

" Again the kingdom of heaven is like," &c.

The year of Christ's ministry 2. By the kingdom of heaven I understand is meant the gospel dispensation; (as it is in several other Parables) or the true and spiritual ministration thereof; in which the special grace and favour of God is comprehended, and extend unto the sons and daughters of men.

Who is meant by the merchant man. To a merchantman. The merchantman may mean, any person who seeks after, or labours for such things that are of an excellent and spiritual nature.

Seeking goodly pearl. Pearls are the choicest things, merchants trade or venture to sea for : Therefore doubtless these goodly pearls that a spiritual merchant seeks, are some of the choicest things of God ; as peace and reconciliation with God, pardon of sin, and eternal life.

Who when he hath found one pearl of great price : by this one pearl of great price is meant our Lord Jesus Christ ; and so I think it is taken by all expositors generally.

Went and sold all that he had : that is he parted with all things, which before he valued, or did esteem to be gain to him, that he might obtain this precious pearl, as Paul speaks, Phil. iii. 8, 9. Whether external riches, honours, pleasures, so far as they are sinful, or carry the heart away from God : he parts with all his sins, his unrighteousness ; moreover, he parts with his own righteousness, also in point of justification, that so he might have Christ and his righteousness to justify him in the sight of God.

" And bought it :" but it is " without money and without price," Isa. lv. 1, 2 ; he came to accept of Christ, or to receive Jesus Christ upon those very terms he is offered in the gospel, viz., freely.

So much briefly by way of explanation of the several parts of this parable.

Thirdly, I shall take notice of two or three points of doctrine from this short exposition, and shall, God assisting, more fully prove and demonstrate the truth of the exposition, and make improvement thereof.

Doct. That a man in seeking after heavenly things, viz., grace and glory, may be compared unto a merchant.

2. I shall show, in what respects a man, in seeking after heavenly things, may be compared to an earthly merchant.

2. Show, that spiritual merchandizes are the most rare, or the most excellent merchandizes in the world.

3. Improve it.

1. A merchant is one that trades or deals for the good things of this world, and he makes it his chief business ; so a man that seeks after heavenly things, he trades or deals in spiritual commodities, and he makes religion his chief business : hence saith Paul to Timothy, " meditate upon these things, give thyself wholly to them, that thy profiting may appear to all men," 1 Tim. iv. 15.

II. A merchant sometimes trades and deals in things of great worth, as here in this parable is expressed, viz., goodly pearl ; what is more valued than gold, silver, precious stones, and goodly pearl ?

So a professor or a Christian, one that seeks those things that are above, trades in such things or commodities, which are of very great worth, as the favour of God, redemption, reconciliation with God, justification, pardon of sin, and eternal life; these are things of the highest value, yea, beyond all computation, what may be compared to them! earthly things are but mere dirt, toys, and trifles to these things; no *onyx, sapphir, chrystal, coral, topaz, or rubies,* may compare to heavenly things, or to the things which the spiritual merchant deals in, and for.

III. A merchant sets his heart, his mind, and chiefest thoughts upon his merchandize; I mean he prefers those things, and in good earnest pursues after them above all things upon the earth.

So a spiritual merchant, or a true Christian, sets his heart and chiefest thoughts upon heavenly things, he " sets his affections on things above, and not on things that are upon the earth: our conversation is in heaven," &c., Col. iii. 1, and Phil. iii. 20, and Rom. viii. 5. Other people mind the things of this world, or the things of the flesh, and labour after the meat that perisheth: but these mind the things of the Spirit, and chiefly " Labour after that meat which endureth unto eternal life," John vi. 27.

IV. A merchant sometimes ventures to sea, and runs many great dangers (in seeking goodly pearls, and after rich merchandizes) both by storms, rocks, and sands, and pirates also. _{A merchant runs great dangers.}

So a true Christian is exposed to great difficulties, and runs many dangers, who ventures out into a visible profession of religion; on the sea of this world; what storms of reproaches, temptations and persecutions is he oft-times exposed unto? Through many tribulations we must enter into the kingdom of heaven.

V. A merchant at first hath not that skill in trading as he attains or gets afterwards: old dealers have more judgment and greater experience, than such who have newly begun to trade.

So a man when he first begins to seek after God, or to mind heavenly things, he hath not that understanding, that knowledge and judgment in the matters of religion, as an old Christian; he is but a babe in understanding, yet by degrees he attains to more light, knowledge, and experience, especially when he seeks after knowledge as after " silver, and searches for it as for hid treasure," Prov. ii. 4.

VI. A merchant ought to know the nature and value of those commodities he deals in and the whole mystery of merchandizing.

So a true Christian or spiritual merchant labours to know the transcendent worth, nature and value of all spiritual things, and the whole mystery of godliness; indeed this knowledge is not easy to attain unto.

The Christian religion is very mysterious; " without controversy great is the mystery of godliness, God manifested in the flesh," &c. We read of the mystery of the faith; " we preach Christ in a mystery, even the hidden mystery," &c., 1 Tim. iii. 16. Some things are to be believed, and are articles of our faith, that are above our reason to comprehend, as the three Persons in the Godhead, and the mystery of the two natures in the Person of Christ: there is also a mystery in the doctrine of satisfaction, and in the doctrine of union with Christ, and in the doctrine of justification. Now every spiritual merchant should labour to know and understand as much as he is able, or God is pleased to reveal of these and other great gospel mysteries; the holy apostles, who were teachers of those mysteries, and stewards of the mysteries of God, confessed that they themselves " knew but in part, and saw things but darkly as through a glass," 1 Cor. xiii. 12. _{A wise merchant is diligent and careful}

VII. A merchant is very careful of his business, when he hath met with loss, lest he run out, and waste his substance, and so at last be undone.

So a spiritual merchant, or a professor of religion, is very thoughtful, and full of trouble, and takes the more care, when he sees, or doth perceive he goes backward rather than forward, or decays in zeal, faith, love, &c., lest he should prove an hypocrite, and so come to nothing.

VIII. A merchant, if he know what pearls be, may be soon, and easily cheated by false and counterfeit pearl. So many a spiritual merchant, if he know not what the person of Christ is, or what it doth consist of, he may easily be cheated of the true Christ, and trust in a false Christ, believe in a false Christ. Some think Christ is but a mere creature, or not God of the essence of the Father, and man of the substance of Mary; and so own and believe in a false Christ; others think the light which is in all men, is the true Christ. And this is from the ignorance of the person of the Son of God. _{Spiritual merchants should take care they are not cheated of the true pearl.}

So some that do not know what true faith in Christ is, are cheated with a false, or a counterfeit faith. Others know not what gospel repentance is, and by this means they take legal repentance for evangelical repentance : therefore it doth behove all Christians to learn wisdom, and to get a good understanding.

Spiritual merchants trade to a far country.   IX. A merchant trades to foreign parts, they fetch their treasure from afar. So a spiritual merchant trades to heaven, which may be called a far country. The church is compared to a merchant-ship, she brings her food from afar ; as a believer lays up treasure in heaven, so by faith and prayer they fetch their treasure from thence.

X. A merchant has his correspondent in those far countries to which he trades, who receives their merchandize, and makes returns of more gainful things and commodities.

Hath also his correspondent.   So all true Christians have their blessed Correspondent in heaven, who manageth all their concerns, viz., the Lord Jesus Christ, who receives all their duties, and makes return of precious mercies. They have " beauty for ashes, and the oil of joy for mourning, the garment of praise for the spirit of heaviness," Isa. lxi. 3.

XI. A merchant is very careful to attend the exchange, or the place where the merchants meet together, and where they hear, and learn how their affairs go abroad, and there have opportunity oft-times either to sell or buy more goods. Moreover, if they neglect, or are remiss in their attendance upon the exchange, it gives just cause of suspicion they may soon break, and so cease to be merchants.

Spiritual merchants should observe exchange of times.   So spiritual merchants are very careful to attend the solemn meetings of the saints, where they hear of and from Jesus Christ, and as they there receive from him, so they make returns of praise to him ; but when any one member grows careless or remiss in their attendance on those days when the Church assembles together, it gives cause to fear such persons are in a decaying condition, and will soon give up that profession they have made of the truth of Christ: " Not forsaking the assembling of yourselves together, as the manner of some is," &c., Heb. x. 25.

XII. Merchants take great care to keep their books or their accounts well, they are often in their counting house.

Spiritual merchants should keep their accounts well.   1. That they may know whether they lose or gain, go forward or backward, which indeed they cannot well any otherwise understand. 2. That they may see a good end of their affairs, and that they are not wronged.

3. That they may have the more comfort in the management of their business.

And thus also do all the saints, they labour to cast up their accounts, i.e., examine their hearts, or try themselves: " I communed with my heart, and my spirit made diligent search." So

1. If professors do not know their hearts, they know not what state or condition they are in, whether they are renewed or not, born again or not, in a state of grace or not.

2. Unless they try and examine their hearts, they do not know whether they grow in grace, or decay therein ; increase in faith, love, and zeal, or decay in those graces, and so are in a withering condition.

3. A man is what his heart is, not simply what his profession is, what his talk is, or what his seeming continuance is, but what his heart is.

4. A man cannot know his own heart unless he search and try it ; nothing is so deceitful as the heart ; it is " deceitful above all things, and desperately wicked, who can know it ?" Jer. xvii. 9.

Spiritual merchandizing the best.   Secondly, I shall show you, these are the best and chiefest merchandize in the world, or no merchandizes like spiritual merchandizes.

(1.) This is the merchandize of wisdom, and the merchandize of it (saith Solomon) is better than the merchandize of silver, and the gain thereof than fine gold," Prov. iii. 14.

Spiritual merchandizes the best.   I. Because the nature of those things these merchants trade in, far excel all the things of this world.

All other things are of little worth to the grace of God, the love of God, union and communion with God, to have God to be our God, and Christ to be our Christ, to trade in gold tried in the fire ; Rev. ii. 3, 18 ; what gold is like that gold ? and white raiment to be clothed, to trade with the riches, the unsearchable riches of Christ ; nay, the pearl of great price, to make such an exchange of all which he have, as to obtain Jesus Christ, and a crown of glory that fadeth not away.

II. All the things of the world are but vanity. "Vanity of vanities, saith the preacher, all is vanity," Eccl. i. 2. But there is real substance in these things, in these merchandizes. "I lead in the way of righteousness, in the midst of the paths of judgment; that I may cause those that love me to inherit substance, and I will fill their treasures," Prov. viii. 20, 21.

III. These merchandizes are best, because they are incorruptible; all other things, even gold and precious stones, are but of little worth, because corruptible, moth and rust corrupteth them, fire may consume them, or thieves may steal them; but neither can moths, nor rust corrupt, fire consume, nor thieves steal these treasures, these goodly pearls. *Earthly things are corruptible, spiritual merchandize incorruptible*

IV. The rareness or scarcity of these merchandizes, or these rich commodities, show their most excellent nature; diamonds, precious stones, especially such that are of a great bigness: things are not only esteemed as most excellent from their great worth, but because they are very scarce, and rare to come at; and such that have them are made exceeding rich by them, they need no greater riches: it is not to be imagined what some precious stones and pearls (they being very scarce) are worth.

Now the things that these spiritual merchants trade for, seek and do obtain, are exceeding rare, or very scarce; hardly one man in a thousand that trade in the world, find these goodly pearls; with the pearl of great price: O how few find the sparkling diamond of true and saving grace, and the saving knowledge of Jesus Christ, justification, and assurance of eternal life. These merchandizes are the best merchandize, this trade is the best trade that any can follow; though they are such commodities that are very scarce, and very few do find them, yet they are to be had. "Surely there is a vein for silver, and a place for gold where they fine it," Job xxviii. 1. "As for the earth, out of it cometh bread, and under it is turned up as it were fire," ver. 5. "The stones of it are the place of sapphires, and it hath dust of gold," ver. 6. Even so there is a place where these pearls are found, a field where heavenly treasure lies hid, though but few have skill to find {them, or seek where they are to be had. "There is a path which no fowl knoweth, and which the vulture's eye hath not seen; the lions whelps have not trod on it, nor the fierce lion passeth by it," ver. 7, 8,

Wicked men who dig in the earth, those vultures of the wilderness, and ravenous lions and other beasts of prey, seek not for, nor do they know where these pearls, and rich treasure is to be had: "The mysteries of the kingdom of heaven are hid from the wise and prudent, and revealed to babes and sucklings," Matt. xi. 25.

V. These merchandizes were bought with a dear price, by the Son of God, he first laid down the full sum that divine justice demanded, and got them into his own hand for his elect; or else they could never have found them, though they have fought for them all the days of their lives: now the great price which was paid for these spiritual good things, tends to show the excellency and incomparable worth and value of them: true, the costliness of some commodities do not discover the worth of them; for some from their fancy may give more for that which they purchase, than it is worth. As such who in getting the world, lose their souls, give more for it than the whole world is worth. But certainly our Lord Jesus well knew (who is the wisdom of God) there is not only a great worth in the soul, which he bought out of the hands of wrath, and divine justice, but also in the blessings of grace and glory, which by the same purchase or price, he procured for his people. Brethren, all spiritual good things which believers trade for, were bought or purchased with the price of Christ's most precious blood; and let none think Christ paid too dear for them, since an interest in God himself whom we lost by sin, is included in this purchase. *Spiritual merchandize cost dear.*

VI. They are soul treasures, such that suit with, and answer all the wants of the precious and immortal soul of man, and therefore are most excellent things in their own nature; nay, they do not only tend to supply, and answer all the wants and necessities of the soul, but also enrich, satisfy, and fatten the precious souls of men; "Wherefore do you spend money for that which is not bread, and your labour for that which satisfieth not; hearken diligently unto me, and eat you that which is good, and let your soul delight itself in fatness," Isa. v. 2, 3. "They shall still bring forth fruit in old age, they shall be fat and flourishing, to shew that the Lord is upright, and there is no unrighteousness in him," Psal. xcii. 14, 15. *Spiritual things suit with the soul, answer soul wants.*

VII. These merchandizes are the best, (and so they prove themselves the wisest of merchants) because of their duration, this shows the excellency of these things they trade in; all the things of this world are but momentary, they are sometimes gone in a moment, and cannot last long, the world passeth *Spiritual things are of an eternal duration.*

away, and all things therein, " The things that are seen, are temporal," 2 Cor iv. 18, but spiritual things, which are not seen with fleshly eyes, they are eternal; they are riches, honours, and pleasures, that abide for evermore. The acts indeed of grace may fail, but the habit of grace can never be lost, a man that is a true Christian, can never be undone, he cannot run out of all and break, because Jesus Christ is his Surety, he hath undertaken for him, and hath obliged himself to supply him with all things he needs; he is a believer's great insurer, other merchants oft-times are undone, one storm at sea may ruin them and bring them to utter beggary.

Christ is a believer's Correspondent.   VIII. This brings me to the next thing, which shows the excellency of these spiritual merchandizes, viz., their correspondent who these merchants trade with, or that manages all their concernments, and is engaged to make them sure and safe returns from afar; I mean from heaven, whither they trade, and from whence all their good things come: now as Jesus Christ is their correspondent, so he is such an undertaker, that they need not fear any thing can miscarry, which is in his hand.

1. From the consideration of that blessed covenant he entered into with the Father for them in eternity, or ever the earth was, which was not only to die for them, (whom the Father gave to him), and pay all their debts (not only that of perfect obedience to the law), but also fully to satisfy divine justice for their breach thereof.

2. And not only so, but to set them up with a sufficient stock of grace, knowledge, and spiritual wisdom, which this trade calls for, or doth require.

3. And if they at any time through weakness, negligence, or temptation, do decay, or waste any of that stock, which is in their own hands, he has engaged by virtue of his covenant, (as he is their Surety), to supply them afresh from that fulness which is in himself.

4. Moreover the promise and oath of God secures them from utter failing, or being undone, " My God shall supply all your need, according to his riches in glory by Jesus Christ," Phil. iv. 19.

5. They also for their further encouragement know the power, ability, wisdom, love, care, and faithfulness of the Lord Jesus Christ, as he is able to help them, and knows how to do it; so his love to his saints, and his faithfulness every way secures them, as doth also that relation they stand in to him, they are his choicest friends, yea, the members of his mystical body; nay, more than all, his people are his spouse, his bride, his wife; and what will not the husband do for his beloved's comfort?

IX. These merchandizes are the best merchandizes, and these merchants the wisest merchants, doth appear in respect of the terms on which they trade.

The blessed terms on which believers trade.   I. All the goods, in which, or for which they trade, are freely given to them, though they are said to buy these things, yet it is, as I said, a buying " without money and without price," Isa. lv. 1, no man can buy other merchandizes without money or money worth; but the great God imparts all his spiritual treasures freely; " Thinkest thou that the gift of God may be purchased with money," Acts viii. 20. Some think they must get some previous qualifications, before they trade with Christ, come to Christ or believe in Christ; and what is this but like bringing something like money with them, they dare not come in their sins and filthiness, but would fain get on some comely dress or garment spun out of their own bowels, I mean their own inherent righteousness, and this they think may render them acceptable to Jesus Christ; but let such fear lest their money perish with them; for all spiritual treasure, or heavenly merchandizes are given freely; " And whosoever will let him take of the water of life freely," Rev. xxii. 17, the poorest and vilest sinner is invited to come to Christ, and such who are far from righteousness; though thou hast no money, thou mayest be received amongst the company of these merchants. O what good news is this for ungodly sinners, for publicans and great sinners! for such Christ loves still to deal or trade with.

Therefore they are the best merchandizes, because these commodities are freely given, it cannot indeed stand consistent with the design of redemption grace, which is to advance the glory of God in his abundant goodness, and to cut off all boasting, and cause of boasting, to admit of any thing of the creature, that looks like money, to procure a right to these things: nay, what we have of our own which we must part with, yea, even, our best is but like filthy rags; and what are filthy rags worth? what can they purchase? what are they good for?

Believers have the best returns.   X. These are the best merchandizes, or this is the best trade, because of the returns, these merchants have from Jesus Christ.

1. They have quick returns; " And it shall come to pass, that before they call I will answer, and while they are speaking I will hear," Isa. lxv. 24. Here is no staying for

the wind, no delay of the ship's return, it is but asking and receiving ; seek and you shall find, find what ? even goodly pearl, nay, the pearl of great price.

2. It is the best trade, because the merchandizes are such rich commodities, the chiefest of all is a pearl of infinite value, as you will hear hereafter. These merchants do not trade for toys and rattles, no, but for the richest pearls and precious stones, things of an inestimable worth.

3. Because the returns are also certain, they are sure of succeeding and of growing rich, truly and eternally rich.

4. Not only rich, but great and noble also ; All these merchants are advanced to mighty honour or dignity ; they are all made hereby " Kings and princes, of whom the world is not worthy," Prov. xii. 26, Psal. xvi. 3 ; they in honour are the most excellent in all the earth, sons and daughters of God, born of God, they walk with God, and have union and communion " with Father and the Son," 1 John i. 2, 3 ; and have the attendance of the holy angels ; they administer to them, wait on them, guard and defend them.

APPLICATION

I. See who are people of the greatest wisdom ; certainly all the wise men of this world are but fools, what do the merchants gain that trade to India ? what are those merchandize to these ? what is their gain to the gain of godliness ?

II. Admire. Is it not strange, since these merchandizes are so precious, and the riches these merchants gain so great, that so few will follow this trade, I mean trade for heaven, or deal with Jesus Christ, or seek for these goodly pearls ! O what folly possesseth the poor ; you have no stock to be earthly merchants, and yet refuse to become spiritual merchants!

3. What reproof also is here to such who will venture their lives, their goods, nay, their souls, for the riches of this world ; and yet will not venture the loss of earthly honour, to gain these merchandizes.

4. Exhort. Be persuaded sinners, to turn spiritual merchants ; labour to recover your lost understanding, and seek after these goodly pearls, viz., an interest in God, pardon of sin, and peace of conscience. O seek after these pearls, and labour after the knowledge of the worth of things, and to know how you may find this God, pardon and peace, which is no otherways to be obtained, but by finding of Jesus Christ, the pearl of great price.

Enlightened persons whilst they seek after goodly pearls, find one pearl, and in finding that they meet with a vast number of other rich pearls also.

3. This is matter of greatest comfort and consolation that can be to all true believers : O how happy are you that are spiritual merchants, who seek goodly pearls, and have found the pearl of great price ! O bless and magnify God ! exalt free grace, who put you upon seeking heavenly treasure : let your lives be lives of praise, and thanksgiving unto God ; and as you have entered upon this trade, never be weary, nor faint in your minds, knowing that your labour shall not be in vain in the Lord ; your gain is great here, but it will be more admirable, and greater hereafter. Amen.

II

Again, the kingdom of heaven is like unto a merchant-man seeking goodly pearls, who when he had found one pearl of great price, went and sold all that he had, and bought it.—Matt. xiii. 45, 46.

I HAVE, my brethren, briefly opened the several parts of this parable, and have also noted one point of doctrine from the first part thereof ; viz., that a man in seeking after heavenly things, may be fitly compared to an earthly merchant. I have prosecuted this, and shall now proceed to another proposition.

2. Doct. That the Lord Jesus Christ (the pearl of great price) is most precious, excellent, or of infinite worth and value. *The second doctrine.*

In speaking unto this proposition.

I. I shall show you, why Christ is compared to a pearl.

2. Show you wherein the excellency, worth, and preciousness of Christ doth consist.

3. Show you, where he is to be sought, and also how.

4. Show you, what buying this pearl doth denote.

5. Apply it.

First, I shall show you, why Christ is compared to a pearl, to the richest pearl.

Why Christ is compared to pearl.

I. Pearls, naturalists tell us, have a strange birth and original. Pliny saith, Shell-fish is the wonderful geniture of a pearl, congealed into a diaphanous stone, and the shell is called the mother of pearl. Now at a certain time of the year this shell-fish opens itself, and takes in a certain moist dew, after which they grow big, until they bring forth the pearl. By which it seems they have their birth from heaven in a marvellous manner.

I hope I may without offence mention this parallel-wise with the birth of the "pearl of great price."

Our Lord Jesus Christ, whose birth according to the flesh, or his conception, was marvellous; God manifested in the flesh. A woman shall compass a man, a virgin, the mother of this transcendent pearl, (as touching his human nature) was overshadowed by the Holy Ghost, and when her time was come, she brought forth the pearl of pearls, viz. Our Lord and Saviour Jesus Christ.

II. Some pearls are of a very great worth. Pliny tells us, that they are the most sovereign commodity throughout the whole world ; moreover, he speaks of one pearl that Cleopatra had, which was of an admirable value.

Our Lord Jesus Christ no doubt is compared to a pearl of great price upon this account chiefly. He is of an inestimable worth and value. God hath many rich pearls ; but Jesus Christ is the richest and most precious of them all ; the holy angels are pearls, and very precious unto God ; and also the saints are pearls in his sight ; " Since thou wast precious in my sight, thou hast been honourable, and I have loved thee," Isa. xliii. 4. Believers or godly persons are called his jewels or choice treasure ; " They shall be mine in that day I make up my jewels," Mal. iii. 17 ; but what are these jewels, these pearls, to this pearl ? All their glory, worth, and excellencies flow from Christ ; he makes them precious. But he in himself, and of and from himself originally and eternally, is precious, and a most excellent pearl, there is none like unto him, neither in heaven, nor on earth ; he is called " a stone, a tried stone, a precious corner-stone, a sure foundation," Isa. xxviii. 16. And in another place he is called " a living stone, disallowed of men, but chosen of God, and precious"—" yea, elect, precious," 1 Pet. ii. 4, 6. He is precious to God the Father, precious to the holy angels, and wonderfully precious to all believers, 1 Pet. ii. 7 ; he is to the Spouse " the chiefest among ten thousands," Cant. v. 10.

III. Pearls have a hidden virtue in them, though but small in bigness, yet great in efficacy, they are rich, and a most sovereign cordial, being (as naturalists observe) good against poison, also do preserve, strengthen, and revive the natural spirits.

Wonderful virtue in Christ the pearl of great price.

Jesus Christ hath a hidden virtue in him, though he be little in the eyes of carnal persons, and vile impostors, yet such who receive him by faith, find wonderful virtue in him ; " I perceive (saith he to the woman that touched him) that virtue is gone out of me," Luke viii. 46.

1. Such who receive this sacred pearl by faith, though they were dead, it immediately quickens them ; and raiseth them from the dead to a state of spiritual life, Eph. ii. 1. There is such a spirit in this pearl of great price, that whosoever receiveth it, are immediately brought to life, though they have lain a long time dead in the first Adam, in the grave of sin.

2. The same Spirit also opens blind eyes ; such who receive inwardly this pearl, have the " Eyes of their understandings enlightened," Eph. i. 18, though they were born blind ; nor is there any besides Jesus Christ can give sight to the blind ; he doth not only raise the dead, but also gives them sight ; " his life is the light of men," John i. 4, 5. This life was originally in the eternal Word, and not only so, but he conveyeth life and light to mankind, both a rational and spiritual life and light ; all men that come into the world receive the light of rational creatures ; but none but such who have union with him, receive the light of grace. " Then spake Jesus again to them, I am the light of the world, he that followeth me shall not walk in darkness, but shall have the light of life," John viii. 12. The light of life, and the life of light is all one. Now as he is Creator he gave man light ; man was created in a state of light by Jesus Christ, (i. e.) in a state of knowledge, of holiness and real joy and comfort ; but this light, this knowledge, holiness, joy and comfort,

mankind loss by the fall; but through Christ, or by this pearl it is restored again; all that receive him have the light of the knowledge of the glory of God in their souls: "God, who commanded the light to shine out of darkness, hath shined in our hearts to give the light of the knowledge of the glory of God in the face of Jesus Christ," 2 Cor. iv. 6. Great light of knowledge was in man at his first creation, and hence the light of God is said to consist in knowledge; "Having put on the new man, which is renewed in knowledge, after the image of him that created him," Col. iii. 10. And as it consisteth in the true knowledge of God; so also in holiness, because the image of God was not only in knowledge, but "in righteousness and true holiness," Eph. iv. 24. No unholy unsanctified person can have fellowship with God: but what saith John: "If we walk in the light, as he is in the light, we have fellowship one with another," 1 John i. 1, 2, 3; not with God only, or with the Father and the Son, but also with one another; but this light of saving knowledge, righteousness, and true holiness, joy and comfort, no man partakes of, but only he that receives this pearl, or partakes of his divine Spirit.

3. Moreover, this pearl inwardly received dissolves and infallibly cures the stone in the heart, I mean, it breaks the hard and stony heart. None ever truly received Jesus Christ, but found this blessed operation or virtue to to be in him; they immediately see the evil of sin, that plague of all plagues, and cry out, O what shall we do; what a good, a holy, a just and gracious God have I offended, resisted, contemned, and rebelled against! *A cure for the stone in the heart.*

4. Such is the virtue of this sacred pearl, that it expels and purges out the poison of sin, which is in the soul; as such who find this pearl are immediately justified, acquitted, and pronounced righteous before God, and for ever freed from condemnation, according to God's ordination and gracious design and purpose. So likewise by virtue of that faith, by which a poor sinner does receive the Lord Jesus, he comes to be sanctified, and the soul purged from the contagion of sin, and cured of that plague, though some of the old relics of it may remain, Rom. vi. 14; yet sin as to its power and dominion is broken, it reigns no more in any person that receives this precious pearl.

5. Such is the hidden virtue that is in Jesus Christ, or in this pearl, that when a man finds it, and partakes thereof inwardly, it fills him with joy and earthly comfort. Therefore it is said, "We rejoice in all our tribulation." The people of Samaria had no sooner found this pearl, Jesus Christ, but it is said, "There was great joy in that city," Acts viii. 8. The soul hath cause of joy, unspeakable joy, considering how happy for ever he is made thereby; for this pearl is made all in all things unto him who receiveth it.

6. Such is the virtue of this pearl, that such who receive it, are presently wonderfully revived, though their spirits were ready to faint, and die away just before; it strangely revives a drooping spirit, Christ "revives the spirits of the humble, and the hearts of the contrite ones," Isa. lvii. 15. There is no cordial can revive a faint and desponding spirit, but Jesus Christ; other cordials may revive the natural spirits, but this revives the precious and immortal soul; it doth not only raise it from the dead and give light, but it enlivens it, and makes it full of activity, and fills it full of sweet consolation.

7. It hath also a wonderful virtue in it to strengthen the heart, and make such strong that receive it, and very fearless, in the midst of all dangers whatsoever, so that they are not afraid what man can do unto them; they are hereby enabled and made strong to perform holy duties, strong to bear heavy burdens, and strong to mortify their inward corruptions, and also strong to resist and overcome all Satan's temptations. Such are "strong in the Lord, and in the power of his might," they are "strengthened according to his glorious power, unto all patience, and long-suffering with joyfulness." Such that have experienced the virtue of this pearl, have been enabled to go through the worst of torments; nay, they have rejoiced in the midst of the flames; "We glory (saith the apostle) in tribulations," Rom. v. 3; not only in their future happiness, but in their present sufferings.

8. Such is the virtue of this pearl, that such that receive it, cannot die; as Christ is compared to a pearl, so to bread, yea to the Bread of life: "This is the Bread that came down from heaven, that a man may eat thereof, and not die," John vi. 50. "He that eateth of this Bread, shall live for ever," ver. 58. It is meant of receiving or believing in Jesus Christ; to eat, to feed upon, to receive, or to believe in Christ, is all one and the same thing.

He who finds this pearl (i. e.) that comes to Christ, feeds on Christ, or applies the Lord Jesus, or the virtue of his obedience, his blood and merits, to his own soul, shall live for ever; that is, he shall not die the second death, Rev. xx. 14, or not die eternally.

9. It hath such virtue in it, that such who receive it, it cures of the burning fever, of

passion, envy, and malice; making the soul mild, peaceable, gentle, and full of pity, mercy, and good fruits, "without partiality, and without hypocrisy," Jam. iii. 17; nay, when once Christ is found and received by a poor sinner, his inordinate love and passion to the things of this world is immediately abated, he becomes dead to the world, and to the lusts of the eyes, and to the lusts of the flesh.

10. Moreover, this pearl is a most sovereign remedy to cure the tympany of pride; it makes the proud humble, laying the soul at the foot of God, even to loathe and abhor himself, and to repent in dust and ashes; and to be ashamed of sin, and of his own righteousness, yea, "confounded, and never to open his mouth more," Job. xlii. 6, Isa. vi. 5, 6, Ezek. xvi. 63,

Thus hath this pearl many most excellent hidden virtues in it, which few ever come to understand, or have the experience of.

IV.   Pearls are of a splendid and oriental brightness, both without and within.

Jesus Christ may well be compared to a pearl upon this account; he being the "Brightness of the Father's glory, and the express image of his person," Heb. i. 3.   He outshines in glory and brightness all the angels of heaven; the beauteous and glorious excellencies of this pearl, *i. e.*, the Lord Jesus Christ, is the same in shining with the Father; being the brightness of his glory, the light of light, the glory of all glory; he is the Father's essential glory. The glory or brightness in any creature, is but a faint resemblance of the being and glory of God.   But more of this hereafter.

V.   Pearls, nay, one pearl of great price enriches him that finds it.   He that meets with such a pearl needs no other riches, but is made for ever, as touching this world.

So they that find the pearl of great price, Jesus Christ, or lay hold on him, are greatly enriched; they are spiritually rich, truly rich, yea, and eternally rich.   We read of the "Unsearchable riches of Christ," Eph. iii. 8.   And whatsoever riches are in Christ, they are his riches that find him, like as a man that finds a pearl: whatsoever that pearl is worth, so far is that man enriched by it, because the pearl is his, he hath the whole interest in it, and right to it; he may say, it is my pearl.

So a believer that finds Jesus Christ may say, Christ is mine, the riches of Christ are mine, they are my riches, I have interest in him.   Thomas cries, "My Lord and my God," and Paul appropriates Christ to himself.   "Yea, doubtless, and I account all things but loss for the excellency of Jesus Christ my Lord," &c., Phil. iii. 8.   It is propriety that makes a thing valuable to a person, and according to the worth of that thing is the person enriched; but though Christ be a pearl, a rich pearl, yet was he a pearl that could not be found (like a pearl that lies at the bottom of the sea) no man could be enriched by him; or if a pearl be found, yet if the man cannot lay any just claim to it, but it is presently seized by the prince or lord of the manor, he would not be enriched by it, nor indeed any ways the better for it.   But he that finds this precious pearl, Jesus Christ, it is his own, this God is his God, and this Christ is his Christ, and his God and Christ for ever.

VI.   Some men when they have found a rich pearl, a pearl of great price, they know not the worth of it; they perhaps think some other pearls are of equal value, or as rich as that, which they have found.

So some, when they have found Jesus Christ, they know not the worth, the riches and excellency of him, but are ready to esteem other goodly pearls equally with Christ, as the pearl of grace, of pardon, and peace.   But certainly this argues great weakness, great ignorance, and that they are strangely beclouded.   For what is grace, the pearl of faith, the pearl of pardon, the pearl of peace, and the pearl of inherent holiness, to the Person of Jesus Christ?   Is there not a vast difference between the person that thou lovest and hast set thy heart upon, and the portion?   Dost thou esteem the portion equal with the person?   This shows thy love may justly be suspected. So it is here, if thou valuest anything above or equal with Christ, nay, though it be grace itself, it will show that thou art not sincere, but hypocritical.   Though grace is a goodly pearl, *i. e.*, the grace of faith, love, humility, temperance, patience, &c., and also though disobedience and inherent holiness are goodly pearls, which all spiritual merchants seek, in seeking of Jesus Christ.   But alas! alas! a Christian who is thoroughly enlightened, doth with Paul, account all these things (though pearls in themselves) but as dung in comparison of the Lord Jesus Christ, I mean the Person of Christ.

Christ excels all spiritual pearls.

Such therefore, that prefer grace, or their own obedience and inherent righteousness, with the Person of Christ, or magnify their righteousness above the righteousness of Christ, or mix it with Christ's righteousness in point of justification, may justly be suspected not to be true Christians, (or at least) but erroneous, if not hypocritical persons.

VII.   This being so, it followeth from hence, that it behoveth him that finds a pearl of great price to know it well what it is, and also its just value, or the true worth and richness thereof; lest he be cheated and part with it for pearls of little value, in comparison of that.

So and in like manner ought a believer to know Jesus Christ, the Person of Christ, the worth of Christ, the excellencies of Christ, lest he be deceived; alas! he may boast of a false Christ, and think he hath found the true pearl, when it is a false, a counterfiet, or a bastard pearl.   Many in these days glory in a Christ within, affirming the light that is in all men, is the true Christ, and deny that the true Christ was ever seen with carnal eyes; or heard with fleshly or carnal ears; nay, affirm that the body of Jesus of Nazareth was but a garment, which the true Christ did wear, or a house in which the true Christ did dwell; and also utterly deny, *The Quakers know not the true Christ.* that Christ is now in heaven above, or that that very body that rose from the dead is now glorified in heaven.   But certainly these men are fools; they pretend to seek for goodly pearls, but know not who, or what the pearl of great price is.   They know not the Person of Christ, their Christ never died, the light within cannot die, nor hath that any blood to shed; being only an inward quality, it hath no bodily substance.   But Paul saith, "He preached how Christ died according to the Scriptures, and that he was buried, and rose again the third day, according to the Scriptures," 1 Cor. xv. 3—8, and that he was seen after he rose from the dead, "first by Cephas, then by the twelve, and after that he was seen of above five hundred brethren at once."   Moreover, there are some who deny Christ is God of the essence of the Father, or the most high God.   Now these men do not know this pearl; that Christ is but of little worth who is not very God, the true God; or can such a Christ save us, for we have no Saviour but God only.   Christ must be God, or he is no Saviour.   It therefore greatly behoveth all Christians to have wisdom and skill, to discern between a pretended Christ, or a false Christ, and the true Christ; as it doth behove a merchant that trades for pearls, to know true pearls, precious pearls from false pearls, or else they may be soon cheated, and utterly be undone.   Also they ought to know the excellencies of Christ, and wherein he is rich, and why he is so wonderfully rich.

A little to open this.

1.   Christ is rich as he is God, the riches of the eternal Godhead are in him.   "For you know the grace of our Lord Jesus Christ, that though he was rich, yet for our sakes he became poor," &c., 2 Cor. viii. 9.   Is God rich?   Is not the whole world, the whole earth, and all things in it, the Lord's?   Even the *Wherein the riches of Christ consist.* cattle upon a thousand hills, so rich is our Lord Jesus Christ; for he is God, therefore all things are his.

2.   Christ is rich in goodness.   "Or despisest thou the riches of his goodness," Rom. ii. 4.   His rich love and favour is infinite.

3.   Christ is rich in wisdom and knowledge.   "In him are hid all the treasures of wisdom and knowledge," Col. ii. 3.

4.   Christ is rich in the grace of redemption.   "By whom have we redemption through his blood, the forgiveness of sins, according to the riches of his grace," Eph. i. 7.

5.   Christ is rich in glory.   "And what is the riches of the glory of his inheritance in his saints," Eph. i. 18.   And again he saith, " That he would grant unto you according to the riches of his glory, to be strengthened with might in the inward man," Eph. iii. 16.

Now that this pearl is a rich pearl, or that Christ is rich, exceedingly rich, as Mediator, appears further. *Christ is rich as Mediator.*

(1.)   By what God hath bestowed on him as so considered, for as Mediator he "is heir of all things, he hath the Heathen for his inheritance, and the uttermost parts of the earth for his possession," Heb. i. 2, Psal. ii. 8.

(2.)   We may know Christ is rich, by considering of the multitudes he hath enriched, even many millions; and yet is not he one farthing the poorer than he was before.

(3.)   It appears Christ is rich, "because it pleased the Father that in him all fulness should dwell," Col. i. 19.   There is in him not only abundance, but also a fulness of redundance; he is not only a fountain that is full, but also overflows.

But because I have spoken fully concerning the riches of Christ in the parable of the marriage-supper, I shall add no more as to this here, but direct my reader to that. *See the parable of the marriage-supper opened, Book III.*

VIII.   Pearls, rich pearls, or pearls of great price, are commonly kept in the possession of noble persons, who are adorned with them, and are known to be honourable and noble persons, by being decked and adorned with precious stones, and rich pearls. No high-born prince but is enriched, beautified, and adorned with the richest pearls.

Christ is the honour and ornament of believers.   So the saints who are noble born, born from above, born of God, are the most excellent in all the earth, and these only are adorned with rich pearls, goodly pearls; grace is as chains of gold, or a necklace of pearl about their neck," Psal. xvi. 3. Wisdom and knowledge, and the fear of the Lord are to be sought for above all things. " For they (as Solomon declares) shall be an ornament of grace unto thy head, and chains about thy neck," Prov. i. 19. "I decked thee also with ornaments, and I put bracelets upon thy hands, and a chain about thy neck," Ezek. xvi. 11. "And I put jewels on thy forehead, and ear-rings on thy ears." Thus all the king's children, or the most excellent in all the earth, are adorned with pearls and diamonds. But though all the graces of the Spirit are as pearls, jewels, and glorious ornaments to believers, yet this one rich pearl, Jesus Christ, renders them more noble and honourable than do all other pearls, whatsoever, with which they are adorned.

Moreover, no person hath, nor ever had one goodly pearl, until they parted with all they had, and received Jesus Christ. Christ first gives himself, and with himself he bestows all other goodly pearls; nor hath any man or woman this pearl, but he is adorned and beautified with all other choice and precious pearls; also the Spirit is first received, which unites the soul to Christ, and then all grace immediately adorn that person, by which he is known to have Christ, and to be an honourable person. " To you that believe he is precious," 1 Pet. ii. 7, or is an honour; and by this believers are known to be the children of God, or the sons and daughters of the King of kings; for none of the base born of this have this pearl, this Christ, nor are beautified with these spiritual pearls; no, they are but beggars, mere slaves, and vassels of sin, and the devil, who are not born of God, though they have never so high an earthly birth, or earthly honour, or earthly riches, yet they are not excellent ones in God's esteem.

APPLICATION

The application.   You young maidens, would you gladly deck yourselves with rich ornaments, or have a necklace of pearls? Here is one, but are you willing to part with all for this pearl, for this Christ? This is that you must do. O labour for Christ, seek and search to find this pearl, to believe in the Lord Jesus, or receive him, so you shall be richly adorned, and become glorious and amiable in the sight of God and all good men.

1 Inference.   2. See what ignorance is in the merchants of this world; they see a worth and value in earthly pearls, but see no worth in this heavenly pearl; they know not the preciousness of Jesus Christ; they cry, " He hath no form nor comeliness, and when we shall see him there is no beauty that we should desire him," Isa. liii. 2.

2 Inference.   3. What fools are sinners, who will venture any danger, and go through all difficulties to get earthly treasure; earthly pearls they will go to sea for them, and be tossed upon the swelling waves, the proud waves, and run a thousand hazards, to obtain gold, silver, precious stones, and rich pearls, yea, and part with all they have for an earthly pearl of great price; and yet they will venture upon no danger, run no difficulties to get this spiritual pearl, though it be of infinite worth, and will make them truly happy, in body and soul both, yea, happy here whilst they live, and happy when they die, and happy to eternity.

3 Inference.   4. Furthermore, what folly and madness is in those sinners, who when they hear that there is such a pearl to be had, and also are told how it may be bought, and they have it for their own, yet slight it, and value it not worth parting with their own righteousness for it, or to account all they have as dung in comparison of it. Poor wretches, they esteem filthy rags above this pearl; nay, and others value their earthly riches, and great possessions, like the young man, in the gospel, before Jesus Christ this precious pearl; and others prize their lusts and abominable sins above this pearl; will not part with one filthy lust, if in so doing they were assured to have Jesus Christ.

Exhort.   5. Sinners, let me exhort you to search for the pearl of great price, "Seek after it as silver, and search for it as for hid treasures," Prov. ii. 4, for then you have a promise of finding it. Read the next verse, " Then thou shalt understand the fear of the Lord, and find the knowledge of God," v. 5. The true knowledge of God lies in our knowing of Jesus Christ; for all knowledge of God as a Creator or a Benefactor, will profit no man to salvation, unless they know him and Jesus Christ, and know the worth of Christ, the excellencies of Christ, in his person, in his offices, and in his work, which they must do, or else they cannot be saved. " For this is life eternal, that they may know thee the true God, and Jesus Christ whom thou hast sent," John xvii. 3.

Inform.   6. This may inform us, that it is no small blessing to have the gospel, and to be under a gracious ministration thereof, since there lies hid in it such a rich and precious pearl. Sirs, what come ye hither for this day? are you not some of those merchants that seek goodly pearls? and is it not the pearl of great price you desire, and long after, and are willing to have upon any terms whatsoever? Well, if it be thus, you will prize the word of God, the gospel of Christ, and the ministry thereof, for here, here he is to be found, as you may further hear hereafter. Some, alas! seek where Christ is not, they seek the living amongst the dead; they seek Christ in the broad way, others think to find him on their beds, by their cold and formal prayers. O know the vein where this gold is dug, the place where this pearl lies hid, and if you find it not presently, yet be not discouraged, if ye follow on to know the Lord, then shall ye know him; remember Christ's gracious promise, seek and you shall find; say within yourselves, we must have this Christ, this pearl, or we shall be undone for ever. "If you believe not that I am he, you shall die in your sins," John viii. 24.

And now, my brethren,

7. You that have found this pearl, rejoice; O blessed are ye for ever, what hath God done for you! how rich are you! you have Christ, and cannot lose him, "He that findeth me findeth life," Prov. viii. 35. You have life because you have Christ.

8. But take heed that none of you are deceived, and place your hope on a   Caution.
false Christ; you heard some know not a true pearl from a bastard pearl, and so by ignorance are undone. O how do many trust in a false Christ, have their faith fixed on a mere creature, their Christ they say is not God most high, but the first creature that God made, and only a God by office. For the Lord's sake, take heed, for there are many false Christs, in our days; and false prophets are also risen up, and have deceived many, yea, a multitude of poor miserable creatures. Some cry up a Christ within, and deny that Christ who is in heaven, i.e., the man Christ Jesus, (as you have newly heard); therefore beware of the error of the wicked, do not let their seeming holiness and outward conversations deceive you. Satan can transform himself into an angel of light, and cause his ministers to seem ministers of righteousness. Therefore know, we are fallen into perilous times, no days have been more evil than these are, therefore watch, and sleep not as others do, lest being led away with the error of the wicked, you fall from your own stedfastness.

But to proceed,

Secondly, I shall now endeavour to show you wherein the excellencies,   *Wherein the worth, and preciousness of the Lord Jesus Christ doth consist.*   *preciousness of Christ's person doth consist.*

First, the great worth, excellency, preciousness, and infinite transcendency of Jesus Christ, consisteth in the excellencies of his glorious person. My   *The chief excellency of Christ* brethren, I told ye that unless a man know a pearl, I mean knoweth what it   *consisteth in* is, he knoweth not the great worth of it. So, and in like manner, unless a   *the dignity* person knows the Lord Jesus Christ, he knows not the worth, the value, the   *of his person.* excellencies, and the preciousness of Jesus Christ. We must know who, or what the person of Christ is, if we would his personal excellencies. "What think ye of Christ?" Matt. xxii. 42. And again our Lord said unto his disciples, "Whom do men say that I the Son of man am," Matt. xvi. 13. Certainly this is a most weighty and great point, that our Lord should take such great care to instruct his disciples into this matter, that they might know how or whom he was.

Secondly, The worth and excellencies of the pearl of great price, i. e., the Lord Jesus Christ, consisteth in his personal excellencies.

Thirdly, Christ's worth and excellencies consist in his offices and work as Mediator.

I. To begin with the first of these, it is acknowledged by all that profess the true Christian religion, that Jesus Christ is the only foundation of our faith, of our hope, and salvation. "Other foundation can no man lay than that which is laid, which is Jesus Christ," 1 Cor. iii. 11.

And it is as necessary to know who, or what Christ is, or what his person   *Needful to* consisteth of, that is to say, who is the true pearl, the true Christ, or he that   *know whom* is the true Saviour: for if any man is at a loss, or doubtful in his mind in this   *Christ is.* case, or that he cannot arrive to a certain knowledge who, or what the person of Christ is, or doth consist of, or mistakes about it, how can he be said to know the pearl of great price, or the worth and transcendency of it?

Moreover, there is an absolute necessity of our knowledge of Christ, and that we should also acknowledge, own, and believe in that individual Person, as he made known himself to himself to his disciples, does appear by those two questions put forth by himself, the one to the Jews, the other unto his own disciples, as I just now hinted.

Inference.   What think you of Christ, whose Son is he?

And unto his disciples, "Whom do men say I the Son of man am?" Peter replied, (intimating some said one thing, and others another. But he, whom do you say I am? Peter then in the name of the rest said,) "thou art Christ." That is, that very person whom he saw with his natural eyes, and who spake unto him, even he was the Christ of God, and Pearl of great price.

Inference.   Christ (my brethren) signifies anointed, and so may refer to his human nature, which the second Person of the Trinity took into union with himself, not that he took any man's person into that union with his own divine person. No, the human nature consisteth in the person of the Son of God, not of itself, but by virtue of the hypostatical union, it consisteth in this person.

Mind well, and observe Peter's further answer, i. e., the Son of the living God, that refers to his Godhead. Moreover, consider what our Lord said, and pronounced upon Peter's answer, i. e., " Flesh and blood hath not revealed this unto thee, but my Father which is in heaven. And I say unto thee, thou art Peter, and upon this rock will I build my Church," &c. That is, upon myself, or upon this very faith of thine, or belief of my person, thus owned, and confessed by thee, viz., I being God and man in one person, God of the essence of my Father, and truly man, of the seed of David, or of the substance of the blessed virgin. Now upon Christ, God and Man in one person, as thus owned, believed in, and confessed by St. Peter, is the Gospel Church built.

The Church built upon Christ as God-man.

Argu. 1.   Arg. 1. And from hence I therefore thus argue, if the gospel church, and every believer, is built upon this Christ, this Rock, or Christ thus acknowledged, owned, and believed in; then it is of absolute necessity that we know his person, i. e., who, or whom the true Christ is; and thus believe concerning him. But the gospel church, and every believer, is thus built, &c., and therefore there is an absolute necessity to know who or whom Christ is, and thus to believe concerning him.

5. If men do not believe, or know, that this individual person is the true Christ, the true Messiah and only Saviour, they must die in their sins; then it is of absolute necessity thus to believe, own, and acknowledge him. But it evidently appeareth, that all such that do not thus believe, own, and acknowledge him, shall die in their sins. Therefore all must thus believe, &c. Pray observe what he saith unto the Jews: " For if ye believe not that I am he, ye shall die in your sins," John viii. 24. Our Lord doth not here so much refer to faith, by which we believe or apprehend him, but the person who is apprehended : as if he should have said; If you do not believe that I am he, i. e., this my individual Person, God and man, or the " Immanuel, God with us," Matt. i. 23, or God in our nature; God manifested in the flesh," 1 Tim. iii. 16, (i. e.) in that particular body of flesh, the divine and human nature making but one person, ye " shall die in your sins."

Such that deny Christ to be God and man in one person deny the Christ of God.

6. It is of absolute necessity thus to believe concerning Christ; for if the Lord Christ, who died for our sins, be truly God of the essence of the Father, and verily and truly man of the same substance of the blessed virgin; then such who deny him so to be, do " deny the Lord that bought them, and so bring upon themselves swift destruction." But the former cannot be denied ; therefore all such who do deny the Lord, (i. e.,) that individual person to be God Man, deny the Lord that bought them, &c.

Furthermore, my brethren, if the denial of the Person of Christ, or who or whom he is, " be a damnable heresy ;" See 2 Pet. ii. 1, then it is of absolute necessity thus to believe concerning him; but the denial of the Person of Christ, or who or whom he is, is a damnable heresy. They no doubt concluded, they were bought by that Christ they preached, but denied his

Christ in some sense bought all men.

Person, who or whom he was. All men were in some sense bought by Jesus Christ, viz., they have the continuance of their lives by his death, or a reprieve for a time thereby from the execution of that sentence they are under.

7. If all our hope of eternal life, or of being saved from hell depends upon our stedfast belief, that the Son of God, or the Second Person of the Holy Trinity, took our nature into union with himself, so as to be God and man in one Person : then it is of absolute necessity thus to believe concerning him. But this is all our hope of eternal life, and of being saved from hell; for if he be not man of that very nature that sinned, (though he was without sin) what ground have we to believe we can be saved by him ? God required man to keep the law of his creation, or the first covenant, and man, or is Surety (one in the same nature) must do it, if we are ever justified. For the law being broken by us, it was " weak through the flesh, and what it could not do, God sending his own Son in the likeness of

sinful flesh.—And for sin condemned sin in the flesh, that the righteousness of the law might be fulfilled in us," &c., Rom. viii. 3, 4.   Moreover, we, or our Surety in our nature must satisfy for our breach of the said law ; therefore, as he must be man to keep the law, and die in our stead, so he must be God to satisfy Divine Justice, which none. but one that could give an infinite satisfaction, could do ; for the satisfaction and atonement made by Jesus Christ, rises from the dignity and worth of his Person, he being God as well as man.

I shall now endeavour to prove that Jesus Christ, or Jesus of Nazareth, was, and is God of the same essence with the Father, or God by nature, and did in his Divine Person exist from everlasting.   *Christ is the most high God.*

1. By plain texts of Scripture.
2. By arguments taken therefrom.
1. The first Scripture shall be that in John ch. i. ver. 1.   *Dr. Thos. Goodwin.*
" In the beginning was the Word."   That is, (as one well observes) the first step, and that " Word was with God ;" that is a second.   " And the Word was in the beginning with God," that is a third ; " And the Word was God," that is a fourth. He might have shut them all up in this sentence, " The word was God, with God in the beginning."   But he puts it into several positive assertions ; yea, and begins with the lowest, namely his having existed, " the Word was," and that in the beginning ; and then that he tells us what he is, i. e. a person distinct from God, (that is, from the Father) " he was with God," and yet was God, that is, of the same essence.

1. A little briefly of his existence, when, and how long.   And then,
2. Of his Person and personal existence, and personal worth and excellencies.   *Concerning the eternal existence of the deity of Christ.*

1. He is a Person who did actually exist before he came into the world, and tabernacled in flesh, or assumed our nature : and that he existed all along the whole time of this world, both in the beginning of it, and before the world was, even from eternity.   " It is strange (saith this worthy author) that the Socinians should so impudently (in the light of the gospel and scripture) say that Christ began then to exist actually, when he was first conceived by the Holy Ghost in the womb of the virgin, and that before he had only existed but in promise, as the day of judgment doth now.   And also such who hold Christ to be but a manifestation of God in man's flesh.   God indeed, say they, was afore, but Christ being but the manifestation of the Godhead in man's nature, existed not until Christ the manifestation of him."   Whereby they not only deny him to be a person who did manifest God ; but also necessarily declare the Christ they own, had no existence until that manifestation of God in man's nature.   Therefore he further adds, " For the existence of that which is only and barely a manifestation, lies only being a manifestation of something that existed afore, but itself not till then.   And this is even as if a man should say and affirm that what other men call the sun, is all one with what we call the day ; and nothing else, which you know, begins in the morning, and ceaseth at night.   And is but the shine and manifestation of the sun when it riseth, and appears above our hemisphere, or this part of the world ; but look as the sun is a body of light that existeth afore it is day with us, and the appearance of it is that which maketh day, so Christ the Son of righteousness is not the bare manifestation of God, but a person that existed with God, yea, and was God ; afore that manifestation of God made by him in this world.   And he is not only the bringing in, or manifestation of life and immortality which was in God ; but he himself was that eternal life which was with the Father, as distinct from him, and was manifested to us, 1 John i. 2.   So that life and immortality is made manifest by his appearance, as of a person that brings it, and manifests it with the manifestation of himself, 2 Tim. i. 13, and who is said to manifest himself unto us as well as the Father," Job xiv. 21.   Thus Reverend Dr. Goodwin.   *Dr. Goodwin on the knowledge of God, p. 52.*

2. We find in another Scripture, that he existed (or was a distinct person from the Father) before he came into the world.   " Wherefore, when he came into the world, he saith, a body hast thou prepared me," Heb. x. 5.—And again he saith, " Lo I come to do thy will, O God," ver. 7.   Here is a person distinct from God the Father, a [me] and an [I], and distinct also from his human nature he was to assume, which he calls a body prepared for him.   A person he is that speaks to God, as one knowing and understanding what he was about to do.

3. We find him to exist before John Baptist ; though John was conceived and born some months afore him, John bare witness of him, " and cried, saying, This was he of whom I spake, he that cometh after me is preferred before me, for he was before me, John i. 15. As God he was before John, and as man he came after John.

4. He existed before the prophets. Job saith, " he knew that his Redeemer lived," Job xix. 25; not that he should live, but that he did then live or exist when he spake those words; he saith not he shall live, he speaks of the Redeemer's life without any distinction of time, past or to come; he liveth, he being God is for ever, or lived from eternity; he is the " Prince of life," Acts ii.; and therefore existed then, and from everlasting. Isaiah saw him; " Woe is me, I am undone, for mine eyes have seen the King, the Lord of Hosts," Isa. vi. 5. That this was Christ, is evident, saith the Holy Ghost, speaking of Christ; " These things said Isaias when he saw his glory, and spake of him," John xii. 41.

5. He existed in the times of Moses: " Neither tempt Christ as some of them did," 1 Cor. x. 10.

6. He existed before Abraham, as he himself testified; " Before Abraham was I am," John viii. 58. Much the same with what God spake to Moses; " I am that I am, before the day was, I am;" so Isa. xliii. 13; I am, signifying the eternity, and uninterrupted being of Christ's divine Person and existence.

7. He was before Noah. For this is he who preached by Noah to the old world, or to those who were disobedient then, whose spirits are now in prison.

8. He existed before the world was made. " Thou Lord hast laid the foundation of the earth (speaking of Christ) and the heavens are the works of thy hands," Heb. i. 10; how could he make all things at the beginning, if he himself was not before all things, did not exist. " The Lord possessed me in the beginning of his ways, before his works of old: I was set up from everlasting, or ever the earth was; when there was no depths, I was brought forth, when there was no fountains abounding with water, before the mountains were settled, before the hills, was I brought forth," Prov. viii. 22, 23, 24, 25, 30. Then was I by him as one brought up with him, and I was daily his delight," &c. See Mich. v. 2. " But thou, Bethlehem Ephratah, though thou be little among the thousands of Judah, yet out of thee shall he come forth unto me, that is to be Ruler in Israel. Whose goings forth have been from of old, from everlasting."

Furthermore, how fully doth the prophet Isaiah show, that there was a blessed council held, and a compact or covenant between the Father and the Son, about the redemption of God's elect. And Paul shows that this council was held before the world began, 2 Tim. i. 9, and that we had in Christ a promise of eternal life before the world was made, Tit. i. 1, 2. Indeed, can any person think that the whole contrivance or platform of our salvation was not laid in eternity between the Father and the Son, &c.

But this could not be if Christ, or the second Person of the Trinity did not exist from everlasting. If there was a promise made to him, and to us in him before the world began, then it follows undeniably, that he did exist before the world begun, but such a promise was then made. *Ergo.*

Another text that proves Christ is God by nature, is that of Paul, Rom. ix. 5. " Whose are the Father's, and of whom as concerning the flesh Christ came, who is over all God blessed for ever, Amen." Compared with Phil. ii. 6. " Who being in the form of God thought it not robbery to be equal with God," &c. So Col. i. 17. " And he is before all things, and by him all things consist, and he is the Head of the body, the church. God manifested in the flesh," 1 Tim. iii. 16. " He is the brightness of the Father's glory, and the express image of his Person," Heb. i. 2, 3.

Arguments to prove the Godhead of Christ. Secondly, Take a few arguments to prove that Christ is the Most High God, which shows the infinite worth, dignity, and excellency of the pearl of great price.

1. Argu. He that hath all the incommunicable names of God most high given to him, is God most high, or the same essence with the Father. But Jesus Christ hath all the incommunicable names of God most high given to him, therefore he is God most high, or of the same essence with the Father.

1. He is called Most Mighty. " Gird on thy sword, O Most Mighty," Psal. xlv. 3.
2. He is called the First and the Last.
3. He is called the only wise God. " To the only wise God our Saviour, be glory and majesty, dominion and power, both now and for ever, Amen," Jude 25.

The title Saviour in the New Testament, is peculiarly given to our Lord Jesus Christ, not excluding God the Father, nor the Holy Ghost.

4. He is called the Mighty God, Isa. ix. 6.
5. He is called the Holy One. " Thou wilt not leave my soul in hell, nor suffer thy Holy One to see corruption," Psal. xvi. 10.

6. He is called the Saviour, nay, our only Saviour.

7. He is called Jehovah. "Jehovah our righteousness."

8. He is called the Everlasting Father, Isa. ix. 6.

9. He is called I Am, John viii. 58. "Before Abraham was I Am," that is, what I am, I will be; and was from everlasting, or a self existence as to his Deity.

10. He is called "God over all blessed for evermore," Rom. ix. 5.

11. He is called the true God. "And ye are in him that is true, even in his Son Jesus Christ, this is the true God, and eternal life," 1 John v. 20.

Now what mere creature or created being, did God ever give such titles unto, or call by such names, which are peculiar to himself alone?

II. Argu. He that hath all the incommunicable attributes of God given, or ascribed unto him, together with God's peculiar works and operations, is the Most High God; but all the incommunicable attributes of God are given, or ascribed unto Christ, together with God's peculiar works and operations, therefore Christ is the Most High God. *All the incommunicable attributes of God are in Jesus Christ.*

1. Argu. Jesus Christ is eternal; he that was before all things were, is eternal. But Christ was before all things were; therefore Christ is eternal, and therefore the Most High God. Prov. viii. 26, Col. xvii., John i. 1, 2, Heb. i. 3.

2. Argu. He that made all things, and laid the foundation of the earth, is the Most High God; but Jesus Christ made all things, and laid the foundation of the earth, *Ergo*, Jesus Christ is the Most High God. John i. 1—3, Heb. i. 8, 10, Rev. iv. 11.

3. Argu. He that upholds all things by the word of his power, "and by whom all things consist," Col. i. 17, Heb. i. 3. He is the Most High God, but Jesus Christ upholds all things by the word of his power, and by him all things consist, therefore he is the Most High God.

4. Argu. Omnisciency is ascribed to Jesus Christ. He that knows all things, and searcheth the heart and the reins, is the Most High God; but Jesus Christ knows all things, and searcheth the heart and the reins; therefore he is the Most High God. "Jesus knowing their thoughts said," &c. Matt. ix. 4. "And Jesus knowing all things that should come upon him, went forth," John xviii. 4. "And Peter said, Lord, thou knowest all things, thou knowest that I love thee; and all the churches shall know that I am he that searcheth the heart and reins, and will give to every one according to his works," John xxi. 17, Rev. ii. 23. He knows not only our external acts, and deeds, but our thoughts, intentions, purposes, designs, ends, and aims, and inclinations of all our hearts.

5. Argu. He that is omnipotent, is the Most High God. But Jesus Christ is omnipotent or almighty in power, and therefore he is the Most High God. Christ is not only called Almighty, but the Almighty. "I am Alpha and Omega, the beginning and the ending, the first and the last, the Almighty," Rev. i. 8.

6. Argu. He that is omniscient, is the Most High God; but Jesus Christ is omnipresent, *Ergo*, therefore the Most High God. "Lo I am with you always to the end of the world," Matt. xxviii. 20. "And where two or three are met together in my name, there am I in the midst of them."

Jesus Christ is said to be equal with God, as well as co-eternal and co-essential.

Arg. 7. He that is co-eternal, co-essential, and co-equal with the Father, is the Most High God; but Jesus Christ is co-eternal, co-essential, and co-equal with the Father, therefore he is the Most High God. "Who being in the form of God, he thought it not robbery to be equal with God," Phil. ii. 5, 6. *Christ is co-eternal and co-equal with the Father.* He did not judge it to be any wrong or usurpation to be acknowledged to be equal with God the Father, being a subsistent in the same nature and essence with him. It is not said, he thought not to do this robbery as to make himself equal with God, as the Socinians would read it, no, but he thought it not robbery to be equal with God; he had not this equality by usurpation, nor by gift, but he was so essentially, and eternally. O what a pearl of infinite price is this pearl!

The fulness of the Godhead dwells in Jesus Christ bodily. From whence I argue.

Arg. 8. He in whom the whole Godhead, or the Godhead bodily doth abide or dwell, is the Most High God, but the whole Godhead, or the Godhead bodily, abides or dwells in Jesus Christ, therefore Jesus Christ is the Most High God. "For in him dwelleth the fulness of the Godhead bodily," Col. ii. 9. Christ was not only a partaker of the divine nature, as the saints are said to do; no, but the fulness of the Godhead, or whole Godhead, or Deity is in him, or the whole essence of God. "There are three that bear witness in heaven, the Father, the Word, and the Holy Ghost, and these three are one," John v. 7. This text hath so baffled many blasphemous heretics, that some of them would not have it to be canonical, alleging it is not in some Greek copies. Yet as a late author notes, St. Cyprian when he argued for the unity of the Godhead in the three Persons, cites this text. And Tertullian (saith he) asserting this to be the Christian doctrine, *i. e.*, that the Father, Son, and Holy Ghost, were each of them God, and yet the Godhead not divided, proved it from this text, *Hi tres unum junt;* and then he remarks from the gender, that they were not *unus* but *unum, i. e.*, not one in person, but one in essence.

Infinite wisdom and knowledge is attributed or inscribed to Jesus Christ, he is wisdom itself, yea, the only wise God, " In whom are hid all the treasures of wisdom," &c.

Christ the only wise God.
> Argu. 9.   He that is all-wise, or infinite in wisdom, or in whom all wisdom is hid, is the Most High God, but Christ Jesus is all-wise, or infinite in wisdom, *Ergo.* Jesus Christ is the Most High God.

The like I might speak of his holiness, he being called the Holy One, and Isaiah heard the angels cry to him, " Holy, holy, holy, is the Lord of hosts," Isa. vi. 15.

Argu. 10.   He that is the Holy One of God, the Holy One of Israel, or infinitely holy, is God most high; but Christ is the Holy One of God, the Holy One of Israel, infinitely holy.   *Ergo,* Christ is God most high.

Divine worship is to be given to Jesus Christ.
> III.   Argu. He to whom spiritual or divine worship, honour and adoration doth belong, even the same divine worship, honour, and adoration that is due to God the Father, is the Most High God; but spiritual worship, honour, and adoration, even the same divine worship, honour, and adoration that belongs unto God the Father, belongs to the Lord Jesus Christ, *Ergo,* he is the Most High God.

It is the will of the Father " That all men should honour the Son as they honour the Father, he that honoureth not the Son, honoureth not the Father," &c., John v. 23.

God the Father doth not command this honour to be given to Christ absolutely as God, but distinctly as the Son in our nature, or as Mediator, *i. e.*, this worship and honour is to be given to Jesus of Nazareth.   It is also to show that no less honour is due to the Second Person of the Trinity, because he took our nature into union with his Divine Person; and so as Mediator, became God's servant.   " And when he brought the first begotten into the world, he said, let all the angels of God worship him," Heb. i. 6.   Adore him, bow down before him.   " Worship him, all ye gods," Psal. xcvii. 7.   And as all the angels of heaven and potentates of the earth, as kings, who are called gods, are to worship him; so the like command is given to the church.   " He is thy Lord, and worship thou him," Psal. xlv. 11, speaking of Jesus Christ; And thus we find all do that are in heaven and earth.

" The four beasts, and four and twenty elders fell down before the Lamb.   And they sung a new song, saying, worthy is the Lamb that was slain to receive power and riches, and wisdom, and strength, and honour, and glory, and blessing.   And every creature which is in heaven, and on the earth, and under the earth, and such that are in the sea, and all that are in them, I heard saying, Blessing, honour, glory, and power, be unto him that sitteth upon the throne, and to the Lamb for ever and ever.   And the four beasts and the four and twenty elders fell down and worshipped him that liveth for ever and ever," Rev. v. 8— 13.   O what wretch upon the earth dares to deny Jesus Christ to be God Most High, or assert he is but a mere creature?   Will God give his honour to another, to a mere creature, or to one who is not of the same essence with himself?

This worship is given to Christ as Mediator, the formal reason of which worship is his divine nature, and his having redeemed us is one special motive of it.   " Thou wast slain and hast redeemed us," Acts. xx. 28.   This is the great motive of this amazing adoration. And as adoration belongs to Jesus Christ, so also doth invocation, which is another branch of divine honour.

Argu. 12.   He to whom we ought to pray or make our supplication, is the Most High God; but we ought to pray, and make our supplication to Jesus Christ, Ergo, he is the Most High God.   All believers come to the Father by him, they address themselves to their blessed Advocate and Intercessor; the first martyr committed his soul to Jesus Christ, " He called upon God, saying, Lord Jesus, receive my Spirit;" again he said, " Lord, lay not this sin to their charge," Acts vii. 59, 60.   Thus also the saints and gospel church were distinguished from all others.   " With all that call on the name of our Lord Jesus Christ, both their Lord and ours," 1 Cor. i. 2.

Jesus Christ hears the prayers of thousand sat one time.
> Arg. 13.   He that can hear distinctly, and answer a thousand thousand persons prayers, all put up the same moment of time, is no mere creature, but the most High God; but Jesus Christ can do this, Ergo, he is the Most High God.   If this be denied, i. e., that Christ can distinctly hear, and answer, so

many prayers, put up at one and the same moment of time, what kind of an Advocate do they make him to be ? or do they address themselves to him as their Advocate at all ?

Arg. 14. He that hath power to forgive all iniquity, or can acquit sinners from vindictive justice, is the Most High God ; but Jesus Christ thus forgiveth sins, Ergo, he is the Most High God. The Jews no doubt were right in that they said, who can forgive sins but God? That is, that hath power to forgive the offence, as it is against God and his infinite justice. " But that ye may know that the Son of man hath power on earth to forgive sins—take up thy bed and walk," Matt. ix. 6.

The Son of man, that is Christ as Mediator, he is God as well as Man, yea, the same Most High God, he hath power to forgive sins.

Arg. 15. He that could raise the dead by his own power, and did raise up the temple of his own body when it was in the grave, and shall also raise up all the dead at the last day, is the Most High God ; but all this Christ hath done, or will do, Ergo, Christ is the Most God. " All that are in the graves shall hear his voice, and come forth," John v. 28, 29. He it is also that raiseth them, quickens them that are spiritually dead, " You hath he quickened," &c. Eph. ii. 1, 2.

Now from the whole I argue thus, if Jesus Christ be the Most High God, then he is a pearl of infinite worth ; nothing sets forth the excellencies and preciousness of Christ, more than the dignity, glory, and excellencies of his person.

But to proceed, he is not God only of the essence of the Father, but truly man, of the substance and very nature of " Mary, and so flesh of our flesh, and bone of our bone," Eph. v. 30 ; indeed if he was not, our finding him could no more enrich us than it might the fallen angels, as I have hinted.

1. He is called Immanuel, God with us, or God in our flesh, i. e., in that particular body of flesh he took in the womb of the Virgin. " Great is the mystery of godliness, God manifested in the flesh," 1 Tim. iii. 16. Not in every man's flesh, no but in that body of flesh only, he taking that very flesh or human nature into an hypostatical union with his own divine person, and so is both God and man in one person. God was manifested in the flesh, I say, in that individual body prepared for him, or in that very flesh that he assumed, or took into union with himself. *Christ is truly man as well as God.*

" A woman shall compass a man," Jer. xxx. 22, that is, by a wonderful conception, by the overshadowing of the Holy Ghost, and hence it is said he was made of a woman, and therefore called the seed of the woman, and the seed of Abraham ; " in thy seed shall all the nations of the earth be blessed."

2. He was conceived of the Virgin, and born of her, and sucked her paps.

3. It is said, " He took not on him the nature of angels, but he took on him the seed of Abraham. Forasmuch as the children are partakers of flesh and blood, he took part of the same," Heb. ii. 14, 16.

4. God sware to David, that " of the fruit of his loins he would raise up Christ to sit upon his throne," Acts ii. 30. Therefore such that deny he took the same flesh, or that his human nature was indeed the seed of David, do render the Holy God to be forsworn ; which is the highest blasphemy to assert.

5. He is the root and offspring of David, David's Lord, and David's Son ; *Inference.* he is the root of David in respect to his Godhead, and the offspring of David in respect to his humanhood ; as he is God he is David's Lord, and as man he is David's Son ; which shows he consists of two distinct natures in one person.

6. It was only a kinsman under the law that had the right to redeem, &c., therefore Christ must be of our very nature, or else he is not one of our brethren, nor our kinsman.

7. Nor could he be our Surety, if not of our very nature ; because it was man made of earth that sinned, and the nature, the justice, holiness, and truth of God, requires to atone for sin, and satisfy divine justice. And, indeed, if this was not absolutely necessary, there had been no need for him to assume our nature, or to be made of a woman, made under the law, even that law that we had broken.

Therefore from hence it followeth, that it is a most dangerous thing, nay, a damnable heresy to deny Jesus Christ to be the Most High God, and man of our very nature. *The dangerous absurdities that follow the denying the deity of Christ.*

Consider (as I have showed) that the chief part of Christ's personal excellency consists in the dignity of his person, or in consideration of who he is.

2. Moreover, that such that deny Christ is the Most High God, or the Son of God by an eternal generation, co-essential and co-equal with the Fa-

Such that
deny the
deity of
Christ ren-
der him to
be a deceiver. ther, render our blessed Lord to be a deceiver, or an imposter, and so justify the wicked Jews, in calling him a blasphemer, in saying he being a man made himself equal with God ; he telling them that he and his Father were one.

3. If you know not his worth, his great price, or the dignity of his person, i. e., that he is truly God, how dare you give that worship to him that is due to God only?

5. To deny Jesus Christ to be the Most High God, renders all that worship him, or give divine adoration to him, to be guilty of gross idolatry, and it is according to their hellish notion, as bad to adore and worship Jesus Christ, as it was in the Israelites to worship the golden calf, or in the heathen who worshipped them who by nature were no gods ; for this must be so if he be not God by nature, but a mere creature.

It also reflects on the care, faithfulness, and holiness of God the Father towards poor mankind, and that he in his word leads us into the sin of idolatry (which his holy nature so much abhors) in requiring all to honour the Son as they honour the Father ; and in saying he was God, and in the beginning with God, and equal with God, nay, the true God, the only wise God, and God over all ; and telling us also that he made all things, and by him all things consist, and commanding all the holy angels to worship him, and that he searcheth the hearts, and tries the reins, and knows all men; what man can from hence but conclude he is bound to give divine worship and adoration unto Jesus Christ ? For would God the Father in his wisdom have left all these things on record in his word, had not Christ been God by nature, or of the same essence with himself ? I desire this may be well considered.

If Christ be
not God most
high, he can-
not be our
Saviour. 6. Moreover, if Jesus of Nazareth is not the Most High God, he cannot be our Saviour, nor ought we to put our trust in him; for none is our Saviour but God alone. " I am God, and besides me there is no Saviour," Isa. xliii. 11, also he saith, " Cursed is the man that trusteth in man, and maketh flesh his arm," Jer. xvii. 5. If, therefore, Christ be no more than a mere creature, or not God by nature, we are cursed of God if we trust in him, or believe in him, and rely upon him for righteousness and eternal life.

7. Furthermore, then also Jesus Christ could not satisfy divine justice for our sins, which were imputed to him as he stood in our law-place; because a finite being, or a mere creature could not satisfy infinite justice, it being from the dignity of his holy person (he being God) that his obedience and death were satisfactory unto God ; and then also it will follow that we are still in our sins, and cannot be justified by his righteousness.

If Christ be
not God, he
cannot bear
our prayers. 8. Besides it must also (if Christ be not the Most High God) be a vain thing to pray to, or call upon the Lord Jesus Christ, because he neither knows our wants, nor can he hear our cries ; and yet we find that the saints did call upon him, and we also daily do it in all our prayers and approaches to the Father in his name, nor ought we any other way come unto God. " No man cometh to the Father but by me," John xiv. 6.

9. Again, if Christ is not God most high, he cannot judge the world at the last day, because he knoweth not the secrets of all hearts ; " For none knoweth and searches the heart but God alone," Jer. xvii. 10. Besides, it is positively said, that " he shall not judge after the sight of the eyes, nor after the hearing of his ears," Isa. xi. 3. That is, he shall not need any to come into witness against any person, or give in evidences against a prisoner, after which all other judges try and condemn guilty criminals.

They that
deny Christ
to be God
over all cast
contempt on
the word of
God, for it
asserts he is
God. 10. Such that deny the Lord Jesus Christ to be Most High God, and man of the seed of Abraham, deny the written Word of God, and cast contempt upon it, and charge the Holy Ghost with a lie, who testifieth in many places that he is really God and truly man in one person.

11. To deny the Godhead of Christ, is to deny him the glory of our salvation. Shall a mere creature share or equally partake with God the Father, in the honour of such a glorious and so great a salvation as the salvation of the gospel is?

Caffins, obj. Obj. Christ is blessed of God, and hath a God, therefore he is not the Most High God.

Answ. If Christ was not man as well as God, this objection hath something in it ; now as he is Man, God-Man, or Mediator, he is called God's Servant, and was sent of God, blessed of God, anointed of God, and hath God to be his God. Sometimes the scripture speaks of him considered as God, or alluding only to his deity ; and sometimes it speaks of him as Man, or Mediator, Luke i. 35, and Gal. iv. 4, and so in those places, God the Father is his God, I say, in respect of his human nature, and as Mediator between God and man; but in respect of his divine nature he is the same one God, though a distinct person from the Father.

Obj. If the Father be the only true God, then Christ is not the true God, but this he himself saith. "That they may know thee the only true God," John xvii. 3.

Answ. The term, only, or alone, the true God, is not to be applied to thee, i.e., the Father, but to God, and then the sense is this, to know thee to be that God, which is the only true God; and as our divines show, this appears from 1 John v. 20, where Christ is said to be the true God, which could not be, if the Father was the only true God, considered distinct from the Son. *(How we are to understand God to be the only true God.)*

(2.) Therefore the term only is not exclusive of the other two Persons in the blessed Trinity, but only of idol gods, which are false gods.

Thus I have showed you, that the transcendent worth and excellencies of Christ the pearl of great price, consisteth in the excellency and dignity of his sacred Person: he being the Most High God co-essential with the Father, I should now proceed to speak to the second thing, viz., further to open more particularly his personal excellencies as God-Man, but that I will leave to the next time.

APPLICATION

I. I infer from hence, that such who deny Christ to be the Most High God, are grand heretics, and so in a fearful state and condition.

II. And as bad heretics they are, and in the like gall of bitterness, who deny him to be man of the seed of David. Both these sorts of deceivers deny the Lord that bought them. Beware therefore of their pernicious principles, and deceitful arguing, who tell you, because the whole lump of the first Adam was corrupted, if Christ took of the nature of the first Adam, he could not be without sin, and so needed to offer up a sacrifice for himself, as the priest under the law did. Thus they argue.

1. Answ. Could not God by the overshadowing the blessed virgin in that hypostatical union, sanctify that part of her nature, which he so took into union with himself.

2. He did not take the person of any man unto union with his divine person, but only the nature of man; for we see not how any one man begotten in the common manner of generation, could be freed from the imputation of Adam's sin and natural defilement thereof; but Christ in respect of his human nature, being no one person proceeding from the first Adam by the common way of natural generation, but being begotten in the womb of the virgin by the Holy Ghost, and the human nature, body and soul, subsisting only in the Person of the Son of God, hence he could not come under the first Adam's sin, as being naturally guilty thereof, but was holy and pure from original defilement.

3. And since the Holy Ghost bears witness that he was of David's seed according to the flesh, and yet born without sin, we ought steadfastly to believe this testimony, and make it an article of our faith, though our weak capacities cannot fully comprehend how this could be, and it argues great pride in any otherwise to think or affirm, because their narrow and dark reason cannot take it in, or their judgments conceive of it, or give a demonstration therof: yet what reason can any give, that he that proceeded not by propagation or in a natural way by common generation, or as being no individual person from Adam's loins (subsisting of himself before the hypostatical union) should be guilty of his sin: either as Adam was a federal head, or otherwise, I see not,

4. Take heed who you hear, you know not how some very near you favour one Caffin's abominable heresies.

5. Let believers comfort themselves with the thoughts of the pre-existence of their Head: "Ye know him that was from the beginning, which ye have heard," &c, 1 John i. 1, 2.

5. O trust in him, and cleave to him, as your joy, chiefest delight, and choicest treasure; "All things being made by him and for him; who was the same yesterday, is to-day, and will be for ever," Heb. xiii. 8.

7. Adore him, say, "Worthy is the Lamb that was slain, to receive power, riches, and wisdom, and strength, and honour, and glory, and blessing," Rev. v. 12.

8. Also admire his love and great condescension in taking our nature into union with his divine person, and live to him all your days.

III

Again the kingdom of heaven is like a merchantman seeking goodly pearls, who when he
had found one pearl of great price, &c.—Matt. xiii. 45, 26.

THE doctrine, my brethren, that I am upon is this, viz., that Jesus Christ, the pearl of
great price, is most precious, excellent, or of infinite worth and value.

I have gone through the first thing, proposed under the second general head of discourse, viz., to show you wherein the infinite worth and excellencies of our Lord Jesus
Christ, the pearl of great price, doth consist, viz., in respect unto his person; he being the
Most High God, or the only begotten of the Father, very God, and yet truly man,
in one glorious Person.

Secondly, I shall now proceed to show you, it doth consist also in other of his personal
excellencies, as also in respect of that honour God hath conferred on him, and in what he
hath made him to be unto his church.

But first let me sum up that which I said the last day, in respect of his person, in one
or two arguements.

The former demonstrations of Christ's glory summed up.   1. Argu. That person who is truly and really God, God by nature, or
the Most High God, co-eternal, co-essential, and co-equal with the Father, is
a most excellent person, and infinitely or inconceivably glorious: but this I
have proved Jesus Christ is, Ergo. And therefore I said the excellencies
of his Person is the chiefest part of his personal excellencies.

Let this always be well considered, viz., that all the perfections of the adorable Deity,
or Godhead of the second Person, are ascribed to Jesus Christ, or to Jesus of Nazareth,
or to Christ, considered as Mediator; and that as he is not Jesus Christ without his hu-
manity: for as the body is not the whole person of a complete man, without the soul, so
the human nature of Christ is not the complete and individual person of Jesus of Nazareth, or the Man Christ Jesus, without his Godhead or divine nature, so that all the perfections of the eternal God, I say, meet in, and belong to the Person of our Lord Jesus
Christ.

I do not mean that God only is in that Person, but that that very Person is God: for that
which constitutes a thing, or is an essential of it, or that of which that thing doth consist,
if that essential part be wanting, that thing cannot be said to be there; we do not say
the body or external part of a man is the man without his soul, but we call it the body
of a man: so Christ is no real person, no Christ without his Deity, because the human
nature which the Son of God took into union with his Divine Person, doth not subsist of
or in itself, (though a human body and soul) but in the Divine Person of the Son of God.

All the perfections of God the Father meet in Chrtst.   So that both natures constitute the Lord Jesus Christ our Redeemer.

2. Argu. He that is eternal, or from everlasting, omnipotent, omniscient,
infinitely holy, infinitely wise, that is, infinitely just and true, infinitely good and
patient, or in whose person all other glorious perfections of the blessed God

shines forth, so that " He is the brightness of the Father's glory, and the express image
of his Person," Heb. i. 2, 3, is a most excellent, and a most glorious Person; but all
these perfections I have proved are in Jesus Christ our Redeemer, therefore he is a
most excellent and a most glorious Person.

Indeed were not Jesus Christ infinitely good, and so the Most High God, we ought not
to make him our chiefest good, nor place our chiefest happiness in him, nor make him to
be the only object of our affections, so as to love him with all our hearts, with all our souls,
and with all our strength. For it would be horrid wickedness thus to do, in giving that
glory of God unto another, which is peculiar to himself. Moreover, was not Jesus Christ
infinitely patient, he could not bear all those horrid reproaches, contempt, and indignities,
that are cast upon him in these (as well as in former) days; how is he degraded in his
Person? In his love, mercy, and patience and goodness? How is his name blasphemed,
his authority, power, and dignity contemned, his ordinances slighted, and his members torn
in pieces and trodden under foot? O what is the patience, long-suffering, and forbearance
of the Lord Jesus Christ!

Heretics, such as are the Arians, Socinians, Eutichians, and Caffinites, blaspheme him,
ungod him, and take the crown off his head, rendering him no more than a mere creature.
The Quakers utterly deny he hath any personal existence, or that he is an individual Person or God-Man, now in heaven above, but strive to make people believe he is nothing

but a mere inward or divine quality of light or power in all men. And profane and ungodly sinners swear and blaspheme his name, and swear by his blood and wounds every day, and O how doth he bear and forbear with all these grand abuses and indignities! Was he no more than a man, and could be revenged upon these blasphemers and contemners of his person, his glory, and his authority, would he not soon do it? nay, had long ago utterly consumed and destroyed them in his anger, certainly he is the Most High God, one endowed with infinite patience, evidently appears from hence.

Secondly, to proceed, the Lord Jesus Christ hath other personal excellencies, considered God-man, now glorified in heaven.

1. His person is the most glorious and ineffable effect of divine wisdom. God's acts or works of creation in making this world, with men and angels, and in indowing mankind with excellent principles of a rational intelligent nature, and a conscience attesting his subjection and subordination, to God and also his works of divine providence, are all glorious effects of his great wisdom and power. But the divine excellencies of the person of Jesus Christ, as the foundation of the new creation, and as the mystery of godliness, were the chief and most ineffable effects of God's glorious wisdom, as reverend Owen showeth—not of his divine person absolutely considered as a distinct person from the Father, *See Dr. Owen on the person of Christ.* or as simply God; for as so considered he is not the effect of divine wisdom and power, but the essential wisdom and power of God; but we speak of him as incarnate, as he assumed our nature into personal union and subsistence with himself.

His conception in the womb of the virgin, as to the integrity of human nature (saith he) was a miraculous operation of divine power, but the prevention of that nature from any subsistence of its own, by its assumption into personal union with the Son of God, in the first instance of its conception, is that which is above all miracles; a mystery it is, and of those dimensions as no creature can comprehend, &c., so far above the order of all creating or providential *The human nature of Christ subsisted not of itself, but in the divine nature.* operations, that it wholly transcends the sphere of them that are most miraculous. Herein God did glorify all the properties of the divine nature, acting in a way of infinite wisdom, grace, and condescension. The depths of the mystery hereof, are open only unto him whose understanding is infinite, and which no created understanding can comprehend. All things were produced and effected by an outward emanation of power from God in creation, "He said, let there be light, and there was light." But this assumption of our nature into hypostatical union with the Son of God, this constitution of one and the same individual person, in two natures so infinitely distinct as those of God and man; whereby the eternal was made in time, the infinite became finite, the immortal mortal, yet continuing eternal, infinite, immortal, is that singular expression of divine wisdom, goodness, and power, wherein God will be admired and glorified unto all eternity. Herein was that change introduced into the whole first creation, whereby the blessed angels were exalted, and Satan and his works ruined, mankind recovered from all dismal apostacy, all things made new, all things in heaven and earth reconciled and gathered into one head, and a revenue of eternal glory raised unto God, incomparably above what the first constitution of all things, in order of nature, could yield unto him.

The mysteriousness of the assumption of the human nature, into union with the divine wisdom purpose, and design of God therein, wonderfully tends to set forth the personal excellencies of Jesus Christ. "The word was made flesh, and dwelt among us," John i. 14, but what word was this? even that which was in the beginning, and which was God; and yet a person distinct from God, and from hence said to be with God, and he also who made all things. "The word was made flesh," not by any change of his own nature or essence (as some heretics assert) nor by any transubstantiation of the divine nature into the human, nor by ceasing to be what it was; but by becoming what he was not, in taking our nature to his own, to be his own, whereby he dwelt among us. *How the Word was said to be made flesh. Dr. Owen.*

Herein shines forth the personal excellencies of Jesus Christ, and this is the glory of the Christian religion, the basis and foundation that bears the whole superstructure, and the root whereon it grows, as the Dr. well observed, natural religion in its first constitution, in the state of pure incorrupted nature, was orderly, beautiful, and glorious; man being made in the image of God, was fit and able to glorify him as God. But whereas what perfection God had communicated unto our nature, he having not united it unto himself in a personal union, the fabric of it quickly fell to the ground, the want of this foundation made it obnoxious unto ruin; God manifested herein that no gracious relation between him and our nature, could be so near and intimate, nor stable and permanent, unless our nature was assumed into personal union and subsistence with himself, on this consideration let us by faith behold Christ, and apprehend him to be, as indeed he is, the power of God, and the wisdom of God unto salvation ; and thus looking upon him let us admire him, as the pearl of great price, who puts a glory upon the whole of our religion, and on all his whole church, and on all who are united to him, " in whom all things consist," Col. i. 17, and who is the " chiefest among ten thousand," Cant. v. 10.

Christ the great re- pository of all divine truth.

Dr. Owen.

Thirdly, the glory and personal excellencies of Christ appear further, in that he is the great storehouse, or repository of all sacred truth, whether truth be considered essentially, or declaratively, the first is God himself, the other is the councils of his will ; as Christ is the same God and essence with the Fa- ther, he is essentially the truth, and as God-man or Mediator, he declareth or maketh known all truth, or the whole council and will of God, " For no man hath seen God at any time, the only begotten, who is in the bosom of the Father, he hath declared him," John i. 18. Christ therefore is the truth (1.) Essential as God, and (2.) Substan- tially in opposition to types and shadows ; and (3.) he is the truth efficiently, as all truth is by him fully and effectually declared ; and also (4.) subjectively, as all divine truth re- lating to the saving knowledge of God, is treasured up in him ; he may therefore well say, I am the truth. And therefore we, if we would know the truth, we must look for it as it is in Jesus.—For

1. Christ is the light of truth, whatever light of grace, love, and truth shines into our hearts, it is as it proceeds from him ; it is made known and revealed by him, " in whom are hid all the treasures of wisdom and knowledge," Col. ii. 3 ; that is, whatsoever is need- ful for us to know, concerning God, or our justification, vocation, sanctification, and eter- nal life ; or of his will, councils, and what we are to believe and practice.

2. In respect of efficacy or power Christ is the truth, it is from the person of Christ, that all divine and efficacious influences and operations of grace proceed : as light, heat, and fruit- fulness, flow from the sun, therefore they who reject the person of Christ, or are not united to him ; or upon whom he hath not yet ever shone, or sent forth his special and most powerful influences, are dead, barren, dark, and undone creatures.

Fourthly, the personal excellencies of Christ shine forth in respect had to his offices as king, priest, and prophet, and in his exercise of each of them. But pray note, that the exercise of all his offices do depend upon the excellency of his person, as being God, and not man only, for his being God gave efficacy to his blessed sacrifice, which he once offer- ed up for sin.

The glory of Christ's kingly of- fice.

1. As being God, he hath all power as a king, to subdue us to himself, and to vanquish all our enemies, whether without or within, as sin, Satan, the world, death, and the grave.

2. And as being God, he only is able to execute his prophetical office.

The glory of Christ's prophetical office.

(1.) For how else could he have took the charge of the church, and every believer from the beginning of the world, and before his incarnation ?

(2.) How else could he now teach, guide, and influence the whole univer- sal church, and every member thereof.

(3.) How else could he have inspired the prophets, the apostles, and all his ministers from the beginning to the end of the world ?

(4.) How else could he give us hearts to understand, as well as understanding to know and do his will ?

(5.) How else could he be with his saints, to teach, guide, and lead them to the end of the world ?

(6.) Else how could he make his own word efficacious and effectual to the souls of sin- ners, or by his speaking make the dead hear, and open blind eyes ?

(7.) How else could he teach the simple, the ignorant, nay fools, so that they shall not err, and make them wiser than the prudent and all the wise men of this world ?

(8.) How else could he teach men, and seal up instruction to them in the night, when deep sleep has seized upon them ? who but God can do these things ?

Put all now together, and then consider what a glorious person Jesus Christ is, as he is a priest, a king, and a prophet.

The glory of Christ's priestly office.

1. What a priest is he that is both the altar, the sacrifice, and the priest also that offers up that sacrifice ?

2. What a priest is he that did sacrifice himself, or offers up himself a sacrifice unto God !

3. What a priest is he, who by the worth of his sacrifice hath by one offering for ever

fully atoned, and satisfied infinite justice for all the sins of God's people, both past, present, and to come, and has left no room for any other atoning and wrath-appeasing sacrifice, to be offered up to God for ever, and also himself sprinkles his own blood, and pleads its virtue now in heaven for us.

Secondly, What a King is he, that is King of kings, yea the Prince of all the kings of the earth, and that gives kings their authority, their power, their wisdom (if they rule well) and their kingdoms also unto them, that can set up one, pull down another at his pleasure.

2. What a King he. is that is king of heaven and of earth, and of hell, that has power and authority over men, angels, and devils, that can subdue in one moment tyrant sin, tyrant world, tyrant Satan, tyrant flesh, tyrant death, and tyrant grave ; that can by one word of his mouth change the heart, enlighten the mind, bow the rebellious will, regulate disorderly affections, deliver from all dangers, scatter all fears, strengthen under all weaknesses, and give courage and undauntedness of spirit to the faint and weak-hearted ones.

3. What a Prophet is he. (1). That knows all the whole will and councils of God (2). That is equal with God in knowledge.

4. What a prophet is he that can give an hearing ear, a seeing eye, and an understanding heart.

5. What a Prophet is he, that teacheth powerfully, effectually, and efficaciously, nay, infallibly ; who in his council, teachings, and instruction cannot err.

Fifthly, the glory, life, and power of the Christian religion, with all the acts and duties which properly belong thereunto, with all the benefits and privileges we receive by it, or by virtue of it, with the whole glory and honour that riseth thereby unto God, have all of them their formal nature and reason (as one well notes) from their respect and relation unto the person of Jesus Christ, nor is he a Christian who is otherwise minded. *The personal excellencies of Christ consists in that great honour that is due to him.*

The person of Christ is the object of divine honour and worship ; I bring not this in now to prove he is God, as before I did) but to discover what excellencies belong and cleave to his person. True, the formal object and reason of divine adoration due to Christ, is his divine nature and its essential infinite excellencies. For the person of Christ having in it the fulness of the Godhead, there is not the less honour due unto him because he assumed our nature, and united it unto himself, than was due to him before, or is due unto the person of the Father, or the Holy Ghost. Wherefore the person of Christ is primarily the object of divine honour, upon the account of his divine nature ; nor was there any divine adoration due to him, were he not truly God, or God over all blessed for evermore. *Dr. Owen on Christ's person, page 112.*

Brethren, I am speaking of Christ in his whole entire person, i. e., the Son of God incarnate, God manifest in the flesh, and I say that his infinite condescension in the assumption of our nature, did no ways divest him of his divine excellencies, though for a time they were vailed from the eyes of men, when " He made himself of no reputation, and took on him the form of a servant," Phil. ii. 6, 7. And let none think they please God the Father, who ascribe all honour to him, and debase the Son. For what saith our Lord ? " He that honours not the Son, honours not the Father." We say the same honour is due to the Son as is due to the Father ; nay, and " this is the will of the Father, that all should honour the Son even as they honour the Father," John v. 23 ; even the same adoration, the same divine worship, the same trust or faith we have in God, we must have in Christ, and the same invocation, and the same love and obedience. " Ye believe in God, believe also in me," John xiv. 1, as God equal with my Father. To ascribe unto any creature anything that is proper and peculiar unto God, or any divine excellency, is idolatry ; therefore we do not honour God the Father with one kind of honour, and the Son, with another ; for that were not to honour the Son even as we honour the Father. And though this honour is to be given to Christ by the Father's command, considered as Mediator, yet originally, upon the account of his oneness in nature with the Father, it is our duty thus to adore, honour, love, and reverence him. *Inference.*

If we are to pray unto Christ, if we are to believe in Christ, trust in him, as on our only Saviour, if we are to love with the same love wherewith we ought to love the Father, if we are to fall down before him, and worship even as we are to fall down before God the Father and worship him, then Jesus Christ is a most excellent and glorious person ; nay, his personal excellencies are infinite and inconceivable. But all these things we are to do, Ergo.

Sixthly, Such are the personal excellencies of our Lord Jesus Christ, that he in his person God-man, is that glorious sluice, conduit-pipe, or conveyance of all those blessings, and that communicable good unto us, which is in God ; *Christ's person the sluice or conduit-pipe of all blessings.*

not one dram of any good thing, any favours, grace, and comfort, either to body or soul, flows from God to us, but it all comes to us through Jesus Christ. So that as the person of Christ considered as God is the fountain of all good, and as he is Mediator, he is the great repository of all good ; even so also he is the sluice or outlet through whom all good is conveyed, or flows from God into our empty vessels, (like as Joseph had all the corn of Egypt in his own possession, so he gave it forth to all that came to him). My brethren, we have no life, no light, no grace, no pardon, no strength, no blessing ; but what we receive immediately from the hands of Jesus Christ ; it is all from God the Father through Christ by the Holy Ghost, even through Christ's merits and his gracious intercession ; and, as we receive all things from God through Christ, so all our returns of praises unto the Father must be in and through Christ ; so that we must always not only give glory unto God the Father and to Jesus Christ, &c., but also give " glory unto God, through Christ for ever, Amen," Rom. xvi. 27.

Beauty is one of Christ's personal excellencies. Seventhly, another personal excellency of Christ is his wonderful beauty and transcendent loveliness, by which means he is represented as the most amicable and lovely object in heaven and earth, attracting and drawing forth our hearts' love and affections to him.

See the parable of the Marriage Supper opened. Divine excellencies in God, are a proper adequate object of our love, but especially divine goodness, that endearing attribute of the Holy God. " God is love—O how great is his goodness," Psal. iii. 19. Now that which causeth his goodness to be admired and prized so much the more by us, is because it comprehends the riches, mercy, grace, and bounty, which answers all our wants and necessities, and tends to make us happy, truly happy here, and eternally happy hereafter.

But wherein doth this beauty, love, goodness, mercy and bounty appear, but in the person of Christ ? It is in Christ that we see God's glorious amiableness, love, goodness, and mercy, so as to desire him, and to set our hearts upon him, above all other things in heaven and earth. " In this was manifested the love of God towards us, because that God sent his only begotten Son into the world that we might live through him. Herein is love, not that we loved God, but that he loved us, and sent his Son to be the propitiation for our sins," 1 John iv. 9, 10. But though God is love, or of a nature infinitely good and gracious, and so the object of all divine love and delight, yet if there be no way for us to attain unto the knowledge of this good God, or as to participate of his goodness, how should we let forth our hearts towards him ? Now it is only in the person of Christ, God's infinite bounty and love to us is manifested, and by whom we come to taste how sweet and consolatory it is ; the love of God can no other way be known to us but by his love in Christ ; this is the cause, the fountain and spring of all our love unto him ; in Christ we know this God may be enjoyed, and that we come to be united to him ; I say it is manifested in and by the person of Christ.

How it appears that we are united to and enjoy God in and through Jesus Christ. 1. Because in him both natures are united, even he is God and man in one person. And so,

2. A door is hereby opened for our union with God ; it is hereby we see ground to hope that we shall taste of the sweetness of his love, and enjoy God for ever.

Furthermore, when the soul takes a view by faith of the goodness of God, as it is manifested in Christ (that is, the essential excellencies of his nature) as exerting themselves in him, the soul reacheth after him with its uttermost desires, longing for his embraces, and it is restless until it attain to a perfect fruition of him.

4. Moreover, in Christ the soul sees God's love is a conjugal or an espousal love, which is the sweetest of all love, it is not only the love of friendship, or of a master to a servant, or of a father to a son, but the love of a bridegroom to his bride, or beloved spouse.

5. Nay, the person of Christ, as it is clothed with all the essential properties of divine nature, all the glory and beauty of heaven shines forth in him. And as we see him clothed with our nature, he appears more clearly to our understanding as a fit and proper object of our love and affections; as being in our nature " he is bone of our bone, and flesh of our flesh," for we cannot attain to such an idea of God, considered as in himself, as we The Beauty and glory of Christ God-man. can as he is manifested in the flesh, therefore God hath condescended to bring forth in Christ an express image of his own person. And as he is thus in respect of his divine nature, so as man now glorified in heaven, what beauty shines forth in him ! God designed to let out, or manifest his infinite and inconceivable glory in the man Christ Jesus. A man, and yet God, a spotless man, a man without blemish, who never knew sin ; in whom all perfections of God and man meet ; that so he might become the proper object of our highest, best, and choicest affections. My brethren, can heaven

and earth make or constitute a glorious and most excellent person, why then here he is; Jesus Christ is the glory of heaven, and the beauty of the earth ; the glory of the upper and of the nether world shine forth in the person of Jesus Christ.

If created light be glorious in the sun, if glory be great in holy angels, much more God's essential glory ; purity, beauty, wisdom, holiness, power, justice, truth, mercy, and goodness, are glorious. No being is glory in the abstract, but God ; and this fundamental excellency shines forth in the person of Christ. "We beheld his glory as the glory of the only-begotten of the Father, full of grace and truth," John i. 14.

1. We have here an object beheld, [Christ] the Son of God ; not Christ only, but the glory of Christ.

2. A specification of that glory, the glory of the only-begotten of the Father, not the glory of a mere man, not the glory of the created sun, not the glory of an angel, but the glory of one out-shining all things, and creatures, i. e., the glory of the only-begotten of the Father.

We beheld, others did not ; we by faith saw his glory, we with our external eyes beheld the person in whom this glory shone forth, though veiled to others. We beheld his glory in his words, doctrine, miracles, and in his transfiguration, resurrection, and in his ascension. My brethren, the excellencies of Christ's person, as the effects of the divine counsel, wisdom, and goodness, beauty and glory, renders Christ's person altogether lovely, Cant. v. 16. The whole book of Solomon's Song is little else save a mystical declaration of the mutual love between Christ and believers, and a great part of it consists in such a description of his Person and personal excellencies, as may render him most amiable and desirable to our souls. "He is fairer than the children of men," Psal. xlv. ii. But do not mistake, his beauty is a hidden beauty, a spiritual beauty, which is only discerned by the eye of our souls, such who can contemplate upon the uncreated glories of the divine nature, cannot but admire him with the psalmist, and say, "Whom have I in heaven but thee," &c., Psal. lxxiii. 25.

Eighthly, Furthermore, that fulness which is in the person of Christ sets forth wonderfully his personal excellencies; "It pleased the Father that in him should all fulness dwell." *The fulness in Christ sets forth his personal excellencies.*

But for the better opening of this, let us consider what Christ is full of.

1. There is in the person of Christ a fulness of divinity. "In him dwelleth the fulness of the Godhead bodily," Col. ii. 9. Not of gifts or operations of the Deity only, which flow from the Godhead (which saints and angels receive in measure) but the Godhead itself, wholly or in the fulness of it ; this fulness is in none but in Christ, in the Father, and the Holy Ghost. *What a fulness is in Christ.*

2. There is in the person of Christ a fulness of the Spirit. (1.) The unction of the Spirit by which the two natures were united in that glorious hypostatical union. (2.) A fulness of the Spirit of unction, he being anointed with the oil of gladness above his fellows.

II. A fulness of merit and satisfaction is in Jesus Christ, he being a complete and perfect Mediator. This appears,

1. He hath paid a full price, or satisfied for all our sins.

2. He hath made a full atonement.

3. He hath obtained our full discharge from the law and justice of God, from sin, wrath, death, and hell.

4. He hath procured a full and complete justification for all the elect.

5. He hath obtained a full remission of sins, or pardon of all our sins, and has it in his possession to give forth to his elect.

6. There is in Christ a fulness of power or authority to give eternal life to all that believe in him, or which the Father hath given unto him.

III. There is in him a fulness of life, he is the fountain of life ; and hence he is called a quickening Spirit. "I am the Way, the Truth, and the Life," John xiv. 5, 16; as he is the original of life, the Prince of life. So that spiritual life we have, is derived from him, no dead sinner can quicken himself. Brethren, both the life of nature, grace and glory, is in and from Christ. And how many thousands hath he quickened, or given a principle of divine life unto,

IV. There is in the person of Christ a fulness of grace, "And of his fulness have all we received, and grace for grace." John i. 16.

1. Grace, favour, or rich bounty ; this he is full of. "Ye know the grace of our Lord Jesus Christ, though he was rich, yet for your sakes he became poor."

2. Grace, (i. e.) that which makes believers gracious, viz., the fruits of the Spirit, the person of Christ is the fountain of all grace which is in the saints. Grace is poured into thy lips," Psal. xlv. 3. His gracious words and gracious deeds proceeded from his gracious heart.

V. The person of Christ is full of righteousness, as the sea is full of water, or the sun is full of light; he is therefore called the "Sun of righteousness," Mal. iv. 2. His glorious robe of righteousness cover thousands of naked sinners.

VI. The person of Christ is full of wisdom and knowledge. "In him are hid all the treasures of wisdom and knowledge," Col. i. 3.

VII. Lastly, In Christ is a fulness of salvation, and not of salvation only, but of all things which do accompany salvation. All these things flow from the person of Christ, and appertain to his personal excellencies as he is Mediator.

In him is a soul-fulness, a seasonable fulness, a suitable fulness, a satisfying, and a soul-enriching, and a soul-fattening fulness.

The excellency of Christ's spirit does consist in his most excellent spirit.

Ninthly, Another personal excellency that is in Christ, is his most excellent spirit. It is said of Daniel, there was a most excellent spirit in him, but what an excellent spirit there is in Jesus Christ, in whose spirit was no stain, no pollution, nothing of natural defilement.

What a spirit Christ is of.

I do not allude to the Holy Ghost that was in Him without measure, but that spirit which appertains to His human nature, or His spirit considered as man; he in this respect was endued "with a spirit of wisdom, of the spirit of counsel, and of might, the spirit of knowledge, and of the fear of the Lord," Isa. xi. 2. His spirit far exceeds the spirits of all men :—For

Christ is of sublime spirit.

I. He is of a sublime spirit, a raised spirit, contemning this world, and all the glory thereof; seeking the glory of his Father alone.

II. He is of a free spirit; free from earthly entanglements, free from the bondage of sin and fervile fear; though he became a Servant, yet he had the spirit of a Son; free from the slavish fear of God, men, or devils; free in all acts of love and bounty, not seeking or asking any thing but the tribute of thankfulness from such he gives his great and glorious gifts and graces unto.

III. He is of a most generous spirit, gave like himself, yet sought not himself, but the honour of his Father, and our good; he takes no advantages against such that slight and despise his bounty, and gracious offers of peace and pardon, but waits still upon them, yea, and gives gifts to the rebellious also, and to stout-hearted sinners, who are far from righteousness; nor doth he seek present revenge on them that hate him, though he could in a moment destroy them all with the breath of his mouth. Also so generous was he, as to give all he had, part with all he had, even with his own life, for our sakes: nay, as to do all that work which was our business, or our work, and to pay all our debts, and suffer all our hell pangs, and bear all our sicknesses and sorrows, all our burdens, nay, and gives his own robe to clothe us, and his own flesh to feed our hungry souls, and his own blood to satisfy our thirsty souls.

IV. Christ is of a strong and courageous spirit; strong to resist temptations, strong to bear afflictions, strong to overcome all difficulties that stood in his way; yea, so courageous, as nothing could discourage him in his work, though earth and hell combine together against him, and his own disciples leave him, and his Father hides his face from him in the hour of his greatest sorrows, straits, and sufferings, as it was foretold of him; "He shall not fail, nor be discouraged, till he have set judgment in the earth," Isa. xlii. 4.

V. Christ is of a holy and heavenly spirit; as in his lips, so in his heart and spirit, there was no guile: "He is holy, and harmless, undefiled, separated from sinners :" he never had one evil thought, as he never spoke one evil word.

VI. Christ is of an humble, of a meek, and of a condescending spirit : "Learn of me, for I am meek and lowly," Matt. xi. 29. "He humbled himself, and became obedient unto death, even the death of the cross," Phil. ii. 5, 6, 7. O that the same mind and the same spirit was in us; shall the prince be meek and lowly in heart, and be content to ride on an ass, and on a colt the foal of an ass, and shall his servant be proud and haughty?

VII. Christ is of a public spirit; not a narrow, base, straightened spirit. Sirs, he was contented to be made a common, or a public head to all his people, and to stand charged with all our sins, and to suffer in our stead, yea, bear that curse and wrath that was due to us for our iniquities; his heart was enlarged toward God, to exalt God, magnify God in all his attributes, and to magnify the law of God, and also to save lost man. "He was cut off, but not for his own sins," Dan. ix. 26. He had no sins of his own, "But for the transgressions of his people was he smitten," Isa. liii. 8. He did not only seek the public good, but did it also with the greatest freeness imaginable, and with the greatest loss and sorrow to himself, both in his name, riches, and life also.

VIII. Christ is of an active and lively spirit. The zeal of God's house even eat him up. He was not only quick in understanding, but quick and lively in all acts of obedience. O the greatness of that work, which he did in a short time, even in the space of three years and a half.

IX. Christ is of a compassionate spirit, full of bowels, love, and pity. "Who can have compassion on the ignorant, and on them that are out of the way," Heb. v. 2. How ready is he to forgive the greatest of his enemies? Even the vilest sinners that fly to him for mercy! He sometimes aggravates the sins of his own people, when it is but to show his abundant grace, love, pity, and pardoning mercy to them, see Isa. xliii. 22, 26, compared with Isa. lvii. 17, 19.

X. Christ is of an obedient spirit. "Lo, I come to do thy will, O God," Heb. x. 7. "It was his meat and drink to do the will of his Father that sent Him," John iv. 34. He was ready to stoop to the hardest thing his Father sent him to do. "Though he was a Son, yet learned obedience by the things which he suffered," Heb. v. 8.

XI. Christ is of a patient and submissive spirit, he bore all things the Father laid upon him patiently, without complaining and murmuring. "As a sheep is dumb before the shearer, so he opened not his mouth," Isa. liii. 7.

XII. Christ is of a faithful spirit. He was faithful to God as a Son, and he is faithful to all his people, in all his promises, and under all those providences which he is pleased to exercise them.

Now put all these things together, and do they not show the most transcendent excellencies, which attend Christ's person?

Tenthly, the personal excellencies of Christ also appears, in respect of those things he is made unto his church and people, he is our only Mediator, our Surety, Testator, God's great ambassador, a King to rule us, a Priest to atone for our sins, a Prophet to teach us, a Foundation on which we build, a Sun to give us light, a Spirit to quicken us, the Way, the Truth, the Life; he is a robe to clothe us, our food to feed us, our Captain to conquer all our enemies (who has overcome sin, the world, devils, death, hell, and the grave for us) a Bridegroom to espouse us, and our heaven to glorify us: he is made of God to all that are in him, "Wisdom and righteousness, sanctification and redemption," 1 Cor. i. 30. In a word his personal excellencies are such, that he is all in all; he is all in sanctification, justification, adoption, union, and communion, pardon of sin, peace, reconciliation, regeneration, vocation, and in salvation.

USE

Now if Christ, the pearl of great price, be so excellent a person, if this be so, if all these and many other most glorious personal excellencies are in him, what happy men and women are they who find Jesus Christ, and have a true interest in him, and right unto him? and what would not any person part with (who knows his infinite worth) to have him to be their own for ever?

2. We may also infer from hence, that but a very few know the Lord Jesus Christ, nor understand whom he is, nor the true worth and excellencies that are in his sacred person.

3. O what fools are they that lay aside this corner-stone, or disallow of this foundation, and build upon the sand, or without a foundation.

4. Moreover, let such tremble who tread this Christ under their feet, and exalt a false Christ above him, a Christ formed out of their own vain imaginations, or strive to ungod him, and render him but to be a mere creature; such a Christ is not worth one farthing, and those that trust in such a Christ shall perish: dare they make a mere man their Saviour, and give the glory of God unto another.

But to proceed to another proposition or point of doctrine, observe.

"And when he had found one pearl," &c.

Doct. 2. That all such who would find Jesus Christ, must seek him.

1. I shall show where they must seek this pearl.

2. When they must seek it.

3. How they must seek for it.

4. Why they must seek it. 5. Apply it.

As to the place where you should seek Jesus Christ the pearl of great price.

First, negatively, not on your beds; thus the spouse sought her beloved; "By night

Where we must not seek Christ.

on my bed I sought him whom my soul loveth, I sought him, but I found him not," Cant.
iii. 1.   Certainly this denotes a cold, lazy seeking; Christ is not found upon the bed of
sloth.

2. You must not seek Jesus Christ in the broad way; the spouse found him not there,
no, she passed from thence, before she found him.   Many seek in dead, carnal, and in in-
vented forms, in that worship, and in such rites and services, that God never instituted.
Pearls are not found in high-ways, or in the broad road, where multitudes pass.

3. You must not seek Jesus Christ within your own hearts; no, he is not there.   All
men naturally are without God, and without Christ, and without the Holy Spirit, and
without hope.

4. You must not seek him on mount Sinai, not by the works of the law, he is not
there.

You must not seek him by doing, or by your own righteousness.

Nor by outward reformation of your lives; you may be reformed, but not meet with
Jesus Christ.

AFFIRMATIVELY

First, pearls must be sought for where they are to be had.   Pliny says, that they are
usually found at the bottom of the sea: so Christ must be sought where he is to be found.

Where we must seek the pearl of great price.   1. You must seek him in the depths, in the great deeps of God's eternal
council, there you may find him, for there he lay hid from everlasting.   I do
not mean you should seek or pry into deep councils that are not revealed, but
in those councils that are now opened in God's word, and in that council held
between the Father and the Son in eternity, there you may find him, and also in that covenant and blessed compact that was between them both, there you shall find mention is
made of him, and meet with him.

II. You must seek him in the depths of eternal wisdom, and in God's glorious purpose
and decree, for there also he lay long hid from the blind world, until God made known
the blessed contrivance of his infinite wisdom.

III. You must seek him in the covenant of grace and of redemption, as the head and
great representative and surety of all God's elect.

IV. You must seek him in the depths of God's eternal love.   If you do not search into the treasures of infinite love, grace, and divine goodness, you will never find this pearl;
do not mistake me, the fountains of these great deeps are now opened, so that you may
by faith dive into this sea, and search for this pearl, and also soon find it.

V. You must seek this pearl in the revelation of God's eternal council, that is the field
where this rich treasure lies hid.   (1.) In the types and sacrifices under the law, there he
is to be found by such who have a piercing sight, and can see through all those dark vales,
which hid him out of the sight of blind and unbelieving men and women.   (2.) You
must seek him in the revelation God made of him in the prophesies of the prophets.   (3.)
and more especially you must seek Jesus Christ in the glorious gospel.   They to whom
the gospel is hid, Jesus Christ is hid, and such that understand the mystery of the gospel,
whose eyes God hath opened to behold the glory of God that shines forth therein, they
find Jesus Christ.   " For God who commanded the light to shine out of darkness, hath
shined in our hearts to give us the light of the knowledge of God, in the face of Jesus,"
2 Cor. iv. 6.

But others to whom the gospel is hid (who think it is only a rule of good manners, or
a new law of evangelical obedience) Satan hath blinded their minds, lest the light of the
glorious gospel of Christ, who is the image of God, shine upon them.   Christ shines not at
all on some of these. and but darkly on others, ver. 3, 4.

VI. You must seek this pearl by believing, by faith: Christ is found by believing, but
such that will not hear the gospel preached, utterly neglect the chief means or way of finding Jesus Christ; for the gospel is an instrument of the mighty "power of God unto the
salvation of every one that believeth," Rom. i. 16.

True unto some it comes "in word only, and not in power," 1 Thess. i. 5; nor by the
efficacious operations of the Holy Ghost: "Now to him that is of power to establish you
according to my Gospel, and the preaching of Jesus Christ, according to the revelation of
the mystery, which was kept secret since the world began.   But now is made manifest,
and by the scriptures of the prophets, according to the commandment of the everlasting
God made known to all nations for the obedience of faith be glory," &c. Rom. xvi. 25, 26.

O how little is the gospel understood, how few by faith search into it, and yet no where else is Christ to be found : true, you may find the gospel preached to Adam, and find the pearl there ; and the gospel preached to Abraham, and find Christ there ; but such who look not on Abraham as a type of Christ, or a covenanting head of all his true spiritual seed, or of all the elect, (distinct from his being a covenanting head to all his natural seed as such ;) may deceive themselves and their poor undone offspring. " If any man be in Christ, he is one of Abraham's seed, and an heir according to promise," See Gal. iii. 16, and 29.

VII. You must seek this pearl in the promises of God, in the promises of the new covenant, or of the Gospel ; for there he is to be found : I do not speak of conditional promises, according to the tenure of the law, or covenant of works, but of the absolute promises ; pray observe well what I say. (1.) You are not to expect that you shall find Jesus Christ upon conditions, which you are to perform as a fit qualification, or as an antecedent condition, that is required of the sinner, in order to the blessings consequent thereupon, by virtue of the promise, and so consequently the benefits and mercies granted are suspended by the blessed God, till those conditions are performed, which conditions the unrenewed sinner hath power to answer, and may, or may not perform. I know some will tell you, that you must have Christ this way, or on such conditions ? why, the conditions are repentance, faith, and sincere obedience ; this they say, but is this gospel ? for if faith and repentance be part of the covenant, or such things which are promised therein ; then they cannot be the conditions upon which we shall have Christ, &c. But a new heart, faith, and repentance, &c., are promised, as part of the matter of the covenant of grace, therefore not such conditions of it. " I will take away the heart of stone, and I will give them a heart of flesh ; I will be their God, and they shall be my people," Ezek. xxxvi. 25, 26. " All that the Father hath given to me, shall come unto me," John vi. 37. Shall come ; that is, they shall believe in me ; " faith is the gift of God," Eph. ii. 8.

(marginal note: Christ must be sought in the promises.)

(2.) If you would find Christ in the promise, be not satisfied with any promise that may come into your minds, unless you can take hold of Christ in that promise, it is Christ received in the promise that relieves the sinner ; without this the promise can do the soul no good.

VIII. You must seek Christ in the way of your duty, in reading, meditation, and prayer, as well as in hearing the word. Certainly seeking of this pearl, seeking of Christ doth take in prayer : seek the Lord while he may be found : seek him by crying to him, calling upon him, and by pouring out your souls before him : if thou criest after knowledge, and lifteth up thy voice for understanding, then thou shalt find it.

God will, Christ will be found of them that seek ; but pray consider that it is Christ who first gives poor sinners a heart to seek him, before he can do this : Christ first seeks us, and finds us, before we seek him, or can find him ; he by his Spirit first apprehends us, and then he enables us to apprehend him ; he opens our eyes to see the worth, the beauty, and glory that is in him, and then we desire him, long for him, pant after him.

Secondly, as I have showed you, where you must seek Jesus Christ, the pearl of great price ; so now I shall show when, or at what time you should seek him.

(marginal note: When we must seek Jesus Christ.)

I. Early. " I love them that love me, and they that seek me early shall find me," Prov. viii. 17.

1. Now to seek this peerless pearl early, is to seek him before and above all other things, before riches, before honours, before pleasures, or any earthly thing, or enjoyment whatsoever. Many seek earth before heaven, earthly pearls above and more than this heavenly pearl, or this world before Jesus Christ. How do many persons enquire after, and earnestly seek for preferment, or to enrich themselves, and add to the substance : say they, O can you tell me how I may improve my stock, improve my trade, and increase my earthly riches ; others they perhaps enquire after a good place, a good service, or a good wife ; these things lie nearest their hearts, and these things they seek before and above the pearl of great price ; nay, never may be think Christ, nor ask after Christ, and so they set a far greater value on these earthly things, than upon the Lord Jesus ; they are not like Moses, who refused to be called " the son of Pharaoh's daughter, and all the glory of Egypt, and the pleasures of sin that are for a season, esteeming the reproaches of Christ greater riches than the treasures of Egypt," Heb. xi. 24, 25.

(marginal note: We must seek the pearl of great price.)

2. To seek this pearl early, " is to seek the Lord while he may be found, and to call upon him while he is near," Isa. lv. 6. God hath set a time, fixed a time, when he will

be found, and to seek him then, is to seek him early; again God hath a time in which he draws near to poor sinners by his word and ordinances, and by the influences and most gracious operations upon their hearts, and they that seek him then, do seek him early.

3. To seek this pearl early, is to seek when God calls. True, God calls once, yea twice, and man perceiveth it not; thus he called Samuel, and though he did not hear, (so as to know whose voice it was) at first calling, yet feeling he did hear before God had done calling of him, he heard and sought the Lord early, but O certainly it is dangerous not to hear at God's first call; he may not call some once, yea twice, nay, and again also; yet let none presume upon frequent warnings, or repeated calls of God; what a caution may that word be, viz., Prov. i. "Because 1 called and you refused"—why, what then, pray read ver. 28. "They shall call upon me, but I will not hear, they shall seek me early, but shall not find me;" early, that is in their affliction, may be as soon as they are sick, and fear they shall die; alas, man knows not his time, therefore his misery is great in the earth.

4. To seek the pearl of great price early, is to seek in due time, " God shall help her, and that right early," Psal xlvi. 5; that is, seasonably, in a due and fit time, when it will most make for his glory and his people's good. So we should in due time, i. e., at such a time when he may receive the most good, when mercy and pardoning grace will be most seasonable and sweet to our souls, as when we come under convictions of sin, and our souls are sick and wounded, and our wounds bleed. O then it is a seasonable time to get Christ, to fly to him, and to believe in him, every thing is beautiful in its season. When a man has just received a grievous wound, O that is the time to get a plaster; or as soon as a person is taken dangerously sick, that is the time to seek a physician, so as soon as thou feel-est the weight of sin, the burden of sin, and thy conscience is awakened, then seek Jesus Christ, then at that very time, and not to delay. This it is to seek Christ early.

5. To seek Christ early, is to seek him in the days of our youth, " Remember now thy Creator," &c., Eccl. xii. 1. Remember his love in finding out a Redeemer, and in send-ing him into the world. O remember that he is a just, as well as a gracious God.

Christ must be sought whilst the Holy Spirit strives with a sinner.   II. The pearl of great price should be sought when the Holy Spirit strives with thee; the time of the strivings, motions, and workings of the Spirit is Christ's time and way of seeking us, and that is the time of our seeking him, Christ came too seek and save that which was lost; all was an act of pre-venting grace; the Holy Ghost comes to enlighten our understanding, to awaken our sleepy consciences, to bow and incline our rebellious wills, and to change our carnal affections; and know, ye sinners, this is the time you should seek, if ever you hope to find the pearl of great price; even when the Holy Spirit begins to act, or move, and to operate upon your hearts : sinners only act Christ-ward, as they are acted, and move, as they are by the Spi-rit and by a divine principle moved. A dead carcase, or a stone, may as soon move of it-self, as a dead sinner can stir, act, or do in a spiritual manner, unless he be influenced and moved by the Holy Spirit.

III.   When we have a full gale of the Spirit.

Christ must be sought when the wind of the Spirit blows.   The time for a merchant to hoist his sails, and set out to sea, is when he has a fair wind; O, says he, now I must be gone, I have been becalmed a great while, but now the wind blows the right way, I have a sweet gale. Even so we should set out on our voyage to seek the pearl of great price, when we have a powerful gale, or strong operations of the word and Spirit upon our hearts. A merchant-man makes four, nay, may be ten times more speed, when he has a full and strong gale of wind, than he can at other times; sometimes may be he makes way, and then he meets with contrary winds, and is drove back again. And thus it is with spiritual mer-chants, that seek the pearl of great price; now perhaps the wind of the Spirit blows, O then they are as it were upon the wing. O how they pray, read, hear, meditate; their souls are filled with love and longings after Jesus Christ : but by-and-by a contrary wind rises, Satan raises a storm, to drive the soul back again, and fill it full of fears and doubtings. Take heed you do not lose a fair wind, and beware of contrary winds raised by Satan, by sin, by wicked relations, and by the world, or by an evil heart.

IV.   You must seek Jesus Christ to-day, even now, " To-day if you will hear his voice, harden not you hearts," Heb. iii. 7; nay, and this the Holy Ghost says, we do not only tell you to-day, this very day you must do it; but God says, to-day, Christ says to-day, " To-day go and work in my vineyard," Matt. xxi. 28; and the Holy Spirit says to-day, if you will hear his voice. And dare sinners say, no, not to-day, it is time enough yet, I will stay till to-morrow : " Boast not thyself of to-morrow, for thou knowest not what a day may bring forth," Prov. xxvii. 1. Some perhaps may make fair promises, and say to-day, I go sir, but go not; like one of the sons bid to go to work in the vineyard. Alas, as I have told you, present promises about closing with Christ hereafter, are but seldom, if ever performed.

V. If some of you are come to the eleventh hour, certainly this is the time, or never, for such to seek Jesus Christ. Some of you are come almost to the end of your voyage, or end of your race, I mean the end of your lives. There are but few sands in your glass, your ship is old, and ready to be broken up. It is, I fear, too late for some to set out now on the seas of temptation, and opposition, to seek the pearl of great price, but if God give a call to any now at the eleventh hour, it is not too late for them; but if Christ be not sought, be not received at this time, such are undone, and shall perish, for ever.

Thirdly, how must the pearl of great price be sought?

I. Diligently. Naturalists tells us, that a choice and rare pearl is not to be found without curious and diligent searching. Pliny saith, they that find such pearls, must run through many dangers, amongst those huge and terrible sea monsters and great rocks. So they that would find Jesus Christ, the pearl of great price, must seek and search with all wisdom, care, and diligence, and endeavour to sail betwixt the dangerous rocks of presumption, on the one hand, and despair, on the other hand: O how many are split, and suffer shipwreck upon one of these rocks, and so never find the pearl, never rightly believe, nor receive Jesus Christ.

Moreover, all ought to take heed of those monsters that are in our seas, I mean among us, i. e., cruel and abominable imposters, who deny the Lord Jesus Christ, who preach up a false Christ, and others who deny any Christ, or utterly cast off all revealed religion, or the whole Christian faith. Some render Christ to be of no value or worth at all; also some deny his imputed righteousness, and make their own righteousness the matter of their justification before God; these men may fitly be compared to huge sea monsters, that make the finding of Christ a very difficult thing.

2. You must seek with much skill and divine wisdom; first to seek in the right way, not by repenting and reformation of life, or by obedience, or inherent righteousness, to think to find Jesus Christ; no, this is not the way to find Christ, if thou wouldst be an honest moral man, thou must reform thy life, and obey all moral precepts; but thou mayest be further from finding of Christ, when that is done, than now whilst thou art a profane and ungodly sinner; for publicans and harlots go into the kingdom of heaven before those who are self-righteous, or sober and civilized persons.—You must know the way to find Christ is by believing.

II. You must have wisdom to know the true Christ, and wisdom to know the right time. Wilt thou apply a plaster to that place, where there is no wound, and put on a robe given to thee as being naked, when thou in thy own conceit, art well clothed.

III. You must seek with full purpose and resolution of thy heart and soul, not fearing what men or devils can do unto thee, though thy wife rages, and is stirred up against thee, to dissuade thee, or a husband, or a father, or mother, or son, or daughter, or neighbours, pretended friends, remember what our blessed Saviour saith, Matt. x. 37; resolve to have Christ, though it cost thee thy life, every sin must die, and self must die, and thou must resist unto blood if called to it.

IV. Thou must seek Christ as one that knowest the great want, need, and necessity of him, as been undone without him; and if thou art an unrenewed person, thou must seek him as one that is without God, and without Christ in the world. *Such that would seek this pearl must know the worth of it.*

V. Again, thou must seek Christ as one who is convinced of that great worth and excellency of him.

VI. Believingly, not doubting, but there is salvation to be had in Christ for the vilest of sinners, also believing his power and willingness to save thee, if thou art helped to come to him, cleaving to him, and resting upon him. *Christ must be sought believingly.*

VII. Seek with longings, breathings, and pantings after him. Joseph and Mary sought Jesus sorrowing from the greatness of their love.

VIII. Seek with an heart inclined, touched with the loadstone of his love; see Prov. ii. 1—4.

IX. Seek constantly and unweariedly, never give over until thou hast found him.

X. Seek him sincerely, not for the loaves, not for secular profit nor applause, nor out of vain-glory; not simply to be saved by him, or for what he has, but for his own sake, what he is, and from a sense of his infinite glory and preciousness; see John vi. 26.

IV

And when he had found one pearl of great price.—Matt. xiii. 45, 46.

THE last day I showed you how Christ the Pearl of great price must be sought.

Fourthly, and lastly, I shall now proceed to show you why he must be sought, or give you the reasons why sinners should seek him.

Christ came to seek sinners, therefore they ought to seek him.

I. Sinners should seek Jesus Christ, the Pearl of great price, because he came to seek them.

1. He sought the salvation of sinners in entering into covenant with the Father for them in eternity: it was to recover those lost sinners which the Father gave him, that caused him to become our Surety, and to enter into that holy and happy compact with God the Father.

2. In his taking our nature upon him, and in coming into this world, it was to seek lost sinners.

3. By his death, in his bearing of our sins upon his own body on the tree, it was to seek and save sinners, and to bring them to God: " For Christ also hath once suffered for sins, the just for the unjust, that he might bring us to God," 1 Pet. iii. 18.

4. Jesus Christ seeks sinners by the ministration of the gospel, wherever the gospel is sent, it is sent to seek and bring sinners home to God; and it may give us ground to believe in those places where the gospel comes, are some sinners which were given to him, and whilst the gospel is continued in a place, certainly there are some yet not called, not found or converted.

5. Christ seeks sinners by his intercession, now in heaven; he doth not only pray or intercede for believers, but for sinners; "He made intercession for transgressors," Isa. lii. 12.

6. Christ seeks sinners by the motions of his Spirit on their hearts and consciences, and when convictions of the Spirit sieze, and are strong upon the sinner's heart, then Jesus Christ may be said to have found the sinner, though the sinner may not have found him.

Why sinners should seek this pearl.

II. Sinners should seek Christ, because seeking him, and finding him, are coupled together: "Then shall ye seek me, and find me, when ye search after me with all your hearts," Jer. xxix. 13. Will any say it is in vain to seek Jesus Christ, they may as well say it is in vain for ministers to preach to sinners, and in vain for them to hear, read, pray; hearing and believing, nay, hearing and living are joined together; for as " faith comes by hearing," so life comes by hearing also: " Hear, and thy soul shall live," Isa. lv. 3. This finding, this hearing, and this believing is all one and the same thing; when seeking of Christ is of no use, preaching will be of no use also. But know, O ye sinners, that seeking of Christ, and finding him are joined together. Therefore it is an indispensible duty for sinners to seek Jesus Christ.

III. Because the promise runs to them that seek: "Seek, and ye shall find, ask and ye shall receive," Matt. vii. 7; though he that seeks not believingly, hath no promise of finding, nor hath he that asketh, unless he ask in faith; yet such who do seek in a right manner, have the promise of God, that cannot lie made to them; " He that seeketh me early, shall find me," Prov. viii. 17.

IV. Sinners should seek Christ, " the pearl of great price," because they are commanded so to do: "Seek ye the Lord while he may be found, and call upon him while he is near," Isa. lv. 6. Again it is said: " Seek ye the Lord, and ye shall live," Amos v. 6. When thou saidst, seek my face, my heart answered, Thy face, Lord, I will seek," Psal. xxvii. 8. God saith, seek me, and will the sinner refuse thus to do ; a duty here is enjoined, and a promise is annexed.

V. Because salvation is only in Jesus Christ; all that seek justification and eternal life, and do not seek Jesus Christ, shall certainly perish: " Neither is there salvation in any other; for there is no other name given under heaven whereby we must be saved," Acts iv. 12. No other name, or thing, not by repenting, nor mourning for sin, no, not by leaving off sin, or reformation of life, not by good works, nor by inherent righteousness, not by being baptized, nor by receiving the Lord's Supper, no, nor by giving to the poor, nor by suffering for Christ or religion ; for there is no salvation to be had but by Christ alone. In the way of duty and of ordinances you ought to seek him, and may meet with him ; but if any rest on their duties, works, or righteousness, nay, on faith itself as the matter by which they hope to be justified and saved, they will certainly perish. It is not faith itself, but Christ that faith receives, or the object faith relies upon, that saves us. Doth my hand that applies the plaster to my wound cure me? No, it is the plaster; nay, the hand of faith is given to us also to apply the balm: "By grace ye are saved, through faith, and that not of yourselves, it is the gift of God; not of works lest any man should boast," Eph. ii. 8, 9. Now since salvation is to be had in none, in nothing, but in Christ, or by the pearl of great price, how doth it behove all poor sinners to seek him.

VI. Sinners should seek Christ, because by nature, or as in the first Adam, they are without him; the merchant before he sought the pearl had it not: "At that time ye were without Christ," Eph. ii. 12. At that time, what time? Why, "when they were dead in sins and trespasses," Eph. ii. 1, 2.

VII. Sinners should seek Christ, because the law condemns them, under God's fearful wrath, and the sentence of death every sinner retains, until they have found Jesus Christ, or do believe in him. "He that hath the Son hath life, but he that hath not the Son hath not life, but the wrath of God abideth on him," John iii. 36.

VIII. Sinners should seek Christ to save them, because the devil seeks to destroy them: "Be sober, be vigilant, because your adversary the devil walketh about seeking whom he may devour," 1 Pet. v. 8.

O how many ways hath Satan by which he seeks to destroy poor sinners! there are many ways by which sinners may perish and be damned, but there is but one way by which they can be saved.

Lastly, Sinners should seek the pearl of great price, from the consideration of that infinite worth and value of him, and that good they will find in him, of which I have largely spoken, and shall now in a few words the application.

APPLICATION

Let me tell you what Christ is to them that find him.

First, O be exhorted to seek him, and delay not. For,

1. He that hath Christ hath life; this the apostle asserts: "He that hath the Son hath life, he that hath not the Son, hath not life," 1 John v. 12. He is the Bread of life, and such that feed upon him shall never perish. "He that findeth me findeth life, and shall obtain favour of the Lord," Prov. viii. 35. *What he hath that hath Christ.*

II. He that finds Christ hath a discharge from eternal death, he is justified, pardoned, sanctified; nay, he hath all things; "All is yours, ye are Christ's," &c.

1. All the things of this life are theirs; that is, so far as God sees them good for them, who would have any earthly thing for his hurt?

2. They have all they have without the curse; wicked men may have more of the things of this world than believers, but they have every thing with a curse, riches with a curse, honours and pleasures with a curse. Nay,

3. The people of God have all they possess with a blessing upon them, every thing is blessed to them, even afflictions, losses, poverty, sickness, and death itself.

III. Whatsoever Christ is made to believers, that he is made to every one that finds him. Two things such should consider, that would find and know how precious a pearl Christ is.

1. What he is in himself.

2. What he is and will be to him that finds him.

1. Whatsoever a great and inconceivable portion is to a man in a natural sense, that is Christ, and much more to him that finds him in a spiritual sense; for he is our portion and inheritance of our souls for ever, Psal. xvi. 5, xxxiii. 26, Lam. iii. 24.

2. What honour and external happiness attends a virgin that is espoused and married to a mighty and excellent prince, what peace, what glory, what satisfaction doth she meet withal? that and much more is Christ to every one that finds him in a spiritual sense, for every believer is espoused and married to him, Rom. vii. 4, 2 Cor. xi. 2.

3. What bread is to a hungry person, or drink to a thirsty person in a natural way, that is Christ, the Pearl of great price, to every soul that finds in a spiritual way; he is the Bread of God, the Bread of life, and Water of life to the soul.

4. What clothing is to a naked man, to the body, that is Christ to the soul that finds him: "Put ye on the Lord Jesus Christ," Rom. xiii. 14. We put him on as a garment in justification, and in sanctification also.

5. What rest is to a weary person in a natural way, that is Christ, and much more, (for his rest is glorious,) in a spiritual way, "Come to me all ye that labour and are heavy laden, and I will give you rest," Matt. xi. 28.

6. What peace is to a troubled and wounded conscience, that is Christ to him that finds him; he gives present quiet, and everlasting peace to the soul that hath him, and knows he hath him.

7. What sight is to one that was born blind, that is Christ in a spiritual way to every soul that finds him.

8. What liberty is to one who has been in bonds, (in prison, in captivity, or slavery) in a natural way, that is Christ and much more in a spiritual way to him that finds him: "If the Son make you free, then are you free indeed," John viii. 36.

9. What millions of gold and silver is to a poor man, not worth a groat in respect of the things of this world, money answering all things; that and much more is Christ to that man that finds him in a spiritual sense.

10. What abundance of corn is to a nation in time of famine, (when its inhabitants were forced to feed on husks) that is Christ and much more to a hungry soul that finds him, who (like the Prodigal) feed on husks which the swine did eat.

11. What a pardon is to a condemned rebel just ready to be executed, that is Christ in a spiritual sense to a condemned sinner when he finds him, who was under the fearful sentence of divine vengeance.

12. What ease and a perfect cure is to a man tormented with intolerable pain, (whether of the stone, gout, or what is worse,) that is Christ to a tormented despairing soul, that finds him: or what a healing and infallible balm, is to a man mortally wounded, that is Christ to a wounded sinner that finds him.

13. In a word, what it is to be perfectly delivered from whatsoever is evil, either here in this world, or hereafter in the world to come, that is and will Christ be to every one that finds him.

14. And what it is to be perfectly possessed with whatsoever is truly, really, and spiritually good; that is or will Christ be to every one that finds him.

Secondly, from hence I infer, that that person that seeks not the pearl of great price, is a notorious fool, or out of his wits; who but a fool or a mad-man would neglect seeking of such a pearl?

Thirdly, how will sinners lament their folly in seeking other things more than Christ, nay utterly neglect the seeking of him.

Fourthly, I infer, that such who have got Christ, or have found this pearl, are the most happy people in the world.

I come now to the last clause of this parable.

" And sold all he had, and bought it."

No marvel he sold all he had to buy such a pearl.

1. I shall show you what may be meant by selling all he had.

2. What may be meant by buying this pearl.

Selling all he had, signifies no more than his parting with whatsoever his heart was inordinately set upon before he found this pearl.

What it is to sell all for the pearl of great price

1. With all his sins and horrid lusts; all that find Christ part willingly with every evil habit, and with every evil act of sin and wickedness, and it is by the Spirit and grace of Christ, he is helped to do this: a sinner finds Christ before he can part with his sins and iniquities.

2. All his old company with whom he took delight, and among whom he oft dishonoured God; he parts also with them with an abhorrence.

3. All his former hopes of heaven, and the foundation on which he built that hope.

He that will have Christ must sell all his own inherent righteousness.

4. All his own external privileges, of which (like Paul when a Pharisee) he might boast.

5. All his own good works, and inherent righteousness in point of justification, he sold also, or parted with. I do not mean he did not now any good works, or ceased being morally just and righteous: no, God forbid, but he parted with them so as not to expect acceptation and justification by those things in the sight of God. Pray see what Paul says he did when he found Jesus Christ; he reckoned up all his legal privileges, and that righteousness he had when a Pharisee, and says, " But what things were gain to me, those I counted loss for Christ," Phil. iii. 7.

Obj. 1. Perhaps some may say, true, he sold all his legal privileges and legal righteousness, but not his gospel inherent righteousness.

Gospel righteousness must be parted with in

Answ. Yea, he parted with all his own gospel righteousness also in point of justification. "Yea, doubtless, and I count all things but loss for the excellency of the knowledge of Jesus Christ, my Lord, for whom I have suffered the loss of all things, and do count them but dung that I may win Christ." point of trust,
or in respect
of justifica-
tion. This is the selling all to have the pearl. St. Paul did not disclaim that righteousness he had before his conversion only, but he speaks now in the present tense, I count all things, &c. He first speaks of what he had and did count gain to him, and also what now he had done, or was wrought in him since a believer and an apostle, he sold all, parted with all his former and present inherent righteousness in point of trust or dependence, or in respect had to his justification before God ; nay, and counted both in comparison of Christ, the knowledge of Christ and his righteousness, to be but dung or dogs-meat, as the word signifies : " And be found in him not having my own righteousness which is of the law, but that which is through the faith of Christ, the righteousness which is of God by faith," Phil. iii. 9.

Whatsoever righteousness we have of our own, it is a righteousness of the law, as the law is in the hand of Christ, as a perfect rule of obedience ; but the righteousness of God is set in direct opposition to the righteousness of any mere creature, and so is the righteousness of faith, placed in direct opposition to works: and from hence it is that Paul saith, " God imputeth righteousness without works," Rom. iv. 6. Faith and works, or grace and works, are opposed one to the other, not only faith and the works of the law, but works as such of what kind soever as done by the creature, are excluded in our justification ; this further appears.

1. See what Paul saith in Rom. iv. " Now to him that worketh is the All kind of
works are
excluded in
our justifica-
tion before
God. reward not reckoned of grace, but of debt," Rom. iv. 4 ; that is, him that worketh with a design to procure justification by what he doth ; this would render salvation to be a debt, let the work be of any kind whatsoever.

2. Because that which is procured by works, is not had by grace : " And if by grace, then it is no more of works, otherwise grace is no more grace, but if it be by works, then it is no more of grace, otherwise work is no more work," Rom. xi. 6. It must be wholly of works, or; else wholly of grace, for these two cannot mix, they being directly contrary one to the other.

3. Because all boasting is excluded; by reason we are justified and saved by faith or grace alone : " By grace ye are saved through faith, and that not of yourselves, it is the gift of God ; not of works, lest any man should boast," Rom. iii. 27, and Eph. ii. 8. If they are works of the moral law, or of the ceremonial law, or gospel works, still it should be of works, and the same reason remain for boasting. But if there is in our justification no room for boasting, there is no room for works ; but there is no room for boasting. Ergo there is no room for works, but all works are excluded in our justification in the sight of God.

Thus it appears he that sells all to have Christ, sells or parts with all his own works and inherent righteousness in justification.

" And bought it."

It is not a proper buying, where the intrinsical value is given, or some- What buy-
ing this pearl
doth denote. thing one man gives to procure another thing, for the sake of which he hath it as a purchasing or procuring condition ; but it is called a buying, because a man in buying parts with something he hath, to receive another thing which he hath not : " but it is a buying without money and without price; that is, without money or money's worth ; and what can that be less or more, but a free giving, and a free receiving : for any other buying is utterly inconsistent with the free grace of God in the gospel ; for righteousness is called a free gift ; Christ is called the gift of God. Faith the gift of God, and salvation or water of life is given freely, and all of God's free and absolute promises without any conditions required of us, to procure any one gospel blessing. The gift of God cannot be purchased with our money, or by any thing we have to give for it : doth God sell his Son and himself to sinners ? pray what doth he receive at our hands : " If thou be righteous, what givest thou to him, and what receiveth he at thy hands," Job xxxv. 7. Before grace, or before God gives us this pearl, what have we to give unto God, but a bundle of unrighteousness ? Doth our filthy rags purchase Christ and his righteousness ? Or doth he receive those rags of us ? No, no, we must cast them away, and all other idols as abominable things. For.

1. He that God gives Christ unto, is righteous by an imputed righteous Christ is a
free gift. ness ; Christ's righteousness is freely given to him, imputed, or counted to be his, as an act of mere sovereign grace.

2. God when he gives Christ to a sinner, gives him his Spirit also, as his own free gift ; and with the Holy Spirit he gives faith the fruit of the Spirit, and so the sinner comes to be renewed, and is inherently sanctified, and by virtue of these free gifts we come to

have a righteous principle planted in us, and are made righteous as an act of God's free grace, inherently righteous.

3. Also every one that hath received this grace, or this free gift, is a righteous person, by a practical righteousness he doth righteousness; the one is a righteousness by regeneration, this is a righteousness by conversation, as the effects of the former; "He that doth righteousness is righteous," 1 John iii. 7; that is, he is in a righteous state through justification; and hath a righeousness planted in him in sanctification. What givest thou unto him? The meaning is, thou givest nothing to him; a free gift is the bestowing of something where there was no obligation lay upon the donor; that is, a free gift which a person is not bound to bestow by any rule or law of righteousness upon any procuring condition or terms required of the receiver; but it is only given freely, as an absolute act of special love and favour; such a gift is Christ, and the Spirit of Christ, and faith to receive Christ.

Obj. But doth not faith, repentance, &c., purchase, or buy the pearl?

Faith doth not purchase Christ. 1. Answ. How can faith, &c., be said to purchase Christ, when it and repentance both are given as a free gift of God? Alas, we receive both these graces at the hand of God, and as a fruit of the Spirit, a man receives the Spirit, and so Christ takes hold of him before he can apprehend Christ, or actually receive him; and faith is not of ourselves, though it is the sinner that believes, as it was Lazarus that lived, and the life he had was his life, but yet it was a life in a supernatural manner given to him.

2. God bids us believe; so Christ bid Lazarus come forth out of the grave; he that commands us to believe, hath promised to give that grace to his elect, by which they shall believe, and Christ takes hold of him; God receives nothing of our hands, but all is given unto us freely.

Obj. But faith is an antecedent condition, and it signifies no more than **Mr. Flavel's discourse of errors. p. 288.** an act of ours, which though it be neither perfect in every degree, nor in the least meritorious of the benefit conferred, nor performed in our natural strength, yet according to the constitution of the covenant it is required of us in order to the blessing consequent thereupon, by virtue of the promise; and consequently the mercies granted in this order, are and must be suspended by the donor, or dispose of them, till it be performed. Such a condition we affirm faith is.

1. Answ. The antecedent condition according to these men, purchaseth the estate or blessings promised; the lawyers reckon it is the purchase money, **What a kind of condition some make faith to be.** saith Dr. Chauncy, the consequent condition gets it, it is the quit rent; which if it be not paid, the Lord can enter and take the estate. So faith, &c., they will have to be the antecedent condition money, deposited and laid down before they have anything of the spiritual estate. And they say it signifies **Faith is no condition nor cause of justification in God's sight.** no more than an act of ours, and pray whose should it be but ours, if the condition to be performed by us? and why is this put in, it signifies no more? Unless the meaning is, that Christ and his righteousness should be shut out, and it should be reckoned under the nature of this condition, merely as our own act, without respect to Christ the author of it, and Christ the true object of it. They tell us it is a negative qualification.——Yet say

It is not perfect in every degree. What's the meaning of that? This insinuates as if it were perfect in some degrees, and imperfect in other degrees. I had **Dr. Chauncy.** thought no grace was perfect in degrees, though it be true as to kind. But they will have it perfect in some degrees, and imperfect in other degrees; pray, in what degree is this condition perfect, and in what imperfect? And whether that be not an imperfect covenant that hath an imperfect condition?

It is not the least meritorious of the benefits conferred, by no means, (i. e.,) by any intrinsical value and worth, either adequate to, or excelling the benefits received.

Answ. No, their meaning is, what they have (saith one) is well worth their money; it is a good bargain: but by their favour (saith he) every federal condition is expacto meritorious; so that they may challenge their bargain upon the performance, if it be but 20 guineas, to purchase an £100. per annum, so that we have only their word for it, that it is not meritorious, when it is so really; the nature of the thing speaks it so to be to the understanding of all men of sense. No, no, do not think to wheedle Christ out of his merits, and God out of his honour, of his free grace, and us out of the comfort of both.

They say, It is not performed in our natural strength.

Answ. No, and yet a condition of a covenant made with man; a most unreasonable thing to require a condition of a covenant, of one that we know hath no strength to perform it. If a rich man should offer an estate of £1000 per year, to a poor man, that he knew was not worth a groat, provided he fetched twenty pounds of his own money, this act would be reckoned a ridiculing this poor wretch. God did not require that small condition of Adam, but that he was actually endowed with strength to perform it. They will say, God gives them ability to perform it; so he did Adam, previous to the covenant. As the rich man may tell the poor sir, I will give you the £20 to pay me for my estate; he will say, well sir, when you give it to me, I will bargain with you, and when I have it, though you gave it to me, 1 shall reckon it my money, as much as if I had raised it myself, or another had given it to me; and if we bargain, yet it is a bargain, and whatever I have of you is debt, and I can sue for it as purchased by me, saith the poor man. Now see how well qualified this condition is.

My brethren, believe it, God makes no such bargain with sinners as this; there is no such buying of this pearl, as these men say,

They say according to the constitution of the covenant, this condition is required of us in order to the blessing consequent thereupon, by virtue of the promise.

This, as our author notes, is a paradox indeed; what do they mean by the constitution of the covenant? is it not according to other covenants by the constitution of their new scheme? is it not by a condition on the creature's part, to be performed, and a promise thereupon annexed? and is not the condition (saith the Dr.) performed *fœderale meritum?* or do this and live, *ordo fœderalis,* and the blessings consequent *ex pacto* therefore a debt; think not to beat us out of our senses, that the blessings of a covenant are only *consequentia ordinis vel porsteritatis;* as one man follows another in a narrow path, or *ordine vel virtute pacti,* in or to a fœderal right and challenge of the benefits as a due debt.

2. How can faith be a condition of the covenant of grace, whereas it is a part or a branch of the said covenant?

Have not they the pearl, who have the spirit and faith given to them? or doth not God give men faith? but contrariwise it is their own act (without the seed thereof being first infused in them) and so Christ is purchased with their money.

3. What condition can he that is dead perform? or are not all before quickened by a vital principle infused into them spiritually dead?

4. Or is there any covenant of grace made with sinners, but that only made with Christ, and in him for all, and with all the elect? And hath not Christ obliged himself to God the Father, to answer all the conditions on their behalf (i. e.) work all their works in them and for them, as an act of free grace alone?

Obj. But our new scheme men we say, the mercies granted in our sense must be suspended by the donor or disposer of them, till the condition (which is faith) be performed.

Answ. You bid poor sinners come and buy, and you say not with the prophet, without money and without price; but they must have a parcel of money first to do it, implying still that sinners must bring faith, &c., repentance, &c., along with them, or there is no Christ for them; and that is as hard to bring as the money of perfect righteousness. For faith is wrought in the soul by the power of God, nay, according to his exceeding and almighty power, and in the same manner that he wrought in Christ, when he raised him up from the dead, as Paul shows, Eph. i. 19. Though we have not Christ without faith, so we have not faith without Christ, and both are promised and given freely; and faith itself is not a purchasing and procuring condition of the blessings promised, but one of the blessings of the covenant, and free and absolute promises of God; " I will be their God, and they shall be my people.—I will take away the heart of stone, and I will give them a heart of flesh.—I will put a new Spirit in them—I will put my Spirit upon them—I will put my law in their hearts, and write it in their inward parts."

If a man must have faith, before he can have Christ, and buy the pearl with that faith, which is his act; then salvation is by works, and, with money, and not without money and price; and that which is worse, if faith be not contained in the free promise, as a part of the covenant between the Father and Son, but men must work it out of their own bowels, or get it as their own money to buy; it is impossible for any man ever to purchase this pearl, but all men must without remedy perish for evermore.

Quest. But doth not the gospel require faith as a condition of justification and eternal life?

1. Answ. Yea as a condition of connexion by way of order, as one thing dependeth on another (as our author observes) in logic, if a creature be a man, he is a rational creature; or if God be the first cause, he is the Creator of all things. And in this sense (saith he) creation is a condition of salvation, if a man be saved, he must be created; so if a man believe, he shall be saved; believing is a condition of connexion, a state of grace, is thus a condition of a state of glory, by way of connexion in the promise, but one is not the federal condition of another, but both come in as the gift of grace. In this sense the covenant contains all the conditions of order and dependence in the exhibition and performance; the hearing the word is the condition of faith, but hearing is not a federal condition; so the giving the Spirit is the condition of our union with Christ and of faith, and faith the condition of our receiving of pardon, and living a holy life—and holiness the condition of seeing God, and of having eternal life; but these kinds of conditions are federal entitling conditions to the promise, but are contained in the promise, and denote the connexion and dependence of one promised benefit with another.

2. Though faith be required of them that are saved, yea, and repentance, regeneration, holiness, and a new heart also; yet these blessings are all promised in the covenant, as part thereof. But faith itself is no federal condition, but only serves to show what God will do for, and work in such that he as an act of free grace will save.

From hence we may see how wofully blind they are, who assert faith, repentance, and sincere obedience are not only federal conditions of justification, but also are the matter or material cause thereof. And this is to buy the pearl indeed with our own money.

Thus having shown what is meant by buying the pearl, I shall run in some few things parallel-wise about buying, though the disparities are great, as hath been showed.

" And bought it."

1. He that buys a pearl, must know where it is to be had, he seeks it and finds it. First, So a poor sinner must know where to find Christ, and he seeks him and finds him, which finding is believing, as I have shown.

2. They that would buy must know the market-day, and repair thither. So must a sinner attend on the word and ministry of the Gospel, that would have Jesus Christ.

3. Buyers commonly ask the price of that they would buy. So sinners should ask the price or terms on which they must have Christ, and that is freely (without money, and without price) or not at all; they must come without money to this market. Good news for the poor.

4. Some come to market only to cheapen, ask the price of, way of buying, and that is all. So do some here; they think it is time enough to buy hereafter, and resolve to keep their sins and the love of the world in their hearts at present.

5. Some that come to buy like not the terms, they are full of money, and scorn to receive all freely; no, they are proud and haughty, it is too cheap for them. So some sinners will have no pearl, no Christ, unless they have it for their money, or on the conditions of faith, repentance, and sincere obedience.

6. Some come to buy too late, the market-day is over. So many (like the foolish virgins,) come too late to buy. See that parable.

7. In buying, some things are parted with, though it be not of any great value in respect of what they receive thereupon. So such who would have Christ the Pearl of great price, must do as Paul did, viz., part with all that is gain to them, or what they have set their hearts upon, or is their own, whether sinful pleasures, riches, or honours, inordinate desires; yea, and all their sins and lusts whatsoever; and also (as I said) with all their old hopes of heaven, and all their own righteousness, good deeds, or good works in point of trust or dependence, or in respect of justification in God's sight. But these terms the young man in the Gospel did not like of, therefore refused this pearl, and many now-a-days are like unto him.

8. Some refuse to buy in the proper season, and afterwards cry out against themselves for their folly. So they that contemn Jesus Christ, or refuse this pearl, out of love to sin, or love to religious or righteous self, will bewail their folly to an endless eternity.

APPLICATION

First, Be exhorted to buy the pearl.

1. You that are poor, and have no money sure will buy, i. e., you will have Christ, for you have nothing to trust to, or depend upon, for eternal life, if you buy not, none will.

15. TREASURE HID IN A FIELD

"Again the kingdom of heaven is like unto treasure hid in a field, which, when a man hath found he hideth, and for joy thereof goeth and selleth all he hath, and buyeth that field."—MATT. xiii. 44.

In two parables in this chapter our Lord compareth the kingdom of heaven to things of small worth or value, viz., grain of mustard-seed, and to leaven, from the nature or quality of those things. But here he makes use of this and that of the pearl, to set forth the kingdom of heaven, by that which is excellent in its own nature, viz., by treasure, that the faithful might prefer the blessings of the Gospel and divine grace, as things of great worth; for what is esteemed by mankind more than treasure of great value?

The design and scope of this parable opened.

2. The kingdom of heaven may be compared to treasure hid, &c., to show that Christ and divine grace, or spiritual riches, are hid from the carnal eyes of the men of this world; and hence it is they have such low and contemptible thoughts of these things, they being of a spiritual and invisible nature in themselves, are not discerned but by him, whose understanding is enlightened by the Spirit of God. "What man knoweth the things of a man, save the spirit of a man that is in him; so the things of God knoweth no man but the Spirit of God," 1 Cor. ii. 11.

3. To show that men who would find Jesus Christ and all spiritual blessings in him, must search with great care and pains after them.

4. To discover that he who finds this spiritual treasure, must part with all that he esteems to be gain unto him, or is valued by him, that he may have, and possess divine riches as his own.

"The kingdom of heaven," &c.

By the kingdom of heaven here, according to all expositors (I have meet with) is meant the word of the kingdom, or the dispensation of the Gospel, together with the grace and favour of God; all grace being dispensed by Christ the Mediator of the new covenant, who is a king, (as well as a priest and prophet), and it also tends to the erecting, setting up, and leading men into Christ's spiritual kingdom here, and unto his eternal kingdom hereafter; and from hence it is called the kingdom of heaven.

"Is like unto treasure," &c.

Though wicked men do generally love riches, or earthly treasure, yet they are ignorant of this, they do not account any thing to be treasure, but such things only which maketh men earthly, rich, and great in this world. But by this parable (and that of the pearl) our Saviour shows us there is better treasure than that which is earthly and visible to the carnal eyes, which tends to make men spiritually rich, and eternally happy.

There is, my brethren, a real and inconceivable worth in Jesus Christ and the spiritual blessings we have in and with him (as you have heard in my opening the parable of the pearl of great price,) this our Lord clearly shows by calling it treasure, that so all might with the greater diligence seek it. Christ is called a pearl, nay, a pearl of great price, and the Word is compared to gold, yea, preferable to much fine gold. Also the apostle calls the knowledge of Christ, and the great mysteries of the Gospel, treasure. "We have this treasure in earthen vessels," 2 Cor. iv. 7. The grace and fulness which is in our Saviour, is called "unsearchable riches," Eph. iii. 8.

"Hid in a field."

The mysteries of the Gospel are called hidden mysteries; they were a long time hid in God, hid in his eternal decree and purpose, and also hid under the shadows and sacrifices of the law. But now by the Gospel are revealed to believers, but yet this treasure in the dispensation of the Gospel is hid still from the wise and learned men of this world. "I thank thee, O Father, Lord of heaven and earth, that thou hast hid these things from the wise and prudent, and hast revealed them unto babes," Matt. xi. 25.

None can find Jesus Christ, know him, and partake of the riches of grace, but such that God opens the mysteries of the gospel unto; the gospel and ministration of it is a large field, in which such must dig deep with utmost care and wisdom, and with a piercing sight, who would find the treasure: some dig in this field, but never find the treasure; they have the outward ministration of the gospel, the cabinet, but find not the jewel: this treasure must be sought "as silver, and searched for as for hid treasure," Prov. ii. 4; nay, men must dig as miners search for golden ore. This field is very broad, very long and mysterious; in it is contained or hid the decree, council, and purpose of God from everlasting; in this field lies hid the covenant of grace, and the mysteries also of Christ's incarnation, the mysteries of God manifested in the flesh, the mysteries of the obedience, death, resurrection, ascension, and intercession of Jesus Christ; the mysteries of election, redemption, reconciliation, justification, adoption, and the mysteries of union, and communion with the Father and the Son, and of eternal life: and all that would find these treasures, must dig deep in this field, and by faith and prayer, if they would find it.

" Which when a man hath found, he hideth."

What hiding this treasure denotes.

1. This shows it is sought and searched for by such that find it. No doubt finding of the treasure denotes the finding of Christ, the worth and preciousness of Christ, or what he is in himself, and what he is made to every one that finds him, or that believes on him. Moreover, he that finds Jesus Christ, or that believes in him, he hides him in his heart, that is, he receives him into his understanding, will, affections, and memory; he that hides not the word of God, the promises of God, and Jesus Christ in the promises, and in the ordinances, discovers to all, that he has not yet found this treasure.

2ndly, Hiding may signify two things: (1.) An high estimation or value such have of Jesus Christ; a man doth not hide or lay up with the greatest care, such things that are of small value. (2.) His care to keep it, lest thieves rob him of it: sin, the world, the flesh, the devil, and impostors, are spiritual thieves, and therefore the godly hide their treasure: Mary laid up all those things the angel told her in her heart; and so David hid the word of God; some men not having hid the true Christ, and treasure of the gospel in their judgments, wills, and affections, have lost that which they seemed to have, by strong delusions, which are sent as a judgment to deceive such, who " Received not the truth in the love of it that they might be saved," 2 Thess. ii. 11, 12.

" He hideth it."

There is a two-fold hiding of this treasure.

1. An evil hiding, which is not intended here.

A little to this.

An evil hiding of divine truth.

I. When a man hath received light and knowledge of Christ and divine truth, or in some degree it is revealed to him, and he (through the power of Satan's temptations, and the evil of his own heart) strives to smother it in his own breast, or conceals what he knows, and stifles his convictions, and that knowledge he hath keeps to himself, and will not make a visible profession of the gospel; this is an evil hiding: now the cause or reason why some do thus, I shall briefly show.

1. Because truth is only discovered to his understanding, they may be much enlightened, but his will consents not, subjects not to the power of it, nor is he in love with it, his affections being not changed, but he prefers some other things above it, or as the apostle hints, such do that receive the truth in the love of it.

2. It may be occasioned through shame; he is ashamed of Christ and of his word, the visible profession of religion exposeth men to reproach and contempt to the people of the world, and it must be the mighty power and efficacy of the Spirit put forth on the heart, that arms a man to despise all shame and reproach he may meet with (for the sake of Christ) by means of his making a visible profession of the gospel. Now this man not being under such a divine power, cannot bear the cross, nor suffer shame for Christ's sake. Nicodemus for some time was under the power of this great evil, he being a master in Israel was ashamed to own Christ publicly, and therefore came unto him by night, John iii. 1, 2. Our Lord shows us, that some are ashamed of him before men, and such he will be ashamed to own and confess before his Father in the great day, Matt. viii. 38. But all sincere Christians are not ashamed of Christ, nor of the cross, and gospel of Christ, they visibly own him, and do not in this sense hide the sacred treasure.

3. It may be through idleness, he is not willing to be at further pains, nor at the charge of selling all he hath to buy this field, or publicly to receive Christ and own him before men; the world is too much in his heart, (as it was in the heart of the young man that came running to Christ) or perhaps his own righteousness is too much valued by him, he cannot part with it in point of trust, that he may win Christ.

4. Moreover, fear may be one cause of the sinful hiding this treasure; he knows not what the losses may be he may meet withal, or what he may suffer for Christ's sake, if he visibly confesseth him before men: it was this which caused the stony-ground hearers to fall away, and deny the truth. " When tribulation and persecution rose because of

the word, they were offended," Matt. xiii. 2. Many in a time of liberty have owned Christ, who have hid their testimony and drawn back in days of persecution.

5. An evil hiding imports a non-improving of their light and knowledge; the slothful servant is said to hide his talent, Matt. xxv. 18, or his Lord's money in the earth, or in worldly cares, and the deceitfulness of riches; he improved not that which he had received.

Secondly, There is a good hiding of this treasure, which may denote. *What it is to hide this treasure.*

1. Such endeavour to the uttermost, whatsoever it may cost them, to make it their own, and will not wickedly conceal nor hide what Christ hath done for them. " Come to me all ye that fear God, and I will declare what he hath done for my soul," Psal. lxvi. 16.

2. They make use of all means to secure it (as I hinted before) and hence they lay it up in the safest place, watching day and night their deceitful hearts, that no corruption within may let in Satan or any enemy to deceive them of this treasure; they keep their hearts shut against all temptations and inordinate affections, they being sensible of the great danger they are in through sinful pleasures, riches and honours, or by means of heresies, errors, or by evil men, and evil company; they will not prefer any thing above it, nor neglect any duty God directs unto, for the securing of it; but as they have received it into every faculty of their souls, and lodged it in the secret recesses of their hearts, so they are daily in the exercise of faith, and of all the graces of the Spirit; and in prayer crying to God continually, to help them to persevere, and keep this treasure against all attempts of enemies whatsoever.

Now the reason why this treasure is and must be hid, is,

1. Because of the value of it; every true believer knows the worth of this treasure, and what is contained in it; who is able to compute the value of the God of truth, and Jesus Christ the pearl of great price, and all his riches. These things show what rich treasure this is, " they buy the truth," Prov. xxiii. 23, (Christ is the truth which they buy,) and sell it not, knowing nothing is to be compared to the excellency of the knowledge of the Lord Jesus Christ. *The reasons why he hideth this treasure.*

2. They hide it, by reason of the power and virtue they find it hath over them; their wills are so powerfully inclined and influenced by the efficacy of divine truth, that they count it their all, or the sum of their happiness; and from hence will sooner part with their natural lives than part with this treasure: " Whom have I in heaven but thee, neither is there any on earth that I desire besides thee," Psal. lxxiii. 25. Will a king part with his crown, or jewels of his crown? No, why this treasure is the believer's crown; now as outward grandeur and glory hath mighty power and influence upon a carnal heart, so true spiritual dignity, riches, and glory, have upon a spiritual heart; and as the causes here are more strong, noble, and powerful than natural causes, so the effects exceeded in their nature also, all natural or moral effects; that which the will thus powerfully inclined doth receive and embrace, that the affections most dearly love and prize; and from hence it is this treasure is hid by every saint of God.

3. They hide it from the apprehension they have of the deceitfulness and evil of their hearts, and of the rage and malice of Satan, who they know will if he can, raise up all the powers of hell and earth to strip them of this treasure. How hath Satan prevailed upon many, by open force taking the gospel in its outward administration from them; and by policy deceiving others, who have parted with this treasure for that which is not preferable to a brass counter, and if it were possible by his hellish delusions would even deceive the very elect.

4. They hide it in their hearts, because it is not only their riches, their honour, but also their food, they live upon it, trade with it; Jesus Christ is the Bread of Life: " They that find me find life, and shall obtain favour of the Lord," Prov. viii. 35. And upon him they live; what is dearer to men than the stay and staff of their life?

5, Moreover, this treasure is the seed of which our Lord speaketh in this chapter; and if the seed be not hid in the earth, it will not root; no more will the word of God, unless it be hid in our hearts. It is also like leaven which must be hid in the meal. So that from hence it appears there is a necessity of hiding of this treasure.

" And for joy thereof goeth and selleth all that he hath, and buyeth that field."

A man that finds hidden treasure rejoiceth. So doth every believer that finds this spiritual treasure; the Samaritans when they found the field, found the gospel, and Jesus Christ hid therein, they rejoiced, " And there was great joy in that city," Acts. viii. 8. Moreover, when the eunuch had found this treasure, " He went on his way rejoicing,"

Acts. viii. 39. The gospel is cause of joy to all that find the rich treasure that is hid therein, for they are enriched thereby, and made for ever, and shall not be poor nor want any good thing while they live on earth, nor to all eternity.

What is meant by selling all.   " And goeth and selleth all that he hath."

He parts with all things, which before he counted gain unto him, whether it was a name among men, or the honours of the world, or unlawful or sinful desires, carnal affections, evil lusts, and sensual pleasures, self-interest, or self-righteousness ; he no more trusteth in that, but esteems it as dung, that he may win Christ, " And be found in the righteousness of God, which is by faith," Phil. iii. 8, 9. This no doubt is meant by selling all he had.

" And buyeth that field."

That is, he maketh the doctrine of the gospel his own, the ordinances and promises of Christ his own, the ministry of the word and sacraments his own ; this is the field where this treasure is hid, he buys wine and milk, but it is " without money and without price," Isa. lv. 1, 2. (i. e.,) he obtains the true knowledge of God and Jesus Christ, or receives the doctrine of free justification, adoption, and pardon of sin, he accepteth of Christ as he is freely offered ; it is the doctrine and dispensation of the gospel, which he purchaseth on those terms which some like not of; he denies himself (being overpowered by divine grace) and takes up his cross, and followeth the Lord Jesus Christ.

I shall say no more here of buying, it being spoken to, in my opening the parable of the pearl of great price.

Doct. Jesus Christ, and the blessings in him, are like to rich treasure, which is hid in the ministry of the gospel, which when a poor sinner finds, he hides, and with joy he parts with all he hath, that he may possess him, and have interest in all those blessings and benefits that come by him, or that are found in him.

In speaking to this general proposition, I shall show,

1. Why Christ (and the blessing of the gospel, which we have in and by him) is called treasure.

2. Show you the nature of this treasure.

3. Show why it is called hidden treasure, or treasure hid in a field.

4. Show from whence it is that such that find this treasure rejoice and sell all for it.

Why Christ and the gospel blessings compared to treasure.   I. Rich treasure is counted a most excellent thing, and therefore it is much desired ; the hearts of mankind naturally run after riches and earthly treasure; Christ and the blessings of the gospel may upon this account be compared to treasure. What is equal in worth and value to the Lord Jesus Christ ? He is called a precious stone ; there are some precious stones of a very great worth ; but O who can compute the intrinsical worth and value of Jesus Christ, the eternal Son of God ; he is also called a pearl, not an ordinary pearl, but a pearl of great price ; he that finds this treasure, hath all ; all things are his, God is his portion, his inheritance, and his exceeding great reward ; pardon is his, peace is his, and eternal life is his ; and from hence all that know the excellency, worth, and preciousness of Christ, desire him above all things. " Whom have I in heaven but thee," Psal. lxxiii. 25. " Neither is there any on the earth I desire besides thee," Phil. iii. 8, 9. Paul counted all things but dung in comparison of Jesus Christ.

Much treasure enricheth him that finds it, it maketh him rich, great, and honourable in this world. So this spiritual treasure makes all that find it very rich ; mankind naturally are poor, and miserable, though they may be rich in gold and silver, or have store of worldly riches, yet they are in a spiritual sense very poor, have nothing to eat but husks, and are clothed with rags ; their bodies may be clothed in cloth of gold, whilst their souls are naked, or clothed in filthy rags. " I counsel thee to buy of me gold tried in the fire, that thou mayest be rich," Rev. iii. 18. Gold is counted the best of earthly treasure ; Christ and his benefits enrich the souls of believers ; this is heavenly gold, and it makes all that find it truly and eternally rich, and also great and most excellent persons in all the earth ; they are raised to the highest honour, they are born of God, born from above, and walk with God ; God honoureth all such that fear him, and who are enriched with this treasure. " Jabez was more honourable than his brethren," &c. 1 Chron. iv. 9. Because he was enriched with grace, or called upon the God of Israel to be blessed indeed. He that findeth wisdom, findeth " Life, righteousness, and honour," Prov. xxi. 21,

III. Much earthly treasure makes men hated and envied by many persons, and are in danger to be robbed by thieves. So a believer is hated and envied by the devil and wicked men, because they are possessed with spiritual treasure, and are made like unto God in holiness, all that are most like to God and Jesus Christ are hated by Satan and by the children of the wicked one; Satan also strives like an old and cunning thief to rob them of their treasure. Poor men do not fear thieves, they have no such occasion as the rich have. So the grand design of Satan by all his wiles, is to deceive and undo the saints of God; what devices hath the devil to rob us in these evil days, of the truths of God, of the doctrine of the gospel, and ordinances thereof, nay, of the true Christ himself; and thus this rich treasure exposeth the saints to many trials and dangers in this world, through the malice of the devil and wicked men.

IV. Such who have much riches, or store of earthly treasure, live high; they feed or fare not as the poor do; also they are more richly clothed and adorned, and delivered from the care and fears which the poor are perplexed with continually. So believers who are enriched with this sacred treasure, live glorious lives; they dwell high, they eat the hidden manna, or feed upon the bread of life, and are clothed in gold of Ophir, or in the rich robe of Christ's righteousness, and have a ring on their hand. *See the parable of the prodigal son.* Moreover, they can trust God, rely upon God, and on his promises; because they are rich in faith, and are delivered from slavish fear which possesseth the hearts of the poor; and indeed such Christians who are filled with doubts and fears, discover they have but a small measure of this spiritual treasure, or are not rich or strong in faith as others are.

V. A man that hath much earthly treasure can do more good to his neighbours than multitudes of others are able to do. So believers who have this heavenly treasure, who are rich in faith, rich in promises, and rich in experience, can do more good than any others; they can give better counsel, and administer more and better comfort to poor disconsolate persons. "The lips of the righteous feed many," Prov. x. 21, they can do more for others by their prayers. "The prayers of a righteous man avail much with God," Jam. v. 16. And if these men and women have the riches of this world, how much good do they do with it above others, how many poor saints and poor ministers do they feed and support under their necessities; while others who have none or but a small portion of this soul-enriching treasure, live to themselves, and do but little or no good so long as they live in the world. It is wonderful indeed to think what abundance of good, some men in this city to my knowledge have done, who are not only enriched with this treasure, but also with earthly riches; may be one man or two have done more than forty who pretend to religion and godliness as well as they, and perhaps as rich in the world as they are also.

VI. He that hath much earthly treasure, values himself accordingly, and rich and honourable are his companions, noble persons are his comforts, and with them he communes every day. So he that hath much of this spiritual treasure, values himself *Psal. xvi. 5.* upon the best and worthiest grounds in the world. (1). In respect to *6,* *2 Cor. vi. 18.* his relation to God, he is a child of God. (2). He hath God for his portion. *Psal. lxxiii.* (3). He is allowed communion with God, he dwells with God, and God *26.* *1 John i 2. 3.* with him, he walks with God, and God with him; he sups with God and Christ, *2 Cor. vi. 16.* and they with him. (4). Because he knows he can never be poor, or be undone, *Rev. iii. 20.* *Psal. xxxiv.* he is assured he shall never want any good thing. A godly man values not himself *9, 10.* from what he knows more than others; for he thinks he knows nothing as he *Psal. lxxxiv.* *11.* ought, nor from what he hath done for God, but from a better ground. Moreover, the godly or such who fear God are his companions; "he hates to walk in the way of the wicked, or to have fellowship with the vile and base-born of this world," Psal. i. 1. "I am a companion of all them that fear thee, and of them that keep thy precepts," Psal. cxix 63.

VII. They that have much earthly treasure are delivered from that contempt, which others are exposed unto; beggars are counted the offscouring of the world. So he who finds this treasure is freed from that contempt which the Word of God casteth upon all wicked men. They are a poor, sordid, and base sort of people, hence called *The parable* tares, vile and abominable ones; when the righteous, who have this treasure, *of the wheat* *and tares.* are compared to gold, and called God's jewels; and indeed these are the rich that have many friends, God, Christ, the Holy Ghost, and all the holy angels of heaven, and all the saints upon earth are their friends, and show themselves at all times so to be to them; what an honour is it to have such friends! and to be attended upon, and ministered to by the holy angels of God!

VIII. Hid treasure is not found without much pains and diligent searching, no more is this spiritual treasure; Solomon shows us how wisdom, that is, Jesus Christ, and spiritual riches, must be sought. "So that thou incline thine ear unto wisdom, and apply thine heart to understanding; yea, if thou criest after knowledge, and liftest up thy voice for understanding; if thou seekest her as silver, and searchest for her as for hid treasures; then shalt thou understand the fear of the Lord, and find the knowledge of God," Prov. ii. 2, 5. Merchants that seek hid treasure, run through a thousand dangers, and stick not at any difficulty. Miners dig through rocks and under rivers to find the golden ore, or to follow the vein of silver, so nothing is too hard to such who seek and search after this hid treasure; they dig in the depths of God's eternal councils and purposes from everlasting, and dig into the covenant of grace, and into the mysteries of God manifested in the flesh, and dig into the mysteries of the gospel, word, and ordinances, and never give over until they have found this treasure.

Where a man's treasure is his heart is.   IX. He that hath much earthly treasure, commonly sets his heart upon it, and it is his chiefest delight, so he that hath found this treasure, sets his heart upon it; God and Christ is his chiefest delight. "Where your treasure is, there will your heart be also," Matt. vi. 21. They that are earthly think of the earth, speak of the earth, they mind earthly things, their hearts are on the world, when they approach near to God with their mouths, and seem to honour him with their lips, because earthly riches are their chiefest treasury; but they that are spiritually rich, whose treasure is in heaven, set their affections on those things which are above, Col. iii. 1, 2. That which is a man's choicest treasure, hath his heart, love, and delight; "Why doth thine heart carry thee away," Job. xv. 12. Why doth thy affection master thy judgment, or why are thy passions too hard for thy reason? the ill treasure of the heart hath power over, and is too hard for the whole man.

X. Such who find great treasure, rejoice; so he that finds Christ, or this spiritual treasure, rejoiceth; he selleth for joy all he hath to buy that field; a believer has cause of joy, he is happy for ever, let what will come, he rejoiceth in his portion, his treasure is safe.

XI. Such who find great treasure, can pay all their debts, so they that find this treasure, can plead a discharge from the guilt of all their sins in Jesus Christ; they see how all their debts are paid. This treasure (that is, Jesus Christ) satisfied the justice of God; though the bare finding of Christ, or believing in him, doth not pay our debts; yet none have their sins so actually paid as they can plead their discharge, but they that receive Christ, or apply the atonement; no man comes out of debt, nor does he know how until he finds this treasure.

"The kingdom of heaven is like to treasure hid in a field," &c.

I shall now proceed to show you the nature of this treasure.

1. It is heavenly, not earthly treasure, as far as heaven excels the earth, so far heavenly treasure, excels all the riches, wealth and treasure of this world, earthly riches is but like dung to this, that is of no value; this is called better substance, better in quality, and more in quantity. Worldly treasure enriches the outward man only, but this enriches the soul; the souls of the wicked are poor and miserable, because their riches suit not the state of their souls, it cannot answer nor supply soul-wants, nor raise their souls to honour; it will not buy soul-food nor soul raiment; no, such as is the nature of the soul, such must be the treasure that enriches it, and the food that feeds, and the raiment that clothes it, that is, it must be of a heavenly, a spiritual and immortal nature and quality.

2. It being heavenly and spiritual treasure, it followeth that it must be incorruptible treasure; gold, silver, and all the best things of this world are corruptible moth; and rust corrupteth it, "Lay up for yourselves treasures in heaven, where neither moth nor rust doth corrupt," Matt. vi. 20. "Your riches are corrupted, and your garments are moth-eaten, your gold and silver is cankered; and the rust of them shall be a witness against you," Jam. v. 2, 3. But this treasure, being incorruptible, is of a blessed nature, it cannot change nor alter, but always abides the same.

3. It is soul-satisfying treasure; the treasures of this world can never satisfy the immortal soul of man; that is still restless, unsatisfied, and craving, "He that desireth silver shall not be satisfied with silver," Eccl. v. 10. Man naturally labours for that which satisfieth not, Isa. lv. 2; that only which is man's chiefest good, tends to satisfy him, and that is the blessed God. And it is from hence that this treasure is of a satisfying nature, for he that finds it comes to enjoy God for his portion, he hath God's love and favour in Jesus Christ, "They shall be abundantly satisfied with the fat things of thy house," Psal. xxxvi. 8. Hence such who find Christ, that blessed gift of God, the living bread, and water of life, thirst no more, but abide satisfied, John iv. 14.

4. It is durable and everlasting treasure, not uncertain riches, which are compared to vapour, "Wilt thou set thy heart upon that which is not?" Prov. xxiii. 5. Wilt thou catch at a shadow or a vapour? if you see a man do thus, would you not think him out of his

wits? children have more wisdom, than to go about to take hold of a shadow; but such fools are the men of the world, they strive to hold fast a shadow, no man can carry any of his earthly treasure out of the world with him; this treasure being everlasting and durable treasure, a believer carries it with him to heaven, or rather goes thither to possess and enjoy it, " Riches and honour are with me, yea durable riches and righteousness; my fruit is better than gold, yea, than much fine gold, and my revenue than choice sliver," Prov. viii. 18, 19. This treasure is better in many respects, and one is, because it is durable; they are not uncertain riches. " Charge them that are rich, that they trust not in uncertain riches," &c., 1 Tim. vi. 17. A man may be rich to-day, and poor to-morrow; nothing is more uncertain than earthly riches, but should a man keep them as long as he lives, yet riches avail not in the day of wrath; they cannot help nor relieve a man on a death-bed, nor when God pours out his wrath upon him. But this treasure will stand him instead in the greatest time of need, as well as it is eternal treasure.

Secondly, I shall show you how it is hid, and why it is called hid treasure, or treasure hid in a field.

I have showed that by this treasure is meant Jesus Christ, with the saving knowledge and benefits of Jesus Christ; now Christ is like hidden treasure,

I. Because he was long hid in God, or covered, and out of the sight of men; that which is kept secret or not discovered, may be said to be hid. " To make all men see what is the fellowship of the mystery, which from the beginning of the world hath been hid in God," Eph. iii. 9. It was in some respects hid from all, but more especially from the Gentiles, they knew nothing of it, it was hid from them. " Even the mystery which hath been hid from ages and generations," &c., Col. i. 26. That is salvation by Jesus Christ. *[marginal note: Why the treasure of gospel is hid, or called hid treasure.]*

II. It was hid from the Jews, who believed not under the law, hid under dark shadows and beggarly elements, so that they could not find this treasure; they could not see Christ in those sacrifices and shadowy ordinances; they were as a cloud, in which the sun of righteousness was hid, and so he is hid from them to this day, though it may seem strange, that they could not see through the sacrifices of poor animals, to the antitype of them; could they once suppose that the blood of bulls and goats could satisfy for the sins of mankind, or their blood could purge the conscience from sin?

III. Christ and his benefits are hid in the dispensation of the gospel, so that very few can find this rich treasure, they have the field, i. e., word and administration of the gospel; but carnal men see not the mysteries of the gospel, it is hid treasure to them, what, be justified by the obedience and righteousness of a poor man, hanged upon a tree, this was accounted to the learned Greeks foolishness, it was hid from them. " We preach Christ crucified, unto the Jews a stumbling-block, and unto the Greeks foolishness," &c., 1 Cor. i. 23; that is, such effect our preaching of a crucified Christ hath both upon the one and upon the other, it lies above their human reason, that that way men should be justified and saved for ever.

IV. This treasure was hid, (and is still) dark, parabolical, symbolical, or tropical expressions uttered by our blessed Lord, many had the field, I mean the parables and similitudes, they were spoken to multitudes, but the treasure hid in them few saw; and it is sad indeed to see how some men mistake the design of our Saviour in many of his parables; it is evident the treasure is still hid from most in our days. I have often cried to God, to help me, that I might understand them, and open them by the help of his own Spirit. But ah, how little do I know !

V. This treasure is hid by the Lord from multitudes, as an act of his sovereign will and pleasure. " To you it is given to know the mysteries of the kingdom of heaven; but to them it is not given." God acts according to his own sovereign pleasure. " Shall I not do what I will with my own," Matt. xx. 15. Is God obliged to send the gospel unto all the nations of the world, because he gives his special favour to some? must he be unjust if he does not afford them to every individual person in the world? Because he opened Lydia's heart, must he open every woman's heart? No no. " He hath mercy on whom he will have mercy, and compassion on whom he will have compassion, and whom he will he hardens," Rom. ix. 18, or hides the mysteries of his kingdom from. " At that time Jesus answered, and said, I thank thee, O Father, Lord of heaven and earth, because thou hast hid these things from the wise and prudent, and hast revealed them unto babes —even so, Father, for so it seemed good in thy sight," Matt. xxi. 25, 26.

The learned Pharisees and Jewish Rabbins had the outward ministration of the gospel as the learned have now, but God did not, and now doth not, reveal the hidden mysteries of his kingdom but to a very few of that sort, and it is only from the good pleasure of his own will he doth this.

Natural
light re-
veals not
the know-
ledge of
Christ the
Mediator. 1. That may be said to be hid which mankind cannot find, without God reveals it to them in a supernatural way : now the knowledge of Jesus Christ and the mysteries of the gospel, mankind naturally, or by the light of nature, cannot know.   And from hence this treasure is hid from most nations of the world.

It is hid from the Pagan world ; they know nothing of Christ crucified, and of salvation by him.

It is hid also from the Mahometan world ; they esteem and honour Mahomet above Jesus Christ, they know him not.

It is also hid from the antichristian world, for though they have the name of Christ, or name of Christians, yet they know not Jesus Christ.

Moreover, it is hid from multitudes of the Protestant world ; true, they walk in the field where it is hid, but many of them never found the treasure ; it is therefore hid treasure.

The Gospel is a sealed book, and though it be given to a man that is learned, he cannot read it because it is sealed, and none can open the seal thereof but the Lord Jesus Christ.

2.   That which needeth many gradations to unfold it, is a hidden thing, but the knowledge of Christ the Mediator, and mysteries of salvation, needed many gradations to unfold it; to our first parents it was made known by that promise, " The seed of the woman shall break the serpent's head."   This was the first discovery of this treasure, which God saw good to make of it.

Then to Abraham God gave a further discovery thereof, telling him that " in his seed all the nations of the earth should be blessed," Gen. xxii. 18.   Afterwards, it was revealed by the types, ceremonies, and sacrifices of the law, which but few could take in, though it was to reveal Jesus Christ the great sacrifice to them ; and then by the prophets he was declared yet more clearly, and that he should be born of a virgin, and die for the sins of his people ; yet how hard was it for any to understand or find this treasure, though God took all these ways, methods, and gradations, to reveal it to them ?

And then when we come to the gospel dispensation, which far exceedeth for clearness all other revelations of Christ and salvation by him, yet what multitudes know him not, find not this treasure, though the light is so clear, yet it is hid from many.   Some think the gospel is but a law of obedience, having the sanction of rewards to such who sincerely obey the precepts thereof, and threatenings of divine wrath to the disobedient.   The mysteries of the gospel are hid still from them ; they cannot find the way of free justification and eternal life, though they have the best and clearest external revelation thereof, of all that were before them.

Christ is
not found
without
much dili-
gence. 3. That which requires our uttermost skill, wisdom, and diligence to search and find out, is a hidden thing : but the true knowledge of Jesus Christ requires our uttermost skill, wisdom, and diligence in searching to find out, and therefore it is a hidden thing.   Pray see what Solomon saith ; " My son, if thou wilt receive my words, and hide my commandments with thee, so that thou incline thine ear to wisdom, and apply thine heart to understanding—Yea, if thou criest after knowledge, and liftest up thy voice for understanding,—if thou seekest her as silver, and searchest for her as for hid treasures—then shalt thou understand the fear of the Lord, and find the knowledge of God," Prov. ii. 1—5.   What is more clear and evident than this, i. e., that our utmost diligence must be used in seeking and searching to find this treasure. Moreover, it must be sought for where it is hid, even in that very field and no where else ; some seek for it within them, but there it is not.   True, in all men there is some dark and blotted remains of the covenant of works, which reproves for sin, as it is against God, and Jesus Christ considered as Creator, but the true gospel silver vein lies not there, that is not the place of this gold where they find it ; Christ is not hid in these secret chambers, (i. e.,) in the hearts of wicked men ; no, that is a false Christ which such have, who cry, " Behold he is in the secret chambers," Matt. xxiv. 26.

My brethren, as men know not the price hereof, so many know not the place thereof, or field where it is hid.   " There is a path which no fowl knoweth, and which the vulture's eye hath not seen, the lion's whelps have not trodden it, nor the fierce lion passed by it," &c., Job xxviii. 7, 8.   These vultures who pretend to have a piercing sight, know not the place of this treasure ; many seek the living among the dead, " he is not here, he is risen," and ascended ; though his word is near, even in the hearts and mouths of believers ; yet the true treasure, the doctrine and saving knowledge of Christ, lies only hid in the gospel, or ministration thereof.

It is hid from many by the devil: " If our gospel be hid, it is hid to them *Satan hides* that are lost—in whom the God of this world hath blinded the minds of them *the treasure* which believe not," 2 Cor iv. 3, 4. Satan, by God's permission, hides this *of the gos-* treasure from many whom he hath deceived with his subtle wiles and delu- *many per-* sions, and in these days hath not only hid from some men's eyes the true doc- *sons.* trine of faith, but from others the true and immediate object of faith also, many relying upon their own righteousness for justification; and others have lost the true Saviour.

" Which when a man hath found, he rejoiceth, and goeth and selleth all he hath," &c. This brings me to the last general head proposed:

Fourthly, I shall show you why he rejoices that finds this treasure, &c.

1. He that finds this treasure, finds the Lord Jesus Christ, the Pearl of *Why a be-* great price, which far exceeds all hid treasure and mountains of prey. How *liever that* do men rejoice when they find a pearl worth ten thousand pounds. I have *treasure re-* read of a pearl of an exceeding great value, but it was but as a bit of dirt or *joiceth.* dung when compared to Jesus Christ. Therefore it is from the worth of this treasure, that a believer that finds it doth rejoice.

II. It may be from the great use this treasure is of to him, (1.) He was *Rev. 3. 17* poor before, and this treasure enricheth him. (2.) He was naked before, but *Luk. 15. 22* by finding this treasure he is gloriously clothed. (3.) He was forced before *Rom. 3.* to feed upon husks, but now he is fed with rare and choice food, he feedeth *25, 26.* on the Bread of life. (4.) He was far in debt before, but now this treasure *Heb. 8. 11.* he sees has paid all he owed to the law and justice of God, and that he is *Eph. 2. 3.* justified from all things, and pardoned for ever. (5.) He saw he was a child *Joh. 3. 18.* of wrath before, but now he is become a child of God. (6.) That he was a *36.* captive and in chains before, but now he is set at liberty. (7.) Condemned *1 Cor. 1.* before, but now sees that sentence is taken off, and that " there is no condem- *30.* nation to him (nor to any that are) in Jesus Christ." (8.) That he was a fool *1 Cor. 2. 4,* before, or without true knowledge and understanding, but now he is become *13.* wise (for Christ is made not only righteousness to them that find him) but wisdom also, 1. objectively; Christ is the wisdom of God, and also he that discovers the great depths of God's eternal wisdom to us. 2. Christ is also made wisdom to us subjectively, we by finding of him are made eternally wise.

III. My brethren, this treasure mainly consisteth in the saving knowledge of God and Jesus Christ. " We have this treasure in earthen vessels," &c., *This trea-* 2 Cor. iv. 7. The apostle doth not only refer in these words to the minis- *sure is the* tration or apostolical office, but to that sight of the knowledge of the glory of *knowledge* God in the face of Jesus Christ, the knowledge of which is life eternal; John *of Christ.* xvii. 3; without this saving knowledge we have no God, no Christ, no grace, no faith, no union with Christ, no actual justification, pardon of sin, peace, not eternal life.

1. It is an experimental, not a mere speculative knowledge, not only a head-enriching, but also a heart-enriching knowledge. *The nature*

2. It is a practical knowledge, such have spiritual acquaintance with God: *of the true* " He that saith he knows him, and keepeth not his commandments, is a liar, *knowledge* and the truth is not in him," Job xxii. 21, 22, 1 John ii. 4. *of Christ.*

3. It is an enlivening knowledge, it is always attended with a principle of divine life; and such " are renewed in knowledge, after the image of him that created him," Col. iii. 10.

4. It is a translating and transforming knowledge, such are changed into the likeness of Jesus Christ, 2 Cor. iii. 18; they are dead with him, and quickened, and raised up to newness of life, Rom. vi. 3, 4, 6; they feel the power of his death and resurrection, and the fellowship of his sufferings, Phil. iii. 10; they find the stream of God's divine love and goodness, and the stream of Christ's love in the efficaciousness and sweetness of his blood and suffering; tasting that the Lord is gracious.

5. It is a knowledge of interest, they can say, " My Lord, and my God," and so a God-endearing, a Christ-endearing knowledge, and therefore it is a knowledge of application; they that thus know Christ, take hold of him, embrace him in the arms of their faith, and can trust in him, and all Christ hath is theirs.

6. It is a self-abasing, a soul-humbling, and a God and Christ-exalting knowledge. " I am resolved Christ shall be magnified in my body, whether it be by life or death," Phil. i. 12.

7. It is a progressive knowledge, a growing and increasing knowledge; " they go from grace to grace, from faith to faith," and are changed " from glory to glory, by the Spirit of the Lord," 2 Cor. iii. 18.

This is the treasure which this man found, and hence he rejoiceth, and hath cause of joy. Without this knowledge no man can love God, nor love Jesus Christ. Love always supposeth knowledge : " What is thy beloved more than another's beloved," Cant. v. 9. Nor can there be true joy unless we have the person, the treasure that is so desirable : " Hope deferred maketh the heart sick, but when the desire cometh it is a tree of life," Prov. xiii. 12. When the desire comes, that is, when the object desired is enjoyed, then peace, and delight, and joy is in that person.

IV. He that finds this treasure, makes the field his own, he secures the field : the doctrine of the Gospel is his own, it is well rooted in him, and thereby he is delivered from all soul-undoing and soul-destroying evils ; and is possessed with all soul-enriching, soul-satisfying, soul-delighting, and soul-ravishing good ; he has in himself a well of living water springing up unto everlasting life, John iv. 14 ; bread to eat that others know not of, and " is abundantly satisfied with the fat things of God's house, and drinks of the rivers of his pleasures," Psal. xxxvi. 8, therefore he may well rejoice.

V. God is his Father, his Portion, his Friend ; Christ is his Saviour, Redeemer, his Bridegroom, his Surety, his riches, his Advocate, nay, his all ; the Spirit is his Comforter, his Guide, his Leader, his Helper, his Strengthener, and his Quickener : the word is his rule, the promises and ordinances are his patrimony ; the angels are his guard, his retinue, and heaven is his inheritance.

He rejoices therefore, and selleth all to buy this field ; if he was possessed of ten thousand worlds, crowns, and kingdoms, yet he would sell them all, part with them all for this treasure.

APPLICATION

1. I infer from hence, that there is a great depth in the Christian religion ; men must dig in this field, and search with enlightened minds, before they can find it ; it is not every one that hath the Bible, or hath the ministration of the gospel, that finds the treasure ; the further we dig into these mysteries, the more we are enriched with the saving knowledge of God and of Jesus Christ. This field is like the water of the sanctuary, where a lamb might wade, and yet a river that no man could pass over, Ezek. xlvii. 5.

2. Let none therefore be wise in their own eyes, in their own conceit, and think they know enough, know all, for such certainly know nothing ; none know anything as they ought to know ; all know but in part, and see darkly as in a glass.

3. We infer, the gospel is a great blessing. O bless God, you who have the field where this treasure is hid, you have the gospel in a clear and gracious ministration thereof, which thousands in the world have not, and so it is impossible for them to find this treasure ; nay, you have the field of the word opened and explained to you, that you may the better discern where the treasure lies hid in it, the types opened, the prophecies opened, the metaphors opened, the parables and similies opened, and the doctrine of the word explained and opened, the sacraments opened ; O what encouragement is here for you to search, when so much is done for your instruction.

4. We infer, that Ministers have need of great light and understanding, or to be men of skill and experience : ignorant preachers are a plague and a curse to a people ; O take heed who ye hear.

Exhort. Be exhorted you that are sinners, to seek this treasure, and resolve to purchase this field.

" With joy he hideth, and goeth straightway and selleth all, and buyeth that field."

Buying, you have heard, only signifieth his parting with all he before counted gain to him.

I. Such that find this treasure will rejoice.

Why he that finds this treasure doth rejoice.   1. Because of the worth of it, and the good he receives hereby.

2. Because of what is contained in it, Christ, grace, justification, pardon, peace, &c.

3. Because he is delivered from all damning evil, and possessed of all true good.

4. Because he cannot be dispossessed of it for ever : God is his God for ever and ever and Christ is his Saviour, and heaven his inheritance.

II. Suppose a man mortally wounded should find a balsam, which being applied, heals all his sores, would he not part with joy, or throw away all his old plasters, which to no purpose he before applied.

III. Or suppose a man was in prison, in chains and fetters, being condemned to die, and meets with a friend that has got his discharge and free pardon, would he not with joy part with his chains and filthy prison, and rejoice and triumph in his liberty? what is sin, the world, self-righteousness, but as chains and fetters, which he that finds this treasure with joy parts with?

IV. Or suppose a man was a captive, and he should obtain a ransom, would he not with joy part with and sell all he had in captivity, and return home? My Brethren, this is the case here, the sinner hath found his friend, that has paid his ransom, and assures him, he is redeemed from sin, wrath and hell, and is set at liberty, made free indeed, free for ever: is not here cause for him to rejoice? and will he not now sell all he hath, part with all his sins, which were as chains in spiritual Turkey, and part with all his old friends, that promised to procure his freedom, with all his old hopes of salvation, peace and justification, and also part with all his old companions, and return to his father's house.

V. Or suppose a poor man was digging in a field, to get his bread, and had nothing but rags to cover his nakedness, and should find vast treasure, a million of guineas, or broad pieces of gold, would he not rejoice, and willingly sell all he had, could he but find a friend to bestow this field, and all the treasure that lies still hid in it, on him, would he not sell or part with his rags, his pick-axe, and his spade, by which means before he thought to live by hard labour, seeing now he is become very rich, and need not dig or work for his bread any more.

Thus it is here, this man was working for life, but clothed with rags, and fed upon husks, but now he hath found Jesus Christ in the dispensation of the gospel, in that blessed field; and this field, this holy doctrine, is by the Lord made his own, and all the rich treasure hid therein; O now he rejoiceth, and he hides it, lays up treasure in heaven, he lays up all (by believing) in the hand of Christ, or commits all to the keeping of the Lord Jesus, in whom all the treasures of wisdom and knowledge, and life also is hid.

USE

Sinners, seek this treasure; the promise is, " If ye seek ye shall find." As to the right seeking, see the foregoing parable of the pearl of great price, where it is largely opened.

2. You that are professors, who conclude you have found this treasure, examine yourselves. O try yourselves, lest you should be deceived.

(1.) If you have found this treasure, you know when, and how you found it; and if it was not by believing in Christ, you have it not, it is no otherways obtained.

(2.) Have you parted with all you had? do you account (with Paul) whatsoever was gain to you but loss for Christ, and esteem it as dung, to be found in him, having his righteousness? &c.

(3.) Do you rejoice in Christ Jesus? are your hearts raised on high? are your affecset upon things above? do you find more joy and gladness in your hearts, than when corn and wine increased? is the light of God's countenance more dear to you than all things in this world, his favour above life to you? Ps. iv. 7.

(4) Where are your hearts? remember what Christ says, " Where your treasure is, there will your hearts be also." The Lord grant it may be with us all thus, and that you may seek this treasure and find it, so will profit redound to you, and glory to God, to whom be praise for ever. Amen.

16. THE TARES OF THE FIELD

I

Another parable put he forth unto them, saying, the kingdom of heaven is likened unto a man which sowed good seed in his field: but while men slept, his enemy came and sowed tares among the wheat, and went his way: but when the blade was sprung up and brought forth fruit, then appeared the tares also," &c.—MATT. xiii. 24, 25, &c.

The scope of the parable. 1. THE design and scope of this parable (as it plainly appears to me) is to show, that though the Lord Jesus Christ and his apostles, and faithful ministers in the primitive times, had lain a good foundation of the church, and sowed good seed, from whence wheat or holy persons sprang up; yet through the remissness of some succeeding ministers, Satan through his malice, by his instruments, (or subtle deceivers) would sow false doctrine or pernicious errors, which would produce evil persons called tares; *i. e.*, men of abominable principles, holding dangerous heresies, and guilty of vile practices, and these would spring up among the wheat.

2ndly. To show that the good and bad should abide together in the world, and not that the tares should be rooted out by persecution, or be cut off by sanguinary laws, but that both should abide together in the field of the world, to the end thereof.

3rdly. That at the last, a discriminating day will come, or a time when the wheat and tares shall be separated or severed from each other, and one be gathered into God's kingdom, and the other cast into hell. So much as to the scope of the parable.

Secondly, We shall proceed to explain the terms and parts of this parable.

The explanation of the parts of the parable. 1. By the kingdom of heaven here is meant the Gospel-church, in which would not only be true believers, but also some hypocrites or ungodly persons; or, 2. The ministration of the Gospel dispensation.

2. The man here spoken of, is the same as in the foregoing parable, viz., the Son of man, the Messiah, Jesus Christ; for it is he that sows the good seed, from whence the wheat ariseth, or godly Christians spring up. See our Lord's own exposition **The man that soweth the good seed is Jesus Christ.** of this parable, ver. 37. " He that soweth the good seed is the Son of Man."

2. The good seed are godly Christians, " the good seed (saith our Saviour) are the children of the kingdom," ver. 38.

3. " The tares are the children of the wicked one," ver. 38, either such **What meant by the good seed.** that are erroneous in their principles, or secret hypocrites.

4. The field is the world; though it may, as some think, also refer to the church. Marlorate saith, by a synecdoche, a part put for the whole, it signi-**What meant by the tares.** fies the church, though this seems doubtful to me, and I rather believe it means this world.

The field is the world. 1. For where is the church put for the world? though the elect before called, are called the world sometimes, as John i. 29, 2 Cor. v. 19, 1 John ii. 2; *i. e.*, the elect amongst Jews and Gentiles.

2. Because tares, when discovered to be such, must not grow amongst the wheat in the church; but ought to be cast out, though they ought to live together in the world. **The sower of the evil seed is the devil.** 5. " The sower of the evil seed (our Lord saith,) is the devil," from whence the tares sprung up, *i. e.*, the children of the wicked one : that is, they are the product either of evil doctrine, or else of the filthy lusts that Satan by his temptations infuseth into the hearts of all unrenewed persons; for all sin and false doctrine is of the devil. " Ye are of your father the devil," John viii. 44, *i. e.*, the produce of his evil seed.

6. The harvest is the end of the world, when time shall be no more, for The harvest is the end of this world. the godly and the wicked to live together, as now they do and shall, until the end thereof.

7. The reapers are the angels. "As therefore the tares are gathered and burnt in fire, so shall it be in the end of the world. The Son of Man shall send forth his angels, and they shall gather out of his kingdom, all things that offend, and them which do iniquity; and shall cast them into a furnace of fire. Then shall the righteous shine forth as the sun, in the kingdom of their Father. Who hath ears to hear, let him hear," ver. 40—43.

1. This shows the woful state of all wicked men and seducers at the day The woful state of the wicked at the day of judgment. of judgment. The angels will find them all out, and bind them up in bundles, and cast them (after the judgment is ended) both body and soul into hell.

2. It also shows the blessed state of the righteous, *i. e.*, such that shall be The happy state of the righteous at that day. found clothed with the righteousness of Christ, and also inherently righteous, being renewed and sanctified by the Holy Spirit.

For none are made, or imputed righteous, in the first sense, who are not truly inherently holy and righteous in the second; there are two or three verses which our Lord opened not, ver. 25—27.

"But while men slept, his enemy came and sowed tares, and went away," ver. 25.

By men sleeping here, no doubt is meant the ministers of the Gospel, or pastors of churches, being remiss and careless in watching against Satan's sowing of tares or evil seed; either the seed of lusts and earthly mindedness, (by which means some professors might be utterly spoiled, and come to nothing) or else the seed of errors and heresies; both are from Satan.

"But when the blade was sprung up," &c. That is, when true believers brought forth the fruits of the Spirit, to show they were wheat.

"Then appeared the tares also," ver. 26. Then some false or corrupt persons appeared and were discerned (by him who is all eye, and perhaps to the angels and men also) to be amongst the saints.

"And the servants of the household came and said unto him, Sir, didst thou not sow good seed in thy field? From whence then hast it tares?" ver. 27.

By the servants are either meant the angels, or else ministers or magistrates; as God is the God of truth, and of holiness, so all errors and evil seed is from the devil.

"The servants said unto him, wilt thou that we go and gather them up?" that is, the tares.

(1.) Some conclude by the servants here, are meant the angels. If to angels, then it may denote that God would not have some judgments to be brought upon the wicked, lest some godly persons fall also with them.

(2.) Some think our Lord refers to Christian magistrates, who have been, and may again be pious persons, and may be ready to cut off by death such offenders, whom our Lord would have lived in the world until the end thereof comes; not but that murders and traitors ought by the sword of justice to be cut off, or pulled up; but not such who are only guilty of divers sorts of errors in matters of faith, or such who many ways are immoral in their lives.

"But he said, nay, lest while ye gather up the tares, ye root up also the wheat with them," ver. 29.

This shows that persecution upon the account of religion, is utterly unlaw- Persecution for religion is utterly unawful. ful, though men may hold grand errors, yet no magistrates have any power to persecute them, much less in the highest degree, so as to put them to death.

1. Because the best of men on earth are not infallible. They do not know but that which they call heresy may be a truth of Christ. "After that way, which they call heresy, (saith Paul) so worship I the God of my fathers, believing all things that are written in the law and the prophets," Acts xxiv. 14. And as good men are not able to distinguish between some truths and errors, so they may think such and such are tares who may be wheat, *i. e.*, gracious and holy persons; and this is the reason our Lord allegeth why they should not root out the tares, "Lest they root out also the wheat with them."

2. Because Jesus Christ is only the king and sovereign of the conscience. None ought to impose upon the consciences of men in matters of religion. They must stand and fall in such cases to their own master.

3. Because it is directly contrary to that golden rule, or true moral precept, "Whatsoever you would that men should do to you, do ye the same unto them." Persecu-

tion is therefore a palpable violation of this holy precept. Would they have others (were they in like power) to persecute them, (for what they believe and practice, according to their light and consciences) no sure, why then they ought not to persecute others; besides, we never find that any Gospel church was a persecuting church, but contrariwise were persecuted.

4. Because such severities have no tending to convince the conscience (if it be erroneous) it may make men to act like hypocrites, *i. e.*, out of fear to do that which is directly against their consciences, and so to sin against God, who alone hath power over it, and will punish those at last accordingly, for obeying man rather than God. When the disciples asked their Lord, whether " they should call for fire from heaven to consume their enemies, (He answered) ye know not what spirit you are of," Luke ix. 54, no more do they who persecute others for their conscience sake.

Yet let none suppose that our Saviour by these words, " Let both grow together until harvest," meant that he would have his people suffer wicked and heretical persons (if Church censures not condemned discovered,) to abide in his church ; no, for that is directly contrary to those by our Saviour, but rules of discipline he hath left in the holy gospel, both in respect of private required. and public offences ; and also in the case of heresy, such ought to come under a just and righteous censure, but for no such evils ; but only for murder, treason, felony, &c., ought persons to be delivered up to the civil magistrate, to suffer corporal punishment. This condemns the church of Rome, and all other people, who are persecutors of men for religion.

Thus having briefly opened the several terms and parts of this parable, I shall proceed to take notice of some doctrinal propositions, from some of the principal things contained therein.

All Divine Grace and Holiness proceeds from Christ. Doct. 1. That it is our Lord Jesus Christ that soweth by his word and spirit the good seed, i. e., that seed from whence all the holy habits, holy acts, and the holy lives of all true believers springs ; all grace and holiness proceeds from Jesus Christ, " Of His own will begat he us by the word of truth," James i. 18. Ministers cannot sow the grace in sinners' hearts, no, they are indeed instruments in Christ's hand, by whom he works, but Christ is the great agent, " Being born again, not of corruptible seed, but of incorruptible, by the word of God," &c. 1 Pet. i. 23. And hence we are said to be " born of the Spirit, and are spirit," John iii. 6. i. e., spiritual. " Which were born not of the will of the flesh, nor of the will of man, but of God," John i. 13.

Believers are a choice and precious people. Doct. 2. Believers are a choice people, choice grain ; they are wheat, the product of choice and precious seed ; or may be compared to wheat ; which is the most precious grain in all the world.

Believers are a choice and precious people. First, I shall show you the saints are a precious and choice people.
Secondly, Show you why they are compared to wheat.
Thirdly, Briefly apply it.

I. By the names given to them they appear to be a choice and precious people.

(1.) They are called the excellent in all the earth, and such that are more excellent than their neighbours, " My goodness extendeth not to thee, but to the saints that are in the earth, and to the excellent, in whom is all my delight," Psal. xvi, 3.

(2.) They are called precious ; " If thou separate the precious from the vile."

(3.) They are called, " The precious sons of Zion, comparable to fine gold," Lam. iv. 2 ; also are often called gold, which is a precious thing.

(4.) They are called honourable ; " since thou wast precious in my sight, thou hast been honourable," Isa. xliii. 4.

(5.) They are called God's inheritance, his portion, his treasure, nay, his jewels, " They shall be mine in that day that I make up my jewels," Mal iii. 17.

(6.) They are called Christ's brethren, also his friends, his love, his dove, his spouse ; all serve to show that they are a very choice and precious people in God's account.

II. They are a choice and precious people, because of the seed from whence they spring ; they are the seed of God, the seed of Christ ; " He shall see his seed," Isa. liii. 11, the seed or product of the Holy Spirit, and of the word ; therefore in respect of their choice and precious birth they are a precious people.

III. In respect of that holy image which is stamped on them ; they bear the image of God, and are like to God, and to Jesus Christ ; the new creature is a glorious creature, a most choice and excellent creature.

IV. In respect had to their union with Christ ; " He that is joined to the Lord is one spirit; every believer is espoused, joined or married to Jesus Christ; they are the beloved, and dear Spouse of this most excellent Prince, and therefore are a precious and most choice people; the church is the Queen of this Prince; " Upon the right hand did stand the Queen in gold of Ophir," Psal. xlv. 9.

V. In respect of those rich robes, Christ hath put upon them the wedding garment, i. e., the righteousness of Christ is a glorious robe; moreover it is said, that " The king's daughter is all glorious within, and her clothing is of wrought'gold," Psal. xlv. 13; inherent righteousness is a rich garment.

VI. In respect to those choice ornaments with which they are adorned. Grace is compared to a crown of gold on the head, and chains about the neck," Prov. i. 9, Ezek. xvi. 12. Now what are these, but the precious graces of the Spirit?

VII. If we consider what an excellent spirit they are of, and how they walk with God every day, and what communion they have with the Father and the Son, it fully shows, they are a choice and precious people in God's esteem.

VIII. Also the precious food they live upon, and the choice and excellent privileges God in his free grace hath bestowed upon them, and what glory they are heirs of, shows they are a precious people.

IX. They are the elect of God, and the price of the blood of Christ, also the workmanship of the Spirit, therefore a precious people.

X. The care God takes of them, and the precious thoughts he hath towards them, and the wonders he hath done, and is about to do for them, tends to make them great, and glorious, and renowned, or a choice people in his sight.

Quest. How the saints come to be a precious and peculiar people?

Ans. 1. They become a peculiar people by virtue of God's special and peculiar love from everlasting; that they who are the people of God, were beloved with a peculiar love, is evident; " The Lord appeared to me of old, saying, yea, I have loved thee with an everlasting love," &c., Jer. xxxi. 3. Our Lord Christ saith, before the 'was made, his delight was with the sons of men, Prov. viii. 31. ' That is, with those that were given him, delight proceeds from love. My brethren, all those blessings which we receive in time, are but the effects or fruits of God's peculiar love to us, before all time, or from everlasting; we must receive all divine favours, either from our merits, God's mercies, from our deservings, or from his peculiar affections, all do not (that is evident) receive alike favours and special blessings; from whence is it? can God's love be purchased? or can sinners deserve anything at his hand? no, no, he had a peculiar love to some from everlasting, and from thence they become a peculiar people; " Therefore with loving-kindness have I drawn thee."

2. They become a peculiar people: by virtue of God's peculiar choice they were elected, (as I told you) as well as beloved from everlasting, " According as he hath chosen us in Him, before the foundation of the world, that we should be holy, and without blame before Him in love,—having predestinated us to the adoption of children by Jesus Christ, according to the good pleasure of his will," Eph. i. 4; all spiritual blessings in heavenly places, in Christ, are according to God's choice of us, ver. 3. Peculiarity, either of state or qualifications, flows from the Father's choice or election; " that his purpose, according to election, might stand," Rom. ix. 11, 13, (he saith) " Jacob have I loved," &c. Either it is of man's free will, or of God's free grace; but " it is not of him that willeth, nor of him that runneth, but of God that shweth mercy," ver. 16.

See how St. Paul argues in this case, " Even so then at this present time also, there is a remnant according to the election of grace," Rom. xi. 5. Well, but may not this election be from foreseen faith, good works, or holiness, no, and if it be of grace, (saith he) it is no more of works, otherwise grace is no more grace; but if it be of works, then it is no more grace, otherwise work is no more work," ver. 6. We do not signalize ourselves by our love and obedience to God, that we are a peculiar people, and have peculiar favours, as it is among men, as when a commander, or soldier acts with much bravery and courage, is promoted to peculiar honour by his prince; no, if it be thus, it is of works, and grace is no more grace.

III. They become a peculiar people, by virtue of that peculiar covenant, made between the Father and the Son, before the world began. Jesus Christ, my brethren, did not engage or covenant with the Father to become a Surety, and to die in the stead of all mankind; no, but only for his own elect; he was not like the first Adam, a head or representative for every individual man and woman in the world, for then all must and would be saved. See St. Paul, " Who hath saved us, and called us, not according to our works, but according to his own purpose and grace, which was given to us in Christ Jesus before the world began," 2 Tim. i. 9. What grace we receive in time, it was in that covenant granted to Christ for us in eternity; and his covenant stands firm, his seed shall endure for ever, it is confirmed by the promise and oath of God, "Who hath sworn to it by his holiness, and will not lie to David," Psal. lxxxix. 27, 28, 29, 35.

IV. They become a peculiar people, by virtue of a special and peculiar price laid down to redeem them. Did God love all men alike, and Christ give himself for all with the same degree of love, and with the same intention, design, and purpose of grace to save all, as he did in respect of some, certainly then all would be saved; for who shall frustrate the absolute design and purpose of Jesus Christ? But this was not so, "His name shall be called Jesus, because he shall save his people from their sins," Matt. i. 21. Not save all people from their sins, no, none but his people, i. e., such that were given to him by the Father. "The Lord hath laid on him the iniquities of us all," Isa. liii. 6. Us all, who were they? Read the 8th ver., "For the transgression of my people was he stricken," John. x. 15. "I lay down my life for my sheep." "Christ purchased the church with his own blood," Acts. xx. 28.

God, in the gift of the Son, acted for his own sovereign pleasure; like as a prince may redeem and save some captives, or pardon some notorious rebels or traitors, and not all, though they as well as the rest deserved to die; all men are guilty of the highest treason against God, and he might justly have left all under wrath; but as an act of infinite, peculiar and sovereign grace, Christ died in the room or stead of some, to redeem and save them.

V. They become a peculiar people, by means of the special and peculiar workings and operations of the Holy Spirit, upon their hearts; is there no specific difference between that grace which is given to some, and that given in common to all? As the gospel is not sent to all, but to one nation and kingdom, and not to another, so the Spirit (where the gospel is preached) works grace in one man, and not in another. "The wind blows where it listeth—so is every one that is born of the Spirit," John iii. 8. The Spirit is a free agent, he opens one man's heart and eyes, and not another; he gives faith, knowledge, and regenerates some, and passeth by others; the Spirit divideth to every man (that is, to every saint) as he will; either God maketh the difference between one man and another; or else men makes themselves to differ; there are, my brethren, special and peculiar operations of the Spirit, and only common operations. "Paul planteth, and Apollos watered; but it is God that gives the increase; neither is he that planteth anything, nor he that watereth anything; but is it God that gives the increase," 1 Cor. iii. 6, 7. To such that are elected, whom God will save, the gospel comes in power, but to others in word only; and were there not such a special power put forth upon some, all would reject the word, and perish for ever. God does no wrong to such that refuse Christ, though he manifesteth peculiar love, to such that truly believe on him; thus by their receiving peculiar grace they become a peculiar people; such as is the cause, is the effect; the effects cannot exceed the cause; the bare preaching the word is not the cause of men's believing, but it lies in the agency of the Holy Ghost; and if the cause of light, grace, and regeneration lay in the power of man's will, or in the power of him that hears the word, then the will and power of man would be more noble and excellent than the new creature, which is but the effects thereof.

There is a common faith, a temporary faith, and a faith that is precious, and special, and only peculiar to God's elect, this cannot be denied, unless men will contradict the Holy Ghost. "Paul, a servant of God, and an apostle of Jesus Christ, according to the faith of God's elect," Tit. i. 1.

"To them that have obtained like precious faith with us, through the righteousness of God and our Saviour," 2 Pet. i. 1.

Observe, this precious faith is given according to the righteousness of God; that is, according to his justice, truth, and righteousness, in performing his promise to Jesus Christ, in behalf of his elect in the covenant of grace and redemption; or else through Christ's righteousness, his obedience, death, and merits, who purchased it for them; it is true in both respects: special faith hath special operations, and they are called the operations of God, and they are peculiar operations to his elect.

VI. They are a peculiar people, by virtue of that peculiar and vital union they have with Jesus Christ; like as a virgin of low degree, by marrying a king, is brought or raised to peculiar grandeur, honour, and greatness; so are sinners that are united and espoused to Christ, raised to special and peculiar dignity, and spiritual grandeur.

VII. It is by the indwelling of the Holy Spirit; the Holy Ghost hath taken up his habitation in these men's hearts, they are his temple, the Father dwells in them, and the Son dwells in them through the Spirit, or by the Spirit; and they walk with God, converse with God, and have communion with the Father, and the Son, and Holy Spirit, and thus they become a peculiar people.

Secondly, Why are the saints compared to wheat? I told you, wheat is the product of a rare and choice seed. So are they the fruit and product of choice love; electing love is choice love; redeeming love is choice love; espousing love is a choice love; but all this may be said of every true believer: and they are also the product of the Holy Ghost: the seed that forms the new creature is the Holy Spirit. *Why the saints are compared to wheat.*

2. The seed of wheat must be first sown in the earth, before it can produce increase; so must the seed of grace be first sown in men's hearts, before they can bear God's image, or bring forth the fruits of holiness unto his praise and glory.

3. Wheat is a profitable sort of grain, to that land where there is plenty of it.

" So the saints and people of God, are a profitable people unto the world; they are the interest of those nations, cities, and places where they dwell; thus was Joseph profitable to Potiphar, everything was blessed which he had for Joseph's sake," Gen. xxxix. 5. So was Laban blessed for Jacob's sake. " The lips of the righteous feed many," Prov. x. 21; " as poor," saith Paul, " yet making many rich; as having nothing, yet possessing all things," 2 Cor. vi. 19. Sodom was safe whilst Lot was in it; " except the Lord of hosts had left unto us a very small remnant, we should have been as Sodom, and should have been like unto Gomorrah," Isa. i. 9.

Happy is that land, that has in it abundance of choice wheat; but much more happy is that land, or kingdom, that hath abundance of choice Christians, or Christ's spiritual wheat in it.

4. Wheat will abide, endeavour and live in the sharpest winter, when some other grain will not. So true believers do abide, endeavour and live in the times of sharpest trials, persecutions, tribulations, and temptations.

" Because I live, ye shall live also; they shall not know when drought comes, neither cease from yielding fruit," John xiv. 19. Cold nor heat injures wheat, but it thrives the better, so spiritual cold nor heat hurts true believers; but as their tribulations abound, their consolations abound also; they being ordained to bring forth fruit, and that their fruit should remain," John xv. 16.

5. Wheat seems sometimes as if it were quite dead; you can in winter hardly see one green blade; so the saints seem sometimes to themselves as if they were almost dead, " I have been afflicted, and ready to die, from my youth up," saith Heman, Psal. lxxxviii. 15. " My hope," saith Job, " is perished;" but though they seem as dead bones, and cry we are dead, yet they have life in their roots.

6. Wheat is sometimes, by reason of unseasonable weather in the spring, very sickly, the colour being changed; so in like manner by reason of Satan's temptations, and the corruptions of their hearts, and evils of the times, poor believers are very sickly and weak, and their countenance is changed.

7. Yet when the sun shines sweetly upon wheat, and God sends dry and seasonable weather, it wonderfully on a sudden revives, (as I have often observed with my own eyes). So when the Sun of Righteousness shines sweetly on believers, they on a sudden revive: " they shall revive as the corn," Hos. xiv. 7. *revive:*

8. Wheat needs weeding; and if it be not, it will soon be grown over with weeds, thistles, nettles, &c. Therefore the diligent husbandman takes care upon that account, though slothful persons too much neglect their fields; so the hearts of believers must be daily weeded, lest the seed of grace be choked, and the weeds of corruption cover their souls, as you heard concerning the thorny ground. "The cares of this world, and the deceitfulness of riches, choke the word, and it becometh unfruitful," Matt. xiii. 22.

Some Christians are too much like the man Solomon speaks of, " I went by the field of the slothful, and by the vineyard of the man void of understanding; And lo, it was all grown over with thorns, and nettles had covered the face thereof, &c. Then I saw and considered it well, I looked upon it, and received instruction," Prov. xxiv. 30, 31. *See the parable of the sower.*

9. Full ears of wheat hang down their heads, being full of corn; so sincere believers are humble, and lowly-minded; they are poor in spirit, being little, nay, nothing in their own eyes: how humble was Abraham? " I that am but dust and ashes," &c. And David,

who cries out, I am a worm and not man.   And Agur, "Surely I am more brutish than any man, and have not the knowledge of a man.   I neither learned wisdom, nor have the knowledge of the holy," Prov. xxx. 2, 3.   And also Job, "I abhor myself," Job xlii. 6. Isaiah cries, "Wo is me, for I am undone; for I am a man of unclean lips," &c. Isa. vi. 5.   Paul also saith, he was "less than the least of all saints," Eph. iii. 8.   That soul that is humble, and nothing in himself, is full of grace.   "I know thy poverty, but thou art rich," Rev. ii. 9.

But proud and haughty professors, are like empty ears of corn, that hold up their heads; they are light, and of a lofty spirit, thinking none more wise and knowing as themselves.

10.   Wheat is not ripe presently, but must have time to grow to maturity, and receive the former and latter rain, before it is fit for the sickle.

So believers are not come to full growth in grace, as to degrees, as soon as they are born again; no, that child would seem a monster, that in a week's time after it is born should grow to the stature of a man; a full assurance is not had presently, nor without time, and much diligence, and such must receive the latter, as well as the former rain of the Spirit; though some are ripe for heaven sooner than others.

11.   Tares oft-times are found to grow amongst wheat, which tends greatly to mar its beauty.   So in the churches of the saints are often found wicked persons, by which means the beauty of those congregations are much marred; and the ungodly of the world vilify and reproach them, as if they were all such; therefore as soon as they are discovered, they are cast out of the church, as the incestuous person was, 1 Cor. v. 1—5.

12.   Wheat, when it is fully ripe, is gathered into the barn; so when Christ sees a believer is ripe for heaven, he gathers it as a flock of corn fully ripe.

13.   Sometimes a harvest seems much in bulk, but there is but a little corn.   So the spiritual harvest may seem much in bulk, a mighty appearance of a great harvest; but there may be but a few sincere believers amongst them.

14.   Wheat dies first, before it rises; "Thou fool, that which thou sowest is not quickened, except it die."   Wheat seems to rot and die before it rises, so the bodies of believers must die, and lie under the clods of the earth, before they are raised at the last day.   But remember, it is the same corn of wheat, the same grain that is sown, that rises again; it is the same I say, as to the matter or substance of it; (though like a grain of wheat, it is not the same as to its beauty and glory) but if it were not the same body, it could not be a resurrection, but a new creation; and then shall not that body that glorified God here be raised to glory; nor the same body of the wicked that sinned be punished, but an innocent body.   And by the same reason it may be denied, it was the same body of Christ that suffered for our sins, that was raised from the dead, and so all our hopes of being saved must perish for ever.

APPLICATION

1.   We infer, that the world is strangely deceived, who look upon believers, or the people of God, as a base and contemptible company, even as the refuses of all things; whereas they are, as you have heard, the most honourable; none so excellent, choice, and precious in all the earth, as they are.

2.   We refer the excellency of divine grace; all men, my brethren, naturally are alike vile, sinful, and odious by sin; there is no difference; it is only that mighty work of the Spirit of God upon the souls of his elect, that makes them so glorious, amiable, and precious in the sight of God; and that our chief comeliness is that which we have in Christ, by having his comeliness, his righteousness put upon us; by which means Christ calls, "His spouse, his love, his dove, his undefiled," Cant. v. 2, 4, 7, and saith, there is no spot in her; "Thy renown went forth among the heathen for thy beauty.   For it was perfect through my comeliness which I put upon thee, saith the Lord," Ezek. xvi. 14.

3.   This should teach all true believers to admire the special and distinguishing love and grace of God to them in Jesus Christ, and to see they lie low at his foot, and ascribe all the glory and praise to him alone.

4.   Moreover, what reproof may this be to the ungodly, who hate the saints, because of that grace and holiness that is in them, and strive to tread them under their feet; alas, it God that is in them, Christ that is in them, which they hate; for as they are men they hate them not, but because they are such men that cannot run to the same excess with them, cannot worship with them, nor have fellowship with them; "They being not of the world, but because Christ hath called them out of the world, therefore the world hateth them."

5. The saints also may learn from hence, to strive to be a choice people, a holy people, a peculiar people, above all other people in the world. Let it appear, my brethren, that we are the product of a choice seed, the offspring of God, such that are born of God, that are the chosen of God, the delight of God, or the wheat of Jesus Christ; the best wheat, not lean wheat, not smutty wheat, some wheat is smutty ; it is black, and needs washing, and so indeed do many of the saints of God, they are not white wheat, but contrarywise, have much filth cleaving to them, many spots, blemishes, and infirmities. Such ought to labour after the sanctification of the Spirit, and mortification of sin; "And to hate the garment spotted by the flesh," Jude 23 ; and get their hearts, their consciences and their lives cleansed by the Spirit, and by faith in the blood of Christ ; " Let us cleanse ourselves from all filthiness of the flesh and spirit, perfecting holiness in the fear of God," 2 Cor. vii. 1.

6. Moreover, by what you have heard, you may try yourselves, and see whether you are the choice, the holy and beloved ones of God, or not ; such that are like wheat, you may go for such, and think yourselves to be such, and yet be mistaken, and not be such ; some are taken to be as wheat, who may be but tares, or chaff in God's sight.

(1.) Are your hearts and lives holy ? Do you differ from others ? Who hath made thee to differ from another ? As there is some wheat better, more fine than others ; so there are some of the saints, who in grace, holiness, and spiritual gifts, excel others ; yet all far excel all unrenewed sinners, both in heart, in principles, and in conversation, and in the end of their conversations also.

(2.) Are you humble, lowly-minded, full of grace, seeing your own nothingness ; and like a full ear of wheat, do you hang down your head in the sense of that inward corruption and filth of your own hearts ?

(3.) Are you profitable to all you converse with ? Do others receive spiritual benefit by you ?

(4.) Do you endure temptations, and thrive under sore trials, and flourish like wheat in a time of drought ?

(5.) Do you love God and Jesus Christ, with your chiefest love and affections, and all that are his members, all that are born of him ? Then no doubt but you are wheat in his sight ?

II

Another parable he put forth unto them, saying, the kingdom of heaven is likened unto a man that sowed good seed in his field, &c.—Matt. xiii. 24, 25. &c.

WE have prosecuted one point of doctrine, from one principal part of this parable, viz. That believers are a choice grain, they are wheat ; the product of precious seed, &c.

I shall now proceed to another point of doctrine.

Doct. 2. The ungodly are a base sort of people ; low and contemptible, tares, good for nothing. The ungodly a base sort of people.

1. That the wicked are a base, low, and a sordid sort of people, appears by the names that are given to them in God's Word ; they are called sons of Belial, unprofitable, or without yoke, rude or untameable.

2. They are called the children of the wicked one.

3. Children of darkness, and children of this world.

4. Infidels, people without faith ; every one that believes not savingly in Christ, is an infidel, though not an infidel in the grossest sense ; he may own a deity.

5. They are the children of the devil ; " In this are manifested the children of God, and the children of the devil," 1 John iii. 10; as the saints are a renowned, an honourable people, by being called the children of God, so the wicked are a sordid, a base and contemptible people, by being called the children of the devil. What adds greater glory to the one, or greater shame and contempt unto the other ?

6. They are " called children of fools, yea, children of base men," Job. xxx. 8. The Hebrew word, as Caryl notes, signifies a man fallen, or failing and withered in his understanding. A fool wants filling, or furniture for his mind ; he is like bare walls, or an empty house. They are children of Nabal, (saith he) a son of Nabal, is of the same signification in holy language, with a son of Belial ; disobedient, rebellious ones, who will not

endure the yoke ; or foolish ones, as having little wit to choose their way, so they make as little conscience of their way ; but as he observes by an Hebrewism, it doth not refer to their parents, as to themselves, base men, as Mr. Broughton renders it, or the most ig- nominious among men ; they are men without honour, who understand not, and so are like the beasts that perisheth.

7.   They are frequently called rebels against God, and haters of God ; " The haters of the Lord should have submitted themselves," Psal. lxxxi. 15. Can a more odious name be given to men, than to be called haters of God ?

8.   They are called devils ; " Have not I chosen you twelve, and one of you is a devil ?" John vi. 70. " The devil shall cast some of you into prison," &c., certainly he means wicked men influenced by the devil.

9.   How often are they compared to brutes ; nay, to the most contemptible of brutish creatures.   They are called dogs, swine, &c. " Cast not your pearls before swine ;" " be- ware of dogs," Mark vii. 6.   Phil. iii. 2.

10.   They are called tares, because it imitates the wheat, and groweth up with it, as if it were the same kind with the wheat ; it should not, saith one, be translated tares, Leigh's crit. but evil seed ; it is that which we call the deaf ears, which grow up with the Sacr. wheat, and cannot be discerned till harvest, and then it appears nought ; for those we call tares, or fitches, are soon discerned, and plucked up ; nor are fitches so con- temptible, being good food for cattle.   Therefore that seed called tares among us, cannot be the tares our Saviour alludes to.

Now since wicked men, particularly hypocrites, who strive to imitate the saints of God, are called tares, or evil seed, it shows they are of no worth, of no value, but hateful in the sight of God.

And though those tares are so much like wheat, whilst in the blade, that they cannot, as Mr. Wilson observes, be discerned ; yet when the harvest comes, they will appear vile and contemptible.

Wicked men   2. The ungodly are a vile, low, and sordid sort of people, doth appear. 1. the seed ¦and In that they are the offspring of the devil, the seed of Satan ; as they are men offspring of the devil. and women, it is true, they are from God, or his workmanship ; but as they are wicked and ungodly, they are from the devil, " Ye are," saith our Lord, " of your father the devil, and the lusts of your father ye will do," John viii. 44 ; hence Cain is said to be of the wicked one, 1 John iii. 12.

He that committeth sin, is of the devil ; not every one that sins, for there is not a just man on earth, that doth good, and sinneth not ; but he that sinneth with full purpose and consent of his will ; or that liveth in a course, trade, or custom of sinning, he is of the devil ; let him be whosoever he will, though he be a king, or one of the greatest poten- tates of the world, and boast never so much of the nobleness of his descent, blood, and family, he is for all that of the devil.   O how may this tend to lower the top-sails of the haughty monarchs of the earth ! Believers (you heard the last day) are the seed of God ; but all wicked men are the seed and offspring of the devil ; they are begotten of him, proceed as it were from his cursed loins.

Wicked men   II. Ungodly persons are a base, a sordid, and contemptible people, appears of a base, from that low, that base, worldly, and earthly spirit they are of ; the apostle and low, earthly spi- gives them their character, " Whose end is destruction, whose God is their rit. bellies, and whose glory is in their shame, who mind earthly things," Phil. iii. 19.   That is, they mind earthly things more than those things that are above ; value their earthly riches, their sinful pleasures, and carnal honours, above God, or Jesus Christ ; nay, preferred their base, sordid, and vile lusts, above all that good which is in the blessed God, or in Jesus Christ. Doth not this show what a poor, base, and con- temptible spirit they are of ?

III. But not only from hence do they appear of a base and sordid spirit, but much more in that they are so much like the devil himself in sensuality and earthly-mindedness ; Wicked men   they show they are like mere animals ; but by their pride, cruelty, malice, are like the envy and hatred of the saints, they show themselves to be mere incarnate devil. devils, or devils in the shape of men ; they have his very image upon them, as they proceed from him ; is the devil an enemy to God, to Christ, to the saints, and to holiness and virtue ?   So are wicked men.   Do devils sin freely, with full purpose, and cannot but sin ? So do wicked men : Do devils do what they can to encourage vice, and all profaneness, and by one means or another strive to hinder or suppress real godliness ?

This is also the great design and endeavour of some wicked men; is the devil so malicious an enemy against the godly, that God seeth it necessary to restrain or chain him up.

The like he seeth in ungodly men, and therefore he restrains them also ; for as the devil is boundless in his rage and malice to mankind, so are many of his emissaries against their fellow creatures.

Doth the devil prompt and tempt men to sin, to make them if he could as vile as himself? So do wicked men entice, tempt, or draw others to sin, and to commit all acts of abomination also. Is the devil swelled with pride ? So are wicked men. Is the devil an accuser of the brethren ? Why, wicked men are in that like unto him. Also thus as wicked men have Satan's name given to them, so they have his hellish nature also in them, and therefore are a base, vile, and contemptible people.

Note also, that pride, malice and envy, are diabolical evils ; and the more proud or malicious, the more like the devil is any man or woman.

IV. Ungodly men are a low, base, and sordid people, if we observe what food they eat or live upon ; princes and noble ones of the earth fare high, they eat the fat, and drink the sweet ; they have all varieties of delicious food ; but the baser sort, such that are ignoble, poor, and contemptible, feed on mere trash, on roots, or mean diet ; even so the saints being noble and high-born souls, kings children, princes, or the most honourable of the earth, you heard they feed on choice food, heavenly food ; they eat at the king's table ; they " eat that which is good, and their souls delight themselves in fatness," Isa. lv. 2.

But the wicked feed on husks, which the swine eat, with which (like the Prodigal) they would fain fill their bellies ; nay, they are said to feed on ashes, and on the wind ; by husks are meant the riches, honours, and sinful pleasures of this world, which can never satisfy the immortal soul of man. *See the parable of the Prodigal Son.*

By feeding on the wind, is meant false doctrine, errors, and airy notions ; and hence it is that this sort are puffed up like bladders with pride and vain-glory, Hos. xii. 1.

V. This further appears by the poor and vile clothing they wear ; noble persons are known by their rich apparel, their excellent robes, and by being decked with jewels, pearls, and precious stones ; if you see a person in cloth of gold, and a crown on his head, you presently say he is a king. Thus the saints, you heard, are in a spiritual manner clothed and adorned. *Ezek. xvi. 12, 13, Psal. xlv. 9, 13.*

But the wicked are clothed with nothing but filthy rags, Isa. lxiv. 6, even the best of them, who live a moral sober life ; for if a believer's own inherent righteousness is in comparison of the righteousness of Christ, but as filthy rags, or filthy garments ; Zech. iii. 5 ; what sordid rags are they that wicked men have on, even the best and most reformed of them ? And as for the rest they are quite naked, and their shame appears to all, and therefore they are a poor, low, wretched, base, and sordid sort of people, and so may well be compared to tares, Rev. iii. 17.

VI. It appears also by the company they keep ; wicked men delight in the baser sort, they cannot tell how to behave themselves amongst such that are born from above ; no, no company pleaseth them but such who have the same swinish and brutish nature, who like a sow love to swallow in the mire and filth and horrid pollution, 2 Tim. ii. 2.

VII. In respect of those filthy and loathsome sores they have on them, they appear a base, a hateful, and sordid sort of people ; they have nothing from the soles of their feet unto their head but wounds, and bruises, and putrifying sores, as well as they are covered with nothing but loathsome rags, Isa. i. 6.

VIII. They are a low, base, and a sordid sort of people, doth also appear in respect of their end, to which they are appointed ; tares are for the fire ; when harvest comes, then the wheat shall be gathered into Christ's garner, and the tares shall be bound up into bundles, and thrown into the fire, and they shall be burned, being good for nothing but to make fuel of ; hence also they are compared to thorns and briars fully dry, which were not created of God, but are the fruit of the curse, Isa. xxvii. 4, Gen. iii. 12.

APPLICATION

1. We may infer from hence, that God doth lay the wicked under the highest contempt.

2. How blind are all ungodly persons ! In a spiritual sense they only see with fleshly eyes, and behold things that are visible and temporal ; but they cannot discern any beauty in spiritual things and objects, because they are spiritually discerned. Moreover, they cannot taste how good God is, they favour not, relish not, heavenly food ; no, nor is it possible they should, unless they had a heavenly nature ; for it is the new man, the new creature, or such that are born of God, who know how gracious and good God is.

3. We infer that sin hath made a fearful change on mankind, and strangely altered his first glorious constitution, marred and spoiled his beauty; how glorious was he when he came out of God's hands! He was made but a little lower than the holy angels; but by sin he is become almost as black and odious as devils.

4. From hence also we may infer, that " a wicked man is loathsome," Prov. xiii. 5, as Solomon saith; and well may the Holy Ghost say, that sinners naturally were cast forth in their blood and filth, " to the loathing of their persons," Ezek. xvi. 5.

5. Moreover from hence we may see the cause why God values them no more. They are of little worth to him, and therefore he hath, for the sake of his own people, his beloved ones, given whole nations of these sordid wretches to the sword, and valued them not, but trod them under his feet as dirt and filth: " I gave Egypt for thy ransom, Ethiopia and Seba for thee; since thou wast precious in my sight, thou hast been honourable, and I have loved thee," Isa. xliii. 4. Well, and what then? " Therefore will I give men for thee, and people for thy life;" and from hence also it is said, he reproved kings for their sakes; " When they went from one nation to another, from one kingdom to another, he suffered no man to do them wrong; yea, he reproveth kings for their sakes: saying, touch not mine anointed, and do my prophets no harm," Psal. cv. 13—15.

The haughty kings of the earth are as filth, or hateful persons in Christ's sight; and he therefore " will come on these princes as upon mortar, and as the potter treadeth the clay," Isa. xli. 25; they shall know that he abhorreth them, and will take vengeance upon them, for all the wrong they have done to his saints and beloved ones, who are as precious to him as the apple of his eye.

6. From hence also we infer, that grace is of a transcendent nature; what a change doth it make in one of these odious, loathsome creatures? O when God gives his Spirit, infuseth grace into the heart of a vile sinner, what a wonderful change doth it produce in such a one! It makes the vile honourable, the deformed beautiful, and the swinish nature a lamb-like nature; the churl liberal, the proud humble, the malicious pitiful; in a word, it turneth the diabolical nature into a God-like and a Christ-like nature and disposition.

7. Let sinners therefore from hence learn to lothe themselves, and attend upon the word of God. O look to Christ! Cry to him that he would work a blessed change in you, that you may find the effects of the blood of Jesus, and the nature of true faith upon your hearts; that though now you are base and filthy creatures in God's sight, being polluted with sin, and in many things resemble the devil, you may find a blessed change, and become beautiful and glorious in God's sight.

8. We also infer from hence, that there is just cause for sinners, when God opens their eyes, to lothe themselves, " Ye shall lothe yourselves in your own sight, for all your evils that ye have committed," &c., Ezek. xx. 43. Grace makes a believer ashamed of his former state, and abominable filthiness, " That thou mayest remember and be confounded, and never open thy mouth any more because of thy shame, when I am pacified towards thee for all that thou hast done, saith the Lord," Ezek. xvi. 63.

Lastly, you that are Christ's wheat, the product of his good seed; or who are believers, praise God and admire his free grace, who hath wrought such a blessed change in your souls who were once as vile, as filthy, and as abominable as others; but now ye are washed, justified, and sanctified, O let God have all the glory! It is he alone that has made the difference, and let it appear you are a choice and precious people; and labour to live to the glorifying of his grace, who hath called you. I shall now proceed to another point of doctrine, 1 Cor. vi. 11.

Doct. The blessed God would have the wheat and tares, i. e., the godly and the wicked, grow together in the field of this world, and both to ripen for the harvest; i. e., the end thereof.

1. He would have his own people abide in the world, though they meet with many sorrows, afflictions, trials, and bad usage whilst they are here, by reason of sin, Satan, and the ungodly that dwell therein, " I pray not that thou shouldst take them out of the world, but that thou wouldst keep them from the evil," John xvii. 15. Our Lord doth not mean afflictive evil, or the evil of afflictions, (unless it be such afflictions that are penal, or in a way of wrath, and divine justice, which none of the godly shall ever meet with; because our blessed Saviour hath born all penal evil, or vindictive wrath, for them) it is therefore the evil of sin; such sin that would or might be ruinous to their souls, he prayed we might be kept from such evil; for the Father heard our Lord always, therefore he granted what he asked of him here.

Quest. But why would he not have his wheat, his saints taken out of the world?

1. He doth not mean that he would have them live in this world always ; no, but so long, even until they are ripe for heaven; wheat is not ripe presently. Believers shall abide here, until they are actually fit and prepared for God's garner above.

Why God would not have his people be taken out of the world.

2, Because they are in some sense the " light of this dark world," Matt. v. 14. Should all the saints be taken out of the world, what a dark world would this be ? Moreover, they are the salt of the earth, ver. 13 ; this world would stink in the nostrils of God, were it not for the saints that are in it, who like salt in some sense preserve it from putrefaction.

See the saints the light of the world, and the salt of the earth.

3. Because they have much work to do for God's glory, and for the good and benefit of mankind in their several generations, whilst this world shall continue.

The saints, especially the ministers of the gospel, are God's witnesses, who stand up for him, witness to his truth, his holiness, justice, mercy, love, faithfulness, &c., to the establishing and comfort of the elect and to the condemnation of the wicked, and the aggravation of their sins.

Quest. But why would God have the tares also to grow in the field of this world, and not rooted out of it ?

Answ. 1. He would not have his church and people to root them out, (were it in their power) for the reason he gives, i. e., lest they root out some of this wheat with them, which I have spoken unto already.

Why God would have the tares not rooted out of the world.

2. God himself will not destroy them, or root them all out of the world presently ; because their sins, like those of the Amorites, may not be yet full, or they may not be fully ripe for the harvest.

3. That God may show his patience, long-suffering, and forbearance towards them, as the apostle shows.

Rom. ii. 4, 5. Rom. ix. 22. 2 Pet. iii. 9.

4. Perhaps some of God's elect may be amongst them, or at least some of their offspring may be such ; for the election of grace runs to many persons, who are the children of ungodly parents ; or such that are here called tares ; an hypocrite, or an abominable wretch, may have a godly child ; the stock therefore must live until the fruit be brought forth ; but no more as to this. Moreover, we may note from the answer given to the servants, (who would pull up the tares).

Doct. That some of the tares are much like the wheat ; or do in some things especially, whilst in the blade, resemble the saints, being not discovered till harvest.

This shows, that by the tares, hypocrites are rather meant than profane persons, who show their sin, as Sodom, and hide it not.

I shall hint a few things to this observation.

1. Hypocrites may own the true doctrine of the gospel, and make a profession of religion, and be taken for saints by the godly, as is showed in the parable of the wise and foolish virgins.

2. They may be under the common illuminations of the Spirit, and partake of the gifts thereof, as is showed by the apostle, Heb. vi. 4, 5, 6.

3. They may be found in the discharge or performance of all external duties of religion ; and particularly they may pray often ; for thus the Pharisees did ; " I pray twice a day," &c.

But having in two parables showed largely how far a hypocrite may go, (and how much he may resemble a true Christian) I shall say no more to it here.

See parable of the sower, and of the Virgins.

III

*Wilt thou then that we go and gather them up ? but he said, nay, lest while you gather up the tares, ye root up also the wheat with them. Let both grow together until harvest.—*Matt. xiii. 28—30.

I HAVE spoken already to one or two points of doctrine, showing both the nature of the wheat and tares.

Doct. 6. We again observe, that the remissness of Christ's ministers and churches, in not watching against Satan and evil men, is of a bad and dangerous nature.

The danger of ministers' remissness or sleeping.

While men slept, the devil sowed his evil seed ; that is through the negligence, slothfulness, or remissness of Christ's ministers and his people ; Satan by his vile in-. struments sowed the seed of errors and heresy in the church, or rather in the field of the world ; from whence many evil men sprang up, to the hurt and prejudice of God's people.

And this evidently appeared in the succeeding ages, next the apostles' time ; O what evil men ! Yea, cursed wolves rose, as St. Paul told the elders of the church at Ephesus there would, " For I know this, that after my departing, shall grievous wolves enter in among you, not sparing the flock," Acts. xx. 29.

1 Tim. i. 20.   What evil men were Hymeneæus, Alexander, Nicolatains, Hermogenes,
2 Tim. i. 15.   and after them Arius and his followers, who denied the God-head of our blessed Saviour ; and multitudes more of cursed heretics also sprang up, which doubtless was through the carelessness of some of Christ's servants, and all chiefly through the malice of Satan, that enemy of God, and of the souls of men, and to show his cruel hatred to our Lord Jesus Christ, and to the doctrine of the gospel, yet no doubt but those wars that rose in the church about the Arian heresies, is condemned, by our Lord in this parable ; it may be feared, some wheat might be plucked up in those times among the tares, by the slaughter of such a multitude.

USE

This may caution all ministers of Christ, and churches, to take heed they sleep not, but watch, and take heed least evil seed be sown amongst them, I mean the seed of error and heresy ; or such doctrine that tends to licentiousness, or to corrupt the doctrine of God's free grace. For,

1. Many may under fair pretences of exalting Christ, sow pernicious and poisonous seed ; and others under a colour of promoting holiness and sanctification, have corrupted the doctrine of free justification by Christ's righteousness alone.

2. By way of council, beware of such men who are lifted up with pride, who to magnify themselves, seem to despise others, perhaps more worthy than themselves.

3. Beware of such that effect novelty, and strive to promote new notions in matters of religion, and all to have themselves admired by the multitude, and unthinking persons.

4. Likewise have a watchful eye, of such that cry up this and that man, and cry down others ; lest the evil seed of the enemy spring up, and prove ruinous to their own and other men's souls ; also lest they prove tares.

5. Moreover. watch such who are subject to wander from their own fold and pasture ; and such also that are ready, on every small occasion, to take offence, and quarrel with their brethren, or to neglect to assemble themselves with the church, Heb. x. 25 ; also such that seem earthly, cold, or lukewarm in the things of God. But I shall add no more to this.

Let both grow together until harvest.

Doct. 7. From hence I note, That both the wheat and the tares, true believers and hypocrites, saints and sinners, do ripen for the harvest.

1. I shall show you how the wheat, or sincere Christians, ripen for the harvest,

2. Also how the tares, or evil men, do ripen also.

I. As Wheat after it is sown hath its ripening time. So have the saints and people of How the   God.
wheat ri-   (1.) They are first rooted in Christ, by virtue of a vital union with him.
pens for the   (2.) Then they spring up.
harvest.   (3.) They ear as it were, and appear full of grace and divine virtue.

(4.) Then afterwards they come to full maturity.

II. Wheat ripens gradually, that it is hardly discerned : so the godly ripen gradually also, it is hardly discerned by themselves or others. He that most complains for want of growth, may be the most growing Christian ; for there is a growing downward in humility.

III. Wheat must have showers to ripen it. So must the saints have the showers of divine or heavenly doctrine, or spiritual dew to ripen them ; one minister by his doctrine planteth, his gift chiefly lieth that way : another he watereth, his doctrine tends most to establishment, growth, or to edification of the saints, and to their comfort and consolation.

" I have planted, and Apollos hath watered," 1 Cor. iii. 6.

I have gathered you to Christ, (as if Paul should say) and Apollos hath built you up, and confirmed you in Christ, with sound and edifying doctrine ; " But God gave the increase," 1 Cor. iii. 7, the new heart ; and all increase of grace is from God ; it is he that blesseth the word and ordinances ; the word of God is the rain, and it comes with power, and is set home upon the soul by the Holy Spirit, there is a divine growth.

Rain is much desired in a time of drought, and much prayed for, and it is a great judgment to have it withheld. So the divine rain of heavenly doctrine is greatly desired by all sincere Christians; " I opened my mouth and panted, for I longed for thy commandments," Psal. cxix, 131; moreover, there cannot be a worse judgment than for God to withhold or take away his word and ordinances from a people ; or to have the word, and yet the soul cannot receive it, or take it in, but like rain that falls on a rock it slides away; this argues the heart is hard ; in time of drought the husbandman cries, O Lord, send rain ! O send a soaking shower to soften the earth ! And to cause the corn to grow and flourish, even so should we cry, when the spiritual rain is withheld from us, Heb. vi. 7, 8.

IV. Moreover, believers grow and ripen for the harvest, by means of the shining and sweet fructifying influences of " the Sun of righteousness," Mal. iv. 2 ; if Christ is withdrawn, or shines not upon our souls, we grow not, flourish not in grace and holiness, but droop, and seem to wither or decay in our souls ; it is Christ that quickens, enlivens, and ripeneth us for harvest ; and such who have most of the influences of the Spirit ripen most ; they flourish while others decay ; " it is from me that all thy fruit is found," Hos. xiv. 8.

V. Some Christians are like wheat smitten or blasted, in respect of their hope, peace, joy, &c., and so seem to languish ; we find God of old smote some with a mildew, Amos iv. 9. O let us fear nothing more than this ! Also some sow sparingly, and so shall reap sparingly, whilst others shall reap plentifully, 2 Cor. ix. 6. " Look to yourselves, that we lose not those things which we have wrought, but that we receive a full reward," 2 John viii. Ministers may fail of a full crop : and members fail of a full crop also.

Quest. What should a believer do to ripen for the harvest ?

Ans. 1. Improve all opportunities, all seasons of grace ; consider well the worth of them ; also how short and uncertain they may be ; some that ripen not, thrive not, neglect gracious seasons and opportunities, or are very careless and negligent in the matter ; they prefer the world above the word.

What believers should do to ripen for harvest.

2. Observe well and cherish all those convictions of your consciences, and of the Holy Spirit, either in respect of sin or duty, lest ye sin them away.

3. Improve all the dispensations and providences of God, or those various trials, afflictions, and temptations you meet with ; the rod feeds as well as the word ; the godly are " like the palm-tree," Psal. xcii. 12, which thrives the more by the weights hanged upon it ; or like camomile, the more it is trod upon, the more it grows and flourishes, Jer. x. 5.

4. Live much in the sense and thoughts of death, and of the judgment day ; O think much of the harvest, i. e., the end of the world ! Deut. xxxii. 29. That will quicken thee to duty, and tend to make thee more serious and diligent in the whole course of thy life.

5. See that you gather day by day, get more strength against sin, and the corruptions of your own hearts, and mortify these inordinate lusts, and give not way to a carnal and worldly frame of heart, Rom. viii. 13 ; " But live in the Spirit, and walk in the Spirit," Gal. v. 16, being spiritually-minded ; these thrive and ripen apace for the harvest : " Abstain from all fleshly lusts that war against the soul ! " 1 Pet. ii. 11.

6. Labour to " add to your faith virtue," &c., 2 Pet. i. 5, 6, 7, to grow in faith, get stronger and more stedfast faith in Jesus Christ ; and grow in love to God, to Christ, and to his saints ; and not only in faith and love, but in humility and patience also ; how did those saints, St. Paul speaks of ripen ? " Your faith groweth exceedingly, and the charity of every one of you towards each other aboundeth." So that we glory in you in the churches of God, for your patience and faith in all your persecutions and tribulations that you endure," 2 Thes. i. 3. This is, my brethren, the glory of Christians ; that they grow in all the graces of the Spirit, and in experience, in holiness, and heavenly-mindedness.

7. The way to ripen for heaven, is to strive against all those things that hinder or obstruct your growth, as thorns and briars ; i. e., the cares of this world, and the deceitfulness of riches, Mat. xiii. 22; we must also labour against spiritual drowsiness, sleepiness, and idleness, in God's service, and against all things whatsoever that tends to hinder our communion with God and Jesus Christ : it is a sign a Christian ripens for glory, when he cannot be satisfied if the face of God be hid, or hath lost sight of it ; they will also not withhold doing good while it is in the power of their hand ; some refuse doing good whilst they live, or leastwise so much good, pretending they purpose to do it at their death. O then, say they, the servants of Christ, the interest of Christ, and the poor saints, shall be remembered.

Alas, it is far better you do it now, for may be then they may not need it as they do now, or perhaps Satan will be too hard for you, and change your purpose before that time comes ; or others may (may be) deceive such to whom you intend to leave something ; " whatsoever thy hand finds to do, do it with thy might," Eccl. ix. 10 ; do it now ; do not defer it; present promises touching what a man, saith he, will do in time to come, seldom ends in real performances.

8. Labour in all things to keep a good conscience, both towards God, and towards man; this was the care of holy Paul, that so whether he was present or absent he might be accepted of God.

9. Labour for a full assurance of faith; when a man has attained to a full assurance he is ripe for heaven; but many may be ripe without this assurance.

Secondly, I shall show you how the tares, or the wicked, ripen for the harvest of sorrow and eternal burning.

Note by the way, as the godly ripen for the harvest of joy, so the wicked ripen for the harvest of sorrow; as the growth of the one is gradual, so also is the other.

How the tares ripen for harvest. (1.) Mercies not improved, but slighted and neglected, ripen the wicked apace for the harvest. God affords a plenteous time or season to gather in, and to lay up, or to provide for another world; but they neglect it, and trifle it away; they have sermon after sermon, but no word fastens upon their hearts; "the gospel comes to them in word only," 1 Thes. i. 5; perhaps they put the word away from them, as that which concerns them not; but may say when they have heard a sermon, there was a word for such a one, and such a one, but did not hear any word that concerned themselves, and so the word becomes to them "a savour of death unto death," 2 Cor. ii. 16,

(2.) When conscience is disregarded, men turning a deaf ear to those checks and sharp rebukes they find in their own breasts, this tends to ripen them for ruin; for as a man uses or deals with his own conscience, (which by light received from God's word reproves for sin) in the same manner he deals with the Holy God himself; for conscience acts, and speaks, and reproves by the command and authority of God. It is God's vicegerent in the soul, and this ungodly sinners shall know one day. Conscience is God's witness in man, and will at the great day come in against all ungodly persons, as being privy to all heart-evil, and all deeds of wickedness done in secret, Rom. ii. 15, 16.

See a poem called War with the devil.

(3.) When a man " being often reproved hardeneth his neck," Prov. xxix. 1, ministers, parents, good men, and his own conscience, often reproves him; and God by many sore providences and disappointments reproves him; but still he is hardened, and Pharaoh-like goes on in his former evil, and wicked courses; O this ripens such persons for the harvest wonderfully!

(4.) When the judgments of God instead of softening, harden the sinner; this was that which ripened Pharaoh and the Egyptians. God brings fearful symptoms of his wrath and displeasure upon this and that man, this and that nation, but they regard it not; may be just whilst the hand of God is upon them, they will cry out, and say, if the Lord pleaseth to spare them, they will amend their lives, &c. But no sooner hath the Lord done it, but they are as vile, as hypocritical, and as abominable as they were before; nay, perhaps worse, " Let favour be showed to the wicked, yet will he not learn righteousness: in the land of uprightness will he deal unjustly, and will not behold the majesty of God," Isa. xxvi. 10. And this made the prophet say, " Lord, when thy hand is lifted up, they will not see, &c., the goodness of God in his sparing mercy works no change in them; but that which should lead them to repentance hardens them in their sins.

" Or despisest thou the riches of his goodness, forbearance, and long-suffering, not knowing that the goodness of the Lord leadeth thee to repentance, but after thy hardness and impenitent heart, treasurest up wrath against the day of wrath, and the revelation of the righteous judgment of God," Rom. ii. 4, 5.

(5.) When the motions of the Spirit, in his common operations, Gen. vi. 3, are quenched; God strove with the old world, and so he strives with sinners now, but they resist the Holy Ghost; but yet he is pleased to exercise patience toward them; but at last he will pour forth his wrath, when they are fully ripe for cutting down; " What if God willing to show his wrath, and to make his power known, endure with much long-suffering, the vessels of wrath fitteth to destruction," Rom. ix. 22.

(6.) The tares or wicked men ripen for the harvest, by letting lusts conceive in them; they readily and freely suffer it to conceive, and then ruminate upon it, and are pleased with the thoughts thereof; either from the profit, or the pleasure and sweetness of it: the lusts of malice seem sweet to some men, as unclean thoughts are pleasant and sweet to others.

(7.) Another gradation or progressive motion to ripening sinners, is when lusts conceived, break forth into acts, or into the abominable commission thereof; " When lust is conceived it bringeth forth sin," &c. James i. 15.

(8.) A third step is, when sins, yea, great sins, are extenuated and rendered small; and little sins perhaps looked upon as no sin, or such that never offended their blind and misguided consciences.

(9.) When sin is delighted in, some men they take pleasure in wickedness, they love their cursed abominations. Sin is a sport unto them, they " drink it in, as the fish drinks water," Job xv. 16; sure such are near ripe for harvest.

(10.) When they are told of their sins, and hellish pollution, and they plead excuses as if the fault was not theirs : but like Adam, say, the woman thou gavest me, she gave me and I did eat : I was drawn in unawares to commit this and that sin; such or such enticed me into their company; sirs, this far from confessing their sins, is but the way to hide and cover them; and certainly this sort are near ripe also for ruin, or for cutting down.

(11.) Such men are certainly ripe for the harvest, who are found glorying in their sin and shame," Phil. iii. 19. Some gloried, how many virgins they have defiled : or, how many whores they have had : and still have others, how craftily they cheated such and such persons ; and others, how many robberies they have committed. Some also glory, how many silly fellows they have drunk down, (as they call it) O to what a degree of sin and wickedness are such beastly wretches arrived, who thus glory in their filthiness !

Lastly, a hardened heart, a seared conscience, final unbelief and impenitence follows, and so they come to be fully ripe for the harvest ; many do not only love all acts of wickedness, and glory in their shame, but draw in others, or are ring-leaders to all profaneness ; and also hate, reproach, and vilify all that are truly pious and religious ; now if any man hates any child of God, because of his likeness to God, or because of his religion and piety ; O to what a degree of wickedness are such grown ! But to close with this, pray take notice, that when neither the Word of God, nor the Rod of God, neither mercies, nor judgments, neither reproof from without, nor the checks of conscience from within, take any place to humble sinners, or leastwise to restrain them from their hellish practices ; but God hath left them to their own hearts' lust, and to walk in their own council; and he says to all reprovers, let them alone, who have hard and impenitent hearts ; these are every way ripe for the harvest.

APPLICATION

See here what different effects the gospel hath upon the children of men ; even as the sun hath in respect of his hot beams, i.e., if it shines upon wax, it softens that ; but if it shines upon the clay, it hardens that ; also it shines upon a garden, and causeth the herbs and flowers thereof to send forth a fragrant scent ; it shines upon a filthy dunghill; and what a loathsome and stink doth the same beams cause or produce ! So the gospel sun makes the hearts of believers soft and tender, but it tends (through sin and Satan's temtations) to make the hearts of some wicked men more hard ; the gospel is a savour of life unto life to some, and the savour of death to death to others ; some bless God for the word, and others blaspheme God and his servants who preach it.

1. We see as the sun that shines on the wheat ripens that; so the same sun shining on the tares ripens them.

2. We also may infer, that no evil is like unto the evil of sin, in respect to the horrid effects of it upon the minds of the children of men. And O what folly, madness, and ignorance is there in their hearts, considering what the effect of sin is which they so much love, and what the fruit of it will be in the end ! for when sin is finished it bringeth forth death.

3. From hence let me exhort sinners to ponder their way ; consider what we are a doing, and whether they are going ; O what will the end of these tares be ? " Where shall the sinner and ungodly appear ?" 1 Pet. iv. 18. Even where the wicked rich man appeared ; " in hell he lifted up his eyes, being in torment," Luke xvi. 23; some men's eyes will never be opened, until they are in eternal flames.

4. O let us try ourselves by what hath been said, and see whether we ripen for heaven or for hell !

5. By way of admiration, we may all stand and wonder at the patience, goodness, mercy, and long-suffering of God ; who lets the wicked alone so long before he cuts them down : you that are tares tremble, but let the saints and people of God rejoice, who are his choice grain, the wheat of Jesus Christ, for they shall not be taken out of this world, until they are ripe for heaven.

IV

Let both grow together until harvest— Matt. xiii. 30.

DOCT. THE harvest will come, which will be a discriminating day ; the wheat then shall be clearly discovered from the tares.

1. I shall show you how fitly the end of the world may be compared to harvest.

2. Show how then the wheat shall be known from the tares, or sincere believers from hypocrites.

Why the end of the world is compared to harvest.

1. The harvest is the time that the husbandman longs for, and hath much patience until it cometh.

So this spiritual or mystical harvest is the day which all the godly long for, and are exercised with patience under all their trials and afflictions until it comes.

2. When the harvest is fully ripe, then both the wheat and tares are severed one from another by the servants of the husbandman.

So all sincere Christians and hypocrites, shall, by the angels, be separated one from another at the end of the world.

3. When the harvest is fully ended, there is no more wheat nor tares growing, or to be found in the field.

So when this world is ended, there will be no people, either godly nor wicked, to be found to live as they do together, now in this world, any more for ever. For as the saints shall be received into God's glorious barn, so the wicked shall be cast into hell.

4. Harvest is a time of great joy to an industrious husbandman, but the sluggard meets then with great disappointment, and is perplexed with grief and sorrow.

So the end of the world will be the day of the saints' joy and gladness ; " everlasting joy shall be upon their heads ; they shall obtain joy and gladness, and sorrow and sighing shall fly away," Isa. xxxv. 10.   The joy of believers then shall far exceed the joy of harvest.

But the wicked and slothful person, who sowed to the flesh, whose heart, doctrine, and life, demonstrated they were tares, when the end of the world cometh, shall reap sorrow, shame, and confusion of face for evermore. " He that soweth to the flesh shall reap corruption, but he that soweth to the Spirit shall reap life everlasting," Gal. vi. 8.

Secondly, how shall the tares be known from the wheat, or hypocrites be discerned from sincere believers, at the end of the world ?

1.   The tares, or ungodly persons, shall then be known by their contemptible bodies ; for though the bodies of the wicked shall be raised immortal, to endure everlasting punishment ; yet their bodies shall not appear glorious, as the bodies of the saints shall ; for the saints' bodies shall be made " and fashioned like to Christ's glorious body," Phil. iii. 21.

And by that the one shall be clearly known from the other.

2.   The ungodly will (no doubt) be known by their company, the saints shall be attended by all the glorious angels ; but the wicked shall have no other retinue than their own condemned companions, viz., ungodly persons and devils ; such company men have chiefly loved and delighted in here, shall be their companions for ever in the world to come ; and by this men may know how it shall go with them in that day.

3.   The wicked will be known by their being naked, or perhaps by that which will be worse than being naked ; but the righteous shall be most gloriously clothed, even in wrought gold ; we cannot conceive how glorious their immortal robes will be in that day.

4.   The wicked will be known by their dismal cries and lamentation. " Behold, my servant shall sing for joy of heart, but ye shall cry for sorrow of heart, and shall howl for vexation of spirit," Isa. lxv. 14.   The consciences of the wicked will accuse, condemn, and terrify them, so that their lamentaion will be exceeding great.

5.   The ungodly will in that day be known from the saints, by that signal act of our Lord Jesus Christ.   " Before him shall be gathered all nations, and he shall separate them one from another as a shepherd divideth his sheep from the goats," Matt. xxv. 32.   This division and act of Jesus Christ will make a full discrimination.

6.   Moreover it will be known by the different placing of the one and the other ; and " he shall set the sheep on his right hand, the goats on the left ;" by these things the tares shall be known from the wheat, when the harvest comes, and the saints return from their graves ; which will make good that word of the prophet Malachi, " Then ye shall return,

and discern between the righteous and the wicked, between him that serveth God, and him that serveth him not," Mal. iii. 18.

Even in this parable our Saviour saith, that the "Son of man shall send forth his angels, and they shall gather out of his kingdom all things that offend, and them which do iniquity," verse 41. Like tares they shall be bound up in bundles, and shall cast them into a furnace of fire, there shall be wailing and gnashing of teeth. From this clause let me note.

Doct. That the wrath of God in hell, or the place of the damned, is like a furnace of fire; into which all ungodly men shall be cast after the judgment day is ended. *The woeful state of the tares or ungodly at the end of the world.*

What is more dismal, more terrifying, and more tormenting, than to be cast into a hot burning fiery furnace ? The torments of the wicked will be intolerable. See that similitude of the fan in Christ's hand, and the parable of the rich man and Lazarus ; "And then shall the righteous shine forth as the sun in the kingdom of their Father," verse 43.

1. We have here a description of the glorious state of believers, called the righteous ; they shall shine. *The happy state of the saints at the end of the world.*

2. The nature or manner how, or to what degree they shall shine, "as the sun."

3. The place where they shall thus shine, i. e. "in the kingdom of the Father."

4. The time when, then, that is, at the end of the world, or at the resurrection day, then shall the righteous shine. Believers have a twofold righteousness.

1. The righteousness of justification, viz., the imputed righteousness of Jesus Christ ; and in this righteousness they shall shine gloriously for ever, for that is the righteousness that carries them to heaven; "Of righteousness, because I go to the Father," John xvi. 10.

2. The righteousness of sanctification, which shall be perfect in that day, and in that righteousness they shall shine gloriously for ever also.

Quest. What need shall the saints have to shine in Christ's righteousness, when they shall be perfectly holy in themselves ?

Answ. Great need and reason there will be for it. *The saints shall shine in the righteousness of Christ for ever.*

1. Because it was not their own inherent righteousness which was their title to heaven, but the righteousness of Christ alone ; therefore they shall boast of, and shine in the righteousness of Christ for ever.

2. Because their own inherent righteousness was imperfect and full of spots whilst they lived upon the earth, and it was made perfect only as an act of Christ's purchase, or the fruit of his merits and obedience to make them meet for that inheritance.

3. Nay, had it been perfect in this life, yet it could not have justified them, nor saved them from hell, (much less brought them to heaven) because it could not have paid off their old score, or satisfied divine justice for original and actual sins, or breach of the holy law of God. For if a man could live now such a holy life, as never to offend God in word, thought, or action ; yet his old sins (unless Christ's righteousness be imputed to him) will cast him into hell.

4. Because the righteousness of Christ is the righteousness of God, i. e., of him that is God and not man only ; it is not the righteousness of a mere creature, therefore that righteousness being put upon the saints, they will shine more glorious in, than in any righteousness, though complete, of mere creatures.

And from hence the saints shall sing praises unto God and the Lamb for evermore, and say, "Worthy is the Lamb that was slain to receive power, and riches, and wisdom, and strength, and honour, and glory, and blessing," Rev. v. 12. Then shall the righteous shine like the sun.

Doct. 1. The great glory of believers is reserved to that time ; now their life is a hidden life, and their glory is veiled.

"Now are we the sons of God, but it doth not appear what we shall be," 1 John. iii. 1—3, "For ye are dead, and your life is hid with Christ in God," Col. iii. 3.

Observe this well, though believers have glory conferred upon them in this world, being now the sons of God, yet their glory doth not yet appear, it is not manifested, nor shall it be until then.

Doct. 2. When the end of the world comes, or at the day of the resurrection, the saints shall shine forth gloriously.

1. Because the saints being God's jewels, are then all made up, or completed every way, and shall shine before wicked men and devils, to the shame and confusion for ever of those wretches.

2. Moreover, as heirs, they then come to a perfect age, and to possess the purchased inheritance, to the praise of God's grace and glory.

3. Then the marriage of the Lamb will be celebrated, and the bride be adorned in all her marriage-robes and rich attire, Rev. xix. 7.

There are degrees of glory. What heart can conceive, or tongue express, the glory of Christ's Marriage-day, or the glory every true believer shall shine more glorious than others ; for some shall " shine as the brightness of the firmament, and those who turn many to righteousness as the stars for evermore," Dan. xii. 3. Our Lord says, they shall shine as the sun, which is far more glorious than the stars; all vessels shall be full, but some shall be greater bodies of light, and so shine brighter than others.

4. Because then the bodies and souls of all believers shall be reunited, both being made perfect ; a curious piece of work, whether a jewel or clockwork never appears so glorious until it is all joined together, and every way perfected ; so the glory of the saints will then every way be full and perfect, both in respect of soul and body too.

5. Because Christ then will appear ; " And when he appears we shall appear with him in glory," Col. iii. 4. " And we shall be like him, for we shall see him as he is," 1 John iii. 4. Then, and in that day, " Our vile body shall be changed, and made like unto his glorious body," Phil. iii. 21, though not in respect of degree, but in quality and similitude. As a star in its quality is glorious, but in degree not so glorious, as the sun ; Christ is God, and in him shall the glory of the Father, nay, the glory of the whole Godhead *How we shall see God in the other world.* bodily, shine forth ; also in him we shall see God, who is invisible to any material or created eyes, we shall see him as he is, we shall behold his glory, and be with him where he is, as he hath asked it of God, so it is granted him, " Father, I will that those also that thou hast given me, be with me where I am, that they may behold my glory which thou hast given me," John xvii. 24, &c., that is, that they may partake of my glory. To behold the glory of God, is to be glorified, but all our glory certainly will reflect from the glory of Christ's person, whose glory will be astonishing.

6. Because then will be the time of " the manifestation of the sons of God," Rom. viii. 19. Then they shall be crowned with glory. Sirs, that will be the saints' coronation-day ; then shall the crown of life, the crown of glory, the crown that fadeth not away, be given to them. " Henceforth there is laid up for me a crown of righteousness, which God the righteous Judge will give unto me at that day ; and not to me only, but to all them also that love his appearance," 2 Tim. iv. 8.

7. Then will be the time of the saints' reaping, as now is the time of their sowing ; and " they that sow in tears shall reap in joy," Psal. cxxvi. 5. They shall reap a full harvest not only of what they have sowed or suffered, but the fruit of that seed which Christ by *A whole Mystical Christ must be glorified.* his obedience and suffering hath sowed ; it will be the harvest (I say, or reaping-time) of Christ's sowing : the time when he shall have his full reward for all he hath wrought ; and not of his own glory, but what he hath wrought for his saints : also it will be the glory of a whole Christ ; not only Christ personally considered, but also Christ mystically considered : the body of Christ then shall be perfect, no one member shall be wanting ; so that then will be the time of Christ and his church's perfection ; and as all the whole body will be complete or perfect, so shall every particular saint arrive to a complete perfection also, both in knowledge, love, beauty, and glory ; and hence it is that they shall shine so gloriously. Christ shall be in the top of his glory, and believers in the top of their glory also.

"Shine as the sun," &c. This denotes the greatness of the glory of the saints. What creature is so glorious as the sun? *Gloria quasi clara*, saith Aquinas, because glory is the bright shining forth of excellency. The glory, excellency, and splendour of believers in that day will be amazing. A little to open this, consider,

Why the glory of the Saints is compared to the glory of the sun. I. The sun is the greatest glory of this world, or far excels in glory all other things.

So the saints shall shine forth in the greatest glory, beyond the glory of Solomon, or all earthly potentates whatsoever.

II. When the sun shines forth in his full strength, all dark clouds and mists are vanquished, and driven away. So when the saints shall shine in their greatest glory, all dark mists of ignorance, and clouds of sin and corruption, shall be expelled from them for ever—no more unbelief nor dark day for ever.

III. The sun is a singular light, and shines with a singular glory, *sol quia solus* ; there are many stars, but one sun ; so the glory of the saints shall be a singular glory ; no glory like that glory, or to be compared to it.

IV. The sun is a pure, bright, and spotless creature, far brighter than the moon or stars. So the glory of the saints will be a pure, bright, and spotless glory ; not like the glory of this world, nor like to the glory which attends the saints while they are here in this mortal body.

V. The glory of the sun is an unchangeable glory ; he alters not, changes not in his glory as the moon doth.

So the glory of the saints in that day will ever abide the same, and never change or be less, because they then shall arrive to a full perfection of glory ; nay, it shall exceed that of the sun, because, (1.) The sun sets or goes out of our sight but the saints' sun shall never go down, their glory never sets. *The glory of the saints shall be full, and never be less.* "Thy sun shall no more go down by day," &c., Isa. lx. 20. (2.) The sun is sometimes clouded, its glory appears not, but the glory of the saints shall never be clouded any more, as it was in this world. (3.) The sun shall then be ashamed. "The sun shall be ashamed when the Lord of host shall reign in Mount Zion, and in Jerusalem, and before his ancients gloriously," Isa. xxiv. 23. That is, the glory of the saints shall so far excel the glory of the sun, that the sun shall, as it were, be ashamed (as such are said to be, when they are outshined) or outdone by others. (4.) The sun is sometimes eclipsed by the gross body of the moon interposing betwixt us and it ; but the glory of the saints shall by no dark body of sin, corruption, or of this world, be eclipsed any more for ever.

VI. The sun is so glorious, that mortals cannot behold it, but their eyes will dazzle. So the glory of the saints will be too great for sinners to behold, it would even put out their eyes, or confound them. O happy believers !

"In the kingdom of the Father." Our Lord here gives us to understand that his mediatorial kingdom shall have an end, and God shall be all in all ; and then also it is said, " The Son shall be subject unto him that put all things under him," 1 Cor. xv. 28. Yet this doth not signify that there is any in- *What is meant by the kingdom of the Father.* equality of essence or power in the Son with the Father ; no, nor that the glory of the Son shall not shine to eternity ; but it only signifies, that as Christ, considered as Mediator did receive his commission and authority from the Father, and so acted all he did in his Fa- ther's name. Even so when all his elect are gathered, and his whole work and office in his mediatorial kingdoms is finished, then the sun will yield up that commission, that power and authority to God the Father, by which he acted as Mediator ; and then comes in that kingdom which is called the kingdom of the Father, and so God shall be all in all ; *i. e.*, there will be a present and immediate communication of God to his saints, different from those mediums by which he manifested *What is meant by the Son's being subject unto God the Fa- ther.* himself to them in the mediatorial kingdom of Jesus Christ. This will be the last act (as I may say) of the Son's obedience and subjection to the Father. As he is God's servant he hereby intimates, that as Mediator he will not fail in his subjection to the Father, even to the last minute or moment of time. But this is so far from lessening the honour of the Son, that it rather tends to magnify his glory, he being no longer then in the state or ca- pacity of a servant, having finished all his work committed unto him to do as Mediator. From hence I might note, that the chiefest glory of the saints will be in the kingdom of the Father, or when the mediatorial kingdom of Christ shall cease, or be ended.

APPLICATION

1. We may infer from hence how vain and foolish a thing it is for any to hide their sin, or cover their iniquities. The day will come that shall discover what men are, and all the thoughts of their hearts, and all their deeds of darkness, shall then be laid open ; for " God will bring every work into judgment, with every secret thing, whether it be good, or whether it be evil," Eccl. xii. 14.

2. It may tend to terrify and awaken all hypocrites, for they shall, when the harvest comes, not only be severed from the wheat, but also be cast into hell, or into a furnace of fire, together with all profane and abominable idolaters, blas- phemers, murderers, and adulterers. They might as well be openly profane, as secretly wicked ; for hypocrites and unbelievers shall have their portion together, with the abominable and profane persons and devils. *The fearful state of hy- pocrites.*

3. This may provoke every one of us to examine and try ourselves, judge ourselves, since the time will come which will try every person : "if we judge ourselves we shall not be judged, nor be condemned with the world," 1 Cor. xi. 31, 32.

O then let us be exhorted to this great work and duty ! Is it not better to examine our own hearts and ways now ; and if sin be in us, or if our hearts are not right with God, to see to it, and judge and condemn ourselves, and fly to Jesus Christ? For there is mercy in him for hypocrites as well as for others, though it be so great a sin in his sight; and no sin more hateful to him.

But what comfort and consolation may this be also to all sincere Christians? **Comfort to saints.** Let such lift up their hearts with joy! O what a blessed and happy condition are they in now! But what will their state be when this life is ended? Such need not to fear death; for, as their souls go then to Christ, so when Christ comes, he will bring them with him; " they shall appear with him in glory." What a harvest of joy, (Col. iii. 4,) shall we, if we are some of Christ's wheat, or true believers, reap at that day! Moreover, it may stir us up to long for this harvest, or to pray for the end of the world. These things being considered, certainly there is nothing may cause greater joy to sincere Christians; the thoughts of this harvest-day may cause us to leap for joy; how doth the husbandman long for harvest, when he reaps the fruits of all his cost and pains!

The signs of Christ's coming are upon us. The signs of Christ's coming, and of the end of the world, are certainly upon us: it is now but a short time to harvest; pray for the latter rain, which will ripen both the wheat and tares for this great harvest-day.

4. And lastly, labour for patience: " Behold the husbandman waiteth for the fruits of the earth, and hath long patience for it, until he receive the early, and latter rain; be ye also patient, stablish your hearts, for the coming of the Lord draweth near," Jam. v. 7, 8. And thus I shall close with this parable.

17. THE MUSTARD SEED

I

Another parable put he forth unto them, saying, the kingdom of heaven is like unto a grain of mustard-seed which a man took and sowed in his field, which indeed is the least of all seeds, but when it is grown, it is the greatest amongst herbs, and becometh a tree, so that the birds of the air come and lodge in the branches thereof.—Matt. xiii. 31, 32. See Luke xiii. 19.

SOME of the parables of our blessed Lord (I told you in the introduction) were prophetical, and so, as I conceive is this, viz., (1.) To discover the great success the gospel would have, **The scope of the parable opened.** and to what glory the church of God should grow in after-times, though it was very small at the beginning; this therefore may be the scope or chief design of our Saviour in speaking of this parable.

(2.) Some conclude our Lord hereby also designed to set forth the nature of true grace, particularly the grace of faith; which though at first it be but very small, yet if it be true grace, or saving faith, it will grow very strong in the end.

But I conclude he chiefly designed hereby to encourage his disciples in respect to that great and wonderful success the gospel and gospel-church should meet with in the world in after-times.

Secondly, as to the parts and terms herein contained.

1. By the kingdom of heaven I understand is here meant the kingdom of grace ; the church, or dispensation of the gospel. Why the church is called the kingdom of heaven is showed largely in the parable of the wise and foolish virgins, to which I refer the reader.

What is meant by the kingdom of heaven.
viz., the gospel church.

2. Like unto a grain of mustard-seed. I find worthy authors do not agree as to what is meant by the grain of mustard-seed in this place.

1. Some say it signifies Jesus Christ. Thus St. Ambrose, as I find him quoted by Mr. Henry Vertue.

St. Luke saith it was sown in a garden, so (saith he) was Christ sown or buried in a garden, and from thence he rose again and became a tree. Christ (saith he), is compared to a grain of wheat, Luke xiii. 19, that fell into the ground, also to wheat because he strengthens man's heart : and " to a grain of mustard-seed," John xii. 24, because he heats the heart of man. Mustard-seed hath a heating property in it. Moreover, he was very little or small in the eyes of the world, though he became great and glorious, and so will remain for ever : but this sense I approve not of, for some reasons which I shall not here mention : indeed he himself runs afterwards to Christ mystical, consisting of head and members.

See Vertue s parables, pag. 206.

2. By his grain of mustard-seed (as hinted before) I judge chiefly is meant the gospel, or the ministry thereof, from whence the church sprang up. Thus Marlorat and our Annotators take it.

" Our Saviour (says the one) tended hereby to let his disciples know what success his gospel should have over all the world, that they might not be discouraged to see the little success it had at present."

Annotator.

(Saith the other), " by this parable the Lord declares what success the gospel should have through the whole world : for the kingdom of heaven was at first very small."

" Which a man took and sowed in his field." By the man here, also is meant Jesus Christ the Son of man, for he sowed the good seed from whence the church sprang up.

Marlorat's. Expost. of Matthew.

" In his field." The field is the world ; the earth is the Lord's, and the fulness thereof. The church grew up out of this world, and grows still in the world.

"Which indeed is the least of all seeds," &c., or the least of seeds which produceth so great a plant. No doubt our Saviour refers to that sort of mustard-seed which was in those eartern countries, which were very small, or the smallest of seeds ; much smaller than ours, and grew much bigger also.

" Which when it is grown, is the greatest herbs." The saints and people of God, though they are the smallest people, or the least or meanest among men, or in the sight of the world, and in their own sight also are as nothing ; yet they having taken root, and begun to grow in the knowledge of Christ, and true Christianity in the primitive time, they shall gradually grow bigger and bigger, and at last become like a great tree, or be the most flourishing and most glorious people in all the world.

" So that the birds of the air shall come and lodge in the branches thereof."

By the birds of the air may be meant the saints. The time of singing of birds is come ; that is, the time when the saints that have been oppressed shall break forth into singing, when the winter is over, or the days of their tribulation are gone. The saints may be compared to birds on divers respects :

The saints are compared to birds.

1. Birds delight in the air, or in the higher region ; so the saints are said " to dwell on high, our conversation is in heaven," Phil. iii. 20, Col. iii. 1, 2, their desires and affections are set on things above.

Saints compared to birds.

2. Birds mount towards heaven as the lark and eagle, &c., so it is said, " They that wait on the Lord shall renew their strength, they shall mount up as on eagles' wings," Isa. xl. 31.

3. Birds want a place of defence and safety when trees are cut down : so when godly princes fall or good magistrates are displaced, the saints are exposed to many dangers.

4. Some birds are made a prey of by fowls of prey, so have the saints been, and will be by the wicked until this tree is come to its full growth, more or less.

5. Birds make sweet music, sweet melody, especially in the spring : so do the saints sing and make sweet melody in their hearts and voices in the ears of the Lord Jesus Christ, but more abundantly shall they sing when the day of Zion's glory cometh in and Babylon is down.

6. Birds suffer much and are almost starved, and many are cut off by fowlers in a sharp winter's season : so in times of persecution the saints have suffered much for want of bread,

their food has been taken away, and many of them have been cut off by the hands of wicked and blood-thirsty men.

" Shall lodge in the branches thereof."

The time shall come when the saints shall with safety lodge in Sion, the church shall grow to that strength and power, that the poor and oppressed ones of Jesus Christ shall be secure in the branches of the church authority and government.

From hence let me note this proposition, viz.,

The gospel church shall become a great and mighty peo-ple. Doct. 1. That though the church and people of God were a very small, shattered, and weak people at first, yet they shall grow to a great height of strength and glory in the latter days ; so that all that love Christ shall be safe under her wings.

1. I shall show you how the church hath been oppressed, broken, and shattered, like a tender branch growing out of the ground.

2. Show how the church shall gradually grow like a tree or tender plant until she comes to her full perfection, that the saints with safety shall lodge in her branches.

3. Apply it.

First, The church was very small at its first plantation in the primitive time. The number of the disciples were but about one hundred and twenty, Acts i. 15.

The church was small at first. Believers in Christ then were the smallest people in the world ; for the whole earth might be divided into three parts.

1. The Jews, who were a great people, even like the sands of the sea for number.

2. The Gentiles, who were left under darkness and ignorance, were more, no doubt, in number, than the Jews.

3. The Christians, and these were but like a grain of mustard-seed comparatively to both the other.

How the church grew. Yet they grow in a short time wonderfully, three thousand being added to them by St Peter's (Acts ii. 4) preaching of one sermon : and after that we read of 3000, and in a few years they increased to a wonderful number, filling many cities and countries. What a vast multitude were put to death for the space of 300 years after Christ, in the ten persecutions under the Roman emperors.

Secondly, I will show you how the church hath been oppressed broken, and shattered like a tender plant sprang out of the ground. This was done three ways, through the rage and malice of Satan.

The ways by which the churches growth was hindered. 1. By false doctrine, that very early crept into the church ; and many, even in the apostles' days, were corrupted hereby.

The first we read of were those false teachers that rose up amongst the Jewish Christians, who taught circumcision, and many other Jewish rites, and mixed the righteousness of the law with the righteousness of Christ in justification ; (1 John ii. 23) ; and also others in the same times denied Christ was come in the flesh, and some declared there was no resurrection, and thereby overthrew the faith of divers Christians ; and some said the resurrection was past, (1 Tim. i. 19, 20). Also the Nico-latains did much harm to the Church of God, which sect rose from Nicholas, who was one *What errors got into the church.* of the seven deacons chose to take the care of the poor in the Church at Jeru-salem (Acts vi. 5, Rev. ii. 15). They asserted polygamy lawful ; that men might have more wives than one, or rather community of women : and many other errors molested the churches, and tended to mar her beauty. And afterwards also rose Arius, whose heresy corrupted thousands, who denied the God-head of our blessed Saviour ; affirming he was a created spirit, and which spirit assumed the nature of man in the womb of the virgin. Moreover, multitudes of other errors broke in ; and soon after Antichrist was revealed, who sprang up out of the apostacy of the Church, as was foretold by St. Paul, 2 Thess. ii. 3. Moreover, until all errors in doctrine and discipline that abound now are vanquished, the Church will not shine in her glory ; but greater light is near.

2. This blessed tree, which sprang from this grain of mustard-seed that was so small at first, was also injured greatly, and its growth obstructed by divisions, contentions, and many other enormities that were in the primitive churches, and in the next ages follow-ing, and this also spoils her growth and glory now.

3. She was also sorely oppressed and vexed by grievous persecutions ; many of her precious branches being that way lopped off, most of the apostles themselves being bar-barously put to death, or suffered martyrdom. Yet, notwithstanding all the wrong the

church sustained by those and other means, she abode visible in the world, though at last was forced to fly into the wilderness from the face of the red dragon, Rev. xii. 6 ; but she hath of late times looked out as the morning, and as fair as the moon, Cant. vi. 10 ; and shall in a little time come forth as clear as the sun, and as terrible as an army with banners.

Thirdly, I shall briefly show how the church shall gradually grow like a tree, or tender plant, and come to her full perfection, when the saints with safety shall lodge in her branches, or under her power and protection. *How or by what means the chu.ch shall grow and become a mighty tree.*

It hath befallen (you have heard) this blessed plant to receive much harm in its growth and beauty, but the predictions, or prophesy of our Saviour hinted in this parable, shall be fulfilled, in spite of all opposition from men and devils, i. e., it shall become a mighty tree ; and the ways by which it will be done, I shall briefly speak unto.

1. " God will arise and have mercy on Sion when the set time is come," Psal. cii. 13. Jehovah hath seemed to many to sleep, and to have neglected his church for a long time, but he will quickly arise or rouse up out of his seeming sleep, and take pity on her as he did in the type, so he will in the antitype, i. e., as he delivered his people out of literal Babylon, so he will save his people and gospel-church from mystical Babylon. *By what means the church shall become great and glorious in the latter days.*

2. He will raise up men, even the kings of the earth, to hate the whore, and to make her desolate, eat her flesh, and burn her with fire, Rev. xvii.

You will see them in a little while deeply engaged in the church's cause, or in behalf of Sion, and he will also stir up his own people, or some of the sons of Sion, to execute his wrath and vengeance upon Babylon, " reward her, as she hath rewarded you," Rev. xviii. 6 ; so that in due time it shall be said, " Come and behold the works of the Lord, what desolation he hath made in the earth," Psal. xlvi. 8. *How Baby-lon shall fall. And the glory of Sion branch forth.*

But this will not begin until the ascension of the witnesses, which will be in one street of the great city, which I doubt not is Great Britain, Rev. xi.

3. It will be done by a farther and more glorious appearance of Jesus Christ, or by the rising of the Sun of Righteousnes ; for the son of perdition shall be destroyed by Christ's bright appearing in the glory of gospel light, which will expel all antichristian darkness, errors, and superstitions, which are still amongst us, 2 Thess. ii. 8.

4. The growth and glory of the church in the latter days, will be effected or ushered in by a more eminent and glorious effusion of the Holy Spirit : the latter rain will come down, and I am persuaded, like that which fell in the primitive times at the day of pentecost. *Miracles shall return again.*

Why may we not expect the returning of God's miraculous working power ? There may be the same need of miracles as there was at first ; what else can tend to remove these great differences that are amongst the Lord's people, I know not, neither am I alone in my apprehensions in this case ; besides, we have of late seen something of this nature ; many cures have been wrought in a miraculous manner, which seem to be but some drops before the shower falls ; moreover, we read that at the fall of Babylon, there shall be apostles and prophets in the church : " Rejoice over her, ye holy apostles and prophets, for God hath revenged you on her, Rev. xviii. 20. The apostolical office was by a special and an extraordinary mission ; nor can we expect any such an office again in the church, without some are called and endowed with the same extraordinary spirit, which I expect will be in a short time. *Extraor-dinary apos tles may be expected again.*

5. It will be effected by virtue of a thorough and blessed union amongst all the Lord's people ; for when God has poured upon the nations of the earth all his fierce anger, and devoured his enemies with the " fire of his jealousy, he will return to the people a pure language, that they may all call upon him with one consent," Zeph. iii. 1—10 ; and then, and not till then, the two sticks shall become one in Christ's hand, and then also will the church appear as terrible as an army with banners, Cant. vi. 10. *A blessed union near among all God's people.*

6. It will be effected by God's setting his king upon the holy hill of Sion, and making him higher in the exercise of his regal power (as King of nations, as well as King of saints) then the kings of the earth, Psal. ii. 6 ; and then " all the kingdoms under the whole heaven shall be given to the people of the saints of the Most High," Dan. vii. 27 ; the stone that shall smite the image on its feet, shall become a great mountain, and fill

the whole earth; which will begin on the ascension of the witnesses, and sounding of the seventh trumpet. Look for these things; though they do not well who boldly prefix the very year; but however, the tenth part of the great city shall fall first, in which the antichristian names of men shall cease for ever.

I shall only add some of the signs of those days, or what things are precedent to them, which our Lord would have well observed; "Now learn the parable of the fig-tree; when his branches are yet tender, and putteth forth leaves, ye know the summer is near: so likewise, when ye shall see all these things, know that it is near, even at the door," Matt. xxiv. 32, 33.

Signs of the glory of the church in the last days.

1. When the enemy comes in like a flood, and without any great resistance seems to threaten to swallow up the church, and swell the banks and bounds of all human power, then the Lord's own arm shall bring salvation, Isa. lix. 16; this, saith an ancient writer, will be one sign, i. e., chap. lxiii. 5, when the world makes invasions and inroads upon the church in several kingdoms like a land-flood, and all things seem to tend to confusion, and the nations are in amaze, and some princes and people fall off to the beasts; the sign, my brethren, seems to be upon us; look abroad, when, since the reformation, was a more dismal face of things?

Gen. xv. 19. 2. Sign, when the enemies of their church are at their height, and their sins are fully ripe, particularly the Romish harlot is lifted up (in one or another kingdom,) in pride and power, saying, I sit as queen, and shall see no sorrow, then the things long looked for draw near.

3. Sign, when we hear of wars, and rumour of wars, and the rushing of nations one against another with a design to overthrow the gospel and kingdom of Christ, which will usher in the great earthquake which shall be upon the ascension of the witnesses, then the time is near.

See Archer's Signs of the last days. 4. Sign, when there shall be an universal defection and darkness in all the churches of the saints, and false doctrine and errors more then usual abound, and deadness, security, and formality increases on the people of God, so that all the virgins seem to be asleep, then is the time near, even at the door. "The sun shall be turned into darkness, and the moon into blood; or, as the prophet Joel saith, "The sun and the moon shall be darkened, and stars shall withdraw their shining," i.e., Joel. iii. 15, the gospel church, that great light of heaven, shall lose some of that light she for many years gave to the world, particularly (from the time of famous Luther) in the doctrine of justification; and many ministers who seemed like stars, shall suck in corrupt principles about that glorious truth, and so withdraw their shining; now this has not been to such a degree until of late years; and then the earth shall be turned into blood, or nothing but blood, blood and slaughter almost everywhere, as if all the earth was like to a common shambles, to quarter out the limbs of sinners. The woman clothed with the sun, had the moon under her feet; what moon is that, but this world in its external and changeable glory?

Jer. xxv. 27.
Jer. xlix 12.
Lam. iv. 21.
Ezek. xxiii. 3.
Psal. xxxiii. 8.
Isa. x. 12.

Sign 5. When the cup of trembling shall be taken out of the hand of Sion, and pass into the hands of her enemies, and they come to drink the dregs thereof, and be drunk, spew, and fall, they shall rise no more. And when the Lord Jesus makes Jerusalem a cup of trembling to all her enemies, Psa. xi. 6, then fire, and brimstone, and horrible tempests, shall be the portion of the cup of those pretended Protestants that have put the saints to grief. But then fearful trembling shall seize upon them; for God has not forgot the blood they have shed: this sign draws near. Also,

Sign 6. When all the churches (as the people in Egypt) groan and sigh under oppression, and break forth into mighty crying unto God with a loud and hideous noise, as a woman in travail, Psa. cii. 5. 6, with bitter mourning, Isa. lxii. 1, and an universal cry to Jehovah, then God will come and avenge his own elect: "He hath a respect to the prayers of the desolate—now will I arise, saith the Lord, and devour at once," Isa. xli. 14.

Sign 7. When the Lord sends forth variety of strange sins and wonders in the heavens, in the earth, Matt. xxiv. 27, and in the waters, strange fish, strange birds, strange monsters, strange hail, thunder, and lightning, and strange and universal earthquakes, and men are filled with fear, looking for what shall come to pass, "lift up your heads, your redemption draws near," Luke xxi. 25—28.

Sign 8. Saith a worthy and ancient author, when God is hammering and squaring fit instruments for his great work, as he hath done in all times of his church's extremities of old, as Moses in Egypt, Joshua, the Judges, Ethniel, Ehud, Sampson, Gideon, Baruk, Sampson, David, Cyrus, Zerobbabel, &c., especially when he makes crooked instruments to strike a straight blow, or unlikely persons to do great things not expected from them, this shows Christ is about to appear in his glory.

Sign 9. When the most knowing and understanding persons in the prophecies shall agree that the witnesses have been slain, and are upon their feet, Mahometan power ceases to be any more a plague to the antichristian party, and so the second is passed away, the time is at the door, Isa. xxvi. 21.

Sign 10. When God riseth up to make inquisition for blood, and puts it into the hearts of some of the ten kings to hate the whore, and a religious war breaks out between the Papist and the Protestant princes, and God takes peace from the earth, so that the breach cannot be made up, lift up your heads.

Sign 11. Before the Sun of righteousness ariseth to build up Sion, Psa. xcvii. 2, 3 ; clouds, great darkness will be round about him, and most will be amazed, and not know what to think ; and from this cloud a fire will break out before him ; sword, pestilence, tempests and whirlwinds, and strange plagues upon the enemies of the church. Sirs, the morning of the day of Christ's power is like to be very cloudy and tempestuous, and full of trouble ; but it is to the enemies of Christ ; and a fire shall burn up and consume them ; but the saints shall be preserved in those times in a wonderful manner.

Sign 12. When the errors of some men, who have prefixed times, shall tend so to blind and harden the world, and also to deceive the godly, that there will remain but little faith in any about Christ's glorious appearance in his wonders ; but most will conclude the time afar off ; then he is just at the door, Matt. xx. 4.

But to proceed, I have showed you how small the church was at first, also the causes of her decay and witherings, until antichrist was revealed, and that she hath of late looked out as the morning, which began about Luther's time ; and how her path hath shone, and shall shine more and more to the perfect day ; with the signs of her near approaching glory.

Now to close ; I shall prove she shall become a great and mighty tree in the last days. " Glorious things are spoken of thee, O city of God," Psa. lxxxvii. 3.

The power and glory of the Church shall be great.

" It shall come to pass in the last days, that the mountain of the Lord's house shall be established in the top of the mountains, and shall be exalted above thee, and all nations shall flow unto it," Isa. ii. 2. That is the time when birds shall dwell in her branches, the mountain of the Lord's house is the regal power and authority of the church ; and this shall be established in the top of all earthly powers, governments, and pre-eminence whatsoever, viz. ; the saints shall have the supreme authority and rule over all powers and governments of the earth ; " And the stone that smote the image became a a great mountain, and filled the whole earth," Dan. ii. 35.

This is expounded by Daniel, ver. 44, " And in the days of these kings, shall the God of heaven set up a kingdom which shall never be destroyed ; and the kingdom shall be left to another people ; but it shall break in pieces and consume all these kingdoms, and it shall stand for ever," See Mich. iv. Some, through ignorance, have thought that this kingdom refers to the gospel-church set up by Christ and his apostles in the primitive time ; but that cannot be, because this kingdom is set up when the government of the Roman monarchy is in its feet. The stone smote the image on the feet ; the Roman power in the apostles' days was in its iron legs, i. e., in its greatest strength : besides, the stone then did not smite, but was smitten by the Romish power for near three hundred years ; the ten toes of the image and the ten horns, refer to the same state of the Romish monarchy, compare this with Dan. vii., " And the kingdom, and dominion, and the greatness of the kingdom under the whole heaven, shall be given to the people of the saints of the Most High, whose kingdom is an everlasting kingdom, and all dominions shall serve and obey Him," Dan. vii. 27, that is, the Lord Jesus Christ.

The saints had never yet all the power and kingdoms under the whole heavens given unto them, but they shall have it in the last days.

" The kingdoms of this world are become the kingdoms of our Lord, and of his Christ," Rev. xi. 15 ; that is, upon the seventh angel sounding his trumpet, they shall become Christ's kingdom.

" Thy people also shall be all righteous, and they shall inherit the land for ever, the branch of my planting, the work of my hands, that I may be glorified," Isa. lx. 21. See here what a glorious tree this mustard-seed will grow unto. " A little one shall become a thousand, and a small one a strong nation. I the Lord will hasten it in his time," ver. 22. " Arise, shine, for thy light is come, and the glory of the Lord is risen on thee," Isa. lx. 1. " And the Gentiles shall come to thy light, and kings to the brightness of thy rising," ver. 3. " Lift up thine eyes round about, and see all; they gather, themselves together, they come to thee; thy sons shall come from afar, and thy daughters shall be nourished at thy side," ver. 4. " Who are these that fly as a cloud, and as doves to their windows ?" ver. 8. Time would fail to give the multitudes of Scriptures which fully confirm this truth, which make good the predictions of our blessed Saviour in this parable.

The glory of the church will appear in those times to consist in these things following.

In what the glory of the church shall consist. 1. In the abundance that shall be added to her; she shall fill the whole earth.

2. In that mighty power and authority; she shall be clothed with the government, being wholly put into the hands of the saints.

3. In that kings shall be converted, and bring their glory unto her; they shall throw their crowns at his feet.

4. In respect of that holiness and purity that shall be in all the Lord's people, both in doctrine, discipline, and conversation; all errors will be vanquished; " Thy people shall be all righteous."

5. In respect to outward peace; oppression shall rise up no more; wars shall cease to the ends of the earth.

6. In respect of love, peace, and union, amongst all the people of God; no more any names of infamy, nor of distinction; all shall be of one heart, and of one way, and all serve the Lord with one consent.

7. In respect had to the glorious presence of Christ; his glory shall then be seen, and shine forth; the latter house shall exceed the glory of the first.

Lastly, In respect of the church's stability, safety, and security; " And the Lord will create upon every dwelling-place of mount Zion, and upon her assemblies, a cloud and smoke by day, and the shining of a flaming fire by night; for upon all the glory shall be a defence," Isa. iv. 5.

APPLICATION

1. We infer, that the love of Christ to his church is very great and wonderful, and he will make it manifest to all the earth; in a short time it will appear he hath not forgotten Sion.

2. Let us learn from hence not to despise the day of small things; see how little and small the church was at the beginning, and to what greatness and glory God will raise her at last: small beginnings may have glorious endings.

Though the church is now low and small, yet God is able to raise her.

3. Let no weak beginner in religion be discouraged; " God will bring forth judgment unto victory," Matt. xii 20. Nor let him that has the smallest talent neglect the improvement thereof; he knows not what it may increase to.

4. Let none proudly overlook nor exult over weak Christians.

5. And let all the saints be of good cheer, and lift up their heads; though now under sorrow and affliction, their redemption draws near.

See the parable of the wise and foolish virgins. 6. Let us cry mightily to God to arise and have mercy upon Sion; be much in prayer; let us fast and pray, pray day and night.

7. Watch; be on your watch-tower; take heed you sleep not, and " So the day comes upon you unawares, while the bridegroom tarried, they all slumbered and slept:" the midnight cry will amaze if you awake not until it is heard.

II

*Another parable put he forth unto them, saying, the kingdom of heaven is like unto a grain of mustard-seed, which is indeed the least of all seeds, &c.—*Matt. xiii. 31, 32.

By the grain of Mustard-seed, chiefly is meant the church of Christ, which was very small at first ; this I have spoken to : but some conclude by it also may be meant true faith : though from the latter part of the parable I doubt whether our Lord does refer to faith or not : yet because faith in another place is compared to a grain of mustard-seed, I shall speak to this second thing, but rather from Matt. xvii. 20, " If ye have faith as a grain of mustard-seed, ye shall say to this mountain, remove hence to yonder place, and it shall remove," Matt. xxi. 21. " Verily I say, if ye have faith, and doubt not, if ye shall say to this mountain, be thou removed, and be cast into the sea, it shall be done."

Faith is compared to a grain of mustard-seed. Some think that it only refers to the faith of miracles ; but sure such have a great and strong faith : for the faith of miracles is in its nature or kind no weak faith. *Faith like to a grain of mustard-seed.*

I conceive, as our annotators observe, it may refer to the grace of faith in any believer. There is nothing too hard which God hath promised for faith, when a believer doubts not ; but certainly, not simply considered as a grain of mustard when it is first sown ; (for our Lord shows, as so considered, it is small and weak) but when it is grown high and strong : nothing is too hard for faith,—for,

1. Is there a mountain of guilt lying upon our consciences ? Faith will remove it, and by enabling us to cast it upon Jesus Christ, (who hath borne our sins,) thrown them into the bottom of the sea. *The power and excellency of faith.*

2. Or is there a mountain of opposition against us, or in our way of following of Christ ? True faith will cast it out of its place.

3. Or is there an evil habit like unto a strong tree deeply rooted ? Faith will pull it up. From hence note,

Doct. True faith or grace in a believer may be small, little, or weak at first ; yet it is of a growing nature ; and it will become strong by exercise, through Christ's watering, and gracious influences.

1. I shall show that true faith is small or weak, at first, in some Christians.
2. That it is of a growing nature.
3. How we may know a weak faith from a strong faith.
4. Apply it.

First, That there is a weak or small faith is evident, " O ye of little faith, wherefore did ye doubt ? why are ye fearful, O ye of little faith ?" Matt. vi. 30, Matt. viii. 26. *There is a weak faith. There is a strong faith.*

There is also mention made of a great faith ; " And Jesus unto her, O woman, great is thy faith," Matt. xv. 8, Rom. iv. 20. Also we read of a strong faith ; " Abraham was strong in faith, giving glory to God." " Be strong in the grace which is in Christ Jesus," 2 Tim. ii. 1.

How weak was the disciples' faith when they feared that the ship would sink to the bottom, where Christ the ever-blessed God was ? also when some of them doubted whether Christ was the true Messiah ; " We trusted it had been he that should have redeemed Israel," Luke xxiv. 21. And others talked of going again to their old trade ; " I go a fishing," John xxi. 3. This shows the weakness of their faith.

Secondly, Faith is of a growing nature, it may become great and strong, though at first but little, like a grain of mustard-seed. *Faith is of a growing nature.*

To what a degree was Peter's faith grown (who before denied his Master ?) " If we this day be examined of the good done to this impotent man, by what means he is made whole, be it known to you all, and to all the people of Israel, that by the name of Jesus Christ of Nazareth, whom ye crucified, whom God raised from the dead, even by him doth this man stand here before you whole," Acts iv. 8, 9. Who more strong now than blessed Peter ? his faith was grown already to a great degree, like a mighty tree.

" We are bound to thank God always as is meet, because that your faith groweth exceedingly, and the charity of every one of you towards each other aboundeth."

Quest. Doth grace grow by infusion of new degrees, or by co-operation with it ? Or is it increased by exercise only ? *How faith grows.*

Ans. I doubt not but both these ways faith may be said to grow and increase. (1)

The Lord Jesus doth increase and strengthen our faith by the influences of his Spirit: "Lord, increase our faith:" and, (2) It also grows by feeding on the word, ordinances, and promises of the Lord Jesus Christ, as a child grows by the nourishment it receives; "As new-born babes desiring the sincere milk of word, that they may grow thereby."

(3.) By a constant use, study, and exercise, faith is increased in believers, until they come to a more perfect stature in Christ Jesus.

Thirdly, What is the nature of a weak faith, and wherein doth it differ from a strong? Heb. v. 14.

I. A weak faith is commonly attended with many doubts and fears; as appears by what our Saviour said unto his disciples, "O ye of little faith, wherefore did ye doubt?" Matt. xiv. 31.

The nature of a weak faith. Christ appears in an ordinance, in a duty, or in providence, and manifesteth himself; but the soul doubts whether it be Christ or not; it may be, saith he, a temptation, or delusion of Satan. Also Christ appears in a promise, and sets some sweet word upon the heart; but yet the weak Christian doubts still whether it be by the good Spirit or not.

Much remaining ignorance is in weak believers. II. A weak faith is attended with much remaining ignorance, or wants clearer light in the mysteries of Christ and of the gospel; they cannot see wherein their great strength lieth, (to wit) in our head, the Lord Jesus Christ; as Sampson's great strength lay in his hair; but weak Christians look for it in themselves. (1.) They see not that abundant grace that is in Christ, and that it is for them that there is in him such a fulness. (2.) They see not so clearly, that the righteousness of Christ is continually imputed to them, or that they always are clothed with that blessed garment. (3.) They cannot discern clearly that Christ is their life, and "that because he lives they shall live also," John. xiv. 19. (4.) They see not their conquest and victory that is in Christ, but look and expect a perfect conquest in themselves over all their enemies; which, while in this body, we shall never find; but sometimes we may be foiled, and have the worst of it; nay, come off with broken bones, as David and Peter did.

III. Ignorance in respect of God's eternal love, the covenant of grace, together with the power, promises, and faithfulness of God.

IV. Ignorance of the suretyship of Christ, and of that blessed union which is between the Lord Jesus and every believer, though never so weak; also they may be ignorant of the nature of grace, and of true faith itself; 1 John. v. 13. They may not know that they do believe, and that they have eternal life. Hence it is that we are exhorted to grow in knowledge as well as in grace, 2 Pet. iii. 18.

V. Weak believers must see and feel; they live more by sense than faith: Weak believers live much by sense. Thomas must see and feel before he would believe; "because thou hast seen, thou hast believed; blessed are they that see not, and yet believe," John xx. 25—29. Thou believest upon the testimony of thy senses, but it is a more noble act of faith, to believe without such a sensible evidence; not to give credit to anything but upon the evidence of our senses, can hardly, in a proper sense, be called faith, it is only what sense confirms, which before we had the relation of, but did not believe.

He that lives by sense has but little faith. Therefore by how much we live by sense and the sensitive evidences, or by seeing or feeling, the weaker our faith is; and from hence some are ready to say, I will open my Bible, and observe what place my eyes are first cast upon, and also desire that God would some way or another, in a visible way, satisfy them about their state and condition; which as it is dangerous, so no doubt but it is from Satan; yet I intend not by this an exclusion of signs or marks of saving grace, or a refix act of faith; but a weak Christian is ready, I say, to give up all his hope, if he finds and feels corruptions bubbling up, and fears they are not mortified. What, saith he, have I so many evil thoughts, earthly thoughts, nay, blasphemous thoughts, and am I so dead in duty, and yet a believer? Though they are grievous to him, and are his burden, and the sickness of his soul, and he cries out for help against them, and will not give the least consent to their quiet lodging in his heart; yet he is ready to give up all his hope; which argues great weakness of faith.

Were my sins crucified, and could I but obtain power against them, and was I in a holy and lively frame of spirit, I could believe; but one that is strong in faith, though they find great deadness, and want of such strength and victory which they desire; yet believe and rest with comfort upon Jesus Christ, knowing that their acceptance and justification rises not from any sensible internal holiness or righteousness in themselves, but from Christ's merits and righteousness only; and, as a presumptuous and impenitent sinner can be no true believer, so he whose faith is grounded on that inherent holiness which is wrought in him, is but a weak believer : for as our own righteousness and holiness adds nothing to our justification before God, so our human frailties cannot diminish anything from it. Yet I deny not but mortification of sin, holiness, and heaviness of spirit, may be evidence to our own consciences of our justification and comfort : " for faith without works is dead," Jam. i. 12, 8, 26.

VI. A weak faith, or one that is weak in faith, cannot either bear the frowns nor smiles of God; for when afflicted, he is ready to conclude it is in wrath, and that God loves him not; and when in a prosperous state, and he enjoys the favour of God, and the light of his countenance, and is in a lively and fruitful frame of heart; he, with David, is ready to say, he shall never be removed; " in my prosperity I said I shall never be moved," Psal. xxx. 6. " Lord, by thy favour thou hast made my mountain to stand strong : thou hidest thy face, and I was troubled," ver. 7. Weak Christians, when fruitful, are ready to say with Leah (in another case) " Now will my husband love me, because I have borne him six sons," Gen. xxx. 20. Now will God love me, because I have done so much good, mortified such and such corruptions, and with holy zeal discharged such and such holy duties. When, alas! it is not for any of these things we are accepted and beloved, but only in Christ, and because he hath, and will love us; it is from himself, and in Christ, and not for the sake of any thing we do, or have done. True, we are beloved, and accepted (in Christ) and when we do well, it is approved by the Lord; but it is not for our doing it, or because we do it. Moreover, infirmities, sins, and corruptions, believers, may offend God, and cause him to hide his face; but pray know they cannot remove his love from us; and though our holiness doth please him, yet our want of such degrees of holiness that are in some, can never provoke him to cast us off, and disown us to be his children : for, as God loved us not for our righteousness, so he will never cast us off for our unrighteousness, if we are his elect children ; and though he afflicts us, yet he will not forsake us ; " My loving-kindness will I not utterly take from him, nor suffer my faithfulness to fail," Psal. lxxxix. 33.

(margin: A weak faith can neither well bear frowns nor smiles.)

(margin: Sins of believers separate them not from God's love.)

VII. Weak believers live more on their hard labour than by faith, or are more for doing than for believing; and have their eye more upon their sore and sickness, than upon their physician ; or more on what they have done and do, than upon what Christ hath done ; and have their eyes more upon that grace that is in them, than upon that grace which is in Christ; they can live, they think, when they are increased in goods ; but cannot live so as to hold up their heads when they can find nothing in themselves. See Hab. iii. 17.

VIII. A weak believer is ready to let go his hold in a storm, or cannot encounter with difficulties. When a storm rose, and tossed the ship, the disciples feared they should perish; Matt. xiv. 30, 31; and when Peter saw the winds boisterous, he began to sink. A storm of temptation, reproach, and persecution, is ready to make them stagger, nay, to fall, as many did in the late persecutions ; which showed their faith was weak.

Quest. From whence is it that some are so weak in faith ?

Ans. Some believers are but new-born, they are but babes in Christ; and can you expect a new-born babe should be as strong as one twenty years' old ?

(margin: The cause why some are weak in faith.)

2. Some are diseased, may be consumptive; distempers cause weakness: a strong man, by a fit of sickness, may be brought to great weakness: so may a strong Christian : he may fall into a consumption of his faith, love, and other graces.

3. Some believers have not such strengthening food as others, or are not fed in such fat pastures: or if they are, yet they cannot digest strong meat, must live upon the milk of the word, Heb. v. 12, 13.

4. Some fall, by some temptation, under the power of some sin: and these strangers devour or consume their strength. Grace is a tender flower, which weeds are ready to choke, or hinder the growth thereof, Hos. vii. 9.

5. And lastly, God may not give to some the like degree of faith which he gives to others: or they may not improve that measure of grace they have by daily exercise.

Secondly, True faith is of a growing nature : that faith that is weak may become strong.

1. We have proved this hath been so in many Christians.

2. And now I shall give you some reasons to prove it shall grow if it be true faith, true grace.

(margin: Faith is of a growing nature.)

1. Because grace is a vital principle, it hath life in it; it is of a fructifying quality, though it be at first but as a grain of mustard seed. (2.) Because this seed is sown in good ground; God hath made the hearts of believers good and upright, they have honest

hearts; " The righteous shall hold on his way, and he that hath clean hands shall wax stronger and stronger," Job xvii. 9. (3.) Because they are grafted into a living stock or root, which is full of sap; " Because I live, ye shall live also," John xiv. 19. (4.) Because undergrowing and strengthening promises, " They shall revive as the corn, and grow as the vine," &c., Hos. xiv. 7. " They shall grow up as calves of the stall," Mal. iv. 2. " The righteous shall grow as the cedar in Lebanon," Psal. xcii. 12. Christ hath promised, he will bring forth judgment in these unto victory.

5. Because they are planted in a very fruitful place, or hill, even on Mount Sion : "Those that are planted in the house of the Lord shall flourish in the courts of our God, they shall bring forth fruit in old age, they shall be fat and flourishing, to show that the Lord is righteous, and that there is no unrighteousness in him," Psal. xcii. 13, 14, 15. (6.) Because they are continually under growing influences, the Holy Spirit daily quickens and operates upon their hearts, and blesseth the word and ordinances unto them : " They that wait upon the Lord shall renew their strength," &c., Isa. xl. 31. (7.) Because " They are ordained to go and bring forth fruit, and that their fruit should remain," John xv. 16. They are not chosen only to believe, but to be fruitful, to be holy, and to continue so as well as to be eternally happy.

USE

1. Counsel. Trust not in your own strength, neither judge of thy strength by the strength of those graces that are in thy own heart, but by the grace that is in Christ.

2. Caution. Do not give up thy hope because thy faith is but small.

Obj. But I fear I have no grace at all; what, such a deceitful heart, and yet have grace ? attended with so many evils in heart and life, and yet have grace ? what such deadness and coldness in holy duties, and yet have grace ? what, so dark and so little sense of divine power, and yet have grace ? what, temptations and unbelief so prevalent, and yet I have grace ? so unworthy, and so unlike Christ, and yet have grace ?

Ans. All this may be, and yet thou have grace, and be a true believer : a little seed may be overlooked, especially when thou hast but a very little light in thy house.

Thirdly, I shall show you in the next place, who they are that have a great faith, whose faith is become a tree.

1. Show how they come by it.

2. The nature or quality of it.

How some come to be strong in faith.
1. God gives some a great faith, or much grace, and great knowledge : some have five talents, and others but two.

2. They have more fruitful showers and shinings than others.

3. They are singled out for special use and services above others.

The quality of a strong faith.
Secondly, The nature of a strong faith is such, that it grows the more by weights and pressures : " The righteous shall flourish like the palm-tree," &c., Psal. xcii. 12.

Nothing can hinder their growth. (1.) The palm-tree is amiable to look on; all its branches shoot upwards, none grow out of the side of this tree ; so all the desires, thoughts, and affections of these are heavenly.

The nature of the palm-tree.
(2.) The palm-tree is very weak when first planted. Pliny says, they therefore planted three or four together, and by that means they strengthen one another ; so those saints that grow strong cleave one to another in all cordial affections, and, like the palm-tree, clasps together in close and sweet communion.

(3.) The palm-tree thrives the more by having weights hung upon it ; and nothing can bend it, or make it grow crooked : though this tree be oppressed, yet it endureth and prospers, saith Ainsworth. So strong believers grow and thrive under all weights and oppressions of sin, the world, the devil, and wicked men without, and false brethren within ; yea, nothing can hinder them from going straight on in their way ; no, though God seems to frown, and good men frown upon them, and strive to discourage them ; yet they grow the more in faith, hope, love, humility, and in patience, though they want sensible comfort from God, and respect and love from the saints.

(3.) A great faith, or a strong believer, will take hold of Christ, though it has not such a particular promise set upon his heart as others have : thus it was with the woman that had the bloody issue, and the woman of Canaan : what promise had they ? and yet with what a strong faith did they take hold of the Lord Jesus ! " I say unto you, I have not found so great faith, no, not in Israel," Matt. xv. 28.

(4.) Much more if it hath but one word from Christ, such believe ; " Speak the word, and my servant shall be healed," Matt. viii. 10, Luke vii. 9, Matt. viii, 8.

(5.) A great faith lays the soul very low in his own sight, yet hath much **A strong believer an humble person.** confidence in Christ: "I am not worthy thou shouldest come under my roof."

(6.) All strong believers were ever very humble. How humble was Abraham, and David ? "I am a worm," Agar, Job, "I loathe myself" Isaiah, "I am undone," &c. Paul, "I who am less than the least of all saints," &c. They have greater light that have a great faith, or have great discoveries of God, of his holiness, love, and goodness, and of their own vileness.

(7.) A great faith, or a strong Christian, will not be discouraged, though **A strong faith will have no denial, nor be discouraged by repulses.** he meets with repulses from Christ, and from his disciples or ministers. What repulses did the woman of Canaan meet with ? first, she cried, " O Lord, thou Son of David," &c. Matt. xv. 22—26. "But he answered her not a word."
2. Then the disciples came and besought him to send her away; but still she cries to him.
3. Then our Lord said, " I am not sent but to the lost sheep of the house of Israel," yet she continues her request, then she came and worshipped him, " Saying, Lord, help me."
4. On this he said, " It is not meet to take the childrens' bread and give it to dogs," What a repulse was that ? " She said, Truth, Lord, yet the dogs eat the crumbs that fall from their master's table," verse 27. Lord, though I am a Gentile sinner, or a dog, yet let me have the crumbs that fall from the table thou hast spread for the children.

" Then Jesus said, O woman, great is thy faith, be it unto thee even as thou wilt," verse 28. Thus it appears no discouragement, no repulses will such who have a great faith regard ; they will have no denial. Such say, with Jacob, " I will not let thee go until thou hast blessed me." A weak faith, if it meets with repulses, or is denied the mercy desired, is ready to give up all hope, and leave off praying. But a strong faith will " wait upon God, that hideth his face from the house of Israel," Isa. viii. 17.

(8.) A great faith, or a strong believer, believes in hope against hope. **A strong Christian, one strong in faith believes in hope against hope.** This did Abraham ; he was strong in faith, and believed when he could not see by any human reason how the promise of God could be accomplished, " And being not weak in faith, he considered not his own body now dead, neither yet the deadness of Sarah's womb," Rom. iv. 18, 19, 20, " but was strong in faith, giving glory to God."

9. A strong faith can live in a famine of the word, or when all outward means fail, weak Christians must have fresh provision every day. A man strong in faith lives upon the fulness of the fountain, and can live when the stream seems dried up ; such bring forth fruit in times of drought ; " They are not careful in years of drought, neither shall cease from yielding fruit," Jer. xvii. 8.

10. A strong Christian can trust God, and wait patiently upon him, **A strong faith can trust God.** though he hath it not given unto him every day ; but weak believers are like to poor men, they must have present money, all in hand, they cannot live upon a bare promise."

(11.) One strong can get up a high hill, when a weak person is ready to faint, and be weary ; so a strong believer, one strong in faith, can ascend courageously up the hill of opposition, and get over the stile of carnal reason, and go through the valley **Isa. xxiii. 4. Isa. lxiv. 7, 18.** of the shadow of death, and not faint ; but the weak are weary by running with foot-men, and how then can they " contend with horses, or live in the overflowing of Jordan," Jer. xii. 5.

12. A believer who hath a great faith, can obey God in the hardest thing, though it be to offer up an only and a beloved son, whereas a weak believer cannot hardly yield in a way of obedience, to precepts very easy ; when opposition is made against him, a strong believer consults not with flesh and blood, nor his own strength, nor who are against him ; but the worth and worthiness of Jesus Christ, and what strength is engaged for him.

APPLICATION

Exhort. Be exhorted to labour for a great faith.

MOTIVES

1. Thou hast strong corruptions that daily beset thee, and a strong devil **Motives to stir up all to labour for a strong faith.** to tempt thee, and a world full of powerful enticements to deceive thee.
2. Consider that the work is great thou hast to do, and it needs great strength, or a strong faith, it is fighting work, and set forth by running of a race ; also it is called wrestling, all which require much strength.

3. Because thou knowest not what sufferings thou mayest be called unto, though we have liberty now, peace now, prosperity now, yet persecution, trouble, and adversity may break in upon us; our way may be rough and rocky, which will be difficult for weak believers to pass through.

4. Because a great faith (as you have heard) tends most to glorify God, or to bring honour to his great name, and it argues also that thou hast the clearer knowledge of God. "They that know thy name will put their trust in thee," Psal. ix. 10.

5. A strong believer meets with the strongest consolation, or with the sweetest comfort; commonly according to the degree of our faith, or measure of grace, is our peace, joy, and consolation. How often do weak believers droop in their spirits, and at every turn are ready to let their anchor, hope, slip? therefore labour after a strong and great faith.

6. Have you not been a great while a gathering, and have had fruitful seasons to grow and gather strength in? what, alas! be always babes in Christ? This is a reproach to the ministry, and a dishonour to yourselves.

1. If you would have a great or strong faith, be sure see your faith is of the right kind, I mean, the faith of God's elect: for if it be not of the right kind, it is not worth improving, for at the best it will be but a strong presumption, and deceive your souls at last.

What we should do to get a strong faith.

2. If thou wouldst have a great faith, pray hard, be much in prayer; he that believes not effectually, will not pray fervently: cry, Lord, increase our faith; this was the prayer of all the disciples.

3. Consult the power, goodness, love, mercy, and faithfulness of God, who hath promised, and cannot deny himself.

4. Take heed of the least sin; for nothing tends more to spoil the growth of faith, and to sow the seeds of doubts and fear in the soul then sin.

5. Give all diligence; the faith of assurance is not easily obtained, attend upon the word and ordinances, give all diligence to make your calling and election sure, that is, sure to yourselves.

Lastly, call to remembrance your former experience, and do your first works, and that is the way to recover lost strength, and to grow in grace. So much to this parable.

18. THE LEAVEN

Another parable spake he, saying, the kingdom of heaven is like unto leaven, which a woman took and hid in three measures of meal until the whole was leavened.— Matt. xiii. 33.

THE scope of this parable, or the design of the Lord Jesus in speaking of it, is doubtless much the same with the former, viz.

The scope and design of this parable.

1. To show the quick and powerful nature of the word of God upon the hearts of men.

2. To show his disciples that the word must be received into the heart before it can operate.

3. To let them know that though the gospel had then but small success, yet in the end it would wonderfully spread and prevail throughout all the world.

Leaven is spoken of in the gospel under a threefold consideration, or as referring to three things:

1. To the doctrine and hypocrisy of the Pharisees; "Beware of the leaven of the Pharisees, which is hypocrisy," Luke xii. 1.

2. To malice and wickedness; "Purge out therefore the old leaven, therefore let us keep the feast neither with the leaven of malice and wickedness, but with the unleavened bread of sincerity and truth," 1 Cor. v. 7, 8. In both these places it is mentioned as an evil and hurtful thing.

3. In this place the kingdom of heaven, or the holy word and gospel, is compared unto it.

From hence we may perceive what different use our Saviour makes of the same thing, which ariseth from the different nature or quality of that which he refers unto, as, in another case, Christ is compared to a thief, and Satan also is compared to a thief; the first in respect of the suddenness and uncertainty of his coming at the last day, the second upon the account of his evil and abominable design, which is to steal, rob, and destroy ; so upon the account of these noble and excellent qualities of a lion, our Saviour is compared to a lion ; and upon the consideration of those evil, ravenous, and devouring qualities of a lion, the devil is also compared to a lion ; and so in several other cases. *Our Lord makes use of one thing for different ends, from the different qualities thereof.*

1. By the kingdom of heaven I understand is meant the gospe-church, or the dispensation thereof.

2. By leaven is meant the Word of God, which our Lord intimates hereby (where it is received and hid in the heart), powerfully works and operates.

"Which a woman hid."

Jesus Christ, no doubt, is meant hereby ; but because it is a woman's work to leaven her meal, he saith, "A woman hid," &c.

"In three measures of meal." That is, but a small quantity, denoting the Word of God was received at first but by a very few persons," Luke xv. 8—10. *See parable of the lost piece of money.*

"Until the whole was leavened." That is, all the whole body of the elect. He shows hereby, that when the Gospel began first to be preached, and in a spiritual way, to leaven the souls of men; it should wonderfully succeed, and never totally cease, until multitudes, even all that shall be saved, were leavened therewith. Note.

Doct. The Word of God may be compared to leaven.

1. I shall show you in what respects the Word may be compared to leaven.

2. Apply it.

1. Leaven is of a diffusive quality. So the Word of God, through the Spirit, is of a diffusive nature, both in respect to every soul that receiveth it, and also in respect of people to whom it comes ; for though at first but a few at Jerusalem, and the regions thereabout, received the Gospel; yet how did it spread and diffuse itself into many nations in a short time ? *Why the Word of God is compared to leaven.*

2. Leaven diffuseth itself gradually; it doth not leaven the whole lump presently. *The Word like to it.*

So the Gospel spread and operated by degrees; as it diffuseth itself into every faculty of the soul at first, so it never ceaseth until the life, and whole man, is leavened therewith. And thus also it shall never cease in the world in its workings and operations, until all nations are spiritually enlightened and leavened with the quickening and saving influences thereof. *Leaven is of a diffusive nature.*

3. Leaven is of assimilating nature : makes all the meal that is leavened to be of one and the same lump. So the Word and grace of God makes the whole soul like itself, or a whole family or nation, where it is once in truth received, the very same people, both in doctrine and conversation. *The Word, like leaven makes meal as of one lump.*

4. Leaven is of a quickening and powerful nature. So is the Word of God "both quick and powerful," Heb. iv. 12. It searcheth and operates, and quickeneth the whole soul, and all that receive it. "Thy Word hath quickened me," Psal. cxix. 50. *The Word like leaven is a quickening nature.*

5. Leaven is hid in the meal which leaveneth. So the Word of God must be hid in the heart, both in the understanding, will, and affection, if the person be spiritually leavened with it. "Thy Word have I hid in my heart, that I might not sin against thee," Psal. cxix. 11. *The Word, like leaven, must be hid.*

It is not enough to receive it into our mouths, or to have it in our Bibles, but we must receive it (in the love thereof) into our hearts, or else Satan will steal it away, or it will not, it cannot work either upon our hearts or lives.

6. Leaven, it is observed, is of a softening nature; though the meal be crushed down hard, yet if the leaven be hid in it, it will make it soft, and mellow. So the Word of God makes the hard heart soft and tender. How soft were their hard hearts made by the Word of God that St. Peter preached to, whom he charged with murdering the Lord of life and glory? O how did *The Word like leaven, of a softening nature. Acts ii. 36.*

they weep and mourn for their great sin and wickedness ! Let a man be never so stout and hard-hearted, if once he is helped to receive the Word of God, he will find his heart broken, and made soft and pliable to the will of God. Sirs, " What must I do to be saved," Acts xvi. 30, saith the jailor. O now he trembles, now he is melted, who before was a hard-hearted wretch, having bitterly scourged Paul and Silas, and put them into the inward prison, and he being not contented with that neither, he made their feet fast in the stocks. But O what a change did the Word make !

7. Leaven secretly and invisibly worketh and altereth the meal, and maketh a change of it, turning it into dough. So the workings and operations of the Word of God are secret and invisible. Our Saviour alludes to this when he compares the workings of the Spirit in regeneration to the wind ; and as the Word works invisibly, so, (as was hinted before,) it makes a mighty change. The Word is that incorruptible seed by which regeneration is wrought in the soul.

The Word like leaven of a changing nature. John iii. 8.

8. A little leaven will leaven the whole lump ; so a small quantity, or but a dram of grace, or one word set home upon the heart of three thousand souls, it will leaven them all, Acts ii. 4.

1 Cor. v. 6.

The Word like leaven, leaveneth the whole lump at once.

9. Leaven answers a great design. It is to prepare the meal to be moulded into a loaf, and so become bread for the family.

So this spiritual leaven, the Word, is by Jesus Christ appointed for a great design ; viz., even to mould and fashion poor sinners for himself, and so fit them for his own use, and that they may be meet and fit matter for his church on earth, and for the church triumphant in heaven. The whole church is by this means made one bread; " For we being many, are one bread, and one body," 1 Cor. x. 17.

APPLICATION

Caution. Let all from hence learn rightly to distinguish between one quality and another. Of that thing our Lord refers to in symbolical and parabolical Scriptures ; for from the sour quality of leaven, (and in some other respects,) false doctrine, hypocrisy, and malice (as you heard) is compared unto it.

But the Word of God hath no unpleasant nor sour quality in it ; but it is the only means by which, through the Spirit, the old leaven, the leaven of malice, hypocrisy, and all false doctrine is purged out.

2. From hence we may infer, what a great difference there is between the godly and the ungodly ; the one are leavened with new leaven, *i. e.*, the Word and Spirit of God ; and they are assimilated into the nature thereof; and the other having the old, corrupt, and sour leaven in them of sin and hypocrisy, remain corrupt, vile, and abominable in God's sight.

3. From hence we also learn, that the Word and Spirit of God works and operates physically. Mere moral suasions can never change the sinner's heart : no the grace of the Word must be hid in the heart by Christ's hand. Leaven put into the meal, and hid there works as physic that is given to a sick person ; for if it was the bare preaching of the Word that leavened sinners, why are not all quickened and changed by it ? Sirs, like as a woman opens her meal, puts in her leaven, so doth the Lord Jesus open the heart of his Lydias, and puts his leaven, his Holy Spirit, into them ; by which means they are renewed, changed, and moulded into the image of the Word.

4. Let us cry to God that he would send his word and holy gospel forth to leaven all the nations of the world ; the whole earth shall be filled with the knowledge of the glory of the Lord, in the latter days, as you have heard in my opening the parable of the mustard-seed ; which occasions me to speak very briefly to this.

Lastly, By what hath been said, let us try and examine ourselves, and see whether we have been and are leavened throughout with this spiritual leaven, the Word and Spirit of God : You have heard what an assimilating nature it is of, and how it diffuseth itself into the whole man, and changes both heart and life.

19. THE DRAGNET

Again, the kingdom of heaven is like a net cast into the sea, and gathereth of every kind : which, when it was full, they drew it to shore, and sat down and gathered the good into vessels, and cast the bad away. So it shall be at the end of the world; the angels shall come forth and sever the wicked from the just; and shall cast the wicked into a furnace of fire ; there shall be wailing and gnashing of teeth.—Matt. xiii. 47—50.

1. THE design of our Lord in this parable, is to discover that in the church there shall be a mixture of good and bad, sincere believers and hypocrites, until the end of the world. *The scope of the parable opeed.*

2. To show that the gospel is appointed as an instrument to gather sinners to Jesus Christ, and into his church, by the preaching thereof.

3. That at the end of the world there will be a full and perfect separation of the righteous from the wicked ; and as the one will then appear very happy, so the other will be very miserable for ever.

"The kingdom of heaven," &c. By the kingdom of heaven I understand is meant the whole dispensation and ministration of the gospel, and so taken here by all expositors I have met with, both the grace dispensed in it, and the means of that grace how dispensed, viz., by the preaching thereof through the operations of the Spirit : the bare preaching, or the external ministration thereof, taketh some, so as to bring them into the visible church ; but none are caught by Christ, but those the Spirit effectually worketh upon : "Many are called, but few chosen." *The parts opened.* *What is meant by the kingdom of heaven.* *Year of his ministry ?.*

"Is like to a net," &c., that is, the ministration of the gospel. *What is meant by the net.*

Doct. The gospel preached may be fully compared to a net.

I. A net is a proper engine or instrument to catch or gather fish : so the gospel, or word of God preached, is a proper instrument to gather sinners out of the world into the church, both visible and invisible. "It pleaseth God by the foolishness of preaching to save them that believe," 1 Cor. i. 2.

II. A net is contrived by the wisdom of men to take fish out of the sea or river, &c., and it is an effectual instrument to that end and purpose : so the gospel, especially by the preaching thereof, is contrived or appointed by the wisdom of God to convert the souls of men, and it is efficacious or powerful to this end, "I am not ashamed of the gospel of Christ, for it is the power of God to salvation to every one that believeth," &c., Rom. i. 16, that is, by the preaching of it, through the operations of the Holy Ghost, it is a proper instrument of God's power. "The preaching of the gospel is to them that perish foolishness, but unto us which are saved it is the power of God," 1 Cor. i. 18.

III. A net is cast into the river or sea before it can take fish, so the word of gospel must be preached that sinners may be converted ; the preaching of the gospel is the casting of this spiritual net, that being the ordinary way or means God hath appointed to work upon the souls of sinners. There are other ways to take fish, but none so effectual and common as that of a net, so there are other ways by which God is pleased to convert sinners, but none are so effectual and common as the preaching of the gospel may be ; where one is by reading or by the rod, &c., converted, hundreds are by preaching.

IV. A net takes fish out of their proper element, where they live and love to be, so the preaching of the gospel taketh such sinners who are truly wrought upon out of that element where they naturally lived and loved to live, viz., out of their sins, their sinful practices and course of life, where once they were, " and drinketh in iniquity as this implies water," Job. xv. 16.

1. Man naturally hath a strong appetite or desire to sin, " What is man that drinketh up scorning like water ?" Job xxxiv. 7, he drinks full draughts of sin, they sin as willingly as a thirsty man drinks, and as naturally as a fish drinks water.

(2.) To drink denotes pleasure and content ; as a thirsty person desires   See Carry 1. drink, so he is pleased with it : so sinners naturally do not only thirst after sin, or to fulfil the lusts of the flesh, but they take delight and pleasure in wickedness ; this shows they are fish in their natural element, and not yet taken out of it, not changed or converted.

(3.) Naturally a man sins with ease even as a man drinks ; it is no pain to a thirsty man to drink, a little matter will persuade him to drink that which he loves.   So sinners need not to be entreated to commit those sins they love and are naturally inclined to.

(4.) Drinking is a frequent act : fish drink every day, yea, continually ; so a wicked man sins often, he sins continually ; he cannot cease from sin ; the cup of iniquity (before he is taken out of the sea of this world) is never from his mouth.

5. To drink iniquity like water, denotes sinners, abounding in sin ; he sins abundantly ; (some men drink till they are drunk, and their reason is gone) ; so sinners drink in iniquity abundantly, till they are intoxicated and deprived of all their reason and spiritual senses ; nay, not only sin away their reason, but their substance, their health, and their souls also.

V. It is the proper work of fishermen to cast their net into the sea to catch fish, it belongs to them ; it is their right ; every man is not allowed to do it, so it is the proper work of Christ's ministers to preach the gospel ; " Follow me, and I will make you fishers of men," Matt. iv. 18, 19.   It belongs to them, and them only, to cast the net of the gospel, that Jesus Christ hath made ministers or fishers of men, viz., such that he hath endowed with grace, and ministerial gifts ; and hath called, and whom his church approveth of, and also hath called forth to attend upon this work and office ; men cannot make ministers of Christ : many are ministers of man's making, not of Christ's making.   Also human learning or knowledge of the tongues will not do it, nor can bishops do it ; no, it is Christ's work only ; nor may any preach that think they are gifted ; for unless they are regularly called by a true church to whom they belong, they are intruders if they take upon them to preach the gospel, " How shall they preach except they are sent," " I will make you fishers of men," Rom. x. 15.   Not to fish for a livelihood, or good benefice, but to catch and save the souls of men.

VI. A net takes fish (when they are caught) out of their proper element, and they die immediately, so those sinners who are indeed taken, or spiritually and savingly wrought upon by the preaching the word, are taken out of that element where they lived, and loved to live before ; i. e., out of a course of sin and wickedness ; and such die presently to sin, and to all the vanities of the sea of this world.   But as a parable does not go upon all four, so pray observe that here is a great disparity ; fish are caught to be destroyed, or devoured ; but the design of God, by the net of the gospel, in taking of sinners, is to save them ; it is not for their hurt, but for their eternal good.

VII. A net must be cast into the sea or river with judgment, by a skilful fisherman ; it requires wisdom to use it to answer the end appointed.   So ministers, Christ's spiritual fishermen, ought to be men of great knowledge, skill, wisdom, and experience. " I being crafty (saith Paul) " caught you by guile," 2 Cor. xii. 16, what was this craft ?   Why, he made no gain of them ; he laid no burden on them, or used not his liberty, but he used far greater wisdom than that to gain sinners to Christ, he being a " Steward of the mysteries of God," 1 Cor. iv. 1.

With what wisdom should ministers preach the gospel, that they may win souls to Christ ? " The preacher, because he was wise, sought out acceptable words, even words of wisdom," Eccl. xii. 10.

They are open dark and obscure texts, and wisely to unfold the deep mysteries of Christ and the gospel ; they must discover the miserable condition sinners are in, the evil also of sin, and the absolute necessity of Christ, and show the way how sinners must be saved, and receive the Lord Jesus, they must not use the words of man's wisdom, but the wisdom of Christ, " My speech and my preaching was not with enticing words of man's wisdom, but in the demonstration of the Spirit, and with power, that your faith should not stand in the wisdom of men but in the power of God," 1 Cor. ii. 4.   He acted not the part

of a philosopher or orator at Athens, but used plainness of speech, and dis- Human elo-
owned human eloquence, and checked all plausible affectations and artifice of quence con-
demned in
words, which the orators of his time used ; he was not for rhetorical flourishes, preaching
or persuasive oratory ; not for the inductions of Plato, nor the sylogisms of the gospel.
Aristotle, nor the subtilties of Seneca, nor the smooth and elaborate blandishments of Cicero.
No, no, he delivered the gospel freely, boldly, and plainly, without rhetorical persuasions,
in the demonstration of the Spirit ; and so ought all Christ's ministers.

VIII. A net is cast where a fisherman hath ground to hope he may take store of fish,
so a minister should preach where multitudes of people are gathered together, when an
opportunity doth present ; thus did our Lord, when he " saw the multitude, he sat down
and opened his mouth," Matt. v. 1, and began to teach them, or to cast in his blessed net;
sometimes he preached in the temple ; and at the last day, the great day of the feast, when
many thousands were together, " He cried with a loud voice, if any man thirst, let him
come to me and drink," John vii. 27.   Yet a minister is to preach to a few, when but a
few will come to hear him ; and may be may catch as many souls then as when he casts
in his net where a thousand are assembled together.

IX. Sometimes fishermen labour all night (as Peter and John did) and take nothing :
it is God that blesses their labour when they succeed well ; but when they succeed not,
they must not be discouraged ; they may prosper well at another time.

So ministers sometimes preach month after month, and not one sinner is converted, and
all the increase is of God, 1 Cor. iii. 6 ; also it is Christ that directs them to cast in the
net on the right side of the ship ; but though but few or none are caught for one season,
yet they ought not to faint or be discouraged, for their labour shall not be in vain in the
Lord ; and perhaps at another season many may be brought home to God.

X. A net takes fish of every kind, some great ones, some small ones ; some good, and
some bad : so the gospel net gathers of every sort, some rich some poor, some great ones,
(but not many of that kind) some little ones, who are despised in the eyes of the world ;
and also some who are great sinners, and some more civilized and sober persons ; some
old, and some young, nay, some good and some bad ; (we have a proverb that they are
not all fish that comes to the net ;) so they are not all true Christians that seem to be
taken by the net of the gospel.   Many prove foolish virgins, or abominable hypocrites.

XI. A fisherman's work is very hard, and he is exposed oftentimes to be tossed on the
tempestuous seas ; so is the work of a minister of Christ, they labour in the word and
doctrine, they labour in their study, and also in the pulpit, and are frequently exposed to
the storms of reproaches, temptations of the world, and to the bitter storms of persecution
of wicked men ; as Paul shows what storms he met withal.

XII. A fisherman sometimes encompasseth a great multitude of fish at one draught;
what a multitude Peter took when his Master bade him cast in the net on the right side
of the ship !   But Peter catched a better draught when he became a fisher of men, even
not fewer than three thousand at one time, Luke v. 4—6.

XIII. A fisherman taketh commonly more small fish than great; so a minister finds
that more of the poorer sort are converted than the rich, more ignoble in the eyes of the
world than noble ; " the poor received the gospel," Matt. xi. 5.   " Ye see your calling,
brethren, how that not many wise men after the flesh, not many mighty, not many noble,
are called," 1 Cor. i. 26.   " Have any of the Pharisees or the rulers believed on him,"
John vii. 48.

XIV. It is not known what fish are caught in the net, until the net be pulled up to the
shore ; so it is not known what sort of persons the net of the gospel hath taken, until the
last day, when Jesus Christ will draw the gospel net to the eternal shore : and then those
who are truly gracious, shall be received by him unto heaven ; and the bad, or all hypocrites, shall be thrown into hell.

Like a net cast into the sea, which taketh of every kind.   By the sea is meant the
world, out of which all believers are taken by the net of the gospel : " I have chosen you
out of the world." The world is

Doct.   This world is, and may be, compared to the sea. compared to
the sea.

I. I shall show you in what respects it may be so compared.   2. Apply it.

1. The sea is a turbulent element, full of commotions, full of swelling and threatening
waves ; so this world is full of commotions ; and I think never fuller than it is at this
time ; certainly those days are upon us, of which our Saviour spake, " the sea and the
waves roaring," Luke xxi. 25.   He alludes to this world, the mystical sea ; and by the
sea and waves roaring, doubtless is meant distress of nations, or those great and amazing

commotions that shall be in the world, and dreadful threats of the enemies of the church; but as the sea is the Lord's, and he made it, so he also alone can and doth master it; he stays its proud waves, and saith, "hitherto shalt thou come, and no further," Job xxxviii. 11, And as God sets bounds and bars to the sea, so he doth to this metaphorical sea; "Thou rulest the raging of the sea; when the waves arise, thou stillest them," Ps. lxxxix. 9. God maketh the stormy sea calm! so did our Lord Jesus Christ, he rebuked the wind and the sea, and there was a great calm.

The winds and the sea obey him; even so the Lord can soon make the swelling sea of this world still and quiet, Matt. viii. 26, 27; "He stilleth the noise of the sea, the noise of the waves, and the tumult of the people," Psal. lxv. 7. "The wrath of man shall praise thee, and the remainder of wrath shalt thou restrain," Psal. lxxvi. 10.

II. The sea is sometimes so tempestuous that fishermen cannot work; so persecution ariseth sometimes so high in these figurative seas, that Christ's ministers have been tossed with the waves into prison, and taken off their work, and others have laboured in great danger both of their goods, liberties, and lives.

III. In the sea are many strange monsters, called sea-monsters; the "Sea-monsters draw out their breasts, they give suck to their young," Lam. iv. 3; so in the sea of this world are many cruel tyrants, who like strange monsters devour mankind. What strange monsters were those four beasts which Daniel saw to rise up out of the sea? The four grand monarchies of the world. But the fourth, the Roman, was the worst, Dan. vii. 3—4. What monsters have the papists been, and their evil offspring. What traiterous, what bloody, what persecuting, what profane, and what hypocritical monsters; what a strange monster is the French tyrant at this day!

IV. The sea is the proper element of fish, both great and small! so this world is the proper element for ungodly sinners of all sorts and kind, who in sin live, sport, and delight themselves.

V. There is no sailing through the sea without the compass, or having skill in navigation; nor without wind, or a fit and proper gale; so there is no sailing through this world to the regions of eternal blessedness above, without the rule or compass of God's word, nor unless we have Christ for our Pilot, and a sweet gale of the Holy Spirit to fill our sails.

VI. There are many sea pirates; so there are also in this world many deceivers, so spiritual thieves and impostors, who are the worst of pirates; and these make our passage through this troublesome ocean very dangerous; many by these deceivers, have been robbed of much treasure.

VII. There are likewise many rocks, dangerous rocks, and sands in the sea, which mariners ought to know, and strive to escape, or they may soon suffer shipwreck; so we who sail through the sea or ocean of this world, ought to know and labour to escape all those spiritual rocks, which many for want of wisdom and care are daily split upon, and perish for ever; there is the rock of presumption on the one hand, and the quicksands of desperation on the other hand, and the nature of both I have elsewhere opened, (see "Every mountain and hill brought low, and every valley exalted," at the beginning of this book.) Paul tells us of some who suffered shipwreck, 1 Tim. i. 19, 20, in his days.

VIII. A ship had need to have a strong anchor; "Hope is the anchor of the soul, both sure and steadfast," Heb. vi. 19; and it enters within the vail, it is cast upward; the rock it must take hold of is Jesus Christ, and to strengthen it we have the promise, the covenant, and the oath of God, Heb. vi. 18. This hope is safe and firm, and secures the soul in the midst of all storms and tempests whatsoever: were it not for this anchor, when the soul like a ship, is tossed with a tempest, it would be broken to pieces. Afflictions, temptations, delusions, and persecutions, are like storms and billows in a troublesome sea.

My brethren, I prosecute this and some other parables according to the analogy of faith, though perhaps farther than the main scope will bear; which tropical writers are allowed to do. The world is in this parable campared to the sea, and our souls (though not here) are compared to a ship. Moreover, here sinners are compared to fish; and this brings me to another proper allusion.

IX. There are in the sea a multitude of fish, but yet but a very few of them comparatively, are ever taken by the fishermen's net. So in this world are a multitude of sinners, but yet very few are ever converted: "Narrow is the way, and straight is the gate, that leadeth unto life, and very few there be that find it," Matt. vii. 13.

X. Several fish that fishermen take (I told you) are not good; and so many sinners the gospel-net takes, who are brought into the church, are not sincere believers. For, as a fisherman sometimes takes fish out of the sea, which he knows not what they are, (as I have heard ;) so ministers know not what kind of persons some are which the church receives : and this is one of the chief things our Saviour signifies by this and some other precedent parable ; viz., that in the church, while this world continueth, there will be a mixture of good and bad.

Quest. But are there not marks or characters whereby good and sincere Christians may be known ?

1. Answ. Yea, the Holy Ghost hath left many characters how we may know ourselves and others; but many hypocrites are so much like sincere believers in many things, (as tares are like to wheat) that it is very hard infallibly to judge who are good and who are bad. Legal convictions and outward reformation of life, seem very much to resemble evangelical conversion; and common illuminations, the special illuminations of the Holy Ghost. Also what outward act of obedience may not a hypocrite perform, which is performed by a true believer ? Moreover, a bad professor may not fall into such gross sins which a true and good Christian may ; so that it is difficult to discern who are upright in heart, and who are not. *It is hard to know a good and sincere Christian from an hypocrite.*

Yet I shall add here a few marks of a good and sincere Christian, whereby he may know himself. *How a sincere Christian may be known.*

1. He may know partly by the doctrine, or good principles of religion he hath received, or by that good, safe, and only foundation on which he builds all his hope, trust, comfort, and salvation, which is Christ ; " For other foundation can no man lay than that is laid, which is Jesus Christ," 1 Cor. iii. 11.

He that builds his faith, his justification, his hope, and salvation, on any thing else than on Christ, on Christ's obedience, merits, and righteousness, is a false professor.

2. He may be known by the goodness of his state ; I mean, by that blessed change that hath passed upon him, it being not a change of his life only, but an effectual change of his heart also.

3. He may be known by that faith and other graces he hath received : where true faith is wrought in any person, there is very grace. Moreover, where true faith is wrought, there the fruits of faith presently appear, and such operations do attend it, that all that obtain it are humble and self-denying persons ; their hearts also are purged *Acts xv. 9.* and sanctified in a gracious manner ; and as to hope, he that hath a true and lively " hope, purifies himself, even as Christ is pure," 1 John iii. 3, and he that has the grace of faith and love, esteems of Christ as most precious, 1 Pet. ii. 7, he is to that soul the " Chiefest among ten thousand," Cant. v. 10 ; and also such dearly love all the children of God. " By this we know that we are passed from death unto life, because we love the brethren," 1 John iii. 14.

4. He may be known to himself by that hatred he hath of all sin ; not only because of the guilt of it, and as it is against his good, but also because of the filth of it, and as sin is against God. This was the cause why Joseph durst not commit folly with his mistress, and why sin makes a true child of God to go mourning all the day. O he wants a clearer likeness and conformity to the image of God, and to Jesus Christ, as holy Paul shows us in respect of himself ; they would be holy as we, as happy, Phil. iii. 14.

5. They may judge of themselves by considering those principles by which they act, and by the main end they aim at in all they do in religious matters ; it is that God may be glorified, and Jesus Christ magnified in their bodies, whether it is by life or death.

6. By the goodness and godliness of their whole lives and conversations, and heavenliness of their desires and affections, as also by the constancy of their course, in their universal obedience to Christ ; they following him always whithersoever he goes, being the same in private, as in public, in whom no changes makes a change, though they may fall into sin, or under temptations, and not be in that good frame at one time, as at another ; and may be also in a withering condition in their own apprehensions, through the prevalency of corruption, temptation, or God's hiding his face from them ; yet they rise, and shall rise again, and revive as the corn. These are some of those signs of good Christians.

Quest. What do you think of them that decry all signs of grace, or marks of justified persons ?

Ans. I think they are under a delusion of Satan ; and such who hearken to them, for want of trying themselves, may soon, with a presumptuous faith and hope of heaven, blindfold fall down to hell : will they contemn the teachings of the Holy Ghost and the holy apostles ? Are there not many signs *Such that decry signs of a justified person detested.*

laid down in God's word, whereby we may and ought to try and examine ourselves?

XI. There are some dead fish in the sea and in rivers which stink abominably; so there are some sinners in the world who lie dead in sin to such a degree, or lie dead in the wicked one, that they stink in the nostrils of God, and in the nostrils of all holy and good men. Moreover, it is observed, that a dead fish always swims down the stream, it goes as the tide carries it; so such men who always swim with the tide, or walk according to the course of this world, and turn as the times turn, who will be of that religion that is uppermost, it is to be feared are dead: for a living fish, it is observed, always swims against the stream; so a living and a true spiritual Christian will swim against the stream of temptations, and opposition of what nature soever; he will not be borne down by the stream of delusions, nor by the stream of persecution; he never changes his course; let what religion soever be countenanced, or set up by authority, he is still the same.

XII. The sea drowns many a man who ventures thereon; so this world drowns and utterly destroys a multitude of sinners, by the snares of the riches, honours, pleasures, and perplexing fears and cares thereof.

XIII. Those that go to sea should look for storms; and not only look for them, but also prepare for them. Moreover, there are many signs by which seamen perceive a storm is near; as by the winds, the working of the sea, and by the gathering of the clouds.

So believers who are sailing through the sea of this world, should look and prepare for storms, afflictions, temptations, persecution, and amazing revolutions: " In the world you shall have tribulation," John xvi. 33.

Our Lord also hath given us warning of them that we might be ready. " These things have I spoken unto you that ye should not be offended in me; they shall put you out of the synagogue; yea, the time cometh that whosoever killeth you will think he doth God's service," John xvi. 1, 2. Likewise God's people perceive storms may be near by observing the signs of the times.

1. When sin, more than ordinarily, abounds.

2. When the clouds gather, and the sea begins to roar afar off: i. e., when the nations in an unusual manner, prepare for war.

3. When general deadness, security, and formality seizeth upon the people of God, all being fallen into a sleeping and slumbering condition, and love grows cold to one another, and the power of religion is much gone.

4. When divisions, animosities, strife, and contentions amongst Christians increase, this hath always been the presage of a storm.

5. When the most knowing and discerning saints and ministers of Christ are in great expectation of some amazing judgments, God hath always given some hints of his dreadful approaches to some of his people.

6. When the price of gospel seasons, gospel liberty, and gospel ordinances, is grown very low, or is but little prized, God commonly brings a storm of one kind or another, and raises the price of them.

7. When strange signs and prodigies happen in a nation, or kingdom, this hath been looked upon as the presage of approaching calamities; and also of that great storm of God's wrath upon Babylon: and what prodigious earthquakes, and commotions, and other amazing signs, have we had in the air, waters, and on the earth, of late years? certainly we are near some great storm, or amazing revolution.

" Which gathereth of every kind."

Every kind may refer to people of every nation where the gospel comes, and the net is cast; as at Jerusalem, (when Peter threw his net into the sea) there were people of many nations; the text says, " Devout men of every nation under heaven, Parthians, Medes, Elamites, Phrygia, Pamphylia in Egypt, Jews, and prosyletes, Cretes, and Arabians," Acts ii. 5, 9, 10, &c., and some of these might afterwards be converted, or at leastwise many of the Gentiles in divers nations were taken by the net of the gospel; (2.) or, some of all degrees and ranks of men; or, (3.) As I hinted, sinners of all sorts, great sinners and small, old and young. (4.) Moreover, it gathers some who prove good, and others who prove bad.

" And when it was full, they drew it to shore," Matt. xiii. 48; that is, when a fisherman hath taken all he concludes his net can take, he draws it to shore; so when the gospel net hath gathered all that God intends to call, to save, and bring into Christ, then it may be said to be full; even when the fulness of the Gentiles is brought in, and the Jews are called, and God is risen up from the mery-seat, and the summer is ended, or the end of the world is come, then the net of the gospel shall be drawn to shore, and never be cast into the sea any more, for time then shall go into eternity.

" And gathered the good into vessels, but cast the bad away ; so shall it be at the end of the world, the angels shall come forth, and sever the wicked from the just," ver. 49.

Our Lord hath opened this part of the parable himself ; when the end of the world cometh, it shall be known what kind of professors the gospel net hath taken ; that will be a discriminating day, and also a time of separation ; the angels shall gather the wheat from the tares, the sheep from the goats, the wise virgins from the foolish, and the good fish from the bad.

The nature of this separation being showed in my opening some other parable, I shall not speak farther to it here.

" And shall cast them into a furnace of fire ; there shall be wailing and gnashing of teeth."

1. The gathering the good into vessels may denote two things : (1.) That the saints, when Christ comes, shall possess the earth, or inherit the earth ; even when the wicked are cut off, this is promised to the meek ; " Blessed are the meek for they shall inherit the earth," Matt. v. 5, that is, peaceably and quietly possess the earth ; " All the kingdoms under the whole heavens shall be given to the people of the saints of the Most High," &c., Dan. vii. 27, which may refer to the thousand years' reign of Christ and the saints upon the earth ; Rev. xx. " The meek shall inherit the earth, and delight themselves in abundance of peace," Psa. xxxvii. 11. This is one vessel into which all sincere believers shall be put. (2.) It no doubt signifies their being gathered into heaven ; that glorious vessel is prepared for them ; " for great is your reward in heaven," Matt. v. 12.

2. The casting of the bad into a furnace of fire, signifies their being thrown into hell, which is sometimes called a furnace of fire, and sometimes a lake of fire and brimstone ; Rev. xx. 15, and very remarkable it is, that thus, or much to the same purpose, our Lord closes with several parables. The wrath of God is often compared to fire, because of the pain and anguish that such feel that are cast into a furnace of fire. " Go into everlasting fire, prepared for the devil and his angels," Matt. xxv. 41. What fire can that be in which angelical nature can be tormented, but the dreadful wrath of God, who is called " a consuming fire ?" Heb. xii. 29. " What fire is that (saith a reverend writer) in which the devils can be tormented ? outward washings may as soon reach the conscience, Heb. ix. 9, as created fire torment an angel,"—yet, as he saith, I deny not when hell is called a furnace of fire, and a lake of fire, but that it imports a fire without, into which the matter, or persons of the wicked shall be cast : moreover, when our Lord speaketh of fire that cannot be quenched, or to a furnace of fire, and of the worm that dieth not, I apprehend he alludes both to the wrath of God within, gnawing and tormenting the conscience, and a created lake or furnace of fire to torment the body of the wicked ; for they shall be in a fire, both in respect of soul and body for ever. *Dr. Goodwin, 3 vol. p. 503.* *See the parable of the rich man and Lazarus.*

APPLICATION

Let all ungodly sinners praise the holy God for the net of the gospel, and that yet it is not gathered to the shore ; it is not yet full.

Christ's fishermen have not yet done fishing ; there are many of God's elect not yet caught, not yet converted, or gathered unto Christ ; and until that time comes, the gospel shall be continued to the world.

But certainly it grows towards evening time ; the day is well spent, and the summer near ended ; it will not be long before Christ will say, " let him that is holy be holy still, and him that is filthy be filthy still," Rev. xxii. 11 ; when all means of making the good better, or the bad good, shall cease for ever.

2. Let ministers also from hence be exhorted to work hard to catch the souls of men, or to bring them to God through Jesus Christ, because we have a fair day to work in ; storms may rise, and the sea of this world be so turbulent, that we may not be able to work : " I must work the work of him that sent me while it is day ; the night comes when no man can work," John ix. 4.

3. It may be of use, by way of lamentation. O how do many of us labour, and yet hardly catch anything ; how few souls come into the net ; it is a great discouragement to a fisherman, when he cannot get one good draught. We have laboured and toiled all night (saith Peter) and have caught nothing. And we may complain, who are spiritual fishermen, almost in the same manner. Also,

4. It may be for reproof to such ministers who labour not ; some fishermen are idle, and mind not the fishing season ; and so are some spiritual fishermen ; they are more industrious to catch a good benefit or maintenance, a good livelihood, than to bring souls to Christ.

5. Prize the gospel, it being ordained to convert and save the souls of men, as an instrument in the hands of Christ ; and look upon ministers as necessary in his hand, as fishermen are needful to cast their nets into the sea.

Moreover, cry to God to bless this fishery, and pray that he would raise up more to labour with this net, and also direct them to cast it on the right side of the ship, for as God speeds the plough of the gospel in convictions, so he doth also the net of the gospel in conversion ; it is God that gives the increase.

6. Terror. Woe to them sinners who are not taken by this blessed net before the season is ended : many will say hereafter as the prophet intimates, " The harvest is past, the summer is ended, and we are not saved," Jer. viii. 20.

7. However, there is comfort to Christ's ministers who labour with this net ; they may say with their Lord, " Though Israel be not gathered, yet they shall be glorious in the eyes of the Lord, and their God shall be their strength," Isa. xlix. 5 ; they shall not say always, we have laboured in vain, and have spent our strength for nought ; for their judgment is with the Lord and their work with their God : their labour shall not be in vain in the Lord.

8. To conclude, this parable looks with a terrible brow upon all hypocrites, and such who seem to be taken in this net ; and yet are not sincere persons, but like bad fish, for such shall be cast into that terrible furnace of fire, where there will be wailing, and gnashing of teeth. Hell is prepared for hypocrites and unbelievers ; let both fear and quake, both profane unbelievers and secret hypocrites ; for as such will be surprized, so they must dwell with devouring fire, and with everlasting burning. So much as to this parable.

20. THE SCRIBE

I

Then he said unto them, every scribe which is instructed unto the kingdom of heaven is like unto a good householder, which bringeth forth out of his treasure things both new and old. —Matt. xiii. 52.

This is the last parable continued in this chapter.

It is brought in by our blessed Lord, upon that answer his disciples gave to a question which he put to them in the precedent verse ; " Jesus said unto them, have ye understood all these things ? they said unto him, yea, Lord," Ver. 15.

The scope. Our Saviour in his preaching sought chiefly the profit and instruction of his own disciples, and to that end he opened and explained to them many parables : moreover, it appears by their answer, they did understand such parables that he put forth, which he explained not.

Ministers should labour to speak so as they may profit their hearers by this holy example of their Lord and Master.

Now they answering that they did understand all those things, he brings in this parable, viz., " Then said he unto them, every Scribe instructed unto the kingdom of heaven," &c.

Seeing then, (as if he should say) ye know and understand all these things, communicate your knowledge of them unto others : do not know for your own profit only, but be like a good householder, "every scribe," &c. Scribes among the Jews were not only clerks but teachers of the law unto the people, "for he taught as one having authority, and not as the Scribe," Matt. vii. 29, Ezra vii. 6. Ezra was a ready Scribe of the law of Moses, who stood upon a pulpit of wood, and read the law of God unto the people, and gave the sense of it to them; now in that Jewish teachers were called Scribes, it may, I *Ministers using of notes justified.* think, clearly hold forth that they did not only study and prepare matter to deliver unto the people, but that they did also commit it to writing, or the heads of what they had so studied, which to me may serve to justify ministers who use notes, that have not the natural gift of memory. I say, I know not but that this may be gathered from hence.

But to come to explain this parable.

1. By Scribes here our Saviour means the true ministers of the gospel, who are furnished with all divine gifts and graces proper for that sacred em- *Ministers called Scribes.* ployment, especially pastors of churches, because compared to a good house- holder that hath a family to provide for, to feed, and take care of.

2. By the kingdom of heaven, is meant (as I conceive) the dispensation of the gospel, or in a remote sense, the gospel church.

3. By an household, is (as I hinted before) intended a spiritual family, or a particular community of Christians, under the special care of a godly pastor.

4. By his treasure is doubtlessly meant his heavenly wisdom, knowledge, gifts, graces and experiences, "We have this treasure in earthen vessels, that the excellency of the power may be of God, and not of us," 2 Cor. iv. 7; which certainly refers to that know- ledge they had of Christ, and the glorious gospel; as to his bringing forth things both new and old, I shall open that in the perfection of that truth or proposition that rises from hence, which take as here followeth.

1. Doct. A good and faithful minister of the gospel ought to be like a rich householder, ever have store of spiritual provision, or have a well-freighted store-house, that he may bring forth all sorts of heavenly food, and not to have his provision to seek when his guests are come together to partake thereof.

Brethren, do not mistake me, God is the chief and proper spiritual householder, minis- ters and pastors of churches are but stewards of God's house. Indeed it is an high honour that is conferred upon them when Christ calls them householders; the family is not theirs, but the Lord's.

In speaking to this proposition, I shall do these things following:

1. I shall show you why pastors or ministers are compared to householders.

2. Show you why they should be well freighted, or have all sorts, and also great store of heavenly provision.

3. Show you what may be meant by their bringing forth of their treasure things both new and old.

4. Apply the whole.

Pray remember that I said before, ministers are but stewards, or deputy householders; as a king, or lord, may have and appoint a deputy householder. Now then,

First, they may be called householders in this sense, because as a deputy *Why minis- ters are called house- holders.* householder is chosen by his Lord to that office; so is every true and faithful minister, or pastor of a church, chosen and called by the Lord to that holy office and employment. Now they are not chosen by the Lord immediately, but mediately, not in an extraordinary manner, as the apostles were, but in an ordinary manner, i. e., by the election and suffrage of the church, as Christ hath directed in his word; for every church hath power, and ought to choose her own minister, or pastor, yet if such are chosen and called that Christ directeth his people to choose, they are such "which the Holy Ghost is said to make overseers," Acts xx. 28; and it is this indeed that gives them this great dignity, name, and office, of being stewards or deputy householders in a spiritual sense, according to the purport of this parable.

Secondly, they may be called householders in respect of that great charge and trust which is committed to them; a steward or householder of a lord or noble person, has the charge of all the family committed unto him, to provide all things necessary for them out of his master's treasure.

So a pastor or minister of a particular church, hath the charge of the said church, and every member thereof, committed unto him, to provide and lay in provision for to feed them with suitable and proper food, though it is all of Christ's own charge; it is his Lord's money which he hath received, I mean all those gifts and endowments which a minister hath, by which he is capacitated to provide for, and feed that household; he received it from Christ. No man hath any spiritual ability of his own to do it; nor would it be to the honour of Christ that he should, at his own proper charge, feed his Lord's household, their talent of bodily strength, natural, or acquired parts and improvements, as well as his talent of time, grace, and all spiritual gifts, are the Lord's; he is but a steward of all these things, and must give an account to him how he hath improved them to the end and design for which they were given to him.

Thirdly, a minister and pastor of a church of Christ may be compared to a steward or deputy householder, in respect of that faithfulness that he ought to manifest in the discharge of his great trust and office, in his minding or having a regard to his Lord's true interest.

"Moreover, it is required in a steward that a man be faithful," 1 Cor. iv. 2.

Wherein the faithful ministers consisteth. Now the faithfulness of a steward or householder consisteth in these things following.

1. It consisteth in his seeking and preferring the honour of his blessed Lord above all things; he is not to seek his own glory, nor his own self-interest; he is not to act so as if his knowledge, parts, and endowments, were his own, that none "may think of men above that which is written, that none of you be puffed up one against another," 1 Cor. iv. 6.

"For who maketh thee to differ from another? and what hast thou that thou didst not receive? why dost thou glory as if thou hadst not received it?" verse 7.

Faithful ministers seek Christ's honour and the glory of God in all they do. Some seem to glory in themselves, as if they fed the people and household of Christ with their own provision, being swelled with pride, or puffed up as a bladder: as if they had something which they received not of the Lord. Now this is not to be faithful to Christ, for it is no less than a robbing of him of his glory, which is that most inestimable jewel which is most prized by him of any thing in heaven and earth.

They also mind Christ's concerns chiefly. 2. The faithfulness of these householders or stewards of Christ doth consist in their great care and utmost diligence, in seeking after, and minding their Lord's concerns and business in his house and family where they are set. "Give thyself up wholly to them," 1 Tim. iv. 15. It ought to be their whole and principal business; none of them should entangle themselves with the affairs of this life. Such that will not leave their own secular affairs, (if the church is able to provide a comfortable maintenance for them,) ought to have this office conferred upon him. Would it not tend to the shame of that steward, that a nobleman hath chosen to be his steward, to take care of his household, and hath also allowed him a sufficient maintenance to employ himself, in some other trade and calling, to enrich himself, when his place and office calls for all his time, strength, and diligence in attending upon it?

Faithful ministers rightly dispense the word of truth. 3. Their faithfulness consisteth in taking care rightly to dispense their master's goods, or to feed Christ's household with such food that he hath ordained or appointed for them, viz., with sound and wholesome doctrine, or with "the sincere milk of the word," 1 Pet. ii. 2.

Not with errors, or airy speculations, or with words of man's wisdom, to please the ears of the people, for that is to starve their souls.

Inference.

"Take heed unto thyself, and unto the doctrine, continue in them, for in so doing thou shalt both save thyself and them that hear thee," 1 Tim. iv. 16.

Inference. They are not to preach Moses, not mere legal doctrine, or jewish ordinance, nor heathenish philosophy, but Jesus Christ, "We preach Christ crucified." Christ must be the main subject of all their ministry.

They must not preach the traditions of men, or human rites and ceremonies, not the decrees of general counsels, but the holy and pure institutions of Jesus Christ.

And not only the duties of men one to another, or the simple principles of morality, but the great fundamentals of Christianity, viz., the saving knowledge of God in Christ, the holy doctrine of the blessed Trinity, the mystery of the incarnation of the second Person, or hypostatical union of the two natures of the person of Christ, the great doctrine of Christ's satisfaction, reconciliation, and of justification by the imputation of his righteousness to all that believe; or that the righteousness of Jesus Christ alone, (excluding all works done by us, or righteousness wrought in us) in the matter of our justification before the holy God; to show the people, that it is Christ's obedience and righteousness only that is their title to heaven, though it is our inherent righteousness, and the sanctification of the Spirit, that tends to make us meet for it.

4. The faithfulness of a minister of Christ consisteth in his declaring the whole coun-

sel of God, and not to keep back anything, because some of their hearers (perhaps) may not approve of it ; for if they do so, that is, seek to please men, they are not any longer to be accounted the servants of Christ ; " For do I persuade men or God? or do I seek to please men? for if I yet please men I should not be the servant of Christ," Gal. i. 10. O, my brethren, how faithful was Paul upon this account? "I have shewed you all things ; again he saith, wherefore I take you to record this day, that I am pure from the blood of all men," Acts. xx. 35. "For I have not shunned to declare unto you all the counsel of God," Acts xx. 26. Even the whole doctrine of faith and practice ; look, saith God to Moses, " that thou make all things according to the pattern which was shewed thee in the mount," Exod. xxv. 40. They must not add to nor diminish from God's word.

Faithful ministers preach the whole counsel of God.

5. The faithfulness of a minister lies in his frequent preaching the word ; for like as a good householder knows it behoveth him to provide meat in due season for the family, and not to put them off with a good meal now and then, but let them have each meal in order day by day, so a minister must provide spiritual food in season even day by day, break the bread of life unto Christ's family. " Preach the word, be instant in season, and out of season, reprove, rebuke, exhort with all long-suffering and doctrine," 2 Tim. iv. 2. No time is out of season properly, but comparatively, i. e., there are sometimes, as on the Lord's day, that is more seasonable for the administration of the word ; yet that should not be all, but they ought to preach the word at other times also ; " Thus Paul preached publicly, and from house to house," Acts xx. 20.

They preach frequently.

The soul stands in need of spiritual food, and ought as duly to be fed as the body ; he therefore is no faithful minister who neglects his care and duty herein, and preacheth the word but seldom, perhaps hardly once in the week : but much less faithful are such that preach but once in a month, or but two or three sermons in a year.

6. His faithfulness consisteth in his care of the whole family, and of every one in particular, so as to know their condition, or how it is with them, whether dead or alive, growing or decaying, weak or strong, healthful or sickly. True, if any be sick in body or mind, or under temptations or desertion, it is their duty to send to their pastor ; " If any be sick, let him send for the elders of the church," James v. 14. A minister cannot be blamed if this be neglected, for he may not know his freedom in some families, where some members may dwell ; besides, should he visit them this day, and find them in health, yet to-morrow some one, or more, may be taken sick, or fall under temptation. Know the state of thy flock, saith Solomon ; but that cannot be, unless he doth oft visit them, or they come to him.

A faithful minister takes care of the whole flock under his charge.

7. The faithfulness of a minister consisteth in his dealing impartially with every one in particular, not preferring one before another, not visiting the rich more than the poor, or sparing the rich when in a fault, because he is rich ; or the poor because he is poor : Levi was not to know his father or mother in judgment. See Paul's charge to Timothy ; " I charge thee before God, and the Lord Jesus, and the elect angels, that thou observe these things, without preferring one before another ; doing nothing by partiality," 1 Tim. v. 21. All things should be done by him without respect had to persons, rich or poor, old or young.

He also deals impartially withal.

8. In his keeping up a good and wise discipline, teaching what the duty of every member is to each other, and that they act according to the rule Christ hath left in his church, towards offenders ; not to suffer that to come into the church which ought to be ended privately, or to enquire whether the offended person hath proceeded according to that rule in Matt. xviii. It is, brethren, a sign of great unfaithfulness in a pastor, should he neglect to stir up the church, to purge out such that are scandalous persons, or not set fit or proper times to do it. Certainly the work of discipline should not interfere with the public worship of God ; but some more fit and proper season ought to be chosen and appointed by the church. The glory of a family lies much in the well and wise governing of it, and in keeping up a careful and strict discipline, and so, no doubt, it doth in a church of Jesus Christ.

A good discipline to be kept up in a church.

9. His faithfulness consisteth in defending the truth against opposers, and such who are seducers ; therefore he ought to be one that is able by sound doctrine to convince gainsayers : for there are some always " Whose mouths must be stopped, who strive to subvert whole houses, teaching things which they ought not," Tit. i. 9—11. Though a minister cannot stop their mouths, or convince them, yet he ought to be able to lay down such arguments that are sufficient to do it : he must not be an ignorant person, not careless of them he hath the charge of : he must not let

A faithful minister defends the truth.

wolves come, and carry away any sheep out of the fold, if it be possible to be pre-vented.

Ministers ought to be humble persons. 10. A minister, or pastor of a church, like a deputy-householder, ought to be an humble person; he being but a servant, should not carry it as if he was lord of the family: will the Lord Christ endure such a steward of his house? What, shall he seek that honour which belongs to his blessed Master, not being lords over God's heritage, but as ensamples to the flock.

The dignity of the pastoral office. Fifthly, yet the office of a minister, or pastor of a church, is an office of dignity, as a steward's office or place in a lord's family or household is; for they represent Christ's person, therefore they are called ambassadors, rulers, angels, &c. Let none from hence slight or despise them; for they that despise you (saith our Saviour) despise me. If therefore any in the family, do cast contempt upon them, let such tremble. Alas! they know not what they do; "Obey them that have the rule over you, and submit yourselves unto them." An householder, though he be but a servant, is to be owned as the chief ruler there under his master; and so ought a pastor of a church: and such that will not be under his just government, after due reproof, ought to be excluded and turned out of the church, as being unruly, and as contemning Christ's authority.

Ministers ought to be well stored with all spiritual treasure. A householder, or a steward of a great family, ought to be one that is well stored or freighted, or to have much of his Lord's treasure committed to him, because he is to provide all things which the whole household needeth.

So ought a minister, who is a pastor of a church of Christ, to have much spiritual treasure in his earthen vessel, i.e., he ought to have much spiritual wisdom, or a competent measure of knowledge, and of all the graces of the Spirit, and be a man of some considerable parts and experience. As appears by those qualifications expressed, 1 Tim. iii., Tit. i., in the case of the choice of them to that office.

1. They should be such who well know or understand the riches of Christ, or the mysteries of God. "Let a man so account of us, as the ministers of Christ, and stewards of the mysteries of God," 1 Cor. iv. 1. If they are ignorant themselves of the divine mysteries of the gospel, how shall they open them unto the people? The Lord's people ought to be fed by pastors "after his own heart with knowledge and understanding," Jer. iii. 15.

2. They ought to be such men that are enriched with the image of God upon their own souls; for if they know not that by their own experience, how shall they explain and open it unto others? Can he in a right manner show what regeneration is, that never felt it in himself? "When thou art converted, strengthen thy brethren;" then, as if Christ should say, thou wilt be able rightly to do it; this made holy David to say, "Restore to me the joy of thy salvation, and uphold me with thy free Spirit; then will I teach transgressors thy ways, and sinners shall be converted unto thee," Psal. li. 12, 13.

3. They ought to be enriched with faith, love, and patience, because these graces will be tried. As to the grace of patience, let it be considered, that he that is a deputy-house-holder will find it a hard matter to please all the family; no doubt but some discontented persons will reproach him, as well as others that are without, therefore he will find great need of a good stock of patience, self-denial, and humility. This brings me to the next general head.

Secondly, I shall show you why a minister who is a pastor ought to be well provided with great store of spiritual riches and heavenly treasure.

Why ministers should be well stored with spiritual things. 1. Because Jesus Christ hath substituted and appointed him to hand out all spiritual provision to others: he hath not only bread to provide for his own soul, but is to provide and lay in for all the household: "Simon, son of Jonas, lovest thou me, feed my sheep," John xxi. 16.

II. Because the household which he is to take the care of, and provide for, may be large; he may have many to feed: a little bread will not serve to feed a great family; also they are King's children, and therefore mean and ordinary food will not serve their turn; they must have rich and soul-fattening food; their souls are born from above, they are nobly descended; their father allows them to eat of the best, even of his most choicest dainties.

Mere trash will serve those base-born sons of nature, or of the first birth, who are born from beneath! but these loathe such diet; they cannot digest it; it would even starve the King's children.

III. They ought to be well stored, because the wants of the household may be great.

Some being also too apt to spend and waste what they have. If the wants of one particular Christian is great, what must be the want of so many that are in some congregations ? " My God, (saith Paul,) shall supply all your needs," Phil. iv. 19. And now it is by the hands of his ministers that God doth supply many of these wants ; he is pleased to give unto them of his divine riches and heavenly treasure to this very purpose ; though it is true there is none but God himself can supply many of the wants of believers, which he doth do by his own Spirit : they are to supply them with divine knowledge, which is one main thing poor Christians need ; " 1 will give them pastors after my own heart, which shall feed them with knowledge and understanding," Jer. iii. 15.

Their hands are often weak, their knees feeble ; their ministers therefore should " strengthen their weak hands, and confirm their feeble knees."

They want comfort also many times, and ministers are to comfort them with the same " comfort wherewith they are comforted of God," 2 Cor. i. 4. God is pleased to comfort his poor ministers, under their troubles and temptations, to the end they might be able to comfort others, that is, by the same methods, arguments, or promises, by which God comforteth them : though all support and comfort is from God, yet he makes use of his ministers to support and comfort them.

IV. They ought to be well stored with all divine and heavenly treasure and experiences, because the family needs various and variety of food, by reason of the various states and conditions they may be in ; partly by reason of their different ages and standing in the house of God ; some being children, some young men, and some fathers : also by reason of their various temptations they may meet with, and be exposed unto.

APPLICATION

1. This may reprehend such churches that choose ignorant and unexperienced men to be pastors. Can such who have none, or but little, of the riches of grace, knowledge, and experiences of God, feed others ? Can they bring out of their treasure things First reboth new and old, who have it not to bring forth ? proof.

Be exhorted to stir up yourselves to pray for your faithful ministers ; we shall speed the better, nay, fare the better, if they are well stored, or filled with divine wisdom and knowledge in the mysteries of God and of Jesus Christ. If you forget your ministers you forget yourselves : do you expect they should feed you, nay, feast your souls, and do you not cry unto God that they may come unto you in the fulness of the blessings of the gospel of Jesus Christ ? For they must receive all that spiritual food wherewith they feed you from God ; if God doth not hand in to them, they cannot hand out unto you.

2ndly. Be exhorted to pity your ministers, and strengthen their hearts and Exhort. hands, and not add grief to them, and lay heavy burdens upon their souls ; some pastors have been heard to say (under temptations) that if they were not in that place and station, they would not be drawn into it, and this by reason of those discouragements they meet with from some persons in the family. Many are never satisfied either full or fasting, no food will please them ; let a poor minister do what he can, and study never so hard for the choicest food, either the matter is not liked, or the manner of the bringing of it forth, viz., it is not brought into them in such rare carved dishes, nor set out with artificial niceties and curiosities as they would have it ; but it argues such are full fed with worse food, and are not sensible of spiritual hunger or want.

Take a few motives to stir you up to pray for, sympathize with, and pity your ministers.

1. Consider that whatsoever offence is taken against a church, or fault that is espied in it, it is commonly charged upon the pastor, though possibly it may be for such things he himself is not a little grieved at, and cannot help it.

2. Consider they are but men, and of like infirmities and weaknesses with yourselves.

3. Consider what temptations they, more than any, meet with, Satan having such implacable enmity against them, because they are the chiefest instruments in pulling down and undermining of his kingdom.

4. Consider what danger they are exposed unto above all in the church in a day of persecution : they then are singled out as the very butts of the wrath and rage of wicked men, against whom they shoot their arrows.

Thirdly, This may inform us who are true and faithful ministers ; they are such who are regenerated persons, holy men, men of great light, knowledge, and understanding in the mysteries of the gospel ; such " that are well instructed unto the kingdom of heaven." It is not men, but God only, that makes gospel-ministers ; I mean, all ministerial gifts and grace is given of God. It is not learning of Greek, Latin, and Hebrew, nor the knowledge of philosophy, or any human arts and sciences whatsoever, that can make a man a true minister of Christ, but those spiritual gifts which are given by Jesus Christ; who, when he "ascended on high, he gave gifts to men: and he gave some apostles, and some prophets, and some evangelists, and some pastors and teachers," Eph. iv. 8, 11. The first were but temporary, serving only the first age of the church, and are long since ceased; only pastors and teachers abide, and must abide in the church until the end of the world.

There are two essentials that tend to make or constitute a man a true minister.

1. The gifts and graces of the Holy Ghost, whereby he is in some competent manner fitly qualified by the Spirit, according to 1 Tim. iii.

2. The probation and election of a particular church.

Yet as to pastors, they ought not only to have these two, but ought also to be orderly ordained by the laying on of the hands of the eldership.

Fourthly, This also shows what a great charge ministers have committed unto them.

1. They have the doctrine of the gospel committed to their charge, to maintain the purity of it without corruption or mixture; as I have noted.

2. The true constitution of a gospel-church, which is and ought to be only congregational, not national, not parochial. Hence the church is compared to an household or particular family.

3. The order and true discipline of the church is committed unto them, i. e., to take care about it, and to instruct the people in the government thereof. I do not say a pastor hath the sole government of it in his own hand; though he is the chief ruler, yet he is not to rule without the church, or some who ought to be chosen as helps of rule and government.

4. The care and charge of the whole church, and every member thereof, is committed to him, as one that must give an account to Christ, the great Shepherd, at the last day.

5. The ordinances of the gospel are committed to every true gospel-minister, which he is bound to see duly administered. Yet some do not say that none but an ordained pastor ought to administer baptism, and the Lord's Supper. Because the first of these was delivered to Christ's disciples as teachers or ministers, not as apostles, or pastors of particular churches; he that is approved teacher they say may baptize by the virtue of the commission, Matt. xxviii. 18, 19, 20; yet if there is a pastor in the church, it only concerns him to administer all ordinances.

But so much at this time.

II

Then said he unto them, every scribe which is instructed unto the kingdom of heaven, is like unto a householder, &c.—Matt. xiii. 52.

Sermon 2.
Nov. 4.
1693.

THE parts of this parable I opened unto you the last time, and took notice of this one proposition; viz.

Doct. That a minister of the gospel is and may be compared to an householder that is well stored with all rich and choice provisions.

1. Why they are compared, and ought to be well stored, we have showed.

2. I shall now proceed further to show why they are compared to an housekeeper or householder, that brings out of his treasure things both new and old.

3. Show you what is meant by things new and old.

I showed you in four respects, why they ought to be well stored.

Christ hath made plentiful provision for his family or household.

V. They ought to be well provided, because Jesus Christ hath made plentiful provision for his spiritual family, which blessed food he hath committed to them to distribute to his household, children, and servants:—his storehouse is always full, which is the holy Scriptures, from whence a minister is to fetch all his provision with which he is to feed God's church.

Christ is a noble householder.

VI. Because their Master is a great King, and all his children are nobly descended; they are sons and daughters of the mighty God of heaven and earth. Shall the children of such a Father, of such a Prince, live, and be fed as poor peasants, or as the baser sort, or like unto mean cottagers?

"In my Father's house (said the prodigal) is bread enough and to spare." He (as if he should say) is no mean person ; he is one that keeps a good house, he hath plenty of provision ; " Wisdom hath killed her beasts, she hath mingled her wine, she hath furnished her table," Prov. ix. 2.

VII. Because of the preciousness of the souls which they are to feed ; certainly this is sufficient to convince all, that ministers ought to be well stored with all sorts of spiritual provisions.

1. Brethren, Jesus Christ saw so great a worth in the soul, that he gave his own life to redeem it ; every one that dwells in Christ's family, that are his children or servants, was purchased with his own blood : this was the argument Paul laid before the ministers and elders of the church at Ephesus.

" Take care unto yourselves, and to all the flock over which the Holy Ghost hath made you overseers, to feed the church of God, which he hath purchased with his own blood."

O what care ought to be taken that such a family be well fed, that were purchased by him, who is God, co-equal and co-eternal with the Father ! What is the nature of the soul, if such be the ransom of it ? And,

2. The soul is so precious a thing, that as Jesus Christ gave himself for it, so he likewise gives his own flesh and blood to feed it : without feeding upon his flesh, and drinking of his blood, the soul cannot live, John vi. 55.

3. Jesus Christ also gives his own righteousness to clothe the soul ; a righteousness which he wrought out in the days of his flesh by his holy life, in conformity to the holy law of God, and his death on purpose to put upon the soul.

4. The souls of believers, my brethren, do partake of the divine nature ; the image of God is formed in them ; therefore most dear unto him : they that touch them touch the apple of his eye : no tender beloved babe can be more dear to an earthly prince, than the saints are to Jesus Christ, therefore ministers should see that they are nobly fed, even with kingly food ; they are not to be fed with the trash of human inventions, nor with gaudy and flesh-pleasing notions or airy speculations : it is not the head that is to be fed, but the heart ; not the ear, but the understanding : it is not the bodies of believers ministers are to feed, but their precious souls.

VIII. Because believers are the members of Christ's mystical body, they are " Flesh of his flesh, and bone of his bone." The church, beloved, is the spouse and wife of Jesus Christ. I am afraid some ministers do not think upon this as they ought ; surely the Lord Christ will take it very ill from such stewards, who instead of providing rich and choice food for his beloved consort, put her off with anything, even with that that comes next to hand, they not giving themselves up to the study of the word ; so that every one might have his portion of right and proper food, as well as in due season.

IX. Ministers ought to be well stored with all divine treasure or spiritual provision, because they are to bring out of their treasure things both new and old.

Whatever they have it is the church's, both themselves and their gifts ; " whether Paul, or Apollos, or Cephas, all are yours," 1 Cor. iii. 22. Be they things new or old, all things are given for the sake of the church ; as the riches and outward wealth some members have, it is put into their hands, and they made stewards of it to give forth to the use of the church, and to the poor thereof ; so are all the spiritual riches, gifts, and grace, which ministers have received : gifted men, fitted by the Lord to preach the gospel, may not preach, or forbear at their pleasure ; no, no, they must administer, they must preach : " As every one hath received the gift, so let him administer one to another as good stewards of the manifold grace of God," 1 Pet. iv. 10. God hath not only set pastors in his churches, but teachers, also ; there are variety of gifts, that so the churches might have variety of food.

Quest. What is that a good householder is to bring forth out of his treasure ? I mean, what it is that a faithful minister is to bring forth.

Ans. By the way this implies, that they have treasure ; ministers should be rich in spiritual things, though many of them may be poor in temporals ; " as poor, yet making many rich." *A minister should be rich in spiritual things, though poor in the world.*

1. They should be rich in divine knowledge, because they are to feed the people with knowledge and understanding, Jer. iii. 15. *With what food ministers should feed the souls of their people.*

1. They must feed them with the knowledge of God, with the knowledge of the holiness and purity of his nature, and with the knowledge of all the other glorious attributes and perfections of his blessed majesty, particularly, that he is most just, as he is most gracious and merciful : from whence rises that absolute necessity of a complete satisfaction to his divine justice through the merits of his Son Jesus Christ.

2. With the knowledge of the holy law of God, that being a transcript or impression of God's holy nature, always and unchangeably the same, so that without we are found clothed with a righteousness every way comporting with that righteousness, we can never be justified in his sight : God neither will nor can make void, violate, or relax the purity or severity of his own law, to save one soul, to the impeachment of his truth, justice, and holiness.

3. With the knowledge of the woful state of mankind, by the fall of our first parents : Also, what the state of man is by grace, and in the state of glory.

4. With the knowledge of sin, both original and actual, knowing the evil of it ; and that it is the plague of all plagues, even worse than the devil or hell itself; and that none but one that is truly God, as well as man, can make a full atonement to divine justice for the evil that is in it.

5. With the knowledge of Jesus Christ, i, e., the necessity and excellency of Christ, in his person and offices, and to understand the purpose and nature of his incarnation, birth, life, death, resurrection, ascension, and intercession.

They should understand or have a true and saving knowledge of the doctrine of justification by Jesus Christ ; the grace of God being the original and efficient cause or spirit of it ; the death of Christ being the meritorious cause, and the righteousness of Christ, in his perfect active obedience and suffering, the meritorial cause thereof ; not that his merits and righteousness purchased or procured such favour and grace, that our inherent righteousness, and sincere faith and obedience, should, with his merits, justify us ; but that all our own righteousness, faith, and obedience, is utterly excluded in point of justification before God, or at the bar of his justice ; and that it is Christ's obedience to the preceptory and penal part of the law, which is the matter or material cause of our justification only : for " as by one man's disobedience many were made sinners : so by the obedience of one shall many be made righteous," Rom. v. 19. Christ's active obedience or righteousness being our only title to heaven, and his bearing the pangs of hell for us, and in our stead, that only which delivers us from hell and eternal wrath ; also that the imputation of the righteousness of Christ is the formal cause of our justification ; and the glory of God, in all his holy attributes, and our eternal happiness the final cause thereof.

6. They ought to know, that every man by nature is alike miserable, even the elect themselves, being all dead in sin, and are by nature the children of wrath as well as others, Eph. ii. 3. They being not actually justified, but contrariwise condemned, until they do believe in Christ, or are transplanted by the Spirit of God out of the first Adam into the second Adam : though all that shall be saved were decretively justified from everlasting and virtually when Christ rose again from the dead, yet they were no more actually justified from eternity, than they were actually glorified from eternity, which was only decretively, or according to God's decree and purpose ; nor no more actually justified when Christ rose from the dead, than they actually ascended unto heaven, when Jesus Christ, as our head, representative, and forerunner, ascended to heaven.

7. They ought to have the clear, full, and saving knowledge of regeneration in themselves, else how can they by experience tell others what it is, or in a right manner feed them with the knowledge thereof ; moreover, they ought to know the nature of true grace in its effects and operations of it on their own souls.

8. With the knowledge of Satan, in his power, policy, malice, and unwearied assaults and temptations.

9. With the knowledge of this world, in the vanities, snares, and allurements thereof.

10. With the knowledge of the covenant of grace ; and how made with Christ for us from everlasting as our covenanting head : and how and when we actually are brought into the bonds of it ; and the nature and stability thereof ; with all the precepts, promises, and threatenings contained therein.

11. With the knowledge of the true church ; I mean, a visible church ; the constitution, the order, government, discipline, dignity, and privileges of it.

How ministers should feed their people with the sacraments.
Secondly, Ministers or stewards of Christ's house must feed them with the holy sacraments.

1. They must show what their duty is ; or what is required of all those that are the fit and proper subjects of those holy ordinances, viz., baptism and the Lord's Supper.

2. The end and usefulness of them.

3. The danger of such that do neglect them, or partake of them, without having those previous qualifications, that are required of all that come unto them.

Thirdly, they should feed Christ's household with their own experiences, or be able to teach others, by telling them what God hath done for their own souls; " Come unto me all ye that fear God, and I will tell you what he hath done for my soul," Psa. lxvi. 16. " That which we have seen and heard declare we unto you, that ye also may have fellowship with us," 1 John. i. 3. They are to " comfort others with the same comfort wherewith they themselves are comforted of God," 2 Cor. i. 3. 4.

Query, what is meant by their bringing out of their treasure things both old and new ?

1. Answer. By old things may be meant all such truths that were from the beginning ; viz., all truths that are purely moral in their own nature, or principles of natural religion ; such as love to God and to our neighbour ; or God to be worshipped, and none else, with divine worship or spiritual adoration. *(What is meant by bringing out of our treasures things new and old.)*

As also that God alone is man's only and chiefest happiness, and that salvation alone is by the seed of the woman ; these were old things, or truths taught from the beginning, held forth by promise and prophecies in the Old Testament.

Not to kill, not to steal, not to commit adultery, not to covet our neighbour's wife, servants, goods, &c., also prayer, praising, and singing of God's praises, are old truths.

Moreover, fasting-days, and days of thanksgiving ; all these things, and some others, they bring out of their treasure.

2dly, They bring out also things that are new. *(What is meant by things new.)*

1. As the actual incarnation, birth, life, death, resurrection, ascension, and intercession, of our Lord Jesus Christ : as likewise the ratification, establishment, or confirmation of the new covenant, and a new order, constitution, and government of God's church being new things, the Jewish church, state, rites, ceremonies, priests, and priesthood, being changed and gone, with many other of old things which were under the law, all things being now become new, 2 Cor. v. 17, 18.

Also new ordinances, as baptism, and the Lord's Supper ; and new church membership ; none being to be admitted into the gospel church, but believers only : the gospel temple being only built up with living or lively stones, 1 Pet. ii. 5, 6. *(What is meant by things new and old, may be meant. Truths formerly delivered. Ministers may preach the same sermon again.)*

2. By old truths may be meant such truths which a minister brought forth formerly ; yet he may put them in remembrance of them again. And thus our blessed Saviour did himself, who, when he first entered upon his ministry, (Luke iii.) preached repentance, and the doctrine of faith ; and he afterwards brought forth the same doctrine, Luke xiii. 3. 5, Mark xvi. 16. This gives ministers authority to bring out, or preach the same truths, the same doctrine, nay, the same sermon again which they preached formerly.

3. By things new and old, may be meant new and old experiences which they have had of God ; they, for the comfort of the believers, tell them what God did for them in former times, when under troubles and temptations ; when they were under darkness and becloudings ; and were persecuted, reproached, and distressed : " I have been young, saith David, but now am old, yet I never saw the righteous forsaken," &c. 2 Tim. iv. 16. 17. Paul also *(By things both new and old may be old and new experiences.)* takes notice of old things, or of former experiences he had of God's presence with him ; " At my first answer no man stood with me, but all men forsook me : I pray God that it may not be laid to their charge ; notwithstanding the Lord stood with me, and strengthened me, that by me the preaching might be fully known, and that all the Gentiles might hear, and I was delivered out of the mouth of the lion ;" hence David saith, " that he would remember the years of the right hand of the Most High."

Then also they bring out things new, i. e., they declare what of late, or at this present time, God had done and doth do for them ; they bring out old promises, and new promises, old wine of consolation, and new wine to refresh the souls of God's people. Brethren, I have told you what choice experiences I had of the love of Jesus Christ unto my own soul, when first in my youthful days he manifested himself unto me ; I was so raised and consoled with sweet tastes of God's love to me, that by the strength of those cordials I have been supported unto this very day ; and doth not the apostle bring out of his treasure old things, when he tells the saints that " Fourteen years ago he knew a man in Christ," 2 Cor. xii. 2. Wonderfully refreshed and transported with what he saw, and heard ; yet what store of new things after that did he bring forth.

APPLICATION

1. We infer from hence, that the Lord Christ hath a family or a household to take care of in this world ; true, all the earth is the Lord's, and all creatures are fed and sus-

tained by him ; there is a common providence over all ; he is the Saviour of all men : but he hath a special love to, and care of his church ; others are not fed as his own people ; he hath not purchased spiritual food for all men on earth ; no, no, he laid down his life for his sheep, for his elect, for his church, and procured all good things for them. " If he that spared not his own Son, but delivered him for us all, how shall he not with him also freely give us all things ?" Rom. viii. 32.

2. We also infer, that Jesus Christ keeps a good house ; he doth not spare of his divine treasure ; as he is very rich, so he feeds his people richly, plentifully, and nobly : he allows them to eat the fat and drink the sweet of his house ; " Eat, O friends, drink, drink abundantly, O beloved," Cant. v. 1. Christ doth not only feed, but feasts his friends ; " Eat you that which is good, and let your soul delight itself in fatness," Isa. lv. 2.

3. I also infer from hence, that it is no small favour and blessing to dwell among the saints in God's house, or to be one of his family ; " I will abundantly bless the provision of my house, and satisfy my poor with bread. I will also clothe her priests with salvation, and her saints shall shout for joy," Psal. cxxxii. 15, 16. This made the prodigal to think of his Father's house, and to desire to return home. God " will give grace and glory, and no good thing will he withhold from them that walk uprightly." If believers did truly and rightly consider of their high and choice privilege, in that they have a place in Christ's house, it would not a little affect and raise their hearts ; " Those that are planted in the house of the Lord shall flourish in the courts of our God : they shall still bring forth fruit in old age ; they shall be fat and flourishing ; to show that the Lord is upright ; he is my rock, and there is no unrighteousness in him," Psal. xcii. 13, 14, 15.

4. It also informs us of the great love of God to his people, in choosing such stewards of his household that are faithful men, men of integrity, who will not suffer any in the family to want so far forth as they have ability to help them ; they having freely received they freely give. They will not make a prey of the flock, not eat the fat, and clothe themselves with the wool, (like some of the shepherds of old) but will feed the flock ; they will strengthen the weak hands, and confirm the feeble knees, and heal those that are sick, and succour such who are tempted, like their great Lord and Master.

5. It may, moreover, inform us of our duties who are of Christ's household, or members of this or that particular church, that we are to abide in our places and station where we are set, and expect to be fed there, and not to wander abroad to seek food elsewhere ; but to consider here is our food in this house which Christ hath provided for us, upon which we may expect a blessing. What account can a steward give of such who make a breach in the family, and will not come where and when he is bound and obliged to hand out to every one their portion of meat in due season ?

Would it not be a dishonour to an householder to find some of his family go to his neighbour's house for bread, as if there was not sufficient for them in his house ? Brethren, doth not this greatly tend to the rebuke of such ? Pray, sirs, you that are good housekeepers, would you not be troubled to see some of your children or servants desert your families, not liking your provision, but go to seek their food at some other house ? Would you not look upon it a great reproach to you ?

6. It also may serve to inform us that ministers should study to provide variety of food for all that they are intrusted to feed ; they are not only to bring out of their treasures continually old things, or the same over and over again, but to make some new discoveries of the same blessed gospel truths ; I do not say they should bring forth any new and strange doctrine ; no, God forbid : by things new that is not meant ; there is nothing new (in one sense) but old ; even the same which we heard from the beginning : all provision is to be fetched out of the word of God ; that only is Christ's great store-house.

2. It may reprove such who dwell in Christ's family, and are daily fed with good and wholesome food ; who are not content with it, but murmur and complain against the steward of Christ's household, like as the Israelites did against Moses, saying, the manna was light bread ; and yet others find much sweetness, strength, and comfort in it.

This argues, that such who thus murmur are diseased and distempered persons ; the full stomach loathes the honey-comb. They are more anxious to feed their heads than their hearts ; many in this age are grown wanton, and know not what they would have, make waste and despise most precious provision.

3. Ministers may learn from hence to see to the nature of that spiritual food with which they feed Christ's family : as to the matter of the provision, it must be Christ ; he is only the bread of life ; it is Christ he must preach ; Christ must be the subject of all

his preaching, " we preach Christ, and him crucified." Christ is a believer's all, and should be the all of gospel-administration ; all is provided and purchased by Christ ; all is enjoyed in Christ ; nothing will do us any good without Christ ; the word and ordinances are but dry bread if we do not meet with Christ in them ; all is to set forth the honour and glory of Christ.

4.   Ministers should see that what they bring forth be hot : cold meat is not so refreshing and sweet as that which is hot ; a minister must preach with life, and holy fervency of spirit ; cold and lifeless preaching, makes cold hearing ; the Lord Christ " preached as one having authority, and not as the Scribes."

5.   Ministers may also from hence know that it is their indispensible duty to give out food to God's people always, even day by day ; for like as a household must daily have provision prepared and set before them, so must the Lord's people have spiritual food continually.   It is not enough to provide one meal in a week for a family, certainly that is the way to starve them, and doth not the soul need to be as often fed ? Or doth it stand consistent with the good, profit, and edification of the household of faith, if this be not done? " Therefore watch, and remember that by the space of three years I ceased not to warn every one night and day with tears," Acts. xx. 31.   Why doth he bid the elders of this church remember what his practice had been, but that they should follow his example in frequent preaching ?   Though trouble arises, or persecution, because of the word, yet ministers must not cease preaching ; if they cannot preach publicly, they must preach in private families, and so from house to house.   " He that withholdeth corn the people will curse him ; but blessing shall be upon the head of him that selleth it," Prov. xi. 26. Certainly it is as great a sin to withhold the food of the word in a time of scarcity, as it is to withhold external food in a time of famine.

6thly, and lastly, this may serve to provoke or stir up all such churches, who have faithful and able pastors and teachers, to bless and praise God they are fed, when perhaps others are almost starved, or pine away for want of such soul-strengthening, refreshing, and feeding doctrine, which is necessary for them ; and this thankfulness of theirs should also be showed by their great love to, and care of their painful pastors, in providing cheerfully a comfortable maintenance for them and their families ; what a shame would it be that such ministers should spend their whole time and strength in providing food for Christ's household, that they should be exposed to want the necessary things of this life for themselves and families, when the church is in a capacity, or able to do it ?   " Who feedeth a flock, and eateth not the milk of the flock," 1 Cor. ix. 7.

Do you not know that " they that wait at the altar are partakers with the altar," ver. 13.

Even so hath the Lord ordained, that they which preach the gospel should live of the gospel.   God may justly blast and not bless churches, who will content themselves with mean and inexperienced teachers, rather than be at the charge of maintaining of an able and profitable ministry, when they are able to do it ; seeing God has ordained that ministers should live of the gospel, and not by the labour of their hands, by going to plow and cart, or by buying and selling, or following of this or that trade.   So much as to this parable.

21. THE RICH FOOL

And he spake a parable unto them, saying, the ground of a certain rich man brought forth
plentifully, and he thought within himself, saying, what shall I do, because I have no room
where to bestow my fruits? and he said, this will I do, I will pull down my barns and build
greater, and there will I bestow all my goods.—Luke xii. 16—18.

LOOK but a little back, and you may see the reason why our Saviour spake this parable, and so see the occasion thereof.

"And one of the company said unto him, Master, speak to my brother, that he divide the inheritance with me," ver. 13.

"And he said unto him, Man, who made me a judge or a divider over you?" ver. 14.

"And he said unto them, take heed, and beware of covetousness; for a man's life consisteth not in the abundance of the things which he possesseth," ver. 15.

The year of Christ's life, 32.

The year of Christ's ministry, 3.

The occasion of this parable.

"And he spake a parable," &c. I might (by the way) note from hence, that ministers should not undertake the work of arbitrators, to terminate matters of civil right and justice: for our Lord refused to do it, and so ought we, it may but expose a minister to reproach, though he act never so justly: but to proceed:

The design and scope of it.

1. Our Lord spake this parable, that all persons might take heed to avoid covetousness, and be admonished of the danger thereof.

2. To discover how uncertain the riches of the world are, and that they tend to entice to sinful mirth and luxury. "Eat, drink, and be merry."

3. To make known the folly that attends such whose hearts are set upon worldly riches.

4. To let all men know, that a man's life consisteth not in the abundance of what he possesseth, i. e., the comfort and happiness of a man's life.

1. But to proceed, I shall speak to the several parts hereof by way of paraphrase.

2. Observe one or two propositions, &c.

"The ground of a certain rich man."

Rich men have ground, they possess much land; poor men have none, they travel to and fro, but tread upon other men's ground; yet nevertheless, in a little time the poor shall have as much ground as the rich: for though a rich man glories of his vast fields, and abundance of land he hath, yet when he dies he will have no more than will bury him; and so much is not denied the poor.

"Brought forth plentifully," Psal. lxxiii. 7. The rich thrive in the world; their riches increase, "their eyes stand out with fatness; they have more than heart could wish." This, for a short time, laid the Psalmist under a temptation, "Behold these are the ungodly, who prosper in the world; they increase in riches. Verily, I have cleansed my heart in vain, and washed my hands in innocency; for all the day long have I been plagued, and chastened every morning," ver. xii. 13, 14.

But he recovered himself by considering the end and design of God therein.

"When I went into the sanctuary of God, then I understood their end—how are they brought into desolation in a moment? they are utterly consumed with terrors; as a dream when one awaketh," &c., ver. 17, 19, 20.

Their seeming happiness is like that when a man dreams, he is a king or a great man, and this pleaseth him, transports him; but when he wakes, he finds himself deceived, it was but a dream ; so this rich man did but dream he was happy, and that he should possess what he had for many years.   My brethren, God gives some wicked men a great portion in this world ; but it is all they are like to have ; they have their good things, their portion, their consolation in this life, " he thought within himself," Psal xvii. 14.   Note,

Worldly men, earthly men, are filled with thoughts, but not of God, no, " God is not in all his thoughts," Psal. x. 4, (nay, as some read it) all his thoughts are, there is no God, or, no such God as concerns himself with the affairs of this world : he is (saith one) a deist, he owns a God in words, but denies his providence.

" He thought within himself." A wise man (as one notes) would have consulted God. Men should ponder well their thoughts before they resolve what to do, " in all thy ways acknowledge him, and he shall direct thy paths," Prov. iii. 6 ; this man by that means might have foreseen it was better for him to have had thoughts of death ; for it appears he had not twenty-four hours to live.

" What shall I do ?" It is not what shall I do to be saved ? No, but what shall I do with my goods ? The difference betwixt a beggar and a rich man is but this ; both are saying, what shall I do ? The beggar saith, What shall I do to get bread, to get a little money ? The other saith, what shall I do now I have it ? Where shall I lay it ? And how shall I keep it ? Both are in perplexity, riches and poverty have sad snares attending them.

The poor and rich cry what shall we do.

Annotator.

" Because I have no room."   Yea, (saith one) enough and to spare : therefore montiture, as Suella tells him, he lies, the poor man's belly, is the rich man's barn : had he thought of that, he might have found barns enough without building any more barns.

See Mr. Livesey's the greatest loss. Eman. see in loc.

" This will I do." Wicked men soon come to a resolution what to do to secure their goods ; but he shows him a graceless wretch ; he does not say this will I do, if God permit, or if God will ; no, I will do it, though he knew not whether he should live till harvest came or not.

" I will pull down my barns." It is wisdom (saith one) to think how to build ; this fool talks of pulling down his barns, when God was about to pull down the barn in which his soul was housed.   When wicked men should think how to build their souls upon Christ, or get a place of security for their souls, they are thinking of building greater barns for their fruits, and warehouses for their merchandizes.

" There will I bestow all my fruits and my goods.   What, spare none for the poor ?" must all be laid up, and none laid out ? the greatest increase is by laying out, than by laying up, " he that gives to the poor, lends to the Lord," Prov. xix. 17.   But not one thought of giving any thing to the poor was in this man's heart, nor one word of any such matter in his mouth ; he designs to keep all for himself.

" My goods." Rich men of the world account their gold, silver, and lands, wares and fruits, their goods ; that which they have to their hurt and ruin of their souls, they esteem their good, nay their chief good ; indeed they know nothing better than what they possess of the things of this world ; therefore they call those things their goods ; and no marvel, because they are their God.

Riches are a wicked man's chiefest good.

Yet earthly things God calls good things : they are good things under a threefold consideration.

1.   In reference to the judgment of worldly men, they so account them ; nay, the best good.

2.   The things of this world are good things, as they are the creatures of God, and come from him.

Earthly things good things in three respects.

3.   In respect of the use of them ; they suit with men's outward necessities ; and being rightly used, they are good things, and a great blessing to them that have them.

It is only the abuse of them which makes them evil and hurtful things ; as when men place their chiefest happiness in them, or set their hearts inordinately upon them, and their whole time is spent about getting, care in keeping, and fear of losing them ; some use not their good things ; though they have them, they have no heart to use them ; and these may be as great fools as they who over-use or abuse them ; yet there is more evil attends the having these good things, than there is good in them, though the temptations of the devil and corruptions of men's hearts : though they are good things in themselves ; yet there are better things, they are not the best good things.

Earthly things are not the best good things

And they that esteem them to be the best good, make them their God, and cast contempt upon God, valuing the creature above the Creator.

" And I will say to my soul, soul, thou hast goods laid up," &c.

A lie ! and a loud one too ; his soul had nothing laid up but horror, wrath, and vengeance.

What he had in his barns was not good for his soul. But we may see what opinion wicked men have of their souls. They think that which suits the body, feeds, clothes, and delights, that will feed, clothe, and delight the soul; as if they had nothing but a sensual soul, a brutish soul. The precious, immortal, and rational soul is forgot: *Bonum corporis animus bonum Deus,* saith one. Sirs, though outward good things satisfy the outward man, yet none but God himself can satisfy the soul or inward man; but the souls of the wicked are forgot and starved, whilst their bodies are fed and feasted.

"Laid up." No, his soul had another portion laid up, even a great heap of wrath against the day of wrath. "Ye have heaped treasure together for the last day," James v. 3. So that he lied again, his soul had not good, but evil laid up; and that not for many years only, but for an endless eternity. Whilst wicked men heap up riches, or the good things of the world for the bodies, they heap up wrath and evil things for their souls. But see how cruel these men are to their souls; for, if their souls cannot live upon that on which their bodies live, they shall starve and perish for ever. But should they feed their cows and sheep with carrion, as they feed their dogs, all would say, they were either fools or mad.

Alas! cows may be fed with carrion, and live on that, grow fat with that, as soon as the precious souls can be fed with earthly good things.

See the parable of the prodigal opened.

"Goods laid up for many years."

O the blindness (saith Austin) of this wretch! *Una nox nonet supererat.* He had not one night to live, and yet projects as if he should never die. Wicked men reckon of living long here; they count of a long time on earth, but forget the length of eternity. Sirs, a thousand years is not a moment compared with eternity.

"Take thine ease," &c.

A guilty, wounded, and condemned soul, cannot have true ease and comfort.

If he speaks to his soul (as it appears he does) he speaks like a fool as he was; for how could his soul have ease, that was under God's wrath, and sentenced to hell flames? Can a graceless soul, a Christless soul, a guilty and condemned soul, a naked, and a wounded, and a starved soul, have any ease? He flattered, and wofully deceived his poor soul.

"Eat, drink, and be merry." What! merry, and just falling into hell! This man is set up as a monument of folly, being branded by the blessed Jesus for a fool, and in this it appeared. Who can eat, drink, and be merry, but he whose sins are pardoned, or who hath an interest in God, a discharge from hell, and a title to heaven? Can a man that is going to die, or to be executed, and so to pass into endless torments, eat, drink, and be merry? The prodigal, when he was returned home to his father, when he was clothed with the best robe, and had a ring put on his hand, and shoes on his feet, was bid to eat, drink, and be merry; and he had cause so to do. But this wretch had more reason to say to his soul mourn, weep, and howl, for thou art undone for ever, and this night thy soul will be in hell.

"But God said unto him." Note, That an ungodly person says one thing, and God says another: he says he is happy, but God says he is miserable; he says he is blessed, but God says he is cursed; he says he shall have peace, but God says his wrath shall smoke against him; he says he shall live many years, but God says he shall not live above one day longer; he says and thinks he is wise, "But God said unto him, thou fool." Better all the men in the world call us fools, reproach and contemn us, than to have God say, thou fool; that man is a fool indeed that God so esteems and calls.

Wicked men are fools in God's account.

"This night thy soul shall be required of thee." The man talked of many years, but God says, no, not one year, not one month, not one week, not twenty-four hours, for this night thou shalt die; for that is meant by requiring of his soul. Wicked men are undone by reckoning wrong; they do not keep their accounts well; they put the evil day far off; they measure their days not by the king's standard, or by just rules and measures. Perhaps they reckon by their present health, their present strength, or by the lives of their progenitors. Their father and grandfather lived to a great age, and so they measure their days accordingly, and conclude they shall live long. But none of these rules are allowed, they are false measures of our days. God sends us to the morning dew, the weaver's shuttle, to the shadow, vapour, a swift post, and to the flower of the field, that to-day is, and to-morrow is burned in the oven.

Men may think of living long when they have not twenty-four hours to live.

"Thy soul shall be required of thee."

Ungodly men must give an account of their souls, and when death comes, they must give that account. Note also, The soul of man is not so his own, but he must give an account to God of it. Moreover, some men are unexpectedly called to God's bar to give this account, or to give a sudden account,

At death men's souls are required of them.

even before they are prepared, or are ready to give up this account; they are at God's call, at his summons, and when he calls all must obey. Likewise God sometimes calls men away without giving them notice or warning of it; and when death comes, all shall know how matters go, and shall go with them in the other world, and to eternity.

"Then whose shall these things be that thou hast provided?"

A rich man when dead, knows not who shall possess his estate, who shall enjoy what he left behind him, or what he got with the loss of his own soul; he may think his wife, his children, or his heirs, or executors, administrators, or assigns, shall have it; but they may be cheated of it, or may die soon after him, and such may have it to whom he would not have given a shilling of what he had whilst he lived: or if his son hath it, he knows not whether his son shall be a wise man or a fool. *No man knows who shall enjoy estate after him.*

As earthly riches are uncertain, so is the life of him that possesseth them.

"So is every one that layeth up treasure for himself, and is not rich towards God."

So what is that? He is a fool, for it was that which God said unto him; but God said to him, thou fool.

"So is every man that layeth up treasure," &c. That is, every covetous man, or earthly worldling, who prefers the riches of this world above spiritual riches, and is not rich in grace, rich in faith, nor rich in good works. He is a fool. *Every covetous man is a fool.* There is only one point of doctrine I shall observe from hence.

Doct. That he (let him be whosoever he will) that labours for, or strives more to lay up riches in this world than to be rich towards God, is a fool.

In speaking briefly to this truth, I shall endeavour,

1. To show who they are (or how they may be known,) that strive more to lay up earthly riches than to be rich towards God.

2. Show how it appears that they are fools.

1. Such are fools, or men of no true wisdom, that choose a base, a low, and ignoble end, above the chiefest, choicest, and most noble end which man is, able, and ought to choose and prefer. Now some men seek themselves, and prefer earthly things above God, the glory of God, and eternal happiness: and *They who labour most for earthly things and are therefore fools.* this is the greatest folly any can be guilty of, and such are therefore fools; for it is far greater folly thus to do, than for a man to choose a brass counter before a pearl of inconceivable worth and value.

2. He that chooses the greatest evil before the chiefest and greatest good, or in the choosing the one rejects the other, is a fool, the greatest fool in the world: but such that choose sin, and reject God, do thus.

How often in the scriptures, upon this very consideration, are wicked men called fools, particularly by wise Solomon: folly is written in the foreheads of all wicked men, if sin be the greatest folly, then sinners are the greatest fools. Now covetousness is one of the greatest sins in the world; and hence it is called idolatry: it is as bad as to adore a graven image. The voice of the heart of an earthly worldling is, that there is more good, more happiness in possessing and enjoying the riches of this world, than to have a portion in God and interest in God, or to have the love and favour of God. Now these men are known many ways.

1. They so pursue the world, that they seldom think of God; God is not in all their thoughts, or rather in none of their thoughts; they desire not to think of God, but the thoughts of God are grievous to them. *How a man is known to be a fool.*

2. Nay, from the great abundance which they possess of the things of this world, and love to them; they say to God, to depart from us, "their bull gendereth, their cow calveth, and casteth not her calf—they spend their days in wealth, therefore they say to God, "depart from us, we desire not the knowledge of thy ways," Job xxi. 14. They like not to approach near God, nor that he by disquieting their consciences should draw near to them.

3. They show God is none of their choice, in that they utterly refuse the means afforded them in order to the finding and enjoying of him, "Wherefore is there a prize in the hand of a fool to get wisdom, seeing he hath no heart to it?" Prov. xvii. 16.

No pains is too much with these men to get and increase their earthly riches; all opportunities and advantages that are in their hands in order to it, are taken hold of, and improved; but a little time cannot be spared to meet with God, or to advance his glory, or the good of his people.

II. Such are fools who prefer the good of their bodies for a short time in this world above the good of their souls and bodies to eternity; should a man only take care to live well for one day, and take no care or regard what becomes of him, or how he lives, all the days of his life after that one day is ended, all would say he is a fool; alas! should a man live an hundred years, that is not as one day when compared to eternity, no, not one hour, not one moment; and yet these men's care is only to live well, and enjoy earthly good for this one moment or while here, but regard not what becomes of their souls and bodies when this life is ended for evermore.

III. Such are fools who esteem the world above the word, nay, reject and set light by the word out of love to the world: " They have rejected the word of the Lord, and what wisdom is in them?" Jer. viii. 9. True wisdom is to walk by a right rule, to a right end; but these men reject the true rule; gain is their rule, and self is their end.

IV. They that let their chiefest thoughts run out after the world, whose chiefest love is set upon their riches, or on earthly things, and whose greatest care and pains is to obtain, and their chiefest fear is of losing them, certainly are fools; for it shows they are blind and ignorant persons, even such that know not what is good, the chiefest good, but weary themselves for very vanity.

V. Such that prefer the world above Christ, and will leave Christ to embrace this present world, are the fools our Lord here speaks of; such a fool was " the young man that came running to Christ," Matt. xix. 22; who when he heard of parting with what he had if he would be saved, left the Lord Jesus, " and went away very sorrowful; for he had great possesssions." Also Demas was another of them, who cast off the Lord Jesus Christ and embraced this present evil world.

VI. Such that prefer sinful gain above the peace of their own consciences, are fools. I mean, such, who to increase their riches, deal unjustly, deceive, defraud, and cheat their neighbours. O what is more precious than inward peace, or than a good conscience? and what is worse than than a gnawing, a guilty, and an accusing conscience? Is not he a fool that wounds himself or seeks to set himself at war and variance against himself; and also thereby fights against his Maker, and murders his own soul? If this man is not a fool, there is none in the world.

VII. He is a fool that prefers corruptible and uncertain riches before those riches that are incorruptible, inconceivable in their worth, and are also eternal.

VIII. He that will let the commonwealth sink, and do that which may ruin and undo a whole kingdom, his children, and posterity, nay, let the church of God sink, and the poor perish, to enrich himself, or rather than he will part with his substance, is a fool, and the mark of a fool is written in legible characters upon his forehead. Many such fools I fear we have now in England. Ah, poor, miserable England ! What monsters hast thou brought forth and nourished in thy borders and bowels ?

Secondly, How doth it appear that earthly and covetous persons are fools ?

How it appears wicked men are fools.

    1. By considering the nature of those things they refuse and slight.

    2. By considering the nature of the things they choose and set their hearts upon.

What worldly men refuse, which proves they are fools.

    1. The things which they refuse are of inconceivable value, the very best things of heaven and earth; things did I say ? consider what is comprehended in them, viz., God the chief good to be their God, and Jesus Christ; they refuse him, an interest in him; they see nothing in him to desire him; they refuse God to be their Father, their Friend, and their Portion and Inheritance, and re-ject the person of Christ, the righteousness of Christ, the love and riches of Jesus Christ. Moreover, they refuse to adhere to the leadings, the guidance and conduct of the Holy Spirit, which strives to renew the image of God in them, and to put the righteousness of Christ upon them, and be an earnest of eternal life and glory to them; and now doth not this show them fools ? They know not what is good, know not how to choose, they dis-cern not a precious pearl from a worthless pebble.

2. They refuse incorruptible things, such riches that are durable treasure that moth nor rust can corrupt.

3. They refuse (though they are ready to perish with hunger) that which is bread, nay, Bread of Life, most rare, sweet, delicious, and soul-nourishing, fattening and satisfying Bread, and all things else that is good and proper food for their souls; which except they eat of they must die and perish for ever; and doth not this show they are fools ?

4. They count those things not worth one serious thought or regard, which all that were truly wise esteemed above all the treasures, riches, and glory of the whole world; nay, more worth than ten thousand worlds.

5. Though they are blind, they refuse eye-salve that would certainly cause them to

see ; and though they are wounded to death, they refuse that balm that would (if applied) infallibly cure them ; and though they are naked, yet they refuse a glorious garment (or a rich robe) to clothe them ; and though they be condemned and sentenced to die, (a grevious death) yet they refuse a pardon ; and though poor, yet they refuse great riches ; and though in slavery, and bound with fetters and cruel chains, yet they refuse liberty, and freedom from bondage and slavery for ever ; and though they are under contempt, and disgrace, and are ignoble persons, yet they refuse to be raised to the greatest honour ; nay, they refuse a crown of glory, and a kingdom that abideth for ever, and are they not fools ? Doth not this show and prove they are fools ?

Secondly, Let us consider what things they are which worldly men choose, and the nature of them, instead of those things, or before those things which they refuse.

1. They choose things unlawful, or such things that are forbidden, and in their choice incur the wrath and displeasure of God, and are thereby proclaimed enemies and rebels, and such that God's soul abhors, for by an inordinate love of riches they are idolators : and the covetous God abhorreth. *The things wicked men choose shows they are fools.*

2. They choose such things that are the portion of reprobates. My brethren, God gives the riches of this world to his enemies, and to such who have their portion in this life, to whom he denies his choicest and chiefest blessings and favours. *Psa. xxii..*

3. They are corruptible things, things which perish in the using, things also that are uncertain. Riches of this world are called uncertain riches ; " Charge them that are rich in this world, that they trust not in uncertain riches, but in the living God," 1 Tim. vi. 17. He that possesseth them to-day, may lose them to-morrow ; they are things that are not : " Wilt thou set thine heart on that which is not ? For riches certainly take themselves wings, and fly away, as an eagle towards heaven," Prov. xxiii. 5. Would a man count himself rich should a great flock of doves settle upon his land, which on a sudden fly away ? But men count themselves rich and happy that have abundance of earthly treasure, though it flies away on a sudden, therefore they are fools.

4. They choose the riches, pleasures, and grandeur of this world, which ruin the souls of all that trust in them, or set their hearts upon them. The world, in its riches, is a cruel enemy to poor mortals, and such who over-prize them do but hug a viper or serpent in their bosoms, and is not this one article of our faith, that the world (as well as the flesh and the devil) is a mortal enemy to the soul ? What, harbour a thief, a treacherous and cruel murderer, in our house, who will soon, if not overcome, lay all the family in their blood, and dead at his foot ! what folly greater than this ! Ah ! how many thousands are now in hell, that the love of this world sent thither, or brought eternal ruin upon.

5. The things wicked rich men choose are but mere vanity or a shadow. " Vanity of vanity, all things are vanity," Eccl. i. 2 ; not vain, but vanity in the abstract, the worst of vanities, and therefore no folly greater than to esteem the riches of this world as a man's best and chiefest happiness ; they weary themselves for very vanity ; should you see a man pursue, or run after, and strive to catch or take hold of a shadow, would you not say he was a lunatic, or a natural, or mere fool ? Such fools are the rich men of this world. Moreover, empty things that cannot satisfy, gold and silver can satisfy no man : " He that coveteth silver shall not be satisfied with silver, nor he that loveth abundance with increase, this is also vanity," Eccl. v. 10. This shows his folly ; he hath abundance, and yet desires more as if he had nothing, and is never content and satisfied with what he hath, and yet counts these things the best of all good ; which shows he is a fool.

6. The love of riches is the root of all evil ; and such " that will be rich fall into temptations and a snare, and into many foolish and hurtful lusts, which drown men in destruction and perdition," 1 Tim. vi. 9. Now if such are the nature and dreadful effects that attend riches, what fools are they that set their hearts upon them ? They do but " Heap up treasure against the last day," James v. 3, or treasure up wrath and divine vengeance. Such that love the world, the love of the Father is not in them ; nay, they are " Adulterers, and adulteresses, the friendship of the world is enmity with God ; whosoever will be a friend of the world, is an enemy of God," James iv. 4. Riches alienate the heart from God, and cause the sinner to war against his Maker : besides, it is hard for any that are rich to enter into the kingdom of heaven ; and therefore rich men, who pursue the world, are fools.

USE

Infer. 1. I infer from hence, that the world is full of folly and madness, what a multitude of fools are everywhere. " When he that is a fool walketh by the way, his wisdom faileth him : he saith to every one that he is a fool," Eccl. x. 3. He that walketh in a covetous way, in a way of eager pursuit after the world, his wisdom faileth him. He saith to every one that observeth him, that he is a fool ; his practice says, though he thinks he is wise.

Infer. 2. We may infer also, that most great men, noblemen, are fools. " Folly is set in great dignity, and the rich sit in low places," Eccl. x. 6. Wicked princes, and such that they advance, are fools ; who pride it in their riches, and vain honour : such that are truly rich, rich indeed, rich in their souls, are in low places : they are neglected, and despised, and counted fools, because poor in this world.

Infer 3. Righteous men only are wise men ; such that contemn the world, or are dead to the world, that see the vanity of the world, that desire not riches, these men only are wise.

Infer. 4. That God counts not as man counts ; he looks not as men look ; they judge the rich and great ones of the earth (though they are wicked) to be wise ; but God says they are fools. See the folly and ignorance of man.

Exhort. Secondly, Be exhorted to pursue more after grace than after gold, and to tread the world under your feet, instead of laying it in your hearts ; and never esteem rich men to be wise men, if they are ungodly or graceless.

2. Bless God that gives you neither poverty nor riches, for snares attend both. Agur was a wise man in his prayer, and let us all learn of him ; but O how few pray against riches ! but it shows their folly, they do not run thus.

3. Fear the danger of riches ; do not rejoice if your riches increase, considering the evils which attend them, and what kind of men do commonly possess them.

Thirdly, This may be matter of comfort to the poor of this world, who are rich in faith. God hath made you rich indeed, blessed you indeed ; others are seemingly rich, but really poor, seemingly wise, but really foolish ; seemingly happy, but really miserable : but you are seemingly poor, but really rich ; and seemingly miserable, but are really happy ; and counted fools by men, but wise in God's esteem. This should therefore satisfy you who have little in possession, but great things in reversion ; for though you seem to have nothing, yet you have all things. Moreover, they who now seem to be rich, and seem to be full, shall be poor and have nothing ; when you, as kings and princes, shall reign in riches, honour, and renown for evermore. You have made the best choice, and shall be known one day to be only wise persons, and all wicked rich men to have been fools, and without true understanding.

22. THE CHILDREN SITTING IN THE MARKETPLACE

And the Lord said, whereunto shall I liken the men of this generation? and to what are they like? They are like unto little children sitting in the market-place, saying, we have piped, and ye have not danced ; we have mourned, and ye have not wept. For John the Baptist came neither eating bread, nor drinking wine, and ye say, he hath a devil. The Son of Man is come eating and drinking, and ye say, behold a gluttonous man, and a wine-bibber, a friend of publicans and sinners.—Luke vii. 31—34.

THE design of this simile was to reprove the froward and base-spirited Scribes and Pharisees, &c. Our Lord discovering hereby, that nothing would touch their hearts, no, not any different means used ; but that they quarrelled at God's messengers, whatsoever methods they took, or behaviours appeared in.

They were not pleased full nor fasting.

" They are like unto little children."

1. Our Saviour compared the people of that generation, viz., the Scribes and Pharisees, and other people, to little children, even to froward children, who are neither pleased with a pleasant nor a mournful noise ; (i. e.) Neither with music nor mourning. Whereby he discovers and detects, (1.) Their ignorance, or weakness in understanding ; for children are weak that way. (2.) Their peevish and quarrelsome temper.

2. He compares his own disciples also to children, who called upon the other, saying, " We have piped to you, and you have not danced, we have mourned, and ye have not lamented."

Our Lord compares his disciples to little children elsewhere, in respect of their innocency or harmlessness, " Verily I say unto you, except ye be converted, and become as little children, ye shall not enter into the kingdom of God," Matt. xviii. 3. And among these children our Lord comprehendeth himself also, who indeed was free from all malice, and of a holy, meek, and harmless spirit.

By the children said here to call upon their fellows, I understand himself and his disciples (together with John Baptist) are meant.

" Sitting in the market-place," our Saviour (as expositors intimate, and also our annotators) refers to a wonted custom of children in those times among the Jews, who having learned the art of music, and being pleasantly disposed, would sit. and play, or " pipe in the market-place," to stir up other children (who had not that skill in music, which some other among them had) to mirth and dancing ; but some being sullen and peevish children, would not regard their music ; and then those pretty children would fall a mourning, or make great lamentation, to see if they could move them to weep ; there was, my brethren, among the Jews, mourning women, viz., such who had the way to make dismal lamentation, enough almost to break the hearts of people ; and perhaps these children might have learned of them to make great lamentation, but they being froward and ill-natured, regarded not their music any more than their mourning and doleful lamentation ; and to those peevish, froward children our Lord compared the Scribes and Pharisees, and other people of that generation, who neither minded that sweet music he and his disciples made in their ears, (when they preached to them the sweet doctrine of peace and reconciliation, enough to charm their ears and their hearts—with God,) nor when they thundered out against them for their sin and unbelief, wrath, and divine vengeance, which might be sufficient to move them to weeping, and bitter lamentation.

There were mourning women among the Jews.

" We have piped unto you, and ye have not danced."

By piping, our Saviour, as I conceive, alludes to the sweet and pleasant way and method of his own and his disciples' preaching, together with the soul-raising doctrine they sometimes did preach to them, it being full of alluring expressions, and gracious promises, making use of such a way that might win, affect, and work upon their hearts, as music affects the ears of some people.

From hence note,

Doct. 1. That the preaching the gospel of peace and reconciliation to sinners, may fitly be compared to sweet and soul-ravishing music.

This I shall but very briefly open.

First, Music is taking to the ear, and it is that which many people are greatly affected with, nay, poor animals ; I mean the beasts of the field are seen to be affected with it. Shepherds in old times, in some countries used music, and would play to their flocks, and perhaps by some shepherds it may be used among us in this nation. So the sweet doctrine of the gospel of God's free grace draws the attention, and wonderfully affects the hearts of all believers who are Christ's sheep.

The doctrine of the gospel is sweet music to some.

That the voice of Christ and his ministers may be compared to music, appears by what is said by God himself concerning the preaching of the prophet.

The doctrine of free grace wonderfully affects the hearts of believers.

" And lo, thou art unto them as a very lovely song, of one that hath a pleasant voice, and can play well on an instrument : they hear thy word," &c., Ezek. xxxiii. 32. But the Jews and Pharisees, yet our Lord's preachings, and his disciples also, was much more like a lovely song, and they had a more pleasant voice than that of the prophets, or made sweeter music ; yet they regarded it not, or were not affected therewith, or charmed thereby, thongh is it said of our Saviour, that "never man spake like this man," John vii. 46. But yet they would not dance after his music, that is, they would not attend upon his word, nor were affected with his soul-ravishing doctrine.

Secondly, music hath its distinct notes, and that makes it melodious, so ministers should preach distinctly, not confusedly, for that makes no music. "If the trumpet gives an uncertain sound, who shall prepare to the battle?" 1 Cor. xiv. 8. It is intelligible and distinct preaching that makes the music, together with the sweetness of the matter uttered.

3. Some that pretend to music, and undertake to play on an instrument, are unskilful, and they make very sorry music; many that hear it, cry, away with it; what a squeaking and an unpleasant noise is this? So some men who pretend to be preachers, make no sweet music; there are too sorts of preachers whose preaching is not musical.

1. Such who seldom or never preach Jesus Christ, for the sum of their ministry is either morality, or the law, or duties of religion; who tell not the poor people what Christ hath done, nor of that peace and reconciliation he hath made by his obedience, and not how, or which way they must be saved, but only press duties and a holy life upon them; and this, too, without showing them the necessity of a changed heart; now these men make but very sorry music.

2. Such who though they may preach Christ, yet it is without such distinctions and a good method which is necessary; but preach confusedly, jumbling things together, confounding justification with sanctification, or Christ's merits; and the believer's inherent righteousness, or grace, and works together; these also make but very sorry music.

Thirdly, he that would make sweet music, must not harp too much upon one string, or have only one distinct note. So a preacher that would make right gospel-music, must not always preach upon one particular gospel truth, but he must touch melodiously upon every string; not preach justification always, as if there was nothing else to instruct the people in, but must insist upon sanctification also; the first as our title to heaven, and the other as our meetness for heaven; nor must a minister, who would make true gospel music, preach only on the promises, but also on the precepts; not of what Christ hath done for us, but also what he wrought in us, and must also be done by us, &c.

Fourthly, it is a curious art to attain to the clear knowledge of music, and to be very skilful, or play well upon an instrument. So it is a most blessed spiritual art, to know how to preach the gospel with all true spiritual wisdom; for as music is a mystery, so is the gospel a great mystery. "We are stewards of the mysteries of God, we speak the wisdom of God in a mystery," 1 Cor. ii. 7. How should this deter men from preaching the gospel, who are ignorant of the gospel? What music can such persons make in the ears of men, that know not the mysteries of God, Christ, and the gospel?

Music is a curious art, so is it truly to know, and rightly to preach the gospel.

Fifthly, some musicians make sweeter music than others, though all may have some skill in it; so some ministers make more sweet gospel music than others, who may be true gospel preachers; some may have clearer light, and more knowledge, and greater gifts and parts than others.

Sixthly, some people, though they hear sweet music, yet know not how to dance after it; and others, though they perhaps do know how, yet will not. So some ignorant people understand not the doctrine of the gospel, though it be clearly preached to them; and others understand more of it than they will receive or practice, will not cry to God for help to believe; and if they do believe, yet are more ready to dance after the promises, than after the precepts.

Some know not music, others know it, but will not dance after it.

Seventhly, a skilful dancer with his feet and body strikes (or imitates) the music very exactly; so true believers can dance so well after gospel music, that they strike every distinct note, or imitate it exactly in their hearts and lives. With the feet of their souls, saith an experienced saint, sir, I could follow you in every thing you have said this day; I find it is true, and experienced it, and live the word; these are sweet dancers indeed; others hear the music, but cannot dance in this spiritual manner.

Who they are that dance we after gospel music.

Eightly, music elevates the hearts of some people wonderfully; so the doctrine of the gospel tends to raise, nay, to ravish the hearts of gracious persons, when they hear of the nature of God's love, Christ's love, and also of the glory and excellency of Christ's person, and what he hath done, and hear what the nature of that peace is which Christ hath made; and hear the covenant of grace, and the promises of God opened unto them.

The doctrine of free-grace like sweet music.

Ninthly, but though music is sweet to some, others love it not, but cry away with it, it makes our hearts sad, &c. So the Jews and Pharisees of old, like many now, love not this gospel music; they did not (and many now do not) love the doctrine of free grace, no, nor to hear a minister's voice, or his music, but cry in their hearts away with it, the thoughts of these things you speak of (say they) tends to make our hearts sad; they love not to hear of the new birth, nor of death and judgment, but cry prophesy to us smooth " things of wine and strong drink," Micah ii. 11.

"We have mourned, and ye have not wept," Matt. xi. 17. John Baptist used a most severe way of preaching, as it is said, he came not eating nor drinking, (because he lived upon locusts and wild honey, and lived a retired life) so he most severely reproved the Jews and Pharisees for their abomin- *What meant by these words, we have mourn- ed to you.* able sins and unbelief; his preaching was as one that mourned, or that made bitter lamentation, his voice was that of one crying in the wilderness, and his doctrine, as it was foretold, burned as an oven. Some think that Malachi speaks of the day of judgment, when he says, " the day cometh that shall burn as an oven." But as reverend Cotton well observed, that prophet there refers to the ministry of John Baptist, that day shall leave them neither root nor branch. *Cotton on the covenant pag. 21, 22.*

The first is, saith he, the root of Abraham's covenant, which John laid the axe at, so that all the confidence they had in Abraham's covenant, temple, and tabernacle, was burned up, and so they had no root left them.

Secondly, saith he, there is something more in it, for with the spirit of burning, the Lord doth cut us off from any power of our natural or spiritual gifts, whereby to lay hold of Christ, and we are cut off from all confidence that we have in our own sufficiency. The Lord also hath cut us off from the righteousness of our parents, &c.

Again he saith, the ministry of John Baptist, which burned as an oven, left the Jews neither the root of Abraham's covenant, nor the branches of their own good works. So cutting them off from the root, he leaveth them no ground to trust to. O what a son of thunder was John! Repent and bring forth fruits meet for repentance, or you shall be cut down. " Now the axe is laid at the root of the trees, and therefore every tree, (every man) that bringeth not forth good fruit, shall be cut down, and cast into the fire." If ye receive not my great Master, down you must go to hell, and know that you, and your church-state, church-membership, suddenly shall be cut down, and rise no more for ever: thus John mourned to them, but they lamented not. Moreover, our Lord himself might sometimes be said to mourn, or preach, or sing a mournful song, as when he said, " Except ye repent, ye shall all likewise perish," Luke xiii. 3, 5. Yet then they did not lament, as the people would not be allured or drawn with the sweet music of his heavenly and soul-raising doctrine of free grace. So neither were they driven by the soul-terrifying threats of God's wrath and divine vengeance, but cried, John had a devil; perhaps they said he had a melancholy devil, he living in the de- sert. " John came neither eating nor drinking, and they say he hath a devil," Matt. xi. 18. *John Bap- tist's severe doctrine to the Jews.*

The doctrine of Christ and of John was the same, but their temper and converse greatly differed. John was a stern and morose man, and our Lord was of a more free and affable spirit and conversation, but these Jews and Pharisees would not give one nor the other a good word.

" The Son of Man came eating and drinking, and they say, behold, a man gluttonous, and a wine-bibber, a friend of publicans and sinners," verse 19.

" But wisdom is justified of her children,"

As their doctrine differed, (one seeming like a lofty song, the other as a mournful song, or like one making great lamentation) so their behaviours and carriages differedmuch also; our Lord was, 1 say, of a more pleasant temper, more free in his conversation, so that they could not say that he shunned the people's company who were sinners, yet they sought all occasions against him, and called him a gluttonous person and a wine-bibber, &c. Though as free from gluttony and drunkenness as John, but though they could not say he was a morose man, yet they blasphemed him, and charged him as bad as they charged the other. *The different tempers of Jesus Christ and John Baptist.*

From hence note,

Doct. 2. That though the ministers of Christ do what they can, or study what ways and methods they can, and live never so circumspectly, yet their persons nor their minis- try shall be accepted of some peevish and froward people.

If neither our Lord, nor his servant John, nor the disciples of our Lord, could get esteem amongst the people (though they appeared different in their temper, carriage, and deportment, yet all harmless, serious, and pious) it is no *No ministers can please all people,* marvel if ministers now cannot give content to their congregations, or to those ill-natured and peevish-spirited people amongst us, nor be free from reproach and infamy ; for what minister is not more or less vilified in these evil days we live in ?

The sad events of those days. 1. For if some live a retired, or a reserved kind of life, and hardly will keep company or converse with people, or very seldom are out of their own houses ; then they are charged to be proud, and contemn the conversation of their brethren and neighbours.

2. If others are more free and affable, and have a free and open converse, and are frequently amongst people ; and perhaps now and then to cheer their spirits, and strengthen nature, may drink a little wine ; then they are charged to waste their time, and spend their money, and, like their Master, are counted wine-bibbers, though their souls abhor it and give no just occasion for any to abuse them.

3. If they preach upon the threatenings of God, or press men to duties of religion and sanctification, or practical holiness, then they are censured to be legal preachers ; and if they preach much upon the doctrine of free grace, free justification, or justification without works, and insist much upon the promises, then they are accused to preach a licentious doctrine, are Antimonians ; so that neither their music nor their mourning will please the people of this generation, no more than it would please that formerly.

APPLICATION

1. We infer from hence, what hard measure Christ's poor ministers meet withal, and what need they have of the prayers of all that love Christ and them, that so they may bear up, and not be discouraged ; and that it is the duty of all Christians not to add to their burden ; but to vindicate them wherein they know they are abused.

2. We infer that no minister can expect to go free of hard censures from evil men, and false brethren ; but though they meet with undue and unjust usage, yet they ought not to be ever troubled or cast down. " For if they have called the master of the house Beelzebub, can they of his house go free ? And if they have done these things to the green tree, what will they do to the dry ?" Luke xxiii. 31.

3. This may also serve to reprove wicked men, who falsely accuse the servants of Christ, charging some to be morose and melancholy persons, if they lead a reserved life ; and others who have more freeness in their conversation, then they are drunkards, and what not ; but let such know (that it is to be feared) had they lived in the days of our Saviour (when he was on the earth) they would have reproached him after the same manner, for they are under the same influences, and of the same spirit.

4. We may infer, that such who are so ready to find fault, and accuse the faithful ministers of Christ, are led by a diabolical spirit ; and being guilty of the same sins with the Jews and Pharisees of old, they may expect the like woful end they met withal.

5. We infer, that such that no ministers can please, or who will not dance after, or kindly accept of the gospel, and delight in it as sweet music, when the doctrine of free grace is preached ; nor tremble and mourn when the threats of God's wrath are thundered out against them, are in a fearful condition ; for such that mercy, and infinite love and goodness, will not draw, nor judgments drive, are certainly like to perish eternally.

6. We infer, that the doctrine of the gospel is sweet to all those who truly believe. O what sweet music is it to them to hear of God's eternal love, and how the wrath of God is over for ever in Christ, and that they are for ever justified and pardoned, that God is their Father, their portion, and that Christ hath espoused, nay, married them to himself for ever.

7. Moreover, ministers may learn from hence, to study all manner of ways to move upon the hearts of sinners, even to preach terror from mount Sinai sometimes, as well as grace and love from mount Sion, or not only to preach on the promises, but on the threatnings, or of hell, wrath, and judgment to come, that such that will not dance may mourn. " But wisdom is justified of her children."

(1.) The plain sense of these words (saith one) is this, viz. It is a proverbial speech, sometimes like that art, *non habit inimicum præter ignorantem*, learning hath no enemies, but the ignorant.

(2.) Grace is justified of all that partake of it.

(3.) Certainly this may also be meant hereby, i.e., that the children of wisdom will justify God in his wise council, in his making use of men of different tempers. God might foresee some might sooner be affected with one, and others with another, &c. Some are for a learned man, who is well acquainted with the tongues, and others for such that only have their gifts and abilities more immediately from God, who know no other language than their own mother tongue, as the disciples of Christ did not, until they were miraculously endowed from on high.

Such that are wise, will not magnify learned men, because they are learned ; nor despise others because they are not learned ; but will justify God in making use of both the learned and the unlearned. And from hence.

8. Let all be exhorted to have an esteem for all Christ's ministers, though they are not of their judgment in some things. I remember the disciples said, " Lord, we saw one casting out of devils in thy name, who followeth not with us," Luke ix. 49, 50 ; but what said our Saviour, " forbid him not, for they that are not against us, are for us." What, though this and that minister follows not us in some things, yet he may be Christ's faithful minister ; do you see in some things more than others ? why others in some other things may see more than you.

Lastly, learn to show yourselves the children of wisdom, and see whether the doctrine of the gospel is music in your ears, and that thou find it so fixed in your hearts, that you spiritually can dance after it, or find all the distinct notes thereof, and live in a holy and exact conformity to it, that all may say you dance well after such that can play well on this blessed instrument ; or so live as to bring glory to God, and honour to your sacred religion and profession, and so shall you not only find joy and gladness on earth, but sing and triumph in endless joys in heaven.

23. FIRE, SALT, AND PEACE

I

For every one shall be salted with fire, and every sacrifice shall be salted with salt. Salt is good: but if salt hath lost its saltness, wherewith shall it be salted? have salt in yourselves, and have peace one with another.—Mark ix. 49, 50.

IT is always necessary, as in parables, so in such dark texts as this is, to consider, and well observe the scope and coherence thereof.

First, This I shall do, and so proceed in my usual method.

Secondly, Open or explain all the terms and parts contained herein.

Thirdly, Observe those points of doctrine that lie most clear in the words.

Fourthly, Apply the whole.

The scope of the words opened. First, To understand the main scope of this place of scripture, we need not look farther back than to the 42nd verse, " And whosoever shall offend one of these little ones that believe in me," &c. By these little ones, are intended, or held forth, humble Christians, or such that are little in their own eyes. And so our annotators on Matt. xviii. 10. The disciples were ready to be lifted up with pride, striving who should be the greatest among them. And the grand design of our blessed Lord, in speaking what we have, ver. 43, to the 48th, seems to be twofold.

1. To teach his disciples humility.

2. To show the necessity of mortification of sin ; the lust of which he doth, by showing, that a right hand, or foot, which offends, must be cut off, and a right eye, that offends, must be pulled out. He doth not, cannot mean the members of the natural body: for so to take it is to render our Saviour to encourage self-murder, which is abominable once to imagine. But by a right hand, foot, and eye, he either means the members of the old man, the body of sin, or else such members that offend in the visible body or church of God : but I conclude he intends chiefly the members of the body of sin, which if not mortified, would expose both the soul and body of such they offend, to eternal flames, Rom. vii. 24. Observe, that the old man, or corrupt nature, is elsewhere compared to the natural body : and every particular sin as a member thereof ; see Coloss. iii. 5, " Mortify therefore your members that are upon the earth :" what these members are he tells us, viz., fornication, uncleanness, evil concupiscence, and covetousness, which is idolatry.

Quest. But what sins are those which are signified by a right hand, a right foot, and a right eye?

Answ. All beleved sins, whether lusts of the flesh, lusts of the eyes, or What is a right-hand sin.
the pride of life.

1. Such sins that seem profitable may be meant by right-hand sins.

2. And all such sins that tend to sensual pleasure, may be meant by right-eye sins. Now it is better to part with these evil lusts, by which the sinner offends God, though they may seem never so profitable to enrich him in this world ; and also better part with such lusts that seem sweet for pleasure, and so dismember the body of sin, than to " be cast into hell fire." Our Saviour, it is to be observed, repeats these words six or seven times, i. e., " Of being cast into hell, where the worm dieth not, and the fire is not quenched." And this no doubt is to confirm the certainty of eternal torments. Many people, he foresaw would hardly be brought to believe, that God will so severely deal with ungodly persons, for living in sin, they being ignorant of that horrid and infinite evil that is in it.

(1.) But did they contemplate upon that fearful anguish or torment our Lord Jesus Christ felt and endured in his soul and body for sin, when he stood in our law-place, as our great and blessed Head and Representative ; they might easily be convinced of their folly and grand ignorance herein.

2. Especially considering the great dignity, and infinite worth of his person, he being God, co-eternal, co-essential, and co-equal wlth the Father. The sufferings of our blessed Lord, my brethren, were a thousand times more than if the whole lump of mankind had been cast into hell, to endure eternal flames of divine vengeance. Alas, what is sorry man, even but as a toad in the sight of God, when once compared to the beloved, eternal Son of God ? Therefore to awaken all men that live in sin, and will not part with them, he repeats these words so often, viz., " Then to be cast into hell, where the worm dieth not, and the fire is not quenched." So much as to the scope of the words.

" For every one shall be salted with fire," [for] is a relative, and refers to what precedes, i. e., every one that will not cut off a right hand lust, a right-foot lust, or pull out a right-eye lust, and so be salted with the spirit, shall be salted with hell-fire, or be preserved in those flames to endure eternal torments.

Quest. How may we know a right-hand sin ? How to know a right-hand sin.

Answ. 1. A right-hand sin is that sin which doth so easily beset the sinner ; they yield as readily to it as they use their right hand.

2. The right hand is the working hand, that cuts, the purse, that seals the wedge of gold, and takes the unlawful gain in trading ; so that is a right-hand sin that tends in an unlawful manner to get riches, or to increase a man's substance.

3. The right hand is held up to keep off the blow that is struck at the body, to defend the body ; so that is the right-hand sin, which for love to, the sinner defends and strives to keep off the blow, when the Spirit of God strikes to destroy the whole body of sin : and he that labours to extenuate sin, or that makes excuses about it, uses his right-hand sin.

4. You know the right hand feeds the body ; so that is a right-hand sin, which feeds the body of sin ; and such use this cursed right hand, that make provision for the flesh, to fulfil the lusts thereof.

5. The right is the beloved hand, that hand which a man is most unwilling to part with ; it is the hand he concludes he shall most need the use of. So a right-hand sin is that sin which a man has his heart chiefly set upon, and is most unwilling to part with ; it is that lust which he thinks will be as great a loss to him as his right hand. Some men think, if in their trading they should deal justly, and honestly, and not exact upon any person, they shall be starved, or be brought to want, as a man that hath lost his right hand.

6. The right hand is a principal member of the natural body : so a right-hand sin is a principal member of the body of sin.

Quest. What is a right-eye sin ?

Ans. 1. A right eye is greatly prized ; what do men value above their What is a right-eye sin. right eye ? So any sin that an ungodly person loves, or greatly delights in, is his right-eye sin.

2. A right eye is, at all times of danger, defended ; how is the hand up to preserve the eyes, especially the right eye ? So a right-eye sin, when it is struck at by the hammer of God's word, how doth the sinner strive to preserve it and plead for it ? he is as ready to defend it as a right eye.

3. The eye is that member that sees the evil object that draws the man into sin. So a right-eye sin is that which is the occasion of committing sin that allures and draws him into sin and folly.

4. The right eye delights the body, by beholding such objects and things that please

the sensual part. So a right-eye sin delights the carnal heart, or fills it with carnal pleasure; so fornication, uncleanness, wantonness, adultery, and the like, are right-eye sins.

Quest. Well, but what if sinners will not part with these sins?

Answ. Why then every such a one must go where the worm dieth not, and the fire is not quenched.

Some would have every one salted with fire, and every sacrifice salted with salt, to mean the same persons, which I believe not. There is a two-fold fire, and all men must be salted with one or the other of them.

(1.) The Spirit of God, that is compared to fire.

(1.) Hell-fire.

First. The Spirit is compared to fire. " Ye shall be baptized with the Holy Ghost and fire." " Quench not the Spirit," Acts ii. 2.

What is meant by salting with fire. Take the words thus, then the sense is this, viz., every one that is not salted with the Spirit, shall be salted with hell-fire.

That the Spirit is, and may be compared to fire, appears by these particulars following.

The Holy Spirit compared to fire. 1. Fire gives light, so the Holy Spirit gives light, or illuminates the understanding.

2. Fire puts such to pain who feel its scorching heat; so the Holy Spirit, in convictions, puts the soul to great pain, and makes the poor sinner to cry out, as those did Peter preached to, who cried out, " Men and brethren, what shall we do?" Acts ii. 37.

3. Fire hath a purging, cleansing, and purifying nature, even so the Holy Spirit purgeth out sin, and purifies, and sanctifies the soul of a believer.

4. Fire burns up all those things which are combustible, so as soon as a man hath received the Holy Spirit, it presently burns up all sinful and sensual pleasures, even all filth, and combustible things of the flesh, world, and devil. Sin, and the corruptions of the heart, are like wood, chaff, and stubble, which when the Holy Spirit takes hold of, it consumes and burns it up.

5. Fire causeth heat, and tends to warm and revive a person who is chilled with cold, or benumbed therewith. So the Holy Spirit causeth spiritual heat and warmth; and such who are in a spiritual sense cold to God, and cold to the things of God, are greatly revived by its sweet influences. " Did not our heart burn within us?" Luke xxiv. 32. How was this, but by the reviving operations of the Spirit upon their hearts? Zeal is like fire which is the product of the Spirit. " The zeal of thine house hath eaten me up," saith David. O how hot and fervent was he (through the influences of the Spirit) in his soul!

6. Fire is of a trying and a refining nature, it tries and refines gold and silver, and makes it more precious. We read of gold seven times refined in the fire. So also the Holy Spirit refines the sons of men. " He is like the refiner's fire, and like fuller's soap, and he shall sit as a refiner and purifier of silver, and he shall purify the sons of Levi," Mal. iii. 2, 3. The Holy Ghost consumes the dross, and makes the souls of God's people more holy, and also refines all the graces of the Spirit. " That the trial of your faith being much more precious than gold that perisheth, though it be tried with fire, may be found unto praise, and honour, and glory, at the appearing of Jesus Christ," 1 Pet i. 7. True afflictions are said to do this, but it is not simply afflictions, but the Spirit of God, in and by afflictions which does it.

7. Fire is of an ascending nature; contrary to other elements, it moves upwards. So the Holy Spirit causeth all that feel its influences and operations, to ascend in their love, desires, and affections towards God, or heavenward.

8. Fire is of a penetrating nature. So the Spirit of God pierces and penetrateth. " The Spirit searcheth all things," &c. 1 Cor. ii. 10.

2dly. Every one that is not salted with this fire, must be salted with hell-fire, which will torment both soul and body for ever.

Quest. What is the nature of hell-fire, and why is hell called a furnace of fire? It is said, that " the wicked shall be cast into a furnace of fire, there shall be wailing, and gnashing of teeth," Matt. xiii. 42.

Why hell is compared to fire. Answ. 1. A furnace of fire (like that which the king of Babylon did heat for the three worthy servants of God) is very terrible. O it is an amazing thing to think of being cast into such a furnace of fire! and is it not more terrible and amazing to think of being cast into that furnace which divine vengeance hath prepared and heated for all ungodly persons, and unbelievers, who slight and reject Jesus Christ.

2. Fire is a very tormenting thing to such who are cast into it, although but endured

one hour, nay a few minutes. Now divines tell us, that the least tortures in hell exceed the greatest that can be devised by men on earth, because the punishment of hell is to satisfy infinite justice. " As is thy fear, so is thy wrath." Fear of hell is not worse than the sorrows and pains feared.

3. Such is the dreadful nature of the fire of hell (as it is tormenting) that it cannot be quenched. How many times doth our Saviour assert this in this very chapter, *i. e.*, as the worm of conscience dies not, so the fire is not quenched. All the tears, yea, Mark ix. 2. floods of tears cannot quench the fire of hell, hence called eternal life. It is not external but eternal fire. There will be no end of the pains and torments of the damned, neither of men or devils.

4. Such is the nature of this fire, that it will torment both the body and soul too. Elementary fire may torment the body, but cannot touch the soul, to hurt or torment that; but the torments of hell will extend to both. Not only shall internal wrath be let out by the accusations of conscience; but no doubt those eternal flames will also torment the whole soul. See the simile of the fan in Christ's hand.

5. It seems also as if this fire will be a dark fire; whereas external, elementary fire gives light.

(1.) Hell is called "utter darkness," Matt. viii. 12.

(2.) And it is also called the blackness of darkness. "To whom is reserved the blackness of darkness for ever," Jude 13. Were it not of this nature, it might seem as if there was some degree of comfort in hell, because light is sweet and comfortable.

Quest. But why is the fire of hell compared to salt?

Answ. 1. Because salt, when applied to a sore or wound in the body, causeth great smart and anguish. So will this fire to a wounded conscience in hell.

2. Because salt is of a preserving nature, so will this fire be like salt to preserve the damned in a state of life. Other fire destroys life, and so puts an end to the torments of such who are burned to ashes in it. But God hath put a different quality into this fire, it shall preserve the objects of divine vengeance from dying, or from being annihilated.

So much as to the first part of the 49th verse.

" And every sacrifice shall be salted with salt."

Some would have every one, and every sacrifice to mean the same persons, as I said before; but I do not believe that our Lord does mean " by every one that shall be salted with fire, and every sacrifice shall be salted with salt" one and the same person.

Pray mind the connexion of the text with what precedes, ver. 47, 48. " If thine eye offend thee, pluck it out, it is better for thee to enter into the kingdom of God with one eye, than having two eyes to be cast into hell fire, where the worm dieth not, and the fire is not quenched." Now mark, " For every one shall be salted with fire." Every one, that is, every ungodly one, (who parts with the Spirit) or will not part with his beloved lusts, shall burn in hell, or be salted with hell fire. " And every sacrifice shall be salted with salt," every one that sacrifices up his lusts, or every saint of God, shall be salted with salt.

Now therefore, by every sacrifice I understand is meant every believer only, and not the ungodly, though the wicked are called God's sacrifice, yet I humbly conceive they are not intended by sacrifices here.

Evident it is, that believers are, and may upon several respects be called a sacrifice.

1. They offer up to God a broken heart. " The sacrifices of God are a broken spirit; a broken and contrite heart, O God, thou wilt not despise," Psal. li. 17.

2. They offer up themselves, both body and soul, as a sacrifice to God. " I beseech you, brethren, by the mercies of God, that ye present your bodies a living sacrifice, holy, acceptable unto God, which is your reasonable service," Rom. xii. 1.

3. All the services of believers are called sacrifices. " Ye also as lively stones, are built up a spiritual house, a holy priesthood, to offer up spiritual sacrifices, acceptable unto God by Jesus Christ," 1 Pet. ii. 5.

Hence praises are called sacrifices. " By him therefore let us offer the sacrifice of praise continually," Heb. xiii. 15.

Moreover distributing to the poor saints is called a sacrifice. " To do good, and to communicate, forget not, for with such sacrifices God is well pleased."

4. Because the saints offer up, or sacrifice every sin and lust to the glory of God; the whole body of sin, and every member thereof, they offer up to be mortified by the Spirit, Rom. viii. 13.

5. Because also sometimes they offer up their lives, or their mortal bodies, as a sacrifice unto God, in the flames, in martyrdom, when called to it. " We are all the day long accounted as sheep for the slaughter," Rom. viii. 36.

So much for the 49th. verse.

"Salt is good, but if it hath lost its saltness, wherewith will ye shall season it ?" Ver. 50.

Salt here refers unto the saints particularly, whom our Lord calls the salt of the earth, " Ye are the salt of the earth," Matt. v. 13. Believers, especially Christ's faithful ministers, are called, or compared to salt.

Saints compared to salt.

1. In respect of that holy and savoury doctrine which they preach, and blessed truths by them professed ; by this means they season the earth, which otherwise would be corrupted with the filth of false doctrine, loathsome, pernicious, and poisonous errors, and destructive heresies.

2. In respect of their savoury words : " Let your speech be always with grace, seasoned with salt,"

3. In respect of their most wholesome and savoury lives and conversations, and good examples they show unto all. Thus they salt and season the earth.

4. Salt preserves things from perishing, so also do the saints and people of God ; were it not for them, the world would stink, and be so loathsome in the nostrils of God, that he would soon destroy it, and tread it down under his feet : " Except the Lord of hosts had left unto us a very small remnant, we should have been as Sodom, and we should have been like unto Gomorrah," Isa. i. 9. Thus the saints, like salt, are of great use and profit to the earth. Salt is good.

5. Salt will not, cannot season all sorts of meat : some is so far gone, being decayed to such a degree. that it stinks like carrion, and is utterly past recovery.

So the saints and people of God cannot, either by their doctrine, or holy conversation, or holy example, season some ungodly ones : they are so vile, filthy, and abominable, that God hath left them, and given them up to their own heart's lust ; and the Spirit will strive with them no more, and they are past all hopes of recovery, and must perish in their sins for ever.

But if salt hath lost its saltness, &c., but if you, my disciples, lose your gracious frame of spirit, or should apostatize from your holy doctrine and principles, or grow carnal and earthly, how, or which way. shall you salt and season others ?

What is meant by salt losing it saltness.

This denotes two things.

1. That gracious persons, or such as are true Christians, and true ministers, may decay in knowledge, zeal, and holiness, by which means they may render themselves incapable to season others with the knowledge and love of the truth.

2. That all such who seem to be true Christians, or appear savoury like salt for a short time, may notwithstanding utterly decay, and fall away (their hearts being never right with God) and so become good for nothing, but like unsavoury salt prove the very worst of men, as such commonly do, who fall into total apostacy, like Julian the apostate, " But it were better for such they had never known the way of righteousness," 2 Pet. ii. 21. They knew the way of righteousness, had some knowledge of it, and professed themselves to be godly persons for a while ; this text therefore doth not in the least intimate, that sincere Christians may, or can totally and finally fall away ; no, it is impossible for the elect to be deceived, or perish in apostasy. " We are not of them that draw back to perdition," Heb. x. 39. Such as have real union with Christ, and are members of his mystical body, are not of them, or of that sort which draw back to perdition ; we are not sons of defection, but God's elect ones : " Christ's sheep shall never perish ; they cannot be like salt which hath utterly lost its saltness, and is become good for nothing," John x. 28.

" Have salt in yourselves."

What is meant by having salt in ourselves.

By salt, in these words, our Saviour no doubt means the true and saving grace of God. Have grace, much grace in your own hearts. Grace is compared to salt.

" And be at peace one with another."

Labour after union, love, and concord one with another ; do not seek or strive who shall be greatest ; seek not the pre-eminence, but be of a sweet, humble, and condescending frame of heart. " A new commandment I give you, that you love one another."

Having thus explained every part of this dark place of Scripture according to that light and knowledge God hath given me, I shall proceed to the observations. There are only two points of doctrine that I shall take notice of, and prosecute from hence.

The doctrine raised.

Doct. 1. That it ought to be the special care of every professor, to have salt in himself, or much saving grace in his heart.

Doct. 2. That it is the indispensable duty of the disciples of Christ, to labour to live in peace one with another.

To both these I purpose to speak in order, but at present shall conclude with a word of application.

APPLICATION

Infer. 1. We may from hence infer, that it is a most dangerous thing for any to live in sin, and harbour base and abominable lusts in their bosoms. Sin may seem sweet in the committing of it, but it will be bitterness in the end.

2. We also infer, that it is no easy thing to be a true Christian, it is as hard as it is to cut off a right hand, or to pull out a right eye: and some men will as soon do the one as the other; they are like that wretched man, who being told by his physician, he must leave off all his evil courses, and reform his debauched life, or he would utterly lose the sight of his eyes, answered and said, then farewell my sweet eyes. He was resolved to keep his lusts, though he lost his sight. There are too many of these, they will not leave their abominable lusts, and beloved sins, though they lose their souls and bodies too, and perish for ever in hell.

3. See how Satan hath deceived miserable mortals: sin is not in vain called deceitful lusts, it is that by which Satan baits his hook, and subtily ensnares the souls of men: the devil is compared to a fowler, and to a cunning hunter, by whose policy many thousands are taken, and devoured, Prov. vi. 5.

4. We also infer from hence, that the future state of the wicked will be very lamentable: who can dwell with unquenchable fire, or in everlasting burnings? Certainly but very few of the ungodly world do indeed believe or give credit to the truth of God's word, nor to what the lip of truth itself has declared; why else should our Lord so often repeat those words, viz., "Shall be cast into hell, where the worm dieth not, and the fire is not quenched?"

But let them believe it, or not believe it, they will one day, to their sorrow, find the truth thereof.

5. How just will the damnation of the wicked be, who choose rather to cleave to their evil lusts, either for the sake of unlawful gain, or pleasure, though they perish, than to embrace Jesus Christ and part with them. Brethren, in the great day men will not be condemned for not doing those things which they had no power to do, but for refusing or neglecting to do that which they might have done; not because they had not new hearts, or the image of Christ formed in them, but because they would not believe or give credit to the veracity of God's word, they having equal power to believe in that manner, as to believe any human approved history; but they will not exercise a human faith. It will be, because they refuse to hear the word of God, or to attend upon the means of grace; in a word, this is the "Condemnation, that light is come into the world, and men love darkness rather than light, because their deeds are evil," John iii. 19. They will not leave their profane cursing and swearing, their lying and cheating, their drunkenness and uncleanness, nor their covetousness and abominable pride, malice, envy, backbiting, and slandering the innocent: no, they love these dark ways rather than the light; and others love themselves, their own works and inherent righteousness, and will trust to that, and not come to Christ that they may have life.

6. We infer also from hence, that there is a necessity of the Holy Spirit in convictions; the Spirit of God is a Spirit of burning, before it is a Spirit of consolation. All those who are not salted with this divine fire, shall perish one day in the fire of hell. And how much better is it for wretched sinners to bear the smart of this fire in mortification, than to be salted in hell, under eternal damnation?

7. From what you have heard, we may also infer, how savoury it behoveth all believers to walk in the whole course of their conversations, and to handle their ministry and holy doctrine so, since thereby they are to season the world, and to prevent them from horrid corruptions and pollutions, that they may not become as filthy and stinking carrion.

8. Moreover, we may see the necessity, and transcendent excellency of divine salt. Sinners, you must be salted with the Spirit, or perish for ever.

Remember eternity is written upon the gates of the broad way, as well as it is on the narrow way; you must come under the power of God's word and Spirit.

Lastly. One word to you that are believers, and I have done; have you found that you are salted with fire, i.e., with the Holy Spirit? All must be salted that are a sacrifice for God: as under the law, "Every oblation, and every burnt-offering was to be salted with salt," Lev. ii. 13.   And so also were their meat-offerings. Happy are you, if you are well salted.

—

II

Have salt in yourselves—Mark ix. 50.

I HAVE opened this, and the preceding verse, and have proposed to speak to two points of doctrine.

First Doctrine.   Doct. 1. That it ought to be the special care of every professor, to see he hath salt in himself, namely, true and saving grace in his heart.

In speaking to this proposition,

> First. I shall shew you, why saving grace is compared to salt.
> Secondly, shew you why every professor should see to have salt in himself.
> Thirdly, shew who they are, that are well salted.
> Fourthly, apply it.

> First, I shall shew you, why saving grace is compared to salt.

Why grace is compared to salt.   1.   Salt (as you have heard) causeth great pain and smart, if it be applied to a green wound, &c.,

So the saving grace of the Spirit doth cause a wounded spirit to smart, or put the soul to great pain. It was a sign that David had grace, or was salted, who cried out in pain, in the sense of his sins, " I am sore pained, I roar because of the disquietness of my heart," Psal. xxxviii. 8.   Also how did those cry out in pain, that Peter preached to, being pricked in their hearts, under the convictions of the Spirit, "Men and brethren, what shall we do ?" Acts ii. 36.   Such who were never wounded under the sense of sin, never felt the smart of this spiritual salt, this pain is very sore.   The spirit of a man may sustain his infirmity, but a wounded spirit who can bear ?

2.   Salt is of a diffusive and searching nature ; if it be applied to meat, or laid on flesh, it will diffuse itself into every part, and search it to the very bone.

So saving grace is of a diffusive and searching nature, it will diffuse itself into every faculty of the soul.   " The Spirit searcheth all things," 1 Cor. ii. 10.

(1.) Grace diffuseth itself into the understanding, and enlighteneth that.   " The entrance of thy word giveth light," Psal. cxix. 130.   Ye that were somtimes in darkness, are now light in the Lord.   " That the eyes of your understanding being enlightened," Eph. i. 18.   Common grace gives some light. We read of hypocrites, who were once enlightened : but special grace gives great light, it enlightens the eyes to see him that is invisible, to see the evil of sin, and the want and worth of Christ, and the vanity of this world.

(2.) Grace diffuseth itself also into the will, it bends the will, and fixes a divine principle there, yea a prevailing, ruling, and reigning principle, so as to receive Jesus Christ, and to make an universal opposition against sin, though it cannot get a total conquest over it.

(3.) Likewise it pierceth into the affections, stirring up an ardent desire after God, and to see that Jesus Christ is the chiefest of ten thousand, and causes the soul to long after a likeness unto him in holiness, meekness, and in humility, &c.

(4.) Grace also diffuseth itself into the conscience, it makes that tender, rightly informing and guiding the conscience by the light and rule of the word.

(5.) Nay it searcheth out every sin, even that sin which is hid, it searcheth every corner of the heart ; it is the candle of the Lord, which searcheth the inward part of the belly.

(6.) It also searcheth out the ends, aims, thoughts, and intentions of a man ; and if hypocrisy be there, it will discover it.   Thus is grace like salt, of a searching nature.

(3.) Salt is of a purging nature, is will cleanse and purge out that filth and corrupt blood which is in the flesh, as is well known to all.

So saving grace cleanseth and purgeth out sin, whether it be in the heart or life, and by this quality saving grace is discerned.

(1.) If we speak of the grace of faith, this is the nature of it.   " He puts no difference between us and them, purifying their hearts by faith," Acts xv. 9.

(2.) If we speak of the grace of hope, this is the nature of it : " He that hath this hope in him, purifieth himself as he is pure," 1 John iii. 3.

(3.) Or if we speak of the grace of love, it is said, that "ye that love the Lord hate evil," and also, " that perfect love casteth out fear :" that is, slavish fear, love purges out this, like as salt purges out corrupt blood that is in the flesh, to which it is applied.

Some men say that they have faith and hope in Christ, and love to Christ, but are as vile, as filthy, and as unholy as ever may be, swearers, liars, drunkards, proud, or covetous persons. Now this shews, they were never salted, they never had true and saving grace ; for grace purges and cleanses the soul, as you have now heard, like as salt purges flesh.

(4.) Salt is of a preserving nature, it preserveth things from corruption and putrefaction : what would become of flesh, and many other things, were it not for salt ? even in a very short time it would stink like carrion, and be good for nothing.

So saving grace preserves a man from sin, and all spiritual filthiness, both of the flesh and spirit.

What was it that preserved Joseph from the sin of uncleanness ? O he was well salted, he had salt in himself, or saving grace in his heart, which made him say, how can I do this great wickedness, and sin against God ? So what was it which preserved good Nehemiah from the sin of covetouness, and from oppressing of the people, as the former governors, had done ? why, he had salt in himself, grace in his heart, therefore, saith he, so did not I, because of the fear of the Lord.

5. Some things must be salted quickly, or it may be too late, they may be so soon corrupted. *Some things must be salted quickly.*

So ought young men and women to be soon, or quickly salted, or seasoned with grace, or they may be so corrupted, and hardened in sin, that God may give them up to their own hearts' lusts, and they become so abominable, that they may be past all hopes of recovery. 'Tis dangerous to delay the salting of flesh, and some other things ; so it is very dangerous to delay looking out for grace ; youth is the proper time, now while it is called today. " Behold, now is the accepted time, behold now is the day of salvation," 2 Cor. vi. 1, 2. Now every soul should see that they are salted with this spiritual salt, before God treads them down as carrion, or as mire of the streets.

6. Sometimes flesh, and other things which are not salted, corrupt presently, the air being corrupt and soultry. So in such a time as this is, persons had *Things not salted corrupt.* need be salted presently, we have very corrupt air, an infectious air, our climate and days are dangerous dwelling in, it is a perilous time, no man can go out of doors, or fall into almost any company, but he may soon be corrupted, either with false doctrine, errors, and heresies, or else with evil and pernicious practices, except he be well salted with grace and saving knowledge.

7. Flesh needeth to be salted, and salted again and again, it is not sufficient that a little salt be scattered upon it : so ought every Christian to be salted often, for a little grace will not do, such is the quality of our nature, and the infectiousness of the air, and the days we live in that we ought to have much grace. " It is good that the heart be established with grace," Heb. xiii. 9. To preserve them from sin, and all manner of corruption.

8. Salt also seasons all things, causing that which is unsavoury to become pleasant and wholesome, " Can that which is unsavoury be eaten without salt," Job. vi. 6.

Now, brethren, grace makes many things to relish and savour well to a child of God.

Ist. It makes spiritual things to savour and taste most sweet to the soul. *What things grace salts.* For although spiritual things are not unsavoury in themselves, yet an unsanctified or graceless heart cannot relish any sweetness in them, their souls being out of taste, they only savour the things of the flesh.

(1) Grace makes the word of God to taste sweet : it made David to say, thy word is sweeter to me than honey, or the honey-comb : and holy Job, to prefer it above his necessary food. " Thy word, saith the prophet, was found, and I did eat it, and thy word was the joy and rejoicing of my heart," Jer. xv. 19. But though it be thus with gracious hearts, yet such who are ungodly, and without grace can taste no good nor sweetness in it. My brethren, how sweet do the promises taste to a man that hath faith ! but what good or spiritual sweetness can a person find in it, who believes not, or that is destitute of faith ? can such feed upon the promises, or taste the sweetness of the word ? no, no.

(2.) Grace makes prayer sweet to a true believer, which hath no taste or savour in it to graceless persons : can they find any sweetness in calling upon God ? is it not unpleasant, nay a burden, and very grievous to them ? without grace, prayer hath no divine relish in it.

(3.) How sweet, pleasant, and savoury is meditation on God, and Jesus Christ, to one that hath much grace ? " My meditation of him shall be sweet in the night-watches," Psal. civ. 34.

(4.) How sweet also is spiritual conference, and Christian converse one with another, to gracious persons. " Did not our heart burn within us, whilst he talked with us, and opened the scriptures ?" Luke xxiv. 32.

(5.) How sweet is the holy supper of our Lord to a Christian, who by faith feedeth on it, or is salted with much grace, much faith, and love to Jesus Christ ?

2ndly. Grace makes afflictions to be savoury, and to relish well to a true believer, which to graceless persons, to such who have no salt in themselves, are very bitter and irksome ; " It was good for me, that I have been afflicted."

3rdly. Grace doth not only cause spiritual things to be sweet and savoury to all godly persons, but it maketh them to be most savoury also.

I say, grace, like salt, makes every true Christian to be savoury.

1. In his words ; grace seasons the tongue. " Let your speech be always with grace, seasoned with salt," Col. iv. 6. It is said of our blessed Saviour, that "they admired the gracious words which proceeded out of his mouth, because he was full of grace," Luke. iv. 22. Solomon saith, " The tongue of the righteous is as choice silver ; but the heart of the wicked is of little worth," Prov. x. 20 ; because not salted with this spiritual salt.

2. Grace maketh believers savoury in their behaviour, deportment, and carriage towards all they are in company with, or converse with : but how light, loose, and wanton are graceless persons in their words, carriage, and behaviour, for want of this salt ?

3. Grace makes holy and gracious persons savoury in their garbs and dresses. As you may know the lightness, wantonness, and unsavouriness of graceless persons by their words, deportments, and behaviour ; so you may also by their garbs and dresses. Like as a bush hung out, shows that wine is sold within ; so by the vain and fantastical dresses some persons wear, you may know that there is a vain, wanton, and graceless heart within. But if ye see women dressed in sober garbs, or in modest apparel, as becoming such who profess godliness, it may show the graciousness of their hearts ; though it is true, some carnal persons may go in modest dresses, like as many professors appear to be that which they are not.

4. Grace maketh Christians to be savoury in their tradings and commerce with all they trade with ; how full of words are some persons, and how will they commend their goods above what they know they ought, may be, tell a company of lies to deceive the buyer. It is easy to discern a holy and gracious person in his dealing and trading in the world, provided he be a man of right principles, and acts to a right end : though it is true, many have got the art to counterfeit a true Christian this way also. In a word, grace makes all true believers savoury unto God, savoury to the saints, and savoury to the world, and also unto themselves.

9. Salt (as Pliny, and other Naturalists observe) is very good to destroy worms that breed in the body of men, women, and children, and also that it is good against the sting of serpents.

Grace is a most sovereign remedy against all sin, which is the sting of the old serpent. Whosoever looks unto Christ by faith, though never so severely stung (as those were in the wilderness by fiery serpents) are all immediately cured ; and indeed to this end is he held up in the gospel, John iii. 14. Also grace, saving grace is the only remedy to kill and destroy the worm of conscience, which breeds out of that filth or corruption that is in the soul, which I understand is that worm (which our Saviour saith in hell, dieth not) it begins to gnaw here in this world, whilst the sinner is alive in the body ; and the pricking and griping pain thereof is sometimes very grievous and tormenting, even according to the degree and nature of that sin or sins which lie upon the conscience, and according to that light which is in the understanding, especially when God lets out conscience to torment the soul.

Quest. Why is conscience compared to a worm ?

What is meant by the worm that dies not. Answ. 1. Because as worms that breed in the body, are bred out of that corrupt matter, or undigested food that nature cannot carry off, either in the stomach, or in the belly ; so the worm of conscience is bred out of the filth of sin and corruption in the soul: for from the greatness of that filth, horrid guilt arises, which the natural powers of the soul cannot purge or cast out.

2. Because as worms in the body are the cause of many sad and mortal diseases : so from this worm of conscience many dangerous diseases of the soul do also arise, as un-

belief, melancholy, frenzy, and desperation : what fearful distempers (by this means) took hold of Spira, and poor Mr. Child!

3. Because as worms bred in the body are very tormenting : so is the pain and anguish which is occasioned by the worm of conscience. No man is able to express what sorrow, pain, and torment those two miserable persons felt and endured, from the guilt of their accusing and condemning consciences.

4. Because as the body in respect of all its natural powers is not able to cure the person, or cast off the pain that rises, or is occasioned by those worms : so all the natural powers of the soul cannot cure a man, or free him of those dolorous pains which rise from the worm of conscience ; no, no, it must be done by the application of some powerful medicines or means made use of, and nothing but the Spirit of Christ, and the graces thereof; especially the grace of faith can do it, by which the blood of Christ is applied unto the conscience.

5. Because as a person who is sorely afflicted, and tormented with worms, without speedy cure must die (for many thousands it is thought do daily die of worms) so except a poor sinner hath not speedy cure of the worm of conscience, he must die, or perish eternally. But such is the excellent nature of this salt, I mean, the grace of faith, which applies the only remedy, that no sooner does a poor sinner believe, but he hath ease, and this worm is destroyed, and he perfectly cured, and to such a degree, that as before his conscience did most sorely torment him, now his conscience (that worm being killed) gives him most sweet joy and peace.

6. Yet as many persons who have worms, and are at times greatly distressed thereby, by taking some medicines, which though they cannot cure them, yet give them some ease for a while ; so by false remedies many sinners have some ease from their tormenting consciences, but soon their pain returns again (unless God suffers their consciences to be seared) and terrifies them more than ever.

10. Salt causes great thirst (as all by experience find) even so the saving grace of God causeth a mighty drought or thirst in the soul after Jesus Christ, the water of life. " As the hart thirsteth after the water-brooks, so my soul thirsteth after thee, O God," Psal. xlii. 1, 2. It is true, some say, that thirsting after Jesus Christ is a previous qualification for Christ, or as a preparation to grace, but certainly they are mistaken ; for it is grace itself that causes this vehement thirst and desire in the soul, by its convictions discovering the sad estate in which naturally it is ; and also by opening of the eyes of the understanding, to see the great necessity and excellency of Jesus Christ. The Spirit (as I told you) being first a Spirit of burning, before it is a Spirit of consolation. God by the Spirit first wounds the soul, and then heals it : and though it is true, the law may convince of sin, yet those legal convictions only torment, and can give no sight of the only cure and remedy which a poor sinner needeth ; but the Spirit of God doth not only convince of sin, but of righteousness also ; doth not only show the soul its disease, but the only cure and remedy also which is by Christ alone, and his perfect righteousness, John xvi. 8, 9.

11. Salt was made use of under the law (as I told you before in the explication) in sacrifices. " Every oblation of thy meat-offering shalt thou season with salt." Again, " In all thy offerings thou shalt use salt," Lev. ii. 13. Which no doubt signified or typified, that we in all God's service must act from a principle of grace, or must be salted with this spiritual salt. " Let us have grace, whereby we may serve God acceptably with reverence and godly fear," Heb. xii. 28. The Hebrew doctors held, that that which was not salted was abominable ; so those duties which are not performed from a principle of grace, i,e., from a principle of faith and love to God, are abominable in God's sight. Hence the scripture saith, that " the sacrifice of the wicked are an abomination to the Lord," Prov. xv. 8, xxi. 27.

So much for the first thing.

Secondly, why should every professor be salted with grace, or have much grace in themselves ?

1. Because there is much corruption, and inward filth in the hearts of the best of saints, which grace, and nothing else, can purge out: possibly some filth may be hid, there may be some sin that a believer hath not yet discovered ; but if he obtain a little more of this salt, it will search it out, and purge it forth also. Alas, a little salt will not search and season much flesh, no, but much must be applied to it : so a little grace (as you have heard) is not enough, it is not sufficient to mortify and overcome all those corruptions that are in some men's hearts ;

Why every believer should be salted with grace.

many Christians are naturally of such a perverse and crooked disposition, so passionate, so peevish, so subject to malice, envy, pride, and covetousness, that they may need, perhaps, ten times more grace than another godly person, who is naturally of a mild and sweet disposition or temper.

2. Every professor hath need to be well salted, or to have much knowledge and grace, because they lie open to so many temptations in these evil and dangerous times, where sin, and all manner of abominations do so abound ; we live in a bad air, a bad climate : so that if men and women be not well salted, they will soon be corrupted; and defiled with the sins of these evil days. How was blessed Joseph corrupted by dwelling in Pharaoh's court, he had learned to swear the court oath, by the life of Pharaoh. " Ye shall not go forth hence, except your younger brother come hither," Gen. xlii. 15. A godly man may abhor one sin, and not be overcome thereby ; but for want of a greater measure of grace, and by dwelling in a wicked place or family, he may be overtaken with another ; like as the children of Isral, when they came into the land of Canaan, and many of the Amorites, &c., dwelling amongst them, they soon learned their evil ways, and served their gods.

3. Because of the great danger all professors are in, to be tainted or corrupted with false and poisonous errors, and pernicious heresies : and now much of this salt of saving grace and knowledge will be a most sovereign preservative against all the danger they are in upon this account. Hence it is the apostle saith, " It is good to have the heart established with grace, and not with meats," Heb. xiii. 9. As they were in danger of being corrupted or tainted with Judaism and Gentilism, &c., so are the saints now with Socinianism, Quakerism, Baxterianism, &c. Alas, how many are sadly corrupted and tainted by some of these errors already, for want of the salt of saving grace and knowledge.

Professors of the gospel lie open to many temptations that are very subject to corrupt them in doctrine, as well as in immoralities ; and it is grace only, like unto salt, which must preserve them from evil principles, as well as from evil practices. " Who can touch pitch, and not be defiled ? with the froward we soon learn frowardness," Psal. cxix. 11. Sin is of an infectious nature ; therefore holy David hid God's word in his heart, lest he should sin against him.

3. All Christians should have much salt in themselves, because they are too subject to decay in holiness and true piety. It is grace only that preserves them in a lively and spiritual frame. " I will put my fear into their hearts, and they shall not depart from me," Jer. xxxii. 40. Grace is put here for fear ; whosoever decays in grace, decays in godly fear, and declines in his faith, love, patience, temperance, humility, brotherly-kindness, and charity (I mean in the exercise of all these particular graces,) if there be but a little sap in the branches, there will be but little fruit.

4. Because according to that degree of grace a person hath, will his peace and comfort be. What is the reason some Christians are so full of doubts and fears, and discomforted, going drooping all the day long ? Alas, it is for the want of faith. Grace, much grace, fortifies the soul against fear, and despairing thoughts. Job having a strong faith could say, though God slay him, yet he would trust in him. What was the cause that the disciples were afraid ? Why, our blessed Lord told them, it was because they had no more faith. " O ye of little faith, wherefore do you doubt ?" Mat. xiv. 31. Their fears and doubts arose from the want of faith. Therefore we should have much grace in ourselves.

5. Because it is by the power and virtue of grace in ourselves that we must perform all our duties. O how heavily do we discharge religious duties ! And how cold, and flat are we, if we are not influenced, quickened, and stirred up by the grace of God in our hearts ! no service indeed is accepted which we perform, unless it be done by the power and assistance of grace. " Let us have grace whereby we may serve God acceptably, with reverence, and godly fear," Heb. xii. 28. How did David cry, that God would quicken him in his ways, which he knew must be done by the Spirit and grace of God in his soul.

6. Because it is by having much grace in ourselves, that we are enabled to bear afflictions, reproaches, and manifold trials which we daily do, or may expect to meet withal. Abraham having much grace, much faith, was enabled to bear up under the greatest trial, even that of sacrificing of his only son Isaac whom he loved. " He staggered not through unbelief, but being strong in faith, he gave glory unto God," Rom. iv. 20. Certainly another child of God, who had not so great a degree of faith, would have fainted at such a

trial, or not have been able to have acted as Abraham did. We know not what trials we may meet with, and therefore we are directed, to "come boldly to the throne of grace, that we may obtain mercy, and find grace to help in time of need," Heb. iv. 16. A weak person is hard put to it, to get up a very high hill, when a man that is strong goes up with much ease.

7. Because grace sweetens the soul, and that not only unto the person himself, but also it renders a man savoury to God, and to all good men. Such who are well salted are a savoury sacrifice unto God ; and the more grace we have, the more sweet and savoury are we in all respects. Indeed it is this that commends religion to the unsavoury world, it makes their hearts, their lips, and their life to be savoury, as you have heard, and therefore we should have much of this spiritual salt in ourselves.

8. Because it is grace that purgeth out that inward filth and corruption that is in the souls of believers, out of which the worm of conscience breeds. My brethren, the soul needs a purge, nay to be purged often, as well the body. We are subject to many diseases, especially to the worm of conscience; if sin be not purged out, conscience will pinch and gripe the soul most bitterly, like as it did Joseph's brethren. "We are verily guilty concerning our brother." Conscience may lie asleep for a while, but a time will come when it will awake and terrify the soul most sorely. But by having much grace, this may be prevented, it will both preserve from, and purge out filth and corruption, by which means a man need not fear he ever shall be afflicted with the worm of conscience.

9. Because the saints are to season others. "Ye are the salt of the earth," Matt. v. 13. Now how should they do this, if they are not well salted themselves? unsavoury professors make an unsavoury world. It is no marvel if the world stink, and is corrupted, if those that should salt it lose their saltness. Therefore should all that profess the gospel have much salt in themselves.

Thirdly, who are they that are savoury Christians, or that have much salt in themselves ? Who they are that are well salted.

I answer, such that are well cleansed and purged from all the inward filth and corruptions of their hearts, or cleansed from their secret faults, and not only from fleshly, but also from spiritual filthiness, 2 Cor. vii. 1. The Pharisees strove to make clean the outside of the cup and platter ; they laboured after external holiness, or to appear to men to be righteous, but inwardly they were as a filthy sepulchre, full of pride, uncleanness, and hypocrisy. But a Christian that is well salted with grace, is cleansed from inward uncleanness. Hence they are said to be pure in heart. "The pure in heart shall see God," Matt. v. 8. They are the sincere ones. "Blessed are the undefiled in the way, who walk in the law of the Lord," Ps. cxix. 1. All that they do is done in uprightness, they allow of no sin, they have no Delilah, no beloved lusts, sin doth not reign nor predominate in them ; grace hath so fully sanctified their souls, there is nothing that they love, and long after, more than heart purity.

2ndly. Such who have a savoury tongue, that watch their words, and keep the door of their lips. Brethren, an unsavoury tongue discovers an unsavoury heart.

1. As a prating tongue, whose tongue runs at random, hardly ever lies still. "In the multitude of words, there wants not sin," Prov. x. 19. This tongue is not salted, it is not seasoned with grace. "The heart of the wise teacheth his mouth, and addeth learning to his lips," Prov. xvi. 23. A fool is known by his much speaking.

Now this salt prevents this evil, he knows when to speak, and when to keep silence; he keeps his tongue as with a bridle.

2. He hath no jesting tongue ; idle talking and jesting is loathed by him ; whosoever are given to vain jesting, and idle talking, have an unsavoury tonge. But grace heals this evil also.

3. They have no bragging and proud boasting tongue. His own lips do not praise himself. How will some glory, and boast of their knowledge, of their parts, of their learning ! "The tongue is a little member, and boasteth great things," James iii. v. The apostle speaks of an unsavoury tongue, a tongue that is not tamed, or not salted with grace. But he that is well seasoned, speaks soberly of himself, he is little in his own eyes, and so speaketh, "To me, who am less than the least saint, is this grace given, that I should preach among the Gentiles the unsearchable riches of Christ," Eph. ii. 8. This shows he was well seasoned with grace.

4. He hath not a lying tongue; no, he abhors lying, and speaks the truth to his neighbour in his heart, he dares not equivocate, as many do.

5. He hath not a back-biting tongue, a detracting tongue. Be sure a backbiter is not

salted, he wants grace, for this is one of the greatest evils a man can be guilty of. Such shall not ascend God's holy hill ; for this is the character of such, " He that backbiteth not with his tongue, nor taketh up a reproach against his neighbour," Psal. xv. 3. An unsalted backbiting tongue God abhorreth. " An ungodly man diggeth up evil, and in his lips there is a burning fire," Prov. xvi. 27. How will he search and dig to find out the faults of his brother out of malice and envy, to reproach him ! This was one of those evils the Gentiles were given up unto.

6. Not a flattering tongue, a dissembling tongue, a fawning tongue. Some will speak smoothly to their neighbour, when deceit is in their hearts ; but a gracious tongue, a tongue seasoned with this salt will flatter no man, but deal faithfully with all.

7. A seasoned and well salted Christian, hath no railing nor scolding tongue. He that 1 Cor. v. 5. is guilty of railing, ought to be cast out of the church.

3rdly. You may know savoury Christians by their savoury discourse, and savoury behaviour. With what modesty, sobriety, and gravity do they behave themselves !

4thly. They are such that are preserved from those vile and abominable evils, and corruptions of the world, in the days in which they live, both in point of doctrine and practice.

5thly. They have a savoury and gracious spirit. " But my servant Caleb had another spirit with him," Numb. xiv. 24. These persons have a heavenly, a serious, an humble, an established, a generous, a patient, and a sincere spirit; and all this is through the nature of this spiritual salt, with which they are seasoned.

6thly. Such perform all their duties acceptably to God, in faith, love, and humility, and with much zeal and fervency of spirit. Grace makes them hot and lively. They do all they do, in God's holy worship with much affection unto God. " The zeal of thine house hath eaten me up."

7thly. They can bear the great heat of persecution and temptation, when others are flyblown, like fresh meat in the heat of summer, they in such a time decay and corrupt, and quickly stink in the nostrils of God, and all good men; when a well salted Christian endures and corrupts not, because he is well salted.

APPLICATION

1. We may infer from hence, that saving grace is the principal thing, as all know salt is. What can we do if we have no salt ? It is so excellent and so needful a thing; and O what can a poor creature do, that has no saving grace in his heart ? O what will become of him in the end ? He will certainly, like stinking flesh, be cast into the kennel of God's wrath.

2. We may also infer from what has been said, that the cause of all those abominable evils which abound in the world, is, because men are not salted, they have not the grace of God in them.

3. Moreover it informs us, wherefore it is that some professors are more savoury than others, they are better salted, they have more salt or grace in themselves. O what a multitude of proud, carnal, earthly, and envious professors are there in these evil days; but the cause is, they are not salted. And hence it is they are so ready to corrupt others, as tainted flesh is subject to taint that which may be sweet that lies by it.

4. Sinners be exhorted to get salt, provide yourselves salt before it be too late, you may in a short time be past all recovery. Salt will not renew you when God hath left you to your own hearts' lusts.

You must know whither you must go for this salt, it is laid up in Christ, he is "full of grace and truth ;" John. i. 14. You must go to him for it, buy it of him, you may have it on easy terms, even " without money, and without price." Isa. lv. 1. Yet know, the market-day may be soon over.

MOTIVES

1. There is no corruption, no sin, or abominable filth, but this salt will purge it out.

2. Being once well salted, you need never fear a total defection, such shall not ever perish. Not that the grace a person hath received will preserve him ; no, but God will continually add more salt, give more grace to such,

3. This salt will preserve you in all times, in all company, in all temptations.

4. It hath one or two properties that commmon salt hath not, viz.,

(1.) It will recover such persons that stink, and are abominable in God's sight.

(2.) Such is the nature of this spiritual salt, that it will never loose its saltness.

(3) You cannot be over salted, no man can have too much grace.

Lastly, It will render you and all your duties most acceptable unto God, even as a sweet smelling savour.

3rdly. Examine yourselves, you that are professors, have you salt in yourselves? are you of a sweet, peaceable, and loving temper, ready to forgive, being meek and lowly in heart, being holy and heavenly, both in heart and life? if so, what comfort may this doctrine administer to you; it is a sign you are those God loved from everlasting, and shall be saved, for grace is the seed of glory.

III

And have peace one with another.—Mark ix. 50.

DOCT. That it is the indispensible duty of the saints, disciples, and members of the church of Christ, to have peace one with another, or to maintain love, union, and sweet concord among themselves.

There are two parts in our text.

1st. A duty enjoined.

2ndly. An excellent virtue commanded, " peace one with another."

1. The person exhorting to this duty, is Jesus Christ.

2. The persons exhorted are his diciples.

In speaking to this great proposition,

First, I shall prove it is the indispensible duty of the saints and members of Christ, to have peace one with another.

Secondly, Give you the reasons of it, or show you wherefore.

Thirdly, Give some directions how to attain, and maintain peace one with another.

Fourthly, Apply it.

First, I shall prove that it is the indispensible duty of the saints and people of God, to live in peace one with another. See what the holy apostle saith, " Endeavouring to keep the unity of the Spirit in the bond of peace," Eph. iv. 3. Endeavouring, this word denotes not only the duty, but the difficulty *It is the duty of saints to have peace among themselves.* in reaching or attaining unto it, and also in maintaining of peace and union. Beloved, Satan and the flesh are great enemies to peace. " The spirit that dwelleth in us, lusteth to envy," James iv. 5. Again, saith Paul, " Fulfil ye my joy, that ye be likeminded, having the same love, being of one accord, and of one mind." To which I might add what he says in another place, " Be at peace among yourselves," 1 Thess. v. 13.

Thus having proved, that this is the indispensible duty of believers, I shall,

Secondly, Give you the reasons why they should be at peace one with another.

1. Because it is a holy precept of our blessed Lord, therefore a great sin not to endeavour after it, or not to live in love and peace. You dread lying, swearing, stealing, drunkenness, &c., because these are abominable sins, hateful to God, and breaches of his holy law. Why, brethren, so it is not to have peace, or not to live in love and peace one with another. " A new commandment I give unto you, that you love one another." It is the will of God, as the apostle speaks in another case, " This is the will of God, even your sanctification;" so I may say, this is the will of God, even that you have peace one with another.

2. Because peace, love, and union, God exceedingly delights in, and also commends in his word, as good and pleasant in his sight; " Behold how good and pleasant a thing it is, for brethren to dwell together in unity," Psa. cxxxiii. 1. Shall we not do that which God thus commends and takes delight in. As he saith, " O do not this abominable thing that I hate;" so let me say, O do this thing that he loves, and delighteth in.

3. This is agreeable to the principles of religion, and true piety, and design of the gospel, and it is also the effect of true grace.

When our blessed Lord was born, the angel proclaimed, " glory to God on high, and on earth peace." Not only peace with God, but also peace one with another. Brethren, hath Christ made our peace with God by his own blood, and shall we not be at peace one with another? God forbid.

This was one design and end of Christ's coming, viz., " He shall turn the hearts of the fathers to the children, and the hearts of the children to the fathers," Mal. iv. 6.

that is, to make all the saints to live in love and peace, and not in strife, contention, and divisions.

4. Moreover, this will be one of the principal blessings of the reign of Jesus Christ in his visible kingdom, there shall be sweet peace and concord among all the saints: " The wolf also shall dwell with the lamb, and the leopard shall lie down with the kid ; and the calf, and the young lion, and the fatling together, and a little child shall lead them. And the cow and the bear shall feed, their young ones shall lie down together ; and the lion shall eat straw like the ox, &c. They shall not hurt nor destroy in all my holy moun- tain," &c., Isa. xi. 6—9. There shall be then no lion-like nor wolfish nature among men any more.

But the saints shall all serve the Lord with oneness of heart, or with one consent. God is now about " gathering the nations, and assembling the kingdoms, to pour upon them his indignation, even all his fierce anger ; for all the earth shall be devoured with the fire of his jealousy," Zeph. iii. 8. Well, but what will be the effect of all this, what will immediately follow ? even the peaceable kingdom of Jesus Christ: observe the very next words, " For then will I turn to the people a pure language, that they may all call upon the name of the Lord, to serve him with one consent," verse 9. Certainly the kingdom of Christ is not yet begun, for our days do not look like to such a time which the prophet speaks of, but it shews what our duty is ; and if the kingdom of Christ be come with power on our souls, this will be one effect thereof, namely power on our sweet, loving, and peaceable spirit, and temper of heart.

5. My brethren, God is the God of peace, and Jesus Christ is the Prince of peace, and the Holy Spirit is the bond of peace, and the Gospel is called the Gospel of peace, there- fore the saints and children of God should labour to have peace one with another ; how else will it appear they are related to such a Father, and are the subjects of such a Prince, and are led and guided by such a Spirit, and feel the divine power of such a Gospel on their own souls? It is said, " The multitude of them that believed were of one heart, and one soul," Acts. iv. 32. Moreover, is said of the saints in the succeeding age after the apostles, that the unity and peace of Christians was so famous, that they had this name or character, viz., " A people that agreed amongst themselves." I am sure this cannot be said to be the character of God's people in this present age, the more to be lamented.   O how are we divided ! what animosities, envyings, and confusions are among us ?

6. Love, peace, and concord, is the property of the new heart; " And I will give them one heart, and I will put a new spirit within you," Ezek. xi. 19. &c. A faithful heart, an honest and sincere heart, a heart not divided between God and idols, not a heart drawing back or revolting from God, yea and a heart united to each other, a loving and peaceable heart ; as they have all one God, one Saviour, one faith, so they shall have sweet communion together ; they shall be united, or have much love, and mutual agreement between themselves, they shall have one heart.

Unum est ens indivisum in se ; unius quidditus, est essendi indivisibilitas.
Others say, that is one which is *indivisum a se, & divisum ab omni alio.*   Such a heart they shall have, a heart undivided in itself, and divided from all things heterogeneal, and of a dividing nature. This oneness of heart may be considered,

Greenhill.

Scaliger's Exercit. 65. Num 2. Suarez in Metaph.

(1.) Respecting themselves, and so first, as it includes the judgment and affections, they shall not dissent and cross one another ; but when truth is in their understanding, the affections shall close with it.

(2.) It denotes also that the will and conscience shall not be divided, or oppose one and the other, as it doth in hypocrites,

(3.) In respect of God ; they shall all look at God as the only and adequate object of their hearts, they shall be content with him alone.

(4.) Moreover, in respect to God's worship, they shall not be for human mixtures in divine worship ; " In that day shall there be one Lord, and his name one," Zech. xiv. 9, Jer. xxxii. 39. By name expositors understand worship, and that shall be one.

(5.) In respect of the saints.

(1.) Their judgment shall be one, *i. e.*, they shall agree in all fundamental, and sub- stantial points of faith.

(2.) One in love and affections : though in some circumstantial things or matters of less moment they may differ, yet they shall all own one another as brethren, and love each other. Now if this be the property of the new heart, how doth it behove us to labour for love, peace, and oneness of heart, and spirit ?

7. Because believers are brethren, this is a great argument why we should live in love and peace together: we may say with Abraham to his kinsman Lot, " Let there be no strife, I pray thee, betwixt thee and me, for we are brethren," Gen. xiii. 8. Discord among brethren is abominable, not only to God, but it is hateful in the sight of all men : we have all one Father, one Lord Jesus Christ, one faith, one baptism ;" Eph. iv. 3 ; and are all of us members of one and the same body : the relation we stand one to another, should stir up to strive after love and peace. Dear children will not quarrel with one another, because it would grieve the heart (should they so do) of their tender, gracious Father, and expose him and his family to reproach.

8. Because hereby we shall answer the blessed purport of the Lord's supper : " For we being many, are one bread, and one body ; for we all partake of that one bread," 1 Cor. x. 17. One loaf is made up of many corns of wheat : so we who are but one body, or members of the same church, should demonstrate this sacred union, by living in love and peace. What, shall we eat of one and the same bread, and not be of one heart, or not be united together in love ? this is to contradict the purport of this holy ordinance.

9. Because this peace and union tends to make our communion most sweet and comfortable to each other. " How can two walk together, except they are agreed ? " Amos iii. 3. Can we have communion with God, unless we are in a state of mystical union with him ? And as this cannot be, so here also, *i. e.*, we cannot have fellowship and communion one with another, unless our hearts are united to each other. Or can our seeming communion be acceptable to God, if our hearts are not united in sincere love and affections ? Moreover, where this is wanting, how are the ways of God, and people of God, exposed to the reproach, and to the contempt of an ungodly world ? But, on the contrary, what saith our blessed Lord, " By this shall all men know that ye are my disciples, if ye love one another."

10. Because this will prevent all those grievous evils, which commonly attend the want of love, viz., strife, contention, and divisions, &c.

(1.) Peace among ourselves prevents Satan in his design, whose work it is to sow discord, and to alienate the hearts of Christians from one another. My brethren, this is the way to counterwork the devil, and to hinder him in one grand design of his.

(2. It will also prevent the loss of much precious time in making up breaches, or to unite such who were at discord one with another.

(3.) It will also prevent the troubles which arise in the church, through that discord, strife, and contention which may be between one member and another ; for, were care taken to maintain love and peace, and things that tend to peace and holiness, we should have but little to do in days of discipline, which often grieve and stumble the weak, and tends to hinder the increase of the churches.

(4.) Moreover, it would prevent those obstructions, of doing much good ; for experience shows, that when the bond of love and peace is broken between one member and another, such things that tend to public good are greatly obstructed ; because all do not draw together, like the horses in Pharaoh's chariot, but heavy burdens are laid upon some whilst others, through offences given, withdraw their hands, and will do but little or nothing.

(5.) It would prevent also the public reproach and scandal, which divisions, and want of love and peace cast upon the ways and people of God ; for thus they without are ready to say, viz., they are full of envy and hatred to each other, or they do not love one another ; can these be the people of God ? " Woe to the world because of offences."

11. It is the indispensible duty of believers, to have love and peace among themselves, because this is that which makes, or tends to make the church formidable, and " terrible as an army with banners," Cant. vi. 10, or like a sheaf of arrows bound up together, which cannot be broken. It was an old proverb, Divide them, and destroy them. " A city divided (saith our Saviour) against itself cannot stand." You have perhaps heard of that aged man, who having many sons whom he called to him on his death-bed, he bid them bring a sheaf of arrows to him, which was done ; and he gave it to his eldest son, and bid him break that sheaf of arrows, which he strove to do, but could not ; then he gave it to his next son to break, but he could not ; then he bid his eldest son take out one single arrow, which he did : said the father to him, break it, and so he presently, and with much ease did : upon which thus spoke the old man, Children, while you abide together in love as one man, you will be like a sheaf of arrows, that cannot, by your enemies be broken ; but if you are divided and alienated from each other, you will be easily broken into pieces.

12. This farther appears, because by this means mutual prayer will not be hindered. Evident it is, that if discord be between a man and his wife, their prayers are thereby

hindered: hence the apostle advises such that are married not to defraud one another, that their prayers be not obstructed: it is said, Acts iv. 24, "That they lifted up their voice with one accord."

Divisions in a family hinder mutual prayer in that family: can we join in our hearts together, if we are not at peace one with another?

13. Because this provokes to sympathy: what then is the joy of one, will be the joy of all; and what is the grief and sorrow of one, will be the grief and sorrow of all; and so hereby we shall be capable to answer that holy precept, "Rejoice with them that rejoice, and mourn with them that mourn." How doth the tender husband sympathize with his dear wife, and the tender wife sympathize with the dear husband in his troubles and afflictions, or the tender parents symyathize with their distressed and afflicted children?

Did believers look upon each other, as being bone of the same bone, and flesh of the same flesh; how would they love and sympathize with one another, and help and relieve each other in all their wants and necessities?

Thirdly, I shall give you some directions, in order to attain and maintain peace, love, and concord with one another.

Directions to peace one with another. 1. Labour after meekness and humbleness of mind; this is a great advancement of peace. "Only of pride cometh contention," Prov. xiii. 10. Were men of an humble, meek, and quiet spirit, and not proud and conceited, they would not make such trouble, or cause and stir up strife and contention, as many times they do. "Let nothing be done through strife and vain-glory, but in lowliness of mind let each esteem others better than themselves," Phil. ii. 3. An humble person will be a peaceable person.

2. Speak well of all your brethren who hold the head, or are sound in the faith, in respect of all fundamental principles, though not in every thing of your opinion in some points of religion: for peace among ourselves ought not to be restrained only to the members of that church we belong unto, but to all the saints, let them be Presbyterians, Independents, or Baptists. I do not mean that it is your duty to hold church-communion with all; no, that cannot be, unless all were of one judgment in all the essentials of church-constitution: for mutual love is not to be the rule of our church-communion and fellowship, but the word of Christ. But though we cannot as yet be all of one judgment in this case, yet we ought not to censure one another but own each other for brethren, and be all united in love and affections. How unchristian-like is it to render them that differ from us odious, as if they were not members of the mystical body of Christ, or belonged not to the universal church? "Speak evil of no man," no, nor speak of the evils of any, except the evil or sin they are guilty of be public, and notorious; and that not then out of an ill purpose, to expose the person out of spite and revenge; for that is most hateful and abominable in the sight of God, and tends to strife and discord. "As much as lieth in you, live peaceably with all men," but much more with all the saints and people of God.

3. If you would have peace one with another, avoid all secret whisperings and backbitings; for indeed nothing more tends to break the bonds of peace, than such unlawful and sinful practice. "A wrathful man stirreth up strife, but he that is slow to anger appeaseth strife," Prov. xv. 18. "A froward man soweth strife, and a whisperer separateth chief friends," Prov. xvi. 28. Now to avoid this evil, be sure you discountenance, nay, sharply rebuke the backbiter; for such who do it not are really guilty, as the proverb is, "The receiver is as bad as the thief."

4. Seek the temporal as well as the spiritual good of all your brethren, especially they that are of the same church or community with you. "Let no man seek his own, but every one his brother's wealth," 1 Cor. x. 24. Do they do so that will not trade with their brother, nor help him in his necessity, when it is in the power of his hands? what, not lend five pounds to thy poor brother, or more or less, which might be of great advantage to him, though thou hast perhaps hundreds lying by thee.

I cannot see how love and peace can be maintained, where those duties of charity, sympathy, and brotherly-kindness are neglected: thou wilt not buy what thou needest of thy brother, but rather of strangers; though by this neglect of thine, and others, it tends to his undoing; and if thou and other friends did trade with him, he might live comfortably. How doth this evil create hard thoughts in one brother against another, and break the bonds of love and peace? They call me a brother, saith the poor man, but I see no brotherly love to be in them. "I seek not mine own profit (saith Paul) but the profit of many," 1 Cor. x. 33. But it will be hard for a man to believe you seek the good and profit of his soul when you do not seek the profit of his body, or external good of his family.

5. If you would have peace one with another, see that you deal with your offending brother according to that rule our blessed Lord hath laid down, Matt. 18.

(1.) Tell him his fault between thee and him alone, but do it gently, sweetly, and not in a rough and angry manner, and labour again and again to convince him of evil ; but if thou canst not prevail,

(2.) Then take one or two more with thee, and see what you and they can do, but with all mildness ; but do not think that their speaking to him is enough, or doth answer the rule : no, no, but you and they must labour to bring him to a sight and sense of his sin ; and be sure all this while discover his fault to no other : at first you should take heed that you conceal his evil, and divulge it to none till you have privately done your duty. But if you alone, nor one, or two more cannot win him, then bring it to the church. Now this rule carefully observed, will greatly tend to peace, order, and concord.

6. If you would have peace among yourselves, make it matter of conscience always to attend the public worship of God in the church to which you belong, and do not hear at such times anywhere else. What though your neighbours feed in a richer pasture than yours is ? will you break the hedge to feed in that pasture which is none of your own ? I must tell you, it is but stolen bread, and it tends to disorder and confusion ; for by the same reason that you go and hear where you please, every member may, and what then will become of that particular church to which you belong ? O what grief and offence is this to your pastor and fellow-brethren ! If this be not prevented, you cannot expect peace one with another. " They went to their own company," Acts iv. 23. I tell you that such actions are a breach of that precept ; " Forsake not the assembling yourselves together, as the manner of some is," Heb. x. 23 ; you must assemble together, not with others that are not of your community.

7. Be sure be impartial in judgment in the discipline of the church ; let none be connived at out of favour, nor others dealt severely with, out of prejudice. Levi was not to know his father nor his mother in judgment.

8. Let no one part of the church meet together as dissatisfied persons, to consult church matters, without the knowledge of the pastor, or consent and appointment of the church : for where this is done, the bond of love and peace is broken.

9. Let no members be received into the church, without general satisfaction taken of their faith and godly conversation ; neither be careless or remiss in receiving of persons, lest such get in among you, who by their turbulent spirits, or ill lives, disturb or disquiet the peace of the church. What sad examples are there in some churches arising from hence, viz., by loose persons getting in among them !

10. Avoid the reception of any persons from other orderly churches sound in the faith, without the consent of that church to whom they belong ; for that is to destroy the just authority and power of Christ in each particular congregation ; nor is it to do as you would be done unto : therefore that church and pastor that is guilty of this evil ought to be discountenanced as violaters of the rules of order and peace amongst the churches of the saints.

11. Let no feuds arise, no strife not dissension upon differing sentiments that may be in some members minds from others about circumstantial matters, either in respect of faith, practice, or discipline ; because all have not attained to the same degree of light and knowledge, in all such cases one member must bear with another, Jude 10. Jam. iii. 14, 16.

12. Let every member avoid the believing a report or charge against any brother or sister, before they know the truth of the matter ; for perhaps such reports may be spread abroad of one member or another, through the envy or malice of some or another that givs way to the devil, and so become like him, viz., false accusers of the brethren ; how was Paul reproached by false brethren, and false apostles ; and also holy Jeremiah, " report, say they, and we will report," Jer. xx. 10.

13. Labour after patience and mutual forbearance one of another, forgiving one another ; if you would have peace among yourselves, see the advice of the apostle, " Let all bitterness, and wrath, and anger, and evil speaking, be put away from you, with all malice. And be kind one to another, tender-hearted, forgiving one another, even as God for Christ's sake hath forgiven you," Eph. iv. 31, 32. O what patience and forbearance doth God exercise towards us, and what a multitude of faults does he pass by and forgive us ! Brethren, we should be like unto him ; " Be ye merciful as your Father in heaven is merciful." Can you expect peace one with another if this be wanting ? and if we do not forgive our brother, neither will God forgive us.

14. If you would maintain peace one with another, take care constantly to visit each other ; the neglect of this tends to break the bonds of love, and alienate one member from

another: what, wilt thou not visit thy brother and sister, that lives near thee, to know how he and she doth? this I must tell thee argues but little love in thy heart to them; such that we dearly love we will see often.

15. Report nothing of the private concerns or matters of the church to strangers, or to carnal persons, especially any thing that is done on days of discipline; the church in this case (as well as in others) is " as a garden inclosed, a spring shut up, a fountain sealed." Cant. iv. 12. This too often disturbs the peace of the church, and breaks the bonds of love. Is it not a shame to any, to divulge the secrets of the family where he dwells? but far greater shame and reproach do these persons expose themselves unto.

16. Do not withdraw thy communion from the church upon private offences, or upon small trifling cases, lest you are found such that slight communion with Christ, as well as grieve thy brethren, and spoil their peace. Is thy meeting with Christ at his table no more valued by thee? therefore until thou hast done thy duty to thy brother, and the church hath dealt with him and excluded him, thou canst not, must not presume to do it. Wilt thou assume the power of the keys, or church authority? beware of this pernicious evil, if you would have peace one with another.

17. Give due encouragement to the exercise of such gifts that are amongst you: first, if you apprehend any brother hath received some competent ministerial gifts; let him freely exercise those gifts privately, and being in time approved, let the church call him forth to preach more publicly; else how shall the church be provided with ministers in future times? or how shall an approved ministry be continued in the church? "As every man hath received the gift, even so let him administer the same, one to another, as good stewards of the manifold grace of God," 1 Pet. iv. 10.

18. Labour to keep up the reputation and honour of your pastor, and do not "receive an accusation against him, under two or three witnesses," 1 Tim. v. 19. Also observe such, who out of prejudice may suggest or insinuate into the minds of unwary members, evil against your minister; for Satan hates no men more, than such who preach the gospel, and have the charge of souls, and of the churches of Jesus Christ; therefore he will not be wanting to render them useless, or to obstruct them in their work; and thereby also disquiet the whole congregation, and put them into confusion. "Smite the shepherd, and the sheep will be scattered." Yet do not wink or connive at any gross enormity in him, for that may soon tear you to pieces. Pious persons be sure will not endure it; for no men more expose the name of God to reproach, and hinder the peace and increase of the church, than scandalous ministers; yet let the rule of the gospel be carefully observed in your dealing with him.

19. Look more at that good that is in thy brother, and speak more of that behind his back, than of those infirmities thou mayest espy in him; let the bright side of the cloud be in your sight, and not the dark. The apostle John commends those virtues that were in the fathers, young men, and children, but not a word of their faults and infirmities; no doubt they had their buts and imperfections, as well as excellent graces. Nay, God himself commends David as a man after his own heart; though he had many weaknesses and infirmities, yet the Lord overlooked all them, and passed them all by; nothing is mentioned save his great wickedness in the case of Bathsheba and Uriah.

20. Get much love one to another; this is Paul's counsel. "Let brotherly love continue," Heb. xiii. 1. This is a blessed way to preserve peace one with another. "Love beareth all things, it endureth all things, it will think no evil:"

"Charity suffereth long, is kind; charity envieth not; love vaunteth not itself, is not puffed up," &c., 1 Cor. xiii. 4.

O what an excellent grace is the grace of love and charity! "Above all things put on charity, which is the bond of perfectness," Col. iii. 14. No Christian is so complete, as he that is full of love and charity; nor can anything tend more to peace and union among brethren. Therefore "above all things, have fervent charity among yourselves; for charity shall cover a multitude of sins," 1 Pet. iv. 8. God out of love, covers a multitude of sin and faults in us; and had we much love and charity towards one another, we should cover all the common weakness and infirmities also, which we see in each other.

Lastly, eye the glory of God, and credit of religion in all things you do, and strive to set God always before your eyes; he takes notice of our carriages and behaviour one to another. O labour to see thy own fault, thine own infirmities, be much at home, and see the beam that is in thine own eye: so wilt thou not be ready to spy the mote that is in thy brother's eye. Grudge not at one another, brethren, lest ye be condemned: behold, the judge standeth before the door," Jam. v. 9. As he always beholds us all, so he will soon come to judge us all. So much as to the doctrinal part.

APPLICATION

1.   From hence we may infer, that the want of peace one with another, may arise from want of grace in our own hearts : " have salt in yourselves, and have peace one with another." No man can have peace with God, peace in his own conscience, that hath not saving grace in his heart ; nor will such who want it be long in peace with their brethren : however the way to have peace with one another, is to get grace or salt in ourselves. Pray remember, that no peace is like that which flows from, or is the product of grace.

2.   Be exhorted to labour after peace, love, and union, among yourselves. " Pursue after it : follow after peace with all men, and holiness without which no man shall see the Lord," Heb. xii. 14.

For motives to this.

1.   Consider the devils can agree to dwell together, even whole legions of them in one man ; and shall not the saints of God agree to dwell together in unity ? Luke viii. 30.

2.   Wicked men also can agree together in wickedness, and to uphold the devil's kingdom : the papists glory in the unity of their church, and the Mahometans agree in their idolatry : and shall not Christians, true believers, and faithful disciples of Christ, agree together in love and peace ?

3.   Consider that Jesus Christ hath taken our nature upon him, and as it was to unite God and man together, so also to unite man and man together in himself, " Ye are all one in Christ Jesus," Gal. iii. 28. " He hath made us to sit together in heavenly places in Christ Jesus," Eph. ii. 6. This should move us to live in love, and to be at peace one with another.

4.   Where there is not love and peace, it will not be long (it may be feared) before there are divisions.

5.   To preserve peace, is the way to disappoint Satan, who is the grand make-bate and disturber of the peace of the saints and churches of Christ.

6.   Consider how dangerous a thing it is to offend any of Christ's little ones, or to judge our brothers : professors may offend Christ's little ones, as well as the profane, " Whoso shall offend one of these little ones, which believe in me, it were better for him that a millstone were hanged about his neck, and he was cast into the sea," Matt. xviii. 6. O how heinous a sin is this !

7.   Love and peace renders the church militant like to the church triumphant ; O what sweet peace and concord is there in heaven !

8.   Consider what a multitude of enemies we have, that strive to divide us and ruin us all, this should caution us to take heed we do not seek to ruin and destroy one another.

Lastly, consider the motives that Paul uses to press this duty, with which, I shall conclude : " If therefore there be any consolation in Christ, if any comfort of love, if any fellowship of the Spirit, if any bowels of mercies ; fulfil ye my joy, that ye be like-minded, having the same love, being of one accord, of one mind," Phil. ii. 1, 2.

24. THE GOOD SAMARITAN

I

And Jesus answered and said, a certain man went down from Jerusalm to Jericho, and fell among thieves, &c.—Luke x. 30.

OUR late annotators upon the holy bible, take but little notice of this parable, more than to show the design of our Lord herein, which is to show who is our neighbour, viz., he that shows us the most favour, pity, and compassion ;   *The occasion and scope of the parable.*

and thereby he clearly shows, that he himself is the only neighbour and friend of our souls : for doubtless this must be comprehended here, as our Lord's grand design in bringing of it in. We have in ver. 25, a lawyer standing up, with great confidence, pleading his justification by the law, thinking himself a righteous person, that stood in need of nothing. This seems to be the occasion of this parable. Also hereby our Lord strives to convince us of the wretched state and condition of all men by nature, and of the evil of sin, which I conceive was one design of it also ; likewise to show, that neither the law, nor Levite priest, nor legal sacrifices, could relieve or help any one miserable and undone sinner.

2.   I shall endeavour (by God's assistance) to open all the parts and terms contained herein.

The parts opened.   First, by the man that went from Jerusalem to Jericho, I understand is meant fallen man, who originally in the first Adam went from God, viz., from a state of peace signified by Jerusalem, that blessed city of peace and safety, where God's habitation was : and not only originally did man go thus from God, but also actually by their abominable practices, and wicked deeds of darkness.

What is meant by thieves.   2.   By "falling among thieves," may be meant that mischief and misery which hath befallen man by sin, Satan, and others enemies of the soul.

What is meant by being stripped.   3.   By " stripping him of his raiment," may be meant all our first or original righteousness. Righteousness being often compared to raiment, or to a garment.

What by being wounded.   4.   By "wounding him," may be intended that sad and fearful privation of the soul in every faculty thereof by sin.

What by being half dead.   5.   By "leaving him half dead," may be meant the spiritual death of the soul, which is half, nay the better half of the man. Man consisteth of two parts, and though a poor sinner be alive in the body, yet he is dead spiritually in his soul, and therefore may be said to be half dead ; not but that the whole man is dead, or wounded unto death by original and actual sin. The sentence of death and condemnation is gone forth against all mankind in the first Adam, all are under the sentence of eternal death, and must perish eternally, unless the good Samaritan pours in his oil and wine. If this be not meant, then it shows that all men are only desperately wounded by sin naturally ; but God's word shows, man is not only wounded, but dead in sins and trespasses.

6.   By " the priest passing that way, and going on one side," may be meant, the law or priesthood of Aaron ; by the Levite may be meant legal sacrifices, and by their both passing by, and not pitying or helping this poor distressed man, may signify that there is no help, no cure, no salvation by the law, nor sacrifices of the law, for undone sinners.

The Samaritan is Jesus Christ.   7.   By " the Samaritan," I understand is meant our Lord Jesus Christ, who is said to pass by and see us in our blood, " Now as I passed by, I looked upon thee, and saw thee polluted in thy own blood," Ezek. xvi. 6, 8.   This was a blessed look indeed, a look of pity and compassion, "when he saw him, he had compassion on him," The Son of God saw us from eternity (he being God) fallen by these thieves, wounded, and in our blood.   " And he went to him,"

Which may refer to two things.

(1)   To Christ's coming into the world to assume our nature. And thus he came where the sinner was, and put himself in our law place.

(2.)   It may refer also to his gracious coming to a wounded sinner by his word and Spirit, in helping him to apply the virtue of his own precious blood to his wounded soul.

What is meant by binding up his wounds.   8.   Binding up his wounds, and pouring in oil and wine, may be meant, Christ infusing of his Spirit and precious grace into his soul; grace, as well as the Holy Spirit being compared to oil.   " The wise virgins took their lamps, and oil in their vessels," Matt. xxv. 4, that is, they had saving grace in their hearts. And that the Holy Spirit is compared to oil, is evident, our Lord is said " to be anointed with the oil of gladness above his fellows," Heb. i. 9.   And as the Spirit and grace is compared to wine, which is not only of a healing, but of a cheering, reviving, and strengthening nature also.

What is meant by setting him on his own beast.   9.   By "setting him upon his own beast," may be intended, or meant, Christ's own doctrine of free-grace.   " Be not carried about with divers and strange doctrines, for it is good that the heart be established with grace," &c. Heb. xiii. 9.   When a man has received the true grace of God, and is by Jesus Christ established in his holy faith and doctrine, that will carry him like a beast to the inn where he is to take up his abode; as a false doctrine carries a man from it. But more of this hereafter.

10. By bringing to an inn, I apprehend is meant a church of Christ, to which the doctrine of Christ carrieth such who subject or yield obedience thereunto, and that the church may be compared to an inn, I shall show you before I have done. *What is meant by the inn.*

11. By the host, that had the charge given to take care of this poor man, may be meant the minister or pastor of the church, to whom the care of all the members of the said church is committed. *What is meant by the host.*

12. By the two-pence given to the host may be meant, as I judge,

(1.) The gifts and graces of the Spirit, which the Lord Christ bestows upon all his ministers.

(2.) Or as some think, the Old and New Testament.

(3.) Others, spiritual and temporal supplies, which are given and allowed by the Lord Jesus to all his faithful ministers, who have the care of a spiritual inn, and of the souls of men and women committed to them.

13. "And when I come again I will repay thee." This no doubt refers to Christ's second coming at the last day; and by repaying the host at his return may signify that glorious reward all true ministers shall receive (when Christ appeareth) in the way of free-grace. *What is meant by his coming again.*

Thus I have briefly opened every part of this parable. Neither do I see any just cause any have to object against this exposition.

I shall in the next place take notice of several propositions or points of doctrine that arise, or may be deduced from the parts thereof, and so give a larger exposition of the whole parable.

Doct. 1. That mankind who are gone from God, are fallen among thieves, viz., Sin and Satan, who have wounded and robbed them, and left them in a sad and lamentable state and condition.

In the prosecution of this, I shall,

First, show you in what respects sin and Satan may be compared to thieves.

Secondly, show you that they are the worst of thieves.

Thirdly, apply it.

I. I shall show you in what respects sin and Satan may be compared to thieves. *Sin and Satan are thieves.*

1. Thieves are enemies to honest men, and of which they are in danger continually. So sin and the devil are enemies to all men, and such enemies that all good men fear, and continually know they are in great danger of being overcome by.

2. Thieves ofttimes in a secret and felonious manner, have taken away all that men had in their possession, leaving them in a very poor and distressed condition, who were very rich before.

So sin and Satan have robbed mankind of all they possessed in the first Adam, which were great riches. God at first invested man with a very great estate, he had abundance of all good things in his possession. He had God to be his God, he had union and communion with God, nay, and the holy image of God stamped upon his noble soul, and blessed peace; besides all the riches of the earthly paradise. But sin and Satan robbed him and all his posterity of all those riches which originally he possessed.

And though believers are restored and enriched by Jesus Christ, yet sin and the devil strive to rob them again, and would do it, was not their treasure put into the hands of a faithful trustee, who keeps a great stock to hand it out to them as their need requires.

3. Thieves many times lead poor travellers out of the king's high-way, into some blind or secret place, and there bind them hand and foot, as well as take away all they have. So sin and Satan have led man out of God's way, and have also bound him with cruel bonds. As, *Mankind led by sin and Satan out of the way, and bound in strong cords.*

(1.) With the bond of ignorance.

(2.) With the bond of of a hard heart. And,

(3.) With the bond of unbelief. "I perceive that thou art in the gall of bitterness, and in the bond of iniquity," Acts viii. 23. As well as robbed him of all that choice treasure which God was pleased to enrich him with in the first Adam.

4. Thieves are a great terror to honest men, and they strive to avoid them as much as they can, and also to defend themselves against them with their utmost power and skill. *Thieves a terror to honest men.*

So sin, the flesh, the world, and the devil, are a great terror to all God's people, who also endeavour to avoid the danger they are hereby in, and continually arm themselves, or rather are armed by the Lord Jesus with spiritual armour, wisdom, and courage, to resist them.

Thieves wait a fit opportunity.   5. Thieves wait a fit opportunity to come upon a person or family, even when they are most secure, or asleep in their beds.

So Satan and other spiritual enemies, watch a fit time when a child of God is most secure, or in a sleepy, or slothful condition. And hence we are so oft exhorted to diligence and spiritual watchfulness. " Watch and pray always, that ye enter not into temptations," Luke xxi. 36.

Sin and the devil the worst of thieves.   II. I shall show, that sin and the devil, &c., are the worst of thieves.

1. They are the worst of thieves, because they are soul thieves, and seek to rob us of our choice and chiefest treasure, as they served our first parents, and all in them. What could excel original righteousness, the image of God, his love and favour, nay, God himself, whom we lost by these thieves, together with the glory of the earthly paradise ?

They are bloody thieves.   2. Because they are such cruel and bloody thieves, murdering thieves ; this poor man, it is said, was wounded and half dead.

They murdered his precious soul, and put out his eyes, and stabbed him at his very heart, mangling every faculty in a bloody and most cruel manner. And as his soul was wounded to death, so these thieves gave his body its mortal wound also, bringing all filthy and tormenting diseases upon that, some of which issue in death at last.

3. They are the worst thieves, because none have escaped them.

None have escaped these thieves, therefore they are the worst of thieves   Pray note, I told you by this man, is meant lost mankind. O what thieves and murderers are these ! Should a company of thieves rob and murder all the people in a great city, or in a vast kingdom, what thieves would they be thought to be ? But lo, these thieves have robbed and murdered, both originally and actually, not only all the people in one city, or in one kingdom, but all in every city and kingdom throughout the whole world, not one escaped, and every particular soul, in the state of nature, lies dead at their feet.

Sin and the devil murdered the Lord Jesus Christ.   4. Nay, and they have not only murdered the whole world of ungodly sinners, but they have also wickedly slain and murdered the Lord Jesus Christ. It was our sins that murdered him, sin was the spear that wounded and pierced his very heart. " He being made sin for us." We could not live again except he bore our sins upon his own body, and human soul, and died a bloody sacrifice for us. " Besides, was by wicked hands that he was delivered up, and was crucified and slain," Acts ii. 23. It was by these thieves, i. e., by the devil and sin, or sinful men, men influenced by sin and the devil ; though it is true, he freely gave himself up into their hands in love to us ; for otherwise it would have been impossible for them to have touched one hair of his head.

Sin and the devil old thieves.   5. Sin and the devil, &c., are the worst of thieves, because they are old thieves and murderers. " The devil was a murderer from the beginning," John viii. 44. He is an old and experienced thief and murderer. And as they began to steal, murder, and destroy betimes, so they have continued in his hellish practice near six thousand years, and still are as bloody, cruel, and merciless as ever, sparing no sex nor degrees of men, neither young nor old, making fearful slaughter by wars, blood, and massacres and devastations in all lands and nations throughout the whole world, to this very day.

They are crafty thieves.   6. They are the worst of thieves, considering their great subtilty, policy, and craftiness. Sin and the devil have many wiles to deceive, rob, and murder poor sinners, too tedious here to reckon up. Sin indeed is the worst deceiver of the two, for it deceived the angels, and turned them that fell into devils. Also these thieves rob, kill, and murder in the day-time ; nay, when the clearest light of the gospel shines forth, they are bold, as well as cunning ; they have perhaps a thousand ways subtily to deceive, beguile, and destroy the souls and bodies of poor sinners ; they commonly assault and set upon unwary sinners under a disguise. " Satan can transform himself into an angel of light," 2 Cor. xi. 14, and pretend to piety, purity, or seeming holiness, and this way he robs and murders multitudes by damnable heresies and false doctrines, putting men to trust in a false Christ, or to rest upon, or trust to their own righteousness for justification and eternal life. Satan is no enemy to counterfeit godliness, nor to a sober life, if he can but persuade men to trust in that, or build all their hopes of heaven on that. And lust is as deceitful as the devil : how often do people change its name, being (as it where) willing to be deceived? covetousness they call industry, thriftiness, and good husbandry, nay sin, as it goes under the name of cove- tousness, some think it is (almost) impossible to find it out. Pride also, though so abominable a thing in the sight of God, is looked upon a decency or a comely dress, because forsooth it is the fashion. Moreover, these thieves, deceivers, and murderers, suit their bait or temptation according to the natural inclination, constitution, and disposition of the sinner's heart, some by sinful pleasures, some by sinful profits, and others by sinful honours ; nay, these thieves are so subtile, that they entice and persuade sinners (who readily yield to them) to open their doors, and willingly let them in, they pretending themselves to be their greatest friends in all the world, and that there is no other way to become rich, great, and to have their lives to be sweet and comfortable to them, but by their adhering to those cursed suggestions which they dart into their evil hearts. Moreover, they labour to put religion and true godliness into a base disguise, rendering it hateful to men, as if it tended only to make their lives burdensome to them, and destroy them with melancholy thoughts, causing them to be mere mums, and to hang down their heads like bulrushes, to fold their arms, and to spend their days in tears and sighing, if not to go beside themselves. These thieves smile in the sinner's face, while they secretly cut his throat, and murder his precious soul; promising them future time to repent, though before that time comes, their souls perhaps are in hell.

How sin deceives sinners.

True godliness rendered hateful.

7. They are the worst of thieves in respect of their power and great strength. Who is a match for them? what mortal is able to subdue sin, and the power of the devil in his own heart ? what great and brave heroes have they conquered? who perhaps were clothed with greater strength than any saint of God hath in these days ; as Noah, Lot, Moses, David, Solomon, Peter, and many more : nay, none but God and the Almighty Jesus can conquer these thieves. Satan is that strong man armed, of whom our Saviour speaketh, " How can one enter into a strong man's house, and spoil his goods, except he first bind the strong man, and then he will spoil his house," Matt. xii. 29. And this must be one stronger than he, which none is but the Lord Jesus Christ, and none but he is able to vanquish and destroy these thieves and murderers.

Sin and the devil are powerful thieves.

You may raise all the town, country, nay the whole land, and yet they cannot save one soul from these thieves; but the Lord Jesus " hath made an end of sin, and utterly spoiled principalities and powers," Dan. ix. 24, Col. ii. 15. He hath and will finally destroy both sin and Satan.

APPLICATION

1. If these enemies are such thieves and bloody murderers, what folly and madness is in those, who so readily, and willingly entertain them in their houses, nay, let them have the chiefest room in their hearts? O how blind are sinners naturally !

2. This shows their folly also who hide their sin, hide their cruel robber and bloody murderer, nay, and have many devices to conceal and cover it, and also make provision for the murderer, or " for the flesh, to fulfil the lusts thereof." O how is this thief fed and cherished day by day, and delighted in, and hugged in their bosoms !

3. Also what infinite love and mercy hath God showed towards us, in sending so great and mighty a Saviour, to vanquish and destroy these thieves and murderers, the whole world had otherwise been lost for ever. Moreover, we may from hence infer, that were not Jesus Christ God, the true Almighty God, he could not have saved us from these thieves. Is a mere man a match for Satan and all the powers of hell and darkness ? the strong man armed keeps all he hath in safety, till a stronger than he comes to lay hold upon him, and binds him. " To this end was the Son of God manifested, that he might destroy the works of the devil," 1 John iii. 8.

4. If sin and the devil are such thieves and murderers, let a hue and cry go out to apprehend them, and let all take care upon their utmost peril, that they hide and conceal them not, nor show them the least favour.

A hue and cry ought to go forth after these thieves.

And that all mortals may yet further be more incensed against them, consider what mischief they have done, which in part you have heard.

(1.) These thieves have caused mankind to cast off the holy God, and to contemn him in their hearts, and to reject his authority over them.

What mischief these thieves have done.

(2.) They have also assumed the very throne of God, (i. e.,) the heart, and there they reign, rule, and bear sway.

(3.) They have (you heard) put the Lord of life and glory to death, our sins were charged upon him ; had not we sinned, Jesus Christ had not suffered ; our entertaining sin and Satan cost our blessed Lord dear.

2ndly. These thieves you have heard, (1.) Have robbed all mankind, and stripped them of their raiment, marring the image of God that was originally formed in us, and have stolen from us jewels of an inestimable value. (2.) They have caused man to become a traitor, and cursed rebel against God, filling their hearts naturally full of rage and en-

Enmity in man's heart naturally a- gainst God. mity against their Maker ; and God hereby they caused to become an enemy to mankind. (3.) They have corrupted our whole nature, both body and soul, bringing nothing but rottenness, and abominable filth upon the precious soul, causing it to become loathsome in the sight of God, wounding every part and faculty, and loading the body with filthy diseases, and tormenting them with gnawing and fearful

Sin a plague to the whole creation. Rom. viii. 20. 21. pain. (4.) They brought a curse upon the creature, nay, upon the whole crea- tion, causing the innocent beast, nay the whole creation to groan and be sub- ject to vanity. (5.) They have caused God to prepare a lake or furnace of fire to cast all into it, who show favour, love to, or entertain these thieves : so hateful are all they who so do, in the sight of God. (6.) These thieves have put all the world into confusion, filling all nations with war and blood, causing one man to kill another. " From whence comes war and fightings ? come they not from hence, even from your lusts that war in your members ?" Jam. iv. 1. (7.) All the plagues, injustice, cruelty, and miseries in the world, are caused by them. (8.) They have caused mankind to violate all the good laws of God, nature, and nations. (9.) The craftiness of these thieves lies in

Sin causes sinners to act like fools or madmen. their blinding the eyes of men, causing them to believe things contrary to reason, as to think they may reap wheat, though they sowed nothing but tares, nay, though they sow not at all, yet may have a great and good crop at harvest : yea, they have so bewitched silly mortals, as to consent to run knives into their own souls, and let out their own hearts' blood, and to persuade them that the pleasure of their sins and lusts is better than all the good that is in God himself, and in his dear love and favour ; nay, to prefer sin, pleasure, and profits here, above a crown of glory in heaven hereafter. Is it not strange that mankind should be so blinded by these thieves, that like the vain Frenchman prefer, as it were, a part in Paris above all the riches and pleasures of paradise. " They say to God, depart from us," Job. xxi, they value the husks that swine eat, above God, and Jesus Christ : they prize sinful profit above peace of conscience, their own filthy rags before Christ's righteousness ; they rob sinners of the power of godli- ness, by setting their hearts more upon morality, or on the base external form of godliness, or on human rites and ceremonies, and many to prize the cabinet, above the jewel ; they promise sinners salvation, though they live wicked and ungodly lives, and sinners are so deceived, that they hardly doubt about it. They tell young people it is too soon to mind heavenly things ; and when any are grown old, they tell them it is to late.

5. If sin be such a thief, what cause of grief is there to see so many to play and sport with it ? " Fools make a mock at sin," Prov. xiv. 9. " They say, are we not in sport ?" Prov. xxvi. 19. But it is bad to sport with such secret, treacherous, and bloody enemies.

6. Sinners, fly to Jesus Christ, get faith in him, who only can save you from these thieves. O get under his wings, " He that is born of God, hath overcome the wicked one." O what compassion is in Jesus Christ, this good and gracious Samaritan ! He sees you wounded, and is come to pour in his oil, and wine, and bind up your wounds, labour to do, as an honest man who is afraid of thieves. Are you hard beset, and in danger by sin and Satan ? cry to Christ for help, cry out, thieves, thieves, Lord help me, save me,

What doors should be shut against these thieves. or I perish, they are too strong for me. 8. Keep the doors shut against these thieves, that neither sin nor Satan may be let in.

(1.) The doors of your eyes, sin sometimes is let in at those doors. Achan saw a " Babylonish garment, and wedge of gold, and he coveted them." Take heed you behold no object with any undue and wanton glance.

(2.) Keep the door of your ears ; do not hear a backbiting or detracting tongue, but show your abhorrence of such ; neither suffer yourselves to be praised to your face by flat- terers, much less let not thy ears hear thy own tongue praise thee, but above all things keep the door of thy heart ; watch this door. " Keep thy heart with all diligence, for out of it are the issues of life," Prov. iv. 23.

1st. Keep thy heart from vain thoughts, or for thinking evil. " Let not vain thoughts lodge in thee." Are evil thoughts grievous to thee, dost thou not approve of them ? canst thou say with David, " I hate all vain thoughts ?" Have they no ruling and reigning power over thee ? dost thou cry out against them, and mourn under them ?

2ndly. Keep thy heart from all unchaste thoughts, all unbelieving, murmuring, distrustful, discontented, distracting and vain-glorious thoughts, lest these thieves get in ; it is easier to keep thieves out of the house, than it is to get them out when they are got in. The heart is deceitful above all things, and ofttimes lets these thieves in: an enemy within, is worse than an enemy without.

(3.) Keep the door of thy lips, watch thy tongue, keep it as with a bit and bridle, (as the apostle James shows) " The tongue no man can tame, it is an unruly evil, full of deadly poison," James iii. 8. Therefore cry to God for help, or else at this door these thieves will get in.

9. Strive to know the advices and craftiness of those thieves. Satan is a serpent for subtilty, a lion for strength, and a dragon for cruelty. And sin also is not in vain called deceitful lusts. The apostle cautions the saints, " Lest any of them be hardened through the deceitfulness of sin," Heb. iii. 13. Those are wise Christians, who have studied Satan's politics : we are not ignorant of his devices.

10. You that are believers, bless God that he hath saved and delivered you from the power of these thieves. O what a mercy it is, that Jesus Christ, the good Samaritan, hath taken compassion of you ; he came where you were, and hath healed your wounds.

Lastly, what comfort and consolation is here for you, that you are out of the reach of those bloody enemies ; you are put into Christ's hands, and are kept by his power, and shall be unto salvation. " Greater is he that is in us, than he that is in the world, he will bruise Satan under your feet shortly," 1 John iv. 4. " Through Jesus Christ, we are more than conquerors," Rom. viii. 37.

O let us love this good and gracious Samaritan, this blessed Jesus, and live to his praise and glory all our days ; who hath done such wonderful things for us ; who hath bound up our wounds, and poured into them oil and wine ; who hath loved our souls with an everlasting love, and hath spread the mantle of his love over us, that we may be rescued from eternal misery.

II

And Jesus answered and said, a certain man went down from Jerusalem to Jericho, and fell among thieves, &c.—Luke x. 30.

I HAVE, my brethren, opened all the parts contained in this parable according to that light and understanding received, and have noted one proposition from them. I have showed what kind of thieves those are, which this certain man fell among, and that all mankind in the first Adam are signified by this man, and that all naturally are half dead ; dead in their souls in respect of any true spiritual life, being wounded in every faculty, and member of the body.

Doct. So that we may infer, that mankind by sin naturally are in a miserable, wretched, and deplorable condition.

1. Their understanding is blinded. 2. The judgment is depraved, so that they cannot make any true judgment of themselves, nor of things. If you see a man that was very wise, to act like a mere idiot, or natural fool, you say his reason is gone; he is broken in judgment, or wounded in his intellectual parts. Thus it is in a spiritual sense with every unrenewed man, their understanding is darkened and full of folly, vanity, blindness, and incredulity ; they esteem husks above bread, and choose a pebble before a precious pearl. Many cry down Judas for selling his blessed Lord for thirty pence. Alas, what do all wicked men much less, who refuse, nay reject the Lord Jesus Christ for the sake of their filthy lusts, or for the unlawful gain of a groat : what think you of them that take abundance of care to deck a sorry cabinet, but take no regard of the jewel, which is more worth than all the world, Matt. xvi. 26 ? See to this, you young men and women, who care not what you bestow to dress and adorn the body, but disregard your precious souls: are not you wounded in judgment ? Suppose your house was all in a flame, and you lay on a soft bed, and one should cry out fire, fire, O arise and save your lives for the Lord's sake, your house is on a flame ; and yet you should lie still and say, it is not midnight, you will not rise yet, it is a great while till day : would not all people that hear of it, say you were mad, or out of your wits ! Sirs, the fire of God's wrath hath taken hold of every unconverted sinner, and they every moment

The state of man by nature is deplorable.

See the parable of the Prodigal son.

are in danger to be cast into hell. But yet most refuse to take hold of Jesus Christ, and return to God, casting off all their wicked ways; no it is too soon, time enough (say they) to-morrow, though before then, perhaps they may be in hell.

The will is wounded to death. 2. The will (that noble faculty) is depraved, and as it were wounded unto death; and it must needs be so, since they are without understanding. As a man that hath his palate spoiled, being possessed with some vicious humour: everything seems bitter according to that humour; so the understanding counts the ways of God grievous and unpleasant; the will acts accordingly, utterly refusing to walk therein, but act cross, contrary to, and in direct opposition to the will and ways of God. O what pride, inconstancy, stubbornness, disobedience, and rebellion is there in the will of wicked men. "Our tongues are our own, and who is lord over us," Psal. xii. 4? This is the voice of the ungodly. "We will not have this man to reign over us," Luke xix. 27.

The affections are also wounded. 3. Their affections, as well as their understanding and will, are wounded to death. O how carnal, vain, loose, and earthly are their affections: "They are lovers of pleasure more than lovers of God," 2 Tim. iii. 4. Their care is more to get an estate, than to get an interest in Christ, treasure on earth before treasure in heaven; they fear more the wrath of man, than the wrath of God, and the loss of their outward liberties, substance, or their natural lives, than the loss of their immortal souls; they rejoice more when they thrive in the world, than to find a gracious work upon their hearts, or to hear the word of God; they mourn for the loss of son or daughter, a husband or a wife, more than for the loss of God. O I have (saith one) lost my only child; and saith another, my dear husband is dead; O my heart will break, I am full of sorrow and heaviness, what shall I do? poor sinner! though these things are cause of grief, yet if thou art in thy sin, I must tell thee worse news, and that which is cause of far greater sorrow, thou hast lost thy God, and thy soul is dead, and what hast thou more? Thou art condemned, even sentenced to be burned alive in eternal flames. Sirs, is it not sad, that a man should be more affected, grieved, and afflicted in his soul, at the loss of a dumb idol, than sinners are for the loss of the true and living God! See Judges xviii. 24, (speaking of Michah) "And he said, ye have taken away my gods which I have made, and the priest, and what have I more? And this you say unto me, what aileth thee?" That which a man's heart is bound up in the love of, and which he esteemeth and prizeth most, is his God; and if he loses it, he cries out, what have I more? If it be a husband, a child, a name, or an estate. But, sinner, know when thou hast God to be thy God, thou wilt see thou canst not be miserable whatever you lose, nor ever be undone, and then all other losses will be patiently borne.

4. The memory is also wounded unto death: how doth that forget what it should remember, and remember that which it should forget; it forgets God, both what he is, and will be to them who find him. God is not in all his thoughts. They forget Christ, and who he is, and what he hath done and suffered for sinners; they forget their own precious souls, their worth, and whither they are going; they forget to pray and to seek God while he may be found; they forget what an evil sin is, they forget to hear and prize the word of God, they forget how short and uncertain their days are, they forget their last end; but they think upon the world, upon their riches, and upon external poverty and afflictions; they remember their pleasures, and those wrongs and injuries some have done to them, so as to seek revenge: is not this sad?

5. Their consciences are wounded, fearfully corrupted, have scarce any spiritual sense or feeling, or are in a drowsy and sleepy state, if not erronius. "Unto them that are defiled, is nothing pure, but their minds and consciences are defiled," Tit. i. 15. Conscience, that like Job's messenger should bring them word that all the rest of the faculties of the soul are dead, is so maimed, stupified, and wounded, that it is dumb, says nothing, or else excuses when it should accuse, and severely rebuke them for their horrid sins. And as all the faculties of their souls are wounded by these thieves, so are their sensitive parts also; their eyes are full of idolatry, their lips are unclean and full of lies, cursing, blasphemy, backbiting, detraction, villifying, reproaching, and abusing their neighbours. Their ears are bewitched with carnal music, and do delight to hear cursed songs and romances, and idle stories, more than to hear the word of God, or of heaven and eternal happiness; their hands are for taking the forbidden fruit, and in many addicted to picking and stealing. "Their throat is as an open sepulchre, the poison of asps is under their tongue, and their feet are swift to shed blood," Rom. iii. 13. They yield their member servants unto uncleanness.

O how sad is the state of wounded mankind by these cursed thieves !

Secondly, but let us consider a little further of their deplorable condition, in respect to the nature of these wounds.

The nature of these wounds.

1. Remember they are soul-wounds. A wound in the hand or foot, is not so bad as a wound in the heart ; these wounds have let out the blood or life of the soul, they reach to the very heart. " This is thy wickedness, because it reacheth unto thine heart," Jer. iv 18.

2. They are poisonous wounds, they are wounds of a sting of a poisonous serpent, the Devil : " The sting of death is sin." When the Israelites were stung in the wilderness with those fiery serpents (saith Mr. Ainsworth) there was thereby a remembrance how sin came into the world by a serpent. O what were those serpents to the old serpents, or those wounds to these wounds ? yet those wounds were very venomous, and the contagion spread itself over the whole body ; so you have heard these wounds have spread over the whole man, both body and soul, and not only over every faculty, but also over every person : our first parents were wounded, and in them every soul that sprung from their lions by natural generation, not one person escaped ; so that the wounds were not only venomous, but also infectious : " By one man's disobedience many were made sinners,—by the offence of one, judgment came upon all men to condemnation." Rom. v. 18, 19.

3. These wounds are extremely painful and tormenting, as all experience, when they come to themselves; as those wounds by those fiery serpents were, they found a fearful inflammation which made them roar out in bitter anguish of pain and misery ; so all poor awakened and convinced sinners feel the smart of sin, or of these wounds, and cry out as those did St. Peter preached to ; " Men and brethren, what shall we do ?" Acts. ii. 39. " How did David cry out in anguish of soul, I am bowed down greatly, I go mourning all the day, for my loins are filled with a loathsome disease, and there is no soundness in my flesh," Psal. xxxviii. 6, 7. The sting of a serpent causes extreme thirst : this shows that all envious or revengeful persons are deeply wounded ; besides that unsatisfiedness that is in men's hearts, after the riches, honours, and pleasures of sin, discovers what drought by sin hath seized all mankind, such a thirst that nothing but drinking of the water of life can allay it.

4. The poison of serpents, as Plutarch notes, gets quickly to the vital spirits, and corrupts the whole mass of blood. So did this sting and cruel wound corrupt the lump of mankind.

5. They are deceitful wounds ; there is a strange insensibleness in sinners, who are mortally wounded, for a great while they feel no pain. I have read of the poison of some serpents, that as soon as a man is stung, he falls into a great laughter, tickled in a strange manner : but no sooner doth the poison come to his heart, but it makes him change his note, crying out most bitterly in dreadful anguish, a fit resemblance of the sting of sin. Poor sinners seem at first to be in sport, and rejoice in their wickedness, and spend their days in pleasure ; but as soon as God brings them to feel the venom and sting at their hearts, their joy is turned into sorrow and extremity of misery ; if they cry not out here, they shall howl hereafter.

6. The wounds by those serpents was present death, unless they looked up to the brazen serpent. So all those sinners who are wounded by these thieves, can expect nothing but present death ; I mean of being cast into hell, except they look up to Jesus Christ, and believe in him.

7. These wounds fester and corrupt, and grow worse, and worse, and it must needs be so, for by these thieves they daily receive fresh wounds ; " so that from the crown of their heads, to the soles of their feet, there are nothing but wounds, bruises, and putrifying sores," Isa. i. 6 ; and so they remain until the good Samaritan closes their wounds, binds them up, and mollifies them with ointment.

8. The wounds of those serpents in the wilderness, could not be healed by any art or wisdom of man : none could find any medicine or balsam that could give ease, or cure those poor wounded and miserable creatures : no, the way of cure was strange, marvellous and supernatural. So no angel in heaven, nor man on earth, could find out a cure for wounded sinners. Our cure is the wonderment of saints and angels ; we could not have help, and live, unless the Son of God dies, and his precious blood be applied to heal our wounded souls.

APPLICATION

1. O what an amazing thing is this, that the world is thus wounded, millions wounded, and yet but few complain of it ; what should be the reason of this ?

Answ. 1. It is because they are dead, dead in sins and trespasses. Can dead people feel pain ? no, you may thrust a sword through their hearts, and they feel not ; were there a principle of life in them, they would soon cry out in bitter pain.

2. How may this tend to incense sinners against these thieves ? what indignation should we have against sin and the devil, who have in such a manner wounded our precious souls ?

3. It may clearly discover, who they are that are spiritually dead. Certainly you that feel no pain, that sin, and yet cry not out under great anguish and misery, are dead : had you life in you, it would be otherwise with you ; therefore such of you that feel the smart and bitterness of sin, and know what it is to offend God, and who cannot commit the least sin, but you find your souls and consciences wounded, it is an evident sign you are spiritually alive.

II. Be exhorted to take heed of these thieves, lest they give you yet more fresh wounds. O beware of all temptations, every sin is a wound.

MOTIVES

Motives to beware of sin.   1. This sting hath stung our blessed Lord to death ; let that enrage your souls against sin, to hate and abhor all iniquity.

2. It lays all ungodly sinners under God's wrath, and the curse of the law ; and if you are not healed, it will make an eternal separation between God and you.

3. Know that this sting, or these wounds (though you may not feel much pain now) yet you will be sensible, and find yourselves tormented in an hour that draws near, if you meet not with a cure. There are four seasons when these wounds will be felt.

When sin as a wound will be felt.   (1.) In a time of common calamity, when you will see sorrow and anguish coming upon you, and you not know whither to fly for succour ; such days are near, that the blind and secure world dream not of. "Then your sins will stare you in the face, and your guilty souls and conscience will terrify you, and God then perhaps will mock when your fear cometh ; because when he called you refused, and set at nought all his reproof," Prov. i. 25, 26.

(3.) At that time when God awakeneneth your sleepy consciences, and lets out conscience to torment and terrify you, and God leaves you to desperation, and under his fierce and divine vengeance ; think on *Francis Spira* and John Child ; you may find such an hour.

(3.) At the hour of death, or at that moment you die : for if while your soul is yet in your body, you do not feel the smart and anguish of sin and wrath ; yet no sooner are you dead, but your soul will be in torment. " And in hell he lifted up his eyes, being in torments," &c., Luke. xvi. 23.

(4.) At the dreadful day of judgement, when both body and soul shall be brought before Christ's tribunal, to receive that fearful sentence, " Depart from me, ye cursed, into everlasting fire, prepared for the devil and his angels." Matt. xxv. 41.

O cry with David, " Lord, be merciful to me, and heal my soul, for I have sinned against thee." Psal. xli. 4, 5.

III. What hath been said, may be for terror to all wicked men : death is near, and it will come on you with its sting, if you are unbelievers ; O fly to Christ for healing ; pray that he will come where you are, and bind up your wounds, and pour in oil and wine.

IV. Comfort. What consolation may from hence arise to all true Christians that are cured of these wounds ; such may triumph over sin, death, devils, and all enemies "O death, where is thy sting ? O grave, where is thy victory ?" 1 Cor. xv. 55. What hurt can sin, death, or devils do me, who am in Christ ? Death hath spent his sting on the Lord Jesus, the sting is taken away from all that believe, and their souls are healed, their issues of blood is dried up, their leprous souls are cleansed ; what have such to do, but with David, to praise and magnify God, and admire the love of Jesus Christ ? " Bless the Lord, O my soul : and all that is in me bless his holy name. Bless the Lord, O my soul, and forget not all his benefits : who forgiveth all thine iniquities ; and healeth all thy diseases." Psal. ciii. 1, 2, 3. Such who are pardoned, are healed ; and they that are forgven may rejoice. " Blessed is he whose sin is hid, whose transgressions are pardoned," Psal. xxxii. 1. They that are at ease, and freed from sin, need neither fear death, nor any danger : though the heavens and the earth shall suddenly shake, and the hearts of sinners tremble, yet they have a place of refuge, and shall be hid in the day of God's wrath.

So much as to this proposition.

" And by chance there came down a certain priest that way ; and when he saw him, he passed by on the other side." "And likewise a Levite, when he was at the place came and looked on him, and passed by on the other side," Luke. x. 31. 32.

Nothing comes to pass by chance.

"And by chance," not that any thing cometh to pass by chance; but the word is used here, to denote such events as fall out to men by the counsel of God, or by his providence. " If a birds-nest chance to be before thee," &c. Ainworth, from the Greek, reads it, if thou meetest with a bird's-nest," Deut. xxii. 6.

" A certain priest," &c.

I showed in the explanation, that by the priest may be meant the law, the priests being the interpreters of it : and our Saviour hereby might show two things.

(1.) That the lawyers, scribes, and Pharisees, were men of no bowels, they showed no pity to the distressed ; though they boasted of their great piety, yet it only consisted in the lesser matters of the law. " They neglecteth mercy and the love of God," they loved not their neighbour as themselves.

(2.) To discover to the lawyer, that the law could not relieve a poor wounded sinner ; that kills, but gives no life, wounds but heals not. " Had there been a law that could have given life, verily righteousness should have been by the law," Gal. iii. 21.

No relief for wounded sinners by the law.

" And behold a certain lawyer stood up and tempted him, saying, Master, what shall I do to inherit eternal life? He said unto him, What is written in the law? how readest thou? And he answering, said, Thou shalt love the Lord thy God with all thy heart, and with all thy soul, and with all thy strength, and with all thy mind, and thy neighbour as thyself. And he said unto him, Thou hast answered aright: this do, and thou shalt live," Luke x. 25,—28.

Thus from the scope of this parable (as I minded) we may easily perceive whom our Lord means by the priest ; he would not say a certain lawyer passed that way (perhaps) because he would not provoke him, but to let him know, that he failed in answering what the law requires, even in respect had to the second Table. Our Lord brings in this parable to show him, that the " law through the weakness that is in man to keep it," Rom. viii. 3, could not give life, or bring to life a poor sinner wounded to death ; and that he loved not his neighbour as the law enjoined all to do: " This do and thou shalt live ;" that is, live and sin not, or perform perfect obedience to the same: for a perfect loving of God and our neighbour, comprehends that complete righteousness the law commands, which nòne since sin entered into the world could do, or ever did, save the man Jesus Christ.

The scope of the parable further opened.

No help, no relief, no justification by the moral law.

Could men live indeed, and sin not, either in word, thought, or deed, and had they never sinned, they might be justified by the law, as Adam was while he stood in a state of innocency : but now we have sinned, all having sinned in the first Adam, Rom. v. 12, and daily do actually sin, and cannot live and sin not : and from hence the moral law cannot afford us any help, but contrariwise it lets fly its dreadful curses against us : " Cursed is every one that continueth not in all things that are written in the book of the law, to do them," Gal. iii. 10. Alas, if men fail in their duty to men, in their love to their neighbour, and thereby break God's holy law, and lay themselves thereby obnoxious to eternal wrath. How far short do all come, in respect had to holiness, and perfect conformity to God, or in their duty and obedience to God, which more immediately the law requires. And thus our blessed Lord clearly showed this lawyer (had he understood whom, or what he meant by this certain priest) that the law leaves every poor and undone sinner in his blood, and bleeding wounds. " For what the law could not do, in that it was weak through the flesh, God sending his own Son, in the likeness of sinful flesh, and for sin condemned sin in the flesh," Rom. viii. 3. It can neither justify, heal, nor save lost sinners. A priest may read the law to the people every day, and expound it, and press them to the strictest observance of it imaginable, yet they still, after all that they can do, abide in their blood and filth : " For if righteousness come by the law, Christ is dead in vain," Gal. ii. 21. But because this is more fully opened in my speaking to some other parables, I shall say no more to it here.

" Likewise a Levite, when he was at the place, came and looked on him ; and passed by."

As the moral law which the priest taught and instructed the people in, could not, did not help any distressed sinner ; so the Levitical priesthood, the sacrifices and offerings thereof (signified by the Levite here) could not take away sin, no, though he should come where the sinner is, and lies in his blood, and offer up a thousand bullocks, ten thousand goats, and ten thousand times ten thousand lambs, yet it would do nothing to help or heal a poor guilty and condemned sinner; therefore it is said, " he passed by on the other side."

Levitical sacrifices and offerings cannot relieve a wounded and guilty sinner.

As no obedience to the moral law performed by any sinful creature, no, though it were a priest himself, can relieve a sinner; so all sacrifices and legal offerings fail in doing it also. " Sacrifices and offerings thou wouldst not," &c., Heb. x. 5. " And when he said, Sacrifices, and offerings, and burnt offering, thou wouldst not, neither hadst pleasure therein —Then said I, Lo, I come to do thy will, O God," ver. 8, 9. It is true, sacrifices were appointed of God under the law; nay, no doubt were from the beginning. Abel offered sacrifices, but all were but types of that great sacrifice, that only can take away sin, i. e., Jesus Christ's offering himself a sacrifice unto God for us; they were shadows of Christ, or Christ in a cloud, he was the substance of them. But,

1. As in themselves they were insufficient to expiate sin: " For it is not possible that the blood of bulls, and of goats, should take away sin," Heb. x. 4. They could make nothing perfect, nor purge the conscience.

2. What a noble creature is man above a beast; if any sacrifice could have appeased God's divine anger, we might think it might rather be our " First-born, or the fruit of our body, for the sin of our soul." But such a sacrifice could not do, it would but be to offer unto God a corrupt thing: nay, should an angel be sacrificed for us, such a sacrifice would fail, because angels are but finite creatures, and owe themselves, and all they have, and can do, to God; they can neither satisfy infinite justice, nor merit any thing for us: it must be a sacrifice of a person of infinite worth and dignity, and that could merit at God's hand, and make an infinite satisfaction for our sins.

3. It was not consistent with the honour of God to be pleased, and his wrath to be appeased with the blood of worthless beasts; how could such sacrifices discover the severity of his justice, and the purity of his nature ? and how would it have been known, that God hath such an infinite hatred of sin, if he had accepted the blood of an abject animal, as an atonement for the sins of the precious, spiritual, noble, and high-born soul of man ? " Was it becoming (saith one) the majesty of God, who had denounced a curse in the law upon the transgressors of it, and published it with thunders, lightnings, and earthquakes, to accept of the manglings of a few beasts in the place and stead of the offenders, who were rational creatures, endowed with excellent faculties ?" No man can reasonably have such despicable thoughts of the majesty, justice, and holiness of God, or the vileness of sin, and greatness of God's provocation, as to imagine, that he should be contented with the sacrifice of a lamb or bullock, or that their blood could pass for an expiation of such abominable crimes man was guilty of.

4. Those sacrifices have, as reverend Charnock shows, " no proportion to the sin of man, the sin of rational creatures is too foul to be expiated by the blood of irrational creatures; nor could the blood of a human body, though the first-born, the strength and delight of man, Mich. vi. 7 : no, the butchery of so poor a creature cannot be any compensation for that, which is a disparagement of the Creator of the world : what alliance was there between the nature of a beast, and that of a man? An inferior nature can never atone the sin of a nature superior to it : there is indeed in the groans of those dying creatures, some demonstration of God's wrath, but no bringing in an everlasting righteousness, nor any vindication of the honour of the law.

Second Volume, p. 856.

5. The often repeating, or the reiteration of those sacrifices, shows their insufficiency. " In those sacrifices there was a remembrance of sin every year," Heb. x. 3. They were the yearly sacrifices ; but in the daily sacrifice there was a remembrance of sin every day. Besides, the Lord declared that he had no delight in them. " Thou desirest not sacrifices,—thou delightest not in burnt-offerings," Psal. li. 16. True, God delighted in such who offered them in faith, beholding a slain Christ in them, or rather beyond them ; but the sacrifice itself was little valued by the holy God ; that sacrifice that God accepteth must be pure and sinless, one perfectly holy, and yet one in our nature : " For he that sanctifieth, and they that are sanctified, must be all of one," i. e., of one nature ; also such a one, in whose sacrifice there was an infinite worth. Jesus Christ, though he " Flesh of our flesh, and bone of our bone," is nevertheless the Most High God, " God and man," in one Person. See the Parable of the Pearl of great price.

Thus neither law, Levite, priest, nor sacrifices, took any regard of this poor man, wounded by these thieves, and lying in his blood.

O what blindness was in the Jews, who thought by their obedience to the law to be justified, and could not discern by those sacrifices, that the Messiah, when he came, must die, or be offered up a sacrifice unto God. But no more at this time.

III

And when he saw him, he had compassion on him, &c.,—Luke x. 33.

Doct. The compassion of our Lord Jesus Christ to poor sinners is very great.
I. I shall prove it.
II. Show what kind of compassion and mercy is in Christ.
III. Apply it.

As the relief, help, and cure of undone sinners, is alone of free-grace; so this parable shows Christ is full of bowels of mercy. "He had compassion on him."

1. Mercy, as you have heard, refers to man in misery. Man before he sinned, partook of divine goodness, but had no need of mercy; but God from eternity foresaw mankind fallen and undone by sin; and divine mercy moved his wisdom to find out a way for his relief and restoration, which was to substitute his Son to be our Surety and Saviour, and to send him into the world, to be the Physician or healer of our souls. *Mercy refers to persons in misery.*

The Son of God early and readily consented to show to man his infinite love and compassion. "His delight was with the sons of men," Prov. viii. 22, 30. *i. e.*, such that the Father gave to him. He delighted in thoughts and acts of mercy. His accepting such an office, and to undertake such a work, sets forth *Christ's compassion great in becoming our Surety.* that great pity and compassion that was in his heart, that he might relieve and recover miserable mankind. He yielded to those terms infinite justice did demand, that so the mercy that was in the heart of God the Father (who is called the Father of mercy) and his own compassion might be let out, and flow forth abundantly, without any wrong or dishonour to the truth, holiness, and justice of God.

2. His mercy and compassion further appears, in that no other way was found which could relieve the miserable creatures.

3. Besides, Christ's compassion is wonderful, because we deserved not the least pity, sinners being obstinate rebels, and enemies to God.

4. His mercy yet further appears, in respect of these things following.

(1.) In that he left his Father, when he lay in his bosom, and laid aside, or veiled his glory, and came into this dark and miserable world. (2.) To be abased, and make himself of no reputation, though he was equal with God; and took upon him the form of a servant, not the form of a prince, or the state and dignity of a mighty monarch, but the state of a servant, and to be in a low and mean condition, having no where to lay his head, who was the Maker, and Lord of heaven and earth. (3.) In his exposing himself to suffering, to shame, and reproach, out of compassion to them that were in misery, naked, wounded, wallowing in their blood. "You know the grace of our Lord Jesus Christ, who, though he was rich, yet for your sakes became poor, that we through his poverty might be made rich," 2 Cor. viii. 9. (4.) Nay, more, he became a curse for us; stood charged with our sins, and bore God's wrath, and the curse of the law for us. "Christ hath redeemed us from the curse of the law, being made a curse for us," Gal. iii. 13. (5). In his pouring out his own blood to heal our wounded souls; *In dying for us.* doth not this show forth the infinite compassion of Jesus Christ, that when he *Christ's mercy in his abasement.* *In suffering shame for us.* saw the sentence passed upon us, and we were, as it were, brought to the place of execution, and the hand of divine justice was up to strike the fatal blow, he cried out, hold justice, stay, thrust thy glittering spear into my heart, I will die for these miserable criminals? He received the stroke of divine wrath due to us, as an act of his love and compassion towards us, our hell-pangs fell upon him, he died that we might live, "In due time Christ died for the ungodly; whilst we were yet enemies, Christ died for us," Rom. v. 6, 8. (6). By his seeking after us miserable creatures, he came where we were, by his word and Spirit, even to that very land, city, town, or village, where his elect lay in their blood and filth; after he had opened the flood-gate of God's infinite mercy, by removing of all those obstacles that hindered it from flowing out, he hath broken up the fountains of the great deeps of divine mercy, to magnify and manifest his own compassion. (7). His pity and bowels appear by his crying to us, and labouring *In using all ways to gather us.* to gather sinners to himself. "How often would I have gathered thy children together, as a hen gathereth her chickens under her wings, and ye would not," Matt. xxiii. 37. There is no creature, saith Bernard, that is moved with greater compas-

sion towards her young, than a hen.   1.   A hen will fly in the face of ravenous birds, that seeks to devour her chickens.   2.   She becomes weak to feed them.   3.   She clucks and calls often, with a mournful voice to them, when they are in danger.   4.   She stands ready prepared, to receive them under her wings.   Sirs, what enemies hath Christ flew in the face of, and how weak did he become to feed sinners ? and how often doth he call upon them to fly to him, and to get under his wings of mercy and gracious protection, seeing them in the uttermost danger ?   " Turn, turn, why will you die, O house of Israel ?" (8).   His compassion, in pitying us when none else did, is marvellous, he manifested his mercy to us.   " When no eye pitied us, to do any of these things unto us," Ezek. xvi. 5, neither priest, nor Levite, then Christ took compassion on us, else we had perished for ever.   (9).   In easing us of all our burdens, as well as in healing of all our wounds ; he doth not aggravate our crimes against us, nor upbraid us with our former abominable re-
In binding up our wounds. bellion, but passeth by and forgiveth all.   (10).   By his pouring in oil and wine, and binding up our wounds ; he leaves us not, but takes care to heal our sores, and to clothe us with a rich robe, and sets us also on his own beast, and carries us to an inn, and provides an host, or a faithful minister, to take the care and charge of us, and by paying all the charges, supplying of all our wants, and
Phil. iv, 19.
Heb. vii. 12.
—17.
John xvi. 33.
Matt. xxviii.
20.
2 Pet. i. 4.
John xvii. 15.
Heb. vii 25.
Isa. lxii. 9.
Phil. i. 6.
Isa. xl.11.
Heb. ii. 14.
Luke xvi. 22.
Inference. giving us his Spirit, succouring us in all our temptations, comforting us in all our tribulations, and keeping us company at all times, and in all states, while we are in this world ; also making such large promises to us, and in his engaging the Father to keep us from the evil, and that none of us may be lost, continually interceding for us, fighting against our enemies, sympathizing with us in all our afflictions, perfecting that grace begun in our souls, carrying his lambs in his bosom, gently leading them that are with young ; charging his angels to minister to us, and to carry our souls to heaven when we die.

Secondly, what mercy, or kinds of compassion, is in the Lord Jesus Christ. 1.   Infinite mercy.   Christ being God, goodness and mercy is an essential property of his nature ; mercy is the effect of his inconceivable goodness, " Thou art good, and doest good," Psal. cxix. 68.   There is in him an innate propenseness to pity and succour such as are in misery, though it is let out according to his sovereign pleasure and the counsel of his will.   2.   Compassion and mercy in Christ, is equal with that goodness, compassion, and mercy which is in the Father, because he is the same God ; I and my Father are one.   2.   It is covenant mercy, and let out in a covenant way, as the result of that holy contract between the Father and himself in eternity. 3.   It is preventing mercy, his goodness and compassion stopped the execution of divine justice ; it prevented the speedy process of justice.   4. Sparing mercy, sinners are spared by the interposition of Jesus Christ, he cries out, spare this, and that sinner, one year longer, though like trees barren that cumber the ground.   5.   It is redeeming mercy, he redeemed us by his own blood. 6. It is renewing, quickening, and regenerating mercy, " Not by works of righteousness which we have done, but according to his mercy he saved us, by the washing of regeneration, and renewing of the Holy Ghost," Tit. iii. 5.   7.   Pardoning and healing mercy, as appears in his compassion to this man, that was wounded by thieves.   8.   Supporting, confirming, comforting, and preserving mercy ; it is the sure mercies of David, because covenant-mercy.   9.   Free mercy, to set up desert or merit, is to destroy mercy.   "I will love them freely." 10. Overflowing or boundless mercy. He is plenteous in mercy; as full of mercy and compassion, as the sea is full of water, or the sun full of light.   11.   Soul-espousing and soul-enriching mercy.   " I will betroth thee to me in loving-kindness and mercy," Hos. ii. 19.   12.   Eternal, abiding, or everlasting mercy.   " The mercy of the Lord endureth for ever," Psal. ciii. 17.   His mercy and compassion fails not.

APPLICATION

1.   Learn to trust in Christ, and call upon him, say with the poor child lately, of four years old, " Lord Jesus save me, Lord Jesus save me."   What is God about to do, and what an unbelieving and Christ-contemning age is this !

2.   Take heed of abusing the mercy and compassion of Christ, he is a Lamb, but when provoked will appear like a lion ; labour to see the need you have of his compassion, how indigent you are, and pray him to pour his golden oil into your empty vessels.

3.   Strive to be like Christ, let us imitate him in mercy and compassion, to such that are in misery, and show that we are good neighbours.

4.   How amiable and lovely doth goodness and mercy render God, and from hence let us fear him.   " There is mercy with thee, that thou mayest be feared."

5. Know, O sinners, your destruction is of yourselves, though your help is in Christ.

6. Dare any say Christ is not willing to save them, to heal them, and ease them of all their pains and sorrows ? Heb. vii. 25.

2ndly. Exhortation. Come to him, venture your souls upon him, he has power as well as compassion. Miss not the day of your visitation; delay not one moment, your wounds stink and are corrupt. He can heal the worst of wounds, or cure the greatest of sin- Heb. vii. 25. ners. Your ignorance is not a hindrance to him. " He hath compassion of the ignorant, and them out of the way," Heb. v. 2.

Lastly. Praise the holy God for sending such a helper, such a Saviour, one willing, able, and mighty to save ; who can speak in a way of righteousness, as well as in a Isa. lxiii. 1 way of mercy and compassion.

" And went to him and bound up his wounds, pouring in oil and wine." Ver. 34.

From hence observe.

Doct. That Jesus Christ is the only Physician of our soul.

Like as a physician heals the diseases of the body, so he heals all the spiritual distempers of our souls.

I. I shall show in what respect Christ may be called a Physician.

II. Prove he is the only Physician of the soul.

1. Christ hath licence, yea full authority from the King of heaven and earth, to be the Physician of our souls ; " For him hath God the Father sealed," John vi. 27. He received a commission, and it was miraculously sealed by the king's broad seal, " This is my beloved Son." Christ authorised to cure our souls.

2. In respect of his great skill, wisdom, and ability : a physician ought to be a skilful person, knowing the nature, kinds, causes, and what will cure all distempers of the body. (1.) The Lord Jesus knows all chronical, habitual, Christ a wise and skilful Physician. inveterate, stubborn, and contumacious diseases of the soul, from such that are acute, occasioned by heat or cold ; I mean by some sudden temptation or infection, by means of the corrupt air or place where cast : he knows the nature of sin, original and actual, and whether deadly or but common weaknesses ; and so the spots of his own people ; he knows whether the disease be radicated and habitual or not, a disease of unregeneracy, or only such as attends a renewed person. (2.) Whether it be the stone of a hard heart, or the timpany of pride, or the consumption of spiritual strength, courage, faith, love, zeal, or of any other grace of the Spirit ; or whether it be the giddiness of the head, for want of a good judgment and understanding in the truths of the gospel, a distemper too many are troubled withal in these times ; or whether it be the feebleness of the knees that cannot bend day and night before the Most High God, nor bear burdens ; or the weakness of the hands, some cannot lift them up to God, nor stretch them forth towards upholding the interest of Christ, the support of his ministers, and the poor saints : he knows all predominant, nauseous, and evil humours, which must be purged out, suppressed, or dispersed, by letting of blood in mortification ; or whether the distemper arises from unbelief, worldly-mindedness, or for want of watchfulness, neglect of prayer, or hearing of the word. Jesus Christ also knows the constitution, or natural inclination of every soul, whether most addicted to this or that sin, or pride, passion, the inordinate love of this word, or of a slothful disposition.

3. The Lord Jesus useth fit, proper, and suitable preparations to dispose the soul to seek after, and receive a cure, i. e., by making the sinner sensible of his state, by the convictions of his Spirit, and putting him upon prayer. Christ

4. Christ, like a wise physician, searcheth the festering wounds of every searches all soul that he undertakes to cure, to prevent the danger that would otherwise men's hearts. ensue upon their being but slightly healed, " They have healed the hurt of the daughter of my people slightly, crying, peace, peace, when there is no peace," Jer. vi. 14. To prevent this Jesus Christ lays open the wound, " I am he that searcheth the heart and the reins ;" that is, the secret thoughts, motions, ends, counsels, and designs of all men's hearts.

5. The Lord Christ, in desperate cases, directs to cut off corrupt members, though it be a right hand, or right foot, and to pull out a right eye ; these rotten members of the body of sin which offend, must be mortified," Mark ix. 43, 44.

6. Christ also, like a gentle physician, deals tenderly with poor wounded and distressed sinners, in binding up their wounds, as appears in this parable, " He will not break the bruised reed, nor quench the smoking flax," Isa. xl. 3, Matt. xi. 28. He calls all that are weary and heavy laden, to come to him. O how ready is he to apply his healing balm to a wounded soul.

7. Jesus Christ makes a right and timely application to sin-sick sinners ; he doth not prescribe corrosives, when he should give cordials, not the terrors of the law to broken spirits but the comfort of free promises ; the oil of gladness, and wine of consolation he knows is proper for such.

Christ tells sinners the worst of their state.   8. Jesus Christ deals plainly with sinners, he will let them know the worst, whether death is like to ensue or not, "If ye believe not that I am he, ye shall die in your sins," John viii. 24. "He that believed not shall be damned," Mark xvi. 16. "Verily, verily, I say into thee, except a man be born again, he cannot see the kingdom of God," John iii. 3. "Except ye repent, ye shall all likewise perish," Luke xiii. 3.

9. Christ, like a faithful physician, often visits sinners, he is ready always at their doors, and at a call ; nay he sits up with his saints all the night of their sorrow and affliction ; " Lo, I am always with you to the end of the world," Matt xxviii. 20.

10. Jesus Christ prescribes rules to his saints, to preserve their souls in health, how to avoid all spiritual surfeits, *i. e.,* all inordinate excess, or use of this world, or enjoyment of the creature, " Take heed lest at any time your hearts be overcharged by surfeiting and drunkenness, and the cares of this life," &c. Luke xxi. 34. To keep good and pious company, and to avoid the wicked ; moreover, to live upon good food, wholesome diet, to hear good doctrine, and not to feed on the wind, or chaff of the idle and airy notions, and to be frequent in prayer. He speak a parable to this purpose, " that man should always pray," Luke xviii. 1. He also directs to reading and meditation, and to holy watchfulness, &c.

11. Christ, like a tender physician, rejoices to see his medicines have the desired effects on sinners, and on the souls of believers, when his word operates, when it abides in them, and when it cleanses and purifies their hearts and consciences, or gives them peace and inward joy and comfort in believing.

12. He gives his cordial to such that are ready to faint. "I had fainted unless I believed," Psal. xxvii. 13. For which cause we faint not. His spirit will raise the dead, as well as revive from deadness.

II. Jesus Christ is the only physician, and exceeds all others.

1. God hath appointed none else ; " There is no other name given under heaven, whereby we must be saved," Acts iv. 12.

2. None else are able to help or save us, they have no healing medicines, not the oil and wine to pour into our wounds, there is nothing can cure sinners but Christ's blood, nor clothe their naked souls but his righteousness. " Whither shall we go ? thou hast the words of everlasting life," John vi. 68. They that depend on any other thing or object, shall perish eternally.

3. Because no sinner, from the beginning of the world to this day, was healed and saved by any other physician, means or medicine. " By the deeds of the law shall no flesh be justified," Rom. iii. 20. " It was impossible that the blood of bulls or goats could take away sin," Heb. 10. 4. "If righteousness be by the law, Christ is dead in vain"—the law kills. Christ is choice, and the best physician, excelling all physicians, Gal. ii. 21. and iii. 21. (1.) In respect of his infinite knowledge, and deep judgment; he cannot be deceived, nor be mistaken about the state of any person, "because he knows all men, and what is in man," John ii. 24. Yea, he knows the nature and cause of all diseases, and so doth none else in the world. (2.) Other physicians sometime, for want of skill or care, kill instead of curing the sick ; but Jesus Christ never undertook the cure of one soul that died under his hand. (3.) Christ can as easily raise the dead to life, as he can heal the living.

(4.) Other physicians are mercenary, do all for money, sometimes are unreasonable, but Christ doth work all his cures freely ; " without money, and without price," Isa. lv. 1, 2. He received nothing of this poor man, but was at all the charge of the inn, and paid the host. (5.) Other physicians will not come to the sick until they are sent for, nor perhaps then neither, if there be no hopes of money ; but Christ came without our sending for. " I am found of them that sought me not," Isa. lxv. 1. (6.) Other physicians cannot bless their physic nor medicines, but Christ can, and always doth, when any cure is wrought ; he quickens whom he will ; he makes his word to prosper to them to whom it

Crist is the poor man's physician.   is sent. (7.) Other physicians attend the rich chiefly, but Jesus Christ is the poor man's physician, such that are poor in this world. The poor receive the gospel, but more especially such who are spiritually poor, little, nothing in their own eyes. The rich he sends empty away. The whole need not a physician. Self-righteous persons Christ came not to call, they are not sick. (8.) Should other physicians, when they come to the sick, be kept out of their houses, and let to stand knocking all night, they would come no more. But though this physician has been many times thus dealt with, yet his mercy is not dried up, nor his patience worn out. " Behold I stand at the door and knock," Rev. iii. 20. (9.) What physician would die to cure his patients, pour forth his own blood to make a balm to heal their distempers? Jesus Christ did thus, he poured out his own blood to heal our wounded souls.

Christ must die if he heals our souls.

> Canst thou be sick and such a doctor by?
> Thou canst not live unless thy doctor die.
> Strange kind of grief, that finds no medicine good
> To asswage her pains, but the physician's blood!

F. QUARLES.

Quest. What way doth Christ heal sick and wounded sinners?

Answ. It is (as you have heard) by his own blood, which was shed to satisfy the law and justice of God, that we are healed of the guilt of sin, by the application of the virtue thereof to our souls, through the Spirit. The word is said to heal us here, i. e., it makes known the only way of our cure, and in its promises gives us encouragement to believe. Faith is likewise said to heal or justify us, but it is only objectively, or in respect of Christ: by faith we apprehend, receive, or apply Christ's blood, merits, and righteousness to ourselves, or to our wounded souls, when we believe we are healed of the guilt and filth of sin. O what a physician is Jesus Christ !

How Christ heals sinners.

> 'Tis either thou must bleed, sick soul, or I ;
> My blood is a cordial : he that suck'd my veins
> Shall cleanse his own, and conquer greater pains
> Than these : cheer up, this precious blood of mine
> Shall cure thy grief, my heart shall bleed for thine.
> Believe and view me with a faithful eye,
> Thy soul shall neither languish, bleed, nor die.

QUARLES.

It must be the wine that flows from the veins of the true vine, and the oil of the true olive-tree, that must be poured into our wounds ; and this applied by faith, purges and purifies our hearts, or works holiness and sanctification in us, and so heals us of all our sores.

APPLICATION

1. We infer, that the ignorance of some men is very great and dangerous. (1.) Such as think their prayers and tears can heal their souls. (2.) Such who apply or trust in their own righteousness. (3.) Such that think their faith is a habit or act, doth heal or justify them, as the material cause thereof ; that God will accept of their sincere obedience, though imperfect, instead of a perfect obedience to the law ; or deny that Christ's righteousness, as imputed to us, is the matter of our justification in the sight of God.

2. Exhort. Sinner, thou art mortally wounded. O fly to this physician ; if Christ heals thee not, thou must die eternally. (1.) Know that Christ can heal thee, let thy disease be what it will. (2.) He is not only able, but also very ready, and willing : " Come unto me, all ye that labour and are heavy laden, and I will give you rest," Matt. xi. 28. (3.) He is now come, and stands knocking at the door. (4.) He will make a perfect cure, yea cure thee for ever. (5.) Thou mayest have a cure, though thou hast no money, no righteousness, no worthiness in thyself, no qualifications, or nothing to recommend thee to him, but art in thy sins wounded, and ready to bleed to death.

3. Trial. Art thou healed, not slightly, but effectually, thoroughly healed ? Try thyself. (1.) Have thy wounds been seared and laid open ? Wast thou ever put to pain by the cutting and piercing convictions of the Spirit ? (2.) Hast thou found thyself sick at heart, sick of sin ? Is sin thy sorrow, thy sickness ? Hast thou been restless, like a sick man, and roared out as David speaks ? Psal. xxxviii. 5, 6. Hast thou found thy wounds stink, i.e., sin loathsome to thee, like corrupt and putrefying sores ? Hast thou not applied some false remedy to cure thy sick and wounded soul ? Hast thou made use of no balm, but the blood of Christ ? Dost thou rest on nothing but a crucified Saviour ? (4.) Hath the portion of physic stayed with thee, i.e., the word, or promises, abode in thy heart ? Some vomit up that dose that is given to them ; so the word doth not abide in some sinners ; nothing will stay with them, such persons are in a dangerous condition. (5.) Doth thy sickness abate, is sin weakened ? Some under the cure, under the word,

grow worse and worse, that is a sign death will ensue, even eternal death. (6.) Doth Christ's physic work with thee? What operation hath the word and Spirit on thy soul? does it purge out thy sins, and cleanse thy heart? or has it wrought a thorough change upon thee? (7.) Canst thou relish or taste a sweetness in the word? When a sick person hath no stomach, cannot eat nor relish his food, it is a bad sign. Dost thou taste that God is good, Christ precious, the word sweeter than honey to thy soul? (8.) Art thou averse to all sin, and hatest vain thoughts, and evil company? (9.) Dost thou cry out to thy physician for help at the least appearance, or return of thy distemper, by a sudden temptation? is thy heart set against all sin, and doth thy will oppose and resist it, so that thou canst say with Paul, "It is no more I, but sin that dwelleth in me," Rom. vii. 17? (10.) Hast thou got strength to walk, to go out into a visible profession, and walk in all the commandments of Christ? (11.) Dost thou make no provision for the flesh, nor feed thy distemper? some do thus. (12.) Canst thou take reproof kindly, or be easily convinced of thy sin, as soon as told of it? and say, "I have sinned against the Lord?" 2 Sam. xii. 13. Some excuse themselves, extenuate, nay, may be deny their sin; but a gracious person will rather greaten his sin, and cry out against his evil heart, than hide or lessen it. (13.) Art thou easy stopped in any undue or disorderly practice, and brought presently to leave it, and turn from it? (14.) Art thou the same in private as in public? (15.) Dost thou mourn most before God, for such evils that appear least before men? (16.) Hath no one sin power over thee, or dominion in thee; Rom. vi. 14, so that thou dost not obey it, but dost make resistance against it? and is the opposition universal, i.e., against all sin? (17.) Dost thou love holiness, is it most amiable in thy sight? and art thou as much in love with the duties of religion and godliness, as with the wages thereof? and is it because God hates sin, that thou darest not commit it? some avoid it, because it causeth shame here, and ruin hereafter. By these things thou mayest know whether thou art cured or not.

4. Terror. How fearful is your state that slight and cast off this Physician, and count his blood as an unholy or useless thing?

5. Caution. Do not delay; will a man mortally wounded say, I will look out for help, for balm to heal me hereafter? O cry those about him, he is insensible, fetch a physician presently. Nothing is more dangerous than delaying looking to Christ.

Take heed you refuse not the remedy, because of the pain of pulling out of a right-eye, or cutting off a right-hand lust.

6. You that are healed, see you ascribe all the glory to Christ, none of it to yourselves, to your care, wisdom, industry, nor to the instruments; what is Paul, or what is Apollos?

IV

Pouring in oil and wine.—Luke x. 34.

DOCT. Christ, who is our only Physician, makes use of fit and proper medicines, to heal sick and wounded sinners.

I. I shall show you, why the blood of Christ is compared to wine.

II. Why the Spirit is compared to oil.

III. What is meant by pouring of it into his wounds.

I. Wine is a precious thing; the best of earthly things is set forth by corn, oil, and wine. We read of wine, as that which cheers God and man: "And the vine said, shall I leave my wine which cheereth God and man?" Numb. xv. 5, 7, 10, &c. Mr. Pool thinks that wine here refers to the wine used in legal sacrifices, and I am of the same opinion; but

How wine cheers the heart of God. — it must then refer chiefly to Christ's blood, which was typified thereby: for God was not pleased with any of those bare sacrifices, but as they were types of Jesus Christ, the substance of them. True, the blood of Christ, the fruit of the true vine, satisfies the justice of God, and it is the only cordial that cheers the heart of man, who drinketh thereof by faith. The healing and comforting virtue of Christ's blood, is meant by wine in this place no doubt.

1. Wine is a choice liquor; so the blood of Christ, that sacred wine, is a most precious thing. (1.) Considering the excellency and dignity of his person. (2.) Considering the end and design of God in pouring of it forth. (3.) In respect of the effects and

virtue of it. (1.) It is pacifying and wrath-appeasing blood. (2.) it is justice-satisfying, and God-reconciling blood. (3.) Redeeming blood : " We are redeemed with the precious blood of Christ," 1 Pet. i. 18, 19. Is the blood of the saints precious to God ? What is then the blood of his own Son? (4.) It is purifying blood, it is that which purges our consciences. (5.) It is purchasing blood, as well as cleansing, we are bought with this price : God purchased the church, and grace and glory for his church, with his own blood, Acts xx. 28. (6.) It is pardoning blood, without the shedding of Christ's blood there is no remission of sin. (7.) It is pleading blood, it cries to God for us : the cry of sin, of the law, and of justice is against us ; but the blood of Christ outcries *The preciousness of Christ's blood.* them, and pleads for us continually, it speaks better things than the blood of Abel. (8.) It is softening and mollifying blood ; it breaks a hard heart, yea, the heart of stone. Hence the Lord applied it to this poor wretch. (9.) It is quickening blood ; it hath a quickening and reviving virtue in it. Unless we drink Christ's blood, we have no life in us, John vi. 33, 34. (10.) It is justifying blood ; justification is not without the blood of Christ : " Much more being justified by his blood, we shall be saved from wrath through him," Rom. v. 9. (11.) It is soul-healing and soul-saving blood. May wine be called precious, much more is the blood of Christ precious. *Christ's blood esteemed above wine.*

2. Wine is highly esteemed by all that know its virtue, so is the blood of Christ ; all believers who know its virtue, value it above all things in this world.

3. Wine, naturalists say, is most excellent to heal sores and wounds, if it be rightly applied : so had not this wine a healing virtue in it, the good Samaritan had not poured it into the poor man's wounds. The blood of Christ only heals our sores, " By his stripes we are healed, Isa. liii. 5.

4. Wine is sweet and pleasant to the taste ; but O how much more sweet and pleasant is the virtue of the blood of Christ, to a believing sinner ! " My blood is drink indeed," John vi. 55.

5. Wine is a restorative, and greatly strengthens decayed nature ; the blood of Christ is the only restorative of our languishing souls ; it quickens and brings to life, as well as strengthens such it hath restored.

6. Wine comforts and cheers the hearts of such that are ready to faint, and are ready to die ; nothing cheers, comforts, and revives a sinking, drooping, and fainting sinner like the virtue of Christ's blood received by faith. " I had fainted, unless I had believed," &c., Psal. xxvii. 13.

II. Why is the Spirit compared to oil ? he poured in oil as well as wine. *What is meant by oil.*

Answ. The Holy Spirit, and the graces of the Spirit, may be compared to oil. *See the parable of the ten virgins.*

1. Oil is of a softening and mollifying nature, and a most sovereign thing to assuage all hard swellings and tumours of the body. So the Spirit and graces thereof soften a hard heart. God complains that the sores of his people " were not bound up, nor mollified with ointment," Isa. i. 6. *Why the Holy Spirit is compared to oil.*

Grace will soon bring down the timpany of pride, and bow the obstinate and rebellious will.

2. Oil is known to all to be of a healing nature, it searches into the bottom of sores : so the Holy Spirit searches the heart of the sinner ; there is no sin, nor secret lusts, but it will find and purge it out, and then heal the wounds those sins had made.

3. Oil expels poison. Pliny saith it is contrary to scorpions, and in a wonderful manner expels dangerous venom ; and secures the vitals from the penetrating power and poison thereof.

My brethren, the Holy Spirit is directly contrary to that old serpent the devil, and it expels all the venom and poison of sin (especially as to its power and dominion in the soul) and it secures that vital principle that is in believers, against all the hellish venom of every sin. " Walk in the Spirit, and ye shall not fulfil the lusts of the flesh," Gal. v. 16.

4. Pliny also tells us, that oil is excellent good to open all obstructions, and so help them that cannot breathe freely, the Holy Spirit, when Christ pours it into a sinners heart, it will open his heart and mouth too, to cry mightily to God. Before grace sinners cannot pray ; they cannot breathe freely, till God " pours out upon them the Spirit of grace and supplication," Zech. xii. 10. No, there is not a sinner in the world can breathe forth his desires to God, until this spiritual oil hath opened all those obstructions they naturally are attended with. " Behold he prays," Acts ix. 19. O know he has received the Spirit of prayer. " We know not what we should pray for as we ought, but the Spirit itself maketh intercession for us, with groanings which cannot be uttered," Rom. viii. 26.

5. Oil, physicians and naturalists say, is good to clear the eyes.   Pliny saith it disperseth mists and clouds, that cause dimness of sight.

The Holy Spirit cleareth the eyes of the understanding, " The eyes of your understanding being enlightened, that you may know what is the hope of your calling," &c., Eph. i.
18.   The Holy Spirit is a Spirit of illumination.

6.   Some oil is exceeding good against shakings, tremblings, and convulsions, which
many are afflicted with.   So the Holy Spirit, the Spirit of faith, is a present remedy
against all the tremblings of the heart in times of dismal calamities.   He that believes and
trusteth in God, God will keep in perfect peace. " At what time I am afraid (saith David)
I will trust in thee."   The Spirit and graces thereof make a believer fearless in evil times,
when fearful convulsions seize upon all others. " Though I walk through the valley of
the shadow of death, I will fear no evil," Psal. xxiii. 4.

7.   The weak joints and limbs of babes, or others (arising from several causes) being
anointed with oil, it will strengthen them greatly; but you must not suppose these virtues
are in all sorts of oil.   Now since some oil hath so many excellent properties in them,
and is good in so many distempers, it is no wonder it is mentioned here, to set forth the
healing virtue of the Holy Spirit, and the saving graces of it : the weak hands and feeble
knees, hereby will be greatly strengthened, as all weak Christians daily experience, so
that they are enabled to leap as an hart.

III.   Why must this wine and oil be poured into the wounds of poor sinners.

Application
of   Christ's
blood neces-
sary.
Answ.   To show that Christ's blood, without the Spirit and grace of the
Spirit, can heal no sinner : we must have the Holy Spirit, and true faith in
Christ, whereby we have his blood and merits applied to our wounded souls,
if ever we are thoroughly healed.

APPLICATION

1.   O the love of our spiritual Physician ! What, heal our wounds by the application
of his blood ! he must pour forth his heart's blood to cure us ; it is not a drop of his
blood, by pricking or opening of a vein will do ; no, he must die, if we ever live again.

2.   When you see wine, remember Christ's blood ; wine is appointed in the Lord's
supper to be poured forth and received by us, to bring to our remembrance how we
came to be restored and healed of all our diseases.

3.   Rest not, presume not on Christ's death, or on the shedding of his blood, unless it
be applied to you by the Spirit, and true faith be wrought in your souls.

4.   He poured in oil and wine.   As Christ prepared the remedy, so he only applies it,
he makes use of our hand, of our faith ; " But faith is not of ourselves, it is the gift of
God," Eph. ii. 8, Gal. v. 22.   Faith is a fruit of the Spirit.

5.   Examine yourselves, whether you have received the mollifying and healing virtue
of this spiritual oil ; and when you see oil, remember the nature of the oil of the Spirit
and grace thereof, and ascribe your health and cure to Jesus Christ.

" And set him on his own beast," Ver. 34.

What meant
by his own
beast
" On his own beast :" I told you his own beast may mean, his own blessed
doctrine of free-grace, or the holy doctrine of the gospel, together with the
precepts thereof : this I conclude may be meant hereby, because the apostle shows, a
doctrine may be said to carry a person in a spiritual way, as a beast doth carry us in an
external way. " Be not carried about with divers and strange doctrines," Heb. xiii. 9.
False and strange doctrines carry a poor shattered professor this way and that way, and
he knows not whither, like a head-strong beast ; but Christ's true doctrine, and holy precepts, carry believers to an inn, i. e., to some true gospel congregation, where Christ takes
care of them.   But O what wild beasts do some men ride upon in these evil days ; what
strange notions and doctrines do they suffer to carry them about, and seldom rest long
anywhere : they are not carried to the inn, where Christ would have them be, but rather
from it, they are unsettled, unestablished persons ; some observing Jewish days, and others
plead for human rites and ceremonies, which profit them not.

The inn may
mean   a
church   of
Christ.
" And brought him to an inn."   The inn I intimated at first, may intend
a true gospel church ; for all know thither the doctrine and ordinances of
Christ do carry believers, when they are at first converted : those that were
healed, or wrought upon by the preaching of St. Peter, were commanded to be baptized,
Acts ii. 26--
40.
and so were carried, or added to the church ; and in the same manner were
they at Samaria, Acts viii. 12, 14.   Christ's holy doctrine and ordinances
carried all believers, as soon as converted in the primitive times, to one inn or church,

or another, where Christ provided an host, or a faithful minister, to watch over them, feed and take care of them.

Doct.   A church of Jesus Christ may be compared to an inn.

This will appear, if we consider these things following.

Why   the
church   is
compared to
an inn.

1.   An inn is a place to entertain travellers, whilst they pass from one place or country to another ; even so a church or congregation of saints is a place to entertain godly Christians, whilst they pass through the wilderness of this world to the heavenly Jerusalem, or from the valley of tears to the mount of joy.

2.   In an inn there is an host, who is to take care of, and make the guests that come thither welcome, and to provide all things for them they need ; so in a church there is a pastor, who is ready to receive all that Jesus Christ brings to this spiritual inn, and to make them welcome, and to feed them like a good householder (or innkeeper) with things both new and old.

3.   An inn ought to be well stored or provided with all things that travellers want, so ought a church of Christ to have whatsoever is necessary to refresh, clear, strengthen, and comfort the souls of the people, who are members thereof.

4.   An inn ought to be well governed, and no disorders be suffered or allowed of : so ought a church of Christ to keep up and maintain a right and godly discipline, and no disorderly person allowed to dwell or abide therein, but be turned out, if they are unruly.

5.   An inn is a place for all sorts of travellers to lodge in, both noble and ignoble, even persons of all degrees and quality, sometimes the king may lodge in an inn.   So a church is a place for all sorts of Christians, both young and old, poor and rich, high and low ; a king, if godly, ought to take up his lodging in it.

6.   An inn is the only place where wounded or sick travellers can find, or meet with comfort and refreshment, and the innkeeper is to receive them, and not let them lie in the street.   So a church of Christ is appointed as a place of refreshment for such believers who are sick or wounded in Spirit, where they meet with convenient food, and sweet repose ; and the pastor, like a tender host, is to minister comfort to them, or " to comfort such who are cast down, with the same comfort wherewith they themselves are comforted of God," 2 Cor. i. 2, 3, 4.   There is in an inn all sorts of food ; a traveller may have whatsoever he pleaseth, either milk or strong meat, so in a church there is food for all sorts of Christians, even for babes, for strong men and fathers ; the milk of the word, as well as such doctrine that is compared to strong meat, Heb. v. 12, 13, 14.

7.   An inn must not refuse such that are desolate ; and though the traveller is very poor, yet if he hath a friend that promises he will pay the host all the charge he is at, he will readily entertain such, so a church is not to refuse the poorest saint, though never so desolate : and it is a shame to that congregation that refuses any such, because Jesus Christ hath engaged to pay all charge and pains they are at, when he comes again.

8.   The door of an inn ought to stand open all the day long, for all comers that want rest and refreshment ; yet care ought to be had of such that are cheats or thieves.   So the door of a church is opened by Christ for all sincere believers who want spiritual refreshment ; but they must come in at the door Christ hath appointed, and not thrust themselves into the church in a disorderly manner ; also it behoveth the pastor and church to examine well all suspected persons, to see they are sincere or faithful, and not hypocrites, or such who are counterfeit Christians, who seek Christ for loaves, or out of and by sinister ends.

9.   An inn nevertheless sometimes, through the ignorance of the host, or such that dwell therein, or for want of care, or through the craftiness of some deceitful persons who pretend they are honest travellers, entertain and lodge evil persons.   So a church ofttimes through ignorance, or want of care in the pastor, or by means of the subtilty and craftiness of some cunning people, let such in who cause great trouble to all that lodge in it, and expose religion to the reproach of the world.

10. An inn is a very desirable place to weary travellers, and also a safe place when thieves are abroad.   So a church of Christ is a desirable place to a soul that is weary and under many weights, being tired out by temptations.   " One thing I have desired of the Lord, and that will I seek after, that I may dwell in the house of the Lord for ever," &c., Psal. xxvii. 4.   He longed for the courts of God's house, as some weary travellers long for an inn.   One day in God's courts was better to David than a thousand : " My soul longeth, yea, fainteth for the courts of the Lord," &c., Psal. lxxxiv. 2.

11. An inn is not a place to abide long in, the traveller takes up his lodging there but for a night.   So the church militant is a place for us to abide in but a short time, i. e.. during

the night of our mortality. Heaven, or the church triumphant, is our lasting dwelling-place; that is, our home, and thither we are a travelling.

Secondly, The church, or spiritual inn, exceeds all inns.

The church excels all inns.   1. In other inns there is nothing to be had without money; if a man has no money, nor credit, he is no guest for them, but a church of Christ feeds all freely; all is at Christ's cost, he pays the host, and bears all the charges of all that come thither, all is of free-grace, we pay for none of the fat things of God's house. "We have milk and honey without money, and without price," Isa. lv. 1, 2. We are bid to "take the water of life freely," Rev. xxii. 17.

2. A man that comes to lodge in an inn, though he hath good entertainment, yet he is not satisfied, nor contented to stay there, but would be gone; but in God's house is all soul-content and satisfaction, and a believer desires to dwell there all the days of his life. Psal. xxvii. 4.

3. An inn is not a traveller's home or dwelling-place; but the church or house of God is a saint's own dwelling-place, it is his Father's habitation, the place where the Lord **God dwells in his church.** desires to dwell for ever; and therefore believers desire to dwell there always likewise. O how sweet is the presence of God and Christ in Sion, and what glory of his shines forth therein!

4. The food of this inn excels all food, and the privileges all privileges, and the rest all rest, and the company all company.

5. In some inns there is no room, it is so full of guests; there was no room for Mary in the inn: but in the house of God and heart of God, there is room enough, though hundreds, nay, thousands come thither, yet there is room: we read of three thousand that came to one of these inns in one day, and all had room enough. Acts ii. 41.

APPLICATION

1. Bless God that there is a place of entertainment, and of spiritual repose and refreshment for poor weary travellers, or for such who are going to heaven. Christ hath well provided for us in our journey, that we may not be exposed to wants, dangers, and necessities, in respect of our souls, while we are in this world.

2. We infer, that great ignorance and folly attend many Christians, who are going to heaven, in that they refuse to take up their lodging in this inn, and rather choose to lie without doors. Hath God provided this place, built his house for all his children to dwell in; and doth "he love to dwell in Zion, and love the gates thereof more than all the dwelling places of Jacob;" and is his presence there, and will "he bless the provision of his house," and have all the saints prized a dwelling in it; and shall any of God's children refuse to dwell therein? this is sad. What, would they rather be "fed as a lamb in a large place?" it is a sign of much ignorance and folly: perhaps they do it to save charge, and to seek their bread where they can find it, God forbid;

3. You that are spiritual travellers, may from hence learn where you should take up your lodging whilst you are on your journey: know Christ hath many inns, and you that are yet without may choose what inn you like best, but be sure see it is one of Christ's inns, one of his churches, and where he dwells.

4. This may caution churches and pastors to take care who they let in, or what travellers they receive and entertain; also to see good order kept, or a right discipline maintained in their respective congregations, that all weary travellers who lodge in them, may take their quiet repose.

There are many other uses which I will leave you to make.

V

And took care of him.—Luke x. 34.

DOCT. Jesus Christ takes care of all them that he heals, pardons, and brings into his church.

Christ takes care of all his saints.   1. He takes care of their souls, bodies, and all things else; he is their Shepherd as well as their physician: "the Lord is my Shepherd, I shall not want," Psal. xxiii. 1. We are put into the hand of Christ to heal, to renew, to quicken, to strengthen, to feed, to comfort, to clothe, to guide and lead us: and all things he hath undertaken to do, and will certainly perform; for many reasons that might be given, some of which here follow.

1. Christus will take care of believers, brought to God, or into his house. Why Christ takes care of his saints.

(1.) Because they are his, they are his own by election, and by free donation, the Father gave them to him; his by redemption, he bought them with the price of his own blood; his by adoption, his by regeneration; they are his friends, his children, nay, his beloved spouse; believers are the bride of Christ.

(2.) Because he entered into covenant with the Father, not only to come into this world to restore, heal, renew, and quicken them, but also to preserve, to keep, and to provide for them all things they want, so long as they are in this world: he hath undertaken to begin the good work; and what says the apostle, "Being confident of this very thing, that he that hath begun a good work in you, will perform it to the day of Christ," Phil. i. 6, or to the day of their death.

(3.) Because he knows their weakness, and how unable they are to help themselves; he knows their impotency, or their inability to stand one moment without him, without his care, his protection and preservation of them. "Without me ye can do nothing," John xv. 5. Ye cannot resist temptations, ye cannot continue in believing and resting upon me: our faith would fail, did not Christ strengthen it day by day; the sap is in the root, that makes the tree to grow. "The branches bear fruit of themselves." Christ also must prune them; all our fruitfulness is from him. "From me is thy fruit found," Hos. xiv. 8.

(4.) Because they have resigned themselves up unto Christ, wholly to rest upon him, and to be cared for by him, taught, justified, pardoned, strengthened, healed, guided, and comforted by him. "The poor committeth himself to thee, thou art the helper of the fatherless," Psal. x. 14. Will a faithful man fail to take care of the poor fatherless children, who are left wholly to his oversight, care, protection, and provision, who have committed themselves to him, and to his care and faithfulness, after he hath also undertaken the care and charge of them? no, he hates the thoughts of betraying so great a trust; much more then will not Christ fail, nor leave any poor helpless saint, who wholly committeth himself to him. "I know whom I have believed, and am persuaded he is able to keep that which I have committed unto him against that day," 2 Tim. i. 12. What was that which Paul had committed unto Christ, but his precious soul, and the souls of all those under his charge? it is said, the saints "gave themselves unto the Lord," 2 Cor. viii. 5. They durst not venture themselves in their own hands, to stand by their own power, or by the power of any inherent grace they had received, but to go to him for all future supplies of grace, and divine aid and assistance.

(5.) Christ will take the care of them, because none else is able; none but the blessed God can keep them, or is capable to take the care of them. As they cannot keep themtelves, so ministers (to whom a charge is given to watch over them) are not able to preserve and keep them from falling, or to support and strengthen their souls; no, though they are never so faithful, yet is not in their power to do it. Christ only is clothed with might, and with everlasting strength to do it, he hath only the ear of God, he only is our Mediator and Intercessor; and what is his business now in heaven, but to take care of his saints on earth, and to intercede to the Father for them? "Wherefore he is able to save to the uttermost all that come to God by him, seeing he ever liveth to make intercession for them," Heb. vii. 25.

(6.) Because believers have many cruel enemies, who continually seek to destroy them, and are also attended with manifold wants, which must be supplied out of his own fulness.

(7.) Because all grace and supplies of whatsoever we want, is put into the hands of Jesus Christ, for him to give forth to us at all times of need. Like as Pharaoh put all the corn of the land of Egypt into the hands of Joseph: and when they came to Pharaoh for bread, he sent them to Joseph, so the Father sends all believers, all his children to his Son, our Lord Jesus Christ, when they need anything for their souls and bodies. "Of his fulness have all we received and grace for grace," John i. 16. "But my God shall supply all your need according to his riches in glory, by Christ Jesus," Phil. iv. 19. See the pearl of great price.

(8.) Because of his promises; he hath made many gracious promises, to help, and take care of his saints at all times, even in afflictions, and when they fall into great tribulations for his sake. "When thou passest through the waters, I will be with thee; and through the rivers, they shall not overflow thee; when thou walkest through the fire, thou shalt not be burnt," Isa. xliii. 2. "Fear thou not, for I am with thee, be not dismayed, for I am thy God, I will strengthen thee, yea, I will help thee, yea, I will uphold thee with the right hand of my righteousness. Again he saith, fear not, thou worm Jacob, and ye men of Israel, I will help thee, saith the Lord, and thy Redeemer. I will open rivers in high places, and fountains in the midst of the valleys," Isa. xliii. 10, 14. 18. " I will never leave thee, nor forsake thee," Heb. xiii. 5. " Verily thou shall be fed." " He will give grace and glory, and no good thing will he withhold from them that walk uprightly," Psal. lxxxiv. 11.

APPLICATION

This may be for reprehension to such who affirm, there is a possibility, that true believers may totally and finally fall and perish for ever; if that be so, then our standing is not by grace, nor by reason we are put into Christ's hand, but it is by our own power, our own care, or by means of our own diligence. My brethren, though we must be careful, watchful, and diligent, yet it is Christ only that keeps us in that watchful and diligent frame of heart; we are not only ordained to believe, but to be fruitful, " And that our fruit should remain," John xv. 16.

2.   This may tend also to reprove such poor, weak believers, who fear they shall fall, and not be able to hold out to the end. O take from hence a sharp rebuke; what hath Jesus Christ taken the care of us, to feed, heal, strengthen, and succour us at all times, and to preserve us unto his heavenly kingdom, and yet do you fear you shall one day perish by this sin, or the other corruption, or temptation ? will you cast such contempt upon the ever blessed and faithful Jesus ? he took care of this poor man he brought to the inn, so he takes care of every one of us; sure you know not, or at least consider not on whom you have believed, and committed the keeping of your souls.

3.   This also may be of use by way of exhortation. " O be persuaded to cast all your care upon Jesus Christ, since he careth for you," 1 Pet. v. 7. It is needless for us to be over-careful, nay, and it is a great evil to be distrustfully careful. Unbelief is the greatest sin ; it renders God unfaithful, who hath promised to keep us by his mighty power, through faith to salvation. Also as you can commit the care and keeping of your souls to Christ, so be exhorted to commit the care and keeping of your bodies, your families, your estates, your liberties, your lives ; and all your secular concerns to him also, can you commit the greater things to him, and not the lesser ?

On the morrow when he departed, he took two-pence and gave them to the host.

This I humbly conceive refers to our Saviour's ascension, when he gave his blessed Spirit and gifts unto men. By the two-pence may be meant, as I intimated, the gifts and graces of the Holy Ghost, which he gave when he ascended on high; it is, my brethren, by virtue of those gifts Christ's ministers are enabled to preach, and to take care of those souls Christ brings to his spiritual inn. It is not human learning that makes men ministers of Christ, but the gifts and graces of the Holy Ghost, the fruit of which is sweet to their own souls, and their work being accepted of God, is a reward to them beyond all encouragement, which otherwise they receive. Yet I will not contend with them, who conclude that by the two-pence is meant also the minister's maintenance. It is clear and evident, that Christ hath provided a comfortable livelihood for the pastors of his churches. " God hath ordained, that they that preach the gospel, should live of the gospel," 1 Cor. ix. 14. Perhaps it may also refer to this, yet ministers should be contented with a small allowance, should not desire hundreds by the year, but according to the riches or ability of the Church, so they ought to hand forth freely to their pastor, and be sure they ought to be delivered from the cares and snares of this life, and their widows and children should be well provided for after their decease.

And gave them to the host, and said unto him, take care of him.

Doct.   The care of the souls of God's people is committed, by Christ, to the pastors of his church, which care shall in a way of free, grace, be well rewarded by Christ at the great day.

I.   I shall prove this.

II.   Show what care they are to take of them.

III.   Why they ought to take this care.

The duty of   I.   Our Lord commands them to feed and take care of those he brings into pastors.   his house.

This appears by these texts. " Simon, Son of Jonas, Lovest thou me ? feed my sheep," John xxi. 16.   Christ will not trust any to feed and take care of them, but such that love him. " Take heed unto yourselves, and to all the flock over the which the Holy Ghost hath made you overseers, to feed the church of God," Acts xx. 28. " Feed the flock of God which is among you, taking the oversight thereof," 1 Pet. v. 2.

II. I shall show you what care he should take of them.

1. He is to study, read, and meditate for them, to enrich his own heart with divine truths, that he may enrich them also. *1 Tim. iv. 13. 14. 2 Tim. ii. 15.*

2. To feed and nourish them with sound doctrine, he must feed them with " knowledge and understanding," Jer. iii. 15. For such pastors God promised to give his people, he is obliged to feed them with the bread of life, that they may be fat and flourishing, and rich in good works.

3. To take the oversight of them, and watch for their souls, or watch over them. *Heb. xiii. 10. 1 Pet. v. 2.*

4. To love the flock with a hearty and sincere love and affection; the church should be dear to him, even be " his joy and his crown," 1 Thes. ii. 20.

5. To do what he can to resolve all their doubts, confirm weak hands, and to strengthen feeble knees, and to carry the lambs (like the great shepherd) in his bosom, &c., and endeavour to settle troubled minds, and succour such that are tempted. *Isa. xxxv. 3. and xl 10, 11.*

6. To be of an humble and condescending spirit in all things. " The servant of the Lord must not strive, but be gentle unto all men," 2 Tim. ii. 24. Not of a contentious spirit, striving about words.

7. To pray for them in private and in public. " God forbid (saith Samuel) that I should sin, in ceasing to pray for you," 1 Sam. xii. 23. Paul made mention of those under his care, day and night, in all his prayers. *1 Thes. i. 2, 11. 2 Tim. i. 3.*

8. To know the state of the flock, and as oft as he can to visit them, especially when sick, or under trouble or temptation; and also to rule them well, with such helps of government Christ hath given. For the power of the keys is given to the church, but a pastor is a ruler or governor therein. *Prov. xxvii. 23. Phil. ii. 19, 20. Ezek. xxxiv. 4.*

9. To administer all the ordinances of Christ to them, according to that order Christ hath left in the gospel. " And to shew himself approved, rightly dividing the word of truth," 2 Tim. ii. 15. Giving every one his portion in due season. " They are to seek out acceptable words, even words of wisdom," Eccl. xii. 10 ; not eloquent words, or words of man's wisdom, but " sound speech that cannot be condemned," Tit. ii. 8, not light and airy expressions, nor new uncouth notions, to please itching and wanton ears.

10. To be laborious, not slothful or idle, giving himself wholly up to his work and business, by preaching and writing, if it be set upon his heart, and to adorn his doctrine and ministry with a sober, and holy life and conversation, so as to be an ensample to the flock ; in these things his care and work lies. *1 Tim. iv. 15. 1 Tim. iv. 12. 1 Pet. v. 3.*

III. I shall give you the reasons why they should take this care of them.

1. Because the care of them in Christ's absence is committed to him ; the good Samaritan went away, and gave the host the charge of this poor man upon his departure ; and Christ commands his ministers to see that they take care of all that are committed to them, " Feed my lambs." *Why pastors should take care of the flock.*

2. He is gifted or endowed with ministerial abilities to this end ; they are given to him to this very purpose, that he may be in a fit capacity to take the care of them. He is chosen and ordained, and hath a competent maintenance allowed him to this end and purpose. He is made a watchman over them by the Holy Ghost, therefore must take care of them.

3. Because of the great worth and preciousness of their souls, whom Christ redeemed with his own blood.

4. Because if any miscarry through their negligence, or for want of giving them warning, Christ will require their blood at the watchman's hand ; they must give an account of their souls. *Ezek. iii. 17. 18, chap. xxxiii. 6, 7, 8.*

5. Because they are Christ's sheep, the elect of God, and members of his body, and are put into his hand to preserve and keep.

6. Because they are subject, like sheep, to go astray, and are in danger to be devoured by wolves and other beasts of prey. " After my departure shall grievous wolves enter in among you, not sparing the flock," Acts. xx. 29.

7. He must be accountable for their souls to Christ at the last day ; and from hence it appears it is his duty to take the care of them.

APPLICATION

1. We infer, it is no small thing to be a watchman, or an overseer of a congregation ; it should be therefore undertaken with trembling, and by men whom Christ by his Spirit hath endowed with suitable gifts and graces for so a great trust. And

2. That they ought to be men of great light and knowledge in the mysteries of the gospel, and in all the main truths thereof. How should they feed others else with knowledge and understanding.

3. Moreover, that it is the duty of the church, and of every member, to pray for them continually, and bear them upon their hearts always. "Brethren, pray for us."

Duty of the church to her Pastor.

4. To behave themselves towards their pastor with due respect and honour, as an ambassador of Jesus Christ, and as a father, and not to rebuke him as an equal. Would it not be a shame in that child, (because he sees infirmities in his father,) to rebuke him, and reproach him before other children : or would other wise and obedient children endure or bear it in such an irreverent brother without severe reproof?

5. It shows the great evil of such, who like cursed Shem, discover their father's nakedness. Let such that so do, fear God's displeasure, and let all act towards their spiritual father, as Shem and Japheth did to their father Noah, who wisely covered his nakedness, by which means they were blessed of the Lord, as well as by their father. Ministers are but men, and men of like passions with their brethren. It is a horrid evil to blame (in an undue manner) the pastor of a church, and far worse to despise and slight him, or speak contemptibly of him, or of his ministry before his face, or behind his back ; for as it is hateful to God, so it may hinder his ministry, and tend to weaken his hand, and lay him under temptations : therefore such who so do, should be laid under severe reproof, and if they repent not, cast out of the church as scandalous persons.

Gen. ix. 23.

6. It is the duty of each member to sympathize with him in all his sorrows, trials, temptations, and afflictions ; to encourage, strengthen, help, and comfort him, and not to join in, or favour such, who by an unbecoming manner reproach him, or slight his ministry, or cast his infirmities at every turn into his face, in the presence of others ; but never in private entreat him as a father, nor let him have the usage of the meanest member, who, if he offends, must be dealt privately with at first, according to Matt. xviii.

7. All ought to attend upon his ministry at all times, and not desert or neglect it on any account at their own will and pleasure ; for it is a duty they owe to God, and also to him ; for as necessity is laid on him to preach, so necessity is laid on them to hear, they must obey him in the Lord.

1 Cor. vii. 9. Heb. xiii. 17.

8. Moreover, it is their duty to visit him, to show they have a dear love and respect for him ; the neglect of which, and their strangeness unto him, is very offensive and discouraging. "The pastor (saith a worthy minister) must not only visit the church, but they are to visit him also."

9. They are bound to minister of their carnal things to him. "Let him that is taught in the word, communicate to him that taught him in all good things," Rom. xv. 27. It is the will of Christ, and "God hath ordained it, that they that preach the Gospel, should live by the Gospel," Gal. vi. 6, 1 Cor. ix. 7, 8. Like as they that feed a flock, eat of the milk of the flock ; his maintenance should be freely and cheerfully handed out to him, with respect and honour, and not given grudgingly nor sparingly, but bountifully, according to every one's ability, and their avowed obligation ; and as his maintenance is of divine right, so such that withhold it, rob God, and may look for a blast in what they have. "Ye have robbed me," Mal. iii. 8. How was that ? Why, in withholding from his ministers, what was appointed for them.

Lastly, (As one well observes,) they are bound to vindicate him under all reproaches and undue reflections cast upon him.

"And whatsoever thou spendest more, when I come again I will repay thee," ver. 35. What thou wantest in this world, I will make up to thee when I appear the second time. Our Lord says, "Behold I come quickly, and my reward is with me, to give to every one according as his works shall be," Rev. xxii. 12. They are all rewards of free-grace, and Christ's ministers shall have a glorious reward when their Lord comes, who are faithful. "They that turn many to righteousness, shall shine as the stars for evermore," Dan. xii. 3. See the latter end of the parable of the wheat and tares, where I have spoken of the reward of Christ's servants. I shall add no more now, but shall close this parable.

25. THE LOST SHEEP

I

And he spake this parable unto them, saying, what man of you having a hundred sheep, if he lose one of them, doth not leave the ninety and nine in the wilderness, and go after that which is lost, until he find it? And when he hath found it, he layeth it on his shoulders rejoicing,—Luke xv. 3—10.

1. THE scope and chief occasion of Christ's speaking this parable, we have laid down in the first and second verses. The Pharisees and Scribes murmured, saying, "This man receiveth sinners." That is, great sinners, notorious sinners, as publicans and harlots; and this offended these self-righteous, proud, and vain-glorious Pharisees; so that the design of our Saviour in speaking of this parable, is to show wherefore he came into this world, which was "not to call the righteous, but sinners to repentance," Matt. ix. 13, or to seek such that were lost, not such that in their own conceit never went astray. Scope of the parable.

2. We shall now open all the parts hereof.

First, By the man having an hundred sheep, is meant the Son of Man, or our Lord Jesus Christ. "The Son of man is come to seek and save that which was lost," Matt. xviii. 11, 12. Thus St. Matthew begins this same parable, for in the next words it is said, "Then he spake this parable. How think ye? if a man have a hundred sheep, and one of them goeth astray," ver. 12. "Doth he not leave the ninety and nine, and goeth into the mountains, and seeketh that which is gone astray?" The parts of it explained.

2. By the hundred sheep, and ninety-nine that never went astray, expositors greatly differ. I find no less than four different apprehensions or exposition about them.

1. Some say by the hundred sheep, is meant the whole number of the elect, whether in heaven or on earth, whether called, or hereafter to be called. They also say, by the sheep going astray, signifies also all the elect, who by nature went astray and are "children of wrath, as well as others, being dead in and trespasses," Eph. ii. 1, 2. Here mention is made but of one going astray (say they) though they went all astray, to let us know the love of Christ to every individual soul of his; that if but one particular soul had been to be redeemed, Jesus Christ would have come down from heaven to have redeemed that one. Moreover, these expositors say, that the ninety and nine signifies all the sheep of Christ who are in heaven, now glorified, whom he left when he came into this world. See Poole's Annot. on this parable.

But this exposition I cannot close with, because it is said, these ninety and nine never went astray; but so it cannot be said of the sheep of Christ, now glorified in heaven, for they once, when they were on earth, went astray. All we like sheep went astray in the first Adam, and we went all astray by actual sins too, until called.

2. Others conclude, by the ninety and nine is meant, such sheep of Christ, who need no repentance comparatively, or in respect of others, who being actually justified by the imputation of the righteousness of Jesus Christ, need not such repentance as unregenerate sinners do, being for ever personally acquitted, and delivered from God's vindictive wrath and justice, and so shall never be lost nor go astray any more.

3. Others by needing no repentance think he means no public confession for offences taken by the church against them; but there lies one or two objections against this sense also.

Object. How can it be said, that God and the holy angels rejoice more over one sinner that returns to him, than over all his saints that are gathered home to him?

Answ. Yet an answer may be given to this objection, *i. e.*, that Christ speaks here after the manner of men. Now a man expresseth more joy over one child recovered from the

329

jaws of death, or escaped with his life, when in a lion's den, than over the rest of his children, who were not exposed to that danger. But then there is another objection, viz.

Object. 2. But these sheep, viz., such saints that are now in Christ, and need no repentance from dead works, as all unrenewed persons do, did once go astray ; but Matthew saith, they went not astray.

The answer to this is, i. e., They do not now go astray, but to take of this the text doth not speak of the present time, but of the time past, "which went not astray," that is, never went astray.

3. Some interpreters say, that the ninety and nine are the holy angels (who be sure need no repentance, because they never sinned) whom Christ left, when by his incarnation he came down from heaven on earth, to work out our salvation : of this opinion it seems was St. Ambrose, Chrysostom, Hilary, &c.

4. Others think thereby both angels and men signified, by an imperfect number (ninety and nine) left in the wilderness, because by man's fall the number of them made to live Hom. **34.** in God's presence was diminished, thus Greg.
In luc. However there are divers objections against both the last expositions.

(1.) It seems clear to me, that the ninety and nine, and the sheep which was lost, were all of one fold, or of the same species, but so are not angels and men.

(2.) Angels I think are no where called sheep in all the scripture. A sheep is (as one observes) a certain image to resemble mankind.

(3.) Moreover, doth God rejoice more over a returning sinner, than over all his holy angels ?

(4.) The holy angels are the friends and neighbours spoken of, who rejoice at the returning home of the lost sheep, and therefore none of the ninety and nine left in the wilderness.

(5.) It seemeth strange to me, that heaven should be compared to a wilderness, and the Quest. evang. angels left therein.
lib. 2. 9. 31. 6. Others understand by these ninety and nine, pharisaical, or self-righteous persons, who themselves just, and are highly opinionated of their own good condition. Thus Aug. "The ninety and nine left in the wilderness, may set forth the proud, who have a wilderness in their mind," &c.

Pharisees meant by the ninety-nine that went not astray.

I am fully satisfied in this last sense ; and the reasons why I take this to be the meaning of our blessed Lord, are,

1. Because it directly agrees or suits with the scope and coherence of the parable ; and what better help have we to find out the true meaning of a parable, than to consider of the drift and scope attentively ? "The Pharisees murmured, saying, this man receives sinners. They did not look upon themselves to be sinners, or such that needed repentance, but were holy and just persons, and so not in a lost state and condition. Well (as if our Lord had said) let it be granted, that you are such that are righteous, and not gone astray, yet these whom you call sinners, you certainly conclude they are lost; and now he adds this parable, "What man of you having an hundred sheep, if one is lost," &c. And this he did to rebuke them, and the same way he took for their conviction, in using other parables upon the like occasion. The Pharisees, I say, looked upon themselves to be such righteous and just persons that needed no repentance, not that there are any who indeed really do need no repentance, but our Lord speaks these words to denote what opinion they had of themselves; you conclude and think you are just persons, and not gone astray ; you are the flock of God, and sheep of the field of Israel. Well, but these persons whom you see me concerned for, and willing to receive, viz., Publicans and harlots, you look upon to be lost sinners, great and undone sinners ; well take this for granted, let it be so, "What man among you having an hundred sheep, if one be lost, doth not leave the ninety and nine, and go to seek that which is gone astray ?" If he will leave all the ninety and nine to seek one, do not blame me, for there are many poor lost and undone sinners, such that have no inherent righteousness to trust in.

2. I take this to be the meaning of our Saviour, because in another place the Pharisees are called righteous ones upon the very same occasion. "Jesus sat at meat with publicans and sinners," Matt. ix. 10, 11; and this the Pharisees reproved him for, and murmured. "And when Jesus heard it, he said unto them, they that are whole need not a physician, but they that are sick ; I came not to call the righteous, but sinners to repentance." Not that the Pharisees needed no physician, but they thought they did not: the objection which our late annotators bring against this exposition, is this, viz., because the holy angels are said to rejoice more over a returning sinner, than over these who needed

no repentance, or these ninety and nine just persons; implying, say they, as if they did rejoice over these self-righteous persons, who rather grieve them, than give cause in any sense to be rejoiced over.

Answ. 1. That it doth not follow in my judgment, that they rejoiced at all over them, from those expressions, " There is more joy in heaven," &c.

2. But suppose it doth imply they did in some respects rejoice over them, why may not the angels rejoice in doing that service they might be employed in towards such persons ? for at that time the Jews who believed not, and the Pharisees were the church of God, and members thereof, and so might be called his sheep, for so were the men of the house of Israel, which church continued until the death of Christ, and the gospel church took place, might not angels rejoice in doing them what service they could, or were employed in, though far greater joy is amongst them, when one poor sinner is brought home to Christ?

Secondly, by the " one sheep that was lost," is meant all God's elect, who are brought to see that they are sinners, lost sinners, before they are convinced of righteousness ; the elect no doubt are that world which the Holy Spirit, first convinceth of sin, and of their lost and undone condition. _{The lost sheep signifies all the elect, who are brought to see their lost estate. John xvi. 8.}

Thirdly, the man going after the lost sheep, signifies Jesus Christ, who, in order to restore lost sinners, came into this world and took our nature on him, and died for us ; as also his sending of his gospel, his ministers, his word and Spirit to convert and turn them to God, as shall hereafter be more fully opened.

Fourthly, Christ finding the lost sheep, signifies his meeting with a sinner, by the powerful convictions of his word and Spirit, for when the word hath fastened upon a sinner's heart and conscience, then Christ may be said to have found the lost sheep.

Fifthly, " He layeth it on his shoulders, rejoicing," ver. 5.

Shoulders denotes the great power or strength of Christ, as it is put forth or exerted in working upon a rebellious sinner, in bringing him home, when Christ is said to " carry his lambs in his arms, and lay them in his bosom," Isa. xl. 10, 11, that implies his great love ; but when he is said to " take them up, and lay them upon his shoulders," that denotes his almighty power : because when a man sets his shoulders to a work, he puts forth the greatness of his strength, the strength of a man lying in his arms and shoulders ; it is not said his shoulder, but his shoulders ; he puts both his shoulders to this work.

Sixthly, " When he cometh home," ver. 6.

Jesus Christ hath two homes.

1. The church upon earth is his home, there he dwells ; Sion is his home and habitation, or dwelling-place for ever.

2. Heaven is his home ; that is, his upper house, palace, or principal place of abode.

Seventhly, " He calleth together his friends and neighbours, saying unto them, rejoice with me, for I have found my sheep that was lost."

1. When Christ brings a lost sinner home, or unto his house or church on earth, he stirreth up all his saints and members there to rejoice ; the saints below rejoice.

2. Also there is joy in heaven amongst the holy angels, when a lost sinner is brought home, see ver. 17. "And I say unto you, there shall be joy in heaven over one sinner that repenteth," &c.

From this parable thus briefly opened, I shall take notice of several propositions, or points of doctrine, and also prosecute them,

Doct. I. That our Lord Jesus Christ leaves all self-righteous persons in the wilderness of this world, and goes after to seek and save such that are lost.

Doct. II. That sinners are lost naturally, even God's elect.

Doct. III. That the Lord Jesus Christ came to seek his lost sheep, and will not give over seeking them, until he hath found them, and will carry them all home to God.

Doct. IV. That Christ's lost sheep cannot go home, or return to God of themselves, or upon their own feet (or by virtue of any power of their own) but must be taken up in Christ's arms, and carried home on his shoulders.

Doct. V. That Jesus Christ, and all his saints below on earth, and also his angels above in heaven, greatly rejoice when one lost sinner repenteth, and is brought home to God.

I shall, my brethren, begin with the first of these observations, and

I. Show you, why this world is compared to a wilderness.

II. Show what kind or sort of people they are, that Jesus Christ leaves in the wilderness of this world, as also what may be meant by his leaving of them.

III. Show why he leaveth them in the wilderness.

IV. Apply it.

This world
compared to
a wilder-
ness. I. This world may be compared to a wilderness ; a wilderness is a vast barren place, which is not tilled, manured, nor sowed ; nothing grows in it, but
comes forth naturally. So, my brethren, the world, I mean the vast and common lump of mankind (or ungodly sinners, who are by our Saviour called the world) are
a barren people. God, the great husbandman, takes no pains with them, but lets them
lie untilled and unsown ; he doth not plough, dig, nor manure, sow, nor plant this wilderness ; mankind naturally are barren and fruitless in their hearts and lives ; nothing grows
but what they bring forth by natural light, or natural powers and princeiples improved.

The Quaker
detected. (1.) By the way, let such that cry up a Christ in all men, see to this. Do
but once fancy that the light within, the light of natural conscience is the
true Christ, and walk up unto it : and O what raptures of joy may such feign to themselves ! They think they have Christ within, and live and sin not, and fancy themselves
perfectly righteous, and justified persons ; when all their righteousness is but the imperfect righteousness of the law, or first covenant.

(2.) Let such also that cry up natural religion, and contemn the revelation of Christ
and his righteousness, look to it : alas, morality is often found to grow in the wilderness
of this world, and it is the proper product thereof ; these men do but strive to paganize
the nation, and labour to make Christians renounce the blessed fruits of Christ's spiritual
garden, to feed with the old Heathen on the grass of the wilderness, and would have us
to put no difference between Christianity and morality, and so cast contempt upon the gospel, as if it were a mere romance.

2. A howling wilderness is not fit place for mankind to inhabit, it is therefore forsaken
of the inhabitants : so the godly cannot live amongst, but separate themselves from the
people of the world. " Come out from amongst them, and be ye separate, saith the Lord,"
&c. 2 Cor. vi. 17. " I have chosen you out of the world," John xv. 16. They cannot
live there, because there is no water, no bread of life, nor water of life.

3. In a wilderness are many pricking briers and thorns ; so that it is hard passing
through it without a scratched face, or being torn or wounded So our Lord himself, and
his disciples, in passing through this world, were torn, abused, and wounded in their names
and persons by the pricking briers and thorns ; the Scribes and Pharisees, the inhabitants
of the wilderness, scratched and wounded them. Wicked men are fitly compared to
briers and thorns : (1.) In that they are the fruit of the curse, and abide under it. (2.)
In that they are good for little, unless it be to make a hedge of : God sometimes, to secure
his own people, causes the wicked of the world to be a hedge or defence unto them ; the
earth helped the woman. (3.) If thorns should chance to spring up in Christ's vineyard,
they are presently cut off by the axe, or dug up by the spade of church-discipline. (4.)
" They must be as thorns thrust away, because they cannot be taken with the hand," 2
Sam. xxiii. 6. What are the briers and thorns, but fuel for the fire ? So shall all the
briers and thorns of this world be thrown into the fire of God's wrath ; " They are near
unto cursing, whose end is to be burned," Heb. vi. 7, 8.

4. In a howling wilderness are many savage and devouring beasts of prey, so that it is
dangerous to pass through it ; and especially if a sheep should chance to stray away, and
be lost in a wilderness, it is by those beasts in eminent danger of being devoured : so in
this world are many wicked men, who are of a savage and cruel nature ; and although
they are in the shape of human creatures, yet they have the nature or qualities of lions,
tigers, wolves, bears, serpents, foxes. A tyrant is compared to a tiger, a lion, a dragon ;
a deceiver or seducer to a wolf ; a drunkard to a filthy swine, a gluttonous person to a
cormorant ; a backslider to a dog, licking up his filthy vomit again ; a flatterer to a pan-
ther, and a crafty persecutor to a fox ; and this makes this world like a wilderness.

5. In a wilderness a man may soon lose his way, unless he hath a knowing and faithful
guide : so a poor Christian may soon lose his way whilst he is in this world, where there
are so many by-paths, and one crying this is the way, and another that is the way ;
wherefore it behoveth all to keep to the unerring rule of God's word, lest they are deceived.

6. A wilderness is a dolesome and solitary place, and it is so called ; even so is this
world ; what can we expect here, but trouble, sorrow, and afflictions ? Also, we are
amongst wild beasts, who by their treachery, cruelty, deceit, flattery, horrid oaths, blasphemy, malignity, and all other detestable evils, render this world like a wilderness. " I
have fought with evil beasts at Ephesus," saith Paul, 1 Cor. xv. 32.

7. A wilderness hath many pits and dangerous places in it, into which a man may soon
fall if he lose his way, especially in a dark night. O what dangerous pits are there in

this world, temptations abroad and at home ; our very tables may be a snare, or pit to us, by which we may be spoiled and undone for ever; nay, our trades may be like a pit of destruction ; a man's wife, his children, his riches, pleasures, honours, may be as snares or pit into which he may fall and perish eternally. Temptations (to such that fall by them) may fitly be compared to a pit, into which a man in a dark night falleth and is lost. O it is dangerous to dwell in the wilderness of this world.

8. Some part of a wilderness hath been turned into a garden or fruitful vineyard : so God hath out of the people of this world, taken his churches and walled them about, that none of the evil beasts can hurt them : all mankind naturally were alike dry and barren, as a wilderness, and brought forth no good fruit. But God hath separated some of this barren ground, to make lovely gardens for himself to walk and delight in.

9. Though a wilderness is dry and rocky, and without water, yet God can turn a wilderness into pools of water, nay, and he hath promised so to do. "The wilderness and solitary places shall be glad for them, and the desert shall rejoice and blossom, as the rose in the latter days," Isa. xxxv. 1. "The whole earth shall be filled with the know-ledge of the glory of the Lord, as the water fills the sea," Isa. xi. 9 : and then the wilderness shall become a lovely garden : O pray for those days.

10. God can spread a table in the wilderness, and bring water out of the rock, as he did of old ; so whilst we are in the wilderness of this world, God feeds' his people with manna from heaven, and makes them drink of that blessed Rock, Jesus Christ, 1 Cor. x. 3.

11. The way to Canaan is through the wilderness ; yet the Lord led Israel safely to the land of promise : so our way to heaven lies through the wilderness of this world ; but Jesus Christ feeds us with heavenly bread, and leads us safely to the true spiritual and antitypical Canaan.

12. Sometimes poor sheep are lost in the wilderness, and on the mountains, and thither the shepherd must go to seek them.

Matthew saith, the man that lost his sheep, left the "ninety and nine, And went into the mountains to seek the sheep that was gone astray." *The world compared to mountains.* By mountains and wilderness is meant the same thing, viz., this world. (1.) Mountains are dry and barren places, like a wilderness. (2.) Mountains are high and lofty: so are the ungodly of the earth, they are proud and haughty in their hearts and spirits. What people were more swelled with pride and self-conceit, than the Pharisees ; yet amongst the Jews who were then as a barren wilderness, or high and lofty mountains, Jesus Christ had some sheep, whom he came to seek, even the lost sheep of the house of Israel. (3.) Mountains are hard and rocky, so are the hearts of all wicked men, and particularly the hearts of the unbelieving Jews. It is said, that our Lord was grieved, because of the hardness of their hearts.

So much as to the first thing.

II. I shall show, what sort of people they are, that Jesus Christ leaves in the wilderness. *What sort of people Christ leaves in the wil-derness.*

1. They are such as looked upon themselves (as you heard) to be the flock of God, the people of God ; and so the Jews indeed were by profession, and by that legal covenant made with Abraham, which was also afterward renewed, when they came into the wilderness, Exod. xx.

2. They were a people that thought they were not gone astray ; for so the Scribes and Pharisees thought of themselves.

3. Such as thought they needed no repentance, not believing they had broken God's holy law, but were pure, holy, and righteous persons.

III. I shall show you what his leaving them in the wilderness does imply, and also why our Lord doth leave them there. *What leav-ing them in the wilder-ness signifies.*

1. Jesus Christ leaving the ninety and nine in the wilderness signifies, his not choosing them, they being none of his sheep, by God's special choice or election, though his flock by that external or legal covenant made with their fathers : "They are not all Israel, which are of Israel ; neither because they are the seed of Abraham, are they all children : but "in Isaac shall thy seed be called." That is, they which are are children of the flesh, these are not the children of God," Rom. ix 7, 8 ; namely, as so considered, or as such.

2. Christ's leaving them in the wilderness denotes an act of preterition, or a passing of them by, not manifesting himself to them, but rather hiding the mysteries of the kingdom of heaven from them.

3. It may also signify his leaving them in a bewildered state, they not knowing in what

a woful, ignorant, and blind condition they were. " And Jesus said, for judgment I am come into this world; that they which see not might see, and that such that see might be made blind," John ix. 39. And thus was Christ a "foundation to build upon for some, and a stumbling-stone, and Rock of offence to others, even to the whole flock or house of Israel." Under which blindness Christ left them, and at last to final unbelief and impenitence, as a just judgment for their horrid pride and contempt of the gospel.

Quest. Why doth Christ leave the ninety and nine in the wilderness, or pass them by?

Answ. (1.) Because they were not lost, i. e., they thought so, or were not lost in their own sight; therefore our Lord told them, If you were blind, ye should have no sin. If your ignorance were simple, and not affected, or you were sensible of your blindness, you would not be so incurable, nor sin with those aggravations, also then you would see great need of me to open your eyes; but because they saw no need of Christ, but looked upon themselves as righteous persons, and never lost or gone astray, he leaves them, or passes by them. " The whole need not a physician, but they that are sick: I came not to call the righteous, but sinners to repentance," Matt. ix. 12.

Why the self-righteous are left in the wilderness.

(2.) Jesus Christ leaves them, because they were not fit and proper subjects of Gospel grace. The design of God is to magnify rich bounty, and sovereign love and favour to such persons that will readily and heartly receive it, as such that see and know they need it, and that will exalt and magnify God in the riches of his free grace towards them: but self-righteous persons can see no need to praise, bless, and magnify God and his free grace, they thinking that they have a fulness in themselves: the Pharisee cries, " God, I thank thee I am not as other men—nor as this publican." God extends his favour to such as will exalt his Son, and his divine goodness; but so doth no self-righteous person; and therefore Christ leaves these in the wilderness.

(3.) Jesus Christ leaves them because they had rejected him, and grew headstrong and unruly, and would not own him to be their Prince and Saviour; though he was the " chief corner-stone," Acts. iv. 11, yet he was disallowed of by these master-builders, and refused as their shepherd.

(4.) Because that flock that consisted of "ninety and nine," a great multitude, was now to be scattered; I mean the church of the Jews was to be dissolved, as a legal and typical church, the date of its continuation being now expiring, or expired; and they refusing to become members of his Gospel-church, he must leave them of necessity, the providence and dispensation of God calls him so to do: remarkable it is, he leaves no man with this flock, " The ninety and nine." When he goes after his lost sheep, as other shepherds were used to do; no, " Moses and the prophets were until John, but the servant abides not in the house for ever." All must be under Christ's teaching, under his feeding, his care, and his government, or else he will leave them. I do not think in this I at all strain this part of the parable.

(5.) Our Lord leaves them, because they were none of his sheep, nor the flock whom he came to gather; it is true, it is said, " He came to his own, and they received him not," John i. 11. How his own? not by the election of grace; not his own by the gospel-covenant, or his gospel-flock; but his own by the legal covenant. Our Lord came not to keep up, support, and uphold the national church of Israel, but to gather all his lost sheep out from among them, and to bring them into a new church state. Now these are some of those reasons, why he left the ninety and nine in the wilderness. And so much as to this first proposition.

APPLICATION

1st. Is this world like to a wilderness? then we may infer, that it is a great mercy the people of God are not utterly destroyed by the ravenous beasts of this wilderness.

2thly. That it behoveth all people that dwell in this wilderness, to enquire the way how they may come out of it, and that is by Christ alone; he must bring them up out of the wilderness: " Who is this that cometh out of the wilderness, leaning upon her beloved?" Cant. viii. 5. Or trusting in, or relying upon a blessed Saviour.

Quest. How do sinners come out of the wilderness?

Answ. 1. In spirit; they receive another spirit: we have not received the spirit of the world, but the spirit which is of God," 1 Cor. ii. 12. That is not a sensual, an earthly, a contentious, a proud, a malicious, a covetous, a self-glorious, a self-righteous, nor a superstitious spirit; but they have received a praying spirit, a believing spirit, a humble spirit, a soul-sanctifying spirit, a God-honouring, and a Christ-exalting spirit.

2. By being born again, or by attaining a new birth, they came out of the wilderness; they are born or brought forth into God's kingdom; delivered out of the kingdom of Satan, and translated into the kingdom of God's dear Son. They obtain a different life, different light and knowledge, a different love, different affections, different fears, different inclinations, and different resolutions, different principles, ends, aims, delight, joy, peace, and different appetite, diet, food, company, and apparel; they wear not their own apparel.

3. They come out of the wilderness, or out of the world, in respect of adoration or worship: the worship of the world is not divine, but devised, not of God, but of man; or much of it is human, and not of divine institution, proceeding from Rome, and not from Jesus Christ.

4. Believing sinners come out of the wilderness, in respect of church constitution; they leave the worldly sanctuary, which is not of God's, but of man's pitching; a mere formal, carnal, and national constitution, built up of dead stones, or consisting not of a people renewed, or made spiritually alive, but are generally profane and ungodly ones, yea, the worst of men. What wretched and abominable persons are allowed to be members of such a church-state; what briers, thorns, and brambles grow in this wilderness.

But enlightened sinners come out of this wilderness into a new constitution, a new church state gathered according to the pattern left by Jesus Christ and his apostles in the New Testament, free from all human mixtures, though not its full glory yet.

5. They come out of the wilderness and worldly sanctuary, or worldly communion, in respect of discipline; the church into which they come, has its government and discipline in itself, or power to receive and cast out by that authority Christ hath left in it, Matt. xviii.

6. In respect of conversation; they walk not as others, in the vanity of their minds, who chiefly pursue the world, and their own worldly interest; they walk not according to the course this world, " nor according to the power of the prince of the air, the spirit that now worketh in the children of disobedience;" see, Eph. iv. 18. Eph. ii. 2.

Quest. But why must not Christ's sheep remain in the wilderness, or in the world, i. e., in the worship of this world? Why all believers should come out of the wilderness.

Ans. 1. Because Christ came to seek them in this world, and to bring them out of it; they are chosen and called out of the world. "I have chosen you out of the world."

2. Because they are not of this world—" because ye are not of the world, the world hateth you," John ix. 19.

3. Because they are redeemed out of this world, or out of every kindred, nation, tongue, and people. Rev. v. 9.

4. Because they are commanded to separate themselves, and come out from among them, or separate from the world in their worship, rites, customs, and human ceremonies, and vain superstitions. " Wherefore come out from among them, and be ye separate, saith the Lord, and touch not the unclean thing, and I will receive you." &c. 2 Cor. vi. 17. " Come out of her, my people, and partake not of her sins," &c. Rev. xviii. 4.

5. Because conformity to this world, in point of worship, customs, evil practices, and in conversation, is forbidden, and it is a great sin to conform to it. " Be not comfortable to this world," &c. Rom. xii. 2.

6. Because the church of Christ is a garden inclosed, or a community of Christians distinct from the world. " A garden inclosed is my sister, my spouse," Cant. vii. 12.

2nly. Doth Christ leave all self-righteous persons in the wilderness? O then let such souls tremble, who trust to their own righteousness.

4thly. And doth he seek sinners, lost sinners? then this is good news to those that see themselves lost and undone, as having no righteousness of their own to justify them.

5thly. Wonder not you that are believers, you meet with trouble in this world; it is a wilderness.

6thly. Let sinners get a good and wise guide to lead them out of the wilderness.

7thly. Let the saints labour to keep themselves clear of the defilements and pollutions of this world, and strive to live above the world, and to get well out of the world, to the heavenly Canaan.

Lastly, It reproves such that remain in the ways and worship of this world; O fly to Sion. And in coming out see you lean upon Jesus Christ as your beloved, as your Saviour, as your guide, your priest, your king, your prophet, &c.

But so much at this time.

II

What man of you having an hundred sheep, if he lose one of them, doth not leave the ninety and nine in the wilderness, and go after that which is lost, until he find it ? Luke xv. 3, 4, 5.

I HAVE prosecuted one point of doctrine, viz., That this world may be compared to a wilderness.

I shall now proceed.

Doct. 2.   That sinners by nature, or as they are in their natural condition, are lost, like lost sheep.

1. I shall show what to be lost doth denote or signify.

What it is to   II.   Show the nature of being lost, or the woful condition such are in.
be lost.
               III.   Apply it.

1. I shall show what to be lost doth denote or signify.

1. To be lost, is to stray away from our proper place, where we were set by the Almighty. As a sheep that is lost is gone from the flock, from the fold, or pasture where it was put ; so sinners are gone astray from God, and from that blessed place and state in which they were created. They are gone out of the way ; we are gone astray like lost sheep.

2. To be lost is to be undone. As we say of a man that falls into the sea, and no help near, or of a man condemned to die, and hath no pardon, he is a lost man, a dead man, dead in law ; so sinners naturally are undone, they are lost, though but few see it, or cry out with the prophet, " Woe is me, for I am undone," Isa. vi. 5.   All mankind are fallen into the sea of God's wrath, and none can help them, no friend, nor brother ; they are as a sheep gone astray, fallen into a lion's den.   Sinners are become a prey to Satan, every man is condemned in the first Adam, and spiritually dead, " dead in sins and respasses," Eph. ii. 1, 2.

II. I shall show the woful state and condition of such that are lost.

The woful   And this in three respects.
state of such   1.   Such is the fearful state of all mankind in the first Adam, that they
that are lost.   have lost God.

2. God hath lost them.

3. They have lost themselves.

They have   First, all mankind in the first Adam have lost God, hence it is said, that
lost God.   the saints at Ephesus were by nature without God. " Being at that time without hope, and without God in the world."

1. We all lost the knowledge of God, all men naturally are ignorant of God, and may say with Pharaoh, " Who is the Lord ? I know not the Lord, that I should obey him." Though they may know there is a God, yet they have lost the true knowledge of the great and holy God. " They proceed from evil to evil, and they know not me, saith the Lord," Jer. ix. 3. They know not the holiness, purity, justice, wisdom, goodness, and faithfulness of God.

2. They have lost the life of God, that blessed life the soul had in the first Adam, and by this means they are said to be spiritually dead, " Having their understanding darkened, being alienated from the life of God, through the ignorance that is in them, because of the blindness of their heart," Eph. iv. 18. Men are alive in their bodies, but without spiritual life in their souls.

3. They have lost the image of God, or likeness to God in holiness and true righteousness. " All have sinned, and come short of the glory of God," Rom. iii. 23. The glory of God, which shone forth in our first parents in the state of innocency, was the image of God ; and by sin instead of that naturally, they, are become like unto the devil.

4. They have lost communion with God. Sin hath so alienated them from God, that they cannot endure his presence. Adam run away from God, would, if he could, have hid himself from his offended Creator. " What fellowship hath righteousness with unrighteousness ? and what communion hath light with darkness ? or what concord hath Christ with Belial ?" 2 Cor. vi. 14, 15. Adam no doubt before he sinned, delighted in, and had sweet friendship and communion with the Almighty, but no sooner had he sinned, but he became a stranger to him, and so are all men naturally. " The carnal mind is enmity against God ; it is not subject to the law of God, neither indeed can be. They say to God, depart from us," &c. Rom. viii. 7.

5. Man hath lost that love and favour of God, which was let out at first, whilst he

stood a perfect and sinless creature. God hates all the workers of iniquity, though I deny not that love, pity, purpose, and good-will of God to his elect from everlasting.

But now let us consider a little the sad effects of this loss.

The sad effects of the least sin.

1. Mankind having lost God, they lost their chief good in whom our happiness alone lieth, and in the loss of which sinners became miserable.

2. By losing God, and sinning against him, all men were brought under the curse; the breach of the law of the first covenant, brought all mankind under the curse, and so they remain until they find Jesus Christ, and are united to him. "For as many as are of the works of the law, are under the curse. Cursed is he that continueth not in all things that is written in the book of the law to do them," Gal. iii. 10. The least sin exposeth the soul to God's eternal vengeance, and lays all mankind under the sentence of wrath and condemnation; nay, and such "who believe not in Christ are condemned already," John iii. 18; and it will, if grace prevent not, plunge the sinner into everlasting perdition and destruction. I say, the least sin, though observe, there is no sin absolutely small or little, who can call sin little, that is committed against a great and infinite God; (though comparatively some sins are greater than others) but one evil thought, or an idle word, deserves eternal wrath. The least sin in some sense is an infinite evil. We ascribe infiniteness to these two (saith a divine) 1st. To the great God, 2nd. To sin. God is infinite essentially, sin is infinite objectively, or in respect of the object sinned against, because injurious to an infinite God, an offence of an infinite majesty, a contempt of infinite authority, an affront to infinite sovereignty, an abuse of mercy, a dishonour to infinite excellency, a provocation to infinite justice, a contrariety to infinite holiness, an enemy to infinite love. "Is not thy wickedness great, and thy iniquity infinite?" Job xxii. 5. Sin therefore, yea, the least sin, deserveth an infinite punishment: O woful condition of lost sinners! Justice requires that the punishment should be according to the offence: a punishment intensively cannot be inflicted upon a mere creature so as to satisfy for it, because a mere creature is not capable of it; therefore what it wants in degrees, must be made up in duration.

Secondly, as sinners have lost God, so God also hath lost them, as a shepherd hath lost his sheep that are gone astray.

But here, first, I must premise one or two things: (1.) That no person, no sinner is so lost to God, but the Lord knows where they are, and in what state and condition they are; he knows the way and course they take, and the thoughts of their hearts. "Thou knowest my foolishness," (saith David,) Psal. lxix. 5; and saith Job, "He knoweth the way I take," Job xxiii. 10. A shepherd knows not where his lost sheep is, neither to what danger it may be exposed; but the Lord knoweth all the evil which hath befallen every sheep in the world: so that in this there is a great disparity. (2.) God doth not search for sinners, as a shepherd doth. A shepherd seeks them where they are not, because of his ignorance, and perhaps may never find them. (3.) No man is gone from God's essential presence, because he is omnipresent, or in all places: though it is said, the Prodigal went into a far country, and was lost, yet he was not gone where God was not; it doth not therefore refer to distance of place, but to distance of the sinner's state. But in the affirmative, when we say, God hath lost the sinner,

1. We mean, he hath lost his love and affection: no doubt whilst Adam stood in a state of innocency, God was the object of his choice, love, and affections, but God lost his heart and chiefest affections when he had sinned, and so he hath lost the love of all mankind; for naturally they love the creature more than the Creator, nay, their sins above God.

What meant by God's losing sinners.

2. God hath lost that glory, that honour which man in his first state gave unto him: like as a son, who rebels against his father, honours his father no more (I mean so long as he abides in his rebellion against him) so sinners instead of honouring of God are said to despise him. "They that despise me shall be lightly esteemed," 1 Sam. ii. 30. "Ye have despised the Lord, saith Moses," Numb. xi. 20; they are called haters of God, contemners of God. "Wherefore doth the wicked contemn God?" Psal. x. 13. So that the honour God ought to have from these creatures he hath lost.

3. God hath lost that service, that homage and worship which belongs to him: men, under apostacy, serve their lusts, serve sin, serve men, nay, serve the devil, and serve not God; they worship not their blessed Creator. "For we ourselves also were sometimes foolish, disobedient, deceived, serving divers lusts, living in malice and envy, hateful, and hating one another," Tit. iii. 3.

4. God hath lost that just and righteous obedience and subjection sinners should yield

unto him ; they will not own him to be their sovereign, " Our tongues are our own, and who is lord over us ?" When a master's commands are not regarded, or a ruler is not subjected to, or what he says is not observed, what says one ? he hath lost all that is valued by him, or belongs to him, so whilst God's authority is contemned, his sovereignty abused, and his commands slighted ; what hath he more to lose, or what greater loss can God sustain (to speak after the manner of men) by his creatures than this ?

Thirdly, sinners have lost themselves.

Sinners have lost themselves.

1. They know not what they have done, they know not what evil is in sin, or what an evil and bitter thing it is to depart from the Lord. " Know therefore, and see that it is an evil and bitter, that thou hast forsaken the Lord thy God, and that my fear is not in thee, saith the Lord of hosts," Jer. ii. 19. When they sin they little think they cast dirt (as it were) in the very face of God, and cross his will, and contemn and despise him in their hearts. Sin is a rebellion against God, sinners take up arms and fight against their Maker and would destroy his very being if they could ; some have wished there was no God, or that they were above God ; they know not what they do.

2. They know not what boundless evils are in their base hearts, nor what they would do, did not God restrain them. He hath lost himself besure, that hath lost the knowledge of himself. " Is thy servant a dog, that he should do this thing ?" 2 Kings viii. 13, (said Hazael to Elisha) he, alas ! knew not the seed of that great wickedness that was in his heart, yet did what the prophet told him, when he became king of Syria.

3. They have so lost themselves that they know not how far they are gone from God, or at what woful distance sin hath set them from the holy God, in respect to their state and condition ; neither do they know what fearful vengeance hangs over their heads ; nor will they believe it when it is told them that God abhorreth them, and all the religion, service, and worship they pretend to perform unto him ; but this is so verily so, " The very prayer of the wicked is an abomination to the Lord." They know not their state and condition, will not believe they are enemies to God, traitors, and rebels, and that they are condemned and under the sentence of everlasting death and wrath, and liable to be cast every moment into eternal flames.

4. The wicked are so far lost (as to themselves) that they know not whither they are going ; they little think or know whither that path they take will lead them ; for they are blind, or in darkness : " And he that walketh in darkness, knoweth not whither he goeth," John xii. 35. Perhaps they think the way they go in, will bring them to heaven, when it is the highway to hell ; the god of this world hath blinded their eyes.

5. They have lost themselves to such a degree, that they know not the way to return home to God ; and from hence they take to by-ways, and following blind guides, who are lost as well as they.

The light within all men will not bring men to God.

(1.) Some think to return home by the light of their own natural consciences, which they call Christ within them. Now (1.) evident it is, that the light that is in all men, is at best but a divine quality : these therefore have lost the true Saviour ; for is Jesus of Nazareth no real person without us ? is he not, though now glorified, of our very flesh and bone ? " Handle and see me, a spirit hath not flesh and bones, as you see me have." And this was after he rose from the dead. Is not the same Jesus that was crucified, now in heaven ? or can the person of Jesus Christ be in the hearts of men and women ? (2) Is the Spirit of Christ in all ? doth not he say, that the world could not receive the Holy Spirit ? (3.) Is that light which is in all men any thing else than some remainders of the law of the first covenant, that was written in the hearts of mankind ? and had not the Jews a clearer ministration of that law than the Gentiles, written in tables of stone ? and if that law could not give them life, was not able to justify the Jews, who walked up in obedience to it ; do these men think to be justified by that dark ministration of the law of the first covenant that was written in the hearts of the Gentiles ? (4.) Do not these people seek to be justified and saved by the works of this law, or light within ? O how far are they lost, who think this way to return to God.

(2.) Others think to return home to God by leading a sober moral life, doing to all men as they would be done unto, which indeed in effect is the same with the former ; for the light in every man's conscience will teach him thus to do : and thus Paul acted also when he was a Pharisee, he kept a moral good conscience then towards God and man ; but all that was nothing to him, when God revealed Jesus Christ to him : see Phil. iii. 5—8.

(3.) Others think to return to God by their prayers and tears, or by their repentance and reformation of life : some it may be feared think, if they cry, Lord have mercy upon me, on a death-bed, and acknowledge their sin, they shall be saved, though they never truly believe in Christ, nor experience the work of regeneration. O how far lost are all these I have mentioned.

(4.) Some think to return to God by the power of their own depraved will, as if a man could change his own heart, or get rid (by any mere moral suasions) of that averseness that is in him to do that which is truly spiritually good, or make his own unwilling will yield and bow to the will of God, without the supernatural operations of the Spirit, as if arguments could prevail upon a dead man to awake and rise out of the grave. I hope many of this sort experience better things than they preach and argue for, or else sad will be their condition at last.

(5.) Some think they were born Christians, and in a saved state, because their parents were Protestants, or that they were made Christians by their baptism; nor is it any marvel when they are told, that " they were thereby made members of Christ, children of God, and inheritors of the kingdom of heaven." Woful doctrine, and a lamentable delusion: let all know assuredly, that if they experience no other regeneration than that they are told they had in their baptism in their infancy, they shall never see the kingdom of heaven. Were their hearts and natures then changed, or the seed of grace then infused into them? sure where the habit of grace is, it cannot be lost, and it will afterwards appear, nay, and that immediately also.

(6.) Moreover, some think if they do continue in that faith in which they were born and educated, they shall certainly go to heaven; these cry up the church, the church, when, alas, it is to be feared they know not what the church, the true church of God is, nor whether that which they are in, and cry up, be a true or false church.

(7.) Some other persons think to return to God, and be justified by their faith and sincere obedience through Christ's merits, making their own faith, gospel-obedience, the material cause of their justification at God's bar.

6. Sinners are so far lost that they are become a prey to Satan, and are under his power and influence, but know it not, though they are taken captive by him at his will: " And walk according to the course of this world, according to the prince of the power of the air, the spirit that now worketh in the children of disobedience," Eph. ii. 2.

7. They are so far lost and gone from God, that they are out of Christ's call by the word, they know not Christ's voice from the voice of strangers: true, if they are Christ's sheep, they shall hear his voice, but not till he gives them hearing ears, and calls unto them by the voice of his Spirit; until then lost sinners do not, cannot hear nor discern betwixt true doctrine and false, so as to hear and believe in Jesus Christ.

8. Sinners naturally are so far lost, as that they know not Christ's wholesome, sweet, and soul-fattening pastures, his flock nor fold; they know " not where Christ feeds, and where he makes his flock to rest at noon," Cant. i. 7, 8. They know not perhaps whether Christ's church be national or congregational, nor who his under-shepherds are; they know not Christ's true ministers from false teachers, men that feed themselves, that feed upon the sheep, but feed not the flock.

APPLICATION

1. Sinners, know what you have done by sinning against God. O bewail your lost state, and see what a condition you are in by nature, by the disobedience of the first Adam. O Adam, Adam, saith one, what hast thou done? Thus mayest thou say, O Adam, what a God is he that thou hast lost, and we in thee? and O how God lost us, and we lost ourselves, both by original and actual sins.

Sinners, labour to be convinced of the evil of sin, and the dismal state you all lost sinners are in thereby.

2. Tremble, ye great sinners, ye scarlet-dye sinners, and crimson-dye sinners: if the least sin exposeth a man to the wrath of God, and unto his eternal vengeance, what will become of you? Sirs, the sins of a wicked man that he thinks not of, or concludes perhaps are no sins at all, even his sins of ignorance, deserve eternal wrath. A man little thinks that his very best duties, his prayers, and that worship he performs to God are sins, and hateful in God's sight. " The prayers of the wicked are an abomination to the Lord, and the ploughing of the wicked is sin," Prov. xxi. 4. Their natural as well as their spiritual actions are sin, because they act not from spiritual principles, nor by a holy and righteous rule, nor to glorify God, or to a holy end, but in religious services are hypocritical, and in all their civil acts they inordinately pursue the world, to gratify their own lusts.

Some I know by ploughing do not understand it literally, but metaphorically. Sin is their trade, as a husbandman's calling is to plough and sow, &c., so " they plough wickedness, and sow iniquity," Job iv. 8.   Ungodly men must pray, though their prayers are full of sin, yet if they pray not they sin worse ; it is the duty of all to pray.   Peter put Simon Magus upon praying to God, " that the thoughts of his heart might be forgiven him," Acts viii. 22.   But if sins of ignorance are so dangerous, and small sins so damnable in their own nature ; what is the nature of great sins ?   If an unrenewed man's righteousness is abominable, what is his unrighteousness ?   If your best be so bad, what is your worst ? Will evil thoughts and idle words damn the soul ? what will horrid oaths, blasphemy, cursed imprecations, actual and abominable adulteries, and other scandalous sins do ?

3. Sinners, for all this do not despair, for here is a Saviour come to seek and save lost and undone sinners.   " Though your sins be as red as scarlet, they shall be as white as snow, though as red as crimson, they shall be as white as wool," Isa. i. 18.   That is, if you close with Christ, if you believe in him, and are turned to God, or are brought home by the good Shepherd of the sheep.

4. O admire infinite love, infinite grace and mercy, that God should send a Saviour, such a Saviour, a great one, one that is " able to save all to the uttermost that come to God by him," Isa. xix. 20, Heb. vii. 25.

5. Know that Christ is come this day by his word, and by his unworthy servant to seek such as are lost, who are " without hope, and without God in the world ;" and is not this good news to such that are lost ? Are you sensible of your undone condition ? are you lost in your own sight ?   If it be so, bless God, for certainly it is Jesus Christ that brings sinners to see that they are lost, as well as he came to seek such ; it is he that opens the sinner's eyes to see his sin, and the state that he is in, and shows him the only way to escape, and be saved for ever.

6. You that were lost, who went astray like lost sheep, but now are returned to the great Shepherd and Bishop of your souls ; what thankful hearts ought you to have, and how ought you to admire distinguishing grace : see that you love this Christ, live to this Christ.   God hath appeared by his preventing grace to you ; therefore let it be in your hearts and minds to ascribe all glory, honour, wisdom, and power unto God, and the Lamb, for ever and ever, Amen.

III

What man having an hundred sheep, &c.—Luke xv. 3—5, &c.

I HAVE opened, by way of exposition, every part of this parable, and have taken notice of several propositions, and have prosecuted two : I shall now proceed to speak unto the next.

Doct. III. That the Lord Jesus Christ came to seek and carry home his lost sheep, and will not give over until he hath found them, and carried them all home.

He will bring them into a state of grace here, and into a state of glory hereafter.   In speaking to this, I shall do four things.

I. Show you what Jesus Christ doth, or the ways he takes in seeking and carrying home his lost sheep.

II. As also further discover, what a condition he finds lost sheep in.

III. Show you, why the Lord Jesus Christ came to seek his lost sheep, and will not give over seeking until he hath brought them all home.

IV. Apply it.

In seeking his lost sheep, divers things are comprehended, which chiefly refer to that state and condition in which he finds them.

What Christ doth in seeking his lost sheep. 1. Christ, in seeking his lost sheep, leaves that glorious place where he was, namely, the glory he had with the Father.   Our blessed Shepherd, the Lord Jesus Christ, was with the Father, considered as God, from eternity ; but to seek his lost sheep he came into this world : and indeed to seek his own elect, who were lost in the first Adam, was one main reason why he came hither. " The Son of Man is come to seek and save that which was lost," Luke xix. 10.   He must come where his lost sheep were, be it never so far a journey : a shepherd goes from the place where he was, in those parts where he hears his sheep are strayed, or lost in the wilderness : so the good Shepherd came into this world, where his sheep were all gone astray. " I came forth from the Father into this world; again I leave this world, and go to the Father," John xvi. 28.

2. To seek his lost sheep, he did not only come into this world, but he did also assume man's nature, and so became Man. This was a wonderful condescension; "Who being in the form of God," Phil. ii. 6, i.e., the second Person in the Trinity, God by nature, very God, existent with the Father, yea, the very express image and character of the Father's person, which denotes a peculiar subsistence, distinct from the subsistence of Heb. i. 3. the Father, thought it not robbery to be equal with God, it being his right by eternal generation, he being co-essential the same God; he judged it not usurpation, he the second Person being a subsistent in the same Divine nature and essence: "But made himself of no reputation, and took upon him the form of a servant, and was made in the likeness of men," Phil. ii. 6. Most willingly he took the nature of man into union with his divine Person, out of love to his lost sheep; not that he "Lost the form of God, or laid his Godhead aside;" no, that he could not do; but he vailed the glory of his Deity, in assuming our nature, to seek and save fallen angels; but he assumed into union with his Person: " For verily he did not take on him the nature of angels, but he took on him the seed of Abraham," Heb. ii. 16. He united not his Person to the angelical nature, to seek and save fallen angels; but he assumed into union with his divine Person the seed of Abraham, that is, the very nature of his elect, or his lost sheep, that he might be fitted or capacitated to accomplish the great work he came about to seek or recover them. For as he was God simply considered, he could not do this, nor simply considered as man; it therefore behoved him to be both God and man in one person. For there was a high and fiery mountain for him to level, which stood betwixt God and his lost sheep, over which it was impossible for him to bring them home to God.

Perhaps you will ask what hill or fiery mountain was this.

I answer, the hill or mount of divine justice signified by mount Sinai, this burning mount he must quench, or make smooth and even with divine love, goodness, and mercy. My brethren, the law and justice of God was such a bar or mount of difficulty to the return of Christ's sheep, that unless Christ satisfies both, he could not bring one lost sheep over this high and soul-amazing mountain; and therefore he wrought out a righteousness for our justification, that suited with the nature of God, his law and justice. For as Adam's sin or disobedience, I mean his first sin was imputed to all his seed, or it was by his disobedience, " That many were made sinners," Rom. v. 18; so it is by the obedience of Jesus Christ, that all in him are made righteous, his obedience being imputed to all them that he seeks, finds, and brings home to God.

A fiery mount betwixt God and lost sinners.

See every valley filled, and every hill and mountain brought low.

3. Jesus Christ to seek, recover, find, and save his lost sheep, laid down his life; for there was a dreadful lake into which his lost sheep were fallen, and out of which the great Shepherd must pluck them, or he could not seek them, so as to save one soul. Now this lake was God's divine wrath, which in the scripture is often compared to fire: now this fire had taken hold of every lost and undone sinner; and this fire, or divine anger, and burning wrath, the Lord Jesus must quench, by bearing of it on his own body and human soul, and so deliver or draw his sheep out of it, or else he could not bring them unto God. " For Christ also hath once suffered for sin, the just for the unjust," 1 Pet. iii. 18; to that end. " That he might bring us to God." Observe it well, he could not bring us to God, unless he suffered for our sins, or bore that wrath that was due to us for our sins in breaking the law of the first covenant. The active obedience of Jesus Christ was not sufficient alone to justify sinners, because we had broken the holy law of God; and God being just (nay justice itself) will have full satisfaction by us, or by our Surety whom he had substituted in our room. And pray note, that to make expiation for sin, there was a necessary concurrence of the two natures in our blessed Redeemer; he must be man, for the Godhead was not capable of that submission and obedience which were necessary and requisite to expiate sin; and he must be man, that the sinning nature might not only actually obey (or pay the debt of actual obedience which we owed to the law) but also bear the punishment or penalty due to us for our sins; and so thereby acquire a title to the satisfaction which is made: for the meritorious sufferings of Christ imputed to believers, are grounded on the union of the two natures, which is (as one observes) as well natural, in his partaking of flesh and blood, as moral, in the consent of their will; as the apostle observes, " That he who sanctifies, and they who are sanctified, are all one," Heb. ii. 11: so (saith he) he that offers, must have communion in the same nature.

Out of a fiery and burning lake Christ draws lost sinners, by dying for them.

Dr. Bates's Harm. p. 121.

And as his human nature was necessary to qualify him for his sufferings to bear God's wrath, so the divine nature was to make them sufficient ; for the human nature considered in itself, could not make satisfaction; but the dignity of the divine person makes a temporal or short punishment to be of infinite worth and value in God's account.   Besides, the human nature would have sunk under the weight of divine wrath, or have been itself consumed in those flames, had not the Deity been personally present, and in union, personally considered with it, to support and uphold it. This the good shepherd hath done in seeking and carrying home his lost sheep.

By virtue of Christ's resurrection, sinners return to God.

4. Jesus Christ, to seek and save his elect, or his lost sheep, rose again from the dead, by which God declared that he was well pleased, and fully satisfied by the payment his Son had made : the prisoner that was charged, carried to prison, and shut up in the prison-house for three days and three nights, is now by the great Creditor, or rather Creator, released, discharged, justified, and acquitted, and all his elect in him, from all sins, debts, dues, and demands whatsoever, both past, present, and to come, due to divine justice ; so that all that are brought home, i.e., who are united to Christ, are for ever freed from wrath and condemnation : and the same blessing is secured for all the elect who are not yet called, Rom. viii. 1. My brethren, had not Christ been able to have raised himself out of that fiery lake (into which his sheep were fallen) and into which he plunged, that fire had never been quenched, both sheep and Shepherd had perished together. But he being God as well as man, it was impossible death or wrath could hold him down ; nor could God in justice keep him in prison, seeing he had received a full satisfaction to his law and justice. This, my brethren, also we ought to know and consider well of, viz., that Christ in obeying of the law, or living in a sinless and unspotted life, and in his dying and rising again, and in his ascension up to heaven, did all as our head, and blessed Substitute, Representative, and Surety.

Christ subdues all the enemies of his elect, that they may return to God.

5. Jesus Christ, in seeking and recovering his lost sheep, must subdue and overcome all our spiritual enemies, who hath all God's elect under their feet: he therefore overcame the world in all its sinful snares, enticements, powers, and temptations. " Be of good cheer, I have overcome the world," John xvi. 33. He overcame the world, and the god of this world, death, sin, and the grave ; Heb. ii. 14, 15 ; so that he might bring his lost sheep to God, both in soul and body : for all these enemies stood in the way to obstruct their returning to God ; he hath therefore " triumphed over principalities and powers," Eph. iv. 8, and led captivity captive, in his resurrection, and in his glorious ascension into heaven.

6. Jesus Christ doth not only thus in his own person seek and endeavour, in all these blessed transactions, the recovery of his lost sheep, but he snbstitutes and appoints his servants or faithful ministers to search also to find them out, and cry aloud to them, and to reveal or make known what he hath done to make their peace with God, and so to discover the only way by which they must come to God : one way therefore by which he seeks them is by the preaching of the gospel; by this means externally he calls them, and strives to gather home his elect. The sheep of Christ know not any other way, but by the revelation of the gospel, of the only way and means of their recovery or restoration : faith is required of such that are saved ; " But how shall they believe in him of whom they have not heard ? and how shall they hear without a preacher ?" Rom. x. 14. But though the preaching of the gospel is the external means Jesus Christ uses to seek and bring home his lost sheep, and which is the ordinary way he hath ordained to work faith in their souls, by which they take hold of him ; yet it is not that will do of itself: for many are called who never are brought home: therefore he, whilst they call by outward preaching, also such that are his own sheep by a more special and powerful voice, I mean, by the influences of his Holy Spirit upon their souls, which is called his voice. " My sheep hear my voice," John x. 5, 27. Others hear it not, because they are not his sheep. Some only hear the voice of his ministers, they do not hear nor know the voice of Christ. Lydia being one of his sheep, " The Lord opened her heart, that she attended on the word that Paul preached," Acts xvi. 14. Christ's voice is powerful, it enlightens the understanding, and inclines and bows the will, and changes the affections ; and thus Christ this way seeks his sheep, and by touching their hearts they believe and come to him.

Christ finds his sheep dead.

II. In what a condition are Christ's sheep when he finds them ?

1. Jesus Christ finds all his lost sheep dead, spiritually dead, " dead in sins and trespasses ;" Eph. ii. 1, and being dead, they must needs be deaf.

But as Lazarus, who was naturally dead, heard the voice of Christ, and came forth out of the grave, so those that are spiritually dead do hear the voice of Christ, his voice makes the dead to hear. "Verily, verily, I say unto, the hour is coming, and now is, when the dead shall hear the voice of the Son of God, and they that hear shall live," John v. 25. He doth not refer to the day of the resurrection, to such that are dead in the grave, for that hour was not then come ; but he means such whom he quickens and raises to a spiritual or divine life by his Spirit, "For the Son quickens whom he will," and he will call and quicken all his lost and dead sheep, first or last ; they it seemed wondered at this saying, therefore in ver. 28, saith he, "Marvel not at this, for the hour is coming, in which all that are in the graves shall hear his voice—and shall come forth," &c. This shows he spoke not of such a death before, but of a spiritual death, "This thy brother was dead, and is alive again ; he was lost, and is found," Luke xv. 34. The Prodigal son was dead, so long as he was in his lost and sinful state and condition.

2. Christ's sheep were fallen into a horrible pit, and he could not bring one of them home, except he draws them by his almighty arm out of this pit. ^{Christ's sheep were in a horrible pit.}
We were all naturally in a deep mire, "As for thee also, by the blood of thy covenant, I have sent forth thy prisoners out of the pit wherein is no water," Zech. ix. 11. No water to wash away sin, no water to drink and refresh the soul ; no, nothing but mire and dirt, and the horrid noise of an accusing conscience, of wrath, and divine vengeance, is to be heard in this horrible pit. He (saith David) "brought me up out of an horrible pit, out of the miry clay, and set my feet upon a rock," Psal. xl. 1. Now what is this horrible pit, but the state of deep alienation from God, in which all lost sinners remain before they are plucked out by Jesus Christ ? and unless they are drawn out of the pit of unregeneracy, they will sink down into a lower pit, nor can they come forth of themselves. "No man can come to me, except the Father that sent me draw him," John vi. 44. This drawing is not the act of men, nor of the servants, but of the Master ; not of ministers, but of the Father.

Jesus Christ finds his sheep blind. As sinners are said to be dead whilst in a state of nature, so also they are said to be blind, "Thou knowest not that thou art blind and naked," &c., Rev. iii. 17. The enemy has put out all their eyes, they are darkness, utterly void of spiritual understanding ; therefore he opens their eyes to see the woful condition in which they naturally are, "That the eyes of your understanding being enlightened," &c., Eph. i. 18. None till then can see the horrid evil of sin, nor what a state of enmity they are in against God. "Having their understanding darkened, being alienated from the life of God, through the ignorance that is in them, because of the blindness of their hearts," Eph. iv. 18. And from hence also it is they cannot see the way home to God, but go every day farther and farther from him. ^{Christ's sheep were blind.}

4. Christ's sheep have lost their fleece ; he finds them shorn and naked ; the enemy hath stripped them of their raiment, I mean of that righteousness and holiness they had in the first Adam : sinners naturally are "like a wretched new-born infant, cast out naked in its blood and filthiness, no eye pitying it," Ezek. xvi. 4, 8. Thus it is when Christ passes by, or comes to seek his lost sheep ; therefore he casts his skirts over them, and clothes them with his own righteousness. ^{Christ's Sheep were shorn.}

5. Christ finds his sheep that are lost in the briers, or in chains and fetters, and cruelly torn and wounded, and were "become meat, and a prey to every beast of the field," Ezek. xxxiv. 8. "Thou art in the gall of bitterness, and in the bond of iniquity," Acts viii. 23. Like as sheep caught in cruel thorns, and pricking briers, are as it were in bonds, as a man bound in chains and fetters, so is every sinner naturally caught, and held fast in the "Bonds of his own iniquity," Isa. lviii. 6 ; and cannot get out, ignorance is as a cruel bond, an hard heart is like another bond, and unbelief binds down every ungodly man and woman, like chains and fetters of iron. Hence the Psalmist says, "They wandered in the wilderness, sat in darkness and in the shadow of death, being bound in affliction and iron," Psal. cvii. 4, 10. And in this woful condition are all Christ's lost sheep when he finds them, and he in compassion looses their bonds, and pours in his oil and wine to heal their wounds. "He hath sent me to bind up the broken-hearted, to proclaim liberty to the captives, and to open the prison to them that are bound," Isa. lxi. 1. ^{Christ's lost sheep caught in briars.}

6. Christ's lost sheep were seized and made a prey of by dogs, lions, bears, and wolves ; and they had torn them in a cruel manner. By these ravenous beasts are meant, the devil and his emissaries ; Satan is called a hungry lion, and some wicked men dogs : and deceivers are compared to wolves, "grievous wolves, ^{Christ's sheep were a prey to evil beasts.}

which spare not the flock," Acts xx. 29. And by these are the lost sheep almost utterly devoured; but the Lord Christ rescues them out of the jaws of these cruel lions, wolves, and dogs, breaking the teeth of the old lion, lioness, and the lion's whelps.

7. Christ's lost sheep (as the fearful effects of original and actual sin) **Christ's sheep were filled full of enmity against God.** were filled with enmity and hatred against God, notwithstanding his great and inconceivable love to them, in sending his Son out of his bosom to die for them, and in their stead, that he might recover them out of the hands of all their enemies, and bring them home again to God, from whom they had wandered. " The carnal mind is enmity against God, it is not subject to the law of God, neither indeed can be," Rom. viii. 7. From hence they naturally show an averseness to return to God, and slight the Lord Jesus Christ. " We will not have this man to reign over us." They resist his word, vex his Spirit, condemn his authority, despise and slight his love, and refuse to come into his bands, and to return to his fold; and until the Lord Jesus changes their rebellious hearts, he cannot bring one of them home. Alas, lost sinners, though such be their woful state (as hath been showed) are not willing to be found, they love to wander; most wretched creatures, they love to sculk with Adam, hiding their heads in the bushes; they had rather abide in the wilderness, and have their sins, and continue in their blood and filth, and in the hands of the devil, than accept the love of their dear and blessed Shepherd: yet seeks them, and never gives over until he hath found them, and made them willing to receive and embrace him with joy.

Christ's Sheep were degenerated into a brutish nature, Tit. i. 12. Jer. x. 34. 8. Christ's lost sheep by sin were degenerated into dogs, wolves, bears, lions, and other ravenous beasts. Sinners are styled evil beasts, as their sensuality and brutish practices demonstrate, they having lost the properties of sheep, and having got the evil qualities or properties of ravenous beasts. Now the Lord Christ takes away or destroys these brutish qualities, and transforms them, restoring a sheep-like nature and disposition to them, making them meek, innocent, and harmless creatures, that so he might, in bringing them home to his fold, make them fit companions for his flock; and all these things he doth in seeking and saving of his lost sheep. So much as to the first and second heads of discourse.

III. I shall in the next place show you why Jesus Christ came to seek **Why Christ doth seek his sheep.** and save his lost sheep, and will not cease or give over seeking, until he hath found, and brought every one of them home to God.

1. Christ seeks them, and will until he finds them, because he loves them: **Christ's love the cause of seeking his sheep.** this is the spring, and efficient cause of all his gracious actings towards them. " Yea, I have loved thee with an everlasting love, therefore with loving-kindness have I drawn thee," Jer. xxxi. 3. In this text we see, that whatsoever Christ doth in the beginning or drawing his sheep to him, it is because he loveth them. Why did he come into this world, and die the cursed death of the cross? was it not out of his endeared love to his sheep? " He loved me (saith Paul) and gave himself for me. Who loved us, and washed us from our sins in his own blood," Rev. i. 5. There was nothing in his sheep he could see, that could move him to come to seek them, or die for them.

They are his sheep. 2. He came to seek them, and will seek them until he finds them, and carry them home, because they are his sheep. " Other sheep have I that are not of this fold, them I must bring," John x. 16.

By election. (1.) They are Christ's sheep by the election of the Father, thine they were, that is, thine, O holy Father, by election. And,

By donation. (2.) They are his sheep also by the Father's free donation. " Thine they were, and thou hast given them unto me," John xvii. 6. To seek them, die **By conjugal affection.** for them, bring them home, and eternally save them.

(3.) They were his by virtue of his cordial and conjugal love and affections, and from hence it is he seeks and will seek them until he finds them, **Christ will seek his sheep, because of his covenant.** because his lost sheep are to be his spouse, his bride, and dear consort for ever.

3. Because of that holy compact or covenant which was between the Father and Son from all eternity. The tenor of which is, that he should redeem all those the Father gave unto him, and bring them home; and from hence Christ said, " Other sheep have I that are not of this fold, and them I must bring." I must by virtue of the covenant entered into with my Father. See what God the Father spake to the Son, " That thou mayest say unto the prisoners, go forth, and to them that sit in darkness, shew yourselves." Again he saith, " Behold these things shall come from afar, and these from the North and from the West," Isa. xlix. 9, 12. Wheresoever the sheep were lost in any land or nation, whether North, East, West, South, the

Lord Jesus was to bring them. "I will bring thy seed from the East, and gather them from the West; I will say to the North, give up, and to the South, keep not back: bring my sons from afar, and my daughters from the ends of the earth," Isa. xliii. 5, 6. "I will give thee for a light to the Gentiles." To what end? observe, "to open blind eyes, and to bring the prisoners, and them that sit in darkness out of the prison house." Now the Son of God, as Mediator, having struck hands with the Father in that blessed covenant, before the world began, to bring home his lost sheep he will perform this his covenant, and will seek and search them out until he hath found them all.

4. He will do it because they were appointed or ordained to eternal life. "God predestinated all them that he foreknew to be conformable to the image of his Son," Rom. viii. 29. And this work belongs to our Lord Jesus Christ; he hath received abundance of the Holy Spirit to pour forth to renew or regenerate all those the Father predestinated. God the Father makes his Son their great trustee; he is the guardian of all God's elect, grace is their portion, and they must have it, because it was given to them in Christ before the world began; (2 Tim. i. 9), and the Lord Jesus is obliged to seek them out, and to give it to them. "All that the Father hath given me shall come unto me," John vi. 37. This purpose of God is absolute and not conditional; no unworthiness in poor sinners shall hinder the accomplishment of God's decree and purpose, as no foreseen works or worthiness was the cause of this purpose. Brethren, Jesus Christ, when he comes to seek and fetch home his lost sheep, He comes leaping over the hills, and skipping over the mountains, like a young hart. No mountain of difficulty on his part shall obstruct him, whatsoever it doth cost him, home he will bring them; nor doth he regard any unworthiness that may be in them; no, though they are enemies to him, and hate him, yea though as vile as sin and the devil can make them in their lost state, such as Manasseh and Mary Magdalene, yet home they shall be brought, the decree and purpose of God must stand. See Ezek. xxxiv. 6. "My sheep wandered throughout all mountains, and upon every high hill. "Thus saith the Lord, behold, I even I, will both search my sheep and seek them out," verse 12. As a shepherd seeketh out his flock in the day that he is among his sheep that are scattered, so will I seek out my sheep and will deliver them out of all places, where they were scattered in the cloudy and dark day. Again he saith, verse 16, "I will seek that which was lost, and bring again that which was driven away, and will bind up that which was broken, and will strengthen that which was sick." This is God's purpose and gracious promise. "The election hath obtained, and the rest were hardened," Rom. xi. 7. The rest contemned God's special grace and favour, and so would these have done, had not divine grace took hold of them, and God by his eternal purpose prevented them by his love and grace, in sending of his Son to seek and save them. Brethren, there is none can hinder God in his eternal purpose. "Who hath saved and called us, not according to our works, but according to his own purpose and grace given to us in Christ Jesus, before the world began," 2 Tim. i. 9. Whatsoever grace we receive in time, is according to God's eternal purpose before time, "For the Lord of hosts hath purposed, and who shall disannul it?" Isa. xiv. 27. Again he saith, "My counsel shall stand, and I will do all my pleasure. I have spoken it, and I will bring it to pass," Isa. xlvi. 10, 11.

Christ will seek his sheep, because of the purpose of God.

5. Christ will, nay must seek, find, and bring home his lost sheep, because he is their shepherd, the good shepherd. What man that hath an hundred sheep, if he lose one will not seek that sheep? If no other shepherd will be remiss herein, or neglect seeking his lost sheep, be sure Jesus Christ, the good shepherd will not fail in this case.

Christ will seek his sheep, because he is their shepherd.

6. Because he died, laid down his life for his sheep, he purchased them out of the hands of justice with the price of his own blood, and therefore will be sure take the pains to seek and search them out, and by his mighty power recover them out of the paw of the lion, and paw of the bear. If he gave himself up to death for them all, how much more will he do all things else that are needful for them? He that gave a thousand pounds for a purchase, will not refuse to part with five pounds to take up and make it sure to himself. And that blood that was shed for them, must be applied and sprinkled upon their consciences. They must therefore be sought and brought home to God by him, "Who gave himself for us, that he might redeem us from all iniquity," Tit. ii. 14. Christ's design in redemption must be answered, it was not only to deliver us from the curse of the law, and out of the hands of divine justice, but also to redeem us from sin, to save us from sin and Satan, and from all enemies of our souls.

Because he died for them. Act. xx. 28.

None else can seek the lost sheep.

7. He will seek and save his sheep, because none else can do it; who can conquer the devil, or pluck them out of the paws of the devil? David was a type of Christ, who delivered a sheep of his flock out of the paw of a lion. Who but Jesus Christ can raise the dead? who else can open blind eyes, or draw them out of that deep and horrible pit, and change their hearts, or infuse sheep-like qualities into them, that were so degenerated as you have heard?

None of Christ's sheep can be utterly lost.

8. Christ will seek his lost sheep, because none of those sheep which God gave to him, can be utterly lost; the holy will of God cannot be frustrated. "And this is the Father's will which sent me, that of all which he hath given me, I should lose nothing." Nothing, no not one, not the least of them. O how faithful was Christ in doing his Father's will, it was his meat and drink, therefore he will be sure to fulfil his Father's will in this matter; for unless he seeks them, renews and calls them, they will be all lost for ever.

APPLICATION

God's wisdom in bringing home the lost sheep.

1. I infer from what hath been said, that the restoration, recovery, and bringing home the lost sheep, is a clear demonstration of the wonderful wisdom of God, since divine justice put such a bar to their return, and must be fully satisfied, or they must all perish for ever. Such is the nature of sin, and such is the rectitude of the pure and holy nature of God, the guilt of sin must be transferred to Jesus Christ (even all the sins of the elect) or it cannot be expiated nor justice satisfied, so that a way might be prepared. Moreover, the law of God put a bar to sinners' restoration, in respect of the want of a perfect conformity to it, in point of actual obedience, and also such bearing the penalty or punishment due to us for our breach thereof, as would appease the wrath of God; so that sinners return to God in a way of righteousness, as well as in a way of mercy, grace, and sovereign love. And from hence it appears, that all the divine attributes shine forth in equal glory and harmony, in the redemption of God's elect; it is by the obedience of Christ that lost sinners are made righteous. "The just must die for the unjust, to bring them to God," 1 Pet. iii. 18. "Christ was wounded for our transgressions," Isa. liii. 5, 6. "He was made sin for us, that knew no sin, that we might be made the righteousness of God in him," 2 Cor. v. 21. He died that his lost sheep might live.

It is a work of infinite love.

2. We also therefore infer, that the recovery of the lost sheep is a work of infinite love, it discovers the greatest love that ever was known or manifested. What, did God so love sinners, as to give his only-begotten Son to redeem these lost sheep with the price of his own blood, and Jesus Christ love them so as to give himself a sacrifice for them. What shepherd, to seek his lost sheep, would die for them? "I lay down my life for my sheep," John x. 17.

It is a work of infinite power also.

3. We may also infer from hence, that the recovery of Christ's lost sheep is a work of almighty power; we needed a Saviour, a great one, or one clothed with Almighty power. Hence, as Jesus Christ "speaketh in righteousness, so he is mighty to save," Isa. lxiii. 1, he is "the power of God, and the wisdom of God," 1 Cor. i. 24. Who but one that was strong and mighty to save, could raise the dead, subdue the devil, death, and all other enemies of our souls? O what grace is here, what pity, what love and compassion hath God showed in Christ! What is man, sorry man, lost and undone man, that God should be thus mindful of him? Nay, thus set his heart upon him, and find out, or devise such means to bring him out of a state of sin, death, and wrath? "Deliver him from going down into the pit, I have found a ransom," Job xxxiii. 24.

4. We may moreover from hence infer, that the ignorance of some men is very great, even such that think the lost sheep may return home by their own good deeds, and good duties, or by their obedience to the moral law, or by living an honest, sober, and just life, or by the power of their own wills, they forget (I speak of the last sort) into what an horrible pit man is fallen, and what a strong lion had the lost sheep in his paws, and how depraved man is in every faculty of his soul, and what enmity there is in his carnal mind," Rom. viii. 7.

2ndly. Exhortation. This may also be improved by way of exhortation: sinners rejoice, the great shepherd is come to seek, to search for, find out, and to save his lost sheep, and he will not (you hear) give over until he hath found all his lost sheep: is not this good news?

Object. Perhaps you will say, it is not good news to all, because he seeks none but such sheep which the Father gave to him.

Answ. It is good news to all that see they are lost, to all that see they are sinners, un-done sinners ; as for such that are righteous, and never went astray in their own conceit, they do not need a Saviour, they being not sick they need not a physician, these indeed he came not to call ; therefore if you are such that never went astray, or never were convinced, or are in a lost and undone condition, it is to be feared you may be some of them which he leaves in the wilderness. But you that are great sinners in your own eyes, may con-clude you are some of them he is come to seek and to save.

3rdly. Comfort. This may be also for comfort to the greatest sinners. "Jesus Christ came into the world to save sinners, of whom I (saith Paul) am chief." It is no matter how great thy sins are, or how long thou hast abode in a wicked course of life ; though thy sins are as red as scarlet, if Christ be come to seek thee and thou fly to him, believing on him, " they shall be as white as snow ; though they be red as crimson, they shall be as wool," Isa. i. 18.

4thly. Admire, praise, and adore the holy and gracious God, in sending such a shepherd to seek and save his lost sheep; "one that is able to save all them to the uttermost, that come to God by him," Heb. vii. 25. Had he sent one of the prophets to seek and save us ; what could he have done? could he have carried the lost sheep over that burning mountain of God's divine justice and fiery law ? or could he have plucked them out of the burning lake of God's dreadful wrath and vengeance ? or could any mere man conquer the devil, raise the dead, or triumph over the grave ? No, no, none but he that was God as well as man, could do it.

5thly. Terror. O what terror may from hence seize upon such who slight this shep-herd, contemn this Christ, and disregard all his love, and tread under foot his most precious blood, as if there was no worth nor virtue in it to wash away sin, or purge the conscience any more than the blood of any other person. Tremble you scoffers, that vilify the true Saviour, and trust to a Christ that cannot save you, a false Christ, a Christ that never died nor hath any blood to shed ; a Christ within, which is nothing more than the law of the first creation, or some remainders of it : if that way, *i. e.*, by living up to that light, lost sinners could be brought home, be justified, sanctified, and eternally saved, Jesus Christ is dead in vain.

6thly. This likewise may tend to reprove all such who discover most horrible ingratitude and unthankfulness, who after all that Christ hath done to recover lost sinners, refuse to submit unto him, to close in with him, believe in him, go with him. How few are there who say with Rebecca in another case, when she was asked whether she would go with Abraham's servant, and become Isaac's wife, " She said, I will go." Ministers ask sinners will you come to Christ, cleave to Christ, go with him, follow your Shepherd whithersoever he leads you ? Will you venture your souls upon him, deny yourselves, and take up your cross and follow him ? But alas ! how few say (and resolve in their hearts) to do this ? What do you say, sirs, that hear me this day ? Will you receive the Lord Jesus, hear his voice ? Is it in your hearts to cleave unto him? Or will you remain in the jaws of devils, polluted in your sins, condemned creatures, and under wrath, and the curse, and so perish for ever ?

7thly. This also should be of use to ministers, and may serve to admonish them to their duty, whose care and labour should be great, to do what lies upon them as their part, to seek after Christ's lost sheep. Let us learn of the great Shepherd ; though we sweat at the work, and spend our strength and spirits ; let us not think it too much, for he sweat great drops of blood, and poured forth his soul to death, to bring home his lost sheep to God.

Lastly. To you that are the sheep of Jesus Christ, " Who once went astray, but now are returned to the great Shepherd and Bishop of your souls," 1 Pet. ii. 25. O remember what the great Shepherd hath done, that he might bring you home into his fold ! O take heed you never go astray any more, neither from Christ, nor from that fold where he hath by his providence put you; be content with your pasture, and be not headstrong, nor wanton, and so foolishly venture to leap over the fold, or break away in a disorderly manner, to get into a pasture that is none of your own. Are you not fed with wholesome doctrine ? Is not the main design of the ministry in this place, to exalt Jesus Christ alone, and the free grace of God in him ? Remember it was Christ that put you into this fold, and you entered into a solemn covenant to feed in this pasture ; and what peace can you have to be in a pasture that is none of your own, nor you were placed in by the great Shepherd ? A shep-herd sometimes sets his dog to fetch out a sheep that is got into another pasture. So Christ may let out Satan to distress your consciences before you are aware, for such an evil, or afflict you sorely sooner or later some other way, that others may fear. Besides, dare any honest shepherd of another flock receive unruly sheep that have broke away from their neighbour's fold, which are none of his own, nor were by the owner committed to his charge? Would not this be looked upon to be a kind of theft, and a dishonest thing, and punishable by the law?

But to conclude, labour to be fruitful to Christ, and thankful to him, who has bought you with his own blood, and brought you home to God, that you may be to the glory of his grace, and live to him all your days.

IV

And goeth after that which is lost until he finds it; and when he hath found it, he layeth it on his shoulders, rejoicing,—Luke xv. 4, 5.

THE point of doctrine which I am upon the prosecution of, is this,

Doct.   That our Lord Jesus Christ came to seek his lost sheep, and he will not give over seeking until he hath found all his sheep that are lost.

I have proposed to do five things in speaking unto this proposition.

I have spoken unto the three first.

Fourthly. I shall now proceed to show you, what the finding lost sinners, or his lost sheep, doth denote or imply.

What Christ's finding his lost sheep denotes.   1. Christ's finding them denotes (as previous to it) his seeking them, and not giving over until he hath accomplished his design and gracious purpose.

Some shepherds seek lost sheep, but soon grow weary, and so give over, despairing ever to find them, and so search after them no more. But thus Christ doth not, he is not weary, nor will give over seeking, and this for two or three reasons.

(1.) Because this shepherd is God as well as man; "And the Creator of the ends of the earth fainteth not," Isa. xl. 28.

(2.) Because he knows where all his lost sheep are, i. e., the place whither they are strayed, and also what a state and condition they are in; and so do not other shepherds, who have lost some of their sheep.

(3.) Because Christ knows, and is sure that he shall find all his lost sheep; "He shall see his seed—and the pleasure of the Lord shall prosper in his hand," Isa. liii. 10. He therefore knows he shall not seek in vain.

2. Christ finds a lost sinner denotes, that the full time is come, in which his word shall be effectual, or his absolute design and purpose of grace shall succeed, in respect to the execution thereof, the design of his death, his end and purpose in sending the gospel. "For as rain cometh down, and the snow from heaven, and returneth not thither, but watereth the earth, and maketh it bring forth and bud, that it may give seed to the sower and bread to the eater," Isa. lv. 10. Ver. 11. "So shall my word be that goeth out of my mouth; it shall not return unto me void, it shall accomplish that which I please, and it shall prosper in the thing whereunto I sent it." The Lord Jesus Christ hath gracious thoughts towards poor sinners, "For I know the thoughts I have towards you, saith the Lord, thoughts of peace, and not of evil, to give an expected end." Jer. xxix. 11. A poor sinner waits, perhaps, under the hearing of the word, year after year, and yet profits but little or nothing, but in hopes and expectation Christ will come at last; and until Christ comes to seek his soul and finds him, all his hearing and praying seems to be without success, but the purpose of Christ shall be accomplished, "Yea, saith he, I have spoken in, and I also will do it," Isa. xlvi. 11. I will come near you, and find you out, Ver. 12. Yea, bring my righteousness near, and my salvation shall not tarry; though you are stout-hearted, rebellious ones, and far from righteousness.

3. The Lord Jesus finding his lost sheep, denotes the powerful convictions of the Spirit, which takes hold of a sinner's heart: when this is done, he may be said to find his lost sheep. "When the Spirit is come (that is, Christ by his Spirit) he shall convince the world of sin," &c., John xvi. 8, 9. Pray note two things here: (1.) That Christ's finding a sinner, is one thing; and (2.) the sinner's finding of Christ is another thing. When Christ finds a sinner, the poor sinner comes to himself (as it is said concerning the prodigal son that was lost) i. e., he sees that he is lost and undone, a vile and wretched creature. True, perhaps he may have some common feeling, or gripes of conscience before, but they go off again, but now they are more pricking, pinching, more strong and effectual, and more

abiding on his conscience: and when a sinner finds Jesus Christ, he comes to see his help, his cure, and only remedy: the first makes him see that he is sick, wounded, lost, and undone; and when he hath found Christ, he sees, knows, and meets with his Physician.

4. Jesus Christ finding his lost sheep denotes, or doth imply, Christ and a sinner's meeting together: now the shepherd sees his lost sheep, and the sheep sees his shepherd; they meet together as the prodigal son and his father met each other. As a sheep that is strayed away never seeth his shepherd, nor meeteth with him, but is alone "as a lamb, and in a large place," until the shepherd finds it; so it is here, though a sinner hears often of Christ, in reading, and in hearing the word preached, yet he never meets with him until Christ finds him. *Christ and his lost sheep meet together.*

5. Christ finding his lost sheep denotes the danger of such souls is over. A sheep or lamb in a large place lost in the mountains, is exposed to many dangers, and may soon become a prey to ravenous beasts, and be torn in pieces; but when the shepherd hath found it, all those dangers are over: so when Christ, the good shepherd, hath found a lost sinner, and it is in his hands, his care is such, that neither sin, devils, the world, nor impostors, can devour or destroy it. *Christ's lost sheep when found secured from all dangers.*

6. It therefore also implies the time of the manifestation of God's special love is come, and that such a lost sheep is one of those the Father gave unto Christ; and because he was beloved from everlasting, Christ is now, according to his covenant with the Father, come to seek and receive him, and actually, manifest his love unto him, and to take care of him. "How is it Lord that thou wilt manifest thyself unto us, and not unto the world?" The reason is because they were his sheep, and the time is now come that they shall know this: before he comes and finds his lost sheep, it is not known to be one of his sheep, or one of God's elect; for before this time he lets such a sinner wander abroad; but in his month he finds it, that is, either the time or month of affliction, or of convictions; he ends it, some are found in or by afflictions; the Lord sometimes takes hold of them, finds them, and brings them to see their lost state by the rod, by this or that affliction which he lays upon them: others he finds by the preaching of the word, by fastening the word, by powerful convictions upon their hearts. And may be the sinner at first is afraid to venture himself into Christ's hand (as a lost sheep when the shepherd hath found it, is afraid of its tender shepherd) the sins of a sinner's heart and life, original and actual, are all laid open before his eyes. "Come see a man that told me all that ever I did," John. iv. 29. The Lord Jesus was come to seek this lost sinner, and now having found her, see how she cries out. Thus the Prodigal son, "Father, I have sinned against heaven, and in thy sight," Luke xv. 18, 19; and being now afraid, he would become a servant, "Let me become as one of thy hired servants." This may not only signify his humility, but his servile spirit; the spirit of bondage seized on him, and he would now do something to procure or deserve his father's love and acceptance. Lord, saith a lost sinner, I have gone astray from thee, and my sins are now set before mine eyes, and I am afraid to come near thee: the soul fears his life may go, he fears divine anger, and is in horror. O, saith he, what will God do with me, who have run from him, and have a long time gone astray? I deserve nothing but hell and eternal wrath; but no sooner doth Christ lay hold of him, and take him up in his arms of love and mercy, and lay him on his shoulders of infinite power, but he sees the compassion of his dear shepherd, "Who gathers his lambs with his arm, and carries them in his bosom," Isa. xl. 11. *Christ's love and care manifested to his lost sheep.*

7. Christ finding his lost sheep, and taking it up in his arms, denotes irresistible grace, such grace that the sinner cannot resist or withstand; not that he forces the will, for that is to destroy the nature of that noble faculty; but he sweetly inclines it, overpowers it, and makes the unwilling will, (that was so naturally) to be willing in the day of this his power. Can a sheep, when the shepherd hath found it, and got hold of it, get out of his hand, (provided he be a strong man) or resist the design and purpose of the shepherd? True, it may struggle a little at first, and make some resistance until it is overcome: so they through Satan's temptations at first, for a short time may make opposition, and struggle under those convictions of the Holy Spirit; but Christ soon overcomes it in such a sweet and gentle manner, that it cannot longer resist his power. Christ doth not leave the depraved will of man (without powerful influences of his irresistible grace) to determine the whole issue of his design and purpose; no, I will work (saith the Lord) and who shall let? *Christ's lost sheep brought home by his irresistible power.*

8. It denotes Christ's removing that enmity that naturally is in every sin- *Christ removes the*

enmity in our hearts against God. ner's heart against God, or his taking away the heart of stone, and giving a heart of flesh, which is the promise of God in the new covenant : " I will take the stone out of their hearts, and will give them a heart of flesh," Ezek. xxxvi. 26. So that Christ finding his lost sheep, is the only way and means by which his sheep comes to find him, and do experience his love, they being by his Spirit united to him ; he clasping his arms of love and mercy about them, makes them willing to go with him, and follow him whithersoever he goeth. Thus Paul, no sooner had Jesus Christ found him (who had with a witness gone astray) but he cries out, " Lord, what wilt thou have me to do ?" Acts ix. 6. Christ finding his disciples Matthew at the receipt of custom, and Peter, James, and John, who were mending their nets, caused them to leave all and follow him : therefore also it implies effectual call, or their special vocation, or his working of faith in their souls ; he helps the lost sinner to hang upon him, cleave to him, and trust in him alone for righteousness, pardon, and eternal life.

Into what a state Christ brings his lost sheep. So much as the fourth general head of discourse.

V. Whither doth Jesus Christ bring, or carry his lost sheep, when he hath found them ; I mean, into what state and condition, and unto what place ?

Answ. 1. He brings them from a state of death unto a state of life ; the sheep of Christ before Christ finds them, lie under the sentence of death, *They are brought from death to life.* with all the rest of mankind ; nay, they were not dead in law only, but they were really dead, or without a principle of spiritual life ; they lay in the wicked one, like carrion in a common shore, or as dead sheep in a filthy ditch, and he brings them to life. " You hath he quickened that were dead in sins and trespasses," Eph. ii. 1, 2. Having now a principle of spiritual life infused into them.

They are brought to a sense of feeling, 2. He brings them to a sense of spiritual feeling : before, though a great mountain of horrid guilt lay upon them, and they are wounded at the very heart ; yet being dead, they felt no pain, never cried out ; but now the least sin is like a sword in their bowels, and they are forced to cry out, " Being pricked at heart, men and brethren, what shall we do ?" Acts ii. 37. And as the jailor did, they *Brought to the sense of seeing.* cry out, " Sirs, what must I do to be saved ?" Acts xvi. 30.

3. Moreover, he brings them (by infusing a vital principle into them) to the sense of a spiritual seeing : " Before they were darkness, but now light in the Lord." They see now the evil of sin, and how they have broken the law of God, and were under wrath and the curse, and come also to behold how vile and filthy they are, and so loathe themselves, crying out, " Woe is me, for I am undone," Isa. vi. 5, 6. And this is effected by their beholding the glory of Jesus Christ, their blessed Shepherd ; *Christ confers lost beauty.* who being come to seek them, he lets them see his glory.

4. Also by this means there is a beauty put upon them. Life infused into a dead person, restores lost beauty. O what a vast difference is there between a dead corpse, a man dead, and a living man ? so a principle of spiritual life causes the soul to shine in heavenly liveliness, in beauty and glory, the image of God being *They taste how good God is.* stamped upon the soul by the Spirit.

5. By this means likewise they come to taste and relish the things of God. Now they " Taste the Lord is gracious. O taste and see (saith David) that the Lord is good." Psal. xxxiv. 8. Alas, dead men cannot taste : as they cannot feel, nor see, so they cannot taste ; no more can dead sinners, carnal persons, taste how good God and Christ is, and his word is, they cannot savour the things of the Spirit : but no sooner does Christ bring them to life, or infuse life into the dead soul, but he finds nothing so sweet to his taste as spiritual things are, especially Christ, and the love of Christ : the very word is *They are brought out of darkness* " sweeter than honey or the honey-comb."

6. Christ brings his lost sheep from the power of Satan unto God ; Satan had the rule in them before, and led them captive at his will. " They walked according to the course of this world, according to the prince of the power of the air, the spirit that now worketh in the children of disobedience," Eph. ii. 2. He effectually before worked in them, governed and acted them ; but Christ hath subdued that strong man armed, and hath rescued them out of his hand, and " hath opened their eyes, and turned them from darkness to light, and from the power of Satan unto God," Acts xxvi. 18. This is Christ's work, though he be pleased to attribute it to his ministers, as the instruments that he ordinarily worketh by, or makes use of. Yet he is the great agent, " who hath delivered us from the power of darkness, and translated us into the kingdom of his dear Son," Col. i. 13. The darkness of ignorance, of unbelief, of sin and misery, to behold the wonderful light and glory of God, in the face of Jesus Christ. And hence we are said to

be called, or brought " out of darkness into his marvellous light," 1 Pet. ii 9.   In his spiritual kingdom, the kingdom of grace, amongst his subjects and servants, where Christ dwells in the heart by his Spirit, and so we are united unto him, by faith that works by love.

7.   Jesus Christ brings them from a state of spiritual bondage, into a state *They are brought into a state of liberty.* of liberty ; he hath loosed their bonds, they were caught in the briars or fetters of sin and the devil ; but he brings them into a state of gospel liberty. " Stand fast in the liberty wherewith Christ hath made you free, and be not entangled again with the yoke of bondage," Gal. v. 1.   He sets them at liberty from the guilt of sin, from the power of sin, and from the curse of the moral law, and from all legal observations, rites, and ceremonies, even from all legal bondage, and slavish fear, and from God's vindictive justice, and his eternal wrath, and this for ever.   " If the Son therefore make you free, ye shall be free indeed," John viii. 36.   Glorious freedom, soul-freedom, and eternal freedom.

8.   He carries them home to God, who as a dear and tender Father embraces them in his arms.   " Like as the Father embraced his prodigal son, *They are brought home to God, who embraces them in his arms.* and fell upon his neck and kissed him."   He did not upbraid him for his former wicked and profane course of life ; he doth not tell him how basely he had wasted his portion on harlots, and never returned until almost starved with hunger ; no, no, not a word of this, but kisses him, and for joy makes a great feast, and calls for the best robe to be put upon him, and a ring on his finger, and shoes on his feet, and commands the fatted calf to be killed, and says, " Let us eat and be merry, for this my son was dead and is alive again, he was lost, and is found," Luke xv. 22, 23, 24.   O take encouragement from hence to fly to Christ, to cleave to Christ ; it is no matter how great your sins are, or how long you have lived in an ungodly course of life.   If now you are helped to return home, or if Jesus Christ become to seek you, and finds you, he will carry you to his Father, who with joy and gladness will also receive you.

9. Christ brings them into a state of union with himself, by which means *Into a state of union with himself.* they are not only made near him, but become also very dear to the Lord Jesus Christ, even as a bride is to the bridegroom.   " But now in Christ Jesus, ye that sometimes were afar off, are made near by the blood of Christ," Eph. ii. 13.   He brings them into the bonds of the covenant, the conjugal knot is tied, he betrothes them unto himself for ever.   Nay, my brethren, he brings them into a state of likeness unto himself, he infuseth divine or spiritual qualities into them, and circumcises their hearts to love him, and delight in him, who before had lost (as you heard) all the properties of sheep, they loving then to wallow like swine in the mire of sin and filthiness.

10. Jesus Christ brings them into a state of justification and reconciliation *Into a state of justification.* with God for ever, as God in Christ was reconciled to them, so they are now reconciled to God, and are pronounced spotless before the throne.   " Being justified by faith, we have peace with God through our Lord Jesus Christ," Rom. v. 1. This also implies a pardon, or free forgiveness of all their sins : such that are justified persons, are pardoned persons, their sins are forgiven, and shall be remembered no more.

11.   Jesus Christ brings them into a state of sanctification and holiness. " God hath not called us unto uncleanness, but unto holiness," 1 Thess. iv. 7. *Christ washeth all his sheep.* The Lord Jesus finds all his lost sheep very foul, polluted, or unclean, and he washes them.   Sheep we know are subject to take filth, especially such that go astray, and they must be washed.   Hence it is said, that his sheep " come from the washing, every one bearing twain, and none barren among them," Cant. iv. 2. They are not only washed in the blood of Christ, or sanctified by the Spirit, but are also made fruitful : they bring forth the fruits of the Spirit, the fruits of righteousness, when Christ hath found them and brought them home to God ; before whilst they were in their lost condition, they brought forth no fruit to him, nor can they bring forth fruit until they are purged, sanctified, and thoroughly washed.   " He saw them polluted in their blood," Ezek. xvi. 6, 7, like a new-born infant, and that was the time of his love ; that is, that was the time of the manifestation of his love : " and then he cast his skirt over them, and covered their nakedness ; that is, he put on them the robe of his own righteousness. " And then I washed thee with water, yea I thoroughly washed away thy blood from thee, and I anointed thee with oil," Ver. 9. He purgeth them from all original, and from all actual pollution whatsoever.   " He hath loved us, and washed us from our sins in his own blood," Rev. i. 5.   They are not Christ's sheep that are not found and carried home, i. e., they are not called and justified, who are not sanctified.

Christ's
sheep
brought into
fat pastures.

12. Christ carries them into good pastures, where he makes them feed and lie down together, and leads them to still waters : those waters that run softly, gently, that cause the soul to possess inward peace and serenity of mind. " And they shall lie in a good fold, and feed in fat pastures," Psal. xxiii. 1, 2, Ezek. xxxiv. 14. This implies, they shall wander no more on the mountains of error and heresy ; Christ leads them out of all idolatry and superstition, out of Babylon and all false worship, they shall no more be defiled with women, that is, by the pollution of false churches, or with harlot-worship ; the church of Rome is called the mother of harlots. Are there no false churches but the Romish church ? yea, there are, no doubt, she hath whorish daughters, though not such vile and beastly harlots as the mother is ; all churches that sprang from her, or are of the like nature, in respect of their constitution, and that retain many of her superstitious names, garbs, rites, and ceremonies, no doubt they are her daughters. Were the gospel-churches national, or did they receive into those churches profane persons ? no, no, they were a separated people, and a congregational, and a holy community, being not conformable to this world ; and into such a church Jesus Christ brings his sheep.

Christ car-
ries his sheep
into his own
fold.

13. And from hence it followeth, that he carries his lost sheep when he hath found them into his own fold, or into some true gospel church ; and indeed no sooner hath Christ found his sheep, but they with the spouse, enquire where he feeds. " Tell me, O thou whom my soul loveth, where thou feedest, and where thou makest thy flock to rest at noon ; for why should I be as one that turneth aside by the flocks of thy companions ? Cant. i. 7. Why should I feed with false churches, who call themselves thy companions, or thy churches ? It is said, " The Lord added to the church daily such as should be saved," Acts ii. 47. " Christ directs all his sheep, to go forth by the footsteps of the flock, and to feed beside the shepherd's tents," Cant. i. 8.

14. And lastly, Christ will carry all his lost sheep home at last, to dwell in heaven with him for ever. " My sheep hear my voice, and they follow me, and I give unto them eternal life, and they shall never perish, nor can any pluck them out of my hand," John x. 27, 28. I will bring them unto the actual possession of eternal life in the kingdom of glory : they shall be all kept by his power, through faith, unto salvation, which faith, as he is the Author of it, so he is the finisher of it also. " Fear not, little flock, for it is your Father's good pleasure to give you the kingdom," Luke xii. 32. By this kingdom doubtless is meant, that state of honour, dignity, and glory to come ; and though the beginning of it may be on earth for a thousand years, yet it refers to that glory they shall possess in heaven for evermore.

APPLICATION

First, from hence we may infer, that Jesus Christ, who is the Shepherd of his sheep, is the best of shepherds, or that there is no shepherd like to the Lord Jesus, he far exceeds all shepherds.

Christ a
wise Shep-
herd.

1. For wisdom. He is called the wisdom of God, the essential wisdom of God, being in him, " In whom the fulness of the Godhead dwells bodily," Col. ii. 9. Denoting the personal habitation of the deity in, and union of it with the human nature. Moreover, he is the wisdom of God in a mystery shines forth in him, as Mediator, in his working out of our redemption. His wisdom appears as he is a shepherd.

(1.) He knows where all his lost sheep are, who are lost and scattered on the mountains, or in the wilderness of this world, other shepherds when their sheep are lost, know not where they are, but Christ doth. " Then spake the Lord to Paul in the night by a vision, be not afraid, but speak, and hold not thy peace, for I am with thee ; no man shall set upon thee, to hurt thee, for I have much people in this city," Acts xviii. 9, 10. There were, it seems, many the Father had given Christ, that dwelt in the city of Corinth ; and though Paul knew them not, nor were they yet called, but abode until that time in their lost state and condition, yet Jesus Christ knew them. " The Lord knoweth who they be that are his," and where they dwell, such wisdom hath he above all other shepherds. (2.) He knows what way to go, and what he must do that he may find them, and bring them all home. (3.) He knows them all by name, as he said to Moses, " I know thee by name," Exod. xxxiii. 12. Some think in the eastern countries, the shepherds gave names to all their sheep, and that our Saviour alludes to that, in John x. 3. " And he calleth his own sheep by name, and leadeth them out." Whatever your name is, by which you are called, Jesus Christ knoweth it full well. (4.) He knows the hearts, nature, state, and condition of all his sheep. (3.) He knows how to heal, to wash, to feed, to lead, and to govern them also.

2. For love he far exceeds all other shepherds ; what shepherd ever so *Christ exceeds all shepherds in love.* loved his sheep, as to lay down his life for them, " He loved us, and washed us in his own blood," Rev. i. 5. What love was ever like to this love ? " As the Father knoweth me, even so I know the Father, and I lay down my life for my sheep," John x. 15. Christ would not only have us to know the sincerity of his love, but also the degrees or greatness of it, and therefore he often compares it to that love wherewith the Father loveth him, and also repeats his laying down his life ; ver. 17, " Therefore doth my Father love me, because I lay down my life, that I may take it up again."

3. For power, he excels all other shepherds, he is the power of God ; or him *Christ a strong and powerful shepherd.* that God hath made strong for himself. In respect of his deity, he is the strong and Almighty God, and as Mediator God-man ; all the divine attributes are united, and equally exert their power in the salvation of the elect. " He was declared to be the Son of God with power, according to the Spirit of holiness, by the resurrection from the dead," Rom. i. 4. Though he was the Son of God from eternity, yet as he was God-man, he was then declared and owned to be the Son of God, and was then known even by his resurrection from the dead, to be the Most High God ; how else could he have raised himself ? for he laid down his life, and took it up again, and now is exalted with power, majesty, and glory, at God's right hand, and " so is able to save to the uttermost all that come to God by him," Heb. vii. 25. No lion, no devil, no powers of hell and darkness, can withstand him ; he is able to rescue his poor lost sheep out of the paw of the old lion. David was, in delivering his sheep out of the paw of a lion, a lively figure of Jesus Christ. " And David said unto Saul, Thy servant kept his Father's sheep, and there came a lion and a bear, and took a lamb out of the flock : and I went out after him, and smote him, and delivered it out of his mouth, and when he arose against me, I caught him by the beard, and smote him, and slew him. Thy servant slew both the lion and the bear," 1 Sam. xvii. 34, 35, 36. David was a valiant and powerful shepherd ; but in this I say, he was a type of Christ, who hath subdued the devil, that roaring lion, and delivered all his lost sheep out of his mouth, who had taken them as a prey in his teeth. Jesus Christ is able to carry home 3000 sheep on his shoulders at one time, nay, 100,000. He hath vanquished all the powers of the infernal lake ; " Hath spoiled principalities and powers, and made a show of them openly, triumphing over them in it," Col. ii. 25. Therefore no poor sinners need to fear, that Christ comes to seek and find, let their sins be never so great ; for he it is " that speaks in righteousness, and is mighty to save," Isa. lxiii. 1.

4. " Jesus Christ excels all other shepherds in care and faithfulness." See *Christ a careful Shepherd.* here in this parable how he is set forth as to his care of one sheep gone astray, he will not lose one soul which the Father gave to him ; what he did in seeking of all his lost sheep, is here expressed, as if he had done it all for one ; he is so careful and so faithful that he will bring home every particular lost sheep ; of all the Father hath given to him he will lose none, he will say at the great day, " Here am I, and all the children thou hast given me."

5. For watchfulness. Though this is comprehended in what I said last, *Christ a watchful Shepherd.* yet in some things it may a little differ : the most careful shepherd that ever was (save Christ himself) must sometimes sleep, and then the sheep are in danger ; but Christ never sleepeth at all, he keeps always awake. " He that keepeth thee will not slumber," Psal. cxxi. 3, 4, 5. " Behold, he that keepeth Israel, shall neither slumber nor sleep." " The Lord is thy keeper, the Lord is thy shade upon thy right-hand." O what a happy case are believers in. How safe are all Christ's sheep, who have such a watchful and careful Shepherd.

Secondly, We infer from hence, that none of Christ's sheep shall want anything which is good, they may all say with David, " The Lord is my Shepherd, I shall not want," Psal. xxiii. 1. (1.) They shall not want seeking if gone astray. (2.) They shall not want pastures to feed and lie down in. (3.) They shall not want folding. (4.) They shall not want healing, he forgiveth all their iniquities, and healeth all their diseases, as David experienced, Psal. ciii. 3. (5.) They shall not want strengthening, he will strengthen them out of Sion. " Be of good cheer, he shall strengthen your hearts," Psal. xxxi. 24. (6.) Nor shall they want quickening, for he will revive their sinking and drooping spirits. (7.) They shall not want comfort in their afflictions and tribulations ; and, which is more than all, they shall not want his own gracious presence, for this Shepherd will never leave them. " Lo, I am with you always to the end of the world," Matt. xxviii. 20. He is with his sheep day and night, he watcheth them " like as the vineyard of red wine," continually, that none may hurt, annoy, or devour them, Isa. xxvii. 2.

How to know who are Christ's sheep. Thirdly, Trial. It may be improved by way of examination or trial. Are you Christ's sheep? see to it. It behoveth us all to search and see whether we are his sheep or not; if you are his sheep, you are either such who are lost, and yet not brought home, or else such that are found, I mean, effectually called. Now none know they are his sheep until he hath found them. Election is only known by special vocation: though Christ knows who are his that are yet sinners and ungodly, yet we do not.

Quest. How may we know who are lost, or not yet found, not called or brought home? Answ. I answer by asking you a few questions.

1. Art thou an ignorant person? dost thou not know (nor ever didst know) what it is to be lost, or to be undone, being in a state of wrath and misery? if not, be sure thou art one of them that are lost.

2. Art thou one that thinkest to return home only by calling or crying for mercy, " Lord have mercy upon me, Christ have mercy upon me?" If it be thus, certainly thou art lost, and in a woful condition: such that are called home believe in Christ, as well as pray for mercy; they see how justice comes to be satisfied for their sins, and see the way to the city of refuge, and run thither.

3. Art thou one that thinkest to return home to God by doing, I mean, by virtue of thy own good works, good duties, and good deeds, as prayer, hearing the word, repentance, and reformation of life, or by acts of charity? if it be thus, it appears thou art lost, and knowest not the way to return home.

4. Dost thou think that that light which is in thee, and in all mankind, or the law of God written in thy heart, is sufficient to guide or light thee home to God? if so, thou art in darkness and lost be sure; for what is that light but some remainders of the law of the first covenant light? and by the deeds of the law, or works and light of the law, can no flesh return home, or be justified in his sight.

5. Or art thou one that resteth on a form of godliness, without the power, " drawing near to God with thy mouth, when thy heart is far from him?" Isa. xxix. 13. May be thou art baptized and become a member of a church, and dost break bread, and art called a saint; but if thou thinkest this way thou art brought home to God, and dost rest on these external privileges, thou art certainly lost and undone.

6. Or art thou a profane person, or a carnal worldling, a drunkard, a swearer, a whore-monger? &c.; thou art lost if it be thus, or if thou livest in any one sin, allowing and loving of it.

7. Dost thou not love nor relish spiritual things, but only savourest the things of the flesh, and findest no sweetness in God, in Christ, nor in his word? if so, thou art lost.

8. Dost thou not love Christ's pastures, but rather treadest down with thy feet such good food that the sheep of Christ feed upon? or despisest thou prayer, hearing of the word, and other gospel-ordinances? be sure then thou art none of his sheep, but art one lost and undone, in respect of thy present state and condition.

9. Or dost thou thrust with the shoulder, and watchest occasions to reproach the sheep of Christ, branding them with the odious name of hypocrites, because of some slips and infirmities thou seest in them? dost thou bite and snarl at the sheep? then thou rather seemest to be a dog, than one of Christ's sheep.

10. Or art thou a self-righteous person, one that never went astray? if so, thou verily art one of them that Christ leaves in the wilderness, and none of them whom he seeks.

Now if thou art one of Christ's sheep, thou mayest know it by these following characters.

Who are Christ's sheep. 1. Thou art one that knows his voice from the voice of strangers. " My sheep know my voice." Thou canst distinguish betwixt his holy doctrine and false or corrupt doctrine.

2. Dost thou know Jesus Christ? " I know my sheep, and am known of mine." They know the person of Christ, and the personal excellencies of Jesus Christ; they know his work and offices as he is Mediator, they know the beauty, the worth and preciousness, and the necessity of Christ.

3. Dost thou love Christ with a great, a sincere and superlative love? Is he " the chiefest to thee of ten thousands?" Cant. v. 10. Hath he thy heart? thy whole heart? Canst thou say, " Whom have I in heaven but thee, and there is none on earth that I desire besides thee, or in comparison of thee? Psal. lxxiii. 25.

4. Dost thou love the sheep of Christ, all the sheep and people of God, not only those

who feed in thy pasture, and lie down in the same fold where thou art, but others also yea, all the saints, even such that differ in some things from thee? He that is a true Christian, loves all the children of God, all in whom he sees the blessed image of their heavenly Father: "By this we know we are passed from death to life; because we love the brethren," 1 John iii. 14. "He that loveth him that begat, loveth them also that are begotten of him," 1 John v. 1.

5. Dost thou love to feed with the sheep of Christ, to feed, fold, and lie down with them? some like their pastures, the doctrine of Christ, the promises of Christ, but they do not love of his ordinances, nor will they come into his fold.

6. Art thou humble and harmless? Sheep are harmless and innocent creatures, they are not envious nor malicious persons. "Concerning malice they are children," Matt. xviii. 2, 3, or like little children; and they are also humble, and lowly in heart, having no conceit or high thoughts of their own wisdom, knowledge, or attainments; but are nothing in their own sight, and think better of others than of themselves.

7. Are you profitable persons? no creatures are more profitable to their owners than sheep, in respect of increase, and also in respect of their flesh and fleece: so Christ's sheep are more profitable to Christ than all people on earth, John xv. 8, they bring most glory to him, they bring forth much fruit, and are very useful to their brethren, friends, and neighbours; they do good to all, especially to the household of faith. "The righteous is more excellent than his neighbour," Prov. xii. 26.

1. Dost thou know that thou wast once lost, and without Christ; and also that he sought thee first, before thou didst seek after him? also dost thou know when, and how thou wast first wrought upon? and dost thou find a great change in thee, and that thou art translated out of the kingdom and power of sin and Satan, into the kingdom of God's dear Son: if thou canst experience these things, no doubt but thou art one of those sheep Christ has found, and carried home to his Father's house.

One word to you that are yet in a lost condition.

What though thou art not yet called, not yet sought for nor found out, yet thou mayest have hopes Christ will meet with thee, because thou art where he hath found many heretofore, and where they found him; they did not presently meet with him, nor did he find them at the first call of the gospel. God called Samuel three times before he knew it was God that called him; therefore wait until his time is come. The poor lame man waited thirty-eight years at the pool before he found a cure.

So much at this time.

V

He layeth it on his shoulders rejoicing.—Luke xv. 5, 6.

WE have showed that Christ's finding a lost sinner, doth imply the work of God's Spirit in convictions and in regeneration. Yet the bare expression of finding his sheep, our Lord foresaw would not fully set forth or evince each act of his sovereign grace upon the soul of a sinner; and therefore he adds, the taking of it upon his shoulders, and so with joy carrying it home.

From whence we have noted this proposition, viz.

Doct. IV. That lost sinners cannot go home to God of themselves, they cannot go home on their own feet, but must be taken up in Christ's arms, and laid on his shoulders, viz., by the almighty power of the Lord Jesus Christ carried home.

When we read of the finger of God, it denotes the power of God's Spirit. "If I by the finger of God cast out devils," Luke xi. 20. But by the arm of God is signified the greatness of his strength, and most powerful operations. "To whom hath the arm of God been revealed?" Isa. liii. 1. That is, his almighty power exerted in working faith in the soul. So by Christ's shoulders is no doubt meant, his efficacious and effectual power put forth in regenerating and converting, or carrying home a sinner unto God, because the strength of a man lies in his arms and shoulders. Now this therefore comprehends (as I conceive,) two things.

1. The mighty power of Christ put forth in the first work of grace upon the sinner's heart.

2. The constant care of Christ in his supporting, upholding, and preserving of a believer

by his mighty power, to the end of their days. "Who are kept by the mighty power of God through faith, unto salvation." For the same power that works grace in us when we are first converted, must preserve us in a state of grace, until it is finally perfected. Hence Christ is said to be "the Author and Finisher of our faith."

In the prosecution of this proposition, I shall endeavour to do two or three things.

I.   Prove the truth thereof by several texts of Scripture.

II. By divers arguments and demonstrations taken therefrom.

III. Improve it.

Irresistible power in bringing home lost sinners.

I.   The first text is that in John xv. 5, "Without me you can do nothing." Can a branch graft itself into a vine, or being severed or cut off from the vine, bring forth fruit? No, all will say, either of these is impossible. So no man can by any power of his own, graft himself into the true Vine, it must be done by Jesus Christ alone; he it is that takes a sinner off of the old stock, the old root, *i. e.*, the first Adam, and by his Spirit unites it to himself. "Without me (that is, without union with me, or except ye be united to me, as branches are united to the vine,) ye can do nothing," ye can bring forth no acceptable fruit to God. Moreover, the branch that is grafted into the stock is passive, it is wholly the work of the husbandman. So a sinner's implantation into Christ, is the alone work of God, that spiritual Husbandman.

Without me, that is, without my almighty arm be made bare, my power exerted, or the power of the Messiah, who is called "the Power of God, and the Wisdom of God."

Another text is John vi. 44, "No man can come unto me, except the Father which hath sent me, draw him." This is not the drawing of ministers (as I have formerly noted) but of the sublime and irresistible influences of the holy God upon the heart, by which he inclines, bows, and subjects the stubborn and rebellious will to believe and receive the Lord Jesus Christ. "My people shall be willing in the day of my power," Psal. cx. 3. Our Lord explains in ver. 65, what he means by drawing in verse 44. "And I said therefore unto you, that no man can come unto me, except it were given unto him of my Father." Unless the Spirit be given, a new heart be given, grace be given, faith be given, or divine power be given of my Father. To these two scriptures I may add another, John i. 13, "Which were born not of blood, nor of the will of the flesh, nor of the will of man, but of God." Not of blood, that is, not by regeneration, or of the blood of Abraham in a lineal way, as if grace or the new birth was the product of nature, or by that legal covenant made with Abraham's fleshly seed as such. "We have Abraham to our father." They concluded they were the children of God, because they proceeded from the loins of Abraham. Not of flesh, **n**ot of the lusts of the flesh, say some; but I rather think he means by flesh, those legal privileges under the law, according to that of Paul, 2 Cor. v. 18, "Henceforth we know no man after the flesh," or esteem not, prefer not any man to be better than others because of their fleshly or legal privileges under the law, compared with what he says in another place, "Though I might have confidence in the flesh, if any other man thinketh that he hath whereof he might trust, I more; circumcised the eighth day, of the stock of Israel, of the tribe of Benjamin, a Hebrew of the Hebrews; as touching the law a Pharisee, and concerning zeal, persecuted the church; touching the righteousness which is of the law blameless," Phil. iii. 4—6. None of these great privileges availed him any thing; regeneration proceedeth not from hence. No man is a son of God by virtue of fleshly or legal privileges, or by means of his own works, or inherent righteousness. Nor of the will of man, or by the power of man's will, or by any act he is able to exert; for before grace or a vital principle is infused, all he can do are but dead works, and please not God. No man can do any thing to oblige God to adopt him to be his child, or procure that great blessing; no, such that have the privilege to become the sons of God, are regenerated by the Spirit. Hence he adds, "but of God," that is, they are born of God. Whatsoever may be the true sense of the former words, by these words it is plain and evident, that God is the efficient or great agent in regeneration, or the procreant cause of all those that are the sons and daughters of God. To be born of God signifies a reception of a vital principle from him, in a supernatural way. Another text that confirms this truth we have in Rom. ix. 16, "So then it is not of him that willeth, nor of him that runneth, but of God that showeth mercy." The grace of God in election and regeneration, was not of Jacob's will, nor is it of any man's own free will, because he chooseth or willeth to become God's child; for naturally no man can will any thing that is truly or spiritually good. It is not of him that willeth or runneth, not from any motion, act, or action, work, desire, inclination, purpose, or endeavour of any man foreseen of God, that he is either elected, renewed, or adopted, but alone of the free love, grace, and mercy of God. "Not by works of righteousness which we have done, but according to his mercy he saveth us by the washing of regeneration, and renewing of the Holy Ghost; which he hath shed on us abundantly, through Jesus Christ our Lord," Tit. iii. 5, 6. The Holy Spirit shed on us, and the effects of it in regeneration, are both ascribed to the free and rich grace, favour, and mercy of God, through Jesus Christ. Compare this with what our apostle speaketh in another place. "Not that we are sufficient of ourselves to think anything as of ourselves, but all our sufficiency is of God," 2 Cor. iii. 5. As if he should have said, let none think that we are able or sufficient, or have power to change men's hearts, though God has made us able ministers of the New Testament; no, we cannot of ourselves without the divine Spirit, do so much as think one good thought, which is the lowest human act. We may see from hence the impotency of man's will unto anything that is truly and spiritually good. He doth not speak here of God as the God of nature, from whom indeed we derive our power of thinking what may be naturally or morally good, but as considered the God of grace, from whom, in a supernatural manner, by the influences of his Spirit we derive our power of thinking holy thoughts. "But we have this treasure in earthen vessels, that the excellency of the power may be of God, and not of us," 2 Cor. iv. 7. The efficacy of the Word preached doth not lie in the hearer, it is not in man, in his will, nor in his care and diligence under the word, nor in the power of the most able minister in the world, that the Word preached becomes effectual; no, no, but it is from God, it is he that gives the increase alone, and so makes one man to differ from another.

The last scripture I shall mention, is Phil. ii. 12, 13. "For it is God that worketh in you, both to will and to do of his own good pleasure." We act as we are acted of God, and move as we are moved by him, in all that we do spiritually, that God accepteth. He bids them work out their own salvation; he speaks to believers whom God hath quickened, and called, justified, and saved; he means no more by working out their own salvation, than their diligent endeavour to discharge all duties of religion God requires in order to the finishing of their Christian warfare; it was Christ who wrought out our salvation, and he alone. Our works or actions work not out our salvation, neither are they the efficient, material, nor the meritorious cause thereof, as the papists argue, for eternal life is the gift of God. "Not of works lest any should boast." Nor doth Paul mean servile or slavish fear, when he says, "Work out your salvation with fear and trembling," but with a holy, filial, or son-like fear of God, implying deep humility, submissiveness of spirit, and a reverential awe of the holy majesty of God, and sense of our duty to him, as to our Father, lest we should grieve or dishonour him. But lest they should think that they had that power which indeed they had not, or on the other hand, be discouraged for the want of power the apostle adds, "For it is God that worketh in you," &c. It is God that gives you a will to do, and helps you then to will and do that which is well pleasing in his own sight, and he will work within you powerfully, effectually, and efficaciously; so that sin, the devil, the world, nor any other thing, shall hinder you in doing that which he requires of you; no difficulties, obstacles, or impediments whatsoever shall obstruct the perfecting the whole work of your salvation, in order to a meetness for eternal life. Grace shall be victorious. "He has ordained us unto eternal life, and also that we should go and bear fruit, and that our fruit should remain," John xv. 16. So that on Christ's shoulders poor sinners shall be carried home to God, even every one of them that are given to him by the Father.

II. I shall further prove and demonstrate the truth of the doctrine laid down, by several arguments drawn from the scripture.

Arg. 1. The first shall be taken from such texts which ascribe the whole work of redemption, regeneration, justification, and salvation to the will and free-grace of God. If the foundation, the rise and original of our salvation, was from sovereign and unconstrained love in God, there being no necessity laid upon him, either to love, elect, or redeem us. If it be free grace, favour, and rich bounty without merit, there being nothing in the creature deserving his love, either absolutely, or comparatively; and also of free grace simply, in respect of motive, there being nothing in us to move his affection; man being not only a lump of deformity, but also a cursed rebel against God. And if regeneration be wholly by the agency of the Spirit of Jesus, and justification alone by his righteousness, and perseverance be by Christ's faithfulness as our Surety; then it is the power of Jesus Christ alone, or upon his shoulders sinners are taken up, and carried home to God. But all these things are certainly so, therefore it is by the power of Christ alone, or upon his shoulders, sinners are taken up, and carried home to God, see Paul, Ephes. ii. 8. "By grace ye are saved, through faith, and that not of yourselves, it is the gift of God." May be some may object, " Though it be by grace and the favour and bounty of God, we are said to be saved, yet it is by faith, and that is man's act, it is man that believes."

Answ.   The apostle, on purpose to anticipate such an objection, adds, that faith is no of ourselves, but it is the gift of God, i. e., though men believe, yet the seed of that faith is God's gift or power to believe is given by God.   " Faith is the fruit of the Spirit," Gal. v. 22 ; it grows not out of the garden of nature, it is more than a mere human faith, it is the faith of the operation of God, a faith of his working. See what he saith in another place, " Who hath saved us, and called us with an holy calling, not according to our works, but according to his own purpose and grace, which was given us in Christ Jesus before the world began," 2 Tit. i. 9. We are called, renewed, and sanctified, wholly by the free grace of God, without any respect had to anything done by us, or wrought in us, as either a motive to it, or that which doth procure it.

Again, he saith, " Not by works of righteousness that we have done," &c.   Tit. iii. 5. Moreover it is said, " Being justified freely by his grace, through the redemption that is in Jesus Christ," Rom. iii. 24.

Rom. iv. 5, 6.   But to proceed, the scripture calls regeneration the forming of Christ in the soul, nay, it is called a new creation, or a new creature, and our being created after the image of God.   " Put on the new man, which after God is created in righteousness and true holiness," Eph. iv. 24. After God, that is, after his image. From hence,

Arg. 2. I argue thus, viz. If the work of grace, the work of faith and regeneration be the forming of Christ, or the image of God on the soul. If it be a new creation, or a new and most glorious creature, then nothing short of infinite power, or the Almighty power of Christ, can create or produce this great and glorious work on a poor, lost, and undone sinner. But all these things are so, they are thus described, therefore the carrying home of a lost sinner is Christ's work, or the product of his irresistible grace, they must be taken up by his arms, and laid on his Almighty shoulders. " This people have I formed for myself, they shall set forth my praise," Isa. xliii. 21. Can man, impotent man, create a fly, or a sorry worm, or put life into the meanest animal ? no, no, much less can he create the image of God, or form Jesus Christ in the soul, and to say man is, or may be a co-partner, or a co-worker with God herein, is to give that glory to mere creature, which belongs to God only, which is abominable. I have, my brethren, often told you, that the new creation, or the creating us anew in Christ Jesus, is one of the highest and most glorious acts of God's divine wisdom and power.

The new   Arg. 3. It is also called a new birth, or a being begotten of God, and
birth wholly   born of God.   " Of his own will begat he us," &c. James i. 18. " And
of God.   every one that loveth him that begat, loveth him that is begotten of him," 1
John v. 1. Now doth a child contribute anything towards its own formation in the womb ? no, no, all must confess it is wholly passive in that case ; and so are sinners wholly passive in regeneration, even as Adam was when God formed him out of the dust of the ground, otherwise the second birth in one main case answers not to the first, nor is it a proper metaphor or allusion.

Lost sinners   Arg. 4. Shall be taken from that opposition which is made by Satan,
in Satan's   and other powers of darkness, against this work of faith and regeneration, or
hands.   the sinner's returning to God. Now evident it is, that all mankind naturally are in Satan's hands, nay, in his chains and strong bonds, he hath power over every lost sinner (as you have heard) " He rules in the hearts of the children of disobedience," Eph. ii. 2. " They are taken captive by him at his will," 2 Tim. ii. 26. And until he is subdued, disarmed, and his power broken to pieces in the soul of a sinner, it is impossible for one poor undone wretch to return to God. Will he be so kind by persuasions to release one of his prisoners ? no, no, he retains his malice and irreconcilable temper against God and man. Or will he regard that great price or ransom that Jesus Christ laid down to atone for sin, and to satisfy divine justice ? No certainly he regards it not, he hath all God's elect in his chains, in his deep dunghill, and there he will hold and keep them all until they are delivered, or redeemed by power.

And now, my brethren, pray consider, is a man in his depraved state, or in his natural condition, a match for the devil, with all his natural powers, or under the highest improvements of common light, knowledge, and attainments ? none sure dare affirm, that any persons can deliver themselves. For if a man who is renewed, and hath the whole armour of God on, cannot encounter with, nor vanquish the enemy, without the special assistance and power of Christ ; how unable is a weak and naked creature to do it ? If a saint with all his spiritual weapons, is no fit match for Satan, certainly a sinner can do nothing to save himself, or to subdue this cruel adversary. He that delivers a sinner out of Satan's hands, must therefore be clothed with greater power than Satan hath, he must be one that is stronger than he, and this indeed our Lord plainly declared to the Jews, when they blasphemously charged him "for casting out devils by Beelzebub the prince of devils; or else how can one enter into a strong man's house, and spoil his goods, except he first binds the strong man, and then he will spoil his goods?" Matt. xii. 29. Hence it appeareth a sinner's deliverance from Satan is the proper work of Christ; he is the person that is stronger than he, and so able to save us from the power of Satan. And this caused the apostle to give thanks to God "the Father, who hath delivered us from the power of darkness," Col. i. 12; it is Christ that "turns us from darkness to light, and from the power of Satan unto God.

Arg. 5. My next argument shall be taken from the consideration of the woful state and condition lost sinners (by nature, by original and actual sin) are in; I told you that they are in a deep pit, an horrible pit, out of which no sinner hath power to come, no, unless he be drawn by an Almighty arm, he must lie there, and perish for ever. *The impotency of fallen man opened.*

In opening the force and strength of this argument, I shall show you the weakness or impotency of undone sinners, lost sinners, to return to God of themselves, unless God's Almighty power be exerted, or unless Christ takes up the sinner on his shoulders. This weakness or impotency of sinners in returning to God, consisteth in three or four things.

1. There is in all men naturally, a privation of power to do that which is spiritually good, an absence, yea (as one notes) a total privation, an absence, not in part and degrees only, it is not only a suspension of acts, as may be when a man is asleep, but an absence, or want of radical power. *Clarkson's serm. p. 475.* "He giveth power to the faint, and to them that have no might," &c. Isa. xl. 29. It is not such an impotency as is in a branch in winter to bear fruit, but such as in a branch that is cut off from the vine, nor is it such an impotency that is in a man very sick, but such as is in a man who is dead, all men are spiritually dead, and so have not the least degree of power to stir, move, or act in a true spiritual way. "When we were without strength," Rom. v. 6

2. It is not only a total privation, in respect of power, in one faculty only, but it is universal in every one of the powers or faculties of the soul; every part is impotent, and wholly depraved, the judgment is corrupted, the understanding is darkened, the will rebellious, the affections carnal, earthly, and sensual; the memory treacherous, thinking of those things it should forget, and forgetting of such things it should remember; the conscience asleep or misled, acquitting when it should charge, and charging when it should acquit: in this woful condition are all lost sinners, as you before have heard.

3. There is not a want of power or ability, or incapacity only, but also an utter incapacity to receive power, as in a dead branch: a branch that is green, and has sap in it, though cut off of a vine (though when it is incapable to bring forth fruit) yet may be grafted in again, and so become fruitful: but this is such an incapacity, as is in a dead, withered, and dry branch; or the incapacity is such as in "stones to become children to Abraham," or in dry bones to live, or to be joined together and animated, and be made the instruments of vital acts: for by these allusions is the state of lost sinners set out by God himself, "Son of Man, can these dry bones live?" The capacity is so remote, there is such a distance betwixt the power and the act, as nothing but infinite power can bring them together, even such a power that brought heaven and earth out of nothing. Hence it is said, we are his workmanship, created and have a new heart put into us, Eph. ii. 10. *See Mr. Clarkson.*

4. Nay, it is worse yet, for there is not only such an incapacity as is in stones to become children to Abraham, or in dry bones to live; for there is not only in sinners an incapacity, as is by those allusions signified, but sinners resist, they being acted and influenced by the devil, and their own evil hearts: though they have no power to do that which is spiritually good, yet they have a diabolical power, by which they can and do oppose and resist the Holy Spirit. "Ye stiff-necked and uncircumcised in heart and ears, ye do always resist the Holy Ghost," Acts vii. 51. Sinners are not able (and yet glory in their power) and as unable they are as unwilling: nay, as our author well observes, "They are not willing to be able," without power, and are unwilling to receive power, and so resist the glorious Agent, the Holy Ghost. It is not (saith Reverend Clarkson) only a physical, a want of power, but a moral privation, i. e., want of will, both unable and unwilling to be able, or to be made willing. "Ye will not come to me that ye might have life," John v. 40. Our Saviour doth not mean, they had power, and would not exert it,

or might believe if they would ; but he showed them the pravity and rebellion of their will ; for in the next chapter he told them that they could not come, " Nor any man except the Father draws him, or except it was given him by the Father," John vi. 44, 65. Lost sinners are averse to God, and all things that are truly and spiritually good. " The carnal mind is enmity against God," &c. Rom. viii. 6.   They are unable to be willing until that enmity is removed : like as some men have an antipathy to some sort of food which others love, they are averse to it ; if you bring it before them they are ready to sound and die away, they hate it, and are prejudiced against it ; it is in vain to persuade them to eat, or to be willing to feed on it ; no, no, they find it is against their nature : so it is with sinners, they have an averseness, an antipathy or enmity against God, and spiritual things.   " The carnal mind is not subject to the law of God, neither indeed can be." Brethren, sinners can no more by any power of their own, return to God, than a blackamore can change his skin, or a leopard his spots," Jer. xiii. 23.   Therefore they must say, ver. 10, " Turn thou me, and I shall be turned."   In conversion there is a twofold act, (1.) Passive, which is the act of God's Spirit, by which he infuseth a vital principle, and gracious habits, or divine qualities in the soul ; and in this act the creature is wholly passive like a patient : Christ, I say, infuses life in the dead soul, as he did in dead Lazarus.   (2.) Active, whereby through the power of that grace, the sinner being quickened, is capacitated to believe, and return to God : being acted, we act ; for the Holy Spirit also influences the same principle, and so moves the soul, and the soul stirs, acts, and moves towards God.   " Draw me, and I will run after thee," Cant. i. 4.   What is this drawing ?   Why certainly both in the soul's first motion to Christ, and in its further motions after him, the Lord putteth forth powerful influences of grace, beyond the arguments of the word, the suasions of his ministers, and the common working of the Spirit, attending the preaching of the gospel.   " After I was turned I repented, and after I was instructed I smote upon my thigh ; I was ashamed, even confounded, &c.   See here first the sinner's heart is turned, and then the sinner returneth, then, and not till then : if Christ sought us not first, and found us not first, and took not us up first by his arms and shoulders of divine power ; we should never seek, find, nor return to him.   And now to descend to particulars.

Conversion   1. It appears that conversion is Christ's work on the soul, it is he that
is of God.   first turns the sinner, he only is the Agent in regeneration, in which the seed of actual conversion is sown in our hearts.

Repentance   2. More particularly it appears, that the sinner cannot repent until the
God's gift.   gift or grace of repentance is bestowed upon him.   " After I was turned I repented."   Jesus Christ must first pour forth the Spirit of grace and supplication upon the soul, before it can in a true spiritual manner mourn for sin.   True, men may get legal repentance, a kind of sorrow, or rather a horror for sin, from the fear and apprehension of God's wrath, and divine vengeance.   Thus Judas repented and confessed his sin, in betraying of innocent blood, and went and hanged himself.

But no man of himself can repent evangelically ; for true gospel or evangelical repentance is the gift of God.   " Him hath God exalted on his right hand as a Prince and a Saviour, to give repentance to Israel, and remission of sins," Acts v. 31.   And in another place Paul saith, " If God peradventure will give them repentance.   It is if God will. Sinners must look up to Christ for grace to repent.   " I will pour upon the house of David, and the inhabitants of Jerusalem the Spirit of grace and supplication."   Well, and what will be the effects of this, or why doth God promise he will do thus ?   See the next words, " And they shall look up unto him whom they pierced, and they shall mourn," &c.   First they look, nay, shall look, grace bends their hearts, overpowers their wills, they shall believe, or cast a believing look up to a crucified Christ ; and then they repent and mourn for their sins, beholding what Christ hath suffered for them.   O then they are in bitterness, as a man mourns, and is in bitterness for his first-born.

Faith is the   3. Sinners have no power of themselves to believe ; they may obtain the
gift of God.   faith of credence, they may get a human faith, or an historical faith, may believe the truth of God's word, believe that there is a God (the devils thus believe) they may believe there is a Christ who died for sinners, and may yield obedience to his external precepts, nay, reform their ways, and do many things ; but not obtain true faith, or the faith of God's elect, or the faith of the operation of God.   " Who hath believed our report ? and to whom is the arm of the Lord revealed ?" Isa. liii. 1.   Faith is not of ourselves, as you heard, " it is the gift of God."   " No man can come to me, except it be given him of my Father," Eph. ii. 8.   Do but see what the apostle saith

about the power of believing in Jesus Christ. " And what is the exceeding greatness of his power to us-ward who believe, according to the working of his mighty power, which he wrought in Christ, when he raised him from the dead," &c. Eph. i. 19, 20. Now, my brethren, it is this way a sinner returns to God, it is by believing, by flying to, and resting upon Jesus Christ ; and such who thus believe, attribute it to the power of God ; not only to his power, but to the exceeding greatness of his power, nay, to the working of his mighty power, and that in the same manner that he wrought in Christ when he raised him 'from the dead. Hence Jesus Christ is called " the Author and finisher of our faith," Heb. xii. 2.

4. Sinners, unrenewed sinners, lost sinners cannot love God, until their Love to Christ is a fruit of the Spirit. hearts and natures are changed: no, but they contrariwise hate him, even wish there was no God : God is not in all their thoughts, they despise and contemn the Holy God. Sirs, divine love is " a fruit of the Spirit : the fruit of the Spirit is love, joy, peace," &c. Gal. v. 22. Moreover, the grace of love, Paul tells the Romans, " Is shed abroad in our hearts by the Holy Ghost," Rom. v. 5. It is a new covenant promise : " I will circumcise their hearts, that they may love me," &c. I will, as if God should say, take away the enmity that is in their hearts against me, and against spiritual things, and make them love and delight in me as their chiefest good, and the beloved object of their soul's affections. The old nature only loves and delights in vanity, in sin, and in the things of this world, and therefore a new heart and a new nature must be given to us before we can truly love God, Jesus Christ, and heavenly things.

5. Sinners cannot hear the word of God to profit thereby, or so hear as to live, unless Christ inclines their hearts, or gives them a hearing ear ; no man can hear to soul advantage, unless the Lord first open their hearts as he opened the heart of Lydia.

6. Sinners cannot pray acceptably, until Christ pour forth on them the The |Spirit given before Sinners can pray acceptably. Spirit of supplication. No doubt Paul prayed before he was converted, when he was a Pharisee, for the Pharisees gloried in their praying twice a day ; but God took no notice of any of Paul's prayers until he was become another man, a changed man, a new man. " When I pray, I will pray in the Spirit," &c. " We know not what to pray for as we ought, but as the Spirit itself maketh intercession for us," &c., Rom. viii. 26.

7. A sinner cannot arrive to any sure hope of everlasting life, until quickened by Christ, and he received the Holy Spirit ; such who have no God, no A lively hope is from God. Eph. ii. 12. Christ, are without hope : " Christ in you the hope of glory," Col. i. 27. If a man be in Christ, Christ is in him ; and " If any man have not the Spirit of Christ, the same is none of his," Rom. viii. 8, 9. And if he be not in Christ, in vain is all his hope and confidence, " And if any man be in Christ, he is a new creature," 2 Cor. v. 17.

APPLICATION

1. Inference. From hence we may see what woful work sin hath made, and what hurt it hath done to poor mortals, certainly there is no evil like the evil of sin, no plague like to this plague, which hath thus divested man of all power of doing anything that is spiritually good.

2. It informs us also of the woful state and misery of men out of Christ, and what a lamentable thing it is to be lost.

3. It informs us also of that great evil of original sin, how weak and impotent is man become hereby. What poor and despicable creatures are men and women naturally ; nay, how great is their deformity. Man is nothing, nay, less than nothing. A non-entity has no sin ; but man is most vile and loathsome naturally, in the sight of God, being filled with enmity and hatred against God, so that there is nothing lovely in him, nothing to draw out the heart of God to love him.

4. It may be of use by way of admiration ; stand and wonder at God's infinite love, favour, and goodness to man. " O what is man, that thou art mindful of him, that thou shouldst magnify the man, and set thy heart upon him," Job. vii. 17, 18, Psal. viii. 4. To send his Son to take our nature upon him, and so become man to die for man ; to be made a curse for so vile a rebel and enemy of God.

5. We may infer, if man be redeemed, reconciled to God, justified and sa- Free-will utterly detected, ved, it must be alone in a way of free grace. God was perfectly happy in himself, the all-sufficiency and independency of God shows, he stood in no need at all of men, nor angels ; and as to his essential glory, there could be no additions made to that ; God

had been as glorious as he is, if man had never been, besides, he was not obliged to man, he owed man nothing; but considering his sovereignty, he might have sent the whole lump of fallen mankind to hell, and have created another race of men more glorious and fit to be the objects of his transcendant love. Or why did he not manifest his pity to the fallen angels, who were more glorious at first than man? Or if men, vile men, lost men, are the subjects of his blessings, and objects of his love and compassion, why as one observes so many men?

he might have passed by more, and chosen fewer vessels of mercy; and if so, many are comprehended in his sovereign love. Why we, and not those in India, and few or none in England? why should we have the gospel here in this isle, and almost all the world lie in the darkness, either of Popery, Mahometanism, or Paganism?

Mr. Clarkson of free-grace, p. 26.

6. Exhortation. O labour to exalt free-grace; God will have all the honour, all the praise, and all the glory of our salvation : we sought not him, asked not for him, found not him first, but he sought us. " I am sought of them that asked not for me, and found of them that sought me not," Isa. lxv. 1.

Arminianism further detected.

7. This may be of use by way of reprehension to such who maintain free-will, and descry and condemn God's sovereign grace and favour to his elect, and to them only.

First. This is that which these men affirm, viz., " That God loved all mankind alike, or with the same love, and gave his Son to die to save every individual person in the world."

Answ. 1. Why then did Christ leave ninety and nine in the wilderness? or wherefore did he not seek them all until he had found every one of them; for though all in one sense were lost, yet some think and believe they were never lost, nor need a Saviour, and such he came not to seek, to save, redeem, and call; they were sinners, i. e., such that saw they had no righteousness to trust to, even the lost sheep of the house of Israel, and lost sheep among the Gentiles, " whom he must bring," John x. 16.

2. Why did not our Lord pray for all, if he died for all, to save all, and loved all with the same love? " I pray not for the world, but for them which thou hast given me, for they are thine," John xvii. 9. There is an elect world, and a world not elected, here he means such that were not given to him, and therefore he prayed not for them. Now would Christ die for them, for whom he would not pray? true " he prayed for them also that were his elect," ver. 20, who then believed not, but should believe in after times, and he prayed for no more that they might be saved; for certainly all that he prayed for so shall be saved, because the Father heard him always; he asks nothing of God but what God granted to him.

3. If Christ died for all, why is not the gospel preached to all? or why have not all the same love manifested to them; if all were reconciled to God by the death of his Son, much more shall all be saved by his life, see what Paul affirms, Rom. v. 18. " And if God spared not his own Son, but delivered him up for us all, how shall he not with him freely give us all things," Rom. viii. 32. It therefore God delivered up his Son to die for all, or every individual person in the world; shall not he freely give to them his gospel, his Spirit, and faith to believe, and whatsoever else is necessary to their salvation? Will a man give the greatest gift, and withhold the lesser, without which the greater can never accomplish the end for which he gave it? As for example, will a man give a million of gold to purchase an estate for another, and not give five pounds to take up that estate, and so make it sure to him? My brethren, there is greater disproportion between God's gift, of Christ to die for us, and the gift of the gospel, and grace to us, no greater gift, greater love than that of God's giving his only begotten Son to die for us; therefore I argue, the lesser gift, the gift of faith, &c., he will not be sure withhold from such and all such that he gave his Son to die in the stead and room of : but the gospel he doth not give to all, nor his Spirit, faith, and other gifts that are necessary to salvation, to many thousand in the world; therefore he did not give his Son to die to save them all.

2ndly. The Arminians affirm, that there is a power in the will of man, to incline him either to choose or refuse, to yield or resist, to embrace Christ and the operations of the Spirit, or reject him and all those operations.

Answ. We say the will of a natural man, or a lost sinner, may and doth resist the common emotions of the Spirit, and offers of grace ; but that special grace which God puts forth upon the soul with an intent according to his own eternal purpose to bring it home to himself, and effectually to call or regenerate, they cannot, shall not resist.

3rdly. They say God doth put forth no other, no greater power in bringing home, or converting such that are saved, than he doth on them that perish, and that the drawings mentioned in the scripture are only moral suasions.

Answ. 1. This is to deny original sin, i. e., the pravity of our natures, or the total corruption and impotency of the creature by nature ; for if he will can incline by moral suasions, under the preaching of the word, as easily to that which is spiritually good, as to that which evil, our nature is not so corrupted as the word of God shows, and our own experience daily evinces. Why then did Paul say, the " carnal mind is enmity against God, and is not subject to the law of God, neither indeed can be," Rom. viii. 7. These men say, the will or mind of man may be subject to the word or law of God, though supernatural or irresistible grace be not infused to incline his will.

2. This also clearly shows, that they do not believe that man is " dead in sins and trespasses," Eph. ii. 1, but lies wounded and maimed only ; and that he without being quickened by a vital principle, may apply the balm of Gilead, or oil of grace to heal and cure himself. They, it is true, say it is of God's grace the will is inclined, but not that God gives power to the will ; no, but that the will had power before, to choose or refuse ; only grace, or moral suasion, excites or stirs up the will, like as a man is roused up out of sleep, by a man's voice telling him the house is on fire over his head.

3. It follows from what they affirm, that a man is not regenerated and born of God, but of the will of man ; nor doth God implant or infuse a principle of grace, or gracious qualities in the soul, especially in the will, to make it willing by his almighty power, removing that enmity and aversion that is naturally in it, for they say, the will needs no such principle or quality to be infused into it ; the will can and does incline itself without any such thing. So that the Spirit's agency in regeneration is denied, and so regeneration itself, for God cannot be said sure, to give us a new heart, a new nature, or form Christ in us, if what they say be true. But if they experience no more than their doctrine leads them to affirm, certainly they are not new creatures, not regenerated, but only reformed men, it being no other thing that is wrought in them than the product of the natural powers of the soul. All they can say is this, viz., the Lord doth not convert us, renew us ; but he helps us to convert and renew ourselves, or inclines us to use our own power.

4. Also according to them it may be said, By the will of man ye are saved through faith, and that of ourselves, it is not the gift of God ; and it is of works, that so men may not boast, see Eph. ii. 8, 9 ; or if what they assert doth not let in boasting, nothing can. But pray remember ye are called and saved alone by grace, and all boasting of the creature is excluded. " Where is boasting then ? it is excluded, by what law ? of works ? nay but by the law of faith," Rom. iii. 37.

5. It appears by what they say, God gives us not the habit of grace, nor power to us to act, and to do of his own good pleasure, but it is of our good pleasure, if we (when the gospel is preached) will believe and return to God, we may ; we need not Christ to open our hearts ; grace is given equally to all, and works physically in none, and that God will convert us and renew us if we will ; but James says, " Of his own will begat he us, by the word of truth."

6. Moreover, it necessarily follows from their notions, that faith and repentance are not given to us, nor are they the gift of God : faith and repentance is given no more to such that do believe and repent, than to such who persevere in impenitency and unbelief. For the grace they cry up all have alike, viz., the gospel and the preaching thereof, and the power and arguments, and moral suasions to excite and stir up the natural powers of the creature ; and so (as one well observes) Christ gave faith no more to Paul than to Judas ; he gave repentance no more to Peter, than to Simon Magus, i. e., he gave it not at all ; for he does no more for any, or gives to any more than this moral grace, and what that can do. True, as the same author notes, they talk of subsequent grace, and of the Spirit, which they after believing do receive ; but this latter grace and gift of the Spirit comes too late to be accounted the cause of conversion : it concurs not with us until we are willing, and do believe ; the determination of the will is before it in order of nature ; and none have the Spirit and after-grace but such who exert their natural power to receive persuasive grace.

7. It appears by their doctrine, that the efficacy of grace, and of the death of Christ, and success of the gospel, depends upon the will of man ; for after all that God doth, or designs to do, he leaves the whole matter to the will of man ; the will determines the whole success, whether it shall be effectual, or ineffectual : so that from hence we may say, that we might be saved we may praise God and Jesus Christ, but that we are saved we may thank ourselves, and glory in our wisdom, care, and diligence. But doth not Paul

say, " The natural man discerns not the things of God, neither indeed can receive them, because they are spiritually discerned ?" Their doctrine is evident doth detract from the glory of Christ, and exalts the creature, descrys free-grace, and magnifies free-will, and so overthrows the glorious design of God in the whole of our salvation, which is to abase sorry man, to humble the creature, that God alone may be exalted.

Object. But doth not the psalmist say, the tender mercy of God is over all his works ?

Anws. 1. He speaks not of eternal, special, or spiritual mercies, but of his common mercies, which are extended to men and beasts, &c. For do God's special tender mercies appear to be over the fallen angels ? they are the works of his hands.

2. If by tender mercies be meant his special grace in the gospel, are they extended to the heathen world ? &c.

Object. But if it as you say, it is in vain for sinners to endeavour to do any thing, if they are so important.

Answ. Man ought to do what he can ; he is able to go to hear the word, he is able to read, hear, and to cry to God ; they may do many things.

2. But they are to acknowledge that Christ only can change their hearts, though they have power, if they exert it, to reform their lives.

3. Let them be in the way ; faith comes by hearing ; God doth work in and by the word : sinners will be without excuse, because they do not what they might do ; besides, we take no power from man, which God hath given to them ; but such that say men may believe to-day, repent to-day, if they use the means, and exert the power they have, may conclude they may use that power to-morrow, and so delay the great work of their salvation ; but let them know to-day, the present time is that time God calls, " This is the acceptable time," Take heed you trust not to power, and to that grace which falls short of salvation, and will suffer you to fall at last into hell, though used, and improved.

Remember it is God that makes one man to differ from another.

To conclude ; you that Christ hath brought home, rejoice, and see you do ascribe all the glory into him ; say, not to us, not to us, but unto thee be the honour, and power, and wisdom, and the glory, for ever and ever, Amen.

VI

And when he cometh home, he calleth together his friends, and neighbours, saying rejoice with me, for I have found my lost sheep.   I say unto you, that likewise joy shall be in heaven over one sinner that repenteth, &c. Luke xv. 6, 7.

SOME understand by his home, his coming to heaven ; but I see no reason to restrain it to that. I rather conclude, that our Lord intends no more than the bringing home, or the conversion of the sinner unto God ; for it refers to the sinner's place, or that place whither he is brought when he is regenerated ; before he went astray, or was a stranger, being estranged from God, or afar off ; but now he is brought to dwell in Sion amongst the saints, for that is called God's habitation, or the place where he dwells. " Now therefore ye are no more strangers and foreigners, but fellow citizens with the saints, and of the household of God," Eph. ii. 19.

The proposition I have proposed to speak unto from hence, is this, viz.

Doct. V. That the Lord Jesus Christ, and his angels in heaven, and also his saints on earth, greatly rejoice when one lost sinner is returned home or God, or truly converted.

He himself rejoiceth when he hath found the lost sheep, *i. e.*, when thorough convictions have taken hold of a sinner, or grace is infused : and when he is effectually converted, or the work is declared, and a confession of that work is made by him, and he is received into the church, the saints and people of God rejoice ; the church is commonly called heaven.

In speaking to this point of doctrine, I shall,

1. Show you who they are that may be meant by Christ's friends and neighbours, also why so called.

II. Why he himself, and his friends and neighbours, do rejoice, when one sinner is returned home to God.

III. Apply it, and so conclude with this parable.

He calleth his friends and neighbours to rejoice ; they are invited to rejoice with him : therefore it is their duty so to do, and they are ready to do it.

1. All expositors agree (that I have met with) that by friends and neighbours are meant the saints and angels, though some conclude it refers to them in heaven only, which I cannot agree to. Saints and angels are the friends of Christ.

See Mr. Neh. Roger's true convert, p. 197. and our annotators on the place.

1. They are called his friends, he himself calleth them so. " I have called you friends," &c. " Ye are my friends if ye do whatsoever I command you." John xv. 14, 15. Abraham was called the friend of God. And believers call Jesus Christ their friend, as indeed well they may. " This is my beloved, and this is my friend, O ye daughters of Jerusalm," Cant. v. 16.

Quest. Why are they called friends ?

Answ. 1. I answer, friends have no enmity in their hearts one to another, but are in a real state of friendship. Hence we say, when two men that were at variance are reconciled, we say they are now friends; the saints are reconciled to God and to Christ, and so are friends.

Why Christ and his saints are called friends.

2. Friends know one another well, they are acquainted and intimate one with the other : so Jesus Christ knows his saints. " I know my sheep, and am known of mine." John. x. 14. He hath a special knowledge of his saints, a knowledge of approbation. " I know Abraham, that he will command his children," &c. Christ saith to hypocrites, I never knew you ; that is, I never approved of you: moreover, every true Christian knows Jesus Christ, i, e., they have a saving knowledge of him, they know his person whom he is, and they know his personal excellencies, also they know his offices, work, and powerful operations on their own hearts : they have an experimental knowledge of the Lord Jesus Christ.

3. Friends have a firm and real love one to another, they are united together in all cordial affections, their hearts are knit to each other, as the hearts of David and Jonathan were one to the other. Their love is hearty, and also abiding. " A friend loveth at all times," Prov. xvii. 17. Christ continues in his love and friendship to them, and they abide in their love and cordial affections unto him, though perhaps not always so hot and fervent, through the flesh, and Satan's temptations.

4. Friends will stick one by the other, and endeavour to keep up the honour of each other : so Jesus Christ sticks to his people, and vindicates them under all undue charges, reproaches, and false accusations, and speaks honourably of them. " Surely they are my people, children that will not lie, and so he was their Saviour," Isa. lxii. 8. Also believers cleave to the Lord Jesus, and study his honour, or labour to exalt and magnify him and promote his interest in the world.

5. Friends give clear proofs of their friendship to each other, in special times when it is needful : so did Jesus Christ ; witness his death; and so he still doth at all times, by succouring them in times of afflictions, temptations, and tribulation, and by strengthening, supporting, and comforting them at all seasons, but especially when they stand in greatest need of such succour, &c. Also they give proofs of their love and friendship to him in a time when others forsake him, they abide with him in times when he is reproached, his authority contemned, his name blasphemed, and his truth trodden under foot.

6. True and cordial friends will venture all they have, or spare nothing that is dear to them, to help and succour, save and relieve each other.

Thus Christ spared nothing, no, not his own life, to help, relieve, and save friends. " Greater love hath no man than this, that a man lay down his life for his friends," John xv. 13. And then the saints when called unto it, have laid down their lives in love to him, to vindicate his honour, name, and witness to his truth.

7. Friends will not soon take offences at one another, but overlook one another's faults ; the Lord Jesus is such a friend that passeth by all the faults and infirmities of his people, and they will not be offended in him (though we read of some that were) " But blessed are ye that are not offended in me."

8. A man takes counsel and advice of his friend ; if a man hath a friend that is an able counsellor, be sure if he wants counsel, he will go to him ; so believers go to Christ for counsel. I bless the Lord that hath given me counsel. " Thou shalt guide me with thy counsel," Psal. lxxiii. 24. Christ is a mighty counsellor, and he gives good, safe, wise, and profitable counsel to all his friends that repair to him for it.

9. A friend imparts his secrets to his friends ; and from hence our Lord told his dis-

ciples they were his friends. " Henceforth I call you not servants ; for the servant knows not what his Lord doth, but I call you friends ; for all things that I have heard of my Father, I have made known to you," John xv. 15. And hence it is said, " The secrets of the Lord are with them that fear him." " We have the mind of Christ." He unbosometh himself unto his friends.

10. Friends sympathize one with the other, they mourn together, and also rejoice together. " In all the afflictions of God's people, he is said to be afflicted." He was grieved for Israel ; if one mourns the other mourns, and if one rejoiceth the other rejoiceth also ; and so here Christ says, " Rejoice with me, for I have found my lost sheep."

1. Neighbours. A neighbour properly is one that dwelleth near us, at the next door, or in the same street, so believers dwell near Jesus Christ. " What people have the Lord so near them ?" We dwell near Christ's heart, and always in his sight, and have his presence.

What meant by neighbours.

2. Our Lord shows who is our neighbour, even he that shows greatest love and favour to us ; so that he is indeed our neighbour, and he esteems such so to be to him, in that they show the greatest love and pity to him in his poor members, but no more as to this.

II. I shall give you the reasons why Jesus Christ and his saints and angels, do rejoice, when one sinner is converted and brought home to God, and that more generally under a six-fold consideration.

1. In respect of God the Father.

2. In respect of Jesus Christ himself, considered as Mediator.

3. In respect of the Holy Ghost, who is the more direct and immediate agent, in the conversion of a sinner.

4. In respect of Satan, who by this means loses his captive, and is vanquished, &c.

5. In respect of the poor sinner himself, considering what infinite good he receiveth hereby.

6. In respect of the ministers of the gospel, the saints and church of God.

1. In respect of God the Father, they rejoice at the conversion of a sinner, because, (1.) they know how pleasing and acceptable it is to him, or in his sight, to see one sinner converted, laying down his arms, and throwing himself at his feet, begging mercy at his most gracious hands. O how doth the heart of God pant after lost sinners ; he longs to see them return to him. " If thou wilt return, O Israel, return to me. His soul was grieved forty years in the wilderness," Heb. iii. 7—10. This God speaks after the manner of men. Now as he is said to be grieved when sinners go astray, so he is glad, he is pleased when they return ; and that which is acceptable to God, is matter of joy to Christ, as Mediator, and to his saints and angels. (2.) They rejoice because God's early love to such a poor sinner is made known or manifested in effectual calling, he being one whom the Father loved from everlasting, and sought out the way how he might discover it ; and now his glorious divine love is accomplished, who gave his Son to die, and to fetch home his lost sheep ; and so his love that was kept secret in his own breast, is now visibly known and magnified to the sinner himself. (3.) Because it is an actual accomplishment of God's gracious covenant and promises made to the Son from eternity, who said, " He shall see his seed, and the pleasure of the Lord shall prosper in his hand," Isa. liii. 10 ; that is, he shall see all that the Father gave him brought home, renewed, born again, or converted, having the image of God stamped upon their souls ; and this must needs be matter of joy to the Lord Jesus Christ, and to his saints and angels. (4.) It is, my brethren, the actual execution and accomplishment of God's decree of election, and of his eternal purpose in Jesus Christ. " Who hath saved us, and called us with an holy calling, not according to our works, but according to his own purpose and grace which was given us in Christ before the world began," 2 Tim. i. 9, that is, he hath brought into a state of grace and salvation, such that he had before appointed or ordained to eternal life. Men do not so much rejoice in what they do decree and purpose, though it be some great and glorious design, as they do when they see their decree, counsels, and purpose hath taken effect, and is accomplished. " For whom he did foreknow, he also did predestinate to be conformed to the image of his Son," Rom. viii. 29. &c. That is, such that he was pleased, as an act of his sovereignty, to set his heart, his love and affections upon, or approve of them, he predestinated to be renewed, changed, or converted to God. There was a twofold purpose of God in his decree of election and predestination. (1.) To bring all his elect seed into a state of grace here, or to renew his own image in them, which is the bringing home of a lost sinner. (2.) To bring them

Christ and his saints rejoice at the return of sinners, in respect of God the Father.

A twofold design of God in election.

all to glory hereafter; that is, he has ordained the end, viz., eternal life, and also the means, and their meetness or preparedness for that great end, which is regeneration and holiness. "According as he hath chosen us in him, before the foundation of the world, that we should be holy, and blameless before him in love," Eph. i. 4. Not chosen us to salvation only, but to be holy also; "Having predestinated us to the adoption of children by Jesus Christ, according to the good pleasure of his will." Not sons or children of God before adopted, and actually regenerated; no, but only predestinated to this gracious end and purpose: and now this being actually done, the Lord Jesus with his saints and angels rejoice, beholding now God's decree and purpose hath taken effect, in the execution of it.

2. The Lord Jesus and his saints rejoice to see one lost sinner converted, in respect of Christ himself. *They rejoice when one sinner is converted, in respect of Christ himself.*

(1.) Because every sinner that is brought to God, or is renewed, is the travel of Christ's soul, not only in his bloody passion and agony, but in bringing forth or renewing the sinner by his Spirit: no woman can rejoice more to see the fruit of her womb, and sore and bitter travail, than Christ and his ministers rejoice to see the travail of Christ's soul, i. e., a babe of grace born to God.

(2.) Because now the Lord Christ sees his kingdom, by the addition of one soul, is increased and enlarged, and Satan's kingdom lessened or diminished; for look as the church of God increaseth, the devil's synagogue decreaseth; when Christ gets one soul, Satan loses one. Now what can be a greater ground for Christ and his saints to rejoice than this?

(3.) Because every sinner that is converted, is espoused and married to the Lord Jesus Christ. "I have espoused you to one husband," 2 Cor. xi. 2. &c. This therefore must needs be cause of joy: and hence it is said, "As a bridegroom rejoiceth over the bride, so shall thy God rejoice over thee," Isa. lxii. 5. True, Jesus Christ knew that this and that sinner was given him by the Father from the beginning, nay, from eternity. But they, alas! abide a long time in a state of enmity against him, and do not love him, but contrariwise hated him and his Father; but now he hath gotten the love, the heart, and the affections of this lost and undone sinner.

Is it not grievous (think you) to the Lord Christ, to see such that he loved from everlasting, and shed his precious blood for, and came to espouse and to betroth to himself for ever, to hate him, despise him, yea, contemn his love, and abuse his patience, and great favour and kindness? Certainly it must needs have such effects upon his tender heart. A young man when he sees himself slighted, and set at nought by one that he loveth as his own soul, cannot but be greatly troubled; but when he hath obtained the love of the person that is the object of his affections, he cannot but be glad, and rejoice, even so doth the Lord Jesus Christ. "Hope deferred makes the heart sick, but when the desire cometh it is a tree of life," Prov. xiii. 12.

(4.) Christ and his saints and angels rejoice, because the conversion of a sinner is the success of his labour; not only in his dying, but also in his interceding. Jesus Christ did not only bleed for sinners, but he also pleads with God for them, that they who are his may be brought home. "And he made intercession for transgressors," Isa. liii. 12. My brethren, the Lord Jesus intercedes to bring sinners into a state of grace; and also when they are brought into such a state, or are renewed, he intercedes with the Father that they may be kept or preserved from falling, or abide in that happy condition to the end. "I have prayed for thee, that thy faith fail not," that is, not finally fail, or that the seed thereof, or the sacred habit may not fail. Every man rejoiceth to see his work prosper and succeed well that is in his hands, and so doth our Lord Jesus Christ.

3. Jesus Christ with his saints and angels, rejoice at the conversion of a lost sinner, in respect of the Holy Ghost. Brethren, each person of the blessed Trinity has their special and peculiar work in the salvation of sinners: the Father loves the sinner, elects the sinner, finds out a ransom, a Saviour, and Surety for the sinner, and entered into a covenant with him from eternity, *Joy in heaven when a sinner repents, in respect of the Holy Ghost.* and sent him into the world, anointed and authorized him to be the only Mediator, and upheld him in doing all his work, and accepted of his undertaking for them, and in their stead, &c. And Jesus Christ hath his work also, who hath wrought out a complete righteousness for all them whom he covenanted with the Father, to bring home them he died for on the tree; "the just for the unjust:" and he exercises all his offices effectually, also to this very purpose. Moreover, the Holy Ghost hath his proper and peculiar work, which is to renew, quicken, call and regenerate, and effectually to sanctify all those the Father elected, and the Son redeemed, or died for, eternally to save from wrath and hell. And now to see the Spirit, that great and glorious agent, doing of his work, which tends to per-

fect and actually to accomplish the whole work of the sinner's redemption, and so make Christ's blood and mediation effectual to the soul, is doubtless no small cause of joy and rejoicing to Jesus Christ, and to his saints and angels. "The flesh profits nothing (saith our Lord) it is the Spirit that quickens," John vi. 63. Christ's flesh alone, had it not been united to his Godhead, could not have profited us any thing; neither doth his flesh in dying profit any man, without the Spirit makes his death and merits effectual unto them; the blood of the sacrifice must not only be poured forth, but also be sprinkled upon the people, &c. From hence therefore Christ and believers rejoice to see the Holy Spirit discharging of his work, in making Christ's death effectual to a poor sinner.

(2.) As the Father rejoiced to see the Son glorifying of him, which was the grand design of the Son in all he did, so Christ and believers rejoice to see the Holy Ghost glorifying of the Son. "He shall glorify me, for he shall take of mine, and shew it unto you," John xvi. 14. The Spirit makes Christ famous, exalts, and lifts up and magnifies the Lord Jesus, he sets the crown upon Christ's head, considered as Mediator: now this was that which our Lord prayed for, "glorify thy Son;" and it was the will, purpose and grand design of the Father thus to do, and therefore both Christ, saints, and angels, rejoice to see the Holy Spirit doing of it, in the conversion of a sinner.

(3.) To see the Holy Ghost bowing the rebellious will, enlightening the dark mind, changing the carnal and earthly affections, giving light to such who sit in darkness, is ground of no small joy; to see the carnal heart made spiritual, the worldy heart made heavenly, the proud heart made humble, a lustful and unclean heart made chaste, holy, and undefiled; to see a passionate heart made meek, an envious heart made pitiful and ready to forgive; to see an hypocritical heart made sincere; in a word, to see a man born again, born of the Spirit, brought forth the second time, not into this world, or Satan's kingdom, but into the kingdom of God's dear Son here, and into the kingdom of glory, is matter or ground of great joy.

Joy in heaven when one sinner repenteth in respect of Satan. 4. Christ, his saints and angels rejoice when a poor lost sinner is returned to God, in respect of Satan, who triumphed over the sinner while he abode in his hands, and under his power.

(1.) They rejoice to see Satan's design defeated, and his work destroyed; he came to deliver sinners from the power of Satan: this was the purpose of Christ in coming into the world; "For this purpose was the Son of God manifested, that he might destroy the works of the devil," 1 John iii. 8. Or dissolve the frame of his kingdom, or overthrown his design; and when one sinner is converted, his power on that soul is destroyed, and he thrown out of that heart, in whom before he ruled, and had the dominion.

(2.) Is it not matter of joy to them to see Satan grind his teeth, to foam, and bitterly to rage, to behold his prey taken from him by almighty power, and he cannot avoid it nor help himself; no, though he raiseth all the powers of the infernal lake, to hinder or withstand it. How doth this torment the devil? 1 will work (saith the blessed God) and who shall let?' What enemy on earth, man on earth, or devil of hell? No, let Satan do his worst, when Christ comes to seek and carry home a lost sinner, he will do it. Sire, the returning of a lost sinner makes hell sorrowful, it fills devils with shame and horror, and therefore heaven and all that dwells above rejoice.

(3.) To see a man, a poor feeble mortal, in the power and strength of Christ, to trample Satan under his feet, and to triumph over him in the name of the Lord, is matter of great rejoicing to Jesus Christ, and his saints and angels.

(4.) To see Satan fly from a poor sinner, and to quit the field, and yield himself conquered, not being able to stand his ground, faith like a shield causing all his fiery darts to rebound back, and a saint, with the sword of the Spirit, conquering hell, and all the powers of darkness, is certainly cause of unspeakable joy.

Joy in respect of the sinner himself. (5.) Christ, and his saints and angels, rejoice when one sinner is converted, in respect of the poor sinner himself, who is brought home.

(1.) To see a poor naked wretch, one who lay wallowing in his blood, cast out to the loathing of his person, like a new-born infant, now clothed with a glorious garment; is not here cause for Christ and his friends to rejoice?

(2.) To see one condemned to die, lying in a deep dungeon, or in a horrible pit, now set at liberty, and brought into a glorious palace, he being one dearly beloved: what cause have all his friends to rejoice, to see this? Why thus it is here, a poor sinner beloved of God, and one comprehended in his eternal decree of election, that lay long in a horrible pit, bound in chains, and condemned to die, is now brought into the king's chamber: thus the spouse speaketh, and every believer may say, the king hath brought me into his chamber, what follows? "we will be glad and rejoice with thee," Cant. i. 4.

(3.) To see a poor creature polluted and covered all over with horrid filth, most loathsome to behold, now washed and made clean, he being one God's heart was set upon ; what cause is this of joy and rejoicing to Christ, and all that dwell in heaven.

(4.) To see one that was a child of wrath by nature, made a child of God by grace ; one that had upon him the very image of the devil, now having the image of God, is surely great cause of joy to Christ, his saints, and angels.

(5.) To see one that Satan, that hungry lion had in his jaws, or one that was a slave and vassal of sin and the devil, set free for ever, is great ground of joy considering the nature of this freedom. "If the Son therefore make you free, ye are free indeed," John viii. 36. That is, you have real perfect, glorious, spiritual, and eternal freedom, from citizenship of heaven, free access to God, and are freed from sin, the law, wrath, death, and hell.

6. To see a poor man out of his wits, or deprived of his senses, stabbing and wounding himself, tearing his clothes, and feeding on husks with filthy swine, brought to his right mind, having his senses restored to him again, and healed of all his wounds; what cause of joy would this be to all his friends ? Thus, my brethren, it is here; the prodigal, it is said, when he came to himself, said, " I will go home to my father." He was not himself before, but like a man out of his wits, as hereafter, when I come to speak to that parable, I shall, God willing, show you. Alas, were not sinners out of their wits, would they do and act as they indeed daily do ? Will men in their right mind destroy themselves ? " O Israel, thou hast destroyed thyself." Will a man in his senses stab his own soul ? choose brass counters, and refuse precious pearls, refuse good and choice food to feed on ashes, husks, and grains that swine feed upon ; or willingly yield himself up to be devoured by a cruel lion ? Or would he contemn God, or refuse God and Christ, and all the good that is in God and Jesus Christ, from love to his sins and filthy lusts ?

(7.) To see a man resisting the Holy Spirit, warring and fighting against his Maker, daring God to damn him, flying in his very face, and in actual rebellion against him, now reconciled and brought into sweet accquaintance and friendship with him ; is not this cause of joy to Jesus Christ, his saints and angels ? to see a vile rebel come in and humble himself to his prince, acknowledging all his by-past treasons, and abominable indignities cast upon the King of heaven and earth, loathing and abhorring himself, and repenting in dust and ashes.

(8.) To see a poor sheep that cost the Shepherd the price of his own blood, bought so dear, to go astray, and expose itself to a thousand dangers, now brought home to his own fold ; is not here cause of joy to the Shepherd, and to all his friends and neighbours ? " rejoice with me, for I have found my lost sheep."

6. There is cause of joy in respect to ministers and members of the church.

(1.) Christ and his angels in heaven, and saints on earth rejoice to see a lost sinner return home to God ; because poor ministers succeed in their great work, as instruments in the hand of God ; hereby it appears that Jesus Christ is with them, owns and prospers them. What can be greater encouragement to them, or tend more to strengthen their hands and hearts ? Was it not matter of joy to Abraham's servant, to see how God had prospered him in his message, when he had prevailed with Rebecca to consent to go with him, to become Isaac's wife ? Ministers are Christ's spokesmen to persuade sinners to receive and embrace the Lord Jesus, and espouse him, who by them is pleased to tender his love unto them. Do not ambassadors of peace rejoice when their embassy is received, and the king's enemies are brought to accept of terms of peace ? A minister is Christ's ambassador, and when one sinner is converted under his ministry, he succeeds in his embassy. This also puts a glory upon the word and blessed Gospel, which is an instrument of God's power, by which he commonly is pleased to work faith in the souls of sinners. " I am not ashamed of the Gospel of Christ, for it is the power of God unto salvation, unto every one that believeth," Rom. i. 16. " It pleaseth God by the foolishness of preaching, to save them that believe." " The Word of God is quick and powerful, sharper than any two-edged sword." Now God owning after this manner his own ordinances, Jesus Christ rejoices with his saints. Moreover, the saints seeing their number increase, and others made fellow-heirs and fellow-citizens with them, they rejoice also.

APPLICATION

1. See how acceptable the conversion of sinners is to Jesus Christ.

2. And is grace received such cause of joy to others ? O then what cause hath a sinner himself to rejoice ? It is said Philip went down to Samaria and preached Christ to them, and they believed and were baptized, both men and women, " and there was great joy in that city."

3. From hence also we may infer, that we ought to rejoice with them that rejoice, or at others good.

4. Moreover, what cause have parents to rejoice, to see their children converted. It is matter of joy to see our enemies converted, and them that hate us : but O how much greater cause have we of rejoicing, when our dear children, or dear relations are renewed, changed, or brought home to God, and made happy for ever ?

5. By way of exhortation. Sinners who would not return to God, if it be cause of such joy to God the Father, to the Lord Jesus Christ, to the Holy Spirit, and to ministers, and to the holy angels ; then labour to return to God ! attend upon the word, cry to him to help you to believe. Certainly the conversion of sinners is a very great thing, it is matter of the highest moment.

6. Ministers also may from hence be stirred up to do their utmost in order to the conversion of sinners : let us not be weary, neither faint in our minds, nor be discouraged, though we meet with reproaches from men, opposition from Satan, and many things that tend to grieve and wound our souls, from the people of God, as the prophet Jeremiah, and the apostle Paul himself did, which made the first to wish his " head was water, and his eyes a fountain of tears," Jer. ix. 1, 2. " Report, say they, and we will report." But if it be so now with some of us, yet let us not be discouraged, since God hath appointed preaching as his great ordinance, for the bringing home, or conversion of lost sinners.

7. We may infer, if the conversion of sinners causeth such joy to Christ, his saints and angels, then when sinners repent not, believe not, that must needs cause grief and sorrow to them. Christ is said to be grieved, because the Jews believed not, or because of the hardness of their hearts : also the Holy Ghost is grieved ; " Grieve not the Holy Spirit," Eph. iv. 30. Angels are grieved, ministers are grieved when sinners contemn God, slight Christ, resist the Spirit, vilify Christ's ministers, and proceed in their ungodly ways, and refuse to return : and the devils rejoice.

Lastly, O how happy are you that God hath called home, who are brought to believe, and are in Christ's hand, and born by his power unto salvation ; you, of all people, have cause to rejoice, for your names are written in heaven.

So much at this time, and thus I close with this blessed parable.

26. THE LOST COIN

Either what woman having ten pieces of silver, if she lose one piece, doth not light a candle, and sweep the house, and seek diligently until she find it ? And when she hath found it, she calleth together her friends and neighbours, saying, rejoice with me, I have found the piece which I had lost. Likewise I say unto you, there is joy in heaven, in the presence of the angels of God, over one sinner that repenteth.—Luke xv. 8, 9, 10.

The intro-   My brethren, it is worth your consideration to note, that our blessed Saviour
duction.   is very intent upon the main or chief matter contained in the former parable, viz., of the lost sheep ; in that he seconds it with this of the lost piece of money : nay, the third time he confirms it, in the lost son.

We seldom or never find him repeating the same thing in different parables ; therefore let me caution all not to think or speak lightly of these parables, or think our Lord used needless representations, expressions, or allusions herein, nor that this parable has but little in it, or that we ought not particularly to attempt to open the several parts thereof, but only mind the chief scope thereof, which is the same with that which goes before (as our late annotators intimate) but certainly he foresaw that the parable of the lost sheep could not fully hold forth some things about the state of lost sinners, or about the seeking of them; therefore he proceeds to this. A sheep is one thing, and a piece of silver is another; also a man doth not light a candle to seek a sheep that is lost, as a woman doth in seeking a lost groat; the one is sought in the clear light of the day, but the other may be lost in a dark house, and cannot be found without lighting a candle: by which is showed, that sinners cannot be found by mere natural light, or by the light in all men, but by a supernatural light, which is signified by an artificial light, i.e., that of a candle. *Why our Lord might add this parable to the former.*

I find but few writers besides Mr. Rogers, who have spoken unto this Parable, but he endeavoured to open every part thereof, whom I purpose not to follow; neither do I think it needful to be so particular on many things as he is, but only to open those things in it which could not be comprehended in the precedent parable: all that I purpose to speak to this, shall be comprehended in one discourse. *See Mr. Neh. Rogers True Convert, an exposition of this chapter of Luke.*

But to proceed.

Our Lord, it is evident, like a wise master of the assemblies, endeavours by a second, nay, by a third blow, to drive the nail, that the matter might be fixed upon their hearts, i.e., the business of his seeking of lost sinners. Therefore the main scope and design of this parable is the same with the former, though part of the matter contained in it is different, viz.,

1. It is to justify his practice in his conversing with great sinners, and in his endeavouring to bring publicans and harlots to repentance. *The scope of the parable.*

2. To reprove the pride and confidence of the vain-glorious Pharisees, who thought themselves righteous, and not in a lost state and condition; and in this and the precedent parable, he seems to grant or suppose it was so, i. e., that they were not lost, but were like pieces of silver in the possession of their owner, they being God's covenant people; he doth not say, that they were not lost, but (I say) he seems to yield to them as if it was so: as if he should say, let it be granted that you are silver or gold, not lost nor corrupted, but are righteous persons; yet these great sinners, you conclude, are lost. "And what person having ten pieces of silver, if one be lost, will not seek it until found."

3. His design herein is to show his great love to such sinners, and so to encourage them to hope for pardon, or to move them to seek for faith and repentance.

4. And also under this parable he shows, what little worth or value is in sinners, as they are in themselves, though they may be some of God's elect. So much as to the scope.

Secondly, as to the division thereof.

1. You have the matter or narration. *The division of the parable.*
2. The application.
3. The confirmation.

1. In the matter or narration, you have an agent described.
(1.) By her sex, a woman.
(2.) By her substance, she had ten pieces of silver.
(3.) What had befallen her, she had lost one.
(4.) Her actions, or what she did thereupon.
1st. She lighteth a candle.
2ndly. She sweepeth the house.
3rdly. She seeketh her lost piece diligently.
4thly. Her good success, she finds it.
5thly. How much she is pleased thereby, " She calleth her friends and neighbours together, and desires them to rejoice with her, because she had found the piece that was lost.

2. You have the application of this, "Likewise there is joy in heaven, in the presence of the angels of God, when one sinner repenteth."

3. The confirmation, " I say unto you." This shows the certainty of it, or that indeed it is so, or a great truth, i. e., " there is joy in heaven," &c. I, the truth itself, the true witness, do say it; that which is spoken by the lip of truth itself, none can doubt of.

In the next place I shall open each part thereof.

What woman? the woman here no doubt signifies the same person mentioned in the foregoing parable, that had the hundred sheep, which we have proved refers to the Lord Jesus Christ, who is often in the scripture set forth by *The parts of the parable opened.*

the feminine gender, by the name of wisdom. " Wisdom hath built her house, she hath hewn out her seven pillars. She hath killed her beasts, she hath mingled her wine, and she hath sent forth her maidens," Prov. ix. 1, 2, 3. Expositors generally agree, that by wisdom here is meant Jesus Christ, who is called the wisdom of God ; and by her maidens, are intended the ministers of the gospel.

But because it belongs to women, or their maids, to light a candle, and to sweep the house ; our Lord made use of this allusion, to set forth what he must do in seeking lost sinners ; and, as Mr. Rogers says, I see no reason to judge but that Christ is meant thereby, as corresponding with the preceding parable, because these ten pieces of silver are said to be the woman's. Now who hath any property in sinners, to call them his, but God, or our Lord Jesus Christ ? for may an angel say they are mine ? or can a minister say they are mine ? no, neither of them can plead any interest in these pieces of silver, or have any property so as to call them theirs ; but the Lord Christ may call them his, " For the earth is the Lord's, and the fulness thereof." Jesus Christ created the world, and all things therein. " By him, and for him they are, and were created," Rev. iv. 11. And he, as Mediator, is heir of all things, all things are put into his hands to do with them, or dispose of them as his own.

"Having ten pieces of silver." Our annotators tell us, that each piece was the quarter part of a Shekel, and of our money it is seven pence half-penny, commonly called a groat, I suppose according to the Roman account, a small piece of little value.

1. By the ten pieces of silver, expositors say, is meant the same species of creatures with the hundred sheep, even all mankind.

But something is here supposed (as I hinted) by way of seeming concession to the Pharisees, which really is not so, viz., that the woman had not lost the nine pieces, or none but one ; for all mankind, or every individual man and woman is lost in the first Adam, though the Pharisees and the greatest part of the people of the Jews (they being God's own covenant-people under the law) thought they were not lost, nor did they judge any among them were vile and undone persons, but profane and notorious sinners only.

2. By the piece that was lost, is meant all God's elect ; and they only are said to be lost because they alone are brought to see and confess themselves to be lost and undone sinners, and so it holds parallel-wise with the lost sheep.

" Pieces of silver ;" this may denote, that man was once (as first created) of some account with God, like as silver is among men and women.

Why a sinner is compared to a piece of silver. (1.) For as silver is a choice sort of metal : so, my brethren, man was once a choice sort of creature, and highly valued by the Almighty.

(2.) Silver stamped for coin, has the image of Cesar, or the image of the prince (whose money it is) stamped upon it, so man, as choice silver coined for God, at first had the image of God stamped upon his soul.

(3.) Money also hath an image stamped upon it by regal authority, even so also by the authority of God, the King of heaven and earth, God's own image was stamped upon the soul of man.

(4.) Money may be defaced, marred, corrupted, or counterfeited by some traitorous person or persons : so Satan and sin, those cursed traitors to the God of heaven, have defaced, marred, corrupted, and counterfeited the king's coin, and to such a degree, that mankind, (I mean all ungodly persons) are become as reprobate silver, as the prophet Jeremiah shows, " Reprobate silver shall men call them, because the Lord hath rejected them," Jer. vi. 3.

(5.) Silver that is corrupted, and mixed with base metal, will not pass for current coin, but it must be melted down, refined, and stamped anew : so every man and woman in the world are so corrupted that they will not pass for current coin with God, no not one piece, until they are melted down, refined, changed, and new coined, and by the Holy Spirit, have the image of God stamped upon them.

From hence by the way let me note,

Man naturally as in himself, is but of very little worth. Doct. 1. Though man was good silver in himself, yet being compared to a groat, it followeth from hence, he is but of very little worth or value ; for being corrupted, mixed with base metal, and abominably counterfeited, he is become like a false piece of money, a brass groat, or rather lead.

What is man naturally good for ? what is sinful man worth ? even just nothing, nay less than nothing ; therefore when our Saviour compares him in this parable to silver, he alludes to what man was at first, as he came out of God's hand.

Let me a little confirm this by God's word.

1. Man naturally is like to unsavoury salt, or salt that hath lost its savour, which (our

Lord saith) " is good for nothing but to be trodden under foot of men," Matt. v. 13.   Indeed not fit to be cast on the dunghil, because it tends to make land barren.

2. Man is called an unclean thing. " We all are as an unclean thing," Isa. lxiv. 6. " They are corrupt, they have done abominable works, they are altogether become filthy," &c., Psal. xiv. 1, 3.   And again, saith the sacred text " How much more abominable and filthy is man," Job. xv. 16.   Sin hath made man most loathsome and abominable in the sight of God.   " The heart of the wicked is of little worth, though the tongue of the just is as choice silver," Prov. x. 20.

3. My brethren, man is compared to a worm, and what is of less value than a worm ? " how much less man that is a worm ?" Mr. Broughton reads it in English, " and the son of man, a vermin." The word, saith Mr. Caryl, signifies, both great and small worms ; are vermin or a worm bred out of corrupt flesh, a carrion worm ? and what is more hateful and loathsome than such worms ? man is a very poor thing, being compared to dust, to vanity, and to a lie.   " Men of high degree are vanity, and men of low degree are a lie," Psal. lxii. 9. " And nations before him are as nothing, and counted to him less than nothing," Isa. xl. 15.   Man deserves not to be called a groat ; no, he is less than a brass counter.

(1.) Look upon his original, he is from the earth, as worms are.

(2.) Look upon him in his natural state ; he liveth upon the earth, on earthly things, as worms do.

(3.) Look upon him as corrupted, and as proceeding from fallen Adam ; he is a worm bred out of corruption.

(4.) Look upon as to his natural powers and ability, and he is as helpless as a worm, he cannot save himself : a worm may save itself from danger, as soon as a man can save himself from sin, wrath, and hell.

(5.) Man as a worm, must shortly return to the earth, and be housed in the earth as worms be.   O how is man by sin degraded ! having lost himself, he is compared to a groat, a leaden groat that once was God's jewel, a most noble and excellent piece in God's sight, made at first but a little lower than the angels.

Again, sinful man, lost man, compared to a small piece of corrupt silver, reprobate silver ; then let me note,

Doct. 2. That the grace, love, and goodness of God, is infinite to sorry man.

Will God set his heart upon man, love a worm, a filthy creature, and send his own Son to seek and save him that is of no worth and value, as in himself ? and what is the nature of the love of Christ, to come to seek the lost groat ; what admirable condescension is this, man who is no better than reprobate silver, or than a corrupt, a poisonous and filthy thing, an enemy, a traitor, and a rebel against God.   Wonder O ye heavens !

Doct. 3. We may also infer, that the excellencies of grace which flow from Jesus Christ are to be admired.

When Christ finds one of these corrupt pieces, a base and vile creature, worse than lead, he by his Spirit and heavenly grace makes it as choice silver, or a most excellent piece, he refines it ; nay, changeth it into pure gold, though it was but corrupt silver when he found it.   " How are the precious sons of Sion comparable to fine gold, esteemed as earthen pitchers !" Lam. iv. 2.   My brethren, Jesus Christ doth not leave the piece as he found it ; no, its being lost, denotes its natural pollution and corrupt state, but he changes the state, the nature and the hearts of sinners, and makes them more pure than gold, and also stamps his own image again upon every piece which he finds.

Doct.   4.   And from hence also we may infer, that all we have, or do receive, is of grace, of rich grace, of free grace.

There was nothing in sinners that could move Jesus Christ to love them, to seek them, and come to save them, but his own pity, grace, and love ; we are of no more worth than a base counterfeit leaden groat.

But to proceed. " If she lose one." I have, in speaking to the foregoing parable, showed you what it is to be lost, how sinners have lost God, and God hath lost them, and how they have lost themselves, and also the woeful state of such ; so that I shall say no more to this now.

My brethren, if one piece, one sinner be lost, Jesus Christ soon hath it upon his heart to seek for it ; also consider, it is better to be one of those pieces which are thus lost, than one that looks upon himself never lost, but in the hand of Christ, or safe amongst his treasure, as the Jew did.   There is one thing to be noted which may afford comfort to lost sinners (as it is hinted in this parable) viz., the piece of money lost was in the house, i. e., it is in the world, it is not lost in the bottom of the sea, it is not in hell, amongst them that are irrecoverably lost, there is hope, and ground of hope, of finding a piece of money lost in our house.

Was it lost in the sea, there was no ground to hope ever to find it again. So sinners that were alive in this world, at present they are in a lost condition, yet they may be **How lost.** found; but those that are in hell are lost for ever.

It is lost, i. e., it hath lost its beauty, its purity, its excellency, it hath lost the image of God.

What is meant by the candle. "Doth not light a candle," &c.

Quest. What may be meant by the candle, and by lighting of it?

Answ. I answer, 1. Christ himself, Jesus Christ is the light of **Christ himself as Mediator is like a candle lighted to seek lost sinners.** the world; and when he came into the world, this candle was lighted. True, in some sense, as he was the light of the world from the beginning, so he was partly lighted (as soon as Adam sinned) in the promise of the seed of the woman, and he gave light to all that were in the house, or that believed under the law; but he never gave so great light as he did when he came into the world.

The gospel or word of God is a candle. 2. The gospel may be meant by this candle, and it is lighted in and by the ministration of it, through the divine influences of the Spirit upon the soul. "Thy word is a lamp (or candle) to my feet, and a light to my paths," Psal. cxix. 105. Christ lights the candle of the gospel, sends his word and the ministry thereof to that nation, kingdom, city, or place, where any of his elect are scattered and lie lost, to seek and search for them, but he himself is the chief and prime light. "I am come as a light into this world."

Also the spirit of a man is as a candle. 3. The candle also may refer to man's spirit, "The spirit of man is the candle of the Lord, searching all the inward parts of the belly," Prov. xx. 27. Hence also David says, "Thou wilt light my candle, he will light my darkness," Psal. xviii. 28. By both these, nay, all these candles, Jesus Christ seeks his lost groat, i. e., lost sinners; he sends his word, his glorious gospel, and puts it into the candlestick of his church, not only to light believers, but also to light sinners; he enlightens also their understanding, or lights their spirit by the light of the Holy Ghost, that so he may find his lost piece of corrupt silver.

From hence I observe,

Doct. 5. The gospel is, or may be compared to a candle, or a light which Christ hath lighted to give light in the night of this world.

This I shall open parallel-wise in a few particulars.

How the gospel may be compared to a candle that is lighted. 1. A candle is not a natural light, but a light contrived or devised by man. So Jesus Christ, as Mediator, was the contrivance of the infinite wisdom of God, he is not that natural light that is in all men (considered as he is Mediator) though he may be said to be the light thereof considered as Creator.

2. What could any people do in a house in the night time, had they not the light of a candle, lamp, or the like? if they have lost anything, they cannot without light find it; work they cannot, and therefore a candle was contrived and made to give light in the night time. So, and in like manner, what could we do in this dark world, was there no Christ, no gospel? what darkness should we be in as to our souls? for the light within all men is but like the light of the moon. Moreover, had not God been graciously pleased to have lighted this heavenly candle, Jesus Christ could not have found one lost sinner. Besides, it is by the light of this candle we must work, and do all which we have to do to glorify God.

3. Darkness is grievous, especially that darkness that may be felt, like the darkness of Egypt. So the spiritual darkness the souls of all men are in naturally, is very grievous "They being alienated from the life of God, through the ignorance which is in them," &c. Eph. iv. 18. What is more lamentable than to dwell always in a dark dungeon and never see light? and this being considered, is it not strange "that men should love darkness rather than the light?"

4. Such who walk in darkness, our Lord says, stumble, as we also find it by woeful experience. So such that never saw the light of Christ, and of his glorious gospel stumble.

5. A candle is a light of acceptation, it is capable to receive light, but it is not a light of information; a candle must be first lighted before it can give light. So the spirit of man is a light of acceptation, it is capable to receive light, but it is the Lord that must light our candle by his Spirit. "There is a spirit in man, and the inspiration of the Almighty iveth him understanding," Job. xxxii. 8.

6. A man "that walketh in darkness, knoweth not whither he goeth." Even so sinners who are in spiritual darkness, know not whither they are going; they perhaps think they are going to heaven, when they are going the direct way to hell.

7. A man in a dark house knows not what company he hath with him, the house may be full of toads and venomous creatures, and thieves may also lurk in some corners of it, who may soon murder him. So sinners who are in darkness, know not what horrid guilt and filth is in their hearts, nor what cursed and abominable thieves they harbour in their house, as sin, the world, and the devil, who alas! are ready to cut the throats of their precious souls, nay, and have mortally wounded them already.

8. "Light is sweet, and it is a pleasant thing for the eyes to see the sun," Eccl. xi. 7. And natural light is sweet and pleasant. O then how sweet is it for the eyes of the soul to see the light of the Sun of righteousness, or to enjoy the spiritual light of this candle!

9. Men should endeavour to work while they have the light, they know not how long it may be before darkness may cover them. Our Lord saith, "I must work while it is day," John ix. 4, or while it was light. Alas! who knows how soon God may remove the candle of the gospel, or blow out their candle, and then they will be in darkness for ever.

10. Light maketh things manifest, and whatsoever doth make manifest is light. What a discovery doth light make of things which those who are in darkness see not. So the light of Christ in the gospel, by the Spirit, maketh many things manifest, or discovers their nature, or what they are which those that are in darkness see not, nor do they know.

(1.) Thereby the evil of sin is discovered to all believers, as the worst of all evils, and plague of all plagues.

(2.) The woeful state and condition of mankind by nature, is also made manifest by this light.

(3.) The vanity, and emptiness of this present world.

(4.) The deceitfulness of our hearts, and the filth and corruption that is therein.

(5.) Also by this light we come to see the infinite wisdom, love, mercy, power, justice, and holiness of God, and all the other attributes and perfections of his ever-glorious and most adorable majesty.

(6.) As also his eternal counsels and purposes of his will about our salvation in eternity, and that blessed covenant that was between the Father and the Son about our redemption.

(7.) It likewise discovers the great glory, beauty, and transcendent excellencies that are in our Lord Jesus Christ, together with the necessity of him, and of union with him, and of faith in him. In a word, all the mysteries of grace, treasures of grace and glory, are made manifest by this candle, or by the light of the gospel.

11. A candle is of great use to kindle a fire, and oft-times it is made use of to do that. So the candle of the word, and blessed gospel, God makes use of to kindle a fire in our souls, which burns up all the combustibles of sin and self, which we find naturally to be in us; and hereby a holy flame is also kindled in our hearts of faith in, love to, and zeal for our Lord Jesus Christ; by which means we are warmed, and have divine heat in our souls, and whereby our hard hearts are melted, and we comforted under all cooling and heart-chilling providences; "Is not my word like fire?" Jer. xxiii. 29.

12. Light dispelleth darkness; so doth the light of the gospel dispel, scatter, and drive away all inward darkness arising from sin, ignorance, and temptations, also the darkness of all errors, false doctrine, and damnable heresies, and human traditions, and superstitions whatsoever.

USE. 1. These things being so, learn to prize the gospel. What a woeful condition are they in who never saw nor had the candle lighted among them; bewail the Pagan, the Mahometan, and Popish world.

2. "Live up in all things according to the light thereof," and let this candle burn all night in your chambers, I mean all your days in your souls.

3. And search your hearts by the light thereof, having your candle first lighted in you by God's Spirit.

But to proceed.

"And sweepeth the house,"

Quest. What is meant by the house?

Answ. Mr. Rogers understands the church of the Jews is meant here, by house; but I conceive that cannot be, because many of God's elect were not lost in that house. Christ came to be a light to the Gentiles, for among them were many poor sinners which he came to seek.

What the house is where this candle is lighted.

2. Because Christ did not come to be a candle or light to that national and typical church, but to remove that external church-state, and to gather a pure Gospel-church out from amongst them and the Gentile nations.   Therefore by the house I understand is meant this world, as Christ is called the light of the world; " I am come a light into the world," that so he may seek in all nations where any of his pieces of corrupt silver are lost.

Why this world is called a house.   1. A house is erected or built by some man; so God, the master builder, who built all things, built this world, he laid the foundation, and hangeth it upon nothing, but is the great pillar thereof himself, by his almighty power.

2. A house, (I mean a rare and magnificient house,) is the contrivance of man's wisdom. So this world is the wise and glorious contrivance of Almighty God.

3. A house that is wonderfully large, hath, or may have a multitude of inhabitants in it; so hath this world.

4. A house of a noble person hath many vessels in it, some of gold and silver, and some of brass, wood, and earth, some for honour, and some for dishonour.   So in this world there are some men and women, who are vessels of gold and silver, I mean, holy and gracious persons, whom God compares to gold and silver, and to precious stones; and also some who are but wood, or like mere earthen vessels of little worth in God's sight.

5. A house in the night, if there be no light, no candle nor lamp lighted, is a very dark place.   So this world, during the whole night of its continuance, had not God sent Christ and the Gospel to give light to it, would have been a dark place, even nothing but thick darkness.

6. Sometimes in a house a piece of money may be lost, and oftentimes is, and it cannot be found without lighting a candle.   Even so, and in like manner, in this world, all God's elect, (signified by this lost groat) before they are called, lie among the rest of undone mankind, and they cannot be found unless Jesus Christ comes a light into this world; no, not by the Son of God himself, unless he be incarnate, and as Mediator, be set up as a glorious light, that by his own mediation he may seek them; and that he might seek and find them, he lights up the candle of the Gospel, *i. e.*, the ministry thereof, and also by his own Spirit lights up our candle, I mean, inspires our spirits, and gives us understanding, &c.

" She sweepeth the house."

What is meant by sweeping the house.   1. Note, There may be, and oft is, much filth in a great house that may cover a piece of silver.   So in this world there is abundance of sin and wickedness, which does cover all God's elect until he comes to light a candle, and sweep the house.

2. Note, A bare lighting of a candle, without sweeping the house, sometimes will not discover a lost piece of silver.   No more will the bare preaching of the Gospel find a lost sinner, until Christ comes with his broom of convictions, and the cleansing influences of his Spirit, to purge the filth of sin, and the filth of the world out of his heart and conscience.

Quest.   What may be meant by sweeping the house?

Answ. 1.   By the broom, or sweeping the house, may be meant the dismal judgments which Christ sometimes brings upon the world, which, though it be a plague and judgment on the wicked, yet it is in mercy to his elect ones, it is that he may seek them by his rod, and that way he many times finds and brings home several of his chosen: for like as a besom is to sweep away the dust and the filth, yet the woman in sweeping designs to spare, nay, to find her lost piece of money, and not sweep that away; even so Jesus Christ sometimes brings the besom of afflictions, and sore judgment upon the world, to sweep away the filth or wickedness of the earth, yet he doth not design thereby to sweep away or destroy his elect seed; no, but to find them, and bring them home by the rod.

2. It also may (as I hinted) intend powerful convictions.   God's amazing judgments do often awaken the conscience of a secure sinner, and these convictions, like a broom, may come upon the soul under the word, and sometimes under the rod; for many are brought home by afflictions, who would not perhaps attend upon the word.

(1.) When the broom comes, it stirs the dust and makes it more discernable; before it may be but little dust or filth appeared in the house.   So under convictions a poor sinner sees the filth of his heart and life.   " Come see a man that told me all that ever I did," John iv. 29, Acts ii. 26, Acts xvi. 30, 31.   " And when they heard this, they were pricked in their hearts, and cried out," and thus also did the jailer.

(2.) Also, under severe judgments, the wicked are discovered to be more vile and abominable, they sin the more, and blaspheme the God of heaven, and grow worse thereby; but such that belong to Christ discover their sin, find out their sin, and are humbled, and give glory unto God.

(3.) Also the broom of church-discipline may be here meant, for the church is in the world, though not of the world. This way much dust and filth is swept away, and Jesus Christ discovers his lost piece; for when the sentence of excommunication passeth against a sinner in Zion, and it doth him good, he being thereby brought to repentance, and his soul humbled, it discerneth that he is one that is a true Christian; but if that censure tends to harden him and he grows worse, this broom sweeps him quite away as filth.

God says that he "will search Jerusalem with candles." He hath more candles than one by which he searches us, he will discover one way or another who are his, and find them all out, either by sweeping providences, or sweeping convictions, or by a sweeping discipline. Therefore I will not exclude the church from being at all meant by the house, which is said to be swept.

"Seeking diligently until she find it."

How Jesus Christ may be said to seek lost sinners, we showed in the preceding parable (to which we refer you.) Christ came from heaven to this end, and took our nature upon him; to this end he became a light unto the world, that he might seek his lost piece of silver. *i. e.*, his elect. He sends the gospel to this end, and sets up that candle; also he sends his ministers as burning and shining lights, to seek and search out lost sinners. John Baptist is called a shining light. He sends likewise his Spirit to convince those who are lost of their sin, and of that woeful condition they are in whilst they abide in the first Adam, and as under the law sentence, and also "To convince them of righteousness; of sin, because they believe not in him; and of righteousness, because I go to the Father," John xvi. 8—10. Christ is discharged of all our sins which were laid upon him. Justice having nothing to lay more to his, nor our charge, as to vindictive wrath, nor the law of God; he is therefore exalted at God's right-hand, and there makes intercession for transgressors; and that way he also seeks his lost Isa. liii. 12. pieces, pleading with God the discharge of all believers, or of all that come unto him by virtue of his own perfect obedience and meritorious sacrifice. Also he sends afflictions, and severe providences upon this and that person the Father gave unto him, using his rod as well as his word, that so he may find such he came to seek and save. He also lights up their candle, *i. e.*, informs their judgments, enlighteneth their understandings, and with his broom he sweeps towns, cities, families, and nations, where any of his elect are; and all this is to find his lost pieces of silver, for so he accounts them, as they are his Father's choice, and his own choice, whom he came to espouse, and make the joy of his heart, and the delight of his eyes for ever.

How Christ seeks diligently to find lost sinners.

Now put all these things together, and it will appear to all, that he seeks them diligently; he seeks, his Spirit seeks, and his ministers seek, and he sets conscience to seek also, and he never gives over seeking, until he hath found all them the Father gave unto him.

1. He is constant in seeking them.

2. He is unweary in seeking them.

3. He spares no labour, no cost, no time, that he may find them.

4. He uses all manner of ways and means, in order to this gracious end and purpose.

5. He hath covenanted with the Father, that he will seek them, even with the price of his blood, so that he may find them.

6. He hath promised his Father, and promised his elect, that he will seek them until he hath found them. "I will seek that which was lost, and bring again that which was driven back, and I will bind up that which was broken, and I will strengthen that which was sick," Ezek. xxxiv. 16. "I will put my fear into their hearts, and they shall not depart from me," Jer. xxxii. 40.

7. He comes over all mountains of difficulties and opposition, and over all mountains of their sins and unworthiness, that he may seek and find them.

8. Nay, and he also causeth them to seek and search after him; he inclines their hearts, bows and bends their rebellious wills, changes their earthly and carnal affections, so that he may find them. All which fully shows, that he diligently seeks them.

"And when she hath found it, she calleth her friends and neighbours together, saying, Rejoice with me, for I have found the piece which I had lost."

The reasons why Jesus Christ, and his saints and angels rejoice, when one sinner is brought to believe and to repent was largely opened in the precedent parable. Consider,

1. God's angels are his friends, and our friends and fellow-servants. Rev. xix. 10.

2. Angels are often made use of for the helping and strengthening of the poor sinners, and of believers; they do many a friendly office, and "minister unto them that shall be heirs of salvation," Heb. i. 14.

3. Angels are much employed to help and succour Christ's poor ministers: an angel brought Elijah meat, and bid him eat, 1 King. xix. 5, 7.   An angel talked friendly with Daniel, and gave him skill and understanding: an angel brought Mary the tidings, how she should conceive and bring forth our Lord Jesus Christ: an angel awakes Peter, and delivered him out of prison, Acts xii. 7: an angel discovered to John those wonderful things contained in the Revelations; nay, angels appeared to the shepherds, and told them the joyful news of the birth of our Saviour, and they also strengthened him in his bloody agony.

Quest. Why are angels so friendly to Christ's ministers?

Answ. 1. Because of the great love they have to Christ, whose servants angels are; they know how Christ bled for his elect, and that he loves them dearly; and therefore what assistance angels can give to ministers, they are ready to afford them, John iii. 29.

2. Because they are the friends of the Bridegroom, and are also employed by him to minister to the saints, and especially to ministers, who are Christ's spokesmen.

3. Because angels know the work of ministers is hard and difficult, and that it is God's work, and that they are workers together with him.

4. Because Satan, or the evil angels do what they can to hinder ministers in the work: now the good angels strive to counterwork the spirits of darkness, against whom they continually war, and so strengthen and encourage Christ's ministers.

5. Because the holy angels know that ministers are hated by the evil angels above all men in heaven or earth, they being their greatest enemies, and striving to overthrow their hellish kingdom.

6. They know how acceptable it is to God, to see sinners converted, and that the whole design of Christ is not answered in his death, until this is done.   Now these things being so, it is no marvel, Christ calls upon them to rejoice with him, at the conversion of one sinner.

" Likewise I say unto you, There is joy in the presence of the angels, when one sinner repenteth."

Hearers should make application of sermons they hear.

1. Our Lord applies his own mysterious doctrine, to teach people how to make application to themselves, of what they hear.

2. This is also all that our Lord said by way of explaining this parable, the rest he left to his ministers inspired by his own Spirit to open.

3. It is also to confirm the truth of what he had spoken, " I say unto you."

" In the presence of the angels."

Angels are spirits, and their name signifies their office, messengers; by nature they are spirits, and have no material bodies, they are endowed with great knowledge, wisdom, and affections also. " They rejoice." But they know not all things, no, not our hearts. " Thou Lord, knowest the hearts of all men," Acts i. 24.   No angel nor devil knows more than by curious observation besides what God reveals to them. " Man (saith one) knoweth much, angels more, God only knows all."   Some think that God may reveal the conversion of sinners to the spirits of just men in heaven, as well as to the angels. Our annotators seem to be of the same mind, but other worthy men will not admit of this.   I will leave it to every man's own conceptions: ye know it is said, " Abraham is ignorant of us," &c., though an answer might be given to that.

Be sure no mere creature in heaven, as a creature, knows what is done on earth : vain and abominable therefore is the practice of the Papists, in praying to the virgin Mary, and to other saints and angels in heaven.   And in vain do such come to God by Jesus Christ, or pray to him, who believe he is no more than a mere creature, and not the Most High God.

APPLICATION

1. I infer, Here is a great cause for sinners to rejoice, and to be encouraged to seek Christ, because he seeks them.   When Christ by his word or rod, is come to seek them, that is the time in which they ought to seek him, and not to doubt of finding him.

2. It may teach sinners also kindly to take rebuke from God, and bear afflictions, because that way Christ sometimes seeks and searches after them, to do their souls good.

3. Also let ministers learn from hence, to be diligent in their work, in seeking and striving to bring sinners to repentance, since their great Master himself is so diligent about this matter.

4. Let us all admire the great love of God, in setting up and lighting of such a candle, as Christ and the gospel is, in this dark world.

5. It may also inform us, that whatsoever light God hath set up in this dark world, it

is for the sake of sinners that are lost, I mean the elect of God, who only are effectually brought to see their lost condition.

6. Let all be exhorted to prize the gospel, which is God's candle to give light to such who are in darkness. O what would become of England, should God take away this candle, or suffer wicked men, and impostors, to corrupt the sacred truths thereof!

7. What encouragement is here for ministers to labour, since angels rejoice to see their success, though there is no calling that men meet with more enemies, and more trouble and disgrace in following; yet none is more honourable, nor esteemed of by Christ, and honoured by the angels.

8. Comfort to believers; as Christ hath found you, so he thereby designed to refine you, new make, change, and anew stamp his glorious image upon you; so that you are now pure gold in his sight, nay, his jewels, who before were like brass, lead, or reprobate silver, Mal. iii. 17. That he might make you glorious pieces, he sought you, and his image shall never be lost in you, nor you be plucked out of his hand. Amen.

So much as to this parable.

27. THE LOST SON

I

A certain man had two sons.

And the younger of them said to his father, Father, give me the portion of goods that falleth to me. And he divided unto them his living.

And not many days after, the younger son gathered all together, and took his journey into a far country, and wasted his substance with riotous living.

And when he had spent all, there arose a mighty famine in that land, and he began to be in want.

And he went and joined himself unto a citizen of that country, and he sent him into his fields to feed swine.

And he would fain have filled his belly with the husks, which the swine did eat : and no man gave unto him, &c.—Luke xv. 11—16.

WE have in this chapter three parables, all showing or holding forth the same thing; the two first I have already spoken unto, viz., the lost sheep, and the lost groat, and now by God's assistance, I purpose to speak to the third, viz., The lost son.

In two respects they do all agree.

1. The sheep was lost, the groat was lost.

The son also went from his father, and was lost.

2. Moreover, they again agree, the sheep was brought home, the groat was found, and the son returned again to his father.

Some will tell you the reason of these three parables is,

1. That a sinner is compared to a sheep, because of that innocent and harmless nature in which man was first created.

2. That sinners are compared to a groat, because God's image was stamped on man in his first creation, and by sin that image was defaced.

3. Sinners are compared to a son, because of that near relation man stood in to God by creation; Adam is called the son of God. Luke in his genealogy saith, speaking of Enos, "which was the son of Seth, which was the son of Adam, which was the son of God," Luke iii. 38. And indeed all men by creation are the children of God, but by sin and transgression, rebels and children of the devil.

Secondly, some of the ancients also (as one denotes) as Augustin, Gregory, &c., say, that in those three parables we may spy a threefold cause of man's fall and apostacy from God.

1. In the sheep's wandering, Satan's suggestions to our first parents.

2. In the lost groat, Eve's yielding to Satan's temptations.

3. In the son's wilful departing from his Father, Adam's voluntary revolting and wasting all his substance; but I think these are too far fetched, nor may they be at all intended by them. I shall therefore proceed. And,

1. Speak a little to the main scope and drift of our Saviour, in speaking of this parable.

2. Open all the parts thereof.

3. Raise divers propositions from several of the principle parts, or things contained therein.

First. To the chief scope, it is the same with both the precedent parables, *The scope of the parable opened.* viz., it was to rebuke the pride and arrogance of the Pharisees, who over-valued their own pretended legal righteousness, and reflected upon our Lord for keeping company with, and showing so much love and favour to publicans and sinners, they concluding they never had transgressed God's commandment, but had faithfully served him.

2. It sets forth man's woeful, actual, and wilful departure from God.

3. His miserable condition, by original and actual transgression.

4. To set forth, and to magnify the great grace, love, and unspeakable compassion of God the Father to the greatest sinner, who by Jesus Christ returneth by an unfeigned faith unto him.

5. To show the envy of the Jews and Pharisees, at God's extended grace and favour to the poor Gentiles, and to such who have been great sinners.

So much as the scope thereof.

But before I proceed to open the parts, let me note one thing by the way, from our Lord's bringing in a third parable to the same end and purpose, i.e., to show the sad and woeful condition of undone sinners.

Doct. That to bring sinners to a sight and full sense of their sins, and of their wretched condition, is no easy thing, so as truly to believe in our Lord Jesus Christ.

1. A little to prove this; and 2. To show the cause and reason thereof.

Men are not easily brought to see their lost state and condition. 1. This appears by Adam's hiding of sin, and making such frivolous excuses about what he had done, when God laid his sin before him. "The woman which thou gavest me, she gave me, and I did eat:" and also by Eve's plea and excuses, "The serpent beguiled me, and I did eat."

2. In that besides the light of conscience, or law written in the heart of all men, which convinceth of sin (I mean, of sin against God as a Creator) he saw need to give his people Israel a written law, that so they might the more effectually be convinced of sin, and of their woeful state thereby.

3. And more especially, in that Jesus Christ doth employ so great and mighty an Agent to this very end, viz., the Holy Ghost, which he said the Father would send in his name. "And when he is come, he shall convince the world of sin," &c., John xvi. 8, intimating that none else could do it effectually. Alas! what can conscience do? What can ministers do? Nay, what can the law do in this matter, unless it is by the Holy Spirit brought home and set upon the conscience? Paul never was throughly convinced "till the commandment came," Rom. vii. 9; that is, till the law was opened, and the spirituality of it discovered to him by the Holy Ghost.

4. David, though a converted man (when fallen under great sin) was hard to be brought to the sight and sense thereof; no, he like others, was ready enough to pass a sentence against another man: "His anger was greatly kindled against the man, who had taken the poor man's lamb," 2 Sam. xii. 3, 7, but was not convinced that he had done the wicked thing, until the prophet Nathan told him positively, "thou art the man."

5. Nay, Peter repented not, nor saw his abominable evil, in denying his blessed Lord, until our Saviour looked upon him. O what a powerful look was that! No sinner indeed is thoroughly convinced, until the Lord Jesus does cast a convincing look upon him: as

much as to say, Peter, what hast thou done? Ah this is worse than to have mine enemies to crucify me.

Quest. How comes it to pass, sinners are so hard to be convinced of sin, and to believe in Christ for righteousness?

1. Reason. It may be because sin is such a bewitching thing, it is of a bewitching nature, and has got deep rooting in the sinner's heart and affections; man is naturally wedded to his lusts, to self-love, and to self-righteousness. *Reasons why sinners are so hard to be convinced.*

2. Reason. It is through their great ignorance, and deep alienation from God; " Having the understanding darkened, being alienated from the life of God, through the ignorance that is in them, because of the blindness of their hearts," Eph. iv. 18.

3. Reason. Because they understand not the nature of God, the justice and holiness of God, nor the nature of the law of God, neither what a righteousness it is which they must have, or be found in to their justification before him, or in his sight. The Jews being blind in respect of those things, how hard was it for them to believe their state was bad, and they guilty sinners, and that their righteousness was good for nothing.

4. Reason. Because mankind are born under a covenant of works, and so think they must be justified, and saved by doing, and not in a way of believing, nay, and that doing a little at last will serve, though they do but cry, " Lord, have mercy upon them, miserable sinners," is sufficient, especially if they can but shed a few tears, or a little reform their lives. What said one lately? she doubted not of her salvation, for she had (she said) done nothing to deserve God's wrath; though the least sin or evil thought is a breach of the law, by which all are liable to eternal vengeance.

5. Reason. It is because the devil hath such hold of poor sinners, and power in and over them, who is so grand an enemy to the salvation of man; all men naturally are in his chains and fetters, and he also is so subtle a deceiver that he beguiles them.

6. Reason. It is also from the deceitfulness of sin, and of the heart of man. But no more as to this.

1. See the folly of such who think they need no other means or power to convince them of sin and righteousness; no, nor to cleanse them from sin, and eternally to save them, and the light within them, and in all men.

2. It may also convince such of their woeful blindness, that think they can return to God when they list, even at the last, and that man's will under the bare preaching of the word can do wonders.

3. It may also tend to stir up all to cry to God, that he would send his Spirit to awaken their sleepy and misled consciences, and throughly convince them of their natural condition.

4. And also to attend on the means of grace, whilst the Holy Spirit strives with them.

5. Moreover this justifies ministers in declaring the same things again and again, the same truths though from different texts.

Secondly, to proceed to the parts of this parable, which I shall divide into two general parts.

1. The state of the prodigal before grace, or his returning to his father.

2. His state upon, and after his returning.

" A certain man had two sons." This certain man represents the great God, the Father of our Lord Jesus Christ; neither let any wonder that God, who is an infinite and immense Spirit, should be compared to a man; for our Lord in another parable directly calls him a man, " My Father is an Husbandman," John vi. 1.

" And the younger said unto his father," &c.

By these two sons there is a great difference among expositors, though all agree about the Father.

(1.) By the elder son, some think our Lord means the holy angels, and by the younger mankind; the good angels (they say) abode always at home with God, but man having all his stock put into his own hand, spent it, and run out all by sin: this is a truth. But the angels cannot be meant here by the elder son; because they are not angry nor grieved at the returning and hearty welcome of any lost sinner that comes to Christ; but contrariwise, it appears by the sequel of both the preceding parables, they do greatly rejoice at the sight thereof; but it is said the elder son was angry to see what entertainment the father gave to his younger brother.

(2.) Besides, they that think the holy angels are meant by the elder son, do also say, they are intended by the ninety and nine sheep that never went astray, or by the nine pieces of silver that were not lost: but this we have refuted, though if the first be granted the last cannot well be denied.

(3.) No doubt all these three parables refer to one species of creatures, and in all of them mainly our Lord designed to rebuke the pride of the Pharisees, for thinking they never went astray, or broke God's commandment, or did ever displease him, so as to need repentance.

2. Some conclude, by the two sons are meant the Jews and the Gentiles; the Jews by the elder, and the Gentiles by the younger.

3. Some affirm, by the elder son the Pharisees are only meant, and by the younger Publicans and great sinners amongst the Jews.

My brethren, I humbly conceive,

Who the elder son is. (1.) By the elder son, more generally the Jews are meant, and more particularly the Pharisees and all self-righteous persons that were amongst them.

(2.) By the younger son I understand the Gentiles, and more particularly great sinners.

1. The Jews kept at home, and were the peculiar people of God under the law, or people in covenant with God; also God was called their Father, by way of that national and legal adoption, God chose and took them for his people.

2. He called them his first-born, which must refer to that legal adoption. "Israel is my first-born." The Gentiles are called the younger son, because not called or brought to partake of the privileges of sons until Christ came, or after the Jews had rejected Christ and the gospel: for if their being called sons doth refer only to what they were by creation, one was not older nor younger than the other.

See Mr. Neh. Rogers. 3. Nor can I see why Publicans and sinners should be called the younger son, if sons only refer to the Pharisees and the Publicans; though one would have the word younger to signify fools; but all younger sons are not fools.

Object. "The elder son told his father, He had never transgressed at any time his commandment;" how can this be said either of the Jews in general, or of the pharisees in particular?

Answ. I answer, it is spoken in respect of what some of the Jews, and particularly the Pharisees, thought of themselves, they concluded they never went astray and were never lost; and so thought they never had broken, or transgressed the law of God. Is not this much with what the young man said, " all these things have I done from my youth, what want I yet?" Matt. xix. 20. And doth not Paul say, that when he was a Pharisee, " as touching the righteousness which is in the law, he was blameless?" Luke. xviii. 21. Phil. iii. 6. This was the opinion they had of themselves, and he that thinks he is blameless, thinks he never transgressed God's commandment: and our Lord might so far yield to them, partly that they might in judgment be further blinded, or perhaps that he might not provoke them at this time.

Object. But doth not the father say to his elder son, " thou art eve rwith me, and all I have is thine;" how can this be said either of the Jews in general, or of the Pharisees in particular?

Answ. 1. I answer, the Jews I told you were all along in covenant with God under the dispensation of the law of Moses, and were accounted a people near to God, while others were said to be afar off.

2. God gave all he had to give (or thought good to give as an act of sovereignty) to the Jews, the elder son; " He gave his statutes and his judgments to Israel, he hath not dealt so with any nation," Psal. cxlvii. They were God's visible church; his worship, his tabernacle, and temple was theirs: " To them was committed the oracles of God," Rom. iii. 2. Nay, see what Paul further says, " Who are Israelites, to whom pertaineth the adoption, and the glory, and the covenants, and the giving of the law, and the service of God, and the promises," Rom. ix. 4. Now pray, what had God more to give under that covenant, or under the dispensation of the law ? the words must be taken with restriction ; for the elder son saith, his Father never gave him a kid, there is somewhat more given to the returning prodigal than ever the elder son received.

" And the younger of them said to his Father, give me the portion of goods that falleth to me ; and he divided to them his living :" that is, let me have that which thou art pleased to give me, and which will please me to receive. Give me ; a saucy and irreverent manner of speaking to a Father; give me, not pray father, if you please give me, or I humbly intreat you Father ; no, but Father give me.

Sinners show they have no reverence to God. Doct. 2. From hence note, carnal men, or the men of this world, carry it towards God unreverently, they have not that holy awe of God upon their hearts which they ought.

" Give me that portion that falleth to me ;" God disposeth unto the sons of men what things they have, as he pleaseth, and according unto his own sovereignty ; and though no man deserveth anything, yet wicked men think there is a portion for them.

" And he divided unto them his living," ver. 12.

God gave the Jews their portion, and the Gentiles what they have ; he divided unto both what they possess.

The Gentiles desire to have what falls to them in this life, they desire a portion here, a present portion ; wicked men would have all in their own hands, or in their present possession, do not desire God to keep it for them, nor a portion in another world, not a portion for their souls, but a portion in this life ; they desire such things as suit with their own carnal hearts, and God giveth to them accordingly ; he answereth them according to the idols set up in their hearts. Hence the psalmist says, " the wicked men have their portion in this life," Psal. xvii. 14 ; as Abraham told the rich man, that he (when on earth) received his good things ; from hence also our Saviour saith of the rich, they have received their consolation," Luke xvi. 23.

Wicked men, or man in his natural state, love not God, they design to leave him, his family is too strict for them ; they love not religion, nor do they value another world ; they would have their heaven here. *Wicked men love not the worship of God and religion.*

Quest. What a portion is it, which the younger son desired (or which a mere natural man would have) which also God divided to them ?

Answ. 1. Even such things which the Gentiles have, and men naturally do enjoy, and account as their portion, viz., riches, honours, pleasures, any, all kinds of earthly things. *What God gave to the prodigal.*

2. Also God gave them the blessings of natural light, they have the works of the law written in their hearts, Rom. ii. 14, 15.

3. They had the knowledge of natural things, and in such things they exceeded all other people of the world. The Greeks sought after wisdom ; that is, natural wisdom, they covet learning, or the knowledge of all human arts and sciences ; and these things God gave them as their portion. They desire the knowledge of the creature, and the natural knowledge of God, and no more.

" And not many days after, the younger son gathered all together, and took his journey into a far country," ver. 13.

Quickly after he had what he desired, away he went : what things grace-less man hath tend to carry his heart from God, or alienate his soul more and more from God ; like Israel of old, Jesurun waxed fat and kicked, " thou art waxen fat, thou art grown thick, thou art covered with fatness," Deut. xxxii. 15. Well, and what then : " Then he forsook God which made him, and lightly esteemed the rock of his salvation." See the evil nature of the things of the world, and how ensnaring they are to the carnal heart of man : " Their bull gendereth and faileth not, their cow calveth, and casteth not her calf," Job xxi. 10, 11. They spend their days in pleasure. But see the effects of these things, ver. 14. Therefore they say unto God, depart from us, we desire not the knowledge of thy ways. As they go from God further and further, so they desire God not to come near them, to trouble or disquiet their consciences. *Wicked men having what their carnal hearts desire purpose to depart from God.*

" He took his journey into a far country."

Quest. What is meant by this far country ?

Answ. The regions of sin ; they take sinful courses, gather up all together which they have, heap up riches, setting their hearts upon them; and the more a man's affections are set upon the things of this world, the further he goes from God : man was born in a state of distance from God, not as to place, no, that cannot be ; no man in this respect can be at a distance from God, nor go from him, who is an infinite, an immense, and an omnipresent Being ; it is or going from God, for he is every where present, but a moral, his heart or soul departs from him : God and sinners in this sense must needs be at a vast distance from one another ; forasmuch as God and sin, are most contrary, or directly opposite, God's way is holiness, a wicked man's way unholiness ; so that he that cleaves to sin, and goes away from God, yea, and every step a wicked man takes, is a going still further from God.

Hence he that returns to God must have his sins turned from him ; the one is done by the sacrifice of Jesus, and the other as the effect of that sacrifice by the Spirit.

Pray observe, the Prodigal went far from his father ; that is, the sinner that goes on in an evil course, or in sinful practices, is gone far from God.

1. He is far from thinking of God ; God is not in all his thoughts ; that is, he is in none of his thoughts, or not at all in his thoughts ; God and his ways are grievous to a wicked man. *How sinners may be said to be sent from God.*

2. Far from union with God : "Because the carnal mind is enmity against God, and is not subject to the law of God, neither indeed can be," Rom. viii. 7.

3. Therefore he is far from having any sincere love and affections unto God : for where enmity and hatred is in a man's heart to any thing or person, it is impossible there should be love to thatthing or person.

4. He is far from desiring after God. That which we hate we desire not : they say to God, depart from us.

5. And far from having communion with God. "Shall the throne of iniquity have fellowship with thee ?" Psal. xciv. 20.   What fellowship hath light with darkness ?

6. Far from having any likeness to God ; naturally man is more like to the devil ; sinners resemble Satan more than the blessed God.

7. Far from adhering to any advice or counsel to return ; no, they are gone so far, that they are out of the call of ministers, they cannot hear them ; and out of the call of godly parents, they cannot hear them : nay, which is worst of all, a sinner is gone so far from God, that he cannot hear when God calls and cries after him.

8. Far from discharging of any acceptable worship or service, to the glory of God ; God hates all their spiritual duties ; the prayers of the wicked are an abomination unto the Lord.   Thus a sinner is gone far from God.

9. Yea, so far as he knows not the way home to God. "What iniquities have your fathers found in me, that they are gone far from me ?" Jer. ii. 3.—"Ye who sometimes were afar off," Eph. ii. 17.

Doct.   Observe, it is the nature of sinners to fly from God, to go from God, or sin is a departing from God.

Every wicked man goes farther and farther still from God : and be sure the farther he goes from him, the farther it will be to return.

" He went unto a far country."

This denotes his choice and voluntary act ; a wicked man sins freely, he sins with a full resolution and purpose of heart, but so cannot a godly man sin ; "ungodly men love darkness rather than light ;" many are like Ahab, they sell themselves to work wickedness.

" And wasted his substance," &c.

Quest.   What may be meant by wasting his substance.

Answ.   1. He wasted his precious time ; that is part of that treasure which God gives to wicked men ; much of his choicest time he might, like a fool, waste and consume to his great hurt.

2. He perhaps wasted much of his outward treasure or earthly riches : for that was part of the portion which he desired : this he might consume and spend on harlots.

3. He might waste his common gifts, and natural powers, parts, and abilities : sinners sometimes lose their wisdom, and exercise of their human reason, and act like fools or madmen : all ungodly persons have lost their spiritual sense, and act more like brutes than rational creatures, and render themselves odious to mere moral man.

4. He might waste, or sin away his conscience, or lose the natural and useful qualities thereof, which reproves for sin, and ofttimes puts a check upon, and stops the sinner in his way and evil courses.

Doct.   A profane sinner is a great waster. He wickedly spends and wastes what God hath given him.   "They consume it on their lusts," Jam. iv. 3.

" And when he had spent all, there arose a mighty famine in that land," ver. 14.

1. Some think by the famine, here is some public and sore judgment that befel him and the whole country, I mean, the ungodly world ; let it be what it will, (1.) His soul is now distressed, he is brought into straits. (2.) You have the occasion of it, a mighty famine. (3.) His great sense, he began to be in want. I conceive the outward wants and straits the Prodigal was brought into, hold forth the distresses, and in a word, the inward troubles which rise sometimes in the mind and conscience of an ungodly sinner.

What meant
by the fam-
ine. 2. Therefore by the mighty famine, doubtless is meant, strong convictions of sin, and apprehensions of God's wrath, not evangelical convictions, but such that rise from the powers of natural conscience, the law of God, and common grace, which many sinners are under, and which sometimes greatly tend to terrify their minds ; so that now all the food their poor souls fed upon, or hopes which they trusted to, is cut off, and they find a famine in their souls.

Doct.   The delights and pleasures of sin are but short ; God can soon embitter, by the sharp convictions of natural conscience, all the sweet and flesh-pleasing enjoyments of sin, and of this world.

A man may have guilt fretting like a tormenting sore, gnawing, or afflicting or terrifying like death, as in the case of Cain, Pharaoh, and Judas ; and yet these may not bring him to himself, nor can they bring him home to God.

Doct. Sin may bring men into straits, but those straits may not bring them from sin to God.

Natural conscience, and legal convictions may distress a sinner, and put him to pain, and stop him for a time in his evil courses ; nay, it may tend to reform his life, but it cannot make him a true penitent, nor change his heart.

" And he began to be hungry."

This shows that he now began to find a great need of comfort, or of food, something to eat, for fear of perishing.

This denotes that a sinner under convictions, may fear he shall perish ; wrath, and hell seem to take hold of him, hunger causes desires, so a sinner may desire to be saved under his straits in afflictions, convictions, and fear of hell, who hath not one drachm of saving grace.

" And he went and joined himself unto a citizen of that country, and he sent him into his fields to feed swine," ver. 15.

By this citizen expositors do conclude, is meant the devil, whose habitation is among men that are ungodly, and who are gone far from God ; he is the chief citizen, and hath divers sorts of work to employ such in, who adhere to him, and close with his temptations and suggestions ; he hath trades that suit with all men's natural tempers, he doth not send all to feed swine, or their sensual appetites ; he sometimes transforms himself into an angel of light, and appears a white devil, a religious devil, and can teach the doctrine of voluntary humility, and persuade men to go naked or bare foot, &c. *(marginal: Who the citizen is, the Prodigal joined himself to.)*

Quest. How may he be said to join himself to Satan, had not he done that before ?

Answ. What though he had, yet his conscience being now awakened, Satan was afraid of losing him, and therefore bestirs himself no doubt, and by suggestions strove to divert his thoughts, and scatter his fears ; and by joining himself to Satan, may be meant his closing in with those fresh and new temptations and suggestions which were darted into his mind ; every time sinners do embrace or yield to Satan's temptations, they afresh join themselves to him, or renew their covenant with death and hell. Satan's great business is, when convictions of sin and wrath have taken hold of a great sinner, to quench that fire, if possible, by one means or another, to divert his thoughts. Thus he sent Cain to build cities, and Felix to send away Paul, that he might hear him preach no more, and this poor wretch he sent to feed swine, knowing by his former practices, his natural and sensual inclinations.

Quest. What may we understand by Satan's fields, and swine ?

Answ. 1. Satan's fields are the ungodly, the multitudes of the wicked, met together to gratify their carnal hearts, and sensual lusts ; these are Satan's fields, where nothing grows but what comes up naturally ; they are fields untilled, not plowed up, nor sown.

2. By swine I understand may be meant two things.

(1.) That vain, wicked, and profane fellows, and impudent harlots, are Satan's swine, and indeed they may in many respects be compared to swine ; and since the Holy Ghost calls them swine, we may safely conclude, that they are partly here intended. " Cast not your pearls before swine," Matt. vii. 6, saith our Lord. Some wicked men are compared to lions, some to dogs, &c., and others to swine, because they have the evil qualities of those brutish creatures. *(marginal: Wicked men are swine.)*

Doct. From hence I note, that profane and sensual men and women are, and may be compared to swine.

1. Swine are an unclean sort of creatures, they love to wallow in mud, filth, and miry places. So this sort of ungodly mortals love their brutish lusts, and to wallow in the mud and mire of filth, and all abominable pollution, sin, and uncleanness. And as it seems pleasant to swine to wallow in the mire ; so it is natural and pleasant to these sinners to wallow in all beastly sins, lusts, and filthiness. *(marginal: Why some wicked men and women are compared to swine.)*

2. Swine are craving, and very greedy creatures : they have, as one observes, no measure in eating and drinking, they will eat until they burst ; so these wicked and ungodly persons are so greedy and unsatisfied, they set no bounds nor measure to their lusts, though they consume all they have : some are mere epicures, gluttonous persons, and others, like swine, will drink until they can neither stand nor go, and wallow in their filthy vomit.

3. Swine, if washed, will soon return to their wallowing in the mire again ; so if any ungodly person is outwardly reformed, or washed from the gross acts of wickedness, their natures being not changed, commonly at one time or other they return again to their former evil and filthy courses ; so that in them (as the apostle noteth) the old Proverb is made good, " The sow that was washed is returned to her wallowing in the mire again," 2 Pet. ii. 22.

4. Swine feed on husks and grains, and tread pearls under their feet ; so these brutish creatures feed on the trash, the husks, and grain of this world, and contemn, nay, tread under their feet the pearls of grace, or all heavenly and spiritual things.

5. Swine feed also on acorns, but never look up to the tree or oak from whence they fall ; so these brutish animals, i. e., ungodly sinners, feed upon those things that God gives them, but never in a due manner look up to God with thankful hearts, from whence they come. Though there is one disparity between natural and metaphorical swine, swine never retain their nature, and it is impossible for them to cease being swine; but metaphorical swine may have their brutish natures changed ; it is imposible for them by the power of divine grace, to become sheep and lambs of Jesus Christ. This shows the fearful and lamentable effect of original and actual sins, and what a brutish and base nature sinful man hath in him, and what a vile contemptible creature he is in God's sight ; also the vast difference there is between a converted person, and a brutish sinner ; the one God esteems as his jewels, or his choicest treasure, and the other to be in his sight, but as mere swine, filthy and abominable.

2ndly. By swine some think also may be meant the Prodigal's own brutish or sensual parts, or sensual appetite.

Quest. What may be meant by feeding these swine ?

Answ. In respect had to the first sense, Satan sending him to keep company with profane and graceless company, and to converse with them.

1. He may be said to feed them by his gratifying their desires, in going amongst them, either to taverns, alehouses, playhouses, whorehouses, &c. This is to feed Satan's swine; such that yield to them, consent to their entice- ments, may be said thereby to feed them. *What is meant by feeding of swine.*

2. They feed them by drinking, sporting, and carousing with them.

3. May be he fed them by diverting them with profane and idle tales, or filthy talk and stories ; for such things those wretches feed upon, and it is as meat and drink unto them. For as the gracious discourse or converse of a godly man, feeds heavenly born persons, so filthy and profane talking feeds the wicked.

4. Perhaps he fed them by spending his money on them, or in their company.

5. And be sure he fed them in gratifying their base and brutish lusts, as such do who keep company with harlots, &c.

Thirdly. As swine may refer to his own sensual appetite, it may mean, that Satan pre- vailed with him to let loose the reins of his lusts, and to deny himself of nothing his sen- sitive part did, or could desire, the devil thinking that way to allay the storm that was rising in his conscience, he perceiving he might be in some danger of losing him by means of that famine, or sore convictions that he felt within, or dread of his future s ate ; for no doubt but it doth denote his fear of perishing for ever. Nay, and from what I say upon this account evident it is, that many a wretched prodigal hath under convictions and sore gripes of conscience, thus joined with, or closed in with Satan's suggestions, to go and feed swine, in both those respects, by which means also for a time, those convictions have gone off.

But no more at this time.

II

A certain man had two sons, &c.,—Luke xv. 11, 12.

I AM, my brethren, upon the opening of several parts of this parable, and have passed through and opened the 11, 12, 13, 14, 15, verses ; I shall now proceed.

Ver. 16. " And he would fain have filled his belly with the husks which the swine did eat, and uo man gave unto him."

You have heard that Satan sent him to feed swine. O what contempt doth our Saviour cast upon ungodly sinners! in that he doth not only compare them to brutish creatures, but to some of the worst of that sort, even to swine, creatures the most nasty and filthy: and then, secondly, What contempt doth he cast upon the service of sin and Satan; it is the feeding of swine, a low and base employment; and as for his wages he is allowed nothing but husks, though almost starved; if for his services he hath anything to eat, it is but husks, such that the devil's swine feed upon.

Christ casts contempt on wicked men, in calling them swine.

Doct. The service of sin and Satan is a base service.

What folly is in wicked men? how blind and deceived are they? they are of a low and base spirit, ungodly, and profane persons; though called nobles, are but such the devil sets to feed swine; nay profane and brutish princes of the earth, are but hoggards; while they serve their lusts, they do but keep at the hog's trough, and feed swine.

1. This may tend to eclipse their glory, and lower their topsails; what signify all their sensual pleasures, and all their bragging and boasting of their grandeur and glory? see what base servitude they love, and are contented with.

2. Who would be in love with the service of the devil? who but fools would serve such a master? What! debase their noble soul so far as make it feed swine; a soul that was created in the image of God, and capable to feed upon heavenly manna, nay, upon Christ, and upon God himself! and shall it be sent by the devil to feed swine, and live upon husks, which swine do eat!

Quest. What is meant by husks?

Answ. You may be sure by these husks, is meant the best that Satan hath to feed his servants. By husks, all generally understand the vanities of this world, as riches, honours, and pleasures, or "the lusts of the flesh, the lust of the eyes, and the pride of life;" whatsoever is of this world, and not of the Father are husks.

Solomon calls them vanity, "all things are vanity;" our Lord calls them husks, hog's meat.

2. Some indeed think by husks, also is meant the doctrine of the Scribes and Pharisees, which was frothy, without substance, and like grains or husks, and then according to them, the prodigal, when the famine was sore upon him, became religious; that is, he left his former loose life, and got among blind Pharisees to get bread of his own, an external and an internal righteousness to feed upon; but all this was but husks, and such food that Satan's slaves feed upon. But I rather adhere to the former sense, because it is said he was sent to feed swine, which must certainly refer to brutish creatures, and brutish lusts.

The doctrine of the Pharisees but husks.

The husks were such things which the swine did eat, not serpents' meat, nor wolves', nor foxes'; Satan hath meat for them, they are all of his herd, and fed by him. But those things that ungodly, sensual, and profane persons feed upon, love and esteem, he fain would have filled his belly with; and it is easy to know what those things are.

"Filled his belly;" that is, eat to satisfaction: but alas, neither riches, honours, or sensual pleasures, can give real peace and satisfaction to a man ready to perish, nor satisfy the precious craving soul in the time of famine.

What is meant by not filling his belly.

1. Because God alone is the only good and proper object of the soul; he is the soul's centre, like as a stone flung out of a sling, rests not until it comes to its proper centre, nor the needle till it comes to its centre, the loadstone; or as Noah's dove found no rest until she returned to the ark: so the soul of man can find no rest nor satisfaction in anything, until it returns to God.

Why none but God can satisfy the soul.

2. The things of this world are only suited to the external part of man, viz., his body, but are no more proper food for the soul than wind, husks, ashes, or gravel stones, can satisfy a hungry stomach.

3. The soul is an immaterial being, and therefore material and external things can never fill or satisfy its desires. Angels may as soon be pleased and satisfied with an earthly palace, external music, and honours from men, as the soul of man can be satisfied with these things.

4. The soul is immortal and eternal; that is, it was created; it was not from eternity, but it can never cease to be, nor shall it be annihilated: therefore mortal and transitory things, delights, and pleasures can never fill its desires, or satisfy it. The more a man hath of any earthly things, the more he desires, whether it be riches, honours, or pleasures.

5. These things are unnatural food to the soul, as flesh is unfit, or unnatural food for sheep, but give it to a dog, and it suits his nature; but sheep, and many other creatures,

will starve and die before they will feed upon it.   Therefore was that man a fool, that
" bid his soul eat, drink, and be merry," because he had gotten abundance of earthly
riches, corn, wine, and oil.

In vain therefore did the poor prodigal labour to fill his belly with these husks : and
woe unto them who never meet with God, never return to God, they must be eternally
miserable if there was no hell to torment them ; for the punishment of the loss of God,
would render them eternally wretched, when all such things are taken from them, which
tend to please the sensual appetites.

What is meant by no man's giving to him.   " And no man gave unto him ;" that is, no man can give that to a hungry
soul, which can fill it, or give rest, peace, and satisfaction unto it.   If the soul
sees its wants, if the conscience be wounded, should a king give that man his
crown and kingdom, yet it would and must be said, no man gave unto him.
Spira's soul felt a famine and if any man should have offered all the gold and silver in the
world, or all earthly pleasures, yet he would have said, no man giveth to me : no doubt
the prodigal had, as to the quantity of husks, no lack : but such was the quality of them,
they could not fill his belly.   Men may have as much silver and gold as Solomon had, and
as many fair houses, vineyards, orchards, pools of water, men-servants, and women-ser-
vants, and men-singers, and women singers, and as many wives and concubines, and conquer as many kingdoms as Alexander the Great, and yet have no satisfaction, cannot fill
his belly, but may cry " all is vanity."   No man giveth to me.

Secondly, As to the other sense, *i. e.*, that by husks is meant the doctrine of the Pharisees, or any religion, any righteousness external or internal, any notions, principles, or
practices, short of Christ the " Bread of life," or the Food of his Father's house, none of
them could fill his belly, or give him peace and satisfaction, when a famine rose in his
soul ; all are but husks or chaff ; all false doctrine, errors, heresies, and human traditions,
devised rites and superstition, may fitly be compared to husks or chaff : " and what is the
chaff to the wheat, saith the Lord."   If therefore the prodigal joined in with Satan's delusions, and became religious in any false way of worship whatsoever, he found no more
satisfaction in any of those ways, than he did in the enjoyment of the sensual things of
this world.

" No man gave unto him."   No man but the Man Christ Jesus can give a hungry soul
to fill his belly ; all false professors. all heretics and self-righteous persons, who boast of
their great enjoyments, joy, and satisfaction, are but like one that being hungry, " dreameth he eateth, but lo, when he waketh, his soul is hungry ! or as a thirsty man, that
dreameth he drinketh abundantly ; but lo he waketh, and his soul is thirsty," Isa. **xxix.**
8.   All who are not united to Christ, planted into Jesus Christ by the Spirit, but are under
the law and covenant of works.   All are under the curse, and are guilty before God and
stand charged with original sin, and with all the guilt of their own actual sins : how then
can they have peace or satisfaction, when God discovers this unto them, by raising a famine in their souls ?

Thus I have done with the state of the prodigal in his lost and undone condition, before he returned to his father.

" And when he came to himself, he said, how many hired servants in my father's house
have bread enough and to spare, and I perish for hunger ?" ver. 17.

" And when he came to himself :" those powerful convictions of the Holy Spirit, which the
prodigal was now under, are termed a coming to himself, intimating as if he had been
beside himself before, or deprived of all his senses, and so indeed are sinners.

Doct.   All ungodly sinners in the world, in a spiritual sense, are deprived of their
Wicked men are beside themselves.   senses, or are without understanding.
Sinners are bedlam lunatics, or void of true sense and reason, as I shall,
God assisting, briefly demonstrate in a short parallel.

1.   The reason of such who are mad, is impaired, they are deprived of their understanding : so all unconverted men are deprived of true spiritual understanding, or void of
spiritual reason, " their understanding being darkened," Eph. iv. 18.

2.   A mad man is furious and rageth, so many wicked are furious and filled with rage
against the godly, as Saul saith, he was mad against the saints ; " being exceeding mad
against them, I persecuted them even unto strange cities," Acts. xxvi, 11.   So all envious,
malicious, and unchaste persons are mad and outrageous on their filthy lusts.

3.   A mad man acteth like an idiot, or natural fool delighting in mischief, they hurt
and wound themselves, and therefore are not trusted with a weapon : so an ungodly sinner is mischievous, he seeks to destroy his soul, and draw others into sin, to ruin them

also ; nay he seeks sometimes to ruin a whole kingdom for want of understanding, by sucking in and spreading of damnable heresies.

4.   Such that are beside themselves, are usually bound, lest they attempt to do further hurt and mischief ; so God binds or puts into chains, or restrains ungodly men, limits their power, lest they should make an utter spoil, or totally destroy his people, and their innocent neighbours.

5.   A mad man will spit in the face of his dearest friend ; so wicked men as it were spit in the very face of God, as the Jews spat in the face of Jesus Christ, and also spit in the face of his ministers, who seek their good.

6.   Such that are beside themselves, tear their very clothes, and refuse any garment to cover their nakedness ; so wicked men delight to go naked and utterly refuse the robe of Christ's righteousness to clothe their poor souls.

7.   A mad man knows not a friend from an enemy, but uses a friend as an enemy : so wicked men take the godly to be their enemies, and use them as such.   " Hast thou found me O mine enemy ?" said Ahab to Elijah, 1 King. xxi. 20.

8.   A mad man hath not wisdom to direct his way, nor is he capable to receive good counsel : so wicked men for want of wisdom to choose their way, run into a lion's den, and are not able, being deprived of true understanding, to receive instruction, but despise it.

9.   Mad men will eat nauseous things, hurtful things, nay poisons, if you give it to them ; so do wicked men, they, like the Prodigal feed on husks, on gravel, and ashes, nay eat poison ; sin is the ratsbane of the soul, which they are greedy of, they drink in iniquity, as the fish drink water.

10.   A mad man cannot judge of the nature of things, of time and occasions ; he will be angry if the sun shine upon him, or if the wind blows : so a wicked man knows not his time, nor the nature and worth of spiritual things, neither the worth of the soul, nor of Christ, but is angry with the ways of God, and cannot abide the heat of his own accusing conscience, he would be saved, but he walks in the way to hell, and is offended at those troubles that befal him, and at those that reprove him.

11.   It is a great cure to recover one that is raving mad, or to bring him to himself ; so it is the work of Almighty God to bring a sinner to himself, or to his right mind, as this poor Prodigal was brought at last.

USE

1.   Wonder not if you are abused, and have violence done you by wicked men ; alas they are mad, or beside themselves !

2.   Pray that God would bind the wicked with cords and fetters, nay, and we have cause to bless God that he doth do it ; for else there would be no living for the godly in the world, it abounding so much with mad men.

3.   Let us also learn from hence to pity wicked men ; mad people are objects of great pity.

4.   Bless the Lord that hath brought you, who were besides yourself, to a right mind ; many never come to themselves, but die distracted, never are sensible of their state until they come to hell.   "And when he came to himself," &c.

Quest.   Do you state the beginning of his conversion here ?

Answ.   There is a twofold work of the Spirit upon a lost sinner ; the first is conviction, " He shall convince the world of sin," &c. John xvi. 8.   The second is, regeneration ; now it was the first of these operations the Prodigal was under when it is said, he came to himself.

1.   From hence note, no legal convictions, or what work soever passeth upon the sinner before the Holy Spirit reproves or convinces him of sin, and of his undone condition, doth, or can bring him to himself ; that is, unto a thorough sight and sense of sin, and of his folly and madness.

2.   Also note, that the effectual and special convictions of the Spirit do bring a sinner to himself, or to his right mind.

" And he said, how many hired servants in my father's house have bread enough ?" &c.

By hired servants I understand are principally meant such who, like the Scribes and Pharisees, work for life, or who are mercenary, who work only for the sake of the reward, and not from a principle of faith in, and love to God in Jesus Christ : no doubt he called to mind what a portion his elder brother had.

Quest.   But had the Jews and Pharisees bread enough and to spare, and were they in his father's house ?

Answ.   1.   Yea, the Jews had bread enough and to spare, they had the moral and

ceremonial law, the worship of God, the covenants, the types, the prophesies, and the promises ; they had not only the moral law as a rule of life, but also as a school-master to
lead them to Christ ; and in the ceremoinal law, and in the types and prophesies they might
(provided their eyes were opened) have seen the Lord Jesus Christ, or have found the
bread of life, and have been sweetly fed and feasted therewith Had not all
God's children, all believers under the law, store of bread, or true spiritual
food ? yea, plenty of good things ; the Jews and Pharisees had in God's house
(I mean in the church of Israel) great plenty ; but they had neither eyes to see it, nor
faith to feed upon it, but became mere mercenary wretches, thinking that they could be
justified by their own righteousness, and understood not the end and design of God in his
giving the law ; "they being ignorant of his righteousness, went about to establish their
own righteousness," &c. Rom. x. 3. I might add also,

Great provision in the church of the Jews.

2.   That the convictions of the Spirit are gradual : a poor sinner may not at first
see so clearly the difference there is between the law and the gospel, as afterwards.

" And I perish with hunger."

Now he saw he was distressed indeed, his convictions were never right, thorough and
effectual until this time : now he saw he was undone, and must perish and be damned for
ever, unless he goes home to his father by Jesus Christ, and feeds upon that which is
bread indeed. His natural conscience was awakened before, being under his sore afflictions
and dismal straits ; but those convictions for a time went off, or were near stifled, by his
joining himself to that cursed citizen, or by closing in with Satan's temptations, either in
striving to fill his belly in a way of sensual pleasures, or by cleaving to some false way
to seek food and satisfaction for his distressed soul.

The Holy Spirit only convinceth of sin and misery.

The effectual convictions of the Holy Spirit bring a sinner under the
spirit of bondage : the prodigal is filled with fear of perishing : thoughts of
hell, death, and eternal wrath, seem to terrify him ; he might not yet be
convinced of righteousness, nor of judgment. Some say, this sense of his perishing state
was the effects or fruit of sharp afflictions. I will not deny but God may make use of
afflictions to bring a sinner to himself ; but no afflictions whatsoever, no more than the bare
hearing of the word preached, without the powerful convictions and illuminations of the
Holy Ghost, can have any such effect upon his heart and conscience.

" I will arise and go to my father."

Something is here implied that is not expressed, viz.,   That he had not only convictions
of sin upon him, but also the knowledge of that blessed way to the Father which is the
Lord Jesus Christ. "I am the way," &c. "No man cometh to the Father but by me."

The Holy Spirit convinceth of the way to the Father.

John xiv. 6.   The Spirit doth not only shew our disease, but also our cure ;
not only our sickness, but the physician ; not only our sin, but a Saviour.

We have here two things to be considered in respect to the poor prodigal.
(1.) His conscience effectually awakend and his judgment informed.   (2.)
His resolution, " I will arise." He was till now without any hope, he was down in the
valley of despair, or had not sought Christ, but on the bed of sloth : but now he says with the
spouse, " I will arise ;" if I abide here in these regions of sin and Satan, I perish for ever,
he now, with David, thought on his ways, and resolves to turn his feet homeward, or towards his father's house.

" And will say unto him, Father I have sinned against heaven and before thee," ver. 18.

Consideration is the fruit and the effect of special convictions, and that begets a firm resolution ; until a sinner finds it thus with him, there is no hope of true and thorough conversion : but where convictions are strong, or when the Spirit hath begun effectually to
work upon the soul, that man comes to a full purpose of heart, he resolves and determines
in spite of devils, earth, and hell ; he will return to God. Moreover, consideration doth
not only put a sinner upon resolving to return, but also upon the uttermost endeavour in
the use of all means God directs in order to his returning, " I will arise and go to my Father," not only rise, but endeavour to go, which doubtless doth denote some knowledge he
had of Christ. " Go to my Father," may be he yet scarcely could say, God was his Father in the Spirit of adoption ; but if he had not some knowledge of God as a Father, in
and by Jesus Christ, he could not have had any encouragement to think of going unto
him ; for out of Christ God " is a consuming fire," Heb. xii. 29.

Mr. Rogers. p. 159.

1. He doth not say he will go to his brother (as one notes) or to his Father's servants, or to his harlots, or to his old companions, no, but to his Father.

There is no help, no succour, no relief for a poor sinner, but in God ; and such that would find it must go to him, in and by Jesus Christ, and this a convinced sinner sees. Though a man, my brethren, hath been a notorious sinner, and consumed all that God gave him on harlots, yet God puts it upon his heart (by his Spirit, when he begins to work upon him) to call him Father. The apprehension that God is a Father, a gracious Father, works most sweetly on a returning sinner, though the habits of grace are all at once infused in the soul, yet the work in order of nature is a gradual work. *(margin: Encouragement for great sinners.)*

1. He came to himself. 2. He considers his perishing condition. 3. He is enlightened so far as to know, that in God are all things he wanted. 4. He resolves to leave his sins, and all his former courses, and his wicked companions, and to go home to his Father.

" And say unto him, Father."

He resolves upon prayer, takes up a full purpose of heart to cry unto his Father for pardon, and humble himself at his feet, and confess all his faults and abominable iniquities. Thus it is with a sinner when God begins to work upon him by convictions ; he considers that God in Christ is a Father, a reconciled God, a merciful God ; and having a deep sense of his sins, and sight of pardon in Christ, he resolves to pour forth his soul unto him. " I will say," &c. There is a purpose, a resolution wrought in the soul before it sets about the work ; a soul's returning to God is a considerate and a deliberate act of the will, nay, of the whole soul, it is no rash, unadvised, or inconsiderate undertaking. " I have sinned against heaven."

Sinners ought to confess their sins, to God, nay, and in that they have sinned against heaven, that is, against the God of heaven, heaven being here put for the God of heaven. *(margin: Sinners ought to confess their sins to God.)*

" And before thee." This must needs refer to God, before thee, or, as in ver. 21. " In thy sight." The Prodigal did not commit all his sins in the presence or sight of his earthly Father. But every sinner commits all his sins before, or in the sight and presence of the great God. *(margin: All things opened in God's sight.)*

Doct. God's eye is upon every man, he sees and beholds their hearts, as well as their actions.

" Against thee, thee only have I done this thing, and in thy sight," Psal. li. 4.

All things are naked and open unto the eyes of him with whom we have to do," Heb. iv. 12.

" Thou knowest my down-sitting, and up-rising ; thou understandest my thoughts afar off. Psal. cxxxix. 2.

Again the Psalmist saith, " Thou hast set our iniquities before thee, our secret sins in the light of thy countenanance," Psal xc. 8.

1. God is omnipresent, he is every where. " Do not I fill heaven and earth ?" Jer. xxiii. 24. No man sins but God is present, he beholds him, and looks on whilst he commits all secret acts of wickedness, which is more than if the eyes of all men and women in the world were present, and beheld him.

It is he that made the eye ; " And shall he that made the eye, not see ? and he that made the ear, shall not he hear ?" Ps. xciv. 9.

1. God doth not carelessly cast his eyes upon sinners ; no, but he observeth and marks diligently all their iniquities, and every circumstance, and all the aggravations of their sins ; " He pondereth all thy paths," Prov. v. 21. *(margin: What an observer God is of men's sins.)*

2. Nay, he keeps (as it were) a book of remembrance of all the sins and iniquities of men and women. " He hath written them in a book, and they are before him," Isa. lxv. 6. Though the sinner has forgot them, yet God hath not. " I remember what Amalek did," &c.

3. He hath them so before him, that he will bring them one day forth, and lay them all before the sinner, Eccles. xii. 14.

4. Yea, he will set them all in order before them ; he will, as it were, sort their sins, set their sins of commission by themselves, and their sins of omission by themselves, also all sins against God, and all sins against men. Moreover, their heart evils, all the pollutions and lusts of their heart, and all the sins of their lips, and of their lives, he will set before them ; likewise how they sinned against light and clear convictions, also in times of prosperity, and in times of adversity ; sins against mercy, and under merciful providences, and in times of affliction, or under judgments. " I will set them in order before thine eyes." *(margin: Ps. l. 21.)*

5. He will also recompense them according to their doings, and sentence them to hell for them.

6. God will not only bring their known and open sins into judgment, but also all their secret sins, even the secrets of all hearts shall be laid open. O think of this ye that forget God, and tremble before him! What a black indictment wilt thou have one day drawn up against thee? O fly to Christ that they may all be blotted out.

" Before thee, or in thy sight." This wounded the poor prodigal to his heart, and this is the cause of the greatest grief to all convinced sinners, viz., that they have sinned against God, sinned in God's sight. " How shall I do this great wickedness (saith Joseph) and sin against God?" It is one thing to be troubled for sin, as it is against us, or as it exposeth the sinner to God's wrath, and to hell-torments, and another thing to be grieved for offending of God, violating his law, resisting his authority, abusing his mercy and patience, crossing his will, grieving of his Spirit, despising his love, contemning his goodness, slighting all his favours, and promises of grace here, and glory hereafter.

The nature of true convictions. " I have sinned." When the Spirit thoroughly convinces a sinner, he will then confess his sin to God. Thus David cries out, " I have sinned," 2 Sam. xii. 13, when he was convinced by Nathan's parable. Thus the woman of Samaria cries out, " Come see a man that told me all things ever I did," John iv. 29. She confesses all her evil. " I said, I will confess my sins unto the Lord," Psal. xxxii. v.

Sometimes indeed it is required, that persons confess their faults one to another, but not as the papists say; for abominable is their auricular confession, none can forgive sins but God; that is, as to his vindictive wrath and justice, or as sin is against the holy God.

III

And am no more worthy to be called thy son, make me as one of thy hired servants.—
Luke xv. 19.

True convictions humble the sinner. I OBSERVE from hence, that the convictions of the Spirit of God tend to humble and abase a sinner, they make him poor in spirit, and lay him at the feet of God; they wound him, and bring him under self-abhorrence.

2. I infer also, that a legal spirit doth at first much attend such convictions, he is for doing something to procure his Father's favour; he did not yet see how he comes to be accepted in Jesus Christ; and thus it was with them St. Peter preached unto, " What must we do?" Acts ii. 37.

The prodigal under the spirit of bondage. 1. It is not the sinner's unworthiness, that he should plead to obtain favour with God, but the worthiness of Jesus Christ, and the free promises of God.

2. It is not our merits, our deserving, no, but the merits of Christ.

3. He should not say, make me as one of thy hired servants, that I may work for life, or do something that I may be accepted in thy sight; but, O Lord, give me faith, and the Spirit of thy Son, a filial, and not a servile spirit; the spirit of adoption, and deliver me from the spirit of bondage. O help me to believe; I am wounded, father, be pleased to apply a proper plaister.

4. It is not our obedience, not what service we can do, but the obedience of Christ. The Lord Jesus was indeed God's hired servant, he has nothing but what he worked for, or obtained by his hard labour. How oft is our Lord called God's servant? and none ever were employed in such difficult service as he was, nor service which brought such honour to God, and good to men. " He took on him the form of a servant," Phil. ii. 7, not of a master. " Though he was a Son, yet he learned obedience by the things he suffered," Heb. v. 8. My brethren, Jesus Christ hath done all that service which procured our justification and acceptance with God.

5. But the prodigal seeing his own unworthiness, shows that he was thoroughly convinced of sin, and of his woeful condition thereby; but in desiring to become as an hired servant, it shows that great darkness was yet in his understanding; though his conscience was thoroughly awakened, yet his mind was not effectually illuminated, and no marvel, seeing he was not yet returned to his father.

" But was yet a great way off." Convictions tend to humble a sinner, though faith may be wanting to comfort him.

6. We can never be so worthy in ourselves, but justice will have something to lay to our charge, until we fly unto Christ; nor ever so unworthy but mercy and the free-grace of God will relieve us, if we plead the atonement and satisfaction Christ hath made. I do not believe he was yet converted, because he did not know whether his father would pardon him or not.

Unworthiness nor worthiness should hinder any from believing in Christ.

" And he arose, and came to his father: but when he was yet a great way off, his father saw him, and had compassion, and ran to meet him, and fell on his neck, and kissed him."

We have here two things to be considered.

First, the actings of the prodigal towards his father, or a sinner's actings towards God. Secondly, God's actings towards a sinner.

First as to the sinner, which is twofold, 1. What he said. 2. What he did: he said, he would arise; and he arose and went, &c.

Secondly, the actings of his Father, or the blessed God.

(1) " His father saw him when he was yet a great way off." (2.) " He had compassion." (3.) " He ran to meet him." (4.) " He fell on his neck and kissed him."

A little briefly to all these by way of explanation.

1. He said he would arise, that denotes his resolution and purpose (as you heard) to look homeward.

2. He rose and went, &c.

1. His rising signifies his using or attending on the means of grace which God hath appointed, in order to faith and union with him; i.e., he now prays in good earnest, he reads, he hears, and meditates, and doth endeavour to his utmost to make a progression Christ-ward, and God-ward; they are the soul's

What the prodigal's rising signifies.

motions, actings, and desires after God in Christ; like as the spouse, " I rose to open to my beloved, I sought him," &c., Cant. v. 5. And as David resolved, " One thing have I desired of the Lord, that will I seek after," &c., Psal. xxvii. 4.

2. It may denote his leaving his former evil practices, and evil company: he now strove to follow on to know the Lord.

Doct. Such who see the want of God's favour, or the want of Christ, will endeavour to set forward to meet with him.

Such will attend upon all ways and means God hath ordained in order to a sinner's meeting with him.

Secondly as to the acting of his father, or God's actings towards a lost sinner.

1. He saw him: he saw him as Christ saw " Nathaniel under the fig-tree." No doubt he was reading or praying when under the fig-tree. God sees all men, he is (as I have showed) everywhere present; but God sees all the motions and workings of our hearts towards him, or all our endeavours after him in prayer, hearing, &c., with special observation and purpose of mercy.

" When he was yet a great way off."

Some sinners may be under great awakening of conscience, and convictions of sin, and may pray, hear the word of God, and look after God, and yet may be a great way from God. And indeed thus it is with every sinner, until he obtains a real union with Jesus Christ: he may have a sense of sin, and of the want of a Saviour, and may sigh, cry, pray, and pour forth many tears before the Lord, and yet God and he be at a great distance. Nothing but God's drawing near to a sinner, by the divine influences of his Spirit, can bring them together: the Holy Spirit is the bond of union; it is not the sinner's approach to God, but God's drawing near to him which doth the work.

" He had compassion." Those, my brethren, that God doth thoroughly convince of sin, and whom he wounds, and that find themselves sick and undone sinners, his bowels move towards, as he wounds them he will heal them. Those that are whole need not a physician, but they that are sick.

" And ran to meet him." A poor distressed, wounded, and sin-sick soul, God doth not only pity, but he makes haste to apply the remedy unto. " I wound and I heal, I kill and I make alive.

God wounds and heals.

Methinks the actings of God towards the prodigal, are much like those actings of his towards the prophet Isaiah, who when he had that glorious vision of God and of his infinite holiness, and saw his own vileness, and that he was undone; one of the Seraphims it is said, flew to relieve him " Then flew one of the Seraphims unto me, having a live coal in his hand, which he had taken with the tongs from the altar; and laid it upon my mouth, and said, lo, this hath touched thy lips, and thine iniquity is taken away," &c., Isa. vi. 6, 7. O see the bowels of God to a convinced and undone sinner, one that sees he perishes without Christ! Ah, saith God to the angel (if I may so speak with reverence) there is my poor servant Isaiah, in a distressed condition; his heart is ready to break, and his spirit fainteth, flee presently, make haste and touch his lips, I will relieve him. So here, the

The bowels of God to convinced sinners.
father ran: if any expressions may move upon a sinner, and melt his heart, they sure are these, and those which God uttered by the prophet Jeremiah; " I have heard Ephraim bemoaning himself thus, thou hast chastised me, and I was chastised as a bullock unaccustomed to the yoke," Jer. xiii. 18. Ver. 10. " Is Ephraim my dear son, is he a pleasant child? for since I spake against him, I do earnestly remember him still: therefore my bowels are troubled for him, l will surely have mercy upon him, saith the Lord." O what a God is this God! what affecting and soul-melting expressions are those? Can your hearts forbear breaking out into tears?

The reason why God is said to run to meet a returning sinner.
" He ran." Should you see a father run to embrace a vile and rebellious son that is returning home, would not every one say, O what a tender and compassionate father is this? The reason why God is said to run to meet and embrace a broken-hearted sinner, I purpose to show you hereafter in the prosecution of one point of doctrine taken from hence.

" To meet him." If God doth not meet a sinner, or move towards a sinner by his Spirit, the sinner can never meet him. A sinner may look towards God, cry to God, but cannot go home until God meets him: it is more than half way, the sinner cannot step one step towards God, until God meets him. Can that which is dead move itself? Sinners are dead, or without a principle of divine life, naturally; and when life is infused, that principle must be stirred up, and the soul must be influenced by the Holy Spirit.

My brethren, in the two former parables we have an account of the wonderful love and compassion of the Son of God. Jesus Christ fetched home the lost sheep on his shoulders, and he found his lost groat; but it is the Father that ran to fetch home his prodigal son, his lost son.

Our Lord Jesus Christ by this shows the great and wonderful love and compassion of God the Father. The Father and the Son have equal love and pity towards perishing sinners: what the Son doth, the Father doth, and the Holy Ghost doth also; nay, it is the Spirit indeed who is the immediate Agent that meets and brings lost sinners home to God: the Father, and the Son act and work in, and by the Holy Ghost.

This was the time of the prodigal's conversion.
Now, and not till now, was the prodigal converted; this was the happy hour the Father's compassionate look pierced his heart, which denotes the infusing of a principle of grace into his soul. When the blessed God, and a convinced sinner meet, or when the sinner sees the pardoning grace of God in Christ, and is helped to put forth an act of faith on Christ, and sees the smiles of God in his promises, the work is done: before he knew not whether his Father would receive him or not, pardon him or not; and where there is no sense or sight of the pardoning grace of God, there can be no act of true faith; though the convictions of the Spirit are a great ground of encouragement to any sinner: for if they are special convictions, they will never go finally off, but end in regeneration.

Let me from hence observe this proposition, viz.,

Doct. That the conversion of a sinner is wholly an act of God's free sovereign grace.

" And he fell upon his neck, and kissed him."

It is by God's looking upon, and meeting with a poor sinner by the influences of his Spirit, and manifestation of his love and favour. " Kissed him."

1. This act denotes God's infinite love and affection to him.

2. That God was reconciled to him in his Son Jesus Christ, and had pardoned all his sins.

3. And not only so, but also a clear manifestation to him of his Fatherly love, and inconceivable favour to him.

It was a custom amongst the Jews, when there was a breach between brother and brother, father and child, or betwixt one friend and another, upon their reconciliation to each

Five sorts of kisses.
other, to kiss one another: we read of several sorts of kisses. 1. A kiss of submission or subjection. " Kiss the Son lest he be angry, and thou perish from the way," Psal. ii. 12, and 1 Sam. x. 1. Thus Samuel kissed Saul, to denote his subjection to him when he was anointed king. It also denotes adoration or worship; they kissed the calves or idols, to show they adored and worshipped them, Hos. xiii. 2.

3. " A kiss of affection;" which is commonly used in these parts of the world, and it

is common for dear relations thus to kiss each other ; and thus Jacob kissed Rachel, and Laban Jacob, &c.

3. A kiss of reconciliation : Joseph's kissing his brethren might not only signify his affections, but that he was reconciled to them, and had passed by all that wrong they had done to him.

4. We read of a holy kiss used amongst the primitive Christians, and was inoffensive in those eastern countries, where friends so frequently used that custom, 1 Cor. xvi. 20, and Rom. xvi. 16.   But I do not think it is expedient amongst us so to do, between men and women, except on some special occasion, as on their departure, or long absence.

We also read of carnal or whorish kisses, likewise of an hypocritical or flattering kiss ; thus Joab kissed Abner ; and a traitorous kiss, thus Judas kissed our Saviour when he betrayed him.
Prov. vii. 13
2 Sam. xv. 5
2 Sam. xx. 9.
Prov. ii. 6.

5. Of a spiritual kiss ; " Let him kiss me with the kisses of his mouth," &c., Cant. i. 2. Let him reveal the doctrine of his free-grace and love to me.

The Father kissing his returning prodigal, or God's kissing a returning and believing sinner, doth signify his special favour and reconciliation to him.

" And the son said unto him, father, I have sinned against heaven and in thy sight, and am no more worthy to be called thy son," ver. 21.

The love of God manifested to a convinced sinner, works notable effects in such a person, the prodigal resolved he would acknowledge his sin, before he knew whether his father would receive him or not, pardon him or not.   But those resolutions sprang from a legal spirit, for then he was to become as an hired servant ; but now not one word of that, no, he had now learned better, having received the Spirit of adoption.

1. The first effect that the sense of God's pardon works upon a believing sinner, is a hearty confession of sin.   " Father, I have sinned."

Doct. True grace upon the manifestation of God's love in forgiveness, produceth a hearty confession of sin.

Yea, the highest expressions of love and mercy do not hinder a believer from making this confession.

2. It works admiration in the soul.   O that God should run to meet me, embrace me, kiss me, pardon such a vile and so abominable a wretch as I have been !

3. An abhorence and detestation of himself, and of sin, thus it was with Job and Isaiah, " I abhor myself and repent," &c., Job. xlii. 5.   " Woe is me for I am undone," &c., Isa. vi. 5.

4. Wonderful contrition, and sorrow of heart ; " Peter wept bitterly."   And it caused " David to water his couch with his tears," Psal. vi. 6.

5. It works deep humiliation in the soul.   " I am no more worthy to be called thy son." Faith hath always this blessed effect, i. e., in sense of pardon ; it tends not to lift up, but to humble a poor believer.   " They shall look upon him whom they have pierced, and shall mourn," &c., Zech. x. 10.   All repentance and humiliation for sin before faith, tends to pride and self-exaltation ; it is legal, and not regarded by the Lord, nor accepted in his sight ; but it is the sense of love and pardon that melts and humbles in the very dust.

Let me speak a little to the first of these effects, viz., that of confession.   What a confession of sin a converted person makes to God.
1. Show what kind of confession it doth produce.
2. Give you the reasons of it, or why they make such a confession.
1. It is a confession or acknowledgment of sin, with great compunction of spirit in the sight and sense of pardon ; it doth not only open our lips but our eyes ; the heart breaks forth when divine grace is poured in, the fear of hell may break the hard heart, but it is divine love and mercy that melts it.   This compunction is according to the greatness of the sin committed.   Why did David confess his sin with so much sorrow, and Peter and Mary Magdalene weep so bitterly, but because their sins had been very grievous and abominable ?

2. It is a confession of sin, as it is against God ; " I have sinned against thee, and in thy sight."   And thus David cries out, " Against thee, thee only have I sinned, and done this evil in thy sight," Psal. li. 4.

3. It is confession of all sins, original and actual, secret and open.   Ver. 5.   " Behold I was shapen in iniquity, and in sin did my mother conceive me."   Paul cries out of " that body of sin and death," Rom. vii. 24.   The woman of Samaria had all her sins set before her, she is ready to confess all her sins to God that ever she did.   " Who can know his errors ?" Psal. xix 12 ; saith David.   Job confesses the sins of his youth : a hypocrite is ready to confess public sins, but not his secret sins, his heart sins ; but a sincere believer confesses all his sins.

4. He confesses his sins with great hatred, abhorrence, and indignation. " What indignation hath it wrought in you ?" 2 Cor. vii. 11. The more God is pleased with him, the more he is displeased with himself for offending him : like a traitor pardoned by his prince, who sought to take away his life but a few days before ; O now he hates himself. So it is here ; " God being pacified towards him, he is ashamed and confounded in his own eyes," Ezek. xvi. 60, 61.

5. It is a confession of sin with all its aggravations ; no lessening or extenuation of sin now, no excuses about it ; not like Adam, " The woman thou gavest me, she gave it me, and I did eat." Legal and servile confessions are commonly deceitful and with extenuations. But see David, " Forgive me my sin, for it is great."

Secondly, Why do forgiven persons, pardoned sinners, confess their iniquities ?

1. God requires this of them, " Only acknowledge thine iniquities that thou hast transgressed against the Lord," Jer. iii. 13.

2. Pity in us is not opposite, but only subordinate to pity in God. Divine love (saith one) doth not destroy but increase duty ; it is a sign of an hardened villain, who being pardoned by his sovereign for the greatest treasons, wipes his mouth as if he had done him no wrong at all ; such men seem to be religious, who boast of forgiveness, but think it below them to confess their transgressions.

3. It flows from the nature of divine love, and sense of God's infinite mercy, considering well the way by which we come to have remission of sin. O saith such a soul, this pardon comes swimming to me through the Red-sea of my Saviour's blood ; though my pardon is freely of grace to me, yet it cost my Lord dear.

4. The nature of pardon itself hath this tendency in it ; the more pardoning grace God shows, the more humility and confession of sins it produceth in our hearts. " Where much is forgiven, there is much love." And which way can it be better manifested, but by the tears of hearty sorrow and confession ? remember Mary Magdalene.

5. Because sin is so hateful and odious to God, shall not we confess those sins by which we have so dishonoured him, since such confessions tend to his glory, being so great and many, yet are all forgiven ?

6. Because herein God hath promised us the sight and sense of pardon. " If we confess our sins, be is faithful and just to forgive us our sins," 1 John i. 9. It may be doubted whether his sins are pardoned, who never confesseth his sins to God ; it appears God cannot let us feel the pardon of our sins to the glory of his justice and faithfulness, if we do not confess our sins. Where is there any promise of the sense of pardon, without grace move us to a confession ? or was any man thus ever forgiven his sins, that never confessed his sins ?

7. Because it tends to the glory of God, that which makes for God's glory, we should always greatly study. " Confess my son, and give glory to the Lord God of Israel," Josh. vii. 19.

(1.) We hereby acknowledge God's omnisciency, that he sees and knows all our former and latter sins and wickedness.

(2.) Hereby also we acknowledge he is a holy God, and hates sin ; we confessing it with utter abhorrence.

(3.) It tends also to the glory of his justice ; we acknowledge that we deserve his wrath and severe displeasure, though he hath received satisfaction for our sins in his Son.

(4.) We give glory to God also, in respect of his infinite love and mercy, by our confessions and acknowledgements of his free-grace, in pardoning all our horrid sins and wickedness committed against him.

8. Because God doth embitter sin to us, he makes sin to appear exceeding sinful in our sight ; he makes us to see the smart of the spear that let out the blood of his Son ; we are wounded with him, and cannot but cry out and confess our sin, though our sore is healed.

Lastly, because not to confess our sins, is to hide them. " He that hides his sin shall not prosper, but he that confesses and forsakes them shall have mercy," Prov. xxviii. 13. Hiding of sin is here set in opposition to a confession of it. " I have hid my sin, as Adam." Sin is covered, saith Mr. Caryl, when it is not confessed.

USE

1. O learn from hence to confess your sins, (1.). This was ever the practice of God's people, and is the character of true believers. (2.) It is a sign you are pardoned, if God's grace, and love works your hearts into due and thorough confession of sin unto him.

2. Let such, who instead of confessing their sins, hide them, fear their state is not good.

3. Ever join faith touching forgiveness with your confession of sin unto God, or in vain is your confession, believe they are all pardoned.

4. Take heed you do not ascribe your pardon to your confessions or humiliation, as that which doth procure it ; no, but only to the blood of Jesus Christ. " Without the shedding of blood there is no remission."

Many, I fear, by their confessions and humiliation for sin, hope to obtain acceptance with God, and pardon of sin ; but this is their great ignorance, for we are only accepted in the beloved. Our acceptation with God, justification, and pardon of sin, is only in Jesus Christ, it is by his obedience and by his blood ; our confession of sin cannot procure it, no nor our leaving of sin, though this we must do ; and all such who see God is pacified towards them, and hath accepted them in his Son, and pardoned all their sins, they will both confess, leave, and loathe all manner of sin and wickedness, as it is an effect of the Spirit and special grace of God received.

But the father said to his servants, " bring forth the best robe, and put it upon him, and put a ring on his hand, and shoes on his feet," ver. 22.

The father said not to him (as many earthly fathers would) son, have you not been a vile wretch, having wasted all I gave unto you upon harlots, and now art come home naked, or in a few filthy rags on your back, and no shoes to your feet ; and being almost starved with hunger, are you returned ? be gone out of my doors ; will I, think you, receive such a vile person as you have been ? no, not a word of any of this, he upbraids him not with his former evil and lewd course of life. God, my brethren, is not like earthly fathers ; no, no, his love and compassion is infinite to returning sinners. " But the father said to his servants," &c.

What is expressed here as done for him, was done for him before, when the Father " met him and kissed him." He was then clothed and adorned. This is done as soon as ever we have union with Christ, and do believe in him ; but all things cannot be expressed at once.

1. Our Lord Jesus would have us know the nature of the love of his Father, as well as his own great acts of rich bounty and mercy to believing sinners.

2. Also that we may know what a rich robe every believing sinner is clothed with, and when also it is put upon the soul. Here is (1.) mention made of a robe. (2.) The nature of this robe, i. e., it is the best robe. " And a ring on his finger," and it is a rich one be sure, a ring of great value, with this motto on it, " My beloved is mine, and I am his." (3.) " And shoes on his feet." That he may walk on thorns and sharp stones, and his feet not be hurt or wounded. " The best robe." He must have change of raiment, more robes than one (as the Lord said unto those that stood by Joshua) " Take away his filthy garments from him, and I will clothe him with change of raiment," Zech iii. 3, 4.

But pray observe the order, the best robe must first be put upon him.

Quest. But who is the author of these favours, and wonderful kindnesses ?

Answ. Why, it is the Father, " the Father said."

Quest. But why is it not expressed, but God said ?

Answ. Because God in Christ is a reconciled God, nay, a Father to all that believe.

The " best robe " is the righteousness of Jesus Christ. Though other robes are glorious, yet this far excels them all. I shall hereafter prove this is the best robe, and that it is first put upon the sinner ; first, in order of nature, though not in order of time ; for all that are justified, are also sanctified. *The best robe is Christ's righteousness.*

" Unto his servants." Expositors differ about who these servants are. Some think the holy angels are here meant, but others think the ministers of the Gospel are only here intended. I humbly conceive,

1. That the ministers of the Gospel may be meant by these servants, they are required ministerially, to bring forth the best robe, or offer the righteousness of Christ unto convinced sinners, and this first of all, there being no previous qualifications required of them in order to fit or prepare them to put it on. *Who the servants are, that are called to bring forth the fatted calf.*

2. But the chief servant is our Lord Jesus Christ, he (as Mediator) is called God's servant ; and it is he who puts the best robe on the soul by his Spirit ; the Father prepared this robe, the Son wrought it, and he by the Spirit puts it upon every returning sinner. True, it is ready for every one of God's elect, i. e., Christ hath it for them ; yet is it not actually put upon any until by the Spirit they obtain a vital union with the Lord Jesus ; for before effectual calling the elect are naked, as all others are.

So much at this time.

IV

But the father said unto his servants, bring forth the best robe, and put it upon him.—Luke xv. 22.

WE have an account of that kind welcome the father gave to his prodigal son, upon his returning home : the son is humbled to the dust ; his rebellion, and that lewd course of life he had lived, now is grievous to him, and he criedout, " Father, I have sinned," &c.

" But the father said to his servants, bring forth the best robe," &c.   The father'sactings towards the son show he was reconciled to him : and he acts after such a manner towards convinced and believing sinners, that they may preceive all their sins and transgressions are forgiven,

" Bring forth the best robe," There are several sorts of robes or garments.

Several sorts of garment.   1.   A natural grament ; Job calls his skin a garment, because as our clothes cover the body, so doth our skin cover the flesh ; while his boils and blotches corrupt, his skin became like a rotten garment ; and when he was healed, skin became like a changed garment, he seemed to be new clothed ; he had before Satan smote him with sores and boils, a whole garment, but saith, " By the force of my disease is my garment changed," Job. xxx. 18.   It became like an old filthy garment ! and afterwards it became like a new and fresh garment.

2.   A civil garment ; that is, the garments with which our bodies are clothed.

3.   A metaphorical or spiritual garment, which is twofold.   There are two sorts of spiritual garments.

(1.)   The garment or robe of justification.

(2.)   The garment of sanctification, or the robe of our inherent holiness.   The apostle alludes to this garment when he says, " having the garment spotted with the flesh, Jude. xxiii.

I told you, by the best robe is meant the righteousness of Christ, which is put upon, or imputed to them that believe in Jesus to their justification before God ; that it iscompared to a robe is evident ; " He hath covered me with the robe of righteousness," Isa. lxi. 10.   " Friend, how comest thou in hither, not having a wedding garment," Matt. xxii. 12.

Two things I shall do here.

First, Show you why the righteousness of Christ is compared to a garment.

Secondly, Show you why it is called the best robe, or prove it is the best robe.

Why righteousness is compared to a Garment.   1.   Garments, are provided to cover our nakedness that our shame may not appear, so the righteousness of Jesus Christ God hath provided to cover our spiritual nakedness, or to hide and cover all our original, and actual filthiness, shame, and deformity ; no sooner had man sinned, but he saw that he was naked.

The Prodigal before he returned home to his father was naked, or clothed, but with filthy rags ; before the elect are united to Christ or obtain a vital union, they are naked, i. e., they have not the righteousness of Christ put upon them, or imputed to them, i. e., they are not actually justified, but are in a state of condemnation, and the wrath of God abideth on them, John iii. 18. 36.

2.   A garment is of great use to the body, it preserves it from many dangers which such that are naked are exposed unto, every thorn otherwise would scratch us and every blow wound us, and every cold blast pinch us, and the hot beams of the sun scorch us, even so the righteousness of Christ desends and preserves our soul from every thorn of the flesh, and temptation of Satan ; also every cursed sin and evil thought (was it not for this robe) would wound us to death, and the law lay us dead before God, and the devil by his fiery darts lay us a bleeding.   Moreover, those cold blasts of winter, I mean sharp trials and afflictions, would chill our souls, and cool our zeal.   Moreover, and the burning beams of God's wrath would scorch and consume our souls.

3.   A garment renders the person that hath it on to be very comely, who before appeared filthy and loathsome ; put a beggar into the king's robe, and he will appear as if he was the king himself ; so the righteousness of Christ put upon a poor sinner, (that was before clothed with rags, and filthy to behold,) appears lovely, and very glorious to look upon. " And thou wert comely, through my comeliness which I put upon thee, saith the Lord," Ezek. xvi. 14.

4.   Some garments discover a man of what rank and quality he is : as a knight of the noble order of the garter is known by his robe : so the robe of Christ's righteousness dis-

covers the saints to be noble persons, *i. e.*, Kings' children, or such who are of the heavenly family, and born of God, or born from above. The high-priest under the law was known by his garment; the ephod was made of fine linen, and set with many precious stones which the high-priest did wear. So the breastplate of judgment was very rich, the ephod was most curiously wrought with bells and pomegranates at the skirts of it. Now the high-priest's garment was a figure of that robe which all the holy priesthood of Christ have on them, viz., the righteousness of Jesus Christ.

5. He that hath a rich robe offered him (who is clothed with rags,) must put off, or be stripped of his filthy garments, to put on that rich and noble robe. So must a sinner be stripped of all his own righteousness, which is as filthy rags. {See the parable of the marriage-supper.}

Secondly, I shall show and prove, that the robe of Christ's righteousness is the best robe. {Matt. xxii. 12.}

1. Comparatively, in respect had to all others.

2. Positively, best in respect of itself, or upon the account of its own great worth.

3. In respect of the esteem of God the Father, he accounts it the best robe.

4. Believers also account it the best robe.

First, It is the best robe in comparison or respect had to that righteousness that the first Adam was clothed with in his innocency, though some think (through ignorance) that it is called the best robe upon the account of its antiquity, *i. e.*, it being the same that Adam was clothed with. But alas! Adam before his fall was not clothed with the robe of Christ's righteousness; no, it was only his own created righteousness. {Why Christ's righteousness is called the best robe.}

Quest. But perhaps you will say, How far doth this exceed the righteousness of the first Adam?

Answ. I answer, so far as Jesus Christ excels in worth and dignity the earthly Adam, or as far as God excels the creature. Christ is God as well as man, therefore his righteousness is not the righteousness of a mere creature, as Adam's was; though Adam was a perfect man, yet Christ is perfect God and man.

2. The righteousness of Christ is more excellent than any the high-priest did wear, and that as far as the substance excels the shadow, or the antitype the type. You will say the man far excels his shadow. Sirs, those garments were but a shadow of this.

3. The righteousness of Christ excels in worth and excellency the righteousness of the holy angels,

(1.) The righteousness of the holy angels is but a created righteousness, and appertains to the first creation; and so of the same nature with the righteousness of Adam in innocency. But this is a righteousness wrought out by the Son of God, and appertains to the second creation. {Christ's righteousness exceeds the righteousness of the holy angels.}

(2.) The righteousness of the holy angels can justify none but themselves, their perfect obedience can merit no righteousness for others; not for us, nor for the fallen angels, because they owe all they are and can do unto God their Creator.

(3.) They are but finite creatures, therefore no obedience of theirs can satisfy infinite justice.

4. It is the best robe in respect of the garment of our inherent sanctification.

(1.) Because our sanctification is not perfect in this life, it is not without spot; where is the saint that in this respect is without sin? There was never any man inherently perfect, or without any stain of iniquity, but the first Adam only, and the Man Christ Jesus. Solomon saith, " That there is not a just man on the earth, that doeth good and sinneth not," Eccl. vii. 20. Paul {Christ's righteousness the best robe in respect of our inherent sanctification.}
no doubt was as holy a man as any of the godly, yet he cries out, " When he would do good, sin was present with him," Rom. vii. 18: and the apostle John saith, " If we say we have no sin, we deceive ourselves, and the truth is not in us," 1 John i. 8.

(2.) Because our own inherent holiness or sanctification cannot justify our persons in the sight of God, nor screen our souls from the scorching flames of God's vindictive wrath and justice.

(1.) The law of God will soon find a flaw, and many spots in this garment.

(2.) Satan can pick holes in it also; therefore we must also say with David, notwithstanding all our own righteousness, " Enter not into judgment with thy servant, O Lord, for in thy sight no man living shall be justified," Psal. cxliii. 2. " If thou shouldst mark iniquity, who can stand?" Psal. cxxx. 3. Paul tells us, " He knew nothing by himself, yet he was not thereby justified," 1 Cor. iv. 4. No, all our works and inherent righteousness are excluded in our justification before God; God imputeth to those that he justifieth, righteousness without works: "It is the righteousness of one," Rom. iv. 6, and it is a righteousness like a garment put upon us, not wrought in us. "It is unto all," offered to all, and put "upon all them that believe," Rom. iii. 22.

Secondly, It is the best robe, not only comparatively, but also positively,

In respect of its own most excellent nature and quality.

The righteousness of Christ is the righteousness of God.   1. In respect of Christ, whose righteousness it is. It is often called the righteousness of God, not the essential righteousness of God, but the righteousness of him who is truly God, perfect God and man in one Person. "But now the righteousness of God without the law is manifested," Rom. iii. 21, 22. "Even the righteousness of God which is by faith," Rom. x. 3. "They being ignorant of God's righteousness," &c. "That we might be made the righteousness of God in him," 2 Cor. v. 21. Some say it is only called the righteousness of God, because he accepteth it; that is, he accepteth of our faith, repentance, and sincere obedience, instead of perfect obedience to the law, through Christ's merits. Christ, they say, hath merited this grace, that our inherent righteousness and good works should justify our persons before God. But this is not gospel, but a piece of new popery we say; and therefore it is called the righteousness of God.

Why Christ's righteousness is called the righteousness of God.   (1.) Because it is a righteousness wrought out by him who is perfect God in our nature, and not that Christ only merited it for us, and so his death only is the meritorious cause of our justification: but Christ's righteousness, i. e., his active and passive obedience, is, we affirm, the matter of justification, or the material cause; and as it is imputed to us, also the formal cause thereof

Christ's righteousness the material cause of our justification.   (2.) It is called the righteousness of God, in opposition, and in contradistinction to the righteousness of mere creatures.

(3.) Because God only found it out in his infinite wisdom, and because also it tends so much to his glory, and likewise because it is his own free gift, and by himself put upon us, or imputed to us.

2. It is the best robe because of the largeness, the length and breadth of it; it is wide enough to cover the whole soul, render the whole soul comely and amiable in the sight of God; it covers all our nakedness, all our sins, deformities, and infirmities whatsoever: it is commonly called the long white robe, it reaches from the head down to the feet, every way complete and perfect before God. And hence it is said, "Ye are complete in him, who is the head of principalities and powers," Col. ii. 10.

3. Such is the excellency of it, that it is a righteousness exactly suiting with and answering the pure nature of God. (1.) The justice of God cannot find one flaw in it. (2.) The truth of God cannot find the least exception against it, in respect of the threats of God against Adam for his disobedience. (3.) The holiness of God beholdeth not the least stain, spot of sin, or blemish in it. Moreover, it exactly answereth that righteousness which the law of God requireth of us to our justification before God, i. e., a sinless righteousness; and therefore it is the best robe.

4. It is the best robe in respect of its duration or stability thereof. Adam's righteousness in innocency was perfect, but not stable nor lasting, but it was mutable, and liable to be lost and rent from him. And O how soon did sin and the devil rob him, and all his posterity in him, of it! What though a man hath a very rich robe put upon him, if he be not certain of keeping it one day, that cannot render him for ever happy. Man, poor man, fell among thieves, and they stripped him of his raiment, as well as left him half dead. "Man in honour abode not one night: but the righteousness of Christ is a durable, a certain, and an everlasting righteousness. It was prophesied that the "Messiah should finish transgression, and make an end of sin, and make reconciliation, and bring in an everlasting righteousness," Dan. ix. 24. A righteousness which cannot be lost; no thieves, no sin, world, flesh, nor devils, can rob a believer of this robe. "Thy righteousness (saith the Psalmist) is an everlasting righteousness," Psal. cix. 142 "My righteousness shall be for ever," Isa. li. 8. He that is once justified, is for ever justified; whom he "justified, them he also glorified," Rom. viii. 30. "There is therefore no condemnation to them that are in Christ Jesus," Rom. viii. 1. Our righteousness and justifictaion is as certain as our salvation, which is, like the covenant, "ordered in all things, and sure," 1 Sam. xxiii. 5.

5. It is a righteousness which hath merited glorious grace, glorious gifts, and glorious privileges, yea, a glorious crown and kingdom. Our justification is not only merited by Christ's death, and suffering, but also by his personal obedience: his doing and suffering, (I newly told you) is the material cause of our justification. But besides what Christ is to

us in justification, he by his perfect obedience, or by what he did and suffered, hath merited all good things for us, yea, wonderful blessings and privileges. The paying the debts of one among men, run out of all, doth not merit the favour and kindness of his creditor. But Jesus Christ by his perfect obedience hath not only paid our debts, and acquitted, and discharged us from wrath and condemnation, but hath brought us thereby into a near relation unto God. Those that are justified are adopted, *i. e.*, made sons and daughters of the most high God; they are the favourites of heaven, and heirs of glory; they are all the King's children, and are accepted, and are most amiable and lovely in God's sight. Sir, no thing, no righteousness can commend us to God, but this only. *{Christ not only paid all our debts, but hath merited wonderful privileges for us also.}*

6. It is the best robe, because it is our only title to heaven, and that which frees and delivereth us from the pangs of hell. We have nothing but Christ's righteousness to plead at God's bar, why we should be saved, and not be cast into hell. Dare any men on a death-bed plead their own righteousness, or their obedience and good works? Certainly if they should, their state would be deplorable; it is the righteousness, the death, and merits of Christ that give believers ease, comfort, and hope at the hour of death, and will give boldness in the day of judgment. *{Christ's righteousness is our title to heaven.}*

7. It is the best robe, because it is that alone which gives a poor sinner, nay, a believer, so much ease and relief at all times, when he is accused and oppressed, either from without, or by enemies within. (1.) When sin presseth sore upon his conscience. Or (2.) when the law lets fly its bitter arrows and curses. (3.) Or when Satan sends forth his fiery darts, and accuses for this and that sin. Or (4.) when death looks grim upon the soul; the righteousness of Christ is, I say, our only plea against them all, and yields a believer sweet help and succour. Jesus Christ made an end of sin, as to its guilt and condemning power, and hath satisfied both law and justice, and vanquished the devil, and taken away the sting of death; so that justice is on our side, and pleads for us, as well as mercy, and death hereby is become a blessing, and no part of the curse to such who have this robe upon them. *{Christ's righteousness put on the soul, gives the sinner ease and much comfort.}*

8. It is the best robe, the best righteousness, because it hath brought the highest and greatest glory unto God, as well as the highest and chiefest good unto man. (1.) It hath in God's contrivance of it exalted and magnified infinite wisdom; and in Christ's working of it out all other of the divine perfections are magnified also; and all the attributes of God meet together in sweet harmony; and also Satan is utterly defeated, his works destroyed, and his kingdom overthrown thereby. *{Christ's obedience brought great honour to God.}*

9. It is the wedding-garment, and therefore the best robe. The wedding-garment of a high-born princess, is always the best and most glorious, being bespangled with jewels, pearls, and precious stones. " Though the king's daughter is all glorious within; yet her clothing is wrought gold. Upon thy right hand did stand the queen in gold of ophir," Psal. xlv. 13.

Glorious within, I conceive, refers to her divine inherent graces and sanctification, and her clothing to the righteousness of Christ, which is elsewhere compared to the sun; "The woman was clothed with the sun," Rev. xii. 1, 2. What created glory is brighter or more glorious than the sun?

10. And lastly it is the best robe, because of the extent of it; it doth not only clothe every believer, but the whole universal church; also rendering the spouse of Christ, or his whole mystical body, amiable, and without spot in the sight of God. It makes them all shine alike in equal glory and beauty before him. *{Christ's righteousness clothes not only every particular saint, but also the whole church of God.}*

Thirdly, it is the best robe in the esteem of God the Father. (1). He calls it the best robe. (2). It is that righteousness which hath satisfied divine justice, and reconciled God to us. " The Lord is well pleased for his righteousness, sake," &c. Isa. xlii. 21. " This is my beloved Son, in whom I am well pleased," Matt. iii. 17. In whom, that is, with all that are in him, or have his righteousness put upon them. The righteousness of Christ, and sacrifice of Christ, is of a sweet "smelling savour unto God the Father," Eph. v. 2.

2. Christ by his righteousness, is mighty to save. " I that speak in righteousness," i. e., in a righteous, spotless nature; I that speak in the righteousness of God, in a righteousness answering the rectitude of God's holy nature, and holy law; and hence mighty to save. The Father hereby is rendered strong, and the Son rendered strong, and the Holy Ghost is hereby also rendered strong, the Holy Trinity is hereby become strong to save.

Fourthly, it is the best robe in the esteem of all the saints and people of God. *{The saints esteem it the best robe.}*

1. It is of this righteousness they make mention only. " I will make men-

tion of thy righteousness, even of thine only," Psal. lxxi. 16. Mine (as if he should say) is not worth mentioning. (1). It is on thine I rely, trust in, and depend upon; it is thy righteousness that relieves, strengthens, and comforts me at all times. (2.) Believers also only glory in this righteousness. "Surely in the Lord shall one say, have I righteousness," &c. In thee shall all the seed of Israel be justified, and shall glory," Isa. xlv. 24, 25. (3). Moreover, the saints count all their own inherent righteousness but as dung, in comparison of this robe of righteousness. "All our righteousness is as filthy rags," &c. "Yea, doubtless, and I count all things but loss, for the excellency of the knowledge of Jesus Christ my Lord; for whom I have suffered the loss of all things, and do count them but dung that I may win Christ: And be found in him, not having mine own righteousness, which is of the law, but that which is through the faith of Christ, even the righteousness of God by faith," Phil. iii. 8, 9. What is more contemptible than filthy rags, or than dung, or dogs'-meat (as the word will bear) he compares such to dogs that feed upon their own works of righteousness as that which justifies them before God; through the saints' inherent righteousness (as considered in itself) is amiable, yet it having many spots and blemishes in it, it is in comparison to the righteousness of Christ of no worth.

APPLICATION

1. I infer from hence, how blind the greatest part of the people of this nation are. O how few speak of this righteousness! how is the church of England apostatized (or many of them) from their ancient doctrine! their people are unacquainted with this righteousness, because their teachers generally are ignorant of it, and little study it, or bring forth this righteousness, that the people might have it put upon them, and be clothed therewith.

2. I infer, that it is the duty of all Christ's servants to bring forth this righteousness to convinced and returning sinners. "And the Father said to his servants, bring forth the best robe."

3. This may also tend severely to reprove all such who slight this robe of righteousness, counting it as a mere fiction, or airy notion. Yet when some of this sort have been laid on a death-bed, they, with the papists, are forced then to fly thither for refuge.

See the simile of putting a piece of new cloth to an old garment.   4. Moreover, it may serve to reprove such that strive to mix their own righteousness with the righteousness of Christ, and so endeavour to put a new piece of cloth upon an old garment. And what is that but to mar or spoil the beauty and glory of the new and glorious robe, and make the old garment worse, the rent worse?

5. By way of exhortation. Let me persuade all returning sinners, convinced sinners, to endeavour to obtain union with Jesus Christ, and to believe in him.

MOTIVES

(1.) Consider how gloriously you will hereby come to be clothed. "And the king will hereby also desire your beauty."

(2.) It will not be for clothing only, and for ornament, but it will be as armour of proof also, or it is armour as well as ornament. Satan can never prevail to wound to death such who have it on. It is as it were a coat of mail, put on the armour of light: Rom. xiii. 12, faith in Christ's righteousness is a shield to defend the soul.

(3.) By nature all are naked, and they so remain, till they obtain a vital union with Christ, or are transplanted out of the first Adam into Jesus Christ.

(4.) Moreover, it is a garment that will keep you warm, as well as preserve you from harm; such shall find spiritual life and heat also in them, in the cold and sharpest seasons of trials and afflictions.

Lastly, For comfort and consolation. Believers, know that you are the most happy people in the world, how low or despised soever you seem to be in the eyes of an ungodly world. Lazarus was more gloriously clothed than the rich man that was clad in purple; do not look as man looks, i. e., on what the body hath on, but see how your soul is clothed. But to proceed.

"The father said to his servants, bring forth the best robe." From hence note, that God the Father is the author of this robe of righteousness.

"All things are of God, who hath reconciled us unto himself by Jesus Christ," 2 Cor. v. 18. (1.) The Father found the way and means by which we come to have this robe. (2.) It is the gift of God; "the gift of righteousness," Rom. v. 17, (3.) It is by God the Father that we are in Christ: "Of him are ye in Christ Jesus," 1 Cor. i. 30.

Our union with Christ is of God the Father. (4.) The Father imputeth the righteousness of his Son to all that believe, and by that way puts it upon them ; the gospel reveals it, and Ministers offer it, and show the necessity and excellency of it. But know ye that no man hath it on without the Holy Spirit's application. Faith is no more than an instrument, i. e., a hand by which the Spirit doth apply it.

V

And put a ring on his hand, and shoes on his feet, &c.—Luke xv. 22.

WE see here what favour the compassionate father showed his returning prodigal, and how welcome he was unto him.

(1.) He calls for the best robe to clothe him. (2.) " A ring to adorn him, and shoes to accommodate his necessity," that he might the better walk in the ways of godliness. (3). The fatted calf to feed and feast him.

From whence I might by way note,

" That whatsoever God sees a returning sinner needs, whether it be for honour, dignity, or to answer his necessities, he will bestow it upon him; " he will give grace and glory, and no good thing will he withhold from such who walk uprightly," Psal. lxxxiv. 11.

The son sought but for room in his Father's family (though it was to be as a servant) when he first came to himself, but the Father gives him the dignity of a son, and the best in all his house.

" And put a ring on his hand."

This is the second favour conferred on this prodigal son. I find the use of a ring in those eastern countries, was significant of several things. *The use of a ring put on the hand among the Jews.*

1. To seal decrees ; the decree was written and sealed with the king's ring.

2. It was used as a badge of honour ; none in ancient times in those countries but noble persons, were allowed to wear a ring. And Pharaoh took his ring from his hand, and put it upon Joseph's hand. Joseph was preferred as the most honourable person in all the land, even next to the king himself, and as a token of this the king put his own ring on his hand. So in the gospel times such that were honourable persons wore rings, as is noted by the apostle James, "If there come into your assemblies a man with a gold ring, you say to him, sit thou in a good place," James ii. 2. 3.

" A ring was worn for ornament, such that were persons of quality, commonly only were decked with bracelets and rings on their hands," Ezek. xvi. 11.

4. A ring, as some hint, was worn as a token of freedom among the Romans ; none were allowed to wear a ring, who were either bond-men or strangers, but such only that were free-born, or purchased their liberty ; and this might perhaps also be a custom among the Egyptians ; for Joseph was a prisoner when Pharaoh sent for him, and Pharaoh putting his ring on his hand might not only signify the honour he now conferred on him, but also given to him as a token or pledge of his liberty, or his discharge out of prison, and that he was now made a free-man of the land of Egypt.

5. A ring was anciently a signet of conjugal love, or a token of unity, yea, of nuptial union and conjunction. From hence St. Chrysostom (as a worthy author notes) saith, that the ring was put upon the prodigal as an emblem of his soul's espousals with Christ.

Now, my brethren, if we consider what is meant by this ring, it may very well be significant of all these things in a spiritual sense ; for no doubt it refers to the glorious and excellent ornament of grace, particularly to the grace of faith, which is often in the scripture compared to gold. Whosoever hath the robe of Christ's righteousness put upon him, is also enriched and beautified with the ornament of precious faith, and all other habitual graces whatsoever. *The ring signifies the ornament of grace.* God speaks of a glorious robe which he had put upon his people, whom he found in their blood and pollution, cast out like a wretched new-born infant : " I spread my skirt over thee ; I clothed thee also with broidered work," &c., Ezek. xvi. 8, 10, and then he saith, " He decked them with ornaments, and put bracelets on their hands," ver. 11. Here it is called a ring, because a ring might signify more than some other ornaments. He, I say, that hath the best robe to clothe him, hath this ring, i.e., precious faith wrought in him, to adorn him ; for he that is a justified person is a gracious person : as the " king's daughter was clothed with wrought gold," Psal. xlv. 9, 13, so she was also all glorious within ; though faith is no part of our justifying righteousness, yet no man is actually justified who hath not true faith given to him. True, God justified the ungodly ; so were all when God first discharged or pronounced them just and righteous persons, without any previous works or acts of righteousness wrought in them ; yet being justified, they are also sanctified, and remain no longer unbelievers or ungodly persons. Were ever any clothed with the best robe that God did not work faith in their souls, or did not put this ring on their hand ? Therefore the outward ornament put on the hand of the returning sinner, signifies the inward adorning of the soul with the graces of the Spirit.

Grace is a seal of glory. 1. Take the ring here for a seal to confirm an absolute decree or purpose, which is like the law of the Medes and Persians, not to be altered. Grace is as a seal of God's eternal decree and purpose in Jesus Christ, signifying, the person who receives it is one that was ordained to eternal life, or it is a seal to him of all those blessings God decreed to give him before the world began ; they that receive the Holy Spirit in the graces of it, are " sealed thereby until the day of redemption," Eph. iv. 30. " In whom ye are sealed with that Holy Spirit of promise, which is the earnest of our inheritance, until the redemption of the purchased possession, until the praise of his glory," Eph. i. 13 14. They, my brethren, who have but one drachm of grace, or the smallest measure of grace, even the weakest faith, are thereby made sure of everlasting life : for grace is the seed of glory, as glory is the harvest of grace. " He that believeth on the Son hath everlasting life," John iii. 36. So that although faith is more than an evidence of our blessed state, yet it is undoubtedly an evidence of it. " These things have I written to you that believe on the name of the Son of God, that ye may know that you have eternal life," &c., 1 John v. 13.

Grace is a sign or signet of honour conferred on believers. 2. Or take a ring (as before mentioned) for a badge or signet of honour. —True grace is an absolute sign of the highest honour that God confers upon any person in this world ; nay, and also of that eternal glory and grandeur he will bring them to in the world to come : the riches of this world, or the greatest fulness of all earthly things, together with temporal glory and grandeur, are no sign that the person that hath them is in the love and favour of God, and shall be great and glorious in the next world ; for the worst and vilest of men are raised up to kingly dignity ofttimes here, even such whom God's soul abhorreth. Lazarus was a nobler and more honourable person in God's sight, than the " rich man that was clothed with purple," &c. Now what man that receives the saving-grace of the Spirit, is born of God, he is an adopted son of God, and is espoused to Jesus Christ, he is a favourite in the court of heaven, and an heir of God ; nay, and by having this ring, being sealed with this ring, he comes to have the image of God imprinted on his soul ; therefore is it a badge of the highest honour. It is, my brethren, a sign of a change of state ; the ring showed that the prodigal, who was before in a state of wrath and death, was now brought into a justified state, or into a state of life : before he was in a state of beggary, but now brought into a state of true nobility. " The righteous is more excellent than his neighbour," Prov. xii. 26. " Jabez was more honourable than his brethren," because he was a gracious person. Or,

Grace the image of God.

Grace signifies a believer's freedom. 3. Take the ring to signify a believing sinner's freedom from slavery and bondage. Grace is a certain sign and pledge of that spiritual liberty and freedom he hath received from Jesus Christ ; he that hath this ring, i.e., faith in Christ, hath on him the best robe, therefore is discharged from bondage and eternal condemnation : he that hath the Holy Spirit is made free by Christ, " If the Son therefore make you free, then are ye free indeed," John. viii. 36. " Where the Spirit of the Lord is, there is liberty," 2 Cor. iii. 17. All those that receive the graces of the Spirit, are free from sin, from the guilt, the power, and punishment thereof ; they are also freed from the power of Satan, and from the condemning power of the law, and from death also as it is a curse, and from the eternal wrath of God in hell. " There is now no condemnation to them that are in Christ Jesus," Rom. viii. 1.

A ring, as some note, is an emblem of eternity, it has no end ; so all spiritual privileges and freedom are eternal.

Grace adorns the soul, as a ring on the hand adorns the hand. 4. Take a ring as an ornament : grace is only that which adorns the soul, or the spiritual ornament of every man and woman who receives it. " A meek and quiet spirit is in the sight of God of great price." What are outward ornaments of the body, but mere vain empty things tending to please carnal eyes ? But grace makes a person lovely in the eyes of God, and Jesus Christ. " Thou hast ravished my heart, my sister, my spouse ; thou hast ravished my heart with one of thine eyes, with the chain of thy neck," Cant. iv. 9. By that one eye, most understand is meant the grace of faith, often called the eye of faith, which is a self-empty-ing and soul-loathing, and self-abasing grace, that which wholly leads out the soul to Jesus Christ, to love him, to exalt him, and to cleave unto him. Our Lord compares the eye of his spouse to the eye of a dove, whose eye is very chaste and always is fixed on its meat. So is the eye and faith of a believer at all times, and in all conditions fixed upon Jesus Christ in every state; and in all he does and suffers for him, he cries with the blessed martyr, " none but Christ, none but Christ." And from hence this eye is a lovely eye in his sight. And then the chain of her neck signifies the complication of all graces; yet faith is the uniting and principle grace of all others.

5. And lastly, take a ring as a signet of conjugal love and union, or an emblem of the soul's espousals to Jesus Christ. The grace of faith particularly is, as I said, the uniting grace, i.e., that faith that works by love. *Grace is a sign or signet of our union with Christ.* No man is married to Christ without faith, though the Holy Spirit is the chief bond of this union, and is that which works faith in the soul. A worthy author, speaking of this ring saith, " that God gives a true penitent faith, by which it is espoused to Jesus Christ; and there are (saith he) six things which conquer in marriages (as is observed by such who write of marriages) which hold good also in our spiritual marriage with Christ, and are signified by the putting on of this ring. *Sedgwick on the prodigal, p. 213.* *Six things concur in marriage.*

1 Mutual consent. 2. Mutual contracting. 3. Mutual obligation. 4. Mutual union. 5. Mutual right and interest. 6. Mutual society and communion.

1. Mutual consent; no person is, or can be espoused and married to Christ without a hearty consent: for as the person must have a true knowledge of Christ, so he must yield to accept of him; for a marriage ought to be a voluntary transaction of both persons, Jesus Christ accepteth of the sinner, embraces the sinner, and the sinner accepteth of Christ, they give themselves to each other: as Christ first chose us, so we chose him, it is a free and ready act of the will. " They gave themselves unto the Lord," &c. *Mutual consent.*

2. Mutual contracting of the soul with Christ, and contraction is done by expression of words proper to marriage, not that I will take thee, &c., but I do take thee, &c. So here, not that I purpose hereafter to accept, take, and receive Christ as the only object of my soul's affection, but I do now receive and take him; though this is not expressed with the words of the mouth, yet it is the voice and expressions of the soul: Christ in his word declares that he gives himself to the soul with all he is, and all he hath; and the soul freely and heartily takes Jesus Christ as its best and dearest beloved, contemning and forsaking all other things and objects for his sake, even whatsoever was gain or dear to him before. *Mutual contracting.*

3. A mutual obligation of Christ to the soul, and of the soul to Christ. Some do call this resignation, and therefore marriage is called a knot or tye, wherein the two persons are mutually limited and bound to each other in a way of conjugal separation from all others in such a relation; and this is called a covenant. Sirs, Jesus Christ obligeth himself to be kind, loving, true, and faithful to the soul; and the soul that marries Christ doth oblige himself to be true, constant, faithful, and obedient unto him. The soul disclaims all other lovers, whether objects or things, that sue for his choicest love, affections, and delight, promising to take up its whole satisfaction and complacency in Christ alone, resting upon him and nothing else for justification and eternal life: I have vowed and cannot go back, saith such a person. *Mutual obligation.*

4. " Mutual conjunction;" that is, they two are now become one; before marriage they were twain, or not thus united; " They two are not flesh:" 1 Cor. vi. 16. Not only one in love and affections, for so a man and his friend, his neighbour or brother may be one; but one flesh. " So he that is joined to the Lord is one Spirit," ver. 17. The divine nature that is in Christ, and Spirit that is in Christ is in that person who is united to him; so that as the soul and body makes but one man, so Christ and believers make but one mystical person, or Christ mystical. What union is nearer and dearer than this? We are said, by virtue of the promises and covenant, " to partake of the divine nature," 2 Pet. i. 4. *Mutual conjunction.*

5. Mutual right and interest in each other, Christ hath by our voluntary obligation and covenant, right to us, and we have right to, and interest in him. Christ hath right as a head, to, in, and over us, to guide and counsel us; he hath the right of sovereignty over us, and our duty is to obey, and be in subjection unto him: but though the wife hath not power or authority over the husband, yet she hath the power of property in her husband. And, my brethren, hereby believers have right to, and inter- *Mutual right and interest.*

est in all Christ hath, as well as interest in his person. "This is my beloved, this my friend, O ye daughters of Jerusalem," Cant. v. 16. They have interest in Christ's righteousness, and in his riches of grace, and his riches of glory. A believer may say with Thomas, "My Lord and my God," and with the spouse, "My beloved is mine, and I am his," Cant. ii. 16. And as Christ endows us with all he hath, as he is our head and husband, so all that we are, have, or can do, Christ hath interest in; all I have (saith the soul) Lord, is thine, my heart, my love, desires, and affections; even all the powers of my soul, and all I can do, all the service I am, or shall be enabled to do for the honour, and glory, and exaltation of thy name, is thine.

Mutual society and communion. 6. And lastly, mutual society and communion. Marriage infers co-habitation as well as co-interest, so Christ and believers dwell together, walk together, sit down together, and sup together, and have mutual love to, and delight in one another. "I will come in unto him, and I will sup with him, and he with me," Rev. iii. 20. "Enoch walked with God three hundred years," Gen. v. 23. And what a privilege and honour is this, "I will dwell in them, and walk in them, and I will be their God, and they shall be my people," 2 Cor vi. 16. The interest of Christ is the interest of believers; the grand work and business of Christ in this world, is the grand work and business of believers, which is Christ's glory, and the good of his church and people, they have mutual promises, mutual privileges; for as God is the Father of Christ, so he is the Father of believers : as Christ is heir of all things, so they are heirs of all things, co-heirs with him. "If children, then heirs, heirs of God, and joint heirs with Christ," Rom. viii. 17. Is there a kingdom promised to Christ? so there is a kingdom promised to them. "Fear not, little flock, it is your Father's good pleasure to give you the kingdom," Luke xii. 32. Is there a throne promised to Christ? so there is a throne promised to them. "He that overcometh shall sit down with me in my throne," Rev. iii. 21. Is there a crown promised to Christ? so there is a crown promised to them. "Henceforth there is a crown of righteousness laid up for me, and not for me only, but for all them also that love his appearance," 2 Tim. iv 8. And as Christ and believers have communion together here, dwell together here; so they shall for evermore dwell together hereafter. "Father, I will that they also whom thou hast given me, be with me where I am, that they may behold my glory," &c., John xvii. 24. Now, I say, this ring may signify all these things, and many more.

APPLICATION

1. O happy souls, on whose hand this ring is put, or who are thus adorned, honoured, freed, sealed, and married to the Lord Jesus Christ!

2. We infer here are most sweet and powerful motives and encouragements for poor prodigals, lost and undone sinners, to labour to return home unto God.

3. We may also infer, that God intends great good, yea most singular mercies and favours to returning sinners; he clothes them, he adorns them, he feeds them, he seals his love to them, pardon to them, peace to them, nay, he espouses and marries them to his own Son; he assures them of his protection, strength, and succour at all times, and in all states, trials, and troubles, and temptations whatsoever. Moreover, he will never leave them comfortless, nor forsake them; he justifies, he adopts, he renews and sanctifies them, he seals the truth of the promises of eternal life unto them.

4. Try yourselves by what hath been said, have you this ring on your hands, *i. e.*, the true grace of God in your hearts? are you adorned therewith?

(1.) Did you ever see the transcendant beauty and excellency in Jesus Christ? is "He the pearl of all pearls," in your eye the chiefest among ten thousand?" is there no beloved like your beloved? is your judgment and understanding brought to an assent and approbation of this Christ? do you see that there is life in him, and that besides him there is no Saviour? do you see he is worthy of your acceptation; do you know that you need him, and must perish, without you get an interest in him.

(2.) Is your will inclined and brought to a ready and hearty consent to embrace him; have you by faith laid hold on him; hath the Spirit of God united your souls to him, and wrought his divine nature and image in you, is your ring no counterfeit ring; is your faith all pure gold, or like precious faith, or the faith of God's elect, what fruits doth your faith bring forth?

But to proceed,

"And shoes on his feet."

This is the fourth favour and great blessing bestowed on the returning pro-digal, his lips were kissed, his back clothed, his hand adorned, and now his feet are shod. Feet are often taken for the instrument or spring of the actions and courses of men.

What is meant by shoes on his feet.

1. Therefore no doubt by feet is meant the will and affections of his soul; for like as the feet of a man carry his body this way or that way, so doth the will and affections carry the soul into obedience to Christ.

Shoes fit to travel in.

2. Shoes are an ornament to the feet. " How beautiful are thy feet with shoes, O princes, daughters," Cant. vii. 1. The daughter of a prince hath commonly rare and costly shoes ; it is an uncomely thing to see a virgin's naked feet, or homely shoes on her feet. To have rich and curious shoes on the feet, tends to the glory of a princess, so for the feet of a Christian, i. e., his will and affections strongly inclined to that which is good, it is his beauty and glory.

Shoes an ornament to the feet.

3. Shoes signify not only a regular will and affection in a believer, but the resolution, readiness, and purpose of the will, &c., to all things that are spiri-tually good, and whatsoever is commanded of God. Joshua was well shod, who said, " I and my house will serve the Lord." And so was David, " I have sworn that I will keep thy righteous precept." St. Paul speaks of these shoes, " And having your feet shod with the preparation of the gospel of peace," Eph. vi. 15. That is, have continually such a resolution and readiness to walk in the ways of the Lord as the gospel calls for, be prepared and resolved always to do or suffer for Jesus Christ.

Shoes denote a prepared-ness or reso-lution to walk in God's way.

4. Shoes were anciently a sign of freedom, and of a comfortable state ; slaves went bare-foot, but when the prodigal comes to have shoes on his feet, it might signify that he was now a free-man, a son, and no more a slave of sin or Satan.

5. Shoes are not only an ornament to the feet and a sign of freedom, but they are also a preservative against cold, and many distempers of the body, as experience shows, so strong resolution of the will, and the raisedness and spiritualness of the affections is an excellent preservative against lukewarmness, and a cold frame of heart ; if you are not shod with the preparation of the gospel, or have not ready resolution of heart to follow the Lord fully, your spirits will soon cool to heavenly things, and one distemper or another will seize upon you.

Shoes pre-serve the feet of the soul from wounds.

6. Shoes on his feet may denote his being fit to travel through any diffi-cult, stony, or thorny paths, where such who are barefooted cannot, dare not venture : so the resolution of the will and spirituality of the affections, causes or helps a Christian to venture through all difficulties in God's ways. A man that wants courage, zeal, and resolution, is afraid to venture through the thorns and briars of the flesh, temptations of Satan, the cares of the world, and the deceitfulness of riches; he is like a man who is barefooted, he sees thorns and pricking briars in his way ; O, says he, I dare not venture further, I shall be wounded : but a man who has excellent shoes on his feet fears nothing, but goes forward ; so he that hath a resolved will and preparedness of heart, his affections raised sublime, and heavenly, he is not daunted, nor faint-hearted, though he meets with never so many difficulties, snares, and temptations from within and from without.

He that is well shod fears neither to tread on stones or thorns.

7. Shoes (saith one) are sometimes put for a mortified disposition to the world : for as shoes keep the feet at a distance from the earth, and with them we trample, so by the gospel preparation, (i. e.,) a ready purpose of the will, and spirituality of the affections, a believer tramples upon all the sinful pleasures, riches, and honours of this evil world, and as shoes strengthen the feet, so hereby the feet of the soul are strengthened. God is said " to keep the feet of his saints," 1 Sam. ii. 9. " Wilt thou not keep my feet from falling ?" Psal. lvi. 13.

Sedgwick.

Doct. God gives a true believer a will to do good, and heavenly affections, by which he is strengthened graciously in his inward man, to walk in a holy course of life, and new obedience.

I. I shall show you what a course, singular life, or holy walking in new obedience is.
II. Why God doth enable them thus to walk.
III. Apply it.

I. It is a different course of life, a singular walking to all other men ; the prodigal before his conversion (saith one) walked with naked feet, wildly, loosely, disgracefully, dangerously ; but now he hath shoes to put on his feet, his heart is not only altered, but his life also ; not only his disposition, but his condition ; not only his condition, but his conversation. Believers are exhorted to " put off

Believers walk in a different course of life from others.

their former conversation," Eph. iv. 22 ; and as they are made free, and become the servants of " righteousness, they have their fruit unto holiness," Rom. vi. 18, 22.

A heavenly course of life. 　　2. They that have these shoes on their feet walk in an heavenly and spiritual course of life ; others are carnally minded, but these are spiritually minded : others have their affections set on things below, but these " have their affections set on things above," Col. iii. 1, 2. Before their feet carried them perhaps to play-houses, to music-houses, and to tippling-houses ; but now their feet carry them into the courts of God's house, and they delight more in praying than they did playing.

In a regular course of life. 　　3. It is a regular course of life. The feet (saith the same author) when shoes are on, are restrained as it were, and confined ; they are kept to a size, and do not squander this way and that way : so a believer walks not loosely nor uncomely, but he takes straight steps with his feet ; he walks by the rule of God's word, not as vain and carnal persons walk, nor according to the course of this world ; but " his conversation is as becometh the gospel of Christ," Phil. i. 27.

In an upright course of life. 　　4. In an upright course of life ; as the shoes keep the feet up on either side, so they are upright-hearted, they walk uprightly ; the living creatures feet (spoken of by Ezekiel) were straight. Ezek. i. 7. The saints are thorough for God, the same in secret as in public ; their whole course is uniform, comely, and beautiful. " How beautiful are thy feet for shoes ?" Cant. vii. 1, saith Christ of his spouse : they act according to those most excellent principles, from faith and love, and according to the state, grace, and dignity attained ; and to high and glorious ends, i. e., that God may be glorified : they seek not their own honour, but the honour of Jesus Christ.

An exemplary course of life. 　　5. Their walk and conversation is an exemplary walk ; it is not only profitable to themselves, but to others also : their path and holy walk gives light and directions to such who walk in darkness. " There is good to be got by him that is made good," saith one ; not by his doctrine only, but by his walk and conversation also : as their lips feed many, so do their lives also.

II. From whence is it, or why doth God put such shoes on their feet, to enable them to walk in such a gracious and religious manner ?

Why believers should walk with shoes on their feet. 　　1. God hath given them a spiritual nature, to the end they might live a spiritual life, that so the goodness of their state may be evidenced by their holy conversation, and goodness of their life.

2. Because it was the design of God in giving of his Son to die, " to redeem them from all iniquity, and make them a peculiar people, zealous of good works," Tit. ii. 14.

3. God hath given them such shoes, because of the difficulty of the way in which they are to walk : great trials, great afflictions, and strong temptations, call for great and strong resolutions, and raised and sublime affections, and holy watchfulness.

4. Because he would prevent their falling, these shoes keep their feet from sliding, and their souls from being wounded. Many who want these shoes, the briers and thorns, or cares of this world, and the deceitfulness of riches wound to death.

5. Because hereby God designs much glory to himself, as well as profit and comfort to their souls ; his grace hereby is magnified in the excellent nature and quality thereof. What can the common principles of nature do, in comparison of the graces of the Holy Spirit in the hearts of believers ? It is one thing to walk as men, and another thing as saints, or men born from above, born of the Spirit.

USE

1st. Exhortation. Get these shoes on your feet, as well as the best robe upon your backs : do not only desire to be justified and saved, but also to walk in an even, upright, and straight path, and to be inwardly sanctified.

MOTIVES

1. They are shoes made by a skilful and excellent workman, viz., the Holy Spirit, and they exactly fit the feet of your souls ; and though they pinch the flesh, yet they are easy to the Spirit : indeed they tend to mortify the lusts of the flesh, which hinder the soul in its spiritual course.

2. They are lasting, and will not wear out ; they are like the shoes of the people of Israel in the wilderness, " which waxed not old for forty years."

3. Your holy conversation will honour your profession, and raise the beauty and glory of religion. By this means, wicked men think it strange that you run not with them to the same excess of riot. Men can better judge of our lives and conversations, than they can of our principles.

4. And otherways your nakedness in part will appear to your shame and reproach.

2dly. Information. This may inform us, why so many are so uncomely in their going or walking. Alas! they want these shoes on their feet, they want holy affections, bowed wills, and Christian resolution; they do not "with full purpose of heart, cleave unto the Lord, nor unto one another in love: "but Daniel purposed in his heart that he would not defile himself with the portion of the king's meat," &c. Did professors purpose not to adhere to any temptation; nor do any unpleasant action, nor neglect any known duty, nor countenance any disorderly person or practice, what comely walkers should we have in our churches.

3dly. Moreover, this may inform us what the cause is so many are hurt and wounded, and halt in the way; alas! their feet want shoes, they are not shod with the preparation of the Gospel of peace; and by this means they give way to a contentious and quarrelling spirit, and disturb their own peace, and peace of the church also. It is for want of these shoes of preparation, that so many neglect their communion to the grief of their pious brethren.

4thly. It may be improved to the comfort of such Christians that are shod with the preparation of the Gospel of peace, who are ready always to every good work. Others are like men that have not their shoes on, they are not ready to comply with this Christian duty, and that Christian duty, but raise up one cavil or another against it: but you who have shoes on your feet, are always ready to every good work, nay, completely armed to oppose the enemy of your souls, and to engage in any difficulty whatsoever, and therefore you shall stand in the hour of temptation.

VI

And bring hither the fatted calf, and kill it: and let us eat and be merry.—Luke xv. 23.

FIRST the father called for the best robe to put upon his returned prodigal, and shoes to put on his feet; and he being well clothed and adorned, and well shod, he now calls for the best he had to feed and feast him.

The poor prodigal when he came to himself, finding he was "pinched with hunger," (being almost starved, and ready to perish) thought of the plenty that was in his father's house, "In my father's house is bread enough, and to spare." He wanted bread; if he could have nothing but bread, it would have satisfied him; he seemed to desire no more than the bread of his father's house; but now he is come home, his father calls for the best he had. "Bring hither the fatted calf, and kill it." Though it was killed before, yet the Holy Ghost intimates as if it was now to be slain, and that particularly too for this one lost son.

Doct. One sinner could not be fed, unless the Lord Jesus be slain and made food for his soul.

Some (as our annotators) take the best robe to mean our inherent righteousness, but I have showed that cannot be the best robe. I should rather (saith he) choose to interpret the killing the fatted calf for the prodigal to represent the "application of the blood of Christ, which is made to every sinner that truly repenteth, and maketh application to God for mercy: and the best robe, the righteousness of Christ, which is reckoned that moment to the sinner that believeth." All indeed that speak of the fatted calf, believe it meaneth the Lord Jesus Christ, sometimes expressed by a lamb, the best of all the flock, and sometimes by a kid, as ver. 29. "And yet thou never gavest me a kid," &c. The reason why I conclude it signifies Jesus Christ, is because he only is the food of our souls, and he that feedeth not on him cannot live, but must perish: and although mention is made of the best robe before (as if he had that on before he fed upon Jesus Christ, or heard of the fatted calf) yet we must know every thing cannot be expressed together; besides, a sinner no doubt is first apprehended by Jesus Christ, before he apprehendeth him: for the Spirit (which is the bond of union, and the seed of faith) is received before the act of faith is exerted, or sensible comfort, joy, and peace, experienced by a believer; for faith is a fruit of the Spirit, and his feeding upon the fatted kid may denote his sensible enjoyment of peace and comfort in believing. The prodigal before fed (you heard) upon husks, on vanity, on the wind, i. e., upon the sinful pleasures, profits, and honours, &c., of this world: but now he is returned to his father's house, he must eat the best, eat that which is good, and his soul delight itself in fatness.

Contin. of Pool's annot.

Fat, fatted, fatness, signifies that which is the best, the most choice and most excellent of every thing; we read of the "fat of wine, the fat of oil, the fat of wheat, the fat of the land," Numb. xviii. 12. "It is said of Asher, his bread shall be fat," Gen. xlv. 18. He shall have the best bread, and abundance of it. "They shall be fed with the fatness of thy house," Gen. xlix. 20, "I will feed them in a fat pasture," Psal. xxxvi. 8, the best, the choicest. So here, the fatted calf, fatted lamb, or kid, signifies the best, or that which excels in its kind.

What is is meant by bringing hither the fatted calf. Bring hither; that is, set before him the best provision of my house; he shall eat the fat, that which is delicious or most dainty food; the very best I have shall not be withheld from him; he shall eat that which is "meat indeed, and drink that which is drink indeed," John vi. 55.

Who the servants are that bring it. You, my servants, my ministers, bring forth a slain Saviour, my fatted lamb, that is killed and roasted in the fire of my wrath, to feed hungry sinners withal; present a crucified Christ before their eyes, that they by faith may feed and feast thereon. Do not feed them with such things that cannot satisfy their precious souls; they shall not eat their own husky bread, nor the trash of their own doings, nor feed upon airy notions, nor upon corrupt and poisonous meat; but upon my fatted Lamb, or upon a crucified Christ, and on what he is made to every one that truly believeth on him.

But more comprehensively, by the fatted kid, or calf, is no doubt meant all the spiritual blessings and choicest refreshments and comforts comprehended in a sinner's receiving of the Lord Jesus Christ. Our heavenly Father allows the best to feed and feast the returned or believing sinner; he is a great King, and therefore the best provision of his house is the very best in heaven and earth.

From hence let me note one or two doctrinal truths.

Doct. I. That a returning sinner, or a believer is not only richly clothed and richly adorned, but also richly fed, he hath the best, the most refreshing, strengthening, and comforting provision of God's house.

II. That no food, meat, nor bread will satisfy, strengthen, cheer, and comfort a poor sinner, but only feeding upon a slain Saviour.

"My flesh is meat indeed," &c., saith our blessed Saviour, no food like a crucified Jesus for poor perishing sinners. "Verily, verily, I say unto, Except ye eat the flesh of the Son of Man, and drink his blood, ye have no life in you. Whoso eateth my flesh and drinketh my blood, hath eternal life," Ver. 53, 54.

I. I shall show you, why God will feed believing sinners with the best of his house, or with a crucified Christ.

II. Prove that this feast, this food, contains the best of all God's house, or what he hath to give unto our souls.

III. Show why feeding upon Jesus Christ is set forth by feeding on a fatted calf, kid, or lamb.

IV. Show you who they are that feed upon the fat things, or best of God's house.

I. Why will God feed sinners with the best of his house, &c.

1. Because no other spiritual food is good for the soul. "Eat you that which is good." Implying that nothing that sinners can meet with short of Christ, or besides Jesus Christ, is good.

(1.) Sinful pleasures, riches, honours, self-righteousness, or moral righteousness, are not proper food for lost sinners. What are these things? they are compared to husks or grains, which the swine of this world feed upon; they are swines' meat, they only feed the sensual part of man, and cannot feed his precious and immortal soul.

(2.) Or what are the traditions and commandments of men, but corrupt food, of which we are bid not to "touch, taste, nor handle?" Col. ii. 21, 22.

(3.) Or what is false doctrine, errors, and heresies, but poisonous food? it will poison, and utterly destroy the souls of such that feed thereon.

All other food forbid. 2. Because all other food is forbidden, it is prohibited, or forbidden meat (as the fruit of the tree of knowledge was to our first parents), upon pain of eternal death, sinners are forbid to feed upon any food, save upon Christ alone, or upon the doctrine of a crucified Saviour, on his obedience, on his righteousness, on his death and merits. If any preach justification and eternal life by any other way, or bring in any other gospel, "Let them be accursed," Gal. i. 9, and let all that receive any other gospel, or feed on any other food, dread the same penalty and eternal danger.

Christ was prepared for 3. Because this food, viz., a crucified or slain Saviour, was provided for returning sinners, or believing sinners, as an act of infinite wisdom, love, and *our food from eternity.* goodness, to feed upon from eternity. " Him being delivered up by the determinate counsel and foreknowledge of God, ye have crucified and slain," Acts ii. 23. Hence, also it is said, " He was a Lamb slain from the foundation of the world," Rev. xiii. 8. O the riches of God's preventing grace! how early did he provide for poor sinners! the plaister was prepared before we were wounded, and the price of redemption before we were brought into slavery, and bread before we were hungry, and a fountain to wash in before we were defiled.

4. Because the Son of God, the Lamb of God, was roasted with the fire, *Christ is made fit food for us.* broken and made fit meat, on purpose to feed believing sinners. God was at no small cost in providing of this banquet for his guests. Should any of you lay out thousands to provide a feast for your friends, surely you would have them eat and feed thereon; you would say, bring hither the fatted calf, and the wine which I have mingled. God hath furnished his table. " Wisdom (that is, the wisdom of God) hath killed her beasts, she hath mingled her wine, she hath furnished her table, and she hath sent forth her maidens," viz., (Prov. ix. 2,) the ministers of the gospel, to make all this known to sinners, and to show how willing God is they should eat thereof.

5. Because believers are the sons and daughters of God, they are the *God's children are fed with the best.* King's children, and shall he deny them to eat of the best in all his house! What father would refuse to let his dear children have the best he hath, especially when he had on purpose provided it for them? It is, my brethren, the children's meat, it was not provided for dogs. " Shall I take the children's bread and cast it unto dogs?" Matt. xv. 26.

Again, our Lord saith, " Give not that which is holy to dogs," Matt. vii. 6. But he that believeth in Christ is a child, and no dog. The prodigal was a son before by creation, but now he is a son of God by adoption; nay, he is begotten and born of God, and so a son by regeneration; and therefore the Father feeds him with the best of his house.

6. Because they are invited to this feast, and are bid to eat; many others *Saints are commanded to eat.* were invited, but they desired to be excused; but the prodigal came, the poor, the halt, and blind came; and what saith Christ to them? " Eat, O friends, drink, yea, drink abundantly, O beloved," Cant. v. 1. Also it is no more *See the marriage feast. Matt. xxii.* than what God hath promised to such he brings into his house. " They shall be abundantly satisfied with the fat things of thy house, and thou shalt make them drink of the rivers of thy pleasures," Psal. xxxvi. 8. And again, he saith, " Eat ye that which is good, and let your soul delight itself in fatness," Isa. lv. 2. Shall God provide thus for believing sinners, and bid them eat; and also knowing what need they have of this food, is it any marvel he saith, " Bring hither the fatted calf? This is his commandment, that we should believe on the name of his Son Jesus Christ," 1 John iii. 23, i. e., this is his command, that we feed on the Lord Jesus Christ. " Eat his flesh, and drink his blood." Fly to him for righteousness, rest upon him at all times for justification, sanctification, for strength, help, support, succour, comfort, and consolation, and for whatsoever we need as long as we are in this world.

7. God will have believing sinners feed on Jesus Christ, or on the best of *God has promised to feed his saints with the best.* his house, for his promise sake; who hath said, " He will give grace and glory, and no good thing will he withhold from them," &c. Psal. lxxxiv. 11. " The young lions do lack, and suffer hunger; but they that seek the Lord, shall not want any good thing," Psal. xxxiv. 10. " He will give meat to them that fear him, he is ever mindful of his covenant," Psal. ci. 5. When a sinner returns to God, he shall have all things whatsoever that are good.

Object. But perhaps some poor child of God may object, and say I want many good things.

Answ. 1. You may call such things good things, which God knows are not good for you; he must be judge, who only knows what is best for us.

2. You may call such things, good things, which though good in themselves, yet are but husks, or dross in comparison of those things that God bestoweth upon you.

3. The poorest saint on earth hath the very best of heaven for his precious *The poorest saint has the best of heaven.* soul, the best clothing, the best ornaments, and the best food. He dwells in the best house or habitation; " For he dwells in God. Thou, Lord, hast been our dwelling-place in all generation," Psal. xc. 1. He hath the best friends, the best company, the best riches, the best honour; he is a child of God, and an heir of glory, he hath the best pleasures, the best peace, and the best privileges, and shall have the best

end ; he has the best retinue or guard to attend him, and wait on him, and to minister to him, viz., the holy angels of God ; and the best promises.   " Godliness hath the promise of the life that is now, and of that which is to come," 1 Tim. iv. 8.

Saints have the best of the earth.   4.   Moreover, whatsoever a believer hath of the things of this world, he hath them without a curse ; those things that the wicked have, they have with a curse ; and not only so, but believers have every thing sanctified to them, and in love ; nay, more, they have also God with them, Christ with them.   Alas ! what are all the things of this world, and no God, no Christ, no pardon, no peace ? " There is no peace, to the wicked, saith my God," Isa. xlviii. 22.   " A little that a righteous man hath is better than the revenues of many wicked," Psal. xxxvii. 16.

Bitter things may be the best things.   5.   What though you have some bitter things, bitter to the body, yet God sees they are best for the soul ; it is hard to persuade a carnal man that Lazarus had better things than Dives.

6.   Besides, all afflictions, trials, sorrows, or bitter things that a child of God meets with, are mixed with sweet ; also their sorrows will be but short, and shall be turned into joy.   Nay, " Their afflictions which are but for a moment, work for them a far more exceeding and eternal weight of glory," 2 Cor. iv. 17.

Spiritual food forfeits not.   7.   If we had perhaps what some others have, it would surfeit us, nay, poison and undo our souls. Men may eat to excess ; drink to excess ; but those things which believers feed upon and enjoy, they cannot have to excess, they are things that neither cloy nor surfeit the soul.   If we had no winter, worms and weeds would spoil the wheat, and destroy our gardens.   So had we no sharp trials, no afflictions, no winterly weather, our corruptions, or the love of this world, might destroy and ruin our souls.

8.   Would you be like the swine of this world, rather feed on their husks and trash, than on the choice food of your Father's house ?   What are all earthly riches, honours, and sensual pleasures, to the riches of grace and glory ?

APPLICATION

1.   This may tend to reprove such ministers who do not as God commands, viz., " bring forth the fatted calf," or the precious Lamb of God for sinners to feed upon ; or that do not preach Christ as the sum and substance of all their ministry.   " We preach Christ crucified," 1 Cor. i. 23.—Philip went down to the city of Samaria, " and preached Christ to them," Acts viii. 5 ; and St. Paul rejoiced that Christ was preached, though some " preached him out of strife and contention," Phil. i. 15.   The great subject all the holy apostles preached, was Jesus Christ, or a crucified Saviour.

How to know true ministers.   2.   By this you may know who are true ministers, from such who are corrupt, or counterfeit, or false teachers.

(1.) Some instead of bringing Jesus Christ or preaching Christ, bring forth the traditions of men, the commandments of men, or the doctrines of men, as the Scribes and Pharisees did.

(2.) Some bring forth the doctrine of merits, that sinners may eat their own bread, as the Papists.   And how many called Protestants, that are counted great preachers, who seldom ever preach Jesus Christ ?   How many sermons may you hear, and not a word hardly of Christ in them ?   I think that word of the prophet, concerning seven women taking hold of one man, may refer to many people in these days : what did they say, why, " we will eat our own bread, and wear our own apparel, only let us be called by thy name, to take away our reproach," Isa. iv. 1.   Many now-a-days are for feeding on their own works, or on their own bread, or to be justified or clothed with their own righteousness or acts of morality, according to the light of their own natural conscience, yet would be called by Christ's name, i. e., be called Christians, to take away their reproach, it being counted a disgraceful thing, or a reproach to be called heathens or infidels, though they are but little better, having no true faith in Christ, nor likeness to him.

(3.) Some bring forth men's own inherent righteousness, their faith and sincere obedience, as that which must feed and justify them before God.

(4.) Moreover, others bring forth the doctrine of the old Heathen, and preach Aristotle, Seneca, and Plato, &c., and feed the people with bread that satisfies not.

And some bring forth other poisonous food, of errors and damnable heresies, instead of bringing forth a crucified Christ.

3.   By this ministers may learn what doctrine to preach ; for as Christ must be received for justification, and the best robe put on, so they must bring forth Jesus Christ still : a crucified Saviour must continually be fed upon, as long as we live, i. e., we must fetch all our hope, strength, and comfort from him always, to the end of our lives.

4. Trial. Sinners, are you come to yourselves? also know that you will not think of returning home to God, until a famine arise in your souls, and you see you have nothing but husks to eat.

(1.) Do you hunger after Christ, long after Christ? do you see that you must perish without Jesus Christ? the prodigal said, I perish with hunger. This caused him to resolve to go home.

How to know we are come to Christ or not.

(2.) What is it which you feed upon? Is it upon Christ, or something else? Something of your own? Or do you only feed your carnal and sensual part, and not consider of your soul's wants.

(3.) Did you ever, "labour for the meat which perishes not?" John vi. 27. They that hunger and see that they are ready to perish, will strive, labour, and do their utmost to obtain bread: the proverb is, that hunger breaks stone walls. What will not men do before they will die with hunger.

(4.) Do you know the way in which you may meet with that meat which endures to everlasting life: and also who it is that must give it to you, if you seek it. "For him hath God the Father sealed," John vi. 27. He that believeth on him shall have this meat; believing and eating is all one thing.

You see what provision the blessed God had made for returning sinners, and what entertainment you shall meet with. Methinks there can be hardly any poor sinner here, but should, in the strength of God, resolve to return to him, in and by Jesus Christ; what, are the sweet embraces of a gracious God not worth regard? He falls upon the neck of returning prodigals, and kisseth such. Also are not the best robe, the ring for the hand, and shoes for the feet, and the fatted calf worth seeking?

But now one word to you that are believers.

1. O labour to admire the rich bounty of your Father: what hath he done to feed, refresh, and comfort our souls; what, hath he not withheld his own Son, not spared his only begotten Son, but delivered him up for us all; "how shall he not with him freely give us all things?" Rom. viii. 32.

2. Can you live one day without feeding upon Jesus Christ; do you every day act faith on him, fetch strength and comfort from Jesus Christ; what is it which bears up, and chiefly revives your spirits, and cheers your hearts; is it the fulness of corn and wine, or the enjoyments of earthly things? or is it not rather the light of God's countenance, his love and favour in Jesus Christ, whose loving-kindness is better than life.

3. Is Christ sweet to you, precious to you? he is so to all that believe. "To you that believe he is precious," 1 Pet. ii. 7. If you have tasted that the Lord is good, that the Lord is gracious. And is he not as good to you still, as ever he was? Can you say that his word is, "sweeter than honey or the honey-comb," Psal. xix. 10. And that you esteem it above your necessary food?

4. What spiritual strength do you find in your souls, against sin and temptations, by feeding upon this meat? Do you grow in strength, in zeal, in faith, and in holiness? This (as you will hear) is strengthening food: the more we eat and feed thereon, the greater strength we shall find in the ways of God, and sin will be weakened and mortified in you, if you live upon Jesus Christ; besides, you will arrive every day to more and greater satisfaction: yea, you shall, "be abundantly satisfied with the fat things of God's house," Psal. iii. 8.

5. Can you feed upon spiritual food heartily? have you a good appetite? Many persons eat not, because they hunger not. "The full soul loathes the honey-comb, but to the hungry soul every bitter thing is sweet," Prov. ii. 7. 7. If it do but feed and nourish, or tend to satisfy its hunger. Some are fed with the rod, and find more nourishment by that than others find in the word.

VII

And bring hither the fatted calf, and kill it; and let us eat and be merry.—Luke xv. 23.

Doct. A believing sinner is not only richly clothed, and richly adorned, but also richly fed: he hath the best of God's house to feed, refresh, strengthen, and comfort his soul.

1st. I have showed you why God will feed believing sinners with the best of his house or with a crucified Christ.

2ndly. I shall now proceed to prove, that this meat, this feast, is the best of all God's house. Fat, fatted, or fat things, we have showed, denote the best of every thing. "Bring hither the fatted calf," i. e., the best I have in my house, that which is meat indeed, &c. And that this spiritual banquet contains the best of God's house, will appear if we consider the cause, spring, or fountain from whence all here cometh, or flows to us, or what they are the choice effects of.

1. The Lamb of God (signified by the fatling in my text) and all these *Spiritual food the best of all God's house.* dainties with him are the best.

1. Because the efficient cause, spring, and fountain from whence they come, is God's eternal, infinite, and incomprehensible love and divine good- *Christ not the cause but the effects of the Father's love.* ness. Jesus Christ, my brethren, is not the cause of God's love, but the effects and fruits of his love: though all other spiritual blessings were purchased for us by the Lord Christ, yet he did not purchase the love of God to us, no, God loved his elect from everlasting, and as the effects and fruits thereof, he sent his own Son to die for us. "God so loved the world, that he gave his only begotten Son," &c., John iii. 16. Divine love in God is an eternal property of his holy nature; God is love. Again, saith the same apostle, "In this was manifested the love of God to us, because that God sent his only-begotten Son into the world, that we might live through him," 1 John iv. 9. Through him, or by means of his death, and by feeding upon him. O from what a choice spring or fountain did this divine feast flow? the cause is great, noble, and amazing, and so is the fruit and effects thereof also; nay, and what we eat of here, was not the product or fruit only of eternal love, mercy, and goodness, but the effects of infinite wisdom also.

The soul of man a choice thing. 2. It is the very best of God's house, if we consider the subject fed herewith, viz., the precious and immortal soul of man, so excellent in its nature is the soul, that nothing but God can satisfy it (God only is the Father of our spirits), Heb. xii. 9, who in a peculiar sense is the cause of its original: and pray view it in its noble faculties, and admirable powers; it is the glory of man, and the envy of devils: it is capable to bear the image of God, and divine union and communion with him; it can contemplate the divine perfections of the majesty of him that formed it, and find out the Creator by the creature; it is in its motions as swift as thought, and capable to receive the Holy Spirit, and to be filled with the fulness of God. How are its rich rooms hanged and adorned with rich and costly jewels? "Like as the carved works of the temple, overlaid with pure gold." The price paid to redeem it shows its great worth, dignity, and inestimable value.

This is the subject that is fed at this banquet, yea, and not only fed, but feasted. "Let your soul delight itself in fatness."

3. It is the best of all our Father's house, if we considder the matter of which this feast doth consist. Is not Jesus Christ the best of heaven and earth? Why it is he that we are called to feed upon, the choice and precious Lamb of God: "he that was with God from all eternity, and was God," John i. 1, 2; yea, co-equal, and co-essential with the Father. My brethren, I may say, and not offend, that God could not give us that which is better, he hath nothing to give that excels that which we are here called to feed upon: for when God gives us Christ, he gives us himself; we feed upon God, enjoy God. "O taste and see that the Lord is good," Psal. xxxiv. 8. Is there any thing greater and better than God himself? he cannot give that which is more, or which excels himself. "I will be your God." God is not our God until we are in Jesus Christ, living in him, and feeding upon him.

4. That it is the best of our Father's house, appears if we consider the nature of the *Spiritual meat incorruptible.* food we are here to feed upon.

(1.) It is incorruptible food. As we are "born again of incorruptible seed;" so our souls are fed with incorruptible food, meat that perishes not. How soon will the best of earthly provision, or choice food corrupt? it will soon breed worms and stink; but this corrupteth not, but endureth for ever: and this is one argument our Saviour useth to exhort us from labouring for earthly food; "Labour not for the meat that perishes, but for that meat which endureth unto everlasting life," &c., John vi. 27. It is well worth our observing, that nothing we have, either to eat, or put on, but perishes in using; but the food of our souls is abiding. "The word of God abideth for ever; and Jesus Christ is the same yesterday, to-day, and for ever," 1 Pet. i. 25, Heb. xiii. 8.

It is precious meat. (2.) "It is a precious food, costly food, yea, food of infinite worth and value." It is worth more than ten thousand worlds, though called a fatted calf, a lamb, or kid. Christ may be called a fatted calf, because he is slighted and contemned by carnal men; but commonly he is set forth by a lamb, as a "Lamb without spot or blemish," 1 Pet. i. 19. "And the Lamb of God," John i. 29. How precious is Christ to God the Father, and to the holy angels, and to all true believers? The spouse says, "He is the chiefest among ten thousands," Cant. v. 10; yet his precious body was broken, and his precious blood was shed that we might live, and be fed therewith to eternal life. That which redeemed, and that which feedeth our precious souls, must needs be a precious thing, and of infinite worth; but Christ both redeemed and feedeth our souls, &c.

(3.) It is, as I have often told you, soul-satisfying food. "Wherefore do you labour for that which satisfieth not?" Isa. lv. 1, 2. Riches satisfy not; *It is soul-satisfying.* pleasures of the world satisfy not; and though earthly food may satisfy the body for a short time, yet we quickly hunger again; but so shall not that soul that eats of this meat. "And Jesus said unto them, I am the bread of life: he that cometh to me, shall never hunger; and he that believeth on me shall never thirst," John vi. 35: that is, he shall never want anything that is truly good; he shall abide always satisfied, having an interest in me: or shall never be perplexed with soul-wants and necessity.

5. It is the bread of life, therefore the best of God's house. He that *See the parable of the marriage supper.* feeds on this meat shall live for ever, and not die. O what food is this? Could some people but meet with bread that would preserve them from death, how would they rejoice? But who (that is wise) would live here always? besides, is not the life of the soul better than the life of the body? And is it not better to live in heaven than on earth, and to be delivered from the second death than the first? Natural death to a believer, is but a passage into life. "I am the living bread which came down from heaven; if any man eat of this bread he shall live for ever," John vi. 51. "This is the bread that cometh down from heaven, that a man may eat thereof and never die," Ver. 50.

6. It is the best food, yea, the best of God's house, because of the choice varieties that are contained herein.

(1.) Redemption. Is not this rare food for the soul to feed upon; what is *Redemption belongs to the gospel-banquet.* more sweet, more delicious? What! redeemed from the curse of the law, and out of the hands of offended justice? What! redeemed from sin, from the guilt, the power, and punishment, and pollution thereof? What! redeemed from slavery, from the bondage of Satan, the captivity and dominion of Satan, who had us once in his chains? and what! redeemed from death, and the power of the grave? "O death, where is thy sting? O grave where is thy victory?" 1 Cor. xv. 6. O what a redemption is this, and how good to feed upon!

(2.) Is not reconciliation sweet food to feed upon? What! reconciled to *Reconciliation is part of this feast.* God? Is God become our Friend and our Father? Is he fully pacified towards us, and engaged in a covenant of peace to be our God, and for us, or on our side, and against all our enemies, and to be our God for ever? What can be more refreshing, more strengthening, or more consolating than this?

(3.) Is not a vital union with Jesus Christ a choice thing? He that feeds on this food, is made one with the Father and the Son. "I in them, and *Union with Christ choice meat.* thou in me, and they may be made perfect in one, and that the world may know that thou hast sent me, and hast loved them, as thou hast loved me," John xvii. 23. Perfect in one; that is, in one body, whereof Christ is the Head: the same Spirit that is in the Head, is in every member, and in his whole mystical body. "He that is joined to the Lord is one Spirit," 1 Cor. vi. 17.

(4.) Is not justification a choice thing, to be acquitted and discharged from *Justification tasteth sweet.* sin and wrath, and pronounced righteous and without sin and spot, by imputation of Christ's righteousness, and to have a right and sure title to eternal life, and for ever freed from condemnation? O how good is this food? Rom. viii. 1.

(5.) Is not pardon of sin precious food? to have all sins, past, present, *Pardon of sin is a precious thing.* and to come (as to vindictive wrath) pardoned for ever. "Their sins and iniquities I will remember no more."

(6.) Is not peace with God, peace of conscience, and joy in the Holy *The peace of God good beyond expression.* Ghost, most delicious food? for how excellent must that be, "which passeth all understanding?" Phil. iv. 6.

So doth the peace of God.

(7.) Is not adoption sweet meat to feed upon? "Because ye are sons, God hath sent

Adoption sweet food.

forth the Spirit of his Son into your hearts, crying, Abba, Father," Gal. iv. 6. The people of the Jews were an adopted people. Israel was called God's son, " To them belonged the adoption," Rom. ix. 4. And from God's promise, the blessings of the spiritual adoption were first given to them; but we that were not sons, but strangers and foreigners, feed on the food of special and peculiar adoption, being " Fellow citizens with the saints, and of the household of God," Eph. ii. 19. " Ye have not received (ye Gentiles) the Spirit of bondage again to fear, but ye have received the

It is a marriage feast.

Spirit of adoption, whereby we cry, Abba Father," Rom. viii. 15.

(8.) Is not a marriage with Christ a sweet thing? Is it not inconceivably consolatory? What! married to Jesus Christ, and sit with Jesus Christ at his table, and eat with him, sup with him, and he with us, at this banquet prepared to

See the parable of the Marriage supper opened.

solemnize the marriage between the Lord Christ, and a poor believing sinner?

(9.) Is not communion with Jesus Christ sweet food? To partake of his love, and to have him to communicate to our souls the fullest and sweetest blessings purchased for us by his blood.

We feed on communion with Christ.

(10.) Is not an assurance of eternal life, sweet, fattening, strengthening, and consoling food? Why, all those things, and many more, are comprehended in our feeding on this fatling, or in feeding on the Lord Jesus Christ.

Thirdly, why is feeding upon the Lord Jesus Christ set forth by feeding upon fatlings, or on slain beasts?

1. Because these fatlings, or fatted beasts, whether a lamb, calf, or kid, are counted the best of all the flesh of beasts: and hence also they were offered up in sacrifice under the law; signifying to us, that the Lord Jesus Christ is the very best and choicest food of all spiritual food for our souls. Those beasts that were ordained for sacrifices were to be clean beasts, and the best of every sort: if a lamb, it was to be the best, a lamb without

Christ the best sacrifice.

spot or blemish, no unclean beasts were allowed of: so Jesus Christ the Lamb of God, was the best of all the flock above and below, a Lamb without spot or blemish, without sin, or the least stain of pollution, either original or actual; for otherwise he could not have satisfied for our sins, nor have fed and feasted our souls, as we by faith do feed upon him.

Christ was slain in our stead.

2. Those beasts under the law that were to be offered up for sacrifices, were to be slain for the sins of the people, and in their stead: so Jesus Christ was slain, and offered up a sacrifice unto God for us, (and in our stead) to atone for our sins, " Even the just for the unjust," 1 Pet. iii. 18.

3. The flesh of the paschal lamb was to be eaten by all the people of Israel, being first roasted with fire; every family were to have a lamb, not one quarter, or piece only, but a whole lamb: so Jesus Christ bore the fiery wrath of God for us, and we must feed upon him, and receive a whole Christ; every sinner must receive a whole Christ into a whole heart; Christ must not be divided, nor the heart of a sinner be divided; we must not take Christ to be our Priest only, but our Prince and Sovereign also, not only to appease God's wrath, and to satisfy his justice for us, but as a Prince to rule and reign in and over us: and every faculty of our souls must be wrought upon, and be renewed, the understanding enlightened, will bowed to the will of God, and to obedience to Christ, and our affections changed, and our whole souls united to him, guided and governed by him.

Beasts under the law were not only ordained or appointed for sacrifices, but also for food; the whole priesthood (as one observes) were to feed thereon; but no stranger in

Lev. xxii. 12, 13, 14.

the priest's family was allowed to eat thereof. So Jesus Christ was not only appointed to be a sacrifice for our sins, but to be food also for our souls. " My flesh is meat indeed, and my blood is drink indeed," John vi. 55. All the saints of God are the antitypical priesthood, 1 Pet. ii. 5. But no stranger, no unbeliever ought, nor indeed can he eat of this spiritual food; nor ought such to be admitted to the Lord's supper (a figure of this feast).

Christ precious to such who feed on him.

4. The flesh of these beasts is very delicious, fattening, sweet, and exceeding good, so is Jesus Christ to them that feed spiritually on him; and if you never tasted him so to be, you are not true believers. " To you that believe he is precious," 1 Pet. ii. 7. " O taste and see that the Lord is good!" Psal. xxxiv. 8. How precious is Christ when a sinner can say, this Christ is my Christ? " My beloved is mine and I am his," or with Thomas, " My Lord, and my God." How good is his love, his promises, his word, and his ordinances unto such persons that believe in him!

Spiritual food streng-

5. The flesh of such beasts is not only sweet and pleasant to the taste, but

is also strengthening food, causing growth in those that feed thereon, until <small>thening.</small> we come to perfect manhood, so believers, by feeding on Jesus Christ, receive soul-strength, and spiritually grow thereby; yea, all thrive and grow in grace, every member of the "mystical body, the whole body having nourishment, increaseth with the increase of God," &c., Col. ii. 19. "Desiring the sincere milk of the word, that you may grow thereby," Act. ii. 2.

My brethren, as the branch lives, grows, and bears fruit, by drawing sap from the root; so believers grow by feeding by faith on Jesus Christ.

6. Meat, as it strengthens, comforts, and nourishes the body, so it preserves life. Hence bread (which comprehends all good things) is called "the stay or staff of life," Isa. iii. 1. So Jesus Christ is the stay and staff, or preserver of the life of our souls, he is ca'led our life, because he purchased it, and his Spirit in us preserves that life which is in our souls; we are preserved also in and by the Lord Jesus Christ.

7. The flesh of beasts, bread, nor any other food, profits any, nourishes, feeds, strengthens, or comforts any man or woman, but such only that eat thereof, it is not enough they see it on the table prepared for them, or take of it into their <small>No man hath life but he</small> hands; no, but if they would be nourished by it, they must eat it, or feed <small>that feedeth</small> thereon: so Christ doth not profit, nourish, strengthen, or comfort any soul, <small>on Christ.</small> but he only that feedeth on him; we must feed upon a crucified Christ. "He that eateth me, shall live by me," John vi. 57. "Verily, verily, I say unto you, except ye eat the flesh of the Son of man, and drink his blood, ye have no life in you," ver. 53. No life, either of justification, of sanctification, nor of consolation. What a noise is there of late, of sinners being justified and united to Christ, before faith, nay without faith? Certainly. they do either not believe that which our Lord here saith, or else they understand him not. Whatsoever federal or virtual union there is between Christ and the elect before faith, we speak not of; but evident it is, no man is personally justified, *i. e.*, acquitted, and pronounced a just and righteous person, unless he obtains a vital union with Christ, and eateth his flesh, and drinketh his blood. No unbeliever is either in a state of life, or hath a principle of life in him. "He that hath the Son, hath life, but he that hath not the Son, hath not life," 1 John v. 12.

8. The flesh of beasts tends to satisfy human nature, allay extreme hunger, and also restores lost strength, and lost beauty. The poor prodigal <small>Feeding on Christ is</small> was near starved before he returned home, and no doubt his strength and <small>satisfying,</small> beauty was gone. But now his craving soul was satisfied, and he was eased <small>and restores lost beauty.</small> of those dolorous and gnawing pains, which before he felt when he came to himself. Believers by feeding on Christ are fully satisfied (as you heard) and their strength is restored, and now they are lively, and of an amiable countenance. The souls of sinners are like Pharaoh's "lean kine, ill-favoured." How wofully doth a man look that is almost starved to death? He is under great and dolorous pains and weakness; but believers are fat and flourishing, comely, and beautiful in God's sight, and eased of those gripes of conscience, which they felt when the Spirit first brought them under strong convictions.

Fourthly, Who are they that eat the best, the fattest, and strongest meat of God's house?

1. Such as feed upon Jesus Christ to the full satisfaction of their souls, "They shall be abundantly satisfied." Some eat, but yet seem to want that <small>Who they are that feed</small> inward peace and satisfaction, which strong Christians have arrived to. Many <small>on the fat</small> believers, though their souls are fed and sustained, yet they are not feasted; <small>things of God's house.</small> they eat, but are not filled, as others are.

2. Such may be said "to feed on the fat things of God's house," as have the sensible enjoyment of Christ's love, and live day by day in the light of God's <small>StrongChristians have</small> countenance, being possessed with, or enjoying strong consolation. There is <small>sensible enjoyments of</small> the life of justification and sanctification, and these all God's children partake <small>Christ's love.</small> of; but the life of comfort and consolation many of them do not enjoy, but walk much in darkness, and under doubts and fears, from the weakness of their faith, or the want of more clear light in the nature of true grace, and of the covenant, of the love of God, and of the suretyship of Jesus Christ, &c.

3. Therefore such as have much clear light and knowledge in the mysteries of the gospel, and a strong faith, feed on the fat things of the house <small>They have much light in</small> of God; for according to the manifestations of the glorious gospel, and the <small>Gospel mysteries.</small> measure of faith; so is our feeding upon Jesus Christ. No man will, nor can eat abundantly, or feed upon strong meat, but such who have a strong faith. The woman of Canaan had a great faith, and she eat the very best of this gospel feast. "O woman,

great is thy faith! be it unto thee even as thou wilt," Matt. xv. 28.   The best I have is
for thee.   So also had the woman who had the issue of blood.   "If I can but touch the
Luke   viii.
44—46. hem of his garment, I shall be whole," Mark v. 25, 28.   Some cannot believe,
though they have many promises made unto them; no, they with Thomas must
see and feel, or else they cannot, will not believe; but this woman had no immediate promise
made her by Christ, but she no doubt, exercised faith in some general promises, and saw
what Christ had done for others who had faith in him; by which means she believed with
the greatest degree of faith.   "Who toucheth me? (saith our Saviour) somebody hath
touched me, for I perceive virtue is gone out of me," Luke viii. 46.   A strong faith fetch-
eth mighty virtue from Jesus Christ, and such are fed with the best food.   Babes cannot
Heb. v. 12, 13. eat strong meat, or but little of it, they must be fed with milk.   But strong
men can eat and digest strong meat: so strong Christians feed upon the strongest, the fattest,
and best food of God's house; they discern more clearly the mysteries of Christ, and of
the gospel; whereas weak Christians must live upon slenderer diet, or on such doctrine that
is more plain and easy to be understood.   "Every one that useth milk is unskilful in the
word of righteousness, for he is a babe.   But strong meat belongeth to them that are of
age, those, who by reason of use have their senses exercised, to discern both good and evil,"
Heb. v. 13, 14.

A strong be-
liever lives
by   faith
alone. 4.   Such who always feed upon Jesus Christ alone, or who eat nothing of
their own, being carried wholly out of themselves to feed upon Jesus Christ
living by faith only.   "Now the just shall live by faith," Heb. x. 38.   But
many weak believers rather live by sense than by faith.   If sin be weakened
in them, and they feel a greater conformity in their souls to God, and are in a lively frame,
then they can live and have some hope and inward comfort; but this is rather to live by
sense, than to live by faith in Jesus Christ.   It is not (saith a strong believer) because grace
lives in me; but because Christ lives (who is my life) that I shall live.   "Because I live,
ye shall live also," John xiv. 19.

5.   They eat the fat, &c., that live by faith upon that fulness which is in Christ.

Such live on
the fulnes of
Christ's wis-
dom. (1.)   Upon that fulness of wisdom that is in Christ; Jesus Christ, saith that
soul, knows what is best for me: though what I meet with is hard to the flesh,
yet he is wise; I need these sharp stripes, these sore trials and afflictions; I
am put into Christ's hand to dispose of me as he sees good, and here I rest
"When he hath tried me, I shall come forth as gold," Job xxiii. 10.   It is not because
God is angry with me, or hateth me, but because he loves me, he doth afflict me.   "As
many as I love I rebuke and chasten," Rev. iii. 19.

On the ful-
ness of
Christ's
strength. (2.)   They that live on the fulness of that righteousness and strength which
is in Christ; though I am weak, yet Christ is strong, and his strength is mine,
it is engaged for me.   "My flesh and my heart faileth, but God is the strength
of my heart, and my portion for ever," Psal. lxxiii. 26.   I have the sense of much sin
and filth in me, but Christ hath a fulness of righteousness in him to justify me, and a
fulness of power to strengthen me; and not only to pardon my sins, but to subdue and
mortify them also.   "In the Lord shall one say, I have righteousness and strength," Isa.
xlv. 24.   I have many spots and blemishes, but I am in him without spot or blemish in
the sight of God.   "Ye are complete in him, who is the head of principalities and powers,"
Col. ii. 10.

Believers
live upon
the fulness
of that grace
that is in
Christ. (3.)   They that live upon that fulness of grace which is in Christ.   O, saith
a strong Christian, my vessel is almost empty, but the fountain is full; "with
thee is the fountain of life."   And from that fountain I shall be replenished
and supplied continually.   "Thou therefore, my son, be strong in the grace
that is in Christ Jesus," 2 Tim. ii. 1.   Do not rely upon that grace that is in
thee, for that may be weak and decay; but fetch all thy support, strength, and comfort
from that grace that is in Jesus Christ.   "When I am weak, then I am strong."   When
weakest in myself, I am strongest in Christ.   "My grace is sufficient for thee, for my
strength is made perfect in thy weakness," 2 Cor. xii. 9.   Christ is full of grace, who is
the head of influence to his whole mystical body.   "And of his fulness all we receive, and
grace for grace," John i. 14, 16.   It was this which caused St. Paul to glory.   What
though a child hath but little bread, a little meat, or but a little money? he matters not.
O, saith he, my father has enough, he is a rich man, a noble man, he hath abundance of all
riches, and of all good things, and I shall not want, because he is my father.   Sirs, should
a multitude of thieves and murderers break into a house, the little children might be afraid,
because they are not able to withstand them; but if they knew their Father could destroy

ten thousand of them with a blast of his mouth, they would not be at all terrified. Why some of God's children are certain of this, they know God can in a moment destroy all their enemies, though their inherent grace and strength is nothing. But now to exercise faith in that strength and grace which is in Christ, is to be strong in the Lord. "Therefore will I rather glory glory in mine infirmities, that the power of Christ may rest upon me," 2 Cor. xii. 9.

(4.) They that live upon the fulness of that love that is in Christ: as he is full of grace, so his love is infinite, unchangeable, and everlasting, nay, it "passeth all understanding;" they know nothing can separate them from the love of Christ," Rom. viii. 35. And thus they that live by faith feed upon the fulness of Christ, and thereby eat the best things, the fat things of God's house. *They live upon the fulness of that love that is in Christ.*

6. I might add, they that live upon the "faithfulness of Christ." I am tempted (saith a poor saint) to decline my profession, or to grow cool in my zeal, nay, to murmur against God, and to think that Christ loves me not; his hand is so heavy upon me, I meet with cross winds, blustering storms that bear my ship almost under water; the gates of hell seem to open themselves against my soul, and the powers of darkness are raised up to destroy me. But Christ is on my side, he is for me, and he hath promised to help me, and he also is faithful. "Jesus Christ, the same yesterday, to-day, and for ever," Heb. xiii. 8. He is the faithful and true Witness. "No temptation hath overtaken you but such as are common to men; and God is faithful, who will not suffer you to be tempted above what you are able, and will with the temptation make way for your escape, that you may be able to bear it," 1 Cor. x. 13. I will not only trust in Christ for strength and support, but will look to him, and expect it from him, because he is faithful; and he hath said, "Fear not, I am with thee, be not dismayed; I am thy God, I will help thee, yea, I will uphold thee, yea, I will strengthen thee," Isa. xli. 10. "I will never leave thee, nor forsake thee," Heb. xiii. 5. This made Jonas when he was in the whale's belly, to say, "Yet will I look again towards thy holy temple," Jonah ii. 4.

7. Such who see suitable promises for every condition, and can rely, and live upon Christ in the promises, let their estate be what it will. "Man lives not by bread only, but by every word that proceedeth out of the mouth of God," Matt. iv. 4. And though they are in darkness, yet they can "stay themselves upon their God," Isa. l. 10. *They live on the promises.*

8. They eat the fat of God's house, who enjoy not only the ordinances, but God with them, and in them. Some are contented with a bare duty, and a bare ordinance, but that is but like dry bread. What is any ordinance if we meet not God with it? But if these believers meet not with God at one time, they resolve to make the more preparation to meet him at another, and ask their souls what the matter may be, why they met not with God at such or such a time; they will not neglect a duty because they met not with God as in times past; they do not find fault with the minister, nor with the ordinance, but with themselves; I was (saith such a person) in a dead and lifeless frame, the cause why I did not profit nor meet with comfort, was in myself. *They live on God in ordinances.*

9. Such who are strong to bear burdens, and can bear up though trodden upon, and suffer contempt and reproach from their brethren, or from the world. These things are signs that such feed high, and are strong in the Lord; no discouragements discourage them, their love to Christ, and to his truth, and ways, is not cooled at all by any of these things; though they have not the love, the esteem, or praise of men, they care not, if they have the love and approbation of God, of which they have comfortable grounds, and see no cause to doubt of it.

10. Such who get power over their inward corruptions, and by degrees find sin weakened in them, and that sin which doth most easily beset them, loses its strength, and grace outgrows the weeds of corruption, yea, and grows the more by means of the cold blasts of temptations and afflictions; so that they are ready to suffer for Christ, having got the world under their feet, and dwell above in sweet communion with God and Jesus Christ. *They get power over their corruptions.*

11. Such who always come to hear the word with a craving appetite, or have a good stomach, these eat the fat of this gospel-feast. Such who are sickly or distempered persons cannot eat strong meat, nor hardly anything will go down with them; so such who have soul-diseases, or are spiritually distempered, can find no appetite to receive the word, it is not sweet to them: and hence this sort are found oftentimes to quarrel with sound doctrine, and dislike and grow sick of their minister, and are better pleased with kick-shaws, I mean with airy and empty *Some saints have always a good appetite to spiritual food.*

notions. Alas, many in these days are certainly surfeited with that great plenty God hath graciously afforded us, and account the heavenly manna but light bread; and so their full stomachs loathe the honey-comb.

APPLICATION

1. From hence we may infer, that God is not like unto sorry man, he performeth to poor sinners all that he hath promised to them.   Men promise, but are often slow in performing, or not so large as in their promises, but thus God doth not.   " Let the wicked forsake his ways, and the unrighteous man his thoughts, and let him return unto the Lord, and he will have mercy upon him ; and unto our God, and he will abundantly pardon," &c., Isa. lv. 7.   God doth not only pardon the sinner, but exceeds in his mercy and good-ness all those thoughts the sinner could have.   What could he do more in a way of mercy God beyond   and love than is here expressed by the Father to the returning prodigal?
man in per-   2. By this example of the Holy God, parents should learn to pass by great
forming of
his prom ses.   sins in their rebellious children, when they return to them, and humble them-selves, and not to be of an irreconcilable spirit towards a prodigal child, who hath spent all on harlots, and by a wicked course of life ; nay, and not forgive him only, but be kind and wonderfully bountiful to him, so as to overcome him with their love and goodness.
Directions to   3. This may inform us, that the pardoning grace of God, and his rich mercy
parents.   and bounty to returning sinners is wonderful, he forgives and upbraideth not.
Information.   4. This may serve to encourage sinners to return to God, though they have been never so vile and abominably wicked.   See, you sinners, what entertainment you shall have, an   how nobly you shall be treated, and be received, if you come unto God by Jesus Christ ; what can you desire more ?   What, shall you have the very best that God hath ? Will he deny you no good thing ?   Certainly some of you that hear me this day will resolve to return to this gracious God.   Can you forbear one moment ?   O let nothing hinder you ; let not Satan persuade you, God will not forgive your sins ; see how he pardoned and re-
Encourage-   ceived this great sinner.
ment.   5. This may also put us all upon the work of self-examination.   Have we tasted how good God is ; have we ever been thus fed and feasted with the best of our Fa-ther's house ; if not, we may conclude that our faith is weak, or that we are but babes in Christ, or do not live by faith, but rather by sense.   Observe those ten particulars I have
Trial.   laid down, and try yourselves by them.

6. Let none henceforth harbour hard thoughts of God, as if he gives grudgingly or spa-ringly unto us, because he gives us no more of the riches of this world.   What, would you have the husks, which is the swine's food ?   God gives us the children's bread, that which is far better than what the wicked of the world have ; and are we not contented ?   Is not God better than the creature ?   Doth he give us himself, and are we not satisfied ?

VIII

And let us eat and be merry.—Luke xv. 23.

" LET us eat and be merry."   This certainly denotes that sweet fellowship and communion every believer hath with God, when he closeth with him in Jesus Christ, or that sweet joy and comfort when he first comes home, or is converted ; he then receives most choice and sensible communion with God and Jesus Christ.   The Father's love is manifested to him, and the love of the Son is manifested to him ; for then he feeds plentifully upon all the blessings of a crucified Saviour.

My brethren, there are three degrees or gradual steps of the happiness of believers.
Three gra-   1. Union with God and Jesus Christ.   The prodigal was now brought into
dual steps of   a state of union with the Father and the Son by the Holy Spirit : here our
the saints
happiness.   happiness begins, this is the first step or spring of it,
                2. Communion.   This is the next, "Truly our fellowship is with the Fa-ther, and with his Son Jesus Christ," 1 John i. 3.
                3. Full and perfect fruition of God for ever : this completes our eternal happiness.
The two first we partake of here, while we are in this world ; the last we shall receive

in the world to come. Union is the spring or way of our happiness. Communion is a sensible taste thereof; and fruition is the fulness and perfection of it.

" Let us eat and be merry." By eating, communion is often set forth in God's word. " If any man hear my voice, and open the door, I will come in unto him, and will sup with him, and he with me," Rev. iii. 20. We will eat together, rejoice, and be merry, *i. e.*, he shall have sweet communion with me, and I with him. The word communion is by some rendered fellowship, by others converse, They are convertible terms, or words of the same import.

Doct. Returning sinners, · or true believers, have communion with the Father and the Son. Let us eat and rejoice together; that is, the sinner with the Father and the Son, and the Father and the Son with him; they have mutual communion one with another.

I. I shall show you what is necessary, as previous to this communion.

II. Prove that there is such communion, and also show wherein it doth consist.

III. Show you the nature of it.

IV. Also show you what the effects thereof are upon the believers heart and life.

V. Apply it.

I. As to what is necessary, as previous to this eating, or gracious communion.

1. No wicked man can have communion with God and Jesus Christ. No wicked " Shall the throne of iniquity have fellowship with thee ?" Psal. xciv. 20. man can have fellowThat is, such that delight in sin and wickedness, no, this cannot be. " What ship with fellowship hath righteousness with unrighteousness? and what communion God. hath light with darkness? Or what concord hath Christ with Belial ?" 2 Cor. vi. 15, 16.

(1.) Can there be communion and sweet fellowship, where there is enmity one against the other ?

(2.) Can that person have communion with God, that hath not the nature of God, or a likeness of God in him ? no, human creatures may as soon have fellowship with filthy brutes, or with swine, as unholy sinners can have communion with God.

2. No person can have communion with God, until he hath union with Union nehim. " Can two walk together, except they are agreed ?" Amos iii. 3. munion. Utter enemies to each other, can have no fellowship together. " The carnal mind is enmity against God," Rom. viii. 7. And God is an enemy to all the workers of iniquity ; his face is set against them, and his wrath is kindled and ready to seize them. Therefore there must be a mutual or reciprocal reconciliation to one another. First, God in Christ is reconciled to his elect, the atonement is made ; and also he is actually reconciled to the person of this or that man or woman that believeth in Jesus Christ. Whilst the prodigal abode in his swinish nature, he was not actually reconciled to his Father ; but now they are united in heart, in love and affections, and so can eat together, or have fellowship one with another.

3. None, it appears from hence, can have fellowship with God that are Regeneranot renewed or born again, or regenerated. The prodigal's heart is now tion neceschanged, he hath got a new nature, and can now taste and relish spiritual munion with things ; sin now is become bitter to him, yea, loathsome and abominable, and God. God is become the object of his love and delight ; he can tell you now that God is good, that root of bitterness, that averseness that was in him unto God and spiritual things, is gone and now he loves as God loves, and hates as God hates ; before he was alienated from the life of God, and also favoured the things of the flesh.

4. None can have communion with God, or with Jesus Christ, until they Marriage have espoused him, or are married to him. Marriage is antecedent to conju- with Christ necessary to gal fellowship and communion. communion

5. Saving knowledge of God in Christ is necessary to this fellowship. The with God. choicest fellowship flows from intimate knowledge and acquaintance persons have of one another ; there may be a remote knowledge where there is no Knowledge of God necommunion ; but to the nearest and choicest communion there is a real and cessary to choice acquaintance. " Acquaint now thyself with him, and be at peace, and this fellowthereby good shall come unto thee," Job. xxii. 21, that is, all true good, that ship. which is the sweetest, even communion with God and his Son Jesus Christ. My brethren, the image of God doth in part consist in knowledge. " And have put on the new man, which is renewed in knowledge, after the image of him that created him," Col. iii. 10.

6. A man must actually be brought into the bonds of the covenant, be- A man must be in the fore he can have communion with God. covenant

Can a sinner eat and be merry, or have fellowship with God, whilst he re- before he mains under the covenant of works, or under the law, or the curse of the law ? hath com-

munion with God. no, evangelical communion is not bottomed upon the legal covenant ; all unbelievers are in the first Adam ; " And as many as are of the law, are under the curse," Gal. iii. 10.   Therefore no unbeliever can eat with God and Jesus Christ, or be merry with them.   Can a condemned malefactor be merry ? or will the king admit him to eat at his table ?   Sirs, a man must have faith, he must believe and see his pardon, or have ground to believe he is freed from the sentence of condemnation, before he can rejoice and have fellowship with God.   No man is actually in the covenant of grace that believes not, nay, he that believes not in Christ, " The wrath of God abides upon him," John. iii. 36.

There must be sincere love to God in him that has communion with God. 7. No man can have communion with God, without sincere love to God. Communion flows from that dear love and affection one person hath to another ; and as love increaseth, fellowship increaseth; and as love decays, communion or fellowship decays or grows cold, also, or it is not so sweet and desirable.   O how was the heart, the love, and affections of the Father drawn out towards his Son, and the heart, love, and affections of the Son set upon his dear Father ? " The Father fell upon his neck and kissed him," and put the best robe upon him, and richly adorned him, and now he eats, drinks, and is merry with him ; now they are united in love, and so have communion together.

8. It is necessary also that a believer knows the nature of that union from whence this communion flows ; there is, as I once told you, a six-fold union.

A six-fold union. (1.)   There is a natural union, that is, between the tree and the branches from whence the tree communicates its sap to the branches ; also between the head and the body, and the members thereof, as likewise between the soul and body, and the food we eat.

(2.)   There is a moral union, which is between one man and another ; they cleave together in cordial love and affections, as Jonathan, who loved David as his own soul.

(3.)   There is a conjugal union, this is that union that is between a man and his wife.

(4.)   There is a political union, which is between a king and his subjects.

(5.)   There is an hypostatical union, which is between the divine person of the Son of God and his human nature.

(6.)   There is a mystical and spiritual union, and this is that union which is between Christ and his church, and every believer ; and it is from hence our spiritual communion flows, though it is set forth by a natural and moral union, yet it is nearer and more intimate, as I shall show you by and by.

II.   I proceed to prove, there is such a fellowship or communion betwixt God and a believing sinner, and shall show wherein it doth consist.

There is a mystical union betwixt Christ and believers. Charnock. 1. They are not only united in love and affections, and in conjugal bonds, but are made one spirit with Christ.   " He that is joined to the Lord is one spirit," 1 Cor. vi. 17.   Not made one spirit essentially, but mystically ; it is as if there was but one soul in two bodies ; the same spirit that is in the head without measure, is in every member in some measure.   " That they all may be one, as thou Father art in me, and I in thee, that they may be one in us," John xvii. 21.

The nature of communion between them. Now where there is such a near union, there must needs be a most sweet communion.   My brethren, true fellowship consisteth in community or communion.   Now there is a fourfold community between Christ and believers.

1. Of enjoyment of each other. 2. A community of affections. 3. Of interest. 4. Of privileges.

1.   They enjoy each other.   Christ is theirs, and they are his.   " I will be their God, and they shall be my people."   " My beloved is mine, and I am his."   God gives himself and all he hath to believers, and they give themselves to him ; also Christ gives himself and all he hath to us, and we give ourselves to him.

(1.)   Christ gives his person to espouse us, and so raises our glory. (2.)   His treasure and fulness to enrich us. (3.)   His righteousness to clothe us. (4.)   His power to uphold and defend us. (5.)   His wisdom to direct us. (6.)   His Spirit to quicken, to renew, to enlighten, and to lead us. (8.)   His love to delight and console us, and his glory to crown us. (9.)   His angels to minister to us.

And we give Christ our hearts. "My Son, give me thy heart," Prov. xxiii. 26.   We give him ourselves, and all we are.   " They gave themselves unto the Lord."   We give our whole souls, strength, affections, even all our faculties and powers, and members of our bodies, our judgments to judge and choose him, our understandings to know him, our wills to close with and obey him, our affections to desire, love, and cleave to him, our thoughts to contemplate on, him, our consciences to be kept awake, and stir us up to serve and live to him, our tongues to speak for him, pray to him, and to praise him, our eyes to look up to him, and to be employed for him, our hands to minister to him in his ministers and poor saints, our feet to travel to his sanctuary, and visit his poor members, &c. Sirs, Christ took our nature on him, " And so he is bone of our bone, and flesh of our flesh," Eph. v. 30. And he gives us his Spirit, his likeness, " And so we partake of the divine nature," &c. 2 Pet. i. 4. Christ's riches is ours, and our poverty was his. " He became poor, that we through his poverty might be made rich," 2 Cor. viii. 9. Christ's righte-ousness is ours and our sin was his. " He was made sin for us, who knew no sin, that we might be made the righteousness of God in him," 2 Cor. v. 21. His blessedness is ours, and our curse fell upon him, " He was made a curse for us, that the blessing of Abraham might come upon the Gentiles through Jesus Christ," Gal. iii. 13. He became a servant, that we might become sons; he bore our cross, that we might wear his crown; he took our shame, that we might have his glory. " The glory thou gave me I have given them," John xvii. 22. He was abused, that we might be exalted; he was crowned with thorns, that we might be crowned with eternal life. Thus there is a community of persons, and of what each other have.

2. There is a community of love and affections. Though this was signified before, yet let me speak to it more particularly because communion consisteth in this.

(1.) God and Christ love believers, and they love God and Christ; they have a mutual love to each other, signified by their eating or supping together. " Thou hast loved them as thou hast loved me. I will love him, and the Father will love him; and we will come unto him, and make our abode with him," John xiv. 23. " Lord thou knowest all things, thou knowest I love thee," John xxi. 17

(2.) Their love runs all in one channel, and it is fixed upon the same objects: what God loves, Christ loves, that believers love also: and what God hates, Christ hates, that believers hate also.

(3.) The nature or quality of their love is the same: Christ loves believers with a strong, a great, a sincere, a constant, a single, or simple love, with a sympathizing love, with a love of complacency, with an unchangeable, and an everlasting love. So the love of every believer to God and Christ is great: it is a superlative love, a sincere, a single, a simple, a constant, a cordial love, and full of delight, and abiding: such as is the cause, such is the effect. " We love him, because he first loved us;" our love is but the fruit and reflection of his love on our souls.

(4.) Christ loves a believer in every state, when poor as well as when rich, in dishon-our as well as in honour, on a dunghill as well as on a throne: when old, as well as young, in a prison, as well as in a palace: so believers love Christ in all states and changes he passed through, when in the manger, when tempted, when betrayed, when spit upon, when scourged, and when hanged on the cross, as well as now he is glorified at the Father's right-hand in heaven.

(5.) Christ loves not the souls of believers only, but their bodies also: yea, and he loves their graces, and all the holy and spiritual duties and services they perform to his glory: so believers love the person of Christ, the offices of Christ, the word of Christ; they love him as he is a Priest, as he is a King, as he is a Prophet, and whatsoever he is in him-self, hath done, is doing, or is made to them; they love his image, his people, his church, his ministers, his poor, his ordinances, his worship, his promises, his interest, and his name, and his kingdom, and long for it.

(1.) He calls them his friends. " Henceforth I call you not servants, but friends: for the servant knows not what his master doeth; but all things I have heard of my Father, I have made known them to you," John xv. 15. And they call him their friend. " This is my beloved, and this is my friend, O ye daughters of Jerusalem," Cant. i. 16.

(2.) They walk together: " Enoch walked with God three hundred years," &c. " I will walk in them," &c.

(3.) They sit together in heavenly places.

(4.) They eat together, as in my text; they sup together, Rev. iii 20, " I will come into him, and will sup with him, and he with me." They feed on his merits, and he feeds upon their duties, and on their graces. " I have eaten my honey with my honey-comb, I have drunk my wine with my milk," Cant. vi. 1. Their graces refresh and delight his soul. " Thou hast ravished my heart, my sister, my spouse; thou hast ravished my heart with one of thine eyes, with the chain of thy neck," Cant. iv. 9.

(5.) They visit each other; Christ visits them in ways of mercy, and they visit him in way of duty.

(6.) Christ loves to hear their voice. " O my Dove, that are in the clefts of the rock let me hear thy voice, let me see thy face ; for sweet is thy voice, and thy countenance is comely," Cant. ii. 14. And they love to hear his voice. " It is the voice of my beloved that knocketh." " My sheep know my voice, and they follow me," &c., John x. 27, that is, they love, approve, and delight to hear my voice.

(7.) Also precious love-tokens pass mutually to each other ; he kisses them " with the kisses of his mouth," Cant. i. 1, which is a token of his love and affection ; and they kiss the Son as a token of their love and subjection. " The Father fell upon his neck, and kissed him."

(8.) They have mutual desires after each other. " So shall the king desire thy beauty," Psal. xlv. 11. And what saith a believer ? " with my soul have I desired thee in the night," Isaiah xxvi. 9.

3. There is a community of interest between Christ and believers.

(1.) They have one and the same design to manage and carry on in the world ; and what is that, but the glory of God, and the good of his church, and of the souls of men ? (1.) Christ's grand design is to glorify his Father, and to greaten his own name ; and this is the main design and endeavour of believers, i. e., to exalt Jesus Christ. " Christ (saith holy Paul) shall be magnified in my body, whether it be by life or death," Phil. i. 20.

(2.) Christ's design is to enlarge his own kingdom in the world, or the increase of his church ; and this is the design and end of believers ; they pray for his kingdom : " Thy kingdom come."—" Do good in thy good pleasure to Sion ; build thou the walls of Jerusalem," Psal. li. 18. Nay, the good of the church they prefer above all things on earth. If, like to David, " I forget thee, O Jerusalem, let my right-hand forget her cunning. If I do not remember thee, let my tongue cleave to the roof of my mouth ; if I prefer not Jerusalem above my chief joy," Psal. cxxxvii. 5, 6. Do some professors do *Reproof to the professors of this age.* this? no certainly. Why it is the property and duty of all believers thus to do ; but do they do this, that hardly ever think of Sion ? do they do this, that by their pride and covetous practices expose her to reproach ? Do they do this, who suffer her to languish and decay, rather than they will spare their strength or treasure to support her ? what hinders the increase of the church or spreading of the gospel ? Is it not self-interest ? Some will lay up hundreds, nay thousands for themselves and children, who grudge a few shillings to uphold the walls of Jerusalem, or to encourage poor ministers at home, or to send them abroad. Some so little regard the interest of Christ, his church and ministry, that were it not for a few faithful persons, his whole interest might fall to the ground for all them. Sad times ! They drive a trade for themselves, and regard not Christ nor his church ; they cannot say with David, " the zeal of thine house hath eaten me up," Psal. cxix. 139. Though he spoke it in the person of Christ, yet it was true no doubt in himself.

Christ's design is the good and comfort of his church. (3.) Christ's design is the good, the comfort and edification of his people, that they may abound in grace and holiness, and in all the fruits of the Spirit : and this is the design of all sincere believers, and thus their interest is one and the same, both strive to pull down Satan's kingdom, and to destroy sin and all sinful practices, with heresies and errors, traditions of men, superstition idolatry, popery, &c. Christ's work is to establish truth, and cause that to flourish : the interest of the husband is the interest of the wife ; that which is the father's true interest should be the child's labour to promote.

2ndly. They also seek and choose the same means, in order to the carrying this interest on ; that way Christ makes use of to promote his own glory, and his churches good, they approve of, and consent to.

(1.) If it be by weak means, they will support and continue it as much as they can, and not say, Christ is able to preserve his own truth, and good of his church, by his own hand another way.

(2.) If it be by persecution, they consent ; if by the rod, they approve of it ; if by liberty, peace, and prosperity, they submit, and are pleased ; or if by ways that may seem hazardous as to their outward state, they complain not, nor go out of God's way ; they are not like Jeroboam, rather than to hazard the loss of his kingdom, set up golden calves at Dan and Bethel.

3rdly. As they mutually agree in the means, so also in the instruments that Christ chooses to promote and carry his interest on, if noble and learned ones, every true Christian is pleased ; but if God lays aside such, chooses few of that sort, but rather the unlearned, or base and contemptible persons to preach his gospel and manage his cause, they are as well satisfied, and will not expose them to the scorn of the world, because they are not endowed with the knowledge of the tongues, or human literature.

4thly. They have also the same friends and the same enemies; he is no friend to Christ, that is an enemy to his people; nor is he a believer's friend that is Christ's enemy. Those that hate thee, and rise up against thee, I hate, saith David. My brethren, why do some men hate his present majesty, our gracious king? is it not because he is a friend to and a favourer of God's people, and why do the godly love him; but because God hath raised him up to favour his righteous cause, and to be a scourge to his enemies? *Christ and believers have the same friends and the same enemies.*

Their interest and end, means and persons (as one observes) are so one and the same, that what is done, said to be done to one, is done to the other. They that despise you, saith our Lord, despise me; and they that receive you, receive me. And they also that persecute the saints, persecute Christ: "Saul, Saul, why persecutest thou me?" Acts viii. 4. And hence the sufferings of the saints are said to be the sufferings of Christ. "They that touch you, touch the apple of mine eye," Zech. ii. 8. Moreover, they that feed, clothe, and visit the poor saints, feed, clothe, and visit Jesus Christ, Matt. xxv. 35. This their interest isone.

4. There is between them communion of privileges also, as is noted by divers worthy men. Christ is called God's child, he is called the holy Child Jesus: so the saints are called the children of God. Christ is the Son of God, and the saints are the sons and daughters of God also: Christ is called God's servant; also the heir of all things, Heb. i. i. 2. And the saints are called the heirs of all things, Rev. ii. 17. Or joint heirs with him. Rom. viii. 17. Christ is God's elect, and they are God's elect in him. Christ was from above, and heavenly, and the saints are said to be born from above, to be heavenly also. Christ is a King and Priest, and the saints are called Kings and Priests also, Rev. v. 10. Christ a Conqueror, so the saints are said to be conquerors. Christ is called a Pearl, and the saints are called jewels: Christ shall judge the world, and the saints shall judge the world with him; they sit with him on his throne; he hath a crown, and they shall be crowned also. Thus they have communion in like privileges, but Jesus Christ hath infinitely the pre-eminence above them. *A communion of, privileges between Christ and believers. See Durham.*

"And let us eat and be merry." Why may not this eating comprehend, or partly refer to the Lord's Supper, every believer that is brought into God's house hath communion with him in that holy ordinance; and of all ordinances they have the sweetest fellowship with God and Christ in this: prayer is an act of homage, praise an act of gratitude; but this is the love-feast, or the chief consolatory dainties of our Father's house. O of what a Lamb do we feed on at this table?

But so much as to the second thing.

III. I shall open the nature of this fellowship and communion between God and Christ, and a believing sinner at this merry and joyful meeting. *It is a most honourable communion.*

1. It is a most honourable and sublime fellowship. What! sit with the Father at his table, the glorious King of heaven and earth, eat, drink, and rejoice with him. What honour like this! what, eat with the King and with the King's Son! and be embraced in their arms, and have the kisses of their lips! What, walk with the King, converse with the King, behold the King in his galleries, nay, be espoused by him, and be led into his chambers, "and into his banqueting-house, and have his left hand under our head and his right hand to embrace us!" Cant. i. 4, 5. ii. 6. Stand and admire!

2. It is a God-glorifying communion. For, my brethren, he manifesteth his glory to us hereby, in his glorious attributes. (1.) His wisdom in finding out the way to raise us to this high fellowship and amazing grandeur, (2.) His power in removing all those impediments that were in the way of it. (3.) His infinite love and goodness. (4.) His justice, in that we are not raised to this happiness, without full satisfaction made to the justice and law of God. (5.) Also, how is mercy, and rich bounty, and free-grace, magnified in admitting of a poor returning prodigal, to such a God glorifying banquet! and then believers glorify God by letting him have their hearts, their whole souls, and their superlative love and affections. *It is a God-glorifying communion*

We by letting out our chiefest affections to God, glorify his beauty, amiableness, and divine goodness.

By a reverential fear of God, we glorify his justice.

By faith and a holy dependence upon him, we glorify his power, all-sufficiency, and faithfulness.

By our humility we glorify him in his majesty and greatness.

By our patience we glorify his wisdom and sovereignty ; and now in the exercise of all these graces of the Spirit, we have communion with the Father and the Son.

It is the highest communion.   3. It is the highest fellowship we are capable of, while we are in this world ; we can have communion with no persons of a higher rank, dignity, or quality. What is it to have fellowship with an earthly king, to eat with him ? &c. To this eating also the greatest love that ever was known was the spring and cause of it, the greatest price also was paid to procure it. Moreover, it is a resemblance of heaven, and prepares us for the fruition of God.

It is soul-profitable.   4. It is a soul-profitable and pleasurable communion. It doth not only tend to the glory of God, but also unto our good ; such that sit under Christ's shadow, find sweet delight ; every step of this fellowship is a paradise. O how sweet are those lips that drop sweet-smelling myrrh ! What a fragrant scent doth he diffuse into our souls whilst he lies in our bosom all night ! they that taste and eat with Christ, or have communion with the Father and the Son, will soon find the sweetest of earthly enjoyments bitter and burdensome ; and be sure those that value not, prize not this fellowship, never tasted how good God is ; the consolations of God are small with them, because they know not what they are, and because earthly comforts are overvalued by them. Until sin be bitter, and earthly enjoyments distasteful, Christ will never be sweet and precious to you ; all is theirs who have Christ. O then let us eat and be merry ! Man's chiefest happiness is in his enjoyment, and feeding on the chiefest good. "Thou hast put gladness into my heart, more than when corn and wine increased," Psal. iv. 7.

It is a free communion.   5. It is a free communion, all is the effects of free grace, sovereign grace. "Lord, how is it that thou wilt manifest thyself unto us, and not unto the world ?" It cannot be purchased ; it is granted to whom the Father pleaseth, and the Son pleaseth ; God gives himself, and Christ gives himself to us freely. "I will heal their backsliding, I will love them freely, for mine anger is turned away from them," Hos. xiv. 4. Freely without any desert, and without bounds or measure. God loves us because he will love us, and he vouchsafes us communion with himself, because he will do it ; it is to magnify his love, and the riches of his free and undeserved grace, according to his own eternal pleasure and purpose in Christ Jesus.

It is an increasing communion.   6. It is an increasing and growing communion. "The path of the just is as a shining light, that shines more and more to a perfect day," Prov. iv. 18. And we grow in faith and love, our communion is more and more ; the more light and knowledge of God and Jesus Christ we have, the more sweet fellowship, joy, and comfort our souls do possess ; the more we grow in likeness to Christ, the more communion we have with him. "They shall go from strength to strength in Zion," Psal. lxxxiv. 7. And from faith to faith, nay, from glory to glory, from a lesser to a greater degree of glory. Grace shall prevail, increase, and be victorious, and therefore this fellowship and communion shall increase and be more sweet every day to such that walk close with God, and daily visit him, and wait upon him in his holy ordinances. If we follow on to know the Lord, we shall know him, i. e., know how good he is, and enjoy his love and favour.

7. It is a soul-strengthening, and a soul-confirming communion, it is feeding upon the fat things of God's house, food that hath strong nourishment in it. It is a vain thing for sinners to question the truth and reality of these things, and to persuade a child of God he is mistaken ; no, no, saith he, I have experienced, and found what I say, I know what I speak, I have tasted how good God is, and the love of God and Christ is. You may as soon persuade me when I have newly drunk a draught of excellent wine, that it was water and not wine, as you can make me think I am mistaken in what I have seen, felt, and tasted, or my soul hath enjoyed of God. O how am I strengthened and confirmed hereby in the belief of this glorious Deity, and in the belief of the blessed Jesus, and in the belief of our true Christianity ! "The joy of the Lord is my strength." The divine presence, his love and favour establisheth my soul in his ways and ordinances, which some contemn and despise. "What we have seen with our eyes, which we have looked upon, and our hands have handled of the Word of life," 1 John i. 1. "For the life was manifested, and we have seen it," ver. 2. As Christ was manifested in the flesh, so he is manifested to the souls of his people. "And that which we have seen and heard, declare we unto you, that ye also may have fellowship with us ; and truly our fellowship is with the Father, and with his Son Jesus Christ," ver. 3. Sirs, if you do arrive to this communion, you will say, O it is sweet, it is satisfying, it is strengthening, and of a soul-confirming nature. But more of this under the next head.

IV. Let us consider the effects of this communion on the soul.

1. This communion you hear is of a soul-strengthening nature; and so it It hath reviving effects. follows from thence, it revives and quickens the soul. "I will be a dew unto Israel:" and what then? "He shall grow as the lily, and cast forth his root as Lebanon; his branches shall spread, and his beauty shall be as the olive-tree," &c., Hos. xiv. 5. This communion is like a dew on tender herbs, it refreshes, quickens, and revives our souls. "They shall revive as the corn, and grow as the vine," ver. 7. The approaches of Christ to us are like the approaches of the sun in the spring on the earth, herbs, and flowers.

It is a soul-satisfying communion. 2. It is a soul-satisfying communion: to eat with God, and sup with him, gives full content and satisfaction to the soul; the soul delighteth itself in fatness. "They shall be abundantly satisfied with the fat things of thy house," Psal. xxxvi. 8. "Blessed is the man whom thou choosest, and causeth to approach unto thee, that he may dwell in thy courts; he shall be satisfied with the goodness of thy house, even of thy holy temple," Psal. lxv. 4. The prodigal eat before, but he was not satisfied, but now he had what his soul desired.

It causeth the soul to contemn the world. 3. It hath such effects on the soul, that it causes it to slight and contemn this world in all its glory, riches and pleasures. "Whom have I in heaven but thee? neither is there any on earth I desire besides thee," Psal. lxxviii. 25. Paul esteemed all things as dung in comparison of the knowledge of Christ, and of communion with him; this made the spouse also to say, "Her beloved was the chiefest among ten thousand."

It is a precious cordial, 4. It is like a strong cordial to a drooping spirit, that bears it up; the reason may be, because it is the soul's first welcome to Christ, and to his Father's house: first love is commonly the sweetest, a believer meets with such a cordial at its first closing with Christ, which he cannot forget as long as he liveth. True, they do not feast on these dainties every day; and should they, perhaps, they would not prize them so much, Paul speaks of what he met with fourteen years ago, 2 Cor. xii. 1, 2, 3; he was not often feasted in that manner.

It causeth the soul to remember God. 5. It makes the love of the Father, and of the Son, and Holy Spirit, to be remembered. "The king hath brought me into his chambers," Cant. i. 4. Well, what then? "We will remember thy love more than wine." Get but a real taste of God's love, of Christ's love, and you will never forget it as long as you live in this world. When I remember these things, I pour out my soul to thee," i. e., Psal. xliv. 4; when I remember what communion I had once with thee. "When I went to the house of God, with the voice of joy and praise."

Communion has soul-abasing effects attending it. 6. It hath soul-abasing effects attending of it; that is, it humbles the soul. Who am I (said Elizabeth) "that the mother of my Lord should come unto me?" Luke i. 43, much more may the soul say, who am I, and from whence is it that my Lord himself should come unto me! O how low did Job lie at the foot of God when he had clear sights of him! "Now I abhor myself, and repent in dust and ashes," Job. xlii. 5. And thus it was with the prophet Isaiah also, he cries out, "I am undone," Isa. vi. 5. The more we see and enjoy of God, the more low we lie at his feet, and are abased before him.

It is a soul transforming communion. 7. Such are the effects of this communion, that it is of a soul-transforming nature; it leaves a divine impression of God's image, of grace and holiness upon us. "We beholding with open face, as in a glass, the glory of the Lord, are changed into the same image, from glory to glory, as by the Spirit of the Lord," 2 Cor. iii. 18. Compare this with Cant. v. 5, "I rose up to open to my beloved, my hands dropped with myrrh, and my fingers with sweet-smelling myrrh upon the handles of the lock." When Moses came down from the mount from conversing with God, his face shone so exceeding bright, that the children of Israel could not behold it.

Communion with Christ makes his ordinances prized. 8. It causes our souls to prize those ordinances in which we meet with this communion; nothing raises the worth of ordinances like this: O, saith the soul, I prize the word of God, and the ministry thereof; I prize prayer, I prize the Holy Supper of the Lord, for I have met with God and with Christ in these ordinances, I have had sweet fellowship with him in them, and what is the cause others do not value them, but set light by them? Alas, they had only the shell, they never tasted God, met with God in them.

It makes us long to be in heaven. 9. It makes the soul to long for heaven. "When shall I come and appear before thee?" if one drop of wine be so sweet, so reviving, so strengthening, so consoling, and so ravishing, saith the soul, what will full draughts of it be, "In thy presence is fulness of joy, and at thy right-hand are pleasures for evermore," Psal. xvi. 11.

It makes a dwelling in God's house prized. 10. It causes the souls of believers to prize a dwelling in the house of God. "How excellent is thy loving-kindness, O Lord ! therefore do the children of men put their trust under the shadow of thy wings, they shall be abundantly satisfied with the fat things of thy house, and thou shalt make them drink of the rivers of thy pleasures," Psal. xxxvi. 7. Also it maketh believers to desire further communion; such certainly are utterly strangers to fellowship with God, that do not pant and breathe after it, and also after greater degrees of. "O when wilt thou come unto me ?" Psal. xlii. 1. How did David long, thirst, and pant for the living God ? so the prophet Isaiah speaks, "With my soul have I desired thee in the night, yea, and with my spirit will I seek thee early," Isa. xxvi. 9.

APPLICATION

1st. Trial. Examine yourselves, have you found fellowship with God ? hath your eating with your heavenly Father, and your supping with Christ had such effects upon your souls, if not enquire, what the cause of it may be.

Why some find no more consolation in Christ. 1. Is not the world got to much into your hearts : are not earthly consolations over-prized by you ?

2. May be you have been too much contented with ordinances, without the God of ordinances ; what is a bare ordinance without God and Christ in it ?

3. May be your faith is weak ; weak believers have but small comfort, are seldom filled with joy, or partake of strong consolation; if you see not Christ is your's, or you have real union with him, your communion cannot be great ?

4. Therefore (as one observes) there is a vast difference betwixt a reflexive or sensible certainty, and a real certainty ; a strong faith hath the advantage and the pre-eminency here : yet you may have a real certainty, for that doth not depend upon the strength of faith, or strength of grace, but upon the truth of it. My condition may be good, and God may be my God, and yet I may not fully know it, or be persuaded of it. Pardon belongs to all believers : all have their sins forgiven, and all are justified, are renewed, all are adopted, all are sanctified; and all have an equal right to glory ; but all do not partake of equal joy and communion with God here in this world.

5. May be thou hast fallen into some sin, or temptation, and hast given way to Satan, or dost not live by faith, live on Christ, on what he hath done, but on what is done and wrought in thee, fetching thy comfort from thy inherent holiness or sanctification. Or,

6. May be Christ hath withdrawn himself from thee for a time ; he will return, and therefore be not cast down nor be discouraged. Or

2ndly. Sinners, may not this make you willing to return home, as this prodigal did ? is not the entertainment you shall have very inviting to you ? believe there is that to be found in God and in Christ which you never yet met with. Moreover, do not blame believers that they so willingly have denied themselves to follow Christ.

3rdly. This commends true religion, faith, and holiness to a blind world; let all take heed they speak not evil of those things they know not, and understand not.

4thly. Learn to know from hence, that the way to true happiness is to obtain union with Christ, and so opens the door to him ; this lets the soul into this sweet and blessed communion, as you have heard.

5thly. What a fearful state are they in that fight or mock at this fellowship, and esteem communion with the works of darkness, and with the workers of iniquity better than this fellowship ! alas, their hearts are carnal, and until they are changed they cannot relish these things. "The natural man receiveth not the things of the Spirit, neither can he know them."

6thly. Happy, thrice happy, eternally happy are you that can say, "Truly our fellowship is with the Father, and with his Son Jesus Christ."

Lastly. O what a difference is there between believers and such who are in their sins ! Moreover, let such who do believe and sup with Christ, nor forget to live to him, to his praise and glory, whilst they live upon the earth.

IX

*For this my son was dead, and is alive again; he was lost and is found.
And they began to be merry.*—Luke xv. 24.

THESE words (as one observes) seem to be an abridgement of the whole parable.

1st. We have his former state expressed under a twofold allusion. (1.) "He was dead." (2.) "He was lost."

2. A twofold account of his present state. (1.) "He is alive again." (2.) "And is found."

3. The consequences or the effects of it upon the hearts both of father and son, and the rest of the family. "And they began to be merry."

True joy flows from grace, or is the fruit of the Spirit, and of divine union and regeneration; and it doth not only cause joy in the soul of a believer, but God the Father, and those that dwell with him in his house are pleased and delighted therewith; also all rejoice together.

"For this my son," &c. (1.) We may observe from hence, that God takes notice of every particular sinner that believes or returns unto him. (2.) Note also, that God sometimes converts great sinners. (1.) "This my son," even he that led such a wicked course of life; great afflictions, straits, and powerful convictions are blessed, sometimes to the conversion of notorious sinners. "This my son was dead and is alive again," (3.) Observe, that grace makes a mighty change upon a sinner; what can be a greater alteration of the creature, than for one that was dead to be made alive? the Spirit puts life into a dead sinner. (4.) That the Lord is not ashamed to be called the God and Father of such that return to him, who have lived very wicked lives before; when he is renewed, the Father calls him his son, owns him to be his child; he is not only (with Zaccheus) a son of Abraham, but by grace and adoption a Son of God. *[margin: God takes special notice of every soul that returns to him.]*

"Was dead," &c.

Doct. An unconverted person is a dead person; or sinners by nature are dead, spiritually dead.

There is a twofold death, viz., a natural death, and spiritual death; the prodigal was spiritually dead. Sometimes the taste of sinners before renewed, called, or regenerated, is set out, (1.) As being fallen. (2.) By one sick. (3.) By one wounded, (4.) By a captive. (5.) By being blind. (6.) By a leper. (7.) By a wretched infant cast out into the open field in its blood. (8.) By one naked. (9.) By one condemned to die, and often by one dead. A man may be considered in a threefold state. (1.) What he was by creation, as considered in the state of innocency, so he was alive. (2.) What his state is by sin or degeneration, and so considered he is dead; this presupposeth he was once alive. (3.) What his state is by regeneration, and so considered he is alive again. "He was dead and is alive again." *[margin: A threefold state of men in this world.]*

I. I shall show in what respect a sinner may be said to be dead, and why said to be dead.

There is a twofold spiritual death.

(1.) In respect of state; as we say a condemned man is a dead man, he is dead in law: thus all unbelieving sinners are dead; the holy law of God lays all under the sentence of death and condemnation; this death passed upon all men in the first Adam.

(2.) Dead, as to a principle of true spiritual life, even truly and really dead in a spiritual sense; as a man naturally is dead when his life or breath is taken away, or his soul departed.

1. This death consisteth in that privation in all the faculties of the soul; they are under a total privation of the life of God, or of original righteousness; the same faculties remain, but the rectitude is gone. Original sin is the extinguishing of the light that was in the soul; like a candle that is put out, the candle remains, but the light is blown out; or like a tree that is dead, the body and arms remain, but the life is gone, its leaves are fallen off, its branches withered, and dead. Even thus it is with all men naturally, they are dead, or without a principle of divine life in their souls; and hence all their works, deeds, and duties of worship which they pretended to perform to God, are called dead works: repentance is called "repentance from dead works," Heb. vi. 1, 2. *[margin: Wherein spiritual death doth consist.]*

Sinners beauty is gone, as is the beauty of a dead man.

Sinners are cold to spiritual things, as a dead man is cold as stone.

2. A dead man's beauty is gone, and his countenance is changed, he looks ghastly : so the spiritual beauty of sinners, by reason of sin, and death in sin, is gone : innocent man was a beautiful creature in God's sight. Virtue puts beauty and glory on the soul ; but sin is the worst deformity, it is that which marred God's image on the soul, so that there remains no more comeliness in the sinner in God's sight, than is in the face of a dead man in our sight.

3. A dead man is as cold as clay, or as a stone : so sinners without a principle of true spiritual life are cold to spiritual or heavenly things as a stone ; and this all unrenewed sinners discover at all times ; there is no divine warmth or heat in them. If you talk to them about spiritual matters, tell them of God, the preciousness of Christ, the sweetness of this world, promises and ordinances : alas ! it is all nothing to them, they are cold to such things ; though it is true, some of them may act from false principles, with some kind of moral heat, and seeming zeal, but Isa. l. 31. it is all from sparks of their own kindling, and not from the spirit of life received from God, and so all they do, or speak, or act, in religious matters, is vain, they being dead to God, but full of life to the things of this world. Talk to them about earthly things, O how warm and lively are they ! then they are in their proper and natural element ; but they are like fish taken out of the sea, if you speak of heavenly things to them.

Men dead in sin breathe not, pray not.

4. Dead men breathe not, there is no breath in them ; so unregenerate persons pray not ; prayer is the breath or spiritual breathings of the new creature : an unregenerate sinner may pray (the Pharisees prayed twice a day) but not from a principle of life, it was not by the Spirit of God : the Spirit of God is a Spirit of supplication, it causes a believer, as soon as ever it is poured Zech. xii. 10. forth on him, to cry Abba, Father, Father. It is one thing to say or read a few prayers, or to have the gift of prayer, and another thing to have the grace and spirit of prayer. Paul before his conversion (no doubt) prayed, but God took no notice of those prayers ; but no sooner did Christ touch his heart, but he poured out his soul, behold (saith the Lord,) to Ananias, he prays, now he breathes forth his desires unto God.

Sinners dead in sin cannot act nor move spiritually.

5. A dead man is without motion, he stirs not, moves not, acts not, all vital motion ceases ; so a man dead in sin can no more move, act, or do anything in a true spiritual manner from a divine vital principle, than a dead man can act or move naturally, and therefore cannot prepare himself in any remote sense, or in any degree in order to obtain the life of grace : nay, it is worse yet with dead sinners, a dead man cannot resist or oppose the almighty Agent that hath power to quicken him ; Lazarus could not resist that power in any respect that raised him from the dead ; but dead sinners (being alive in their bodies, and the spirit of Satan being also strong in them at first) resist and oppose the motions of the Spirit, their carnal minds being filled full of enmity against God, and against the word and workings and influences of the Spirit, they for a time may make resistance. " Ye will always resist the Holy Ghost," saith Stephen, Acts vii. 51. Therefore know, it is one thing for men to act by natural or moral principles, and another thing to act from a vital principle. " Ye will not come to me that ye might have life," John v. 40. This shows the averseness or rebellion that is in the will, and not the power of it in moving the soul to come to Christ. From hence it appears, that greater power is required to be exerted to raise a dead sinner, or to quicken one dead in sin, than in raising one that is naturally dead,

Greater power required to quicken and raise a dead sinner, than one that is naturally dead.

or that which God puts forth in creating the world ; for there was no devil then to oppose him, nor in his creating man, there was no rebellious will to resist him ; but there is, when he begins to create us again in Jesus Christ, the heart of the sinner opposes, the will opposes, and the devil oppose, and makes oppositions against the Spirit and operations of God : though in the day of his power the will is made willing. " If God will work, who shall let ?" " The wind bloweth where it listeth," John iii. 8.

6. A dead man cannot speak, he cannot praise and magnify God. " The dead cannot celebrate thee. The living shall praise thee," &c., Isa. xxxvii. 18, 19. So unrenewed sinners, dead sinners, cannot perform any acceptable service to God, though God requires duties of them, and they owe him honour, worship, and praise, must hear and pray, &c., yet they bring no glory to God ; all people are to pray, praise, nay, sing the praises of God, yet none but the living, i. e., the saints of God pray and sing his praises acceptably, to his glory ; for how can he sing with grace that has no grace in his heart ?

7. Such that are dead cannot feel, see, hear, taste, nor smell ; so all the spiritual senses

of the soul are gone: though guilt, like a mountain, lies upon him, he feels it not; though sin, like a sword, pierces his soul, he cries not out, nor feels any pain. Also he is so blind that he sees no beauty in Christ, nor good in divine things; and so deaf that he cannot hear the voice of the Lord Jesus in the word; they are like the deaf adder; neither can they taste any sweetness in the word, that is as honey and the honey-comb; and their smelling also is quite gone, they smell not the savour of Christ's sweet ointments, nor of his garments which are as myrrh and cassia, they savour only the things of the flesh, and taste the sweet or worldly gain, honour, and pleasure.

8. A dead man soon stinks and is loathsome: so it is with dead sinners, they stink in the nostrils of God, and all gracious persons; and all their brave ornaments and odours are but the perfuming of a dead corpse. " Their throats are as an open sepulchre." Their breath is loathsome, or their prayers abomination to the Lord. Moreover, a dead man is not fit to remain above ground, but to be buried; so wicked men are good for nothing but to be cast into hell.

USE

O mourn over the dead, over your dead sons, dead daughters, dead husbands, and dead wives, and dead neighbours.

2. See what sin hath done; O what evil is in it? it hath slain the soul, nay, the whole world, &c. What fools are sinners who love their sins, that have murdered their souls, and exposed them to eternal wrath.

3. I infer, that we live among the dead, converse with the dead; and yet how few mourn over them: in some families many lie dead, and hardly any that there is not one or more dead. O lament! people converse with the dead, and yet are not afraid; the pestilence that fills houses with the dead is dreaded, but this plague, i. e., sin that slays millions, and lays all men dead and full of the tokens, yet very few either fear it, or strive to escape from it: when there was but one dead in a house in the land of Egypt, what sorrow or lamentation was there? But for these that are spiritually dead, few are concerned.

4. This may reprove such that say, mankind by nature are not dead, but only maimed or wounded, and so need not to have a vital principle infused to quicken them: these men assert that the will is not so dead to spiritual things, but that only moral suasions may incline it so powerfully to that which is spiritually good, as to turn and convert the sinner; which error I have in other parables detected.   See the lost sheep.

5. Yet here is comfort for the dead; Christ, that quickening Spirit is come to make the dead to live, he can raise the dead. " You hath he quickened, that were dead in sins and trespasses. Even when we were dead in sin, he hath quickened us together with Christ." Eph. ii. 1, 4. Such that are dead may in a moment be raised to life. " The dead shall hear the voice of the Son of God, and they that hear shall live," John 5, 25.

" This my Son was dead, and is alive again."   Saints are made spiritually alive.

Doct. He only lives in a true spiritual sense, that hath received a principle of divine life from Christ.

A believing and a true penitent person is a living person: saints are alive, though sinners are dead.

I. Let me open the nature a little of this divine life, and prove that believers are alive

1. Before he was dead, but now life is infused into his soul: Can a dead man live until his soul returns again into him? My brethren, what the soul is to the body, that is the Holy Spirit to the soul; I mean it is the vital principle, or that which makes him a living man. Adam was no living person till his soul was created and breathed into him. Therefore as the body without the soul is dead, so is the soul without the Spirit of Christ. Some may ask, can these dead bones, dead sinners live? yea if Christ please, " for the Son quickens whom he will."   Who are alive spiritually.

2. Life infused, is stirring, it is not without motion; so where there is true spiritual life, that soul will be moving Godward and Christward; they are full of spiritual activity. Sirs, according to the nature of that life possessed, such is the nature of the motion and actings of the creature; for all creatures act according to that principle by which they live.

3. Such that live in a spiritual sense, they are sensible, they see, they hear, they feel, they taste, they hear and know the voice of Christ, the call of Christ, they hear the joyful sound, or the soul-ravishing melody in Christ's banqueting-house. " There was music upon the returning of the prodigal to his father's house," Eph. i. 18. In God's house is mirth or spiritual melody; and what is that but singing " Psalms, hymns, and spiritual songs?" It is a pity any of the family should not like it; they do not only hear,

but also see " their understanding is enlightened ; they see what sin is to loathe it, what the world is so as to die to it ; what Christ is, so as to cry out, he is " the chiefest among ten thousand," and that he is "altogether lovely," Cant. v. 10, 16. They also feel, the least sin makes them cry out, the very thoughts and words are a burden to them ; I mean words that drop unadvisedly, or too hastily from their lips. Moreover, they taste and know the Lord is gracious, "that the Lord is good," Psal. xxxiv. 8 ; and daily feed upon the feast of fat things which others relish not, nor can taste any sweetness in ; and they also smell the sweet odour of Christ's myrrh, cassia, and frankincense ; all the graces of the Spirit are as sweet spices or perfumes to them.

4. Spiritual life influences the whole man ; the whole man is quickened .thereby, wherever it is, even all the faculties of the soul, and members of the body are governed by this life ; their tongue speaks for God, prays to God, and praises God, &c.

5. They relish spiritual things, and are spiritually minded ; also they " live in the Spirit, and walk in the Spirit," Rom. viii. 11, Gal v. 25, Rom. viii. 14. They live in Christ, they live with Christ. and they live to Christ ; for the grand work and design of the Spirit, is to glorify Jesus Christ, and this is the great tendency of this life : such strive to magnify Christ, and exalt him above all in heaven or earth. Moreover, there is heat and warmth in their souls ; " Did not our heart burn within us ?" Luke xxiv. 32.

6. Lost beauty, even the image of God, is restored to them, they partake of the divine nature ; the new creature is a glorious creature, it being " created after the image of him that created it," 2 Pet. i. 4. This life makes them lively and holy, and causeth them to delight in God, and to walk with God, and to live on high, i. e., in communion and fellowship with the Father, and with his Son Jesus Christ, 1 John i. 2, 3.

7. Such who partake of this life breathe freely, unless they are distempered, fallen sick, or are under temptations : I mean, unless they are fallen into sin, or are disordered in their spirits : they pray always, and go to God as to their Father, and cry Abba, Father ; they love God as a Father, and love the habitation and provision of his house. And thus it was now with this poor prodigal, and therefore the father said, " This my son was dead, and is alive, was lost, and is found." What it is to be lost and to be found, I have opened in the parable of the lost sheep, and shall add no more to it here.

APPLICATION

1. O what a change doth grace make ! and O what power is that which God puts forth when a sinner repenteth ? It is God that raiseth the dead.

2. Bless God for Christ, and magnify Jesus Christ, " who came that we might have life," and have it more abundantly. Sirs, we come to have this life by Christ's death ; it is a life purchased for us, as well as a life infused in us.

3. Trial. Try yourselves.

(1.) What spiritual life, warmth, heat, and zeal do you find in your hearts ? is God, Jesus Christ, and religion, preferred above all things by you ? Are religious duties your delight ? Do you make religion your main business? then certainly you are spiritually alive.

(2.) Do you remember the time when you were dead and cold to spiritual things, seeing no worth and value in them ; and can you remember how, and by what means, and near the time when this mighty change was wrought in you ?

(3.) Is sin, every sin dead in you, as to its ruling power ? and is the least sin like a thorn in the flesh to your souls, or as a heavy burden ? if so, no doubt but there is life in your souls. Are you dead to this world, and to all the sinful profits, honours, and pleasures thereof ? and are you also dead to your own righteousness, dead to the law, and that dead to you, by your espousing of Jesus Christ ?

(4.) Do you breathe freely and continually, that is not only a sign of life, but also of health ; not that you are only in a good state, but in a lively frame. Some persons, though alive yet breathe with difficulty, they meet with obstructions ; and others fetch their breath short, being weak and faint, and have lost their appetite : so some cannot pray freely, and others make very short prayers (though long prayers always may not be expedient, nor the best) but when a child of God finds it difficult to pray, it is a sign he is sick or distempered in his soul.

(6.) What faith have you ? Faith is the life of the soul. " The life which I now live in the flesh, I live by the faith of the Son of God," Gal. ii. 20. None have Christ but such that believe truly in him. " He that believes hath the Son," John iii. 36. " And he that hath the Son hath life, and he that hath not the Son hath not life," 1 John v. 12.

(7.) Is the Spirit of Christ in you ? the Spirit of Christ is the life of faith, that which gives life and vigour to faith ; the Spirit is the vital principle in the soul.

(8.) Are you spiritual, holy, and heavenly minded? "They that are after the Spirit, do mind the things of the Spirit," Rom. viii. 5.

Exhort. O prize this life! what is natural life to true spiritual life? yet how is natural life valued? What will not a man give for his life? O then esteem this life!

1. It is a dear bought life; it cost Christ the price of his most precious blood.

2. It is the life of the soul; and O how precious is the soul, the subject of this life! and what a fearful death was it under before!

3. It is secure, it is a life a believer cannot lose; men nor devils cannot take away this life. "Because I live, ye shall live also," John xiv. 19. Men may as soon deprive Christ of life, as any one that is in him, of this spiritual life.

4. It is the seed, and the assurance of eternal life. Believers, by having this life, have eternal life in them; eternal life in the seed, in the principle, in the earnest, in the promise, and in their head.

5. It tends therefore to peace, to comfort, and joy, through the Holy Ghost; O what consolation is here to believers!

6. It is a growing and an increasing life; such grow in faith, love, humility, &c., and in saving knowledge; here is cause of mirth, "And they began to be merry."

"Now the elder son was in the field; and as he came and drew nigh to the house, he heard, music and dancing."

This elder son, I told you, was the Jews and Pharisees, they were in the field of this world, working for life, doing to be justified. But when they came near the gospel-church, in the ministration and dispensation thereof; they heard that the Gentiles and great sinners were returned to God, and that he pardoned them, and made them sing for joy of heart, and rejoice in the abundance of gospel blessings. At this the elder brother, the Jews and Pharisees were offended, and seem to be angry, that great sinners, and vile Gentiles, should be esteemed above them, or fed and feasted with gospel dainties. But see how sweetly the Father reproves him, answers all he had to say in a precious mild way, "Son thou art ever with me, and all I have is thine." These expressions, I suppose, make some think by the elder son, the holy angels are meant; but that cannot be, because they are not of the same kind or species with sinners: nor are they angry when a sinner repents, but contrariwise, as I have showed, do rejoice to see it. Nor can the older brother signify godly men: for they never are offended, nor angry when sinners repent and come to God, but also do rejoice.

By being ever with God must refer, I humbly conceive, to whatever God speaks of under the law, of the Jews, and of Jewish ordinances, rites, and privileges; which ever only referred to the end of that dispensation, or until the gospel-church took date. And plain it is, some of his words show him to be a Pharisee.

"These many years do I serve thee." He is called a son, but had a servile spirit.

"Neither transgressed I at any time thy commandment." Thus the Jews and Pharisees gloried. "All these things have I done from my youth up," said the young man.

"And all I have is thine." All must be taken here with restriction (as in many other places of scripture) i. e., all I have thought good to give to you my people of the fleshly seed of Abraham, or stock of Israel, legal rites, blessings, and privileges. "To whom pertaineth the adoption, the glory, and the covenants, and the giving of the law, the service of God, and the promises," Rom. ix. 4. Nay, Christ also was sent to them, offered to them, and he was theirs, as concerning the flesh. Now what had God more (if I may may so speak) to give under that dispensation to this elder brother? "What could be done more for my vineyard, than I have done?" or be given more to them: but for their sins in rejecting of Christ, they lost all, and were cast off, and the younger brother, i. e., the poor Gentiles, were received and grafted into Christ, even all that believed, or received the Lord Jesus, though never so great sinners; and therefore the Father saith, it was meet that we should make merry and be glad: "For this thy brother was dead, and is alive again; and he was lost, and is found."

And thus I shall close with this parable.

28. THE PERSISTENT WIDOW

I

And he spake a parable unto them, to this end, that men ought always to pray, and not to faint ;

Saying, there was in a city a judge, which feared not God, neither regarded man ;

And there was a widow in that city, and she came unto him, saying, avenge me of mine adversary.

And he would not for a while, but afterwards he said within himself, though I fear not God, nor regard man ;

Yet because this woman troubleth me, I will avenge her, lest by her continual coming she weary me.

And the Lord said, hear what the unjust judge saith.

And shall not God avenge his own elect, which cry day and night unto him, though he bear long with them?

I tell you that he will avenge them speedily.   Nevertheless, when the Son of Man cometh, shall he find faith on the earth ?—Luke xviii. 1—8.

Year of
Christ 33

Of his ministry 4.

The time when preached.
Feb. 2. 1701.

MY brethren, I enter upon this parable at a season when the subject may appear to all very seasonable, what is at this time more necessary than extraordinary prayer, or crying unto God ?   We seem to be in an evil and amazing hour, what God is about to do with England, with other nations, and with his own people, we know not, we are in a cloud ; things look black abroad, and bad at home.

But to proceed.

In what parables the main scope only should be observed.

My brethren, there is in this parable little more than the main scope and drift of it to be opened, it so much (with some other parables) differs from the generality of the parables our Lord spoke.   Indeed, such parables that are taken from the actions of wicked men, as that of the unjust steward, and this, &c., it is only the main scope that should be chiefly minded.

Now the main drift and design of our blessed Saviour in speaking this parable, is in the general expressed in the first verse, " He spake a parable to this end, that men should always pray," &c:

1.   Therefore one grand design of it is, to provoke the people to prayer, viz. ;

The scope.
(1.)   To be fervent in prayer ; this is signified by crying, " Who cry day and night to him."

(2.)   To be constant in prayer, " Men ought always to pray."

(3.)   Not to be weary, or give over praying, " And not to faint."

(4.)   To patience in waiting for the answer of prayer, " Though he tarry long," &c.

2.   Our Lord's design herein is to show his saints, that all those wrongs and injuries they sustain in this world, from the hands of wicked men, shall be avenged, and that in the mean time their afflictions and persecutions should stir them up to fervent prayer.

3.   And to assure us also, that though God doth seem to delay, to avenge his own elect for a time, or to answer their prayers ; yet he will assuredly at last appear for their help, and against their enemies, though they think it is long before he doeth it.

4.   That if God's people do cry unto him day and night, and not faint, he will avenge them speedily ; he never tarried long, when a mighty spirit of prayer was poured forth upon them.

5. To show nevertheless, that when Christ comes to avenge his elect upon their enemies, in the last days, but very few will believe it will then be done.

" Shall the Son of man when he comes find faith on the earth ?" That is, faith as to his coming to execute judgments on his church's enemies ; he refers to this, not to the grace of faith. These five things, I conclude, take in the sum of his whole design, in speaking this parable.

As to what is contained in the several parts of this parable, and how to be improved, I shall in the next place speak briefly to that. *The parts of the parable opened.*

1. We have an account of a judge, and of his character, viz., an unjust judge, one " that feared not, neither regarded man ;" a worse judge cannot be.

2. An account of a widow, poor widows commonly go to the walls, and are unjustly dealt with, and abused with their poor fatherless children.

(1.) A relation of her condition (which is implied) she was wronged by her enemy. Widows (like poor afflicted Sion) have adversaries, or meet with enemies, and are ill-treated, as I hinted.

(2.) An account of her actions, or what she did. (1.) She came to this unjust judge, to be avenged of her adversary. (2.) Her importunity, she would not let him rest ; she it seems follows him, and cries to him again and again, saying, " Avenge me of my adversary."

(3.) An account of her success at last ; though he would not at first, yet at last he did it.

(4.) The reason why he resolved in himself to do it, or grant her request, i. e., lest by her continual coming she weary him.

3. We have the improvement our blessed Saviour maketh of this action of the unjust judge, viz., " And shall not God avenge his own elect ?" that is, shall not God much more do it ?

1. Because the judge was a person that feared not God, nor regarded to do that which was just to men ; he was an unjust judge, but God is a righteous judge.

2. He did it for a woman that perhaps was a stranger to him, or one that was no ways related to him ; whereas the saints are God's own elect, such that he hath redeemed ; his children are such that he loves dearly.

3. Also very likely the unjust judge was under no promise nor engagement to this widow ; but God hath laid himself under many gracious promises to his people, to appear for their help, and to save them when they cry to him.

4. The unjust judge regarded not his honour, name, nor credit ; for he regarded not man, valued not what men spoke of him : but God's name and honour is dear to him. " Shall not the judge of all the earth do right ?" With him the fatherless find mercy ; and he is the revenger of the widow's cause ; " For the Lord your God is God of gods, and Lord of lords, a great God, a mighty and terrible God, who regardeth not persons, nor taketh reward ; he doth execute the judgment of the fatherless and widow," &c. Deut. x. 17, 18. Poor Sion who sits as a desolate widow, he judgeth. " A Father of the fatherless, and a judge of the widows, is God in his holy habitation," Psal. lxviii. 5.

5. The unjust judge had no bowels to pity, nor sympathize in his heart with the widow ; but God is full of pity and bowels. " As a father pities his children, so the Lord pitieth them that fear him," Psal. ciii. 13.

And therefore (as if our Saviour should say) you may be sure from hence, God will avenge his own elect. Shall a wicked graceless man, by reason of earnest importunity, appear to help a poor widow ? What greater reason have you to believe that God will avenge his own elect, that cry day and night to him, and who have none else to help and relieve them ? and though (for reasons known to himself) he may seem to tarry long, yet if they cry to him, and cease not, he will at last avenge them with fury, and that speedily, though but few on earth will believe that he will do it then, or at that very time when he will come, and appear clothed with vengeance against his enemies to do it.

Now from the words thus opened, several propositions, or points of doctrine may be noted.

Doct. I. That prayer is a great duty, and ought continually to be performed. *The doctrines raised.*

Doct. II. That the people of God, like a poor widow, are greatly wronged and abused by an ungodly world, or by wicked men.

Doct. III. That God will hear the cry of his people, or his elect ones, and at last execute vengeance on their enemies, though he seems to delay.

Doct. IV. That at that very time when Christ comes to execute judgment on his peoples' enemies, but very few, or none of them, will believe it.

My chief design is to speak to the first of these propositions, as taking in the main scope and design of this parable ; and I shall show,

I. That prayer is a great duty, and ought continually to be performed.

II.   Show what is meant by praying always.

III. Prove that prayer is an indispensable duty.

IV.   Show that prayer tends much to the glory of God, and to the profit of his own people, and others also.

V. Show what prayer tends to the honour of God, and is profitable to us, and others.

What prayer is.   I. Show you what prayer is, or what it is to pray.

1.   Prayer is the pouring forth of the soul to almighty God, by the help, assistance, and the influence of the Holy Spirit. Hence the Spirit of God is called the spirit of supplication. " I will pour upon the house of Jacob, and the inhabitants of Jerusalem, the spirit of grace and supplication," &c. Zech. xii. 10.   Hannah prayed to the Lord, and what did she say ? " I have poured out my soul before the Lord," 1 Sam. i. 15.

My brethren, I understand not that reading out of a book, is any more praying, than the reading a sermon out of a book is preaching.   When I pray, I will pray with the Spirit : that is, my spirit shall pray by the aid and assistance of the Spirit of God.   And hence Paul saith, " We know not what to pray for, but as the Spirit helps our infirmities," &c. Rom. viii. 26.   It is called a wrestling and striving with God.   " Jacob wrestled with the Lord, he wept and made supplication," &c.

2.   There are several sorts of prayer, but all from the same Spirit.

Several sorts of prayer. Ejaculatory prayer.   1.   There is ejaculatory prayer, which is nothing else than the lifting up of the soul to God upon a sudden emergent occasion, or at any time, which some sorts, but lively expressions of our desires to him ; it may be vocal, or only by some secret sighs, desires, groans, and workings of the heart to God, and those darts often reach heaven as well as the loud cries and voices which a thousand people hear.   When Hannah prayed, though her lips moved, yet her voice was not heard. This sort of prayer is to be valued, (1.)   Because we may be beset by some sudden temptation of Satan, and then may send up to God our prayers and sighs, when we have no place to retire unto to put up vocal prayer.   (2.)   Because we may pray thus when we walk the street, or in our work, or among evil company, even at all times.   (3.)   And this is the way to keep our hearts with God continually, and a sovereign means to get our affections off of the world, and delivered from snares, and also to keep up our communion and converse with him always.

Vocal prayer.   2.   There is vocal prayer ; that is, to pray with our heart and voices ; but if we are alone, it is best our words be not loud, lest it proceed from hypocrisy ; that God that knows our sighs and groans can hear us, though our voice be not heard.

Social prayer.   3.   There is social prayer ; that is when many join together with one heart in those prayers that are put up by one mouth : for it is confusion for many to speak in prayer together ; though we read in social singing all joined together, not only in heart, but in their voices also, which tends to make the melody the more sweet : but we read of no such sort of praying.

Family prayer a great duty.   4.   There is family prayer, which ought to be daily performed, if possible, twice or thrice a day.   We read that " David prayed three times a day." The same also did Daniel, Dan. vi. 10.   Such therefore who pray not so much as once a day, are either under great temptations, or in a dying state, or else are no true Christians.   The prophet invokes God to pour forth his wrath upon the families that call not upon his name, Jer. x. 25.

It appears that Cornelius prayed in his house or family always ; it was, no doubt, his constant practice, Acts x. 2, 3.

Secret prayer.   5.   There is secret prayer, or closet prayer, when a man gets by himself alone in secret, and pours forth his heart to God ; and this sort of prayer our Saviour exhorts us to ; nor can a true believer live without it, though being found in this we ought not to neglect family duty any day : one duty should not displace another. " When thou prayest, enter into thy closet, and when thou hast shut thy door, pray to thy Father," &c.

Extraordinary prayer, when to be found in it.   6.   There is also extraordinary prayer ; and the special times for extraordinary prayer, are these following.

1st. When we are afflicted.   " Is any afflicted ? let him pray," James v. 13.   What, only then ?   No, no, not only when afflictions are upon us, but at such a time more than ordinarily, to be much more in prayer, or pray mightily to God.

2ndly. When we are tempted or buffeted by Satan. Thus Paul in an extraordinary manner prayed, when he had that " thorn in the flesh, the messenger of Satan to buffet him. For this I besought the Lord thrice, that it might depart from me," 2 Cor. xii. 8 ; that is, many times : how often that thrice might be, we know not ; he means he cried often and earnestly to God. *When we are tempted, we must be much in prayer.*

3rdly. When we look for, and suddenly expect to be called to great sufferings. Our blessed Saviour just before he suffered, was all night in prayer, and in prayer he prayed, that is, in an extraordinary manner. When we look for suffering, or are in trouble, or under persecution, we should cry mightily to God. " Call upon me in the day of trouble," &c., Psal. l. 15., that is, more than at other times. *So when great sufferings are expected.*

4thly. When the enemies threaten us, and seek to invade us, or come in like a flood upon us, then we would in an extraordinary manner pray and cry to God. Thus did Jacob, when he heard his brother Esau was coming to meet him with four hundred armed men, to cut off the mother with the child ; he was all night wrestling with God in prayer, and prevailed, Gen. xxxii. 24, 26. Thus also did Jehoshaphat and all Israel ; and the like did Hezekiah, when Sennacherib invaded Judah. Also Esther and Mordecai, when all the Jews were in danger to be cut off in one day, 2 Kings xviii. 10, 15. *When we are threatened, we should pray much to God.*

5thly. When heavy judgments are upon us, or upon the land. " If I shut heaven that there be no rain, or if I command the locusts to devour the land, or if I send the pestilence among my people," 2 Chron. vii. 13. O that is a time to pray more than ordinary. " If my people humble themselves, and pray, and seek my face, and turn from their evil way ; then I will hear from heaven, and will forgive their sins, and heal the land."

6thly. In times when great and wonderful things are expected, or strange revolutions for the church's deliverance may be near, then mighty prayers should be made. Thus did Daniel, when he understood by books, that the seventy years captivity was near expired, he then set himself to seek the Lord by prayer and fasting, Dan. ix. 3, 4. *When great things are expected we should pray mightily.*

7thly. When we are going about some great work for God, or desire that he would put forth his miraculous working power, as in healing the sick, or casting out unclean spirits ; then we must fast and pray, or be more than ordinary in prayer. " This kind goes not out but by prayer and fasting," Matt. xvii. 21. *When we are going to do some great thing or to ask some great things of God.*

3. I shall show you of what parts prayer consisteth. Prayer, my brethren, consisteth of three parts. *Prayer consisteth of three parts.*

Confession.

Supplication or intercession. Thanksgiving.

(1.) When we pray, we should confess our sins, and the sins of God's people, even all the manifold evils of our lives, and our unprofitableness unto God : thus we find all the Lord's people ever did, and thus our Lord teacheth us to do.

(2.) We must humbly entreat God, or supplicate him graciously to give or vouchsafe to us whatsoever it is we need, or his people need : even lay all our wants, and the wants of our families, and of the church of God, and of the land in which we live, before him ; and intercede for help, and all supplies from him.

(3.) Also give God thanks, and bless his holy name for all those good things we daily receive from his merciful and bountiful hands.

My brethren, as we must pray to God for what we have not, so we must praise him for what we have.

So much as to the first thing, viz., what it is to pray.

II. I shall show you what is meant by praying always.

1. Negatively ; not that we should do nothing else but pray, for that would take us off from many other indispensible duties, both civil, moral, and religious.

2. Affirmatively. 1. Our Lord means, no doubt, that there is no time or season when we can have an opportunity, but we ought to pray ; we must neglect no proper praying time. He is said to dine, or eat bread with us continually, that feeds with us at our table every day, and at every meal. And from hence it is said, David told Mephibosheth, Jonathan's son, that he should " eat at his table continually," 2 Sam. 9. 7. He did not mean, he should do nothing but eat. *To pray every day, is to pray always.*

2. To pray always, is to pray every day. Hence our Lord saith, God's elect cry to him day and night : which may refer, as some think, to morning and evening, without neglecting of it once, if in health, or able. *To pray in all things we enter upon.*

3. In everything, according to that of St. Paul, " In everything by prayer and supplication, and giving of thanks, let your request be made known," &c. Phil. iv. 6. We should set about nothing, enter upon no enterprise, but we should seek to God for wisdom, directions, and a blessing upon. " In all thy ways acknowledge him, and he shall direct thy paths." Whether it be in temporal or spiritual matters, and then thou mayest be said to pray always.

To pray always, is to pray in every condition.   4. To pray always, is to pray in every condition, age, or state we are in, when child, a young man, or apprentice, or a journeyman, a single man, or a married man ; if rich or poor, if in health, or sick; if in prosperity or in adversity, we must pray.

To pray always, is to have a heart always to pray.   5. To pray always, is to have a heart to pray, or to be in a praying frame of heart, nay, and not to neglect it, though not in so good a frame at one time as at another ; we must not do as some children, who having mispent the day in play, steal to bed for fear of being chid or whipped. If a workman's tools, be blunt, he must see to set a new edge on them. If new sins are committed, we must apply Christ's blood by fresh acts of faith, and being joined by prayers and tears, sue out for a sense of pardon.

To pray always, is to pray as long as we live.   6. To pray always, is never to cease or give over praying ; we must not cease praying until we cease living ; neither should our constant performance degenerate into lifeless formality. " I will call upon thee as long as I live."

III. I shall prove that prayer is an indispensible duty.

Prayer a moral duty.   1. Prayer is a moral duty, or a branch of natural religion. Mankind are taught and moved by the light of nature to pray, and to sing the praises of God. When the mariners were in that storm with Jonas, though heathens, " they cried to their gods." It is a proverb, " If a man cannot pray, send him to sea." But, I fear, there is at sea more cursing and swearing than praying now-a-days.

Prayer brought under divine institution.   2. But prayer is not only a moral duty, but is an ordinance instituted and appointed of God. Mind my text, " Men ought always to pray." Not only the saints, but also all men ; but more especially our Lord put his disciples upon prayer, " Ask, and ye shall receive."—Again, he saith, " Watch and pray, that ye fall not into temptation," Matt. xxvi. 41. " Watch and pray always, that ye may escape all those things that shall come to pass," Luke xxi. 36.

3. That in the doing of which, God hath made gracious promises unto his people, is a great duty, but O what a multitude of precious promises hath the Lord made to the prayers of his people ! Therefore prayer is a great duty.

4. That which God hath owned, and wonderfully confirmed and crowned with his miraculous appearances, is a great duty; but God hath wonderfully owned, confirmed, and crowned the prayers of his people with his miraculous appearances, therefore prayer is a great and indispensible duty.

5. If God will be sought to by us, that he would do whatsoever he hath promised to us, then prayer is a great duty ; but this he hath positively said he will be.

6. If the prayers of God's people be his delight, and also a great duty, it is a great sin to restrain prayer from God; and prayer is a great and indispensible duty; but this is so.

IV. I shall show you, that prayer tends greatly to the honour of God, and to the profit of our own souls, &c.

Prayer is a God-honouring duty.   1. Prayer is a God-honouring duty, because it is part of his holy worship ; and not only so, but it ought to be mixed with all other ordinances, all duties of sacred worship ought to be mixed with prayer ; nay, we should not enter *Prayer ought to be joined with all duties.* upon any civil or earthly business, without seeking first to God by prayer, but much more careful we should be to begin every part of God's worship with it. Before we preach we ought to pray, prayer ought to be joined with preaching, baptism ought to be administered with prayer ; first we should look up to God. Laying on of hands must be with prayer. The Lord's supper must be with prayer. " Every thing is sanctified by the word of God, and prayer." Hearing, reading of God's word, meditation, and watching must be with prayer. And as prayer should be used in every ordinance, so also in all trials, temptations, afflictions and troubles whatever ; nay, in eating and drinking, or what ever we do else, we should pray, and so we may expect a blessing from God, and all ordinances, mercies, and afflictions to be sanctified to us, and not otherways ; therefore prayer must needs tend to the honour of God, and our good.

By prayer we own and acknowledge the sacred Deity.   2. By prayer we acknowledge the holy and most sacred Deity, or divine being, and majesty of heaven, and that he is God only, and none else, and thereby we glorify him also in every one of his blessed attributes.

(1.) By prayer we own and acknowledge God's omniciency, (i. e.,) that he sees and knows our hearts, thoughts, desires, and all our wants and necessities whatsoever they be, and declare hereby, that we doubt not of the glorious perfection of the divine majesty. By prayer we acknow-ledge God's omnisciency.

(2.) Prayer tends also to glorify God in his infinite power, omnipotency, and all-sufficiency : we declare hereby, and doubt not, but as he sees and knows all our hearts and wants, so also that he is able to supply them, and do all things for us,—" and nothing is to hard for thee," Jer. xxxii. 17.   We hereby declare, that there is nothing too hard for God to do and work in us, and for us : and though men and devils, and the powers of hell and darkness combine against us, faith and prayer magnifies the God of power, and raiseth the glory of omnipotency.

(3.) Prayer tends to magnify God's infinite wisdom, hereby we acknowledge, that as God is able to help us, to strengthen us, to pardon us, to save us in or out of trouble ; so he also knows how to do it, and also at the best Prayer mag-nifies God's infinite wis-dom. and most seasonable time ; that he is wiser than man, though never so crafty, and can turn their wisdom into foolishness, and counterwork Satan in all his devices, and defeat all the policy of hell, and all powers of darkness.

(4.) Prayer tends to glorify God's mercy, love, and infinite goodness to us ; for he knows how to blast all hellish politicians in those designs of theirs, carried on with the deepest subtilties for many ages, and can bring all to nought in one moment : so his love, mercy, and pity to his people is such Prayer mag-nifies God's love and mercy to his people. (which we plead with him in prayer, he being our Father) that hereby we declare that sense and apprehension we have of his goodness, that we cannot doubt of succour and pity from him.   And indeed this our blessed Lord himself clearly informs us of in this parable : for if an unjust judge will avenge a poor widow that cries unto him, how much more will God (as if our Saviour should say) avenge his own elect, who is so full of bowels, love, and compassion to his children, or to them which fear him ? God is good and gracious, as well as just and righteous, and he also is our Father and dearest Friend ; and, as so considered, we direct our prayers to him, and this also by the rule he hath given us, " Our Father which art in heaven," &c.   Who can make supplication (with strong confidence) to one that he believes is void of bowels, love, and pity ? True, the widow is said so to do, as was heard, but not to the honour of the judge, in respect of his pity to the woman, but because he would not be troubled with her.

(5.) Prayer tends to magnify and raise to honour God's faithfulness in performing of his own gracious promises, and in making good his holy cove- Prayer mag-nifies God's faithfulness. nant.   " I know the Lord will maintain the cause of the afflicted, and the right of the poor," Psal. cxl. 12.   This we plead, and this we are obliged stedfastly to believe.   " He is faithful that hath promised, and he will do it," 1 Cor. i. 9.

(6.) By prayer we glorify God, in respect of his sovereignty over us; we hereby show, that all our hope and help is in God ; and also that all creatures and things are at his disposal : " For thine is the kingdom, the power and the glory, for ever and ever."   Amen. Thou mayest do what thou wilt (even according to the good pleasure of thine own will) with us, and with all the nations of the earth.   " And all the inhabitants of the earth are reputed as nothing; and he doth according to his will in the armies of heaven, and among the inhabitants of the earth ; and none can stay his hands or say, what doest thou," Dan. iv. 35.   And this he will make all haughty tyrants of the earth to know in due time, as well as he caused Nebuchadnezzar to know it, before he had done with him.   I might also add the like in respect of the other attributes of God, but shall close at this time.

II

He spake a parable, that men ought always to pray, and not to faint &c.—LUKE xv. 1—8.

DOCT. That prayer is a great duty, and ought continually to be performed.

I am upon the fourth head proposed, viz. That prayer tends to the honour of God, and to the great profit and advantage of our own souls.

This I am upon, and have showed how it tends to glorify God in all his blessed attributes.   To proceed,

(7.) By prayer we confess we are poor depending creatures, and cannot help ourselves, save ourselves, nor direct our paths, nor deliver ourselves from dangers feared, and that all our wisdom, strength, and succour, is from God, and hereby we give glory to God. "Neither know we what to do, but our eyes are up unto thee," 2 Chron. xx. 12. While we acknowledge our own weakness and inability to do any thing as of ourselves, and also can, and do rely believingly upon the great God in every state and condition, we advance the name and glory of God. And thus by prayer we magnify God, or the glorious Deity, as essentially considered; so hereby also in the second place we glorify God, as he is, personally considered. (1.) We by prayer glorify God the Father in all his perfection.

Prayer tends to glorify God the Father. (1.) In prayer we acknowledge that relation he stands in to us through Christ, viz., as our gracious Father; not only a great, a wise, a holy, a just, a merciful, and a faithful God, but a tender Father also; and that as he is so considered, he is the first and efficient cause, fountain, and spring of all that good we want, and do receive from the glorious Deity.

(2.) That he is in heaven, i. e., that he is exalted above angels, men, or devils, and that his kingdom ruleth over all, and as far above all as the heavens are above the earth: what need the children of such a Father fear?

(3.) That he is a living Father, and the Father of mercy, and of all strength, comfort, and consolation, knowing the wants of all his children, caring for them, feeding, clothing, correcting, teaching, and succouring them all, and that continually in all fatherly bowels, wisdom, and compassion knowing all our necessities, and hearing all our cries and prayers we put up to him.

(3.) By our holy and reverential approaches to him by faith, filial fear, and child-like affections; and thus, (and in many other respects,) we glorify God the Father in prayer.

Prayer tends to glorify God the Son. 2. Hereby we glorify also God the Son, or lift up and advance his honour. (1.) In that we call upon his name, as he is Mediator, and so own that the Son is the same God, or one in essence with the Father, and that he is the immediate object of all divine worship. We by him come to God, believe in God, and worship God, and give the same honour to the Son, that we give to God the Father.

(2.) In that we always come unto God in the name of our Lord Jesus Christ, as our only Mediator and "Advocate with the Father," 1 John ii. 1, 2, 1 Tim. ii. 5; *i. e.*, that it is for his sake, and through his merits alone, that the Father hears and answers all our prayers, and supplies all our wants.

(3.) We glorify Jesus Christ, in that we confess we come to God for nothing but for what Christ hath purchased for us by his blood, and is laid up for us in him, as the fountain of life, that is, with the Father. "With thee is the fountain of life," &c., Psal. xxxvi. 6. "It pleased the Father, that in him all fulness should dwell," Col. i. 19. And thus we, as God hath exalted him as Mediator, do lift up his glory, "In whom are hid all the treasures of wisdom and knowledge," Col. ii. 3.

(4.) In that we hereby also acknowledge, that we receive all things we need, by virtue of his intercession.

(5.) Also in that we in prayer confess and declare the great love, power, care, and faithfulness of our Lord Jesus Christ; believing that he both knows our wants, and *Heb. vii. 25.* is ready and able to help and save us to the uttermost, and all that come to God by him, and so acknowledge that all the divine perfections and attributes of the Deity, are equally in the Son as in the Father; he being the same one and "ever blessed God over all," Rom. ix. 5. Amen.

3. Prayer tends also to glorify the Spirit, or God the Holy Ghost.

Prayer tends to magnify the Holy Ghost. (1.) In that we confess we cannot pray acceptably, without the assistance of the Holy Spirit, nor know we what to pray for. "No man can call Jesus Christ, Lord, but by the Holy Ghost," 1 Cor. xii. 3. That is, no man can call on Jesus Christ aright, (*viz.*, truly own and acknowledge him, believe in him, cry to him, or so call on his name as to advance his glory) who is not renewed, influenced, and assisted by the Holy Spirit. "Likewise the Spirit also helpeth our infirmities, for we know not what we should pray for as we ought; but as the Spirit itself maketh intercession for us with groans that cannot be uttered," Rom. viii. 26.

(2.) In that all fervour, life, heat, and spiritual warmth in prayer, is from and by the Holy Spirit. How cold and flat are those prayers which are not put up to God by the influences of the blessed Spirit? This we find and do acknowledge, and so magnify the Holy Ghost in prayer.

(3.) It is by the Spirit that our faith in prayer is strengthened, and we attain to a lively hope, and are also helped to wait patiently upon God, until we receive those things we ask of God.

(4.) The Holy Spirit is magnified, in that it is by him we call God Father: he is the Spirit of adoption, and so helps us to cry Abba, Father. My brethren, we pray to the Father in the name of the Son, and by the Holy Spirit; and thus glorify all the three persons of the Trinity in this great and holy duty of prayer.

Secondly, as prayer tends thus to the glory of God, so likewise it is profitable to our own souls, to others, and to the whole church of God. *Prayer tends to our own profit.*

1. God hath appointed prayer as the way or means, in and by which he will supply all our wants. "If ye abide in me, and my words abide in you, ye shall ask what you will, and it shall be done unto you," John. xv. 7. That is, whatsoever may be for the glory of God, and our own good. "Every one that asketh receiveth," &c., "Ask, and ye shall receive, that your joy may be full," John. xvi. 24. O what a blessed ordinance is this, by which God gives every thing we stand in need of to us! "And whatsoever ye ask in my name, that will I do, that the Father may be glorified in the Son," John. xiv. 13; i. e., Whatsoever is according to the will of God, I will do it, signifying his oneness in essence with the Father. Compare this with 1 John. v. 14.

2. It is by prayer, our faith (and all the graces of the Spirit) is increased and strengthened: "Lord, increase our faith." This was the prayer of all the disciples, they prayed to the Lord Jesus, so did the woman of Canaan, "Lord, help." And the poor man, " I believe, Lord, help mine unbelief," or, help me against my unbelief; for that he meant. He that would obtain a stronger faith, must pray to the Lord Jesus, or to the Father in his name. *Prayer is the way to have our faith increased.*

3. By prayer or crying to God, we come to have an evidence of pardon. Thus David, " I acknowledge my sin to thee, and mine iniquity have I not hid. I said I will confess my transgressions unto the Lord, and thou forgavest the iniquity of my sin, Selah. For this shall every one that is godly pray unto thee in a time that thou mayest be found," &c. Psal. xxxii. 5. 6. *Prayer is the way to have an evidence of pardon.*

Confession, you heard, is one branch or part of prayer. For this (that is, for pardon of sin, or for this reason, this motive) I prayed to the Lord, and he pardoned me." And let every one that is godly, that hath sinned, do the same, and they shall receive the same blessing also, " forgive us our trespasses;" &c., apply the blood of thy Son to our souls, and give us the sense and sight of pardon, let us know that our sins are forgiven. My brethren, prayer is the way to obtain this great gospel-blessing, and therefore most profitable to us.

4. God hath made many gracious promises to his people, but the way to have those promises made good to us, is by our praying and crying to him. " I will nevertheless be enquired of by the house of Israel, to do it for them," &c. God will bring us upon our knees, before he will give us the mercy or good things which he hath promised. And this our Lord signifies in this parable. Before his own elect are delivered from their enemies, they must cry mightily to him, and faint not. Show me that saint or godly man, who did not this way receive the good things promised from the hands of God. God promised Abraham a son, but he entreated God for that son: God promised Jacob that he would surely be with him, and bless him; but he wrestled with God, prayed and cried to him to be blessed. Thus David received the promise: and Daniel also, though God promised to return the captivity of his people, yet how did he cry to God that he would do it, even just when the time was come! Dan. ix. 2. 3. 4. *Prayer is the way to have the good things God hath promised.*

5. Prayer is the way to escape Satan's temptations, or to be delivered from his assaults, or strengthened when assaulted. Paul prayed thrice, when he had the messenger of Satan to buffet him, and the enemy prevailed not; he failed not of help and succour. " My grace is sufficient for thee, for my strength is made perfect in weakness," 2 Cor. xii. 9. Our Lord directeth us to pray, " lead us not into temptation," not into a way of temptation, nor suffer us to fall in a temptation. *Prayer is the way to be succoured in a time of temptation.*

6. Prayer is the way to prevail with God to divert judgments, or to escape the wrath and rage of our enemies. Thus God delivered Jacob from the wrath of his brother Esau: he cried unto God, and prevailed: and, as the answer of prayer, God defeated the wicked design of bloody Haman against the Jews : and thus was the counsel of Ahithophel overthrown. David prayed, Lord, turn the counsel of Ahithophel into foolishness ; and the Lord heard him. How were the Philistines *Prayer is the way to have the wrath of man defeated.*

overthrown by the prayers of Samuel and all Israel: also the mighty hosts that came against Jehoshaphat. 1 Sam. vii. 7—10.

7. Prayer, importunity in prayer, is the way to get the loaves, and to have God to avenge us of our adversary.

Prayingsouls shall be hid in the day of God's wrath. 8. Prayer is the way to be hid in the day of God's wrath, nay, and to have a mark set upon us, that the destroying angel may spare us. "Set a mark upon the foreheads of the men that sigh and cry for all the abominations that are committed in the land," Ezek ix. 5. God gave commission to the angels to slay utterly old and young, even all besides those on whom the mark was, and to begin at his sanctuary. All must fall or be cut off, besides those crying and praying persons, in the day of some of God's sore judgments. "Seek the Lord, all the meek of the earth," &c., "may be ye shall be hid in the day of the Lord's anger," Zeph. ii. 3. Moreover our Lord directeth us to "watch and pray always, that we may escape all those things that shall come to pass, and stand before the Son of Man."

Prayer is the way to have fulness of joy. 9. Prayer is the way to have or obtain fulness of joy. "Hitherto ye have asked nothing in my name; ask, and ye shall receive, that your joy may be full," John xvi. 24. This is the way to meet with God, and to enjoy the light of his countenance, and to have all our doubts, darkness, and sorrow removed. We must do as David did, even cry, "Lift up the light of thy countenance on us," Psal. iv. 6. And again, "restore to me the joy of thy salvation," Psal. li. 12. We have no more peace, no more light, no more strength, no more joy, because we pray no more. Our clouds would soon be dispelled, our fears vanquished, our doubts resolved, and our souls comforted, did we pray more than we do.

10. Prayer is profitable to us, because this is the way to be prepared to meet with God in his ordinances. My brethren, we are to approach near to God at his table this evening. Have you prayed? Have you endeavoured to prepare yourselves? This of prayer is one of the principal ways to do it. We read, many in Ephraim and Manasseh had not prepared themselves; but "Hezekiah prayed for them, the good Lord pardon every one that prepareth his heart to seek God," 2 Chron. xxx. 18, 19.

Prayer is the way to have every thing sanctified. 11. Prayer is the way to have every thing sanctified unto us. "Every thing is sanctified by the Word of God and prayer," 1 Tim. iv. 5. You cannot expect that any thing should be blessed to you without prayer. You should pray that your trading, your buying, your selling, your health, your relations, your meats, your drink, your clothes, your liberties, and lives, as well as all spiritual good things, should be blessed and sanctified to you. This is the way to have everything do us good. "In every thing by prayer, &c., let your request be made known to the Lord."

Also it is the way to know such truths we are ignorant of. 12. Prayer is the way to have God make known those truths to us, that we may yet be ignorant of: "What I know not teach thou me." God led his people of old by prayer and supplication; and this is the way he leads them still.

To succeed well in all things. Lastly, this of prayer is the way to be directed by the Lord, and to succeed well in all our undertakings. "In all thy ways acknowledge him, and he shall direct thy paths," Prov. iii. 6.

Thus I have showed you how profitable prayer is unto us ever, to our bodies and souls, and to the whole church of God. But to proceed.

Fifthly, I shall show you what prayer it is that tends so much to the glory of God, and to our own good and advantage.

They are the prayers of a godly man that glorify God. 1. In respect of the persons praying, you must know it must be a gracious or godly person: "God heareth not sinners." The prayers of unconverted men tend not to the honour of God, their prayers do not glorify God: the man whose prayers are accepted, must be renewed or regenerated, or one that is in Jesus Christ. "The prayers of a righteous man availeth much," &c., James v. 16. Though he be a man of infirmity (or a man as Elias was, of like passion) they are the prayers of such a person that tend to glorify God, and to his own profit. The prayers of "the wicked are an abomination to the Lord. When ye make many prayers, I will not hear you, your hands are full of blood," Isa. i. 15.

Sincere prayers glorify God. 2. They must be prayers put up to God in sincerity; the person must be one that is upright in heart. "The prayers of the upright are his delight," Prov. xv. 8. They must proceed from a pure heart, a sanctified heart, a heart sprinkled with the blood of Christ; and also put up to God in godly sincerity; not hypocritical prayers, of one whose heart and tongue agrees not. "My prayer also is pure," Job. xvi.

17. Prayers are then pure, when the heart is clean, and sanctified by the When prayers may be said to be pure.
Spirit.

3. When we ask according to the will of God. " This is the confidence
we have in him, that if we ask anything that is according to his will, he
heareth us," 1 John v. 14. (1.) Either those things God hath commanded us to pray
for. Or (2.) Whatsoever things are prophesied of, or foretold, God will do for us, or for
his people : to pray for the accomplishing of such things, is according to the will of God.
(3.) Or what things he hath promised to give unto us.

4. Our prayers tend to the honour of God, when our ends and aims are purely to glorify him, or to advance his name and interest in the world.

5. When our prayers are the breathings forth of the Holy Spirit in our hearts. Prayers
that tend to the glory of God, and which shall be heard, are such that are put up by the
assistance of the Holy Ghost. " Praying always with all prayer, and supplication in the
Spirit," Eph. vi. 18. The Spirit helps us to indite those prayers that we put What it is to pray in the Spirit.
up by God, and also stirs up, or excites our spirits, and strengthens our faith :
it is the Holy Spirit that helps us to act and exercise its own graces in prayer,
and also gives us boldness to cry, Abba, Father. We must not only pray for the gift of
the Spirit, but also for the graces of the Spirit : when the soul melts in prayer, and the
affections are raised and strengthened, and our doubts and fears are scattered, we may be
said to pray in the Spirit.

6. It is the prayer of faith that tends to glorify God, when we act faith in The prayer of faith brings glory to God.
the power, mercy, goodness, faithfulness, and in the promises of God. As
unbelief dishonours God, so a strong faith tends to the honour of his holy
name. Thus Abraham glorified God, " He staggered not at the promise of God through
unbelief, but was strong in faith, giving glory to God," Rom. iv. 20. Nothing is too hard
for prayer, when it is put up by faith in God. " Let him ask in faith, nothing wavering,"
James i. 6. Let not a man that doubteth of the power, love, or faithfulness of God,
think to receive any thing from God's hands, or of bringing any glory to him. " It is
the prayer of faith that saves the sick," James v. 15.

7. Prayer that tends to bring glory to God, must be fired with zeal and Fervent prayer glorifies God.
holy fervency. " The effectual fervent prayer of a righteous man availeth
much," &c., ver. 16. Cold lukewarm prayers will never do any execution upon our enemies, neither on sin, Satan, nor the world, nor stir up the Almighty to appear for our help
and succour ; we must cry, " And shall not God avenge his own elect, that cry to him
day and night ?"

8. It must be argumentative prayer, or prayer that fills the mouth with Argumentative prayer honours God.
arguments to plead with God. This was the prayer that always prevailed
with God. " I will (saith Job) fill my mouth with arguments," Job xxiii. 4.
Thus Jacob prayed also, " Thou sayest I will surely do thee good," &c., Gen. xxxii. 12.
Again, he saith, " O God of my father Abraham, &c., which saith unto me, return unto
thy country, and to thy kindred, and I will deal well with thee. I am not worthy of the
least of thy mercies, &c. See what arguments he used to prevail with God. The like
did Joshua ; " O what wilt thou do for thy great name ?" Josh. vii. 9. What arguments
did the church also make use of : " We are thy people," Isa. lxiii. 16. " Where is thy
zeal, and thy strength, and the sounding of thy bowels, and of thy mercies towards me ?
are they restrained ? Doubtless thou art our Father, O Lord, thou art our Redeemer, &c.
We are thine, thou never bearest rule over them," ver. 19. Thus Jehoshaphat pleaded
with the Lord also : " O our God, wilt thou not judge them ? We have no might against
this great multitude that cometh against us, neither know we what to do, but our eyes are
upon thee," 2 Chron. xx. 12.

9. They are prayers put up to God in the Spirit of adoption, which tend Prayer put up in the Spirit of adoption glorifies God.
to the honour of God : we must not come to God, as unto a just, and sin-re-
venging God, or as unto an angry Judge, but as to our Father in Jesus Christ,
or to a God in covenant with us. " Our Father which art in heaven," &c.
" We have not received the Spirit of bondage again to fear, but the Spirit of adoption,
whereby we cry Abba, Father," Rom. viii. 15. Such prayers God is well pleased with,
and they tend to his glory.

10. They are prayers put up with humility, with self-loathing, and self- Humble prayer honours God.
abhorrence ; we must lie low before the Lord. " I that am but dust and
ashes," &c., saith Abraham. " I abhor myself," saith Job ;" Job xlii. 5 : not like the
prayer the proud Pharisee made, who boasted he was not like other men.

Watching unto prayer, in and after prayer, tends to the honour of God.

11. They are prayers with watching; it is not enough to pray, but to watch as well as to pray. A man that was a great professor, who fell lately into a great sin, confessed he prayed, but he did not watch; such prayers God will not hear, nor will they glorify him, neither be profitable unto us. Satan will be too hard for us, if we do not watch as well as pray; he always watcheth against us, he sleeps not. Hence St. Paul exhorts the saints to watch unto prayer," Eph. vi. 18. "Watch and pray always," saith our blessed Lord. Watching may be considered as threefold.

What we must watch.

(1.) We must watch our hearts in all their inclinations; our hearts are deceitful, and should be watched continually. "Who can know his errors?

(2.) We must watch the Lord in all his dispensations, we must observe his various providences, under which we, and his people are exercised.

(3.) We must watch Satan in all his temptations: we must watch before prayer, in prayer, and also after prayer, that we are not hindered from praying, nor obstructed in prayer, our souls being carried away with wandering thoughts; and after prayer call to mind how we prayed, and for what: that we may wait to receive it, we must pursue our prayers.

Prayer must be with thanksgiving.

12. Prayers that tend to the glory of God, and our good, must be with thanksgiving; we should never pray for what we want, but also give thanks to God for what we have received. "In nothing be careful; but in everything by prayer and supplication, with thanksgiving, let your request be made known unto God," Phil. iv. 6. Shall we be always a craving of God, and not make return of praise to him? Should you be asking this and that favour of your dear friend that has done much for you, and never acknowledge his former kindness done you? Sure that could not be the way to prevail with him: no, but he may say, I will find you first more thankful for what I have already done for you.

Sixthly, I shall a little farther open the matter of prayer, or show you wherein the matter of prayer does consist.

God's word shows us what we should pray for, as well as after what manner.

What we should pray for.

1. More generally, the main thing that we should pray for is, that God would glorify his own holy name. "Hallowed be thy name." This is the first petition we are directed to put up unto God. Now the name of God (1.) signifies the being or essence of God. The name of the God of Jacob is all one with the

What it is to seek God's honour, or his glory in prayer.

God of Jacob. (2.) The name of God denotes his holy attributes, his wisdom, power, holiness, goodness, justice, love, faithfulness, &c. and we must pray that God would glorify all his perfections, and blessed attributes, for his own honour, our good, and the ruin of his enemies. (3.) By the name of God sometimes is meant his word; but by whatsoever God is called, or made known to us, that is his name; and since God is made known, or chiefly manifested to us in and by Jesus Christ, our Lord Jesus is the name of God; and hence he is also called the Word of God: and we must in prayer desire God would glorify his Son, or advance the honour, and raise the glory of Jesus Christ; for his name is upon him, and his design is to exalt, extol, and make him very high. Note,

(1.) We can add nothing to the essential glory of God; but when we pray, we desire God would declare or make known his own glory, and do whatsoever may tend thereunto.

(2.) That we may be helped to do whatsoever may tend to the glory of God, or to raise the honour of Jesus Christ.

(3.) Hereby also we are taught to lie low before the Lord, and be abased to the very dust before him.

(4.) To acknowledge all things to come from God, and also to trust in him, rely upon him, and to confess that nothing is too hard for him to do.

We must pray for God's kingdom to come. Ps. xciv. 3.

2. The second thing that we should make the matter of our prayer is, that God's kingdom might come; hereby we acknowledge God is a great King, above all gods, a glorious, a just, a wise, and righteous King, and also that he hath a kingdom which is not yet come, or least-wise not in its full glory, as it shall come in the latter days. We pray that God would pull down, or overthrow Satan's kingdom, and that his own kingdom may shine forth more visibly in glory and splendour in this world, and also come with greater glory into our souls.

3. The next thing that should be the matter of our request, and humble petition unto God, is, "That his will may be done." (1.) That the will of God may be done by us, and others. (2.) That the will of God may be done on us, or we submit to whatsoever he is pleased to exercise us under.

God's will, my brethren, is the rule of all he doth, and he being infinitely good, can will nothing but what is just and righteous ; and therefore we should pray we may be helped willingly and cheerfully to submit unto it in all things.

4. We should pray for whatsoever God engaged to our blessed Lord, in the covenant of grace or redemption, to give unto us.

5. And also for all those things that Christ hath purchased for us, and which are treasured up in him as our Head, blessed Trustee, and Mediator, and for all things that God hath promised to give us, and which also Christ Jesus intercedes for, or pleads with God as our Advocate and High-priest, to give unto us. But all things must be prayed for, as to measure, manner, and time, as God in wisdom seeth good to bestow them upon us ; not what, nor in what measure, or at what time we think best, but to leave all to the divine will.

6. Chiefly we should pray for spiritual things, or for supplies for our souls; *Chiefly to pray for spiritual things.* this being according to that directory prayer our Lord taught his disciples. There is but one petition respecting our outward wants, " Give us this day our daily bread." Certainly it is unlawful to pray for riches, or great abundance of outward things, seeing we are bid to pray to God, to give us day by day bread to eat. Solomon's request was well pleasing to God, who asked wisdom, not riches, honours, nor the life of his enemies. As undue endeavours after riches are sinful, so to pray for them is sinful. We read of one of the wisest of men that prayed against riches. (1.) If we *When we sin in praying or endeavouring after riches.* pray for temporal things, with preference to spirituals, or in an equal degree. (2.) Or if we pursue them by unjust means, or in an undue manner. (3.) Or ask them, that we may consume them upon our lusts. (4.) Or seek to obtain them to the hurt of others, or in neglect of the poor, or to the prejudice of the church or kingdom. (5.) Or to lay them up, and neither be willing to give them to such that need them, or not with a resolution to part with all, when God calls us so to do ; then thus to pray for outward things, or endeavour after them, is very sinful, and it argues gross ignorance of the divine being, and of what is for our good (God being a pure spirit) we must desire nothing above a likeness to him. For, (1.) That which renders us most like to God, and tends most to our happiness here, and eternally hereafter, we should always chiefly pray for, and endeavour after. (2.) That which is contrary to the divine will, or a transgression of his holy word, is sinful, and to be abominated ; but to love the world, and chiefly to desire the things thereof, is contrary to the divine will, and a transgression of the holy word ; therefore it is sinful and abominable. " Love not the world," &c. Such that love the world above God, are such that hate him.

7. We should pray to be contented with our present state, and with such *We must pray to be contented with our present state.* things as we have, not with what we once had, or with what others have, but with what we have now, though but food and raiment, or though we want that, because God knows what is best for us, and wisely orders all things for the good of our souls.

8. We should pray to be delivered from all evil, all temptations : that is, that we be not brought into the way of temptation, nor fall in the hour of temptation ; and that we may be enabled here to glorify God, and made meet for glory for ever hereafter.

Seventhly, I shall lay down a few arguments or motives to stir us all up to be constant and fervent in prayer.

1. Prayer is the way of our access through Christ to the Father, hereby *By prayer we have access to God.* we daily visit the blessed God, it is by prayer we have access to him ; and sure if we love God, we will visit him often.

2. Prayer is (saith one) the golden key of heaven, but it will never open the door without faith. It is the tree of the promises, but the fruit will not fall unless it be shaken by the hand of faith.

3. They that restrain prayer from God, are estranged from God, and at last God will be a stranger unto them, and not know them when they cry to him in their distress.

4. May be many Christians receive no more from God, because they ask no more of God. " Ye have not, because ye ask not," James iv. 2, or because they ask amiss, or not such things that are according to the will of God.

5. Consider how much it tends (as you have heard) to the glory of God. Prayer gives that glory to God which is due to his holy name.

6. It argues such are converted souls that are praying souls, or that they have divine life in them, " Behold he prays," Acts ix. 11.

7. It is also an argument, that such are in a state of health that breathe freely, in like

manner it is an argument, that such have healthy souls (or are in a state of spiritual health) that pray freely, or breathe forth freely their desires unto God. Some cannot breathe without difficulty, or do fetch their breath secret; so some find it hard to keep up in a constant course of prayer, and others prayers are too short, though long prayers are not always most prevalent with God.

8 Prayer is that which God delights in, if it be the prayers of godly persons, and their voice is sweet also unto Jesus Christ. " O my love, &c., let me hear thy voice, for sweet is thy voice, and thy countenance is comely," Cant. ii. 14. Will you deny God that, and Christ that, which he is so much pleased with ?

9. Prayer hath done or obtained wonderful things (as you have heard) it has defeated the council of the wicked, and it also consumed the captains and their fifties, it stopped the clouds from raining for three years and a half. It opened heaven again, and it rained. O what power hath this ordinance with God, that thus shut and opened heaven ! It hath made hungry lions, as harmless as lambs, nay, made them become guardians of their intended prey; it hath opened the earth, and quenched the violence of fire, the " two witnesses," Rev. xi. 6, this way smote the earth as often as they pleased. What was the fire that went out of their mouths, but the answer of their prayers ? It hath stopped the sun in its race, and the moon in the valley of Ajalon, and also caused the sun to go back, as well as not to move at all ; and it also hath, and can, when joined with faith, remove mountains of difficulties. Prayer is like an amazing engine, or battering ram, that beats down towers and strong holds, and lays all even before it ; it makes hell quake, haughty tyrants to fear, and devils to tremble. O be much in prayer ! it hath put to flight the armies of the aliens, and cast out devils, and obtained great deliverances, having opened the prison, and caused gates of brass to give way, and let out the prisoner.

The wonders that prayer hath done

Josh. x. 12.
Isa. xxxviii.

Acts 9.

10. Prayer is an evidence of the truth of grace, of a changed heart. The Spirit of grace is a " Spirit of supplication," Zech. xii. 12 ; and also it is the way to have all grace, knowledge, and spiritual gifts to increase, and the word to run and to be glorified. By this means the word hath a door of utterance, and also a door of entrance into the sinner's heart, causing the soul to love the word, to believe and obey it, and to contemplate thereon, and esteem it above thousands of gold and silver.

USE

Therefore see you pray always, and not faint ; and let such that give over praying, be ashamed ; indeed we should never cease praying until we cease living, and as a man dies, or lives not when he breathes not, so he dies in his soul that prays not.

III

And shall not God avenge his own elect, which cry to him day and night? &c.—Luke xviii. 7, 8.

In these words,
1. We have an account of an act done. Avenge, &c.
2. An account of a glorious agent, viz., the great God.
3. The subject for whom this act is done, viz., his elect.
4. The motive moving God to do it for them, viz., their cries, " who cry to him day and night."
5. A confirmation, it shall be done. (1.) " I tell you," Christ says it. (2.) God's will, he will do it ; it is God's purpose, his decree ; he will avenge his own elect.
6. The manner how, &c., speedily, suddenly, unexpectedly, as to the time when, and manner how.
Doct. 1. God's people have adversaries that wrong them, which they cannot, must not avenge themselves upon.
Doct. II. That God will at last, though he seems long first, avenge his own elect, though when he doth it, few will believe it, or then look for it.
I shall, my brethren, speak a little to both these.
I. Show how, or wherein God's people are, and have been wronged, injured, and abused.

II.   Show you after what manner God will avenge them.

III.   Give you a few of the reasons why God will do it.

IV.   Show when he will do it.

1.   Wicked men have, and do wrong the saints and people of God in their names.   O what scandalous, bitter, and reproachful words have they spoken against the saints !   " As with a sword in my bones, mine enemies reproach me," Psal. xlii 10.   " My soul is among lions, even among them that are set on fire, even the sons of men whose teeth **God's elected** are as spears, and arrows, and their tongues a sharp sword," Psal. lvii. 4.   **wronged in their good name.**

Few think how some words cut and wound the children of God, as a spear thrust into their heart : how did the prophet Jeremiah complain, as well as " David, their tongue is as an arrow shot out ! it speaketh deceit ; one speaketh peaceably with his mouth, but in his heart he lieth in wait," Jer. ix. 8.   Some smite openly, and others secretly.   " I am in derision daily, every one mocketh me." xx. 7.   " I have heard the defaming of many : report, say they, and we will report."   And this made him say " I will speak no more in the name of the Lord," verse. 10   How do reproaches weaken the hands, and afflict the heart of a faithful servant of God ! It is often from open enemies, and sometimes from false brethren, and that is worst of all.   Moreover, how was our Saviour himself reproached, e. i., called a gluttonous person, a wine-bibber, and a friend of Publicans and sinners (as if he encouraged them in their ways of wickedness) because he kept company with them, or allowed them to come into his presence, that he might do their souls good, and preach faith and repentance to them, who came to seek such that were lost.   Paul also, and other apostles, were sorely reproached.   " If a man smite you on the face," &c., 2 Cor. xi. 20, 21.   " I speak as concerning reproaches ; which he compares to smiting on the face.—Also when he reckons up his afflictions, mentioneth this as one ; " In reproaches, in necessities," &c., 2 Cor. xii. 10. And again he saith, reproached, but yet true.   Our Lord also saith, " they shall speak all manner of evil against you falsly, for my sake," Matt. v. 11.   **God's people**

2   God's people are also wronged and injured, in respect of the holy doctrine they preach, sacred religion they profess, many censuring and condemning them, as if guilty of errors and heresy, and as factious persons.   " But this I confess unto thee, that after the way which they call heresy, so worship I the God of my Fathers, believing all things which are written in Moses and the prophets," Acts xxiv. 14.   Again it is said to him, we desire to hear of thee, what thinkest thou of this sect, we know that everywhere it is spoken against," Acts xxviii. 22.   It is no new thing for God's people to be called sectarians and such that love singularity ; the primitive Christians were separates, i, e., they separated from the Jewish worship, and from the idolatries of the Gentiles ; and from hence were vilified and censured as a bad and odious sort of people.   **wronged in the doctrine they preach, rendered heretics.**

3.   Their sincerity was also questioned, and they censured as deceivers and hypocrites.   Thus was holy Job charged, and not by his enemies only, but by his friends also ; our Saviour was called a deceiver ; " We remember the deceiver said," &c. Matt. xxvii. 63.   " Thou art a Samaritan, and hast a devil," John viii. 48. 52.   Again they said, we know that thou hast a devil.   Again " thou hast a devil, and deceivest the people."   Hard words ! and as our Saviour was called a deceiver, so was his servant Paul, " as deceivers, yet true," &c., Cor. vi. 8.   What could they say that was worse, or more hard to bear ?   **God's people called hyocrities and deceivers.**

4.   God's people were, and still are wronged, in respect of their liberties, and just rights, as men, and as Christians, as it was some years since here, and is now in France, and othes places, contrary to the laws of God, nature and nations.   **Wronged in their liberty and just rights.**

5.   They have been, and still are wronged by cruel threatenings, " Behold, Lord, their threatnings," &c. Rev. xiii. 6.   How do the wicked belch out oaths, and blaspheme against all that dwell in heaven, or in the church of God !

6.   Nay, how often have God's elect, and dear children, been wronged by persecution, spoiling their goods, gnashing at them with their teeth, yea, biting and tearing them to pieces, casting into loathsome prisons and dunghills, thinking no death bad enough for them ! How have thousands been barbarously murdered, by hanging them, burning them alive, roasting then alive, pulling or flaying off their skins alive, boring out their eyes, drawing them to pieces with horses, and all other inhuman and cruel deaths which man devils could invent ! These have been some of those sorrows, wrongs, and injuries which God's elect have met with from their enemies,   **God's elect wronged by bloody persecutors.**

besides, thousands have suffered in bloody massacres, thirty thousand at one time, and more than two hundred thousand at another, but about sixty years since by bloody papists, and not far from us, even in Ireland, and our own poor Protestant Country, both men, women, and children.

II. I shall show you how, or after what manner God will avenge his own elect, for all the wrongs they have suffered.

1. By famine, sword, and pestilence. It is true, the sin-revenging God

How and after what manner God will avenge his people on their ene- mies.

hath this way already poured out his wrath upon his peoples' enemies, as also by sudden and fearful deaths upon many of their bloody persecutors, as approved histories show, but those forementioned judgments will, in these latter days, be more dreadful than any, (except the amazing wrath and vengeance of God, that was poured out upon the Jews, to the utter desolation of the city, of Jerusalem and their temple, to avenge the wrongs done to our blessed Lord, his apostles, and dear children, for wrath came upon them to the uttermost). But this way, that is, by the sword and famine, and by the pestilence, will God destroy Babylon, and contend with all the enemies of his church and people. " Therefore her plagues shall come upon her in one day," (that is, in one year) " death, mourning, and famine, and she shall be utterly burnt with fire ; for strong is the Lord God that judgeth her.

God will take vengeance of his churches enemies, by thunder, and lightnings, and earth- quakes.

2. As leading to this, God will send dreadful earthquakes, thunder, lightning, and great hail, such that never was seen or known before, which may be daily expected to come to pass, from the God of vengeance, as a just recompence upon his peoples' enemies, or to avenge his own elect, that cry unto him.

3. God will avenge them, by setting their enemies one against another ; he will take peace from the earth, and fill the wicked with rage and fury ; so that they shall kill one another, as they have part already done. And power was given to him that sits thereon, to take peace from the earth, and that they should kill one another ; and there was given to him a great sword. God will set ruler against ruler in Babylon. " My people, go out of the midst of her, and every man delivered his own soul from the fierce anger of the Lord ; lest your hearts faint, and ye fear, for the rumour that shall be heard in the land : a rumour shall come in one year, and after that in another year shall come a rumour and violence in the land, ruler against ruler.—For nation shall rise up against nation, and kingdom against kingdom, and there shall be famine and pestilence, and earthquakes in divers places," Matt. xxiv. 7. May be this prophecy is begun ; O look up ! the days of vengeance draw near. " Blood e'er long shall come out of the winepress, up to the horses bridles, for the space of a thousand and six hundred furlongs."

A mystical earthquake upon the church's enemies.

4. God will avenge his own elect upon the tenth part of the city, or mystical Babylon, by a mighty and terrible, mystical earthquake, which will make the hearts of the enemy in that street of the great city to tremble, and there shall be slain of the names of men seven thousand, " and the remnant will be affrighted, and give glory to the God of heaven," Rev. xi. 13. And so the second woe will pass away, seven is a number of perfection ; it is a certain number put for an uncertain.

The ten kings shall execute God's ven- geance on Babylon.

5. God will put it into the hearts of the ten kings (or some of them) to hate the whore, " and to make her desolate and naked, and they shall eat her flesh, and burn her with fire," Rev. xvii. 16. They will be kings of those kingdoms that formerly gave their power to the beast, or owned the pope, and popish church; but the Lamb by his word, or sword, that goes out of his

The saints shall be in- struments in it.

mouth, shall overcome them, and God's own people also shall join with them (or with some of them) and they shall be God's battle-axe, by whom he will cut down their enemies. " Come out of her my people," &c. " Reward her even as she rewarded you, and double unto her double, according to her works, in the cup which she hath filled to you, fill to her double," Rev. xviii. 4. They will be some, or all of the Protestant princes, and the saints in conjunction with them, by whom God will avenge himself and his people, on his and their adversaries.

God will come forth clothed with vengeance.

6. In a word, God will also, in a way perhaps which we know not of, by his more immediate hand, break forth in dreadful wrath upon the enemies, and make an utter end of all the persecutors of his church and people ; he will arise and devour them. " I have for a long time holden my peace, I have been still, and have refrained myself; now I will cry like a travailing woman, I will destroy and devour at once," Isa. xlii. 14. O how dreadful will that God appear,

when he comes forth clothed with wrath and vengeance! " He will put on righteousness as a breast-plate, and an helmet of salvation upon his head, and he put the garment of vengeance for clothing, and was clad with zeal as a cloak," Isa. lix. 17. What a man of war is the Lord! and how terrible will our God appear, when he comes forth in fury, thus armed! " The Lord will rise up, as in mount Perizim; he will be wroth, as in the valley of Gideon, that he may do his work, his strange work, and bring to pass his act, his strange act," Isa. xxviii. 21. The land shall be soaked with blood—" For it is the day of the Lord's vengeance, and the year of recompence for the controversy of Sion," Isa. xxxiv. 7, 8. And hence it is said, " He will roar out of Sion," Joel iii. 16. Little do the tyrants of the earth know what days of vengeance upon them are near, neither how they will " come on princes as on mortar, and as he that treads the clay," &c.

III. Why will God avenge his own elect, or execute vengeance upon their enemies?

Answ. 1. Because his people's enemies are guilty of blood. Shall mur- derers escape the just vengeance of God? nay, they have murdered the saints, the best of men; yea, they have murdered thousands, if not millions. What murderers are they who have shed the " blood of the saints, and the blood of the martyrs of Jesus!" The sentence of the moral law is, the murderer shall die. " He that sheds man's blood, by man shall his blood be shed," Gen. ix. 6. Some- times murderers escape long, so have these, but they shall be taken at last, and with ven- geance die. O it is a righteous thing with God, to avenge the wrongs of his people! "He will give them blood to drink, because they are worthy." *{Why God will avenge his own elect.}*

2. Because vengeance belongs to the Lord, it his his right to execute it. " Vengeance is mine, saith the Lord," Rom. xii. 19. " To me belongs ven- geance," Deut. xxxii. 35. " O Lord God, to whom vengeance belongs, show thyself," Psal. xciv. 1. God's people are not to avenge themselves; and when he makes use of them as instruments, or as an axe in his hand, it is he that is the Agent, it is God that takes vengeance, let whosoever be the instruments. *{Vengeance belongs to God alone.}*

3. God will avenge his people upon their adversaries, to make good his promises unto them, and his threatenings denounced against their enemies. " I will bear the indignation of the Lord," &c., until he plead my cause, and execute judgment for me," Mich. vii. 9. " Now shall she be trodden down, as the mire in the streets," verse 10. How many times hath the Lord said, he will execute his wrath, and pour out his wrath on Sion's enemies! " Thy nakedness shall be discovered (speaking of Babylon) thy shame shall be seen, I will take vengeance, and will not meet thee as a man; no, but as a terrible God," Isa. xlvii. 3. " Be strong, fear not, behold your God will come, even God with a recompence, he will come and save you," Isa. xxxv. 4. These words refer to the time of the church's deliverance, and the setting up his king- dom. " When sorrow and sighing shall fly away," verse 10. " The Lord will take ven- geance on his adversaries, and he reserveth wrath for his enemies," Nah. i. 2. *{God will avenge his elect, to perform his word.}*

4. Because they are so near and dear to the blessed God; and besides, it is for his own holy Name-sake that they suffer, and have always been exposed to the rage of their enemies. How doth it grieve a tender father, to see his dear children torn into pieces, and burned alive before his eyes! and much more the compassionate and tender husband is afflicted, and in bitterness of soul, to see his beloved wife abused and mangled in a most barbarous and inhuman manner, whilst he looks on. And how would such a father or husband avenge the blood of such relations (were it in their power) on such murderers! Now the love and bowels of our heavenly Father far exceed the love and pity of any earthly father to his children, and so doth the love and compassion of Jesus Christ to his church, which is his spouse, and en- deared wife, for whom also he poured forth his own blood. O Sirs, from hence be sure he will not spare her bloody enemies, in the day of his wrath! especially considering it was alone, for his sake, they have suffered all those lamentable sorrows and miseries. *{God will avenge his elect, be- cause they are so near and dear to him.}*

5. God will avenge his own elect, to convince the world how grievous to him it hath been, to behold all that violence and cruelty wicked men have done unto his own people, and to discover their horrid murders, and to convince them of the detestable sin of perse- cution, tyranny, and oppression, and likewise to clear the innocency of his people. " Be- hold the Lord comes to execute judgment upon all, and convince all that are ungodly a- mong them, of all their ungodly deeds, and hard speeches, which ungodly sinners have spoken against him."

6. God will do it, because it is the vengeance of his temple. " Her foundations are fallen, her walls are thrown down, for it is the vengeance of the Lord," Jer. l. 15. " De-

clare in Sion the vengeance of the Lord God, the vengeance of his temple," verse 28. Moreover, because it is the time of the Lord's vengeance. "These are the day of vengeance," Luke xxi. 22. As there are days of mercy, so the days of vengeance will come, when mercy will be turned into fury.

God will avenge his people because the wicked's day must end, and the saint's day must begin.

7. Because the harvest of the wicked will be then fully ripe for cutting down, and the time when the wicked shall be utterly cut off, and rooted out of the earth; they shall have their time, the full time that is set for them: but when the last period is expired of their time, and the "set time also is come for God to favour Sion," and to give his people the kingdom, then with vengeance the other shall fall, that God may exalt the other.

Because of the prayers and cries of God's elect.

Lastly, God will avenge his own elect, because they cry to him both day and night. This is one reason and argument which our Saviour gives, why God will do it, as it is expressed in this parable. Shall not the prayers of the Lord's people be answered? Will he never remember their sighs and cries? See what he himself saith, "For the oppression of the poor, for the sighing of the needy, now will I arise, saith the Lord, I will set him in safety from him that puffeth at him," Psal. xii. 5. What a multitude of prayers are there on the file in heaven, that shall all be answered in God's own time, put up to him by his people in every age; and besides, the cry of the blood of the slain saints, nay, their souls are said to cry to God. "I saw under the altar the souls of them that were slain for the word of God, and for the testimony which they held.—And they cried with a loud voice, saying, How long, O Lord, holy and true, dost thou not judge and a- venge our blood on them that dwell on the earth!" Rev. vi. 9, 10. This is one, and not the least reason neither, why God will avenge his own elect; their prayers and cries shall be answered, though God seems to tarry long.

IV. When will God avenge his own elect on their enemies?

When God will avenge his people.

Answ. 1. When the beast's forty-two months are fully expired, so long God hath determined the wicked shall have; Antichrist must have his full time to reign, but when those long months are ended, and the saints' 1260 days or years of suffering, and the whole time of their distress is run out, then the days of vengeance will begin. In a word, when the "second woe is passed away, and the seventh angel begins to sound his trumpet," then the enemy shall fall, and the "kingdoms of this world shall become the kingdoms of our Lord and his Christ," Rev. xi. 14, 15, 16. Which I, with many other servants of God, believe will suddenly be accomplished.

2. When the sins of his enemies are full. When the sins of the Amorites were full, God drove them out, and gave Israel the land of Canaan, Gen. xv. 16: so the enemies of Sion must fill up the measure of their sins, and the saints also must fill up the measure of their sufferings which are behind; and when both these are done, God will destroy the one, and deliver the other.

3. When Babylon is in great expectation of recovering her lost children, or some that fell off from her, and she begins to say, I sit a queen, and shall see no sorrow, then the time comes, "How much she glorified herself, and lived deliciously, so much torment and sorrow give her; for she saith in her heart, I sit a queen and am no widow, and shall see no sorrow; then her plagues shall come in one day," Rev. xviii. 7, Isa. xlvii. 8. The enemy shall seem very secure, just when her ruin comes. Thus was Nebuchadnezzar and Belshazzar his son, when judgments came upon them, Dan. v. 21, 22, 23.

4. A little before that very time that God riseth up to execute his judgments on his enemies, he will assemble the nations, or stir them up one against another in war, so that they shall strangely weaken one another, and waste their people and treasure. "Therefore wait upon me, saith the Lord, until the day that I rise up to the prey; for my determination is to gather the nations, and that I may assemble the kingdoms, to pour upon them mine indignation, even all my fierce wrath; for all the earth shall be devoured with the fire of my jealousy," Zeph. iii. 8. Well, and then what will follow? Mark the next words, "For then will I turn to the people a pure language, that they may all call upon the name of the Lord, to serve him with one consent." Then no more distinction of names, Presbyterians, Independents, Baptists. &c. No, all shall become one church; perhaps this may be effected at the ascension of the witnesses, Rev. xi. 11.

5. When the people of God, or the virgins seem to be all asleep, or secure, and yet by some sudden and amazing Providence are awakened, to put up a mighty cry to God, then will the time come; look not for it until you see a mighty spirit of prayer poured out upon the people of God, or many of them. Yet,

Lastly, By what our Saviour here saith, just when God begins to avenge his people upon their enemies, they will be very low in their faith and expectation, as to the time of their deliverance. " Shall the Son of Man when he comes, find faith on the earth ?" They will not believe it will be then.

APPLICATION

1. Let none despair of God's mercy touching his people's deliverance, it will come, the vision will speak ; though it tarry, yet wait for it.

2. We infer, that God hath not forgotten his poor people ; it is for wise ends he seems to delay his coming to avenge them on their enemies.

3. From the whole, let us all be put upon most fervent prayer, yea, pray and not faint ; and also exercise faith in our prayers, touching the church's deliverance, and the utter ruin of her enemies.

4. By what hath been said we may also infer, that there is much reason for us to believe the days of vengeance are very near.

5. Let all that be yet in Babylon haste out speedily, and every one deliver his own soul.

INDEX TO SERIES ONE

Additional Studies on the Parables

LESSER PARABLES OF OUR LORD   **William Arnot**

Discover the many rich truths embedded in the lesser-known parables. Included also are 26 studies from First Peter as well as ten lessons of grace illustrated from nature.

0-8254-2121-7   464 pp.   hardcover

THE STUDY OF THE PARABLES   **Ada R. Habershon**

(Foreword by Sir Robert Anderson) A complete treatment of the purpose, interpretation, and application of parables. Includes useful appendices, outlines, and charts.

0-8254-2852-1   392 pp.   paperback

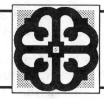 # Classic Commentaries for Bible Study

STUDIES IN LEVITICUS   **Samuel H. Kellogg**

(Foreword by Cyril J. Barber.) Kellogg staunchly defends Mosaic authorship and ably treats Jewish ceremonial law in all its practical aspects. A classic study of the "law of the priests," the typology of the tabernacle, and the laws governing the daily lives of God's people.

0-8254-3041-0   574 pp.   paperback
0-8254-3043-7   574 pp.   deluxe hardcover

COMMENTARY ON THE PSALMS **Joseph Addison Alexander**

Relying on strong exposition of the Hebrew text, Dr. Alexander provides the pastor, student, and layman with a solid foundation for interpretation and exposition of the Psalms. The reader will find in this well researched and clearly focused work a well-spring of interpretive and suggestive material of every Psalm. *Commentary on the Psalms* includes "a literal version of the Hebrew text" and is loosely based on Hengstenberg's *Commentary on the Psalms*.

0-8254-2140-3   568 pp.   paperback
0-8254-2141-1   568 pp.   deluxe hardcover

COMMENTARY ON THE PSALMS   J. J. Stewart Perowne

(Two volumes in one; Foreword by Walter C. Kaiser, Jr.) A classic exegetical work which highlights the sheer beauty and grace of language in the book of Psalms. Perowne provides a complete background for every Psalm along with detailed exegesis and commentary. Includes notes on the Hebrew text, the ancient versions, and other English translations. The best of evangelical scholarship is combined with profound spiritual perception to offer Bible students a trustworthy storehouse of insights into the Psalter.

0-8254-3485-8	1144 pp.	paperback
0-8254-3486-6	1144 pp.	deluxe hardcover

COMMENTARY ON EZEKIEL   Patrick Fairbairn

(Foreword by Peter M. Masters.) One of the most valuable works on this important Old Testament book. Fairbairn discusses the person, position, and circumstances of Ezekiel as well as looking at some of the more distinctive features of his prophetic character. This verse-by-verse commentary is a welcome addition to Old Testament studies.

0-8254-2627-8	512 pp.	paperback
0-8254-2630-8	512 pp.	deluxe hardcover

COMMENTARY ON ZECHARIAH:
HIS VISIONS AND PROPHECIES   David Baron

(Foreword by Walter C. Kaiser, Jr.) W. H. Griffith Thomas called this ". . . the best available book on Zechariah." A thorough exposition of this prophetic book.

0-8254-2277-9	566 pp.	paperback
0-8254-2216-7	566 pp.	deluxe hardcover

COMMENTARY ON MATTHEW   John A. Broadus

One of the finest volumes ever produced on the Gospel of Matthew. John A. Broadus, perhaps one of America's greatest biblical scholars, offers a balanced commentary which contains a straightforward exegesis of the text. In addition, a gold mine of practical insights will provide the reader with a deeper understanding and application of this "gospel of the King!"

0-8254-2283-3	610 pp.	paperback
0-8254-2284-1	610 pp.	deluxe hardcover

COMMENTARY ON ROMANS   Frederic Godet

Even a beginner Bible scholar will discover scriptural concepts made practical in Godet's *Commentary on Romans*. Godet also inspires the more experienced Bible scholar to adjust his focus to varying theories, by which he will gain insight into deeper Bible truths.

Godet brings new insights, fresh discoveries of truth in his verse-by-verse exposition and challenge. His masterful exposition of the Greek text explains and clarifies each concept that he sets forth. You will find this commentary to be the study aid for which you have been looking to explain in a concise manner, the God-breathed doctrinal truths of Romans.

0-8254-2732-0	544 pp.	paperback
0-8254-2715-0	544 pp.	deluxe hardcover